Nineteenth-Century
Literature Criticism

Guide to Gale Literary Criticism Series

For criticism on	Consult these Gale series
Authors now living or who died after December 31, 1999	CONTEMPORARY LITERARY CRITICISM (CLC)
Authors who died between 1900 and 1999	TWENTIETH-CENTURY LITERARY CRITICISM (TCLC)
Authors who died between 1800 and 1899	NINETEENTH-CENTURY LITERATURE CRITICISM (NCLC)
Authors who died between 1400 and 1799	LITERATURE CRITICISM FROM 1400 TO 1800 (LC) SHAKESPEAREAN CRITICISM (SC)
Authors who died before 1400	CLASSICAL AND MEDIEVAL LITERATURE CRITICISM (CMLC)
Authors of books for children and young adults	CHILDREN'S LITERATURE REVIEW (CLR)
Dramatists	DRAMA CRITICISM (DC)
Poets	POETRY CRITICISM (PC)
Short story writers	SHORT STORY CRITICISM (SSC)
Black writers of the past two hundred years	BLACK LITERATURE CRITICISM (BLC) BLACK LITERATURE CRITICISM SUPPLEMENT (BLCS)
Hispanic writers of the late nineteenth and twentieth centuries	HISPANIC LITERATURE CRITICISM (HLC) HISPANIC LITERATURE CRITICISM SUPPLEMENT (HLCS)
Native North American writers and orators of the eighteenth, nineteenth, and twentieth centuries	NATIVE NORTH AMERICAN LITERATURE (NNAL)
Major authors from the Renaissance to the present	WORLD LITERATURE CRITICISM, 1500 TO THE PRESENT (WLC) WORLD LITERATURE CRITICISM SUPPLEMENT (WLCS)

ISSN 0732-1864

Volume 115

Nineteenth-Century Literature Criticism

Excerpts from Criticism of the Works of Novelists, Philosophers, and Other Creative Writers Who Died between 1800 and 1899, from the First Published Critical Appraisals to Current Evaluations

Lynn M. Zott
Project Editor

WITHDRAWN
FAIRFIELD UNIVERSITY
LIBRARY

GALE®

THOMSON
GALE

Detroit • New York • San Diego • San Francisco • Cleveland • New Haven, Conn. • Waterville, Maine • London • Munich

Nineteenth-Century Literature Criticism, Vol. 115

Project Editor
Lynn M. Zott

Editorial
Jenny Cromie, Kathy D. Darrow, Elisabeth Gellert, Edna M. Hedblad, Jelena O. Krstović, Michelle Lee, Jessica Menzo, Thomas J. Schoenberg, Lawrence J. Trudeau, Maikue Vang, Russel Whitaker

Research
Nicodemus Ford, Sarah Genik, Tamara C. Nott, Tracie A. Richardson

Permissions
Debra Freitas

Imaging and Multimedia
Robert Duncan, Lezlie Light, Kelly A. Quin

Composition and Electronic Capture
Carolyn Roney

Manufacturing
Stacy L. Melson

© 2003 by Gale. Gale is an imprint of The Gale Group, Inc., a division of Thomson Learning, Inc.

Gale and Design™ and Thomson Learning™ are trademarks used herein under license.

For more information, contact
The Gale Group, Inc.
27500 Drake Rd.
Farmington Hills, MI 48331-3535
Or you can visit our internet site at
http://www.gale.com

ALL RIGHTS RESERVED
No part of this work covered by the copyright herein may be reproduced or used in any form or by any means—graphic, electronic, or mechanical, including photocopying, recording, taping, Web distribution, or information storage retrieval systems—without the written permission of the publisher.

This publication is a creative work fully protected by all applicable copyright laws, as well as by misappropriation, trade secret, unfair competition, and other applicable laws. The authors and editors of this work have added value to the underlying factual material herein through one or more of the following: unique and original selection, coordination, expression, arrangement, and classification of the information.

For permission to use material from the product, submit your request via the Web at http://www.gale-edit.com/permissions, or you may download our Permissions Request form and submit your request by fax or mail to:

Permisssions Department
The Gale Group, Inc.
27500 Drake Rd.
Farmington Hills, MI 48331-3535
Permissions Hotline:
248-699-8006 or 800-877-4253, ext. 8006
Fax 248-699-8074 or 800-762-4058

Since this page cannot legibly accommodate all copyright notices, the acknowledgments constitute an extension of the copyright notice.

While every effort has been made to secure permission to reprint material and to ensure the reliability of the information presented in this publication, the Gale Group neither guarantees the accuracy of the data contained herein nor assumes any responsibility for errors, omissions or discrepancies. Gale accepts no payment for listing; and inclusion in the publication of any organization, agency, institution, publication, service, or individual does not imply endorsement of the editors or publisher. Errors brought to the attention of the publisher and verified to the satisfaction of the publisher will be corrected in future editions.

LIBRARY OF CONGRESS CATALOG CARD NUMBER 84-643008

ISBN 0-7876-5979-7
ISSN 0732-1864

Printed in the United States of America
10 9 8 7 6 5 4 3 2 1

Contents

Preface vii

Acknowledgments xi

Literary Criticism Series Advisory Board xiii

Christopher Pearse Cranch 1813-1892 1
American poet, journalist, and artist

Vuk Stefanović Karadžić 1787-1864 75
Serbian folklorist and language reformer

Charlotte Smith 1749-1806 116
English poet, novelist, translator, and author of children's books

Alfred, Lord Tennyson 1809-1892 231
English poet and dramatist
Entry devoted to In Memoriam

Literary Criticism Series Cumulative Author Index 383

Literary Criticism Series Cumulative Topic Index 473

NCLC Cumulative Nationality Index 483

NCLC-115 Title Index 487

Preface

Since its inception in 1981, *Nineteenth-Century Literature Criticism* (*NCLC*) has been a valuable resource for students and librarians seeking critical commentary on writers of this transitional period in world history. Designated an "Outstanding Reference Source" by the American Library Association with the publication of is first volume, *NCLC* has since been purchased by over 6,000 school, public, and university libraries. The series has covered more than 300 authors representing 29 nationalities and over 17,000 titles. No other reference source has surveyed the critical reaction to nineteenth-century authors and literature as thoroughly as *NCLC*.

Scope of the Series

NCLC is designed to introduce students and advanced readers to the authors of the nineteenth century and to the most significant interpretations of these authors' works. The great poets, novelists, short story writers, playwrights, and philosophers of this period are frequently studied in high school and college literature courses. By organizing and reprinting commentary written on these authors, *NCLC* helps students develop valuable insight into literary history, promotes a better understanding of the texts, and sparks ideas for papers and assignments. Each entry in *NCLC* presents a comprehensive survey of an author's career or an individual work of literature and provides the user with a multiplicity of interpretations and assessments. Such variety allows students to pursue their own interests; furthermore, it fosters an awareness that literature is dynamic and responsive to many different opinions.

Every fourth volume of *NCLC* is devoted to literary topics that cannot be covered under the author approach used in the rest of the series. Such topics include literary movements, prominent themes in nineteenth-century literature, literary reaction to political and historical events, significant eras in literary history, prominent literary anniversaries, and the literatures of cultures that are often overlooked by English-speaking readers.

NCLC continues the survey of criticism of world literature begun by Gale's *Contemporary Literary Criticism* (*CLC*) and *Twentieth-Century Literary Criticism* (*TCLC*).

Organization of the Book

An *NCLC* entry consists of the following elements:

- The **Author Heading** cites the name under which the author most commonly wrote, followed by birth and death dates. Also located here are any name variations under which an author wrote, including transliterated forms for authors whose native languages use nonroman alphabets. If the author wrote consistently under a pseudonym, the pseudonym will be listed in the author heading and the author's actual name given in parenthesis on the first line of the biographical and critical information. Uncertain birth or death dates are indicated by question marks. Single-work entries are preceded by a heading that consists of the most common form of the title in English translation (if applicable) and the original date of composition.

- The **Introduction** contains background information that introduces the reader to the author, work, or topic that is the subject of the entry.

- A **Portrait of the Author** is included when available.

- The list of **Principal Works** is ordered chronologically by date of first publication and lists the most important works by the author. The genre and publication date of each work is given. In the case of foreign authors whose works have been translated into English, the list will focus primarily on twentieth-century translations, selecting those works most commonly considered the best by critics. Unless otherwise indicated, dramas are dated by first performance, not first publication. Lists of **Representative Works** by different authors appear with topic entries.

- Reprinted **Criticism** is arranged chronologically in each entry to provide a useful perspective on changes in critical evaluation over time. The critic's name and the date of composition or publication of the critical work are given at the beginning of each piece of criticism. Unsigned criticism is preceded by the title of the source in which it appeared. All titles by the author featured in the text are printed in boldface type. Footnotes are reprinted at the end of each essay or excerpt. In the case of excerpted criticism, only those footnotes that pertain to the excerpted texts are included. Criticism in topic entries is arranged chronologically under a variety of subheadings to facilitate the study of different aspects of the topic.

- A complete **Bibliographical Citation** of the original essay or book precedes each piece of criticism.

- Critical essays are prefaced by brief **Annotations** explicating each piece.

- An annotated bibliography of **Further Reading** appears at the end of each entry and suggests resources for additional study. In some cases, significant essays for which the editors could not obtain reprint rights are included here. Boxed material following the further reading list provides references to other biographical and critical sources on the author in series published by Gale.

Indexes

Each volume of *NCLC* contains a **Cumulative Author Index** listing all authors who have appeared in a wide variety of reference sources published by the Gale Group, including *NCLC*. A complete list of these sources is found facing the first page of the Author Index. The index also includes birth and death dates and cross references between pseudonyms and actual names.

A **Cumulative Nationality Index** lists all authors featured in *NCLC* by nationality, followed by the number of the *NCLC* volume in which their entry appears.

A **Cumulative Topic Index** lists the literary themes and topics treated in the series as well as in *Classical and Medieval Literature Criticism, Literature Criticism from 1400 to 1800, Twentieth-Century Literary Criticism,* and the *Contemporary Literary Criticism* Yearbook, which was discontinued in 1998.

An alphabetical **Title Index** accompanies each volume of *NCLC*, with the exception of the Topics volumes. Listings of titles by authors covered in the given volume are followed by the author's name and the corresponding page numbers where the titles are discussed. English translations of foreign titles and variations of titles are cross-referenced to the title under which a work was originally published. Titles of novels, dramas, nonfiction books, and poetry, short story, or essay collections are printed in italics, while individual poems, short stories, and essays are printed in roman type within quotation marks.

In response to numerous suggestions from librarians, Gale also produces an annual paperbound edition of the *NCLC* cumulative title index. This annual cumulation, which alphabetically lists all titles reviewed in the series, is available to all customers. Additional copies of this index are available upon request. Librarians and patrons will welcome this separate index; it saves shelf space, is easy to use, and is recyclable upon receipt of the next edition.

Citing *Nineteenth-Century Literature Criticism*

When writing papers, students who quote directly from any volume in the Literary Criticism Series may use the following general format to footnote reprinted criticism. The first example pertains to material drawn from periodicals, the second to material reprinted from books.

Kim McQuaid, "William Apes, Pequot: An Indian Reformer in the Jackson Era," *The New England Quarterly,* 50 (December 1977): 605-25; excerpted and reprinted in *Nineteenth-Century Literature Criticism,* vol. 73, ed. Janet Witalec (Farmington Hills, Mich.: The Gale Group, 1999), 3-4.

Richard Harter Fogle, *The Imagery of Keats and Shelley: A Comparative Study* (Archon Books, 1949), 211-51; excerpted and reprinted in *Nineteenth-Century Literature Criticism,* vol. 73, ed. Janet Witalec (Farmington Hills, Mich.: The Gale Group, 1999), 157-69.

Suggestions are Welcome

Readers who wish to suggest new features, topics, or authors to appear in future volumes, or who have other suggestions or comments are cordially invited to call, write, or fax the Project Editor:

Project Editor, Literary Criticism Series
The Gale Group
27500 Drake Road
Farmington Hills, MI 48331-3535
1-800-347-4253 (GALE)
Fax: 248-699-8054

Acknowledgments

The editors wish to thank the copyright holders of the excerpted criticism included in this volume and the permissions managers of many book and magazine publishing companies for assisting us in securing reproduction rights. We are also grateful to the staffs of the Detroit Public Library, the Library of Congress, the University of Detroit Mercy Library, Wayne State University Purdy/Kresge Library Complex, and the University of Michigan Libraries for making their resources available to us. Following is a list of the copyright holders who have granted us permission to reproduce material in this volume of *NCLC*. Every effort has been made to trace copyright, but if omissions have been made, please let us know.

COPYRIGHTED MATERIALS IN *NCLC*, VOLUME 115, WERE REPRODUCED FROM THE FOLLOWING PERIODICALS:

American Literature, v. 21, January, 1950. Copyright 1950, renewed 1978 Duke University Press. All rights reserved. Reproduced by permission.—*American Transcendental Quarterly,* n.s. 1, March 1987. Reproduced by permission.—*Critical Review,* v. 39, 1999. Reproduced by permission.—*Dalhousie Review,* v. 51, Summer, 1971 for "Tennyson's 'In Memoriam' as Love Poetry" by Joanne P. Zuckermann. Reproduced by permission of the publisher and the author.—*European Romantic Review,* v. 9, Summer, 1998. Reproduced by permission.—*Journal of English and Germanic Philology,* v. 77, 1978. Reproduced by permission.—*Papers on Language and Literature,* v. 8, Spring, 1972. Reproduced by permission.—*Philological Quarterly,* v. 56, Summer, 1977 for "The Chiastic Structure of 'In Memoriam, A.H.H.,'" by James Kilroy. Reproduced by permission of the author.—*PMLA,* v. 84, March, 1969. Reproduced by permission.—*Princeton University Library Chronicle,* v. 53, Autumn, 1991 for "Charlotte Smith's Letters and the Practice of Self- Presentation" by Sarah Zimmerman. Reproduced by permission of the author.—*Review of National Literatures: The Multinational Literature of Yugoslavia,* v. 5, Spring, 1974. Reproduced by permission.—*SEL,* v. 38, Autumn, 1998. Reproduced by permission.—*Studies in the American Renaissance,* 1977; 1978; 1992. All reproduced by permission.—*Tennyson Research Bulletin,* v. 3, November, 1981; v. 6, November, 1993. Both reproduced by permission.—*University of Toronto Quarterly,* v. 45, Winter, 1976; v. 52, Spring, 1983. Both reproduced by permission.—*Victorian Poetry,* v. 1, April, 1963 for "Circle Imagery in Tennyson's 'In Memoriam'" by James G. Taffe; v. 18, Summer, 1980 for "Computers and Style: The Prosody of 'In Memoriam'" by Robert Dilligan; v. 18, Summer, 1980 for "'In Memoriam': Twentieth-Century Criticism" by Joseph Sendry; v. 34, Spring, 1996 for "Tennyson, Lincolnshire, and Provinciality: The Topographical Narrative of 'In Memoriam'" by Patrick Scott; v. 36, Summer, 1998 for "Producing the 'Far-Off Interest of Tears': Tennyson, Freud, and the Economics of Mourning" by Gerhard Joseph. All reproduced by permission of the respective authors.—*Victorian Studies,* v. 7, December, 1963; v. 18, March and June, 1975. Both reproduced by permission.—*Western Folklore,* v. 30, January, 1971. Reproduced by permission.—*Women's Writing: The Elizabethan to Victorian Period,* v. 2, 1995 for "Thorns and Roses: The 'Sonnets' of Charlotte Smith" by Deborah Kennedy; v. 7, 2000 for "Charlotte Smith and 'Mr. Monstroso': An Eighteenth-Century Marriage in Life and Fiction" by Judith Stanton. Both reproduced by permission of the publisher and the respective authors.—*The Wordsworth Circle,* v. 24, Summer, 1993. Reproduced by permission.

COPYRIGHTED MATERIALS IN *NCLC*, VOLUME 115, WERE REPRODUCED FROM THE FOLLOWING BOOKS:

Anderson, John M. From *Seeing into the Life of Things: Essays on Literature and Religious Experience.* Fordham University Press, 1998. Copyright © 1998 Fordham University Press. All rights reserved. Reproduced by permission.— Butler, Thomas. From *Papers in Slavic Philology 2: To Honor Jernej Kopitar 1780-1980.* Edited by Rado L. Lencek and Henry R. Cooper, Jr. University of Michigan, 1982. Copyright © 1982 by University of Michigan. All rights reserved. Reproduced by permission.—DeFalco, Joseph M. From an introduction to *Collected Poems of Christopher Pearse Cranch.* Scholars Facsimiles Reprints, 1971. Copyright © 1971 by Scholars Facsimiles Reprints. All rights reserved. Reproduced by permission.—Fry, Carrol L. From *Charlotte Smith.* Twayne Publishers, 1996. Copyright © 1996 by Twayne Publishers. All rights reserved. The Gale Group.—Gransden, K.W. From *Tennyson: 'In Memoriam.'* Edward Arnold (Publishers) Ltd., 1964. Copyright © 1964 by Edward Arnold (Publishers) Ltd. All rights reserved. Reproduced by permission.—Haogwood, Terence Allan. From an introduction to *Beachy Head with Other Poems,* by Charlotte Smith. Scholars Facsimiles Reprints, 1993. Copyright © 1993 by Scholars Facsimiles Reprints. All rights reserved. Reproduced by permission.—Hawley, Judith. From *Women's Poetry in the Enlightenment: The Making of a Canon, 1730-1820.* Macmillan Press Ltd., 1999. Copyright © 1999 by Macmillan Press Ltd. All rights reserved. Reproduced by permission.—Hoeveler, Diane Long. From *Gothic Feminism: The Professionalization of Gender from Charlotte Smith to the Brontës.* The Pennsylvania State University Press, 1998. Copyright © 1998 by The Pennsylvania State University Press. All rights reserved. Reproduced by permission.—Holton, Milne, Vasa D. Mihailovich. From *Songs of the Serbian People: From the Collections of Vuk Karadzic.* University of Pittsburgh, 1997. Copyright © 1997 by University of Pittsburgh. All rights reserved. Reproduced by permission.—Ivic, Pavle. From *Papers in Slavic Philology 2: To Honor Jernej Kopitar 1780-1980.* Edited by Rado L. Lencek and Henry R. Cooper, Jr. University of Michigan, 1982. Copyright © 1982 by University of Michigan. All rights reserved. Reproduced by permission.—Johnson, Rob. From *Post-Structuralist Readings of English Poetry.* Cambridge University Press, 1987. Copyright © 1987 by Cambridge University Press. All rights reserved. Reproduced by permission.—Koljevic, Svetozar. From *The Epic in the Making.* Oxford University Press, 1980. Copyright © 1980 by Oxford University Press. Reproduced by permission.—Little, Greta D., and Joel Myerson. From an introduction to *Three Children's Novels by Christopher Pearse Cranch.* The University of Georgia Press, 1993. Copyright © 1993 by University of Georgia Press. All rights reserved. Reproduced by permission.—McKinsey, Elizabeth. From *The Western Experiment: New England Transcendentalists in the Ohio Valley.* Harvard University Press, 1973. Copyright © 1973 by Harvard University Press. All rights reserved. Reproduced by permission.—Miller, F. DeWolfe. From *Christopher Pearse Cranch and His Caricatures of New England Transcendentalism.* Harvard University Press, 1951. Copyright © 1951 by Harvard University Press. All rights reserved. Reproduced by permission.—Rogers, Katharine M. From "Romantic Aspirations, Restricted Possibilities: The Novels of Charlotte Smith," in *Re-Visioning Romanticism: British Women Writers, 1776-1837.* Edited by Carol Shiner Wilson and Joel Haefner. University of Pennsylvania Press, 1994. Copyright © 1994 by University of Pennsylvania Press. All rights reserved. Reproduced by permission.—Rosenberg, John D. From *Tennyson: In Memoriam.* Macmillan and Co., Ltd., 1970. Copyright © 1970 by Macmillan and Co., Ltd. All rights reserved. Reproduced by permission.—Stolz, Benjamin. From *Papers in Slavic Philology 2: To Honor Jernej Kopitar 1780-1980.* Edited by Rado L. Lencek and Henry R. Cooper, Jr. University of Michigan, 1982. Copyright © 1982 by University of Michigan. All rights reserved. Reproduced by permission.—Stula, Nancy. From *Transient and Permanent: The Transcendentalist Movement and Its Contexts.* Massachusetts Historical Society, 1999. Copyright © 1999 by Massachusetts Historical Society. All rights reserved. Reproduced by permission.—Ty, Eleanor. From *Unsex'd Revolutionaries: Five Women Novelists of the 1790s.* University of Toronto Press, 1993. Copyright © 1993 by University of Toronto Press. All rights reserved. Reproduced by permission of the publisher.

PHOTOGRAPHS AND ILLUSTRATIONS APPEARING IN *NCLC*, VOLUME 115, WERE RECEIVED FROM THE FOLLOWING SOURCES:

Cranch, Christopher, portrait.—Title page from "Elegiac Sonnets," written by Charlotte Smith, illustration. The University of Michigan Library. Reproduced by permission.—Smith, Charlotte, stipple engraving in oval frame, photograph. National Portrait Gallery. Reproduced by permission.—Title page from "In Memoriam," written by Alfred Tennyson. Special Collections Library, University of Michigan. Reproduced by permission.—Tennyson, Lord Alfred, photograph. Courtesy of The Library of Congress.

Literary Criticism Series Advisory Board

The members of the Gale Group Literary Criticism Series Advisory Board—reference librarians and subject specialists from public, academic, and school library systems—represent a cross-section of our customer base and offer a variety of informed perspectives on both the presentation and content of our literature criticism products. Advisory board members assess and define such quality issues as the relevance, currency, and usefulness of the author coverage, critical content, and literary topics included in our series; evaluate the layout, presentation, and general quality of our printed volumes; provide feedback on the criteria used for selecting authors and topics covered in our series; provide suggestions for potential enhancements to our series; identify any gaps in our coverage of authors or literary topics, recommending authors or topics for inclusion; analyze the appropriateness of our content and presentation for various user audiences, such as high school students, undergraduates, graduate students, librarians, and educators; and offer feedback on any proposed changes/enhancements to our series. We wish to thank the following advisors for their advice throughout the year.

Dr. Toby Burrows
Principal Librarian
The Scholars' Centre
University of Western Australia Library

David M. Durant
Joyner Library
East Carolina University

Steven R. Harris
English Literature Librarian
University of Tennessee

Mary Jane Marden
Literature and General Reference Librarian
St. Petersburg Jr. College

Mark Schumacher
Jackson Library
University of North Carolina at Greensboro

Gwen Scott-Miller
Assistant Director of Materials and Programming
Sno-Isle Regional Library System

Christopher Pearse Cranch
1813-1892

American poet, journalist, and artist.

INTRODUCTION

Recognized by contemporaries for his poetry, essays, and landscape paintings, Cranch is best remembered today as the member of the New England Transcendentalist movement with a sense of humor, depicting Ralph Waldo Emerson and other leading members of the group in caricature. He was considered a dilettante by many contemporaries because his interests and talents covered a variety of fields, including painting, literature, and music. He was associated with the Hudson River School of painting and was, for a time, a member of the American expatriate colony in Italy.

BIOGRAPHICAL INFORMATION

Cranch was born in Alexandria, Virginia, on March 8, 1813, the youngest son of thirteen children. His father, William Cranch, was a judge and his mother, Nancy Greenleaf, was the niece of John Quincy Adams. Cranch attended Columbian College (now George Washington University), graduating in 1832, and the Harvard Divinity School, graduating in 1835. Although he was never ordained, he worked for several years as an itinerant minister, traveling from Maine to Virginia and eventually to what was then the West—Illinois, St. Louis, and Cincinnati. There he joined the staff of the *Western Messenger,* a journal whose purpose was to spread Transcendentalism into that part of the country. In 1837-38, he moved to Louisville and filled in for *Western Messenger* editor James Freeman Clarke, who spent two winters in New England. During these years Cranch struggled with his own perceived inadequacy for the ministry, a career he considered his duty to pursue, and his attraction to literature and art. His personal struggle was exacerbated by the ongoing conflict between conservative Unitarianism and Transcendentalism, and in 1843 Cranch left his ministry. In October of that year Cranch married New Yorker Elizabeth de Windt and the couple settled in New York City. In 1844 Cranch published *Poems,* a collection of his pieces reflecting the Transcendentalist outlook.

Cranch soon began drifting away from Transcendentalism and concentrating more on his painting, becoming associated with the Hudson River School. Beginning in 1846, the Cranchs spent three years abroad, during which time they made the acquaintance of Elizabeth Barrett and Robert Browning, whom Cranch greatly admired. They returned to New York in 1849 where they took up residence in the city, although they summered in Niagara, the Hudson River, the Berkshires, and the Catskills, where Cranch could find inspiration for his landscape painting. On a return visit to Europe in 1853, Cranch met James Russell Lowell and the two became life-long friends. Cranch spent the next ten years in Paris painting, writing children's books, and translating Vergil's *Æneid.* Although his paintings sold, his income as an artist was not sufficient to support his family. When an inheritance at last brought him financial stability, Cranch abandoned art and concentrated once again on literary pursuits. In 1880 Cranch returned to Europe for two years, accompanying his daughter Caroline, a promising painter, so that she might be exposed to the work of the European masters. He published three more collections of poetry, the last in 1887. Cranch died in Cambridge, Massachusetts, in 1892.

MAJOR WORKS

Cranch's first poem was published in 1836, a parodic ballad entitled "Childe Christopher," followed by "Correspondence" (1839) and "Enosis" (1840), often anthologized as an example of Transcendental poetry and warmly praised by Emerson. Beginning in 1836, Cranch became a regular contributor of both poetry and prose, most of it religious in nature, to the *Western Messenger,* and he continued to write for the magazine even after he had returned east. His poems "To the Aurora Borealis" (1840) and "Enosis" were recommended by Emerson to Margaret Fuller, editor of the new Transcendentalist journal *The Dial*; both pieces appeared and Cranch was the chief contributor of poetry to the magazine for the first two issues. He continued to write for *The Dial* from 1840 to 1844, and also contributed Transcendental poetry to the *Harbinger, Graham's, Godey's,* and the *Democratic Review.* His most famous prose pieces were his review of Emerson's *The American Scholar* (1837) and "Transcendentalism," a defense of the movement, written in 1841. Both pieces were written for the *Western Messenger.*

Cranch's first poetry collection appeared in 1844 and was titled simply *Poems.* Although he continued to write for periodicals, he did not produce another book for nearly 30 years when he published *Satan: A Libretto* (1873), well received by critics but ignored by the public. The following year Cranch published *The Bird and the Bell, with Other Poems,* a collection whose title poem had been written many years earlier with advice and assistance from Robert and Elizabeth Barrett Browning. His final volume of poetry, *Ariel and Caliban* (1887), brought the total number of sonnets published over the course of his career to nearly 100.

In addition to his poetry and essays, Cranch's best known works are his children's tales, *The Last of the Huggermuggers* (1856) and its sequel *Kobboltozo* (1857), and his translation of Vergil's *Æneid* (1872) into blank verse.

CRITICAL RECEPTION

Critical assessment of Cranch's work is mixed. In his own time, he was called a dilettante; his detractors believed that although he was talented in many fields, he pursued none with the intensity required to become great in any of them. Emerson gently acknowledged a similar sentiment in a letter to Cranch: "I have always understood that you are the victim of your own various gifts; that all the muses, jealous of each other, haunt your brain." Edgar Allan Poe, who despised the Transcendentalist movement, granted Cranch faint praise as "the least intolerable of the school of Boston Transcendentalists," although he later conceded that Cranch was "one of our finest poets." The assessment of Cranch as a dabbler followed him into the twentieth-century. J. C. Levenson, calling him a "minor talent," claims that the poet was "locked in a world of banal conventionality." Yet Joseph M. DeFalco believes he is one of the five greatest Transcendentalist poets and one of the few Transcendentalists with a sense of humor.

Even critics unimpressed with the complete body of Cranch's work single out one or two poems for distinction. Levenson suggests that the pair of sonnets entitled "The Garden" represents the best of Cranch's poetry, while Greta D. Little and Joel Myerson consider "Correspondence," which draws heavily from Emersonian philosophy, to be among his finest. Little and Myerson concede, however, that the conventional criticism of Cranch is well-founded: "Like many people who have spread their abilities over a number of fields, Cranch failed to make a significant name for himself in any one of them." Even Cranch himself acknowledged that: "I have wooed too many mistresses; and the world punishes me for not shutting my eyes to all charmers but one."

PRINCIPAL WORKS

Poems (poetry) 1844
The Last of the Huggermuggers: A Giant Story (fairy tale) 1856
Kobboltozo: A Sequel to The Last of the Huggermuggers (fairy tale) 1857
Æneid of Vergil [translator] (poetry) 1872
Satan: A Libretto (poetry) 1874
The Bird and the Bell, with Other Poems (poetry) 1875
Ariel and Caliban, with Other Poems (poetry) 1887
Three Children's Novels (fairy tales) 1993

CRITICISM

Southern Literary Messenger (review date 1845)

SOURCE: "*Poems* by Christopher Pearse Cranch." *Southern Literary Messenger* 11, no. 5 (May 1845): 295-99.

[*In the following anonymous review, the critic provides a mixed reading of Cranch's* Poems.]

In spite of the matter-of-fact character ascribed to our nation, we have every day instances that the soil of Uncle Sam's great farm is not only fertile in producing merchants, whose possessions are those of princes, statesmen and military heroes, who, by the way, in these peaceful times, earn epaulets and laurels bloodlessly enough; but also numberless writers of greater or less distinction, and in every class of literature.

Among the latter, none are more numerous than the (so-called!) poets, (verily, *bellua multorum es capitum!*) the height of whose ambition it frequently is, to contribute "stanzas" and "lines" on so-and-so to some magazine with a colored fashion-plate. In process of time, these effusions accumulate on the hands of our young composers, and they presently discover a publisher sufficiently venturous to issue their labors in an elegant form, the gilding, after all, being reckoned upon, rather than the contents, to secure a sale.

The worst feature in the works of our American poets—I speak of the larger proportion—is that they write too much and with too little care: they are satisfied with appearing frequently before the public, flattering themselves that to do so is to be on the high road to fame; quite overlooking the fact, that it is the *quality,* not the *quantity,* of the goods they bring, which will obtain them purchasers in the great market of authors' wares.

The English have the right of it in this respect; they bend the whole power of their genius to the production of two or three compositions, which at once secure the author a brilliant reputation. This once grasped, they issue volumes, to the matter included in which they pay little regard, provided in the midst appear one or more of these real gems, the beauty of which, they are quite confident, will blind the eyes of their readers to all defects occurring in the minor productions. Thus, in a recent edition of *Barry Cornwall,* a large proportion of the verses were such as we would have expected to see over the signature "anonymous" in a daily newspaper: yet withal, we did not regret a moment having purchased the volume when we came to discuss such exquisite morsels as make their appearance at intervals: thus also, in Bulwer's "Eva, &c.," but seven pieces, in our estimation, compose the book, the remainder being evidently inserted to swell the space between the covers of the publisher; yet we do not know any volume of like size; nay, nor any five, issued within the last six years, for which we would be willing to exchange our unadorned copy; supposing always, (which the muse forbid!) that none other was to be obtained.

We were inclined to regard the little volume of poems before us with a favorable eye, so soon as we saw the author had not taken refuge behind the arts of the binder and engraver, which always remind us of the charms the enchantress Alcina, in "Orlando Furioso," assumed to conceal her deformities, and attract enamored knights to her palace by the grace of her outward seeming.

Our author certainly makes a fair beginning; in fact, we are of opinion he has, unlike the arrangement of the Roman legions according to Livy, placed his best performance in the van. Whether this order is to be preferred, it is not our present design to call in question. We regard with something more than horror, those peevish and harsh critics, who, as vultures are said sometimes to treat an animal on its last legs, flap around, tear out the eyes, and croak warning in the ears of their victim, who, if suffered to take his own course, would soon die a natural death.

We introduce this simile, however, merely to show that we are not of a captious disposition; not because we think the subject of the present review in danger of sharing the last mentioned fate.

To acknowledge the truth, we were so pleased with the very beginning of his first poem, that we at once re-turned to the title page and endeavored to call to mind some former production, to which the autograph of our poet—he gives his name in full, "Christopher Pearse Cranch"—had been attached. If he has written (and published) anything of note hitherto, however, it has escaped our attention.

"College Lyfe," (the title of our favorite,) is written in imitation of the Old English: the dialect in which, more or less modified, Chaucer, Sir Tristrem, and a host of old ballads, have been handed down to us. We have many objections to this style of composition; not only because it savors somewhat of affectation, but because, in the present polished state of our language, as Selden says in his quaint way, of those who kiss a lady's hand after her lips, it is like the fashion of little boys who, when they have eat the apple, fall to and eat the paring.

Besides, we never see a word lengthened a syllable by the addition of the prefix "y," without being reminded in a lively manner of the ache we once caused our eyes by reading Spenser's Fairie Queene in venerable black-letter.

Mr. Cranch, however, has handled his subject in so admirable a sort, that we are quite disposed to forgive him any pains he may have, by chance, recalled. Take for instance the three first stanzas:

"There stands upon a hille, al verdantlie
Y-clad with trees, and grasse, and waving graine,
An edifice, ne very haught and highe,
Ne lowe; of bricks y-built, joli and plaine;
Beseemeth such an house there to remaine.
A spire decks the roofe, which to the eyne
Of wandering wighte, who there his course hath ta'en,
Beneathe Dan Sol doth often glitterynge shine;
And al beyonde the walles are groves and meadowes fine.

"There often have I whilom conned my taske,
Intent on booke with no huge pleasaunce fraughte,
Withouten hope of drinke from luscious flaske.
To speede upon his waye one labouringe thoughte;
A looke as drye, perdie, was never boughte!
Ofte have I nodded, filled with drowsie sleepe,
Which Morpheus from his sombre land hath broughte,
And ofte would starte, and vigyl fain would keepe,
Yet that same sleepie god still o'er my braine dyd creepe.

"Then, ere I could againe my booke resume,
O fatale finisher of al my joye!
The glib-tongd bel would tingle through the roome,
O cursed bel, my peace thus to destroye!
No elfin spirite me then mote so annoye,
Ne goblyn ghoste with hellish puissance,
Ne byrchen swytch y-drad by idle boye,
Ne to the hen-peckt wighte hys wyfe's keen glance,
More troublous seemes than this, my miserie to enhance."

Who that has been to college, does not fancy himself in the presence of his alma-mater again, while reading the first verse, or fails to recall the peculiar wandering of thought, (here, after some "luscious flaske") and drowsiness, which even the hardest student must at some time in his life have experienced over a "booke with no huge pleasaunce fraughte;" or to sympathize with the "luckless youthe," startled into consciousness of the existence of such things as recitation-rooms and college discipline, by the sound of the bell he anathematizes as more vexing than "byrchen swytch, y-drad by idle boye."

Our author, who is tolerably fair in the division of his subject, after giving three stanzas to matters relating to "bookes," introduces two, replete with the noises incident to dormitories surrounding a "campus."

We give the last of these:

"Ne noyse alone of merriment was hearde.
There met the eare oftimes straunge mingled soundes,
Not like the liquid notes of woodlande byrde;
More like a packe, methinks, of hungrye houndes,
Yelping a chorus ere they slippe their boundes;
Fyddels y-crackt and huskie flutes were there,
Such discorde as the very aire astoundes!
That man must praye for deafnesse who would heare
The chaos straunge and loude that filleth al the aire."

The description of doings in the refectory is highly humorous, and partaking as much of the reality as it is possible for words to make it. The remainder of this little poem is devoted to the pursuits of the students (?) during hours of recreation; such as wanderings through woods and fields, and—which college lads are prone to undertake—the plundering of trees, &c.: "Small gripes," he writes with no less truth than quaintness, "dyd conscience give, those tymes I trow."

One more verse, and we are done with his "college lyfe."

> "Sometymes we wandered by a sylvan streame,
> That made soft murmurings on a summer's daie;
> Along it's bankes how often dyd we dreame,
> And see its dark green waters glyde away,
> Kyssing the flowers which to their brinke dyd straie
> There too, huge scarped rocks dyd hie appeare,
> And from the sunne dyd shelter it alwaie;
> Here as we sometymes strayed, wel mote we heare
> Sweete sounde of distant bel, or mil-wheel plashyng neare."

The beauty of this extract, it requires no encomium from our pen to make evident; the last line is particularly harmonious and faithful in description.

In what section of country the college, of which our poet here treats, is situated, we have no means of knowing; that it lies somewhere in the South is apparent from his mentioning, among other "lyttel flies" which annoyed them, certain "*mosquitoes* highte." This is a matter of no consequence however; the sketch presented us is one evidently drawn from realities—aye, and well drawn too.

We wish we could continue to write in the same strain of praise of Mr. Cranch as a poet, but our character as an impartial and discriminating reviewer, might be justly questioned, did we follow this course.

In good truth, as we advance into the volume, his productions, far from appearing more attractive even manifest less genius and poetry in their composition than those which have gone before; and what is still more remarkable, being arranged chronologically, we are compelled to infer that our author has become not a whit better poet in *ten years* than he was at first. Even the sonnets concluding the work, (of which more hereafter,) bear out our remark, the dates affixed being 1836-37 and 38.

Our author, however, differs in one marked particular from the multitude of those who publish works formed, like his, of a collection of minor pieces; he does not weary the reader from the first with "Lines to Miss———," nor "verses on a Lock of Julia's Hair;" and such other insipidities as find their way into our magazines. He does not even, (which is a matter of curiosity in a poet!) condescend to mention the "gentle passion" in any wise, until he arrives at the *eighty-seventh page,* where the pronoun "*she,*" (who? the lines are entitled "a Bouquet,") is often introduced. Catching inspiration at once from the new emotion, he devotes the five mortal stanzas, (of eight lines each!) on the succeeding pages, to the subject of "Love," in the first couplet of which our poet notifies the world that he has fairly enrolled himself under the banner of Cytheræa, by confessing,

> "There is no blessedness in life
> Apart from blessed love!!"

We will spare our readers the rest, with the exception of four lines, which certainly are not bad. Speaking of love he says:

> "It lifts the burden from the soul,
> And puts the staff in hand:
> The gloomy clouds behind us roll,
> And all before is dawn, and fairy-land."

We cannot say we like the three additional syllables to every eighth line. Before we dismiss this piece, we would ask the writer, (with all due submission,) in what portion of the world he finds "scented air snowing with scattered blossoms, &c?" We of course understand the idea he means to convey, but as far as our horizon reaches, the air never snows.

The lines on the following page, "To E———," (a single instance!) and "on separation," with those we have quoted above, comprise the extent of Mr. Cranch's toying with the tender passion.

But although we have taken a long stride—having arrived at the ninety-second page—it is not our intention to abandon in so summary a manner the matter contained in the intervening leaves. We commended our author so highly in the opening of our review, that it is only just he should learn to appreciate our praise, by the discovery that we are not blind to his faults.

Passing over several errors of small consequence, we would call attention to the following lines:

> "Amid the dark blue firmament,
> There hung the seven-stringed lyre on high,
> But a reckless comet *came* rushing by
> And swept it as he *went* (!!)"

Was ever passage less nobly expressed? First, a comet in spite of all bounds and orbits, which last the astronomers tell us are defined, becomes "reckless," and "sweeps" the constellation of the "lyre" as it rushes by.

The following verse affords the most extraordinary example of poetical license we ever remember to have noted.

> "And deep amid the o'er arching trees,
> A low-toned waterfall was gushing;
> *Unseen, beneath a stream went rushing*
> *And mingled with the breeze.*"

"Beneath"—beneath what? And who ever heard of a stream "mingling with the breeze."

We have always thought few things more ludicrous than the (gravely expressed) opinions of visitors to Niagara, contained in the book kept there for that purpose. We do not know whether our author's lines on the above subject made their first appearance in the pages of that volume of miscellanies; at all events they are worthy of a conspicuous position among the rest.

> "Down, down forever—down, down forever,
>   *Something falling, falling, falling,*
> Up, up forever—up, up forever,
>   Rest never,

>   Boiling up forever,
>   Steam-clouds shot up with thunder-bursts appalling."

This brief extract requires no comment. The *up and down* mode of expression used, the "boiling," "never resting," "steam-clouds shot up," and above all the "*something*" which we are to imagine falling—falling—falling, (by jerks as it were!) compose a passage unequalled in bathos, and which leaves the mind in a perfect whirl of doubt, bewilderment and falling waters!

Omitting a number of pieces of no great merit, we will now present to our readers **"Night and the Soul"**; lines certainly replete with quiet beauty, and which forcibly remind us of some of Longfellow's. We give nearly the whole.

"Night and the Soul."

> "I went to bed with Shakspeare's flowing numbers
>   Within me chiming,
> As I sank slowly to my pleasant slumbers,
>   My thoughts with his were rhyming.
>
> "Out of the window I saw the moonlight shadows
>   Go creeping slow;
> The sheeted roofs of snow,—the broad white meadows
>   Lay silently below.
>
> "A few keen stars were kindly winking through
>   The frost-dimmed panes,
> And dreaming chanticleer woke up and crew
>   Far o'er the desolate plains.
>
> "But soon into the void abyss of sleep
>   My mind did swoon;
> I saw no more the broad house-shadows creep
>   Beneath the silent moon."

He then wakes—the sun shining brightly. The thoughts of our author are as true as gracefully expressed.

> "Why does the night give to the spirit wings,
>   Which day denies?
> Ah, why this tyranny of outward things
>   When brightest shine the skies?
>
> "My soul is like the flower that blooms by night,
>   And droops by day;
> Yet may its fruit expand, though in the light
>   Night-blossoms drop away."

Again, in **"The Poet,"** Mr. Cranch writes as he really feels and, consequently, with success. Take the two verses below as examples.

> "And these he loves;—and with all these the heart
> Of frail humanity, which, like a tremulous harp
> Hung in the winds, not oft from storms apart,
> Sobs or rejoices; and when tempests sharp
> Sweep the tense strings, a 'sweet, sad music' bears,
> Where others list no voice, nor heed the dropping
>   tears.

> "Who scorns the poet's art, deserves the scorn
> Which he would heap on others' heads; that man
> Knows not the sacred gift and calling born
> Within the poet's soul when life began:
> Knows not that he *must* speak, and not for fame,
> But that his heart would wither else within its flame."

It is difficult to credit that the author of the last two selections, ever penned lines like those "to Niagara!"

We notice a peculiarity in the compositions of Mr. Cranch, in which, however, he is not alone. Many of his articles begin with much promise, but conclude rather lamely.

Thus the first four lines of his **"Endymion"** are not unattractive.

> "Yes, it is the queenly moon
> Walking through her starred saloon,
> Silvering all she looks upon:
> I am her Endymion."

Yet the conclusion is evidently inferior.

The **"Star-gazer,"** which we regard as a parable in some sort, deserves a hasty glance.

> "Star after star looked glimmering down,
> As in the night he sat alone,
> And in the firmament of mind
> Thought after thought upon him shone."

This is certainly well turned. The "Star-gazer," who, we suppose, represents *en masse* the servants and disciples of science, sits alone and unnoticed, patiently awaiting the day when the darkness around him will be dispelled; the moment arrives at last.

> "They slept, and would not wake until
> The distant lights that fixed his gaze
> Came moving on, and spread abroad
> The glory of a noontide blaze.
>
> "And then they started from their dreams,
> And slowly oped their leaden eyes,
> And saw the light whose splendors now
> Were darting through the morning skies.
>
> "Then turned and sought for him whose name
> They, in their sleep, had mocked and cursed;—
> But he had left them long before,
> The vision on their souls had burst," &c.

The **"Thunder-gust," "Beauty and Truth," "Enosis," "The Ocean,"** and several of the sonnets with which he closes his volume, are worthy of perusal, and exhibit some poetic talent.

We have mentioned his sonnets before, and cannot refrain from treating our readers to a selection or two.

"Morning."

> "The earth was wandering in a troubled sleep,
>   And as it wandered, dreaming tearful dreams,

> Then came the sun adown his orient sleep,
>   Making sweet morning with his golden beams;
> A parent, bending o'er his child he seems,
>   Kissing its eyes, lips, cheeks, with warm embrace;
> So kisseth he the mountains, woods and streams,
>   And all the dew-like tears from off its face.
> O joy! That father's smile is like no other—
>   The child is folded in a parent's arms,
> And looks up to the sky, its blue-eyed mother,
>   And laughs, with light upon its waking charms.
> Ah, happy earth; what tender care hast thou!
> There is no midnight cloud, or dream upon thee now."

This description is really charming; if Mr. Cranch would publish lines no worse than the foregoing in future, he need never anticipate remaining unread and unknown.

It is seldom our author descends to a style of composition so sprightly as the following, yet so abundant in ease and grace, and happy in illustration.

"The Violin."

> "The versatile, discursive Violin,
>   Light, tender, brilliant, passionate or calm,
> Sliding with careless nonchalance within
>   His range of ready utterance, wins the palm
> Of victory o'er his fellows for his grace;
>   Fine, fluent speaker, polished gentleman—
> Well may he be the leader in the race
>   Of blending instruments—fighting in the van
> With conscious ease and fine chivalric speed;
>   A very Bayard in the field of sound,
> Rallying his struggling followers in their need,
>   And spurring them to keep their hard earned-
>   ground.
> So the fifth Henry fought at Azincour,
> And led his followers to the breach once more."

As an antithesis to his sonnet entitled **"The Violin,"** we subjoin that on **"Trumpets and Trombones;"** breathing nothing but military glory!

> "A band of martial riders next I hear,
>   Whose sharp brass voices cut and rend the air.
> The shepherd's tale is mute, and now the ear
>   Is filled with wilder clang than it can bear;
> Those arrowy trumpet notes, so short and bright,
>   The long drawn wailing of the loud Trombone,
> Tell of the bloody and tumultuous fight
>   The march of victory and the dying groan;
> O'er the green fields the serried squadrons pour,
>   Killing and burning, like the bolts of heaven;
> The sweetest flowers with cannon smoke and gore
>   Are all profaned, and Innocence is driven
> Forth from her cottages and woody streams,
> While over all red Battle fiercely gleams."

In conclusion, we would say that, on the whole, we consider the little volume before us, better entitled to a place on the shelves of a library than many works of a similar character; and perhaps we have dealt more harshly with the author's inferior productions than the general tone of his writings would seem to justify; κακιον ειναι το αδικειν του αδικεισθαι[1] says Plato.

It is a pity our author has allowed poems so unworthy as one or two we have noticed, to appear by the side of others of infinitely greater merit.

We are ignorant of the age of our poet, but, supposing his **"College Lyfe"** to have been written at college, (which at least is probable,) the number of years intervening between the date of this piece (1834) and the present year, being *ten*; and eighteen, (a fair average,) assigned as his *then* age, we have him at the present date about twenty-eight or thirty; the very period of life when a man's genius, of whatever kind it be, will show itself most conspicuously.[2] We would advise Mr. Cranch then, not to be discouraged if his poems do not at once meet with the favor his own affection for his offspring and the good will of his personal friends may have induced him to anticipate.

He exhibits in many places genius of no ordinary stamp, and which, if cultivated and brought nearer to maturity, will assuredly give him an elevated position among our American poets.

After all, we can entertain few fears for the success of a poet who expresses himself so gracefully, and in so modest, yet dignified a strain as the following, with which we will close our review.

"Sonnet."

> "I'll love the sonnet then for its own sake,
>   And calmly hold my quiet course along.
> Like clouds and sky seen on some lonely lake,
>   Far from the crowded world, my humble song,
> Although reflecting truth and loveliness,
>   May be unknown, save to a cherished few;
> Yet shall I never love my pen the less,
>   Nor cease to wreathe my little lyre anew
> With the wild wood-vine, and the simple green
>   Of Nature. Yes, the soul *must* sometimes speak,
> And though its numbers flow almost unseen,
>   It hath within itself, nor harsh, nor weak,
> A harmony that will at times have vent,
> Though all untuned the while, the poor, dull instrument."

Notes

1. "It is worse to be unjust, than to suffer injustice."

2. Mr. Cranch is a son of Judge Cranch, and was born at Alexandria, D. C., in March 1813. He was graduated at Columbia College, D. C., in 1831, and is now about 32 years of age.—[Ed. Mess.]

J. C. Levenson (essay date 1950)

SOURCE: Levenson, J. C. "Christopher Pearse Cranch: The Case History of a Minor Artist in America." *American Literature* 21, no. 4 (January 1950): 415-26.

[*In the following essay, Levenson suggests that Cranch's indolence resigned him to a career of mediocrity as a writer and an artist.*]

> A great literature is more than the sum of a number of great writers. . . . The continuity of a literature is essential to its greatness: it is very largely the function of secondary writers to preserve this continuity, and to provide a body of writing which is not necessarily read by posterity, but which plays a great part in forming the link between those writers who continue to be read.
>
> —T. S. Eliot.

Christopher Pearse Cranch (1813-1892) is mentioned today in a number of different contexts ranging from the Hudson River School of painters to the American expatriate colony of Italy, but he is most interesting in the context of New England Transcendentalism. The Transcendentalist movement, to which our American tradition owes so great a debt, drew a large part of its liberating energy from the sheer weight of numbers, and through Cranch one can get directly at the constructive role of the minor figure in a genuine literary and artistic movement.

Cranch may seem a somewhat remote New Englander although he passed his most formative years in that section and later, when he had reached his threescore and ten, made his pilgrimage back to Cambridge to die; actually he was a son of the provincial tradition in one of its most cosmopolitan strains, and his life is a constant affirmation of that lineage. He was born in Alexandria, then a part of the District of Columbia, the son of William Cranch, chief justice of the District Court. His father had been a Harvard classmate of John Quincy Adams and had obtained his judicial office by one of John Adams's midnight appointments in 1801. Equally conservative in his Unitarianism and his Federalism, Judge Cranch had his wife and children kneel about him daily for their family prayers and maintained, south of Mason and Dixon's line, an island of strict New England observance of the Sabbath. Within the passage of a generation the old judge was to suffer the shock of learning that his son Pearse was indulging in the new intellectual radicalisms of the day; indeed, his informat may have been his friend and classmate from Quincy, former President Adams, who made a caustic comment in his journal at about this time on the unexpected frivolity of the youngest Cranch. The gulf between the generations became clear when, in 1841, the father wrote the son as strong a letter as only a Federalist judge in Democratic times knew how and drew from the prodigal a reply which was perhaps the most courageous act of his life. Pearse Cranch protested to his father:

> Somehow the name "Transcendentalist" has become a nick-name here for all who have broken away from the material philosophy of Locke, and the old theology of many of the early Unitarians, and who yearn for something more satisfying to the soul. It has almost become a synonym for one who, in whatever way, preaches the spirit rather than the letter.[1]

He went on to defend Emerson, the epitome of all that was dangerous, and ended defiantly: "All Unitarians should be of this school."[2]

We have very little information to help us with the problem of how the Boston-Washington-Federalist tradition that so early took its stand against any new views whatever managed to become involved with Transcendentalism. As far as we know, Pearse Cranch passed an exceptionally uneventful youth in Washington, and there is no reason to suspect that he learned anything dangerous at Columbian College there. The answer seems to lie in the fact that his older brother Edward was, when Pearse graduated in 1832, already preparing to succeed their father in the law and that Pearse was not interested in medicine. The only gentlemanly profession left open to him was the ministry, and so he packed his carpetbag and made his way north to the Harvard Divinity School. There he fell in with heterodoxy almost at once: among his classmates were Cyrus Bartol and Samuel Osgood; John Sullivan Dwight and Theodore Parker became his particular friends. We have a story from Edward Emerson that shows how quickly he slipped from a proper high seriousness of purpose: he and Dwight, we are told, used to spend so much time playing duets in their room at Divinity Hall that "their outraged friend, Theodore Parker, who disliked music, was driven in self-defense to saw wood outside their door."[3] This anecdote records Cranch's first step away from the creed of his ancestors and toward a Transcendentalist independence.

With his time spent so ill at the Divinity School, it is natural that later Cranch should have had professional difficulties. Although licensed to preach after his graduation in 1835, he never did well enough in any one place to be ordained. His wanderings in search of a pulpit took him as far north as Bangor, where he was for a time assistant to Frederic Hedge, and as far south as Richmond, Virginia. There, where the elder William Ellery Channing had learned his radicalism, Cranch learned *his* radicalism, too, the love of fine company whose interests were music and literature. The year 1836, the *annus mirabilis* of Transcendentalism that produced Emerson's *Nature* and so many of the lesser manifestoes, was a climax in Cranch's life in that he turned west to grow up with the country. This climax was not very great: his first stop in the West was St. Louis, where he became assistant to his cousin William Greenleaf Eliot. Eliot established in St. Louis the first Unitarian Church of that city and a family that was to produce the renegade Anglo-Catholic poet quoted at the outset of this essay; Cranch's destiny was only to move on once more.

These were hard times for a young man of artistic bent trying to get started in a profession for which his calling was none too sure. In the midst of his distress Cranch wrote sadly and a little pompously, in a letter of August, 1837:

> I have *never* been accustomed to give full vent to my feelings and thoughts: I cannot do it. . . . In general, I am reserved, *secretive*, proud, indolent, but above all *diffident*. This besetting diffidence lies at the root of all my reserve, and keeps me again and again silent and seemingly cold. . . .[4]

Had he only known it, Cranch was on the threshold of his great opportunity. In Louisville, James Freeman Clarke was becoming restless, and someone was needed to fill his pulpit temporarily so that he might take his excursion back east. In assuming Clarke's pulpit Cranch also undertook responsibility for Clarke's magazine, the *Western Messenger*. It was this episode that offered him the first real opportunity to employ his hitherto frustrated literary talents.[5]

The *Western Messenger* was a periodical less of the West than of New England. Even in its earliest days, when it was seeking out Western poets and Western writers, Easterners made up the overwhelming majority of its contributors. It lived up to its title as a journal of religion and literature: published side-by-side in one issue, for example, were an article called "Brief Review of Trinitarian Proof Texts" and a sketch, "Foot-Prints on the Sea-Shore," "by the Author of Twice-Told Tales." Although it reviewed all the newest books by Emerson, Brownson, Ripley, and Alcott, its articles indicate that there was, nevertheless, a slight cultural lag in Louisville; they were mostly polemics in the rear-guard action of the Unitarian controversy. The taste of the editors was scarcely infallible since they offered in the same number of the *Messenger* Emerson's "Rhodora" and Cranch's **"Lines on the Death of an Aged Relative,"** which begin:

> She hath passed away—her soul hath fled,
>   That meek, pure-hearted one;
> She is numbered with the sainted dead;—
>   Her Pilgrimage is done.[6]

This questionable taste of the editors is responsible for the one thing for which Cranch is most frequently remembered: as a parlor game he and Clarke used to draw caricatures to illustrate particularly fantastic lines from Emerson, such as the famous "I am a transparent eyeball" passage of *Nature*. (To illustrate this passage, Cranch drew a cartoon figure, all legs and eyeball, gazing over the sunlit vistas of a spreading New England landscape.) Cranch's sense of humor did not have the courage of its convictions, and he spent the rest of his life disclaiming any intent to ridicule. It is all too easy to believe his disclaimers since about this time he preached on the great eclipse of 1838, denouncing the low masqueraders of Cincinnati who celebrated the occasion of God's handiwork so impiously by revels.

At the moment of America's greatest movement to the frontier Cranch found the West too full for him and took his solitary way back to Boston. This was one of the great pilgrimages of his life, and almost as soon as he was settled, he wrote excitedly:

> New England is the place of places for all sorts of views. Things new and old are brought to light, and have their advocates and believers, and deniers. We have one Miller here, an ignorant preacher, who teaches that the world is coming to an end in 1843. We have another man who is zealous as a flaming fire in lectures upon English grammar!—defying his antagonists like a second David. We have had lectures on the Turks by a Turk; on Switzerland by a German, the lamented Dr. Follen; on Geology, on carbonic acid gas, on Eastern customs, on storms, on Shakespeare, and on the Smithsonian legacy. . . . In fact this Boston is a very Athens.[7]

In the excitement Cranch came to the conclusion that he was not made for the ministry and decided to drop it. He thought seriously of joining the experiment of Brook Farm; though he never quite brought himself to that, he did manage to visit the little band there as often as possible and help their morale with his flute-playing and singing, which often brought tears to their eyes. He even overcame his "besetting diffidence," and having heard of the "New Magazine" that was projected, screwed up his courage sufficiently to submit a couple of poems to Emerson.

These two poems were printed in the very first issue of the *Dial*. The first of them, **"To the Aurora Borealis,"** is, for the first half at least, uniquely brilliant in Cranch's work, worthy of the praise that Emerson so lavishly bestowed. The other poem, **"Gnosis,"** is, unfortunately perhaps, far more representative of Cranch and of Transcendental poetry in general, so that it is through this latter poem that one can best approach a critical estimate of Cranch's work:

> Thought is deeper than all speech,
>   Feeling deeper than all thought;
> Souls to souls can never teach
>   What unto themselves was taught.
>
> We are spirits clad in veils;
>   Man by man was never seen;
> All our deep communing fails
>   To remove the shadowy screen.
>
> Heart to heart was never known;
>   Mind with mind did never meet;
> We are columns left alone
>   Of a temple once complete.
>
> Like the stars that gem the sky,
>   Far apart though seeming near,
> In our light we scattered lie;
>   All is thus but starlight here.
>
> What is social company
>   But a babbling summer stream?
> What our wise philosophy
>   But the glancing of a dream?
>
> Only when the sun of love
>   Melts the scattered stars of thought,
> Only when we live above
>   What the dim-eyed world hath taught,
>
> Only when our souls are fed
>   By the fount that gave them birth,
> And by inspiration led,
>   Which they never drew from earth,
>
> We like parted drops of rain,
>   Swelling till they melt and run,
> Shall be all absorbed again,
>   Melting, flowing into one.[8]

The theme of **"Gnosis"** is a recurrent one in the work of Cranch and his contemporaries, expressing as it does the atomistic side of Transcendental social theory. The epistemological revolution ultimately derived from John Locke had led to the issues of romantic philosophy whereby the individual came to question his own and the world's existence so profoundly as to neglect such intermediate groupings as society offered. The homely reference of Emerson's imagination in a poem like "Each and All" could save him from such an implicit solipsism, but Cranch had no such resource.

Cranch's limitations are again revealed in his attempts to use the Emersonian dialectic, most noticeably in the brace of poems which he called "Inworld" and "Outworld." Together these poems make up a kind of Kantian reverie on the great epistemological dilemma in which Man and the Over-Soul, alone in the universe, debate the thesis that "Nothing is, if thou are not."[9] Emerson had the ability so to express his contradictions in symbols as to force an unconscious synthesis in the mind of his audience; Cranch's efforts in the same mode fall flat just because of his limited powers of expression, so that his product is a little more than the inanity of an unresolved contradiction.[10]

Cranch's intellectual grasp of the richness and uses of symbolism was far less competent than Emerson's. Emerson saw in the fact "a double, a quadruple, a centuple" meaning, whereas Cranch usually saw in the fact only a one-to-one correspondence to some spiritual truth. So he tended to limp through his verse explicitly philosophizing far more often than he employed even his limited command of the symbol. As late as 1873, in an article called **"Symbolism and Language,"** he was still serving a much-watered broth from Emerson's *Nature* as news and promising of Emmanuel Swedenborg that "the time is coming when this great seer will be recognized as one of the most resplendent lights of modern thought."[11] But, for Cranch, symbolism and correspondence meant a much too simple progression from the world of substance to the world of idea so that in his highly mechanical poem, **"Correspondences,"** he could offer lines like:

> Every thought that speaks to the senses was meant for
>   the spirit:
> Nature is but a scroll, God's handwriting thereon.[12]

Devotee of Emerson that he was, he went too often to the schools of Felicia Hemans and Henry Wadsworth Longfellow for his technical inspiration.

Cranch was deceived, as many a young Transcendentalist poet was deceived, into putting too great reliance on his "genius" as against his "talent," on "nature" as against "reason," on "Reason" as against "Understanding":

> Speak not, reason not—but live;
> Reins to thy true nature give,
> And in each unconscious act
> Forth will shine the hidden fact.[13]

Unfortunately, this program did no more for his command of language than it did for his mastery of the Emersonian dialectic. For Cranch, Reason and Understanding were uncannily alike. It is pitiful to read in one of his best scanned poems the ludicrous cliché, "my wild, broken verse."[14] The reason his "wild, broken verse" reads so tamely is not far to seek: if we inspect his bravest intuitions, we find that Cranch's inner world, like that of the **"Blind Seer"** of his poem,[15] is a world of *thought* and thought alone, at least so far as he is able to express himself. Locked in a world of banal conventionality, his philosophical poetry was one day to degenerate into a grim parody of his early work.[16]

The unrelieved ordinariness of Cranch's mind concealed the fact that he was a man who had feelings and a very real love of nature. He was never able to unify the modes of experience sufficiently to give us what we call "metaphysical" poetry; his responses to life and the natural world tended to remain in a totally different category from the conceits of his philosophical poetry. This is by no means to say that he was devoid of sensitivity. Thus, with the feeling of liberation that he got by coming back to Boston in 1840, he wrote in his journal:

> What should we be but for the gentle teachings of this green summer time? I feel that I am at God's school, when I sit on the grass, under the elms, and look about me, and think upon Nature's impersonality. Man has not broken into the charmed circle in any way. Least of all does Nature imitate the obtrusiveness of our moral codes. She reads her mysterious fables, but we are not pestered by the word "application" at the bottom of the picture.[17]

Thirty-five years later he published his pair of sonnets called **"The Garden"**:

> Nought know we but the heart of summer here.
> On the tree-shadowed velvet lawn I lie,
> And dream up through the close leaves to the sky,
> And weave Arcadian visions in a sphere
> Of peace. The steaming heat broods all around,
> But only lends a quiet to the hours.
> The aromatic life of countless flowers,
> The singing of a hundred birds, the sound
> Of rustling leaves, go pulsing through the green
> Of opening vistas in the garden walks.
> Dear summer, on thy balmy breast I lean
> And care not how the moralist toils or talks;
> Repose and Beauty preach a gospel, too,
> Deep as that sterner creed the Apostles knew.
>
> Is there no praise of God amid the bowers
> Of summer idleness? Still must we toil
> And think, and tease the conscience, and so soil
> With over careful fingering the flowers
> That blow within the garden of the heart?
> Still must we be machines for grinding out
> Thin prayers and moralisms? Much I doubt,
> Pale priest of a thorn-girded church, thy part
> Is small in this wide breathing universe.
> Least can I find thy title and thy worth
> Here, where with myriad chords the musical earth
> Is rhyming to the enraptured poet's verse.
> Better thy cowl befits the cloister's gloom;
> Its shadow blots the garden and its bloom.[18]

"The Garden" represents the best of Cranch's poetry. As so often in this period, the form of the sonnet with its strict requirements served to make a writer who was less than a master craftsman aware of technical problems that he was unable to formulate for himself. Further, Cranch here succeeded in fusing sensation, emotion, intellectual structure, and expression into an organic poetic whole. The internal rhythms declare that here Cranch wrote with an integration beyond the reach of his usual self: the first lines of the second sonnet invite comparison without embarrassment with "The Collar," by George Herbert; yet the Transcendentalist piety of Cranch calls him, not to duty, but to the languor and repose reflected in the rhythm of the whole and dominant in the first sonnet. In its moral and rhetorical development, **"The Garden"** is a rewriting and reversal of the great Herbert poem, not unworthy of its model.

In these two sonnets Cranch passionately expressed the stand that he resolved on at the end of his great pilgrimage to Boston. In 1841, while he was recovering from some slight illness, he amused himself with paints and brushes and discovered that it was landscape painting to which he wanted to devote his life. When he gave up the ministry for this, he renounced much more than a pulpit he had never won. In taking the path of "repose and leisure," he squared himself against all the worldly demands implicit in the dominant tradition of his social world.[19] He rejected not only the role of "pale priest of a thorn-girded church" but his very livelihood. He said with Emerson, "Why so busy, little man?" With Hawthorne, he openly defied his ancestors. With Alcott, he undertook a long "apprenticeship to leisure." When he came to marry, he offered his wife, not the security and status of a ministerial position, but the opportunity to keep a boardinghouse in New York so that he might paint. Without any financial justification whatsoever he elected himself into the leisure class and betook himself to Europe. Tilting at the windmill of "the Protestant ethic," he revolutionized his New England conscience; and what is more, for the rest of his life he kept writing to his older brother, Edward, urging him to quit the bar and join him in his indolence.

In his attitude toward the arts Cranch compensated for the "besetting diffidence" that he had felt as a minister. Just as he was overconfident about his natural gifts as a writer, so, in painting, he was always sure that he needed only a couple of lessons and that he could carry on with his newly chosen métier from there. There seems to be no way of learning directly whether this breezy confidence was justified. His landscapes are not listed in the museums, and the most complete records do not disclose that even a single one of them has been sold on the American market. All that we know of his painting, to which he devoted the best fifty years of his life, is the appraisal of Henry Tuckerman, whose estimate might serve for Cranch's poetry as well:

> There is, perhaps, a want of emphasis in the landscapes of Cranch, especially in the details of rock and foliage; but in the more ethereal elements, he often exhibits a skill and feeling which win the spectator; his clouds, atmosphere, and all the traits which bear generalization, evidence the hand of one in true though often vague relation with nature, especially in her loveliest and most serene moods.[20]

Although Cranch's service to American art is not to be learned about in museums, there is perhaps no better memorial to the quiet courage and profound earnestness which he lent to a movement of greater artists than himself than his own poem, **"Ars Longa, Vita Brevis."** This poem is superb autobiography, for which the mediocrity of the verse is its own poignant commentary. The poem starts with Cranch's recollection of the "lonely read" on which he started with but a few companions:

> To live for Nature, finding truth
>   In beauty, and the shrines of art;
> To consecrate our joyous youth
>   To aims outside the common mart.

While he often "turned aside and lingered long," his comrades moved on more purposefully, and some, enjoying "blithe self-confidence," achieved their highest aims; some even won recognition from the very public that had rejected them. Neither kind of success ever came for Cranch.

> And still though oft I bind my sheath
>   In fields my comrades have not known;
> Though Art is long and life is brief,
>   And youth has now forever flown,
> I would not lose the raptures sweet,
>   Nor scorn the toil of earlier years;
> Still would I climb with eager feet,
>   Though towering height on height appears.
> And up the mountain road I see
>   A younger throng with voices loud,
> Who side by side press on with me,
>   Till I am lost amid the crowd.[21]

Cranch's significance, just as he so candidly remarked, did decline as a younger generation brought reinforcements of new blood and strength; yet, had his achievement been even slighter than it was, Cranch would deserve remembrance as a private in the ranks of those who struggled for the birth of American art. The magnanimity with which he accepted his being "lost amid the crowd" underscores for us the devotion he was able to bring as a minor talent to the making of a great literature.

Notes

1. Leonora Cranch Scott, *The Life and Letters of Christopher Pearse Cranch* (Boston and New York, 1917), p. 50.

2. *Ibid.*, p. 51.

3. Edward Waldo Emerson, *The Early Years of the Saturday Club, 1855-1870* (Boston and New York, 1918), p. 47.

4. Scott, *op. cit.*, p. 35.

5. It is interesting to note, as a sidelight on Cranch's career, the progress he made in the periodicals he wrote for, since his progress was to be significant of the Transcendental movement in general. His first vehicle was the *Western Messenger, Devoted to Religion and Literature*; later he would write for the *Harbinger, Devoted to Social and Political Progress*;

eventually his work was to be printed in the *Galaxy, an Illustrated Magazine of Entertaining Reading.* The subtitles describe the path of a great intellectual Odyssey.

6. *Western Messenger,* VII, 199 (July, 1839).

7. Scott, *op. cit.,* pp. 47-48.

8. *Dial,* I, 98 (July, 1840).

9. *Dial,* II, 288-290 (Jan., 1842). Because of the printer's cuts, "Inworld" had appeared without its mate in the previous issue (II, 271-272).

10. This persistent disproportion between conception and rendering is evident not only in his lyric poetry but in the trials he made of other literary modes. The two children's books on which he put at least some financial hopes are *The Last of the Huggermuggers* (Boston, 1855) and *Kobboltozo* (Boston, 1857). These fantastic tales fail to achieve the circumstantial interest of Gulliver, or even of *Jack-o'-the-Beanstalk,* much less the satirical interest of which they are capable. The island on which the last of a great-hearted race of giants wither and die through the machinations of a mean-spirited dwarf is fine scaffolding, but the plot is not solidly executed; only a minor figure among the shipwrecked visitors, that Barnum-like Yankee Zebedec Nabbum, really engages the imagination of the reader. Equally unmemorable is Cranch's contribution (*Aeneid,* 2 vols., Boston and New York, 1872) to the series of epic translations by Longfellow, Bryant, and Bayard Taylor, all of which appeared within a single lustrum. Cranch chose blank verse as the medium for Vergil's epic in order to escape "that seductive siren Rhyme" whose "jingling chains" had imprisoned Dryden. His translation is literal, his language clear, his scansion unexceptionable, but there is a pervading lack of elegance; he banished the *heroic* with the couplet.

11. *Galaxy,* XVI, 375 (Sept., 1873).

12. *Dial,* I, 381 (Jan., 1841).

13. *Dial,* II, 484 (April, 1842).

14. In "Memory," *Western Messenger,* VI, 183 (Jan., 1839).

15. *Dial,* II, 47-48 (July, 1841).

16. This was to be his challenge to Darwinian philosophy in "Survival of the Fittest":

"Raise your scientific lore,
    Grant us larger definitions,
Souls are surely something more
    Than a bundle of cognitions."

And this is a sample of his commemoration verse from "The Victories of Peace":

"Boast not when musketry rattles
    O'er corpses of landsmen and seamen.
Gains that are greater than battles
    Come with the ballots of freemen."

Both poems are in *Ariel and Caliban, with Other Poems* (Boston and New York, 1887), pp. 100, 107.

17. *Dial,* I, 379 (Jan., 1841).

18. *The Bird and the Bell, with Other Poems* (Boston, 1875), pp. 290-291.

19. It is interesting that there is but one grating word in each of these sonnets that comprise Cranch's confession of faith—"moralist" in the former, "moralisms" in the latter.

20. *Book of the Artists, American Artist Life* (New York, 1867), p. 461. As against the paragraph devoted to Cranch by H. T. Tuckerman, S. G. W. Benjamin gives him a sentence in his *Art in America, a Critical and Historical Sketch* (New York, 1880), saying that he "has exhibited in his Venetian landscapes a correct perception of color, while his method lacks a firmness of drawing, and shows traces of foreign influence more than that of many of our artists who studied abroad at this time" (p. 76).

21. *Ariel and Caliban,* pp. 90-91.

F. DeWolfe Miller (essay date 1951)

SOURCE: Miller, F. DeWolfe. "Christopher Pearse Cranch—Poet, Painter, and Humorist." In *Christopher Pearse Cranch and His Caricatures of New England Transcendentalism,* pp. 3-28. Cambridge: Harvard University Press, 1951.

[*In the following excerpt, Miller assesses Cranch's modest reputation as artist and writer.*]

The character of Christopher Pearse Cranch presents no anomalies and no particularly difficult paradoxes. The even moral tenor of his long good life reveals him as a man to whom it was so natural to be good that no especial praise is suggested. Diffidence was his most marked characteristic, and the trait of course found its way into much of his work. We are bound to conclude that he would have made more mistakes had he been less timid. He did not have the vigor and vinegar which disposed his friend Theodore Parker toward barn-burning. On the other hand he did not have the great reserve of moral strength that enabled Emerson, his elder and master, to meet a storm of incrimination with placid composure. His temperament is rather to be compared to that of his lifelong intimate, John Sullivan Dwight, who resigned his pulpit like Cranch and became the gentle arbiter of America's taste in music.

Though it apparently never occurred to Cranch to be otherwise than good, he could have done otherwise than he did. In the early few years of service as a missionary Unitarian minister, he could have fallen in with the orthodox element and lived a comfortable—and probably anonymous—life. He chose instead the unpopular cause of transcendentalism. And it is by no means certain that he gave up the ministry because of the resulting insecurity. Landscape painting, to which he turned, was far more precarious, especially for a man of thirty who had had almost no previous training.

The latitude of behavior afforded an artist who resided in New York, Italy, and France, he of course never took advantage of. The history of his life is thus lacking in the dramatic element and sensationalism which biographers were seeking in the decades immediately following the appearance of *The Life and Letters of Christopher Pearse Cranch,* published by his daughter in 1917, when the reaction against everything Victorian was at its height. The biography was prepared accurately and well, but through a shift in emphasis it creates an illusion of the comfortableness for which the twentieth century (partially through envy, no doubt) has so derided the nineteenth. One literary historian, reading it too hastily, actually got the impression that Cranch was a man of "ample means."

The modest and diffident quality in Cranch's personality is the most difficult aspect of his character to explain. From youth to old age he was so handsome that nearly all who wrote about him were impelled to mention his appearance. Poe, who thought Cranch's profile "hard and disagreeable," was the only dissenter, but even the admitted that Cranch was "not unhandsome," though his description in the Literati article is not accurate enough to assure us that he knew Cranch well. There is evidence quite ample that of all the New England Brahmins Cranch was, if not the most striking, certainly one of the most handsome.

If his appearance gave him no grounds for modesty, neither did the variety of his talents, which were so diverse that he was looked upon as a colorful figure. His gentle humor, his flute and his plaintive singing, his ironic sketches and illustrated parodies—these casual things, added to his gradually accumulated knowledge of art and music and the literature of several languages, made him good company among those who were accustomed to the best, though what he himself preferred was the single companionship of a friend like Clarke, Dwight, Parker, Story, or Lowell. James Russell Lowell was so fond of him that when Cranch begged poverty as the reason for not going to Boston for a visit at the time of Lowell's half-century birthday, Lowell offered to "stump the rusty" for the trip from New York. "Cranch always reminds me of Clough," he told Norton, as warrant of his desire to have Cranch with him.

Since a man with such capacities and bearing as Cranch's would have no apparent reason to be personally or intellectually shy, this quality in him can be explained only in the terms of inheritance. George William Curtis explained it thus; and Lowell said that Cranch had gifts enough for three—only his foolish fairy left the *brass* out when she brought her gifts to his cradle.[1]

Yet Cranch's cradle was a good one, for through several generations it had united musical and artistic talents with strong character. The family was English for many generations back, though there was a tradition (which could have originated in jest) that the somewhat rare name Cranch was anglicized from the German family of painters, the Cranachs.[2] Richard Cranch, the grandfather, immigrated to America, where he became a lifelong friend of John Adams, he and Adams having married the remarkable Smith sisters, Mary and Abigail. Self-educated, he was well versed in theology, and ultimately became a judge and received an honorary degree from Harvard. The next generation, the cousins William Cranch and John Quincy Adams, went to Harvard together and were very intimate in early life. In 1801 William Cranch was appointed by John Adams to a judgeship in the District of Columbia, and despite his strong Federal politics, was made chief judge of the District Circuit Court by Jefferson in 1805. He held this position until he died in 1855 with one of the longest and most consistent records in the history of the nation. He is remembered among other things for his nine volumes of reports of cases argued before the Supreme Court, covering the era of John Marshall's most vital opinions on constitutional questions.

William Cranch married Nancy Greenleaf, whose sisters were the wives of Judge Thomas Dawes and Noah Webster. She bore him thirteen children in twenty-three years and lived to be seventy-seven. Some of the children were not so resilient. Three died in infancy and three others shortly after reaching maturity. John, an older brother of Christopher Pearse, became a portrait painter. Emerson in the journal of his first trip abroad recorded the conversations with him in Italy as the greatest experience of the trip, next to meeting Carlyle. Edward, another older brother, spent his life in Cincinnati, a lawyer who along with his other avocations designed and decorated pottery. Though they saw each other infrequently, Edward and Pearse (the family used Cranch's middle name) were intensely devoted to each other throughout their lives.

Among the sisters there was Elizabeth, who married a cousin, Rufus Dawes, romancer and poet who catered to the annual and gift-book tastes; and Abby (named for Abigail Adams), who married her cousin William Greenleaf Eliot, Jr., and became the grandmother of T. S. Eliot.[3]

Cranch was the tenth child and was given the old family name, Christopher Pearse, after the brother before him, of the same name, died in infancy. He was born on March 8, 1813, in a section of the District of Columbia which has since been ceded back to Virginia and is now a part of Alexandria. Virginia librarians sometimes claim him, and he is represented in *The Library of Southern Literature,* but he is actually no more southern than Poe was the "Bostonian" which he early acclaimed himself. Cranch was quite New England.

Although the family was Unitarian in belief, its religious regimen revealed the tenacious pattern of Puritan habits and standards. Some of the children exhibited a very strong sense of religious duty,[4] but none of the daughters became minister's wives and none of the sons ministers, save for

Pearse, whose decision was at the best perfunctory. He was graduated at Columbian College (now George Washington University) in 1832 at the age of nineteen before he even considered the ministry. On the advice of his father and the urging of his cousin William Eliot, he made the decision which was to take him among the transcendentalists. After hasty tutoring in German, he entered the Harvard Divinity School, where he was instructed by the two Henry Wares and by Palfrey, "orthodox" ministers of the unorthodox Unitarian faith. The most notable divinity students there in his time were Theodore Parker and John Sullivan Dwight—and Cranch himself. Some of the other ministerial candidates later developed transcendental leanings, but among those who were in school at that time, it was these three friends who became the most outspoken adherents of the movement which began to make itself felt shortly after Cranch completed his training and entered the ministry in 1835.

Cranch and Parker were close friends until the latter's death, but it was between Dwight and Cranch that an almost idyllic friendship developed. Born in the same year, they never lost contact with each other after their love of music made them friends at the Divinity School. They both preached transcendentalism from the pulpit and they both left the pulpit, one to devote himself to music and poetry and translation, the other to painting and poetry and translation. They spanned a good part of the century together, and died within a twelvemonth. After their beards had grown white, Cranch's daughter Caroline painted their portraits, the one for love, the other for the Harvard Musical Association.

Dwight was ordained after a few years, but Cranch, whose diffidence may have made him a poor pulpit orator (though Dwight and his congregation thought otherwise), was never settled. Engaged by the Unitarian Association, he was a missionary at large, preaching for periods of varying length in churches from Maine to Richmond and as far west as Illinois and St. Louis. The first winter he spent snowbound in Andover, Maine, where he consoled himself by writing a ballad, **"Childe Christopher,"** in parody of "The Ancient Mariner," and by illustrating it with marginal sketches.[5] In this good-humored (if not particularly *good*) protest against having been sent into a land of Philistines, so cold that the very logs "Did beg for to be burned," there can be discerned the first indication that he might not follow the pattern expected of a son of Judge Cranch. For a few years to come, however, he was to counter these mundane impulses by writing to Dwight of the glories of the pulpit and rededicating himself in his journal to his duties.

The next year (1836-37) had much in store for him. During the summer in Richmond, Virginia, two cultured, older Jewesses by sympathy and flattery seem to have quickened very greatly his poetic impulses. A second and different experience came that fall. Aged twenty-three, he had yet done no more than conventional reading in philosophy, but he responded with immediate eagerness to Emerson's *Nature,* which he found in St. Louis after he arrived in December. He absorbed this little book, and then read *Sartor Resartus,* which had been published some months earlier. He went on to the third and least important of the transcendental books of the year, his cousin William H. Furness's *Remarks on the Four Gospels.*

In December and January he wrote a long letter to Edward, exalting this rich reading. The letter can be said to be a prose draft of his poem **"Enosis,"** one of the most famous though hardly the best of the poems of the transcendental movement. "Enosis" was not actually composed until three years later, but the letter makes it clear that the ideas and much of the phraseology of the poem were developed at this time.[6] It was recently pointed out that **"Enosis"** has suffered considerably in interpretation because subsequent anthologists perpetuated an error made in an anthology of 1882 which printed the title as "Gnosis" ("knowing"), a word vaguely appropriate for a part of the poem, but misleading for the piece as a whole.[7] **"Enosis"** ("communion") was inspired directly by an application of ideas which Cranch found in *Sartor Resartus* and applied to his lifelong desire to achieve an ideal rapport, both spiritual and intellectual, with some favored friend—in this case, his brother Edward. Cranch deplores the barriers, psychological and materialistic, which block the idealized, even mystical, relationship between two souls. The experience is just as elusive and, if achieved, just as fleeting as Shelley's mystical union with "awful Loveliness" and Keats' yearning after an idealized beauty. The psychology of the poem fascinated William James, with whom it was a favorite; and a line from it has supplied the title of a recent poem—"A Temple Once Complete," which is one of the best poems in Edd Winfield Parks' *Predestinate Iron* (1948).

The tripping meter of **"Enosis,"** borrowed apparently from the hymns he gave out on Sunday, though unsuitable, could not spoil entirely the images and idea which have made the piece famous. This and another poem evoked warm praise from Emerson and won Cranch an invitation to come for a visit with him at Concord—alone. Two years later (five years after the poem was actually conceived) some of the same ideas and symbols appeared in Emerson's "Over-Soul," but if there was any debt, as there probably was not, Emerson had already justified it in a letter to Cranch, in words which should do much to make reasonable the account books which critics keep: "If my thoughts have interested you, it only shows how much they were already yours."

Cranch had hardly finished reading the new transcendental books when he began to contribute frequently to the *Western Messenger,* a New England magazine which like many a New England schoolteacher and minister of the day, had a western address. Since youth, Cranch had occasionally sent things to the newspapers, but his first magazine appearance had been in the *Knickerbocker* in the fall of 1836. For the *Messenger* he now produced both prose and poetry, and he unfortunately exhumed some juvenile writings from his portfolio. Jejune religiosity marked most of these productions. For two or three years the prose was largely uninspired arguments for Unitarianism. Far superior was his review of Emerson's *The American Scholar*; and his defense of transcendentalism in 1841 can still be read quite profitably.

In poetry he was early disposed toward the sonnet, a form which he ultimately mastered and in which his best work was at least equal to the best sonnets of any of his American contemporaries with the possible exception of Jones Very. Sonnets were frequent among the poems he gave the *Western Messenger*; and though the subtitle committed the magazine to both religion and literature, the religious note in Cranch's contributions was heavy. His personality, however, began to show signs of a slight shearing, for at the same time that he was publishing banalities in the *Messenger* he was writing fairly good nature poems unencumbered with a moral, and these he soon began to send off to the *Southern Literary Messenger*, as if to hide them from his fellows or himself. At a time when according to Clarke most of the poetasters were imitators of Shelley and Byron, Cranch's favorite was Wordsworth.[8] In his worst moments, however, he could be guilty of a near-parody of the popular Mrs. Hemans.

Between 1836 and 1839 Cranch spent something less than two years in the "West," never remaining in one location much more than a season. In the absence of editor James Freeman Clarke he prepared at least two numbers of the *Messenger*, which had begun to support the liberal side of the second Unitarian controversy and thus had become the first of the several transcendental magazines. In January 1839, shortly before he left the "West" for good, he was in Louisville with Clarke, who had just returned from Boston, exultant over the words and work of the new seer, Emerson. But, as the pages of the *Messenger* show, neither Clarke nor Cranch could be always serious, and they were soon drawing funny scraps about the man they would allow no one else to censure. Cranch's sketches were far the better, and soon after he departed on a six-month trip ending in Boston, Clarke sent the news of the drawings on ahead, and Cranch was called on for more and more cartoons.

In the winter of 1839-40 he attended Emerson's lectures on "The Present Age" and in visits to Theodore Parker discovered that his views coincided almost exactly with those of the "learned Theban" or, as Cranch at other times called Parker, "the very athlete of scholars."[9] Cranch, enjoying himself immensely now, wrote to his admiring sister Margaret:

> We have transcendental and aesthetic gatherings at a great rate—and they make me sing at them all. I have worn my Tyrolese yodlers almost to the bones. People ask if I am not a German!—in fact I am quite a singing lion. My *flute* is unknown altogether—and my guitar almost as much . . . Sunday evenings I go into Ripleys about 9 and eat baked potatoes & drink ale. Sometimes I go to the oratorios—sometimes to lectures—sometimes to parties—So we keep it up.[10]

His drawings, he told her, had passed from house to house through the city, so that he heard reports of them wherever he went.

He wrote and sent to Emerson two poems (**"Enosis"** and another) for the newly projected *Dial* and then went on to Maine to preach transcendentalism to the heathen. Among the Philistines he met one cultured young married woman, whom Dwight had warmly recommended to him. Cranch was astonished and a little bewildered when after a few meetings together, playing the flute, singing, and reading German, he and Mrs. Little blurted out their mutual love. The consequences were not dreadful. He soon returned to Massachusetts, where he could write to Dwight that he was healing quickly, though he feared for the one he left behind, who "had never had her feelings drawn out in full sympathy before."[11]

Cranch was by this time outspoken in his support of the liberal point of view. Although he finally accepted and gloried in the name "transcendentalist," he at first objected to it—and on very good grounds—as nothing better than a nickname. His father became alarmed when as far off as Washington he got hints of his son's inclinations; and Cranch, preaching at Quincy, "gave out quite a stream of transcendentalism" and provoked John Quincy Adams to one of the most famous of all the "common-sense" utterances on the "hurly-burly innovation."[12]

In August of 1840 Cranch responded to Emerson's invitation and spent a few days with him at Concord. It was an ill-chosen time for Cranch, who during that month suffered the first attack of an illness—a nervous depression of some sort—which chronically annoyed him for three years. Despite Cranch's silence, Emerson talked a good deal, "read poetry—of his own—of his anonymous young lady correspondents, and of old Ben Jonson's." They walked a great deal, went huckleberrying, and saw Walden Pond.[13]

The next summer, while at home in Washington, he discovered to his delight that he could paint a little in oils. Painting seemed to relax him during the spells of depression when he could neither write nor think. A shocking letter from Dwight,[14] who had been forced from his pulpit because of his transcendental leanings, precipitated Cranch's decision not to become ordained, and to look about for something else to do—but it was two years yet before he made a final decision.

In the meanwhile he became one of the most frequent and important contributors to the *Dial*. Brook Farm, another transcendental adventure, he observed with personal interest, though he never did become a member. He visited the "Hive" at least twice, and by his presence made a permanent impression, especially on the younger members of the colony.

In the course of his duties he found himself at Fishkill-on-the-Hudson, in the home of John Peter De Windt, whose seven daughters were descendants of John and Abigail Adams and therefore Cranch's cousins. His cousin Elizabeth wanted tutoring in German, and after a few lessons they were engaged. In October 1843, two years later, they were married, with Charles Fenno Hoffman as Cranch's groomsman. A gift of a thousand dollars from the wealthy father-in-law enabled the young couple to furnish a boarding house in New York, where Cranch could set up a studio. Among the boarders were William Henry Channing and family, Margaret Fuller, and Caroline Sturgis, transcendentalist friends all.[15]

He had ceased his contributions to the *Dial*, but he later continued his transcendental connections by sending the *Harbinger* some poetry and prose, and he contributed a bit to Channing's magazine, the *Present*. However, his poetical composition was much reduced by the necessity of learning to paint, and most of the little he did write went to magazines which paid him small sums—*Graham's, Godey's,* the *Democratic Review*—and to the gift annuals. In 1842, before he had published a volume of poetry, he had been generously represented in the first edition of Griswold's famous anthology, *The Poets and Poetry of America.*

In 1844 the most distinguished publishers of belles lettres in America, Carey and Hart, brought out his first volume, a thin, neatly printed book of selections, **Poems**, by Christopher Pearse Cranch. Poe, whose critical work in prosody originated in his analysis of Cranch's **"My Thoughts,"** said that the volume was most unmercifully treated and much injustice in his opinion done the poet, the "least intolerable of the school of Boston transcendentalists," whose poetry was among the *"truest"* in America. Though none of the reviews contained any more superlative praise than Poe's later articles on Cranch, certainly none of them were as unmerciful as Poe was in his sarcastic treatment of some of Cranch's conceits.

The emphasis in the little book of poems is on the inner life as against the crass utilitarianism to which the New England group were consistently opposed. In the weaker poems the thought is so sentimentalized that the reader is almost bound to be ironically affected when he reaches **"Field Notes,"** in which Cranch addresses himself to the select few:

> Him we will seek, and none but him,
> Whose inward sense hath not grown dim;
> Whose soul is steeped in Nature's tinct,
> And to the Universal linked;
> Who loves the beauteous Infinite
> With deep and ever new delight,
> And carrieth where'er he goes,
> The inborn sweetness of the rose,
> The perfume as of Paradise;
> The talisman above all price;
> The optic glass that wins from far
> The meaning of the utmost star;
> The key that opes the golden doors
> Where earth and heaven have piled their stores;
> The magic ring—the enchanter's wand,—
> The title-deed to Wonder-land;

> The wisdom that o'erlooketh sense,
> The clairvoyance of Innocence.

The light measures in which all of the transcendentalist poets framed their thoughts if not immediately successful frequently made the poem ridiculous. The poet who presumes a title deed to the Universal is in danger when he dallies with the perfume of Paradise. Cranch's lines, however, are successful within their limits. He sustains both mood and imagery and does not lapse into the mechanical banalities found in a comparable passage in Emerson's "Woodnotes":

> Caesar of his leafy Rome,
> There the poet is at home . . .
> In the wood he travels glad,
> Without better fortune had,
> Melancholy without bad.

Poems, 1844, of which five hundred copies were printed,[16] was no more salable than was Margaret Fuller's prose account, *Summer on the Lakes,* published in the same year. This he anticipated, but one of the reasons for publishing—to increase his magazine market—was thwarted by the fact that he soon went abroad, where he was absorbed in landscape painting.

In his new profession Cranch received very little formal training. Thomas Cole and Asher B. Durand, the leading landscape painters of the era, gave him "useful hints," and he took a few lessons from John Greenough in Boston. His brother John reports that he did no copying during his apprenticeship, having preferred to learn directly from nature.[17] In this he may well have been following Durand's advice, though he did not in later years follow Durand's precedent of completing the entire picture out of doors.

In 1846, having received some sort of financial backing—apparently from Mr. De Windt—the Cranches departed rather hastily for Italy where they remained for three years, lacking not for good New England company. The country was swarming with Yankee artists, writers, and travelers, some of them transient and some rather fixed. The Cranches went over with their young friend George William Curtis, soon to become famous; and they sailed the same day that Margaret Fuller departed by another route for Italy. William Wetmore Story, who back in Boston had practiced his pencil on Cranch's profile, was in Italy, about to give up law and become a sculptor. He was wealthy and generous and his presence made life more pleasant for the Cranches. He thought so much of Cranch that he offered to share his purse: "Let us spend together and make life as happy as we can."[18]

The Cranches lived in Rome and in Sorrento, finally going to Florence in December 1848 for their last six months abroad. There they were on friendly terms with the Brownings, both of whom helped Cranch revise the longest poem he had written. **"The Bird and the Bell,"** which was to become the title poem of a volume published many years later, was a symbolic polemic opposing authoritarian religion. The bird's clear and spontaneous notes are tokens of a free and natural worship, while the clangor of the bell summons men to worship by habit and command. One of the transcendentalists, Brownson, after a series of theological handsprings became a Roman Catholic at last, but as the rest of the group objected even to the mild restrictions of a liberal faith like Unitarianism, they would naturally not be well disposed toward the formalism of the Roman church. Prompted by Parker, who begged an illustrated letter from abroad, Cranch had, before he wrote the poem, sketched out in rhymed prose and in india-ink drawings many of his objections to the religious practices in Italy.[19]

In 1849 the Cranches returned to New York with the two children, George William and Leonora, who had been born in Italy. During the three years abroad Cranch had sold pictures totaling $2000—less than $700 a year. His earnings in New York for 1850 were "over $800." Judge Cranch, who had worked through all his debts, sent him $250; and about the time the third child, Caroline Amelia, was born in 1853 he inherited $400 from an uncle. When Judge Cranch died in 1855 Pearse's inheritance was less than $70. If Mr. De Windt was continuing his aid, it could not have been great, for Cranch continued to allude to his precarious position on up until 1870, when after her father's death Mrs. Cranch was made beneficiary of a trust which in 1890 amounted to about $54,000 and earned about $3,600 annually.[20]

As early as 1844 Cranch was represented in the annual exhibits of the National Academy of Design, but his paintings passed with only cursory notice. Upon returning to New York he immediately sold three Italian scenes to the American Art-Union, which soon thereafter purchased a newly painted Hudson River landscape. In the spring of 1850 he was represented in the National Academy with five pictures which received what he considered "favorable notice." The criticism actually was not enthusiastic, but he at least had emerged from a horde of artists; his name appeared in the notices along with men like Durand and Kensett; and he was made an associate in the Academy that summer. The picture which was considered his best was a landscape, "The Deserted Hut at Sunset," which was described as a quiet lake, shut in by hills, with an old hut in the foreground.[21] This of course was a conventional subject, though a dead tree (which appeared *ad infinitum*) was a much more frequent gothic vestige than a decayed building.

Upon his reintroduction in New York Cranch took a position as a kind of major mediocrity in landscape painting. None of the critics charged him with being servilely imitative; some noticed a degree of individuality; but none ever remarked any particular strength. The critic who was warmest would more than likely turn out to be the one who found absolutely no place in art for work like W. S. Mount's "Eel Spearing"!

He busily spent the next four summers exploiting the favorite scenes of the Hudson River School—the Catskills, the Berkshire Hills, Lake George, and Lake Mohonk, and of course Niagara and the Hudson. He occasionally went on painting junkets with other "Hudson River" men. In the summer of 1852 he took his family to Lenox, where he rented the small red house which the Hawthornes had moved out of the previous November. They had just settled themselves in the rooms where *The House of Seven Gables* had been written, when they were called to Fishkill. When they arrived they found that Mrs. De Windt, her son-in-law, the landscape designer Andrew Jackson Downing, and Hawthorne's sister had been drowned in the burning of a river steamer.

The following year they received a letter from Story (enclosing one each from the Brownings), begging them to come abroad. The Cranches suddenly decided to beat winter across the Atlantic. They sailed for Paris, and intending to remain for a year or two stayed ten. The family lived in Paris, while Cranch foraged during the summer for subjects. He went several times to Barbizon to join the artists who were crowding the Forest of Fontainebleau. During two summers he visited Switzerland, and one winter he spent in Rome. He made two trips to Venice and, residing in the rooms which Félix Ziem had previously occupied, made Venetian pictures somewhat after the manner of Ziem's popular work. After the Civil War these became Cranch's most popular paintings.

The year 1855 was a happy one. Lowell sought him out in Paris and made a lifelong friend of him; with Lowell he visited Story in London, saw the Brownings several times, and was entertained by Thackeray; he hurried back to Paris for the birth of Quincy Adams Cranch, the fourth and last child; he exhibited two pictures of Niagara in the Universal Exhibition;[22] and late in the year he published his first book for children.

But a vague melancholy clouds the rest of the Paris decade. Ada Shepard, the clever young woman who was shortly to become a governess in Hawthorne's family, was much impressed by the gentle, handsome Cranch, the happy home life, and the good music and musicians which one could usually expect in the home.[23] Appearances deceived her. Despite good friends—Henry James, Sr., and his family, and Frank Boott among many others—Cranch was not happy. "One must be of good stuff to be always merry," he wrote Edward at a time when he thought he was seldom merry. In depressed mood he would ask Curtis whether to come home. Of Lowell, who was busy with a new professorship, a new wife, and the new *Atlantic,* he would pitifully beg another letter.[24]

Cranch's story for children, *The Last of the Huggermuggers,* was followed by a sequel, *Kobboltozo,* published well in advance of the 1856 Christmas season. The first story, though late on the market, had been quite successful, and the publishers offered Cranch $500 for the next, and probably got a bargain, for the books were reprinted frequently and were referred to at the end of the century as familiar favorites. Illustrated by Cranch, they were beautifully printed and bound, and the sequel was widely advertised. Cranch prepared a third book the following year, but an international depression intervened, and the book was never published, unless bits of it appeared among the prose and poems which he supplied for *St. Nicholas* and other children's magazines up until the last year of his life. *Huggermugger* and *Kobboltozo* were allegorical tragedies about benevolent giants and envious dwarfs, which set no new standard. They survived longer than most juvenile literature of their time, but they were forgotten after sixty or seventy years.

Cranch with his family returned to America in 1863. George, sixteen years old, went immediately to a military school and the father went immediately to work. The Venice scenes were at once more popular than anything Cranch had yet painted, and by virtue of them he was made a full member of the National Academy in 1864. During the nine years after his return from abroad he enjoyed a minor sort of success, exhibiting a number of oils and water colors in the Academy each year and getting two and three times the price he had asked before.

The Hudson River School and subsequent landscape painters whose names are loosely associated with it enjoyed a rather wide contemporary vogue, but they were soon almost forgotten. If they were revived from oblivion in the early twentieth century, it was only for obloquy; however, with what may be termed the neonationalistic spirit of the past two decades, a certain historical interest has been developed. In 1945—the same year in which universities throughout the country began almost suddenly to offer programs in American civilization—the Art Institute of Chicago and the Whitney Museum of American Art in New York prepared an elaborate exhibition of the Hudson River School. Fifty nineteenth-century painters were represented, yet Cranch was omitted.[25] This neglect seems quite arbitrary, for no matter how strictly the term Hudson River School is limited, Cranch is among the group. He began his career among them, set up his easel alongside theirs, and was counted among them by his contemporaries. He perhaps yielded more to foreign influences than many of them did—especially later in his career—but several of his fellows also learned much abroad. Some of the artists represented in the 1945 exhibition received no more attention than he among their contemporaries, and have received little or none since. The intrinsic worth of all but a few of the Hudson River pictures is at best questionable, so that present interest in them is in the main historical. Valued thus, Cranch should not have been neglected if as many as fifty painters were to be represented. Like those of many contemporaries, his pictures have scarcely any market value today; the museums have only a token canvas or two, and in some cases none at all.

In his paintings Cranch seems to have attempted only once the humor which inspires the rough transcendental sketches and is less successful in his later poetry. In 1869 he exhibited in the Academy a satirical picture which, out of deference to the public, he called "A Visit to the Studio." In writing to Lowell, who had seen it and ordered a copy, Cranch used a more specific title, "The Geese; or the Critics," and reported that it had been much complimented.

At about this time Cranch began as a personal amusement to translate the *Aeneid* into blank verse. As the work progressed it became earnest, and with the aid of three young friends and the criticism of Lowell he completed the whole, which was published in 1872 in an edition uniform with Longfellow's *Dante,* Bryant's *Homer,* and Taylor's *Faust.* It was a faithful and accurate translation, in the placid measures and diction which he had already mastered. The book was quite favorably reviewed by men who had had much experience in translation, although the epic quality was not Cranch's and it therefore could not inform his work. New editions were called for and the translation was issued both in very cheap and in expensive large format editions, and it was listed as in print until recent years. It was not so successful, however, as Conington's earlier octosyllabic translation, done in the manner of Scott and Byron. Longfellow later urged Cranch to complete his Virgilian work, and he subsequently translated the *Georgics* in blank verse and the *Eclogues* in hexameters, but he was never able to find a publisher.[26]

When he began work on the *Aeneid,* Cranch's composition of original poetry and prose was very considerably accelerated. Though he was abroad when the *Atlantic* was established, he was represented in the first volume, and he continued with some degree of regularity to contribute to it until his last years. He was never a prolific writer, but after 1869 he wrote more than he had ever done before, and his name thereafter appeared from time to time in most of the prominent national magazines. This renewed interest in literature marked a decline in painting, which he all but abandoned when he moved to Cambridge in 1873.

A transcendental poem, *Satan: A Libretto,* came out in a thin volume in 1873, received good reviews, and passed without a sale. The following year Cranch published his largest collection, *The Bird and the Bell, with Other Poems.* The inconsonant moods and subjects in this potpourri of thirty years' work represent Cranch at his best—which is frequently in sonnets—as well as in his most commonplace philosophizing.

"The Bird and the Bell," composed three decades earlier, had more recently been among the poems and papers which Cranch had read before the Radical Club, a group of aging transcendentalists and some latter-day recruits who were sound and solid enough to risk the dangerous name. The meetings of this club amounted to something vastly better than pretentious discussions beyond the scope of the participants, but Cranch in a bit of humorous verse admitted that after the talk of Higginson, Longfellow, Weiss, and Emerson and others they went home with the universe still firm on its base, and he also admitted that the *Tribune* was prone to write *Hic Jacet* over their reports (which occasionally informed the public of little details such as the fact that Emerson sat in a chair that came over on the *Mayflower* while he listened to Cranch's parody of his poetry).[27] Life in Cambridge was sometimes mellow and pleasant. There were occasional invitations to meetings of the Saturday Club, and at the great birthday dinners and breakfasts Cranch was present, with testimonial verse in hand. At the Whittier dinner, a newspaper reporter looked over the forgathered great of New England and marked Cranch, among all these poets, as the most poetic looking, Emerson the most venerable.[28]

Mr. and Mrs. Cranch during these years endured some personal sorrows. Shortly after the War the oldest son died of a fever, and later the other son, who had joined the crew of the *Surprise* for a round-the-world trip, fell from the rigging, struck the deck, and fell into the sea. It was months afterwards when the parents learned of the fact, and of the terse log, "Ship kept her course." Caroline, whom the parents in 1880 had taken for a two-year painting trip abroad,[29] began in 1884 to give Cranch grave concern for her nervous health.

William Dean Howells in his idealized reminiscences gives this account of Cranch:

> Of like gentleness, but of more pensive temper, with bursts of surprising lyrical gayety, was the poet Christopher Pearse Cranch, who came to live in Cambridge rather late in my own life there. I had already met him in New York at a house of literary sympathies and affiliations, where he had astonished me by breaking from his rather melancholy quiet and singing comic character songs . . . [Later] I heard him at Longfellow's supper table sing the old Yankee ballad, "On Springfield Mountain there did dwell." The tragical fate of the "young man" who was bitten by a rattlesnake on his native hill took a quality from the pathetic gravity of the singer which still affects me as heartbreakingly funny. It was a delightful piece of art in its way, and Cranch could not only sing and play most amusing songs, but was as much painter as he was poet. I especially liked his pictures of Venice for their simple, unconventionalized, unsentimentalized reality, and I like and printed many of his poems . . . I recall his presence with a tender regard, and I would fain do my part to keep his memory alive, for I think he did things that merit remembrance.[30]

Lowell and, by inference, several others told Cranch that he had talents which should be appreciated. "Get rid of your whoreson modesty," Lowell advised,[31] but Cranch could do no more than continue to write poems in which he consoled himself that men who please "the public's facile thought" will be soon forgotten, while the artist who is "Scornful of fashion and heedless of chances" will be known only after the grave closes over him. He was pathetically unaware that his "fashion" and even his liberal theology were already recorded history.

As he grew older he pondered much the question of individual as well as literary immortality, vacillating sometimes between opposite convictions. From this shearing impulse come two of his better sonnets. **"The Pines and the Sea,"** first published eight years after "Dover Beach," is not weakened when read along with Arnold's poem, though "Dover Beach" is more comprehensive in purpose than the shorter sonnet in which the doubt of the poet is concerned only with immortality. In **"If Life Be Final"** Cranch struggles to affirm immortality by making the alternative, mortality, appear abhorrent. The argument is identical with that which was already on record in Emerson's yet unpublished journals: "July [1855]. The blazing evidence of immortality is our dissatisfaction with any other solution." Whatever the reader's view of this assumption, he will admit the cogency of Cranch's imagery as he compares mortal man with madrepore.

These two sonnets appeared in Cranch's final volume, **Ariel and Caliban** (dated 1887 but published late in 1886), which brought the total number of Cranch's collected sonnets to ninety-eight. The title poem in the volume allows Ariel to ameliorate the condition of Caliban and to give him some hope for the future. It thus is in the same tradition with **Satan,** Cranch's best longer poem, in which he had blithely and perhaps blindly served up again the optimism of the transcendentalists in their youth. **Ariel and Caliban** as a whole has more unity and finish than the preceding collections. It was genially reviewed by old friends—Hedge, Curtis, Higginson—who said what one would expect good friends to say in old age. Woodberry, however, who was neither a friend nor of Cranch's generation, admitted in the *Atlantic* the merit of his soft nostalgic tones.

Cranch was the chief performer at the memorial service held for Robert Browning at King's Chapel in Boston, where the crowd was so great that Lowell, who was a bit late, could not make his way to the church. Cranch gave his reminiscences of Browning, and concluded with a sonnet:

> Themes strong—verse bloodwarm with the limbs and veins Of life at full-flush . . .[32]

What Santayana called New England's Indian summer of the mind had long since passed when the last tenacious leaves began to fall in clusters in the early nineties. Cranch had not long since helped the photographer pose Lowell for his last photograph and then become his pallbearer,[33] when he himself died on January 20, 1892.

Shortly before Cranch's death Holmes wrote to Whittier that he had been looking over the headstones in Griswold's cemetery, *The Poets and Poetry of America.* In commenting on five of the poets who still survived, he said that Cranch's "poetical gift has too rarely found expression."[34] Much earlier, when Cranch had not seen Emerson during the long years abroad, Emerson wrote, "I have always understood that you are the victim of your own various gifts; that all the muses, jealous each of the other, haunt your brain."[35] This was intended as a compliment, but the word "victim" has the tone of consolation. Both Holmes and Emerson were generous, at least. We cannot conclude that if Cranch had concentrated his energies or had written much more poetry, he would have been a better poet. His English contemporaries, William Morris and Samuel Butler, had a wider range of similar talents, and the achievement of each was far greater. Holmes rightly says that the volume of his poetry is small. Besides the translation of the *Aeneid* there were fewer than two hundred and fifty poems in the three collections, and most of them were short. The four longer poems taken together are comparable in bulk to a short play. By writing much, Cranch might have hit upon two or three more memorable poems, but we would expect little general improvement save in form and polish. And it was not for lack of these that he failed.

The comments on Cranch that have been made here, and those that can be gleaned elsewhere will do little more than verify and amplify an estimate that has already been made. Henry James, Jr., in masterful cadences has given a description of his friend Cranch which is at once delicately appreciative and soundly critical:

> Christopher Pearse Cranch, painter, poet, musician, mild and melancholy humourist, produced pictures that the American traveller sometimes acquired and left verses that the American compiler sometimes includes. Pictures and verses had alike, in any case, the mark of his great, his refined personal modesty; it was not in them at least, for good or for ill, to emphasise or insist.[36]

The comical sketches concerned with the transcendental movement have heretofore been known only through two published samples and through the descriptions of them found in the lives and letters of his contemporaries. Since they are a unique, accurate, and delightful commentary on one of the most important movements in American intellectual history, they may serve to give Cranch a bit more of the appreciation he so deeply desired. The incisiveness lacking in poem and painting was here exhibited in impromptu drawings, some of them hastily done, none of them meant for the public. Cranch, with his sense of rightness and fitness and finish, much of which was the common property of his age and climate, managed never again to be so bold as he was in these youthful pencilings.

Notes

1. Horace E. Scudder, *James Russell Lowell* (Boston, 1901), II, 96; Curtis, "Editor's Easy Chair," *Harper's Monthly,* LXXXIV (1892), 800-801; Lowell, *Complete Writings* (Boston, 1904), XIV, 325.

2. The tradition was related to me by two different members of the family. See F. P. Stearns, *Cambridge Sketches* (Philadelphia, 1905), p. 126.

3. The best record of the Cranch family is found in the Greanleaf genealogy, a manuscript volume deposited in the State House in Boston.

4. See Scott, chap. i, and the William Cranch Papers in the Manuscript Division, Library of Congress.

5. The only copy I have discovered is in another hand and does not have the marginal drawings. It is in the Boston Public Library.

6. CPC to Edward Pope Cranch, St. Louis, December 22, 1836, and January 2 and 9, 1837.

7. Sidney E. Lind, "Christopher Pearse Cranch's 'Gnosis': An Error in Title," *Modern Language Notes,* LXII (1947), 486-488.

8. James Freeman Clarke, "Ars Critica. A Conversation on Modern Poetry," *Western Messenger,* VII (1839), 105-112. This article, signed "C. F. J." at the end and "C. J. F." (both anagrams of Clarke's initials) on the cover, is actually a criticism of Cranch's poetry, with emphasis on the poem "True Beauty," which Clarke had "stolen" from Cranch's portfolio and published, unaware that it had recently appeared in the *Southern Literary Messenger.* Cranch's preference for Wordsworth is made apparent in his letters dated during these years.

9. MS Autobiography, pp. 45-48, which copies directly from his journal entries concerning the visits.

10. CPC to Margaret Cranch (Mrs. Erastus Brooks), Boston, February 23, 1840.

11. CPC to John Sullivan Dwight, Portland, Me., May 13, 1840; Quincy, Mass., June 19 and August 16, 1840.

12. Scott, pp. 49-51; *Memoirs of John Quincy Adams* (Philadelphia, 1874-1877), X, 344-345.

13. CPC to Dwight, Quincy, Mass., August 16, 1840.

14. See Cranch's reply, Washington, D. C., July 22, 1841.

15. MS Autobiography, p. 90.

16. Record Books, II, 34, Carey & Hart MSS, in Historical Society of Pennsylvania collection. The manufacturing costs were only $164.80, but the book was printed and bound with taste.

17. MS entitled "Reminiscences of a Landscape Painter", John Cranch to Rufus W. Griswold, Washington, June 7, 1855, in Boston Public Library; and MS Autobiography.

18. Scott, p. 181. In March 1843, Story did three pencil sketches of Cranch, all presently among the Scott Papers.

19. CPC to Theodore Parker, Rome, Italy, January 21-March 8, 1848.

20. CPC to William Cranch, New York, January 11, January 25, March 24, and April 4, 1850, and January 17, 1851; Scott, p. 191; William Cranch's will, 1855, Probate Court, Washington, D. C.; John Peter De Windt's will, 1870, Surrogate's Court, Dutchess County, Poughkeepsie, N. Y.; and January 1, 1892, statement of the trustee to E[lizabeth] D[e Windt] Cranch, in Cranch papers, Boston Public Library.

21. *Bulletin of the American Art-Union,* II (1849), 45, 46; *Transactions of the American Art-Union,* 1850; see for an example of criticism, *Literary World,* VI (1850), 423-425.

22. Scott, pp. 201, 213-218; CPC to Lowell, Paris, August 17, 1855, Harvard College Library. This letter reveals that Hiram Powers had recommended Cranch to Lowell.

23. Ada Shepard to H. C. Badger, Paris, September 17 and 23, 1857. Through the combined courtesy of Robert L. Straker and Norman Holmes Pearson I learned of these allusions to Cranch in the unpublished letters, transcriptions of which Prof. Pearson has made.

24. Scott, pp. 242, 243; CPC to Lowell, Paris, January 14, 1858, Harvard College Library.

25. See Frederick A. Sweet, *The Hudson River School* (Chicago, 1945).

26. CPC to the editors of the *Critic,* Cambridge, Mass., August 31, 1890, in the Massachusetts Historical Society.

27. See Mrs. John T. Sargent, *Sketches and Reminiscences of The Radical Club* (Boston, 1880), pp. 406-407; and an unidentified newspaper clipping in Cranch's scrapbook of clippings.

28. Unidentified newspaper clipping in Cranch's scrapbook of clippings.

29. There is an oral tradition that while they were abroad Henry James, Jr., was so attentive to Caroline that she had reason to believe his intentions were serious. After maturity their paths could have crossed in Cambridge in 1874, in London in July and August 1880, and possibly but not probably in Venice the next spring. However, in October 1880 James made it clear that none of the numerous rumors about him had any foundation. (See p. 35 in Robert C. LeClair's "Henry James and Minny Temple," *American Literature,* March 1949.)

30. From "Some Literary Memories of Cambridge," *Harper's Monthly,* CI (1900), 823-839; included, with some revision, in *Literary Friends and Acquaintance* (New York, 1900).

31. Scott, p. 256.

32. See *The Browning Society; Boston; In Memoriam* (Cambridge, n.d.).

33. *Cambridge Tribune,* XIV, 1 (February 20, 1892). This was a Lowell memorial issue, but it came out after Cranch's death and contains an editorial on Lowell and Cranch's friendship, a complete text of A. W. Steven's memorial address on Cranch, and other Cranch material.

34. S. T. Pickard, *Life and Letters of John Greenleaf Whittier* (Boston, 1894), II, 756.

35. Scott, p. 281.

36. *William Wetmore Story and His Friends* (Boston, 1903), I, 110-111.

Joseph M. DeFalco (essay date 1971)

SOURCE: DeFalco, Joseph M. Introduction to *Collected Poems of Christopher Pearse Cranch,* pp. vii-xx. Gainesville, Fla.: Scholars' Facsimiles and Reprints, 1971.

[*In the following excerpt, DeFalco discusses Cranch's writing career and the critical response to his work by his contemporaries.*]

By any estimate Christopher Pearse Cranch must be ranked as one of the five major American Transcendentalist poets. Although he lacked the profundity and originality of Emerson, and although he never achieved the brilliant insights of Thoreau, at his best he approaches their more significant productions in poetry; in his ordinary efforts he is at least equal to Channing and Very. Most histories of American literature give Cranch only brief attention, and many assign him the pejorative label of "dilettante." Certainly Cranch was a lover of the arts, and certainly he had diverse talents. One of the few transcendentalists who possessed a keen sense of humor, he brilliantly caricatured some of Emerson's ludicrous expressions. Perhaps this aspect of his character has affected later judgments of his work, but it is a gross misrepresentation to consider him a mere dabbler because of his lighter moods. The profession of art was a serious matter for Cranch; for almost a half century he labored to achieve success in poetry and painting. Public accolades were few, but he lived to see three collections of his poetry published and his paintings placed in some of the better galleries and exhibitions in New York and Paris.

The youngest son of thirteen children, Cranch was born on March 8, 1813, in what is now Alexandria, Virginia. His family came from New England, and his father, William, was a lay Unitarian preacher and a Harvard classmate of John Quincy Adams. Appointed in 1805 by Thomas Jefferson as Chief Justice of the United States Circuit Court of the District of Columbia, the elder Cranch served in that post for over fifty years. Cranch's mother, Anna Greenleaf, was a niece to Abigail Adams, and his aunt Rebecca Greenleaf was married to Noah Webster. A complete genealogy of the Cranch family would yield the names of some of the leading lights of the spiritual and intellectual life of New England and the nation in the nineteenth century. Perhaps the outstanding issue from this lineage in the twentieth century is T. S. Eliot, a grandnephew of Christopher Cranch.

Cranch entered Columbian College (now George Washington University) in 1829, and three years later at age nineteen was graduated. The following year he entered the strongly Unitarian-oriented Harvard Divinity School.

Among his classmates and friends who later achieved prominence in various fields were Theodore Parker, Samuel Osgood, and John Sullivan Dwight. Cranch spent the first years after graduation from the Divinity School traveling from place to place as a substitute for established Unitarian ministers and as an organizer for the American Unitarian Association. He preached in various New England communities; in Richmond, Virginia; Washington, D.C.; and in 1836 he went west to St. Louis, Cincinnati, Peoria, and Louisville. In Louisville he occupied the pulpit of James Freeman Clarke and assumed the temporary editorship of *The Western Messenger*. Under Clarke the *Messenger* had become the voice of liberal Unitarianism in the West. Cranch's own views harmonized with those of Clarke; over the next three years he was called upon several times to guide the *Messenger* in place of Clarke. During his association with the *Messenger* Cranch contributed a variety of prose pieces and several dozen poems. Even after he returned to the East and Channing became the editor of the *Messenger*, Cranch continued to submit items for publication. He was writing other kinds of poetry at the time, but most of his *Messenger* poems are conventionally religious in character. Few of them reveal the imaginative range that he displays in his better transcendental poetry, and none of them suggests that he was turning away from orthodox Unitarianism. In the January, 1841, issue, however, he published an essay in defense of transcendentalism; this public expression fairly marks his private turn away from Unitarianism.

Cranch's credentials as a transcendental poet were validated by no less an authority than Emerson. He sent two of Cranch's poems to Margaret Fuller for publication in the first issue of *The Dial* (July, 1840), and later that summer he entertained Cranch at Concord. In the fall he sent several more poems by Cranch to *The Dial*. With this auspicious beginning Cranch became an acknowledged member of the transcendental fraternity. He was the chief contributor of poetry in the first two volumes of *The Dial*, outstripping many of his better-known colleagues in number of contributions.

Cranch's transcendental education began some time before his initial appearance in *The Dial*. He had already read and avidly assimilated the ideas he found in Emerson's *Nature* (1836), and he attended a course of lectures given by Emerson in Boston. He was equally impressed with the views he found in Carlyle's *Sartor Resartus*. In a letter written to a correspondent early in 1840 he ranks Emerson along with Carlyle and "other stars of the age." At the same time he was no naive follower of such "stars." He notes in the same letter that Emerson's views were not popular and were considered "heretical by most persons, and by as many, downright atheism, mysticism, or perhaps nonsense." Cranch was too deeply committed to allow public opinion to sway him from his idealistic course; eventually his persistence cost him his pulpit and his confidence in his ability to find a suitable profession.

The transition from liberal Unitarian to transcendentalist was not an easy one for Cranch; there is evidence that he underwent a personal crisis before he effected the change. In a letter written to his father around the time that his poems were to appear in the first issue of *The Dial*, Cranch is decidedly defensive in his response to his father's concern that he had succumbed to the blandishments of the "Transcendental sentiments of the German Theologians." He reassures his conservative parent that the views of the "New School" are not far removed from the true spirit of Unitarian Christianity, and he goes on to divorce Emerson's doctrines from those of Kant and Fichte. Whether Emerson would have concurred with this line of defense is open to question, but there is no inconsistency with sound Emersonian doctrine in Cranch's plea for a break from the "old theology of the early Unitarians" and for adherence to a strong individualism. His summary is worthy of the master himself: "What my intellect receives must accord with the blessed revelation to my heart and conscience." His father's response is not recorded; he would have been a most obtuse jurist not to have detected the advance stages of a new idealism that was to lead his youngest son far from his own orthodox views of Unitarianism.

By early 1841, when he was preaching at the church of Frederic Henry Hedge, the founder of the Transcendental Club, Cranch began to suffer from some sort of mental depression. He characterized his difficulty as "trouble in my head and brain," and it lasted for several years. It seems beyond coincidence that his "trouble" arose when he began to see that he could not espouse Emersonian views and at the same time preach from a Unitarian pulpit. The news that John Sullivan Dwight, his close friend, had been forced to resign from his church because of his liberal views must have confirmed many of his own fears and underlined the need to seek a profession in which he could make a living and not compromise his ideals. Although he was a steady contributor to *The Dial*, poetry offered little hope in terms of compensation. His only alternative was painting. He had enjoyed painting and drawing since childhood; his talent delighted his friends on many occasions. His decision to become a serious painter terminates his commitment to the ministry and begins a search for recognition in the arts that lasted to the end of his life.

Much of Cranch's gloom and anxiety over his future was dispelled in the fall of 1841, when he met Elizabeth DeWindt, the woman he married. She was a cousin of Cranch's and the great-granddaughter of John Adams. Her family home was at Fishkill Landing on the Hudson River, where during the courtship and for many years after their marriage Cranch painted and sketched. Some of Cranch's better landscapes in the manner of the Hudson River School of painting derive from the subjects he found there. By the time he married in 1843, Cranch already was devoting most of his energy to painting. His career as a poet continued; he published in a few well-known magazines and in several gift annuals during these years.

The major event of Cranch's career as poet after leaving the ministry occurred in 1842, when Rufus Griswold selected his work for inclusion in *The Poets and Poetry of*

America. Cranch had not yet published his first volume of poetry, but his inclusion in the anthology placed him among the established poets of his day. The young Cranch must have been elated over his appearance in the famous anthology; if the event seemed to foretoken a wide reputation as a major poet, it misfired. Years later the older and sometimes melancholy Cranch of *The Bird and the Bell* looked back upon the anthology somewhat ruefully in **"The American Pantheon."** Thinking of his own fate, no doubt, he labels those whom fame has passed by as *"Dii minores* of a voiceless past."

Poems, Cranch's first volume of collected poems, appeared in May, 1844, two years after Griswold's anthology. He dedicated the work to Emerson, but the poems within the volume better attest his regard. With the exception of **"The True in Dreams,"** all of the *Dial* poems are included. Most of the other pieces are of the same order: strong lyrical expressions of the transcendental spirit. The highly Emersonian **"Enosis"** appears, and so does **"Correspondences,"** an almost direct poetical translation of Emerson's doctrine of that name. The brilliance of the transcendental pieces made little impression on the public; the volume failed to advance Cranch's reputation as a poet. There is no question that the poems are of mixed quality, for they range from the *Dial* poems to the juvenile **"College Lyfe."** A reviewer for *Graham's,* who treated Cranch rather gently, summarized his view of the weakness of the volume as "lack of nerve, the absence of that power and knowledge which are conferred by the rough discipline of the world, the want of true depth and intensity."

The *Graham's* reviewer was writing about the productions of a youthful Cranch; by the time another collection appeared, the tone and content had shifted considerably. The occasion of the change is not difficult to surmise. Two years after *Poems* appeared, Cranch decided to move to Europe to further his career as a painter. He well knew that the idiosyncracies of the artistic marketplace were such that an American artist painting in Europe increased his opportunities for sales and enhanced his possibilities of gaining recognition. Practical necessity thus dictated the move, but Cranch derived a maturity from the European experience that evidences itself quite unexpectedly in the poems of this period. Freed from the rather narrow provincialism of New England transcendental influences, Cranch's poetry exhibits a wider range of creativity and maturity than would seem possible from his earlier efforts.

Cranch's "expatriate" years on this first trip to Europe were spent mainly in Italy. The first years were passed in Rome; the last year was broken up into shorter stays in Naples, Sorrento, and Florence. These years reflect a diminished production of poetry and a commensurate increase in painting. One cannot examine the poetry written during the Italian years without concluding that the effort expended for the one profited the other. Whatever else it did for him, the experience Cranch gained in Italy gave him some of that worldly discipline recommended by the *Graham's* reviewer. His focus and subject matter in poetry shifted to a broader, more comprehensive and humanistic emphasis upon man and the subjection of mankind to social and political forces. He had given some attention to these matters in America, as evidenced in his **"Sonnet on the Mexican War,"** published in *The Harbinger* not long before he sailed for Europe, but Italy, with its Roman Church and the political oppression of its people, gave him an objective context in which to view the suppression of the human spirit. As the later **"The Bird and the Bell"** demonstrates, his response was at once critical and direct.

During the three years that Cranch lived in Italy, he furthered his artistic education by touring all of the major galleries, meeting and talking with the many practicing painters and sculptors who lived there, and by generally absorbing the aesthetic atmosphere of the country. Many enduring personal and professional relationships were established on this trip. George William Curtis accompanied the Cranch family on the voyage to Europe, and a friendship that began at Brook Farm crystalized into an association that lasted until Cranch's death. After Curtis became a distinguished essayist and editor of *Harper's Weekly* and *Harper's Magazine,* he was able to assist Cranch professionally on a number of occasions. Cranch's friend, William Wetmore Story, was already in Europe, and they maintained their close relationship. Among those with whom Cranch associated were Hiram Powers and Horatio Greenough, both noted American sculptors of their day. Margaret Fuller visited, and through her the Cranches met the Robert Brownings. While living in Florence, the Cranches visited at Casa Guidi several times; Browning dropped in at Cranch's studio at times. Browning and Cranch shared mutual interests in music and painting; Cranch was impressed with Browning's poetical accomplishments. Some of Cranch's later poetry reflects the Browning influence; from letters we know that the Brownings read and offered advice on revision of Cranch's **"The Bird and the Bell."** Cranch recorded many of his feelings about Browning in his **"Memorial to Robert Browning"** (1890).

In the spring of 1849, the Cranches returned to America. They remained until 1853, when once again practical necessity drove them back to Europe. Cranch had sold some paintings while living in Italy, and he sold a few more during this American interlude. His sales were always disappointing; they rarely provided him and his family with more than a marginal existence. Some financial assistance was provided by his family and that of his wife, but this was never enough to give the Cranches a sense of financial security. Cranch's publication of poetry during this interval was slight; all but a few of those pieces that he did place were published by his friend, John Sullivan Dwight, in *Dwight's Journal of Music.* Cranch seems to have had little regard for these poems, for he did not collect them in his later volumes. Longfellow, however, felt that several of the Italian pieces were of sufficient merit to include them in his *Poems of Places* (1877).

When the Cranches returned to Europe, they established themselves in Paris. This time they remained for ten years.

Once again Cranch set about painting and sketching in earnest, touring galleries, and making new acquaintances and renewing old ones. He saw Browning again, but that relationship was never to prove any more rewarding than it already had. Of more lasting importance was the friendship that began in these years with James Russell Lowell. On one memorable occasion Cranch, Lowell, and Story were invited to dine with William Makepeace Thackeray at the Garrick Club in London. After dinner Thackeray read to them from the last installment of "The Newcomes." The incident left a lasting impression on Cranch, who recorded it in some detail in his **"Autobiography."**

The London excursion was one of several that took Cranch away from Paris. Visits to Barbizon, Switzerland, and to Rome were undertaken in order to seek out fresh subjects for his painting. But even the Forest of Fontainbleu, where the Barbizon School of painting was being spawned, failed to provide him with that elusive ingredient that would have made him an important landscape painter of his time. Many of the scenes that he painted provided him with subjects for his poetical compositions. The poems in the later collections recall some of these experiences in terms as vivid as any painting he might have composed.

When Cranch returned to America in 1863, the country was in the midst of the Civil War. A staunch supporter of the Northern cause, Cranch registered in his poetry his intense reaction to the war and to Lincoln's death. Some of his war poems were published in contemporary periodicals; these and others were brought together under the title **"Poems of the War"** in *The Bird and the Bell.* Cranch continued to paint in the years after the war, but by the mid-seventies he had all but given over serious painting in favor of poetry and prose writing.

In 1872 Cranch published his highly successful translation in blank verse of Virgil's *Aeneid.* The work appeared in the prestigious series of translations published by James R. Osgood. Included in the series were such landmarks of American scholarship as Longfellow's translation of Dante's *Divine Comedy* and Bryant's translations of the *Iliad* and the *Odyssey.* Cranch was an adept translator; in addition to Latin he translated a number of poems from German and French. Some of his translations remain unpublished. As successful as his *Aeneid* was, publishers still remained tuned to the contemporary market. Included in the unpublished material are translations of Virgil's *Georgics* and his *Eclogues.*

One of Cranch's more remarkable poems, *Satan: A Libretto,* appeared in 1874 as a separate work. Although it failed to attract much notice, Cranch thought so highly of it that he revised it and included it under the new title of **"Ormuzd and Ahriman"** in his final collection, *Ariel and Caliban.* Taken from the Zoroastrian designations of the contending forces in the universe, the new title is a better indicator of the major premise of the work. Both versions announce the old Emersonian doctrine of the essentially privative nature of evil. Cranch's reconstruction of the transcendental non-dual universe this late in the century seems anachronistic, but much of the charm of Cranch's poetry is his perennial optimism. Although his impatience with social inequities and his bitterness in the war poems offset the optimism to a degree, his belief in a final transcendental reconcilement never wavered.

Some of the poems that Cranch included in *The Bird and the Bell* (1875) had appeared as early as 1852; the majority represent the work published and written in the years just prior to 1875. Many of these later pieces appeared in *The Atlantic, The Independent,* and *Dwight's Journal of Music.* The critical reception of Cranch's work in these years could not be called enthusiastic, but he did enjoy a reputation of sufficient stature to allow him to place his work with relative ease.

In 1880 Cranch left his Cambridge, Massachusetts, home, where he had lived since 1873, and set out on what was to be his final visit to Europe. This time he toured for two years in England, France, and Italy. The primary purpose of the trip was to give his daughter Caroline an opportunity to study the paintings of the European masters. Because she was well on her way to becoming a first-rate portrait artist, Cranch felt that she needed to free herself from purely American and contemporary influences in order to complete her art education. For the sixty-seven year old Cranch, though, Europe held few surprises. His letters suggest that he retained his enthusiasm for continental life and that his appreciation of art remained keen; still, unlike his earlier visits this time there were no new views to gain and no fresh subjects to stimulate his imagination.

Ariel and Caliban (1887), the last collection of Cranch's career, brought together many of the poems that Cranch published in various periodicals over the twelve years since *The Bird and the Bell.* Although the poems are the products of his later years, in many ways the subjects and moods are reminiscent of his youthful first collection. The craftsman has matured considerably; if this last collection contains no brilliant or imaginative outbursts, it nonetheless reveals some of the best examples of Cranch's mastery of the techniques of poetry. The overall temper of the collection is philosophical, exhibiting in the individual pieces an air of objectivity acquired from long experience. The vigorous social criticism of *The Bird and the Bell* is here melioristic, and, as the title poem and the concluding **"Orhmuzd and Ahriman"** reveal, Cranch's final views are conciliatory and optimistic.

Cranch died on January 20, 1892. His career was decidedly uneven, although he never gave up the quest for recognition in the arts. George William Curtis, who paid his friend a final tribute in his "Easy Chair" column of *Harper's Magazine,* in his summation of Cranch's career suggests the irony implicit in the life of a man who was near-brilliant and many-talented but who remained, essentially, a failed artist: "He was, indeed, an artist in various kinds. The diamond which the good genius brought to his cradle, it broke in many parts." . . .

Elizabeth R. McKinsey (essay date 1973)

SOURCE: McKinsey, Elizabeth R. "Christopher Pearse Cranch." In *The Western Experiment: New England Transcendentalists in the Ohio Valley,* pp. 34-41. Cambridge: Harvard University Press, 1973.

[*In the following excerpt, McKinsey provides a brief overview of Cranch's career as a Transcendentalist writer in the West.*]

Christopher Pearse Cranch, like Clarke, was twenty-three when he went west in 1836. He shared a sense of dedication to the Unitarian mission, but had no definite role into which to fit himself. He went not to fill a particular pulpit but to visit his cousin, William Eliot, the Unitarian minister in St. Louis, and he stayed in Cincinnati (where his older brother Edward was a lawyer) as "minister at large." This meant he would establish some sort of ministry among the poor, outside the formal structure of the church, and would be expected to act as substitute in pulpits empty because of travel or illness. Otherwise he was completely free to determine the particular forms of his work, to read, write, travel. Taking advantage of this freedom, he spent some time preaching in Peoria, Illinois, and more time in Louisville, working with Clarke on the *Messenger,* and taking full responsibility for it when Clarke was absent.

More a free spirit than Clarke, without the same ambition for power or obsession with order, Cranch was not destined to undergo the same kind of disillusionment. The tenth child and youngest son, Cranch had not been pressured to succeed in the way oldest or only sons often are. He was fathered by a gentleman of the old school, a devout New England Federalist, but he grew up in the suburbs of Washington where he had great freedom to roam. The father's position, too, may have contributed to the son's sense of freedom: although a Federalist, he held a Jeffersonian appointment to the Circuit Court, having broken out of the confines of party and section. Young Cranch was encouraged to pursue all his many interests: painting, music, philosophical study, and frequent visits to the Senate to listen, enraptured, to the utterances of Clay and Webster. He would have liked to continue such a varied existence, certain that there was more of life in painting and poetry than in conventional professions; but there was no secure living to be got in the arts. Needing gainful employment of some sort, he settled upon the ministry and set off for the Harvard Divinity School. There exposed to German Romanticism, he soon aligned himself with those young idealists who would be called Transcendentalists. Cranch was unique among them, however, in his sense of irony and playfulness, even vis-à-vis the movement. Perhaps his not having grown up amidst the tensions of crumbling Federalism, the Unitarian controversy, and the Puritan heritage of New England freed him from the high seriousness of many of his colleagues. In any event his delightful caricatures of Emerson and Transcendental ideas, extravagant but never insulting or irreverent, provide comic relief from the philosophical issues.

Also relatively carefree was Cranch's approach to his own life. He took a pulpit in Richmond, Virginia, immediately after his divinity school graduation, but intended no permanent commitment. Although he "should prefer settling here to almost any other place," he was "possessed of the Western mania in some degree"[1] and soon set off for St. Louis, yielding to his restlessness.

The western years that followed constitute a classic example of the *Wanderjahre*: positively pursuing a noncommittal, experimental life, Cranch was happy as a dilettante preacher, poet, and philosopher. "Living in a dusty, noisy law-office, and sleeping in the same on a most extemporaneous couch-bed, without a pillow," he was free to be "a regular loafer" or to pick up and travel at a moment's notice.[2] The *Messenger* provided a convenient and appreciative artistic outlet, publishing many of his poems, parables, and critical and philosophical articles. It was an indispensable apprenticeship, even though the poetry that resulted was, as Perry Miller pointed out, largely banal and maudlin.[3]

Though Cranch could handle his freedom in a way that Clarke never could, he was unable to control it—his indulgence as the baby of the family grew into self-indulgence and restlessness; even in the freedom of the West he was not satisfied. "Still I dream of travelling, night after night it is the same. I am a second Peter Schlimmel [sic] with his seven-leagued boots. If I ever get crazy, I suppose it will be on this subject, possessed with the demon of perpetual motion."[4] Traveling constantly through the West, he was never quite satisfied; his "Lines" on the prodigal son are indicative of his state of mind,[5] but he could never "come home." Indeed, apart from the erotic aspect, the similarity between Cranch and Byron is striking. Many of Byron's characteristics describe Cranch equally well: "relies on his absolute self against all institutional . . . trammels on the display of individuality," "passionate and willful," "capable of taking an ironic attitude toward his own foibles as well as those of other men."[6] Both were artists, dedicated to Truth. Even in their shyness and extraordinary handsomeness, the likeness holds. Never compromising his individual integrity (not only an ideal, "self-reliance" was an intimate part of Cranch's character), ever wandering in search of experience and intensity, he was a "good," American version of the Byronic hero.

Part of Cranch's restlessness was the gnawing feeling that he was far from the world's artistic and philosophical centers. As he complained in his first letter from the West, "Truly, I am in a desert in more ways than one."[7] Although he soon positively enjoyed western life and felt himself and his colleagues very much a part of the New School, his review of Emerson's "American Scholar" address betrays his longing, however subtle, to be at the fountainhead of the new impulses. "Would that we had been in the church of old Harvard when the thinker, the orator, the poet charmed the multitude to silence."[8]

Cranch was propelled to perpetual motion by his constant fear of stagnation. Whenever he lost his intensity he despaired. "I stop at times and wonder at myself, and fear.

At times so alive, so excited, so full of one or another faith or aim; and at others so dead, immovable, ennui-ish, a dumb beast, a clod, an animal."[9] This is more than just a recognition of the human rhythm of activity and rest; it points up Cranch's paralysis, paradoxical as it may seem, in spite of his frenzied motion, and hints at the compulsiveness of his wandering. Chained to his ideal of freedom, he was unable to commit himself to a single pulpit, indeed to the ministry as a career. He wrote in defense of the New School, "Their sympathies embrace the secluded scholar, the active preacher, the devoted schoolmaster, the enthusiastic artist, the true poet—every man who feels that life should not be a mechanical routine, but be filled with earnestness, soul and spiritual energy."[10] Mortally afraid of a routinized life, he was attempting to be all these men at once—the preacher, the poet, the artist.

Providing fuel for the fire of his restiveness was his second demon, an extraordinary diffidence; perhaps it was easier for him to move on than to deal intimately with people. His self-consciousness and great sensitivity (born also of self-indulgence) may have made him a poet and a Transcendentalist, but they made everyday life a trial. It is interesting that his own shyness prevented his perceiving Clarke's lack of self-confidence: Cranch envied his colleague's "independence of character . . . It does me good to be with him."[11] As he had hoped, Cranch learned the West's lessons—"boldness" and "an habitual independence"—on at least the elementary level, although he eventually gave up preaching and formal association with large groups. Learning to use his humor to communicate with people, he developed a real facility for entertainment; this later made his visits to Brook Farm memorable events. "His powers of entertainment were almost unlimited: he had a good baritone voice; he played piano, guitar, flute, or violin as the occasion came; he read from his own poems or travesties; and his ventriloquism, which embraced all the sounds of nature and of mechanical devices . . . held the younger members spellbound."[12] But he recognized—for he experienced it painfully—that the logical extension of man's individuality is his eventual isolation.

> We are spirits clad in veils
>   Man by man was never seen:
> All our deep communing fails
>   To remove the shadowy screen.
>
> Heart to heart was never known:
>   Mind with mind did never meet:
> We are columns left alone,
>   Of a temple once complete.[13]

To compensate for such existential isolation, Cranch clung to his ideals of transcendence and communion; through artistic expression he tried to restore the "temple once complete."

After less than two years of aimlessness in the West, the tensions underlying his restlessness rose to a level demanding some kind of resolution. Cranch wrote to Clarke in the spring of 1838, "Well, here I am—again a wanderer—another, and still another parting have I endured. For nearly three years it has been my lot to rove about from place to place, North, South, East and West—making friends and parting from them—verily I am growing aweary of such an intinerant way of living. It hardly seems the appropriate destiny for one who has so much of that quiet home-loving propensity which phrenologists term Inhabitiveness."[14] By the next year his inhabitiveness prevailed and he was ready to settle down. Without clearly defined work to do, lacking identification with a particular community, with his extreme self-consciousness, Cranch was frightened by the dissipation inevitable in continued lack of commitment. Having provided no place for him to "hang his hat," the West also failed to give him any sense of coherence or identity. Ready for commitment and responsibility, he therefore turned back to the East. "Think I shall candidate at the North," he wrote, "and settle there. Heartily tired am I of wandering. I want a home, quiet steady work, and a wife. I shall not find them this side of the mountains."[15] He returned to the East "Tuesday next," in February 1839.

Like Clarke, Cranch did not articulate his identity crisis; yet he was never able to strike a satisfactory working compromise with life, even after returning to the familiarity and relative stability of the East (as Clarke did do in Boston). His disquiet continued; two years after his return he was still unsettled, searching, the future "a cheerless blank . . . Conscious of capabilities, yet unable to choose, unable to decide what I am to work at, as first and foremost. Where am I to go? What am I to do?"[16] Despite his eventual marriage[17] and his decision to give up the ministry in order to devote himself primarily to painting, he was always dissatisfied and never very productive. Remaining a Unitarian, clinging to Transcendentalism as a means of self-definition as well as embracing it philosophically, he did not identify completely with either group; he really was too self-reliant to relinquish his identity to any group, cause, or creed, no matter how freely conceived, but he was unable to achieve integration on his own.

Writing for *The Dial*, publishing scattered volumes of poetry and, after "some instruction" from Thomas Cole and Asher Durand, concentrating on landscape painting, he remained artistically and personally unfulfilled, finally unable even to turn his sense of humor to account; he drew almost no more caricatures and his playful poems became pathetic. Transcendentalism provided some comfort but no solution. Cranch spent the rest of his life a restless wanderer—in New England, New York, Europe, dabbling in his paints. Having failed during his "prolonged adolescence" in the West to find the tools with which to work out the commitments of adult life, "he ultimately proved one of the most futile and wasted talents" of the age.[18]

Notes

1. Cranch to John S. Dwight, 15 June 1836, Scott, *Life and Letters of Cranch*, p. 26.

2. Cranch to Clarke, Feb. 16, 1839, *ibid.*, p. 45.

3. Miller, *Transcendentalists*, p. 385.

4. Cranch to Catherine Myers, 24 Nov. 1838, Scott, *Life and Letters of Cranch*, p. 43.

5. Cranch, "Lines," *Western Messenger*, 4 (Sept. 1837): 62-63.

6. These quotations are from M. H. Abrams' Introduction to Byron in *The Norton Anthology of English Literature* (New York: Norton, 1962), II, 252-258. That Cranch himself identified with Byron to some extent is evident in his poem "Childe Christopher."

7. Cranch to Catherine Myers, 29 March 1837, Scott, *Life and Letters of Cranch*, p. 32.

8. *Western Messenger*, 4 (Nov. 1837): 184-188.

9. Cranch to Catherine Myers, 24 Nov. 1838, Scott, *Life and Letters of Cranch*, p. 42.

10. Cranch, "The New School in Literature and Religion," *Western Messenger*, 6 (Nov. 1838): 47.

11. Cranch to his sister Margaret, 15 Oct. 1837, Scott, *Life and Letters of Cranch*, pp. 39-40; see also p. 35.

12. Lindsay Swift, quoted *ibid.*, p. 52. Erikson has pointed out the possibilities of identity formation based on one's sense of humor, in lectures and in writing of Gandhi's playful streak in *Gandhi's Truth* (New York: Norton, 1969).

13. Usually called "Gnosis," these lines are titled "Stanzas" in Miller, *Transcendentalists*, p. 385.

14. Cranch to Clarke, *Western Messenger*, 5 (June 1838): 183.

15. Cranch to Clarke, Feb. 16, 1839, Scott, *Life and Letters of Cranch*, p. 44.

16. Cranch to John S. Dwight, June 8, 1841, *ibid.*, p. 70.

17. He married Elizabeth DeWindt, Oct. 10, 1843, after a two-year engagement.

18. Miller, *Transcendentalists*, p. 179.

David Robinson (essay date 1977)

SOURCE: Robinson, David. "Christopher Pearse Cranch, Robert Browning, and the Problem of 'Transcendental' Friendship." *Studies in the American Renaissance* (1977): 145-53.

[*In the following essay, Robinson examines Cranch's friendship with Robert Browning and its effect on Cranch's poetry.*]

The thirty year interval between Christopher Pearse Cranch's first collection of verse, ***Poems*** (1844), and the successive publications of ***Satan*** (1874) and ***The Bird and the Bell*** (1875)[1] is marked by many apparent changes in a man characterized as one of the most restless of the Transcendentalists.[2] Much of this period was spent overseas, where Cranch, in the company of numerous other American intellectuals, was establishing himself as a successful, if not brilliant, landscape painter, and somewhat later in America, as an accomplished translator of the *Aeneid*.[3] But the themes to which he returned in his later poetry are remarkably similar to those of the early poems which won the praise of Emerson, and even Poe.[4] What is striking, however, in the second collection, ***The Bird and the Bell***, is the personal flavor of many of the poems which are written to, or about, the literary figures Cranch had come to know in Europe. While the early poems have rightly been characterized as poetic paraphrases of Emersonian doctrine,[5] some of the later poems seem to test that doctrine in the vivid terms of a man whom Perry Miller characterizes as "a social being."[6]

Despite his social graces, and his continuing reputation as "the most delightful of the Transcendental group,"[7] Cranch was haunted by a conviction of loneliness, marred and imperfect friendship, and even rejection by others. One can note a hint of this feeling in **"A Friend"**:

> We smile and clasp the hands
> With merry fellows o'er cigars and wine;
> We breakfast, walk, and dine
> With social men and women. Yes, we are friends;
> And there the music ends![8]

These may appear wistful, even maudlin sentiments until they are put in the context of one of the most striking, and puzzling, poems in the same volume, **"Veils."** The poem begins with the memory of a friendship that transcends ordinary social bounds:

> Once we called each other friends.
>   'T was no formal greeting
> When we clasped each other's hands;
>   Soul with soul came meeting.

(100)

Here the clasp of the hands, the sign of merely formal friendship in **"A Friend,"** is the outward sign of a deeper communion of souls. But, turning away from the past, the poet depicts the current dissolution of this tie:

> Other friends now come between,
>   Other love outstrips me.
> Can my light be then so dull
>   That they all eclipse me?
> Often have I longed for you;
>   Often have I wondered
> Why we two, whose thoughts were one,
>   Ever should be sundered.

(100)

The presence in the volume of so many other poems of personal reference raises the question of an actual biographical source for the poem, and perhaps intentionally, Cranch provides enough evidence to identify Robert Browning as the unnamed friend and subject of the poem.

Cranch, through an introduction by Margaret Fuller, had met Robert Browning in Florence, in December 1848, and was immediately impressed by his "true, social, healthy, open, frank nature," that of a man "entering into life and associating with men, while inwardly delicate and poetic."[9] When Browning returned Cranch's first visit with calls to his home and studio, Cranch called them "good, long, real and not formal visits."[10] After another visit of Browning to his studio in January 1849, he called him "a most genial man to whom I feel drawn exceedingly."[11] In these early meetings, at which Elizabeth Barrett Browning was sometimes present, Cranch saw Browning as someone beyond social formality, and was drawn to what he felt was the inner delicacy, or "soul," of the poet. As Cranch was to recall later in his **"Personal Reminiscences"** of Browning, "The natural feeling of remoteness in our first admission to the society of two such distinguished poets was soon dissipated by their frank and genial hospitality. We saw them often, and it is needless to say that the privilege of this acquaintance gave added charms to our residence that winter in Florence."[12]

The impact of these meetings was all the greater for Cranch when one considers his feeling that he "knew" Browning before meeting him through his writings. Thus in **"Veils,"** the relationship is depicted as having begun before any actual meeting.

> Long ago I loved your books,
>   (They first drew me to you);
> Loved you better than you thought;
>   Ere I saw you knew you.
>
>   (100)

Cranch himself dates the beginning of his knowledge of Browning in the mid-1840s in his **"Reminiscences"** of 1892: "My first acquaintance with Browning's works dates back to over forty-five years ago, when I was one of a comparatively small circle of the readers and admirers of the first of his books known in America. I well remember with what fresh delight and enthusiasm we read them."[13] Cranch is recounting in personal terms the impact of Browning on the Transcendentalists, one of the earliest phases of his growing American popularity. This regard for Browning's poetry was no transient enthusiasm for Cranch, who wrote in a letter of 1853 that "He is, in my opinion, the great poet of the day. I don't know anyone teeming with such rich life and thought as Browning."[14]

There is more, however, than the parallels of the relationship depicted in **"Veils"** and these 1848 and 1849 meetings to indicate Browning as its subject. Cranch closes the poem with the realization that the friendship can only continue in a realm totally apart from society, the imaginative realm where they first met as poet and reader:

> You and I will speak in dreams
>   Loves not unrequited,
> As we met ten years ago,
>   Happy and united.
>
>   (105)

The specific mention of the meeting "ten years ago" is significant in light of the date Cranch affixes to the poem, "Rome, 1859." The growing possibility that the ten year period refers to the 1848-49 meetings of Cranch and Browning is confirmed by further evidence of their last meeting. Again in later years, Cranch briefly recalls the meeting: "I met Browning again in London in 1855—also in Paris—and in 1859 in Rome. But he was then moving much in aristocratic society, and we saw less both of him and his wife."[15] The reference is brief, but its lack of explanation is revealing. Cranch does not explain the apparent drifting apart because he himself fails to understand it. He only knows his own exclusion in favor of the "aristocrats" whom he feels do not really "know" the poet.

> There are those who cling to you
>   As their lamp and fuel,
> Or who wear you on their fronts
>   Like a glittering jewel;
>   . . . . .
> Happy if they can be seen
>   With you closely talking,
> Proud, if arm in arm with you
>   In the street they're walking.
>
>   (101)

The time between the first and last meetings of Cranch and Browning were years of accelerating fame for both Brownings, which certainly accounts for the social success Cranch observed from without. *Men and Women* had been published in 1855, and the popularity of both the Brownings was growing. With poetic success came social success, and Browning's love for Rome's society was confirmed in the winter of 1858-59, when, as Louise Greer notes, "Browning was caught up in the social whirl which his wife considered much giddier than that of Paris, and hardly spent one night at home in a fortnight."[16] Cranch himself was in Rome at this time, painting and seeking buyers for his works, but also caught in the round of parties and balls that made the city such an attraction to foreigners. "Every evening this week past has been occupied with visits or parties, except one,"[17] he wrote his wife in January 1859. The immediate threat of war in Rome, and his eventual decision to return to America a few years later, prevented Cranch from returning, and, sadly, from meeting Browning again. Whatever prevented their satisfactory communication in Rome—the impenetrability of social forms, differing social circles, or in Cranch's words, "Time and space and circumstance" (102)—the split left Cranch to continue his relation with Browning only through Browning's works.

Whatever biographical interest the relation holds for us, it poses a much more important poetic problem, especially in light of Cranch's poetic career. It is significant that **"The Bird and the Bell,"** the title poem of the volume containing **"Veils,"** was read in manuscript and criticized by both Brownings, whose poetic opinion Cranch valued highly.[18] More important, however, is the obvious allusion of the title of **"Veils"** to Cranch's most widely popular poem, **"Enosis."** The second and third stanzas of **"Enosis," probably its most memorable, pose in abstract terms the actual problem Cranch later faced in his relation with Browning:

> We are spirits clad in veils;
>   Man by man was never seen;
> All our deep communing fails
>   To remove the shadowy screen.
>
> Heart to heart was never known;
>   Mind with mind did never meet;
> We are columns left alone
>   Of a temple once complete.[19]

The "veils" of this poem are unmistakably the veils Cranch faces in his relation with Browning. But in **"Veils,"** the metaphors of **"Enosis"** become less symbolic, and more literally descriptive. Thus the "shadowy screen" of **"Enosis"** becomes the shaded window barring Cranch from his friend:

> Time and space and circumstance
>   Barred me from your presence.
> Then behind your veils you seemed
>   Some dim phosphorescence.
> Half-transparent window shades
>   Told where you were sitting,
> And your astral lamp, half blurred,
>   Threw your shadow flitting
> Up against the curtain-folds.
>
> (102)

The similarity of both the theme and imagery of the two poems suggests a conscious echoing by Cranch, and as a result, a testing of transcendental doctrine. If **"Enosis"** suggested an Emersonian solution to the abstract question of isolation, **"Veils"** tests that solution emotionally in a concrete social situation.

The personal problem developing in the two decades between **"Enosis"** and **"Veils"** was what one critic has called Cranch's "extraordinary diffidence," an intense personal shyness that "made everyday life a trial."[20] One can, of course, account for Cranch's reputation as an engaging social personality in terms of a need to compensate for his deeper shyness, but, whatever its other causes and results, it has poetic and philosophical ramifications. The transcendental doctrine of the unity of man, which stressed an ultimate personal communion beyond ordinary social contact, offered Cranch a theoretical solution to his loneliness. Shyness or diffidence, viewed ideally, only meant the recognition of the infinity of the soul of each individual, ultimately unknowable in a social context because of its infinite nature. Interpreters of **"Enosis"** have tended to stress the opening despair and isolation of the poem rather than its closing affirmation, seeing it, in Levenson's terms, as an expression of "the atomistic side of Transcendental social theory."[21] Perhaps Cranch speaks more honestly of isolation than communion, or perhaps his images of isolation conform more readily to a modern view of human relations. His intention, however, was to depict the superficial isolation of individuals in order to emphasize their deeper, or higher, unity. Thus the poem turns when Cranch attacks the superficiality of society: "What is social company / But a babbling summer stream?" (*Poems,* p. 51). After this question, Cranch spends the last three stanzas establishing a communion transcending social intercourse, culminating the poem in a final image of unity rather than isolation:

> We like parted drops of rain
>   Swelling till they meet and run,
> Shall be all absorbed again,
>   Melting, flowing into one.
>
> (*Poems,* p. 52)

In abstract terms, then, Cranch affirms Emerson's "great discovery that there is one Mind common to all individual men; that what is individual is less than what is universal."[22]

But can one live out such a philosophy? The question plagued Emerson, who struggled against guilt for his "coldness," and almost every other Transcendentalist made at best a partial truce with the dilemma posed by the unsatisfactory nature of social relations and the unrequited need for human contact. Transcendental communion answered the problem philosophically, but how rare was the person who could, in Thoreau's unforgettable image, "talk across the pond to a visitor on the opposite side."[23]

Cranch's more concrete approach to the problem in the later poem, **"Veils,"** suggests the emotional cost of trying to maintain a transcendental friendship. The three part structure of the poem suggested by Cranch's spatial divisions offers an opening meditation on the possible causes of the friendship's end (ll. 1-44), and a closing attempt to respond to the breakup (ll. 97-124), but centers on the actual social exclusion that signals the end of the friendship. Cranch pictures himself waiting for Browning who, "When the guests are gone" will "come / Where I'm waiting lonely" (102). The vision is one of restored communion, a reference to the four year interval (1855-59) since their last meeting.

> We will pace his garden-walks,
>   Of the past discoursing.
> All his heart will open, free
>   From convention's forcing
>
> (103)

But instead, Cranch feels a "chill between his [Browning's] words" as he asks him to return "to-morrow" (103). The pain he feels as a result is not, as he depicts it, the result of a social snub, but rather a realization that there is less in the relation than he expected or hoped. Again, fashionable society is the problem for Cranch, coming between real communion between the two men. Thus he begins the final section of the poem with a bitter admission of the "veils" between them:

> "Were we far from fashion's forms
>   In some desert gloomy,

>   You might learn to know me then;
>   For you never knew me!"
>
>   (104)

The poetry of **"Veils"** is far inferior to that of **"Enosis,"** but the pain of loneliness seems more real, or at least more accessible. Perhaps for that reason, Cranch's final attempt to return to the purely ideal communion of poet and reader as a source of solace fails to convince even himself:

> "I will read your books again;
>   They at least will lead me
>   Into walks where we may meet,
>   Though you do not need me."
>
>   (105)

The final despairing line of this quatrain carries far more emotional weight than the earlier attempt at self-comfort. Similarly, the images of "cold estrangement" and "Loves not requited" in the last lines of the poem overshadow the "fancy" and "dreams" (105) which are left as alternatives to an actual relation between the men.

After reading **"Veils"** in the context of the friendship of Cranch and Browning, one cannot but be struck by the following brief passage from Cranch's late reminiscences after Browning's death:

> At the time I first knew him he was thirty-seven years old. He wore no beard or moustache, and his hair was nearly black. This was his appearance the last time I saw him. The later photographs of him, with gray hair and full gray beard, do not help me in the least to a recollection of his face.[24]

This is Cranch in old age recalling as fact what, in earlier years, he only feared:

> "I will fancy you the same
>   As in that bright weather
>   Ere this cold estrangement came,—"
>
>   (105)

Notes

1. Christopher Pearse Cranch, *Poems* (Philadelphia: Carey and Hart, 1844); *Satan: A Libretto* (Boston: Roberts, 1874); *The Bird and the Bell, with Other Poems* (Boston: James R. Osgood, 1875). Cranch's volumes of poetry have recently been collected in a facsimile edition, *Collected Poems of Christopher Pearse Cranch,* ed. Joseph M. De Falco (Gainesville, Fla.: Scholars' Facsimiles and Reprints, 1971).

2. Elizabeth R. McKinsey, *The Western Experiment: New England Transcendentalists in the Ohio Valley* (Cambridge: Harvard University Press, 1973), pp. 36-39.

3. *The Aeneid of Virgil Translated into English Blank Verse,* trans. Cranch (Boston: James R. Osgood, 1872).

4. Emerson greeted Cranch's submission of two poems to the *Dial* in 1840 with a letter of acceptance calling them "true" and "brilliant" and "one more authentic sign—added to four or five I have reckoned already—of a decided poetic taste, and tendency to original observation in our Cambridge circle" (Leonora Cranch Scott, *The Life and Letters of Christopher Pearse Cranch* [Boston: Houghton Mifflin, 1917], p. 59; hereafter cited as *Life and Letters*). Poe offered grudging, but impressive, praise, considering his contempt for the Transcendentalists, calling Cranch, "one of the least intolerable of the school of Boston transcendentalists," possessing an "unusual vivacity of fancy and dexterity expression." Poe's liking for Cranch was so out of character that he concluded that Cranch "has at last 'come out from among them [the Transcendentalists],' abandoned their doctrines (whatever they are)." Poe's sketch of Cranch is included in "The Literati of New York City" (1846); see *The Complete Works of Edgar Allan Poe,* ed. James A. Harrison (New York: Thomas Y. Crowell, 1902; rpt. ed., New York: AMS Press, 1965), 15:69-72.

5. Perry Miller calls his contributions to the *Dial* "resolute attempts to turn Transcendental metaphysics into poetry" (*The Transcendentalists: An Anthology* [Cambridge: Harvard University Press, 1950], p. 385). J. C. Levenson, noting the Emersonian themes of Cranch's earlier poems, concludes that "Cranch's intellectual grasp of the richness and uses of symbolism was far less competent than Emerson's" ("Christopher Pearse Cranch: The Case History of a Minor Artist in America," *American Literature,* 21 [January 1950]: 421).

6. Miller, *The Transcendentalists,* p. 179.

7. Miller, *The Transcendentalists,* p. 179. The most well-known sketch of Cranch is that of Van Wyck Brooks who characterizes him as "the all-attractive entertainer" to the friends he visited in the commune at Brook Farm (*The Flowering of New England, 1815-1865* [New York: E. P. Dutton, 1936], p. 250).

8. *The Bird and the Bell,* p. 59; hereafter cited in the text by page.

9. *Life and Letters,* p. 156.

10. *Life and Letters,* p. 157.

11. *Life and Letters,* p. 157.

12. Cranch, "Personal Reminiscences," *In Memoriam; Memorial to Robert Browning* (Cambridge: Browning Society of Boston, 1892), p. 49; hereafter cited as "Personal Reminiscences."

13. "Personal Reminiscences," p. 48.

14. *Life and Letters,* p. 215.

15. "Personal Reminiscences," p. 49.

16. Louise Greer, *Browning and America* (Chapel Hill: University of North Carolina Press, 1952), p. 65.

17. *Life and Letters*, p. 237.

18. *Life and Letters*, pp. 157-61.

19. *Poems* (1844), p. 51. First published as "Stanzas" in the first issue of the *Dial*, 1 (July 1840): 98.

20. McKinsey, *The Western Experiment*, p. 38. McKinsey's characterization of Cranch is supported both by the evidence of his problematic friendship with Browning, and by Hazen C. Carpenter's discussion of his somewhat unsuccessful attempts to maintain a relation with Emerson. His letter of 1855 to Emerson, complaining of his "need of a voice and touch that come near to me in my solitude" is quoted at length by Carpenter in "Emerson and Christopher Pearse Cranch," *New England Quarterly*, 37 (March 1964): 34.

21. Levenson, "Cranch," 420. Paul O. Williams, "The Persistence of Cranch's 'Enosis,'" *Emerson Society Quarterly*, No. 57 (4th Quarter 1969): 44, concurs, arguing that "such laments for lost organic unity were common among transcendental poets." Carpenter, the exception here, stresses the affirmative ending of the poem (24).

22. *The Early Lectures of Ralph Waldo Emerson*, ed. Stephen E. Whicher, Robert E. Spiller, Wallace E. Williams (Cambridge: Harvard University Press, 1959-72), 2:11.

23. *The Writings of Henry D. Thoreau* (Princeton: Princeton University Press, 1971-), vol. 1, *Walden*, ed. J. Lyndon Shanley (1971), p. 141.

24. "Personal Reminiscenses," p. 49.

David Robinson (essay date 1978)

SOURCE: Robinson, David. "The Career and Reputation of Christopher Pearse Cranch: An Essay in Biography and Bibliography." *Studies in the American Renaissance* (1978): 453-72.

[*In the following essay, Robinson surveys critical and biographical literature depicting Cranch as a Transcendentalist, poet, and painter.*]

Christopher Pearse Cranch assured himself at least a small place in American literary history through his caricatures of Emerson's *Nature,* which suggested that the Transcendentalists shared a certain sense of humor about their common enterprise, and even about their leader Emerson. But just as his drawings suggest a different mood from the high moral seriousness usually associated with Transcendental philosophy, Cranch's entire career as a minister, poet, and artist encompasses a variety of interests and pursuits which, taken together, deepen our appreciation both of his own talents, and of the movement which he consistently and enthusiastically championed, even at some cost to himself. Henry James' observation that "there were certain chords in Emerson that did not vibrate at all"[1] could not be applied to Cranch, who was at various times in his life a minister, a Unitarian missionary to the West, an important force behind the *Western Messenger,* the pioneering literary and theological journal of the Ohio Valley, a theological controversialist, a poet, a writer of children's fiction, a translator of Virgil, a champion of music in America, especially that of Beethoven, an avid follower of theater and opera, and a professional painter of some repute. Emerson, who encouraged Cranch in his poetic pursuits, publishing two of his poems in the first issue of the *Dial,* later gently accused him of dilettantism, saying "I have always understood that you are the victim of your own various gifts; that all the muses, jealous each of the other, haunt your brain."[2] Perry Miller, who clearly saw Cranch as an antidote to the unrelieved moral intensity of most of the Transcendentalists, characterized him as "one of the most delightful of the Transcendental group—if only because he alone had a feeling of frivolity." But, Miller adds, "he ultimately proved one of the most futile and wasted talents."[3]

Miller's mixture of attitudes toward Cranch exemplifies the attitude of many of the literary historians who have dealt with him. The legacy of Cranch's sporadic career as a poet, of his life so varied in activity, and of an almost universal testimony to his unusually great personal charm, has led to an historical estimate of Cranch as a failed poet whose major historical interest lies in his personality. While his humor has been hailed as a sign of healthy detachment from Transcendentalism, he has also been judged a dilettante, not committed to his literary pursuits firmly enough to be successful. The assessment of Cranch's literary artistry has thus been inseparable from assessments of his relation with Transcendentalism. While Cranch certainly belonged with that movement, and counted his relationship with Emerson and association with the *Dial* among his most fulfilling achievements, the fact of that association has tended to draw away attention from his poems themselves, replacing it with attention toward his place in the movement. In this essay, I will attempt to review the major directions of the published work which is devoted to, or which touches upon, Cranch's work and career, both to assess what has been done, and to suggest what still remains a fruitful area of inquiry. . . .

Cranch the Transcendentalist

As the variety of the preceding catalog of Cranch's literary and artistic endeavors confirms, he was a many-sided individual. His historical reputation, however, arises out of his early championing of Transcendentalism, and his continuing part in that movement. Cranch assumed a place as one of the earliest expounders of Transcendentalism because of his association with the *Western Messenger* from 1835 to 1837, the first periodical which could be labeled Transcendental. Later in 1839, he returned from the Ohio Valley to New England, where he began to associate with others in the Transcendental movement, including Emerson, and contributing to the *Dial* from its very first issue. His close friendship with J. S. Dwight also gave him a connection with Brook Farm and its periodical, the *Harbinger*. Cranch was not as completely committed to the creation of a new American literature as Emerson was, nor as committed to social reform as was Dwight, and from one perspective, his association with Transcendentalism was only one phase on his road to personal and intellectual maturity. But his contribution to the movement was real, and its effect upon him was profound.

The general biographical portraits of Cranch usually center around his relations with Transcendentalism, and provide a basis for any study of that relationship. Leonora Cranch Scott, the daughter of the poet, publishes much of the basic information about her father's life in *The Life and Letters of Christopher Pearse Cranch,* including Cranch's correspondence with Emerson in the early 1840s, which is of special significance. Scott's work is supplemented by F. DeWolfe Miller's biographical sketch in *Christopher Pearse Cranch and His Caricatures of New England Transcendentalism,* a work based on the earlier biographical material in his more comprehensive dissertation. Miller briefly sketches Cranch's career at the Harvard Divinity School, his years as a minister, missionary, and journalist in the Ohio Valley, his return to New England, and the establishment of his ties with Emerson. Other biographical portraits of Cranch which focus upon his relations with Transcendentalism can be found in Frederick Coburn's "Christopher Pearse Cranch," *Dictionary of American Biography* (New York: Scribner's, 1930) 4:501-502, and in "Christopher Pearse Cranch," *The Library of Southern Literature,* comp. Lucian L. Knight (Atlanta: Marlin and Hoyt, 1907), 15:99. Cranch is included in the latter collection because he is a Virginian by birth, although as Miller points out, "he is actually no more southern than Poe was the 'Bostonian' which he early acclaimed himself. Cranch was quite New England."[4] Frank Preston Stearns' *Cambridge Sketches* (Philadelphia: J. B. Lippincott, 1905) offers one of the most interesting biographical essays on Cranch, approaching him less from the point of view of literary or artistic history than as a fascinating social figure. While Stearns cannot be relied upon heavily for complete factual accuracy, he does offer such memorable glimpses as Thackeray reading aloud to Cranch in a London chophouse, or Emerson meeting Cranch at the Concord Railway station with "an old cylinder hat which had evidently seen good service, and yet became him remarkably," or Cranch singing Bret Harte's "Jim" in a deep, rich, and sonorous voice (pp. 123-25). Aside from such anecdotes, Stearns offers a fuller discussion of Cranch the artist than most of his other biographers interested in him primarily because of his connection with Transcendental concerns.

In studies of the Transcendental movement itself, Cranch is usually given at least brief mention. Octavius Brooks Frothingham's early *Transcendentalism in New England* (New York: Putnam's, 1876) notes Cranch's contributions to the *Dial* and later to the *Harbinger*. Harold Clarke Goddard's *Studies in New England Transcendentalism* (New York: Columbia University Press, 1908) refers to Cranch as "one of the most picturesque figures of the period" (p. 37), and William R. Hutchison notes his "happy but relatively unproductive career as a painter and dilettante after leaving the ministry" (*The Transcendentalist Ministers* [New Haven: Yale University Press, 1959], p. 198n.). Lawrence Buell (*Literary Transcendentalism* [Ithaca: Cornell University Press, 1973]) sees Cranch, J. S. Dwight, and Ellery Channing as among those Transcendentalists whose temperaments were "closer to the purely artistic temperament than Emerson" (pp. 42-43), and who were thus troubled by the demand for forceful prophecy that Emerson's aesthetics seemed to place on them. Henry A. Pochmann offers a brief biographical sketch of Cranch, and also notes his translations of German verse in *German Culture in America: Philosophical and Literary Influences, 1600-1900* (Madison: University of Wisconsin Press, 1957), pp. 449, 769. Cranch's German translations are also noted variously in Stanley M. Vogel's *German Literary Influences on the American Transcendentalists* (New Haven: Yale University Press, 1955). Perry Miller's treatment of Cranch in *The Transcendentalists* contributes one of the most enlightening analyses of Cranch's career and his relationship with the Transcendental movement. In introducing excerpts from Cranch's prose and poetry, including his early *Western Messenger* review of Emerson's "The American Scholar," Miller depicts Cranch's early conception of the religious nature of Transcendentalism, and what Miller feels is his turn toward "unabashed aestheticism" (p. 385) in his later career, as exemplified in his sonnet pair entitled **"The Garden."** Lawrence Porter's "Transcendentalism: A Self-Portrait," *New England Quarterly* 35 (March 1962): 27-47, attempts to recreate the Transcendentalists' conception of themselves as a group, focusing on their private expressions of that conception rather than their public stance. Porter notes Cranch's seeming lack of clarity about Transcendental goals as revealed in his letters, and also cites his satirical drawings as evidence of a certain distance between himself and the group.

Cranch's relationship with James Freeman Clarke and the *Western Messenger* is of itself an especially fascinating area of study, both for what that relationship meant to Cranch, and for what the periodical itself tells us about Transcendentalism. There is evidence of a warm friendship between the two men in Clarke's *Autobiography, Diary and Correspondence,* ed. Edward Everett Hale (Boston: Houghton, Mifflin, 1891), and anyone interested in this phase of Cranch's career would do well to consult Clarke's description of his own motives for undertaking his missionary assignment to the West. Essential background information on the *Western Messenger* is available in several places, but a definitive study of the journal remains to be written. W. H. Venable's early study, *Beginnings of Literary Culture in the Ohio Valley* (Cincinnati: Robert Clarke, 1891), devotes a section to the *Western Messenger,* calling it "an eastern messenger—the organ of New England liberalism in the Valley of the Ohio" and arguing that it was "even more literary than religious" in its character (p. 72). Ralph Leslie Rusk's *The Literature of the Middle Western Frontier* (New York: Columbia University Press, 1925) also notes the contribution of the journal to American literary history, singling out Cranch's poetical reference to Wordsworth ("To my Sister M., with Wordsworth's Poems," *Western Messenger* 4 [February 1838]: 375-76) as evidence of the growth of romanticism in American literature. In *The Periodicals of American Transcendentalism,* the basic study of all the Transcendental periodicals, Clarence Gohdes discusses the *Western Messenger,* calling particular attention to Cranch's early reviews which championed Emerson's controversial addresses, and to Cranch's essay **"Transcendentalism"** (*Western Messenger* 8 [January 1841]: 405-409). More detailed information on the journal, and on Cranch's hand in editing it, can be found in Charles E. Blackburn, "Some New Light on the *Western Messenger,*" *American Literature* 26 (November 1954): 320-26.

The most thorough and suggestive study of the *Western Messenger* and those who founded and sustained it is Elizabeth R. McKinsey, *The Western Experiment: New England Transcendentalists in the Ohio Valley* (Cambridge: Harvard University Press, 1973). McKinsey's study treats not only the *Western Messenger,* but the larger experiment from which it was born—the attempt of several young Unitarian ministers with decided Transcendental leanings, Clarke, Cranch, and William Henry Channing, to carry liberal religion to the Western frontier. McKinsey is concerned above all with the reasons for the ultimate failure of their experiment, since all of them eventually abandoned their plans. Were these personal failures on the part of the young ministers themselves, or did their failure reflect the peculiar limits of the Transcendental movement? In answer, McKinsey points to the nature of the Transcendentalists' hopes for the West as an explanation of their failure: "From the outset, the problem for the *Western Messenger* editors was of course that there were two Wests—their ideal and the rough-and-tumble frontier reality" (p. 53).

McKinsey devotes part of her essay to an individual analysis of each of the three men's careers, and her portrait of Cranch raises several important questions about the complexity of his psyche. She stresses the contrast between his graciously charming social presence and a private self that was tormented by a feeling of isolation, and a haunting fear of being unable to establish fulfilling relationships with others. Her analysis is thus a corrective to the temptation to regard Cranch's superficial social successes as evidence of an excessively casual or overly simplified pattern of social relationships.

After returning to New England from the West, Cranch found himself caught in the midst of the social and theological controversy that surrounded Emerson and the Transcendentalists. There is evidence that Cranch was in some sense ignorant of the vehemence of the conflict from the distance of the Ohio Valley—or at least that he was unaware of what consequences his growing Transcendental credentials could have for him in terms of his intended career as a Unitarian minister. As his 1840 letter to Dwight reveals, Cranch felt excluded by the established Unitarians, his name "expunged from the list of *safe* men."[5] But he was welcomed by the Emersonian circle, and Emerson himself welcomed his contribution of two poems, **"Stanzas,"** later retitled **"Enosis,"** and **"To the Aurora Borealis"** to the newly founded *Dial.* It had been the *Western Messenger* which first published some of Emerson's early verse. If Cranch's earlier contributions to the *Western Messenger* had initiated his relationship with Transcendentalism, his contributions to the *Dial* confirmed his place in the movement.

Cranch's submission of poems to the *Dial* initiated a correspondence with Emerson, which is largely reprinted in Scott's biography. The letters reveal Emerson's real pleasure in the poems, and also contain a certain measure of cordiality, which, it is fair to say, Cranch hoped would develop into a deeper friendship. For the full account of Cranch's relation to the *Dial,* Cooke's *An Historical and Biographical Introduction to Accompany The Dial* is an essential beginning document. Cooke devotes one volume of his study to the origin and history of the *Dial,* and a second volume to the individual authors who contributed to it, including an essay on Cranch which still stands as one of the better brief introductions to his life and work. Although Cooke's interest in him clearly centers around his poetic contributions to the *Dial,* he also recognizes that "His profession was that of a painter, and to that his heart was given" (2:6). Cooke's essays on the *Dial* contributors have recently been reprinted by Kenneth W. Cameron as "Memorabilia of the Transcendentalists in New England," *American Transcendental Quarterly,* no. 27 (Summer 1975). Cooke concludes his study with a compilation of "Titles and Contributors" to the *Dial,* a survey which is updated and corrected in Joel Myerson, "An Annotated List of Contributions to the Boston *Dial.*" Myerson also adds further essential information in "The Contemporary Reception of the Boston *Dial,*" *Resources for American Literary Study* 3 (Autumn 1973): 203-20, which notes reprints of several of Cranch's *Dial* pieces (**"Stanzas," "To the Aurora Borealis," "Musings of a Recluse"**) in various periodicals reviewing the *Dial.*

Myerson's dissertation, "A History of the *Dial* (1840-1844)" (Northwestern University, 1971), abstracted in *Dissertation Abstracts International,* 32:4573A, has superseded Cooke's earlier work as the most complete history of the *Dial.* Myerson's study falls into two parts, one devoted to a history of the journal itself, and the other concerned with its contributors. The study also contains much bibliographical information of interest to students of the period. Another more recent dissertation, Donald F. Warders' "'The Progress of the Hour and the Day': A Critical History of the *Dial* (1840-1844)" (University of Kansas, 1973), abstracted in *Dissertation Abstracts International,* 34:7790A, offers a critical approach to the *Dial* which stresses the journal's theological context, and argues for its place in the process of the secularization of American thought.

The most significant study of Cranch's relation with Emerson is Hazen C. Carpenter, "Emerson and Christopher Pearse Cranch," *New England Quarterly* 37 (March 1964): 18-42. Carpenter sketches the Cranch-Emerson relation from its inception through what he describes as a long barren period in which Emerson's coolness to Cranch was evident, and was the source of some pain for Cranch. Perhaps most significantly, he prints a portion of a March 1855 letter to Emerson in which Cranch complains of his "need of a voice & touch that come near me in my mental solitude" (34), a letter which Carpenter doubts that Emerson ever answered. Carpenter goes on to describe the apparent rebirth of the two men's friendship later in life, and to discuss briefly some of Cranch's later essays on Emerson. The importance of Carpenter's essay is the strong case it makes for seeing Cranch as a man who was more haunted by a feeling of isolation than his superficial social graces made apparent. Our understanding of what went wrong in the Emerson-Cranch relationship is deepened by William M. Moss, "'So Many Promising Youths': Emerson's Disappointing Discoveries of New England Poet-Seers," *New England Quarterly* 49 (March 1976): 46-64. Moss puts Emerson's relationship with Cranch into the larger context of his dealings with several other young poets who began in promising fashion but who eventually disappointed Emerson's hopes in one way or another. Cranch's situation is thus paralleled in Emerson's relations with Jones Very, Henry Thoreau, William Ellery Channing II, and Charles King Newcomb, with Emerson in each case taking a more professional view of the young man than he might have preferred. As Moss sees it, Emerson's enthusiasm for Cranch "was neither as intense nor as long-lasting as his enthusiasm for the others," for Cranch, "though more polished than some, lacked the fire of inspiration" (55).

Cranch also had his own perspective on Emerson, and although he revered him as an intellectual leader, he was sensitive to his faults. For a sense of his later attitude toward Emerson, one should consult his **"Ralph Waldo Emerson,"** *Unitarian Review* 20 (July 1883): 1-19, and an even later essay, **"Emerson's Limitations as a Poet,"** *Critic*, n.s. 17 (27 February 1892): 129. In the latter, Cranch responds to the question of whether any American poet ranks with the greatest English poets. Cranch's answer is that Emerson does not, although he is careful to note that "in almost all his prose he is a poet" and his prose is his greatest achievement. What is lacking in his verse, Cranch argues, is "one essential element, the sensuous." The short essay as a whole is a perceptive analysis of Emerson's strengths and weaknesses, which has been largely confirmed in the continuing criticism of Emerson in our century. These later essays on Emerson should be compared with Cranch's early *Western Messenger* review of Emerson's "The American Scholar" (*Western Messenger* 4 [November 1837]: 184-88), partially reprinted in Miller, *The Transcendentalists*, pp. 178-80.

Cranch's other major connection with Transcendentalism arises from his close friendship with John Sullivan Dwight, and his resulting connection with the Brook Farm experiment of which Dwight was a leading member. Cranch himself never joined the group, although he visited the farm often, and considered joining it as his correspondence with Dwight indicates (see Scott, pp. 88-89). Yet his visits to Dwight, which are recorded in most of the histories of the Brook Farm experiment, have established a certain historical image of Cranch which pervades many of the biographical estimates of him. Perhaps the best-known such sketch of Cranch is Van Wyck Brooks' description of him as an "all-attractive entertainer" to those he visited at Brook Farm in *The Flowering of New England, 1815-1865* (New York: E. P. Dutton, 1936), p. 250. Brooks' characterization of Cranch is one of several such descriptions based in part on John Thomas Codman's early study, *Brook Farm: Historic and Personal Memoirs* (Boston: Arena, 1894). Codman describes Cranch's abilities as a musician—he came to visit Dwight always bringing his flute—and also notes his animal imitations which delighted the children of the commune. Much the same story is told in Katherine Burton's *Paradise Planters: The Story of Brook Farm* (London: Longmans, Green, 1939) and Edith Roelker Curtis' *A Season in Utopia: The Story of Brook Farm* (New York: Thomas Nelson, 1961). A more detailed sketch of Cranch as a visitor to Brook Farm is offered in Lindsay Swift's *Brook Farm: Its Members, Scholars and Visitors* (New York: Macmillan, 1900), pp. 257-59. Swift notes Cranch's variety of talents, exhibited in his entertaining visits to the commune and his contributions of poetry to the *Harbinger*, but also notes that "perhaps, it was true of him that versatility was fatal to achievement" (p. 258), furthering the perception of Cranch as a dilettante who never realized his potential fully in any creative medium.

George William Curtis' graceful encomium in the "Editor's Easy Chair" (*Harper's New Monthly Magazine* 84 [April 1892]: 800-801) reflects the impression of Cranch from one who first met him at Brook Farm "when the Arcadian Company was gathered in the little parlor of the Eyry." Curtis concludes with the observation that Cranch's was "a long and lovely life, and if great fame be denied, not less a beautiful memory remains." Several contemporary glimpses of Cranch can be gleaned from Curtis' early letters to John Sullivan Dwight published in *Early Letters of George William Curtis to John S. Dwight*, ed. George Willis Cooke (New York: Harpers, 1898). Curtis sends news of Cranch in New York in 1843-44 to Dwight at Brook Farm, mentioning two early landscape paintings ("very striking") but later expressing doubts about his painting a scene from Tennyson's "The Lady of Shalott."

Cranch the Poet

Cranch's poetical career can be said to have begun during his association with the *Western Messenger*, a periodical which provided him with a convenient and receptive outlet for his poetry. Real recognition of his poetry, however, began with Emerson's acceptance of his contributions to the *Dial*. In accepting the poems, Emerson called them "one more authentic sign—added to four or five I have reckoned already—of a decided poetic taste, and tendency to original observation in our Cambridge circle" (Scott, p. 59). Cranch continued his contributions to the *Dial,* and to various gift books, and brought out his first collection of verse, *Poems,* in 1844. Curiously, it was about the time of the publication of *Poems* that Cranch was deciding to devote his energies to a different art, painting, as his vocation. *Poems* was to meet with little attention after its release, and this reception, combined with the thirty-year interval which preceded his next volume of verse, relegated Cranch to a somewhat smaller role in literary history than he might otherwise have attained.

Cranch was able to find admirers within his own circle of Transcendentalists, and to attract at least a degree of respect from the Transcendentalists' most bitter critic, Poe. Poe's notice, along with an early review of *Poems* by John Sullivan Dwight in the *Harbinger,* stand as the most important and perceptive of the early critical assessments of Cranch's poetry. Poe's essay on Cranch ("The Literati of New York City," *Godey's Lady's Book* [May 1846], included in *The Complete Works of Edgar Allan Poe,* ed. James A. Harrison [New York: Fred DeFau, 1902], 15:69-72) concerns itself primarily with Cranch's formal strengths and weaknesses, and Poe seems to recognize Cranch as an accomplished poet despite his skepticism about Transcendental philosophy. After calling Cranch "One of the least intolerable of the school of Boston transcendentalists," he goes on to say that "I believe that he has at last 'come out from among them,' abandoned their doctrines (whatever they are) and given up their company in disgust." It is hard to tell whether Poe is writing for effect here, or whether he honestly suspects that Cranch's removal from Cambridge and presence in New York indicate a falling away from Transcendentalism. But he goes on to note in *Poems* an "unusual vivacity of fancy and dexterity of expression, while his versification is remarkable for its accuracy, vigor, and even for its originality of effect." Although Poe is bothered by some of Cranch's "absurd conceits" (as he is by some of Donne's), and what he calls Cranch's lack of coordination of thought and meter, he nevertheless offers him higher praise than any of the other Transcendentalists. Cranch is also discussed in "The Rationale of Verse," *Southern Literary Messenger* 14 (October, November 1848): 577-85, 673-82, where Poe calls him "one of our finest poets" (673), and uses him as one of several examples in his development of a theory of scansion and rhythm.

Dwight's review of *Poems* in the *Harbinger* (1 [26 July 1845]: 105-107) stands as one of the most probing analyses of Cranch's strengths and weaknesses as a poet. There is praise in the review, as we might expect given the close friendship of the two men, and their shared philosophical views, but there is also an honest recognition of Cranch's limitations. Dwight suggests his major reservations about Cranch's poetry when he says, "The temperament of the poetry is passive," a term which points to Dwight's perception of a lack of force or positive will in the poetry. In short, Cranch's poetry has a "grace" from which "you would not expect great energy, strong determinations of the will, or the kind of eloquence that excites the will in others." Dwight is unwilling to separate this aesthetic quality from the moral character of the poet, so he adds a further observation:

> There is nothing in him which could by any possibility tyrannize over others. You feel that here is a gentle nature, a good sincere true brother, who had rather sit silent hours and days than *impose* the influence of his speech, and who would suffer all the consequences of inaction, rather than *take* the lead as some do wherever others are passive enough to let them. He would rather court the shade than *claim* regard.
>
> (106)

One wonders, after reading such a description, whether Dwight's personal friendship with Cranch was not taking over here, and whether the passage is not inspired as much by Cranch's personal qualities as by his poetry. It is also striking to note the remarkable similarity between this portrait of Cranch and Emerson's earlier description of the Transcendentalist as one willing to wait indefinitely in passive expectation rather than act without the proper motivation: "I can sit in a corner and *perish,* (as you call it,) but I will not move until I have the highest command."[6]

It is clear from Dwight's language that he is not entirely convinced that a lack of force is a fault, and that he feels that Cranch's passivity is preferable to a misguided or clamorous force. Thus Cranch's strength as a poet originates in the same source as his weakness. His passivity bespeaks a corresponding receptivity to the central Transcendental concept of the unity of the universe. Dwight therefore attributes Cranch's appeal to his perception and poetic communication of this unity: "The breath which makes his harpstrings vibrate is the Unity of nature; not merely the superficial unity of the parts with one another, but the unity of nature and the soul. The key to every unity lies in the living Passion, the soul of man. That key he grasps by a poet's instinct, by a lover's feeling, if not by a scientific formula" (105-106). Dwight's early critique in some ways predicts the development of Cranch's critical reputation, for while the complaint about his lack of force has developed into the view of Cranch as the dilettante whose potential never flowered into a mature poetic voice, his stress on Cranch's fundamental perception of a monistic unity has been echoed in the view of Cranch as a singularly direct translator of Transcendental philosophy into poetry. Cranch's ability to represent the poetic qualities of Transcendentalism also probably brought him the recognition of inclusion in the first edition of Rufus Wilmot Griswold's *The Poets and Poetry of America* (Philadelphia: Carey and Hart, 1842), and his inclusion in that anthology may well have been helpful to him in securing publication of *Poems* by the firm of Carey and Hart which published Griswold's anthology.

Although Cranch continued to write verse after the publication of *Poems,* he was increasingly absorbed in painting, and did not bring out a poetic volume for thirty years. The adverse effect of this long silence on Cranch's reputation has been mentioned above, but it should also be remembered that when Cranch began again to publish volumes of verse in the 1870s, Transcendentalism was a waning movement. William Dean Howells greeted **Satan: A Libretto** (1874) with moderate praise, noting Cranch's distinctly "liberal" idea of evil in his character Satan, and the theological modernism of the book (*Atlantic Monthly* 33 [March 1874]: 370-71), and George Parsons Lathrop called **The Bird and the Bell** (1875) the representative of "a long term of artistic life with its successes and half-successes and its various endeavor in search of the ideal" (*Atlantic Monthly* 37 [February 1876]: 244). But even had Cranch's volumes embodied successes alone, as they surely did not, his themes and preoccupations, as well as his style, were fast falling out of fashion. Lathrop rightly notes, however, that Cranch's most effective poems were his shorter portrait sonnets, such as **"To J[ames] R[ussell] L[owell] on his Fiftieth Birthday."** They reflect not only the variety of his literary friendships, but his increasingly keen eye for individual qualities. This preference for Cranch's shorter poems is confirmed by George E. Woodberry's later review of *Ariel and Caliban* (*Atlantic Monthly* 59 [March 1887]: 417-18). Cranch's later attempts to write longer poems such as *Satan*, **"The Bird and the Bell,"** or **"Ariel and Caliban"** were, to varying degrees, failures, but the shorter personal and occasional poems of these years will continue to have interest for the student of the period.

After the comments of contemporary reviewers, there is little noteworthy critical analysis of Cranch's poetry until he began to attract occasional attention in academic criticism in the 1950s. Such comments as were made about him in the early part of the century dealt largely with his life and his part in the Transcendental movement (noted above), and even recent criticism has tended to be heavily biographical. J. C. Levenson's 1950 essay on Cranch as a representative minor artist ("Christopher Pearse Cranch: The Case History of a Minor Artist in America," *American Literature* 21 [January 1950]: 415-26) remains one of the best treatments of Cranch's artistic career, emphasizing his small but well-deserved place as one of the sustaining secondary artists in the American tradition. Levenson's examination of some of Cranch's earlier verse in the *Dial* is a step toward establishing the relative importance of his earlier poems, and his praise of the sonnet pair, **"The Garden"** (it "represents the best of Cranch's poetry") is a reminder of the value of Cranch's often-neglected later work. What stood in the way of higher achievement, Levenson feels, was Cranch's incomplete grasp of the nature of symbolism—he was not able to "unify modes of experience" with the same power as his chosen leader, Emerson. Perry Miller acknowledges Levenson's influence in his anthology *The Transcendentalists*, which reprints several of the *Dial* poems as well as **"The Garden."** Miller follows Levenson in seeing that poem as indicative of a certain element of Cranch's character, and of the Transcendental movement as a whole, which prefers the claims of literature over religion, and of repose over action (p. 385).

Marilyn R. Nicoson's recent dissertation, "The Inworld and the Outworld in the Poetry of Christopher Pearse Cranch" (University of Pittsburgh, 1974), abstracted in *Dissertation Abstracts International,* 36:1507A, offers an analysis of Cranch's poetry based on the terminology of the poems **"Inworld"** and **"Outworld"** published in the *Dial* 2 (January 1842): 288-91. Nicoson argues that Cranch's greatest poetic achievement is in his later poetry, rather than in the better-known earlier verse, and argues that he achieves in that poetry a final vision of harmony between his conceptions of the inworld and the outworld. In a related article, "Christopher Cranch and His Three Muses," *Concord Saunterer* 9 (December 1974): 1-11, she refers to the terms "inworld" and "outworld" as "the foci of his developing vision," inworld meaning "his inner world of self, thought, and intuitive knowledge—and 'outworld'—the actual world where reality limits the fulfillment of his inward desires." Nicoson's article lays the groundwork for a fruitful and long-neglected perspective on Cranch, one which admits his close ties to Emerson but which stresses that this closeness "does not imply that Cranch's transcendental leanings were derivative." Her portrait of Cranch leaves one finally with a firm impression that he was a man of independent mind and implacable convictions, whatever impressions of diffidence he may have left on others. Nicoson's discussion of his personal confrontation with his admitted literary and artistic "failure" late in life is as moving and revealing a glimpse of the inner man as we have yet seen in the literature.

Cranch's early poetry receives some attention in Helen Hennessy, "The *Dial*: Its Poetry and Poetic Criticism," *New England Quarterly* 31 (March 1958): 66-87, where Hennessy stresses the representative quality of Cranch's poetry to Transcendentalism, and calls **"Correspondences"** the "most extraordinary statement of the transcendental view of nature." Cranch's best known poem, published as **"Stanzas"** in the *Dial* 1 (July 1840): 98, and later entitled **"Enosis,"** is the subject of two essays. Sidney E. Lind's "Christopher Pearse Cranch's 'Gnosis': An Error in Title," *Modern Language Notes* 62 (November 1947): 486-88, notes the persistent misspelling of the title of the poem as "Gnosis" (knowledge) rather than **"Enosis"** (unity). After Longfellow published it in *The Estray* (1847) as **"Enosis,"** it appeared thereafter as either "Stanzas" or "Gnosis," the error also perpetuated in George Willis Cooke's *The Poets of Transcendentalism* (1903). Paul O. Williams' "The Persistence of Cranch's **'Enosis,'**" *Emerson Society Quarterly,* no. 57 (IV Quarter 1969): 41-46, deals with Cranch's growing frustration over his persistent identification with that single poem. Its popularity with anthologists often prevented reprinting and wider readership for his other poems. One of Cranch's later poems, **"Veils,"** is the focal point for David Robinson's discussion of Cranch's relationship with Robert Browning in "Christopher Pearse Cranch, Robert Browning, and the Problem of 'Transcendental' Friendship," *Studies in the American Renaissance 1977* (Boston: Twayne Publishers, 1978), pp. 145-53. Robinson argues that Browning is the unnamed figure whose loss of friendship Cranch is lamenting, and links the poem with both Cranch's personal sense of isolation in later life and with the larger question of the idea of friendship among the Transcendentalists.

In his *Musical Influence on American Poetry* (Athens: University of Georgia Press, 1956) Charmenz S. Lenhart deals with the influence of music on Cranch's verse, noting at the outset his close relation with J. S. Dwight, a pioneering music critic, and his close association with music circles in America. Lenhart's specific attention is directed to **Satan: A Libretto,** and to Cranch's introduction to the poem linking the poem to the musical form of the libretto. Donald Stauffer's survey, *A Short History of American Poetry* (New York: E. P. Dutton, 1974), briefly treats Cranch in the context of Transcendental poetry, and suggests that Cranch's experimental **"Correspondences"** anticipates Whitman's overturning of the traditional poetic line. Stauffer also notes a "clarity and directness" in Cranch's verse "so rarely found among the others" of the Transcendentalists (p. 109).

As the foregoing survey indicates, there has been relatively little close reading of Cranch's poetry, and very little critical evaluation that has not been biographical in its orientation. Certainly Cranch's poetry will not support the extended reading given the more accomplished poets of the period, such as Emerson, Whitman, or Dickinson, but the final evaluation of his place in literary history demands a closer reading of his literary productions.

Cranch the Artist

Cranch's turn from a career as a preacher and poet to that of a painter happened with remarkable quickness in 1841. Suffering from a debility which he told Dwight was "of a kind to depress and render unelastic both mind and will," he complained that "Thought, eloquence, and poetry desert me" (Scott, pp. 68-69). He picked up painting as a diversion, having been forsaken by language, and found in it not only therapy for his illness, but a life's work. His speculations on its possibilities as a profession are illuminating, especially in what they reveal about his attitudes toward the ministry: "I have attempted nothing but small sketches as yet, but long to launch into something larger. Why may I not pursue it eventually as a profession? It is a precarious one, I know, to earn a livelihood by, but not less so than that of a minister, a free speaker—I mean, in the present crisis of things" (Scott, p. 68).

From the middle 1840s to the 1870s, Cranch's reputation as a painter slowly widened. His strength was in landscape painting, and he devoted his early work to American landscapes of the Hudson Valley mode, and to Italian scenes. His career in painting had led him abroad where he was associated with William Wetmore Story and other Americans living in France and Italy. Henry James, in his history of those early expatriates, recalls him as "painter, poet, musician, mild and melancholy humorist, [who] produced pictures that the American traveller sometimes acquired and left verses that the American compiler sometimes includes" (*William Wetmore Story and His Friends* [Boston: Houghton, Mifflin, 1903], 1:110). Like Dwight, James sees in Cranch's painting and poetry a certain lack of force, about which he is ambivalently critical: "Pictures and verses had alike, in any case, the mark of his great, his refined personal modesty; it was not in them, at least, for good or ill, to emphasize or insist" (1:110-11). F. DeWolfe Miller's brief section on Cranch's career as a painter is the best published discussion of this phase of Cranch's career (*Christopher Pearse Cranch and His Caricatures,* pp. 18-22). Miller makes a strong argument for Cranch's historical association with the Hudson River School, although he notes that Cranch has been neglected by the art historians of the period. Cranch's painting also receives brief notice in Cooke's introduction to the *Dial* (mentioned above), which lists and dates some of Cranch's individual paintings. Frank Preston Stearns (*Cambridge Sketches*) discusses Cranch's artistic career in broad terms, referring specifically to certain of his paintings, and suggesting that Cranch "never became a mannerist" but that his similarity of subject and of treatment "bordered on the commonplace" (p. 122). Stearns also suggests that Cranch's brother-in-law, an art critic whom he does not name, disparaged Cranch's work, costing him a good deal of popularity. He also tells of Cranch, late in life, setting himself against the vogue of Velasquez in Boston in 1873, and embarking on a trip to Paris, late in life, to save his daughter's artistic taste and talent from being ruined by more provincial Boston tastes and fashions. In "Return from Arcadia: The Journey of Christopher Pearse Cranch," *New Bulletin* (Staten Island Institute of Arts and Sciences), 13 (February 1964): 63-70, Mabel Abbot and Gail K. Schneider describe an 1847-48 Italian sketchbook of Cranch's which was originally given to George William Curtis and has since come into the possession of the Staten Island Institute. Cranch's work as a painter and his relation to the Hudson River School of painting are discussed in Willie Vale Oldham Quade's masters thesis, "Christopher Pearse Cranch and John Cranch: Nineteenth Century Artists" (George Washington University, 1969), which includes photographs of several of Cranch's paintings.

Cranch maintained a lively interest in other fine arts besides painting, notably music and theater. Part of his close friendship with Dwight was based on their shared interests in music. Henry Pochmann (*German Culture in America,* p. 767) notes that the two of them, along with Margaret Fuller, formed an early Beethoven cult which took the lead in recognizing the composer. There is also passing mention of Cranch in George Willis Cooke's *John Sullivan Dwight: Brook-Farmer, Editor and Critic of Music* (Boston: Small, Maynard, 1898). Cranch's love for the theater is noted in Lucile Gafford, "Transcendentalist Attitudes Toward Drama and the Theatre," *New England Quarterly* 13 (September 1940): 442-66.

Despite the general concensus that Cranch's literary career was damaged by his dabbling in other arts, it is hard to criticize, or to regret, his wide cultivation. Whether he was, as Emerson said, "a victim of [his] own various gifts," and whether his artistic career robbed him of greater literary achievement, we cannot say, though the closer one examines the record, the more he is convinced that Cranch was not suppressing literary impulses in his turning to painting. It is clear, however, that art was both a psychological and an economic salvation for Cranch, offering him deep personal satisfaction and the means of livelihood that could not have been obtained through letters alone.

Conclusion

This survey of Cranch's career, and of the critical estimates which have grown up around it, should suggest that close attention to Cranch's poetry and prose is still the most essential task that remains for those whose interest has been pricked by this delightful, yet melancholy man. Such a reading will not, I suspect, produce any large-scale revisions of the general view that Cranch was a man of enormous talent but small achievement, but it might suggest that he was less a failure, than a man whose ambitions were modest and largely personal rather than public. The value of a fresh and close look at Cranch's poetry will be the light it sheds on the personal aims of a man whose career spanned America's cultural coming of age, from the early aspirations of Transcendentalism to the expatriatism of American aesthetes in the middle nineteenth century.

Each phase of Cranch's career sheds light on part of that cultural awakening. His early prose exemplifies the interplay of Unitarian sectarianism and romanticism out of which Transcendentalism emerged, and Cranch's perspective on the controversy that ensued between Unitarians and Transcendentalists is a valuable one. The relation between his spiritual goals and his aesthetic tastes is similarly indicative of the merging of these two sensibilities in many of the other Transcendentalists. Cranch's later work, still largely overlooked, suggests the delicate historical link between Transcendental moral concerns, and the more purely aesthetic concerns of a later generation of Americans, and furthers our sense of a context for figures like Dwight, Lowell, Story, and even James and Howells.

Much of what Cranch published will not repay extremely close attention, but much of it will. The problem is that few discriminations have been established as yet, so the distinction between former and latter groups of his work has to be made through firsthand investigation.

Notes

The completion of this essay was made possible through grants from the General Research Program and the College of Liberal Arts Research Program, Oregon State University, which the author gratefully acknowledges.

1. Henry James, *Partial Portraits,* ed. Leon Edel (Ann Arbor: University of Michigan Press, 1970), p. 30.
2. Leonora Cranch Scott, *The Life and Letters of Christopher Pearse Cranch* (Boston: Houghton Mifflin, 1917), p. 281.
3. *The Transcendentalists,* ed. Perry Miller (Cambridge: Harvard University Press, 1950), p. 179.
4. *Christopher Pearse Cranch and His Caricatures,* p. 7.
5. Myerson, "Transcendentalism and Unitarianism in 1840: A New Letter by C. P. Cranch," *CLA Journal* 16 (March 1973): 366.
6. *The Collected Works of Ralph Waldo Emerson,* ed. Robert E. Spiller and Alfred R. Ferguson (Cambridge: Harvard University Press, 1971-), 1:212.

Shelly Armitage (essay date 1987)

SOURCE: Armitage, Shelly. "Christopher Pearse Cranch: The Wit as Poet." *American Transcendental Quarterly* n.s. 1, no. 1 (March 1987): 33-47.

[*In the following essay, Armitage discusses the role of wit, as defined by Emerson, in Cranch's poetry.*]

> You were not born to hide such gifts as yours
> 'Neath dreary law-books, nor amid the dust
> And dry routine of desks to sit and rust
> Where clerks plod through their tasks on office-floors.
> Let duller laborers drudge through daily chores,
> And do what fate for them makes fit and just.
> You bravely do your work because you must;
> And when released, your genius sings and soars.
> Such humor your pen hath ever run
> In pictures or in letters all unforced,
> As Hogarth, Lamb, or Dickens might have done;
> Finer than any noted wit, who, horsed
> Upon the public's favor, waves his blade
> Like Harlequin, and makes his jests his trade.
>
> *Ariel and Caliban,* 1886

It is difficult to read this sonnet from his last collection of poems other than autobiographically, for Christopher Pearse Cranch (1813-1892) rejected both the practice of law and the ministry for the life of a poet, painter, essayist, and writer of children's stories. Indeed, Cranch upturned a number of bushels in an effort to let his light shine; in 1888, he wrote his brother, Edward: "One thing I am sure of . . . I should have been a composer" (Scott 358). Friends and critics would have argued to the contrary, for though they admired Cranch's many gifts, they unanimously criticized his pursuit of all of them: Lowell said Cranch's foolish fairy left the brass out when she brought her gifts to his cradle (XIV 325); Emerson wrote he was the victim of warring muses which haunted his brain (Scott 280); Henry Tuckerman noted a want of emphasis in his landscape painting (461); F. DeWolfe Miller called for less of the humor that made his poems jejune (10); and William Wetmore Story wished for more humor in his lachrymose children's stories (Meigs 208). Following this precedent, modern critics tag Cranch a "dilettante" for his failure to achieve distinction in any of these arts.[1]

Yet, as the opening sonnet suggests, Cranch's is a well-intended halfness. In order for genius to "sing and soar," one must escape "dry routine" and "daily chores." The emancipator? Wit—that swift play and flash of mind which delights by expressing the dissimilar and incongruous. This was Cranch's habit throughout his life: to "horse upon the public's favor" in pictures, letters, and in poetry. His caricatures of Emerson and the transcendentalists and his journal and letters each reckon with the incongruities of language. More important to this study, Cranch's wit is the consistent element in his otherwise various poems. To this extent, he make "jests his trade."

A "well-intended halfness" is the central term in Emerson's definitive essay on wit, "The Comic." First delivered in Boston on January 30, 1839, as "Comedy," and published in *The Dial* in October 1843, the essay undoubtedly was read by Cranch who by 1838 had become an Emerson proselyte and who published alongside him in *The Dial* from 1840 to 1844. Emerson writes: "The essence of all jokes, of all comedy, seems to be an honest or well-intended halfness; a nonperformance of what is pretended to be performed, at the same time that one is giving loud pledges of performance. The balking of the intellect, the frustrated expectation, the break of continuity in the intellect, is comedy" (205). What Emerson describes, according to opinions of his time, is the traditional realm of humor and wit. Humor deals with incongruities of character and circumstance as wit does in those of arbitrary ideas.[2] Because he is not concerned with formal definition, but instead with the consequences of various incongruities, he interchanges the terms "humor," "wit," and "comedy," taking the generator of wit—the intellect—and extending it to the plane of humor and comedy:

> This is the radical joke of life and then literature. The presence of the ideal of right and truth in all action makes the yawning delinquencies of practice remorseful to the conscience, tragic to the interest, but droll to the intellect. The activity of our sympathies may for a time hinder our perceiving the fact intellectually, and so deriving mirth from it; but all falsehoods, all vices seen at sufficient distance, seen from the point where our moral sympathies do not interfere, become ludicrous. The comedy is in the intellect's perception of discrepancy.
>
> (206-207)

By yoking the intellect's perception to life *and* to literature, Emerson's "radical joke" further suggests the interrelationship of action, perception, and expression and the role of the writer and audience. He implies that both the writer (or actor or speaker) and the audience participate in expression as a result of the intellect's perception: the wit writes and the audience is bemused. Communication is the key, that is, the re-linking of the network between intellects originally broken by the disparate character or event. Therefore, the wit, who sees similarities in dissimilar things, uses paradox, play on words, surprising diction, epigrams, comparisons, etc., to unite writer and audience. His "well-intended halfness" is not disjunctive but connective. Furthermore, this comic perception has yet another positive effect on the perceiver (whether he be writer or audience): "A perception of the Comic seems to be the balance-wheel in our metaphysical structure. . . . It appears to be an essential element in fine character. We feel the absence of it as a defect in the noblest and most oracular soul. The perception of the Comic is a tie of sympathy with other men, a pledge of sanity, and a protection from those perverse tendencies and gloomy insanities in which fine intellects sometimes lose themselves" (207-208).

As we shall see, Emerson's "The Comic" is an apt description for the role of wit in Cranch's work; initially, however, we should note how wit functioned in his life. From the time he attended Harvard Divinity School in 1832 until his decision to leave the ministry in 1843, Cranch battled the eccentricities of a sharp intellect cloaked in the expectations of the Unitarian ministry. During this period, wit was his salve as he attempted to balance his misgivings about the ministry and his doubts about himself and his future. Born of auspicious parentage, his father the chief Justice of the District Court in Alexandria and former classmate of John Quincy Adams, Cranch was the youngest of thirteen children in a firmly religious but loving family. When one brother chose medicine and the other law, there was but one gentlemanly profession left to Cranch; and after graduating from Columbian College and Harvard Divinity School, he was licensed to preach. Sent as a missionary at large to congregations in Bangor, Portland, Andover, Richmond, Louisville, and St. Louis, Cranch simultaneously got his first taste of homesickness and of a job ill-suited to him. Typically, Cranch drew on his wit to offset his melancholia, and in one response to a friend, John Sullivan Dwight, he wrote from Andover, Maine: "If you have a spark of sympathy and kindness for me will you put this note up for me in some Christian church in the civilized country I have left: 'A man abiding in the wilderness desires the prayers of his friends for his liberation and return'" (Scott 21-22). He further told Dwight that he was a "tropical animal" who might be frozen by later generations and viewed as "a rare specimen of a departed race of animals" (Scott 21-22). Snowbound that winter in 1837, he wrote **"Childe Christopher,"** a parody of "Childe Harolde," complete with marginal sketches. He protested in another letter to James Freeman Clarke that it was so cold "that the very logs do beg to be burned," and, describing his life among the "Philistines," he enclosed a draft of a sermon on which he had drawn devils in the margins (F. D. Miller 8).

These seemingly whimsical scribbles were in fact Cranch's release from an intense period of soul-searching and depression. During his tenure in Bangor in 1837, he wrote his sister Margaret:

> My eyes are turned so habitually on myself, that almost every action of my life is divested of freedom. Nothing goes from me that has not passed under the eyes of self, and is not referred to the opinion of others around me. I am not free enough; I am not bold enough for a minister of the Word of Life. Over and over again I

chide my timidity, my reserve, my sensitiveness. I want what might be called spontaneousness. I must mingle among men and women more. I must converse freely about everything. I must think more of my fellow man and less of myself. I must not feel detached from society but as forming a stone in the arch, helping support the building. The minister should not be a standing, placid lake, embosomed by mountains and gazing on the stars; but a quick, deep, active strong-moving stream winding among men, purifying and gladdening the world.

(Scott 40)

Ironically, the traits Cranch describes at the end of this passage were characteristic of his wit, not his methods as a minister. A poor orator, hemmed in by a role that prompted intimidating introspection and magnified what he saw as faults, Cranch's wit—necessarily a product of detachment or "aloofness," as Emerson called it—allowed him to distance himself while achieving the spontaneousness and supportiveness he desparately sought. But he wanted most what he could not muster in the pulpit: public expression. In a letter to Miss Julia Myers, he indicates that his battle was to free his expressive self through an exciting belief:

In Richmond many, many things were in my heart, but I could not trust to common spoken language to utter them, and indeed I know not if it is much easier to do it on paper. I have never been accustomed to give full vent in words to my feelings and thoughts; I cannot do it; I have at times, under the influence of a temporary excitement of the organ of language, joined with other causes, and for a brief period my diffidence was driven out by self-possession, and my inertness by a short-lived vigour, and words came with ease and aptitude which surprised myself. But this is only at times. A besetting diffidence lies at the root of all my reserve, and keeps me again and again silent and semingly cold, when no one could tell how deep and strong the stream which ran hidden within.

(Scott 35)

Thus, Cranch's task was to find some means of expression analogous in its attending philosophy and language to the "unforced" humor he wrote of in the sonnet from *Ariel and Caliban.* Moreover, Cranch sought a publicly successful means of communicating rather than a private one, and between 1837 and 1844 several events led to a solution. First, while in Louisville, he was encouraged by two elderly Jewesses to write poetry, and he began publishing religious and Wordsworthian stanzas in the *Western Messenger* and the *Southern Literary Messenger,* respectively. At the same time he took up this means of expression, he discovered a new philosophy, for in 1837, shortly after arriving in St. Louis to fill the pulpit and the editor's chair of the *Western Messenger* for Clarke, he read Emerson's *Nature.* His reaction to Emerson and his ideas was recorded in his review of "The American Scholar" in the November, 1837, number of the *Messenger* where he referred to Emerson as a man of genius, a bold deep thinker, and the concise original writer. He compared the style in "The American Scholar" to that of *Nature,* "that bright little gem in our literature" ("**Emerson**" 184). Later, he wrote to Emerson of the influence of *Nature* on him: "I have long wished to express my deep gratitude for the instruction and delight I have derived from all your productions, published and spoken. I utter no hollow compliments or vain imaginings when I say that I have owed to you more quickening influences and more elevating views in shaping my faith, than I can ever possibly express to you" (Scott 58). And, again, to Emerson: "Your books are wells of deep truth, which I feel I can never exhaust. . . . There are no writings of the day which have so captivated me, and afforded such matter for profound thought as yours" (Scott 60-61). A measure of these profound thoughts was found in "The Divinity School Address," which Cranch reviewed in the *Messenger* in the issue following his "American Scholar" review. Cranch again praised Emerson's "original genius," defending his attack on historical Christianity. Cranch was impressed by what he called Emerson's plea for the spirit of Christianity, and shortly afterward wrote his father in defense of his newly adopted philosophy:

Somehow the name "Transcendentalism" [sic] has become a nickname here for all who have broken away from the material philosophy of Locke, and the old theology of many of the early Unitarians, and who yearn for something more satisfying to the soul. It has almost become one who, in whatever way, preaches the spirit rather than the letter.

(Scott 50)

By 1842, Cranch was publishing poetry of a primarily transcendental spirit. And he wrote Emerson: "I become more and more inclined to sink the minister into the man, and abandon my present calling in toto as a profession. . . . A clergyman's life is the life of a slave. He cannot be a man. He cannot own a soul, and a mouth of his own" (Scott 60). Thus, by 1843, Cranch had solved his personal dilemma of diffidence and lack of inspiration and appropriate expression. He decided to leave the ministry; in its stead he turned to the "new philosophy" rather than to the old religion, and, rather than writing sermons, made poetry his mouthpiece.

If there was not a new god, at least there was a prophet of the new religion. In **"The Prophet Unveiled,"** Cranch recorded the enthusiasm of a new convert:

We have heard him speak; upon his eye and tongue,
Dropping their golden thoughts we mutely hung.
Aurora shootings mixed with summer lightning;
Meteors of truth through beauty's sky still bright'ning
Phoenix-lived things born amid stars and flashes;
And rising rocket-winged from their own ashes;
Pearls prodigally rained, too large and fast;
Rich music-tones too sweet and rare to last—
Such seemed his natural utterance as it passed.
And yet the steadier light that shone alway,
Looked through these meteors in their rapid play,
And warmed around us like the sunlight mild,
And Truth in Beauty's robes stood by and smiled.

(645)

What is remarkable about the poem, other than its exuberance and evidently concrete reference to a lecture Cranch had heard, is the language.[3] Imagistic, allusive, and metaphorical, the poem suggests the power of the prophet; his words are "Aurora shootings mixed with summer lightning"—pearls of truth, music, meteors, regenerative "golden thoughts" that make the audience hang upon the prophet's words. The result for the young proselyte turned poet is his own evocative language. Earlier, Cranch had praised the "rare beauty" of Emerson's style, noting that its hallmark was an obscurity and an "irreverence or impiety to the common ear" ("**New School**" 37). What Cranch recognizes is Emerson's sometimes shocking style as he defined it in *Nature*: "Wise men pierce this rotten diction and fasten words again to visible things; so that picturesque language is at once a commanding certificate that he who employs it is a man in alliance with truth and God" (17). Moreover, Cranch has discovered that this power of the poet—to surprise through uncommon comparisons, unusual diction, paradoxes, etc.—is also the realm in which he is most fluent. It is the realm of "the comic" or wit. As Emerson revealed to Cranch both in *Nature* and in the copy of "The Poet" he sent to Cranch in 1844, the poet, like the comic writer, derives his perception from the intellect. "The sensual man conforms thoughts to things; the poet conforms things to his thoughts. The one esteems nature as rooted and fast; the other, as fluid, and impresses his being thereon. To him, the refractory world is ductile and flexible; he invests dust and stone with humanity, and makes them the words of reason" (29). Also like the comic writer, the poet is "a person in whom powers are balanced." What of comedy's "well-intended halfness"? The poet by ulterior intellectual perception, gives words "a power which makes their old use forgotten, and puts eyes and a tongue into every dumb and inanimate object." Thus, Cranch's turn to poetry gave him a public arena for his native wit. The necessary proclivities were the same; indeed, through wit, the poet could hope to awaken and inspire his audience to his most earnest perceptions.

If Cranch could not quite hitch his wagon to a star as Emerson so neatly did, he nevertheless used his wit to instruct as well as delight. The very fact that he conceptualized Emerson's outrageous diction in the caricatures indicates his recognition that bold thoughts sometimes border on the ridiculous. By rendering Emerson's figurative language in a literal sense—the cartoon—Cranch dramatized the power of Emerson's wit—a feat which Cranch claimed was both entertaining and instructive.[4] Not surprisingly, in Cranch's own poetry his wit accomplishes like ends; always its purpose is to prick the audiences' recognition of a truth. An example is "**The Humming Bird**" included in his first collection, *Poems*, in 1844. Cranch begins whimsically enough:

> Tell us, tell us, whence thou comest,
>   Little thing of rainbow wing;
> Tell us if thou always hummest:
>   If thou canst not sing.

Yet the poem soon evokes lost youth and innocence, suggesting nature's mystery:

> When a boy I often dreamed,
>   Wondering what thou wast and whence,
> For thy quivering winglets seemed
>   Scarce like things of sense.

Finally, the poem focuses on the narrator rather than the bird, implying a nostalgic comparison:

> But like a suspected lover,
>   Darting off into the sky,
> Ere we could with truth discover
>   Half thy brilliancy.
>
> I'll not blame thee, little thing,
>   That thou wast then a mystery,
> When life and thought were in their spring,
>   And fancy wandered free.
>
> For I was like thee, gentle bird,
>   As wild and gay, as strange and shy,
> And all my hours were with the flowers,
>   Beneath a summer sky.

(26)

The most fascinating use of wit occurs in poems dealing with the role of the seer and his audience. Indeed, in each of Cranch's three volumes of poems there are numerous works that deal with this theme. Moreover, unlike many of his other poems which are purely lyrical or experimental or are modeled after familiar forms, Cranch's poems on the poet are distinctively witty. In his first volume in which most of the poetry is Wordsworthian or transcendental in sentiment, four poems deal with the seer: "**The Poet**," "**The Artist**," "**The Blind Seer**," and "**The Star Gazer**." In "**The Poet**," Cranch posits Emerson's characteristics of the poet, and he optimistically describes his role:

> Thus hovering, bee-winged, over every floor,
>   And gathering all the nectar from its bosom,
> And e'en midst broken hearts, in grief's dark hour,
>   Stealing a sweetness from the poison blossom,
> He garners up the honey of his thought,
>   And yields unto the world whate'er his soul hath wrought.

(39)

These lines hardly pack the import of Emerson's "man's relation to nature, his power over it, is through the understanding, as by manure," but Cranch has his poet's honeyed thoughts come even from *poison* blossoms. Nevertheless, in a review of the 1844 *Poems*, the writer for *Graham's* correctly observes: "The volume has a lack of nerve, the absence of that power and knowledge which are conferred by the rough discipline of the world, the want of true depth and intensity." By the time the next volume appeared, *The Bird and the Bell* (1875), Cranch had that added dimension, for he had lived abroad in both Italy and Paris. Deriving a maturity from his European experience and freed from the rather provincial influences of New England transcendentalism, Cranch's poems in this volume exhibit a wider range and creativity. Unlike the predominantly philosophical poems of the first volume, these poems are on topical subjects such as the Civil War and the nation.

In this context, the role of the poet or seer takes a different turn. In **"The American Pantheon,"** Cranch jibes at what had initially pointed to his poetic greatness—his inclusion in Rufus Griswold's *The Poets and Poetry of America* (1842) two years before his first book of poems was published. He had claimed in **"The Poet"** (1838):

> Time's wreaths await him: far in future ages,
>   Twined in their amaranth beauty they are shining,
>   And blessings rained upon his fragrant pages,
>   And tears from kindred hearts, quenching, repining,
>   With warm sympathy and smiles of joy
>   Embalm a sacred life which Time cannot destroy.
>
>   (608)

But in **"The American Pantheon"**:

>   When Rufus Griswold built his Pantheon wide,
>   And set a hundred poets round its walls,
>   Did he believe their statues would abide
>   The test of time upon their pedestals?
>
> A hundred poets! Some in Parian stone,
>   Perchance! and some in brittle plaster cast;
> And some mere busts, whose names are hardly known—
>   *Di minores* of a voiceless past.
>
> So while around this Pantheon wide I stray,
>   Where poets from Freneau to Fay are set,
> I doubt not each in turn has sung some lay
>   The world will not be willing to forget.
>
>   (217-218)

Cranch cleverly undercuts the notion of the wide Pantheon by using a Latin phrase—supposedly appropriate to the Pantheon—to debunk it. These poets not only are forgotten, but they are "*di minores* of a voiceless past," suggesting they failed even in their own time. Cranch indicates that both those set in the white stone of Paros and those plaster-of-Paris poets will perish. Cranch gives us the reason in his clever rhyme of "stray" and "lay": by aligning these in rhyme, he suggests their relationship—one that emphasizes the disparity between the poets' songs and a wandering bard. In this case, one of their own members is straying—a word intended to suggest a double meaning. Cranch is both casually strolling among the ruins of this pantheon and escaping, while the other poets are "set." Why does he stray? The world is willing to forget these so-called permanent fixtures of poetic prowess. Thus, through rhyme, word play, irony, and imagery, Cranch suggests the poetic immortality he touted in his youth is tenuous.

In the same volume, Cranch chooses a more humorous tone to carry a like theme. This time, the poem offers more insight into the interrelationship of the public (or audience) and the poet. He writes in **"The Thrush in a Gilded Cage"**:

> He glanced at freedmen, operas, politics,
>   And other common topics of the day;
> But not one brilliant image did he mix
>   With all the prosy things he had to say.
>
> At least I hope that one I long had known,
>   In inspired books that built his fame,
> Would breathe some word, some sympathetic tone,
>   Fresh from the ideal region whence he came.
>   . . . . .
>
> Simple enthusiast! why do you require
>   A budding rose for every thorny stalk?
> Why must we poets always bear the lyre
>   And sing when fashion forces us to talk?
>
> Only at moments comes the muse's light,
>   Alone, like shy wood-thrushes, warble we.
> Catch us in traps like this dull crowd to-night,
>   We are but plain, brown-feathered birds, you see!
>
>   (156)

One need but compare this poem to **"The Prophet Unveiled"** to get a notion of Cranch's changing opinion of the success of the seer with the audience. In fact, the poem may be about Emerson, though this is merely supposition. Nevertheless, the poem pursues the disastrous effects of the gilded cage—the trap of the dull crowd—by the same clever use of diction, rhyme, and imagery cited in Cranch's poems above. But to this poem Cranch adds the interesting transformation of the narrator from a member of the audience to one who, as a poet, identifies with the plain brown bird, the failed poet. At the beginning of the poem, the persona is a member of the audience, disappointed that the poet mixes no brilliant images, but speaks "prosy things" instead. Then he speaks to the "simple enthusiast"—chastises him, really—as if he were another member of the audience and yet, himself, for in the same stanza the persona identifies himself also as a poet. Finally, after his shift to the "we"—the poets taxed by uninspiring audiences—shifted affiliation indicates not the criticism of the poet heard in the first stanza, but criticism of the audience.

Other poems in this collection address the problem of perception and communication, and conclude that communication has been lost from the human realm and resides only with the animals. In **"Bobolinks"** and **"Bird Language,"** Cranch playfully links the spontaneity of nature's creatures with the ability to communicate. In each case, the persona in these poems fails to understand the animals, but because of his youthful and joyful attitude, can appreciate the fact that communication exists. In this emphasis, Cranch suggests that man has lost the ability to communicate for several reasons. One, as indicated in **"The American Pantheon,"** is fashion, or endlessly changing tastes. Another is the influence of science, which would solve mysteries and, hence, interfere with the domain of the poet. In **"Luna Through a Lorgnette,"** science's snooping telescope cancels mystery, romance, and the ideal—indeed, this invention prompts a new perception:

> Ah, farewell my boyish fancies!
> Farewell, all my young romances!
> As that orb that shone Elysian
> On my young poetic vision,
> As that cresent boat which lightly
> Tilted o'er the cloud-rack nightly,
> I again can see her never,
> Though I use my best endeavor.
> On me once her charms she sprinkled,
> Now her face is old and wrinkled.
> As Diana chaste and tender,
> Can I now as once defend her?
> She is full of histories olden
> Wrapped up in her bosom golden.
> Sorceress of strange beguiling,
> Thousands perished by her smiling—
> Girls kept waking, old men saddened,
> Lovers lost, and poets maddened.
> Now the well-armed eye of Science
> Bids her magic spells defiance;
> Moonstruck brains by moonlight haunted
> Telescopes have disenchanted.
> Talk not of the brow of Dian.
> Gentle bards you may rely on
> What I've seen to-night; 't is clearly
> Known the moon's constructed queerly,
> Full of wrinkles, warts, and freckles,
> Gilded cracks and spots and speckles;
> As if in wandering through the void,
> Her face were marked with varioloid.
> Then her cheeks and eyes so hollow,
> That I'm sure the bright Apollo
> Ne'er would know her for his sister,
> Nor Endymion have kissed her.
>
> (47-48)

In a perfect illustration of the "Machine in the Garden," Cranch shows in his jog-trot verses how technology destroys myth. In this way, the poem is a beautiful example of the effects of nineteenth-century industrialization, for, though the telescope was developed long before, Cranch depicts the plight of poetic vision in an era of search for greater efficiency, progress, and concreteness. Indeed, the poet juxtaposes romanticism and realism, handily playing off classical images of the moon and her attendants with the wrinkles, warts, and freckles the well-armed eye of Science sees. Ironically, the poem also suggests that the role of comic perception is like that of the scientist: the wit, like the scientist, attends to the parts and magnifies them, whereas the poet or the romanticist sees the whole from afar. Thus, Cranch, the wit, uses this "well-intended halfness" to dramatize these two visions. The poem ends on a humorous note, suggesting that once his perception is changed, the romantic seer can recapture the mystery, but only through illusion:

> Cold astronomers may show thee
> Rough in feature, fair I know thee;
> At thy critics thou art laughing;
> In spite of all their photographing,
> In their rigid prose detailing
> Every spot and every failing.
> I will be thy enamored poet,
> Though my friends may smile to know it;
> For my dreams do scorn alliance
> With these prying thieves of science.
>
> (49)

The way in which Cranch varies the voice in the poem—that is, the two levels of diction, one formal and the other, informal—suggests that though the persona remains the moon-struck lover, poetry itself is changing. There is a distinct difference between the astronomers with their rigid prose and the "enamored poet" who is the persona. This change is exemplified further in Cranch's last collection of poems, *Ariel and Caliban* (1886). Though the poems reflect much of the philosophical proclivities of the young Cranch in *Poems,* these themes of perception and communication, poet and audience are worked out in contemporary terms. Still fascinated with the effect of progress on perception and expression, Cranch writes a series of poems on technological advances, called **"The Seven Wonders of the World."** Typical of Cranch's chicanery, he makes the last "wonder" **"The Fireplace,"** whereas the others are the printing-press, the ocean steamer, the locomotive, the telegraph and telephone, the photograph, the spectroscope, and the microscope. Obviously, these inventions constitute new ways of seeing and communicating, and the question is how do these improvements affect tradition? In **"The Printing-Press,"** Cranch writes:

> In boyhood's days we read with keen delight
> How young Aladdin rubbed his lamp and raised
> The towering Djin whose form his soul amazed,
> Yet who was pledged to serve him day and night.
> But Guttenberg evoked a giant sprite
> Of vaster power, when Europe stood and gazed
> To see him rub his types with ink. Then blazed
> Across the lands a glorious shape of light.
> Who stripped the cowl from the priest, the crown from
>   kings,
> And hand in hand with Faith and Science wrought
> To free the struggling spirit's limed wings,
> And guard the ancestral throne of sovereign Thought.
> The world was dumb. Then first it found its tongue
> And spake—and heaven and earth in answer rung.
>
> (142)

Progressing chronologically, Cranch compares the Djin with Guttenberg's powerful sprite, the rubbing of the lamp with the rubbing of the types with ink. The wish granted, then, is that the world may speak; indeed, the strongest line in the poem is "The world was dumb," ironically an echo of "in the beginning was the word." This untapped power—indeed, a democratic spirit—is tapped because of technology, and unlike that of **"Luna Through a Lorgnette,"** the tone of this poem is as serious as the implications are. In fact, Cranch sees in these inventions a chance for improved communication. In **"The Telegraph and Telephone,"** he says:

Fleeter than time, across the Continent,
. . . . .

The new tuned earth like some vast instrument
Tingles from zone to zone; for Art has lent
New nerves, new pulse, new motion—all to each,
And each to all, in swift electric speech
Bound by a force unwearied and unspent.
. . . . .

We for all realms were made, and they for us.
For all there is a soul, an ear, a mouth;
And Time and Space are naught. The mind is all.

(145)

The manner in which Cranch connects these instruments to Art indicates that the "swift electric speech" makes communication the power of all; moreover, this power is boundless. Thus, technology enhances man's senses and intellect: it gives him an ear, a mouth, a soul. It cancels time and space and allows the mind to be all. What more Emersonian notion could be stated? Indeed, here technology acts as a medium for the oversoul, allowing man to be part and parcel of the universe.

Yet, Cranch is ambivalent, for, as he shows in **"The Poet's Soliloquy,"** life in a world speeded by technology and industrialization has its dear costs. Bemoaning what the "practical public demands" have done to the "Parnassus of beauty and truth," he says:

> We have striven, have toiled,
> Have pressed with the foremost to sing to the men of
> our time
> The thought that was deepest, the lay that was lightest
> in rhyme.
> We are baffled and foiled.
> The crowd hurries on intent upon traffic and pay;
> They have ears, but they hear not. What chance to be
> heard has the poet today?

(231)

The title is a tip-off to Cranch's answer to this dilemma: art must be its own reward; the poet must sing unto himself. Yet, if this is true, then the role of the poet as wit is negated by fashion, progress, scientific innovation—but, most of all, by a schism between himself and his audience. If the reason for wit (as in Cranch's case) is both entertainment and instruction through dramatizing life's discrepancies, then a poet who must sing only to himself has failed. Perhaps fittingly, Cranch's last published poem, **"The Birds on the Wires,"** is his most sceptical:

> Perched on the breeze-blown wires the careless birds
>   Whose chattering notes tell all the wit they own.
> Know not the passage of the electric words
>   Throbbing beneath their feet from zone to zone.
>
> so while mysterious spheres enfold us round,
>   Though life's tingling chords we press so near,
> Our souls sit deaf to truth's diviner sound.
>   Ourselves—not Nature's wondrous voice we hear.

(Scott 345)

Gone is the joyous and youthful curiosity of **"Bobolinks"** and **"Bird Language"** in the 1875 collection where the poet, like a child, harkened to the language of nature, despite his inability to understand it. Here, the language is dissident. The birds are "careless" on the "breeze-blown wires," and their chatter is "all the wit they own." They "know not" the very thing they hold and are ignorant of "electric words"—the wisdom of science. Cranch slides from the personification of the birds as people into a full translation and comparison in the second stanza. The poet says "we" are deaf to truth. Like the birds and their chatter, we listen only to ourselves, not to the outside world. The birds unwittingly hold the "electric words" in their grasp; we are enfolded by mysterious truths, "life's tingling chords we press so near." But there is an irony in these last lines. If Nature, as represented by the birds of the first stanza, is a chattering, senseless entity, then no "diviner sound" exists. The self alone, as in the case of **"The Poet's Soliloquy,"** can provide no truth and neither can Nature. Thus, communication which is essential to knowledge and truth is muted by the indifference of Nature and the isolation of the individual. The fact that Cranch suggests in his comparison that "electric words" are like Nature's "tingling chords" suggests an affinity between man's efforts to speed communication (via science) and the self-evident truths of the natural world. Significantly, both fail because of the careless listener.

Here, then, is Cranch's ultimate achievement as a wit. He perceives the discrepancy and seeks to communicate it through a "well-intended halfness"—hence the use of poetic techniques to awaken the reader to his meaning. Moreover, despite the revelation, in this and the other poems discussed, of Cranch's gradual loss of faith in the possibility of "aurora shootings mixed with summer lightning"—the essential spark between poet and audience—this poem evidences that he was still, at the end of his life, attempting to master techniques that would crate this communication. To the end, Cranch evidenced both a sharp wit and consternation over his ability to express himself to people. He still was sending devils to his brother Edward—this time traced on a pottery jar—in 1883. In 1889, he wrote Mrs. Scott the "Chronicles of the Land of Nod" in which he enumerated scenes in his story. He began: "1. And it was the season of summer in the Land of Manhattan. And it waxed exceeding hot." And he ends: "19. And they who took afternoon naps said perpetually, 'Blessed be the man who invented sleep.'" And "20. And when they awoke from their slumbers they said, 'Lo, this is the Land of Nod, of which the Prophets of old did speak'" (Scott 362). A year later, he confessed to his brother, Edward: "I must confess to terribly agnostic views about it all—death." At the same time, he sent along a little sketch of "The Grasshopper is a Burden," which shows a man in bed, looking horrified at a large grasshopper on his knees. That drawing is an apt illustration of the wit of the comic and how essential it is to the wisdom of the poet.

Notes

1. The term "dilettante" is used in particular by Joseph M. DeFalco in the introduction to Christopher Pearse

Cranch, *The Collected Poems* (vii), and by Perry Miller (381). This is such a popular view of Cranch that scant critical attention has been paid to either of his two careers, poetry or landscape painting.

2. Generally, humor is distinguished from wit in this way: humor implies a sympathetic recognition of human values and deals with human frailties; with is primarily intellectual and is expressed in phraseology, plays upon words, surprising contrasts, paradoxes, diction, etc. The *New English Dictionary* defines wit: "that quality of speech or writing which consists in the apt association of thought and expression calculated to surprise and delight by its unexpectedness."

3. Emerson in December of 1839 delivered the first three lectures in his series of ten on "The Present Age" in Boston's Masonic Temple. The lecture referred to in the poem must have been his introductory lecture on this topic on December 4 or one of the two on "Literature" delivered December 11 and 18, for Cranch wrote Miss Julia Meyers on February 4, 1840 that he had attended "Mr. Emerson's on the Age."

4. See F. DeWolfe Miller, 38. A much more detailed argument could be made about Cranch's conceptualization of poetic diction as a result of his caricatures. He managed to focus, for example, on passages from "The American Scholar" and "Nature" which are crucial to Emerson's philosophy of perception, action, and expression. In addition, Cranch's other art forms, such as his landscape painting, for example, open up interesting questions about the role of these other arts in his conceptualization and renderings as a poet.

Works Cited

Cranch, Christopher Pearse. *Collected Poems, 1835-1892.* Ed. Joseph M. DeFalco, Gainesville: Scholars' Facsimiles and Reprints, 1971.

———. "Mr. Emerson's Oration." *Western Messenger,* IV, 183-184.

———. "The New School in Literature and Religion." *Western Messenger,* VI, 37-42.

Emerson, Ralph Waldo. *The Portable Emerson.* Ed. Carl Van Doren. New York: The Viking Press, 1946.

Lowell, James Russell. *Complete Writings.* Boston: 1904.

Meigs, Cornelia, ed. *A Critical History of Children's Literature.* New York: The Macmillan Company, 1953.

Miller, F. DeWolfe. *Christopher Pearse Cranch and his Caricatures of New England Transcendentalism.* Cambridge, Massachusetts: Harvard University Press, 1951.

Miller, Perry. *The Transcendentalists: An Anthology.* Cambridge, Massachusetts: Harvard University Press, 1950.

Scott, Leonora Cranch. *The Life and Letters of Christopher Pearse Cranch.* Boston: Houghton Mifflin, 1917.

Tuckerman, Henry. *Book of the Artists, American Artist Life.* New York: 1867.

Julie M. Norko (essay date 1992)

SOURCE: Norko, Julie M. "Christopher Pearse Cranch's Struggle with the Muses." *Studies in the American Renaissance* (1992): 209-27.

[*In the following essay, Norko discusses Cranch's personal struggle in choosing between a career in the ministry, which he believed was his duty, and art and literature, which he found more appealing.*]

In may 1874, Ralph Waldo Emerson wrote a letter to Christopher Pearse Cranch containing his assessment of the younger man's talents: "I have always understood that you are the victim of your own various gifts; that all the muses, jealous of each other, haunt your brain, and I well remember your speech to the frogs, which called out all the eloquence of the inhabitants of the swamp, in what we call Sleepy Hollow in Concord, many years ago."[1]

The critical assessments of the individual who entertained children with sounds of barnyard animals at Brook Farm and adults with Emersonian caricatures have not varied significantly in the past century. In *The Flowering of New England,* Van Wyck Brooks depicts Cranch as a man "having ample means and mundane tastes, [who] had gradually 'sunk the minister in the man' and followed the call of the Muses . . . a man who had taken Emerson at his word and planted himself on his instincts, wherever they led him."[2] In *The Transcendentalists,* Perry Miller concludes with a mixture of admiration and disappointment: "One of the most delightful of the Transcendental group—if only because he alone had a feeling for frivolity—he ultimately proved one of the most futile and wasted talents."[3]

While these depictions touch on important aspects of Cranch's character (his humor, his variety of talents, and his self-acknowledged failure to excel at poetry, painting or music), they seem too simplistic. Cranch has usually been reduced to a spokesman for Emerson and the Transcendentalists, a derivative poet, an unexceptional artist, and above all, a dilettante. F. DeWolfe Miller claims that he became the "true pattern of a Transcendentalist of the New England fashion."[4] While evidence from Cranch's correspondence supports this conclusion, we often ignore Cranch's struggle, and assume that he effortlessly divorced himself from the ministry in order to devote himself to "unabashed aestheticism."[5] This struggle helps to account for the often overlooked melancholy strain in one of the more lighthearted Transcendentalists. Cranch spent a large portion of his early years attempting to ignore or unsuccessfully reconcile his concept of duty with his natural inclinations. He was "closer to a purely artistic temperament than Emerson"[6] even before he left the ministry to pursue a career in the arts. His prose of the period after he accepted the call to preach Unitarianism in the Ohio Valley demonstrates the development of the tension between vocation and inclination. In the prose, missionary zeal confronts his love of art, poetry, and music. These conflicting interests foreshadow his eventual movement from religion to aestheticism.

Although born in Alexandria, Virginia, as the tenth child and youngest son of William and Nancy Greenleaf Cranch, Cranch inherited a "New England" sense of responsibility. William Cranch, friend and cousin of John Quincy Adams, served as assistant justice, and later chief justice of the Circuit Court of District Columbia. According to F. DeWolfe Miller, William Cranch, "though one of the eminent lay Unitarians of his day, was in character as true a Puritan as the Post-Revolutionary period produced . . . God's immanence and man's duty to God were real truths for him."[7] Cranch's recollections support this description; he speaks admiringly of his father as "one of that noble fraternity of quiet thinkers and workers, of all times and professions, who are content to do their duty thoroughly and well, careless of shining honors and fame."[8] According to Elizabeth McKinsey, Cranch was not forced to succeed as is often the case with oldest and only sons.[9] While this assessment may be true, the devotion to duty admired in the father impressed the son and was adopted when he became a minister.

The family moved to an area of Alexandria named the "Village" in 1832. Cranch recalls it as the place where "I first began to amuse myself with drawing, and in learning to play on the flute. And it was there that I first attempted my first versification, a paraphrase from Ossian."[10] The phrase, "began to amuse myself," indicates Cranch's early attitude toward the arts. According to Cranch, his father's artistic inclinations were always associated with leisure and with his propensity for order. He remembers his father's days of leisure when he would sometimes spend a morning "tuning his piano or parlor organ, in a thorough and methodical way.[11] Although William Cranch had a deep love of poetry, art, and especially music, his son received no formal training in these areas. Perhaps William Cranch's classification of the arts as leisure activities explains not only why Cranch could not be formally trained in them, but also why he could not seriously consider a career in them. Leonora Cranch Scott describes her father's predicament: "At that time in America painting and music as professions were generally very lightly regarded. When my father was about to decide upon a profession, he considered the ministry the only one left him to his taste. His brother Edward was a lawyer, and for a doctor he seemed entirely unfitted."[12] It appears that the elder Cranch also shared this general opinion. After his son's graduation from Columbian College in 1832, he urged Cranch to select one of the three learned professions. Based on the recommendation of his father and his cousin (and future brother-in-law), William G. Eliot, Jr., who was then a divinity student at Harvard, he decided on the ministry. "Of the three professions, this was most to my taste; and as it accorded with my father's inclination, I decided to go to Cambridge and Theological School."[13] The diffident nineteen-year-old had not yet clearly articulated his own "inclination," and relied mainly on the advice of others to choose the ministry.

While Cranch's decision apparently was largely motivated by the wishes of other individuals, once he committed himself to the ministry, he conscientiously attempted to prepare himself for his duties at Harvard. His daughter assesses her father's Harvard days in *The Life and Letters of Christopher Pearse Cranch*: "The atmosphere was very religious and prayerful, and my father earnestly strove to work conscientiously. . . . He could always do better with his pen than in extemporaneous speech. But nevertheless, he persisted."[14] Cranch's instruction, from men like John Palfrey, Dr. Henry Ware, Sr., and Dr. Henry Ware, Jr., reinforced the Unitarian belief in man's accountability to God.[15] Nothing in Cranch's correspondence indicates that he did not accept this idea. Miller describes the resulting tension that haunted Cranch as long as he remained in the ministry: "Cranch developed while he was at divinity school a kind of self-conscious devotion to his appointed work, a devotion that was not of the same spirit that became his when during the years of supply preaching, he was quickened by his contacts with the new philosophy."[16] The tension between religious duty and an inclination toward the arts became more pronounced after Cranch became a preacher and left "cultured" Boston. Although a novice minister, who had not yet defined where "self-culture" ended and duty began, Cranch began to intuit a conflict of interests that he carried with him throughout his public ministry.

After his graduation from Harvard in 1835, Cranch served as an itinerant preacher in Providence, Dover, Andover, and Richmond. His divorce from "civilized," Unitarian-controlled Boston underscored the tension between self-fulfillment and occupation. Evidence indicates that he truly believed in the necessity of a "more liberal and rational"[17] religion than the faith he saw in Andover, a town which contained a seminary devoted to the protection of orthodox calvinism.[18] Indeed, according to one of his parishioners, he preached "'spiritual sermons' . . . that were much liked by liberal members of the congregation,"[19] but he continually voiced doubts about his suitability for the ministry. In a letter to John Sullivan Dwight in 1836, he expresses concern about the insubstantiality of his faith:

> I would to heaven that I understood more clearly the great laws of that invisible world within my mind. I would that my faith could support itself more trustingly upon the knowledge of my mental operations—their laws and relations and connections with the world without . . . my conceptions of the ideal True, which I feel to be something more than vain and empty imaginings, are crushed in the bud.[20]

Although he lightheartedly asked Dwight to post a note requesting prayers for his return from the "wilderness" of Andover,[21] Cranch's complaints moved beyond merely his dissatisfaction with the lack of culture in the town. They reflected an internal struggle, a crisis which would become more pronounced as he slowly realized the necessity for a stable faith in order to excel in the duties of his chosen vocation.

The conflict between religion and aestheticism appeared again in Richmond, where Cranch indicated a degree of satisfaction with the ministry and another form of satisfaction prompted by the beauty of the natural world. He recognized the empowering aspects of his position, viewing the pulpit as a lonely throne that impressed upon him the importance of the Unitarian ministry for the dissemination of liberal religion. He writes to John Sullivan Dwight: "It was glorious to arrest the attention of a passer-by, or a door-lingerer . . . to catch his eye and a new inspiration at the same moment, to blaze right at him and to hold him like the Ancient Mariner to his seat, and address him in an appeal, which it almost seemed as if Providence had brought him expressly to hear."[22] However, in the same letter, he describes a different kind of inspiration, the inspiration to write a sonnet on one of the local flowers, the *magnolia grandiflora*: "Something in the powerful and delightful fragrance that carries the imagination so into the dark and deep forests of Florida and the banks of the Mississippi."[23] Cranch confronted two sources of inspiration: direct, from the works of nature, and indirect, from the effect of his preaching on the listener. It is in Richmond that Cranch first began to compose poetry with some assurance, and he sent his brother a sonnet entitled **"To the Magnolia Grandiflora"** in 1836. Cranch's belief in the necessity of "duty" and "action" soon pitted his inspiration to create art against his inspiration from the pulpit.

Considering his doubts about his ministry and his discomfort with the "wilderness" on the Eastern seaboard, why would Cranch have seriously considered his next move to the Ohio Valley? Again, family influenced Cranch's career decisions. His brother Edward lived in Cincinnati, and his cousin William Greenleaf Eliot, who was preaching in St. Louis, urged him to come West. Eliot, a man whose "life was a consecration to the highest ideals of duty,"[24] had helped to found the *Western Messenger*, a periodical promoting Unitarian interests in the West. Miller cites the purpose of the *Messenger* as "identical with Cranch's ideal for his own life at that date."[25] Robert Habich offers insight into the motives of Cranch's fellow laborers in the vineyard, claiming that the opportunity to shape a society free from the weight of tradition enticed idealistic young Unitarians.[26] They saw the West as an area where the seed of liberal religion could take root in untrammeled ground. The presence of his cousin and James Freeman Clarke, who had aligned himself with this magazine "devoted to Religion and Literature" in the West, must have further facilitated Cranch's move. Therefore, claiming that he had been "possessed by the Western mania to some degree,"[27] Cranch arrived in St. Louis near the end of 1836 and supplied his cousin's pulpit.

When Cranch "settled" in the West, he immediately began contributing to the *Western Messenger*. He steadily produced prose and poetry and edited the periodical twice during his years in the Ohio Valley. In the "General Preface" to the first volume, the editors declared the periodical "devoted to the spread of a liberal and rational religion." In light of the purpose of the magazine, Cranch contributed primarily religious poetry and verse that hinted at his evolving Transcendentalism and demonstrated his propensity for creative expression over didactic prose.

These artistic inclinations, the nomadic nature of his ministry, and increasing insecurities about his suitability for such a life complicated Cranch's years in the West. The exigencies of the missionary situation, as well as certain personality traits, compounded this insecurity. Cranch spent from 1836 to 1839 travelling in the West, usually spending less than a season in any place. In a letter of August 1837, he describes himself as "reserved, *secretive*, proud, indolent, but above all *diffident*. This besetting diffidence lies at the root of all my reserve, and keeps me again and again silent and seemingly cold, when *no one* could tell how deep and strong the stream which ran hidden within."[28] In this year he attempted to further consecrate himself to his task by requesting that James Freeman Clarke ordain him. As Cranch searched for a course of action to correct the flaws that interfered with his religious obligations, wholehearted devotion appeared to him to be the best method. Clarke wisely ignored Cranch's request, and Cranch himself would later express relief in avoiding the "ordination noose."[29]

When Cranch compared himself to ministers like Clarke, he usually detected his own inadequacy. In mid-1837 Cranch supplied the pulpit for Clarke and also took over responsibility for writing and editing the *Messenger*. In October 1837, Cranch praises Clarke in a letter to his sister. He claims that Clarke

> possesses in a marked degree that which I am perpetually conscious that I am most deficient in—that is, boldness—an habitual independence and disregard for the opinion of men . . . My eyes are turned so habitually on myself, that almost every action of my life is divested of freedom . . . I am not free enough; I am not bold enough for a Minister of the Word of Life. Over and over again I do chide my timidity, my reserve, my sensitiveness. I want what might be called *spontaneousness*. And I think the West is the school where this want is to be supplied . . . I must think more of my fellow man and less of myself. I must not feel myself detached from society, but as forming a stone in the arch, helping to support the building. In the West it is especially necessary that no member of society should forget his relations and isolate himself. He must step out from the charmed circle of his own peculiar tastes, habits, feelings, and sympathize with, and help, all around him. This is the minister's office by preeminence. The minister should not be a standing, placid, lake, embosomed by mountains and gazing on the stars; but a quick, deep, active, strong-moving stream, winding about men, purifying and gladdening and fertilizing the world.[30]

The above statement seems more indicative of Cranch's insecurities with the ministry than Clarke's position in

Louisville.³¹ Just one month after this yearning for "spontaneity," he labeled himself "much the child of impulse, though not wholly so, I hope."³² Cranch continually found himself without "boldness" in terms of the Unitarian mission, while the "impulse" toward art did not waver during his years in the West. According to his daughter, Cranch felt "unfitted" for his position as he constantly struggled to "prepare himself for his duties." She writes: "it was endeavoring to fit a square peg into a round hole; his poetic effusions, his love of painting and of music all calling him away from sermonizing, which he was strongly urged to follow and to crush the rest."³³

The indirect association which he began with the Transcendentalists through the *Western Messenger* quickened his aesthetic impulses in the midst of his struggle. Miller labels Cranch as a "seedling transcendentalist" before he moved west.³⁴ This unconscious Transcendentalism gradually solidified in the years that he spent in the Ohio Valley. He began to seriously write poetry between the publication of Thomas Carlyle's *Sartor Resartus* in the spring of 1836 and Emerson's *Nature* in the autumn. Men like Clarke and books like *Nature* and *Remarks on the Four Gospels* by his cousin William Henry Furness exposed him to iconoclastic ideas and a budding movement more eclectic and more suited to aestheticism than to Unitarianism. By the time Cranch left the West, he was a full-fledged advocate of this movement.³⁵

Cranch's prose contributions in 1837 to the *Western Messenger* reflect his struggles to "consecrate" himself. Most of the prose from that year consisted of arguments for Unitarianism as members of the religion worked to defend their doctrine against the accusations of orthodox Calvinists. Cranch used parables to figuratively express these doctrines,³⁶ but he usually concentrated on the necessity for self-denial in order for men to realize higher purposes. In one of his first prose pieces appearing in the *Messenger* in July 1837, a nature parable called **"The Ant Hills,"** Cranch uses the natural world, in this case—the "little world of a sand heap"—to share a moral with the human world. He moves the emphasis from individual needs and places it on God's "higher law of Nature."³⁷ Mirroring *Pilgrim's Progress*, Cranch creates an Interpreter who provides the answers to the confused Christian. In another parable in the November issue, **"The Balloon,"** Cranch emphasizes the need for self-denial by comparing man with a hot air balloon. While he realizes the necessity of the body as a balance to the spiritual element in man which "urges the soul to rise to God and duty," true faith requires a rejection of those impulses. "But let him throw away the weights he bears, and he instantly rises, and will continue to rise, till the spirit within him finds its place high in its native element."³⁸ The tension between the heavenly and the earthly aspects of Cranch's personality and its effect on individual salvation and happiness prompted his discussion of the conflict in his prose.

In the expository prose of 1837, Cranch stressed that religion's role in societal change as well as individual salvation further necessitated duty to God and self-denial. In November 1837, Cranch extended his concept of duty to include good actions in **"Duties and Responsibilities of Unitarian Christians."** Unitarians adopted the notion of their religion as a "city set upon a hill which cannot be hid."³⁹ This metaphor places great importance upon the ability of correct actions to influence others. Outward forms assume an essential role as standards used to judge Unitarians for inner truth. In conjunction with this, Cranch emphasizes traditional forms like the Lord's Supper and the Sanctuary. He explains the special responsibility of Eastern Unitarians in the West: "How great therefore is the responsibility of those of us who have come from a part of the country where religious institutions flourish! What a duty is imposed upon them to see that those institutions be not neglected and downtrodden in this Western Valley."⁴⁰ Cranch's awareness of the possibility and necessity of missionary work in the West prompted him to make such statements. But underneath these bold assertions of the importance of duty were insecurities about his faith. The emphasis on responsibility reminds us that Cranch, the role model for the missionary, also struggled with his responsibility as a role model.

In 1837 Cranch's early affinity with the Transcendentalist movement exposed him to another cause. In the November issue of the *Western Messenger*, Cranch reprinted large sections of Emerson's "American Scholar" address. He praises the speech as "full of beauties, full of original thought and illustration."⁴¹ His admiration for Emerson's thought and his pervasive self-abnegation combine as he wistfully concludes "would that we had been in the church of old Harvard, when the thinker, the orator and poet charmed the multitude to silence in such a strain as that we have here so imperfectly reviewed."⁴² Why did Cranch support statements that foreshadowed the Oversoul and Emerson's radical self-reliance? It is obvious that he did not view Emerson's doctrines as irreconcilable with the true spirit of Unitarianism; he welcomed the free thought as consistent with the spread of liberal religion and devotion to Truth. In addition, he instinctively felt the rightness of Emerson's statements. In 1840 Emerson wrote Cranch in response to Cranch's immoderate praise of *Nature*: "If my thoughts have interested you, it only shows how much they were already yours."⁴³ This man, who did not value his own inclinations in 1837, attempted to apply these Emersonian truths to his own duties in the Unitarian mission. When Cranch quotes Emerson's "Only so much do I know, as I have lived,"⁴⁴ he views this statement as a damning appraisal of his inactivity in the missionary life.

Cranch continually focused on the importance of action, as prompted by men like Emerson and Carlyle, in 1838. From Louisville in November, he writes to Catherine Myers:

> As I have often said when egotizing, I am a bad mixture of the oyster and the spirit, the unexcitable and the excitable, . . . or of whatever other strange contrarieties and extremes you please. . . . At times so alive, so excited, so full of one or another faith and aim; and at other, so dead, immovable, ennui-ish. . . . I hope it may not always be so. It is a great hindrance to me in

my walks and undertakings in life to be such a Janus with a double head, looking two ways and going neither. It is truly a "mortal coil," this body. . . . Yet we are encompassed around by Spirit. The solemn morning light, the presence of Duty, the voices of friends, the existence of vice in the world—every feeling—every thought . . . all our proving it to us . . . in every word embodying our inmost *Me*.[45]

In the same letter, he discusses his attitude toward travelling: "If I ever get crazy, I suppose it will be on this subject, possessed with the demon of perpetual motion . . . by the dull prosaic methods of conveyance usually esteemed in fashion upon this nether planet."[46] In this comment, Cranch indicates his progressive dissatisfaction with the itinerant life. He yearns for another form of travelling, a transcendence into the world of the Spirit. This transcendence results from his reading of Keats' *Endymion*: "This will transport you to every spot in air, earth, ocean, but this dull surface we plain mortals grovel upon."[47] This correspondence also mentions his meeting with one of Keats' nieces from Louisville. His description of her offers some insight into his slowly-shifting self-definition. She possessed the "poet's dark, soul-like eyes and diffident manner."[48] He uses the same term, "somewhat diffident,"[49] to describe Elizabeth Barrett Browning ten years later in Florence. Cranch lends the term some importance by associating it with artists, and yet he criticizes his own "diffidence" as a detriment to his work in the West. Through the application of this term to himself, he aligns himself with the artists. His inclination is to see himself in such a light, but the "Duty" that he mentions in the letter reminds him not only of his spirituality but also of his earthly mission.

The tension between individual fulfillment and vocation appears in Cranch's prose from 1838. In **"Letter on Travelling, & c,"** we see the different aspects of Cranch's personality. He begins:

> Well, here I am—again a wanderer—another, and still another parting have I endured. For nearly three years it has been my lot to rove about from place to place, North, South, East and West—making friends and parting from them—verily, I am growing aweary of such an itinerant way of living. It hardly seems the appropriate destiny for one who has so much of that quiet home-loving propensity which phrenologists term inhabitiveness. But so it is—it is a discipline—perhaps a salutary one. But I don't sit down to egotize.[50]

Despite Cranch's wish to avoid the self, he soon launches into a romantic description focused on his reaction to a ride on the Mississippi. He concludes: "I could have sat for hours and gazed—but there were none to share my feelings."[51] After a long-winded description of modes of traveling, he echoes the same sentiment in his letter to Catherine Myers:

> For myself, I have tried all these modes, (including sleigh and *sled* riding) so long and so far, that even my night dreams are consumed in repeating them over and over again in my imagination, and strange places, mountains and rivers, and long roads whirl through my brain—with strange ways of passing through them, till like the flying fiend in Milton, I fancy the demon of perpetual motion and migration hath wholly possessed me.[52]

He abruptly shifts tone in the next sentence as he reminds himself of the purpose of the essay: "But I was about to say that there seem to me to be some advantages which may be derived from this much traveling." Cranch restricts his sentence to suit his attitude toward the subject as he claims the chief advantage lies in the realization that man is a "passive thing, leaning against the arm of God—entirely in His hands who is father of all."[53] The more controlled structure and tone of the second sentence indicates Cranch's divorce from uninhibited self-expression and the adoption of the dutiful sentiments of the Unitarian ministry.

Similarly, in the August issue of the *Messenger*, Cranch's varying sentence structure betrays his attachment to subjects focused on the self as opposed to subjects focused on religion. He identifies himself with the "wandering pilgrim" in **"A Ride over the Mountains,"** and begins the essay with a description of a pastor's sermon: "He preached well. The manner, the spirit, and delivery of the discourse all pleased me . . . I think we have good reason to hope that the light of a sound theology and of liberality still dwells and is diffused in this place."[54] A shift from the impersonal "we" to "I" parallels the increasing intensity of his language and tone in his description of the Hawks nest and the Kanawha river. The statement above contrasts markedly with his description of Hawksnest:

> It was a deep wall of fathomless atmosphere which was before me. I shuddered as I thought where one single step would take me. I felt my insecurity and I felt my insignificance . . . But the distant view—the spirit of beauty and stillness which pervaded everything—the mountain forests—the foaming river wandering far from its far mountain home, the sunset clouds around and above, calmed down the momentary thrill of fear. I gathered some springs of pine, and some moss which grew at the verge, with some pieces of the rock itself, as memorials, and was hurried away . . . It was a place to kneel and worship in alone.[55]

The driver's box replaces the throne of the pulpit and becomes the elevating instrument as he tours his majestic surroundings. He concludes his essay with these two sentences:

> Long shall I remember these scenes—yet with a sweet confused dreamy feeling—a lingering sense of undefined beauty—more cherished perhaps than any sharp outline.
>
> I will conclude with saying that I arrived in Cincinnati, without any accident. I shall be here a month or two.[56]

In the previous prose pieces, Cranch chooses an inspired and unrestricted manner to discuss his aesthetic impulses and a terser and nonemotional method to express his feelings about preaching. The manner in which Cranch describes the work involved in his occupation, and the more expansive style which he employs to speak of natural beauty, betrays his prejudices toward the aesthetic realm. Appreciation of natural beauty as opposed to religion served as an emotional stimulant, but his obligations to the ministry pulled him from complete acceptance of his inclination.

Cranch tries to convince others and himself of the importance of self-restraint in the parables of 1838. In **"The Lightning and the Lantern," "The River of Death," "The Fountain in the Desert,"** and **"The Three Mountains,"** he adopts the traditional motif of the pilgrimage in order to describe the necessary toil of the faithful Christian. In **"The Lightning and the Lantern,"** a wanderer, like Cranch, commits himself to an offered lantern rather than the flashes of lightning that intermittently shed bright light on the darkness. The Interpreter concludes: "It is only the steady light of habitual religion, seen and felt and followed at *all* times, which can be 'a lamp to our feet and a light to our paths.' Good feelings—religious excitements—revivals—can do us no good unless they can be arrested, and made to minister to constant and habitual good *works*."[57] Even an emotional experience of religion must be contained and controlled. Feelings or inclinations cannot be unbridled; for Cranch all must be subjected to an overarching sense of duty.

In **"The Three Mountains,"** Cranch discusses the Mount of Instruction, Mount of Transfiguration, and the Mount of Crucifixion. Experiencing all three mountains leads to salvation. After the Christian has witnessed Religion as "Truth and Beauty," in the Mount of Transfiguration, the narrator counsels him "to be strong, self-denying, active, resigned. Religion must be to him something more than merely a sermon and a dream of Beauty. The Soul's Calvary must be the Soul's gate to Heaven." Cranch stressed the importance of enduring "the hard duties and trials of life" in order to achieve salvation.[58] As indicated by his correspondence, the virtues of self-denial and action are the same virtues that Cranch hoped to cultivate in the West. His attempts to reject aesthetics and consecrate himself for the ministry became his Calvary. He constantly recognized the difficulties of the Christian experience, especially as related to his own experience in the West, and his prose became the attempt to work through these difficulties by justifying them as a service to a greater good.

Cranch also betrays his insecurities about his aesthetic impulses and his profession by using metaphors from music. Here he describes the importance of expression in strengthening thought and feeling: "Expression calls back thought on the feelings, and fixes it, and takes its impress in the mind and heart—makes it echo and reverberate like sound in the deep chambers of the soul, till we have caught the *key note* of the new harmony that comes chiming in upon us."[59] According to Cranch, this process explains the need for prayer, which strengthens religious feelings. It is also the reason that poets, musicians, and painters need their respective means of expression. Cranch links prayer with his three aesthetic interests and uses them to make his case. Through expression, "we then begin to feel a certain faith in the reality of what we have uttered, which before we had not."[60] Could this statement reflect Cranch's own insecurities about the ministry? As in his earlier letter to Dwight, the response of others to his faith, rather than the faith itself, served as its validation. Near the end of his tenure in the Ohio Valley, Cranch wavered between service to the Unitarian God and service to the Muses. In 1838 he did not have the inner strength or outward support to accept his "tastes" as a career. Instead, he continued to chastise himself for wavering in his devotion.

In 1839 circumstances forced Cranch, along with many other of the young missionaries, to assess the success of his ministry in the West. Of course, he immediately detected his so-called faults, and therefore began the year with a resolve to correct his supposed flaws. In the first entry from his 1839 journal, he asks God for a firmer faith and chides himself for his inactivity and indifference:

> All things must become more *real* to me. I must 'see into the life of things.' I must *realize*. The great end of life is to *realize*. At present I only *dream*. Half of my existence seems to be *dreaming*. A deadly *Indifference* hangs over me—like a lethargy. It is partly temperament & partly habit of mind—I think. I must break this egg shell—out of this prison I must forth. I must realize, & the way to realize, is to give up dreaming and go to acting & working. As to needed knowledge, will it not "come round," as Emerson says, to him who works and truly lives?[61]

Cranch applies Emerson's doctrines to his failure in the Unitarian mission. He also uses Carlyle to criticize his passivity:

> I want faith in my former impressions & convictions, and aspirings. I want Faith that I am a *Spirit*. . . . I must not be afraid of my thought, if it is an earnest and true one, to myself . . . I must be an independent feeler. I am not now natural enough. I am afraid of those around me. They'll think me affected, strange, undignified or lax in principle. Must not mind them. Do what is right and natural. Obey my higher instincts. In a word—I must begin to *Live*. Then I shall begin to *Realize*—then to think, feel, act, grow.
>
> The ministry to the Poor, may be a great thing for me. A stern discipline, but a salutary.
>
> God grant me faith and patience, and the spirit of self-sacrifice![62]

Cranch's attempts to break free from the judgment of others were paralyzed by a superimposed belief in the importance of "discipline" for authentic vocation. Howe labels Unitarian character development as a "peculiar mixture of moral conditioning, emotional stimulation, and learning to keep busy."[63] Cranch's constant attempts to "think, feel, act, grow" illustrate his awareness of that standard. However, his western experiences led him to the inevitable conclusion that he did not possess the abilities to promote the Unitarian mission in the West.[64] When James Handasyde Perkins offered to replace Cranch in his position ministering to the poor in Cincinnati, he accepted. Rather than merely criticizing his failure to live up to a standard, he maturely assessed his talents and admitted his unsuitability for the position. He bowed to men like Perkins:

> He will make the most efficient minister to the poor, that could be found in the country. He is already fitted for it. I am not. The time that I should spend in learning, he would spend in acting—and acting on the broadest foundation, & with the most earnest & devoted spirit. It will release *me* from my position—a position I have been standing in less than from my own will, than from the urgency of my friends. I feel that though this ministry would be a glorious discipline to myself, yet I am unfitted for it by taste and habits; while with Perkins, it seems to be the very sphere for which everything predestines him.
>
> Still some such discipline I must have. But where shall I *now* go? The West is all open before me. Shall I remain this side of the Mountains, or not? I must decide quickly.[65]

Cranch's admission of failure and acknowledgment of his dissatisfaction with his imposed vocation freed him to return to the East. Upon acceptance of the weakness of his faith, he moved back to the established center of Unitarianism to find a "home, steady work, and a wife."[66] Nevertheless, he did not completely give up the ministry, only his missionary wanderings. Still, he continued to search for a "discipline" and to criticize his lack of action and his failure in devotion to duty. In February he lamented "this dreadful indifference which hangs upon me—! . . . I am dissatisfied with myself, and almost everything about me." He looked to action to remedy this deplorable condition. "Action—a habitual daily fixed routine of duty can alone deliver me from the body of this death. I feel now as if I were letting my powers run to waste. It must not be."[67]

Cranch could not formally reject the ministry and accept his aestheticism until he found a way to reconcile a career in art with his sense of duty. In Washington City in April 1839, he records his pastimes:

> Occasionally draw, & india-ink and flute, . . . or amuse myself with the piano forte. My passion for music is such that I sometimes wonder tis not all-absorbing. No enjoyment of my existence is greater. When I sit down at twilight to the piano forte, and roam over the soul like chords of that glorious instrument, I can feel what *perfect beauty* is. What *God* is. I can feel what the language of angels must be. That language *must* be music. What else can it be?[68]

He adopted art as a method of perceiving a higher truth. Yet he refused to devote himself to the cultivation of the arts, continuing to believe in an imposed view of a "profession" as weightier than "talents" and "tastes." He adds in the same entry: "I must learn to renounce, more than I do, many of my talents & tastes in music & drawing, for instance, & give myself more to my profession. I am behind bad in this. I am too desultory—too indolent, too *unclerical*."[69]

The necessity for action and self-denial haunted Cranch's prose in early 1839 as he confronted personal and professional crises in terms of faith and vocation. In the January 1839 issue of the *Western Messenger,* he prompts men "more by the actions than by the feelings that we must discern the Regeneration of the human soul. We consider man's deeds a test of his religion."[70] He continued to renounce self-fulfillment and self-reliance. In the April *Messenger,* he cautiously advises Unitarians that "the only safe rule in searching for religious truth, is to leave fruitless speculations, and not attempt to be wise beyond what is revealed and written."[71] In July, he contends that men should "'be still' and wait, trusting in God and faithful to duty, and in due time, all will be revealed."[72] In his prose Cranch cannot yet divorce faith from suppression of self.

However, the more imaginative prose marks a shift in Cranch's emphasis from God's role in the world to the interaction between Nature and the autonomous self. When he does discuss God's power in the universe, he uses metaphors. In the parable, **"Prayer Without Ceasing,"** Nature speaks to the narrator: "And is not this beautiful mist that is stealing up, and this breath of the opening flowers that steals up with it, the silent orisons of Nature to her God?" The narrator responds poetically: "I look abroad on the awakening landscape, as the golden light comes from afar, kissing the earth as a mother kisses her waking child."[73] In his last parable for the *Western Messenger,* he uses a metaphor to compare man to a "spiritual Harp." Although the Interpreter adds that "its place in this life is a state of trial and discipline," the man who keeps his harp in "tune by labouring with God," will participate in Heaven "in the thousand varied strains of the celestial Hymn."[74] Linking music with religion provides a way for Cranch to express his aestheticism without participation in "unclerical" activities.

Cranch finally began to come to some sort of reconciliation, at least unconsciously, with his aestheticism. This is evidenced in his June contribution to the *Messenger.* He submitted **"Dreams"** in January 1839, the same month in which he struggled against his propensity to dream rather than act. However, in this piece, he describes dreams as "Poetry" manufactured by the creator in order to demonstrate man's connection to the spiritual world. He asks: "may it not be, that dreams are one way in which the spiritual gains access to the spirit's ear . . . the invisible element which enwraps our being, streams inward to the imprisoned spirit, to remind it of its glorious birth, nature, and heritage?"[75] Instead of a faculty which restricts necessary action, he aligns dreaming with the Imagination, which reveals spiritual realities. In July, Cranch supports the "romantic in the soul" in **"Leaves from My Omnibus Book."** The soul that pauses before Nature "looks on life and the world with an angel's eye, not with a dreamer's. It is allied to faith, to lofty enthusiasm, to all things beautiful and holy." He carefully qualifies his praise, dividing these natures into false and true romance. "It is only a false, morbid romance which steals away from life and duty and action, and creates its own world, which it peoples with its own idle dreams."[76] Duty is still present, and still qualifies his aestheticism. Cranch must eventually accept such a qualification or reject his past.

After Cranch left Cincinnati, he led a life very similar to the one he had led in the West, with one major exception. His proximity to the cultural centers of the East allowed him to devote more time to the arts as leisure activities, and directly exposed him to the heated debate over Transcendentalism. In Boston in February 1840 he describes his life as "a sort of dissipation,"[77] where he takes advantage of the cultural atmosphere. However, Cranch produced very little prose in the few years before he seriously began to consider leaving the ministry. In the same letter, he relates: "I have had no invitations from the Muse in a long time."[78]

The few pieces of prose he wrote for the *Western Messenger* and the *Dial* indicate that he had fully accepted Transcendentalism, perhaps explaining the new freedom in his prose from the restrictions of religion. In **"Grandfather's Spectacles,"** he contrasts the worn-out theology suiting "old eyes" with "some newer and more living form of faith." He concludes: "let us then leave the old for the old, and take what is good and true out of the new forms, and we shall be suited, and get along comfortably and peaceably."[79] The last statement—"get along comfortably and peacefully"—reflects Cranch's new ideals for his life at that date. His involvement in the Transcendentalist controversy came about because he could not understand how a liberal religion could reject any "free seekers after truth."[80] As he defended freedom of expression, he began to accept it as a possibility for himself. In a **"Sign from the West,"** he states his satisfaction with the discourse of Andrew Wylie, "one who, if he lived here, would go about branded with the nickname 'Transcendentalist,' a terror to women and children—the more as having crept out of an unlooked-for quarter."[81] He aligns himself with men like Emerson and Wylie who supported "Intuition" and rejects the expression of Christianity only as a creed. Cranch's prose hints at his eventual decision to trust completely in his own Intuition.

The movement from duty to inclination and practical action to spiritual knowledge appears in the prose of these years. In **"Musings of a Recluse,"** he stresses the needlessness of "watching, guarding, and arranging our actions . . . Is not the difference between spiritual and material things just this; that in one case we must watch the details, in the other keep alive the high resolve, and the details will take care of themselves?"[82] Cranch had shifted his devotion from duty to religion to duty to self. In **"Glimmerings,"** published in the *Dial* in January 1841, Cranch's acceptance of human knowledge as "but approximation" freed him from certain obligations that weighed heavily on him while he lived in the West. In this piece, he stresses nature's importance to the soul's rejuvenation. "Least of all does she imitate our obtrusive moral codes. She reads her mysterious fables, but we are not pestered by the word 'application' at the bottom of the picture."[83]

This shift helps to explain Cranch's movement toward the arts as a career. But what else accounted for Cranch's decision to leave the ministry in 1843, and why did he wait so long? In 1840 Cranch first began to experience the symptoms of an illness that plagued him for three years. According to Scott, "to occupy himself while he had some distemper which prevented him from writing or thinking for the time being, he turned to painting."[84] Cranch called this painting a "great solace and delight"[85] but he did not consider abandoning the ministry with that discovery. In 1841 Cranch was located in Washington and was completely self-absorbed with painting. Therefore, he barely realized that Parker and Dwight had accepted views which made it impossible for them to remain in the ministry. With the realization that these views mirrored his own, and would force him to follow the direction of his friends, he began to consider painting no less a precarious profession than the ministry and also one more suited to his talents. He shares this discovery with Emerson:

> I have been spending the summer at the South, and have lately taken very vigorously to landscape painting, which I am strongly tempted to follow in future instead of sermon writing. It is an art I have fondly looked at from boyhood. Whether I turn artist or not, I become more and more inclined to sink the minister in the man, and abandon my present calling *in toto* as a profession. Verily our churches will force us to do it whether we will or not.[86]

However, Cranch was content to wait until forced to leave. He explains his position in a letter to Dwight from Burlington, Vermont, in 1842:

> I am determined not to give up preaching unless compelled to by health, and by want of sympathy and encouragement from without. I like my profession in many respects, and have grown accustomed to it. I should never get bread in any other way; and I know not if, upon the whole, any other sphere of life would bring me any more inward peace and satisfaction than this. I am resolved, therefore, to submit as far as I can do so without compromising my views and feelings, to such usages and forms as the profession ordinarily carries with it, and to wait for things to grow better and more rational.[87]

Between 1841 and 1843 Cranch found that the Unitarian Association's awareness of his affiliation with the "heretical" Transcendentalists made a permanent place for him more unlikely. In May 1843 he writes again to Dwight of his ambition to enter "life as a whole man—an individual man; and if possible, of working and earning money in some way suited to my tastes."[88]

Therefore, with the support of his new wife, Cranch decided to devote himself to a career as illustrator, landscape painter, and author. He describes his new cause in aestheticism that stands apart from "everyday" duty:

> Here in this quiet, subdued, mellow light, the harsh world is shut out, and approached only when duty and common everyday interests summon us to action, which

only prepares us for the next day's absorbing labor, at the end of which we only find ourselves weary without knowing why. And is not the artist, too, working for truth and goodness as well as beauty? I have an inward feeling that my time is not misspent, though I may never attain to eminence. If I can, in the remotest degree, by my labors, bring the thoughts of nature and the dreams of paradise into a single soul, I have done some good, I have spoken some truth.[89]

Cranch realized that "common" duty and "higher" inclinations usually did not lead in the same direction. Therefore, he found a way to infuse painting with a greater duty by linking the exposure of others to "truth and goodness" with inclination. A combination of factors, including his increasingly unpopular position in the Unitarian Church, his illness, and encouragement from his friends, Emerson, and his wife, prompted his formal separation from the ministry. He came to his own private reconciliation between art and religion.

Like Emerson, Cranch faced a conflict between vocation and inclination. Emerson's "inability to satisfy simultaneously the conventions of his youth, the demands of humanitarians, his own temperamental inclination, and the ethical ideals of English Romanticism" caused a tension that he could not resolve in his early career.[90] Cranch's distance from the center of Unitarianism, his stoic temperament, and a lack of confidence in his usefulness without the ministry allowed him to publicly avoid these problems while in the West. However, the prose demonstrates Cranch's insecurities and his struggle to find a niche in an unsuitable profession and an alien society. After he left the West, the tension between self-consecration and self-fulfillment continued to plague him.

In 1850 Cranch expresses this dichotomy between professionalism and aestheticism in a letter to his brother:

> I don't like to think that your theory, or your life, should be all sacrificed, made up of nothing but duty. Or at least I want to hear some time that your duty and your inclinations both point in the same direction. O, why were you not an artist; or a literary man, or an editor, or a farmer; or anything for which God and nature fitted you, rather than a lawyer?[91]

Henry A. Pochman also associates Cranch with Fuller and a few other Transcendentalists in his cultivation of the arts.[92] And according to David Robinson, "art was both a psychological and an economic salvation for Cranch, offering him deep personal satisfaction and the means of a livelihood that could not have been obtained through letters alone."[93] Are Cranch's sentiments similar to other artists' in the period? Did other artists feel that "economic and psychological salvation" was discouraged through an imposed sense of duty to society or others? Where does devotion to self end and responsibility to society begin? Contrasting attitudes toward inclination and duty in different artists with the "conventional" views of nineteenth-century society might help us to better understand the literary branch of the Transcendentalist movement.

Notes

1. Leonora Cranch Scott, *The Life and Letters of Christopher Pearse Cranch* (Boston: Houghton Mifflin, 1917), p. 281.

2. Van Wyck Brooks, *The Flowering of New England, 1815-1865,* rev. ed. (New York: Modern Library, 1941), p. 258.

3. *The Transcendentalists,* ed. Perry Miller (Cambridge: Harvard University Press, 1950), p. 179.

4. F. DeWolfe Miller, "Christopher Pearse Cranch: New England Transcendentalist" (Ph.D. diss., University of Virginia, 1942), p. vi.

5. Miller, *The Transcendentalists,* p. 385.

6. Lawrence Buell, *Literary Transcendentalism* (Ithaca: Cornell University Press, 1973), p. 42. Buell links Cranch with a group of Transcendentalists who moved beyond Emerson in pursuing aesthetic interests.

7. Miller, "Cranch," p. 10.

8. Scott, *Cranch,* p. 11.

9. Elizabeth B. McKinsey, *The Western Experiment: New England Transcendentalists in the Ohio Valley* (Cambridge: Harvard University Press, 1973), p. 34.

10. Scott, *Cranch,* p. 6.

11. Scott, *Cranch,* p. 14.

12. Scott, *Cranch,* p. 67.

13. Scott, *Cranch,* p. 19.

14. Scott, *Cranch,* p. 20.

15. Daniel Walker Howe, *The Unitarian Conscience: Harvard Moral Philosophy, 1805-1861* (Middletown: Wesleyan University Press, 1988), p. 107. Howe describes the Unitarian religion as a "means of self-culture." This self-culture is the attention to sentiments and duty resulting from the realization of man's obligations to God. Proper action discharges this obligation.

16. Miller, "Cranch," p. 31.

17. See Scott, *Cranch,* p. 23.

18. See Daniel Day Williams, *The Andover Liberals: A Study in American Theology* (Morningside Heights, N. Y.: King's Crown Press, 1941). Williams discusses Andover's shift from conservatism to liberal Christianity in the nineteenth century.

19. Scott, *Cranch,* p. 30.

20. Francis B. Dedmond, "Christopher Pearse Cranch's 'Journal 1839,'" STUDIES IN THE AMERICAN RENAISSANCE 1978, p. 130.

21. Scott, *Cranch,* p. 21.

22. Scott, *Cranch*, p. 25.
23. Scott, *Cranch*, p. 27.
24. Scott, *Cranch*, p. 31. Leonora Cranch Scott uses these words to describe Eliot.
25. Miller, "Cranch," p. 65.
26. Robert D. Habich, *Transcendentalism and the Western Messenger* (Rutherford, N.J.: Fairleigh Dickinson University Press, 1985), pp. 25-48.
27. Scott, *Cranch*, p. 26.
28. Scott, *Cranch*, p. 35.
29. See Miller, "Cranch," p. 131.
30. Scott, *Cranch*, pp. 39-40.
31. See McKinsey, *The Western Experiment*, pp. 23-24.
32. Scott, *Cranch*, p. 41.
33. Scott, *Cranch*, p. 32.
34. Miller, "Cranch," p. 31.
35. F. DeWolfe Miller, *Christopher Pearse Cranch and his Caricatures of New England Transcendentalism* (Cambridge: Harvard University Press, 1951), pp. 12-13.
36. Buell, *Literary Transcendentalism*, p. 116*n*.
37. *Western Messenger*, 3 (July 1837): 841-42.
38. *Western Messenger*, 4 (November 1837): 156.
39. *Western Messenger*, 4 (November 1837): 158.
40. *Western Messenger*, 4 (November 1837): 163.
41. *Western Messenger*, 4 (November 1837): 184.
42. *Western Messenger*, 4 (November 1837): 188.
43. Scott, *Cranch*, p. 59.
44. *Western Messenger*, 4 (November 1837): 186
45. Scott, *Cranch*, p. 42.
46. Scott, *Cranch*, p. 42.
47. Scott, *Cranch*, p. 43.
48. Scott, *Cranch*, p. 44.
49. Scott, *Cranch*, p. 156.
50. *Western Messenger*, 5 (June 1838): 183.
51. *Western Messenger*, 5 (June 1838): 184.
52. *Western Messenger*, 5 (June 1838): 185.
53. *Western Messenger*, 5 (June 1838): 185.
54. *Western Messenger*, 5 (August 1838): 339.
55. *Western Messenger*, 5 (August 1838): 340-41.
56. *Western Messenger*, 5 (August 1838): 342.
57. *Western Messenger*, 5 (September 1838): 374.
58. *Western Messenger*, 6 (December 1838): 97.
59. *Western Messenger*, 5 (September 1838): 375.
60. *Western Messenger*, 5 (September 1838): 375.
61. Dedmond, "Journal," p. 138.
62. Dedmond, "Journal," p. 139.
63. Howe, *The Unitarian Conscience*, p. 113.
64. Miller, "Cranch," p. 97.
65. Dedmond, "Journal," p. 143.
66. See Scott, *Cranch*, p. 45.
67. Dedmond, "Journal 1839," p. 144.
68. Dedmond, "Journal 1839," p. 144.
69. Dedmond, "Journal 1839," p. 144.
70. *Western Messenger*, 6 (January 1839): 151.
71. *Western Messenger*, 6 (April 1839): 401.
72. *Western Messenger*, 7 (July 1839): 192.
73. *Western Messenger*, 6 (January 1839): 152-53.
74. *Western Messenger*, 6 (February 1839): 269-70.
75. *Western Messenger*, 7 (June 1839): 99.
76. *Western Messenger*, 7 (July 1839): 197.
77. Scott, *Cranch*, p. 48.
78. Scott, *Cranch*, p. 48.
79. *Western Messenger*, 8 (July 1840): 120.
80. Scott, *Cranch*, p. 51.
81. *Dial*, 1 (October 1840): 163.
82. *Dial*, 1 (October 1840): 188.
83. *Dial*, 1 (January 1841): 397.
84. Scott, *Cranch*, p. 66.
85. Scott, *Cranch*, p. 66.
86. Scott, *Cranch*, p. 60.
87. Scott, *Cranch*, p. 79.
88. Scott, *Cranch*, p. 80.
89. Scott, *Cranch*, p. 83.
90. Henry Nash Smith, "Emerson's Problem of Vocation: A Note on the American Scholar," *New England Quarterly*, 12 (March 1939): 60.
91. Scott, *Cranch*, p. 179.
92. Henry A, Pochman, *German Culture in America* (Madison: University of Wisconsin Press, 1957), p. 449.

93. David Robinson, "The Career and Reputation of Christopher Pearse Cranch: An Essay in Biography and Bibliography," STUDIES IN THE AMERICAN RENAISSANCE 1978, p. 470.

Greta D. Little and Joel Myerson (essay date 1993)

SOURCE: Little, Greta D., and Joel Myerson. Introduction to *Three Children's Novels by Christopher Pearse Cranch*, pp. ix-xxxvi. Athens: The University of Georgia Press, 1993.

[*In the following essay, Little and Myerson offer an overview of Cranch's literary career, focusing on his stories for children.*]

Christopher Pearse Cranch's reputation has not fared well over the years. Henry James, who knew him, called Cranch a "painter, poet, musician, mild and melancholy humourist, [who] produced pictures the American traveller sometimes acquired and left verses that the American compiler sometimes includes."[1] And Perry Miller, in his anthology of *The Transcendentalists,* described Cranch as "one of the most futile and wasted talents" among the group.[2] If both James and Miller slight Cranch's work as a writer and artist, they both also ignore his contribution to children's literature. We hope that the republication of *The Last of the Huggermuggers* and *Kobboltozo: A Sequel to The Last of the Huggermuggers,* along with the first publication of **"The Legend of Doctor Theophilus,"** will help to bring Cranch and his writings for the young back into public view.

Cranch was unique among the Transcendentalists in that he was born a southerner, in Alexandria, then in the District of Columbia, on 8 March 1813.[3] His father was a judge who had married a niece of his lifelong friend John Quincy Adams, and Cranch counted Noah Webster among his uncles. With this background, it was natural for Cranch to look toward New England for his future after he was graduated from Columbian College (now George Washington University) in 1832.

Cranch attended the Harvard Divinity School, where he became friends with Theodore Parker, and, planning to become a minister, he went to Providence, Rhode Island, to preach after his graduation in 1835. He passed the winter in Andover, Maine, where he wrote his first extended literary work, **"Childe Christopher,"** a poetic parody of "The Ancient Mariner" with himself as the title character.[4] The following summer he traveled to Illinois, and then on to Cincinnati, where his brother Edward had settled.

At Cincinnati, Cranch was given an opportunity to use and hone his literary talents when he was invited to join the staff of the *Western Messenger,* a journal devoted to spreading the word of Transcendentalism in the West. Cranch's work was appreciated, and when the *Messenger*'s editor, James Freeman Clarke, left Louisville for New England in the winter of 1837, Cranch moved to Louisville and edited the magazine. He substituted for Clarke again the following winter, and when Clarke returned in January 1839, he told Cranch the latest news from Boston, including the activities of Ralph Waldo Emerson, whose writings Cranch had read and praised in the pages of the *Messenger.*

Cranch's activities on behalf of the *Western Messenger* had whetted his literary appetite, and he became more and more attracted to Transcendentalism in general and Emerson in particular. Because Cranch had not been in any hurry to be ordained, it is fair to say that the ministry as a career held less interest for him as his literary activities and talents became more valued. In 1839 both of Cranch's talents came to the forefront. Cranch the artist began the **"New Philosophy Scrapbook,"** containing caricatures of contemporaries, most notably those based on passages from Emerson's writings, the best known of which is the long-legged, barefoot, dinner-coat-clad transparent eyeball.[5] In that same year Cranch the writer composed one of his best poems, **"Correspondences,"** which was deeply indebted to Emerson's ideas for its philosophical content.[6]

Cranch returned to New England in the fall of 1839. He visited his old Divinity School classmate Theodore Parker at West Roxbury, and Parker found him "full of spontaneous fellowship," though he recognized Cranch's dilettantish attitude would not make him "a man who the world will use well."[7] In December Cranch moved to Boston, where he attended a meeting of an informal group, the Transcendental Club, on the fifth. The meeting was held at the house of George Ripley, who would later organize the Brook Farm community, and among those present were the educator Bronson Alcott, the historian George Bancroft, the famous Unitarian divine William Ellery Channing, Emerson, the feminist Margaret Fuller, and Parker.[8] Of all this heady company, it was Emerson whose presence was most important to Cranch.

Cranch had followed Emerson's career with interest. He had read *Nature* soon after its publication in 1836, and had told his brother that it had sent him "athinking."[9] He had reviewed Emerson's address on "The American Scholar" in the *Messenger,* calling it "beautiful and masterly," and had privately described the Divinity School Address as "the utterance of a seer and a prophet, a word of profound truth."[10] Moreover, his cousin William Henry Furness was a childhood friend of Emerson's, and his brother John had met Emerson when both were in Rome in 1833.[11] And after arriving in Boston, Cranch attended Emerson's lecture series on "The Present Age," which he called "a treat whose worth I can find no words to express."[12]

On 2 March 1840, Cranch sent two of his poems to Emerson, **"To the Aurora Borealis"** and **"Enosis,"** the latter having been written in Cranch's Boston hotel room while he was attending Emerson's lectures.[13] He asked Emerson to be the poems' "godfather" by placing them in the *Dial,* a new journal started by the Transcendentalists and edited by Margaret Fuller. And he expressed his "deep gratitude" for Emerson's ideas and his pleasure in Emerson's writings, concluding: "I utter no hollow compliments or vain imaginings when I say that I have owed to you more quickening influences & more elevating views in shaping my faith, than I can ever possibly express to you."[14] Emerson praised both poems to Fuller, and they appeared in the *Dial* for July 1840.[15]

Over the next few years, Cranch served as an itinerant preacher (but still put off his ordination), drew more caricatures of his contemporaries,[16] and contributed more poetry to the *Dial*. His closeness to Emerson and the Transcendentalists was simultaneously a boon to his poetry (he had a total of eighteen poems published in the *Dial*) and a curse to his ministry. John Quincy Adams heard Cranch preach in August 1840 and complained that he "gave out quite a stream of transcendentalism, quite unexpectedly."[17] The reformer Lydia Maria Child warned, after hearing Cranch preach a few months later, that he was "unconscious of the evil that lies under his very whiskers!"[18] By November 1840, Cranch wrote a friend that he had not had a paying preaching engagement for two months, for which he blamed the "sapient owls" of the Unitarian Association, who had "expunged" his name from "the list of *safe* men"; he had, he concluded, "the misfortune to have associated with Emerson, Ripley & those corrupters of youth, and have written for the Dial, and these are unpardonable offences."[19]

By 1842 Cranch had traveled to New York, where he met and fell in love with Elizabeth de Windt. He also became involved in the New York artistic scene, and particularly the Hudson River School of painters. He and Elizabeth were married in October 1843 and they settled in New York. Although his **Poems** (which was dedicated to Emerson) was published in May 1844, the book served almost as a postscript to his early poetic career. The move to New York and his new life as an artist both physically and aesthetically separated him from the Transcendentalists, and when he and Elizabeth embarked on a European tour in August 1846, Cranch put this part of his life behind him—the ministry for good, but the writing, as it turned out, only temporarily.[20]

The Cranches spent three years abroad, living for extended periods in Rome, Sorrento, and Florence, where they met and became friends of Elizabeth and Robert Browning. George William Cranch was born in March 1847 and Leonora Cranch was born in June 1848. Cranch continued his painting, but apparently earned only $2,000 for his work during this period. On this trip, as was true until the 1870s, the Cranches depended at least in part for their support on gifts from their fathers.[21]

The Cranches returned to New York in August 1849, living in the city but summering in places where Cranch could paint, such as the Catskills, the Berkshires, Niagara, and the Hudson. In the summer of 1852, they moved into the house at Lenox that the Hawthornes had vacated the previous fall. Caroline Amelia Cranch was born in May 1853. That October, the Cranches returned to Europe. It was there that Cranch met and began his lifelong friendship with James Russell Lowell. The next ten years were quiet ones, spent in Paris, with Cranch painting. A fourth and final child, Quincy Adams Cranch, was born in August 1855.

Upon their return to America in July 1863, the Cranches stayed in the New York City area, living at various times in the city, up the Hudson at Fishkill, or out on Staten Island. Cranch continued painting, and while his work was exhibited and sold, it did not fully support his family. Following the settlement of his father-in-law's estate after his death in 1870, Cranch achieved financial stability. No longer needing to maintain the pretense that his painting supported the family, he gradually began to leave that behind him as he returned to a literary career.

Cranch had never given up writing completely, publishing poetry and prose throughout the time he had concentrated on his painting. In 1872 he published his translation of the *Aeneid,* and the following year the family moved to Cambridge. There Cranch joined in the literary and social clubs of Boston and Cambridge, and saw other surviving friends from the Transcendentalist period. He published **Satan: A Libretto** in 1874 and **The Bird and the Bell, with Other Poems** the following year.

In 1880 the Cranches made their final trip to Europe, traveling there for two years. After returning to America, Cranch continued writing poetry, publishing his last book, **Ariel and Caliban,** in 1887. He died peacefully on 20 January 1892.

Cranch is today best known for his spirited caricatures of Emerson and other Transcendentalists. Like many people who have spread their abilities over a number of fields, Cranch failed to make a significant name for himself in any one of them. He himself was aware of this problem, and in the 1870s he expressed it in this fashion: "It is my misfortune (as regards worldly & pecuniary success) to have too many sides—to have been born (and educated) with a diversity of talents. . . . I have wooed too many mistresses; and the world punishes me for not shutting my eyes to all charmers but one."[22]

The publication of **The Last of the Huggermuggers** and **Kobboltozo** came about as the result of a number of circumstances. After a downturn in his literary activities in the late 1840s, Cranch began to write more and more during the early 1850s. For two years he served as a correspondent for the *New York Evening Post,* but most of his work was poetry. As an expatriate writer—and a relatively unknown one at that—Cranch would have had little opportunity to publish his writings in America had he not had an agent or friend working for him abroad. That friend was George William Curtis, who had sailed to Europe with the Cranches in 1846. The friendship among the three was firm and lasting, and the Cranches named their firstborn after him. After his own return to America, Curtis had established himself as a best-selling popular author with such travel books as *Nile Notes of a Howadji* (1851), *Lotus-Eating, A Summer Book* (1852), and *Potiphar Papers* (1853). He also helped found *Putnam's Monthly Magazine* in 1853 and contributed the "Editor's Easy Chair" column to each issue of *Harper's Monthly Magazine* from 1854 to 1892. It was Curtis who used his connections with publishers on Cranch's behalf; as early as 1851 he had written his friend with this advice: "Keep on, and have a store of ammunition ready to let fly, and especially to send me everything you want to sell, and if I can not buy it, I can perhaps persuade others."[23]

Cranch availed himself of Curtis's assistance, and allowed him to place a number of his poems in New York and Boston periodicals. In the winter of 1854-1855, he wrote a children's book, which he described as "amusing, with some pathos at the end," drew illustrations on wood that could be used by an engraver, and sent everything to Curtis "to get a publisher for it."[24] Cranch had confidence in the book, since he had already tried it out on his children, eight-year-old Georgie and seven-year-old Leonora, with success. He told a friend that "the germ of it was conceived in inventing something to amuse" the children. Cranch read Georgie "the chapters as I wrote them, which amused and excited him, but always made him cry at the end over the sorrows of the poor giant."[25]

Curtis also liked the story, calling it "unique and droll," and he sent it to Appleton's. But their report, as he quoted it to Cranch in June, was a negative one: "'We do not think that the story, although well written, would do to sell by itself. Fairy tales do not possess very great attractions to parents in search of books for their children, or if they do wish them, they more frequently look for a volume containing a variety, than for a single story.'" Curtis promised to continue seeking a publisher, vowing to send it to Ticknor and Fields, then if necessary to the Harpers.[26]

Other publishers must have agreed with Appleton's, for it was not until November that Curtis was able to report having success. The book had been accepted by the Boston firm of Phillips, Sampson, who were, coincidentally, the publishers of Emerson's *Representative Men* and *English Traits*. Curtis wrote that it was "to be done in the best and most costly manner." The publishers considered the sale "doubtful, (publishers always do)," but Curtis jocularly added "I don't believe you will make more than a million by it." He also enclosed a newspaper clipping with an advertisement for the book, described as intended "for large as well as small children," with illustrations "uncommonly spirited and beautiful."[27]

Unfortunately, the book was accepted and put into production too late to fully capitalize on the large volume of a sales associated with the Christmas season, appearing as it did on 22 December.[28] His friend William Wetmore Story wrote to Cranch that "at 5 oclock of the day ***The Last of the Huggermuggers*** was published, 300 copies were sold, & that Phillips & Sampson said that if the holiday had been a little farther off, they could easily have sold 10,000."[29] Cranch was delighted with this news, and he wrote James Russell Lowell of his anticipation at receiving a bound copy: "Huggermugger is coming—is coming to cheer our eyes—we shall see ourselves in print—clear large beautiful print, with our own illustrations engraved:—and across the great waters we hear the approving clapping of little hands and know that we are known among the juvenile gentry."[30]

Story, rather than Curtis,[31] was apparently the one who encouraged Cranch to write a sequel to ***The Last of the Huggermuggers***, for in April 1856 he wrote Cranch that he had "promised on your behalf to Phillips, Sampson & Co. that you will write them another story with illustrations of about the length of ***Huggermugger***, and send it to them in July. So bestir your stumps." Still, as had often happened in Cranch's career, there were reservations about his work. Story reported that "your friends did not think it [***Huggermuggers***] up to your mark. We all know that you can do much better if you choose to put your energies to work; and now you must do so. You must invent a new story, and tell it in a livelier and sharper way."[32]

Cranch wrote ***Kobboltozo: A Sequel to The Last of the Huggermuggers***, and that fall he reported to his brother Edward that it was "much better in subject, style, and in the designs." In fact, he went on, "Phillips & Sampson are much delighted with it, and say no expense will be spared to make it the most splendid book ever published in Boston," which news he found "pleasant and encouraging."[33] But to Lowell, Cranch complained, somewhat humorously, about the way in which books had to be fancified to ensure a good sale: "In what typographic dandyism and display will my bantling appear! P. & S. standing as godfather over it, decking it at the baptismal font with lace and gold and baubles—as if it were a Prince Imperial . . . But I dare say infantine America loves such things—the way gingerbread nowadays must be gilt—and every dog eared story book must blaze with illuminated letters—why dont they bind it in diamond-dusted and ruby spangled covers at once! The children of this generation go for *luxe (looks)* more than they did in our young days."[34]

Cranch, not wishing to lose sales again, sent in ***Kobboltozo*** early enough for it to appear in time for the Christmas season, and it was published on 10 December.[35] The book also appeared in time to be reviewed, although as a Christmas book aimed at a juvenile audience, it received short and general notices. Typical of the comments on ***Kobboltozo*** was the praise of it as "a very attractive and amusing book" in a two-sentence review in the *Boston Daily Advertiser*.[36] Reviewers had remembered ***The Last of the Huggermuggers***, and the one in the *Boston Daily Evening Traveller* noted that everyone who read the first book will "rush to devour this one"; both were "capital stories, admirably illustrated."[37] And the reviewer in the *Boston Daily Evening Transcript* called Cranch's books "two sterling additions to the literature of childhood."[38]

Cranch's two children's books proved to be a financial windfall for him. ***The Last of the Huggermuggers*** sold "perhaps 12 to 1400 copies," even though it was published so late in the season,[39] and Cranch received a $500 payment through Lowell in late 1856.[40] At about the same time, Curtis sent Cranch another "$200 from Phillips, Sampson 'on account of Hugg. and Kobbo.'"[41] Ironically, Cranch earned at least as much from these two children's books as he had earned annually from his painting during his trip abroad in the 1840s.

The success of **Kobboltozo,** which had been placed on sale early in the 1856 Christmas season, gave Cranch reason to hope for further success with his children's books. Curtis advised him to write more stories for the Christmas market: "Your name thus becomes associated with the holidays. Children will think of Santa Claus and Cranch as brothers."[42] Cranch apparently took Curtis's advice, for in March 1857 he wrote to his longtime friend Mrs. Mary Preston Stearns of his plans for the next holiday season: "I have written a tale with an amusing shell and spiritual kernel with the motto 'For the young a story, for the old an allegory', which I am a good deal pleased with. I am preparing it and a fairy story for next Christmas."[43] The story he mentions must be **"Doctor Theophilus,"** which ends with "For the young, a magic-story. For the old, an allegory." **"Burley-bones"** is almost certainly the fairy story.

In July, Curtis conveyed the bad news that Phillips, Sampson would not be publishing a new Cranch story for Christmas. Cranch later explained to his brother that his work was "declined by the publisher on account of squally times beginning—and not for any fault of the stories."[44] Even without seeing them, Curtis offered to print the stories himself, "in my own 'Schoolfellow'—a magazine we publish for children, and a very popular affair for the young people."[45] However, the magazine ceased publication in 1857 without printing Cranch's stories. Curtis wrote in September that he had the manuscripts and blocks, which he would try to sell.[46]

The publishing market continued to struggle, and neither book was printed. Phillips, Sampson itself went bankrupt in 1859.[47] Consequently, Cranch's career as a storyteller gave way to his painting for the rest of his stay in Europe.

In 1863, when the Cranches returned to the United States, Cranch devoted more of his time to writing, especially poetry—some explicitly for children. His poems for children appeared in the leading children's periodicals of the time: *Riverside Magazine for Young People* and *St. Nicholas.* Many of these poems had been destined for a volume of children's poems to be called *Father Gander's Rhymes,* but no such collection ever appeared.

Cranch also began trying to publish his storybooks again. In 1866 he showed **"Burley-bones"** and the accompanying illustrations to Lowell, who wrote to Charles Eliot Norton that he hoped to get James T. Fields to publish the story.[48] Cranch wrote to Lowell in January 1867, asking him to inquire of Ticknor and Fields about the **"Burley-bones"** manuscript: "I fully understood that it was accepted, and would be published, sometime or another, in 'Our Young Folks'—But I am inclined to think that Fields intends to do nothing about it."[49] Cranch went on to mention that Henry Oscar Houghton (of the firm Hurd and Houghton) was thought to be looking for illustrated stories, and asked Lowell to show him **"Burley-bones"** and the illustrations for **"Doctor Theophilus."**

In 1869 the two earlier books were reissued by Lee and Shepard, and Cranch suggested that Lowell approach them about the two manuscripts.[50] In May, he complained: "My unfortunate stories with the unfortunate blocks are I suppose still in limbo, in Boston. Mr. Woodman who undertook so enthusiastically to recommend them to Lee and Shepard has written no answer to a letter I sent him long ago. It's of no use I suppose writing again to him. They are doomed to be stillborn. . . . I can learn nothing about the other story and the illustrations—**"Dr. Theophilus."**"[51]

The Theophilus manuscript continued to elude him. On 31 January 1870 he wrote Lowell:

> And will you just rummage once more in your drawers, for my missing Ms. **"Dr. Theophilus"**—I can't help thinking it has slid into some chink, or been covered up out of sight, somewhere about your study.
>
> Mr. Fields, I am told, states that he knows nothing about the Ms.
>
> I am sorry to put you to this trouble. And if you shouldn't find it, the loss will not be irreparable—as I have a rough copy of the same—only the missing one is an improved edition.[52]

We cannot know whether Cranch ever found his manuscript; there is no evidence it was ever published. In any event, by the next year, Cranch had turned his attention to translating Virgil's *Aeneid.* Although his poems for young people continued to appear occasionally—the last in *St. Nicholas* for August 1891—he did not return to writing children's fiction. ***The Last of the Huggermuggers*** and ***Kobboltozo*** were reprinted several times in the nineteenth century, but after that 1870 letter, no further references concerning **"Doctor Theophilus"** or any other children's fiction have been found.

Although Cranch's fiction for children is better known, he also wrote a number of poems for young people as well. They appeared on the pages of *St. Nicholas, Hearth and Home,* and *Riverside Magazine for Young People* from 1869 until his death in 1892.

Many of these poems reveal the storytelling skill and sense of humor that characterized his two children's books. **"The Painter's Scarecrow"** tells of an independent young woman whose painting is repeatedly interrupted by rude, disruptive boys. Without a male protector and unable to find a policeman to help her, she creates a scarecrow to insure her privacy.[53] **"A Chinese Story"** tells of two near-sighted men who challenge one another to read the inscription on a distant marble tablet. Both men cheat, and their misdeeds are exposed when the tablet is replaced by a blank slab. The priest to whom they appeal for a judgment says:

> "I think, dear sirs, there must be few
> Blessed with such wondrous eyes as those you wear.
> There is no tablet with inscription there!
> There was one, it is true; 't was moved away,
> And you plain tablet placed there yesterday."[54]

Cranch often wove lessons into the fabric of his poems and his fiction as well. **"Burley Bones,"** the tale of a "big young fairy who had idle habits, and who got into difficulty" because he did not know the value of work, is the fairy story which Cranch originally prepared for Phillips, Sampson in 1857 and later believed to be accepted for publication in *Our Young Folks*.[55] An abridged version of the story appeared in *Hearth and Home* in 1871.[56] Burley Bones drinks punch and becomes drunk, embarrassing himself before Whirligig, the fairy maiden he wishes to woo. He is taken in by the kindly Deacon Hollyhock and his wife, Mrs. Pansy, but the ungrateful fairy repays their kindness by destroying their garden. Hollyhock takes him to the fairy court, and Burley Bones is sentenced to hard work in the garden for a year. He finally recognizes the error of his ways and becomes "quite a respectable and useful fairy." He is rewarded by a second encounter with Whirligig, who sees the remarkable change in him. They marry and live happily in the garden. Cranch uses his story-telling skills to teach a moral lesson: "And I conclude with the hope that all who read this may be as good and useful in their day and generation."

The fantasy which is characteristic of his fiction can also be found in his poetry. In **"The Coal-Imp,"** when Cranch lights his fire, a spirit trapped in the coal appears. The artist captures his likeness on paper and asks how he got there. The spirit complains of his imprisonment and is released:

> Then, taking the poker, I punched
>   A hole in the half-burnt mass—
> When the fire leaped up, and the Imp flew off
>   In a laugh of flaming gas.[57]

In **"How Willie Coasted by Moonlight,"** Willie is lured outside in the cold for an eerie ride with his "uncle" from Lapland. They go faster and faster down a hill with no end until they seem to be flying through the air and around the stars. A meteor flashes by knocking him off his seat and he wakes to find it was all a dream.[58]

Cranch's enjoyment of language play also shows up in his children's poetry. In **"Four Charades"** he composed four word puzzles for young readers. Each stanza suggests one syllable of the two-syllable words, and the third is a clue for the whole word.[59] The answers—*carpet, bargain, picnic,* and *nightmare*—were given in a later issue. **"Phaeton"** shows Cranch's penchant for wordplay as well as the interest in classical literature displayed in his poetry for adults. It is the story of the sun's charioteer, Phoebus Apollo, and his son, Phaeton.

> So, one day, Phaeton
> Said to his sire, "I'd like to drive your Sun—
> That is myself—dear sir, excuse the pun,—
> Twelve hours through space. You know you
>   promised once
> Whatever I might ask." "I was a dunce,"
> Apollo said. "My foolish love for you,
> I fear, my son, that I shall sadly rue."

Pressing his case, Phaeton goes on,

> "Father, you swore it by the River Styx,—
> You know you did,—and you are in a fix."

Jupiter must save the earth from destruction by sending a thunderbolt to stop Phaeton's wild driving. Cranch interjects:

> (but wait—
> Here in parenthesis I'd like to state
> This may have been a *telegram*; for then
> Lightning dispatches were not known to men,
> But only used by heathen gods)[60]

Although Cranch had planned a volume of poetry for children, the project—like **"Burley Bones"** and **"Doctor Theophilus"**—never reached fruition. The book, the aborted *Father Gander's Rhymes,* included a number of fantasy poems featuring animal characters. Selections from the proposed book were eventually published in *Riverside Magazine for Young People* with illustrations prepared by Cranch.[61]

Cranch is best remembered today for ***The Last of the Huggermuggers*** and ***Kobboltozo.*** His fantasy adventures for children hold a special place in the history of American children's books. For the practical-minded audience of nineteenth-century America, fantasy did not yet hold a major place. Hawthorne had introduced the notion of fairy tales in his *A Wonder Book* and *Tanglewood Tales,* but the fantastic adventure story was only beginning to emerge. Early publications for children were dominated by a concern for secular education in the works of Samuel Goodrich ("Peter Parley") and Jacob Abbott or religious education in the works published by the Sunday School Union and the American Tract Society. All these individuals and groups were opposed to fantasy stories or fairy tales that appealed to children's imaginations. Hawthorne and Cranch, however, had close ties to the Romantic movement in the United States and welcomed the added respect being granted to the imagination.

Cranch particularly was able to combine the genre of the fantasy tale represented by Hans Christian Andersen and the Brothers Grimm with the adventure story, especially the Robinsonades patterned after Defoe and Swift. In telling of a meeting between ordinary folk and make-believe giants and dwarfs, Cranch recalled the tradition of *Gulliver's Travels,* but added a new dimension to it. The stories are aggressively American, with only a subtle message about moral character woven into the plot.

The realistic and thoroughly practical Americans enter the island world of fantasy—giants, dwarfs, witches, magic shellfish—and emerge unaffected. They retain control of themselves and of their lives. Readers are impressed by their ingenuity, not their piety or even by the power of supernatural forces. Although similar to the Robinsonade genre, *Huggermuggers* focuses more on the opportunistic ingenuity of Jacky Cable and Zebbedee Nabbum than on Cable's instinct for survival. Their plan to capture the giants and make them the main attraction of a P. T. Barnum show is born of self-interest, not self-revelation. Thus Cranch helped pave the way for pleasurable, non-instructive reading among young people.

The two stories also display his talent and affection for humorous wordplay. Cranch had fun using puns to name his characters: Mark Scrawler, the historian; Kobboltozo, the cobbler; Hammawhaxo, the carpenter; Stitchkin, the tailor. Nevertheless, his friends complained that the story was "too lachrymose" and urged him to write "in a livelier and sharper way."[62] Cranch himself thought the sequel "was much better in subject, style, and in the designs."[63]

Indeed, the plot of *Kobboltozo* is more cohesive and the theme more explicit. The focus has shifted from the adventurers to the dwarfs and their efforts to become giants themselves. The dwarfs are unable to grasp the message given them by the king of the sea:

> He that is a dwarf in spirit
> Never shall the isle inherit.
> Hearts that grow 'mid daily cares
> Grow to greatness unawares;
> Noble souls alone may know
> How the giants live and grow.

The dwarfs' refusal to work together tears their community apart and the Americans must teach the dwarfs how to live in harmony. In this story, Cranch is more direct in his use of physical size to represent moral character. He also reveals more clearly the mark of his Transcendentalist ties in the antimaterialistic message.

Although the advice of his friend arrived too late to have much impact on *Kobboltozo*, Cranch seems to have taken it to heart in writing **"The Legend of Doctor Theophilus; or, The Enchanted Clothes."** Story had urged him: "Don't begin till you have settled all your plot in your mind; and if you can, let it hold a double story, an internal one and an external one, as Andersen's do, so that the wiseacres shall like it as well as the children. Read 'The Little Tin Soldier' of Andersen's, 'The Ugly Duckling,' 'The Emperor's New Clothes.' You *can* do this and you *must*."[64] The influence of Story's advice can be seen in the subtitle and further in the closing lines: "For the young, a magic-story. For the old, an allegory." The attention to clothes also reveals Cranch's interest in Thomas Carlyle and *Sartor Resartus*.

The opening chapter of **"Doctor Theophilus"** is reminiscent of Dickens's *Bleak House,* where the fog in Chancery Court represents the stagnation of the British legal system. However, Cranch's target is the medical profession in particular and reverence for the past in general. He uses puns to speak of Fogland's inhabitants as "Foggies or old (as we often spell the word) Fogies." Theophilus's foes are Dr. Sangsue (a leech), Dr. Musophof (hater of light), and Dr. Status-quo. His failure to heed the lesson of the encounter with his patient Godfrey shows the danger of the doctor's inaction. He is so wrapped up in his books and his work that he cannot see his peril. At last Theophilus discovers the enchanted clothes and does battle with the magician who made them, conquering him with one blow from the Bible.

Children will enjoy the doctor's cleverness in outsmarting his enemies as he destroys the Grand Panjandrum, and they will recognize the danger inherent in the good doctor's desire for fancy clothes. Children will immediately know that the energized clothes are magic, especially when the suit has tantrums. The news that his suit resembles the robes of the Grand Panjandrum will alert young readers that the magic clothes are dangerous. But the exact nature of that danger will be a surprise. Unlike the emperor's clothes, the doctor's clothes have too much substance. Instead of revealing the wearer's vanity, these clothes set out to ruin the good doctor and his reputation.

It is our hope that this book will introduce children, both young and old, to American fantasy in one of its early manifestations. Jacky Cable, Zebedee Nabbum, and the gentle giants have a place in American children's literature. Although overlooked, they helped define the genre in the new world, bringing brash American ways into the fantasy world of Huggermugger Island. Furthermore, this volume introduces the long-lost story of Dr. Theophilus and his nemesis, the enchanted clothes. The story-telling talents of Christopher Pearse Cranch have brought these characters to life with gentle humor and a now seldom-heard message of cooperation and harmony.

Notes

1. Henry James, *William Wetmore Story and His Friends,* 2 vols. (Boston: Houghton Mifflin, 1903), 1:110.

2. *The Transcendentalists: An Anthology,* ed. Perry Miller (Cambridge: Harvard University Press, 1950), p. 179.

3. Biographical information is drawn from Leonora Cranch Scott, *The Life and Letters of Christopher Pearse Cranch* (Boston: Houghton Mifflin, 1917); F. DeWolfe Miller, "Christopher Pearse Cranch: New England Transcendentalist," Ph.D. dissertation, University of Virginia, 1942; F. DeWolfe Miller, *Christopher Pearse Cranch and His Caricatures of New England Transcendentalism* (Cambridge: Harvard University Press, 1951); Joel Myerson, *The New England Transcendentalists and the* Dial: *A History of the Magazine and Its Contributors* (Rutherford, N.J.: Fairleigh Dickinson University Press, 1980), pp. 133-39; and Robert D. Habich, *Transcendentalism and*

the Western Messenger: *A History of the Magazine and Its Contributors, 1835-1841* (Rutherford, N.J.: Fairleigh Dickinson University Press, 1985). For a survey of the scholarship on Cranch, see David Robinson, "Christopher Pearse Cranch," in *The Transcendentalists: A Review of Research and Criticism,* ed. Joel Myerson (New York: Modern Language Association, 1984), pp. 123-30.

We are grateful to the Andover-Harvard Theological School, the Cornell University Library Department of Rare Books, the Houghton Library of Harvard University, and the Massachusetts Historical Society for permission to quote from materials in their possession.

4. The manuscript of this poem, at the University of Wyoming, shows it to be a decidedly juvenile effort. This was clearly Cranch's apprenticeship period: F. DeWolfe Miller describes the verses of this time as marked by "jejune religiosity," and even his friend John Sullivan Dwight called his poetry "always beautiful, but feeble" (*Cranch,* p. 10; Dwight to Cranch, 12 August 1837, typescript copy, Massachusetts Historical Society).

5. Reproduced in Scott, *Cranch,* opposite p. 40, and Miller, *Cranch,* figure 3.

6. See Hazen C. Carpenter, "Emerson and Christopher Pearse Cranch," *New England Quarterly* 37 (March 1964): 18-42. "Correspondences" was published in the *Dial* 1 (January 1841): 381.

7. 12 October 1839, Parker, "Journal," 1:250, Andover-Harvard Theological School.

8. See Joel Myerson, "A Calendar of Transcendental Club Meetings," *American Literature* 44 (May 1972): 205.

9. Cranch to Edward Cranch, 22 December 1836, in Miller, "Cranch," p. 53.

10. "Emerson's Oration," *Western Messenger* 4 (October 1837): 184-89; entry of ca. 15 July 1838, "Manuscript Autobiography," in Miller, "Cranch," p. 81.

11. 5 April 1833, *The Journals and Miscellaneous Notebooks of Ralph Waldo Emerson,* ed. William H. Gilman, Ralph H. Orth, et al., 16 vols. (Cambridge: Harvard University Press, 1960-1982), 4:156.

12. Cranch to Julia Myers, 4 February 1840, in Scott, *Cranch,* p. 47.

13. "Enosis," which was influenced by Cranch's reading of *Nature,* appeared in the July 1840 *Dial* as "Stanzas." Its later title of "Gnosis" resulted from editors' misreadings of the German-style typography of its title in Cranch's *Poems* (see Miller, *Cranch,* p. 9; Miller, "Cranch," p. 105; Sidney E. Lind, "Christopher Pearse Cranch's 'Gnosis': An Error in Title," *Modern Language Notes* 62 [November 1947]: 486-88).

14. Cranch to Emerson, 2 March 1840, Collection of Joel Myerson.

15. See Emerson to Fuller, 3 March 1840, *The Letters of Ralph Waldo Emerson,* ed. Ralph L. Rusk and Eleanor M. Tilton, 8 vols. to date (New York: Columbia University Press, 1939; 1990-), 2:258; Emerson to Cranch, 4 March 1840, *Letters,* 7:374.

16. One of the best that has survived shows a man lying on a couch, sipping wine while his wife glowers at him as she polishes his boots. A copy of the *Dial* is under the couch and the caption is a line from Caroline Sturgis's poem "Life": "Why for work art thou striving, / Why seeks't thou for aught? / To the soul that is living / All things shall be brought." See *Dial* 1 (October 1840): 195, for Sturgis's poem. The drawing is reproduced in both Scott, *Cranch,* opposite p. 60, and Miller, *Cranch,* figure 17.

17. *Memoirs of John Quincy Adams,* ed. Charles Francis Adams, 12 vols. (Philadelphia: J. B. Lippincott, 1874-1877), 10:345.

18. Child to Augusta King, 21 October 1840, Department of Rare Books, Cornell University Library.

19. Cranch to John Sullivan Dwight, 17 November 1840, in Myerson, "Transcendentalism and Unitarianism in 1840: A New Letter by C. P. Cranch," *CLA Journal* 16 (March 1973): 366-67.

20. A month before he left New York, Edgar Allan Poe portrayed Cranch in his "Literati of New York City" as "one of the least absurd contributors" to the *Dial,* who had since then "reformed his habits of thought and speech" (*Godey's Lady's Book* 33 [September 1846]: 18-19).

21. Elizabeth's father died in 1870, leaving them a sizable estate valued in 1890 at $54,000, with an annual interest of $3,600 (see Miller, *Cranch,* p. 17).

22. "The Book of Thoughts," commonplace book, 1872-1879, quoted in Francis B. Dedmond, "Christopher Pearse Cranch's 'Journal. 1839,'" in *Studies in the American Renaissance 1983,* ed. Joel Myerson (Charlottesville: University Press of Virginia, 1983), p. 149n.

23. George William Curtis to Cranch, 23 June 1851, typescript copy, Massachusetts Historical Society.

24. Cranch to Mary Preston Stearns, 10 August 1855, in Scott, *Cranch,* p. 215.

25. Cranch to George Luther Stearns, 25 December 1855, typescript copy, Massachusetts Historical Society.

26. George William Curtis to Cranch, 19 June 1855, typescript copy, Massachusetts Historical Society.

27. George William Curtis to Cranch, 21 November 1855, copy, Massachusetts Historical Society.

28. It was advertised as "nearly ready" in the 18 December *Boston Daily Evening Transcript,* and as published on that day in the 22 December *Boston Daily Advertiser.*

29. William Wetmore Story to Cranch, 24 December 1855, quoted in Cranch to James Russell Lowell, 27 January 1856, Houghton Library, Harvard University. In her transcript of Story's now-lost letter, Scott reports the sales as "nine hundred copies" (*Cranch*, p. 218).

30. Cranch to James Russell Lowell, 27 January 1856, Houghton Library, Harvard University.

31. Story wrote Cranch on 20 July 1856 that "I took upon myself to advise & direct as best I could for your advantage, although you had put the matter into George Curtis' hands, especially as he was at a distance and in love, 2 facts which interfere with business transactions" (typescript copy, Massachusetts Historical Society).

32. William Wetmore Story to Cranch, in Scott, *Cranch*, pp. 220-21.

33. Cranch to Edward Cranch, 14 September 1856, in Scott, *Cranch*, pp. 222-23. Story also found the book good, writing to Cranch that it was "a great step in advance of 'Huggermugger'" (20 July 1856, typescript copy, Massachusetts Historical Society).

34. Cranch to James Russell Lowell, [Fall? 1856?], Houghton Library, Harvard University.

35. *Boston Daily Advertiser,* 10 December 1856, p. 2.

36. *Boston Daily Advertiser,* 12 December 1856, p. 2.

37. *Boston Daily Evening Traveller,* 16 December 1856, p. 4.

38. "Knick," "Juvenile Books and Periodicals," *Boston Daily Evening Transcript,* 20 December 1856, p. 1.

39. George William Curtis to Cranch, 28 December 1856, typescript copy, Massachusetts Historical Society.

40. Lowell had written Cranch in August about sending him $500 from "my Boston publishers," but he had not received it by November. But a letter from John Sullivan Dwight the next month reports that "Lowell tells me they have just sent you solid cash" (Cranch to James Russell Lowell, 24 November 1856, Houghton Library, Harvard University; Dwight to Cranch, 7 December 1856, typescript copy, Massachusetts Historical Society).

41. George William Curtis to Cranch, 28 December 1856, typescript copy, Massachusetts Historical Society.

42. George William Curtis to Cranch, 28 December 1856, in Scott, *Cranch,* p. 228.

43. Cranch to Mary Preston Stearns, 30 March 1857, typescript copy, Massachusetts Historical Society. Mrs. Stearns, the wife of antislavery crusader Major George Luther Stearns, met Cranch through Frederic Henry Hedge when the latter was pastor of a Unitarian church in Bangor, Maine, in 1836-1837. They became lifelong friends.

44. Cranch to Edward Cranch, 12 November 1857, in Miller, "Cranch," p. 290.

45. George William Curtis to Cranch, 18 July 1857, typescript copy, Massachusetts Historical Society.

46. George William Curtis to Cranch, 14 September 1857, typescript copy, Massachusetts Historical Society.

47. The firm suspended business in September 1859, within a month after the deaths of both partners, Moses D. Phillips and Charles Sampson (see Emerson, *Letters,* 5:172n).

48. James Russell Lowell to Charles Eliot Norton, 30 May 1866, in Miller, "Cranch," p. 309.

49. Cranch to James Russell Lowell, 28 January 1867, Houghton Library, Harvard University.

50. Cranch to James Russell Lowell, 16 December 1868, Houghton Library, Harvard University.

51. Cranch to James Russell Lowell, 10 May 1869, Houghton Library, Harvard University.

52. Cranch to James Russell Lowell, 31 January 1870, Houghton Library, Harvard University.

53. *St. Nicholas* 5 (September 1878): 714-15.

54. Originally published in *Lippincott's Magazine of Popular Literature and Science* 11 (April 1873): 398-99, this poem was plagiarized and appeared under the name of W. J. Bahmer in *St. Nicholas* 15 (September 1888): 839.

55. Cranch mentioned the fairy story in a letter to Mary Preston Stearns, 30 March 1857, and again in a letter to James Russell Lowell, 28 January 1867 (see above).

56. Scott cites a description of the old de Windt home, which she claims is the opening of the fairy story "Burley-bones" (see *Cranch,* p. 203). Nothing resembling this passage occurs anywhere in the text published in *Hearth and Home.*

57. *St. Nicholas* 2 (February 1875): 220-21.

58. *St. Nicholas* 3 (January 1876): 168-70.

59. *St. Nicholas* 5 (April 1878): 406.

60. *St. Nicholas* 11 (February 1884): 288-90.

61. Four installments of Father Gander's rhymes, including a preface and some ten poems, appeared in *Riverside Magazine for Young People* 4 (1870): 60, 117, 152, 360. That number is about half of the twenty poems Miller indicates were originally planned ("Cranch," p. 320).

62. William Wetmore Story to Cranch, 18 April 1856, in Scott, *Cranch,* pp. 220-21.

63. Cranch to Edward Cranch, 14 September 1856, in Scott, *Cranch,* p. 223.

64. William Wetmore Story to Cranch, 18 April 1856, in Scott, *Cranch,* p. 221.

Nancy Stula (essay date 1999)

SOURCE: Stula, Nancy. "Christopher Pearse Cranch: Painter of Transcendentalism." In *Transient and Permanent: The Transcendentalist Movement and Its Contexts*, edited by Charles Capper and Conrad Edick Wright, pp. 548-73. Boston: Massachusetts Historical Society, 1999.

[*In the following essay, Stula examines Cranch's career as an artist who successfully translated Emersonian philosophy and Transcendentalism into a visual medium.*]

In September 1841—just six years after completing his studies at Harvard Divinity School—the young Unitarian minister Christopher Pearse Cranch (1813-1892) confessed to Ralph Waldo Emerson: "I become more and more inclined to sink the minister in the man, and abandon my present calling *in toto* as a profession."[1] Cranch's inspiration to abandon the ministry stemmed from his having "very vigorously" taken up landscape painting. Today, however, Cranch is best known as a poet linked with the New England Transcendentalists; that his involvement with the new philosophy led him from a fledgling career as a Unitarian minister to a career as a landscape painter is seldom considered.[2]

Despite the recent interest among literary historians in Cranch as a disciple of Emerson, his career as an artist has not been recognized and his paintings have received almost no attention. Perhaps this lack is partially due to the fact that the majority of Cranch's surviving paintings remain hidden away in private collections. Also responsible, however, are suggestions by scholars that Cranch was a dilettante. The scholarship of American Transcendentalism, greatly influenced by Perry Miller's *The Transcendentalists: An Anthology* (1950), has unfortunately accepted Miller's pronouncement that Cranch was one of "the most futile and wasted talents. . . . [H]e gave up the pulpit, not . . . to take on serious work, but to become, by deliberate intention, a dilettante."[3]

Clearly this was not the case. Christopher Cranch considered painting his "chosen life profession,"[4] and during his forty-five year career as a landscape painter, he met with success. He was elected "Academician"—the highest rank an artist could attain—at the prestigious National Academy of Design in New York. Along with fellow Hudson River School artists, he contributed to major American exhibitions, very often to critical acclaim.[5] Cranch was also among an elite group of Americans in Paris in the 1850s to gain entrance to the highly competitive Salon; notwithstanding the formidable competition and absence of any connection to the French atelier system, he succeeded in having his *American Sunset* hung "on the line."[6] He exhibited at three Paris Salons as well as at the 1855 Exposition Universalle. In addition, Cranch wrote extensively on the role of art and the artist within the context of Transcendentalism; these writings comprise a coherent theory of art.

Despite his successes, Cranch's name is quite unknown among art historians today. Perhaps we may blame Cranch himself for not assuring his fame: in Henry James's words, it was not in his nature "to emphasise or insist."[7] Cranch's diffidence, more than any aesthetic qualities or deficiencies in his paintings, worked to insure his obscurity. Cranch was in fact a gifted painter. Possessed of a receptive mind, he was able to give voice to a wide range of ideas current in the philosophical climate of nineteenth-century America, of which Emersonian Transcendentalism was a significant part.

We are thus faced with the need not merely for revision, but for an initial consideration of Cranch as an artist who was a Transcendentalist. Cranch was the only New England Transcendentalist who painted and his landscapes readily lend themselves to a reading of Emersonian philosophy made visual. His most intense association with Transcendentalism extended into the late 1840s, a period which coincides with a fruitful time in his career as a painter. These paintings must be viewed in the context of his Transcendental interests.[8] While Cranch's well-known caricatures of the late 1830s and early 1840s provide us with the most explicit link between Emersonian philosophy and his landscape paintings (for in drawing these caricatures, Cranch explored the visual potential of Transcendental ideas), only his paintings will be treated here.[9]

This essay will grapple with the question of what constitutes a Transcendental painting, if indeed such a thing exists. Many scholars have accepted luminist paintings (such as those produced by the American artists Fitz Hugh Lane, John Frederick Kensett, Sanford Robinson Gifford, and Martin Johnson Heade) as visual corollaries to the writings of Emerson and, by extension, to Transcendental philosophy.[10] The relationship of luminism to Transcendentalism, however, is tenuous.[11] Instead, I will propose that Christopher Cranch, rather than any of the luminists, is the more appropriate link between American landscape painting and Transcendental thought.

Cranch's first career was in the Unitarian ministry. Upon graduating from Columbian College in 1832 he was confronted with having to choose between the three "learned professions." Settling on the ministry, he enrolled in Harvard Divinity School along with John Sullivan Dwight and Theodore Parker and graduated in the summer of 1835. Although Cranch was never ordained, he set out as a supply preacher on the eastern seaboard, an undertaking that involved substituting for the permanent preacher at various parishes. Despite an inborn diffidence, Cranch became acclimated to preaching. During his first year he was exhilarated with his new career: "I have had some most glorious moments in the pulpit, moments which have carried with them an excitement I do not remember ever to have experienced elsewhere, or ever so deeply."[12]

Cranch's exhilaration was short-lived. Experiencing doubts as to his suitability for the Unitarian pulpit, he complained: "I cannot forget myself. . . . Nothing goes from me that has not passed under the eyes of self. . . . I am not free enough." His journals from these years are consumed with pledges to improve himself, to be bolder: he realized that his inborn reserve and diffidence "keeps me again and again silent."[13] Increasingly, the Unitarian ministry proved inhibiting. While his thoughts still flowed on paper, he had difficulty speaking publicly. He found himself virtually unable to preach.

The problem lay in what he termed his lack of "spontaneousness," and the cure, he decided, was to be found in the West. Encouraged to travel to St. Louis by his cousin William G. Eliot, he commenced his ministry at large in 1836, substituting first for Eliot and then for James Freeman Clarke in Louisville. Cranch was especially content with his situation in Louisville, for he was able to combine preaching with his love of writing, which he did as contributor to, and substitute editor of, *The Western Messenger*. In fact, he was so satisfied that he considered permanent settlement in the West and even suggested that Clarke ordain him. Three months later, however, Cranch was once again on the road and in February of 1839 he returned permanently to the East.

Before heading west, Cranch had some insight into the "new views" of Unitarianism, but it was during his years in the Ohio Valley that he blossomed as a Transcendentalist. Cranch and Clarke had known each other briefly as students at Harvard Divinity School, but in the West Cranch discovered in Clarke a soul sympathetic to those liberating views that had been labeled "Transcendentalism." Self-doubt and dissatisfaction with his career had been exacerbated by the restrictions that the Unitarian ministry placed on him. It is not surprising that by 1838 Transcendental precepts consumed Cranch's language; by 1840, recognizing that his theological views had undergone a complete metamorphosis, he burned twenty-four sermons and believed "others will follow before long. They are old clothes. I feel myself too large to get into them again. I do not stand where I stood a year ago."[14]

Transcendentalism was a Romantic impulse. By the 1830s Unitarianism had lost its "emotional appeal" for many of the younger generation. Young Christopher Cranch wanted to trade dry, rational Unitarianism for something "more satisfying to the soul," something that would allow him to express his religious views freely.[15] Initially he sought emotion and intensity. To appreciate the wonder of God's creation entailed breaking away from convention and routine—what Thomas Carlyle called "Custom."

Cranch credited his rapid conversion to Transcendentalism to two primary influences: Thomas Carlyle and Ralph Waldo Emerson.[16] He read Carlyle's *Sartor Resartus* (1836) and was most inspired by the religious pantheism he encountered in the chapter "Natural Supernaturalism." There Carlyle encouraged a transcendence of mundane appearances in order to recognize the miraculous in nature, even when "Custom" persuades us that "the Miraculous, by simple repetition, ceases to be Miraculous." Cranch first read Emerson's *Nature* (1836) shortly after it was published, and for him it was an eye-opening experience which he likened to a sunrise. He would re-read *Nature* several times over the course of his life. But it was Emerson's "Divinity School Address" (1838) that "drew the dividing line between the old and the new school of Unitarianism" and defined Transcendentalism for Cranch. He wrote of Emerson's address: "To some of my contemporaries it was dangerous heresy, to me it was a gospel of truth." Even though some considered Emerson's doctrines heretical, as "downright atheism, mysticism, or perhaps nonsense," Emerson remained for Cranch the "master mind of New England."[17]

While Cranch was not as radical in his views or as outspoken as Emerson, he did encounter opposition as a result of his ties to Transcendentalism.[18] In the spring of 1840, when Cranch delivered the commemorative poem he had written for the Quincy, Massachusetts, bicentennial, he publicly pleaded the case of Transcendentalism.[19] In so doing he attracted the attention of several prominent Quincy citizens, including his father's cousin John Quincy Adams. By June, news of Cranch's Transcendental tendencies reached his father, William Cranch (1769-1855), the chief justice of the Circuit Court in Alexandria, Virginia, and Christopher had to defend his radical new views.

In his letter to his father Cranch played with semantics, avoiding any commitment to that dangerous term "Transcendentalism," which he craftily assigned to the German school:

> I know very little about this system of philosophy. . . . of Kant, Fichte, Hegel, Schelling, etc., which is what I suppose to be the Transcendental philosophy, has always, from the very slight idea I have of it, struck me as a cold, barren system of Idealism. . . .
>
> But somehow the name "Transcendentalist" has become a nickname here for all who have broken away from the material philosophy of Locke, and the old theology of many of the early Unitarians. . . . It has almost become a synonym for one who . . . preaches the spirit rather than the letter.
>
> The name has been more particularly applied to Mr. Emerson.

Nevertheless, Cranch reassured his father that Emerson "seems to be very far from Kant or Fichte. His writings breathe the very spirit of religion and faith. . . . [T]here is nothing in anything he says, which is inconsistent with Christianity." He added: "Since we cannot avoid names, I prefer the term 'New School' to the other long name."[20]

Cranch finally met Ralph Waldo Emerson in Boston in the winter of 1839-1840 when he attended the first three of Emerson's ten lectures on "The Present Age." That March, Cranch initiated a correspondence with Emerson, sending him two poems for inclusion in the premier issue of *The Dial*. In his letter he expressed his gratitude: "I have owed to you more quickening influences and more elevating views in shaping my faith, than I can ever possibly express to you."[21] Emerson likewise was impressed with the young poet; he praised Cranch's verse and invited him to

Concord to "compare notes a little farther, to see how well our experiences tally."[22] Cranch was one of the "many promising youths" about whom Emerson was enthusiastic.[23] For the next year at least they remained in contact, but by October 1841. Emerson's estimation of Cranch's work appears to have fallen and he distanced himself from the young poet. Despite the ensuing one-sided relationship, Emerson's writings remained an unceasing influence on Cranch.

From his first reading of *Nature*, Cranch became interested in exploring Emersonian concepts and phraseology through visual means, initially through caricature. Conservative Unitarians criticized the heretical ideas of Transcendentalism, but the popular audience objected more to the language of Transcendentalism, describing it as odd to the point of being incomprehensible. In his essay **"Transcendentalism,"** published in the *Western Messenger,* Cranch defended the language of the Transcendentalists, but his defense is in essence recognition that inarticulate passages did exist.[24] He too found humor in the wording, and these phrases provided material for the caricatures he and James Freeman Clarke began drawing in the 1830s. Emerson's phrase "Almost I fear to think how glad I am!", for example, provided Cranch with the image of Emerson dashing across a lawn, stepping in puddles, and waving his arms—simultaneously running scared and exhilarated.[25] But perhaps Cranch's most famous image is his caricature of Emerson's line in *Nature* "I become a transparent eyeball" (figure 1), which earned him the reputation of being the most playful of the Transcendentalists. Emerson is depicted as an enormous eyeball, optic nerve tied in a ponytail, perched atop a minuscule body in top hat and tails.[26] Cranch's sarcastic prophesy to Clarke—"We are linked in celebrity, and thus will descend to posterity as the immortal illustrators of the great Transcendentalist!"—ironically had come to pass: this image has been reproduced more often than Cranch's other caricatures or any of his paintings.[27]

The details of their history notwithstanding, the significance of these caricatures is that, in choosing to create images from Emerson's key phrases, Cranch located his conception of Transcendentalism in the realm of the visual. It was probably a combination of the very material quality of the words Emerson used as well as Thomas Carlyle's graphic method of presentation in *Sartor Resartus* that convinced Cranch of the suitability of visual images to the expression of Transcendental ideas.[28] Cranch realized that the graphic actuality of language is precisely where the fusion between text and image occurs and similarly allows images to grow from the text. The expression of Transcendental philosophy through visual means, initiated in his caricatures, ultimately found the ideal vehicle in landscape painting. Before committing himself to a career in painting, however, Cranch first had to reach a crisis point.

The controversy surrounding Transcendentalism, combined with the demands of the Unitarian ministry, seriously affected Cranch; he suffered a mental and physical breakdown of sorts. Because of his affiliation with the Transcendentalists, he was unable to find pulpits to supply. By the summer of 1840, shortly after his poems appeared in the *Dial,* Cranch complained that "Most of the religious societies were afraid of the 'New Views.' The pulpits were barred against me."[29] Continuing to encounter opposition from his ties to the new philosophy, and oppressed by the limitations of the Unitarian ministry, he lamented "a clergyman's life is the life of a slave. . . . He cannot own a soul, and a mouth of his own." Cranch vowed never to be ordained. Confiding in John Sullivan Dwight that his career goals were changing, Cranch searched for alternatives to preaching and even expressed interest in joining Ripley's Brook Farm. The continual worry that the Unitarian churches were "ridding themselves of all their best ministers" hastened Cranch's abandonment of the Unitarian ministry.[30]

The search for new vocations and rejection of the ministry was characteristic of the Transcendental movement. Emerson had left the ministry in 1832 to write and lecture. George Ripley and John Sullivan Dwight also gave up preaching for other pursuits. Cranch ultimately abandoned the ministry, but the break with his first career was neither easy nor well defined, occurring sometime between 1841, when he declared that he had "given up everything but the . . . glorious brush and palette," and 1844, when he claimed that he was "completely free from the clerical yoke."[31]

Nevertheless, trading a career in the ministry for one in the fine arts has been viewed as an unusual, if not extreme, conversion. Julie M. Norko, in her 1992 article, proposes that Cranch viewed art and religion as "conflicting interests" that ultimately resulted in his "movement from religion to aestheticism." But the conflict, I would argue, is not between religious duty and aestheticism, or "vocation" and "inclination," as Norko suggests, but rather between the new views Cranch had adopted and steadfast Unitarianism: Transcendentalism, in fact, could be aligned with the fine arts in its opposition to mainstream Unitarianism.[32] For Cranch, preaching and painting were not separate activities but simply two sides of the same coin: celebrations of God in Nature. Painting, like prayer, became an act of devotion, and thus, Cranch's goals remained constant.[33] Released from the Unitarian ministry, Cranch allowed nature to take on the role of the pulpit and continued to express his new religious views through prayer, poetry, and painting. As a result, theology and painting intertwine.

The alignment of religion with art was commonplace in the nineteenth century. Landscape, according to the American art critic James Jackson Jarves in his *Art-Idea* (1864), was "the creation of the one God—his sensuous image and revelation, through the investigation of which by science or its representation by art men's hearts are lifted toward him." Art led men to God, so artists could in some measure replace preachers. Barbara Novak, referring to the artists of the nineteenth century as "priests of the natural church," observes that "since artists were created by God and generously endowed by him with special gifts, the powers of revelation and creation extended to them too." In fact Cranch would exclaim: "I feel, while painting, the joy of a Creator, as if I were the Spring, making the trees put out leaves and . . . calling up clouds and lighting them with sunset glories."[34]

Perry Miller implicitly supported the link between painting and religion in his alignment of Transcendental literature with religion. According to Miller in *The Transcendentalists,* after Unitarianism rendered theological disputation obsolete, the Transcendental "revival of religion had to find new forms of expression instead of new formulations of doctrine, and it found them in literature"—or in Cranch's case, in painting. "The self-consciously literary character of the movement should not deceive us into regarding it as no more than a school of aestheticians," Miller cautioned; "worship remained the controlling motive." Like Thoreau writing of the daily trials of life on Walden Pond and Emerson on nature, Cranch too was attempting in his landscapes, in Miller's words, to "create a living religion without recourse to . . . the obsolete jargon of theology."[35]

Cranch recognized that the role of the artist—like the poet or preacher—was to give his audience insight into "the light of that truth," which was God manifested in Nature. In an essay published in the *Western Messenger* in 1838, Cranch addressed the need for a creative outlet which would align itself with religious aims. Emphasizing the close relationship between religion and art, he grappled with art theory, maintaining that the artist not only strengthens his own religious feelings through the act of expression but also makes spirituality available to his audience. Given the fusion of God and nature in nineteenth-century American culture, George William Curtis's comment that "some beautiful landscapes that I saw of [Cranch's] . . . made my heart 'babble of green fields' to itself for some days afterwards" demonstrates Cranch's success in his mission.[36]

That Curtis was a Transcendentalist confirms Cranch's ability to speak to a Transcendental audience. In fact, several members of this community, including Margaret Fuller, John Sullivan Dwight, and Theodore Parker, admired Cranch's work. Both Curtis and Fuller would praise Cranch in their published reviews of his paintings, and Parker owned Cranch's *Cascades of Tivoli,* which he lent to the Boston Athenaeum for exhibition in 1850.

One of Cranch's first attempts at landscape painting is *A River View of Upstate New York* (1843), painted at the height of his immersion in Emersonian Transcendentalism.[37] He presents us with a pristine landscape broken only by the inclusion of a few tiny figures: a hunter stands on the shore with his dog while Native Americans pass below in a canoe. It is in every way a scene of man in harmony with nature, embracing Emerson's view of nature as commodity, in which the physical needs of man are supplied (the hunter and fishermen), and as beauty and spirit. The foreground consists of a rocky promontory and a storm-blasted tree; the latter, having fallen across the chasm, provides a natural bridge, facilitating the viewer's access into the scene. The fortuitously placed log and large rocks not only offer the viewer access into the landscape but a secure place to stand as well, encouraging direct contact with nature.

Cranch maintained that we "must enter the great temple of the invisible and spiritual through the door of the visible." Here Cranch attempted to transcend sensual "understanding," as defined by Samuel Taylor Coleridge in *Aids to Reflection* (1825), in order to access "Reason,"—an extension of Emerson's moral sentiment which was the direct and immediate knowledge of the spiritual. Once we enter into Cranch's image of the beauty and power of God in nature, we transcend sensuality. Like George William Curtis, whose admiration of Cranch's landscape led him to remember actual landscapes, and finally to relive his own past experiences in nature, we too transcend the visual before Cranch's painting. Internalizing such scenes of nature, the Transcendental viewer becomes mesmerized, so to speak: "We fall into trances and almost abnormal spheres of life when we yield ourselves to her [Nature's] power." Then, "locked to the heart of Nature."

> [we] feel the same spirit thrilling through her and us. We breathe the same breath, we are filled with the same joy with which the Infinite Fountain of Love inspires her . . . as these revelations of God are incessant, a flowing river of delight and instruction; so the soul of man shall be a corresponding receiver thereof, and his interior nature be a true reflection of the Kosmos—the immense world of beauty that forever shines around us.

John Sullivan Dwight, like G. W. Curtis, a viewer well versed in Emersonian concepts, noted of Cranch's work, "Were there not these still mirrors to reflect the beauty of the heavens to us, it might be lost to eyes so seldom lifted upwards."[38]

Cranch's *River View* offers us the tranquility necessary for such reflection. Sailboats glide across the calm river under a blue sky accented with fair-weather cirrus and cumulus clouds. But Cranch's image is not the "still mirror" which so aptly describes luminist painting: here the light appears cool and palpable as it settles over the distant mountains, but one is aware of Cranch's short, curling brushstrokes, which cause the light to circulate and shimmer over the landscape. The image as a whole is not still or quiet.

As mentioned above, several scholars have linked American luminism with Transcendental philosophy as the luminist vision finds a corollary in Emersonian precepts, specifically to certain phrases found in Emerson's *Nature*.[39] The absence of brushstroke, for example, is a particularly fitting parallel to the absence of ego suggested by Emerson's description of becoming a "transparent eyeball" and allowing the currents of the Universal Being to circulate through him. When the artist's labor trail of brushstrokes is invisible—as it is in luminist painting—then, as Emerson wrote, "all mean egotism disappears." The stillness and expansiveness inherent in Emerson's imagery, "my head bathed in blithe air and uplifted into infinite space," find a visual equivalent in the hard, cool light of the luminists' landscapes and in the dominant horizontality of their compositions.

It is significant, then, in light of the alignment of luminism with Transcendentalism, that Cranch, who was immersed in Emersonian philosophy, did not produce luminist paintings. Only on rare occasions did he employ the extended format featuring the strong unbroken horizon line favored by the luminists. His delicate, rounded brushstrokes create a pattern offering quite the opposite effect from that achieved by the magically invisible stroke of luminist painters. Their crystalline clarity is traded for a soft shimmering or vibrating effect in Cranch's work. His landscapes are not composed of the spare outlines favored by Lane and Kensett, but rather are diverse to the point of appearing crowded. His paintings are filled with activity and sound.

The fact remains that Cranch, who did not participate in luminism, was both a painter and a Transcendentalist who endeavored to render visible Transcendental ideas. Cranch's brand of Transcendentalism bypasses the "transparent" aspect to celebrate a nature that is sound-filled and motion-filled—the nature Emerson called "ecstatic." The luminist emphasis on the "transparent," with its compositional structure privileging the horizontal and its absence of brushstroke, causes these landscapes to become quiet and still. In effect, time stops. This militates against the flux, the continual shifting and metamorphosing that Emerson celebrated as one of nature's methods. The stoppage of time plays no role in this aspect of Emersonian Transcendentalism where perpetual motion and change are evident everywhere in the natural world. As Emerson noted, there was "every hour, a picture which was never seen before, and which shall never be seen again."[40] It is this facet of Transcendentalism—in which the galvanizing flow of energy as the Universal Spirit moves through nature, or moves nature through us—that we see characterized in Cranch's landscapes. It is not surprising that Cranch found his voice in the Emersonian celebration of the energy in nature, for motion—wandering and searching—was a defining element in his personality and his career. Cranch's search for a vocation and inspiration were in essence his search for a voice.

The New-York Historical Society's *Landscape* (1849) (figure 2) provides a visual counterpart to the flux in nature that Emerson celebrated. The scene is energized with activity, sound, and endless variety. A bald mountain looms large over the right side of the composition and is balanced by a smaller peak at the left; both are echoed in several rounded mountain peaks in the far distance. Deciduous and evergreen trees encircle a calm lake which erupts into a waterfall; it, in turn, dashes down either side of the large rock that obstructs the stream in its center. In the foreground is a storm-blasted tree trunk that lends an element of the sublime to the richly varied scene; its presence recalls the past violence of some storm and all of its attendant motion and thunder. The sublimity is balanced—in the Emersonian sense of the inherent balance of polarized forces in nature—by the calm sky above.[41]

But the scene as a whole is fictitious. It is not a transcription of an actual American view but rather a composite of several landscapes, and in this sense it is conceptual. Emerson had experimented with the possibility that nature may exist only in our minds, a projection instilled in us by God, and Cranch too had remarked upon the power of the mind independent of matter.[42] In a parallel manner, a conceptual approach informs his image. Conceptual attitudes often bore two-dimensional results and Cranch's *Landscape* does in fact contain passages that militate against the compositional devices that attempt to locate the objects in deep space. Here Cranch attempted a Claudian composition[43] featuring a central pool of water framed by trees, all infused with a golden light; however, the conceptual underpinnings of this scene become apparent: the calm lake in the middle-ground tilts towards the picture plane and the distant mountains flatten in the hazy light and push forward. This wavering back and forth between two- and three-dimensionality warps the Claudian construct and militates against any sense of tranquility in the scene, or in the mind of the viewer.

The sound- and motion-filled nature that Cranch celebrates corresponds to Emerson's belief that "when God speaketh he should communicate, not one thing, but all things; should fill the world with his voice; should scatter forth light, nature, time, souls, from the centre of the present thought; and new date and new create the whole." In keeping with the rush of sound as God's voice and varied presence fills the world, Cranch's paintings and poems are rarely silent. **"Field Notes,"** written in 1842, celebrates the wealth of sounds and species in nature. Cranch's choice of words for their phonetic qualities reinforces his portrayal of a sonorous Nature:

> Heareth wisdom musical in a low-toned waterfall,
> Or the pine grove's breezy rush,
> Or the thrilling of a thrush, . . .

Or, of the endless variety of nature:

> Vines that creep and spikes that nod,
> Golden-helmet, golden-rod,
> Orchis, milk-weed, elder-bloom,
> Brake, sweet-fern and meadow broom. . . .[44]

In his paintings, including *Landscape* (figure 2) and *Landscape with Waterfall* (1851) (figure 3), sound is transmuted into visual activity as a sign of the continual flux in the natural world. In the painting from 1851, the dominant motif—a waterfall, which is the epitome of sound and motion—sets the tone for the scene. Placed against the picture plane, the cataract begins to invade the viewer's space, in essence moving sound into the foreground. The waterfall supplants the calm Claudian coulisse entirely.

At first glance the composition of *Landscape with Waterfall* appears Claudian, but on close observation one senses again a deviation. The river, viewed on an acute angle, twists the composition so that the river banks appear parallel to each other, retreating into the distance in a semicircular motion. The vanishing point appears to be located at the extreme left of the composition, at a point on the horizon hidden from view by the birch trees. Thus the resulting landscape appears to be in motion, oddly and slowly revolving.

During the late 1840s and 1850s Cranch was repeatedly drawn to certain motifs that include this "split waterfall." That motif is featured in the New-York Historical Society *Landscape* and *Landscape with Waterfall*, discussed above, as well as in *Autumn Landscape with Boy Fishing* (1845, not illustrated). Given Cranch's immersion in Transcendental philosophy during these years, these landscapes can be read as visual expressions of Emersonian concepts of flux, polarity, and unity in variety. Because such images were intended to be "read" by the viewer, iconography is privileged over technique and other formal issues.

During these years, Cranch was fascinated by the writings of Emanuel Swedenborg. In his journal entries from 1839 through the 1870s he grappled with Swedenborgian concepts.[45] In *Heaven and Its Wonders and Hell* (1758) Swedenborg took care to label natural symbols; he supplied links between individual species of trees, for example, and very specific moral attitudes.[46] Echoing Swedenborg's belief that every object in nature was attached to a moral law, Cranch, in his poem **"Correspondences,"** likened Nature to "a scroll,—God's handwriting thereon," thus forging a relationship between word and image.[47] Like Swedenborg, Cranch endeavored to pierce through the externalities of nature to locate underlying spiritual messages. Certainly the correspondence theory was predominant in his mind when he began painting in the 1840s; it was not long before he was able to translate Swedenborgian concepts into visual form. While Cranch demonstrated little of Swedenborg's interest in assigning such specific attributes to natural forms, the emphasis on allowing external, sensual form to stand in for spiritual truths had ramifications on Cranch's iconography.

A "transcendental landscape," then, might be replete with natural symbols, such as the waterfall. The split waterfall motif—best described as a stream that invariably splits around a central rock causing the water to rush around both sides before ultimately rejoining—appears to have held special significance for Cranch. A clue to the symbolism and emotional significance of this favored motif may be found in the last stanza of Cranch's **"Enosis"** (1840). In these lines he celebrates the inherent, though sometimes obscured unity between two kindred souls, perhaps between himself and Ralph Waldo Emerson:

> We like parted drops of rain
> Swelling till they meet and run,
> Shall be all absorbed again,
> Melting, flowing into one.[48]

The stream of water in the landscape, in an identical manner, when separated, will flow around an obstacle and ultimately be reunified.

For Cranch, the split/reunified waterfall, like the drops of rain flowing into one, can be read as a symbol of Transcendental friendship. While the waterfall is encountered almost exclusively in the landscapes of the 1840s and early 1850s—the period of Cranch's immersion in Transcendental philosophy—it appears in only one later painting: the *Landscape* Cranch painted as a gift for Emerson in 1874 as a testament to his lasting influence.[49] This image, above all else, must be read as a statement of the philosophical debts he owed Emerson and as a visual manifestation of his words.[50]

It is significant that Cranch, after abandoning the waterfall motif for almost two decades, reinstalled it as the dominant motif in this landscape. The painting, which today still hangs on a wall in Emerson's house in Concord, Massachusetts, is a sunset landscape. The central body of water, colored by the setting sun, flows toward the viewer before cascading over a wall of large rocks in the foreground. The effect is that of the split waterfall. Painted several years after Cranch and Emerson lost contact, this landscape can be read as Cranch's attempt at renewing their friendship. This intention is apparent in the motifs Cranch chose: one strong, well-branched tree stands above the rest and towers over the landscape. The stream below, which breaks over the rock passage forcing the water into small streamlets, each separate from the other but composed of the same stuff, are ultimately reunited. The composition is balanced and Claudian: trees on the rocky banks frame the lake and waterfall. A golden light—warm, palpable, and in motion—envelops and unifies the scene. Cranch's palette and technique developed sophistication over the years; here his stroke is quite painterly, a result of his contact with Barbizon painting in the late 1850s, and he experiments with the interaction of reflected colors imbuing the foreground objects with a red hue as the sun sets behind them.[51]

Cranch's feeling for light, evidenced throughout his career in his landscapes, emerged in his poetry as well. **"The Artist,"** published in the *Dial*, is one who "breathed the air of realms enchanted" and "bathed in seas of dreamy light."

> A sky more soft than Italy's
> A halcyon light around him spread;
> And tones were his and only his,
> So sweetly floating o'er his head.[52]

Other poems, including **"The Ocean"** (1844), in which Cranch likens mankind to "Spirits bathing in the sea of Deity," contain passages in which the senses are transcended. **"The Music of Nature"** (1836), begins with such a passage:

> I wandered with a calm surprise
> Half on the earth, half on the air,

> And sometimes I went gliding where
> The ocean meets the skies.
> O, it was sweet to roam away!
> No cumbrous limbs to clog the motion.[53]

These lines approach the light-filled clarity of the "transparent eyeball" aspect of Transcendentalism, yet even Cranch's closest approaches to luminism are not quiet or still. When gliding "half on the air," or transcending the body and senses, as he does below, there remains a concern with motion and sound that breaks the characteristic silent stillness of luminism:

> Whilst slept the limbs and senses all,
> Made everything seem musical;
> How could I cease to hear?[54]

As with Cranch's paintings, in which brushwork militates against any sense of tranquility, the concern with sound and motion in his poetry dilutes the power of the quiet mood evoked.

When Emerson first encouraged Cranch to break away from the Unitarian ministry to pursue landscape painting in 1841, he championed self-reliance.[55] Asserting his Romantic belief in the sacredness of the individual, Cranch broke away from institutional religion and pursued his inner calling to celebrate God's work as a painter of nature. Yielding to Emerson's precept to "insist on yourself," Cranch asserts his presence in painting through the application of paint and through his arrangement of landscape elements. Applying paint in curving motions with his characteristic light stroke, Cranch achieves a roundness of form and a constant, albeit subtle, surface activity. He is present in all of his images. (Conversely, the luminists, through the suppression of brushstroke and rejection of conventional composition, became, in essence, "invisible.")

For Cranch, as for Emerson, traces of the artist's life experiences, such as were carried in brushwork and compositional structures, were an essential part of true art. Nevertheless, in America at mid century, it was commonly understood that an artist must not assert himself in landscape painting to a degree that would cause the image to deviate from truth to God's creation. Cranch never privileged technique over content, which for him was the poetry or religious spirit in nature. Instead his presence was meditative, his "spirituality" was "of the still, contemplative sort; breathings, aspirations," detectable in his "constant tendency to converse with the essence and souls of things through the outward form."[56]

In his essay **"On the Ideal in Art,"** published in 1845, Cranch refuted the popular Lockean notion that art is merely the skillful "imitation" of nature. He argued instead that visible nature must pass through "the refining fire of human genius, before she takes her highest degree," developing Emerson's idea that "thus is Art a nature passed through the alembic of man." Cranch acknowledged that "No one denies that Nature is the material basis of Art, that Nature must be accurately imitated"; however, it is "the Mind, the Soul, after all, which perceives nature; the eye is but an optical instrument." No artist can be completely objective and imitative in the Lockean sense, but neither can he tamper with God's Nature: "Let us strive to imitate Nature: but there will be unconsciously imparted to the imitation a treatment which is strictly our own. Nor is this departing from Nature. For there is an ideal as there is an actual Nature." He accepts that while attempting accurately and truthfully to transcribe the landscape onto his canvas, his conception, as well as the mark of his brush, will remain visible. His characteristic brushstrokes and complex compositional structure should then be read as an assertion of self and of the image of nature in the artist's Mind and Soul.[57]

Ultimately, Cranch's art is a function of the compromise that "Art is neither wholly material nor wholly spiritual," but rather "the beautiful child of the wedlock between Nature and the Soul; and she is the more beautiful, the more she bears a resemblance to both parents."[58] Straddling the line between the real and the ideal in his theory of landscape painting, Cranch spoke as a New England Transcendentalist whose philosophy was located a distance from the materialism of John Locke—which stressed reliance on the senses, and correspondingly on the imitation of nature—and somewhat closer to the idealism of Kant—which emphasized the processes of the mind, of which imagination was a large part. These were issues that concerned Cranch as an artist over the course of his life.

Cranch's method had always required an intense communion with nature which was itself an act of devotion. Allowing nature to sink into his soul, he extracted its essence in "rare landscapes of soft mellow tone."[59] His early landscapes of the 1840s and 1850s, the period when he was most closely associated with Transcendentalism, are encyclopedic and necessarily fictitious views that included every natural phenomenon imaginable in an effort to reveal the flux and endless variety in nature. In his later paintings, Cranch sought out quiet, arcadian landscapes—scenes of Venice bathed in light and tranquil views of the Hudson River (see figure 4)—that cultivate a mood of contemplation and a spirituality stemming from Transcendentalism. Yet all of his landscapes support an intimate dialogue between man and nature.

Rather late in his career, Cranch published an essay, **"The Unconscious Life,"** in which he continued to promote a form of painting that would rely on the imagination to filter sensory information received from its models (nature) but that was also the result of various unconscious, intuitive processes. This essay was published in 1890—just two years before his death—but it found its genesis in his **"Commonplace Book"** circa 1876, reflecting the direction Cranch's Transcendentalism took in the 1870s and 1880s.[60] Cranch explored the implications of the unconscious in directing the painting process. As paintings are often "injured, if not spoiled, by being overlabored," he sought to locate the truest image in the "first fresh impression" without regard for technique or composition. In this context, even the roughest oil sketch would be valuable as a record of direct contact with God in nature. The unconscious allows the artist to intuit truth in nature, thus taking on the role of Emerson's moral sentiment, through these first impressions. An unfinished sketch would enable us to feel "how small things may suggest the greater—the drop of water image the firmament."[61]

Over the years Cranch's painting style and technique gained sophistication, and his brand of Transcendentalism developed into a system in which painting and theology function as one. Nevertheless, one aspect of his life as an artist remained unchanged. Cranch, the Transcendentalist, was in communion with God when he painted his landscapes and sketched outdoors. Breathing the fresh air, opening his heart and mind to the beauties of the landscape, he received the moral sentiment. Transcribing nature onto canvas became an act of devotion, an integral part of the intimate relationship he found with the Universal Spirit in Nature. Christopher Cranch was unique in that he painted as a Transcendentalist. Whether he was painting the Grand Canal in Venice or a cedar tree in Fishkill, his goals were inherently religious. While Transcendentalism can be found, to a limited degree, in his paintings—that is, in his approach and in his iconography—it remains that for Cranch the very act of painting the landscape was Transcendentalism.

Notes

1. Christopher Pearse Cranch to Ralph Waldo Emerson, Sept. 12, 1841, in Leonora Cranch Scott. *The Life and Letters of Christopher Pearse Cranch* (Boston and New York, 1917), 60.

2. Recent scholarship has focused on Cranch as a Transcendentalist within the context of his relationships with Ralph Waldo Emerson. Theodore Parker, and the Transcendental circle in general. J. C. Levenson was among the first to write about Cranch in "Christopher Pearse Cranch: The Case History of a Minor Artist in America." *American Literature* 21(1950):415-426. Hazen C. Carpenter, in his article "Emerson and Christopher Pearse Cranch," *New England Quarterly* 37(1964):18-42, traced the often one-sided relationship between the two Transcendentalists: Elizabeth R. McKinsey's study *The Western Experiment: New England Transcendentalists in the Ohio Valley* (Cambridge, Mass., 1973) offered insight into his psyche. These essays were followed by a series of articles published in the 1970s and 1980s by: David Robinson. "The Career and Reputation of Christopher Pearse Cranch: An Essay in Biography and Bibliography," *Studies in the American Renaissance 1978,* ed. Joel Myerson (Boston, 1978), 453-472; David Robinson, "Christopher Pearse Cranch, Robert Browning, and the Problem of 'Transcendental' Friendship," *Studies in the American Renaissance 1977,* ed. Joel Myerson (Boston, 1977), 145-153; Joel Myerson, "Transcendentalism and Unitarianism in 1840: A New Letter by C. P. Cranch," *CLA Journal* 16(1973):366-367; Francis B. Dedmond, "'A Pencil in the Grasp of Your Graphic Wit': An Illustrated Letter from C. P. Cranch to Theodore Parker," *Studies in the American Renaissance 1981,* ed. Joel Myerson (Charlottesville, 1981), 345-357; Francis B. Dedmond, "Christopher Pearse Cranch: Emerson's Self-Appointed Defender," *Concord Saunterer* 15(1980):6-19; Francis B. Dedmond, "Christopher Pearse Cranch's Journal, 1839," *Studies in the American Renaissance 1983,* ed. Joel Myerson (Charlottesville, 1983), 129-150: and Shelly Armitage, "Christopher Pearse Cranch: The Wit as Poet," *American Transcendental Quarterly* 1(1987):33-47. Most recent is Julie M. Norko's 1992 article, "Christopher Pearse Cranch's Struggle with the Muses," *Studies in the American Renaissance 1992,* ed. Joel Myerson (Charlottesville, 1992), 209-228. Recent monographs of Transcendental periodicals—*The Western Messenger, The Dial,* and *The Harbinger*—also contain substantial discussions of Cranch's role.

3. Perry Miller, *The Transcendentalists: An Anthology* (Cambridge, Mass., 1950), 179. It is unclear why Miller did not view Cranch's painting as "serious work," but his pronouncements have had ramifications on Cranch's reputation. Lawrence Buell, for example, quoting Miller, refers to Cranch as a "would-be artist." *Literary Transcendentalism* (Ithaca, 1973), 42, n. 42.

4. Christopher Pearse Cranch, "Autobiography," unpaginated, unpublished MS, private collection.

5. Cranch exhibited widely during his career. For a listing of exhibitions in which he participated see James Yarnall and William H. Gerdts, *The National Museum of American Art's Index to American Art Exhibition Catalogues* (Boston, 1986). Cranch belonged to the group of New York-based artists who later came to be known as the "Hudson River School." These landscape painters exhibited at the National Academy of Design, spent summers sketching along the Hudson River, and congregated at the Century Club in New York City. As a group, their paintings typically combined precisely observed detail with the ideal elements of the Claudian composition. Cranch was one of the least well known participants in the Hudson River School, but his work deals with the same issues and functions within the same parameters as that of the other Hudson River artists.

6. "On the line" refers to the exhibition practice of honoring certain paintings with a prime location on the wall, that is on the "line" that is eye-level. On the other hand, those paintings considered inferior by the hanging committee were "skied," meaning that those painting were hung close the ceiling, far above the visitor's eye level and easily overlooked.

The Paris Salon was held every other year during Cranch's stay in France (1853-1863), and his paintings were accepted for the Salon every year it was held: 1855, when he exhibited two landscapes; 1857, when he exhibited four paintings: and 1861, when he exhibited one landscape. Cranch returned to New York in 1863.

7. Henry James, *William Wetmore Story and His Friends* (Boston, 1903), 1:110.

8. In a letter to John Sullivan Dwight, dated July 22, 1841, Cranch wrote: "A friend of mine here, who paints very sweet landscapes, offers to give me some instruction in the practical parts of painting, and then I can go on of myself. I am all impatience to begin." In the same breath, he continues: "Do you ever see Emerson? His last book has been a living fountain to me," thus confirming the concurrence of Emersonian inspiration with the urge to paint. Cranch to Dwight, July 22, 1841, Cranch Papers, Massachusetts Historical Society.

9. These caricatures can be found in the collections of the Houghton Library at Harvard University, the Massachusetts Historical Society in Boston, and the Albany Institute of History and Art in Albany, New York. For an in-depth treatment of Cranch's caricatures, see F. DeWolfe Miller's excellent study *Christopher Pearse Cranch and His Caricatures of New England Transcendentalism* (Cambridge, Mass., 1951).

10. Through the suppression of brushstroke and rejection of conventional composition, the luminists become, in essence, invisible. This elimination or suppression of self causes the artist to become transparent and allows the "currents of the Universal Being" to circulate through him as well as through the viewer without mediation. A visual corollary is provided to Emerson's "a light shines through us upon things and makes us aware that we are nothing, but the light is all. Emerson, "The Over-Soul," in *Selected Essays,* ed. Larzer Ziff (New York, 1982), 208.

11. In fact, so tenuous is the link between the luminists and Transcendentalism that Elizabeth Garrity Ellis observed that, while it is unlikely that luminist Fitz Hugh Lane (1804-1865) knew Cranch's caricature of Emerson's "transparent eyeball," "Cranch's top-hatted creature towering over field and hills . . . has nonetheless dominated discussions of the luminist paintings [Lane] produced from the mid 1850s until his death in 1865," thus suggesting a link between Lane's paintings and Emerson. Ellis, "Cape Ann Views," in *Paintings of Fitz Hugh Lane* (Washington, D.C., 1988), 19.

Most recently, however, an article published by Mary Foley in *The American Art Journal* puts forth a stronger case for Lane having some familiarity with Emerson's ideas. Until the publication of her article, only the fact that Lane's name had been found on a list of members of the American Union of Associationists tied him with a group of former Brook Farmers. Elizabeth Garrity Ellis. "Fitz Hugh Lane and the American Union of Associationists." *The American Art Journal* 17(1985):89. Foley discovered Lane was also active in the Gloucester Lyceum after 1848, where he was appointed to the board of directors in September 1849. The fact that Emerson lectured at the Lyceum encourages the possibility that Lane may have heard him lecture or may even have spoken with him. Mary Foley, "Fitz Hugh Lane. Ralph Waldo Emerson, and the Gloucester Lyceum," *The American Art Journal* 27(1995-1996):99-101. While Lane may have heard Emerson speak in Gloucester, there is still no evidence that connects Lane with Transcendentalism on a deeper level.

12. Cranch to John Sullivan Dwight, June 15, 1836, in Scott, *Life and Letters,* 26.

13. Cranch to Margaret Cranch (sister), Oct. 15, 1837, in Scott, *Life and Letters,* 40; Cranch to Julia Myers, Aug. 10, 1837, in Scott, *Life and Letters,* 35. Cranch's 1839 "Journal" begins with a New Year's resolution on Jan. 8, 1839: "I must begin to *Live* more in earnest, than I have done. . . . At present I only *dream*. Half of my existence seems to be *dreaming*. A deadly *indifference* hangs over me—like a lethargy." "Journal." Cranch Papers. Massachusetts Historical Society.

14. Journal entry of 1840, transcribed in Cranch, "Autobiography."

15. Cranch to William Cranch, July 11, 1840, in Scott, *Life and Letters,* 50.

16. "Carlyle was an early love with me . . . [as was] Emerson. To these two great minds, among others, I was mostly indebted for the change that gradually took place in my theological belief. . . . These two leaders marshalled me the way my natural tendencies were impelling me." Cranch, "Autobiography."

17. Thomas Carlyle, *Sartor Resartus* (Boston and New York, 1897), 235; Cranch, "Autobiography"; Cranch to Julia Myers, Feb. 4, 1840, in Scott, *Life and Letters,* 47.

18. In Maine, during the winter of 1840, Cranch wrote: "I came across some people who called Emerson crazy and sneered at . . . 'transcendentalism.' . . . I spoke in defense. I long to utter my mind to these Philistines, but I anticipate some squalls here. If it comes to this I shall clear out of Portland pretty quick" ("Autobiography"). Once labeled a Transcendentalist, Cranch encountered difficulty in finding pulpits to fill. He voiced his frustration to John Sullivan Dwight through sarcasm: "Let me advise you . . . to repent of your heresies, to renounce R. W. E. and all his evil works and return to good old fashioned Unitarianism." Cranch to Dwight, Apr. 20, 1840, Cranch Papers. Massachusetts Historical Society.

19. Cranch's poem was published as *Poem Delivered in the First Congregational Church in the Town of*

Quincy, May 25, 1840, the Two Hundredth Anniversary of the Incorporation of the Town (Boston, 1840).

20. Cranch to William Cranch, July 11, 1840, in Scott, *Life and Letters,* 49-51.

21. William Cranch to Ralph Waldo Emerson, Mar. 2, 1840, in Scott, *Life and Letters,* 58.

22. Emerson to Cranch, Mar. 4, 1840, in Scott, *Life and Letters,* 60. Emerson praised "Enosis" and "Aurora Borealis" as "true" and "brilliant" and "one more authentic sign . . . of a decided poetic taste, and tendency to original observation in our Cambridge circle" (5n). Cranch was unable to go immediately to see Emerson so the visit did not take place until August. A letter from Cranch to Emerson dated Sept. 12, 1841, refers to additional visits "enjoyed with you under your roof and occasionally in Boston." In Scott, *Life and Letters,* 60-61.

23. Emerson exclaimed to Margaret Fuller that Cranch, along with Henry David Thoreau and William Ellery Channing comprised "the best club that ever made a journal." Quoted in William H. Moss, "'So Many Promising Youths': Emerson's Disappointing Discoveries of New England Poet-Seers," *New England Quarterly* 49(1976):55. Moss also notes that "Emerson had followed this same pattern several times before in his relationships with young poets" at first enthusiastic and later disenchanted with their productions (47).

24. "Truth dawns like light upon nations," Cranch explained. "All who are true . . . feel its coming, though they only *feel,* in dim, vague glimmerings of imagination and hope, but cannot *think* their dream into shape—much less speak it. . . . They are like infants who have but a confused inarticulate language of their own." "Transcendentalism," *Western Messenger* 8(Jan. 1841):405-409.

25. The original of this caricature in the archives of the Houghton Library. Harvard University, has been torn; the remaining portion, from Emerson's feet to his neck, is on the reverse of Cranch's "disagreeable things" cartoon (many thanks to Jennie Rathbun at the Houghton Library for locating this item). A "reconstruction" appears in F. DeWolfe Miller, *Christopher Pearse Cranch and His Caricatures of New England Transcendentalism* (Cambridge, Mass., 1951).

26. Several versions of this caricature exist: one, in the Houghton Library at Harvard University; a second version in the Albany Institute of History and Art in Albany. New York; a third in Cranch's 1839 "Journal," Cranch Papers, Massachusetts Historical Society, in which the name Ralph Waldo Emerson inscribed over the walking eyeball has been crossed out.

27. Cranch to James Freeman Clarke, May 20, 1839, Cranch Papers, Massachusetts Historical Society. While Cranch's caricatures have a wide audience today, it remains unclear just who their intended audience was in the 1830s and 1840s. Cranch confessed to Clarke that he lent to his cousin William Henry Furness "my Emersonian scraps . . . and it seems by sundry external signs upon them . . . that they have been considerably thumbed and pocketed. Great men have looked upon them." But it is not clear whether Emerson ever saw the caricatures.

28. In 1839, according to his "Journal," Cranch wrote a "Sartorish letter" illustrated with images that have what Cranch called "a sense—a Carlylean graphicness and truth. There can be a touch of comicality in them too—to give them a relish." Cranch, Jan. 9, 1839, "Journal," Cranch Papers, Massachusetts Historical Society.

29. Cranch, "Autobiography." Cranch complained of not having had a preaching engagement in the previous two months because "My name is expunged from the list of *safe* men. . . . I have the misfortune to have associated with Emerson, Ripley, & those corrupters of youth, and have written to the Dial, and these are unpardonable offenses." Cranch to John Sullivan Dwight, Nov. 17, 1840, in Myerson, "Transcendentalism and Unitarianism," 366-367.

30. Cranch to John Sullivan Dwight, July 22, 1841, Cranch Papers, Massachusetts Historical Society. Cranch made several visits to Brook Farm in West Roxbury, Massachusetts, and although supportive of the venture, he never became a member: "I have . . . no plans; or prospects, save of the vaguest sort. I want to see something of Ripley's establishment, and know if there is any work held out there to me in which I can earnestly engage." Cranch to Dwight, July 22, 1841, Cranch Papers, Massachusetts Historical Society.

In the 1830s and until the early 1840s, before Cranch began to paint, he contributed poetry and essays to the various Transcendental periodicals: the *Western Messenger,* the *Dial,* and the *Harbinger.* This involvement not only demonstrated his commitment to Transcendentalism but also points to his increasing need for an outlet for his "new views" outside of the Unitarian pulpit. For a complete discussion of Cranch's involvement with Transcendental periodicals, see Robert D. Habich, *Transcendentalism and the "Western Messenger": A History of the Magazine and Its Contributors, 1835-1841* (London and Toronto, 1985); Joel Myerson, *The New England Transcendentalists and the Dial: A History of the Magazine and Its Contributors* (London and Toronto, 1980); and Sterling F. Delano, *"The Harbinger" and New England Transcendentalism: A Portrait of Associationism in America* (London and Toronto, 1983).

31. Cranch to Julia Myers, Aug. 2, 1841, in Scott, *Life and Letters,* 67; Cranch, "Autobiography."

32. Norko, "Christopher Pearse Cranch's Struggle with the Muses," 210. Norko proposes as her thesis:

Cranch spent a large portion of his early years attempting to ignore or unsuccessfully reconcile his concept of duty with his natural inclinations.... His prose of the period after he accepted the call to preach Unitarianism in the Ohio Valley demonstrates the development of the tension between vocation and inclination. In the prose, missionary zeal confronts his eventual movement from religion to aestheticism.

(210)

Furthermore, Norko provides support for her view of painting as not only "inclination" but "amusement" for Cranch with the observation that Cranch's father would only tune his piano on "days of leisure": "Perhaps [father] William Cranch's classification of the arts as leisure activities explains not only why Cranch could not be formally trained in them, but also why he could not seriously consider a career in them" (210). That few opportunities for "formal training" in painting existed in America in the 1830s notwithstanding, Norko never mentions a detail of critical importance: Christopher Cranch's older brother John was an artist who toured Italy with Thomas Cole and whose drawings can today be found in the collection of the Metropolitan Museum of Art, New York.

33. Further support for this alignment of nature and God can be found in the writings of the Hudson River School artists, of which the best known is Asher B. Durand's "Letters on Landscape Painting" (published in *The Grayon* in 1855), as well as in contemporary art criticism.

34. James Jackson Jarves, *The Art-Idea,* ed. Benjamin Rowland, Jr., (1864; Cambridge Mass., 1960), 86; Barbara Novak, *Nature and Culture: American Landscape and Painting, 1825-1875* (New York, 1980), 9; Christopher Pearse Cranch, "The Painter in the Woods," *Sartain's Union Magazine* 10(Jan. 1852):44-45.

35. Miller, *The Transcendentalists,* 9. Miller cautioned that "unless this literature be read as fundamentally an expression of a religious radicalism in revolt against a rational conservatism, it will not be understood" (8). He also observed that "This inherently religious character of New England Transcendentalism has not been widely appreciated, mainly because most students are not acquainted with all the writings ... [and] because all the insurgents strove ... to put their cause into the language of philosophy and literature rather than of theology" (8-9).

36. Christopher Pearse Cranch, "Expression, the Mother of Sentiment," *Western Messenger* 5(Sept. 1838):375; George William Curtis to John Sullivan Dwight, Dec. 22, 1845, in *Early Letters of George Wm. Curtis to John S. Dwight: Brook Farm and Concord,* ed. George Willis Cooke (New York, 1898), 237.

37. This image can be found in Nancy Stula, *Lured by the Muses: Christopher Pearse Cranch, 1813-1892* (New York, 1997).

38. Christopher Pearse Cranch, "Ralph Waldo Emerson," undated, unpaginated MS. Cranch Papers, Massachusetts Historical Society; Cranch, "Painter in the Woods," 44-45; John Sullivan Dwight, review of Cranch's *Poems* [1844], *The Harbinger* 1(July 26, 1845):105-107.

39. John I. H. Baur identified luminism in his 1954 article "American Luminism: A Neglected Aspect of the Realist Movement in Nineteenth-Century American Painting," *Perspectives U. S. A.* 9(1954):90-98; but Barbara Novak, in *American Painting of the Nineteenth Century: Realism, Idealism, and the American Experience* (New York, 1969), first stressed the links between luminism and the transparent and tranquil aspect of Transcendentalism. More recently, Novak has stated: "There is perhaps little direct influence. But we can claim affinity. Luminism is the purest visual formulation of mid-century transcendental philosophy." *Nineteenth Century American Painting: The Thyssen-Bornemisza Collection* (New York, 1986), 30.

40. Emerson, *Selected Essays,* 44. Barbara Novak, in a footnote to her discussion of luminism in *American Painting of the Nineteenth Century,* acknowledges that several scholars (including John McCoubrey and John Kouwenhoven) have "put forth the idea of flux as the essentially American quality."

If a dominant American quality is, as I maintain, not flux but an absolute in time and space that fortifies the constant existence of both thing and thought, it is perhaps because we have indeed had an awareness of flux that has engaged us even more intensely in a search for the underlying absolutes.... For Emerson, the task seems to have been to find that unity beneath the flux.

(300n)

41. This painting was completed just after Cranch's return from Italy in 1849. While the Italian landscape and ruins had been a source of associations, the pristine wildness of the Catskills and Adirondacks put Cranch in touch with the power of God. The sublime, with its attendant rawness and power, spoke of Creation itself.

42. In his "Commonplace Book," circa 1872, Cranch wrote: "If Mind has this tendency and this power of making a magic lantern of itself, with eyes ... to see its own hidden pictures thus made real—does it not argue a power independent of matter ... ?" Cranch, "Commonplace Book," 26, Cranch Papers, Massachusetts Historical Society.

43. "Claudian" composition refers to the compositional structure employed by the French artist Claude Lorraine (1600-1682). This landscape structure consists

of framing trees, a middle ground punctuated by water—usually a central coulisse—and a distance bathed in a golden light. Nineteenth-century American artists found Claude's compositions especially well suited to conveying the aesthetic of the beautiful. Cranch, as a young art student, studied Claude's *Liber Veritatis* in the Library of Congress, admiring his landscapes for their "truth" and "ideality." Cranch to John Sullivan Dwight, June 9, 1841, in Scott, *Life and Letters,* 71.

44. Emerson, *Selected Essays,* 188: Christopher Pearse Cranch, "Field Notes," in *Poems* (Philadelphia, 1844), 82-86. This poem is dated July 1842.

45. Cranch delved into Swedenborg's *Arcana Coelestia: or Heavenly Mysteries Contained in the Sacred Scriptures* (Boston, 1794) very early, in 1839, and while he denied that he had become a "Swedenborgian," the theologian's influence is nonetheless apparent in several of his poems of this period as well as in his paintings. In his "Commonplace Book." circa 1872. Cranch continued to graple with Swedenborg: "All depends on which side we approach him. If on the philosophical, common sense side he is a help to us. . . . [T]hrow out his contradictions of statement and then strain his philosophical creed through the seive of Reason . . . and Swedenborg become a great light in our hands." Cranch, "Commonplace Book," 11, Cranch Papers. Massachusetts Historical Society.

46. Swedenborg set forth that "Vines and laurels correspond to affection for truth . . . while olives and fruits [trees] correspond to affection for good." *Heaven and Its Wonders and Hell* (New York, 1900), 79.

47. Christopher Pearse Cranch, "Correspondences," *Dial* 1(Jan. 1841), 381.

48. Cranch, "Enosis," in *Poems,* 51-52.

49. This oil on canvas, c. 99′ x 12′, is owned by and can be seen at the Ralph Waldo Emerson House in Concord, Mass.

50. Cranch's letter to Emerson, dated Apr. 27, 1874, which accompanied the painting, is transcribed in Scott. *Life and Letters,* 280-281.

51. Cranch spent ten years in France, from 1853-1854, and during this decade he was inspired by the painters who worked in the area around Barbizon and in the Forest of Fontainebleau. This group of painters often took unassuming landscapes for their subjects and developed an approach characterized by broad brushstrokes that obliterated fine detail.

52. Christopher Pearse Cranch, "The Artist," *Dial* 3(Oct. 1842):225. When published in 1844 with his collection of *Poems,* "halcyon" was replaced so that line 12 reads: "Their wealth of light around him spread."

   In an 1872 entry in his "Commonplace Book," Cranch sings a "Prayer to the Sun-God . . . I worship thee—Joy of the Universe! Today, by thy light, let me paint as I never painted before, And the joy of thy light, And the joy of my work, shall be my best reward! N.Y. Feb. 7 1869." "Commonplace Book," 6-7. Cranch Papers, Massachusetts Historical Society.

53. Cranch, "The Music of Nature," in *Poems,* 14-20. The poem is dated June 1836. In an undated manuscript entitled "Dreams," Cranch described a similar sensation, but one in which he cannot transcend the senses as walking on air required extreme physical exertion: "I have a strange vivid dream, now and then, of walking in the air. I don't mean that flying sensation some have, but a plain rising and stepping, only accomplished by strong effort of will and usually just a few feet above the heads of my companions. . . . I sink only when I relax my will and muscular effort." "Dreams," undated, unpaginated MS, Cranch Papers, Massachusetts Historical Society.

54. Cranch, "The Music of Nature," 20.

55. Emerson wrote to Cranch in Oct. 1841: "that the beauty of natural forms will not let you rest but you must serve and celebrate them with your pencil, and that at all hazards you must quit the pulpit as a profession, I learn without surprise. . . . The Idea that rises with more or less lustre on all our minds, that unites us all, will have its way and must be obeyed." Emerson to Cranch, Oct. 10, 1841, in Scott, *Life and Letters,* 62.

56. John Sullivan Dwight, review of Cranch's *Poems,* 105-107. Of Cranch's nature. Dwight wrote: "There is nothing in him which could by any possibility tyrannize over others. You feel that here is a gentle nature . . . who would rather sit silent hours and days than *impose* the influence of his speech, and who would suffer all the consequences of inaction, rather than *take* the lead" (106).

57. Christopher Pearse Cranch, "On the Ideal of Art," *The Harbinger* 1(Aug. 23, 1845):170-171; Emerson, *Selected Essays,* 47; Cranch. "On the Ideal of Art," 170-171. For Cranch, genius was the artist's "God-given privilege of infusing . . . Imagination into the dead materials it has collected together, breathing upon dry bones and clothing them in the garb of life and beauty."

58. Cranch, "On the Ideal of Art," 170-171.

59. Cranch, "The Artist," 225.

60. Christopher Pearse Cranch, "The Unconscious Life," *Unitarian Review* 33(Feb. 1890):97-122. Excerpts from the first draft of this essay are found in Cranch's "Commonplace Book" entry for Nov. 11, 1876, Cranch Papers, Massachusetts Historical Society. An essay also titled "The Unconscious Life" was read before the Sunday Club of Boston on Oct. 12, 1880 (Minutes of the Sunday Club, Cranch Papers), before the essay was published in the *Unitarian Review.*

61. Cranch, "The Unconscious Life"; Cranch, "Painter in the Woods," 44-45.

FURTHER READING

Biography

Kane, Paul. "Christopher Pearse Cranch." In *Poetry of the American Renaissance: A Diverse Anthology from the Romantic Period*, p. 165. New York: George Braziller, 1995.

    Brief biographical sketch of Cranch accompanying a selection of his poetry.

Scott, Leonora Cranch. *The Life and Letters of Christopher Pearse Cranch*. Boston and New York: Houghton Mifflin, 1917, 395 p. Reprint. New York: AMS Press, 1969, 395 p.

    A collection of Cranch's correspondence, as well as biographical details on his life, compiled by the author's daughter.

Criticism

Dedmond, Francis B. "'A Pencil in the Grasp of Your Graphic Wit': An Illustrated Letter from C. P. Cranch to Theodore Parker." *Studies in the American Renaissance* (1981): 345-57.

    Includes the text of an 1848 letter, complete with several caricatures, from Cranch in Rome to his friend Theodore Parker.

Dedmond, Francis B. "Christopher Pearse Cranch's 'Journal. 1839.'" *Studies in the American Renaissance* (1983): 129-49.

    Reprints Cranch's 1839 journal written when he was substituting for James Freeman Clarke in his Louisville pulpit and as editor of the *Western Messenger*.

Delano, Sterling F. "Christopher Pearse Cranch's *Address Delivered Before the Harvard Musical Association* (28 August 1845)." *Resources for American Literary Study* 17, no. 2 (1991): 239-53.

    Provides the full text of Cranch's address, suggesting that critical attention to the significance of music in the Transcendentalist movement is long overdue.

Habich, Robert D. "1837-1839: 'A Living Mirror of the Times.'" In *Transcendentalism and the "Western Messenger": A History of the Magazine and Its Contributors, 1835-1841*, pp. 82-126. Rutherford: Fairleigh Dickinson University Press, 1985.

    Outlines Cranch's importance to the magazine and credits him as the most talented of the Transcendentalists after Emerson and Thoreau.

Koster, Donald N. "Some Other Important Transcendentalists." In *Transcendentalism in America*, pp. 64-76. Boston: Twayne, 1975.

    Praises Cranch's sense of humor but labels him a dilettante.

Miller, Perry. "Christopher Pearse Cranch (1813-1892)." In *The Transcendentalists: An Anthology*, pp. 178-80. Cambridge: Harvard University Press, 1950.

    Discusses Cranch's review of Emerson's *The American Scholar*, calling Cranch a "futile and wasted talent."

Myerson, Joel. "Transcendentalism and Unitarianism in 1840: A New Letter by C. P. Cranch." *CLA Journal* 16, no. 3 (March 1973): 366-68.

    Reprints the full text of a letter from Cranch to John Sullivan Dwight with inferences to the controversy involving Unitarianism and Transcendentalism.

Additional coverage of Cranch's life and career is contained in the following sources published by the Gale Group: *Dictionary of Literary Biography*, **Vols. 1 and 42.**

Vuk Stefanović Karadžić
1787-1864

(Also referred to as Vuk Stefanović, Vuk Karadžić, and Vuk) Serbian folklorist and language reformer.

INTRODUCTION

Karadžić's contributions to Serbian culture stem from his interest in developing a national literature and language that would reflect and preserve the language, songs, and stories of Serbia's peasantry. His career is defined by two main areas of scholarship: the collection of Serbian folklore and the reform of Serbian language. Karadžić edited and published numerous collections of folksongs, folklore, and customs, as well as a Serbian grammar and dictionary. Because of his extensive documentation of the folk culture and the vernacular language of the Serbian people, Karadžić is affectionately known by his first name, Vuk, in his native country.

BIOGRAPHICAL INFORMATION

Karadžić was born on November 6, 1787, in Tršić, Serbia, then under Turkish rule, in a village not far from Belgrade. His parents, Stefan and Jegda Joksimovic, were peasant farmers whose five previous children had all died in infancy. They named their sixth child Vuk, or wolf, to protect him from death. Little is known about Karadžić's early childhood except that he taught himself to read and write and briefly attended school at the monastery of Tronosa. His most valuable education came from living at home where he learned the folk customs, rituals, and songs that would inform his early writings. In 1804, a Serb uprising against the Turks resulted in a period of Serbian liberation that lasted until 1813. During this time Karadžić went to Austria where he attended school, learned German and Latin, and was exposed to Western culture. In 1808, Karadžić began to suffer from pain in his legs, feet, and hands; an undiagnosed illness affecting his left leg forced him to walk with a crutch for the rest of his life.

In 1813, when the Turks again conquered Serbia, Karadžić fled to Vienna. It was shortly after his move to Austria that Karadžić attracted the attention of Jernej Kopitar, an Austrian censor, by submitting an article written in the Serbian popular language. Kopitar became Karadžić's friend, advisor, and supporter; not only did he praise and publicize Karadžić's work but he also suggested directions for future scholarship. In 1814, Karadžić published his first collection of folksongs and a grammar to help readers understand his materials. Based on the positive response to these two works, Karadžić published another volume of folksongs the following year. In 1818 Karadžić traveled to Russia to seek intellectual and financial support for his research and writings, and then returned to Serbia to gather additional material for the second and third volumes of an enlarged, four-volume collection of folksongs. In 1823, Karadžić visited Jacob Grimm, who had written a positive review of the third volume of the folksongs, and who introduced him to Johann Wolfgang von Goethe. Between 1828 and 1832, Karadžić worked for Prince Milos Obrenovic, who had led a successful overthrow of the Turks in 1815. Karadžić's duties included teaching French to Obrenovic's sons, translating Napoleonic Laws into Serbian, and writing Serbian history. Karadžić's work for Obrenovic, and by extension for Serbia, ended in 1832 when Karadžić's alphabet and folksongs were condemned by the Orthodox Church as subversive and vulgar. The opposition to his work failed to discourage Karadžić, however, and in 1833 when he was permitted to re-enter Austria, he published the fourth volume of his expanded folksong collection in violation of the Church's ban. By 1835, much of the opposition to his work had subsided, and Karadžić was awarded a pension for service to his country. The pension and the official recognition that accompanied it enabled Karadžić to travel, collect material, and revise his earlier collections of Serbian folklore, culture, and history. Karadžić died in Vienna in 1864.

MAJOR WORKS

Karadžić's interest in folk life and folklore developed from his own upbringing as the son of peasant-farmers, as did his development of a Serbian language based on the vernacular. His work can be categorized into two overlapping areas: language reform and collections of folk material. Karadžić wrote *Pismenica serbskoga iezika* (*Grammar of the Serbian People*) in 1814. He substantially revised the handbook by 1818, the same year he published his *Srpski rječnik* (*Serbian Dictionary*), the first dictionary of spoken Serbian. Karadžić's work focused on the language of the peasantry, the people with whom he identified, as opposed to the more formal language of Church Slavic tempered with Russian. His first two collections of Serbian folklore, *Mala prostonarodnja slaveno-serbska pjesnarica* (*A Simple Little Slaveno-Serbian Songbook*), and *Narodna srbska pjesnarica* (*A Serbian Book of Folksongs*), were published in 1814 and 1815 respectively. These oral narratives, recorded from immigrants living in Srem, rather than written from memory, were Karadžić's first foray into the collection and publication of folklore and established the focus of his scholarship; from that point on, he began to travel extensively and collect material in a more methodological fashion. Karadžić's primary research resulted in an expanded and considerably different collection of these two early works. This new collection was published in four volumes between 1823 and 1833: *Zenske pjesme* (1824; *Women's Songs*); *Pjesme junačke najstarije* (1823; *Oldest Heroic Songs*); *Pjesme junačke srednjijeh vremena* (1823; *Heroic Songs of the Middle Period*); and *Pjesme junačke novijih vremena o vojevanju za slobodu* (1833; *Heroic Songs of Recent Times of the War for Freedom*). Publication of the first volume, *Women's Songs,* was delayed because the Austrian government feared Karadžić's writing would encourage hatred of the Turks and sedition against the Turkish government. Thus volumes two and three preceded the first volume by one year. Another folk collection, *Srpske narodne poslovice* (*Proverbs*), followed in 1836. Karadžić's two areas of research yielded a vivid picture of Serbian life and customs and his work helped to define a Serbian national literature and literary culture.

CRITICAL RECEPTION

Karadžić is considered a major force both in the development of Serbian language and in the collection of Serbian folklore. These two areas—linguistic and folkloristic—are the focus of the majority of scholarship on Karadžić. Early folklorists, notably Jacob Grimm, praised Karadžić's collections and commitment to his country's folk culture. Their reaction has informed most of the contemporary scholarship on Karadžić. Many critics, including Yvonne R. Lockwood, Albert B. Lord, Nikola R. Pribić (see further reading), and Pavel Ivić, concentrate on Karadžić's importance in the development of Serbian, Yugoslavian, and Balkan folklore studies. Some folklorists focus on the role of Karadžić's informants and the oral tradition, as does Svetozar Koljević (see further reading). Other scholars are interested in Karadžić's work with linguistics and language reform. Included in this category are such critics as Thomas Butler and Benjamin Stolz who assert the importance of the relationship between Karadžić and Jernej Kopitar in the development of Karadžić's *Grammar of the Serbian People* and *Serbian Dictionary.* Duncan Wilson (see further reading) has produced a comprehensive English-language study that provides an examination of Karadžić in the context of the history and politics of Serbia and its neighbors. Together these works reassert the importance of Karadžić's contributions to Serbian culture.

PRINCIPAL WORKS

*Mala prostonarodnja slaveno-serbska pjesnarica [*A Simple Little Slaveno-Serbian Songbook*] (songs) 1814
Pismenica serbskoga iezika [*Grammar of the Serbian People*] (handbook) 1814
Narodna srbska pjesnarica [*A Serbian Book of Folksongs*] (songs) 1815
Srpski rječnik [*Serbian Dictionary*] (dictionary) 1818
†*Pjesme junačke najstarije* [*Oldest Heroic Songs*] 2nd vol. (songs) 1823
Pjesme junačke srednjijeh vremena [*Heroic Songs of the Middle Period*] 3rd vol. (songs) 1823
Zenske pjesme [*Women's Songs*] 1st vol. (songs) 1824
Pjesme junačke novijih vremena o vojevanju za slobodu [*Heroic Songs of Recent Times of the War for Freedom*] 4th vol. (songs) 1833
Srpske narodne poslovice [*Proverbs*] (folklore) 1836

*Spelling for Karadžić's Serbian titles may vary in the critical works, depending upon the author's transliteration.

†Karadžić collected and published his expanded folksongs in four volumes. The first volume was published after volumes two and three.

CRITICISM

Yvonne R. Lockwood (essay date 1971)

SOURCE: Lockwood, Yvonne R. "Vuk Stefanović Karadžić: Pioneer and Continuing Inspiration of Yugoslav Folkloristics." *Western Folklore* 30, no. 1 (January 1971): 19-32.

[*In the following essay, Lockwood considers Karadžić's impact on Serbian culture, and notes his continuing influence on the study of folklore.*]

Vuk Stefanović Karadžić did more to revolutionize Serbian culture than any other individual before or since. His two greatest contributions—language reform and collections of folk literature—with their very foundation in peasant culture, had great impact on all Serbian culture. From an illiterate peasant background, Vuk taught himself to read and write and went on to reform the written language, changing it from Church Slavonic to one based on popular Serbian. Having been raised in a peasant environment, Vuk had close association with oral literature in his early years. This peasant upbringing determined Vuk's attitude toward his collections of folksongs, tales, and proverbs. His attitude toward peasant culture, in general, differed greatly from that of the urban intellectual's of his day, whether the latter regarded peasant life and its manifestations as backward and crude or with romantic idealization. Vuk hardly considered peasant life romantic; it was simply a way of life and the only one he knew for many years. With a realistic outlook that is part of peasant culture, Vuk regarded oral literature as one of many expressions of the Serbian people.

Karadžić was born in 1787 during Turkish rule in the village of Tršić, Serbia, near the Bosnian border. His parents were well-to-do peasants from Hercegovina. They had already lost several children before he was born and, consequently, named him "Vuk" (wolf) as a preventive measure.

It was believed that witches feared wolves and that the name would serve as a charm against them and the evil eye. Vuk remained with his parents throughout his childhood. His father wanted him to become a merchant. With the help of an uncle, Vuk taught himself to read and write. For a short time he attended school at a nearby monastery. However, during Turkish occupation, the monks had no time for teaching; instead, they and their students, including Vuk, farmed the land and tended stock. Vuk soon returned to his father's home.

Vuk's thirst for knowledge grew; he constantly sought help from people who knew more than he. Finally, at age seventeen, he received his father's permission to go to high school. However, the instructors determined that Vuk was already well educated and refused him admission. Then Vuk went to Croatia, at that time part of the Austrian Empire, and taught himself German and Latin. This was his first contact with western culture. Serbia had been cut off from western Europe for many years while under Turkish rule. As part of the Ottoman Empire and also a country predominantly Eastern Orthodox, Serbia had little contact with the West prior to the nineteenth century. Although it is not known who his associates were in Croatia, western influence was great enough that Vuk soon realized he was not meant to be a merchant.

After some time, Vuk returned to Serbia, settling in Beograd, where he associated with local intelligentsia. Utilizing their influence, he was able to enroll in school. He contracted a serious illness which left him a cripple, walking only with the use of a cane for the rest of his life.

Having been liberated in 1804, Serbia again fell to the Turks in 1813, after a short-lived period of independence. At this time Vuk fled to Vienna. This period was the most significant in his career; it was during this time that he began his lifework. He submitted an article for publication to the Austrian censor, Jernej Kopitar, a Slovenian by ethnic origin. Kopitar was impressed because Vuk had written the article in the vernacular language rather than the language used by many of his contemporaries, i.e., a language greatly affected by Church Slavic and Russian. Until then, this had seldom been attempted. Kopitar made a special effort to meet Vuk. He saw Vuk as a living source of Serbian contemporary language and history, and one of the rare intellectuals closely associated with oral literature and folk customs. Vuk, on the other hand, saw Kopitar as everything he himself was not—a great learned person and member of the intelligentsia. There was mutual respect and fondness, and a great friendship developed. Vuk had no plans for his future and, therefore, when Kopitar made suggestions, Vuk followed them. Vuk wrote about this period:

> Kopitar recognized that I am a man of the folk and that I am different from all Serbs whom he had seen and met up to that time. . . . Little by little he convinced me to write down not only folksongs but a dictionary and grammar. . . . The first influence and beginning of my collection of folksongs and language reform came from Mr. Kopitar alone.[1]

In 1814 Vuk published his first work, *Mala prostonarodna slaveno-srpska pesnarica,* a collection of 100 lyrical and 6 epic songs which he had learned at home as a child and had written down from memory. Then, in order that readers could better understand the songs, he compiled a small grammar of the Serbian language, which he published in the same year. Thus, in a single year, from a single impetus, Vuk launched both aspects of his important career.

Stimulated by the success of his first publications, Vuk collected more folk songs in Srem, where many Serbs had gone to escape the Turks. In 1815 he returned to Vienna and published *Srpske narodne pjesme,* a volume containing 101 lyrical and 17 epic songs, his first publication based on collected materials rather than personal recollections. At first Vuk did not fully realize the impact of these collections on people such as Kopitar, Jacob Grimm, and Goethe. Kopitar himself translated the first volume for Goethe,[2] and Grimm even learned Serbian in order to read the songs, some of which he also translated.[3] When Vuk realized the enthusiasm with which his songs were received, he was inspired to do even more serious work. He became very conscious of writing down songs in the dialect sung, admitting that the language in his first two volumes was not "pure folk."[4] In one of his many letters to Kopitar from the field, Vuk wrote that the third collection would be printed in the language just as people spoke.[5] By 1816 Vuk had broadened his interests and began to collect everything he heard associated with folk life and customs. He had no knowledge of what was being done in Europe at the time, but received guidance from Kopitar. In regard to proverbs, for example, Kopitar told him to seek only "pure" Serbian proverbs and to make explanatory notes.[6] Kopitar's influence remained a strong force throughout Vuk's career. It was Kopitar who suggested that Vuk go on to collect other genres of oral literature, write an orthography of the Serbian language, compile a dictionary, and translate the Bible.[7]

In 1818 Vuk's dictionary, *Rječnik,* was published. Besides being the first dictionary of spoken Serbian, it was the beginning of his work in noting folk customs. Within its pages there are many descriptions of folk life, especially in the later revised edition, which makes it an indispensable reference book.

In 1818 Vuk married a simple, illiterate German-Austrian. The same year he went to Russia. In the course of the trip he met many scholars in literature and philology in both Poland and Russia. As a result of contacts he made, he was awarded an annual pension from the Russian government for translating he promised to do.

In 1820-21 Vuk spent time in Serbia collecting material. He returned to Vienna to publish the first volume of folktales and a third collection of songs. In 1821 he published the tales, *Narodne srpske pripovijetke,* but he was informed that the Austrians did not dare publish the folksongs. Apparently, Vuk's opponents had convinced the

Austrian officials that with the songs in this third volume, Vuk was trying to provoke the Serbs into battle against the Turks. In so doing he would have helped the Greeks, who had just rebelled against their Turkish rulers.[8] The Austrian police were also very suspicious of Vuk because of his close tie to Russia and the pension he received from the czar.[9] As a result, Vuk went to Leipzig where he published the third volume of *Srpske narodne pjesme* in 1823. It was at this time he had his first opportunity to meet Goethe and visited Jacob Grimm, whom he had met earlier in Vienna. He was surprised and flattered that German scholars knew of him and his work.

In 1828 Vuk was called back to Beograd to help translate Napoleonic Laws from German to Serbian. Unfortunately, he made an enemy of the chief of police, who was able to use his power to obstruct Vuk's work in many ways. Moreover, Vuk was opposed by the hierarchy of the Serbian Orthodox Church, who interpreted his language reforms as acts against the Church. The powerful body of officials maintained that the only language was Church Slavonic and the folk used a degenerated form of it.[10] Finally, in 1831, Vuk was expelled from Serbia. However, the attempts to stop Vuk's work were not successful until he was accused of being a Russian spy. Incongruously, at the same time he was accused of being an Austrian hireling working against Russia and Serbia.[11] Much earlier his enemies had been suspicious of his close ties with Kopitar, an official of the Austrian government.[12] Suspicion increased when Vuk's collections were published, and subsequently he was accused of trying to ridicule the Serbian people because the songs were presented in the "vulgar" vernacular. Vuk went to Zemun, then a part of Hungary, and tried to go to Austria, but in view of the charges against him, Austrian officials were cautious. During 1832 he was kept under constant police surveillance and not allowed to travel outside of Zemun.[13] Finally he was granted permission to enter Austria. He returned to Vienna and in 1833 published the fourth volume of *Srpske narodne pjesme.*

In spite of opposition, Vuk did not cease his work; he continued to travel and collect wherever he could. During a visit to Montenegro he completed his collection of proverbs, *Srpske narodne poslovice,* published for him in 1836 by Peter Petrović Njego`s, Prince Bishop of Montenegro, against the orders of the Serbian Orthodox Church.

The opposition against Vuk gradually subsided until, in 1835, King Miloš of Serbia awarded him a pension for having been of great service to Serbia. In the period from 1837-45 Vuk traveled and collected extensively. He died in Vienna in 1864 leaving reams of unpublished material.

Vuk devoted the greater part of his life to collecting and compiling data. He spent months at a time away from his family traveling about or living in an area near his informants. He constantly worked on the collections. In many respects, his task was a thankless one. He was always penniless, barely having enough money to publish his collections in addition to feeding his family. Except for the recognition by a few scholars, his works encountered great criticism from his contemporaries. His field work, however, was a labor of love; in a letter to Kopitar he described collecting folksongs as his dearest work.[14]

Vuk was interested in the total picture of folk life and all its manifestations, every expression of material and nonmaterial culture. His main objective in the published collections of folksongs, tales, and proverbs was to present a form of vernacular language as a norm in order to create a Serbian literary language.[15] Vuk said: "In folksongs there is the purity and sweetness of our language. When our literary people realize this they will not spoil and insult the purity of their folk and their language but will trouble themselves to learn it from folksongs."[16]

He regarded oral literature as a diachronic portrayal of Serbian folk life as well as an example of great creative skill.[17] In reference to his volumes of folksongs he wrote, "these books will grow in importance and value as the honest mirror of our pure folk language, folk thoughts and customs, folk spirit and life and folk history and will last as long as our people and language."[18] With regard to his collection of proverbs Vuk made a similar statement: "the readers will find examples of our pure folk language, folk philosophy or science and knowledge of life in the world. . . ."[19] He was anxious to have his works translated into foreign languages. Convinced of their intrinsic beauty, Vuk wrote letters to friends asking them to translate his songs so the world could enjoy them. He was pleased when he heard that different people in France, England, and the United States were also interested and had translated songs. Vuk's incentive to work with Serbian oral literature was somewhat influenced by nationalism and Romanticism, although he remained realistic and stressed his primary aim of inducing language reform. This constructive aspect is important when considering Vuk's work. Although nationalism was the underlying incentive for language change, his sense of purpose distinguishes him from many of his contemporaries. It also shaped the nature of his work so that he has left a valuable folkloristic legacy, rather than the altered, unannotated versions of the Romantics.

Careful analysis and reading of Vuk's many published volumes of collections and articles reveals something about his focus, methodology, and theories. The most important collection he made is of lyrical and epic folksongs in four volumes entitled *Srpske narodne pjesme.* In volume 1 Vuk included many footnotes either explaining the meaning within a song or the custom associated with it. The locality in which the song was collected is noted; sometimes the notation is very general, stating only the republic, but at other times the village is also specified. Variants are also given. Vuk's introduction in this volume brings out many of his theories. In his chatty style, he discusses his ideas and defends his work. Volumes 2 and 3 have fewer explanatory texts, but in the introduction to volume 4, Vuk notes the origin of most of the songs in the entire series including biographical data on all informants, the songs received from each, and his criteria for evaluating songs and informants.

Another important work, *Život i običaji naroda srpska,* deals with folk life and customs. The incomplete manuscript was found among his possessions and published posthumously. It is a report of different customs, beliefs, and holiday celebrations in Serbia. Vuk, naturally, was not using modern methods of field workers today and, therefore, there is much one can say in criticism. For example, he described some games, never stating which sex participated, when the game was played, nor the particular areas of Serbia where he made his observations. However, no one before him had attempted such a task in Serbia. Where he got the idea is not apparent in the literature, but for its time the collection is unique.

The first publication of proverbs, *Narodne srpske poslovice,* came out in 1836. Vuk followed the advice of Kopitar; almost every entry has an explanatory note—often a rewording, sometimes an associated tale, or occasionally just a note of the area in which it was collected. As part of this publication Vuk did include lists of informants' names according to geographical area, but these are not correlated with the proverbs and were given only to acknowledge those who assisted him. With only a few exceptions, Vuk also followed Kopitar's advice about printing only "pure" Serbian proverbs. He included some Biblical expressions and a Slovak proverb and justified their inclusion by saying they were used by the people.[20]

Vuk was convinced about his own qualifications for collecting oral literature. He wrote:

> In order to differentiate between . . . songs, one must know and understand songs well, and that is difficult for our contemporary literary people. . . . If our folksongs only originate from simple folk it is not possible to assume that each of our literary scholars, without any preparation in this field, can understand the songs. . . .[21]

He continued that he himself was born and raised in a home where an uncle and grandfather, both *guslari,*[22] also lived and that every winter people from Hercegovina came to winter with them. It was during this time that he heard many songs. But he said, "For twenty years I have collected songs and still I find parts in them I do not understand."

Vuk traveled much during his career, especially in Serbia, Dalmatia, Montenegro, and among the Serbian refugees in southern Hungary. He regarded the Balkans as a culture area which should be studied as a whole and regretted that he did not go also to Bosnia-Hercegovina, Macedonia, Bulgaria, and Albania.[23] This attitude also distinguishes Vuk from those early collectors who, prompted primarily by nationalistic concerns, collected only from a single people, without regard for outside influence.

Vuk gathered his collections in two ways: he himself did the field work or he received them from others who collected for him. When Vuk went into the field it was not unusual for him to remain there for many months, thus anticipating the extended period of field work used by most modern folklorists. (But, unfortunately, not by most modern Yugoslav folklorists, who more commonly limit field work experiences to very short periods.) With a few exceptions, there is no mention of Vuk's field methodology. In the fourth volume of *Srpske narodne pjesme,*[24] he wrote that the informant sang the song several times while he wrote as fast as possible. When Vuk had it down, the informant once again sang as Vuk checked his notes. Without modern recording equipment, this method was probably the most accurate possible. He encountered the same problems in the field that modern scholars do; people suspected that he asked for songs as a joke or to pass idle time and would tell him they did not know songs. When this happened, Vuk resorted to the ploy of using children because they lacked this self-consciousness. As the children sang, the elders corrected and scolded them for not singing properly; little by little the adults loosened up and sang.[25]

Vuk obviously recognized the importance of context. In an early letter to Kopitar he wrote that "proverbs are difficult to collect because one must wait until he hears one spoken."[26] He compared collecting proverbs with songs and folktales, stating explicitly that the methodology must be different. One can ask an informant for a song or tale, but for proverbs one can only listen carefully and wait until a proverb is used.[27]

This sketchy evidence indicates that Vuk was cautious and patient in his field methodology and also realized the importance of remaining in one area for extended periods of time.

Early in his career, Vuk established friendships with persons in Serbia and Srem who periodically sent him songs they had heard. In at least one case, such a friend turned over to him a substantial collection made prior to their meeting.[28] Vuk not only contacted people personally, but also, in the introduction of the fourth volume of his folksong collection, he asked readers to send in songs, promising them acknowledgment in resulting publications. He received many songs in this manner, but he used only a small fraction of them. Of the 479 songs in the first three volumes of the second edition of *Srpske narodne pjesme,* Vuk stated that no more than 33 were collected by others.[29]

Vuk recognized the significance of variants and individual creation; the role of gifted singers was one of his main considerations from the very beginning. He wrote that a song varies according to the person singing. He continued: "The songs did not immediately become as they now are, but rather one presents it as he knows it and after him the next one does the same. From mouth to mouth it grows and is embellished and sometimes it is shortened and even spoiled."[30]

Vuk made the distinction between "singer-creator" and "singer-carrier," i.e., active and passive bearers.[31] For example, his father, Stefan, did not concern himself with songs to any great degree, but he did know some. His grandfather, Joksim, and his son, Vuk's uncle Toma, on the other hand, knew many songs and Vuk knew them to compose new songs about recent historical events. When one knows fifty different songs, he said, it is easy to compose more new songs.[32] With this statement he forecast the important work of Albert B. Lord on epic song creation.[33]

Vuk also made a distinction between good and bad singers. While there were numerous singers who knew many songs, it was difficult to find one who knew them well and clearly (dobro i jasno). One of his best informants was Tešan Podrugović. Vuk wrote that he had never met anyone who knew as much as he.[34] Podrugović played the gusle well, but because he could not sing he recited the texts. Vuk felt that such informants are best because they are careful and give thought to the order of sequence. Each of Podrugović's songs was judged good, "because he understood and felt the songs and thought about what he said." Podrugović was Vuk's example of a good singer.

A bad singer, according to Vuk, often sings without giving any thought to what he sings. Vuk thought every folksong was "pretty and good" (lijepa i dobra), but it was important to have a good singer who knew the song. Vuk continued this discussion by comparing good and bad songs and singers.[35] A bad singer poorly remembers a song and spoils it. On the other hand, a good singer makes a choice either to improve a bad song or to forget it if it is not worth repeating. Vuk's reference, then, to "good" and "bad" singers seems to refer more to whether the singer was a good or bad informant than unprofessional value judgments.

In stating how a song should be judged, Vuk makes it clear that historical fact should not be sought in folksongs, but the narration should make "common sense."[36] As an example, he cites some of the epics from the Marko Kraljević cycle in which there is a rifle motif. Vuk points to the absurdity of this since there were no guns during Marko's time. However, Vuk was not fully aware of the ways in which oral literature is dynamic. Although he realized that songs change from one informant to another, he did not perceive the element of change through time.

The classification Vuk gave his folksongs and tales is still used by modern Yugoslav scholars. In his first publication of folksongs in 1814, Vuk stated, "all songs which are not ten syllables and cannot be sung to the gusle are called women's (ženske) songs by the simple Serbians."[37] Elsewhere he said that most of the songs in the collection were sung in a feminine voice, but that a few were songs sung in a masculine voice accompanied by gusle.[38] Grimm distributed an announcement about the second part of this collection in 1815 stating that among the songs called "ženske" by Vuk, some seemed to fit the description for the German heldenlieder. Vuk, henceforth, divided his songs into two categories: ženske and junačke (heroic), the latter being the Serbian equivalent of heldenlieder.[39] In the introduction of volume 1 of **Srpske narodne pjesme** he applied this classification.[40] He defined heroic songs as sung by men with gusle, performed especially for others, the words being more important than music. Ženske songs were defined as songs sung usually by duets but sometimes by a single singer. They were performed by women, girls, and men, especially young, unmarried men, and the music was more important than the song texts.

In his classification of folktales Vuk uses the terms muške (men's) and ženske.[41] He likens ženske to Märchen, saying the tales are full of fantasy and impossible situations. On the other hand, muške tales have no fantasy; all that is related is possible.

Both these classifications are very general. Vuk realized this and said that there were many songs and tales which did not fit either category.[42] However, he did not discuss new definitions.

Vuk said that proverbs could be divided into two main groups: those repeated the same way as heard and those which vary.[43] However, he did not use this classification in his proverb collection. Instead, he listed the proverbs alphabetically.

Vuk's classifications and definitions are not wholly accurate. Despite his intermittent contact with Kopitar and Jacob Grimm, Vuk was well out of the mainstream of ideas and had little theoretic basis on which to work. However, one encounters in the literature frequent examples of Vuk's abilities as a professional folklorist. In one discussion, Vuk questioned whether folksongs which do not fit standard meter are actually "errors" of the informant as some foreign scholars believed.[44] Although he did not attempt to answer the question, his awareness of the situation displayed considerable insight. In another instance, Vuk questioned an informant about the meaning of a sword with eyes, which appears in an epic.[45] Vuk assumed the reference to be to jewels, however he also recorded the folk interpretation. Examples of this kind point out that Vuk was not an ordinary nineteenth-century collector and compiler of oral tradition.

The most discussed and criticized aspect of Vuk's work is his policy of correcting and editing his material. As previously mentioned, Vuk was greatly harassed by his contemporaries and accused of purposely ridiculing the Serbian people because he did not correct the songs he collected. Vuk defended his use of the folk language by stating, "these are not my ideas; it is the truth told the way it really is."[46] In the same article he answers one of his chief enemies, who had asked why in one song he did not correct a word to conform to the official Serbian. Vuk stated he did not want to spoil the speech, because that was how the folk spoke. Elsewhere Vuk singles out the grammatical errors in a particular folksong.[47] He said that the people of that area use gross deformities in their speech, but he published the song that way regardless.

All this would imply that Vuk did not alter his texts but published them just as he collected them. But, unfortunately, this was not the case. Ljubomir Stojanović pointed out that Vuk's corrections are most obvious when comparing the same songs published in the first and later editions.[48] In later editions there are noticeable changes: (1) more corrections in language than Vuk admits to; (2) the text is fuller; (3) a change in word order, substituting one word for another and addition of exclamations, all made to make verses smoother; (4) a change from one dialect to another. This latter point was also discussed by S. Matić.[49]

Vuk's process of selection eliminated some need for alterations. He stated that when an incident is commonly related in folksongs and there are a large number of good songs, it is foolish to publish the bad ones.[50] This idea appears over and over in his letters and articles. However, it should be clarified that he apparently collected everything he heard and selected only for publishing. It is suspected that modern scholars do the same thing, even if advocating differently.

Vuk published a collection of folktales which are closer to the source than others published at that period, but he also gave them the stamp of his personal style. According to Maja Bošković-Stulli, Vuk cleaned up elementary written formulas, and he used new words and constructed compound sentences from the simple ones used by the informant.[51]

The contradiction between what Vuk said and what he actually did to oral literature is difficult to resolve. The constant harassment he was under may have weakened his ideals. One should also keep in mind that Vuk's greater concern was language and establishing a standard literary language based on the vernacular. The changes he made in the language were relatively minute in comparison to how others would have corrected it. It is only in the context of his own time and intentions that his work can rightfully be judged.

Vuk's impact on subsequent scholarship, up to and including the present day, has been phenomenal. He was the primary impetus to folklore collecting in the Balkans. He was followed by a great number of other collectors, but with little improvement over his methodology. Some recent publications of proverbs, for example, contain merely page after page of proverbs without the contextual information that Vuk thought necessary. Subsequent collections of Serbian folksongs do no more than supplement Vuk's work; his collection remains the basic and most complete source. In Croatia, stimulated by Vuk's activity in Serbia, an equally valuable collection of Croatian folksongs was compiled (the Matica Hrvatska collection). Modern day scholars continue to study his collections; even present-day guslari utilize Vuk's collections to learn epic songs. The number of articles that exist about Vuk's work in folklore alone is unbelievably large. A journal, *Kovčežić Prilozi i Gradja o Dositeji i Vuku,* is published on his work. After his death, the Serbian government received all unpublished notes and manuscripts, and from 1891-1902 his entire collection was published in nine volumes.[52] In 1964, the centennial of his death, the Yugoslav government began to republish his entire works under the title Sabrana Dela Vuka Karadžića. This new series contains valuable supplementary studies on Vuk's works by leading modern Yugoslav scholars.

Vuk Stefanović Karadžić remains an inspiration for modern Yugoslav scholars; his collections still provide material for modern folkloristics. Perhaps the most significant aspect of Vuk's importance as a folklorist is that, although all of his limitations were imposed by the historical milieu in which he worked, his contributions have far transcended time and place.[53]

Notes

1. "Pravi uzrok i početak skupljana našijeh narodnijeh pjesama" (The Real Cause and Beginning of the Collection of Our Folksongs), reprinted in *O književnosti i književnicima,* ed. Dušanka Perović (Beograd, 1964), 14-15.

2. Ilija Kecmanović, *Vuk-Njegoš-Svetozar Marković* (Sarajevo, 1949), 45.

3. D. H. Low, trans., *The Ballads of Marko Kraljević* (Cambridge, 1922), p. xiv.

4. Kecmanović, 44-45.

5. *Pisma* (Letters), ed. Dž. Gavela (Beograd, 1947), 21.

6. Miloslav Pantić, "Vuk Stefanović Karadžić i naše narodne poslovice" (Vuk Stefanović Karadžić and Our Popular Proverbs), in *Srpske narodne poslovice* (Sabrana Dela Vuka Karadžića) (Beograd, 1965), 579.

7. *Pisma,* 7, 15.

8. *Pisma,* 73.

9. *Pisma,* 135.

10. Vuk Stefanović Karadžić, "Prosta i istinita istorija" (A Simple and True History), reprinted in *O književnosti i književnicima,* ed. Dušanka Perović (Beograd, 1964), 106-7.

11. *Pisma,* 152-54.

12. Kecmanović, 12.

13. *Pisma,* 133, 154.

14. *Vukovska prepiska* 1 (Vuk's Correspondence) (Beograd, 1907), 362.

15. Maja Bošković-Stulli, "O narodnoj priči i njezinu autenticnom izrazu" (About the Folktale and Its Authentic Wording), *Slovenski Etnograf* 13 (1959): 110.

16. "Pravi uzrok i početak skupljana našijeh narodnijeh pjesama," 19.

17. Kecmanović, 42-43.

18. "Objavlejenije na prvu, drugu i treću knjigu narodnih pesama bečkoga izdanja" (An Explanation to the First, Second, and Third Volume of Folksongs of the Vienna Edition), reprinted in *O srpskog narodnoj poeziji* (Beograd, 1964), 170.

19. *Srpske narodne poslovice* (Sabrana Dela Vuka Karadžića 9), ed. Miloslav Pantić (reprint; Beograd, 1965), 357.

20. Pantić, 579.

21. *Srpske narodne pjesme,* 4 (reprint; Beograd, 1953), p. xxx.

22. Singers of epic songs, so called because they accompany themselves on the *gusle,* a bowed, one-string instrument.

23. Kecmanović, 47.

24. P. xiv.

25. 4, p. xvi.

26. *Pisma,* 146.

27. Pantić, 578.

28. *Pisma,* 13.

29. Kecmanović, 43.

30. *Srpske narodne pjesme,* 1, p. xxvii.

31. Ibid., 4, pp. xxiii-xxiv.

32. Ibid., 1, p. xviii.

33. *Singer of Tales* (Cambridge, 1960).

34. *Srpske narodne pjesme,* 4 pp. x-xi.

35. Ibid., 4, pp. xxvii-xxix.

36. Ibid., 4, pp. xxviii-xxix.

37. "Napomene u prvoj knjizi pjecnarice, 1814" (Comments in the First Book of Songs, 1814), reprinted in *O srpskoj narodnoj poeziji* (Beograd, 1964), 46.

38. "Predgovor prvoj knjizi pjecnarice, 1814" (Introduction to the First Book of Songs, 1814), reprinted in *O srpskoj narodnoj poeziji* (Beograd, 1964), 44.

39. N. Banašević, "Ranija i novija nauka i vukovi pogledi na narodnu epiku" (Earlier and Newer Science and Vuk's Views on the Folk Epic), *Prilozi za književnost, jezik, istoriju i folklor* 30, s.v. 3-4 (1964): 174.

40. P. xvi.

41. Vojislav Čurić, "Predgovor" (Introduction), *Antologija narodnih pripovedaka,* ed. Živan Milosavac (Beograd, 1960), 8.

42. Ibid.

43. *Srpske narodne poslovice,* 46.

44. "Povodom 'opita sličnorečnosti' Luke Milovanova Georgijevića" (On Examination of the Poetic Composition of Luka Milovanov Georgijević), reprinted in *O književnosti i književnicima,* ed. Dušanka Perović (Beograd, 1964), 33-42.

45. *Srpske narodne pjesme,* 2, p. 106.

46. "Pravi uzrok i početak skupljana našijeh narodnijeh pjesama," 20.

47. "Napomene uz pjesme bečkog izdanja" (Comments to the Songs of the Vienna Edition), reprinted in *O srpskoj narodnoj poeziji* (Beograd, 1964), 225.

48. Ljubomir Stojanović, *Život i rad Vuka Stefanovića Karadžića* (The Life and Work of Vuk Stefanović Karadžić) (Beograd-Zemun, 1924), 105-8.

49. "Vukov odnos prema ekavskim pesmama narodnim" (Vuk's Relation to Ekavian Folksongs), *Naš Jezik* 9, s.v. 3-4 (1958): 93-101.

50. *Srpske narodne pjesme,* 4, pp. xxix-xxx.

51. Pp. 111-15.

52. Kecmanović, 45.

53. After this article was already in press, there appeared a new and relevant study on Vuk, *The Life and Times of Vuk Stefanović Karadžić* by Duncan Wilson (Oxford, 1970). It is the first full biography in English. Particularly important for folklorists are the translations of Vuk's writings in which he stated his views on traditions and collecting and a discussion of his relationship to other collectors of oral literature.

Albert B. Lord (essay date 1974)

SOURCE: Lord, Albert B. "The Nineteenth-Century Revival of National Literatures: Karadžić, Njegoš, Radičević, the Illyrians, and Prešeren." *Review of National Literatures: The Multinational Literature of Yugoslavia* 5, no. 1 (spring 1974): 101-11.

[*In the following essay, Lord traces the chronological development of national literatures in Serbia, Slovenia, and Croatia during the nineteenth century, examining Karadžić's contributions as a leader in orthography and the collection of narratives.*]

Although the roots of modern literature in Serbia, Montenegro, Croatia, and Slovenia go much further back, the early and mid-nineteenth century saw the emergence of a number of heroic figures who shine as beacon lights at the beginning of a renewed and intensified literary activity which continues to the present day. In Serbia, Vuk Stefanović Karadžić (1787-1864) is the first of the group not only in age but also in date of published work. Karadžić's ***Mala prostonarodna slaveno-serbska pesnarica*** (***Little***

Slaveno-Serbian Songbook for the Common Folk) appeared in Vienna in 1814, a year after the second great writer in this pantheon, Petar II Petrović Njegoš (1813-1851) was born in Montenegro. Njegoš's first poems came out in 1834, a year before the manifesto of the Illyrians was published in Zagreb under the title *Danicza Horvatzka, Slavonzka y Dalmatinzka* (*The Croatian, Slavonian, and Dalmation Day-Star*). Its leading light, Ljudevit Gaj (1809-1872), was slightly older than Njegoš, and the oldest of the Illyrian group which included three other authors worthy of notice with him: Stanko Vraz (1810-1851), a Slovene who moved to Croatia, Ivan Mazuranić (1818-1890), and Petar Preradović (1818-1872). The leading Slovenian poet, France Prešeren (1800-1840), was younger than Vuk but older than all the other writers mentioned. He began to write poetry in 1824, the same year in which the youngest of the authors considered in this article, Branko Radičević (1824-1853), was born in Serbia. Branko's first poems appeared in 1843.

The most intense activity of our writers covers only a few decades. The thirties and forties of the last century were the most productive, although Vuk and Prešeren were working very successfully during the twenties and Vuk was still publishing in the fifties. It is a curious fact that four of the eight figures we are considering died of tuberculosis between 1849 and 1853, Prešeren first in Slovenia in 1849, followed by Vraz and Njegoš in 1851, and Radičević two years later. Vuk Karadžić died at the age of seventy-seven in 1864. The Illyrians Gaj and Preradović both died in 1872, but Gaj's main contributions were made in the thirties and forties, and Preradović alone was active throughout the sixties. The last of the eight, the Illyrian Mažuranić, lived until 1890, thus being, next to Vuk, the longest lived of the group, spanning most of the nineteenth century, but the majority of his literary work belongs to the thirties and forties. After that, he went into public life and wrote very little indeed during the ensuing years. We have thus briefly set the chronological parameters for the interweaving of the appearances in time of the Serbian and Slovenian poets and their early works and the beginning of the Illyrian Movement, which was identified with national revival as well as pan-Slavism in Croatia.

1 LANGUAGES

The very significant accomplishments of these giants fall into several categories. The first problem that required solution was the need for a literary language and a reformed orthography. In Serbia Vuk Karadžić led such a movement. In the same year (1814) in which his first songbook was published, there appeared his **Pismenica serbskoga iezika** (**Grammar of the Serbian Language**), which saw a second edition as **Srpska gramatika** (**Serbian Grammar**) in 1818, together with, that same year, the first edition of his **Srpski rječnik** (**Serbian Dictionary**). He entered into controversy with those who advocated the artificial Slaveno-Serbian language favored by the church. He himself was on the side of the language as spoken by the majority of the people, the living language written as spoken, and in an orthography in which each sound was expressed by a single letter and vice versa. Vuk's publishing of the oral literature of the Serbs, their songs and stories, also played a large role in the establishing of a literary language. By mid-century Vuk and his followers had carried the day and Serbia had a literary language suitable to the needs of a vital literature. It had already produced great works.

In Croatia the movement toward language and orthographic reform was begun by Ljudevit Gaj. We have already noted the appearance in 1835 of the *Danica hrvatska*. The literary language of Croatia at this period tended to be German, or Latin. It is symptomatic that Gaj's first work in 1826 was a translation into German of a Latin manuscript of 1799-1800 *Die Schlösser bei Krapina* (*The Castles in Krapina*) and that his first original work in prose was a short story in German "Kowotschka, der Räuberhauptmann" ("Kowotschka, the Robber Chieftain"). His first book in Croatian (1830) was significantly *Kratka osnova horvatsko-slavenskoga pravopisanja* (*Short Fundamentals of Croato-Slavic Orthography*). Others of the Illyrians had begun their literary careers writing in German, such as Petar Preradović, whose sonnets to his homeland written in Milan in 1843 were in German and entitled "An mein Vaterland." But already the following year he published his famous Croatian poem "Zora puca, bit će dana" ("The Dawn Breaks, It Will Be Day") in the journal *Zora Dalmatinska* (*Dalmatian Dawn*) which had just been started. By the middle of the nineteenth century the Croats also had a viable literary language and orthography. It is remarkable that the literary language chosen by Vuk and by the writers of the Illyrian Movement in Zagreb was neither the dialect of Zagreb nor that of Belgrade but that of the oral literature in Herzegovina.

The language problem in Slovenia concerned the Slavic tongue itself, as was in part the case also in Croatia, as we have seen. Slovenian was disappearing under the dominion of German which was the language that the Slovenian intelligentsia both read and wrote. France Prešeren and his close friend Matija Čop worked tirelessly to extend the use of Slovenian in literature as well as in speech, and to increase the scope of that language that it might be a proper vehicle for the best of literary productions. Their efforts were centered around the journal, or almanach, *Kranjska čbelica* (*The Beehive of Kranj*), begun in 1830. No small credit for their success is due to the poems of Prešeren himself, living proof that they were of the literary quality of the Slovenian language. (For more on the literary languages of Yugoslavia see Professor Butler's article in this volume).

2 COLLECTIONS OF ORAL LITERATURE

A second category of activity which was undertaken in the period under consideration was the collecting and publishing of oral literature, or folk verse and prose. Here too Vuk Karadžić led the way from 1814 onward and the four volumes of folk songs that appeared before his death were to become the classical collection not merely for Serbia but for a wider circle as well. The story of how Vuk was led to his collecting is a long and complex one, starting with a few songs given to Alberto Fortis, an Italian natural scientist, towards the end of the eighteenth century, whose book which incidentally contained them was translated into German. They eventually came to the attention of Herder and Goethe, and one of them, the famous Moslem woman's song, or ballad of the wife of Hasanaga, was translated into German by Goethe. When Vuk arrived in Vienna, he was befriended by the Slovenian Slavist Jernej Kopitar, who was in touch with the Herder group. Kopitar persuaded Vuk to write his grammar and work on a dictionary and also to put down in writing some of the folk songs. From this influence came the first little volume in 1814 of which I have spoken earlier. A second volume, this time written down from others not merely from Vuk's own memory, followed in 1815, and the major volumes later to form the classical collection began to appear in 1823. They contained lyric and ritual songs, ballads and epics, ranging from the so-called mythological songs to songs of more recent history in Montenegro and in Serbia. There were songs of Kosovo, the battle in 1389 in which Car Lazar as well as the Sultan Murat were killed and the way opened for Turkish invasion. Songs of the hero Marko Kraljević are well represented, and there are many *hajduk* songs. Of special interest to Vuk himself was a group of songs, written down chiefly from Filip Visnjić, which dealt with events in the abortive uprising of the Serbs under Karadjordje against the Turks. In Serbia itself others were to follow Vuk, including his contemporary Vuk Vrčević and later in the same century such figures as Bogoljub Petranović. Njegoš also collected epic songs in Montenegro, as did his romantic tutor Sima Milutinović Sarajlija, from whom Njegoš also acquired a taste for cosmic imagery. The intent of all those, especially in the last century, who made these collections was to set down the history of Serbia or Montenegro as it was reflected in the epic. Many of them also composed poems of their own in the style of the folk epic.

Collecting in Croatia came somewhat later, but in 1850 *Bosanski Prijatelj* (*The Bosnian Friend*), under the editorship of I. F. Jukić Banjalučanin, published a number of folk epics, and Luka Marjanović in 1864 brought forth a book of poems. In 1879 the Matica Dalmatinska Society published a *Narodna pjesmarica* (*Popular Songbook*). The year before that Valtazar Bogišić of Cavtat, the lovely town south of Dubrovnik on the Dalmatian coast, collected poems that he had found in earlier manuscripts and brought them together into a volume. Thus the way was prepared for the series of volumes of collected songs from the archives of the Matica Hrvatska in Zagreb, the first volume of which appeared in 1896.

Although Moslem epics had been collected as early as the first quarter of the eighteenth century, that group was not published until as recently as 1925 by Gerhard Gesemann. Kosta Hörmann's collection of Moslem songs came out in 1889, and the great Marjanović collection from northern Bosnia appeared in 1898 in volumes III and IV of the Matica Hrvatska series.

The popular poetry, especially the Vuk collection, had an important impact on Croatian, Serbian, and Montenegrin literature. It was widely imitated, and its form was influential in shaping the style of literary poetry, both narrative and lyric, throughout the century and even later. Some of its subjects—Kosova, Marko Kraljević, the *hajduks*, the songs of the Serbian uprising, for example—were taken up by literary narrative poets and by the dramatists, especially Jovan Sterija Popović and, in the sixties, Laza Kostić. The Illyrian Petar Preradović used their themes, as did many others down to the present day. Finally the great poet Njegoš made rich use of them in his masterpiece *Gorski Vijenac* (*The Mountain Wreath*).

There is another activity of Vuk Karadžić that deserves mention here, namely his ethnographic and historical writings. The Serbian uprising in which he had been personally involved fascinated him, and he wrote, among other things, biographies of some of its leaders. He also published admirable ethnographic descriptions of the *Boka Kotorska* and of Montenegro in which he caught the spirit of those regions.

3 ORIGINAL WRITINGS

A third category of writing, surely the most significant, was purely literary. The poetic genres blossomed in Montenegro with Njegoš, in Serbia with Branko Radičević, in Croatia with the Illyrians, Ivan Mazuranić, Petar Preradović, and Stanko Vraz, and in Slovenia with France Prešeren. As was the case earlier in Dalmatia at the time of the Renaissance (1500-1650), so in the national revival in the nineteenth century, poetry was the main, almost the sole literary vehicle.

The earliest of the poets of this group is France Prešeren in Slovenia (1800-1849). His poems were of great importance in forming the literary language as well as in providing a model for others to follow. Born in a small town, Vrba, educated in Vienna, he returned to his homeland finally, to a modest law practice in Kranj, and to writing. He had a great lyric gift; the shorter forms, such as sonnet and ballad, were most congenial to him, although he did write one epic, "Krst pri Savici" ("Conversion at the Savica"), of about five hundred lines. An unhappy love affair motivated a famous "Sonnet Wreath" published in 1834, of fifteen sonnets, the last of which consists of the first lines of each of the preceding sonnets, which then form an acrostic of the name of his beloved, Primicovi Julija. In addition the last line of each sonnet becomes the first of the following. There is much more than unrequited love in these sonnets. Some of the sonnets speak of the history of the Slovenes, and Prešeren, while lamenting his country's unhappy past, is filled with hope for the future.

"Krst pri Savici" appeared two years later (1836). Not only had his love for Julija been futile, but his best friend and close associate Matija Čop (1797-1835) had been drowned while swimming in the Sava, and Prešeren's sorrows were doubled. Yet during this period, he wrote the epic. Its introduction relates the capture of the fortress Ajdovski Grad by the Christians under Knez Valjhun. Of the pagan defenders only their leader Črtomir remained alive after the battle. The second and longer part of the poem tells first of Črtomir's love for the daughter of the guardian of the temple of the goddess Ziva on the island in Lake Bled, and then it goes on to describe Črtomir after the battle of the first part standing by the waterfall of the Savica. He is approached by a priest and his beloved Bogomila, who has become a Christian. Together they persuade Črtomir also to be converted, and he kneels with the priest beside the Savica. Once again Prešeren had sought solace from his personal griefs in the history of his land, for whose future he had great hope.

Contemporary with Prešeren in years of writing, if in age thirteen years younger, was the Montenegrin Prince-Bishop Petar II Petrović Njegoš. A fine, if somewhat prolix, account of his life and works was written by Milovan Djilas a few years ago, *Njegoš, Poet, Prince, Bishop* (New York, 1966). Djilas describes admirably the scene in which the young Petar takes over, in typical tribal setting, the office of Prince and Bishop of Montenegro, acclaimed by the leaders of the several Montenegrin tribes. Njegoš was well read and well travelled. He had been to Russia for the sake of his tiny country, and we have a moving account by Ljubomir Nenadović of his encounter with Njegoš in Naples, where he had gone, as elsewhere, for some relief from tuberculosis. Njegoš is in many ways the most remarkable of this group of rather extraordinary writers.

He was preeminently a narrative and dramatic poet, although within his historical stories lyric moments are not lacking. Serbian lyricism came into its own with Branko Radičević (1824-1853), whose poems appear first in 1847, the same year as Njegoš's major work, *Gorski Vijenac* (*The Mountain Wreath*). Njegoš's poetry is solidly based on the folk epic, which he himself had collected and imitated. He wanted to present the history of Montenegro in that manner and his earliest works, such as the "Svobodijada" in 1834, did just that. In 1845 Njegoš's *Srpsko ogledalo* (*Serbian Mirror*) appeared, his own collection of the folk epic of Montenegro with some additions. But *The Mountain Wreath* is his most arresting work, a poetic drama written around an historical event of the latter part of the eighteenth century, the killing of the Moslemized Montenegrins by their Christian brothers under Prince-Bishop Danilo, the central figure in the drama. It opens with a monologue by Danilo in which he debates with himself the steps that his people are about to take. The drama ends with the gathering of his men after the massacre. The contents of the poem-drama are varied, but through it all one sees the ethos of Montenegro depicted by a sensitive philosopher-poet. The men gather about their leader, some with tales of incidents at home that had delayed them. One returns from Venice with an account of the confusion and corruption of that city. They have a final meeting with the Moslem leaders, one of whom gives a lyrical description of Stambol. The men sleep on Mount Lovćen and the next morning recount their dreams. Many elements of Montenegrin folklore are used tellingly by Njegoš. And from time to time, in the fashion of Greek tragedy, a Chorus comments. The Kosova legend and the deeds of its hero Miloš Obilić play a large role in the thinking of the actors. It is an extraordinary poem.

More surprising perhaps than *Gorski Vijenac* is a philosophical epic entitled *Luca mikrokozma* (*The Ray of the Microcosm*). With elements of both Dante and Milton clearly in its background, together with Balkan dualistic thought, the narrative tells of the flight of the soul into the heavens. The influence of his tutor Milutinović in celestial imagery is strong in it. We would not have expected from the warrior prince-bishop, who was ever defending Montenegro from the Turks, the depth of religious philosophy that Njegoš displays in these two works.

Njegoš's last work was another poetic drama, perhaps somewhat more unified than *Gorski Vijenac*. It deals with the impact in Montenegro of the arrival of an imposter pretending to be fugitive Russian Czar Peter III. *Lažni car Šćepan Mali* (*The False Czar Stephen the Little*) presents also a dramatic and moving picture of the Montenegrin heroic milieu and legendary heroism in times of stress, but it does not reach the heights of *Gorski Vijenac*.

The account of Vuk and Njegoš and their times would not be complete without a word about one of Serbia's most beloved poets, Branko Radičević. Like Vuk, he went to Vienna, where he came to know many of Vuk's friends and became a staunch supporter of Vuk's language and orthographic ideas. Branko's erotic lyrics shocked many with their frankness, but the intensity of his lyricism and the grace of his language marked his poetry with distinction. His satirical narrative poem "Put" ("The Journey") took its author on an imaginary journey on Pegasus over parts of Serbia. In it are hidden references to the literary controversies of his day that were seething in the circles of writers and scholars. The battle for reformed orthography is set forth in amusing and imaginative fashion, and the satire is scathing. Byronic also are his romantic epics, such as "Hajdukov grob" ("The Hajduk's grave") which is a model of the genre, depicting the last stand of a *hajduk* and his beloved, pursued by the Turks and finally cornered on the verge of a cliff, whence they leap together to their deaths. This period in Serbia would have been much less colorful without Branko's poetic genius.

Lyric, narrative, and dramatic poetry were also cultivated at this time in Croatia by the group which called itself the Illyrians. We have spoken of their beginning with Ljudevit Gaj and the *Danica hrvatska* in 1835. The most outstanding figure in their circle was Ivan Mažuranić, who wrote topical poetry about the Illyrians, but whose two main works were remarkably different one from the other. He was born on the coast in Novi Vinodolski and early became an enthusiast for the Dubrovnik renaissance poetry. He became so well versed in it that he was able to write in seventeenth-century Dubrovnik style his own version of the two cantos in Gundulić's epic "Osman" that Gundulić had left unfinished at the time of his death. The intriguing thing about the missing cantos is that they are not at the end of the epic but in the middle of it. Gundulić had left some of the romantic threads of his complex story unresolved and Mažuranić's attempt to tie them together became the standard one, though he was not alone in trying to solve the mystery. Mažuranić's most famous poem, however, was quite different and, some think, alien to both his love for the Dubrovnik past and his involvement in the Croatian literary scene, for it is concerned with an event in Gacko in Herzegovina. Be that as it may, *Smrt Smailaga Čengića* (*The Death of Smailaga Čengić*) shows the fine lyric and narrative talent of its author, particularly the former. Mažuranić's depiction of the heroic band that gathers to assassinate Smailaga for his brutal treatment of the raya when he attempts to extort tribute from them is reminiscent of Njegoš, but his use of several meters, his effective employment of literary figures of speech, and the sonority of his verse mark the lyric poet. The scene in which the priest gathers the band about him and gives them courage on the eve of the ambush is one of the finest in the poetry of this period.

The Illyrians advocated not only national revival and language reform but also pan-Slavism, especially, but not exclusively by any means, for the Balkan Slavs. They tried to convince the Serbs and Slovenes to join them in this endeavor, but both groups felt that they already had their own national literatures by this time in the works of Vuk and Prešeren especially, and were loath to accede to the wishes of the Illyrians. One Slovene was an exception. This was the poet and man of letters Stanko Vraz. He had begun writing in German and in his native Slovenian, but under the influence of the Illyrians he moved to Croatia and turned to writing in the Croatian literary language which was just being formed. His gift also was lyric. One of the most significant contributions that Vraz made, however, to the whole movement was the establishing of a new literary journal *Kolo* in 1842. The quality of this new periodical was far above that of Gaj's *Danica hrvatska*. It included articles on other Slavic literatures and reports on the latest writings in them. It was one of the most important vehicles for the best in Illyrian writing.

The poetic work of the last of our group, another Illyrian, Petar Preradović, was not only lyric and narrative but also dramatic. He was an army officer, and his first verses were in German. He joined the Illyrian movement under the influence of Ivan Kukuljević Saksinski, and the first Croatian poem, already mentioned above, "Zora puca, bit ćé dana" ("The Dawn is Breaking, It Will be Day") was a personal manifesto as well as a regional one. Famous among his poems are "Putnik" ("The Traveller"), telling of one wandering in a foreign land, and "Djed i unuk" ("Grandfather and Grandson"), which breathes the romantic spirit of times when men saw the folk epic and the one-stringed *gusle* as symbols of the heroic and the heritage of the past. Philosophic epic is represented in his longer poems "Prvi ljudi" ("The First Men") and "Prvenci" ("The First Ones"), but more significant are his two poetic dramas, "Marko Kraljević" and "Vladimir i Kosara." The latter is a dramatic presentation of a tale told in the Ljetopis Popa dukljanina of the twelfth century, a story of love and intrigue and tragic betrayal and vengeance, that became a favorite in nineteenth-century drama by others as well as Preradović. "Marko Kraljević" is a complicated play about the coming of Marko to save his people when they are oppressed, one of the aspects of his legend that later writers found attractive. Preradović was thus a versatile poet and his contribution to the Illyrian movement and to Croatian poetry in general was a distinguished and lasting one.

With the efforts of these remarkable men of the early and mid-nineteenth century the modern literature of the Serbs, Croats, and Slovenes had its very distinguished beginnings. Many of their poems are still vital and moving for they set forth human sorrows, longings, and triumphs against odds in a living and vibrant language and with true mastery of poetic art.

Svetozar Koljević (essay date 1980)

SOURCE: Koljević, Svetozar. "The Singer and the Song." In *The Epic in the Making*, pp. 299-321. Oxford: Oxford University Press, 1980.

[*In the following essay, Koljević focuses on the singers of Karadžić's collected oral epics and popular songs.*]

The general picture of chronology, geography and achievement of Serbo-Croat oral epics seems to be fairly clear in its main outlines. The first Slav singers in the Balkans used their cithers as disguise in espionage near Constantinople in the seventh century and they gave their name to the professional practitioners of this art in the Hungarian language. But their pagan world survived only sporadically in some of the village customs in much later times. Medieval Christian Serbia, however, gave a much stronger imprint to the whole tradition of the epic art: its history provided some of the major later themes and motifs, its monastic literature left the heritage of several major legal and moral concepts as well as a few skeletons of much older Eastern legends, its frescoes kept in vivid memory the outward appearance of the medieval feudal lords, their gowns, rings, and pitchers. During the Turkish conquests and the dissolution of this medieval world in the fifteenth century, the feudal professional singers cultivated their distinctive 'Serbian manner' in their retreat in Hungary at least until the middle of the sixteenth century. The same 'manner' was absorbed into the much more popular and plebeian forms of epic singing in the Christian urban setting of some prosperous cities along the Adriatic coast. It was in this environment that the old feudal *bugarštice* were written down as they were dying from the end of the fifteenth to the end of the eighteenth century. Their debris left a rich bequest of themes and motifs, stock phrases, formulas and formulaic expressions, stylistic and narrative devices to the flourishing tradition of decasyllabic village singing.

On the other hand, the irrefutable early sixteenth-century evidence makes it clear that the epic songs about the Battle of Kosovo (1389) were widely cultivated among the Christian population in the central Balkan area spreading from old medieval Serbia to Herzegovina and Bosnia, all the way to the western Turkish frontier with Croatia. For obvious political and cultural reasons these popular village songs could not be recorded, but this area, particularly the region of Herzegovina and Montenegro, is generally assumed to be the cradle of decasyllabic village singing. The earliest collection of these songs—which an unknown German wrote down, probably in or near the military camps along the northern Balkan Christian frontier in Slavonia—dates from about 1720 and its linguistic features as well as some of its subjects reflect the long travels of the epic voice through many regions, from old medieval Serbia and the Adriatic coast, to Herzegovina, Bosnia, and Croatia. This evidence also shows that many Croatian and Moslem singers must have contributed a great deal to the oral epic diction in Serbo-Croat, but as their respective cultures were dominated by urban centres which provided different modes for cultural expression, it was only among the Serbs that oral epic singing absorbed for a long time most of the available artistic national talent. The central function which epic singing had in Serbian village life and the enormous pressure of historical circumstance, particularly on some of the greatest singers, explain perhaps how the debris of the 'high' monastic medieval culture could come so fully alive in the 'low' social setting of the later epic songs. The shape and the ornamentation of some humble products of nineteenth-century village craftsmen mirror clearly what actually happened. Their chairs and flasks, for instance, often embody in an impressively simplified design their grand medieval ancestors. Thus the finely-wrought and yet sturdy village chair of Berane (Ethnographical Museum, Belgrade) reflects the medieval design of such lofty objects as the throne in the fifteenth-century Church of the Ascension in Leskovec near Ohrid. (See Pl. 5.) And the crude specimen of a popular nineteenth-century flask (Ethnographical Museum, Belgrade) was obviously inspired in its form by medieval pitchers—such as the fifteenth-century one in the Museum of Applied Art in Belgrade, or the earlier one which Moses holds on a fourteenth-century fresco painting in the monastery of Dečani.[1]

The most extensive and valuable body of decasyllabic oral epics, which were collected by V. S. Karadžić, represents a similar kind of achievement. But these epics also bear the social and historical imprint of the First and the Second Serbian Uprisings, 'the first of the great nationalist movements of the nineteenth century'.[2] And it is, of course, significant that the geography of the oral epic song in its golden age shows that the greatest poems come from the areas in which epic singing was most intensely and widely cultivated. 'At the present time', claims Karadžić writing in 1823,

> heroic songs are most widespread and most lively in Bosnia and Herzegovina, in Montenegro and in the hilly southern regions of Serbia. In these regions even today there is a *gusle* in every house, and particularly in the shepherds' summer huts in the mountains. And it is difficult to find a man who does not know how to play the *gusle,* and many women and girls know it too. In the lower regions of Serbia (along the Sava and the Danube), the *gusle* are more rare in people's houses, but I still think that in every village (particularly on the left bank of the Morava) one could be found.[3]

On the northern banks of the Sava and the Danube, in Srem, Bačka, and Banat, which were more prosperous and had been for a long time under the Austrian and Hungarian rule, only blind men had the *gusle* and sang oral epic songs. Apparently, 'other people were ashamed to hang blind men's *gusle* in their houses'.[4] And it is this distribution which explains, in Karadžić's opinion, the difference in the poetic achievement in various areas:

> the epic poems in Srem, Bačka, and Banat are worse sung than in Serbia, in Serbia along the Sava and the Danube they are worse sung than further inland, especially in Bosnia and Herzegovina. In the same way, as we move westwards from Srem through Slavonia to Croatia and Dalmatia, heroic songs are more and more cultivated by the people.[5]

This geographical picture shows that heroic songs were most widespread and best sung in the heart of the central mountain ranges in Herzegovina, Bosnia, Montenegro, and Serbia, as well as along the military frontiers of Slavonia, Croatia, and Venetian Dalmatia.

This agrees with the general directions of the major Balkan migrations from the fourteenth to the nineteenth century—the migrations which were so extensive that in this period 'almost all the population in the area from the Canyon of Veles on the river Vardar (Macedonia) to the Mountain of Zagreb (Zagrebačka gora, Croatia) changed its abode'.[6] (See Map 4.) Hundreds of thousands of people were moved by force from Serbia all over the Turkish Empire during the fifteenth century: during the single decade after the fall of Constantinople (1453) over three hundred thousand Serbs were displaced in this way.[7] During this heavy depopulation of Serbia in the fifteenth century the bulk of the refugees moved along the central Dinaric mountains to the regions which, a little later, supplied most of the Serbian migrants moving to the areas of the Slavonian, Croatian, and Dalmatian frontiers. The second wave of Serbian migrations during the great Turco-Austrian wars in the seventeenth century left dozens of villages completely uninhabited and many towns with only a handful of people in them. Austrian reports on the demographic situation in Serbia from the beginning of the eighteenth century show that the number of deserted settlements exceeded that of inhabited ones: at this time there were probably only about one hundred thousand people in the whole of Serbia (four to five per square kilometre).[8]

These migrations supplied a vast army for the Hungarian, Austrian, and Venetian military frontiers. The nineteenth century, however, marked the beginning of vast movements in the opposite direction: the extent of the repopulation of liberated Serbia is reflected in the fact that in the area of the river Morava and the river Drina about eighty per cent of the total population at the beginning of the twentieth century had come from somewhere else.[9] The linguistic and thematic impact of these migrations on the art of oral epic singing can hardly be overestimated: it explains why this art had to be not only 'anachronistic' but also 'anatopistic' from the moment when the first two complete songs were written down in the middle of the sixteenth century.[10]

For the singer and the song followed these main historical streams, and not only their social status but also the range of their voice was affected. The pre-Christian Slav singers in the Balkans seem to have been ordinary people sharing in a popular entertainment, but in the early Christian times they were already known as professionals in Hungary and among some other nations. In the monastic literature of feudal times there are references to 'the devilish songs' of common people,[11] to the lascivious 'harmful songs of youthful desires', to the collective epic singing about themes of public importance, to the various forms of royal and feudal entertainment by professional singers.[12] The evidence of strong epic traditions, absorbing hagiographical legends and apocryphal material, in the patrician setting of Bar is also significant.[13] However, the whole world of medieval feudal song—performed by foreign and native *jongleurs,* by various types of medieval entertainers, singers, actors and drummers, by wandering scholars ('dijaci') and composers of popular religious songs ('začinjavci')—was mainly absorbed either into the literary or into the oral culture in the sixteenth century.[14] The new type of popular epic singer was a different man in a different social setting.

To begin with, he might have been just any peasant, farmer or fisherman, in any rural area under the Turkish rule, or in any village or city on the Christian side of Turco-Christian frontiers. More specifically, he was often an outlaw, a border raider, a soldier, a gifted articulate man often from a distinguished village family in a patriarchal community, a slightly bohemian or artistic 'misfit', a village 'character', a self-made merchant, a clever shepherd, a blind man or woman making a living by his art. However, the popular image of the *guslar* as a blind visionary is exaggerated, even if it is a true description of Filip Višnjić, the most popular and perhaps the only true professional among Karadžić's best singers. But how did the personality, the biography, and the social setting of the greatest singers affect their art? There is sufficient evidence about some of the greatest of the nineteenth-century singers to suggest in outline some answers to this question.

Karadžić's family history is in itself significant. The family of the great collector came originally from Herzegovina, the heart and cradle of Serbo-Croat decasyllabic heroic songs. They lived at Tršić, near Loznica, in the hills of north-western Serbia, where the neighbouring monastery provided not only the initial education for the greatest Serbian man of letters, but also ammunition for the Serbian rebels and fighters against the Turks. And it is not surprising that Karadžić himself, one of the few literate laymen in his country, served as a clerk in the rebels' army during the First Serbian Uprising. When this Uprising was crushed in 1813, Karadžić crossed the river Sava and emigrated, with tens of thousands of his compatriots, to Austrian territory. It was here—near the monastery of Šišatovac—that he recorded many of his songs. And it was from his father that he wrote down the few fragments of Kosovo poems, perhaps among the finest in the language, and certainly central in the general epic landscape of the whole tradition.[15] His father was a pious and serious farmer—perhaps not too serious to indulge in epic song-making, but certainly serious enough not to admit to the indulgence. Karadžić—who made it clear on many occasions that poems were improvised rather than memorized[16]—seems to have believed his father when he told him that he was not responsible for the songs, because they were, in fact, old grandfather's responsibility.[17] There was also an uncle in the family who was capable of making up heroic songs as soon as the occasion arose—for instance, four or five days after Smail-bey Begzadić was killed.[18] This song is not a particularly significant achievement, but it is a clear and adequate description of a contemporary event of public importance. There are no jarring notes in it and this suggests a correspondence between the whole of the traditional epic diction (its formulas, its stylistic and narrative devices, its basic moral concepts) and the popular response to history as well as the way in which it was immediately understood and interpreted.

This situation will soon change, but it can be most clearly demonstrated in the life and work of Filip Višnjić, Karadžić's most popular singer. He was a man who carefully collected first-hand information from the Serbian rebels about the battles in which they fought and which became the subjects of his songs.[19] At the same time, however, he was a man 'who could move his audience to tears'.[20] This can be explained, in so far as such things can be explained, by his command of the epic language and by his imaginative gifts, but it might also have something to do with his own personal experience of history. He was born in Bosnia, 'on the other side of the river Drina',[21] and it was in his native part of the country, in the vicinity of Bijeljina, that he came to witness some of the common forms of Turkish terror. When he was twenty, blind after smallpox from the age of eight, a group of Turks raped one of the women in his uncle's household, where he lived after the death of his father. In revenge the family killed a Turk and 'hanged another one on a plum tree by his horse's halter'.[22] As a result all the members of the family were tortured and most of them killed. What survived this punishment was the story of his heroic uncle

Marko, the head of this large farming household, who 'sang through the town of Zvornik as he was going to the gallows'.[23] Homeless Filip, a very gifted young man, travelled for years and lived on his voice. He sang to the Christian rayah in many Bosnian villages and to the crowds on popular feast days at the monasteries. But he also cultivated a special repertoire for 'the great Turks' whom he entertained when his travels took him to towns.[24] During the First Serbian Uprising his native region was sometimes a major battlefield: in 1809, for instance, the Serbian rebels crossed the river Drina and, under the command of Stojan Čupić and Luko Lazarević, who were to become great heroes in Filip's songs,[25] besieged Bijeljina and fought some severe battles in this region. When they were forced to retreat, Filip joined them. Stojan Čupić, who had risen from the position of a servant to that of a great captain of the rebels' army, gave Filip a white horse for his song 'The Battle of Salaš'. The song described one of the major battles in 1806 and Stojan Čupić is presented in it as a man of immense courage and equal sensitivity for the social position and suffering of his peasants.[26] During 1810—after Višnjić's retreat to Serbia—his song kept up the spirit of the twelve hundred rebels, besieged in Loznica and exposed to Turkish fire and poisoned water supply. They waited for twelve days for the relief which was led by Karađorđe himself, the chief commander of the Serbian armies. After the Serbian victory Višnjić's song moved Karađorđe who, 'a man of few words', came to talk to him.[27] After the Uprising was crushed in 1813, Višnjić crossed the river Sava and came to live in Srem. He had a hut in a farmer's courtyard and some stools for the villagers who would come to listen to him during the winter. In summer he travelled round the villages in the whole area and wherever he came he was well-received and richly rewarded for his songs. The peasants in his own village Grk remembered him for a long time; when he died in 1834, they carved a *gusle* on his oak cross.

The nature of Višnjić's achievement becomes clearer in the light of his personal and historical fate. It is the fate of a blind seer who experienced some of the most atrocious forms of Turkish terror in his young days and found himself at the heart of one of the greatest historical national upheavals. But it is also the fate of a persevering and widely travelled craftsman who learned his art in the large central areas of oral epic singing where he mastered its full range. For Višnjić sings about Stefan Nemanja, St Sava, Marko Kraljević, the outlaws and the border raiders and, above all, about the greatest captains and the common soldiery of the First Serbian Uprising. Moreover, he also sings about Sultan Murad, the Great Dahijas, many Turkish and Moslem heroes, their mothers and wives—often at considerable length and sometimes with a vocabulary which reflects his appreciation of their human involvement in tragic history. This is why his dramatic sense of history, his intense feeling for concrete detail, his visionary image of the whole landscape and his imaginative response to the human impact of gory realities are so impressive.

His blindness explains why in his songs St Sava claims that his father Stefan Nemanja spent his treasure not only building churches and monasteries but also, among other things, 'giving alms to the crippled and to the blind'[28]—a detail not to be found in blind Stepanija's version of this poem who did not respond so quickly to the occasion of interweaving a moving personal element into a traditional epic tale.[29] And this ability is not mirrored only in Višnjić's long list of monasteries which Nemanja built, including many Bosnian ones which Nemanja did not build but which Višnjić, a widely travelled singer, knew. It is even more clearly demonstrated in Marko Kraljević's bequest of his treasure—part of which is again to be given 'to the crippled and to the blind':

> 'Let the blind walk the roads of the world
> And let them sing of Marko in their songs'.[30]

Besides, as blind professional singers were much more dependent on their public performances, often at the monasteries on great festivals, and as they were generally much more influenced by hagiographical literature, it may be also Višnjić's blindness which accounts partly for his outstanding sense of the miraculous—sometimes according to the epic standard, but often quite exceptional in its frequency and in the importance of its epic function. Thus, for instance, the ominous dream at the beginning of 'St Sava and Hasan Pasha' is a standard epic narrative device, but the melting of the Pasha's sword when he tries to slash the relics of St Sava, the fire which burns his tents, the Pasha's blinding and the crippling of his arms and legs, his wailing for mercy, the abbot's prayer and the miraculous healing of the Pasha are much more in keeping with the song's distinctly hagiographical tenor which is usually characteristic of blind singers.[31] Some of the miraculous elements in the story about the death of Marko Kraljević—particularly the appearance of the *vila* and her prophecy of Marko's death—are also according to the epic standard. But the ominous stumbling and weeping of Marko's horse, the evocation of ancient beliefs in the miraculous properties of water, Marko's reflection in a well which forebodes his death—these give the whole tale a visionary colouring which is not common in the songs about Marko.[32] And the heavenly omens in 'The Beginning of the Revolt Against the Dahijas' as well as the stars, 'trapped' in a dish of water which mirrors the headless bodies of the Turkish rulers, are certainly quite unique in a story about a contemporary historical subject.[33]

But in Višnjić's poems the visionary and the miraculous—and in this he is different from many other blind singers—often illuminate the historical and the immediate which are given with exceptional factual accuracy. For Višnjić is above all the singer of contemporary history and his descriptions of the beginning of the Serbian revolt and many of the historical battles—at Čokešina (1804), near Salaš (1806), in the field of Mišar (1806), at Loznica (1810)—are not only broadly true to historical facts but also distinguished by a lively sense of many particular details. The shortage of ammunition in 'The Battle of Čokešina' and the subsequent use of guns as clubs, the bleating sheep and the lowing cattle which are driven away from their homeland in 'The Battle of Salaš' and many other of Višnjić's great scenes are unique both in their physical precision and their imaginative sense of the Serbian soil and history.[34] Moreover, Višnjić's sense of realistic detail ranges from the heroic and the tragic to the genuinely comic and humorous. Such are the moments when Ilija Birčanin frightens the powerful Dahija out of his wits as he throws at him the bag with the tax-money which he had collected, when the cowardly Captain Ćurčija explains that he cannot afford to fight a stronger enemy because he is not like a willow-tree, once cut, to sprout again, when Bey Ljubović challenges Bajo Pivljanin to a duel and threatens, if the challenge is refused, that he will send his enemy raw wool and a distaff to make a shirt and a pair of pants for himself.[35] Similarly, we well may ask why it is that the hands of the great Serbian captain Anto Bogićević tremble so that he cannot write a message requesting help for besieged Loznica. Is he so frightened of the Turks, or is he illiterate and frightened of paper—or perhaps just an old man with trembling hands?[36]

The interplay of such vivid realistic elements with the invocations of Kosovo itself, with the visionary and miraculous illuminations of history suggest an almost medieval imaginative genius flourishing in the setting of much later times. Višnjić's ability to merge such diverse and often anachronistic elements into a unified vision of his tales make him an exemplary epic singer. In short, his 'darkened sun' is as much a heavenly omen as it is the result of the fog of gunpowder in Mačva and this is perhaps why he succeeded—to paraphrase his favourite image—in 'tying the red flame into the skies'.[37] And last but not least, it was perhaps his singing to 'the great Turks' in Bosnia that enabled him to master their moral and psychological idiom and push the frontiers of the epic drama so far as to include the great and humane Turkish characters, like Sultan Murad and Old Fočo, within the scope of his vision.[38] In short, the maturity of his epic voice—that of a young blind boy, a victim of Turkish terror, a professional singer and craftsman, an entertainer of the Serbian rebels and an elderly exiled man—was not unearned.

A different but equally significant historical and biographical pattern is reflected in the life of Tešan Podrugović, the greatest of Karadžić's poets—for he did not sing but used to 'speak' his poems. He was born in the village of Kazanci in Herzegovina and he also travelled quite extensively, at first making his living as a trader. He was a huge man—as big as a man and a half (*po drugog čoveka*); hence Podrugović instead of Gavrilović which was in fact his original family name.[39] His courage equalled his stature: as a young man he was unperturbed when a group of Turks tried to rape one of the girls in his household and everyone ran away. He killed one of the Turks and drove away the others, so that at the age of about twenty-five he had to leave his home and take to the woods. As an outlaw he made a name for himself; when the Serbian Uprising broke out he crossed the river Drina and joined the rebels. He distinguished himself in the battles near the river Drina, but when his captain did him an injustice, he left the Serbian army so that he should not have to kill his superior. Before the defeat of Serbian rebels in 1813 he crossed the river Sava and came to live in Srem in utter poverty.[40] Karadžić found him making his living by cutting reeds and selling them in towns—a reticent and serious man, with a strange sense of humour, 'scowling' as he told his often funny stories.[41]

'He was clever and, for an outlaw, an honest man';[42] and it was at this time, when Podrugović was about forty, that Karadžić recorded twenty-two poems from him. 'I have never found anyone who knew the poems as well as he did. Each of his poems was a good one, because he—particularly as he did not sing but spoke his poems—understood and felt them, and he thought about what he said.'[43] He had a large repertoire and knew, in Karadžić's opinion, at least another hundred poems apart from the recorded ones; moreover, Karadžić claims that if Podrugović were 'to hear the worst poem, after a few days he would speak it beautifully and in proper order which was characteristic of his other songs, or he would not remember it at all, and he would say that it was silly, not worth remembering or telling.'[44] However, Karadžić's recording of Podrugović's songs in the monastery of Šišatovac in Srem was suddenly interrupted. About Easter time in 1815 the news came that the second round of fighting against the Turks in Serbia had just started; it was, Karadžić tells us, 'as if a hundred thorns had got under his skin'.[45] And it was with great effort that Karadžić kept him for a few more days to write down some more of his poems before Podrugović left for Serbia to 'fight the Turks again'.[46] Obviously, he had more important business on hand than the most enlightened man in Serbia of his time could understand.

However, in the summer of the same year, he left the Serbian army again, went to Bosnia, killed a bey and became an outlaw. A little later he tried to get back to Serbia, but on his way he quarrelled with some Turks in an inn. He killed a few of them and, himself wounded, tried to escape. However, the Turks caught up with him and as he had no ammunition, he defended himself by throwing stones as he retreated up the mountain. With two more wounds he managed to escape, but they went bad and he had to return to a village in which he died a few days later.[47]

Podrugović's courage and suffering, his physical stature and his irascible temper, his grand sense of personal, family, and national honour, his love of funny stories defying his experience of history suggest the characteristic figure of a great outlaw who becomes a fighter for national independence at the beginning of the nineteenth century. Besides, his personal fate and character also explain his imaginative attachment to certain themes. His sense of patriarchal loyalties—which turned him into an outlaw at the age of twenty-five—is clearly mirrored, for instance, in the poems in which the ideals of family village life dominate the heroic feudal scene. Thus in 'Dušan's Wedding' Miloš

Voinović, the historical military commander who represented the emperor in his dealings with Dubrovnik, is turned into a shepherd who rides a horse covered by a bearskin and defends his imperial uncle in spite of the latter's credulity and slanderous insults. His outstanding stature, cunning and courage, and above all his skill in outwitting his enemies and making fools of them are clearly the reflections of Podrugović's own personality. A sense of patriarchal values also dominates his great song about the Battle of Kosovo in which Tsaritsa Milica obtains Tsar Lazar's blessing to have one of her brothers stay with her, but each of them feels in duty bound to die in the battle. Similarly, when a Turkish girl helps the wounded King Vukašin and accepts him as her brother-in-God but is betrayed by her own brother, Marko Kraljević will kill the treacherous brother when he offers King Vukašin's sword for sale ('Marko Kraljević Knows His Father's Sword').

However, Podrugović's greatest heroes—like Miloš Voinović who can jump over three horses with three fiery swords on them, or Marko Kraljević who plays by throwing his mace into the clouds and catching it again—are not only men of uncommon physical strength. They also illustrate Podrugović's unique sense of realistic comedy which often takes place within the framework of exalted heroic ideals. Thus Karadžić's claim that Podrugović liked to tell funny stories with a scowl defines the comic tenor of **"Marko Kraljević and Ljutica Bogdan"** in which two hot-headed Serbian heroes come to blows and frighten each other so much that their final reconciliation reflects above all their desire never to meet again.[48] An equally rich and often much more complex sense of comedy pervades, as we have seen, Podrugović's greatest songs about Marko Kraljević: **"The Wedding of Marko Kraljević"**, **"Marko Kraljević Knows His Father's Sword"**, **"Marko Kraljević and the Daughter of the Arab King"**, **"Marko Kraljević and Musa Kesedžij"**, **"Marko Kraljević and Demo of the Mountain"**. For it was in the traditional songs about Marko Kraljević and his exploits that Podrugović found the richest scope for the expression of his own genius—the genius of great comic dignity, of a hot-headed, irascible and clumsy, but also exalted sense of personal and communal honour. And, finally, it is also significant that this great outlaw has left us several of the classic lines about 'the bad craft' of outlawry,[49] about the 'bitterness' of the outlaws' fate, about the skill and courage of the man

> Fit to overtake and run away
> And stand his ground in terrible places . . .
> Who fears no one but God Himself.[50]

To sum up, Karadžić's greatest epic poet, who knew that fighting was more important than singing, created the heroes who have to face—and use—the tricks and treacheries of history and Realpolitik to defend the dignity of human life on this earth.

The links between the singer's personal fate, his interest in particular themes of the epic heritage and his ability to make them live as poetry can also be discerned in the four outstanding songs—running to almost three thousand lines—which Karadžić recorded from Old Milija (Starac Milija). The honorary title of 'starac' was not the privilege of 'just any elderly man', but of 'the wise man and the sage who knew the tradition', who was held in high esteem, next to the village chief.[51] This suggests that Karadžić's recording of Old Milija's songs took place when a wise and, as we shall see, tough man was breaking under the burden of old age, personal misfortunes and drink. For Old Milija was also, like Podrugović, born in old Herzegovina, in the vicinity of Kolašin (now in Montenegro) and, like Podrugović, he was also involved in a fight against 'some Turks', which forced him to leave his native area.[52] Unlike Podrugović, however, he was not twenty at the time, but at least in his fifties. This is not the age when a farmer would easily leave his land; and there is no doubt that some great trouble must have driven Old Milija to escape to Serbia.[53] When Karadžić met him in 1822 in Kragujevac, the souvenirs of this trouble were still vivid: 'all his head was scarred with cuts', Karadžić tells us.[54] Besides, Karadžić had great difficulty getting in touch with the gifted, decrepit singer: the efforts of the head of the Serbian administration in the district of Požega were not sufficient to secure his presence. So in the autumn of 1822, when Karadžić came to Serbia on the invitation of its ruler Prince Miloš Obrenović, the illiterate Prince himself gave strict orders to his head clerk 'to have Milija brought alive or dead'[55] and make special arrangements for normal work on Milija's farm in his absence. When Old Milija turned up, he was so weak with old age and his wounds that he was unable, and unwilling, to sing without 'slivovits'. As soon as the drink was brought, he would pour it all into his own flask and disregarding the custom of offering it to other people present, he would start sipping and singing. People in the audience often teased him about this and asked him what the 'slivovits' was like. 'He used to answer, shuddering and frowning: "Awful, my son, so bad, it couldn't be worse; Heaven forbid that you should drink it!"'[56] The recording itself did not go smoothly: Milija was unable to sing his songs with the required pauses. So he drawled out his phrases as best he could and Karadžić wrote as fast as he could, and this had to be repeated several times for each song. Four songs took more than fifteen days to write down. Finally, one of the loitering local louts—'such as can be found in many courts, worrying only about how to turn everything into a joke'[57]—persuaded Milija that all his harvest would go to the dogs if he went on wasting his time with such an irresponsible and mad fellow as Karadžić who cared, obviously, only for songs.[58] Milija soon disappeared—having collected his fee from the Prince's office—in the utmost secrecy. When Karadžić enquired about him again a year later, he was already dead.[59]

Milija's personal misfortune which struck him in old age and drove him away from home is mirrored in all his poems in the imagery of ravaged homes when the heroes are far away or terrible miseries which befall them on their long journeys. In **"Banović Strahinja"**—running into eight hundred and ten lines, probably the greatest single epic poem in the language—the hero's home is devastated, his mother and his love are captured, while he feasts far away with his in-laws. This provides not only the moving force of the narrative, but also the most important inner link of Ban's sympathy with a noble-minded old Turkish dervish, a solo drinker like Milija himself.[60] For the two enemies understand each other much better than any of their friends: the old dervish had been humanely treated as Ban's prisoner a long time ago and he touches Ban to the quick when he tells him his story of his return to his ravaged home in which elder had come to grow in the doorposts. In **"The Wedding of Maksim Crnojević"**—one of the outstanding poems in the epic tradition, running to 1,226 lines[61]—the hero is disfigured with smallpox while his father is far away in Venice, looking for a bride for him. The universal catastrophe—the quarrel and the slaughter of the wedding party with far-reaching historical consequences—also occurs on their journey, far away from home. The long journey which takes Marko Kraljević, Miloš Obilić, and Winged Relja of Pazar to Captain Leka's castle results in the tragic maiming and blinding of the prospective bride who insults her great Serbian suitors (**"Captain Leka's Sister"**).[62] And in 'Captain Gavran and Limo'—with its magnificent image of the loot equally divided among the living and the dead outlaws—there is also a very long journey which takes the Montenegrin fighters to north-western Bosnia and the frontier area near the town of Bihać.[63] Long journeys are not, of course, uncommon in the epic tradition, but no other singer makes them a source of personal tragedies in all his poems. It is in this sense that Milija's songs embody a vivid awareness of his own personal tragedy as well as a wider concept of patriarchal village culture, the assumption that being far away from home is one of the main sources of misfortune and misery in human life.

Karadžić's description makes it clear that Old Milija tried to extinguish his sense of misfortune and misery in drinking, just as the old Turkish dervish does in **"Banović Strahinja"**. Besides, Milija's representation of Marko Kraljević, a notorious drinker in the songs of many other singers, is outstanding, not perhaps because Milija's Marko drinks a whole 'tub' of wine and gives one to his horse, but because this enormous amount of wine makes the horse red up to his ears and Marko only to his eyes![64] And when the wedding party in 'The Wedding of Maksim Crnojević' comes to the sea, everyone does what he likes best:

> Every drunkard tips up his flask.[65]

The number of drunkards suggested shows that a common element in the tradition must have been exceptionally near to the singer's heart.

Finally, the poetic genius of the unfortunate old drunkard saw everything on a magnificent scale. His Strahinić Ban is not only richly dressed like so many other epic heroes: the rosy colour of his clothes surpasses that of the sun, their redness is redder than water—presumably at sunset.[66] In **"Captain Leka's Sister"** Marko Kraljević appears all in gold and his horse is covered in lynx fur;[67] Miloš Obilić has 'three storeys' of rich clothes on him;[68] the Winged Relja of Pazar makes both of them look shabby by his appearance.[69] The gold shirt which the mother-in-law gives to the prospective bridegroom in **"The Wedding of Maksim Crnojević"** has a serpent's head under the throat with a precious stone so brilliant that the groom will need no candle when he takes his bride to their bedroom.[70] Moreover, the cruelties of Milija's heroes and heroines are on the same scale: no other epic heroine ever dared insult the three great Serbian dukes as Captain Leko's sister did, no other epic hero was as generous as Strahinić Ban who spared the life of his unfaithful love. This is why it has sometimes been claimed—not perhaps with any reliability and certainly with little sense of what Old Milija's art is about—that the behaviour of his heroes and heroines suggests a certain decline of patriarchal moral norms in actual life, characteristic of Milija's times and perhaps of his own personal experience.[71] Be that as it may, in Milija's songs we are faced with a tragic range and intensity which endorse the broken moral patterns and reveal an outstandingly generous and perceptive poetic mind.

Far less is known about Karadžić's other singers. But it is worth noting that Old Raško—the singer of several of the best poems with motifs from Serbian medieval history, such as the splendid, if highly controversial 'Building of Skadar' and the universally acknowledged 'Uroš and the Mrljavčevići'—was also born in Kolašin, in old Herzegovina, and came to Serbia at the beginning of the First Serbian Uprising.[72] Stojan the Outlaw—the singer of 'The Wedding of King Vukašin', one of the greatest poems with medieval heroes—was also born in Herzegovina. But when he came to Serbia and gave up outlawry, he ran into trouble for having killed an old woman who, he believed, was a witch who had 'eaten' his child.[73] His idea of women and witches may go some way towards explaining his interest in such characters as the faithless Vidosava, the villain in the story of 'The Wedding of King Vukašin' and one of the greatest 'bitches' in the Serbo-Croat epic tradition.[74] It is also noteworthy that the greatest of Karadžić's Montenegrin singers Đuro Milutinović, the singer of the two best poems from this area, 'Perović Batrić' and 'The Piperi and Tahir Pasha', was a blind man who brought a letter from the Montenegrin Prince Bishop to Karađorđe in 1809 and stayed in Serbia.[75]

To sum up, the existing evidence about Karadžić's greatest singers—and it is evidence recorded by an outstandingly shrewd and objective observer, whose sober judgement is illustrated by everything he wrote, including his historical writings, his great dictionary and grammar—seems to point not only to the basic routes of the Serbian migrations but also to a very lively interplay of the oral epic traditions with the personal involvement of the singers in the burning issues of contemporary history. But if this is a major part of the picture there is also another vast and important area which tells a completely different story and which is not usually fully recognized. It is the area of the great epic songs of blind, pious old women who did not move about and were sometimes linked with particular monasteries. Their greatest achievements are to be found in the songs about medieval feudal times and their sense of the distant past seems to be stronger and sometimes more accurate than that of other singers. So, for instance, 'Momir the Foundling'—a great song originating perhaps from a *bugarštica* which derived its story from Byzantine sources and, ultimately, from *1001 Nights*—was recorded from 'blind Živana who sat in Zemun'.[76] Two more songs about Marko Kraljević—one of them being 'Marko Kraljević and Alil-aga', one of the finest in Karadžić's collection—were written down from the same singer.[77] Blind Jeca who, apparently, also 'sat' in Zemun was the singer of 'The Death of Duke Prijezda', deservedly one of the best-known poems in the language, the greatest example of a tragic feudal drama in the Serbo-Croat oral epic tradition.[78] One of the very few songs about the Battle of Kosovo in Karadžić's collection, 'Tsaritsa Milica and Duke Vladeta', was written down from blind Stepanija of whom we know only that she was born in Jadar in Serbia.[79] Karadžić also notes that he received a variant of this song—'almost the same as this one'—from another source.[80] What 'almost the same' exactly means is difficult to say—but does it suggest a higher degree of memorizing than we usually find in the tradition? And last but not least Lukijan Mušicki, a learned versifier and the abbot of the monastery of Šišatovac in Srem, recorded—or had someone record for him—from a blind woman in the neighbouring village of Grgurevci some of the finest poems about feudal times in Karadžić's collection: 'The Downfall of the Serbian Empire', 'The Kosovo Girl' and 'Marko Kraljević Abolishes the Wedding Tax'.[81] 'The Kosovo Girl' is one of the finest songs in the tradition and it is astoundingly accurate in historical detail—the communion of the Serbian army on the eve of the battle, and the representation of the silver gilt rings, feudal gowns with monograms and circular ornaments, the scarves woven with gold threads and given in token of betrothal. S. Radojčić—one of the most distinguished Serbian art historians—has checked these details against the evidence of contemporary Byzantine military tracts, Serbian monastic literature and medieval fresco painting. This has led him to claim that their survival can only be explained by the assumption that the poem was memorized by generations of singers and repeated 'like Paternoster—with or without understanding—but accurately, line by line'.[82]

Of course, this need not have been the case. But even if generations of singers memorized only stock phrases, formulas, and clusters of formulas hardly ever running beyond a few lines, even if they learned only how to handle some specific narrative and stylistic structures, this does not imply merely the command of a poetic language. This language itself was a way of memorizing history, many of its physical details, actual events and social concepts. At the same time this language was not being mastered in the abstract, but within narrative structures which were a way of responding to history and interpreting its significance. These narrative structures were open to change and adaptation, they could absorb new concepts and new material; and it was in a dramatic interplay of the past and the present, the imaginative interplay of anachronistic and anatopistic features, that the singers created their greatest achievements. For the oral epic singing at its best was both a way of coming to terms with history and a means of getting out of it. This is why its ultimate significance cannot be grasped in the analysis either of the technique of its composition or of the diverse historical sources of its social concepts, motifs, and themes. For a song about fighting is not the same thing as fighting or even as the recording of an actual response to it. Similarly, songs about great defeats, vassalage, outlawry, or rebellions attempt to grasp in language not only their historical but also their moral significance. They interpret the actual in terms of what it means as a challenge to the human spirit and to the whole tradition of oral poetic language in which it expresses itself. This is why the way in which diverse stylistic and narrative devices, the whole anachronistic heritage of the historical material embedded in the nature of the oral epic convention itself, has to be the object of inquiry: what sense—if any—does the Serbo-Croat oral epic language at its best make of what it remembers of several centuries of the Balkan history?

Notes

1. See V. Han, 'Putevima narodne tradicije od srednjovekovnih fresaka do folklornih originala', *Zbornik Svetozara Radojčića,* Filozofski fakultet, Belgrade, 1969, pp. 391-8.

2. D. Wilson, *The Life and Times of Vuk Stefanović Karadžić 1787-1864,* p. 28.

3. 'Predgovor', *Karadžić,* i, p. 529.

4. Ibid., pp. 529-30.

5. Ibid.

6. *Enciklopedija Jugoslavije,* vii, p. 506.

7. See ibid.

8. See ibid.

9. See ibid., pp. 506-7.

10. See above pp. 49-58.

11. See V. Latković, 'O pevačima srpskohrvatskih narodnih epskih pesama do kraja xviii veka', *Prilozi za književnost, jezik, istoriju i folklor,* xx (1954), p. 188.

12. See above pp. 12-15.

13. See above pp. 16-19.

14. See V. Latković, op. cit., pp. 191-2.

15. See above pp. 160-1, 164-7.

16. See below p. 322.

17. Karadžić refers to his father as 'a pious and earnest man who cared little for songs except in so far as he memorized them, almost accidentally, from his father Joksim and his brother Toma, who not only knew

many songs and were glad to sing and tell them, but also made up songs themselves' ('Predgovor', *Karadžić*, iv, p. 374).

18. See ibid., pp. 374-5.

19. 'Višnjić told Lukijan Mušicki how he began his songs about the Uprising. He asked the fighters, he said, as they were coming back from the battlefield: "who was their commander", where they fought, "who was killed, who they fought against". This is to say—he collected his material. The singer did not tell Mušicki how he turned the dry details into poetry. He himself was not aware of the secret.' V. Nedić, 'Filip Višnjić', *Narodna književnost*, p. 331.

20. L. Ranke, *A History of Servia and the Servian Revolution*, London, 1847, p. 76. See also below pp. 322-3.

21. V. S. Karadžić, 'Predgovor', *Karadžić*, iv, p. 365.

22. V. Nedić, 'Filip Višnjić', *Narodna književnost*, p. 324.

23. Ibid.

24. Ibid.

25. Both these heroes figure in the famous 'Battle of Loznica' (*Karadžić*, iv, No. 33) and 'Luko Lazarević and Pejzo' (*Karadžić*, iv, No. 34). Stojan Čupić also figures in 'Čupić's Boast' ('Hvala Čupićeva', *Karadžić*, iv, No. 36) and in 'The Battle of Salaš' (*Karadžić*, iv, No. 28).

26. See above pp. 286-7 and below pp. 340-1.

27. V. Nedić, 'Filip Višnjić', *Narodna književnost*, p. 325.

28. 'Dijeleći kljastu i slijepu', 'Sveti Savo', *Karadžić*, ii, No. 24, l. 42.

29. See above pp. 142-3.

30. '(Treći ćemer) kljastu i slijepu, / Nek slijepi po svijetu hode, / Nek pjevaju i spominju Marka'. 'Smrt Marka Kraljevića', *Karadžić*, ii, No. 74, ll. 110-12.

31. See 'St Sava and Hasan Pasha' ('Sveti Savo i Hasanpaša'), *Karadžić*, iii, No. 14. For the miraculous element in the songs of blind singers see above pp. 107-9 and, particularly, pp. 161-2.

32. See 'The Death of Marko Kraljević', *Karadžić*, ii, No. 74, ll. 12-14, 49-66.

33. See 'The Beginning of the Revolt Against the Dahijas', *Karadžić*, iv, No. 24, ll. 1-68.

34. See above pp. 280-95 and below pp. 340-2.

35. See 'Bajo Pivljanin and Bey Ljubović' ('Bajo Pivljanin i beg Ljubović'), *Karadžić*, iii, No. 70, ll. 14-19.

36. See 'The Battle of Loznica', *Karadžić*, iv, No. 33, ll. 291-2.

37. See above p. 267.

38. See above pp. 292-4.

39. See V. S. Karadžić, 'Predgovor', *Karadžić*, iv, p. 364.

40. See V. Nedić, 'Tešan Podrugović', *Narodna književnost*, pp. 344-6.

41. See 'Predgovor', *Karadžić*, iv, p. 364.

42. Ibid.

43. Ibid., pp. 364-5.

44. 'Predgovor', *Karadžić*, iv, p. 378.

45. Ibid., p. 364.

46. Ibid.

47. See V. Nedić, 'Tešan Podrugović', *Narodna književnost*, p. 346.

48. See 'Marko Kraljević i Ljutica Bogdan', *Karadžić*, ii, No. 39, ll. 12-37, 113-16.

49. See above p. 246.

50. See note 10, p. 246.

51. M. Lutovac, 'Ibarski Kolašin', *Srpski etnografski zbornik*, lxvii (1954), p. 114.

52. 'Predgovor', *Karadžić*, iv, p. 366.

53. Lj. Zuković suggests that Old Milija was, if not a 'real outlaw', at least 'an outlaw of the Montenegrin type, i.e. from time to time he joined an outlaw company and when the danger was over, he returned home' ('Vukov pjevač starac Milija', *Putevi*, xi [1965], p. 604). Zuković's argument rests partly on the interpretation of Karadžić's note that Old Milija 'escaped to' ('dobežao'), not just 'came' or 'moved' to Serbia.

54. 'Predgovor', *Karadžić*, iv, p. 367.

55. See ibid.

56. Ibid.

57. Ibid.

58. See ibid.

59. See ibid., pp. 367-8.

60. See above p. 136.

61. 'Ženidba Maksima Crnojevića', *Karadžić*, ii, No. 89.

62. 'Sestra Leke kapetana', *Karadžić*, ii, No. 40.

63. See above p. 240-2.

64. See 'Sestra Leke kapetana', *Karadžić*, ii, No. 40, ll. 56-63.

65. 'Ko l' bekrija, naginje čuturom', *Karadžić*, ii, No. 89, l. 594.

66. 'The cloth was redder than the water, / The cloth was pinker than the sun' ('Što od vode čoha crvenija, / A

od sunca čoha rumenija'), 'Banović Strahinja', *Karadžić,* ii, No. 44, ll. 24-5.

67. See 'Sestra Leke kapetana', *Karadžić,* ii, No. 40, l. 54.

68. 'Tri kata haljina', ibid., l. 144.

69. See ibid., ll. 187-92.

70. See 'Ženidba Maksima Crnojevića', *Karadžić,* ii, No. 89, ll. 791-8.

71. See P. Bakotić, 'Starac Milija', *Školski vjesnik,* xii (1962), No. 8, p. 26.

72. See 'Predgovor', *Karadžić,* iv, p. 368. For the discussion of 'Uroš and the Mrljavčevići' and 'The Building of Skadar' see above pp. 138-41, 147-151.

73. See above p. 127 and particularly note 10 on that page.

74. See above pp. 128-31. There is also an example of a treacherous wife in Stojan the Outlaw's song 'Vuk Jerinić and Zukan the Ensign': Hajka, Zukan's 'faithful love', takes hold of a broken sword and helps Zukan's enemy to slaughter her husband (see 'Vuk Jerinić i Zukan barjaktar', *Karadžić,* iii, No. 54, ll. 209-17).

75. See 'Predgovor', *Karadžić,* iv, p. 369.

76. Ibid., p. 370. See also above pp. 115-17.

77. See above pp. 199-201. The other song which Karadžić recorded from blind Živana is 'Marko Kraljević and the Twelve Arabs' ('Marko Kraljević i 12 Arapa', *Karadžić,* ii, No. 63).

78. See above pp. 89-91 and below pp. 337-8.

79. See 'Predgovor', *Karadžić,* iv, p. 372. See also above pp. 170-1.

80. 'Predgovor', *Karadžić,* iv, p. 372.

81. See above pp. 161-2, 171-2, 203-4.

82. S. Radojčić, 'Kosovka djevojka', *Uzori i dela starih srpskih umetnika,* p. 239.

Pavle Ivić (essay date 1982)

SOURCE: Ivić, Pavle. "Kopitar and the Evolution of Vuk Karadžić's Views on the Serbian Literary Language." In *Papers in Slavic Philology 2: To Honor Jernej Kopitar 1780-1980,* edited by Rado L. Lencek and Henry R. Cooper, Jr., pp. 99-107. Ann Arbor: University of Michigan, 1982.

[*In the following essay, Ivić explores Jernej Kopitar's considerable influence on Karadžić's work.*]

The extent of Jernej Kopitar's contributions to the work of Vuk Karadžić is reflected in three facts: he persuaded Vuk to begin writing systematically; he defined the main points of Vuk's program of work (publishing folk poetry, a grammar, a dictionary, and a translation of the Holy Bible); and he suggested to him fundamental views on the literary language, the alphabet and orthography.

Vuk accepted Kopitar's views (Kopitar 1857: passim) that every nation ought to use its own language in literature, that the field of use of the Church Slavonic language among the Serbs should be restricted to the Church, that the mixture of language types such as that practiced by the *slaveno-srpski* writers of the time was impermissible, and that the task of the grammarian is not to prescribe language, but merely to describe it. In the same way, Vuk accepted and implemented the phonemic principle in the alphabet and orthography, which Kopitar had summarized in the formula, "No sound may have more than one sign, and no sign more than one sound" (in 1813; Kopitar 1857: p. 249). Kopitar's ideas about language bear witness to his lucidity and to his adoption of the most positive ideas of the age, while the program of Vuk's work indicates Kopitar's ability to select what was essential, which made it possible for Vuk not to waste his energy on minor matters but to concentrate on issues in which his efforts would bear the most significant fruit.

In the early period of Vuk's activity, along with the above viewpoints which were undoubtedly well-founded, several other, more specific and partly less justified attitudes appeared, also linked in a way with Kopitar.

Vuk wrote in Ijekavian, although the vast majority of Serbian writers of the time used the Ekavian dialect. Vuk did this because he preferred his native dialect and because it was easier for him to write in this way, but he found his arguments for doing so in Kopitar, who had often toyed in his writings with the idea that all dialects should attain the rank of literary languages, as was once the case in ancient Greece (e.g., Kopitar 1857: pp. 278, 307, 349). This Romantic dreaming, to which Vuk gave an apodictic formulation (Karadžić 1894: I, 157), in no way suited the needs of a modern literary language in the process of formation. The Greek model was an anachronism in an age when the main medium of culture was the printed word, which demands a broad market for books, and when literary languages were functionally much more polyvalent than in Greece before the generalizing of the Koine. Had Vuk, by some miracle, implemented Kopitar's vision for the Serbs, it would have brought the Serbian literary language into a state of regional division, harmful both culturally and politically, and Vuk would not have been remembered for his accomplishments in forming the standard language but for the harm which he caused to its formation. As for Vuk's insistence on the Ijekavian dialect, it is no simple matter to determine the extent to which it helped and the extent to which it harmed the Serbian nation and its culture. If Ijekavian, under Vuk's influence, could have been generally accepted, it would have been of great value because it would have secured greater unity of the literary language for the Serbs in different regions. History has shown, however, that this was not possible, and it is difficult and inappropriate to guess what might have happened if Vuk had accepted Ekavian. Nevertheless, it is clear that his Ijekavian harmed his own struggle most of all. Of everything which he proposed, Ijekavian was the least acceptable to the majority of Serbian intellectuals (and in general to the majority of Serbs) and later turned into one of the most frequently mentioned and most successful arguments of his antagonists.

In the earlier phases of his work, Vuk frequently stressed that "we must take grammar from shepherds and plowmen" (e.g., Karadžić 1894: I, 159), because only the language of simple rural folk is unspoiled, while people in towns speak badly and authors from an urban environment write in a language full of mistakes. In this case, too, Vuk, born in the countryside and brilliantly aware of his native speech, chose what was closer to him and easier for him, at the same time discrediting what his antagonists, advocates of the "cultivated" language, were proud of. In this too, Vuk relied on Kopitar, who often had pointed out that Slovene was spoken well only in the countryside, whereas the language of town-dwellers, and especially the language used in books, was debased by the influence of German. Vuk applied a similar view to the conditions of the Serbs and gave the problem the sharpened aspect of a social clash. We can guess that he had had painful experience with the arrogance of certain members of the "upper class" in the Vojvodina, who saw in him an uneducated peasant boy. Psychologically, the conversion of his weakness into a virtue and of his opponents' advantage into a drawback is understandable. This move might also have looked like a skillful tactical maneuver, but it did not prove to be so: it distanced the Serbian intellectuals from Vuk and was frequently castigated and ridiculed. It was rightly claimed that the language of a modern culture cannot be based on the possibilities of expression of those who lack that culture, and that the literary languages of all advanced nations are founded on the speech of the educated circles of society.

Kopitar counted the Catholic speakers of Štokavian, e.g., the Slavonian Šokac population and the Dalmatian writer Andrija Kačić-Miošić, among the Serbs, on the basis of linguistic criteria. In the age of Romantic enthusiasm for ethnicity, language was considered practically the only determinant of nationality, and Kopitar was well aware of the linguistic proximity of all speakers of Štokavian and of the differences which marked them off from Čakavian and Kajkavian speakers (the latter, again on the basis of language, he considered Slovenes). Vuk's acceptance of this opinion was to have serious consequences later on: it aroused strong resistance in the Croats, who saw in Vuk's claim to the Štokavian Catholics an aggressive nationalist attitude and stressed quite rightly that that population did not consider itself Serbian. The discord which ensued did harm to the relations between the two peoples.

Kopitar is responsible for one more move of Vuk's, which, in all fairness, affects only a detail, but one which played a great historical role. Kopitar early began to be carried away by the dream of a common alphabet for all Slavs and a synthesis of the cyrillic and latin alphabets. He even suggested to the Germans that they should include a few cyrillic letters in their alphabet (Kopitar 1857: 243-256). We should be so much the less surprised, then, that in his review of Vuk's first grammar he expressed the idea that the Serbian alphabet should be supplemented with the letter *j* (Kopitar 1857: p. 313). Vuk accepted his advice, thereby giving his opponents an argument which served them perhaps better than any other. The Serbian public in any case suspected that Kopitar, a loyal Catholic trusted by the Viennese Court, wished to separate the Serbs from the Orthodox tradition, using Vuk as a means. This suspicion was cherished and fanned by the high-ranking Orthodox clergy, who were in the forefront of the resistance to Vuk's reforms, mainly because they wanted to preserve the influence of the Church in culture and to defend the link between the Serbs and Russia, which was seen as the protector of Orthodoxy. The Serbian public was oversensitive because of the frequent attempts of the Austrian authorities to subject the Serbs to the Catholic Church. Thus, the latin *yod* (*j*) looked like a tool by which Kopitar wished to separate the Serbs from their Orthodox Russian brethren. For this reason, the *yod* became the main subject of attacks on Vuk's alphabet and the main obstacle to its adoption. This alphabet would certainly have been accepted more easily and rapidly if Vuk had used the letter *i* or *ǔ* instead of *yod*. These two letters had already been used in the Serbian cyrillic alphabet, but Vuk had exiled both from the alphabet, only to introduce the sign *j* unnecessarily.

The ultimate fate of Vuk's five controversial ideas mentioned here was not the same for all. Vuk clung faithfully only to the use of *yod*; there is no sign that he ever thought of deviating in this detail. In connection with Ijekavian, he went through a period of hesitation about 1830, when he was living in Serbia, probably as a result of feeling the extent to which Ekavian predominated in the ruling circles of the new state. But on his return to Vienna, again separated from the Serbian environment, he returned to his native Ijekavian dialect. As for the three other points, Vuk later revised his stand.

Vuk at first deviated from the opinion that all the speakers of Štokavian were Serbs, but he later returned to this claim. Evidently under Kopitar's influence, Vuk in his first grammar of 1814 divided the Serbian language into three dialects, one of which he defined as "Slavonian." This is in fact the Ikavian dialect spoken by a Catholic (and Moslem) population, and not a Serbian one. In 1817 and 1818, however, he had already changed this classification, not mentioning the Slavonian dialect. Much has been written on Vuk's possible motives for leaving it out (e.g., Rešetar 1907: 2-3; Belić 1948: 109-111; Ivić 1971: p. 270). But one point has not been emphasized to date: Kopitar himself had arrived at the realization of the linguistic unity of the Serbs and Croats. He expressed this for the first time in 1822, and more fully in 1836 (Lencek 1976: 46-47). It can be supposed, however, that even before 1822 he had begun to think about this: it had seemed to him unjustified to consider the dialect of a Catholic population Serbian if Serbian and Croatian were one language. Nevertheless, in 1849, when Kopitar was no longer alive, Vuk returned to the opinion that all speakers of Štokavian were Serbs, at the same time determining only Čakavian speakers as real Croats. Here too Vuk was not original, but followed the opinion of the most outstanding expert in Slavic languages of the time, Fran Miklošič, who, to the end of his life, distinguished between the "Serbian" language (i.e., the Štokavian dialect) and the "Croatian" language (i.e., Čakavian). Clearly, with the advantage of hindsight, Miklošič and Karadžić were wrong, as indeed Kopitar himself was once. Respectfully but polemically, the Zagreb philologist Bogoslav Šulek replied to Vuk in 1856. In his rejoinder of 1861, Vuk changed his original opinion considerably, admitting that there could be Croats among the Catholic Štokavian speakers, and allowing that the confession of a particular faith might play a role as one criterion for national determination.

The ideas that the language of an uneducated rural population might form the model for the literary language and that dialectal pluralism could exist in the literary language were never explicitly corrected by Vuk. He supported them eloquently at the beginning, and later silently, abandoning them unnoticed at the end.

It was in 1821 that Vuk first demanded a selective attitude from writers toward the dialects of the simple people: "If writers have any power in language, I think that it consists in this, that in grammatical matters which are undecided among ordinary people, they choose what is correct." This is Vuk's first mention of grammatical correctness as a concept independent of the dialectal authenticity of a linguistic form.

We have very few statements by Vuk on the literary language or at least very few new attitudes dating from the 1820s and the first half of the 1830s. This was the period of Vuk's hardest work and intellectual maturing. Expanding his knowledge and experience, he gradually outgrew his intellectual dependence on Kopitar. In lively contact with the processes of formation of the Serbian literary language, he had the opportunity to better understand the phenomena of the literary language and the needs of Serbian society in that sphere. He certainly reflected on the reaction of the Serbian public to his writings; he was too wise not to become concerned about why not even his friends approved of him in some matters.

In 1836 Vuk introduced into his language the writing of the letter *h* in words of Slavic origin (until then he had written *h* only in international loanwords and in foreign names). Vuk made this change only when he had made sure that the consonant *h* was pronounced in the living dialects of Dubrovnik, Boka Kotorska, and Montenegro. This was the first time he had applied his new idea of the literary language as a selective combination of the features of various dialects. Such an approach is in conflict with his earlier viewpoint that writers should use authentic folk dialects. Nevertheless, Vuk remained loyal to his principle that nothing must enter the literary language which does not exist at least somewhere in folk dialects (it is understood that this principle does not refer to vocabulary, although Vuk did not stress this point specifically). The distance between this and Vuk's former concepts of the literary language is best illustrated by his claim of 1836 that if there is something "more beautiful and correct" in Boka Kotorska than that which is spoken elsewhere, "it should be taken into the general Serbian language," although there were no more than thirty thousand inhabitants of that region. On the other hand, Vuk in 1836 repeated the idea that every writer ought to use his own dialect. But this, as the context shows, was only his defense of his own practice of writing in Ijekavian: he was not prepared to renounce his native dialect nor was he able to impose it on Ekavian speakers; therefore he allowed dialectal pluralism in literature (reduced in reality to the difference between two types of reflex for the vowel *ě*). Vuk failed to notice here that his new vision of the literary language as a selection of features from various dialects excluded the freedom of writing in any actual dialect. Besides, in Vuk's 1836 formulation, his liberal attitude toward dialects was accompanied by a considerable restriction: writers were to use their own dialects *for the time being,* until the public became well acquainted with the features of the dialects, and then a general literary language would be formed itself with time, according to the rules by which literary languages were formed in other nations too.

In 1839, Vuk introduced further changes into his literary language, the most important of which was the writing of *tje* and *dje* instead of *će* and *đe* in cases where dental plosives were followed by short *ě*. Vuk found support for this too in the dialect of Dubrovnik; as early as 1822 he had mentioned that this feature was present in Sarajevo and other Bosnian towns. He accompanied his innovation with the explanation that this was "the urban, gentlemanly (*gospodski*) variety" of the Ijekavian dialect. This was a break with his theory of peasant dialect as the model for the literary language. The whole course of the discussion until then had shown that this attitude was untenable in principle, and Vuk reached out to urban dialects outside the Vojvodina, as soon as he had the opportunity, as models to which the literary language should conform. (It should not be forgotten that the towns of the Vojvodina were the main strongholds of his antagonists and that in order to discredit them he had often stressed that people made more language mistakes in the Vojvodina, particularly in the towns, than anywhere else, and that the writers in those places erred the most.) His altered attitude toward rural speech is also typified by the passage dated 1839 in which Vuk instructs his opponent Svetić to first "study the *spoken* language" (Vuk's italics)—thus the *spoken,* not the *rural* language—if he wishes to write well.

An analysis of the changes which Vuk introduced into his language in 1836 and 1839 (Ivić 1966) shows that his interventions were directed toward archaizing the literary language to a certain extent, bringing it closer to the other Slavic literary languages, increasing the measure of grammatical consistency in the language and, as we already pointed out, giving it a base in certain urban dialects. The same criteria can be discerned even in the long lists of "corrupt" forms spoken by "the vulgar," which were rejected by Vuk in 1845. That year, Vuk also introduced the concept of "general correctness," but he did not define it. The context shows, however, that the above-mentioned criteria stand behind this concept, especially loyalty to older forms and inner grammatical correctness—both elements considered relevant even today in issues of accepting linguistic phenomena into literary languages.

Vuk's translation of the New Testament in 1847 brought a clarification of his attitudes to vocabulary. In his foreword he gave lists of words which he had used in the translation, although they were not used in the vernacular. He included 86 Church Slavonic words and 84 words which he himself had made up in the spirit of the folk language. Vuk showed by this very clearly that he understood that the vocabulary of a folk language is not sufficient to supply the needs of a literary language.

In conclusion, we can contend that Vuk, remaining firm in his fundamental point of view that the popular language should be the basis of the literary, corrected his view in the following ways: (1) he abandoned the idea that rural dialects are better than urban as a model for a literary language; (2) the Romantic liberal attitude toward dialectal pluralism in literature was replaced by a conscious striving toward linguistic unity, not on the basis of a single local dialect but a selection of the features of various dialects, executed according to sociolinguistic and internal linguistic criteria. (Indeed, Vuk more or less tolerated the coexistence of the Ekavian and Ijekavian varieties in the literary language until the end of his life, but this was evidently a historical inevitability.)

In both cases, Vuk was on the right road. His attitude toward the Serbian literary language was sober and responsible. He was right in deviating from Kopitar's advice in some matters. Although Kopitar's knowledge of linguistics was far greater than Vuk's, Vuk better understood what a literary language is. This was natural. Owing to historical circumstances, and perhaps because of his personal characteristics, Vuk was in a different position from Kopitar: not of dreaming about the literary language of his people but of creating and nurturing it. Vuk had all the traits of a fighter capable of winning and putting his ideas into practice. This means that he was not only a visionary but also a realist.

Works Cited

Belić, Aleksandar 1948. *Vukova borba za narodni i književni jezik.* Beograd: Prosveta.

Ivić, Pavle 1966. *Dva aspekta Vukovog dela.* Vukov Zbornik, Beograd: Srpska akademija nauka i umetnosti, Posebna izdanja t. 400, 63-71.

Ivić, Pavle 1971. *Srpski narod i njegov jezik.* Beograd: Srpska književna zadruga, kolo LXIV, knjiga 429.

Karadžić, Vuk 1894-1896. *Skupljeni gramatički i polemički spisi Vuka Stef. Karadžića.* Beograd: Državno izdanje. I, 1894. II/1, 1894. II/2, 1895. III/1, 1896, III/2, 1896.

Kopitar, Barth. 1857. *Kleinere Schriften.* Erster Theil. Wien: Friedrich Beck's Universitätsbuchhandlung.

Lencek, Rado 1976. *A Few Remarks for the History of the Term "Serbo-croatian" Language,* Zbornik za filologijui lingvistiku XIX/1, 45-53.

Pogačnik, Jože 1973. *Kopitarjeva zamisel o kulturnozgodovinskem razvoju pri južnih Slovanih.* Referati za VII medunarodni kongres slavista u Varšavi. Novi Sad: Filozofski fakultet u Novom Sadu, 121-139.

Thomas Butler (essay date 1982)

SOURCE: Butler, Thomas. "Jernej Kopitar and South Slavic Folklore." In *Papers in Slavic Philology 2: To Honor Jernej Kopitar 1780-1980,* edited by Rado L. Lencek and Henry R. Cooper, Jr., pp. 109-21. Ann Arbor: University of Michigan, 1982.

[*In the following essay, Butler examines Jernej Kopitar's support of Karadžić and the importance of both to South Slavic folklore studies.*]

Jernej Kopitar's role in promoting the collection and popularization of South Slavic folklore, as well as the establishment of a scientific basis for its investigation, has never been adequately examined nor sufficiently appreciated. When the Slovene's name is mentioned within the context of folklore it is usually in connection with his encouragement and support of the activities of Vuk Karadžić (1787-1864), the foremost collector and publisher of Serbo-Croatian folksongs, as well as the reformer of the Serbo-Croatian literary language.

Scholars have tended to regard Kopitar's strong support for Vuk's folklore activities within the framework of a larger interest, namely, the establishment of a new Serbian literary language based on the spoken language of the peasantry. The responsibility for this distorted focus on the Slovene's contributions to the folklore field must, at least in part, be laid at the door of Kopitar himself, for on many an occasion, in reviews and articles, he pointed to the high aesthetic quality and expressive language of the folksongs as proof of the superiority of Vuk's new literary language over the "macaronic language" (mixed Serbian and Russian Slavonic) of his opponents. The following paper will attempt to offer a more accurate picture of Kopitar as a folklorist by examining his development in this field as a separate phenomenon, without reference (as much as this is possible) to any of his other interests in the area of *slavica*.

Jernej Kopitar had outstanding assets for a South Slavic folklorist. First, he was a true man of the people; the son of peasants, he grew up on a farm and spoke only Slovene for the first nine years of his life. In his autobiographical sketch, written in 1839 and included in his *Kleinere Schriften,* Kopitar tells us that he knew "not a syllable of German" when he left his native village of Repnje and went to Ljubljana to attend the gymnasium.[1] Kopitar knew the rural Slavic agricultural milieu in a way no city dweller ever could; he understood Slavic folk ways because he had lived them, and throughout his scholarly career he maintained an interest not only in the folksongs but in the folk customs as well. He also never lost his instinct for what was authentic folklore and what was false.

Kopitar's work as the secretary to Baron Sigismund Zois, from 1799 to 1808, certainly contributed to his development as a scholar. While living in Zois' house he played an active role in the efforts of a Zois-led group to revive the Slovene literary language on the basis of Adelung's principles, which stressed the spoken language as the ultimate arbiter of correct usage ("schreib wie du sprichst").[2] During this period Zois and his brother gleaned hundreds of words in the fields of botany and mineralogy from among the country folk; and the poet Valentin Vodnik, who was preparing a German-Slovene dictionary, copied down Slovene folksongs as well.[3] Although Kopitar's *Selbstbiographie* offers no information on the subject, it does seem possible that young Jernej made folksong-collecting forays into his own native region during this period. This would have been a natural thing for him to do, not only in competition with Vodnik, but also in sympathy with the romantic enthusiasm for everything "folk" then prevailing in Europe.

Kopitar's classical education, plus his natural facility in learning foreign languages, also contributed to his development as a folklorist. Not only was he able to read the Homeric epic poems in the original Greek, but he was also able to read Macpherson's *Ossian* and the modern Greek folksongs as well. Perhaps the single most important "event" in the Slovene's development as a folklorist was his reading of Goethe's translation of the "Hasanaginica," published in Herder's *Volkslieder* in 1778. A poetic jewel in its own right, Goethe's "Klaggesang von der edlen Frauen des Asan Aga" made such a deep impression on Kopitar that he referred to it in his Slovene *Grammar* (1808)[4] and continued to refer to it in his writings on Serbo-Croatian folklore in subsequent years. In an age when all of Europe was awakening to the value of its folklore, this exquisite Moslem ballad was like a single Slavic nugget that continually enticed the young scholar with the thought that somewhere in the Balkans there was a "mother lode" of folksongs which would prove that the Slavic bards were the equal, if not the superiors, of their Germanic and Celtic counterparts. And not only were Kopitar, Zois, and Vodnik interested in Slavic folksongs, but the Patriarch of Slavic linguistics himself, Josef Dobrovský, wrote to Kopitar from Prague (in answer to an earlier letter), enquiring about the existence of South Slavic folksongs and folk ways.[5]

When Kopitar moved to Vienna in 1809, he asked his newfound Serbian and Croatian friends whether they knew any songs like the "Hasanaginica" or the poems in Kačić-Miošić's *Razgovor ugodni*.[6] In a letter to Dobrovský from Vienna in 1809, the Slovene writes, "First of all, I asked my new Serbian friends about the Serbian folksongs, such as those about Kraljević Marko, etc."[7] In that letter he also included a pair of Croatian folksongs he had taken down from a Croatian border guard. During the early years in Vienna he began to study Serbo-Croatian seriously, making a chart of the differences between "Serbian" and his native tongue. (About this same time he became convinced that there was no essential difference between Serbian and Croatian.[8]) In 1810, at the wedding in Vienna of his former student Bonazza (Zois' nephew), Kopitar met the Croatian Bishop Maximilian Vrhovac. He asked Vrhovac's help in finding the Croatian folk treasure, and he eventually persuaded the Bishop to send out a circular letter to all his parish priests asking them to write down words, folk expressions, folksongs, and customs, and ordering them to keep a notebook of all old Slavic books and manuscripts in their parishes.[9] But this attempt was largely unsuccessful, and Vrhovac sent the Slovene few songs.

Kopitar then decided to try the Serbs. On 24 June 1811 he wrote the head of the Serbian Orthodox Church in Austria, Bishop Stefan Stratimirović, asking for the name of a Serb with whom he could correspond regarding *serbica*.[10] Stratimirović put him in touch with the archimandrite Lukijan Mušicki, who was a lover of folklore and a poet as well. In a letter to Mušicki in 1811 Kopitar mentioned Goethe's translation of the "Hasanaginica" and comments on the song's "depth of feeling." He also discussed the puzzling (for non-Moslems) question of Hasan Aga's wife's refusal to visit her wounded husband in his tent ("a ljubovca od stida nije mogla"). And in this same letter he also continued his quest for authentic examples of folksongs: "If only a better Kačić would turn up among the Illyrians, one who would collect the most beautiful songs of every type, then the Serbs and Croats would have a treasure like perhaps no one else!"[11] Kopitar's hopes for maintaining a scholarly correspondence with Mušicki were largely unsatisfied, the Serb being a poor correspondent.

In his early review articles too, Kopitar referred to the need for a skilled collector of South Slavic folklore. In an article entitled "Slavische Sprachkunde," published in the Vienna periodical *Annalen für Literatur und Kunst* (II, 1811, 52-68), while reviewing a new Croatian grammar, he suddenly stops and exclaims: "One more time! The Croats have such beautiful folksongs that Goethe and Herder translated several of them in the collections of their immortal works. Can no one be found who will collect them in a more critical and more complete way than did Kačić?"[12] In the same article Kopitar also cites the first lines of four folksongs from a Jesuit songbook, included with a Croatian evangelium first published in 1619.[13] The Jesuit gave the first lines of the peasant songs to show the airs to which he wanted church hymns sung ("Poszejal szem basulek, poszejal szem, draga ljuba," "Igralo kolo široko," etc.). Kopitar asks: "Does anyone know whether these four folksongs have been preserved among the people?"[14] Later scholars, including Vatroslav Jagić, followed the Slovene scholar's lead, using the old church hymnals as sources for the history of Slavic song.[15]

Kopitar's persistent search for a qualified collector of South Slavic folklore was finally crowned with success when he met Vuk Karadžić in 1813. A refugee from the recently suppressed Serbian uprising against the Ottoman Empire (more precisely, against some renegade local rulers called the *dahije*), Vuk had written a pamphlet in which he discussed the causes for the failure of the Serbian *ustanak*. Since Kopitar was by now the Censor for all Slavic books in the Austrian lands, Vuk's manuscript came into his hands for approval. In Vuk's own words: "This manuscript of mine came into the hands of Mr. Kopitar, as Censor, and when he recognized from it . . . that I was a man of the people, and that I was different from all the Serbs he had seen and known . . . he came to my place to see me."[16] Now we do not know precisely what it was in Vuk's pamphlet that drove Kopitar to seek him out, but it was most likely Vuk's language, which would have been closer to spoken Serbo-Croatian than the language of Kopitar's Serbian friends Davidović and Frušić (the editors of the new Serbian newspaper in Vienna, *Novine Serbske*), and certainly purer than the written language of Dositej Obradović, whose works the Slovene had already reviewed.[17] It is also possible that in his pamphlet Vuk quoted some lines from the Serbian epic poems about the uprising. Whatever the cause of his initial interest, Kopitar quickly ascertained that Vuk knew Serbian folksongs and that he had access to other Serbs who knew songs, and so the Censor soon convinced him to begin preparation of a small book.

Vuk's first book of songs, **Mala prostonarodnja slaveno-serbska pjesnarica,** was published in Vienna in 1814. That same year the German folklorist Jakob Grimm came to the Austrian capital as a member of the Hesse-Cassel delegation to the Vienna Congress. It was Kopitar who met Grimm and told him of Vuk's songbook and persuaded the German to study Serbo-Croatian so that he might be able to read the songs in the original. Grimm wrote a review of the **Pjesnarica** for the *Wiener allgemeine Literaturzeitung* in 1815, at Kopitar's suggestion.[18] In his review Grimm disclaimed his own competence to judge the purity of the **Pjesnarica**'s language (to which Kopitar commented, in a footnote: "It is highly correct!"), but instead he analyzed the meter and the imagery of the songs, comparing them to German folk verse. Grimm's thoughtful review was the first scholarly critique of Serbo-Croatian folklore.

In persuading a scholar of the German's caliber to review Vuk's **Pjesnarica,** Jernej Kopitar not only enhanced the prestige of the songs among educated Serbs and Germans, but what is even more important he managed through Jakob Grimm to establish South Slavic folklore collecting on a scholarly basis from the very start. Grimm's concern for purity (authenticity) of language, his request for details concerning the singers, the music of the songs, and the circumstances of their recording—all these essential elements helped shape the framework within which future South Slavic folklore collecting would be carried out. Grimm also sent Vuk (via Kopitar) a circular on the proper method for collecting folklore, one which he had recently printed for use throughout the German-speaking lands.[19] The German folklorist's influence on Slavic folklore collecting was not confined to the South Slavic area alone, however; Max Vasmer has shown that Grimm also had a strong influence on nineteenth-century Russian folklorists, including Hil'ferding, Afanasyev, and Snegiryov.[20] It does not seem an overstatement then to say that Jernej Kopitar's enthusiasm for Slavic folklore, which led him to seek out Jakob Grimm and persuade him to study Slavic languages and folklore, had a profound effect on the collection and preservation of folklore in the Slavic world.

Vuk's second book of songs, **Srpske narodne pjesme** (1815), was reviewed by Kopitar himself anonymously, since the book was dedicated to him.[21] The reviewer begins by stating that this book contains the first and only examples of pure Serbo-Croatian published to date. He shows the breadth of his Balkan interests, as he compares the Serbian songs to the modern Greek: "Only the peasants and the hajduk poets, who can neither read nor write, express themselves in pure Greek, as here in pure Serbian." The reviewer compliments his protegé for reproducing the songs exactly as they were sung, reflecting for example the dialect differences between Bačka and Hercegovina. He also compliments Vuk for giving the music for some of the songs (here Vuk was helped by the Polish composer Mirecki), and for giving biographical details about the singers.

Kopitar showed his classical background in his review, as he compared the singer Filip Višnjić's "Početak bune protiv Dahije," a song about the beginning of the Serbian uprising in 1804, with Homer's *Iliad*: "It is twice as long as Homer's catalog of ships in the *Iliad*!" the excited Slovene exclaimed. In this review and elsewhere he began to refer to the Serbian epic poets as "Homeriden," and in 1819 he wrote the German scholar F. Wolf, author of *Prolegomena ad Homerum* (1795), to advise him that a study of the Serbo-Croatian epic songs would be a useful approach to understanding the composition of the Homeric epics themselves.[22] This insight anticipated the direction of later scholars such as Murko, Parry, and Lord.

Having established through Vuk the existence of a rich store of Balkan Slavic song, and having promoted the publication of two books of these songs, Jernej Kopitar began to concern himself with their poetic translation into German. He hoped that such a translation might convince European scholars and literati of the wealth and beauty of Slavic folklore. In reviewing Vuk's second songbook, the Vienna Censor had asked whether "some Goethe might also transplant these magnificent flowers onto the German Parnassus." Kopitar did not mention that he himself had already translated into German 107 songs from Vuk's *Pje-*

snarica, and had sent them to Goethe with a "Vorbericht" in which he advised the great poet that Vuk Karadžić, the collector and publisher of these songs, was a refugee from Serbia, and that it was only after he had seen Herder's *Volkslieder* and Goethe's translation of the "Hasanaginica" that he was persuaded to write down the songs.[23] The Slovene, who signed himself simply "Kop.," without giving any further clue to his identity, probably hoped that the renowned poet would rework his simple prose translations into a poetic German. This Goethe did not do, but he did keep the translations, and they did serve a useful purpose later, as we shall see.

Kopitar also tried to get his friend Jakob Grimm to do a poetic translation of the songs. He hounded Grimm to no avail, since the German folklorist did not believe it possible to translate poetry successfully. (On the other hand, Grimm did translate two songs for Goethe's journal *Über die Kunst und Alterthum,* and he is also believed to have translated the nineteen Serbo-Croatian songs in F. Förster's *Sängerfahrt* [1818], although this has been the subject of some dispute, some scholars preferring to ascribe the latter translations to Kopitar.)[24] Kopitar even tried to persuade Mušicki to do a German version of the **Pjesnarica,** but this attempt also failed.[25]

But as was the case with his years-long quest for a collector of the songs, Kopitar's search for a translator was eventually successful. A Fräulein Theresa Albertine Louisa von Jakob, later known to the literary world by her acronym Talvj, inspired by Grimm's review of Vuk's 1823 (Leipzig) edition of the folksongs, as well as by Goethe's connection with the Serbo-Croatian lore, sent Goethe her own translations of a few of Vuk's songs. Goethe accepted the translations for publication in his journal and suggested that she do a full book of songs. He sent her Kopitar's 107 translations to help her on her way.[26] Now Talvj is said to have known both Russian and Church Slavonic, languages which she learned during the course of several years spent in Russia with her schoolteacher father.[27] Yet she did not know Serbo-Croatian, and so she wrote Kopitar on 23 May 1824, seeking the Slovene linguist's aid:

> Your Excellency may pardon the boldness with which I, a complete stranger, propose a correspondence of which I have a very definite need. The impossibility to find here . . . advice on the Serbian language and . . . the lack of tools . . . all of this gives me the courage; and the actual part which your Excellency played in furthering Vuk's own undertaking gives me the hope that you will not refuse to give your kind attention to my translations.[28]

An examination of Talvj's correspondence with the Vienna Censor in the period 1824-1826, and a comparison of her translations with the 107 translations first sent to Goethe by "Kop.," will show that she was closely dependent on both Kopitar and Vuk in the preparation of her two-volume *Volkslieder der Serben* (Halle, 1825-1826). She nagged Kopitar and Vuk to send her more German prose translations of the folksongs, and she also borrowed heavily from the German translations published by the Slovene in Hormayr's *Archiv.*[29] But even while imploring their advice and guidance, she also complained bitterly when Kopitar did not allow her "muse" sufficient freedom. She preferred freer and more Germanized translations, at least in the beginning of her translating activity, while the Slovene, like Grimm, wanted a close and nearly literal rendition. Although Kopitar refused to allow her to mention his name in the foreword to her book, denying her translation of the protection of his "scholarly authority" (her words), she did manage to acknowledge his role in a later edition of the book, which appeared several years after the scholar's death.[30]

Kopitar's efforts to gain Serbo-Croatian folklore a European audience were further enhanced by the publication of English and French editions of the songs, based on Talvj's German translations. John Bowring (*Servian Popular Poetry* [London, 1827]) had been in correspondence with Kopitar and had received two volumes of the songs in the original Serbo-Croatian. But this was hardly necessary, because he simply pirated Talvj's work, barely acknowledging his debt to her. Elise Voiart (*Chants populaires des Serviens recueillis par Wuk Stephanowitsch et traduits d'après Talvj, I-II* [Paris, 1834]) freely acknowledged her debt to Talvj, as the title of her book indicates.

The Talvj, Bowring, and Voiart editions of the Serbo-Croatian folksongs represented the culmination of the Slovene scholar's efforts in the folklore field, and the fulfillment of a task he had pursued over the course of some twenty years: to find the missing mother lode of South Slavic lore; to have it published in the original; and then to have the songs translated so that they might reach the broadest possible audience. It is true that he had a simultaneous interest in the establishment of a new Serbo-Croatian literary language based on the spoken language of the peasantry, but this was a separate goal; and while the two interests were inevitably intertwined at times (the beauty of the songs serving as a justification for the new literary language), still it would be an injustice to Jernej Kopitar not to view his folklore activities independently, as a pioneering effort which influenced not only the scholarly level at which South Slavic songs were collected and studied, but which also affected (through Grimm) the level of folklore scholarship in Russia as well.

Notes

1. Jernej Kopitar, "Selbstbiographie," in *Kleinere Schriften, I* (cited hereafter as *KS*), ed. Franz Miklosich (Vienna, 1857), p. 3. Note that the German form of Kopitar's given name, Bartholomäus, appears on his writings.

2. Johann C. Adelung, *Deutsche Sprachlehre zum Gebrauche der Schulen in den könig. preuss. Länden* (Berlin, 1781), p. 577.

3. Nestor M. Petrovskij, *Pervye gody dejatel'nosti V. Kopitara* (Kazan', 1906), p. 29.

4. Bartholomäus Kopitar, *Grammatik der slavischen Sprache in Krain, Kärnten und Steyermark* (Laibach, 1808).

5. Dobrovský wrote Kopitar in 1809: "Gibt es erweislich alte Volkslieder? Sind sie 4 oder 8-sylbig? . . . Wer hat sich in Liedern (oder der Poesie) vor andern, früh oder spät ausgezeichnet? Gibt es Fabeln oder Räthsel? Gibt es gedruckte Sammlungen von Sprichwörtern?" In *Pis'ma Dobrovskogo i Kopitara v povremennom porjadke,* ed. Vatroslav Jagič, *Sbornik ORJaS AN,* 39 (St. Petersburg, 1885), p. 28.

6. Kačić-Miošić (1704-1760) published the first edition of his *Razgovor ugodni naroda slovinskoga* (A Pleasant Discourse about the Slavic People) in Venice in 1756. Kačić enlivened his history of the Slavs with poems about famous battles and leaders. Most of these poems are of his own composition, and although they have a folk style they also have elements such as rhyme which distinguish them from the true oral epic. For a while Kopitar believed, as did others, that Kačić had taken these songs from the folk bards. In a review of Dobrovský's *Slovanka* he said of Kačić's *Razgovor*: ". . . worin viele serbische Heldenlieder vorkommen und der daher unter allen mit lateinischen Buchstaben gedruckten Büchern allein auch von Orthodoxen Serben gelesen wird." (In *Wiener allgemeine Literaturzeitung* [hereafter *WALZ*] II (1814); *KS,* p. 287.) In a letter to Vuk, dated 27 May 1814, he urged the Serb to republish Kačić's songs but in a Serbian text: "Die Krainer schreiben mir: Es gehört die Beharrlichkeit eines Vuk dazu, um aus der schlechten und fehlervollen Orthographie des Kacsich den serbischen Text herzustellen. . . . Kein Volk wird dann so schöne Volkslieder aufzuweisen haben, als das Serbische." (*Vukova prepiska* [ed. Ljub. Stojanović] I, p. 134.) Vuk stalled Kopitar by pointing out that since Serbs had already read Kačić in latin letters he doubted they would buy the same book again in cyrillic. (*Vukova prepiska,* I, p. 136.) But within nine months Kopitar figured out that Kačić's songs were not authentic folk songs, but his own. On 21 March 1815 he wrote to Vuk: "Eben sehe ich, dass Kačić nicht gesammelt, sondern sie alles selbst gemacht hat, und zwar im serbischen Metro, aber dazu noch gereimt. (*Vukova prepiska,* I, 143-44.) And just three days later he wrote Dobrovský: "Video Cacichium plerasque ipsum fecisse, modis quidem serbicis, sed tamen a se . . . factas etc." (*Pis'ma Dobrovskogo i Kopitara,* op. cit., p. 401.)

7. Ibid., 35-36.

8. On 1 February 1810 he wrote Dobrovský: "Kroatischer und Serbischer Dialekt sind synonyma." (*Pis'ma Dobrovskogo i Kopitara,* op. cit., p. 87.)

9. Bishop Vrhovac's circular letter of 26 June 1813 is cited by Matthias Murko in his *Deutsche Einflüsse auf die Anfänge der böhmischen Romantik* (Graz, 1897), p. 10. Murko quotes Vrhovac's circular: "Omnes cuiusvis generis cantilenas croaticas aut slavonicas cum adnotatione, quantum constaret, quando, et a quo . . . opportune colligat et haec omnia ad me successive transmittat." The full circular was first published in *Danica ilirska* in 1837 (no. 24). It was later republished in *Kolo,* IX, 43-46.

10. *Novye pis'ma Dobrovskogo, Kopitara, i drugix jugozapadnyx slavjan,* ed. Vatroslav Jagič, *Sbornik ORJaS AN,* 62 (St. Petersburg, 1897), 779-80.

11. Ibid., p. 786.

12. *KS,* p. 46.

13. *Szveti Evangeliumi, koteremi szveta czirkva katholiczka szlovenszko-horvaczka sivée* (Czeska Ternava, 1694), 12th edition.

14. *KS,* p. 47.

15. See Vatroslav Jagić's article "Gradja za slovensku narodnu poeziju," in *Rad JAZU,* XXXVIII (1876), 33-137.

16. Quoted from Vuk's article "Pravi uzrok i početak skupljanja našijeh narodnijeh pjesama," republished in Vuk Karadžić, *Skupljeni gramatički i polemički spisi,* III, ed. L. L. Djordjević (Belgrade, 1896), p. 66.

17. Kopitar wrote several early articles designed to bring the works of Dositej Obradović to the attention of the Austrian reading public. He translated "Bruchstücke" from Obradović's autobiography, *Život i priključenija,* including the "letter to Haralampije" (Dositej's manifesto on the new Serbian literary language); he also published a "Vollständiger Auszug" from the same work, and wrote a eulogy to the Serbian "Anacharsis" after Obradović's death. All three Kopitar pieces are reprinted in *KS,* 49-56, 79-94, and 113-120.

18. Jakob Grimm's review of the *Pjesnarica* in *WALZ* in 1815 was republished in his *Kleinere Schriften,* IV, 427-36 (1869 edition). In his very thoughtful review Grimm touches upon the connection between a scarcity of written culture and a rich and vital folklore: "Unter allen slawischen Völkerstämmen sind diese Serben mit ihrer sanften, überaus singbaren Sprache, zum voraus begabt mit Lied, Gesang, und Sage, und es scheint, als ob der gütige Himmel ihnen ihre Bücherlosigkeit durch einen Haussegen von Volkspoesie stets habe ersetzen wollen"; op. cit., p. 436.

19. Jakob Grimm, "Circular wegen Aufsammlung der Volkspoesie" (Vienna, 1815).

20. Max Vasmer, in *Bausteine zur Geschichte der deutsch-slavischen geistigen Beziehungen,* I (Berlin, 1939), writes concerning Grimm's influence on the Russian folklorists: "Was die Sammlung Hilferdings (Onežskije byliny) besonders wertvoll macht, ist die genaue Beachtung der Eigenart der einzelnen Liedersänger und die treue Beibehaltung der sprachlichen Form. Beides hatte Grimm in seinen Besprechungen von Vuks Serbischen Liedern gefordert"; op. cit., p. xxxi.

21. Kopitar's review appeared in *WALZ* in 1816, 314-33. It is also in his *KS*, 347-69.

22. Max Vasmer, op. cit., p. xxxix, quotes Kopitar's letter to F. A. Wolf, dated 26 March 1819: "Nirgends gibt es noch heute zu Tage treffendere Pendants zu Ihren Homeriden, als in Serbien und Bosnien."

23. Jevto Milović, *Übertragungen slavischer Volkslieder aus Goethes Briefnachlass* (Veröffentlichungen des Slavischen Instituts an der Fried.-Wilhelms-Universität Berlin, 28) (Leipzig, 1939), p. viii.

24. The "neunzehn serbische Lieder" in Förster's *Die Sängerfahrt: Eine Neujahrsgabe für Freunde der Dichtkunst und Malerei* (Berlin, 1818), are included both in the collected works of Jakob Grimm (*KS*, IV [1869], 455-67) and of Jernej Kopitar (*Jerneja Kopitarja Spisov II del*, 1 knjiga [Ljubljana, 1944]). Rajko Nahtigal, editor of the latter volume, gives a long discussion (72-75) of the dispute over the authorship of the nineteen translations in Förster's book.

25. Vuk wrote to Mušicki, relaying to him Kopitar's suggestion that the archimandrite should translate the poems "for the honor of the Serbian nation and language." *Novye pis'ma*, p. 798.

26. The Kopitar-Goethe-Talvj connection is discussed by Jevto Milović (op. cit., p. xi).

27. For information on Talvj's life see Irma E. Voigt, *Life and Works of Mrs. Theresa Robinson* (Talvj) (Chicago, 1913).

28. See Jevto Milović, *Talvjs erste Übertragungen für Goethe und ihre Briefe an Kopitar* (Vëroffentlichungen des Slavischen Instituts an der Friedrich-Wilhelms-Universität Berlin, 33) (Leigzig, 1941), p. 36.

29. Kopitar published his translation of Višnjić's "Početak bune protiv Dahije," ("Der Aufstand der Serbier gegen die Dahijen"), in Hormayer's *Archiv für Geographie, Historie, Staats- und Kriegskunst*, in January 1818 (republished in *Jerneja Kopitarja Spisov II del*, knj. 1, 28-45); in March of that same year he published three more translations of epic songs from the Serbian uprising: "O bitki srbskoj s Turcima na Salašu"; "O bitki srbskoj s Turcima na Mišarskom polju," and "O smrti Mehe Orukčića" (republished in ibid, knj. 1, 45-72). Kopitar's translations are accompanied by interesting notes which show that he was not a mere dilettante but a scholar who had studied the cultural background of these songs as well. For example, in one note he reminds the reader that the Bosnian Turks are not real Turks, but Serbs who profess the Koran: "they seldom know any Turkish, but just Serbian" (ibid., p. 67). Kopitar also sprinkles his commentary with references to the ancient Greek epics; for example, in a note to "O smrti Mehe Orukčića," where the singer hails the land of Pozerje, home of the hero Miloš Stojčevič, the Slovene writes: "Wir enthalten uns hier aller Parallelen mit der dankbaren altgriechischen Sitte, auch den Geburtsort des Helden zu preisen; sie ist in der Natur der Sache gegründet" (ibid., p. 71).

30. In the introduction to the third edition of her *Volkslieder der Serben* (Leipzig, 1853), published nine years after Kopitar's death, Talvj wrote: "Ich würde nicht den Muth gehabt haben, meine Versuche dem Publikum zu übergeben, wenn nicht der ausgezeichnete slavische Gelehrte Kopitar aus Liebe zur Sache übernommen hätte, mein Manuscript durchzusehen" (op. cit., I, p. xxxviii).

Benjamin Stolz (essay date 1982)

SOURCE: Stolz, Benjamin. "Kopitar and Vuk: An Assessment of Their Roles in the Rise of the New Serbian Literary Language." In *Papers in Slavic Philology 2: To Honor Jernej Kopitar 1780-1980*, edited by Rado L. Lencek and Henry R. Cooper, Jr., pp. 151-67. Ann Arbor: University of Michigan, 1982.

[*In the following essay, Stolz considers Jernej Kopitar's support of Karadžić and asserts that their collaborative effort developed a Serbian literary language.*]

The scholarly literature on Jernej (Bartholomäus) Kopitar and Vuk Karadžić is so voluminous—and so much has been added already on this subject by competent investigators right here at this conference—that anyone who approaches the topic runs the risk of mere repetition, with slight reinterpretation, or of loose speculation and reckless theorizing. Still, the contribution of Jernej Kopitar and Vuk Karadžić to the rise of the modern Serbian literary language retains its fascination, for it is surely one of the most dramatic stories of individual intervention in the history of any literary language, Slavic or non-Slavic. The roles of Kopitar and Vuk deserve reexamination, for the impact of their collaboration can now be more accurately and dispassionately measured. Recent research, the increasing availability of published source materials connected with Vuk's career, and the evolution of the Serbian (and Serbo-Croatian) literary language in the two hundred years since the birth of Kopitar have placed all of us in a relatively favorable position.

Both men rose from South Slavic peasant origins, but beyond that their backgrounds diverged sharply: Kopitar, a learned Slovene Catholic with a classical education, was one of the greatest Slavists of his era; Karadžić, an Orthodox Serb who was to become his brilliant protégé in Vienna, had only a sporadic formal education and had functioned as a scribe and civil servant in unlettered rebel Serbia prior to the collapse of the first Uprising in 1813. Kopitar's romantic attitude toward vernacular language and folklore and his particularly strong interest in Serbian are evident in his correspondence as well as his publications, much of it dating from before his meeting with Vuk. It is clear that Kopitar owed a great deal to his European contemporaries and precursors: Herder, Grimm, Dobrovský, Schlözer, and Adelung. He cites Schlözer in support of his notion that truly vernacular-based literary languages are a prerequisite for culture among the emerging nations: "Culture does not begin among the peoples until they write in their own languages."[1]

Earlier, in his Slovene grammar Kopitar had mused along Herderian lines on the history of the Slavs. "One can think what the same religion, the same literary language—and why not also [living] under a single leader, a Slavic Vladimir ('World-ruler')—might have done even earlier for this gigantic nation?" He goes on to list a number of disadvantages suffered by the Slavic peoples: (1) the Great Schism, with the resultant split of Christianity into Eastern and Western churches; (2) the introduction of the Latin rite in those Slavic lands under the Western church, preventing the use of the Slavic tongues for liturgical purposes; (3) the subjugation of the Slavs (whom he describes as "peaceful farmers who in their innocence had forgotten to think ahead about war") by Magyars, Turks, Mongols, and Germans—with the result that "on the throne and in all state functions the language of the foreign conquerors rules, while the poor native language is banished to the huts of the conquered, who are declared bondsmen."[2] The situation, Kopitar tells us in a footnote, obtains for all the Slavs, except for the Russians, among whom the language of the folk is also the state language. A long discussion of orthographic problems ensues, with reference also to the difficulties engendered by the two alphabets, roman and cyrillic. Chaos reigns in the use of the roman alphabet in the West, including those Slavic languages where it is employed. "Only [let there be] an intelligent and strong leader and this anarchy too will vanish."[3]

Kopitar, despite certain misconceptions, had a keen awareness of the linguistic situation among the Serbs and Croats. He credited Dositej Obradović with being the first Serbian vernacular writer, and knew his works intimately; and as Censor for Slavic books in the Austrian Empire, he read and reviewed the works of later Serbian writers, criticising and praising them according to their mastery of the written vernacular. Kopitar's "Patriotische Phantasien eines Slaven," published in 1810, encapsulates his views on a number of important language issues three years prior to his meeting with Vuk. Dositej Obradović, among others, had noticed the close similarity of the West Balkan Slavic dialects; Kopitar echoed this, pointing out that while the Serbs as yet had neither a grammar nor dictionary of the vernacular language, "those of the Catholic Slaveno-Serbs [i.e., speakers of the three 'Illyrian' dialects—Ragusan, Bosnian, and Slavonian] are also usable here."[4] Vuk Karadžić was a Serbian nationalist and populist with an essentially rationalist outlook acquired through reading the works of Dositej Obradović. Vuk (like Kopitar) shared Dositej's conception of language, not religion, as the primary determinant of nationality. In meeting Kopitar, Vuk was drawn into the orbit of German Romanticism and became convinced of the need for a radical language reform among the Serbs—and one that would unite them with their Roman Catholic brothers. Ambitiously espousing Kopitar's program, he immediately undertook in turn the collection of verbal folklore and the compiling of a grammar and dictionary of the vernacular language.

A number of earlier researchers agree on the crucial role Kopitar played as Vuk's mentor. In essence, they say with varying degrees of emphasis what Aleksandar Belić wrote: "Jernej Kopitar made Vuk Karadžić the man that he was. All the ideas which Vuk set forth on the necessity of introducing the vernacular (*narodni jezik*) were also Kopitar's or were derived from his ideas. Vuk's reform was the work of the two of them, in which the primary initiative and the fundamental idea, and the whole plan, were given by Kopitar."[5] The Slovene Matija Murko had earlier expressed much the same thing: "Kopitar so to speak created the whole Vuk Karadžić . . .";[6] and elsewhere Murko called Kopitar "the man who found, taught, led, and supported Vuk Karadžić."[7] Rajko Nahtigal, the leading Slovene linguist of his day, wrote: "Without Kopitar, his help, support, and instruction, there would not have been the great reform work . . . by his genius student Vuk Stefanović Karadžić."[8] Vatroslav Jagić, whose critical judgment of Kopitar's career was both severe and humane, considered the collaboration with Vuk in the period up to the publication of Vuk's **Rječnik** (1818) to be Kopitar's most significant achievement, standing above all his polemics and critiques.[9] Quite naturally it is possible to find observers who would prefer to deemphasize Kopitar's role. N. Banašević, while admitting the importance of Kopitar in "the crystallization of Vuk's aspirations,"[10] disputes the notion that without him Vuk would have amounted to nothing. S. Nazečić[11] interprets Kopitar's guidance as an important but not overriding factor, arguing on the basis of letters and documents that Vuk in addition to his native intelligence had the experience, knowledge, and ambition that prepared him to accomplish the projects which he tackled in such swift succession after his arrival in Vienna.

Obviously there is a danger in viewing Vuk's journey to Vienna as a kind of linguistic Hegira, or in treating Kopitar and Vuk as if they were central characters in G. B. Shaw's "Pygmalion"—or Cyril and Methodius. The reality is never as simple as it is made to seem in textbooks. Nevertheless, even a cursory reading of Kopitar's and Vuk's relevant works, as well as their extensive correspondence, offers convincing evidence of the enormous part played by Kopitar in Vuk's emergence as a man of letters and language reformer. And at the same time it confirms Vuk's inherent strength and talent. To ask whether Vuk in fact followed the course set by Kopitar or whether and to what extent Vuk's own goals were achieved poses a different set of questions altogether. Ultimately, as we shall see, Kopitar's indirect role as a liaison between Vuk and the leading European scholars, intellectuals, and literati was to prove every bit as important as his direct influence upon him.

On many occasions public and private, Vuk himself credited Kopitar with launching his career. Sreznevskij asked Vuk how he became a man of letters. "Oh," he said,

"Here's what I think: Without this wooden leg, and without my good wife, and without the noble Kopitar, I wouldn't have been a *književnik*; and it also helped that I loved to travel. . . . But the main reason I became a *književnik* will always be Kopitar. In that regard I owe him, if not everything, then much, very much."[12]

Vuk's private correspondence with Kopitar is replete with gratitude for Kopitar's continuing guidance. In one of his earliest letters to Vuk, Kopitar spurs him on (Vienna, 21 March 1815): "Are you going ahead with collecting for the ***Song Book***? . . . With the ***Song Book*** as well as with the ***Grammar*** you are on the only true path. . . . Look for everything on Kraljević Marko. Also, about the ***Grammar*** (which I haven't been able to read through yet), collect for the second, third, etc., editions; it will go through twenty more, and even after our death will be called *Vuk's **Grammar***."[13] Vuk responds (Novi Sad, 18/30 March 1815) after answering about collecting folk songs: "I'm thinking about the grammar too, and have noted down some small points, and some of the learned Serbs have urged me to attend to it again; but that will be hard for me to undertake except at your place in Vienna, for without you neither the grammar nor the song book would ever see the light of day."[14]

Vuk's conscious effort to satisfy his mentor's taste for vernacular Serbian is apparent in a letter written a year later from Šišatovac (10 March 1816):

> This is the third year since I became acquainted with you. Since that time I have begun to go back and to get closer to the folk speech, and I still haven't come to the right place. The second part of the song book is purer than the first, and the grammar; but the third part of the grammar and the Serbian dictionary will be written and printed just exactly the way the people speak. It's a difficult thing when something gets twisted into a man's head from childhood!"[15]

And a week later Vuk, still in Šišatovac, writes joyfully (17 March 1816):

> Last night I received your letter and the review of the song book. Lucky Serbs, to have such a friend and admirer of their language and literature! But as for myself I can say nothing! . . . The dictionary will already be done in ten days (that is, all the words will be put in order); then I'll leave it here and go to Serbia especially on account of the dialects; from Serbia I intend to return (if the Serbs don't kill me) in July, and then I'll come to Vienna so that we can print it (the dictionary); without you nothing can be."[16]

Kopitar, in a letter to Jakob Grimm of 23 May 1829, expresses his high esteem for the young Leopold von Ranke, who had just finished his *Die serbische Revolution* with Vuk as his informant; Kopitar is careful to reaffirm Grimm's leading role as Vuk's intellectual sponsor in Germany: "He [Ranke] will make his fortune, and soon, and a brilliant one. Moreover, the Serbs also owe him such a real debt of gratitude. But you are and remain our first patron."[17] Demonstrating his constant solicitude for Vuk, Kopitar keeps Grimm informed of Vuk's activities. In letters of 1832 Kopitar discusses Vuk's difficulties in getting his translation of the New Testament published. Even Kopitar cannot help in Vienna, so strong is the opposition of the Serbian church:

> Catholic police believe a schismatic monk more than an otherwise irreproachable Catholic Censor! But it is really so, and the situation here can't be helped. . . .[18] Here is Vuk's answer. See if you can't help him (and me) somehow get the New Testament into print; for Turkish Serbs, since the Christian Macaronians [Kopitar refers here to the Serbian Church authorities who favor the Russian Church Slavonic and *slaveno-srpski* traditions of the Vojvodina] . . . are still too strong.[19]

On the death of the formidable Metropolitan Stratimirović, in October 1836, Kopitar again writes to Grimm:

> The Serbian Metropolitan Stratimirović has died at the age of seventy-nine, after having the day before hospitably entertained Prince Miloš! . . . He slandered me and even the good Vuk quite unscrupulously to Austria as a *Russoman,* to Russia as a *Uniatoman!*[20]

The details of Kopitar's background and world view relevant to his influence upon Vuk can scarcely be hinted at in a paper of this length. Although much of the story of their collaboration has been told elsewhere, a great deal of research remains, for example, to properly illuminate the nuances of their mutual relationship, which was obviously productive and unusually altruistic. For the sake of brevity, therefore, it seems appropriate merely to list Kopitar's chief contributions to Vuk's emergence as a language reformer: (1) The Herderian notion that the language of folklore could serve as a model for a vernacular-based Serbian literary language; (2) the conviction that a radical reform of the Serbian alphabet and orthography was needed; (3) the notion that the language of the existing Serbian writing tradition was "macaronic," "Russo-Slavo-Serbian jargon"—a bastardized form of Russian Church Slavonic, eighteenth-century Russian, and Serbian—and therefore not a true descendant of Old Serbian; (4) a practical program to overcome the existing deficiencies—published collections of folk songs, a grammar, and above all, a dictionary of vernacular Serbian.

Kopitar's collaboration with Vuk on the dictionary (published in 1818) was no doubt his most important scholarly contribution to Vuk's success. His help in Vuk's translation of the New Testament might also be mentioned, but although the manuscript was ready in the 1820s, its publication was suppressed until 1847. The ultimate success of Vuk's efforts, however, resulted not so much from any theoretical indoctrination, scholarly training, or direct aid Kopitar provided but rather indirectly from the latter's effectiveness as an agent for Vuk and his work among the leading scholars of the day, and especially the Germans. Vuk was fighting against tremendous odds and powerfully entrenched opponents. Kopitar correctly understood that for Vuk to succeed in his revolutionary task he would need the prestige and legitimacy of European recognition.

He and Vuk may not, however, have realized how many years would pass before this recognition took effect in Serbia and how oblique and in certain ways mixed the results would be. In any case Vuk sensed that time was on his side, and that Serbian youth would be the key to the installation of his vernacular-based language as the literary norm.

Only a decade after his fateful meeting with Kopitar, Vuk Karadžić was famous throughout Europe, was a member of academic and learned societies, and held an honorary Doctor of Philosophy degree. Kopitar did not engineer these honors for Vuk, but his connections helped make them possible. Shortly after Vuk's arrival in Vienna and his discovery by Kopitar, Vuk had made the acquaintance, through Kopitar, of the likes of Jakob Grimm, Wilhelm von Humboldt, and Friedrich Schlegel, who had come to the Congress of Vienna with German diplomats. (Grimm would subsequently write laudatory reviews of Book III of Vuk's folk songs and the dictionary as well as an introduction to the German translation of Vuk's grammar, which he not only extensively edited, but for which he even found a publisher.) In 1819, after the publication of his folk songs, his grammar, and his dictionary had brought him European renown, Vuk traveled to Russia. Stopping on the way in Cracow he was granted membership in the Towarzystwo naukowe krakowskie. In Moscow he was made a member of the Moskovskoe obščestvo ljubitelej russkoj slovesnosti, and at St. Petersburg won a gold medal from the Russian Academy for his dictionary. Among the luminaries whom he met in Russia were Karamzin and N. P. Rumjancev. During his visit to Germany (March 1823-March 1824) Vuk saw Grimm again, met Vater in Halle, received an honorary doctorate at Jena, and was accorded a reception by Goethe himself. A short list of foreign scholars, writers, poets, and statesmen (besides those mentioned earlier) whom Vuk met in Vienna, on his travels, or corresponded with, includes Dobrovský, Šafárik, Hanka, Palacký, Wieland, Ranke, Talvj, Šiškov, Vostokov, Griboedov, Gnedič, Polevoj, Köppen, Žukovskij, Sreznevskij, Nadeždin, and Pogodin. Janeff's claim that without Grimm and Goethe, Vuk would have amounted to "only a small episode in the history of Serbdom"[21] is of course tendentious and inflated, but the importance of such contacts is not to be underestimated.

Leopold von Ranke is an interesting case in point. The brilliant young German historian came to Vienna in 1827 with the purpose of studying the recently acquired Venetian archives. Kopitar introduced him to Vuk, and from their acquaintance sprang von Ranke's *Die serbische Revolution*. Written on the basis of the author's detailed conversations with Vuk and access to his papers, it is often considered their joint work. First published in Hamburg in 1829, this famous history of the Serbian uprisings was to go through numerous printings and two revised editions during von Ranke's lifetime, and was translated into Serbian, Russian, and English. Its huge impact upon European knowledge of Serbia and the Balkans is generally recognized. As Vladimir Stojančević puts it in his introduction to a recent Serbian translation, "*Die serbische Revolution* had the same significance for the political understanding of the 'Serbian question' in European politics as Vuk's collections of songs had for the knowledge of the culture of the Serbian people in the world."[22]

Vuk looked to Russia as well as Western Europe for support in his struggle to gain acceptance in his native Serbia, and was well aware of the importance of scholarly connections, east and west, as a means of promoting his own works (in the original and in translation) as well as those of associates well disposed to his cause. In 1825 Vuk writes to V. G. Anastas'evič (1775-1845, a Russian bibliographer and translator) announcing that he is forwarding a copy of his Serbian grammar "edited in German by the famous German philologist and grammarian Jakob Grimm."[23] In the same year he asks P. I. Köppen whether Talvj has sent him a copy of her translations of his folk songs, *Volkslieder der Serben*; in letters of 1826 and 1829 Vuk informs Köppen that he has sent copies of Šafárik's *Geschichte der slavischen Sprache und Literatur* ("which I received from the author for forwarding to you") and Ranke's *Die serbische Revolution*.[24]

In fact Vuk, who frequently proclaimed his desire to turn Serbia into an educated European country (even offering to teach Prince Miloš to read and write!), was at pains to use not only Western Europe but also Russia as models. Vuk's **Prvi srpski bukvar,** published in Vienna in 1827, has a special foreword for Russians explaining the phonetic values of the various letters in his new orthography. And while holding up the European example of high literacy, he is quick to point out that the Russians had given up the traditional names of the letters a century before as a hindrance to the mastery of reading:

> Let us not take as a model peoples of other faiths and races, but the Russians, who are of one faith and race with us. A hundred years ago, when they separated their language and alphabet from the church language and alphabet, they recognized that the *names* of our letters were difficult, too difficult, for learning to read; therefore even then in their schools in place of *az, buki, vjedi* . . . they began to teach *a, be, ve* . . .[25]

His long and friendly association and correspondence with I. I. Sreznevskij attests to the success of his "Russian" strategy. By the 1840s Vuk's efforts had begun to make real headway among the Serbs. Sreznevskij writes in July 1842, ". . . I am sincerely delighted that the Serbian government has begun, as it ought, to appreciate your merits . . . ; with time, God grant, they will take the path you have laid out and will cease to be ridiculous in the eyes of people who understand the importance of nationality, national education, and literature."[26]

In 1847 Vuk expressed his amazement to the Russian historian V. I. Grigorovič at the favorable notice his own work had received: "Really! Have you read in Part IV of the *Srpski ljetopis* of last year, 'Neke čerte iz" povĕstnice našeg" povĕstnice našeg" kn'ižestv'? I never hoped that something like this would be said in this *Ljetopis* during my lifetime."[27] What Vuk referred to was a wide-ranging article by the editor of the journal, Jovan Subotić, in which Vuk is described as a successor to Dositej Obradović, and in which nearly all aspects of Vuk's work—including his orthography—are singled out for praise. Serbian folk songs, writes Subotić, are not just *Volkslieder* but *Nationlieder*, and stand closer to the poetry of the ancient Greeks than does the poetry of any educated European nation. The Serbs, he claims, appreciated their songs long before Goethe dreamed of the Hasanaginica, and before Talvj was even born. When they were published by Vuk in Serbian,

> And when after that learned Europe exclaimed not only about the inherent value, but about the form of communication, the language in which the songs were sung, then our learned men also saw that it was possible to write in the vernacular (*narodni jezik*) in such a way that it pleased Europe. Now it was useless to say that books could not be written in the vernacular; and if a teacher was found who said that, then the student couldn't believe him, for on the opposite side stood much greater authority. . . . Dositej introduced the vernacular into books, and Vuk showed us which vernacular it was; Dositej showed us that we should write books in the vernacular, and Vuk showed us how we should write. . . . At the beginning Vuk exaggerated in his language, and under the guise of the vernacular took everything that was common. But this was on the one hand natural, for what reform at the beginning hasn't gone to the opposite extreme, and on the other hand necessary: for if something was to be gained, everything had to be sought. But still that served a good purpose in that it immediately became clear what was not needed and what was. And he himself has long since drawn his compass more narrowly, and on the other hand has broadened the territory of the vernacular. Now Hercegovina is not the Serbian Paris, but Hercegovina is everywhere Serbian is spoken—that is, all the lands in which Serbs live and speak Serbian seem suitable for his attention.[28]

The year 1847 has often been cited to mark Vuk's triumph, the final victory of his vernacular-based literary language among the Serbs. Four major works were published in that year which supposedly enshrined Vuk's language as the norm: Njegoš's *Gorski vijenac*; Radičević's *Pjesme*; Vuk's translation of the New Testament; and Daničić's *Rat za srpski jezik i pravopis*. But is the language of these works sufficiently uniform, or close enough to Vuk's previous writings, and especially to his normative works, to be called Vukovian? With the exception of Daničić's, the answer is no, as modern linguistic research has conclusively shown. Njegoš's poetic language was original, idiosyncratic, and contained numerous regional as well as Russian and Church Slavonic elements. Radičević, a disciple of Vuk's, nevertheless composed his poetry in a vernacular which bore significant traces of his native dialect. Vuk's New Testament displays a language which had evolved in many ways and which looked far different from the raw West Serbian vernacular of his 1818 dictionary. Nevertheless, the publication of these works, like the favorable reaction toward Vuk's reform by Jovan Subotić, indicates that by the late 1840's the balance had begun to tip decisively among the Serbs toward acceptance of a vernacular-based literary language which, if not identical to Vuk's in orthography or phonology, or even lexicon, was far closer to the Vukovian norm than to the various *slaveno-srpski* models of the fading Vojvodina tradition. Despite the efforts of Duro Daničić, Vuk's jekavian reflex (even in its somewhat moderated last stage) never took root in the Belgradecentered Serbian literary language; and although Vuk's radical orthography was grudgingly permitted for use in state editions in 1860, it was not officially adopted for public education until 1868. Kopitar died in 1844, and Vuk twenty years later. Vuk lived to see a vernacular-based language installed as the literary language. But was it really his language, or was Vuk himself part of a resurgent vernacular tradition? I believe the latter is correct, but I also believe that Kopitar and Vuk hastened the evolution of the Serbian literary language in the direction it ultimately took. Vuk, who in Skerlić's words "gave Serbian nationalism a West Serbian character,"[29] was aided as much by the European recognition he gained through Kopitar as by any other factor.

What led to the abandonment of the *slaveno-srpski* tradition of the *Prečani*, the educated transriparian Serbs of Hungary, and to the acceptance of a vernacular-based literary language? Although there was a hiatus in written literary activity during the Ottoman occupation followed by a revival under strong Russian influence in the Vojvodina, there existed among the Serbs an unbroken vernacular tradition which was manifested in non-literary and literary genres and in written as well as oral modes of expression. Outside Serbia, Gavril Venclović's poetic works, written in the early eighteenth century but only recently published, reveal a mastery of vernacular Serbian; and Dositej Obradović's literary production in the late eighteenth century, if it does bear the mark of a learned Russian influence, nevertheless represents the strongest pre-Vukovian model of the vernacular literary tradition. These are not isolated examples. Both before and during Vuk's career as a language reformer there were Serbs who wrote in the vernacular with varying degrees of success, a fact which Kopitar and Vuk both acknowledged. Moreover, Vuk himself had written in the vernacular during the Uprisings, thus following a Serbian usage for administrative and diplomatic correspondence that was at least seven hundred years old. This indigenous vernacular tradition, combined with the massive illiteracy that prevailed among the population of Serbia proper, formed a barrier to the spread of the Russian-influenced *slaveno-srpski* tradition of the Hungarian Serbs—and a powerful support for a language reform along Vukovian lines.

The historical preconditions for the success—such as it was—of Vuk's reform were two in number. The first was the resurgence under Miloš Obrenović of Belgrade as the administrative center of the semi-autonomous *pašaluk* after the second Uprising and of the autonomous Principality of Serbia in 1833; with a restored "national capital" there occurred a concomitant shift of cultural power southward from Budapest and Novi Sad. The second was the exposure of the next generation of Serbian youth to European universities, where they were introduced not only to Romanticism, nationalism, and democratic ideas, but also to the prestige and legitimacy of Vuk's vernacular-based literary language, which it had won through his published works in the original and in translation, and to the recognition also accorded the heroic Serbs, for example, in von Ranke's *Die serbische Revolution*.

Ljubomir Nenadović (1826-1895) is a striking example of this transitional generation in new Serbia, the first generation of European-educated urban intellectuals centered in Belgrade. The son of Prota Matija Nenadović, a prominent figure in rebel Serbia, he was born in the same north Serbian ekavian village (Brankovina) and attended school there and in Valjevo and then in Belgrade, where he studied for five years at the gymnasium and lycée. In 1844, at the age of eighteen, he began his years as a wandering scholar and writer. Early in his first year abroad Ljubomir writes from Prague to his former classmates at the Belgrade lycée. Evoking the muses to compose two poems which express greetings to his friends and homesickness for Belgrade, Nenadović describes a few of the wonders of Prague. Significantly, the only person he mentions in the letter is Pavel Šafárik, "who is truly among the best of men, and whom I recommend to you as comrades that you respect him."[30] Šafárik, the noted Slovak philologist and ethnographer, had long taught at Novi Sad before moving to Prague, and knew the South Slavic world intimately; he and Vuk had first met at Varadin in 1820 and had enjoyed a cordial and mutually supportive professional relationship ever since.[31]

After a year at Prague, Nenadović moved on to the universities of Berlin, Heidelberg, and Paris. Though he never took a final examination at any of these institutions, he seems to have pursued his studies with some interest, reading Czech and Serbian folk poetry (Vuk's collection), Branko Radičević, the Dubrovnik poets, philosophy, religious history, and Slavic philology (he translated Mickewicz). Without a diploma he returned to Belgrade from revolutionary Paris in 1848 and became a professor at the gymnasium. In 1850 he founded the journal *Šumadinka* and plunged into the publishing of a great quantity of material, including his father's strongly vernacular memoirs, and numerous translations.

Ljubomir Nenadović is best remembered for his mastery of the vernacular language and for his effortless, unselfconscious prose style. While Nenadović's orthography was traditional, he shared with his Serbian contemporaries the ekavian reflex and the lack of /h/. Otherwise he is basically Vukovian in his lexicon (despite an occasional borrowing) and grammar, but his syntax gives a more modern impression than Vuk's. As Miodrag Popović writes:

> Nenadović's letters from abroad (*putopisi*) signaled a new era in Serbian literature. The links between living speech and the writer's word are even somewhat more obvious than in Vuk's work. Both writers, that is, have the same vernacular (*narodni govor*) as their point of departure; but Vuk's written style is more studied, more polished, heavier, while Nenadović's is more spontaneous, closer to the reader. Vuk, with his prose on the Serbian Uprising and his translation of the New Testament, introduces the vernacular (*narodni jezik*) into literature as early as the 1820s, but it took Nenadović to make the urban reader fond of literary prose in the vernacular. . . . Vuk writes, Nenadović talks (*priča*); Vuk is closer to the village, Nenadović to the city, Vuk's work is a monument to the Serbian language, while Nenadović is the beginning of the urban era in the development of the vernacular literary language (*narodni književni jezik*).[32]

Quoting Ljubomir Nenadović himself from his *Pisma iz Nemačke*:

> The same is true of human reason and writing. . . . You should just let the pen go along the paper; line after line will come by themselves. Writing is like yarn, it comes from the brain like a thread from the skein; not every skein need be silk, it can be made of nettles as well. Words are bricks, and style is architecture; not every building need be symmetrical, not every piece of writing need have a system. To write: that is the same as having a conversation with yourself. When you write, you do nothing more than photograph your thoughts. Not all photographs have to be beautiful.[33]

It has been observed that it is not the normative grammarians who establish and consolidate literary languages, but good writers. The works of Ljubomir Nenadović and other popular writers of the new Serbia established once and for all the post-Vukovian norm which was to culminate in the distinctly modern "Belgrade style" of the early twentieth century and the extensively elaborated, constantly evolving Serbian literary language of the present day. How these same writers might have written had Vuk never met Kopitar is an entirely different question, the answers to which can only be guessed at. Clearly, however, without the sponsorship of European scholars and intellectuals, the intervention of Vuk Karadžić would never have won European prestige and legitimacy, and the language of the second generation of modern Serbian writers, even if essentially vernacular in its base, would have been markedly different in lexicon, phonology, morphology, syntax, and especially orthography. And finally, without the international acclaim achieved by Vuk with Kopitar's guidance, it is debatable whether modern Serbian and Croatian would have developed in tandem, with the result that we can speak today of a Serbo-Croatian literary language and not just Serbo-Croatian dialects.

Notes

1. Rajko Nahtigal, ed., *Jerneja Kopitarja spisov*, II del, 1 knjiga (Ljubljana: Akademija znanosti in umetnosti, 1944), p. 6; translations into English are mine (B.A.S.) throughout the present article.

2. Bartholomäus Kopitar, *Grammatik der slavischen Sprache in Krain, Kärnten und Steyermark* (Laibach/Ljubljana, 1808), p. xvii.

3. Kopitar, p. xxvi.

4. Bartholomäus Kopitar, *Kleinere Schriften,* ed. Franz Miklosich (Vienna, 1857), p. 67.

5. Aleksandar Belić, *Vukova borba za narodni i književni jezik: rasprave i predavanja* (Belgrade: Prosveta, 1948), p. 198.

6. Matija Murko, *Izbrano delo,* ed. Anton Slodnjak (Ljubljana, 1962), p. 277.

7. Matyáš (Matija) Murko, *Rozpravy z oboru slovanské filologie,* Práce Slovanského ústavu v Praze, svazek IV, ed. Jiří Horák (Prague, 1937), 27-28.

8. Nahtigal, p. xiii.

9. Vatroslav Jagič, ed., *Enciklopedija slavjanskoj filologii,* 1 (St. Petersburg, 1910), p. 196.

10. Nikola Banaševic, "Kako je Vuk postao književnik," *Kovčežić: prilozi i građa o Dositeju i Vuku,* 1 (1958), 44-45, 54.

11. Salko Nazečić, "Vukova staza," *Izraz: časopis za književnu i umjetničku kritiku,* 6 (1964), 628, 629.

12. Izmail I. Sreznevskij, "Vuk Stefanović Karadžić. Biografska i bibliografska skice," trans. Miloš M. Moskovljević, *Srpski književni glasnik,* 52 (1937), 388, 390.

13. Ljubomir Stojanović, ed., *Vukova prepiska,* 1 (Belgrade, 1907), p. 143.

14. Stojanović, 144-45.

15. Stojanović, 156-57.

16. Stojanović, 159-60.

17. Max Vasmer, ed., *B. Kopitars Briefwechsel mit Jakob Grimm,* Abhandlungen der Preussischen Akademie der Wissenschaften, Philosophisch-historische Klasse, 7 (1937), 62-63.

18. Vasmer, p. 92.

19. Vasmer, p. 94.

20. Vasmer, 160-61.

21. Janko Janeff, *Südosteuropa und der deutsche Geist* (Berlin: Fritsch Verlag, 1943), p. 132.

22. Leopold Ranke, *Srpska revolucija,* trans. Ognjan Radović (Belgrade: Srpska književna zadruga, 1965), p. 9.

23. S. A. Vinogradov, E. P. Naumov, and G. P. Čekanova, "Iz perepiski Vuka Karadžiča s russkimi učënymi," *Slavjanskoe istočnikovedenie* (Moscow: Nauka, 1965), p. 189.

24. Vinogradov et al, 187, 189, 195.

25. Vuk Stefanović Karadžić, *Prvi srpski bukvar* (Vienna, 1827, repr. Belgrade, 1978), p. 2.

26. P. T. Gromov, ed., "Perepiska V. S. Karadžiča s I. I. Sreznevskim," *Razvitie kapitalizma i nacional'nye dviženija v slavjanskix stranax* (Moscow: Nauka, 1970), p. 328.

27. Vinogradov et al, p. 200.

28. Jovan Subotić, "Neke čerte iz" po věstnice serbskog" Kn'iževstva," *Serbskij lětopis*", vol. 75, part 4 (1846), 104-124, esp. 118, 121-23.

29. Jovan Skerlić, *Istorija nove srpske književnosti* (Belgrade, 1914), p. 274.

30. Savo Andrić, "Pismo Ljubomira Nenadovića iz Praga 1844 godine," *Zbornik Istorijskog muzeja Srbije,* 8-9 (1972), 119-25.

31. Ljubomir Stojanović, *Život i rad Vuka Stefanovića Karadžića* (Belgrade, 1924), 187, 287, 291-92.

32. Miodrag Popović, *Istorija srpske književnosti: Romantizam,* II (Belgrade: Nolit, 1972), p. 269.

33. Ljubomir P. Nenadović, *Pisma iz Nemačke* (Belgrade: Srpska književna zadruga, 1922), p. 10.

Milne Holton and Vasa D. Mihailovich (essay date 1997)

SOURCE: Holton, Milne, and Vasa D. Mihailovich. "Introduction: Vuk Stafanovic Karadžić and *Songs of the Serbian People.*" In *Songs of the Serbian People: From the Collections of Vuk Karadžić,* pp. 1-12. Pittsburgh: University of Pittsburgh Press, 1997.

[*In the following essay, Holton and Mihailovich provide an overview of Karadžić's work, with an emphasis on his collection of oral folksongs.*]

The oral poems translated herein are taken from a single work of collection undertaken by one man, Vuk Stefanović Karadžić (1787-1864), a scholar and linguist living in the city of Vienna in the early years of the nineteenth century. He began his work in 1813, around the time of the collapse of the first Serbian insurrection against the Turks.

Vuk Stefanović Karadžić was born in 1787 in the village of Tršić in Western Serbia, the son of a Serbian peasant. A sickly child, he was given the name Vuk (Wolf), supposedly to ward off evil spirits. As a youth he became involved in the service of the *hajduk*[1] rebels against the Turks and later in the first insurrection. Later he attended briefly the famous high school at Sremski Karlovci and then studied for a time at the new *velika škola* (later university) in Karadjordje's Belgrade. But he soon left Belgrade and, after an illness that left him crippled for life, went to Vienna in 1810. It was here that he met Jernej Kopitar, a Slovene scholar of some distinction who was then living in Vienna, where he occupied the post of official censor for Slavic literatures.

Kopitar was only three years older than Vuk but much more intellectually sophisticated, and he soon assumed the role of mentor. Both in his official capacity and as a result of his absorption of Herder's ideas of the importance of "popular"—as opposed to literary—cultures as the legitimate expression of national character, Kopitar was committed to the support of the language and culture of the Slavic peasants in the Balkan lands. It was his belief, and the policy of his government, that the encouragement of the Slavic populations of the empire in their nationalist aspirations would protect them from Russian influence even as it would commit them to the protection of the Habsburgs. Kopitar, who read an essay written in the vernacular Serbian by Vuk, recognized in the younger man the ideal advocate for that vernacular.[2]

Kopitar proposed a three-part program for the young scholar: the establishment of a vernacular grammar, the writing of a dictionary, and—most important for our purposes—the collection of the oral songs of the people, for he had become aware that Vuk remembered many of them.[3] Certainly Kopitar was right, for with his encouragement and assistance, Vuk would first produce a grammar of the vernacular Serbian language in 1815 and a Serbian dictionary three years later. In these works he reduced the complex Slavo-Serbian alphabet from forty characters to thirty, following the then radical principle of the elimination of all unpronounced letters. These works, both of which were of crucial importance to South Slavic linguistics, letters, and history, and neither of which Vuk could have completed without Kopitar, attracted the hostility of the Orthodox Church fathers, who, although recognizing the importance of a vernacular literary language, saw Vuk's radical reforms as attempts that played into the hands of the Austrians and Catholics by turning Serbian loyalties away from Russia, her religion, and her language.[4]

As the imperial authorities perhaps also recognized, Vuk's commitment to the vernacular was radically subversive. For in a sense what Vuk had undertaken was a redefinition of South Slavic nationalism—or indeed of the Serbian nation itself. No longer was that nation, or people (the two words are one in Serbian, ever since Vuk, in his 1818 dictionary, offered one word, *narod,* to bear both meanings), defined by a shared Orthodox Christian faith and the literary tradition that faith had generated. For the nation Vuk reified in his grammar and dictionary, and later in his collections of songs, was much more broadly based, the great *raja*[5] of the Balkans, oppressed and on the edge of rebellion, a potential for disorder in Ottoman lands, yet attracting only occasional support from Vienna. It was the language spoken by that *raja* that Vuk privileged by establishing its textuality. And it would be the poetry of that language that Vuk would offer to give legitimacy to the language itself.

Thus, in a sense Vuk redefined the South Slav nationality. He provided it with a realistic and viable identity, which would survive the censorship of his collections in Vienna, the early years of Obrenović rule,[6] and Vuk's own exile from Belgrade after 1832. In his years of exile, the 1830s and 1840s, he traveled in Croatia, Dalmatia, and Montenegro, came to know the peoples of those lands, and attempted to minimize their linguistic differences from the Serbs. Then—after the Obrenovićs themselves were exiled to Vienna in 1842—he received the financial support of Miloš's son and successor, Prince Mihailo. Vuk would also be supported by the "Illyrian" movement centered in Zagreb, which would demand more independence for all the empire's Slavs. Thus Vuk was an honored figure at the Pan-Slav Congress in Prague in 1848.

After that year of revolution Vuk's assumptions, and his Serbian language, were taken up by a new generation, the generation of the United Serbian Youth movement, which throughout the second half of the nineteenth century rejected the traditional culture of the Serbs in Austria and south Hungary and turned to that of the people in the Balkan homeland.

Duncan Wilson has pointed out that there are two aspects of Vuk's importance, that of the radical reformer and that of the conservative—the conservator of the heritage of oral singing in the Balkans. He has observed that while Vuk's countrymen often overemphasize the first, it is the second that has received the attention of foreign scholars. Certainly, it is the latter aspect that is the more important for our purposes; Vuk was responsible for the collection of the oral poetry that was to become the foundation of the literary culture of the South Slavs. But it was also that work which, by providing the exotic and romantically heroic flavor fashionable in literary circles of the time, attracted the attention of Europe's leading writers, generated translations—and fakery—in English, French, German, Russian, and Polish and, more importantly, helped bring Serbia and the Balkans to the European consciousness.

Even before he had undertaken his grammar, just after the crushing of the first insurrection in 1813 and the flight of yet more refugees into the Srem (the Austrian lands between the Danube and the Sava whose population was then composed mostly of South Slavs), Vuk had also begun to gather from his own memory and from the recitals of relatives and other Serbian exiles a collection of Serbian oral poems, mostly lyrics. He published his first collection, ***Mala prostonarodnja slaveno-serbska pjesnarica*** (*A Simple Little Slaveno-Serbian Songbook*) in 1814.

Vuk then moved into the Srem and prepared a second collection, where he met the *guslari* and *guslare* (for there were women singers), who would serve him as sources: Tešan Podrugović, a Bosnian Serb freedom fighter of prodigious size and memory; Filip Višnjić, a blind *guslar*; and "the blind Živana," an old woman who would give him "The Kosovo Maiden" and other songs. The songs Vuk heard from these singers were the basis for a second collection, ***Narodna srbska pjesnarica*** (*A Serbian Book of Folk Songs*), published in Vienna in 1815, in which the first of the "heroic" songs, the long narrative histories in *deseterac,* the ten-beat line of the peasant songs, especially songs of the Battle of Kosovo, of Marko Kraljević, and of the insurrection appeared.

In his work of collecting, Vuk received the encouragement of Lukijan Mušicki, then archimandrite of the monastery at Šišatovac in Srem, who had taught at Sremski Karlovci during Vuk's years in the school there. But it was Vuk's friend Kopitar who showed the collection to the renowned German scholar, Jakob Grimm, then attached to the German diplomatic delegation in Vienna. It was through Grimm that Vuk would meet Goethe and that his collections would establish the fame of Serbian poetry throughout Europe.

Vuk also journeyed east into the Banat to collect more songs from other refugee *guslars* and *hajduks*. It was these singers who can be seen as the authors of the songs, for they never sang from texts; their songs were memorial reconstructions set out in *deseterci*. It is not clear what is meant by "knowing" a song—whether to "know" a song was simply to have the ability to correctly set forth a narrative line and the skill to set it forth in one's own lines, or whether to "know" described an act of memorization of prescribed linguistic structures, or whether the true meaning lay somewhere between these extremes. It is clear, however, that to a great or lesser extent, each singing was a compositional and not purely a recitational act, for each singer sang the songs differently (indeed Vuk himself often collected many versions of a single song). So in a certain sense, regardless of the "age" of the songs, what Vuk was collecting were early nineteenth-century folk songs, all of which, after having been passed on from generation to generation, had passed through the minds and memories of their singers and had been reformed according to their tastes or experience and in the vocabulary of their own cultures.

Vuk's two most important singers had been encountered in Šišatovac as early as 1815. The first—the first singer Vuk heard as an adult—was Tešan Podrugović, a huge man of about forty years who as a youth in Bosnia killed a Turk who had raped a girl in his family. He fled to become a *hajduk,* then joined the first insurrection under Karadjordje. He fought bravely, but quarreled with his commanding officer and left the army to cross the Danube into the Austrian Srem after the Turks recaptured Serbia. He made a living there as a gatherer of reeds. Vuk made his acquaintance through Obrad, Lukijan Mušicki's cousin, shortly before Easter of 1815, a week after the beginning of the second insurrection under Miloš Obrenović. Vuk was barely able to restrain him from a return to the fighting, and he soon departed to join the other rebels. However, in the summer he left the army again, killed a bey,[7] and again became an outlaw in Bosnia. There he got into a fight in an inn, where he was beaten by some Turks and died shortly thereafter. Podrugović recited (he did not sing) his songs to Vuk, many of them very funny, with a straight face, never smiling. He knew hundreds; Vuk had a sense that many remained unsung. He collected twenty-two songs from Podrugović, notably comic songs and *hajduk* songs, of the experience that he knew so well. Vuk called Podrugović "the first and the best" of his singers.[8]

Shortly after Podrugović had departed with his unsung songs, Vuk met his second singer, a successful *guslar* (the only professional singer Vuk would encounter) named Filip Višnjić. Višnjić, who had been born in Bosnia in the vicinity of Bijeljina and had been blinded by smallpox at eight, had fled after his father died, members of the family were tortured and killed, and his uncle Marko was hanged for killing a Turk who had raped a member of the family. Višnjić became a professional singer, singing both to Turks and Christians, and traveled as far south as Skadar, then came to Serbia in 1804, found himself in the midst of the battles of the first insurrection, crossed into the Srem in 1810, and settled in the village of Grk. There he was well received and well paid for his singing. Vuk met him when Višnjić was about fifty years old, well-off and successful as a *guslar* who regularly performed in public. He was perhaps Vuk's most popular singer and was remembered by the villagers for years afterward. When Višnjić died in Grk in 1834 he was buried with a *gusle* carved on his cross.[9]

Višnjić was extremely capable as a singer. His songs—notably songs of the first insurrection—were worked with new formulas, perhaps the most accomplished of the songs collected by Vuk. Vuk transcribed from him a total of nearly forty songs—over ten thousand lines all together. It was this transcription that formed the nucleus of what was to be Vuk's extensive and monumental collection, ***Narodne srpske pjesme,*** published in Leipzig between 1823 and 1833, the so-called Leipzig edition.

There would be other singers. There was "the blind Jeca," a woman singer whom Vuk met in Zemun and who sang "The Death of Duke Prijezda" for him;[10] there was "the blind Stepanija," who gave him both a version of "The Building of Skadar" and "Tsaritsa Milica and Duke Vladeta." There was an unnamed blind woman from the village of Grgurevci from whom Vuk took three of the finest of the Kosovo songs, "The Fall of the Serbian Empire," "The Death of the Mother of the Jugovićes," and "The Kosovo Maiden."[11] Indeed, it is strange to discover how many of the historical songs, and many of them among the finest, were sung by blind and presumably illiterate women singers, whose access to their material must have been either mnemonic or purely imaginative.

There were other great male singers as well: "Old Milija," whose "Banović Strahinja," perhaps the single greatest of the poems, reflected the tragedies of his own life; "Old Raško" (in the patriarchal culture of Vuk's Serbia the attribution of "old" was honorific and not merely descriptive), the singer of several of the medieval songs: Stojan the Outlaw, who, in prison in Serbia for having killed a woman who (he said) "ate" his child, in 1820 gave Vuk the magnificent "The Wedding of King Vukašin";[12] and several others. These were the true authors of the heroic songs; in the final analysis Vuk was really only their editor and collector.

The fruits of Vuk's work as a collector of the oral songs came between 1823 and 1833 in the now famous and greatly expanded Leipzig edition. For in spite of his recognition abroad Vuk had difficulties at home. The Office of the Censor in Vienna, probably provoked by the Orthodox clergy in Austria, denied permission for Vuk's *Narodna srbska pjesnarica,* so it was in Leipzig that the book appeared. In this edition were many new songs that Vuk had more recently collected. And with its four volumes Vuk established the arrangement of the poems that was to become the basic pattern of all subsequent editions. Volume 1 (1824) presented the *Ženske pjesme* or **Women's Songs,** the lyric poems, usually not in *deseterci,* short, mythic narratives, many of pre-Christian origins, and the round dances. The second volume (1823)[13] was identified by Vuk as the *Pjesme junačke najstarije,* or the **Oldest Heroic Songs,** the narrative and historical songs in *deseterac* that—because they made no mention of firearms—Vuk regarded as the oldest. The third volume (1823), *Pjesme junačke srednjijeh vremena* (**Heroic Songs of the Middle Period**), consisted mainly of *hajduk* narrative songs and other songs set during the years of the Turkish occupation. A decade later there appeared Volume 4, *Pjesme junačke novijih vremena o vojevanju za slobodu* (**Heroic Songs of the Recent Times of the War for Freedom**), where were collected the songs of the Montenegrin and Serbian insurrections.

After the Leipzig edition Vuk, with the uncertain patronage of Prince Mihailo Obrenović, then exiled to Vienna, traveled south, to Montenegro and its Bay of Kotor, to Dubrovnik and Lika on the Dalmatian coast, places he had not visited before, known for their oral songs. His search there for other *guslari,* for new poems, and for variants of poems he had already heard was in preparation for what would be a definitive "Viennese" edition of the collection—some 1,045 poems—entitled *Srpske narodne pjesme* and published again in four volumes, in 1841, 1845, 1846, and 1862.[14]

There have been many subsequent editions of the songs—a somewhat bowdlerized edition by Ljubomir Stojanović in 1891-1901 (it was reprinted between the world wars); an annotated edition by Djurić, Matić, Banašević, and Latković in 1953-1954; Nedić's edition of the Viennese edition in 1969; and an edition with the "objectionable" poems separated in a volume not publicly sold, in 1973-1974.[15] For the Serbs, *Srpske narodne pjesme* constitutes the "classic anthology" (in the Confucian sense) of Serbian oral poetry.

Vuk Karadžić was neither the first nor the last to collect or to transcribe the oral songs of the Balkans. As Koljević tells us, there are references to the singing of the South Slavs throughout the seventeenth century. But much earlier, as early as the twelfth century, at least one hagiography and several of the Dukljanin's chronicles may have been based on oral narrative songs. There is a transcription of a fragment of a Slavic oral song, transcribed by Ruggiero Pazienza, a court poet of the Queen of Naples, in the village of Gioia del Colle in southern Italy in 1497; it is extant in the fifth volume of an eight-volume courtly epic, *Lo Balzino,* the manuscript of which is presently located in the City Library in Perugia.[16]

Around 1555 a *bugarštica,* a heroic song conducted in the "long line" of fourteen to sixteen syllables and associated with a courtly tradition of oral performance, entitled "Marko Kraljević and his Brother Andrijaš," was transcribed on the island of Hvar, then the richest Venetian community in Dalmatia. In 1568 Petar Hektorović, a nobleman from the same island, published in Venice a poem written in the long line of the *bugarštica,* a fisherman's eclogue (then popular in Italy), which contained transcriptions of several of the oral songs sung by his fishermen companions on a fishing expedition. And many other *bugarštice*—recounting the collapse of the Serbian Empire at the end of the fourteenth century and the events of the subsequent Turkish occupation—were transmitted and published in the towns along the Adriatic Sea and elsewhere in the seventeenth and eighteenth centuries—by Nikola Ohmučević, a merchant, later by the poet Ivan Gundulić, by Djuro Matijašević, a cleric (all citizens of Dubrovnik), and by others living in or around Kotor in the Bay of Kotor, another major Venetian colony and a city long important to Serbs, and elsewhere.

These *bugarštice* were poems that exemplified the degeneration of an older poetic form prevalent in feudal court poetry and then surviving as a form of popular entertainment in various cities and towns along the Adriatic coast. No longer feudal poetry, the *bugarštice* had become urban poems, essentially bourgeois in their assumptions. They described banquets and toasts, concerned themselves with the appropriateness of manners and clothing, showed familiarity with money, and demonstrated an awareness of a greater world and its political realities. But the *bugarštice* still contained elements—motifs, stylistic devices, even stock phrases and formulaic patterns, which belonged to their courtly predecessors and may originally have been mnemonic in function.

However, it was not the *bugarštice* but the *deseteračke pesme* (*deseterci*), the songs conducted in ten-syllable lines, being sung at the time in the patriarchal peasant villages of the Serbian, Bosnian, and Montenegrin uplands, even in Croatia, that were Vuk's concern. The *deseterci* were products of a different culture, not urban but peasant, not bourgeois but patriarchal, and as such they told their stories in a different vernacular—less sophisticated, perhaps, more metaphorical and less accurately realistic in representations of things like money and banquets and fine clothes. But their shorter line gave for a certain economy of epithet, and the narrative moved more cleanly. The motifs and patterns and phrasings surviving in the *bugarštice* were tightened and simplified in the *deseterci*. Also, the heroes of the *deseterci* seemed to live in a less ordered world, a world of violence and uncertainty, of pragmatic values and compromise, the world of the uplands, not in the more ordered world of the songs sung on the civilized coast.[17]

The *deseterac* line is dominantly trochaic, end-stopped, and unrhymed (occasionally internal rhyme is employed). Most important, each line is divided into two parts by a strong caesura, which always occurs after the fourth syllable. This line has a rhythm known to every Serb. It is so familiar, and so charged with association, that—like those written in the *bugarštica*—the poems themselves are identified by their special metrical norm.

The *deseterci* were also transcribed and translated.[18] The earliest extant transcriptions of the *deseterci* songs were set down in Perast (then an aristocratic Venetian community in the Bay of Kotor on the Adriatic) around the end of the seventeenth century, and appeared beside *bugarštice*. Then, around 1720, songs sung by Slav soldiers near Vienna were transcribed—very imperfectly—in a manuscript in which 217 lyrics and epics were collected; this manuscript, the "Erlangen manuscript," was discovered in 1913 in the Erlangen University library and is of great value if one wishes to consider the changes brought about when the presumably courtly songs, having passed to the uses of a bourgeois merchant society, then fell into the hands of Slavic peasants and outlaws under the domination of a foreign power.

Later in the century, in 1774, an Italian traveler and scholar, Alberto Fortis, who had taken an interest in the Italian translations of MacPherson's *Ossian,* traveled to the Dalmatian islands and there translated into Italian two songs, one of which is today known as the *Hasanaginica* or "The Wife of Hasan Aga." They were then translated by Goethe into German and appeared in Herder's *Volkslieder* (1778, 1779), which generated the first enthusiasm among newly romanticized European readers. Walter Scott made an English version ("The Wife of Hasan Aga") of the *Hasanaginica* from the German.[19] Madame de Stael declared herself "ravie"; Prosper Mérimée produced a fraudulent French version of a heroic song; and Pushkin followed Mérimée. But by this time Vuk had begun his collection, which coincided with the first insurrection. And then, as we have said, his **Narodna srbska pjesnarica** caught the attention of Jakob Grimm, then Europe's greatest comparatist.[20]

Grimm and his brother translated nineteen of Vuk's songs for Forster's *Sängerfahrt* in 1818. Then the daughter of a German university professor from Halle, Fräulein Theresa Albertina Luisa von Jacob, an enthusiastic disciple of Goethe, with his encouragement translated slightly less than half of Vuk's first collection into German (using her initials "Talvj" as her nom de plume), beginning in the 1820s. Talvj was the first to translate Vuk's transmissions of the Serbian songs into a major European language.[21] Again there was a spate of retranslation. The first into English seems to have been that of John Gibson Lockhart, Scott's biographer, in an anonymous and privately printed collection of 1826 entitled *Translations from the Servian Minstrelsy: to Which are Added Some Specimens of Anglo-Norman Romances* (Lockhart, the editor of the *Quarterly Review,* acknowledged his role as retranslator in that journal in 1845).[22] But by far more important is Sir John Bowring's *Servian Popular Poetry* of 1827; in it appear English versions of some 107 "songs and ballads,"

translations made, presumably, from Talvj's German versions but with reference to Vuk's Serbian texts.[23]

So it was Vuk Karadžić who shaped—for his own European literary world, but, more importantly, for many Serbs—a new sense of nationality. He did this in a collection of songs in a language that he had also made it possible to read (through his grammar and dictionary) and that would serve as the vernacular of a newly forming literary tradition. If the importance of such an undertaking had been recognized even before its achievement by others, it was Vuk to whom we owe that achievement. There is no person in the cultural history of the Balkans whose work is more entirely beneficent than Vuk. Had its history been different, had Vuk's definition of nationality ultimately obtained, the history of the Balkan people of our own time might well have been more benign than that brought to them by other visions.

Notes

1. Outlaw brigands living in bands in the highlands of the Balkans, some of whom may have been politically motivated to rebellion against Turkish rule.

2. Much of the biographical information in this section is taken from Duncan Wilson's remarkable biography, *The Life and Times of Vuk Stefanović Karadžić: 1787-1864* (Oxford: Clarendon Press, 1970), and from George Rapall Noyes and Leonard Bacon, eds. and trans., *Heroic Ballads of Servia* (Boston: Sherman, French, 1913). Antun Barac's *A History of Yugoslav Literature* (Belgrade: Committee for Foreign Cultural Relations, 1955, and Ann Arbor: Michigan Slavic Publications, 1973), and, of course, Svetozar Koljević's authoritative work on the epics in English, *The Epic in the Making* (Oxford: Clarendon Press, 1980), subsequently cited as "Koljević," have been of inestimable critical value.

3. Duncan Wilson, *The Life and Times of Vuk Stefanović Karadžić,* 2-3; subsequently cited as "Wilson."

4. See Wilson, 2.

5. The *raja* were the Christian peasantry of the Balkans under the Ottoman Empire.

6. The second modern Serbian dynasty, established by the leader of the second insurrection, Miloš Obrenović, who ruled from 1815 to 1839 and from 1858 to 1860. The first dynasty began with Karadjordje.

7. A "bey" (beg) is a Turkish district governor.

8. See Wilson, 106-8; Karadžić's introduction to the Leipzig edition, vols. 1 and 4; and Koljević, 311-14 et passim.

9. See Wilson, 110-11, and Koljević, 306-10 et passim; see also Karadžić's introduction to volume 4 of the Leipzig edition.

10. See Koljević, 89-90.

11. See Koljević, 319.

12. See Koljević, 127.

13. The second and third volumes were published in 1823 before the first, in 1824.

14. Koljević, 345. V. Nedić reproduced this edition, correcting only misprints, in *Srpske narodne pjesme*, Belgrade: Prosveta, 1969.

    Throughout his life—or at least until he received the support of Prince Mihailo—Vuk suffered from lack of money, so he did not confine his literary activities to his collections but collaborated with Leopold von Ranke on a history of contemporary Serbia (which contained accounts of the insurrections) in 1828 and a first description of Serbia's now famous monasteries in 1821. Moreover, also on Kopitar's advice, he undertook a translation of the New Testament into vernacular Serbian.

15. Ljubomir Stojanović, ed., *Srpske narodne pjesme*, by Vuk St. Karadžić, 9 vols. (Belgrade, 1891-1901); Vojislav Djurić, Svetozar Matić, Nikola Banašević, Vido Latković, eds., *Srpske narodne pjesme*, by Vuk St. Karadžić, 4 vols. (Belgrade, 1953-1954); Vladan Nedić, ed., *Srpske narodne pjesme* 4 vols. (Belgrade: Prosveta, 1969), and *Srpske narodne pjesme iz neobjavljenih rukopisa Vuka Stef. Karadžića* (Serbian Folk Poems from the Unpublished Manuscripts of Vuk Stefanović Karadžić) 4 vols. (Belgrade, 1973-1974).

16. See Koljević, 11-28. We are much indebted to Koljević for the following discussion.

17. Koljević discusses the *bugarštice* in his chapter entitled "The Grand Stammer"; see Koljević, 31-68. The *bugarštice* are presented in English translation in an anthology by John S. Miletich entitled *The Bugarštice: A Bilingual Anthology of the Earliest Extant South Slavic Folk Narrative Song* (Urbana and Chicago: University of Illinois Press, 1990).

18. Translators of the *deseterci* have over the years remained undecided whether to reproduce the line itself or to suggest its cultural resonance. Over the nearly two hundred years during which English translators have attempted the *deseterac*, very few have agreed upon an appropriate metrical procedure. Some English translators have sought the nearest English equivalent in associative force; they have generally translated into heroic couplet or blank verse, sometimes into ballad stanza. Still others, fearing that the *deseterac* would prove a metrical form too rigidly invariable for the English ear, especially when in translation it must be unaccompanied by the counterrhythms established by the *gusle,* sought complex and variable solutions. The most recent English translations of the heroic songs, the distinguished translations by Anne Pennington and Peter Levi collected in *Marko the Prince: Serbo-Croat Heroic Songs* (New York: St. Martin's Press, 1984), make no attempt to establish a metrical equivalent for the *deseterac.*

    The strong caesura has remained a problem for the English translator as well (albeit less so than for translators into other languages). Some leave it unmarked; some space so as to render two half-lines as in Anglo-Saxon; some, especially translators who have recently attempted the *deseterac* itself, have divided the ten syllables into two half-lines organically defined and have broken the lines syntactically, or at breath pauses.

    In our own translations we have attempted to conform closely to the syllabic and caesural conventions of the *deseterac* and have at the same time attempted to reduce its monotony, a monotony relieved in the performance of the Serbian poems by conducting the translations in a meter that, especially in the second half-lines, is a highly variable iambic (more natural to the English ear). And we have attempted to conform to a "plain" style, that of the *guslars.*

19. For a discussion of Walter Scott's translation see D. H. Low, "The First Link Between English and Serbo-Croat Literature," *Slavonic Review* 3 (1924): 362-69.

20. See Koljević's introduction to Pennington and Levi's *Marko the Prince,* xiii-xvii. See also Dragutin Subotić, *Yugoslav Popular Ballads: Their Origin and Development* (Cambridge: Cambridge University Press, 1932), 165ff.

21. See Subotić, *Ballads* 165ff., and his "Serbian Popular Poetry in English Literature," *Slavonic Review* 5 (March 1927): 628-46.

22. See Subotić, *Ballads* 243-44.

23. See Subotić, *Ballads* 225-43.

FURTHER READING

Biography

Wilson, Duncan. *The Life and Times of Vuk Stefanović Karadžić 1787-1864: Literacy, Literature, and National Independence in Serbia.* London: Oxford University Press, 1970, 415 p.

The only book-length biography of Karadžić in English. This cultural biography offers an examination of Karadžić's work in social and historical context, and provides English translations of Karadžić's correspondence.

Criticism

Cooper, Jr., Henry R. "Kopitar and the Beginning of Bulgarian Studies." In *Papers in Slavic Philology 2,* edited by Rado L. Leneck and Henry R. Cooper, Jr. pp. 55-64. Ann Arbor: University of Michigan, 1982.

Examines the contributions of Jernej Kopitar to Karadžić's work as it relates to Bulgarian folklore studies.

Fisher, Laura Gordon. Introduction to *Marko Songs from Hercegovina a Century After Karadžić,* pp. iii-x. New York: Garland Publishing, 1990.
 Provides an overview of nineteenth-century Serbio-Croation folksong collections and their characteristics. Fisher acknowledges Karadžić's importance in the development of such studies.

Koljević, Svetozar. "Repetition as Invention in the Songs of Vuk Karadžić." *Oral Tradition* 7, no. 2 (1992): 349-64.
 Studies repetition and variation in the oral folksongs collected by Karadžić.

Pribić, Nikola R. "Vuk Stefanović Karadžić—Founder of Comparative Balkan Folklore." *Synthesis: Bulletin du Comité National de Littérature Comparée de la République Socialiste de Roumanie* 2 (1975): 107-11.
 Examines Karadžić's contributions to the collection and study of Balkan literature.

Additional coverage of Karadžić's life and career is contained in the following source published by the Gale Group: *Dictionary of Literary Biography,* **Vol. 147.**

Charlotte Smith
1749-1806

(Full name Charlotte Turner Smith) English poet, novelist, translator, and author of children's books.

The following entry provides an overview of Smith's life and works. For additional information on her career, see *NCLC,* Volume 23.

INTRODUCTION

A popular and prolific novelist and poet in her own time, Smith is remembered today for her sentimental novels and her role in the late eighteenth-century revival of the sonnet form which influenced such prominent figures of Romanticism as William Wordsworth and Samuel Taylor Coleridge. In both prose and poetry, Smith went beyond the usual concerns of the woman writer to explore the social, political, and intellectual issues of her time—issues conventionally assigned to male writers.

BIOGRAPHICAL INFORMATION

Smith was born on May 4, 1749, to a wealthy London family who owned estates in Sussex and Surrey in addition to their London townhouse. Her mother, Anna Towers Turner, died three years after Smith's birth, leaving a maternal aunt to raise her while her father, Nicholas Turner, traveled abroad and nearly exhausted the family's funds. Educated at schools in Kensington and Chichester, and by private tutors at home, Smith was an avid reader and began composing poetry at an early age. Her father's eventual return and remarriage to a wealthy woman prompted an arranged marriage for Smith at the age of 15 to Benjamin Smith, the son of a prosperous West Indian merchant. Her young husband was extravagant, abusive, and profligate. He quickly drove the family into debt and depended on his wife to appeal to his father for more money. In 1783, he was incarcerated in debtors' prison, where Smith herself soon joined him. She began writing out of financial necessity in an effort to support her many children. When her father-in-law died in 1776, his will, intended to provide for his grandchildren and protect the estate from his unreliable son, ironically had the opposite effect. The complexity of the will left Smith and her children unable to collect their much-needed inheritance. Smith continued to write in order to provide for her children and to preserve their social standing, always believing her career as an author was merely a temporary necessity until the estate was settled. She obtained a legal separation from Benjamin in 1787, and although her hus-

band hid from creditors in Scotland, he would often secretly return to England to claim Smith's book earnings as well as the interest on her marriage settlement—both of which he was legally entitled to receive. During these years Smith helped to establish her children in marriages and careers, struggled with her many creditors, and begged publishers for advances on her books. She never achieved the financial stability that would allow her to retire. Her "temporary" literary career lasted for 22 years and her father-in-law's estate was not settled until after her death in 1806.

MAJOR WORKS

Smith's first publication, *Elegiac Sonnets, and Other Essays* (1784), was a collection of various poems she had written over the years and rather hastily assembled while her husband was in debtors' prison. In 1785 when Benjamin fled to France to escape his creditors, Smith accompanied him. While there she translated into English Abbé Prévost's novel *Manon Lescaut* (1785), publishing the work upon her return to England the following summer. After her separation from her husband in 1787, Smith turned to novel writing in an attempt to generate income to support her large family. Her first novel, *Emmeline* (1788), met with both popular and critical acclaim and was quickly followed by *Ethelinde* (1789) and *Celestina* (1791). Considered by some critics a blending of elements of both the sentimental novel and the Gothic novel, these first three works all feature virtuous young heroines in distress, a standard feature of the sentimental genre, along with the poetic landscape descriptions characteristic of the Gothic.

Smith's fourth novel, *Desmond* (1792), proved a turning point for Smith's career as she changed focus from the subject of proper female conduct that marked her first three novels to political issues, specifically those inspired by the French Revolution. Many critics, in fact, believe that *Desmond* was a direct response to Edmund Burke's *Reflections on the Revolution in France*. Her succeeding novels also dealt with political concerns, although none with the stridency of *Desmond*. In all, Smith produced ten novels from 1788 to 1798.

Smith also produced several books for children—primarily didactic works designed to teach such virtues as charity, fortitude, and humility—and two more volumes of poetry. Her long poem *The Emigrants* (1793) was, like *Desmond*, inspired by the French Revolution; the work urged sympathy for the unfortunate refugees displaced by the events in France. Her final work of poetry, *Beachy Head with Other Poems* (1807), was published posthumously.

CRITICAL RECEPTION

Smith's books—particularly her sonnets—were well received by her contemporaries. Wordsworth described her as "a lady to whom English verse is under greater obligations than are likely to be either acknowledged or remembered." Coleridge credited Smith and William Lisle Bowles with popularizing the sonnet form in the late eighteenth century, and later critics acknowledge her efforts not only to revive the sonnet form but to adapt it to the mood of contemporary England. But in the years between her death and the modern revival of interest in her work, Smith was largely forgotten, and the attribution for the revival of the sonnet was generally assigned to Bowles. However, scholar Brent Raycroft insists this recognition rightfully belongs to Smith and suggests that critical neglect of her work can be attributed to "the deep-set prejudice against admitting women into the mainstream of literary history," as well as to Smith's politics, which Raycroft describes as "somewhere between liberal and radical," in contrast to Bowles's conservative affiliation.

Many modern critics focus on the autobiographical elements in Smith's work, particularly her sonnets, which tend to be uniformly melancholy. In her own time, Smith's rival Anna Seward criticized what she considered Smith's constant complaining, calling the sonnets "everlasting lamentables." But modern scholars find wider implications in Smith's plaintiveness than Seward did. Deborah Kennedy, while conceding that the tone of Smith's sonnets is relentlessly gloomy, claims that writing about the effects of oppression on women was an act of defiance against the patriarchy. Critics also consider that many elements of Smith's novels are based on characters and incidents from her life. Judith Stanton, who has edited Smith's 430 letters, claims that the letters "reveal how very autobiographical her fiction is." Stanton maintains that Smith's husband Benjamin served as the model for many of her degenerate, albeit charming, male characters. Katharine M. Rogers, however, suggests that the circumstances of Smith's life did not aid her in producing fiction, but rather interfered with her ability to incorporate the ideals of Romanticism into her novels. "Perpetually weighed down by family cares, she could not escape to or even maintain faith in an ideal world," Rogers explains.

Many scholars have pointed out that by incorporating autobiographical incidents and characters in her fiction, Smith was critiquing social and cultural issues that affected all women. Diane Long Hoeveler asserts that the real concerns of Smith's first novel are inheritance, property ownership, and social status. She believes that *Emmeline* is a testament of how difficult it is for women to navigate in a social system that defines them as "appendages, dependents . . . to the 'main chance,' the patriarch." Terence Allan Hoagwood has objected to the concentration on the details of Smith's personal misery that has informed much of the criticism of her work from shortly after her death to the present. Carrol L. Fry also emphasizes the larger issues in Smith's work, claiming that "in all her novels after 1791, Smith adapts the conventions of fiction to present social and political issues from a republican perspective" in order to help educate her female readers.

Some feminist critics rank her on a level with Mary Wollstonecraft in criticizing the effects of patriarchy on women's lives, although she was not as overtly radical as Wollstonecraft. Eleanor Ty has studied the contradictions in Smith's first novel *Emmeline,* and suggests that her feminism, less explicit than that of her more radical peers, "is manifested in more subversive ways." According to Ty, "Through narratives that seem to contradict each other, through the conflation of seemingly 'pure' and corrupt characters, or the depiction of apparently kind-hearted figures who turn out to be not so benevolent, Smith questions the moral and social values of her contemporary society."

PRINCIPAL WORKS

Elegiac Sonnets, and Other Essays (poetry) 1784; enlarged edition 1786; enlarged as *Elegiac Sonnets* 1789; enlarged edition 1792; enlarged edition 1795; enlarged as *Elegiac Sonnets, and Other Poems* 2 vols. 1797

Manon Lescaut by Abbé Prévost [translator] (novel) 1785
Emmeline, The Orphan of the Castle 4 vols. (novel) 1788
Ethelinde; or, The Recluse of the Lake 5 vols. (novel) 1789
Celestina: A Novel 4 vols. (novel) 1791
Desmond: A Novel 3 vols. (novel) 1792
The Emigrants: A Poem, in Two Books (poetry) 1793
The Old Manor House: A Novel 4 vols. (novel) 1793
The Banished Man: A Novel 4 vols. (novel) 1794
The Wanderings of Warwick (novel) 1794
Montalbert: A Novel 3 vols. (novel) 1795
Marchmont: A Novel 4 vols. (novel) 1796
A Narrative of the Loss of the Catharine, Venus, and Piedmont Transports, and the Thomas, Golden Grove, and Æolus Merchant Ships, Near Weymouth, on Wednesday the 18th of November Last (journalism) 1796
Minor Morals, interspersed with Sketches of Natural History, Historical Anecdotes, and Original Stories (children's stories) 1798
The Young Philosopher: A Novel 4 vols. (novel) 1798
The Letters of a Solitary Wanderer (novel) 1800
Conversations Introducing Poetry, Chiefly on Subjects of Natural History, for the Use of Children and Young Persons 2 vols. (fictional dialogues and poetry) 1804
Beachy Head, with Other Poems (poetry) 1807
The Natural History of Birds, Intended Chiefly for Young Persons 2 vols. (non-fiction) 1807

CRITICISM

British Critic (review date 1807)

SOURCE: "*Beachy Head,* with Other Poems" *British Critic* 30 (August 1807): 170-74.

[*In the following review, the author laments the death of Smith and praises her posthumous poems as some of her best work, particularly noting the composition and tone.*]

Most sincerely do we lament the death of Mrs. Charlotte Smith. We acknowledged in her a genuine child of genius, a most vivid fancy, refined taste, and extraordinary sensibility. We could not, indeed, always accord with her in sentiment. With respect to some subjects beyond her line of experience, reading, and indeed talent, she was unfortunately wayward and preposterous; but her poetic feeling and ability have rarely been surpassed by any individual of her sex. Her sonnets in particular will remain models of that species of composition; and, as Johnson remarked of Gray's Elegy in a Country Church-yard, had she always written thus, it were vain to blame and useless to praise her. It remains to take notice of these posthumous poems. The first is on **"Beachy Head,"** and in blank verse. Blank verse is of late becoming a favourite style of composition. We are inclined to suspect that this proceeds either from idleness, or from a conscious want of powers. But a vast deal more is required in blank verse than youthful poets may at first imagine. We are by no means satisfied with the regular and correct structure of the verse, we require both classical taste, strong poetical fancy, a judicious arrangement, and melodious rythm.

Mrs. Smith has demonstrated in this her first poem, that she could adorn any branch of poetry upon which she chose to exercise her powers. This poem is distinguished by great vigour, and, by what was the characteristic of the author's mind, a sweet and impressive tenderness of melancholy. It is a very charming composition. We would not disgrace our page by any hypercritical cavil on little oversights and inaccuracies, but confidently appeal to the subjoined specimen in vindication of the praise which we have given to this poem.

> "Ah who is happy? Happiness! a word
> That like false fire, from marsh effluvia born
> Misleads the wanderer, destin'd to contend
> In the world's wilderness, with want or woe—
> Yet *they* are happy, who have never asked
> What good or evil means. The boy
> That on the river's margin gaily plays,
> Has heard that Death is there.—He knows not Death,
> And therefore fears it not; and venturing in
> He gains a bullrush, or a minnow—then,
> At certain peril, for a worthless prize
> A crow's, or raven's nest, he climbs the boll
> Of some tall pine; and of his prowess proud
> Is for a moment happy. Are *your* cares
> Ye who despise him, never worse applied?
> The village girl is happy, who sets forth
> To distant fair, gay in her Sunday suit,
> With cherry-colour'd knots, and flourish'd shawl
> And bonnet newly purchas'd. So is he
> Her little brother, who his mimic drum
> Beats till he drowns her rural lovers' oaths
> Of constant faith and still increasing love;
> Ah yet awhile, and half those oaths believ'd,
> Her happiness is vanished; and the boy
> While yet a stripling, finds the sound he lov'd
> Has led him on, till he has given up
> His freedom and his happiness together.
> I once was happy, when while yet a child
> I learn'd to love these upland solitudes,
> And, when elastic as the mountain air,
> To my light spirit, care was yet unknown,
> And evil unforeseen:—Early it came
> And childhood scarcely passed I was condemned
> A guiltless exile silently to sigh,
> While Memory, with faithful pencil, drew
> The contrast; and regretting, I compar'd
> With the polluted smoky atmosphere
> And dark and stifling streets, the southern hills
> That to the setting sun, their graceful heads
> Rearing o'erlook the Frith, where Vecta breaks
> With her white rocks, the strong impetuous tide,
> When western winds the vast Atlantic urge
> To thunder on the coast—Haunts of my youth
> Scenes of fond day dreams, I behold ye yet
> Where 'twas so pleasant by thy northern slopes
> To climb the winding sheep-path, aided oft
> By scatter'd thorns, whose spiny branches bore

Small woolly tufts, spoils of the vagrant lamb,
There seeking shelter from the noon-day sun;
And pleasant, seated on the short soft turf
To look beneath upon the hollow way,
While heavily upward mov'd the labouring wain;
And stalking slowly by, the sturdy hind
To ease his panting team stopp'd with a stone
The grating wheel."

The second poem in the volume is the Truant Dove, from Pilpay, very interesting and very elegant; but as it is not original, we say no more than that it will well repay the reader's attention. The third is the Lark's Nest, from Æsop, which is precisely in the same predicament, except that it indicates, what does not often appear in this writer's productions, much playfulness and genuine humour. The next is an original poem, named **"The Swallow,"** and this we give at length.

"The Swallow."

"The gorfe is yellow on the heath,
    The banks with speedwell flowers are gay,
The oaks are budding; and beneath,
The hawthorn soon will bear the wreath,
    The silver wreath of May.

"The welcome guest of settled spring,
    The Swallow too is come at last;
Just at sun-set when thrushes sing,
I saw her dash with rapid wing,
    And hail'd her as she pass'd.

"Come, summer visitant, attach
    To my reed roof your nest of clay,
And let my ear your music catch
Low twittering underneath the thatch
    At the gray dawn of day.

"As fables tell, an Indian Sage,
    The Hindostani woods among,
Could in his desert hermitage,
As if t'were mark'd in written page,
    Translate the wild birds song.

"I wish I did his power possess
    That I might learn, fleet bird, from thee,
What our vain systems only guess,
And know from what wide wilderness
    You came across the sea.

"I would a little while restrain
    Your rapid wing that I might hear
Whether on clouds that bring the rain
You fail'd above the western main,
    The wind your charioteer.

"In Afric does the sultry gale
    Thro' spicy bower, and palmy grove
Bear the repeated cuckoo's tale?
Dwells *there* a time, the wandering quail,
    Or the itinerant dove.

"Were you in Asia? O relate
    If there your fabled sisters woes
She seem'd in sorrow to narrate;
Or sings she but to celebrate
    Her nuptials with the rose.

"I would enquire how journeying long
    The vast and pathless ocean o'er,
You ply again those pinions strong,
And come to build anew among
    The scenes you left before;

"But if, as colder breezes blow
    Prophetic of the waning year,
You hide, tho' none know when or how,
In the cliff's excavated brow,
    And linger torpid here;

"Thus lost to life, what favouring dream
    Bids you to happier hours awake,
And tells, that dancing in the beam,
The light gnat hovers o'er the stream,
    The May fly on the lake.

"Or if, by instinct taught to know
    Approaching dearth of insect food,
To isles and willowy airs you go.
And crouding on the pliant bough
    Sink in the dimpling flood.

"How learn ye, while the cold waves boom
    Your deep and ouzy couch above,
The time when flowers of promise bloom,
And call you from your transient tomb,
    To light, and life, and love?

"Alas! how little can be known
    Her sacred veil where Nature draws;
Let baffled Science humbly own,
Her mysteries understood alone
    By *Him* who gives her laws."

"Flora," which succeeds, has been printed before, in *Conversations for the Use of Children and Young Persons*; so has the next poem, called **"Studies by the Sea."** This is followed by the **"Horologe of the Fields, addressed to a Young Lady, on seeing at the house of an acquaintance a magnificent French Time-piece."** This is a very elegant and well-timed composition, intimating that many of the simple productions of nature will, to those who well observe them, mark the periods as they pass, as well as these costly and splendid toys. Such, for example, as the Nymphæa, the Hieracium's various tribe, the Star of Bethlem, the Arenaria, Silene, and others, which contract or expand their flowers at different hours of the day. The next poem is entitled **"Saint Monica,"** which is followed by a Walk in the Shrubbery, Hope, Evening, Love and Folly, from Fontune, and a trifling Jeu d'Esprit, on the Aphorism, "L'Amitie est l'Amour sans ailes."—Notes are added to all the poems, but of no material value.

We take our leave of this author with unseigned regret and sympathy. Her life was embittered by sorrow and misfortune, this gave an unavoidable tinge to her sentiments, which, from the gay and the vain, and the unfeeling, may excite a sneer of scorn and contempt; but in the bosoms of those who, like Charlotte Smith, with refined feelings, improved by thought and study, and reflection, have been compelled, like her, to tread the thorny paths of adversity, will prompt the generous wish, that fortune had favoured her with more complacency; and will induce the disposition to extenuate such portions of her productions, as sterner judgment is unable to approve.

Sarah Zimmerman (essay date 1991)

SOURCE: Zimmerman, Sarah. "Charlotte Smith's Letters and the Practice of Self-Presentation." *Princeton University Library Chronicle* 53, no. 1 (autumn 1991): 50-77.

[*In the following essay, Zimmerman discusses Smith's constant efforts to present herself to her readers and publishers as a woman attempting to support her children through her writings.*]

In a letter to her publishers written in March 1797, Charlotte Smith requests changes to a portrait for a new edition of her *Elegiac Sonnets,* the collection of poems which had already undergone seven editions since its initial appearance in 1784.[1] The engraving provided a visual counterpart to the verbal self-portrait that her writings comprised. Smith was sharply aware that her continuing success was generated largely by her readers' sympathetic response to a figure of herself as elegiac poet. The alterations represent subtle refinements in a practice of self-presentation which had helped to make her, by the time she wrote the letter, one of the most popular English writers of the late eighteenth century.[2] "In regard to my picture" she wrote,

> I do not return it because I very much doubt whether the faults that I see in the engraving can be alterd—The face is too long; that must remain so I know My family & such friends as I have shewn it to, think there is a want of spirit in the eyes—If that can be amended it may, & I will send up the picture with the book Under the portrait is to be this motto from Shakespeare which perhaps may be set about immediately
>
> Oh! grief has changed me since you saw me last
> And sorrowing hours with times deforming hand
> Have written strange defeatures in my face.[3]

The letter offers us a vivid glimpse of a writer whose profile has been obscured since her death in 1806. Shortly thereafter, a reviewer worried about the longevity of the fame that she had so obviously worked hard to earn. He recalled that "during the *whole* course of her literary career, she was embarrassed in her affairs, entangled in *legal difficulties,* and sometimes enduring the pangs of penury, and that HER PEN was not only a mental but a pecuniary resource; which, if we consider its various and successful exertions, ought to have proved as PERMANENT as it was PROLIFIC."[4] The reviewer's doubt about the endurance of Smith's reputation proved prescient, but recently there have been signs of a revival of interest: two of her novels have recently reappeared in print,[5] and a limited but steady stream of criticism is increasing.

By providing us with documents from her practice of self-portraiture, the seventeen letters by Smith in the Princeton University Library aid contemporary readers in retracing her cultural figure. They are addressed to her various publishers, except for two, which were written to the Reverend Samuel Greatheed, who helped Smith to sell an edition of *Elegiac Sonnets* by subscription.[6] The letters, found in four different collections in the Library, comprise a scattered group with a cumulative import which seems out of proportion to their number.[7]

In the 1797 letter to her publishers, we find Smith paying minute attention to the production of her works, a process which she oversaw repeatedly, from the proposal of a new idea, through negotiations with her publishers, to the presentation of the volumes themselves, including their illustrations. The letter is exemplary of the care that she took with her epistolary prose. For Smith, letter-writing was not only an expected accomplishment for an eighteenth-century author but also a way to win the support of persons who could help her.

Smith was persistent and shrewd in her dealings with publishers, but aware that she—and the family she supported—depended primarily upon a general audience, and her greatest effort went into turning her life into appealing reading material. In the 1797 letter, she strikes a Shakespearean pose to allude to her own particular circumstances. In her works, Smith repeatedly adopted gestures familiar to her readers from literary tradition in order to tell—in a reassuring guise—the story of a late-eighteenth-century woman supporting her children by writing.[8] Although *Elegiac Sonnets* includes translations of sonnets by Petrarch, Goethe, and Metastasio in which a male speaker addresses a female lover, Smith's own poems exclude the subject of erotic love to protect her self-portrait as a mother who wrote only to support her family.

Smith's letters are written by a steady hand that consistently adorns certain letters with a flourish, a style that avoids the appearance of either harshness or frivolity. In all of her correspondence we find a writer at work, managing a prolific career of more than twenty-two years during which she published, on average, one book each year. The Library's letters elaborate the circumstances in which her works were written: she apprises her publishers of the progress of her volumes, requests advances and, occasionally, more time. The group of letters spans a period nearly as long as Smith's career. The earliest dated letter was written in January 1788, four years after *Elegiac Sonnets* first appeared, and the latest letter was written in June 1804, just two years before her death.

The Library also holds three prints from engravings of the portrait by George Romney that Smith mentions in the 1797 letter to her publishers.[9] A fourth print in the Library may have been drawn from the same portrait. The group of portraits provides visual evidence to support Smith's implicit contention in the letter that, in engravings, small alterations produce significant effects: her expression changes from a dejection bordering on listlessness to the "spirited" gravity that she wanted to convey.

The letters provide us with detailed accounts of how Smith managed a career of continual self-presentation, but they are also important works in themselves. In her published writings Smith claims to write directly from her own experience. Her letters employ a similar rhetoric of actuality, as she tells various readers parts of the story that she rehearses at length for a general audience. In what follows, I will argue that Smith's letters are emblematic of her published writings in that, in her correspondence, she borrowed gestures from literary convention to present her case directly to her readers, a practice that she maintained in the works themselves. In all of her writings, Smith adopted the familiarity of epistolary prose to give her distressed circumstances a human face.

. . . . .

In her letters and published writings, Smith left distinct outlines of her life for readers to follow. Her critics have found circumstances that lend themselves to narration.[10] Smith's birth in 1749 into a prominent family that owned property in Surrey and Sussex was followed, three years later, by her first and perhaps her greatest tragedy. Charlotte's mother died in childbirth, leaving three children in the care of their father and aunt. A minor poet himself, Charlotte's father encouraged his daughter's early enthusiasm for reading and writing, but her fashionable education prepared her primarily for an advantageous marriage, an event which came early, when she was fifteen. Her brief engagement to Benjamin Smith, a suitor chosen by Charlotte's guardians, was followed by a married life of increasing instability. Her husband's gambling and brutality brought financial ruin to a growing family and led to the couple's separation.

Even before she left her husband, Charlotte found herself responsible for her children's—and often her husband's—support. She began to write for publication in an effort to maintain the family's social standing until her father-in-law's estate could be settled. Richard Smith had attempted to ensure a comfortable existence for his daughter-in-law's family by leaving the bulk of his property to her children, but his complex will provoked a legal battle about which one critic recalls, "The Jarndyce case itself was not a greater godsend to the Chancery Bar."[11] The estate was settled shortly after Charlotte's own death, thirty years later.

In 1783, Benjamin Smith was sentenced to serve seven months at the King's Bench for debt.[12] In an attempt to raise money for her husband's release, and to support, at the time, nine children, Charlotte approached a prominent London publisher and bookseller, James Dodsley, with a small selection of poems. Dodsley declined to publish the collection, but offered to print them at cost in exchange for any profits generated. In an early show of her business acumen, Smith refused his proposal only to return with permission to dedicate the volume to the poet William Hayley, patron of William Blake, along with the confidence to have the poems printed at her own expense.[13] She was rewarded for her daring by the immediate success of

Elegiac Sonnets and Other Essays. In the course of ten subsequent editions, the collection grew from a slim volume of twenty-five sonnets with three other poems to a two-volume set with ninety-two sonnets and twenty-seven poems. As successive editions of the sonnets appeared, Smith published two other volumes of poetry, eleven novels, two translations from the French, four works for young readers, a journalistic narrative of a shipwreck, a book of natural history, and a history of England. An autobiographical thread can be traced throughout the works, emerging in characters who resemble Smith in the novels and works for children, and, most recognizably, as the first-person speakers in her poems.

In a review of her long poem, *The Emigrants,*[14] a critic for *The European Magazine* describes Smith as a poet "whom we can discover almost at the bottom of every page, as we may the portrait of some of the most renowned painters in the corner of their most favourite pictures."[15] Smith's fate in literary history, however, has been to fall somewhere between periods conventionally defined by Thomas Gray and William Wordsworth. Her features were still easily recognizable to the generation of writers that followed her. Although he pointedly distanced himself from most of his eighteenth-century predecessors, William Wordsworth acknowledged Smith's significance to his poetics.[16] In an explanatory note to his "Stanzas Suggested in a Steamboat off St. Bees' Heads, on the Coast of Cumberland," he memorializes a poet already fading from public view in 1835: "The form of stanza in this Poem, and something in the style of versification, are adopted from the **"St. Monica,"** a poem of much beauty upon a monastic subject, by Charlotte Smith: a lady to whom English verse is under greater obligations than are likely to be either acknowledged or remembered."[17] Coleridge turned to Smith's poetry in his attempt to theorize the sonnet.[18] In his introduction to a collection of sonnets printed and circulated privately in 1796, he argues that, since Smith and William Lisle Bowles were the poets who "first made the Sonnet popular among the present English," he is "justified" in "deducing its laws from *their* compositions."[19] Smith herself declined to theorize her writings. Instead of producing poetic manifestos, she found herself from the time of her first publication having to justify her reasons for writing.

. . . . .

Most of Smith's volumes open with prefaces in which she addresses her readers directly, telling them her own story in an attempt to win their sympathy and their readership. In a letter to her publisher, Thomas Cadell, Sr., she announces her decision to publicize her circumstances:

> I think it necessary to say that in the preface I mean to touch on the hardship of my situation—Who after waiting *nine* years while the Estate of Richard Smith the Grandfather was at [?] now, that all his debts are confessedly clear'd—& Effects arising every day, am no better off than before because Mr. Dyer whose children have an 8th share (& that partly conditional, in the property) opposes any division till his youngest child is of age, who is abt. Seventeen—tho he has not the

shadow of pretence for it. I am driven almost to despair by these circumstances; and the conduct of Mr. Smith—who lives upon the interest of my fortune, with a Woman he keeps, leaving me to support as well as I can his seven Children who are in England.[20]

In all of her writings, Smith presents her case to the public: in the prefaces, letters, poetry, prose works, and even in the novels, she depicts herself as a woman wronged by a profligate husband and by a society that excuses his financial abandonment and his emotional and physical abuse. By offering an account of indigence in the language of sensibility, Smith presented herself as a sympathetic figure to a public familiar with tales of women's suffering from the sentimental novels that followed the example of Samuel Richardson's *Clarissa*.[21] In **Elegiac Sonnets,** Smith assumed a role that was already available—the heroine of sensibility—but she revitalized the story by providing her readers with details from her own life—an on-going plot. The prefaces that open most of her works became, in effect, a serialized autobiographical narrative.

In the preface to the first edition of **Elegiac Sonnets,** she predicted that her readers will be "the few, who, to sensibility of heart, join simplicity of taste."[22] Smith presented herself as a woman who had entered the literary marketplace only when she found herself responsible for supporting her family. She confided to her readers,

> Some very melancholy moments have been beguiled by expressing in verse the sensations those moments brought. Some of my friends, with partial indiscretion, have multiplied the copies they procured of several of these attempts, till they found their way into the prints of the day in a mutilated state; which, concurring with other circumstances, determined me to put them into their present form.[23]

Smith seems to speak candidly, but her account follows an established convention of denying a desire to publish writings which were written exclusively for the pleasure of friends. Her disclaimer, however, provided Smith with more than the appearance of a becoming modesty: it offered a necessary justification for her prominent position in the literary marketplace. A year after Smith's death, a critic described the precarious position of women writers in late-eighteenth-century England: "The penalties and discouragements attending the profession of an author fall upon women with a double weight; to the curiosity of the idle and the envy of the malicious, their sex affords a peculiar incitement: arraigned, not merely as writers, but as *women,* their characters, their conduct, even their personal endowments, become the subjects of severe inquisition." Smith's case was complicated by her active involvement in a legal battle, a circumstance which she publicized to win sympathy and support from her readers. The critic recalls: "Mrs. Smith individually created enemies by the zeal and perseverance with which she endeavored to obtain justice for her children, on the part of men who hated her in proportion as they had injured her."[24]

Despite her candor about her financial situation, Smith was sharply aware of the need to remain a sympathetic figure. In her preface to the sixth edition of **Elegiac Sonnets,** she reassures her readers that "notwithstanding I am thus frequently appearing as an Authoress, and have derived from thence many of the greatest advantages of my life, (since it has procured me friends whose attachment is most invaluable,) I am well aware that for a woman— "The Post of Honor is a Private Station.'"[25] Smith's rhetorical agility is exemplified in the way that she praises the institution of domesticity even as she submits another edition to the public.

In both her letters and her published writings, Smith was careful to placate potentially censorious readers. Writing to Thomas Cadell, Sr., in one of the Library's letters, she explains "I should not Sir trouble you with this history, but to account not only for steps if lost must still be compell'd to take, but to shew you that I cannot afford to lose the smallest profit that may arise from my *exertions*; which but for these difficulties, I should never make."[26] A letter in the Library from William Hayley to Smith's daughter, Charlotte Mary, suggests that Smith made no distinction between her "public" and her "private" writings. Shortly after Smith's death, Hayley worried: "I fear your mother was rather displeased by the very honest advice I ventured to give her against an idea of printing a volume of her letters—However excellent her Letters might be & they certainly excelled in that brand of literature I thought the measure of printing her letters in her life-time not suited to the dignity of her literary character."[27]

The letters themselves provide evidence that she considered them publishable. In both her correspondence and in her published works, Smith relies on practices of narration and description to win an audience. Writing to her publisher, Thomas Cadell, Sr., in one of the Library's letters, Smith turns her sure sense of plot to her own pressing circumstances. In an attempt to persuade them not to relinquish her earnings to her husband, she tells them a "story" which is worth quoting at length:

> The reluctance I ever feel to give *you* farther trouble, who have already so much and who have voluntarily undertaken so much on my account; has prevented me mentioning my renewd apprehensions abt. Mr. Smiths taking the residue of what may be in *your* hands, on my behalf—but now it becomes necessary for me to inform you that abt. a month since, he wrote to me to say, that as he had *taken* his passage for Barbados, he beg'd to see his children before he went.
>
> As I could not doubt an assertion so positive; and as many of our joint friends to whom he had represented his sorrow at being parted from his "dear Wife and children"; thought I *ought* to comply with this request; I not only assented to it, but instead of sending his children to meet him at the Inn as he suppos'd I should, I hired a post chaise and met him myself at Godalming, desirous not only to convince him I had no malice against him; but to conceal his journey from his numerous creditors in Hampshire and Sussex—concluding he would only stay a day or two and then return to sail for the West Indies.
>
> But I soon found reason to repent my credulous folly— Tho my house is so small & I have eight children at

home & am therefore forced to put a tent bed up in my little Book room; he took possession of it, & treated me with more than his usual brutality—threatening to sell the furniture, the Books and every accessory which I have since saved from the rapacity of his Creditors. This is the situation I have been in for three weeks; yet I have borne it with patience, in hopes of obtaining what I at length got him to do, a deed providing out of my fortune for his three younger children; born since the death of their Grandfather, who has given to the rest some provision. But within these two or three days a new fit of frenzy has seizd him; he has broke open all my drawers where my papers were; taken away several sign'd receipts for the Sonnets (of which Heaven knows what use he may make;) and foul copies of many things I am writing, all of which he has taken with him; and he openly declared a resolution of demanding of you, the money you hold of mine. To day he is gone—to London; & there is reason to suppose may make immediate application to you—I now believe him capable of *any* thing, and therefore relying entirely on you, beg the favor of you if you have any apprehensions of his having the *power* to take the money; that you will be so good as to pay it into the hands of your own Banker, or any confidential friend; and on your informing me that you have done so, I will instantly forward to you a receipt in full of all demands—And I am informed that on your producing such receipt to Mr. Smith he can have no power to molest or trouble you—I shall be extremely uneasy till I hear from you or Mr. Davis on this matter—as he appears careless of every thing, & totally regardless of the infamy that must attend on such an action—From his own account he is connected with persons in Town, who are engaged in the desperation of gaming houses, and I know not what—& from such a Man so acquainted I and my family have every thing to fear.[28]

Smith's apprehensions were prescient, but even she could not foresee how long she would have to evade her husband's claims. His "circumstances" remained desperate until his death, which came just six months before her own.

Smith's letters and published works share a vocabulary of sensibility. In letters to her publishers, she often interjects requests for better financial terms and advances into narrative accounts that read like novels. In one of the Library's letters, she writes to Cadell and Davies to propose a price for *Celestina,* her third novel, of "£50 a volume," and requests that the transaction be completed as quickly as possible. She explains that although "the Ballance if any will be but small, it will be of service to me now, as I am straining every reserve to keep up appearances till my daughters establishment with a Man of fortune who has been some months attach'd to her is secured." She describes her situation with a disarming frankness, but concludes with a distinctly literary phrase: "For this, as it is worth every thing to me & my other children, I would spare no exertion; & indeed it is well worth every effort; as the one of few things that wd. give a new colour to my hitherto dark & sad destiny—."[29] For her, letters are an occasional genre: she presents her publishers with a dated document informing them that, while she has "never been more distressed," it is in their power to help her. Smith's writings deliberately confuse conventional distinctions between autobiography and fiction in order to add the interest of "real life" to the appeal of familiar literary forms.

Smith recognized that her success was partly due to the believability of her self-portrait. An unidentified poet published a "Sonnet to Mrs. Smith" in *The European Magazine* rapturously lamenting the circumstances that inspired her:

> Than thine no tenderer plaints the heart can move,
> More rouse the soul to sympathetic love;
> And yet—sad source! they spring from REAL WOE.[30]

Smith also used the pale tints of pastoral to "colour" the circumstances of her life for public presentation. She sketches a natural setting for her self-portrait: a landscape comprised of details culled from her indigenous surroundings and the familiar props of pastoral tradition. At the back of each volume of poetry is a section of "Quotations, Notes, and Explanations" in which she cites allusions to other authors, provides short biographies of poets mentioned, and descriptions of plants and animals. In the notes, Smith addresses her readers directly and verifies her personal knowledge of the scenes and events in the poems. In *Elegiac Sonnets,* a landscape with carefully documented botanical and ornithological detail is peopled by an incongruous crowd: the shepherds and nymphs of pastoral tradition share the countryside with local poets Thomas Otway, William Collins, and William Hayley, and with Smith herself.

The notes elaborate a common ground for the sonnets and become increasingly important in later editions. Some of them, in fact, seem to be prose accompaniments to the poems. The note to **"Sonnet XLIV," "Written in the Church-Yard at Middleton in Sussex,"** is nearly as long as the poem itself:

> Press'd by the Moon, mute arbitress of tides,
> While the loud equinox its power combines,
> The sea no more its swelling surge confines,
> But o'er the shrinking land sublimely rides.
> The wild blast, rising from the Western cave,
> Drives the huge billows from their heaving bed;
> Tears from their grassy tombs the village dead,
> And breaks the silent sabbath of the grave!
> With shells and sea-weed mingled, on the shore
> Lo! their bones whiten in the frequent wave;
> But vain to them the winds and waters rave;
> *They* hear the warring elements no more:
> While I am doom'd—by life's long storm opprest,
> To gaze with envy, on their gloomy rest.[31]

In the note, the sonnet's imagery is recycled into a brief, self-sufficient narrative. The information provided seems, at best, incidental to the poem, but the note manages to situate an event which could take place anywhere within Smith's local landscape. "Middleton," she informs us,

> is a village on the margin of the sea, in Sussex, containing only two or three houses. There were formerly several acres of ground between its small church and

the sea, which now, by its continual encroachments, approaches within a few feet of this half ruined and humble edifice. The wall, which once surrounded the church-yard, is entirely swept away, many of the graves broken up, and the remains of bodies interred washed into the sea: whence human bones are found among the sand and shingles on the shore.[32]

Although the scene is horrific in the generality of its details—the very namelessness of the dead suggests a universal destruction that borders on the apocalyptic—the note locates the event within a familiar setting, and thereby enhances the poem's autobiographical appeal.

In many of the sonnets, a speaker elliptically laments the fate that led her away from the early pleasures of her native countryside only to cast her back into the landscapes in which she wanders, drawn to solitary expanses but estranged from their serenity. Most of the poems depict a speaker who resembles the elegiac figure of the frontispiece portrait, wandering in a landscape which seems to be Smith's own rural Sussex. Her claims for the authenticity of her writings require an attention to natural detail. **"Sonnet II," "Written at the Close of Spring,"** rehearses the story in its most succinct form:

> The garlands fade that Spring so lately wove,
> Each simple flower, which she had nursed in dew,
> Anemonies, that spangled every grove,
> The primrose wan, and hare-bell, mildly blue.
> No more shall violets linger in the dell,
> Or purple orchis variegate the plain,
> Till Spring again shall call forth every bell,
> And dress with humid hands her wreaths again.—
> Ah! poor humanity! so frail, so fair,
> Are the fond visions of thy early day,
> Till tyrant passion, and corrosive care,
> Bid all thy fairy colours fade away!
> Another May new buds and flowers shall bring;
> Ah! why has happiness—no second Spring?[33]

"Sonnet II" opens Smith's collection with a clear but unacknowledged echo of the second stanza of Gray's "Ode on a Distant Prospect of Eton College." Standing where he can view the landscape of his childhood, Gray's speaker mourns the period when he was "A stranger yet to pain." Smith, too, posits an Edenic state from which she was banished to become a mother and a popular writer. Her autobiographical narrative traces a fall from a pastoral world into the arena of the literary marketplace. Her marriage is the unmentioned turning-point in her story, after which began a decline in her social and economic position. There can be no "second spring" for a mother who must support a family by her writing in late-eighteenth-century England.

While she displayed a surprising frankness about her circumstances, Smith recognized that she must temper their details before presenting them to an audience. The story of Leonora in *The Letters of a Solitary Wanderer* has seemed to many of her critics a pastoral version of Smith's childhood. Having lost her mother early in life, Leonora turns to a feminized natural world. She recalls, "Accustomed to wild and romantic scenery from my earliest remembrance, and being suffered, till I was seven years old, to be almost as free as the birds that inhabited the woods where I wandered; I was educated till then by nature, and have ever since been enthusiastically attached to my first instructress." In Leonora's narrative, Smith offers an account of her own fascination with natural history, an interest which became her trademark. She seems to be explaining her own interest in her natural surroundings as Leonora explains: "There are some very common plants of which I am particularly fond, because they were cultivated in a border that I was allowed to call my garden; and the wild flowers which grew on our hills, now give me, when I see them in other places, a sort of melancholy gratification."[34]

Smith's credibility as a natural historian was important to maintain the rhetoric of actuality that characterizes her writings. Her claims to write from personal experience are supported by her assiduous documentation of natural detail in the sonnets. In one of the Library's letters, she asks her publishers to make typographical changes in order to preserve her trademark accuracy, worrying, "Since I have got Smiths Tour, I find I have made some mistakes in regard to the names of the plants, which names I should be very sorry to print incorrectly. I cannot recollect the page but I *** out I have somewhere written Rododendron Alpinum. It ought to be Rhododen*drum* Ferrugineum."[35] Later in the letter in which she requests changes to her portrait, she threatens to omit a poem contributed by a friend if she cannot confirm its natural details. She predicts that compiling the notes to her new edition of ***Elegiac Sonnets*** "will take at least three days, as I will not be told as I was before (by Dr. Darwin & another judge) that I was deficient in correctness of natural History." She explains:

> In some very beautiful verses of my poor friends, there are some descriptive lines of the scenery & natural productions about Lisbon which for want of being accustomed to study such objects are I am sure represented by wrong names & in other respects incorrect—Nothing is more easy to correct without injury to the Poetry or Spirit—but I have not been able to obtain any history of Portugal to enable me to do this—& I am afraid I must omit the Poem on that account—if you know of any such book as relates to the plants & trees of Portugal & could borrow & send it me, I could perhaps please myself in the alterations I wish.[36]

The explanatory notes that appear at the back of each volume of poetry juxtapose references to Milton and Gray with citations from Erasmus Darwin and Linnaeus. Smith's writing can be described as lyric realism: her first-person speaker in the poems is a natural historian who carefully observes the world around her and who strongly resembles Smith herself. Walter Scott admired the way she "preserves in her landscapes the truth and precision of a painter." He confirms her own conviction about the importance of maintaining her scrupulous attention to detail by finding it "remarkable that the sea-coast scenery of Dorset and Devon, with which she must have been familiar, is scarce painted with more accuracy of description, than the tower upon a rugged headland on the coast of Caithness, which she could only become acquainted with by report."[37]

Smith's insistence on botanical accuracy extended from her verse to the accompanying illustrations. In the letter concerning her portrait, she also requests changes to an engraving for **"Sonnet XXXVI"**:

> I believe I shall be able to send off the book entirely ready for the press on Wednesday evening, but not to lose any more time about the last drawing I return it herewith & beg the favr. of you to say, that I am charm'd with the landscape part which is the prettiest thing I ever saw in my life, but I think the figure of the Nymph too fat—It takes off all that pensive look which becomes such an ideal being & looks more like the plump damsel of the Dairy than a Naiad—Nor do I like the bracers; they look too modern—& take off the classical appearance which such a figure ought to have A very little alteration wd. do away all these objections & I dare say Mr. Corbould wd. have the goodness to name to the engraver these little remarks, so as to have them, (the changes) made without altering the drawing—which is so very pretty in point of scenery that it cannot be better—I hope the engraver will take care of it for me—& instead of flowers round the head a reedlike wreath, or what represents acquatic plants was substituted, I think it would be more characteristic—.[38]

In the process of critiquing the illustration, Smith defines the qualities that characterize her writings: a "pensive" tone combined with "characteristic," plausible detail. By cataloging her poems' natural details, she emphasizes their veracity, and, by logical extension, validates the story of her life that she presents to her readers.

Smith's success enabled her to support her family, but her on-going legal battles and the need to provide for her husband and children kept her just ahead of her creditors. Evidence of the strain of her prolific writing and publishing began to emerge as an increasing bitterness and a new bluntness about the sources of her misery in her letters and published writings. In 1795, Smith's favorite child, Anna Augusta, died giving birth. In one of the Library's letters, she remarks, with an uncharacteristic flatness, "The Trustees have refus'd me not only assistance for my daughter while she lived, but wherewithal to bury her."[39] In the year that she found herself unable to afford her daughter's funeral, Smith published the seventh edition of **Elegiac Sonnets**, her eighth novel, and her first work for children.

The success of **Elegiac Sonnets** brought Smith a measure of celebrity, but she was continually aware that her children's welfare depended upon maintaining her popularity. In one of the Library's letters, Smith requests an extension, citing her need to protect "an encreasing reputation" which "I am of course very unwilling to risk," arguing that it would be better "to be a few weeks later than to send an hurried or incorrect performance abroad." Mindful, as always, that her success was her source of bargaining power, Smith adds:

> It may perhaps be not unpleasant to you to hear that my literary acquaintance & of course my fashion is daily encreasing I have been introduced among others to Mr. Sheridan who complimented me very highly on both the Novels—& indeed I have reason enough to be proud of [the?] attention I daily receive—.[40]

Smith was under the continual necessity of turning her "fashion" to immediate account. In a letter to a publisher written in 1789, she proposes a collection of "tales" to the publishing house of Robinson and urges favorable financial terms by mentioning her "reputation": "I shd. perhaps want some advance before the delivery of the book, which may & probably will be in April, but certainly none, till the Books were in considerable forwardness & approved by the first literary Judges."[41] Robinson, apparently, declined her proposal.

. . . . .

Smith's works were widely reviewed in the periodicals of the day, including *The Gentlemen's Magazine, The Monthly Magazine, The Analytical Review,* and *The European Magazine.* Her dramatic public figure elicited lavish praise and sharp censure, and occasional parody. Samuel Egerton Brydges, essayist, editor, and bibliographer, was Smith's ideal reader: he championed her cause by confirming and enhancing her self-portrait. In his *Imaginative Biography,* he retells her story, adding his own flourishes: "Sorrow was her constant companion; and she sang with a thorn at her bosom, which forced out strains of melody, expressive of the most affecting sensations, interwoven with the rich hues of an inspired fancy."[42]

Smith proved an equally tempting figure to satirists. In an essay on "The Sorrows of Mrs. Charlotte Smith," Viscount St. Cyres dryly observes that "contemporary critics had a certain case against her":

> Take, for example, her sixty-second sonnet, written "while passing by moonlight through a village, while the ground was covered with snow." The reader inevitably pictures her hurrying back to her cottage near Chichester, intent on a change of boots and a cup of tea; and it comes as a serious shock to his nerves when she informs him that really
>
> I wander, cheerless and unblest,
> And find in change of place but change of pain.
> For me, pale Eye of Evening, thy soft light
> Leads to no happy home; my weary way
> Ends but in sad vicissitudes of care:
> I only fly from doubt—to meet despair.[43]

Although St. Cyres relishes her potential for parody, he recognizes clearly that "quite an appreciable proportion of her tears was due to purely literary requirements."[44] Although he claims, in apparent outrage, that "No other grief that ever sighed has worn so much crape and bombazine," he assesses Smith's practice of self-presentation shrewdly: "Mrs. Smith was a servant of the public, and her many-headed master called for a melancholy tune."[45] St. Cyres realized that Smith's apparent candor and self-assurance obscure the fact that she was writing under the pressure of immediate economic necessity, and that her self-presentation was shaped in response to popular demand and according to the roles available to a woman writer in late-eighteenth-century England.

Despite her precarious position, however, Smith refused to limit herself to subjects considered safe for women writers. In the course of telling her own story, Smith chronicled social abuses that produced other victims and became an advocate for various political causes in her writings. Smith drew the wrath of conservative critics by protesting English marriage laws, the trade in African slaves, and the plight of the poor in England. In her first long poem, *The Emigrants,* she pleaded the case of exiles from post-revolutionary France, whom she recognized as the victims of a cause that she had initially supported. Smith used the rhetorical techniques that she had learned in presenting her own situation to publicize the circumstances of others; her prominence and her popularity made her a particularly effective spokesperson.

In 1795, Smith suspended work on her ninth novel, *Marchmont,* to lend her name to a particular cause. In November of that year, a storm destroyed six ships off the coast of Portland, taking nearly 250 lives. In an effort to raise money to support two survivors of the disaster—appropriately, a mother and her child—friends of the victims asked Smith to prepare an account of the event for sale by subscription. Narratives of shipwrecks were a popular genre, and their marketability could be enhanced by a prominent author. Working from the accounts of survivors and witnesses, Smith prepared *A Narrative of the Loss of the Catherine, Venus, and Piedmont Transports, and the Thomas, Golden Grove, and Æolus Merchant Ships, Near Weymouth, on Wednesday the 18th of November Last.*[46] After her death Smith's earliest biographer, her sister Catherine Anne Dorset, recalls: "She was always the friend of the unfortunate, and spared neither her time, her talents, nor even her purse, in the cause of those she endeavoured to serve."[47]

Smith's fourth novel, *Desmond,*[48] drew her earliest and harshest reviews from conservative critics incensed by its sympathy for radical political reform in England and France.[49] In her preface, Smith makes an argument in support of women's education in which she implicitly defends her own stance as woman author and public figure:

> But women it is said have no business with politics—Why not?—Have they no interest in the scenes that are acting around them, in which they have fathers, brothers, husbands, sons, or friends engaged?—Even in the commonest course of female education, they are expected to acquire some knowledge of history; and yet, if they are to have no opinion of what *is* passing, it avails little that they should be informed of what *has passed,* in a world where they are subject to such mental degradation; where they are answered as affecting masculine knowledge if they happen to have any understanding; or despised as insignificant triflers if they have none.[50]

The position that Smith defines for women is, of course, one that she had adopted herself: that of the "informed" and "knowledgeable" observer of the "scenes that are acting around them," a task for which Smith's own education had not prepared her. In writing her own *History of England,* Smith makes a gesture toward redressing the inequalities in men's and women's education by arranging her account "in a series of letters to a young lady at school."[51]

In her two long poems, *The Emigrants* and **"Beachy Head,"** Smith provides panoramic views of her contemporary surroundings from the perspective of a first-person speaker who chronicles and comments on the events, both natural and human, that unfold in front of her. Her practice of observing and describing the natural world and her reputation for scrupulous attention to detail made Smith a believable witness. Politically conservative critics were alarmed by a female speaker who could arouse sympathy and anger on behalf of other "unfortunates" by pleading her own cause. Smith's success in raising financial relief for survivors of a natural disaster seemed to indicate a similar capacity to aid those victimized by their social environment. In **"Beachy Head,"** a poem left unfinished at her death in 1806, Smith's speaker extends her line of sight beyond the contemporary political scene to document historical event. In her last works, Smith herself assumed the role of natural and social historian, in *A Natural History of Birds* and the unfinished *History of England.*

. . . . .

In *Elegiac Sonnets,* Smith introduces herself as a heroine of sensibility, a role that becomes politicized as she begins to chronicle her contemporary world and to protest the abuses she witnesses. In **"Beachy Head,"** Smith begins to articulate a final stance: by climbing a cliff that overlooks the sea, the speaker in **"Beachy Head"** finds that she can not only see farther, but also to other points in time. From this elevated position, she can chronicle the events of individual lives, national history, and geologic time. In the landscape she describes, she discovers not only the traces of her own life, but the evidence of successive generations that preceded her, from before the Norman conquest. In her last poem, Smith's speaker shifts her attention to focus on the history inscribed in the landscape which she had originally described as the setting for her own story. The poem has few autobiographical references, and its lengthy explanatory notes are filled with accounts of contemporary and historical events. The speaker herself seems to become nearly transparent in long, blank verse paragraphs that build minutely observed details into panoramic views. But even as she becomes an almost impersonal narrator her position becomes more integral. As long passages of description are broken by recollections from her own life, we are continually reminded that the scenes that we are viewing are presented from her perspective. We are intermittently recalled from views of war and natural change to the speaker who remembers them.

In her last poem, we find Smith sketching the profile of a figure who represents a new role for herself: she is a mediating figure whose "knowledge" and "understanding" are responsible for what we can see. The speaker imagines "Contemplation," as a figure who "High on her throne of rock, aloof may sit, / And bid recording Memory unfold / Her scroll voluminous."[52] This emerging figure lends the capacity and resources of an individual "Memory" and the practices of description, narration, and persuasion developed in a lifetime of letter-writing and publication to a new task: the work of cultural recollection.

Notes

1. Quotations from *Elegiac Sonnets* are taken from a copy of the eighth edition held by the Department of Rare Books and Special Collections, Princeton University Library: *Elegiac Sonnets and Other Poems*, 8th ed., 2 vols. (London: T. Cadell, Jr., and W. Davies, 1797). The Library holds copies of several other editions: *Elegiac Sonnets*, 4th ed., "corrected" (London: J. Dodsley, H. Gardner, J. Bew, 1786); and *Elegiac Sonnets*, 5th ed. (London: T. Cadell, 1789). The Graphic Arts Collection of the Princeton University Library holds a copy of the first Worcester, Massachusetts, edition, printed by Isaiah Thomas (1795). This edition has a full-leather, gilt-stamped binding made by Henry B. Legge for Thomas. The volume has colored illustrations and wove paper, features that required processes still in their early, experimental stages in America. The Library also holds copies of *The Romance of Real Life* (1787), *Emmeline* (1788 and 3rd ed., 1789), *Ethelinde* (1789), *Celestina* (1791), *Desmond* (1792), *The Emigrants* (1793), *The Old Manor House* (1793 and 3rd. ed., 1822), an extract from that novel printed separately as *Rayland Hall; or, The Remarkable Adventures of Orlando Sommerville* (1810), *The Wanderings of Warwick* (1794), *Montalbert* (1795), *The Banished Man*, 2nd ed. (1795), *Marchmont* (1796), *The Young Philosopher* (1798), *The Letters of a Solitary Wanderer* (1800-1801), and *Beachy Head* (1807).

2. In her introduction to *The British Novelists* edition of *The Old Manor House* (London: F. C. and J. Rivington, 1810), vol. 36, p. iii, Anna Laetitia Barbauld recalls: "Her *Sonnets*, which was the first publication she gave to the world, were universally admired. That species of verse, which in this country may be reckoned rather an exotic, had at that time been but little cultivated. For plaintive, tender, and polished sentiment the Sonnet forms a proper vehicle, and Mrs. Smith's success fixed at once her reputation as a poet of no mean class." Stuart Curran credits Smith's sonnets with generating not only a vogue for the genre, but also "the beginnings of Romanticism," and "the rise of a definable woman's literary movement." See his *Poetic Form and British Romanticism* (New York: Oxford University Press, 1986), pp. 30-32. For a fuller discussion of Smith as one of a group of women authors writing within the social and cultural context of British Romanticism but producing an alternative poetics, see his essay "The I Altered" in *Romanticism and Feminism*, ed. Anne K. Mellor (Bloomington: Indiana University Press, 1988), pp. 185-207.

3. Smith to Thomas Cadell, Jr., and William Davies, 5 March 1797, General Manuscripts [Misc.] C 0140, Rare Books and Special Collections, Princeton University Library. Unless otherwise noted, all of the letters cited are held in this collection. They are reproduced with Smith's spellings and punctuation intact.

4. Review signed "J. M." in *The European Magazine* 50 (November 1806): 338-341.

5. Editions of Smith's works currently in print include *The Old Manor House*, ed. Anne Henry Ehrenpreis (Oxford: Oxford University Press, 1989). An Oxford University Press edition of *Emmeline* is no longer in print. *Emmeline* and *The Old Manor House* are available in the Pandora Press *Mothers of the Novel* series: *Emmeline, The Orphan of the Castle*, intro. Zoë Fairbairns (London: Pandora, 1988); *The Old Manor House*, intro. Janet Todd (London: Pandora, 1987). Garland Press reprints of *Desmond, The Old Manor House*, and *The Young Philosopher* are currently unavailable.

6. The letters to her publishers include one letter to the publishing house of Robinson; one letter to Dodsley; thirteen letters to Thomas Cadell and to his successors, Thomas Cadell, Jr., and William Davies, along with a letter to Smith from them. The Cadells and Davies were Smith's principal publishers.

Beginning with the first edition of *Elegiac Sonnets*, Smith's works emerged from Britain's most prestigious publishing houses. Thomas Cadell, Sr., was acquainted with some of the leading literary figures of the day, including Samuel Johnson and David Hume, and began what was considered the premier publishing house in Great Britain. Joseph Johnson published Smith's *Conversations Introducing Poetry, A Natural History of Birds,* and *Beachy Head.*

Joseph Johnson would have been a significant figure for Smith not only because he was William Cowper's first publisher, but because he was at the center of a group of intellectuals and political radicals that included Joseph Priestley, Thomas Paine, William Godwin, Henry Fuseli, William Blake, and Mary Wollstonecraft. Johnson employed Wollstonecraft as a literary critic for the journal he founded in 1788, *The Analytical Review*, in which she reviewed several of Smith's works. See Ian Maxted, *The London Book Trades 1775-1800* (Folkestone, England: Dawson, 1977).

For a discussion of Smith's relationships with her publishers, see Judith Phillips Stanton, "Charlotte Smith's 'Literary Business': Income, Patronage, and Indigence," in *The Age of Johnson: A Scholarly Annual*, ed. Paul Korshin (New York: AMS Press, 1987), pp. 375-401.

7. For an extensive list of Smith's correspondence, which is dispersed primarily among libraries in the United States and Great Britain, see Stanton, "Charlotte Smith's 'Literary Business'."

8. For a detailed discussion of Smith's "literary business," see Stanton, "Charlotte Smith's 'Literary Business'."

9. In his discussion of the letters by Smith held by the Huntington Library, Alan Dugald McKillop attributes the portrait to George Romney. See his "Charlotte Smith's Letters," *Huntington Library Quarterly* 15 (November 1952): 237-255.

10. The most comprehensive account of Smith's life and writings is Florence Hilbish's critical biography, *Charlotte Smith, Poet and Novelist* (Philadelphia, 1941). Unless otherwise noted, biographical material is taken from Hilbish's account, which remains the primary biographical resource for Smith's readers.

11. Viscount St. Cyres, "The Sorrows of Mrs. Charlotte Smith," *Cornhill Magazine,* n.s., 15 (November 1903): 684.

12. Hilbish, *Charlotte Smith,* p. 85.

13. The Library holds several letters from Hayley and from William Cowper to and about Smith.

14. *The Emigrants: A Poem* (London: T. Cadell, 1793).

15. Unsigned review in *The European Magazine* 24 (July 1793): 42.

16. Wordsworth urged anthologists to include more of Smith's sonnets in their collections. He penciled his name onto a list of subscribers to the fifth edition of *Elegiac Sonnets* in the copy he owned as a student at Cambridge. For a description of his marginalia in the collection, see the essay by Bishop C. Hunt, Jr., "Wordsworth and Charlotte Smith," *The Wordsworth Circle* 1 (Summer 1970): 85-103. His essay offers an extensive, detailed analysis of Smith's significance to Wordsworth.

17. *The Poetical Works of William Wordsworth,* ed. Ernest de Selincourt and Helen Darbishire, 2nd ed., 5 vols. (Oxford: Oxford University Press, 1952-1959); vol. 4, p. 403.

18. Smith has also been credited with an influence on Keats. See Burton R. Pollin, "Keats, Charlotte Smith, and the Nightingale," *Notes and Queries* (May 1966): 180-181; and George W. Whiting, "Charlotte Smith, Keats, and the Nightingale," *Keats-Shelley Journal* (Winter 1963): 4-8.

19. Coleridge, "Introduction to the Sonnets," reprinted in *The Complete Poetical and Dramatic Works,* ed. James Dykes Campbell (London: Macmillan, 1938), pp. 542-544.

20. Smith to Thomas Cadell, Sr., April 1792.

21. A first edition of *Clarissa,* with marginalia by Lady Bradshaigh and Richardson, is in the Robert H. Taylor Collection, Princeton University Library.

22. Smith, *Elegiac Sonnets,* vol. 1, p. iv.

23. Smith, *Elegiac Sonnets,* vol. 1, p. iv.

24. Unsigned article in *British Public Characters of 1800-1801* (London: Richard Phillips, 1807), p. 63. For a contemporary account of the problematics of being a woman novelist in Smith's day, see Katharine M. Rogers, "Inhibitions on Eighteenth-Century Women Novelists: Elizabeth Inchbald and Charlotte Smith," *Eighteenth-Century Studies* 11 (Fall 1977): 63-78.

25. Smith, *Elegiac Sonnets,* vol. 1, p. xii.

26. Smith to Thomas Cadell, Sr., April 1792.

27. William Hayley to Charlotte Mary Smith, 1 November 1806.

28. Smith to Thomas Cadell, Sr., 14 January 1788. In a later letter, Smith resumes the story of her husband's returns. Roughly two years later, on 22 August 1790, she writes to Cadell proposing to sell her copyright to him: "Alas!—it is my poverty and not my will, that has forced me to do it, & while Mr. Smith's circumstances remain as they are, I do not know whether it is not better to sell entirely *all* my literary property—which, when once bought and paid for no claimant against him can, as I am well informed affect—Whereas I am much afraid that there are circumstances wherein every thing really mine wd. be given up, during his life to the use of Mr. Smith's Creditors." Smith to Thomas Cadell, Sr., 22 August 1790, Robert H. Taylor Collection [RT Co1], Princeton University Library.

29. Smith to Thomas Cadell, Sr., 22 August 1790, Taylor Collection. In a letter to Cadell and Davies, she closes a careful line of reasoning with a direct appeal for sympathy: "I cannot therefore but think, that as Mr. Cadell voluntarily offer'd me 10 Gs. for 6 Sonnets, vis from Sonnet LIV. to Sonnet LIX. that the same Sum cannot be too much for a larger & more varied addition to the present edition of a second vol. If you are of this opinion, it would confer a singular obligation on me, if you would send me the money to day, for strange to tell, yet unhappily it is true, I have never been more distress'd." Smith to Cadell and Davies, 31 May [?], General Manuscripts [Misc.], C 0140.

30. *The European Magazine* 10 (August 1786): 125. This sonnet appears in a group of poems signed by a "constant Reader," "W. P.," which includes "Advice to Mrs. Smith. A Sonnet."

31. Smith, *Elegiac Sonnets,* vol. 1, p. 44.

32. Smith, *Elegiac Sonnets,* vol. 1, pp. 101-102.

33. Smith, *Elegiac Sonnets,* vol. 1, p. 2.

34. *The Letters of a Solitary Wanderer,* 5 vols. (London: T. N. Longman and O. Rees, 1802); vol. 4, pp. 96-97. Smith assumes the role of natural historian most fully in a late work, *A Natural History of Birds, Intended Chiefly for Young Persons,* ed. T. C., 2 vols. (London: J. Johnson, 1807).

35. Smith to Cadell and Davies, n.d. (1796).

36. Smith to Cadell and Davies, 5 March 1797.

37. Sir Walter Scott, *The Miscellaneous Prose Works,* 28 vols. (Edinburgh: Robert Cadell, 1849); vol. 4, pp. 64.

38. Smith to Cadell and Davies, 5 March 1797.

39. Smith to Cadell and Davies, n.d. (1795?).

40. Smith to Thomas Cadell, Sr., 22 August 1790, Taylor Collection.

41. Smith to Robinson, 28 September 1789, John Wild Autograph Collection, C 0047, Princeton University Library.

42. Brydges, *Imaginative Biography,* 2 vols. (London: Saunders and Otley, 1834); vol. 2, p. 101.

43. St. Cyres, "Sorrows," p. 688.

44. St. Cyres, "Sorrows," p. 687.

45. St. Cyres, "Sorrows," pp. 689, 696.

46. *A Narrative of the Loss of the Catherine, Venus, and Piedmont Transports, and the Thomas, Golden Grove, and Æolus Merchant Ships, Near Weymouth, on Wednesday the 18th of November Last* (London: Sampson Low, 1796).

47. Catherine Anne Dorset, in *The Miscellaneous Prose Works of Sir Walter Scott,* vol. 4, p. 55.

48. *Desmond, A Novel,* 3 vols. (London: G. G. J. and J. Robinson, 1792). For a discussion of the novel within the context of British women novelists of the 1790s, see Diana Bowstead, "Charlotte Smith's *Desmond*: The Epistolary Novel as Ideological Argument," in *Fetter'd or Free? British Women Novelists, 1670-1815,* ed. Mary Anne Schofield and Cecilia Macheski (Athens, Ohio: Ohio University Press, 1986), pp. 237-263.

49. Wordsworth is often mentioned as the only Romantic poet to have visited the continent in the early, heady days of political ferment. It seems significant, then, that on his way to France in 1791, Wordsworth should have visited Smith in Brighton. She gave Wordsworth letters of introduction to her acquaintances, including Helen Maria Williams, who by that time had already published works sympathetic to the revolutionary movement, her *Letters Written in France,* and a poem, *A Farewell for Two Years, to England.* Wordsworth gives a brief account of the meeting with Smith in a letter to Richard Wordsworth, dated 19 December [1791]. See *The Letters of William and Dorothy Wordsworth, The Early Years, 1787-1805,* ed. Ernest de Selincourt, rev. Chester Shaver, 2nd ed. (Oxford: Clarendon Press, 1967), pp. 68-69.

50. Smith, *Desmond,* Preface, p. iii.

51. *The History of England, from the Earliest Records, to the Peace of Amiens; in a Series of Letters to a Young Lady at School,* 3 vols. (London: Phillips, 1808). According to Hilbish, *Charlotte Smith,* pp. 213-215, only volumes one and two are written by Smith.

52. Smith, *Beachy Head, with other Poems* (London: J. Johnson, 1807), p. 8.

Matthew Bray (essay date 1993)

SOURCE: Bray, Matthew. "Removing the Anglo-Saxon Yoke: The Francocentric Vision of Charlotte Smith's Later Works." *The Wordsworth Circle* 24, no. 3 (summer 1993): 155-58.

[*In the following essay, Bray examines the increasingly pro-French version of the history of English-French relations.*]

Charlotte Smith initially opposed the British war with France for humanitarian reasons. In her polemical blank-verse poem, **The Emigrants** (1793), for instance, Smith argues that her fellow country men and women should derive national pride from "acts of pure humanity" toward French ecclesiastical emigrés displaced by the Revolution rather than from "the deafening roar / Of Victory from a thousand brazen throats, / That tell with what success wide wasting War / Has by our Compatriots thinned the world" (33-34). During the Napoleonic era, however, Smith's opposition to the war moved beyond mere humanitarian pacifism. From 1798 until her death in 1806, she articulated an increasingly seditious vision of England's historical and political ties to France, a vision that went against the patriotic Anglo-Saxonism that consumed England during the early years of the war. I wish here to trace the development of Smith's Francocentric vision of English History—of English history as *French* history—paying special attention to the remarkable military history section of her final major poem, **"Beachy Head"** (1807, posthumous).

My first two examples come from works that Smith ostensibly wrote for children: **Minor Morals, interspersed with sketches of natural history, historical anecdotes, and original stories** (1798) and **History of England, from the earliest records, to the peace of Amiens; in a series of letters to a young lady at school** (1806). Through the book's authoritative teacher Mrs. Belmour, **Minor Morals** strongly opposes the idea that the physical barriers between nations should carry any ideological significance: "Nor could the Omnipotent implant in the inhabitants of two divisions of the earth parted from each other only by a few leagues of water . . . a *natural* antipathy, so that, from mere hatred and detestation of each other, the study of whole generations of these men should be mutual annoyance, and their whole ambition to sweep each other from the earth" (2nd. ed. 1799, 7-8). She proceeds to critique further the anti-French, nationalist mindset of the English by asserting that England was first "peopled from Gaul"; therefore, "we can trace our origin no farther back than to the people [the French] we hate and despise" (17). Thus Smith's opposition to the war with France acquires a new ideological dimension here: not only is war inhumane but also, the English should realize that in fighting the French they are in fact futilely battling themselves.

The emergence of a patriotic Anglo-Saxonism in England during the first decade of the 19th century found expression in historical account such as Sharon Turner's popular *History of the Manners, Landed Property, Government, Laws, Poetry, Literature, Religion, and Language of the Anglo-Saxons* (1805), in the spate of national epics that emphasized King Alfred's central role in the formation of English character, in anti-Napoleon broadsides, and in the manifold sermons, military histories and poems occasioned by Nelson's victory and death at Trafalgar. Although the argument that contemporary English liberties stemmed from Anglo-Saxon institutions had been used since the Civil War to justify constitutional arguments for either a stronger parliament or monarchy, by 1805 it was tied to a generalized patriotism, one complacent with contemporary English institutions and with the supposed coherence of English liberty over the past millennium.[1] In her ***History of England*** (3 vols. 1806), Smith first mimics and then subverts this nationalistic Anglo-Saxonism.

Like contemporary patriotic poets and historians, she begins conventionally by stating that "the rudiments of those laws which made this country the cradle of freedom" can be found in Anglo-Saxon England. Smith declares that demonstrating this continuity has been "so ably executed by our historians" that she only aims "to abridge their more elaborate accounts" (I. 79). Her "abridgement" consists, however, of an ironic account of Anglo-Saxon England as a brutally militarist land where the average working man had no say in his government, where slavery was a fact of life, and where marriage was a transaction in which women functioned solely as economic tokens. In constructing this counter-history, moreover, Smith appropriates and augments the historical narrative of David Hume, the one major British historian who dissented from the dominant seventeenth and eighteenth-century view of Anglo-Saxon England as the cradle of English liberty (Simmons 38).

Of the Wittenagemote, or the national council of the Anglo-Saxon Heptarchy, which the majority of historians took to be the precursor to the House of Commons (Hill 65-122, passim), Smith writes: ". . . it is doubtful whether that rank of men which we call the Commons . . . formed a part of this assembly . . . it is not probable that the Saxon conquerors, who thought nothing glorious or honourable but the profession of arms, should admit those to a share of the government who were engaged in trade or commerce, or employed as tillers of the land. . . . The landed property of England was in the hands of a few; and these, most likely, formed the national assembly of those limits."[2] When the possession of slaves is added to the generally unrepresentative nature of the Wittenagemote, "All the evidence we possess agrees that they had no liberal ideas of general freedom" (I: 81). Smith characterizes the Anglo-Saxons as "extremely credulous and bigoted": in their houses of mourning "drinking and riot prevailed," they educated their children solely for war, and marriage was primarily an economic exchange in which a bride "was frequently purchased of her guardian" by her intended husband (I: 82-3). If there exists any connection between Anglo-Saxon and modern England, Smith seems to suggest, then it is a continuity of barbarism, ignorance and oppression.

A highly compressed, loco-descriptive meditation on war, poverty, history and human happiness, **"Beachy Head"** carries Smith's subversive historiography to its logical conclusion. It does so by reversing a central emphasis of patriotic Anglo-Saxonism: the notion that the Norman Conquest imposed a short-lived, tyrannical "yoke" upon nascent Anglo-Saxon liberties. Going completely against this anti-Norman grain, Smith exalts the Normans' valor and piety, making their deeds the centerpiece of her account of English military history (lines 117-167). Thus **"Beachy Head"**'s "proudest roll by glory fill'd" (167) begins not with the earliest English military victories that other contemporary accounts featured,[3] but instead with an extensive, celebratory history of the Normans, beginning with the Rollo's conquest of Normandy and Brittany and ending with William the Conqueror's defeat of the Anglo-Saxon heptarchy.

In her note to this passage, Smith describes how Rollo, after Charles the Simple granted him Normandy and Brittany, ". . . added the more solid virtues of the legislator to the fierce valour of the conqueror—converted to Christianity, he established justice, and repressed the excesses of his Danish subjects, till then accustomed to live only by plunder. His name became the signal for pursuing those who violated the law." (p. 148) She fills in the gap between Rollo and William with a second incident illustrating the Normans' Christian nobleness. In 983, a small party of Normans, returning from a pilgrimage to Jerusalem, helped to liberate Salerno from Islamic rule; this act initiated the chain of events that led to the Norman sovereignty over Naples and Sicily (pp. 148-50).

Unlike the early history of the Normans, Smith does not relegate the Norman Invasion of England to the footnotes. She first emphasizes the Normans' military prowess. The "One not inglorious struggle" England made could not repel "The war song daring Roland sang . . . with astounding voice" and thus "the Saxon heptarchy, / [was] Finish[ed] for ever" (133-8). Smith, however, goes beyond depicting the Norman's superior military might by also describing their humility and piety in victory, perhaps in satiric contrast to the loud boasting that nearly all of England voiced after Nelson's victory at Trafalgar. William constructed a holy pile at Battle Abbey, where "to appease the heaven's wrath for so much blood, / The conqueror bade unceasing prayers ascend, / And requiem for the slayers and the slain" (140-42).

It is worth recounting how potentially dangerous such a positive account of Norman history was in the post-Amiens period. For the English, the Norman Conquest immediately brought to mind fears of a second French conquest by Napoleon. Thus, in the contemporary imagination, William the Conqueror equalled Napoleon, and the Normans represented the modern French, poised to invade England at any moment. One satiric handbill from 1803, "Bonaparte's Ten Commandments," cites Napoleon's desire to become "future *Conqueror* of the base English," while another "[Napoleon's] Epitaph" refers to his "boasted *Conquest*" (emphases added).[4] W. T. Fitzgerald's poem, "Britons, to Arms," declares that, after the English fleet crushes Napoleon, "ENGLAND [will] *never know* INVASION more."[5] The Letter "I" in "The Loyalist's Alphabet" (1804) stands for "Invasion once stood," another direct reference which implicitly contrasts the successful Norman Invasion to the imputed failure of a Napoleonic Invasion (Ashton, 241).

Contrary to this spate of patriotic propaganda, Smith invokes the Norman Conquest not to bury it in the past as an example of the disastrous consequences of national irresoluteness, but to praise it and, by unavoidable historical analogy, to praise Napoleon. And if lauding the Normans was risky, then equally dangerous was Smith's assertion that the Saxon heptarchy was finished "for ever." This pointed statement could not fail to carry significant ideological weight in the spring of 1806, when Smith submitted the poem to her publisher,[6] suggesting as it does that the supposedly enduring Anglo-Saxon institutions championed by the patriotic historians and poets were extinguished as well, that modern England, by implication, could really only trace itself back to the Normans—to the French. Furthermore, not to decry past occupations of England as tyrannical and unnatural was tantamount to advocating a new French invasion during the tense, post-Amiens period during which Smith wrote **"Beachy Head."**

Smith pushes her seditious historiography yet one step further in her note on the Normans, the longest by far of any that she writes for **"Beachy Head."** Here, after recounting the establishment of Normandy and their victory over Saracens at Jerusalem, Smith traces the Norman advance in the tenth and eleventh centuries down through the Italian peninsula, where they made an alliance with the Pope and "became the sovereigns both of Sicily and Naples." Immediately after making this statement, Smith declares that "How William . . . possessed himself of England, is too well known to be repeated here" (but she gives a detailed account anyway) (pp. 149-150).

The latter of this narrative resonates strongly and, I would suggest, intentionally with contemporary European history.

On September 27, 1805, Napoleon announced his conquest of Naples and, in early 1806, Joseph Bonaparte declared himself the "King of the Two Sicilies."[7] With Napoleon's troops poised to sail across the Channel as late as August, 1805, fear of invasion, though temporarily assuaged by Nelson's victory at Trafalgar, would still have been prominent in the minds of English men and women in early 1806.[8] The strong parallel between Norman and recent French history suggests that William's "well-known" conquest of England may find a logical historical repetition—with England falling after Naples and Sicily—in an imminent Napoleonic conquest.

It seems unlikely that Smith did not have in mind this parallel because of her pointed selection of Naples and Sicily out of the scores of Italian city-states that the Normans subdued in the tenth and eleventh centuries—many of these more powerful than Naples—and because of her rearrangement of historical chronology: the Normans in fact did not conquer Sicily until 1072, six years after the conquest of Anglo-Saxon England.[9] Smith's repeated emphasis on the cooperation of the Normans with papal authority and on William's Christian piety may, furthermore, also have a parallel among Smith's readers with Napoleon's own alliances with the Vatican and his coronation by Pope Pius VII on December 2, 1804.

After presenting this dangerous account of the Norman history, Smith more carefully satirizes the manifold apostrophes to English naval power that appeared after Trafalgar: e.g. *The British Flag Triumphant! or the Wooden Walls of Old England!* (1806). Declaring initially that France would be presumptuous to hope "that ever thou again, Queen of the isles! shalt crouch to foreign arms," Smith further mimics hyperbolic assertions of national power in the remainder of this section: England is the "Imperial Mistress of the obedient sea" who will "now undaunted meet a world in arms" (144-5, 151, 153). And yet the only *specific* event recalled within this mimicry of nationalistic discourse is the French victory over a combined English and Dutch fleet in 1690 off of Beachy Head:

> England! 'twas where this promontory rears
> Its rugged brow above the channel wave,
> Parting the hostile nations, that thy fame,
> Thy naval fame was tarnish'd, at what time
> Thou, leagued with the Batavian, gavest to France
> One day of triumph. . . .
>
> (154-59)

Within this passage, Smith suggests that England's claim to military fame is limited to its naval exploits when the narrator immediately qualifies "thy fame" with "thy *naval* fame," perhaps implying that England has almost desperately celebrated its victories at sea in order to cover over the fact of its inadequate army, which had been all but useless for checking France's European conquests. Or, as John Thelwall said in *The Triumph of Albion,* "the Sea redeems The Land's disasters" (192-93). On land as well as at sea, France's contemporary triumphs were hardly rare: Napoleon himself viewed Trafalgar merely as a "painful incident" (Lefebvre 194).

By presenting events from "the proudest roll by glory fill'd" that were, in fact, significant defeats, this section of **"Beachy Head"** continues to chip away at the nationalistic version of England's military glory. Moreover, the Norman Invasion and the lost battle directly off Beachy Head seriously challenge a belief in the inviolable integrity of England, since they represent French victories both within England and perilously close to England. Smith further discredits the notion of England's mythical invulnerability by pointing out, in another note, that it was only French ignorance of the English coast and failure to communicate effectively among themselves that prevented them, in 1690, from taking "all the advantage they might have done from this victory" (p. 153). One hundred and sixteen years later, this note implies, the French under Napoleon do not suffer these handicaps of intelligence and organization.

By the time Smith recounts the Battle of Beachy Head, she has violated in all possible ways the implicit code in the growing patriotic discourse of the era. **"Beachy Head"** never invokes the key figure of King Alfred, the supposed progenitor of English liberties, and, indeed, does not discuss Anglo-Saxon England at all, except to narrate its ultimate defeat. Nor does it allude to Nelson's victories at the Nile and Trafalgar, a commonplace in contemporary verse accounts of England's military history such as *The Triumph of Albion* (9-19). The poem, in fact, never mentions any specific English victories, highlighting instead the disastrous Battle of Beachy Head. Finally, and most seditiously, she places a glorified account of William the Conqueror and the Normans at the center of her narrative.

Smith does not, moreover, limit her attention to the relationship between England and France to military history. The inciting incidents in **"Beachy Head"** is the prehistoric geological separation of England from France, the time when

> . . . the Omnipotent
> Stretch'd forth his arm, and rent the solid hills,
> Bidding the impetuous main flood rush between
> The rifted shores, and from the continent
> Eternally divided this green isle.
>
> (6-10)

Lines 117-166 of **"Beachy Head"** effectively place this geological division into an historical epic framework. Smith's emphasis upon the Norman Conquest as the founding event of English history and her drawing of implicit parallels between the Normans and the modern French suggest that the paradise lost during the divisive wars between England and France since the Norman Conquest—a division that exacerbates their physical separation by the English Channel—will be regained when England recognizes its common political and historical ties to France. Napoleon, as the second conqueror of England, may be the messiah who will forcibly bring about this recognition. Thus, far from echoing the popular hatred of the "Norman Yoke," Smith, in her later works, calls for a removal of the ideological Anglo-Saxon yoke that allows the English people to support an untenable division with France, the country from whence they came and with whom they may again soon unite.

Notes

1. On the constitutional arguments, Chapter 3, "The Norman Yoke," in Christopher Hill, *Puritanism and Revolution: Studies in Interpretation of the English Revolution of the 17th Century* (1958) 50-122 and J. G. A. Pocock, *The Ancient Constitution and the Feudal Law* (1967). On patriotic epics of the early 1800s, Stuart Curran *Poetic Form and British Romanticism* (1986) 161-62. On Sharon Turner's patriotic Anglo-Saxonism, Clare Simmons, *Reversing the Conquest: History and Myth in Nineteenth-Century British Literature* (1990) 55-60.

2. This passage closely follows Hume's assessment; see *The History of England, from the Invasion of Julius Caesar to the Revolution of 1688,* 6 vols. (1762) I:146.

3. E.g., John Thelwall, *The Triumph of Albion* (1805) in Donald H. Reiman, comp. *John Thelwall: Ode to Science; John Gilpin's Ghost; Poems; The Triumph of Albion* (1978).

4. Quoted in John Ashton, *English Caricature and Satire on Napoleon I* (1888; rpt. 1968) 159, 177.

5. The *Northampton Mercury,* July 23, 1803, quoted in Colin Pedly, "Anticipating Invasion: Some Wordsworthian Contexts," TWC [*The Wordsworth Circle*] 21:2 (Spring, 1990):64.

6. Florence May Anna Hilbish, "Charlotte Smith: Poet and Novelist (1749-1806)," diss., U of Pennsylvania, 1941, pp. 217-18.

7. Mack Smith Denis, *A History of Sicily: Modern Sicily after 1715* (1968) 336-40. The French did not, however, fully conquer Sicily at this time, despite Joseph's decree.

8. Georges Lefebvre, *Napoleon: From 18 Brumaire to Tilset 1799-1807,* trans. Henry F. Stockhold (1969) 188-94.

9. David C. Douglas, *The Norman Achievement: 1050-1100* (1969) 235-41.

Terence Allan Hoagwood (essay date 1993)

SOURCE: Hoagwood, Terence Allan. In an Introduction to *Beachy Head with Other Poems,* by Charlotte Smith, pp. 3-11. Delmar, N.Y.: Scholars' Facsimiles & Reprints, 1993.

[*In the following essay, Hoagwood describes the content of Smith's poetry as surpassing the usual poetic concerns to embrace social, political, and intellectual issues.*]

Charlotte Smith, an influential poet and extraordinarily successful novelist, was the author of sixty-three volumes, altogether,[1] including bestseller novels with social themes (saliently feminist and politically revolutionary themes) and books of widely-admired poetry, of which the volume here reprinted was her last. Admirers of her work included Sir Walter Scott, Queen Caroline, William Wordsworth, and Samuel Taylor Coleridge. Smith regarded her own poetry as more important than her fiction; she not only established anew for English literature the importance of the sonnet and the sonnet sequence (in ways that were formative for the subsequent work of Wordsworth and Coleridge, by their own admission), but she also developed other genres in aesthetically and intellectually influential ways. For example, her use of the topographical and narrative meditation in blank verse (as in *The Emigrants* of 1793 and **"Beachy Head,"** reprinted here) was revolutionary and influential.

Characteristically, in these poems, landscapes (especially the coast, the sea, the rising sun, and the turbulent waters between England and France) furnish Smith with symbolic imagery, with which she represents the stormy political times of democratic revolution and its aftermath, in iconographic form. Wordsworth's *The Prelude,* Swinburne's *A Forsaken Garden,* and Eliot's *Four Quartets* display the ways in which her genre—and frequently her particular symbols—shaped major poetry to come after her.

Smith's concerns, however, were not specialized poetic concerns; they involved, rather, some larger social, political, and intellectual goals. As Florence Hilbish has written, in her exemplary scholarly biography, Smith contended across her career that "poverty and ignorance [were] due to unjust laws," and she also advocated democracy, which included abolition of privileges owing to birth, sympathy for the American colonists, and the French, hatred of war and prejudice; humanitarianism towards the prisoner, beggar, insane, and slave."[2] In the period of the democratic revolutions, the counter-revolutionary war, the treason trials, the Gagging Acts, censorship, and imprisonment of authors and publishers for dangerously democratic utterances, Smith's ability and determination to persist in the fictional and poetic projection of these contentions, with integrity, consistency, and (in her poetry) artistic excellence, amount to a remarkable achievement even within a large view of the history of English literature.

This achievement, however, has been largely screened from the public view. With a few exceptions—preeminently Hilbish—writing about Smith has been limited chiefly to the genre of the short biographical narrative, typically in the form of encyclopedia articles and introductions to her novels.[3] Like other genres, this one has its conventions, and in Smith's case the conventions have operated lugubriously to cover her historical importance and her social vision under a dark blanket of overbearing personal misery. Her mother died when she was three years old; to facilitate his remarriage to a wealthy woman, her father arranged her marriage at age fifteen to an abusive profligate, whom she followed into debtor's prison, "amidst scenes of misery, of vice, and even of terror."[4] Prisoners twice attempted to effect their escape by blowing up the walls of the prison. Leaving her loveless, violent, and exploitative husband, she lived as a single mother, and, according to Anna Barbauld, she saw the deaths of six of her twelve children (her first baby died while her second was being born).[5] While raising those of her children who did survive, she was on occasion reduced to sleeping in the public road.

With rare exceptions, scholarly and critical accounts of Smith have been dominated by the melancholy recitation of these unhappy personal circumstances (and others, including some long-standing legal problems that kept her in penury and frustration). Anne Henry Ehrenpreis, one of the best scholars to write about Smith in the fifty years since Hilbish's book appeared, advises readers in these terms: "for details of her miserable life, see my introduction to *The Old Manor House.*"[6] The tradition of enveloping her work with a morose concentration on her miserable life goes back a very long way: within four years of Smith's death, for example, Barbauld wrote that Smith had "lost her mother when very young," was "plunged into the cares of married life" while a teenager, suffered "vexation" and "perplexities," and generally underwent a life of trouble that "gave to her writings that bitter and querulous tone of complaint which is discernible in so many of them."[7]

The theme of the biographical parable was thus established by 1810, and it has been carried on from that day to this.[8] In 1834, Sir Walter Scott expresses admiration for Smith's novelistic skill (especially her use of language and her skill at characterization) but he also reproduces a biographical memoir written by Mrs. Dorset, a surviving sister of Charlotte Smith. What is probably the most sustained and unmitigated example of the genre (the morose biographical parable) was published by Julia Kavanagh in 1863; Kavanagh begins with a tone impressively calculated to dampen enthusiasm: "There are lives that read like one long sorrow, and that leave little save sadness and disappointment behind them when they close in death. Such a life was that of Charlotte Smith, full of cares while it lasted, and once it was over, doomed to fade away from memory."[9] That is surely one of the least inspiring introductions to a major author one could readily find. Kavanagh continues: upon her marriage, Smith was moved to a "house in one of the narrowest and dirtiest lanes in the City, and in which the sun's beams had never shone" (p. 189); her husband was "foolish, ignorant, pleasure-seeking, and dissipated," and (when she was living with her vicious husband in the house of her father-in-law) the sound of the elder Smith's creaking shoes made Charlotte hide whatever she was doing (p. 190). Kavanagh reports that Charlotte Smith was in prison for a while, and that from the time of her imprisonment until her death, "her life was a succession of cares, with few respites" (p. 190).

My point about this genre (the mournful parable of Smith's miserable life) is that it is doubly misleading, obscuring the meanings of both her life and her art.[10] Barbauld's negative judgment about the "bitter and querulous tone of complaint" that is supposedly discernible in Smith's writings established a tone that many others have repeated. If it were true that Smith merely (or chiefly) complained about her personal sufferings (and it is not true), it seems to me that it would still be odd to register surprise or disapproval at the fact. I remember recently hearing a Benefits Officer of a private corporation indicating candidly that she did not object to the sickness, pain, and suffering of the helpless people she heard from, so much as their constant whining about it.

Smith, however, did not produce self-absorbed whining; she produced vigorous, intelligent, positive, and even profound social criticism in imaginative forms. Smith was not reduced to the shrunken privacy of personalistic sadness, which is what the mythos of self-pity would imply; instead, she was unusually industrious *and* she maintained an unusually large vision of social and cultural issues. As I have said, Smith wrote sixty-three volumes altogether; this massive productivity is not consistent with chronic self-pity.[11]

A second way in which the traditional and generically miserable short story of her life obscures her meanings has to do with her works' intellectual content. If we understand her poetry as referring principally to her self, to her unique and private sorrow, then we remain deaf to its larger meanings. Smith's poetry characteristically adopts a symbolic form, rather than openly political polemic, a fact which should not surprise us, when we recall that during this period Paine, Thelwall, Holcroft, Tooke, and dozens of other authors and publishers were convicted and imprisoned for the promulgation of social views like Smith's. This shift of socio-political polemic into figurative form can be understood as one of the major tendencies of the literary culture of Romanticism: Wollstonecraft's turn to fictional form, in *Wrongs of Woman,* and Thelwall's turn to poetic symbolism, as in his *Hope of Albion* (written after his trial for treason) are two obvious examples; and so are Joanna Baillie's displacement of French Revolutionary politics and war into exotic analogies (as in *Constantine Paleologus*), and Byron's displacement of contemporary European conflicts into historically removed settings (as in *Werner*) or mythic symbols (as in *Heaven and Earth* and *Cain*). Even more clearly than these writers, Smith embeds her historical vision in the symbolic form of her ostensibly topographical poems.

Smith's characteristic imagery includes conventional political icons from the revolutionary movements, though some of her later readers have been stunningly willing to take them literally and only literally: these images include sunrises, floods, earthquakes, feudal ruins, and springtime renewal. She writes in plain prose (in the preface to her novel ***Desmond***) that "the political passages dispersed through the work . . . are, for the most part, drawn from conversations to which I have been a witness, in England, and France." Smith is not moping but taking a progressive and defiant position when she writes the following sentence, in the same preface: "But women it is said have no business with politics—why not?"[12] In the dedicatory preface to her poem, *The Emigrants,* Smith writes not of her personal sorrow or her miserable private life, but rather the "reciprocal hatred so unworthy of great and enlightened nations" and her work's ambition "to humanize both countries . . . and at length annihilate the prejudices that have so long existed to the injury of both."[13] To interpret Smith's fiction *or* her poetry as if it were privatized moping about her miserable life is to obscure not only the truth of her productive life, but also the meanings of her socialized themes.

As Mary Anne Schofield has said, Smith's works include tales "of political exploitation and imprisonment that deftly teach insurrection and revolution"; her work is positive, vigorous, and even optimistic in its purposes, revolution (obviously) implying optimism. All her adult life, Smith meant "to show her readers how to deal with despotic, domineering men, especially tyrannical fathers." What Schofield calls Smith's "strength of mind and character" enables her to show "her readers that they do not have to accept the lies men offer, that they have a right to their own minds, selves, and lives." Schofield points out that "Smith exposes the myths which have proliferated in the pages of the century's fictions—the notions of female dependency and . . . entrapment." Further, in her poetry Smith presents this activist treatment of her society's present with a sophisticated treatment of its past, layering the present over its determining history. In poems like **"Beachy Head,"** Smith raises the subject from the merely particular (the landscape, and anecdotes from local lore) to the level of societal and historical change. She writes of a civilization undergoing revolutionary change, and not merely her private sorrows. Smith does not wallow hopelessly in a self-regarding slough of despond; instead, she devotes a substantial life's work to a complex representation of a legal, political, and economic structure that oppresses women, enslaves the poor, and violently opposes evolutionary change in the direction of freedom.

Beachy Head: With Other Poems was already in press when Charlotte Smith died (in 1806). In the title poem, as in ***The Emigrants,*** she produces a substantial and symbolic representation of historical and social themes, in an ostensibly topographical meditation and reminiscence. To be acquainted with the iconography of the revolutionary period will help us to interpret the poem, which begins with reference to the counter-revolutionary (Napoleonic) war that was in progress while she wrote. The opening emphasis on the "awful hour / Of vast concussion" means something more than a weather report; she is writing about the war, and not about the sensitive appreciation of nature. Looking over the channel toward France, the poem envisions a glorious sunrise (p. 2), and the sunrise is of course an icon of revolutionary hope, here as it is likewise (to mention only three examples), in William Blake's well-known print, *Albion Rose,* or in Wordsworth's *Prelude* ("bliss was it in that dawn to be alive . . ."[14]), or in Swinburne's book of poems on the European revolutions, *Songs Before Sunrise.*

No special code of iconography should be necessary to enable us to appreciate the fact that (as on pp. 4-5) Smith's poem attacks imperialism and affirms "the sacred freedom" of all humanity. The poem refers openly enough to "modern Gallia" and to the Italian and Spanish responses to the Napoleonic war; and when, in the concluding portion of the poem, the speaker turns to the question of the value of "visionary" projections, the worth of "dreams," surely her contemporary readers (including Wordsworth, who visited Smith in 1791, on his way to revolutionary France) would have understood that this discourse of dream and disillusion involved not an individualistic or psychological preoccupation, but rather the political history of England and Europe during the revolutionary decades and their aftermath.

In this way, a synopsis of **"Beachy Head"** sounds like a synopsis of Wordsworth's *Prelude*: the poem moves from the topics of tyranny and war to the topics of sympathy and compassion, and it concludes with an exemplary narrative about a solitary vagrant and a meditation on visionary hopes, disillusionment, and the restorative power of imagination. The poem's explicit treatment of the imagination's power to deal positively with political disillusionment is only one of the ways in which Smith's poetry bears comparison with Wordsworth's. The poem's language is both colloquial and dignified, sometimes imitating natural speech and sometimes rising to Miltonic tones. The imagery offers a literal level as an appreciation of nature, and a figurative depth involving both political history and the poetic imagination.

All of these features have long been associated with the poetry of the *Prelude*; but I would emphasize that it was Smith's poetry that influenced Wordsworth's, in the first instance, rather than the other way around; in fact, it was his admiration of her poetry, and particularly the **Elegiac Sonnets.** that led him to visit her in 1791. To appreciate her poetry's power and excellence requires our understanding of its relationships in its troubled historical moment. Smith's poetry represents the historical period's largest social and political concerns. If we are still learning to read that cultural history in its symbols, surely the availability now of some of her finest poetry—including this, her great, last book—makes possible some instruction and delight that have, in my judgment, been obscured for far too long.

Notes

1. Florence Hilbish, *Charlotte Smith: Poet and Novelist.* (Philadelphia: University of Pennsylvania Press, 1941), p. 3.

2. Both Gina Luria (in her introduction to Smith's novel, *Desmond* [New York: Garland, 1974], p. 9) and Mary Anne Schofield (in her introduction to Smith's novel, *Marchmont* [Delmar, NY: Scholars' Facsimiles & Reprints, 1989], p. 6) quote likewise this passage from Hilbish's *Charlotte Smith,* which is still the best source for information on Charlotte Smith.

3. In addition to Luria's introduction to *Desmond* and Schofield's introduction to *Marchmont*, the following are among good examples of biographical essays on Smith: Anna Barbauld, "Mrs. Charlotte Smith," in *The British Novelists; with An Essay; and Prefaces, Biographical and Critical, by Mrs. Barbauld,* vol. 36 (London: F. C. and J. Rivington, 1810), pp. i-viii; Sir Walter Scott, "Charlotte Smith," in *Biographical Memoirs of Eminent Novelists,* vol. 2 (Edinburgh, 1834); Julia Kavanagh, "Charlotte Smith," in *English Women of Letters: Biographical Sketches,* vol. 1 (London: Hurst and Blackett, 1863), pp. 187-93; "Charlotte Smith," in *Dictionary of National Biography,* ed. Leslie Stephen and Sidney Lee (1917; rpt. London: Oxford University Press, 1921-22); Anne Henry Ehrenpreis, Introduction to *The Old Manor House* (London: Oxford University Press, 1969); Ehrenpreis, Introduction to *Emmeline: The Orphan of the Castle* (London: Oxford University Press, 1971); Bernard Smith and Peter Haas, "Charlotte Smith," in *Writers in Sussex* (Bristol: Redcliffe, 1985); Mary Anne Schofield, Introduction to *Montalbert* (Delmar, N.Y.: Scholars' Facsimiles & Reprints, 1989); "Charlotte Smith," in *British Women Writers: A Critical Reference Guide,* ed. Janet Todd (New York: Frederick Ungar, 1989); Virginia Blain, Patricia Clements, and Isobel Grundy, "Charlotte (Turner) Smith," in *The Feminist Companion to Literature in English: Women Writers from the Middle Ages to the Present* (New Haven: Yale University Press, 1990); Jonathan Wordsworth, Introduction to *Charlotte Smith: Elegiac Sonnets 1789)* (Oxford: Woodstock Books, 1992).

Blain, Clements, and Grundy report that an edition of Smith's letters, by Judith Stanton, is forthcoming. Stuart Curran informs me that his edition of the poetry of Charlotte Smith is forthcoming from Oxford University Press. For studies of Smith's fiction, see Roger D. Lund, "The Modern Reader and 'The Truly Feminine Novel,' 1660-1815," in *Fettered or Free? British Women Novelists. 1670-1815,* ed. Mary Anne Schofield and Cecelia Macheski (Athens: Ohio University Press, 1986), pp. 398-425. One of the very few studies of Smith's poetry, since Hilbish's book, is Stuart Curran, "The I Altered," in *Romanticism and Feminism,* ed. Anne K. Mellor (Bloomington: Indiana University Press, 1988), pp. 185-207.

4. I quote Smith's own description, from Barbauld's "Mrs. Charlotte Smith," p. iii.

5. Barbauld, "Mrs. Charlotte Smith," p. 5.

6. Ehrenpreis, Introduction to *Emmeline,* p. viii. The excellent biographical introduction to which Ehrenpreis refers appears in her edition of Smith's novel, *The Old Manor House.*

7. Barbauld, "Mrs. Charlotte Smith," pp. i-ii.

8. Stuart Curran writes that "Charlotte Smith made a virtual career out of self-pity" ("The I Altered," in *Romanticism and Feminism,* ed. Mellor, p. 198).

9. Julia Kavanagh, "Charlotte Smith," in *English Women of Letters: Biographical Sketches,* vol. 1 (London: Hurst and Blackett), p. 187.

10. On the art of biography, and particularly on the tendency to concentrate on personal emotion in the privacy of the subject's psyche (often to the point of slighting the public positions and contributions of a writer), I am indebted to three important books by Reed Whittemore: *Pure Lives* (Baltimore: Johns Hopkins University Press, 1988); *Whole Lives* (Baltimore: Johns Hopkins University Press, 1989); and *Six Literary Lives* (Columbia: University of Missouri Press, 1993).

11. At my request, Kimberly Hoagwood (a psychologist) reviewed the facts of the case and confirmed that, from a psychological point of view, the fact of that much productivity is itself sufficient to rule out the possibility that Smith suffered from chronic self-pity. I would like to thank Dr. Hoagwood for generously making her expert judgment available on this matter.

12. I quote Smith's preface to *Desmond,* from the facsimile edition with an introduction by Gina Luria (New York: Garland, 1974).

13. Smith, *The Emigrants* (London: T. Cadell, 1793).

14. William Wordsworth, *The Prelude,* ed. Jonathan Wordsworth, M. H. Abrams, and Stephen Gill (New York: Norton, 1979), p. 396.

Eleanor Ty (essay date 1993)

SOURCE: Ty, Eleanor. "Contradictory Narratives: Feminine Ideals in *Emmeline.*" In *Unsex'd Revolutionaries: Five Women Novelists of the 1790s,* pp. 115-29. Toronto: University of Toronto Press, 1993.

[*In the following excerpt, Ty discusses Smith's first novel, suggesting that although Smith was constrained by financial considerations and the need to please her readers, her critique of patriarchy is as powerful as those of her more radical peers.*]

Like Wollstonecraft's *Mary, a Fiction* and Inchbald's *A Simple Story* Charlotte Smith's first novel, **Emmeline; or, The Orphan of the Castle,** may be considered a pre-revolutionary novel because of its composition and publication date of 1788. Yet in this early work Smith already demonstrates a strong feminist sensibility because she, like Wollstonecraft, Hays, and Inchbald, does not hesitate to criticize patriarchy and its ideals, especially the belief in the male figure of authority. Unlike the other more radical and outspoken writers we have examined, Smith often takes an oblique approach in her critique. The reasons for this caution or indirectness are financial and practical: the subsistence of Smith's family depended on the popularity of her work, and so her novels were written to please and entertain a general public, rather than to offend. Smith's experience with the translation of *Manon Lescaut,* for example, taught her that English morals were not as liberal as French, and therefore not all topics were acceptable to the English public.[1] Because of her pecuniary straits, she had to be careful of the subject matter and tone of her compositions.

What I want to demonstrate, however, is that **Emmeline** is by no means merely a light, delightful, and, by implication, rather innocuous piece of fiction, as some contemporary readers seemed to believe. Sir Walter Scott had praised it as a 'tale of love and passion, happily conceived, and told in a most interesting manner.'[2] Sir Egerton Brydges called it an 'enchanting fiction with a new kind of delight' and wondered about the author: 'How a mind oppressed with sorrows and injuries of the deepest dye, and loaded with hourly anxieties of the most pressing sort, could be endowed with strength and elasticity to combine and throw forth such visions with a pen dipped in all the glowing hues of a most playful and creative fancy, fills me with astonishment and admiration.'[3] However, its criticism of patriarchy, of the customs of marriage and domestic life, is as vehement as those levelled by more forthright and radical feminists such as Wollstonecraft and Hays. In fact, the novel is a rich blend of romance, sexual politics, and social critique. While I agree with Jane Spencer, who notes in *A Dictionary of British and American Women Writers 1600-1800* that Smith's 'feminist interests are evident in her attempt, particularly in the later novels, to portray strong heroines whose fortitude and intelligence show them to be the equals of men,'[4] I would argue that Smith's feminism is not limited to just the portrayal of role models or 'strong heroines'; rather, it consists of a questioning of the basis of patriarchal ideology. In **Emmeline, Desmond,** and **The Young Philosopher** Smith examines and deconstructs the traditional definitions of domestic felicity and the ideal wife, as they would be presented in the mid-1790s by conservative writers such as Jane West and Hannah More. Mary Anne Schofield says that Smith 'displays her tendency toward unmasking and realism,' and 'uncovers several romantic conventions in **Emmeline.**'[5] It is this rejection and yet, at the same time, conscious employment of romantic convention that create much of the tension in Smith's fiction. She challenges accepted eighteenth-century notions of the importance of woman's sexuality in male/female relationships but seems as if she is perpetuating existing ideologies. Through textual strategies such as multiple plots and double discourses Smith rewrites these concepts, revealing the weaknesses of the ideal, and the constraints on female subjectivity and desire.

Read in the light of Mikhail Bakhtin's notion of heteroglossia, or double-voiced discourse,[6] **Emmeline** becomes a complex narrative containing both a 'dominant' story and other 'muted' stories, what Sandra Gilbert and Susan Gubar identify as a 'palimpsest.'[7] The dominant story, that of the sweet, helpless orphan Emmeline, conforms to the conventions of the romance: the young heroine, relying on her beauty and goodness, survives the trials and tribulations of her entrance into the world and finally marries a worthy and wealthy suitor.[8] But behind this dominant story are two muted ones which do not fit into the fairy-tale-like, happily-ever-after mould. Mrs Stafford's history shows the plight of an intelligent woman of the eighteenth century who is united to an insensitive brute whom she has to respect as husband and authority figure, while Lady Adelina's case examines adultery from the point of view of the so-called 'fallen' woman. Both tales demonstrate the need for reform in the existing social and marital customs. As well they serve to balance or undercut the romance of the dominant narrative.

The female protagonist, Emmeline, is very close to a paragon of virtue, and as Egerton Brydges noted, she is very much like Smith's other heroines. Brydges comments on Smith:

> What are the traits which characterize every heroine delineated by her pen? An elevated simplicity, an unaffected purity of heart, of ardent and sublime affections, delighting in the scenery of nature, and flying from the sophisticated and vicious commerce of the world; but capable, when necessity calls it forth, of displaying a vigorous sagacity and lofty fortitude, which appals vice, and dignifies adversity.[9]

This description of Smith's female characters suggests a valorization of a number of qualities which have also been praised by the other women novelists of this study: simplicity, closeness to nature, personal rather than public or social values, morality, and strength of character. As I have argued in the case of Inchbald's dichotomy of nature and art, the tendency to prefer the natural, the affective, or the unsophisticated reveals an affinity for the traditionally feminine, and in the light of Burkean politics of the 1790s, may also suggest a non-conformist attitude towards the male-dominated world ruled by the Law of the Father. Like Wollstonecraft, Hays, and Inchbald, Smith demonstrates a hesitancy to endorse fully the symbolic or the public sphere, particularly as that world is depicted as greedy, shallow, and artificial.

Like Inchbald's two Henry figures, Emmeline grows up in virtual exile, away from the corrupting influences of society. Up to the age of sixteen Emmeline is brought up by a housekeeper 'in a remote part of the county of Pembroke,' in 'an old building' which belonged to 'the ancient family of Mowbray' (1). This isolation from the materialistic and self-seeking society, combined with her intelligence and 'intuitive knowledge' (2), makes her into a heroine who is capable of thinking and acting independently of conventional societal values. We admire Emmeline from the outset because of her spirited nature. In the all-important question of marriage, for example, she unfailingly makes the right decisions. At the beginning of the novel, though believing herself penniless and friendless, Emmeline nevertheless rejects young Frederic Delamere's professions of love for her even though he is the only son and heir of Lord Montreville. Her thoughts of becoming Delamere's wife show her sound understanding and judgment:

> Splendid as his fortune was, and high as his rank would raise her above her present lot of life, she thought that neither would reconcile her to the painful circumstance of carrying uneasiness and contention into his family; of being thrown from them with contempt, as the disgrace of their rank and ruin of their hopes; and of living in perpetual apprehension lest the subsiding fondness of her husband should render her the object of his repentance and regret.
>
> The regard she was sensible of for Delamere did not make her blind to his faults; and she saw, with pain, that the ungovernable violence of his temper frequently obscured all his good qualities.
>
> (73)

Notice that neither rank nor fortune, the values of conventional society, entices Emmeline into 'carrying uneasiness and contention into [Delamere's] family.' She does not wish to let worldly ambition affect familial ties and at the same time is level-headed enough not to be blinded by youthful passion.

In contrast to Emmeline are a number of silly girls in the novel, such as Miss Ashwood, who

> had learned all the cant of sentiment from novels; and her mama's lovers had extremely edified her in teaching her to express it. She talked perpetually of delicate embarrassments and exquisite sensibilities, and had probably a lover, as she extremely wanted a *confident* . . . Of the 'sweet novels' she had read, she just understood as much as made her long to become the heroine of such a history herself.
>
> (229)

This passage shows that Smith understood the conventions of romance and was not entirely unaware of the ideological implications of art, of the fact that literature can 'interpellate' the reader, offering the reader the position which is most obvious, that of the 'subject in ideology.'[10] In *Emmeline* Smith attempted to create a heroine who, although constrained by her position as a female with no family or fortune, is able to act according to her sense of honour and self-esteem rather than according to the values of the bourgeois or aristocratic world.

One reader who felt that Smith's heroine was a bit too faultless and perfect was Jane Austen, whose character Catherine Morland is a deliberate inversion of Emmeline.[11] Emmeline, with no formal education, only with her 'uncommon understanding, and unwearied application,' 'acquired a taste for poetry, and the more ornamental parts of literature' (2, 4). At sixteen 'her understanding was of the first rank' (6). Later she even teaches herself to draw miniature portraits and to sing, with her voice 'soft and sweet'

(41). In *Northanger Abbey* Austen makes fun of Emmeline's flawlessness by making her heroine unable to learn anything before she was taught, unable to play any instrument, and deficient with the pencil.[12] This deliberate parodic treatment, however, does not mean a total condemnation of Smith's works. Parody can often reveal a grudging admiration for the master text.[13] Indeed several scholars have shown how Austen was in fact indebted to Smith and other lesser-known female authors of the 1790s.[14] Nevertheless, Austen's criticism does raise an interesting question of authorial awareness on Smith's part.

Because of the details of Smith's own marriage and other life experiences, we know that the author herself could not have endorsed whole-heartedly the model of docility, submission, and self-sacrifice represented by a heroine such as Emmeline. For in her characterization of Emmeline, Smith adheres to almost all the accepted notions of the ideal woman, one that West and More would have approved of. One could read the character of Emmeline almost as a deliberate exaggeration of the conventional notions of the feminine since she is frequently referred to in epithets of perfection, from the discourse of romance novels, which verge on the ludicrous. For instance, she is an 'angelic friend' (445), one possessing the 'lovely purity' of character (388); Godolphin, her suitor, in ecstatic happiness, pronounces her to be 'adorable, angelic goodness . . . best, as well as the loveliest of human creatures' (446); he is enchanted by her 'softness,' thrilled that he is dear to her 'angelic bosom' (488). In her infallibility, her purity, and her self-sacrificing attitude towards both Delamere and Adelina, Emmeline comes close to the incarnation or all the qualities that Virginia Woolf would later term the 'angel in the house' figure:

> She was intensely sympathetic. She was immensely charming. She was utterly unselfish. She excelled in the difficult arts of family life. She sacrificed herself daily . . . in short she was so constituted that she never had a mind or a wish of her own, but preferred to sympathize always with the minds and wishes of others. Above all—I need not say it—she was pure.[15]

Woolf explains that it was this figure who haunted her when she came to write, and speaks of the necessity of murdering this angel or phantom: 'Had I not killed her she would have killed me . . . For . . . you cannot review even a novel without having a mind of your own, without expressing what you think to be the truth about human relations, morality, sex.' According to Woolf, if women are to be this 'angel in the house' figure, they cannot write because they 'must conciliate, they must . . . tell lies if they are to succeed.'[16]

I suggest that the dilemma Woolf articulates is precisely the problem which faced Smith as she wrote her many novels. As a woman living in a predominantly patriarchal society, Smith was aware of the subject-position expected of her; she was conscious of the need to sympathize and sacrifice, to 'conciliate' and 'tell lies.' Yet her experiences as wife and mother, as sole supporter of her large family, taught her how difficult it was to sustain this role and even perhaps made it necessary for her to act otherwise in order to survive. In *Emmeline* we see how she works out this predicament by presenting us with multiple versions of the feminine. Consistent with the model of female psychological maturation proposed by such a feminist as Nancy Chodorow, Smith does not confront or 'murder' the 'angel in the house' figure; instead, she attempts a compromise and an accommodation.[17] In her first novel she portrays the 'angelic' figure as well as two other non-stereotypical ones which are more in keeping with her own experiences as a woman and wife in a male-dominated society.

The heroine of the dominant story, Emmeline, embodies all the traditional, proper 'feminine' virtues. In the area where she grew up, for example, the 'ignorant rustics' saw Emmeline as possessing 'the beauty of an angel, administering to their necessities and alleviating their misfortunes, looked upon her as a superior being, and throughout the country she was almost adored' (5). Emmeline's friend Mrs Stafford asserts that Delamere will nowhere meet with 'a more lovely person, a better heart, a more pure and elegant mind' than Emmeline's (62). The narrator comments that unlike others who are 'attentive to pecuniary or selfish motives' Emmeline 'was liable to err only from the softness of her heart' (97). In many instances we are shown her generosity and her sympathy: with Mrs Stafford, who is in difficult financial straits; with Lady Adelina, who needs a nurse and a friend; even with the infatuated Delamere. It is almost as if Smith consciously tried to depict her heroine after a paragon for public approval.

Just as Richardson's *Pamela* uses elements of the Cinderella fairy tale, so Smith's *Emmeline* employs this story of a poor girl turning princess in her novel. Indeed the dominant story can be read as a theme of 'virtue rewarded.' Like Fielding's Tom Jones, Emmeline is a fortunate 'foundling' in many ways. In the beginning she is believed to be an illegitimate, penniless orphan, the 'natural daughter' of Mr Mowbray (1); but by the end, through some papers discovered in ancient caskets, she is recognized as the legitimate 'heiress to a large fortune' (472), the rightful 'princess' and owner of Mowbray Castle. Her aunt, Lady Montreville, who seems always ready to call Emmeline by 'harsh and injurious appellations' (55), and who is full of 'pride and malignity' (133), is a fairly close recreation of the wicked stepmother. Though Emmeline does not attend a ball, like Cinderella, she is swept off her feet by a dashing young prince from the Isle of Wight, Captain Godolphin. Godolphin, noble, generous, and patient, acts as Emmeline's knight in shining armour and escorts her through her difficult period of trials and adjustment. His unselfish nature is demonstrated early on in his friendship with Emmeline: upon discovering that 'his heart was irrecoverably gone,' he avoids her in order 'not to embitter *her* life with the painful conviction that their acquaintance had destroyed the happiness of *his*' (304). He also successfully wards off Emmeline's inappropriate suitors, the gallant Chevalier Bellozane and the impetuous Delamere.

This charming romance, which affirms the belief in moral goodness, the belief that passive female suffering will be ultimately rewarded, is doubtless the aspect of the novel that so delighted contemporary readers like Hayley[18] and Brydges. However, this fairy-tale-like narrative is not the only story in **Emmeline.** Without destroying the appeal of the sentimental tale, Smith nevertheless undercuts it or renders it ironic with the more realistic or 'literal' stories of two unhappily married women. In essence, the 'muted' stories of Mrs Stafford and Lady Adelina deconstruct the myth of the princess as exemplified by Emmeline. Their presence in the novel calls into question the very feminine ideals that Emmeline seems to represent for those around her. For example, female 'purity,' so highly extolled as a virtue in Emmeline, does not become an issue in Lady Adelina's case. Lady Adelina has violated the codes of what Mary Poovey terms the 'proper lady' by not conforming to the ideal of the tractable female, and by flaunting her sexual desire in her adulterous relationship with George Fitz-Edward.[19] But in Smith's novel the detection and the punishment of the sexual transgression are not the key issues. Rather, through the disinterested concern of Emmeline for the so-called 'fallen' woman, readers are given an example of the positive effects of female generosity, benevolence, and charity. Smith outlines the social and psychological reasons behind Adelina's infidelity and, in so doing, makes her readers sympathetic allies rather than judges of her case.

Smith is careful to suggest that it is the circumstances surrounding Adelina's matrimony and domestic life which are responsible for her subsequent action, and not an inherent 'weakness' or susceptibility to depravity in woman that causes the adultery. At fifteen, Adelina, 'just out of the nursery, where [she] had never been told it was necessary to think at all' (211), consents to wed the first gentleman who dances with her at the request of her father. Note that the age of Adelina and the motives of marriage closely parallel the details of Smith's own life. The gentleman's love for her is compared to his fondness for a 'favourite hunter or a famous pointer' (213). 'Neither a friend or a companion . . . not even a protector,' Trelawny 'was hardly ever at home' (216). The 'young men of fashion, who call themselves his friends . . . make love to [her], with as little scruple as they borrowed money of *him*' (214). Adelina complains that his conversation 'consisted either in tiresome details of adventures among jockies, pedigrees of horses, or scandalous and silly anecdotes about persons of whom nobody wished to hear' (217). Like the author's husband, Benjamin Smith, he gambles away their fortune, goes abroad to flee his creditors, and leaves Adelina to fend for herself.

This situation, somewhat similar to what Smith herself experienced in marriage, sets the stage for Adelina's extramarital relationship. In her despair Adelina turns to George Fitz-Edward, who tenderly alleviates Adelina's physical, emotional, and, eventually, sexual needs. His appearance at a moment of vulnerability, when she feels abandoned and disillusioned with her husband, makes his actions seem more heroic than usual in Adelina's eyes. Her 'partiality' for him increases until she feels that 'it was no longer in [her] power to live without him' (219, 222). The liaison results in Adelina's pregnancy, and her attempt to hide from Fitz-Edward, from her own 'family, and from all the world' (224). That Smith did not want her readers to think she condoned Adelina's actions is shown in her careful attempt not to be lenient towards Adelina. When Emmeline meets Adelina, she has become a sincere, almost 'extravagant,' penitent,[20] wishing only 'to remain, and to die . . . unknown' in seclusion (224). Throughout the novel Smith does not have Adelina see Fitz-Edward again, and only in the last pages of the novel, after the death of Adelina's husband, does she suggest a possible reunion between them.

However, Smith's sympathetic treatment of Adelina, the fact that she allows the heroine to befriend her,[21] as well as the similarities in the depiction of the 'pure' and the 'fallen' woman suggest a challenging of conventional dichotomies. One example of Smith's subversion of Puritanical values may be the perhaps unintentional lexical confusion of descriptions of Emmeline and Adelina. Both characters are described in practically the same terms, suggesting affinity rather than obvious or distinct differences. For instance, Emmeline is alluded to as the 'lovely orphan' (250); while Adelina has a 'lovely figure' (227). Adelina is full of 'sorrow' and 'regret,' and possesses a 'great sensibility of heart' (227), while Emmeline, too, has a 'tender and susceptible mind' (73), and is frequently depicted as 'melancholy and repining' (72). One could argue that these repetitive passages are clichés from sentimental fiction, but Smith may be using these analogous portraits to question the stereotypical binary opposition of the traditionally 'good' and 'bad' woman, or of the angel and whore figures.[22] Despite her infidelity to Trelawny, for Smith, Adelina is as 'pure' as the virginal Emmeline.

Another subversive strategy is in the conclusion of the Adelina subplot. By not dooming Adelina to a tragic death or to a life of prostitution, the conventional endings for the unfaithful wife who dares defy patriarchal rules of propriety,[23] Smith is implicitly giving a critique of the society and of the literary conventions which support the belief that a woman who expresses admiration, and subsequently, sexual preference for a man to whom she was not legally bound, is in fact a depraved 'monster.' For Lady Adelina, while not 'virtuous' in the traditional sense, is not 'corrupt' either. Her example shows that the distinction between good and evil, purity and iniquity, madonna and temptress, is in fact a more complex issue than the question of mere sexual chastity.

In addition, her affection for Fitz-Edward asserts the presence and validity of female desire, which is a notion contradictory to the ideas espoused by conduct books and by writers such as Gisborne, More, and West. These and other traditional thinkers believed that a wife should have no desires of her own, but should be 'like a Mirrour which hath no image of its own, but receives its stamp from the face that looks into it.' A woman must not only obey her husband, but must bring 'unto him the very Desires of the Heart to be regulated by him so far, that it should not be lawful for her to will or desire what she liked, but only what her husband should approve and allow.'[24] In depicting Adelina's love for a man who is not her husband, Smith is defying these beliefs in female subservience and submission to the male authority figure in her home. Implicitly, she is also opposing the belief in the necessity of the effacement of female desire in matrimony.

Similarly, the history of Mrs Stafford challenges the plausibility of a woman's achieving happiness or domestic felicity solely through marriage and the traditional family. Specifically, her case examines and rejects what Burke would later defend as the notion of the benevolent patriarch as the best ruler of the household. Like the author herself Mrs Stafford is married to one who is not her intellectual equal. In fact, the story so strongly resembles the experiences of Charlotte and Benjamin Smith that biographical studies of the author's life have tended to quote directly from *Emmeline* for illustrations of Smith's own life.[25] One contemporary critic censured Charlotte Smith for mixing life with art. The poet Anna Seward wrote the following after reading the first novel of her rival literary lady: 'Whatever may be Mr. Smith's faults, surely it was as wrong as indelicate to hold up the man, whose name she bears, the father of her children, to public contempt in a novel.'[26] Seward's charge of Smith's 'indelicacy' may be true, but it is precisely the exposition of the unpleasant 'truth' of many domestic arrangements that Smith desired. The Stafford sub-plot not only illustrates the inadequacy of the patriarchal ideal, but also illustrates a woman's economic and social helplessness, and her total dependence on the whims of her husband once she embarks on the marital state.

Like the other revolutionary writers discussed in this book Smith was aware of the illusory pleasure of marriage and was wary of idealizing it as the ultimate goal for every woman. Though many of her own novels have the conventional ending of matrimony, this closure must be read in the context of her own life, as well as the digressive tales or sub-plots of the other female characters in the novels. The inclusion of Mrs Stafford's unhappy conjugality in *Emmeline* makes visible women's frustrations and disappointments. Trapped as a writer as her characters are trapped as women, Smith may not have invented a new ending for her heroine, as Williams did, for example, but she does articulate her dissatisfaction with the social, economic, and psychological reality of marriage. Through Mrs Stafford, Smith demonstrates some of the difficulties encountered in the construction of female subjectivity. Mrs Stafford's subject-position as wife is antithetical to her subject-position as an adult capable of reason and judgment. For as wife in the social order of the eighteenth century she has to submit to the caprices of her husband, even while recognizing their foolishness. Like Geraldine Verney's situation in Smith's most radical novel, ***Desmond***, Mrs Stafford's narrative demonstrates that by social and legal definition, a wife was virtually a piece of property to be disposed of as the husband wished.

Mrs Stafford's tale can be read as a 'double-voiced discourse' because of a potentially radical critique behind its seemingly conservative façade, sentimental discourse, and moralistic lesson. While seeming to extol traditional female virtues of compliance, self-sacrifice, and acceptance of woman's lot, the story actually decries the injustice of the power relations structured in matrimony. Mrs Stafford's problem is as follows: despite possessing a 'very superior understanding,' a mind 'originally elegant and refined . . . highly cultivated, and embellished with all the knowledge that could be acquired from the best authors in the modern languages' (43), Mrs Stafford is forced to submit to the caprice of her husband, who, 'ever in pursuit of some wild scheme,' was 'fond of improvements and alterations' which never amounted to anything but expense and disappointments for his family (44, 190). Though he is married 'to a woman who was the delight of her friends and the admiration of her acquaintance,' Mr Stafford grew 'irritable in proportion as his difficulties encreased' and 'sometimes treated his wife with great harshness; and did not seem to think it necessary . . . to excuse or soften to her his general ill conduct' (177). At one point Mrs Stafford, like the author herself, is reduced to either following 'her husband to a prison, or prevail[ing] on him to go to the Continent while she attempted anew to settle his affairs' (301). Like Wollstonecraft in *The Wrongs of Woman* Smith lets her heroine speak at length about her afflictions, demonstrating that the woman is affected not only by the degradations of her physical conditions—her clothing, food, and shelter—but that she has to undergo mental and spiritual agony as well.

Perhaps the greatest disappointment in Mrs Stafford's marriage is the descent from an upper-middle-class society to that of her husband's lower-middle-class or commercial circle. Mrs Stafford explains:

> . . . born with a right to affluence and educated in its expectation, with feelings keen from nature . . . to be compelled . . . to solicit favours, pecuniary favours, from persons who have no feeling at all . . . I have endured the brutal unkindness of hardened avarice, the dirty chicane of law . . . I have been forced to attempt softening the tradesman and the mechanic, and to suffer every degree of humiliation . . . Actual poverty, I think, I could have better borne.
>
> (458)

While Smith makes an impassioned plea on behalf of herself and her heroine, this appeal is limited in its scope to a specifically middle-class sensibility. Here Smith is not advocating a total system of reform which would benefit all who are oppressed, but targets her criticism to a specific social and cultural phenomenon which often circumscribed middle-class women.

Reviewing *Emmeline* in the *Analytical Review*, Mary Wollstonecraft called Adelina 'a character as absurd as dangerous' because of her adultery and her subsequent melodramatic repentance, and contrasted her with the admirable Mrs Stafford and her 'rational resignation.' At this time, relatively young and inexperienced herself, Wollstonecraft praised Mrs Stafford for turning 'to her children instead of to romance' when disappointed in her husband.[27] While Mrs Stafford does seem to be a model of 'resignation,' as Wollstonecraft suggests, the fact that Smith embeds her disagreeable experiences in the midst of a conventional romance draws the reader's attention to the shortcomings of both the literary practice of ending with a matrimonial celebration, and the socio-cultural custom of viewing marriage as the answer to every single woman's search for fulfilment. That both Adelina's and Mrs Stafford's experiences, which are in the background, influence Emmeline's story, which is in the foreground, is revealed by the heroine herself. At one point when Delamere tries passionately to persuade her to meet and marry him secretly, she refuses as 'she had lately seen in her friends, Mrs Stafford and Lady Adelina, two melancholy instances of the frequent unhappiness of very early marriages; and she had no inclination to hazard her own happiness in hopes of proving an exception' (230). This comment is an ironic reminder of quotidian reality and hard truth amidst the easy flow of fantasy which seems to characterize the rest of the novel.

Finally, one other aspect of the novel which has often been regarded as Smith's specialty is the use of Gothic elements. In *Emmeline* the Gothic castle with its dark and mysterious passages, the secret papers in ancient caskets, and the tyrannical uncle suggest a similarity to perhaps the most highly developed romance of the 1790s, Ann Radcliffe's *The Mysteries of Udolpho,* which was written a few years later. Indeed Smith has been regarded as a forerunner of the genre of Gothic romance.[28] However, the use of the Gothic in *Emmeline* is rather scant and is different in many ways from how it is used by Radcliffe and her followers. Whereas Emily St. Aubert is transported from a pastoral, idyllic landscape to the terror of the castle in Udolpho, Emmeline begins in Mowbray Castle and is restored to it as its rightful owner by the end. For Emmeline, unlike other abducted maidens in unfamiliar surroundings, the castle represents a place of comfort and familiarity: 'There she had passed her earliest infancy, and had known, in that period of unconscious happiness, many delightful hours which would return no more' (36). When she leaves the castle, which was 'still frowning in gothic magnificence' with 'its venerable towers . . . the ruins of the monastery . . . the citadel . . . covered with ivy,' (37), it is with sadness and melancholy. For Emmeline the castle is not a prison; rather, it is a haven or, as one critic says, 'a refuge from . . . power.'[29]

It is only with the intrusion of males from the public or symbolic world of the Father that the castle poses any danger to the heroine. Kate Ellis suggests that 'Terror appears in *Emmeline* when she is confronted with sexuality, and thus with a need to assert herself,'[30] but I think terror stems from male invasion and not from female sexuality itself. When besieged, Emmeline eludes those who would assault her virtue by deliberately running into dark, bewildering passages which are known to her. In Smith's novel it is the men who are frightened of the dark. For example, Lord Montreville's French valet, Millefleur, missing a turn, blunders 'about till the encreasing gloom, which approaching night threw over the arched and obscure apartments, through windows dim with painted glass, filled him with apprehension and dismay' (14). When he encounters Emmeline, he attempts to molest her, but she flies 'hastily back through those passages which all his courage did not suffice to make him attempt exploring again' (15). With Delamere, Emmeline similarly escapes from his attention by running 'lightly thro' the passage, which was very long and dark' (33). Emmeline deliberately lets her candle 'fall after her' to confuse Delamere and leave him in 'total darkness' (33). This ability to negotiate the dark long passages of the castle, which are often associated with the feminine, the female body, the mysterious, and the chaotic, suggests an affinity to what Kristeva calls the 'semiotic' or the pre-symbolic world. This capability to function in dark and mysterious passages may also imply a knowledge of or, at least, a certain connection with female sexuality and the body. Implicitly Smith may be pointing out Emmeline's latent female desires or sexuality while depicting her as a seemingly 'pure' and 'angelic' heroine. Appropriately, the castle is where Emmeline experienced youthful 'unconscious happiness' (36) with her care-giver and substitute mother, Mrs Carey. With the death of this mother figure Emmeline is displaced from the cosiness of the feminine Gothic castle, and thrown into the male-dominated world of power and greed.

In psycho-linguistic terms we can read the castle as the place without the Father, where male power, male desire, and even male logic cannot penetrate. The long, darkened corridors where Emmeline moves without a light, 'feeling her way' (31) until she reaches what she believes to be safety is analogous to the area Irigaray describes in 'La Mystérique,' the 'place where consciousness is no longer master, where, to its extreme confusion, it sinks into a dark night that is also fire and flames.'[31] By making her heroine agile at escaping from male predators in a landscape they are unfamiliar with and terrified of, Smith suggests a realm of 'other' which is not dependent upon the symbolic authority of the Father. Emmeline triumphs over her would-be assailants, but the victory is short-lived and rather limited because soon after these incidents she is expelled from the familiar world of Mowbray Castle. The dark passages offer a temporary refuge, but one cannot stay there forever. In a sense, Emmeline has to be educated and exposed to the world outside with its symbolic representation and masculine values before she returns to the castle as its legitimate owner.

In her use of the Gothic, Smith, like Radcliffe, Wollstonecraft, and Inchbald, makes connections between politics and terror, the incompatibility of human reason and a society based on fear and tyranny.[32] In *Emmeline* she hints effects of male domination, arbitrary authority, and the misuse of power as her heroine is forced to flee from one threatening man to another. Paradoxically it is mostly outside of the maternal, dark, and mysterious castle that Emmeline is at risk. Without parental protection, Emmeline is persecuted by the unwanted attentions of the steward, Maloney; young Delamere; the rich old banker Mr Rochely; the handsome but presumptuous Bellozane; and a host of other suitors. She is kidnapped by Delamere at one point but escapes injury because of high fever and her determination not to yield to his impetuosity. However, unlike the novels written after the French Revolution, **Emmeline** does not offer a consistent parallel between castles and tyrants, between domesticity and monarchy. The authority figure in the novel, Emmeline's uncle, is not a complete tyrant or villain like Radcliffe's Montoni. Lord Montreville does show compassion for Emmeline on several occasions, even to the point of defending her against the snobbery of his wife (183), but Smith depicts him as avaricious, self-centred, and, if not cruel, certainly an inadequate patriarch. He claims to possess Mowbray Castle and embezzles the sum of 'four thousand five hundred a year' (433) from the orphan heroine, though almost inadvertently. His legal and financial adviser, Sir Richard Crofts, conceals the truth of Emmeline's birthright from him, thus leading to believe she has no legitimate claim to the estate. However, the fact that Montreville cared so little about his affairs as to trust everything to the cunning Crofts may suggest a subconscious wish to believe in, and a willingness to comply with, the lucrative propositions of his lawyer.

On the whole, the novel is not as radical or forthright as those written by Wollstonecraft, Hays, or even Inchbald. Feminism in **Emmeline** is often manifested in more subversive ways, as we have seen. Through narratives that seem to contradict each other, through the conflation of seemingly 'pure' and corrupt characters, or the depiction of apparently kind-hearted figures who turn out to be not so benevolent, Smith questions the moral and social values of her contemporary society. The explicit challenge to patriarchy was to culminate in a work written four years later, **Desmond, a Novel.**

Notes

1. The celebrated English critic, George Stevens, severely censured Smith for her choice of an immoral work. He believed that the passion in *Manon Lescaut* was an apology for licentiousness and ought to be condemned. As a result of this outcry Smith withdrew the work. See Florence Hilbish, 'Charlotte Smith, Poet and Novelist (1749-1806)' (PHD diss., University of Pennsylvania, 1941), 118-19.

2. As quoted by Anne Henry Ehrenpreis, 'Introduction,' *Emmeline; or, The Orphan of the Castle,* by Charlotte Smith (London: Oxford University Press 1971), vii. Subsequent page references are to this edition.

3. As quoted by Hilbish, 'Charlotte Smith, Poet and Novelist,' 131

4. Jane Spencer, 'Charlotte Smith,' in *A Dictionary of British and American Women Writers 1600-1800,* ed. Janet Todd (London: Methuen 1984), 289

5. Mary Anne Schofield, *Masking and Unmasking the Female Mind: Disguising Romances in Feminine Fiction, 1713-1799* (Newark: University of Delaware Press 1990), 150

6. M. M. Bakhtin, *The Dialogic Imagination: Four Essays,* ed. Michael Holquist, trans. Caryl Emerson and Michael Holquist (Austin: University of Texas Press 1981), 324

7. As quoted by Elaine Showalter, 'Feminist Criticism in the Wilderness,' in *The New Feminist Criticism,* ed. Elaine Showalter (New York: Pantheon 1985), 266

8. This plot summary fits a number of novels written in the eighteenth century, including, for example, Samuel Richardson's *Pamela,* Frances Burney's *Evelina,* and Jane Austen's *Emma* and *Mansfield Park.*

9. Egerton Brydges, *Imaginative Biography* (1834), 2:95-6, as quoted by Anne Henry Ehrenpreis, 'Introduction,' *Northanger Abbey,* by Jane Austen (Harmondsworth: Penguin 1972), 14

10. See Catherine Belsey, *Critical Practice* (New York: Methuen 1980), especially chapter 3, 'Addressing the Subject,' for a further discussion of this topic.

11. Several critics have noted that Catherine Morland is a parody of Smith's Emmeline, among them, Anne Henry Ehrenpreis, in her 'Introduction' to *Emmeline,* xi; and Mary Lascelles, *Jane Austen and Her Art* (Oxford: Oxford University Press 1939), 60-3.

12. See the first chapter of *Northanger Abbey.*

13. Linda Hutcheon suggests that 'parody is a form of serious art criticism' and 'has the advantage of being both a re-creation and a creation, making criticism into a kind of active exploration of form' (*A Theory of Parody: The Teachings of Twentieth Century Art Forms* [New York: Methuen 1985], 51).

14. See, for example, Kenneth L. Moler, *Jane Austen's Art of Allusion* (Lincoln: University of Nebraska Press 1968); Frank W. Bradbrook, *Jane Austen and Her Predecessors* (Cambridge: Cambridge University Press 1966); Marilyn Butler, *Jane Austen and the War of Ideas* (Oxford: Oxford University Press 1975); William H. Magee, 'The Happy Marriage: The Influence of Charlotte Smith on Jane Austen,' *Studies in the Novel,* 7, no. 1 (Spring 1975), 120-32; and Eleanor Ty, 'Ridding Unwanted Suitors: Jane Austen's *Mansfield Park* and Charlotte Smith's *Emmeline,*' *Tulsa Studies in Women's Literature* 5, no. 2 (Fall 1986), 327-29.

15. Virginia Woolf, 'Professions for Women,' reprinted in *Virginia Woolf: Women and Writing,* ed. Michèle Barrett (London: Women's Press 1979), 59

16. Ibid., 59, 60

17. According to Nancy Chodorow, 'a girl usually turns to her father as an object of primary interest from the exclusivity of the relationship to her mother, but this libidinal turning to her father does not substitute for her attachment to her mother. Instead, a girl retains her preoedipal tie to her mother . . . and builds oedipal attachments to both her mother and father' (*The Reproduction of Mothering: Psychoanalysis and the Sociology of Gender* [Berkeley: University of California Press 1978], 192-3). On the basis of Chodorow's theories Mary Poovey suggests that 'it may well be the case that woman's psychological relation to authority may involve accommodation rather than confrontation; in other words, it may be more in keeping with her psychological development to identify with and accept a number of role models instead of trying to usurp the place of her authoritative forebears' (*The Proper Lady and the Woman Writer* [Chicago: University of Chicago Press 1984], 254).

18. Hayley was quoted as observing that *Emmeline*, 'considering the situation of the author, is the most wonderful production he ever saw, and not inferior, in his opinion, to any book in that fascinating species of composition.' Hayley is quoted in a letter of J. C. Walker to Bishop Percy, 16 September 1788, in John Nichols, *Illustrations of the Literary History of the Eighteenth Century* (1848), 708, as noted by Ehrenpreis, 'Introduction,' *Emmeline*, vii.

19. See the first chapter of Poovey, *The Proper Lady and the Woman Writer.*

20. Jane Spencer, in *The Rise of the Woman Novelist: From Aphra Behn to Jane Austen* (Oxford: Basil Blackwell 1986), says that 'Adelina proves herself not really ruined by this one error by the extravagance of her repentance' (128).

21. Eva Figes, who sees similarities between Smith's *Emmeline* and Frances Burney's *Cecilia,* points out that the incident with Adelina illustrates the difference between Smith's and Burney's fictional worlds. Figes observes: '. . . no Burney woman would have been allowed to be friends with a pregnant woman . . . Smith's heroines constantly express active sympathy for women in distress' (*Sex and Subterfuge: Women Novelists to 1850* [London: Macmillan 1982], 64).

22. The kind of feminist criticism that seeks to identify stereotypical portraits of women has been labelled 'feminist critique' by Elaine Showalter in 'Toward a Feminist Poetics' and 'Feminist Criticism in the Wilderness,' both reprinted in Showalter, ed. *The New Feminist Criticism.* One early example of this type of feminist criticism is Mary Ellmann's *Thinking about Women* (New York: Harcourt 1968).

23. One classic case is Defoe's Moll Flanders, who is seduced by an older brother, but marries the younger brother, Robin. Moll subsequently becomes a prostitute and thief. In Inchbald's *A Simple Story* Miss Milner is unfaithful to Dorriforth and is exiled to die unloved and alone in Scotland. In Smith's *Emmeline* another adulterous figure, Lady Frances, who, because of vanity and boredom, embarks openly on an affair with Chevalier de Bellozane, is disciplined for her indiscriminate actions by a '*lettre de cachet,* which confined her during pleasure to a convent' (525).

24. Edwin Hood, *The Age and Its Architects,* as quoted by Poovey, *The Proper Lady and the Woman Writer,* 247

25. See, for example, the first chapter, 'Formative Influences,' of F. Hilbish's 'Charlotte Smith, Poet and Novelists,' where she cites Mr and Mrs Stafford's 'history' as the experience of Benjamin and Charlotte Smith (88-91, 95-9).

26. Quoted by Ehrenpreis, 'Introduction,' *Emmeline,* viii

27. Mary Wollstonecraft, *Analytical Review* 1 (1788), 333

28. See, for example, J. M. S. Tompkins, *The Popular Novel in England 1770-1800* (London: Constable 1932), 266, 375, who first pointed out that Radcliffe was profoundly indebted to Smith. Similar views are expressed in James R. Foster, 'Charlotte Smith, Pre-Romantic Novelist,' *PMLA* [*Publications of the Modern Language Association of America*] 43 (June 1928), 463-75; and Ehrenpreis, 'Introduction,' *Emmeline,* xi.

29. Spencer, *The Rise of the Woman Novelist,* 194

30. Kate Ferguson Ellis, *The Contested Castle: Gothic Novels and the Subversion of Domestic Ideology* (Urbana: University of Illinois Press 1989), 86

31. Luce Irigaray, *Speculum of the Other Woman,* trans. Gillian Gill (Ithaca, NY: Cornell University Press 1985), 191

32. David Morse, in *Romanticism: A Structural Analysis* (Totowa, NJ: Barnes and Noble 1982), argues that 'the gothic is a field of discourse saturated with political connotations and addressing itself to issues raised in the work of Godwin and Paine: the incompatibility of reason and humanity with a society based on domination and fear; the critique of secrecy and the insistence that healthy society must be based on frankness, openness and sincerity; the suggestion that in a society governed by despotism and permeated by religious hypocrisy and bigotry natural human impulses will become warped and distorted; the conviction that relationships between individuals on any basis other than that of freedom and equality must necessarily be alienating, even for . . . those who coerce and manipulate' (3).

Katharine M. Rogers (essay date 1994)

SOURCE: Rogers, Katharine M. "Romantic Aspirations, Restricted Possibilities: The Novels of Charlotte Smith." In *Re-Visioning Romanticism: British Women Writers, 1776-1837,* edited by Carol Shiner Wilson and Joel Haefner, pp. 72-88. Philadelphia: University of Pennsylvania Press, 1994.

[*In the following essay, Rogers explores Smith's limitations as a female writer incorporating the ideals of Romanticism in her novels.*]

Charlotte Smith wrote her novels in the 1790s (from ***Emmeline*** in 1788 through ***The Young Philosopher*** in 1798), at the time when Romanticism was just beginning to vitalize English literature. She shared the Romantics' intense relationship with nature and was drawn to their ideals of political and sexual freedom. But she could not pursue these ideals as freely as her younger contemporaries Blake and Wordsworth, partly because the novel is more restricted than poetry by actual circumstance, more because, as a woman writing about women, she could not claim the boundless power of the Romantic imagination.

Even though the novel was in some ways unreceptive to Romanticism, however, its development in the later eighteenth century into feminized sentimental and Gothic forms both prepared the way for and shared characteristics with the new movement. Some of what might be considered Romantic features of Smith's work came from the tradition in which she was writing. From mid-century, these novels had affirmed the value of subjectivity by focusing on the consciousness of their protagonists and consequently setting feeling above institution and law. Sensitivity became an essential attribute of superior people, and it alienated them from the obtuse society around them; sentimental novels typically display sensitive characters suffering in a crass world. This suffering was best displayed in young women, socially powerless and therefore dominated and exploited by unworthy established authorities. From the contemporary Gothic tradition, Smith took exotic adventures, which she used in a mechanical way, and wild natural settings, which she developed to better effect than any of her contemporary novelists.

All her sensitive characters share her own intense responsiveness to nature, which she explicitly identifies as romantic. Mrs. Stafford and Emmeline are "romantic wanderers" because they like to take walks through an unspoiled forest, and vulgar Mrs. Ashwood sneers at Emmeline's "pretty romantic notion of contemplation by moonlight" (*Emmeline* 147, 202). Mrs. Glenmorris looks forward to "wild romantic solitude" in northern Scotland (***Young Philosopher*** 2: 77), as does Celestina, whose worldly suitor tries to keep her near him by deriding her plan as "wild, romantic, unpleasant" (2: 236). Enthusiasm for wild scenery and use of natural description to heighten the emotional effect are equally prominent in the novels of Ann Radcliffe (published 1789-97), but Smith's backgrounds are more authentic and more sensitively adapted to her characters' moods.[1] In Radcliffe, natural scenery functions as a self-consciously picturesque backdrop, invariably sublime and intended to elicit generalized religious awe; and it signifies the finer sensibility of those characters who can respond to Nature's grandeur. In Smith at her best, it seems to flow from and amplify the emotions of characters in a particular situation.

Typically, her natural descriptions are called forth by her characters' state of mind. Temporarily cheered by the hope of meeting Marchmont's family, Althea can appreciate the signs of early spring in the desolate manor house she has been banished to: "the faint tinge of fresh green" in the ruined garden, some red buds on the long-neglected fruit trees, a few surviving crocuses (2: 90-94). Celestina goes off by herself to contemplate a sublime sunset in the Hebrides:

> The sun was already declining in an almost cloudless sky, and gave the warmest splendour to the broad expanse of ocean, broken by several islands, whose rocky points and angular cliffs caught the strong lights, in brilliant contrast to the lucid hue of the heath with which their summits were cloathed, and which on the northern and eastern sides threw a dark shadow on the clear and tranquil bosom of the sea. The sea birds, in swarming myriads, were returning to their nests among the ragged precipices beneath her.
>
> (3: 28)

She thinks how Willoughby would share her delight and how, with him, she could enjoy spending her life even in so desolate a setting. When her hopes of marrying Willoughby wane, with the waning year, she finds a bleaker solace in Nature.

> The sun, far distant from this northern region, was as faint and languid as the sick thoughts of Celestina: his feeble rays no longer gave any warm colouring to the rugged cliffs that rose above her head, or lent the undulating sea that sparkling brilliance which a few weeks before had given gaiety and cheerfulness even to these scattered masses of almost naked stone, against which the water incessantly broke. Grey, sullen, and cold, the waves now slowly rolled towards the shore, where Celestina frequently sat whole hours, as if to count them, when she had in reality no idea present to her but Willoughby lost to her for ever.
>
> (3: 40)

Geraldine, traveling through a war-torn area of France to meet her unspeakable husband, describes "one of those cold, damp, gloomy mornings, which impresses a dreary idea that the sun has forsaken the world.—The wind sighed hollow among the half stripped trees; and the leaves slowly fell from the boughs, heavy with rain—The road, rough, and hardly passable, seemed leading us to the dark abode of desolation and despair" (***Desmond*** 3: 289). The long opening sequence of ***The Banished Man*** makes even more effective use of natural conditions. Smith's characters are fleeing by night from their castle, which will soon be overrun by the French Revolutionary army; they cannot see their enemies or know their future. The whole scene is drenched with water—torrential rain that makes it impossible to see, marshy ground that they cannot depend on, and a river that they must cross without knowing where the ford is. The amorphous watery confusion both heightens their anxiety and symbolizes the uncertainty of their fate.

Smith and her characters turned to Nature in the manner of the major Romantic poets, to respond to their emotional needs and help them to articulate their feelings. But there is a significant difference: they could not count on finding consolation there. Wordsworth knew that "Nature never did betray / The heart that loved her" (*Tintern Abbey* ll. 122-23); Byron's Childe Harold found an unfailing "pleasure in the pathless woods" and solaced his troubles by mingling "with the Universe" (Canto 4, stanza 178). But Smith's repeated conclusion, in her own person and through her characters, is that Nature cannot cure human misery. Leaving her castle, Emmeline is offered a set piece of sublime landscape—a rushing mountain stream a ruined monastery and a castle "still frowning in gothic magnificence," a rugged seashore, and a rich autumnal valley set off by "blue and barren hills." But, despite being "ever alive to the beauties of nature," all Emmeline feels is that she is leaving the only home she has ever known (37).

We can approach a definition of Smith's Romanticism by contrasting her with Ann Radcliffe, who wrote at the same time and in the same genre, but who was (despite Byron's admiration) much more conservative. As Smith's use of natural description was more innovative, so her interpretation of the conventions of the sentimental novel approached far closer to Romantic radicalism. Both women created sensitive heroines who recoil from crudity and resist attempts to coerce them into loveless marriages, but who also consistently exert rational control over their impulses. Radcliffe, however, lays more emphasis on control; well-conducted Emily in her *Mysteries of Udolpho* is constantly exhorted to control her sensibility. Smith's heroines, on the other hand, sometimes luxuriate in theirs. In her first letter, which opens Volume 2 of **Desmond,** Geraldine Verney presents herself as a unique sufferer: "Is it, that I set out in life with too great a share of sensibility? or is my lot to be particularly wretched?" (2: 1). Without any troubles like Geraldine's to justify her conclusion, Rosalie at eighteen had "already . . . acquired that painful experience that had made her fear she should taste of unalloyed happiness no more" (**Montalbert,** 1795, 1: 25).[2]

Sensitivity leads Smith's characters to the alienation from a crass society that marked Romantic heroes. Inability to fit in, a comic or blameworthy trait in Fielding's or Smollett's novels, becomes a distinction in Romantic literature. Although none of her characters are self-conscious rebels and outcasts like Cain or Prometheus, they do not fit smoothly into the established social order, any more than she herself did.[3] Alone in the woods on a still November evening, Orlando contrasts Nature's quietude with man's anxious activity, runs through the various careers open to a young man, and concludes that all are pointless, if not pernicious (160-61). Rosalie, the heroine of **Montalbert,** who is supposed to be the daughter of the local vicar, feels alien from him and his family, who, though presentable enough, are commonplace. She goes off whenever she can to read or draw by herself, for she has long been "conscious, that such sort of people as she was usually thrown among, people who only escape from dullness by flying to defamation, were extremely tiresome to her, though she saw that nobody else thought so, and suspected herself of being fastidious and perverse" (2: 137). Her timid self-doubt is not justified, of course; the Romantic heroine really is superior to the commonplace, conventional people around her.

Smith's heroines (after her first, Emmeline) are also distinguished from Radcliffe's by being more ready to commit themselves to love than was strictly compatible with contemporary standards of feminine prudence and propriety. In **The Old Manor House,** timid, inexperienced Monimia declares, without having consulted any older authority: "I do not know, Orlando, why I should be ashamed to say that I love you better than any body else in the world; for indeed who is there in it that I have to love? If you were gone, it would be all a desert to me" (43). Shortly after meeting Montalbert, Rosalie engages herself to him without any thought of consulting her parents, even though he is a Roman Catholic and her supposed father is a Church of England clergyman. She then agrees to a clandestine marriage by a priest for fear of losing Montalbert; Smith censures her lightly, but does not punish her with remorse as was customary at the time. Althea feels a strong interest in Marchmont shortly after meeting him and before he has made any declaration to her; this soon develops into an "extreme concern" that instigates her to help him even though she knows the world would disapprove (**Montalbert** 2: 148); and she accepts his declaration of love while knowing that there is no hope of marriage or of her family's consent.[4]

Smith often calls her characters "romantic," almost always to show their superiority to commonplace people. The word was used throughout the eighteenth century to mean reaching beyond the bounds of reason and common sense, but in the earlier period it generally suggested fatuous wishful thinking or quixotism. Smith, however, typically applies it to idealistic characters whose principles rise above expediency and whose aims rise above mercenary prudence. FitzEdward, a hardened young rake in **Emmeline,** dismisses Delamere's intention of marrying a penniless girl of uncertain birth, rather than seducing and abandoning her, as "a boyish and romantic plan" (**Emmeline** 52). When Rosalie refuses to marry a crass but rich young clergyman, her supposed father accuses her of "affecting . . . fine romantic airs." Her supposed mother exhorts her "to follow, like a reasonable woman, the advice of those who know better what is fit for you than you do yourself" and ridicules the idea of women's marrying "just according to their own romantic whims" (**Montalbert** 1: 57, 61, 74-75).

The most Romantic lover in Smith's novels is Desmond, who adores the unhappily married Geraldine Verney. He is aware that a love that finds total satisfaction in serving a woman and contemplating her virtue from a distance would be considered "romantic, and even ridiculous" by ordinary people (*Desmond* 2: 241). His hard-headed friend Bethel doubts that an erotic passion can be at once intensely pure and intensely ardent and warns against cultivating one that cannot be lawfully fulfilled.[5] Bethel advises Desmond to distract himself from a passion that can only serve to render him miserable by finding some other woman worthy of his love or, if he has "become, through the influence of this romantic attachment, too fastidious for reasonable happiness," to go abroad and seek relief in a change of scene or a pleasant liaison (1: 188-89).

Even after he seems to have lost Geraldine forever, Desmond insists on the superior value of his love: it "may be very true, and very reasonable" that, "if I could once determine to look out for some other enjoyments than those my romantic fancy had described, I might yet find as reasonable a portion of happiness as any human being has a right to expect"—but he cannot, because he has envisioned a higher degree of felicity: "I know there are a hundred, nay, a thousand other plans and people, with whom other men might sit down contented; but I have made up a '*fair idea*,' and losing that, all is to me a blank." He goes on to marvel that a man of Bethel's fine mind, who knows Geraldine, "cannot comprehend the delight of living only for one beloved object, though hopeless of any other return than what the purest friendship may authorise" (3: 214-16). Smith presents her hero and develops her plot to indicate that Desmond's "unreasonable" attitude, his refusal to settle for what is attainable, is to be accepted as admirable. Desmond's total commitment to his passion and Smith's insistence that it is not quixotic and morally questionable, but, rather, idealistic beyond the reach or even the conception of ordinary people, makes him a Romantic hero, even if not so forceful and exciting a one as Manfred or Heathcliff.[6]

The sentimental novelists consistently affirmed that women should not be forced to violate their feelings in choosing a husband, but they agreed that, once married, a virtuous woman had to repress her feelings as necessary to fulfill her conjugal duty. The sacred institution of marriage took precedence over personal feelings, except for extreme radicals and Romantics. Although Smith never explicitly asserted that it was unjust to keep people bound forever to an unequal bargain or that love should take precedence over legal bonds, she filled her novels with deserving people (of both sexes) permanently chained in marriage to odious spouses. In her time, it was shocking even to hint that some marriages should be dissolved; only Mary Wollstonecraft was bold enough to declare, in *The Wrongs of Woman*, that a woman whose marriage had been destroyed by a vicious husband had the right to find emotional and sexual fulfillment with another man.

Smith did shock her contemporaries by her presentation of Lady Adelina Trelawny in *Emmeline*. Adelina, overpersuaded in early youth to marry a man who abuses and deserts her, yields to a congenial lover and becomes pregnant. Overwhelmed by guilt and fear of the brothers she has supposedly dishonored, she retreats into seclusion, suffers from critical illness and insanity, and longs for death until her child gives her the will to live. All the while, however, she has the unhesitating sympathy and support of the virtuous heroine; and in the end there is a hope that she will marry her lover.[7] This was a liberal position in a world where moralists like Hannah More defined Christian forgiveness of an adulteress as isolating her from society to spend the remainder of her life meditating on her sin (*Strictures* 1: 47-49). Even Mary Wollstonecraft (in her prudish youth) condemned Smith for making Adelina too attractive and romantic and insufficiently reformed (*Analytical Review* 27). Without explicitly justifying Adelina's sin, Smith's detailed account inevitably suggests the absurd injustice of giving it overwhelming importance, imposing the responsibility for an entire family's honor on a desperate young woman, expecting anyone not to prefer a loving, attentive man to one who broadcasts his total disregard for her.

Although Smith does criticize women who yield to unlicensed love, she often endows them with good qualities that completely overshadow their failure in chastity. Emily Cathcart in *Celestina,* seduced as a girl and now a kept mistress, is noted for her generosity rather than her unchastity, as she supports her destitute sister and strives on her deathbed for the moral salvation of her lover; she is "amiable, unhappy" (4: 80), rather than sinful. Mrs. Vyvian, Rosalie's real mother, is treated with total sympathy even though she gave birth to an illegitimate child: we hear only of her beautiful character and her sufferings at the hands of the hard-hearted husband she was bullied into marrying to cover her supposed disgrace. The fact that Mrs. Vyvian sees her own situation in that of Rosalie, who has been imprudent although not seduced, suggests a more daring sexual message than Smith is prepared to make explicit—that is, that a heroine might violate the law of chastity and still attain a happy ending; in short, that unchastity need not be punished by lifelong remorse and domestic oppression.[8]

In *Desmond,* Smith daringly placed an adulterous passion at the center of her plot. The novel is set in the early stage of the French Revolution, and Smith draws a pointed parallel between despotism in the nation and in the home. The French have thrown off the oppression of king, aristocracy, and church, but Geraldine Verney remains the slave of her worthless husband.[9] When she must obey his order to follow him into war-torn France, she consoles herself with the thought that even "the wildest collection of those people, whose ferocity arises not from their present liberty, but their recent bondage," will not "injure *me,* who am myself a miserable slave, returning with trembling and reluctant steps, to put on the most dreadful of all fetters[.]—Fetters that would even destroy the freedom of my mind" (3: 71). Unfortunately, Geraldine's insight into her oppression does not liberate her—or Smith—sufficiently to nerve her to resist it. Smith goes no further than to hint that there is something unhealthy and mechanical in Geraldine's rigid obedience, motivated by duty and not at all by love, and presumably fueled by guilt for not loving and a masochistic satisfaction in behaving correctly with no reward in view (3: 72, 271).

Yet the circumstances Smith presents cannot fail to lead to a questioning of English marriage law. How can any law make Verney's atrocious exploitation of Geraldine morally right, or require her to be loyal and loving to a man who insults her even as he exorbitantly demands her services? How can the tie that binds Geraldine to Verney be more sacred than Desmond's idealistic devotion? If the representation "of a man capable of . . . a passion so generous and disinterested as to seek only the good of its object" is the height of morality, as Smith claims in her Preface (ii), marital fidelity is clearly a lesser value. Smith further qualifies Geraldine's orthodox saintliness by supplying two sympathetic female characters who are not so rarified. Madame de Boisbelle, also married to a worthless husband, is allowed to have an affair with impunity; and Fanny Waverly, Geraldine's sister, freely condemns their selfish, stupid mother and her attempts to keep ideas out of her daughters' minds. In her lenient treatment of sexually transgressing women, in her repeated representation of extramarital relationships that are more loving and responsible than the corresponding marriages, Smith implies, in true Romantic fashion, that love is more sacred than law.

Although Smith never explicitly condemns the excessive power that a husband held in marriage, she reiterates the injustice of primogeniture, an almost equally sacrosanct part of the family property system. All of her female and most of her male protagonists are dispossessed in favor of less worthy brothers. Typically, the men are younger brothers whose selfish, irresponsible older brothers squander the inheritance that by rights belongs to the whole family (Orlando in *The Old Manor House,* D'Alonville and Ellesmere in *The Banished Man,* Montalbert, George Delmont in *The Young Philosopher*). Sisters, of course, are routinely sacrificed to the interest of their brothers, a point Smith hammers home in ***Desmond.***

Smith's enthusiastic faith that the French Revolution promised universal liberation, personal and sexual as well as political, was shared by all the Romantics. Robert Southey, for example, reminisced that the Revolution had seemed to open up "a visionary world": "Old things seemed passing away, and nothing was dreamt of but the regeneration of the human race" (Abrams, *Norton Anthology,* 5th ed. 2: 14). In its early, idealistic stage, the Revolution seemed to verify the Romantics' hopes for limitless human improvement in a new society cleansed of the old corruptions.

It was daring for a woman, who was not supposed even to express opinions on public affairs, to defend the French Revolution; and Smith went so far as to make her hero attack the great Edmund Burke's "elaborate treatise in favor of despotism," *Reflections on the Revolution in France* (2: 62; cf. 3: 209). The action of ***Desmond*** runs from June 1790 to February 1792: that is, after the abolition of the special privileges of the church and the aristocracy but before the September Massacres, the trial of the King and Queen, and the Reign of Terror. Smith filled her book with political discussions, in every one of which an enlightened, virtuous character defends the Revolution against opponents who are either unthinking or self-interested and corrupt. The Revolution did more than simply reform abuses in France: in showing what the people could accomplish, it brought light to the world. Desmond declares that its success "involves the freedom, and, of course, the happiness, not merely of this great people, but of the universe" (1: 106-7). English "*soi-disant* great men who love power" had better recognize that "the hour is very rapidly approaching, when usurped power will be tolerated no longer" (1: 178).

Desmond's intelligent but cynical friend Bethel counters his enthusiasm with the traditional eighteenth-century view that it is not so easy to reform human nature. Bethel has not yet noticed any success produced by the new modes of government in France, his personal experience indicates that politicians are inevitably selfish and insincere, and he has not seen enough steadiness and virtue among the Revolutionary leaders to be confident that their admirable principles will be put into practice (1: 197-98). But this reasoning does not puncture Desmond's Romantic optimism; instead, he convinces Bethel that the Revolution is a "great and noble effort for the universal rights of the human race." However, as he sees hostile reactionary forces arising in all the surrounding nations, Bethel cannot agree with Desmond's optimistic hope "that uncemented by blood, the noble and simply majestic temple of liberty will arise on the site of the barbarous structure of gothic despotism" (2: 52-53).

Writing ***The Banished Man*** after the atrocities of the Revolution had begun, Smith still did not abandon her faith in its ideals (Preface, 1: x). But by the time she wrote her last novel, she had given up hope for a reformed society in Europe, agreeing with Bethel "that liberty having been driven away to the new world, will establish there her glorious empire" (***Desmond*** 2: 55). In ***The Young Philosopher,*** Glenmorris confirms this glowing vision. He had settled in America after arriving there by accident in the middle of the Revolutionary War and admiring the Americans' determination to be free.[10] After returning to England and being overwhelmed by troubles, he cannot wait to bring his family back to America, where nature and cultivation are happily combined, without the corruption, the false values, the mental restrictions, and the exploitation that have marked all previous civilized societies:

> To cultivate the earth of another continent, to carry the arts of civil life, without its misery and its vices, to the wild regions of the globe, had in it a degree of sublimity, which, in Glenmorris's opinion, sunk the petty politics and false views so eagerly pursued in Europe, into something more despicable than childish imbecility.

... When he reflected on the degradation to which those must submit, who would make what is called a figure in this country; that they must sacrifice their independence, their time, their taste, their liberty, to etiquette, to forms and falsehoods, which would to him be insupportable, he rejoiced that he had made his election where human life was in progressive improvement.

(4: 201-2)

In America Glenmorris will not have to "see a frightful contrast between luxury and wretchedness . . . daily witness injustice I cannot repress, and misery I cannot relieve." There he can study "the great book of nature" instead of corrupt European society, "where all greatness of character seems lost" and where it is impossible "to study human nature unadulterated by *inhuman* prejudices" (4: 391-92). It is a grand Romantic vision of human society as it ought to be, and, at the end of the book, Delmont and the Glenmorrises go to America, the only place where free, enlightened characters can be at home.

However, George Delmont, the Young Philosopher, is an idealist who has managed to remain uncorrupted by English society. Educated by an enlightened mother according to the principles of Rousseau's *Emile,* he has been brought up to form his own opinions, "which he never was flogged out of . . . at Eton" (1: 34). Even as a child, he was an individualist who often wandered off by himself, "threw himself down under a tree with some favourite book, then fell into a reverie as he listened to the wind among the branches, or the dashing of the water against the banks, where, among the reeds and willows crowding over the Thames," he avoided both the crude mirth of his schoolfellows and the mechanical pedantry of his lessons (1: 49-51). As he generously relieved needy people, he not only glowed with indignation against those who had oppressed them, but looked beyond the individuals to the systems that made the oppression possible. "From detestation against individuals, such as justices and overseers," this remarkably penetrating young analyst "began to reflect on the laws that put it in their power thus to drive forth to nakedness and famine the wretched beings they were empowered to protect; and he was led to enquire if the complicated misery he every day saw . . . could be the fruits of the very best laws that could be framed in a state of society said to be the most perfect among what are called the civilized nations of the world" (1: 54). In earlier books Smith had occasionally related corrupt lawyers to the corrupt institutions that nourished them; here she has moved to a full-scale radical attack on the legal system itself.[11]

"Early taught to have on every point an opinion of his own," Delmont considered his career options and "determined to yield his freedom to none of those motives which the love of power or of wealth might hold out to him, but to live on his little farm unfettered by the rules he must submit to if he entered into any profession." Aware that this decision will bring ridicule and blame on him, Delmont nevertheless thinks it more valuable to be a farmer than a judge "condemning wretches legally to die on the gallows," or a bishop sitting in Parliament and voting for war, or a general presiding "at these human sacrifices," where men destroy each other without even daring to ask why (1: 92-94). When Orlando reached the same conclusion in **The Old Manor House,** it might be attributed to old-fashioned sentimental retirement from the world; but here it is definitely Romantic defiance of convention.

In contrast to the conventional moralists of his time, who preached that woman's supposedly natural inclination to comply with those around her was an amiable feature of her character, Delmont wishes that his sweet and compliant sister were less pliable, fearing "that her character would not be formed on reason and conviction, but on the sentiments and conduct of those among whom she might be thrown" (1: 95). He deliberately chooses his own company. Having long discovered that associating with his neighbors "was a very great waste of his time, as well as a needless trial of his civility," as soon as he was grown up and his own master, he decided to "recover the portion of his days thus unnecessarily given to persons whom he could not discover were at all the better, while he felt himself a great deal worse." He realized that this decision would make him enemies, but as he had no ambition "to be chairman at a quarter session, or foreman of a grand jury, . . . he quietly submitted to invidious remarks he did not hear." However, though he had freed himself from the constraints of meaningless forms of politeness, he did not impose his exacting standards on his sisters; for he made "it the rule of his life, as well in trivial as on material occasions, never to trench upon the liberty of others, while he guarded against being cheated out of his own" (1: 119-21).

Medora, the heroine of **The Young Philosopher,** is a less satisfactory example of natural reason and rectitude. She is presented as "entirely the child of nature," and she is a more plausible example than such highly socialized children of nature as Frances Burney's Evelina and Camilla. Medora has "not one idea . . . that she blushes to avow," not because she is too "innocent" to have any desires, but because she is free of prudery and unaware of sexual competitiveness. She will later, we are assured, develop a mind and character like that of her enlightened mother, Mrs. Glenmorris (1: 244-45). But Medora fails to display any mental or moral quality that would distinguish her from her contemporary heroines. All Smith's heroines show this discrepancy between aim and achievement. She recognized this problem herself, complaining in **Marchmont** that she had to conform to conventions that dictated that heroines must be very young, and that very young women must not distinguish themselves by independence of mind or freely expressed passion; indeed, *any* strongly marked qualities were considered out of place in a young woman (1: 177-79). Smith was also unable to create a fable that would make real the Romantic attitudes and qualities of her characters, resorting instead to tired Gothic devices: Medora is abducted, and Mrs. Glenmorris goes insane from her anxiety at Medora's disappearance.

Mrs. Glenmorris does, however, voice Smith's eloquent expression of Romantic values. Most people, she says, condemn as "wildly romantic" anyone who "ventures to feel or to express themselves out of the style of common and every day life. But why is it romantic?" She would not like to see Medora let her imagination outrun her reason and make herself "either useless or ridiculous" by bewildering "herself among ideal beings":

> but if affection for merit, if admiration of talents, if the attachments of friendship are romantic; if it be romantic to dare to have an opinion of one's own, and not to follow one formal tract, wrong or right, pleasant or irksome, because our grandmothers and aunts have followed it before; if not to be romantic one must go through the world with prudery, carefully settling our blinkers at every step, as a cautious coachman hoodwinks his horses heads; if a woman, because she is a woman, must resign all pretensions to being a *reasoning* being, and dares neither look to the right nor to the left, oh! may my Medora still be the child of nature and simplicity, still venture to express all she feels, even at the risk of being called a strange romantic girl.
>
> (2: 13-15)

This is a vision of the emotional freedom, intellectual independence, and openness to new ideas that the Romantics insisted was the natural birthright of every human being. We might wish for more bold and full portrayals, but Smith does show young women protesting against mental limitations (Fanny Waverly), celebrating gains in human liberty (Geraldine Verney), and feeling sexual love outside the bonds of strict propriety (most of her heroines). Neither Smith nor anyone else before Charlotte and Emily Brontë created fully realized Romantic female characters.

Mrs. Glenmorris is protesting against the limitations imposed by a narrow conception of reason that equated it with prudence and a common sense acceptance of things as they are. Thus circumscribed, reason directs us to accept the status quo as the only possible reality, to resist any change as risky, and to dismiss hopes for radical improvement as fanciful. Romantic imagination, as its opposite, liberates the mind to conceive of something better than what presently exists, to dare to strive for and possibly achieve radical improvement.[12] Smith's younger contemporary Jane Austen, who had made fun of romantic excesses in her youth, came to see the value of romance, by which she meant much what Mrs. Glenmorris did. Anne Elliot "had been forced into prudence in her youth, she learned romance as she grew older" (*Persuasion* Ch. 4). That is, Anne learned to trust her own feelings and judgment, to venture beyond common sense and prudence, to try for what might be better rather than to settle for what she already knew. Smith's and Austen's claims for the Romantic imagination are comparatively modest, but they point toward the human longing for something better than the life that is reasonable for us to expect—a longing that Emily Brontë was to express with consummate beauty fifty years later: for a world "where life is boundless in its duration, and love in its sympathy, and joy in its fulness" (*Wuthering Heights* Ch. 16).

Yet, of course, Smith was not a fully committed Romantic: she did not find transcendence in Nature, she insisted that passions must be curbed, and she did not believe that imagination led to a more real world than sense. If the Romantic imagination was sublime and spellbinding, it was also self-assured to the point of arrogance. Wordsworth's imagination displaces the evidence of his senses to reveal an invisible world of infinite potentiality that is the proper home of humanity (*The Prelude* 6: 593-609). Blake asserts even more decisively that his imagination creates a world more real than the one around us. Women, socialized to be receptive, compliant, and conventional, could not develop such confidence in their individual judgment. As a woman, Smith could not make the enormous claims of men possessed by the Romantic imagination. She had to work within the social world she knew, with characters bound by mundane circumstance. She questioned conventional thinking and established institutions, but she could not cast them aside altogether.

Smith's form further tied her to the actual life around her, since the novel requires a strong emphasis on things as they are. As Robert Kiely points out, a romantic novel is something of a contradiction in terms, a battleground on which the claims of imagination and the self collide with those of "reason and the public welfare" (25). The battle rages in Smith's novels, where she claims to aim at probability more than at "the wonderful and extraordinary" (Preface to ***The Banished Man*** 1: x), but has one heroine imprisoned in a tower and two others abducted. She constantly calls up romance in her novels in order to deflate or discredit it, as when ridiculous Clarinthia purposely falls in love so as to be sure of "opposition from her family, and . . . such imaginary miseries as might establish her in her own opinion the 'heroine of a tale of sympathy'" (***Ethelinde*** 5: 85). But for five volumes Smith puts Ethelinde herself, the exemplary heroine, through very similar "imaginary miseries."

Often, however, Smith effectively juxtaposed romance and realism in order to bring out the contrast between idealistic aspirations and the limitations of actual life. In ***The Old Manor House,*** Romantic elements emphasize the disparity between the unworldly, unselfish hero and heroine and the sordid world they must live in. Romantically named Orlando (who, however, was named after his ancestor to curry favor with the ancient cousin who controls the family property) wants to marry Monimia because she is lovely and he loves her, regardless of her social inferiority and their lack of money. Their love is all-important to them, but the financial constrictions that prevent their marriage are worked out in grinding detail. Monimia is a princess locked away in a tower of the old manor house, and her knight Orlando climbs up to her by a concealed staircase; but both exist in the prosaic context of mean-minded, absurdly self-important Mrs. Rayland and the servants who flatter and outsmart her. "Sanguine and romantic" Orlando loves to contemplate "visionary prospects" (138); but for most of the book he is constrained by petty authorities and irksome circumstances.

As a woman novelist focusing on women, Smith was further limited by the conventions of feminine propriety. Romantic abandon was out of the question for heroines if they were not to forfeit readers' sympathy. Moreover, letting her heroines abandon themselves to passion would mean giving up the claim to rationality that feminists had worked so hard to establish throughout the eighteenth century. Nor would it have been realistic to show women liberated as men could be. The Young Philosopher has been educated to think for himself and acts according to his own views of morality. His sisters neither feel his need for independence, since they have never been encouraged to develop their own ideas, nor would be able to defy convention if they did feel it. They have to listen to their unpleasant great-aunt and sit with boring company, while George blithely goes off to his friends. He claims the right to escape social intercourse that would be disagreeable to himself and not useful to anyone else (1: 257); they have no such option.

Like Radcliffe, who was also concerned with female dignity, Smith never abandoned rational standards of conduct. Byronic heroes who reject all convention and social obligation to pursue their grand, resistless passions may be attractive or, in Smith, sympathetic; but they must be reprehended. Delamere, the original hero of *Emmeline,* makes no attempt to restrain his passions and repeatedly distresses the heroine by heedlessly pursuing her; he forces Emmeline to lock herself in her room to escape his temper tantrums and grandly dismisses her fears of scandalmongers, refusing to see that a young woman's reputation was more vulnerable than a male aristocrat's. Emmeline, in contrast, invariably maintains rational control and judiciously weighs possibilities. Even when she feels most warmly toward him, she is not subject to "that violent love, which carrying every thing before it, leaves the mind no longer at liberty to see any fault in the beloved object, or any impropriety in whatever can secure it's [sic] success, and which, scorning future consequences, risks every thing for it's present indulgence" (149). In the end, he gets himself killed in an unnecessary duel, and she is provided with a suitably self-disciplined young man. Clinging Montague Thorold and overbearing Vavasour, the unwanted suitors who harass Celestina, are closer to the conventional romantic lover than Willoughby, the hero, who seriously considers a prudential marriage for the sake of his family. Smith's ideal heroes show their love by thoughtfulness and consideration, not, like Thorold, by flamboyant offers to die for their beloved. Even Desmond demonstrates infinite consideration more than fiery passion. He is the most Romantic of Smith's major characters, yet, far from pursuing his emotional needs at all costs, he constantly restricts his actions so as to avoid embarrassing or distressing Geraldine.

None of Smith's approved characters recklessly follow their impulses. Orlando is deeply in love with Monimia and dreads a long separation from her, but when Warwick, about to elope with Isabella, tempts Orlando to elope with Monimia at the same time, he resists out of consideration for his parents (*Old Manor House* 333-35). After he has married her, he learns that poverty is miserable even if one shares it with a dearly loved wife: "the romantic theory, of sacrificing every consideration to love, produced, in the practice, only the painful consciousness of having injured its object" (517).

Smith's moral ideal is the person who quietly fulfills his or her obligations. Her admirable characters are mindful of the claims of reason and family responsibilities, although most of them commit themselves to an unalterable romantic attachment. Even George Delmont, the Young Philosopher, embarrasses himself to pay his brother's gambling debts. This insistence on consideration for and responsibility to one's family came from Smith's life circumstances more than convention. As a mature woman with an inadequate husband and a family of children to bring up, she was painfully aware that stable family life was more important than romantic raptures. Perpetually weighed down by family cares, she could not escape to or even maintain faith in an ideal world. In an amusing sequence in *The Banished Man,* her alter ego, Mrs. Denzil, complains that she must devise a tender dialogue between two idealized lovers while worrying about bills and struggling to meet her publisher's deadline in order to pay them, meanwhile fretting about the destruction of her garden by the neighbor's pigs (2: 225-28). In such a setting, a woman could not see herself as a prophet in the manner of Blake and Wordsworth. As a hard-working professional whose works had to meet the bills, she was tied to this world. Romanticism enhanced Charlotte Smith's response to natural beauty, strengthened her feminism, enlarged her interests; but it could not provide her, or most women, with a consistent world view.

Notes

1. There is one embarrassing exception when, in *The Old Manor House,* Smith made injudicious use of a secondary source and placed the St. Lawrence River in a subtropical landscape. It is also true that she sometimes wrote minutely, even pedantically, detailed descriptions more suggestive of James Thomson than of Wordsworth.

2. Other sensitive characters who suffer in an unsympathetic society are transparent alter egos of Smith herself: a succession of irreproachable middle-aged matrons afflicted by irresponsible husbands and dishonest lawyers (Mrs. Stafford in *Emmeline,* Mrs. Elphinstone in *Celestina,* Mrs. Denzil in *The Banished Man,* Leonora in *The Letters of a Solitary Wanderer*).

3. Smith constantly presents herself as excluded from privileged circles, dropped by her prosperous, conventional friends. As Stuart Curran points out, alienation is the prevailing theme of her *Elegiac Sonnets* and *The Emigrants* ("The 'I' Altered" 200-201).

4. Emmeline, Smith's first heroine, is more concerned about propriety than any of her later ones: there is

more emphasis on her self-command, and she delays tiresomely in confessing her love for Godolphin. She is pointedly differentiated from "a romantic girl" by her ability to distinguish between true love and the mixture of liking, gratitude, and pity that she feels for Delamere (*Emmeline* 73). Goethe's *The Sorrows of Werther* is mentioned with disapproval in *Emmeline*, with sympathy in *Celestina* and *Desmond*.

5. Smith herself, remembering that she is writing a realistic novel, concedes that Desmond's feeling is not *quite* so pure as he intends; he would like physical fulfillment.

6. Celestina, the heroine of Smith's preceding novel, anticipates Desmond's unalterable constancy in her refusal to consider loving any man other than Willoughby, even though she believes they can never marry and she has another devoted and eminently acceptable suitor. In contrast to the lesson inculcated by Richardson, Celestina "found it impossible . . . to transfer to another the same attachment" she had formed for Willoughby (*Celestina* 4: 158). Her attitude would be considered (foolishly) romantic by some, but not by anyone who understood her motives (4: 300).

7. In pointed contrast, another woman in the book, Lady Frances Crofts, who commits adultery without the excuse of love, is punished by being immured for life in a convent.

8. Cf. the hero's widowed grandmother in *Ethelinde*, a common law wife who is presented with utmost sympathy. The only person who receives Orlando kindly when he returns, destitute, to his former home is a kept mistress, who is sensible and generous (*Old Manor House*). Smith also presented a series of virtuous men married to unworthy wives who are in love with the admirable heroine (Sir Edward Newenden and Ethelinde, Walsingham and Rosalie in *Montalbert*, and Eversley and Althea in *Marchmont*).

9. This is no hyperbolic metaphor. Geraldine speaks of herself as the "property" of Verney, and soon afterwards Desmond attacks the institution of Negro slavery (3: 148, 161*-64*); husbands and slaveowners shared many of the same powers over their subjects. See Diana Bowstead's analysis ("Charlotte Smith's *Desmond*") of the connection between political and sexual oppression in *Desmond*.

10. In *The Old Manor House*, Smith had argued effectively for the American Revolutionaries. Stupid Mrs. Rayland and corrupt General Tracy scorn and condemn the "rebels." Orlando, though fighting in the British army, comes to realize that the Americans are fighting for their just rights.

11. Marchmont is imprisoned for debt, and the system that imprisons him is an indictment of "a country boasting of its enlarged humanity and perfect freedom" (*Marchmont* 2: 22). He protests that it does little good to punish individual villainous attorneys, when "no radical cure can be administered" to legal abuses, lest it endanger "the sanctity of the laws" (4: 39-40). Appalling Lawyer Vampyre is the more appalling because he is a "*legal* monster" (4: 180, Smith's italics).

12. For a discussion of (Romantic) imagination in some of Smith's contemporaries, see Katharine M. Rogers, *Frances Burney: The World of "Female Difficulties."*

Works Cited

PRIMARY WORKS

Abrams, M. H. et al., eds. *The Norton Anthology of English Literature.* 5th ed. New York: Norton, 1986.

Smith, Charlotte. *The Banished Man.* London: T. Cadell and W. Davies, 1794. 4 vols.

———. *Celestina.* 1791. Ann Arbor: University Microfilms, 1972.

———. *Conversations Introducing Poetry: Chiefly on Subjects of Natural History.* 2 vols. London: Sampson Low, 1799.

———. *Desmond.* 1792. New York: Garland Press, 1974. 3 vols.

———. *Emmeline: The Orphan of the Castle.* 1788. London: Oxford University Press, 1971.

———. *Ethelinde, or The Recluse of the Lake.* London: T. Cadell, 1789. 5 vols.

———. *The Letters of a Solitary Wanderer.* London: Sampson Low, 1800-02. 5 vols.

———. *Marchmont.* 4 vols. 1796. Delmar, NY: Scholars' Facsimiles and Reprints, 1989.

———. *Montalbert.* 1795. Delmar, NY: Scholars' Facsimiles and Reprints, 1989. 3 vols.

———. *The Old Manor House.* 1793. London: Oxford University Press, 1969.

———. *The Young Philosopher.* 1798. New York: Garland Press, 1974. 4 vols.

SECONDARY WORKS

Curran, Stuart. "Romantic Poetry: The 'I' Altered." In Mellor, ed., *Romanticism and Feminism.* 185-207.

Rogers, Katharine M. *Frances Burney: The World of "Female Difficulties."* Hemel Hempstead: Harvester Wheatsheaf, 1990.

Deborah Kennedy (essay date 1995)

SOURCE: Kennedy, Deborah. "Thorns and Roses: The *Sonnets* of Charlotte Smith." *Women's Writing: The Elizabethan to Victorian Period* 2, no. 1 (1995): 43-53.

[*In the following essay, Kennedy discusses the autobiographical content of Smith's* Elegiac Sonnets.]

In her book on sensibility, Janet Todd traces the development of the figure of the melancholy poet, which had become a common literary type by the mid-eighteenth century.[1] The models were men of feeling like Thomas Gray and Edward Young; there were no popular female equivalents until Charlotte Smith published her aptly named *Elegiac Sonnets* in 1784.[2] Although other women had written melancholic poems, no one had produced an entire collection in this vein. Lady Mary Wroth's sombre sonnets of 1621 (neglected until recently) might provide a parallel, except that Wroth's, unlike Smith's, focus on unrequited love.[3] As well, in the early eighteenth century, Anne Finch wrote a number of melancholic poems, which form one part of a diverse collection that included many satires. In her brilliant pindaric ode "The Spleen", Finch presents spleen—a catch-all word for depression and nervous illness—as a serious and debilitating medical condition—one for which she herself was treated.[4] Smith, however, resists a medical model, directing attention to external rather than internal factors, implying that it is things in the world that cause a woman to feel melancholic. Written in a dignified and serious tone, Smith's sonnet series establishes woman's right to position herself as a subject, foregoing silence in order to articulate her discontent.

The *Elegiac Sonnets* first appeared in a small volume in 1784, and Smith added to the many subsequent editions, until by 1800 the book had become a two-volume collection of 92 sonnets, plus miscellaneous poems. The popularity of her sonnets in the 1780s marked the beginning of Smith's successful career as a poet and novelist. Her sonnets renewed interest in the genre, which then would remain popular throughout the Romantic period. Since my purpose here is to analyse the coherent voice of the autobiographical persona in her sonnet series, my study will necessarily exclude those pieces in Smith's collection which are based on Petrarch's sonnets and on Goethe's *Werther*, as well as sonnets attributed to male and female characters in her own novels, where they were originally published.

The title *Elegiac Sonnets* signals the mood of these poems rather than their occasion, for Smith was not mourning either a deceased person or an absent lover; instead, she mourned her own self and the loss that she felt in living a life she regarded as a "rugged path" she was "doom'd to tread" (**"Sonnet 1"**:2). It is worthwhile to note that in a 1991 study called *Silencing the Self: Women and Depression*, Dana Crowley Jack found that "as women describe the pervasive impact of depression, they most frequently call on the metaphor "loss of self" to describe their inner experience."[5] Twenty years earlier, Phyllis Chesler argued in *Women and Madness* that "women are in a continual state of mourning—for what they never had—or had too briefly, and for what they can't have in the present".[6] Although in the sonnets Smith does not indicate what it was that made her own life so difficult—the reader simply must accept the speaker's assertion of discontent—her personal circumstances became well known to her reviewers and thus to her readers.

Smith had been a gifted child who grew up in affluence, but her life was circumscribed after an early and bad marriage to an irresponsible and promiscuous man who wasted both of their fortunes. In fact, Smith began preparing the sonnets for publication while accompanying her husband to debtors' prison in 1783. Fortunately, the *Elegiac Sonnets* were enormously popular, and Smith's writing became the main means of support for her family. She separated from her husband and fought a long legal battle to secure for her children their inheritance from their paternal grandfather.[7] In her novels, and more explicitly in the prefaces to them, she directly criticised the inefficiency and injustice of the patriarchal legal and financial systems. But in her poems, she alludes the causes, and simply expresses her despair.

The protagonist in Smith's autobiographically-based sonnets defines herself as a melancholy woman, with "pensive" thoughts and a penchant for gloomy or nocturnal scenes. However, far from being generic, the settings are actual places like "The River Arun" and "the South Downs", sites of her happy childhood in Sussex, from which she hoped to gain some sort of healing influence. For example, in **"Sonnet 68"**, **"Written at Exmouth, midsummer 1795"**, the speaker pleads for a balm from nature: "Fall, dews of Heaven, upon my burning breast, / Bathe with cool drops these ever-streaming eyes" (1-2). Smith is atypical in actually seeking *relief* from her misery. As the title of Thomas Warton's "The Pleasures of Melancholy" (1747) suggests, there was a long literary tradition of prizing melancholy as a contemplative mood and therefore distinguishing it from a serious depression or madness. The well-known "Bluestocking" Elizabeth Carter wrote a poem on this subject, "Ode to Melancholy", and regarded it, in Amy Reed's words, as a "harmless pleasure"[8]—as we see in these lines, "Thou sweetly sad ideal guest, / In all thy soothing charms confest, / Indulge my pensive mind"[9]—which is something quite different from Samuel Johnson's experience of "melancholy" as a debilitating mental illness.[10] **"Sonnet 32"**, whose very title, **"To Melancholy"**, would have raised certain expectations in readers, is a rare instance in which Smith conforms to the "pleasures of melancholy" school, echoing Carter's sentiments and language in these lines: "O Melancholy!—such thy magic power, / That to the soul these dreams are often sweet, / And soothe the pensive visionary mind!" (12-14). Primarily, however, in Smith's poems, as in Finch's, melancholy is an affliction which is devoid of pleasure. Yet, by taking advantage of the literary taste for melancholy, both Smith and Finch created texts that used, but departed from, convention and drew attention to the state of women's mental health and happiness, while simultaneously validating woman's right to self-reflection.

While the *Elegiac Sonnets* do not glorify melancholy, neither do they present the speaker as an enfeebled victim: there is none of the fainting or shivering that one often finds in female characterisations in the eighteenth and nineteenth century, subjects studied by Roy Porter and Elaine Showalter, respectively.[11] The Victorians, according to Showalter, may have blamed biology rather than an oppressive social system for women's deviant behaviour or apparent mental instability, but the condition of Smith's speaker is not medicalised and she is not depicted as weak or unstable, but as dissatisfied. In fact, a reader might be impressed with the speaker's strength, reflected in the liberating image of a woman wandering in nature, thinking about her life, even though those thoughts centre on her unhappiness. The wandering is perhaps almost as important as the reflecting, since the spatial freedom of movement is symbolic of and correspondent to the non-spatial freedom of thought. Smith gets woman out of doors, just as Mary Wollstonecraft (though without the same calm and controlled persona as Smith) would advise in *Vindication of the Rights of Woman*—where she repeatedly encouraged women "to acquire strength, both of mind and body"[12]—and just as she would demonstrate in *Letters from Sweden, Norway and Denmark*, all exemplifying Ellen Moers's argument that "a whole history of literary feminism might be told in terms of the metaphor of walking".[13]

Inevitably, though, the image of wandering is constrained by the speaker's awareness of her usual confinement, and in **"Sonnet 3"**, **"To a Nightingale"**, Smith provides a particularly poignant image of her own desire for freedom: "Ah, songstress sad! that such my lot might be / To sigh and sing at liberty like thee" (13-14). Although it was the male bird which was known for its song, Smith followed literary convention in making her nightingale female after the mythological Philomela. Using alliterative phrasing in her memorable rendering of the "songstress sad" who will "sigh and sing", Smith creates an image of herself. In Anne Finch's poem, "To the Nightingale", she looks to the (female) bird as a model for poetic inspiration, but she is more concerned with emulating its fluency than its freedom. The line "Free as thine shall be my song, / As thy music, short or long" (5-6), exemplifies the desire of Finch's speaker for the bird's virtuosity[14], whereas Smith's seeks a spatial freedom: "to sigh and sing at liberty, like thee". In his conversation poem entitled "The Nightingale", Coleridge contests the literary convention of the "melancholy" nightingale, insisting that those who actually take the time to go outside and hear the real bird will think of it as "the merry Nightingale" (42)[15], but Smith identifies with it as a figure of female suffering and yearns above all for its liberty.

In **"Sonnet 4"**, entitled **"To the Moon"**, the speaker walks alone at night, seeking comfort by gazing at the moon:

> *Alone and pensive, I delight to stray,*
> *And watch thy shadow trembling in the stream,*
> *Or mark the floating clouds that cross thy way,*
> *And while I gaze, thy mild and placid light*
> *Sheds a soft calm upon my troubled breast.*
>
> (2-6)

As mentioned before, the scene itself is not a unique one. For instance, in Milton's "Il Penseroso", the speaker enjoys similar moonlight walks: "I walk unseen / On the dry smooth-shaven green, / To behold the wandering moon" (65-67), but Milton's pensive man differs from Smith's persona in that he does not ask for relief from his melancholy thoughts, but rather finds spiritual elation through his meditative solitude, seeking to be dissolved "into ecstasies" (165)[16]—a here and now fulfilment unavailable to Smith. Similarly, in the poem "Mirth and Melancholy" by Margaret Cavendish, the character of Melancholy is content with her solitary life, dwelling "in quiet and still peace".[17] These two seventeenth-century poems, Milton's of course the most influential, present the conventional view that melancholy is a state valuable in itself—a sombre and reflective mood.

Later novels of sensibility often perpetuate this convention. For instance, in Ann Radcliffe's *Romance of the Forest* (1791), Adeline, the literate, sensitive, and virtuous heroine, experiences melancholy as a delicate emotion, softened by her response to nature's beauty and her religious faith. Like Smiths's protagonist, Adeline, too, enjoys solitary walks in the forest, where she composes poetry as a proper outlet for her melancholy: "At the decline of day, she quitted her chamber to enjoy the sweet evening hour . . . she closed [her] book, and yielded to the sweet complacent melancholy which the hour inspired".[18] Adeline's poem "Night" includes an enraptured tribute to melancholy:

> *Then let me stand amidst thy glooms profound*
>   *On some wild woody steep, and hear the breeze*
> *That swells in mournful melody around,*
>   *And faintly dies upon the distant trees.*
> *What melancholy charms steal o'er the mind!*
> *What hallow'd tears the rising rapture greet*[19]

While she may have been capitalising on the figure of the melancholic female popularised in Smith's sonnets in the 1780s, or even influenced by Smith's novel **Emmeline** (1788), Radcliffe reasserts the "pleasures of melancholy", which run counter to Smith's articulation of despair.[20] In *The Romance of the Forest*, the problems of the victimised heroine are always cushioned by a demure narrative whose "sweet complacent melancholy" has little in common with Smith's strongly voiced complaint about "murder'd Happiness" (**"Sonnet 47"**:8).

Many of Smith's poems might well be called elegiac because the protagonist looks to death as an end to a hopelessly sorrowful life. For example, at the end of the sonnet to the moon, the speaker imagines escaping her troubles by actually going to the moon, a place where "the wretched may have rest" in its "world serene" (8, 13), a world which is emphatically female, as Peggy Dunn has pointed out.[21] Smith takes this one step further in **"Sonnet 90"**, entitled **"To Oblivion"**, by feminising oblivion as the "Sister of Chaos and eternal night" (5). In **"Sonnet 44"**, the speaker describes an almost apocalyptic scene in which a raging sea causes such damage that graves are opened and the beach becomes a clutter of shell, bones and seaweed. Smith explains in a note that this is a real place, the village of Middleton near Sussex: "The wall, which once surrounded the church-yard, is entirely swept away, many of the graves broken up, and the remains of bodies interred washed into the sea; whence human bones are found among the sand and shingles on the shore"[22]:

> The wild blast, rising from the western cave,
> Drives the huge billows from their heaving bed,
> Tears from their grassy tombs the village dead,
> And breaks the silent sabbath of the grave!
>
> (7-8)

The scene is presented from the point of view of someone actually observing the destruction. The speaker, enthralled by the seaquake, only laments that she is an observer, gazing "with envy on their gloomy rest" (14), as if she would prefer to be part of the "warring elements" (12), rather like Wordsworth's Lucy—a being "rolled round in earth's diurnal course / With rocks, and stones, and trees".[23] She describes the bones being whitened by the waves, in desacralising imagery that blends the human and the natural elements. Fascinated by what seems like a ritual purifying, the speaker welcomes the storm that forces the sea to swell across the land. On the one hand, **"Sonnet 44"** is a morbid poem, but, on the other hand, it has a liberating quality because the speaker's envy upon gazing at the frenzied elements seems like a projection of her own desire for some type of release of energy—perhaps creative or sexual. In "The Laugh of the Medusa", Hélène Cixous suggests a correspondence between the body of woman, her writing and nature, and at one point she writes, "we are ourselves sea, sand, coral, seaweed, beaches, tides, swimmers, children, waves . . . More or less wavily sea, earth, sky—what matter would rebuff us? We know how to speak them all".[24] Charlotte Smith expresses a somewhat similar sentiment, paradoxically contained in the rigid form of the sonnet, as she, too, seeks an identification with the apparently free forces of nature.

In these poems, death means the end of pain, and although her anticipation of death may imply the possibility of a Christian afterlife, Smith usually stops short of making explicit references to that possibility (see **"Sonnet 48"** as an exception). Instead, it is the death-wish itself, shorn of religious consolation, that recurs throughout the sonnet series. In **"Sonnet 12"**, the speaker sits alone on a cliff and imagines herself as a shipwrecked mariner whose only relief could come from drowning. Using another analogy in **"Sonnet 36"**, Smith compares herself to a wanderer in a forest, who finds an occasional "rose" along a path of "thorns and roughness" (3). But her life has become so unbearable that she looks forward only to death, the "tranquil shore, / Where the pale spectre Care pursues no more" (13-14). Though Smith never attempted suicide, as far as we know, but, rather, seemed to exhibit a great deal of strength in her personal and professional life and perhaps maintained her mental health by articulating her disconent in her poetry and prose, her world-weariness has a suicidal edge to it, and like a suicide threat it carries a tone of defiance. Mary Robinson, in her despairing "Stanzas" (1797), strikes a similar pose, but situates her speaker in an urban setting, rank with corruption and class conflict:

> In this vain, busy world, where the good and the gay
> By affliction or folly wing moments away;
> Where the false are respected, the virtuous betrayed,
> Where Vice lives in sunshine, and Genius in shade;
> With a soul-sickened sadness all changes I see,
> For the world, the base world, has no pleasure for me!
>
> . . . . .
>
> And, oh! with what joy to the grave I would flee—
> Since the world, the base world has no pleasures for me.
>
> (1-6; 53-54)[25]

Robinson explicitly attacks social and political injustices, turning her poem outward to rail against the world, rather than, like Smith, concentrating on the inner world of her pain without mentioning the causes of her suffering.

The *Elegiac Sonnets* are also elegies for the happier days of childhood, as Smith emphasises the gulf between past and present. In the fifth sonnet, **"To the South Downs"**, which is explicitly autobiographical, she imagines visiting the hills where she played as a child and asks:

> Ah! hills beloved!—your turf, your flow'rs remain;
> But can they peace to this sad breast restore,
> For one poor moment soothe the sense of pain,
> And teach a breaking heart to throb no more?
>
> (5-8)

Memory may provide momentary relief, but her own disappointments make her pessimistic about other children, who might seem as happy as she had once been. Even watching children play, she can think only of the troubles that await them: in **"Sonnet 27"** she painfully contemplates "the thorns that lurking lay / To wound the wretched pilgrim" (7-8), recalling the theme of Thomas Gray's bleak "Ode on a Distant Prospect of Eton College".[26] Smith's sonnet ends, however, with a maternal response: she weeps for the children, saying, "for their future fate how many fears / Oppress my heart—and fill mine eyes with tears!"; on the other hand, Thomas Gray, a bachelor, is soothed by the sight of the children playing, even though he is conscious that they live in ignorant bliss. Smith conveys neither the resignation that Gray feels, nor the pleasure that Wordsworth later conjures from childhood recollections. In fact, to return to **"Sonnet 5"**, after she recalls the happy memories of her beloved hills in Sussex, she wants to forget all of the troubles that plagued her adult life, but she realises that, "Ah! no! when all, e'en Hope's last ray is gone, / There's no oblivion—but in death alone!" (13-14). As mentioned earlier, the absence of religious consolation contributes to the sense of despair and to the existential ethos of the poems. Smith does not pretend to find succour, and hers seems a bleak vision, yet the very publication of the sonnets can be viewed as a victory for feminism in its early stages.

Stuart Curran argues that Smith's work attracted writers like Wordsworth and Coleridge because of the "dynamic of an isolated sensibility".[27] They respected her ability to promote the value of the individual consciousness in an alienating world. An important difference, however, is that Wordsworth could engage freely in an imaginative quest by assuming the role of the poet-prophet or the male visionary, whereas Smith had always to face the real constraints of a life defined by the social expectations of domesticity and propriety imposed on a woman. Smith did not become the acknowledged mother of a tradition, a fact belatedly registered by Wordsworth, fittingly in a footnote to one of his minor poems, where he wrote that she was "a lady to whom English verse is under greater obligations than are likely to be either acknowledged or remembered".[28] After her death, William Lisle Bowles, whose *Fourteen Sonnets* of 1789 were derivative of her own, had the good fortune to be the surviving sonneteer from this period and became credited with the revival of the form. Other female poets such as Helen Maria Williams, Mary Robinson and Anna Seward, though celebrated to varying degrees in their turn for their works of verse and prose, were also quickly forgotten, and it was not until Felicia Hemans that a female poet's fame outlived her. In general, women writing poetry in this period, no matter how talented, had little prospect of a posthumous reputation because of the inferior status accorded women's writing.

If Smith did not win for her "mournful pages" (45) an audience in "distant ages" (48), as she had hoped in her poem **"To My Lyre"**, she did earn a favourable reputation in her own lifetime; but it involved her in something of a double bind, since the public image that grew out of the autobiographical sonnets overshadowed the poems themselves. Although the sonnets make no explicit references to her family's financial and legal difficulties, the prefaces to the sonnets and to her novels do, so Charlotte Smith the poet became Charlotte Smith the suffering woman, the melancholy star of her own poetry. Critics hardly ever reviewed her poems without commenting directly on her personal life. They chivalrously leapt to the defence of the respectable gentlewoman-in-distress, neglecting Smith's technical and imaginative achievements as a poet. She was a fine writer, her critics said; but they spent most of their time offering their condolences to her as a woman struggling to support many children and to maintain her upper-middle-class status. Reviewers preferred dealing with the wronged gentlewoman rather than the existential poet:

> *We are sorry to see the eye which can shine with so much poetic fire, sullied with a tear; and we hope the soothings of the Muse may wipe it from her cheek.*[29]
>
> *The present volume is said to have been composed under the heavy pressure of difficulties, and amid heart-rending sorrows. It pains us to hear so frequently of this lady's misfortunes . . .*[30]

One reviewer hopes her tears will be wiped away—somehow; the other admits to being almost wearied by hearing of her misfortunes. Although reviewers tended to subordinate their interest in the poems to their interest in her life, this at least meant that she became known as a woman who had been wronged by society, and thus her public reputation drew attention to the inequitable nature of the legal system and the effect it had on a woman who was powerless to control the assets that she was better qualified than her husband to control. In a way, Charlotte Smith called for a Mary Wollstonecraft to vindicate the rights of woman more directly; and, conversely, Wollstonecraft probably found some of her own melancholy reflected in the sonnets: she knew Smith's poems well and quoted from them in both her *Female Reader* and her first novel, *Mary, A Fiction*.

The characteristics of Smith's poetic persona, which have been outlined here, are symbolised by the central image in this sonnet series, namely, the archetypal image of the rose and its thorns, which appears first in the opening sonnet. For Smith, it is the thorns that prevail relentlessly through her life. While acknowledging that, like the typical melancholic writer, her poetic sensitivity means she will suffer more, Smith weighs the pros and cons of her vocation. On the one hand, the gift of poetry has been a positive element in an otherwise difficult life—the Muse has "smiled" on her "rugged path" (1-2), and she describes with a flourish how the Muse "still with sportive hand has snatched wild flowers, / To weave fantastic garlands for my head" (3-4). But then she reveals another side to wearing this poet's crown, for while she wears the roses on her head, thorns fester in her heart. Here Smith does violence to the image of the garland, chopping the stems and thorns off the roses. She evokes the symbolism of the thorn in the heart[31], but it requires her to act aggressively against the coherent image of the rose garland. This symbolic destructiveness in the centre of the sonnet ("Which while it decks the head with many a rose, / Reserves the thorn to fester in the heart" (1:7-8) resonates through the entire poem, unsettling the reader who expects either resignation or consolation.

Smith makes the point again in **"Sonnet 77"**, where she first dazzles readers with the picture of a poet's garland made of "rainbow-light" (13), and then concludes with the deflating remark that "soon at Sorrow's touch the radiant dreams dissolve" (14). The poetic highs of "fantastic garlands" and "rainbow-light" brutally collide with and make her more sensitive to life's difficulties, and resenting this, she quotes and mocks Pope's line, "those paint sorrow best who feel it most".[32] Her opening poem, in which she presents herself as a garlanded poet, is primarily a lamentation, not a celebration. Nevertheless, it seems that when Smith states "But far, far happier is the lot of those / Who never learned her dear delusive art" (5-6), she is rejecting the state of melancholy itself rather than the art of poetry, and insisting that her readers should not glorify a stance of melancholy because that would be to envy the misfortunes that led her to write poems of despair.

Smith's attitude to her poet's garland is ambivalent in the first sonnet, but she elsewhere acknowledges that her ability to write poetry at least gave her an outlet for the pain she felt. In the preface to the first and second editions of the ***Elegiac Sonnets*** she explained that, "some very melancholy moments have been beguiled by expressing in verse the sensations those moments brought".³³ Acknowledging that writing the sonnets beguiled "some very melancholy moments", Smith attributes a therapeutic value to writing poetry, a point she remembers in her last poem, **"To My Lyre"**, where she states that her lyre soothed "each adverse hour" (35) and

> *In cheerless solitude, bereft*
> *Of youth and health, thou still art left,*
>   *When hope and fortune have deceived me;*
> *Thou, far unlike the summer friend,*
> *Did still my falt'ring steps attend,*
>   *And with thy plaintive voice relieved me.*
>
>   (37-42)

Smith's lyre soothed her because through the "plaintive voice" of her poetry she was able to confront and express her discontent, which brings us once again to the central image. In the sixth sonnet, **"To Hope"**, the image of the rose reappears, and this time the speaker states twice that she is left with the thorns, not the blossoms. In the first half of the sonnet she writes, "wilt thou renew the wither'd rose, / And clear my painful path of pointed thorn?" (3-4); and she later laments "Lo!—the flowers fade, but all the thorns remain" (11). By using the image of the rose as a symbol of her suffering, Smith implies that the truth about her experience, if not woman's experience in general, can be found in the thorns—harshness, and pain—not in the flowers associated with femininity.

Further, the "thorn" festering "in the heart", as Smith describes it in **"Sonnet 1"**, represents the passive suffering or typical inner-directed female response to pain, which is in contrast to the typical outer-directed male response to pain through acts of verbal or physical aggression. As Phyllis Chesler explains in *Women and Madness,* "unlike most men, [women] do not express their hostility physically—either directly, to the "significant others" in their lives, or indirectly, through physical and athletic prowess. It is safer for women to become "depressed" than physically violent".³⁴ Smith's "thorn" festering "in the heart" can be viewed as an emblem for the depressed state of mind that results from women's passive suffering, and it is through this imagery that Smith alludes to the psychic and physical damage that is done to women in a world that delimits their freedom in every area of their lives. She illustrates this in **"Sonnet 9"**, with an image of penetration that is even more explicitly violent than the image of the thorn. At the end of the sonnet, the poet's breast is stabbed again and again: "Thro' whom each shaft with cruel force is felt, / Empoisoned by deceit—or barb'd with scorn" (13-14). The shaft, the force, the poison, the deceit, the barbs and the scorn—these words represent violent penetration, forceful intrusion on a private world.³⁵

Inevitably, then, the thorns are a phallic image representing the patriarchal oppression that is the real cause of the speaker's misery. Smith did not name her oppressors, but she condemned them, by choosing not to be submissive and silent. The depressive and sometimes violent imagery that gives her work its funereal cast depicts the effects of this oppression on woman's body, mind and very life. It is ironic that while the sonnets show oppressed and depressed womanhood, their publication constituted an act of self-assertion and empowerment for Smith. In *The Elegiac Sonnets,* Charlotte Smith publicly and famously deplored her lot, articulating with dignity her rejection of a world that she discovered was a path of thorns.

Notes

1. Janet Todd (1986) *Sensibility: An Introduction* (London: Methuen).

2. Quotations from Charlotte Smith's poetry are taken from Charlotte Smith (1993) *The Poems of Charlotte Smith,* ed. Stuart Curran (Oxford: Oxford University Press). Line numbers will be given in parentheses.

3. Lady Mary Wroth (1992) *The Poems of Lady Mary Wroth,* ed. Josephine A. Roberts (Baton Rouge: Louisiana State University Press).

4. Finch complains of her sickness in these lines: "O'er me, alas! thou dost too much prevail: / I feel thy force whilst I against thee rail: / I feel my verse decay, and my cramped numbers fail" (73-75), quoted from "The Spleen", in Anne Finch, Countess of Winchilsea (1987) *Selected Poems,* ed. Denys Thompson (Manchester: Carcanet), pp. 40-44. See also Katharine M. Rogers (1989) "Finch's "Candid Account" vs. Eighteenth-Century Theories of the Spleen", *Mosaic,* 22, pp. 17-27.

5. Dana Crowley Jack (1991) *Silencing the Self: Women and Depression* (Cambridge: Harvard University Press), p. 29.

6. Phyllis Chesler (1972) *Women and Madness* (New York: Doubleday), p. 44.

7. See Florence M. Hilbish (1941) *Charlotte Smith, Poet and Novelist* (Philadelphia: University of Pennsylvania).

8. Amy Reed (1962) *The Background of Gray's Elegy: A Study in the Taste for Melancholy Poetry 1700-1750* (New York: Russell & Russell), p. 222.

9. See Elizabeth Carter (1990) "Ode to Melancholy", reprinted in *British Women Poets 1660-1800: An Anthology,* ed. Joyce Fullard (Troy, New York: Whitson), pp. 412-414; lines 4-6.

10. See Roy Porter (1985) ""The Hunger of the Imagination": Approaching Samuel Johnson's Melancholy", in *The Anatomy of Madness* Vol. 1, eds W. F. Bynum, Roy Porter & Michael Shepherd (London: Tavistock), pp. 63-85.

11. See Roy Porter (1987) *Mind-Forg'd Manacles: A History of Madness in England from the Restoration to the Regency* (Cambridge: Harvard University Press), pp. 104-109; and Elaine Showalter (1981)

"Victorian Women and Insanity", in *Madhouses, Mad-doctors, and Madmen: The Social History of Psychiatry in the Victorian Era,* ed. Andrew Scull (London: Athlone), pp. 313-336.

12. Mary Wollstonecraft (1988) *A Vindication of the Rights of Woman,* ed. Carol H. Poston (New York: Norton), p. 9.

13. Ellen Moers (1985) *Literary Women* (New York: Oxford University Press), p. 130.

14. Anne Finch (1987) "To the Nightingale", *Selected Poems,* pp. 67-68.

15. Samuel Taylor Coleridge (1974) "The Nightingale", in *Poems,* ed. John Beer (London: J. M. Dent), pp. 160-162.

16. John Milton (1957) *Complete Poems and Major Prose,* ed. Merritt Y. Hughes (Indianapolis: Odyssey), pp. 72-76.

17. Margaret Cavendish (1972) "Mirth and Melancholy", in *The Women Poets in English: An Anthology,* ed. Ann Stanford (New York: McGraw-Hill), pp. 56-59.

18. Ann Radcliffe (1986) *The Romance of the Forest,* ed. Chloe Chard (Oxford: Oxford University Press), p. 83.

19. Radcliffe, *The Romance of the Forest,* p. 84.

20. Many of Smith's characters in *Emmeline* are amateur versifiers: the hero Godolphin recites a sonnet also called "Night", though his mood is at least momentarily "wretched" and "hopeless"; see Charlotte Smith (1987) *Emmeline* (London: Pandora), p. 439. The melancholic scenes and poetry in Smith's novels require a separate, detailed study. For a brief discussion of the use of poetry in novels by Radcliffe and Smith see Mary A. Favret (1994) "Telling Tales about Genre: Poetry in the Romantic Novel", in *Studies in the Novel,* 26, pp. 153-172.

21. Peggy Dunn (1993) "Charlotte Turner Smith (1749-1806): The Absorption of the Female Voice", a paper delivered at the Second Annual Conference on Eighteenth- and Nineteenth-Century British Women Writers, University of Washington, May 1993.

22. Charlotte Smith (1993) *The Poems of Charlotte Smith,* p. 42, note.

23. William Wordsworth (1976) "A Slumber Did My Spirit Seal", in *Wordsworth Poetical Works,* ed. E. de Selincourt (Oxford: Oxford University Press), p. 149.

24. Hélène Cixous (1976) "The Laugh of the Medusa", *Signs,* 1, p. 889.

25. Mary Robinson (1992) "Stanzas", in *Women Romantic Poets 1785-1832,* ed. Jennifer Breen (London: Dent), pp. 73-75.

26. Thomas Gray (1977) "Ode on a Distant Prospect of Eton College", in *Poetical Works,* ed. Roger Lonsdale (Oxford: Oxford University Press), pp. 20-23.

27. Stuart Curran (1988) "The I Altered", in *Romanticism and Feminism,* ed. Anne K. Mellor (Bloomington: Indiana University Press), p. 200.

28. Wordsworth, *Poetical Works,* p. 724, note.

29. *Critical Review* (1786), pp. 467-468.

30. *Monthly Review* (1797), p. 458.

31. Her "thorn in the heart" reminds one of the Christian images "thorn in the flesh" (2 Corinthians 12:7), and "crown of thorns" (Mark 15:17).

32. Anne Finch uses a related image in her poem "To the Nightingale": "the unhappy poet's breast / Like thine, when best he sings, is plac'd against a thorn" (12-13).

33. Charlotte Smith (1993) Preface to the first and second editions of the *Elegiac Sonnets,* in *The Poems of Charlotte Smith,* p. 3.

34. Phyllis Chesler (1972) *Women and Madness* (New York: Doubleday), p. 45.

35. Kathleen Hickock has noticed the image of a rose's thorns used as a sexual metaphor in a poem by Edith Nesbit (1858-1924). In "Maidenhood", Nesbit writes that the virgin must exchange her crown of lilies for the thorny crown of love, adding, "Who knows what fears beset her innocence / Who, trembling, learns that thorns will wound some day, / And wonders what thorns are, and why, and whence?" Hickock remarks that "the appeal of the floral imagery (blossoms, lilies, the rose) is overpowered in the poem by the fear of thorns. It does not seem far-fetched to consider the flowers female and the pricking thorns phallic". See: Kathleen Hickock (1984) *Representations of Women: Nineteenth-Century Women's Poetry* (Westport: Greenwood), p. 47.

Carrol L. Fry (essay date 1996)

SOURCE: Fry, Carrol L. "The French Revolution in Charlotte Smith's Works: *Desmond, The Emigrants,* and *The Banished Man.*" In *Charlotte Smith,* pp. 64-88. New York: Twayne Publishers, 1996.

[*In the following excerpt, Fry discusses Smith's innovative use of contemporary political events in her novels and poetry.*]

> Bliss was it in that dawn to be alive,
> But to be young was very Heaven![1]

So wrote Wordsworth of the early days of the French Revolution after he arrived in Paris in 1791, the times that Charlotte Smith describes in volume 3 of ***Celestina.*** While he is in France, Willoughby mentions "hearing, and *but* hearing, at a distance, the tumults, with which a noble struggle for freedom at this time (the summer of 1789) agitated the capital, and many of the great towns of France" (III, 181). Later, in the digression that tells his life, Bellegarde praises the "glorious flame of liberty"—the fall of the Bastille—which released him from the prison where he was held by his father's lettre de cachet, one of the hated tools of the French monarchy.[2] Bellegarde's story demonstrates what could happen to a "victim of despotism" during the ancien régime, and the old count is the pattern aristocrat to English liberals. A few years later, the language of this passage would have attracted the wrath of the *Anti-Jacobin* and other reactionary voices; but in 1791, the year **Celestina** was published, the reviewers took no notice. Most British liberals believed the French were simply achieving the freedoms that the British had long enjoyed, freedoms that the youthful Wordsworth had seen as "a gift that rather was come late than soon."[3]

But Smith would go on to take the novel to a level of political discourse that this developing genre had not seen. It is a curious fact that she was nearly the only British novelist to address the contemporary events in France that would leave Europe in flames for 20 years and forever change the course of history.[4] In **Desmond**, published in 1792, Smith's hero articulates a moderate republican position. **The Emigrants** (1793), a long, meditative poem, reflects disappointment with the violence that had marred the revolution and asks for tolerance toward French refugees; but the author's republican views remain unchanged. Finally, **The Banished Man** (1794), while one of Smith's most self-indulgent and least successful works when judged as art, remains an interesting insight into British liberal thought after the French experiment in democracy resulted in anarchy and terror. In the latter two works, Smith condemns the leadership of the revolution but upholds the original ideals.

Desmond stands as a turning point in Smith's career. All of her novels following 1792 contain political commentary and criticism of social injustice. Gone is the focus on proper female conduct and domestic problems as central issues. Smith would continue, however, to use the techniques she had established in her first three novels. Her characters fit the nature/art dichotomy, and she uses polarities of thought similar to the *concordia discors* concept. She decorates the novels with her poetry, and she continues to use landscape description to establish scenes or reflect the mood of characters. Although she makes her distaste for gothic paraphernalia all too apparent in asides and prefaces, she felt she had to include the sort of gothic thrills that she had used in her early novels and that Ann Radcliffe and others popularized. But in all of her novels after 1791, Smith adapts the conventions of fiction to present social and political issues from a republican perspective. Although **The Banished Man** and later works show her disappointment with the revolution in France, her republican principles remained intact throughout her life. Her prefaces and occasional textual comments suggest that she used her novels to bring otherwise unavailable political issues (as well as information ranging from history to botany) to her largely female audience. Her political novels evidence a different sort of didacticism from that of her early works.

Desmond, a novel

Desmond is a historical novel, of sorts. The dates of the letters that compose this epistolary work track the recent history of the early 1790s. The first letter is dated June 9, 1790, and the final one February 6, 1792. The author's Preface carries the date June 20, 1792. Thus, the novel's action covers the period following the fall of the Bastille on June 14, 1789, through the early days of reform, the bringing of the royal family and the National Assembly to Paris, the nationalization of the church, the initial war with Prussia and Austria, the attempt of Louis XVI and his family to escape, and the development of the French constitution.

Desmond articulates, then, the early euphoria that British liberals felt at the success of the revolution. Ironically, if Smith sent her final copy to the publisher in June, the book must have arrived in bookstores at nearly the same time the Parisian mob massacred approximately 1,200 prisoners on September 2-6, 1792, an event that dismayed many of those in England friendly to the revolution. But the positive reviews, which began appearing in September, show that the reaction against the revolution had not set in. A reviewer for *The Critical Review*, for instance, notes the lack of balance in Smith's presentation of political ideas but concedes that "history may confirm the sentiment and confute ours."[5]

Smith satirizes both the smug conservatism of the British ruling classes and the reactionary ire of the French aristocracy. Against these positions, she juxtaposes the favored liberal views of Desmond, her hero. He is another of her Werther characters, a man dominated by passion. In the context of the novel, Smith balances Desmond's republican ideas against the comments of Bethel, the young man's chief correspondent, who provides something like a center point. But **Desmond** differs from Smith's other novels in that the hero's actions as a Werther character prove to be the norm, despite the fact that his views (or at least his rhetoric) are somewhat more liberal than Bethel's.

Thus, on one level **Desmond** is a novel of ideas, with various speakers contributing to the interplay of political dialogue. On another level, the novel offers much of the appeal of Smith's earlier works. Smith blends the discussion of politics with the story of Desmond's hopeless love and gothic melodrama to keep her readers' interest. She enlists sympathy for republican ideas by putting them in the mouth of conventional characters from the sentimental tradition.

The plot grows from Lionel Desmond's attachment to Geraldine Verney. Desmond is a well-to-do young British landowner who has just come into his patrimony. In this epistolary novel, the hero addresses most of his letters to Erasmus Bethel, his friend and mentor. Geraldine is another autobiographical character: a woman whose family pressed her into marriage with a feckless husband. As the story progresses, Desmond tries to help Waverly, Geraldine's brother, a hopelessly scatterbrained and constitutionally indecisive young man, by taking him to France. There Desmond fights a duel to save Waverly from a disastrous marriage and is wounded. Desmond later lives incognito near Geraldine in England, to protect her, and then goes to France when Mr. Verney tries to sell his wife to the unscrupulous Duc de Romagnecourt, a corrupt French aristocrat who has fleeced Verney in high-stakes gambling. Desmond arrives in time to save Geraldine in a blood-and-thunder sequence with enough gothic thrills for the most avid devotee, and Mr. Verney is conveniently killed, leaving Desmond free to wed his Geraldine.

The love story is quite different from Smith's earlier novels of didactic sensibility. Desmond is in love with a married woman, and he consistently defends his feelings against Bethel's criticism. Moreover, while in France, he has an affair with Josephine Boisbelle, the sister of his friend Montfleuri, a French aristocrat with republican sentiments. Like Geraldine, Josephine is a married woman, separated from her émigré husband. She nurses Desmond after his duel and bears his child.

Smith's comments in the preface show her concern as to how her readers might respond to Desmond's passion for a married woman: "In sending into the world a work so unlike those of my former writings . . . I feel some degree of the apprehension which an Author is sensible of on a first publication."[6] She goes on to defend her hero's behavior: "No delineation of character appears to me more interesting, than that of a man capable of such a passion so generous and disinterested as to seek only the good of its object; nor any story more moral, than one that represents the existence of an affection so regulated" (ii). But she does not mention the affair with Josephine Boisbelle. Were there no political discussions in the work, the love story would seem revolutionary enough for British fiction of the 1790s.

The letters from Desmond describing his political discussions provide the central focus of the novel. In the preface, Smith acknowledges that the political content of the work may offend some and attributes the ideas she presents to "conversations to which I have been a witness, in England, and France, during the last twelve months."[7] She also acknowledges her republican bias when she adds that "if those in favor of one party have evidently the advantage, it is not owing to my partial representation, but to the predominant power of truth and reason, which can neither be altered nor concealed" (ii-iii). Smith's assumption of reason's infallibility echoes the thinking of Thomas Holcroft, William Godwin, and other British republican writers.

The Desmond/Geraldine love story provides the structure of the novel and the opportunity for Desmond to move from place to place and report his conversations to Bethel. His friendship with Montfleuri leads to discussions with both liberals and conservatives on the continent, and he corresponds with the Frenchman when he returns to England. Through these letters, Smith gives her readers insights into both political issues and recent historical events. Despite a spirited defense in the Preface of a woman writing on politics, Smith must have felt insecure in undertaking such subjects. She puts most of the political discussion into the mouths of male characters. Apparently, she felt that while her audience might accept political novels from women writers, the actual ideas were best spoken by male characters.

DESMOND AS HISTORICAL NOVEL

Desmond reflects the rush of events in France and the polarities of response those incidents inspired in Great Britain. The events of 1789 and 1790 caused little trepidation there. British liberals had long deplored conditions in France. Six years before the Bastille's fall, William Cowper wrote in *The Task*,

> There's not an English heart that would not leap
> To hear that ye [the Bastille] were fall'n at last; to know
> That ev'n our enemies, so oft employ'd
> In forging chains for us, themselves were free.[8]

Cobban quotes a letter from *The Analytical Review* published after the Bastille's fall that seems typical of the British reaction: "As men, and as Britons, we most sincerely wish them success; and pray that no dissentions amongst themselves may obscure the glorious prospect before them."[9]

Britain, though, had more radical thinkers. Dissenters believed that the Test Act kept them from full political participation, since those who could not subscribe to the "Thirty-Nine Articles" of the Anglican faith were not eligible for government service and there were ambiguities regarding freedom of worship. These individuals, and others concerned about the corruption all too common in government, wanted parliamentary reform. Many organized groups existed, and they became the meeting places for reformers. Agendas varied for those who attended, ranging from the more radical who wanted to do away with monarchy and aristocratic titles to moderates who focused on reforming the parliament.[10]

In 1789 the London Revolutionary Society, named for the Glorious Revolution of 1688, planned a commemoration of the anniversary of the revolution, and on November 4, Dr. Richard Price, a Unitarian minister, presented a sermon entitled "A Discourse on the Love of Our Country." Price celebrated the gains in toleration achieved in 1688 and praised the revolution in France. His conclusion was heady stuff for its time: "Tremble all ye oppressors of the world! . . . Restore to mankind their rights; and consent to the correction of abuses before they and you are destroyed together."[11]

The speech touched off a war of pamphlets. Edmund Burke responded with *Reflections on the Revolution in France*, published in November 1790, attacking Price specifically and republican principles in general. Mary Wollstonecraft replied within a month with *A Vindication of the Rights of Men,* a republican response to Burke's conservative broadside. But the event that polarized the debate was the publication in March 1791 of *The Rights of Man* by Thomas Paine (a second volume followed in 1792). Both Paine's and Wollstonecraft's titles come from the French General Assembly's *Declaration of the Rights of Man and the Citizen* on August 26, 1789.

Paine, an accomplished propagandist,[12] attacked Burke's defense of monarchy in a work with great popular appeal, by one estimate selling more than two million copies.[13] Paine's book won him friends in Paris, where he was elected to the General Assembly, taking his seat in 1792. But he was tried for sedition and found guilty in absentia in England, an ominous note for the British revolutionary movement. Dozens of books and pamphlets appeared siding with Paine or Burke (primarily the latter as repression deepened).

Desmond is a fascinating historical novel in its own right. But the work is also a shot fired in this war of pamphlets, books, and magazine articles, and it is the only novel to address the subject. Smith attacks Burke through the comments of Desmond and Bethel. Thus, the Burke/Paine controversy is part of the recent history that the novel reports, as well as a central point in the discussion of ideas.

If, as was her usual practice in producing a novel, Smith spent approximately one year in composing *Desmond,* it is possible that she adapted the novel's discussions to events as she wrote it. Her surviving letters provide no evidence, so whether she might have responded to current events cannot be proved. Yet the novel is a unique amalgam of fiction, events of the day or very recent history, and political discussion.

One looks in vain for a specific reason for the sudden change in Smith's work. Her letters provide few clues. She does write to Joel Barlow on November 3, 1792, complementing him on his tracts "Advice to the Privileged Orders" and "Letter to the National Convention" (Huntington). An American, Barlow was a well-known sympathizer with republican France, and perhaps he is the sort of person to whom Smith's sister, Catherine Anne Dorset, refers when she mentions that at Brighthelmstone (Brighton) Smith "formed acquaintances with some of the most violent advocates of the French Revolution, and unfortunately caught the contagion, though in direct opposition to the principles she had formerly professed."[14] William Hayley, her mentor, was of the republican camp. And Smith's acquaintance with Helen Maria Williams,[15] a friend of the revolution in its early stages whose *Letters from France,* which presents an idealized view of revolutionary reforms, is the only other solid evidence of connections with those sympathetic to the revolution.

Smith borrowed from Williams's *Letters* in **Desmond** at several points. The two writers certainly express similar ideological views on the French Revolution, but there are more specific points of comparison. In 1785 Williams became friends with the wife of the Comte du Fosse, who had married against his father's will, leading to persecution similar to that which Smith's Montfleuri describes in **Desmond** and Bellegarde in **Celestina.** Both of Smith's characters are aristocrats who support the revolution and utter the same sentiments as those that Williams reports from du Fosse. Also, Smith's portrayal of happy peasants dancing on the village green at Montfleuri's estate closely resembles passages in Williams's letters describing a visit to du Fosse's estate. A more precise bit of borrowing is the passage in **Desmond** in which the hero reports on "the furious manner in which the carriages of the *noblesse* were driven through the streets, where there are no accommodations for the foot passenger—and where the proud and unfeeling possessors of those splendid equipages . . . have been known to feel their rapid wheels crushing a fellow creature . . ." (I, 108). The passage goes on at some length, as does a similar report in the *Letters*: "One subject of complaint among the aristocrates [sic] is, that, since the revolution, they are obliged to drive through the streets with caution. . . ."[16]

Williams first went to France in July 1790 and returned to England in September; later that fall she began publishing her *Letters*. Textual parallels suggest that Smith read the first volumes of the *Letters,* and perhaps her acquaintance with that work gave her ideas for the development of Montfleuri and Bellegarde as characters. Certainly Smith's and Williams's political sentiments run parallel. Both admire the Comte de Mirabeau,[17] express views consistent with republican moderates on parliamentary reform and war, and defend the general effectiveness of the British constitutional system, if improved.

Two Perspectives On Dining With A Footman: Political Dialogue In *Desmond*

In her review of **Desmond** for *The Analytical Review,* Joseph Johnson's publication, Mary Wollstonecraft praises the novel's subordinate characters because they are "sketched with that peculiar dexterity which shoots folly as it flies."[18] Wollstonecraft alludes to the variety of individuals with whom Desmond reports dialogues, showing that the folly Smith describes comes from both British conservatives opposed to the revolution and aristocrats in France.

The dialogue begins when Desmond visits the Fairfax home while waiting for Waverly to arrive for their projected tour. General Wallingford decries the National Assembly as "a collection of dirty fellows" who have "abolished all titles and abolished the very name of nobility" (I, 60). Mrs. Fairfax's addition to the discussion is especially interesting because it reflects the kind of sensibility that Smith and other British liberals had come to reject: "Heavens! how my sympathizing heart bleeds, when I reflect on the numbers of amiable people of rank, compelled thus to the cruel necessity of resigning those ancient and honorable names which distinguished them from the vulgar herd!" (I, 63). In Smith's later poetry and novels, true sensibility brings empathy for victims of social injustice. Mrs. Fairfax is a false sentimentalist.

Desmond expresses satisfaction with the overthrow of the feudal system. But Mrs. Fairfax's response focuses squarely on the basic fears of the English middle class: "Good Heaven! I declare the very idea is excessively terrific; only suppose the English mob were to get such a notion, and in some odious riot, begin the same sort of thing here!" Desmond's response is that of British moderate republicans: "Perhaps there may never exist here the same *cause*: and, therefore, the *effect* will not follow" (I, 68-69). He goes on to demonstrate that the British and French aristocracy are quite different and that many of the abuses being corrected in France do not exist in England.

Smith does not allow the withers of British aristocracy to go unwrung, however. Lord Newminster is a republican's portrayal of the aristocrat, a rude, ignorant lout to whom the middle-class Fairfaxes compulsively genuflect. In one scene, he comes into the Fairfax home while the family is having tea, stretches out on a sofa with his boots on, and embraces a dog, cooing "Oh! thou dear bitchy—thou beautiful bitchy—damme, if I don't love thee better than my mother or my sisters." He then feeds the dog chocolate, crying, "[W]as it hungry? . . . was it hungry, a lovely dear?—I would rather all the old women in the country should fast for a month, than thou shouldest not have thy belly full" (I, 57). The double-edged satire hits not only the bad manners of the aristocrat but the toadying attitude of the middle-class Fairfaxes to a titled boor.

Desmond's letters report similar debates with conservatives in France. When a young abbé defends the old way, Montfleuri responds by saying that "the antiquity of an abuse is no reason for its continuance" (I, 123) and lectures the abbé on the *taille*, the *gabelle*, tax farming, lettres de cachet, and other abuses. Smith follows with a long passage that amounts to a history lecture from Montfleuri, tracing the events that led to the Revolution, replete with quite erudite allusions to Millot, Voltaire, Rousseau, and others. Part of Montfleuri's lecture involves references to the French king, Henry IV, a name that appears often in the writings of British republicans.[19] The founder of the Bourbon line stood as a symbol for liberals of the good king.

A visit to Montfleuri's uncle, the Count de Hautville, provides an opportunity for another lengthy conservative/liberal dialogue, capped by an interesting allusion to James Boswell's *Life of Samuel Johnson,* which had been published in 1791. Smith must have read the *Life* either immediately before beginning **Desmond** or during the book's composition. In a bit of historical irony, Johnson's attacks on republicans made him a target of opportunity in the pamphlet wars long after his death. Under the date of 1763, Boswell writes, "He [Johnson] again insisted on the duty of maintaining subordination of rank." He then quotes the Great Lexicographer as follows:

> Sir, there is one Mrs. Maccaulay in this town, a great republican. One day when I was at her house, I put on a very grave countenance, and said to her, "Madam, I am now become a convert to your way of thinking. I am convinced that all mankind are upon an equal footing; and to give you an unquestionable proof, Madam, that I am in earnest, here is a very sensible, civil, and well-behaved fellow-citizen, your footman; I desire that he may be allowed to sit down and dine with us." I thus, Sir, shewed her the absurdity of the leveling doctrine. . . .[20]

Mrs. Catherine Maccaulay remained "a great republican" from 1763 until her death, ironically in the year of the *Life*'s publication. She wrote a number of histories of England (particularly of the Stuarts) from a republican perspective, and even wrote one of the many pamphlets by republicans attacking Burke's *Reflections.*

Smith alludes to Johnson's antirepublican sentiments during a conversation between Desmond and de Hautville, a typical aristocrat of the ancien régime. Desmond asks de Hautville "whether you really think, that a dealer in wine, or in wood, in sugar, or cloth, is not endued with the same faculties and feelings as the descendant of Charlemagne" (I, 236). In a passage that echoes Johnson's put-down of Mrs. Maccaulay, de Hautville asks why Desmond's footman is a servant if they are equals. Smith explains in a footnote that this question had previously been called unanswerable. But Desmond has a ready response:

> Because—though my footman is certainly so far upon an equality with me, as he is a man, and a free-man; there must be a distinction in local circumstances; though they neither render me noble, or him base—I happen to be born heir to considerable estates; it is his chance to be the son of a labourer, living on those estates.—I have occasion for his services, he has occasion for the money by which I purchase them: in this compact we are equal so far as we are free.—I, with my property, which is money, buy his property, which is time, so long as he is willing to sell it.—I hope and believe my footman feels himself to be my fellow-man; but I have not, therefore, any apprehension that instead of waiting behind my chair, he will sit down in the next.—He was born poor—but he is not angry that I am rich—so long as my riches are a benefit and not an oppression to him. He knows that he never can be in *my* situation, but he knows also that I can amend *his.*
>
> (I, 237-238)

The lecture goes on for almost two more pages, concluding with a quotation from Voltaire that supports the speaker's conclusions.

The word "compact" explains Smith's answer to the vexing questions that the existence of a servant class must have posed to British republicans. Smith no doubt agreed with the views of Rousseau, the author of *The Social Contract,* that the third essential duty of government is to fill citizens' wants. But not as a gift. In his *Discourse on Political Economy,* Rousseau writes: "This duty is not, we should feel, to fill the granaries of individuals and thereby to grant them a dispensation from labor, but to keep plenty so within their reach that labour is always necessary and never useless for its acquisition."[21]

The letter from de Hautville's estate is rich in ideological dialogue of the day. Desmond, for instance, carries on a discussion with a member of the high clergy, who execrates the General Assembly not only for its confiscation of church property and establishment of civil status for clergy but also for leveling the incomes of all ecclesiastics, an action that increased the income of local priests but greatly diminished that of the hierarchy. This long letter is another example of Smith's practice of matching recent historical events with fictional scenes, as it is dated September 30, 1790, about two months after the Assembly's reconstitution of the church.

DESMOND, BURKE, AND PAINE

Desmond abounds with references to the controversy that arose over Burke's *Reflections*. The first appears in a letter dated January 8, 1991, two months after the publication of the book. After reading the *Reflections*, Desmond writes to Bethel, "I own I never expected to have seen an elaborate treatise in favor of despotism written by an Englishman, who has always been called one of the most steady, as he undoubtedly is one of the most able of those who were esteemed the friends of the people" (II, 62). The tone of disappointment may arise from Burke's opposition to the British war with the American colonists, an opposition shared by Smith and other republicans. But Desmond goes on to accurately, if hyperbolically, predict, "I foresee *that a thousand pens will leap from their standishes* (to parody a sublime sentence of his own) to answer such a book" (II, 63) In an April 10 letter, Desmond writes, again to Bethel, "Leave him then, my friend, to waste in swinish excess, sums, which he has earned by doing dirty work, at the expence of those who are now called the 'swinish multitude,' hundreds of whom might be fed by the superfluities of his luxurious table" (II, 114).

Smith attributes the phrase "swinish multitude" to Burke. She uses it satirically in a variety of contexts in ***Desmond*** and other works that follow, as did many republican writers. *Politics for the People: or A Salmagundi for Swine,* a republican magazine published in 1794 and 1795, used "swinish multitude" as something of a logo, publishing satirical poems and essays signed by "Old Hubert" or "a brother grunter." There were many other responses to "swinish multitude," including "The Rights of Swine: An Address to the Poor" (1794).[22] The satirical sallies on his unfortunately chosen phrase characterize Smith's attacks on Burke in the novel, which come up again and again in the dialogues between Desmond and Bethel. The attacks become more vitriolic as the novel progresses, with Desmond labeling the British statesman "the champion of the placeman—and the apologist of the pensioner" (III, 209).

References to Paine's *The Rights of Man* turn up on schedule from a historical perspective when Bethel sends Desmond a copy with a letter dated March 18, 1791, the month when the book appeared, noting that it is written by an "obscure individual, calling himself the subject of another government" and that it "could never have attracted so much attention, or have occasioned to the party whose principles it so decidedly attacks, such general alarm, if there had not been much sound sense in it, however bluntly delivered" (II, 92). Desmond answers on April 10, responding that he is "forcibly struck with truths, that either were not seen before, or were (by men, who did not wish to acknowledge them) carefully repressed" (II, 115-116). Desmond goes on to predict the attack that will be (and was) mounted against Paine and notes that "those who feel the force of his abilities, will vilify his private life, as if that was any thing to the purpose" (II, 117). Smith, who would have written the passage a few months after volume 1 of *The Rights of Man* appeared, thus acknowledges the ad hominem attacks on Paine's marital difficulties and his failure as an exciseman before immigration to America. In the same letter she predicts the government's sedition trial of Paine in 1792 by having an effete British lordling whom Desmond meets in France cry, "I wonder they don't punish the author, who, they say, is quite a low sort of fellow." He goes on to articulate, as does Mrs. Fairfax in England, the underlying fear of the privileged classes in England: "I hope our government will take care to silence such a demagogue, before he puts it into the heads of *les gens sans culotes* [sic], in England, to do as they have done in France, and even before he gets some of the ragged rogues hanged—*They* rights! poor devils, who have neither shirts nor breeches!" (II 121).

Part 2 of *The Rights of Man* appeared in February 1792, and Paine's attack on the monarchy provoked government reaction. Wilson and Ricketson report that "Prime Minister Pitt undertook a smear campaign against the character of Paine and initiated court action which eventually resulted in the libel conviction."[23] Thus, Smith's letters in ***Desmond*** dated April 1791, may be reactions to the events that continued into the spring and summer of 1792. It is worth noting that ***Desmond*** appeared at almost the same time that Paine left England for France, with a writ out for his arrest.

Other historical milestones come up in the letters between Bethel and Desmond. In a letter dated June 28, 1791, Bethel notes "the flight of the King of France and his family" being reported in England, and on July 2, Desmond responds, calling attention to the "magnanimity shown by the French people, on the re-entrance of the King into Paris: This will surely convince the world that the *bloody democracy* of Mr. Burke, is not a combination of the swinish multitude, for the purposes of anarchy, but the association of reasonable beings, who determine to be, and deserve to be, free" (III, 89). He goes on to compare the moderation of the French people in receiving the returned king with what might have happened had the monarchists succeeded in overthrowing the revolutionary government.

Also, war with Austria and Prussia impended in 1791, the date of the final letters in the novel. Desmond takes note of this possibility, deploring the actions of the "Northern

Powers" but asserting that such actions will hardly "destroy the lovely tree that has thus taken vigorous growth in the finest country in the world." He goes on to regret that despite the pacific intentions of the French toward their neighbors, "its root must be manured with blood" (III, 207-208). The tree metaphor was rather common in France at the time. Doyle notes that in 1789, peasants planted liberty trees on land owned by aristocrats. "They called them *Mays,* from a much older tradition, festooned them with symbols of seigneurialism, and claimed that if they stood for a year and a day their lord's rights would be extinguished."[24]

Some of the most interesting letters reflect differences between Bethel and Desmond. Bethel's given name, Erasmus, alludes to the author of *The Praise of Folly,* a work that proposes a sane, balanced view of life, and the name suggests his political position. Bethel speaks with the authority of experience (Smith tells his history in a long letter at the outset) and reason. In a letter dated July 6, 1791, Bethel begins by suggesting that Desmond is "far gone . . . in what are called (but, I think, improperly called) the *new doctrines,* that you would contest this opinion with me," and goes on to praise the English constitution, which though flawed, is "undoubtedly the best in the world." He insists that "it may, I believe, be truly asserted, that in no age or country, has there existed a people, to whom general happiness has been more fairly distributed, than it is among the English of the present day." Moreover, he reads trouble on the horizon in France. He hopes the French will find a government superior to the British, but, "I am compelled to say," he writes, "that the proceedings of the National Assembly, since the death of Mirabeau, gives [sic] me too little reason to believe they will." He regrets the absence of "some great leading mind" to guide the revolution, because "[t]he *despotism* of superior ability is, after all, necessary; and it is the only despotism to which reasonable beings ought to submit" (III, 101-103). Bethel's republicanism is of the most moderate sort, and he lacks Desmond's passion.

Desmond soon answers, with a criticism of the English constitution. He quotes Boswell's *Life* on the subject of the British Parliament, in which "any question, however unreasonable or unjust, may be carried by a venal majority," and he goes on to answer Bethel's assertion that the British system brings general happiness more effectively than any other by saying that "this rather proves that their condition is very wretched, than that ours is perfectly happy." He deplores British attitudes toward slavery, and concludes with a statement that ends up not very far from that of Bethel and seems a good summation of British liberal—as opposed to radical—thought of the period:

> I think that our form of government is certainly the best—not that can be imagined—but that has ever been experienced; and, while we are sure that practice is in its favor, it would be most absurd to dream of destroying it on theory.—If I had a very good house that had some inconveniences about it, I should not desire to pull it down, but I certainly should send for an architect. . . . But I should be very much startled if my architect was to say, "Sir, I dare not touch your house—If I let in more light, if I take down those partitions, and make the other changes you desire, I am very much afraid that the great timbers will give way, and the *party-walls* crush you beneath their ruins"
>
> (III, 165*-166*).[25]

Neither Bethel nor Desmond articulates a specific political agenda, and their comments about change differ more in Desmond's impassioned rhetoric than in substance. Both support moderate reform, and the dialogue between them provides a springboard for Smith's presentation of republican ideas.

Desmond And Fictional Conventions

Despite the ideological tone of ***Desmond,*** Smith relies on the fictional conventions that she had both inherited and created in her earlier novels. Moreover, she juxtaposes opposites as she does in those works, cues the reader with the repetition of words and the evocative language of the sentimental novel, and includes a bit of gothic melodrama at the conclusion.

In volume 3 Desmond follows Geraldine to France, where she has been lured by her husband. In scenes that would do justice to Radcliffe at her best, Desmond rescues her from banditti who glower "with the terrific look which Salvator gives to his assassins" (III, 274-275).[26] The scenes abound with ruined castles, hollow groans, and all the paraphernalia of the developing gothic mode—considerably intensified from Smith's earlier novels.

Smith's characters are cut from the cloth of the sentimental-gothic tradition and the nature/art dichotomy. Geraldine admires Desmond because he "has so much taste, and so much genuine enthusiasm" (II, 217). Despite his revolutionary fervor, Desmond can admire a picturesque ruin on Montfleuri's estate, even though it reflects the ancient tyranny of the church, commenting to Bethel, "I, who love, you know, every thing ancient, unless it be ancient prejudices, have entreated my friend to preserve this structure in its present state—than which, nothing can be more picturesque" (I, 171). Both Geraldine and Desmond display the alienation of the hero and heroine of sensibility. Desmond, for instance, confesses in one of his letters to being "a strange, eccentrick being, and not much like any other" (II, 233). Like the conventional sentimental characters in so many other novels, both Geraldine and Desmond eschew the materialist lifestyle, and both respond to the needs of the unfortunate. Geraldine, for instance, writes to her sister that the "only pleasure I have lost in losing high affluence, is that of having the power to befriend the unhappy, to whom I can now give only my tears" (II, 197). The properly disposed reader would respond to Desmond and Geraldine as fellow sentimentalists.

In his powerful feelings, at least, Desmond is a lineal descendant of Delamere and Sir Edward Newenden, an "English Werter" (III, 60), as his friend Bethel calls him. In the *concordia discors* of reason and feeling, Desmond fails to control his passion. When he follows Geraldine into the countryside, he writes to Bethel that "much eloquence will be necessary to supply the defect of *reason,* which I know you will think my conduct betrays" (II, 233-234). But, as he later writes, "I find, that seven-and-twenty is not the age of reason, or, at least, where the heart is so deeply concerned" (II, 235-236). When Smith has him quote Saint-Preux from *La Nouvelle Héloïse,* Desmond's identification with passion is complete: "'There are,' says St. Preux, in those enchanting letters of the incomparable Rousseau, 'but two divisions of the world, that where Julie is, and that where she is not'" (II, 240). He goes on to compare his feelings for Geraldine to these sentiments.

Other characters reflect an excess of passion over reason. Perhaps Smith panders to a British audience's cultural assumptions about the French or perhaps she shares them. But her Gallic characters, Josephine Boisbelle and her brother Montfleuri, are at the mercy of their passions. Although Josephine writes no letters, the novel suggests that she initiated the affair with Desmond. And while Montfleuri may follow sweet reason in his politics, his letters after meeting Fanny Waverly, Geraldine's sister, demonstrate a stereotypical Gallic impetuosity.[27]

Smith counterpoises Desmond's apparent excess of passion with Geraldine (who remains a dutiful wife despite her obvious attachment to Desmond) and Bethel. The latter expostulates with Desmond throughout the novel over his conduct, and the word "reason" recurs consistently in his letters, identifying his position for the reader. He advises Desmond, for instance, to "sit down for some months, at least, quietly in Kent, where I hope you will recover your reason" (III, 85). Desmond's powerful feelings contrast with what the younger man calls Bethel's "cold and calm philosophy" (I, 161). Later, when the Duc de Romagnecourt arrives in England, insisting that Geraldine accompany him to France, she fears that Desmond will challenge the Frenchman. She reasons that if she persists in refusal, Romagnecourt will go away. But, she writes to her sister, "nor would Desmond be persuaded that I ought patiently to endure this transient evil—I saw consequences attending *his* applying to Monsieur de Romangecourt, of which I could not bear the idea without terror" (III, 19). The fiery Desmond has already fought one duel at this point and seems ready for another.

Smith's presentation of a Werther figure who becomes the moral norm of the work reflects the dawning of a romantic sensibility in Great Britain and on the continent. Schama writes:

> The drastic cultural alteration represented by this first hot eruption of the Romantic sensibility is of more than literary importance. It meant the creation of a spoken and written manner that would become the standard voice of the Revolution, shared by both its victims and its most implacable prosecutors. The speeches of Mirabeau and Robespierre as well as the letters of Desmoulins and Mme. Roland and the orchestrated festivals of the Republic broadcast appeals to the soul, to tender humanity, Truth, Virtue, Nature, and the idyll of family life.

Schama goes on to quote Mercier: "'Reason with its insidious language can paint the most equivocal enterprise in captivating colors but the virtuous heart will never forget the interests of the humblest citizen. Let us place the virtuous statesman before the clever politician.'"[28] Charlotte Smith's novels never display the distrust of reason that characterizes French radical thought, but in *Desmond* and the novels that follow, the feelings become an ever more important guide to her virtuous characters.

"THE SACRED FLAME OF LIBERTY BECOMES A RAGING FIRE": *THE EMIGRANTS*

Since the Preface to *Desmond* carries a date of June 1792, we can assume that the novel could not have reached bookstores or circulating libraries until at least late summer. By then the swirl of events in France had taken a new direction. In early September, the Parisian mob killed approximately half of the 2,600 people held in nine prisons, nearly all of the deaths outright murders or executions after proceedings in kangaroo courts.[29] The Jacobin clubs—revolutionary groups that met across France—insisted on the removal of the king and the establishment of a republic. And after the king's attempted escape, despite the attempts by moderates in the Assembly to justify keeping Louis on the throne, radicals demanded that he be brought to trial, a demand supported by the ever more powerful Parisian mob. The trial and subsequent execution of Louis XVI took place in December 1792 and January 1793. The *sans culottes* of Paris dominated the Legislative Assembly, sometimes by terror, and the nation veered toward chaos.

Long before the Reign of Terror, thousands fled the country. By 1791, half of the officer corps had left France. Many stayed on the French borders, and Koblenz was a center of émigré activity. A far larger number of aristocrats, terrified at the castle burnings in the countryside, and priests who refused to accept the civil constitution of the clergy (designated as "refractory") also left. The émigrés were a source of concern in the Assembly from the beginning, and on November 8, 1791, it passed a decree threatening them with a death penalty if they did not return by January 1. Many of these emigrants came to England, where they sometimes received a cool welcome.

English liberals were shocked at the turn of events. Charlotte Smith's poem *The Emigrants,* the Dedication for which is dated May 10, 1793, at Brighton, less than a year after the publication of *Desmond,* is a response to the changed situation.[30] It expresses the disappointment that British republicans must have felt at the chaos in France, attempts to enlist readers' sympathy and understanding for émigrés, and warns of what can happen if people are denied liberty too long.

Undoubtedly, Smith spoke with both the Chevalier de Faville, her son-in-law, and other exiles during the months before Augusta's marriage. Thus, *The Emigrants* is in part a plea for tolerance of those who fled the troubles in France, albeit a rather cool one. Smith demonstrates ambivalence in her feelings about those who fled France, however, and in some respects, the poem can be read as another entry in the pamphlet war.

In her dedication to William Cowper, Smith notes that in Britain, "those who are the victims of the Revolution, have not escaped the odium which the undistinguishing multitude annex to all the natives of a country where such horrors have been acted." The phrase "undistinguishing multitude" is surely an ironic allusion to Burke's "swinish multitude." She continues in a passage that reflects the uneasiness republicans must have felt in a time of building repression:

> . . . by confounding the original cause with the wretched catastrophes that have followed its ill management; the attempts of public virtue, with the outrages that guilt and folly have committed in its disguise, the very name of Liberty has not only lost the charm it used to have in British ears, but many, who have written or spoken, in its defence, have been stigmatized as promoters of Anarchy, and enemies to the prosperity of their country.[31]

The author sets the poem on the beach at Brighton on "a morning in November, 1792." She establishes the meditative and elegiac mood by writing "Alas! how few the morning wakes to joy! / How many murmur at oblivious night / For leaving them so soon" (I, 8-10). As in *Elegiac Sonnets,* Smith establishes herself as narrator and generalizes about the woes of the world before introducing a group of émigrés.

> Behold, in witness of this mournful truth,
> A group approach me, whose dejected looks,
> Sad Heralds of distress! proclaim them Men
> Banish'd for ever and for conscience sake
> From their distracted Country, whence the name
> Of Freedom misapplied, and much abused
> By lawless Anarchy, has driven them far
> To Wander. . . .
>
> (I, 95-101)

She makes her republican sympathies and ambivalence about the French emigrants apparent when she notes that their sole hope is that German armies may scourge France, "that pleasant land" (I, 104), and continues, "Whate'er your errors, I lament your fate" (I, 107-108).

In the lines that follow, she introduces four clerical figures: a monk, a high churchman, an abbé, and a parish priest. Smith's republican principles do not permit her to describe them with much sympathy. The monk, "in a moping cloister long comsum'd" (I, 114), had thought that "To live on eleemosynary bread, / And to renounce God's works, would please that God" whom he worshiped (I, 118-119). Next she describes the high official of the church who "declines / The aid he needs not" (I, 125-126), while he looks back to what he had lost, services "Where, amid clouds of incense, he held forth / To kneeling crowds the imaginary bones / Of Saints suppos'd, in pearl and gold enchas'd" (I, 132-134). In France, he was believed "To hold the keys of Heaven, and to admit / Whom he thought good to share it" (I, 137-138). The higher clergy in France was almost exclusively composed of younger sons of the aristocracy.[32] Thus, this priest can afford to decline aid. She next describes the abbé (a priest who would serve in a well-to-do family) in only marginally sympathetic fashion. She then praises the selfless devotion of the parish priest, but notes that he "Taught to the bare-foot peasant, whose hard hands / Produced the nectar he could seldom taste, / Submission to the Lord for whom he toil'd" (I, 172-174). She goes on to establish a tone of disapproval that he has left and some justification for the violence in France:

> . . . even such a Man
> Becomes an exile; staying not to try
> By temperate zeal to check his madd'ning flock,
> Who, at the novel sound of Liberty
> (Ah! most intoxicating sound to slaves!),
> Start to license[.]
>
> (I, 190-95)

Smith includes disclaimers in footnotes, noting that "nothing is farther from my thoughts, than to reflect invidiously on the Emigrant clergy," but the description of them strikes a decidedly negative tone.

She introduces two other émigrés, an aristocrat and his wife. The latter dreams of the glories of Versailles, where "Beauty gave charms to empire" (I, 226). Neither she nor her husband in their "high consciousness of noble blood" can see the true cause of the revolution, because "luxury wreathes with silk the iron bonds, / And hides the ugly rivets with her flowers" (I, 278-279). Smith asks of the aristocrat,

> . . . could *he* learn,
> That worth alone is true Nobility?
> And that *the peasant* who, "amid the sons
> Of Reason, Valour, Liberty, and Virtue,
> Displays distinguish'd merit, is a Noble
> Of Nature's own creation!"
>
> (I, 239-44)

In a footnote that reflects the growing mood of repression in Great Britain, Smith credits James Thomson for the quoted lines (from his adaptation of *Coriolanus*), noting that many now view the egalitarianism of Thompson's lines not as "commonplace declamation but sentiments of dangerous tendency."

Smith describes tax farmers (*fermiers generaux*) who have also become émigrés and ". . . unlamented sink, / And know that they deserve the woes they feel" (I, 294-295). She then addresses "Fortune's worthless favorites" in England, "Who feed on England's vitals" (I, 315-316), and in a passage whose tone foreshadows Thomas Carlyle's *The French Revolution: A History* and Charles Dickens's *A Tale of Two Cities* writes,

> Study a lesson that concerns ye much;
> And, trembling, learn, that if oppress'd too long,
> The raging multitude, to madness stung,
> Will turn on their oppressors; and, no more
> By sounding titles and parading forms
> Bound like tame victims, will redress themselves!
>
> (I, 332-37)

The phrase "raging multitude" in this passage refers once again to Burke's "swinish multitude" and warns that when the masses are treated as "swinish," they are likely to react as did the French.[33]

Book 2 opens on the South Downs in Sussex and is dated April 1793. The narrative reflects the changes that time had wrought. Smith again establishes the persona from *Elegiac Sonnets* as narrator, noting that, like her, the emigrants have known better times; and while she asks for tolerance and humanity in their treatment, most of Book 2, like Book 1, reflects the reaction of British republicanism to the chaos in France. She asks what promise the young year will bring those "who shrink from horrors such as War / Spreads o'er the affrighted world" (II, 45-46). Referring to French moderates, she observes that they see the "Temple, which they fondly hop'd / Reason would raise to Liberty, destroy'd (II, 48-49). She refers to "The headless corse of one, whose only crime / Was being born a Monarch" (II, 54-55) and to the war that had begun in February 1793. She hopes that when France revives, a free people will choose a king, speculating that such a ruler will be like the much-admired Henry IV.

But Smith still speaks for the original goals of the revolution, while the world "shrinks, amaz'd, / From Freedom's name, usurp'd and misapplied" (II, 80-81), and sees tyranny the greater evil. Before rejecting liberty, the reader, she writes, should consider the "black scroll, that tells of regal crimes / Committed to destroy her" (II, 88-90). Book 2 contains a lengthy description of the horror of war in France and closes with a meditation on the human condition:

> . . . my soul is pained
> By the variety of woes that Man
> For Man creates—his blessings often turn'd
> To plagues and curses: Saint-like Piety,
> Misled by Superstition, has destroy'd
> More than ambition; and the sacred flame
> Of liberty becomes a raging fire,
> When Licence and Confusion bid it blaze.
>
> (II, 412-19)

In this poem, Smith, as she observes in her Preface, imitates the blank verse style of Cowper's *The Task*. But *The Emigrants* resembles *Elegiac Sonnets* in its description of natural scenery, the general tone of melancholy, and the ubiquitous autobiographical persona. *The Emigrants* stands apart from early editions of *Elegiac Sonnets,* however, in its powerful political statement. While the poem's ostensible subject is the unfortunate plight of those who have left France, it offers at best a mixed sympathy. The aristocrat has failed to understand what caused his fall, as have the refractory clergy she describes. Much of the poem is an apology for the early phases of the Revolution, mixed with the disappointment of a British republican that it had failed, resulting in yet another tyranny.

The Banished Man

Smith's seventh novel,[34] published in 1794, a year after *The Old Manor House* and within months after *The Wanderings of Warwick*, is one of her least satisfying from an artistic standpoint. It is her seventh novel in six years, and during the same time period she had published *The Emigrants* and three editions of *Elegiac Sonnets,* a remarkable production under any circumstances, but especially impressive considering the author's family obligations. In *The Banished Man,* however, she seems written out. The novel has a numbingly long autobiographical digression, in the form of Mrs. Denzil's story, and an aimless plot. Also, the text of the first edition is riddled with typographical errors.[35] The only real interest the work holds is the author's interpretation of events in France and the British reaction to them.

The story again reflects recent history, beginning in October 1792, in Austria near the French border at the castle of the Baron de Rosenheim. The baron is away, and the baroness and her daughter fearfully await the arrival of the French troops after their victory over the Prussian-Austrian army. Smith may refer to the battle at Valmy, in the passes of the Argonne, on September 20 of that year, although it did not precipitate the sort of wholesale retreat the novel describes. The baroness hears groans outside and eventually discovers the Chevalier d'Alonville and his father, the Viscount de Fayolles, both of whom had fought against the revolutionary forces. Fayolles is fatally wounded, and after his death, d'Alonville escorts the ladies to Koblenz, where they rejoin their husbands.

After d'Alonville returns to the castle and retrieves an important legal document for the baroness, he meets the Marquis de Touranges, an embittered aristocrat searching for his wife and mother and accompanied by the Abbé de St. Remi. He also meets Ellesmere, a young Englishman with whom he forms a friendship. After traveling about the German states, the group eventually goes to England with Ellesmere.

While d'Alonville ponders his future, he visits Ellesmere's family, meets Henrietta Denzil, another autobiographical character, and falls in love with her daughter, Angelina—a parallel, of course, to Augusta Smith. But d'Alonville feels he has to visit his brother in France, who has gone over to the revolutionary side and adopted the name du Fosse.[36] D'Alonville is caught, but his brother saves him, hoping to convert him to the revolution. D'Alonville steadily refuses and eventually, with his brother's help, escapes and returns to England, bringing jewelry given him by du Fosse for safekeeping. He briefly serves as a tutor to the children of Lord Abedore, fights a duel with a rake who has designs on Angelina, and marries his true love. With Mrs. Denzil, the couple then move to the continent, where they can live on d'Alonville's modest income from the sale of the jewelry given him by du Fosse, who was guillotined during the Terror.

Despite the work's artistic flaws, it has historical interest in its treatment of incidents of the time. Like **Desmond,** the novel describes recent events, the action beginning in 1792. The Abbé de St. Remi, for instance, tells of Madame de Touranges being held in prison during the September massacres, spattered with the blood of the slain, and released by the whim of the mob. Coblenz, where d'Alonville spends some time, was an important rallying point for emigrants, and the description of their community rings true. In volume 2, d'Alonville's captivity in Paris and his experience of seeing from his prison window 11 prisoners (three of them women) guillotined resembles contemporary accounts. The times were stormy in Paris in 1793, with the mob gaining ever greater control of the Assembly.

Smith introduces another historical allusion in Carlowitz, the Polish patriot whom d'Alonville and Ellesmere meet in Dresden. The revolutionary fervor of the times inspired a movement toward greater freedom in Poland, and the Poles were able to establish a constitutional monarchy in 1791. Later, Russia, Prussia, and Austria invaded. From the spring of 1794 until the fall, the Poles, led by Kosciusko, put up a determined resistance.[37] But the superior armies of the enemy and the nation's internal class divisions brought about eventual defeat, and the three powers partitioned Poland out of existence.

The Polish revolution would have been in progress as Smith wrote **The Banished Man.** Thus, the novel is yet another instance of the author's introduction of topical material. The peaceful revolution in Poland was inspired by the American and French experiments in democracy. However, we hear very little about Carlowitz's specific philosophy. He insists, "While I have any remains of strength I must use it, though my country exists no longer" (I, 163), but he addresses no issues. The Polish people and their friends abroad must have known that national extinction would be the result of defeat, and the novel surely reflects liberal sympathy for Polish Jacobinism during the days in 1794 when Poles fought for independence. Thus, the Carlowitz character instructs readers on current history.

In addition to using Carlowitz to introduce contemporary historical events, Smith juxtaposes his political liberalism against d'Alonville's hatred of republicanism and gives the Polish patriot the most stirring arguments. Even d'Alonville is nearly convinced, saying, "Had I been a Polonese, I might have thought and have acted as you have done. Had you been a native of France, you would have seen her monarchy exchanged for anarchy infinitely more destructive and more tyrannical, with the same abhorrence as I have done" (I, 164). And so it goes, when Carlowitz eventually makes his way to Paris seeking help for his

ELEGIAC SONNETS,

BY

CHARLOTTE SMITH.

THE FIFTH EDITION,

WITH ADDITIONAL SONNETS

AND OTHER POEMS.

LONDON:
PRINTED FOR T. CADELL, IN THE STRAND.
M.DCC.LXXXIX.

country. D'Alonville meets him on his way back to England after his adventure in France, where the Pole was imprisoned for debt. Carlowitz tells of his disappointment:

> I thought I should have found in the new land of freedom, persons in whom I should meet congenial sentiments, and be admitted to serve the cause in which my whole soul was engaged; but how cruelly I was disappointed, you may imagine, when I tell you that I quitted almost immediately a place where I saw and heard actions and language more inimical to the cause of the real liberty and happiness of mankind, than could have proceeded from the united efforts of every despot that had ever insulted the patience of the world.
>
> (II, 163)

But Carlowitz remains a republican, and at the end of the novel, Smith describes him engaged in friendly discourse with d'Alonville: the Pole convinced that "worth alone is true nobility and true honor" and intent on returning home to "rouse the dormant or timid virtue of his country" (II, 172); d'Alonville remaining equally adamant against republican philosophy. Ellesmere, who had been wounded in battle on the continent, speaks the position of the author.

He adheres "to that system of government as the best under which his own country had become the most flourishing in the world," but "he seldom thought the bold assertions of Carlowitz were carried too far" (II, 172-173). Through Ellesmere, Smith sums up the views of moderate British republicans in a letter to d'Alonville: "*You* think, that even in its first germination it [the French Revolution] threatened to become the monster we now see. . . . I still think, that originating from the acknowledged faults of your former government, the first design, aiming only at the correction of these faults, at a limited monarchy and a mixed government, was the most sublime and most worthy [purpose] of a great people" (II, 321).

Smith provides an amusing political polarity in Sir Maynard Ellesmere, who is a Tory of the old school, and Mr. Nodes, "whose money was obtained by making buttons." Much to the disgust of Sir Maynard, Nodes "impudently built a better house than Eddisbury Hall itself; placed a bust of Franklin in his vestibule; . . . had Ludlow among his books, quoted Milton to his companions, and drank to the rights of man" (II, 151). He also has pictures of Richard Price and Joseph Priestly in his house, two heroes of the British republican movement. Nodes seems the sort of republican one might have met at meetings of the local revolution society.

The conservative magazine *The British Critic*, which reviewed few novels, took note of **The Banished Man,** welcoming Smith back into the fold of correct politics. "We must not close this article," the reviewer writes, "without congratulating the lovers of their King and the constitution, in the acquisition of an associate like Mrs. Charlotte Smith. . . . She makes full atonement by the virtues of **The Banished Man,** for the errors of **Desmond.**"38 Both the fact that such a magazine would review Smith's novel at all and the tone of respect for the author demonstrate Smith's status, even though the political views expressed in her novels had damaged her reputation.

Yet the reviewer surely responds only to the sentiments of the novel's hero and ignores those of Carlowitz and Ellesmere. The political dialogues in **The Banished Man,** while not so effectively embedded in the plot as are similar passages in **Desmond,** demonstrate no real difference in the writer's politics. D'Alonville is the most charismatic character in the work, and he expresses political principles appropriate for a French émigré. Smith balances liberal against reactionary views, however, and the tone of the work favors the liberal.

Smith is never specific in her republicanism, and she creates no real political agenda. Her ideas come from Rousseau, Voltaire, Diderot, Montesquieu, and certainly John Locke. She valued liberty and hated tyranny. **Desmond, The Emigrants,** and **The Banished Man** show sympathy for the early ideals of the French Revolution and with the reform movement in England. Her heroes express the sentiments of moderate British republicanism; and one suspects that while Charlotte Smith might not care to dine with her footman (if she had had one), she would certainly have defended him as a fellow citizen and member of the social compact.

Notes

1. *The Prelude,* XI, 108-9, in Knight, 352.

2. A lettre de cachet could bring imprisonment without trial for the person against whom it was issued. Smith, by the way, does not criticize that instrument when Lord Montreville places his erring daughter, Frances Croft, in a French convent via the same device in *Emmeline,* published three years earlier.

3. *The Prelude,* IX, 247-48, in . . . [*The Poetical Works of William Wordsworth,* ed William Knight (London: Macmillan, 1896)], 315.

4. Allene Gregory, in *The French Revolution and the English Novel* (Port Washington, N.Y.: Kennekat Press, 1965), refers to only one British novel that was actually set in France during this time, *The Bastile, or The Adventures of Charles Townley* (1789), and Tompkins cites only *Lindor and Adelaide* (1792), which she describes as a conservative reaction.

5. *Critical Review* 2 (September 1792): 100.

6. Charlotte Smith, *Desmond, a Novel* (New York and London: Garland, 1974), I, i. Further references will be cited in the text.

7. Neither Smith's early biographers nor her letters mention a visit to France at this time. But in a letter to Joel Barlow dated November 18, 1792, she asks him to deliver a note to a friend in Paris and to make an enquiry there for she is "trying to go over in March or April—an enquiry which is so important in this plan on which my *rebellious* heart is set" (Huntington). This and other letters suggest that Smith hoped to leave England.

8. From *Poetical Works,* 4th ed., H. S. Milford (London, Oxford University Press, 1967), V, 388-392.

9. Alfred Cobban, ed., *The Debate on the French Revolution: 1789-1800,* 2d ed. (London: Adam and Charles Black, 1960), 55.

10. Conservative journals, such as *The Anti-Jacobin,* express a level of paranoia in discussing these groups reminiscent of McCarthyism in the United States in the 1950s. Surviving papers suggest that most members were moderate in their reform agenda. But some radical elements had connections with French officials. According to Mary Thrale, "The French were aware of the LCS [London Corresponding Society] and planned that a conquered Britain should have Thomas Hardy as Minister of Police and another prominent LCS member, John Thelwall, as one of the five members of an English *Directoire.*" See *Selections from the Papers of the London Correspond-*

ing Society, 1792-1799 *(London: Cambridge University Press, 1983), xv.

11. Cobban, 64.

12. Paine, an Englishman, had traveled to America in time to help persuade the colonists to establish a new nation with works such as *The American Crisis* and *Common Sense.*

13. Samuel Edwards, *Rebel: A Biography of Tom Paine* (New York: Praeger, 1974), 121.

14. Dorset [*The Lives of the Novelists,* ed. Sir Walter Scott (London and New York: Dent and Sons, n. d.)], 322. Clifford Musgrave notes that the Duc d'Orléans (who later took the name Phillipe Égalité) was in Brighton in 1790, temporarily exiled by Louis XVI because of his republican sentiments. Brighton seems to have been a resort for Anglophile French for several years before the revolution, many of whom, no doubt, brought the radical thought of the continent to the city. See *Life in Brighton from the Earliest Times to the Present* (London: 1970), 105-106.

15. That Smith was acquainted with Williams can be demonstrated by one of Wordsworth's letters. He mentions stopping to see Smith in Brighton before leaving England for France in 1791. He reports that Smith treated him cordially and gave him a letter of introduction to Williams. See Ernest de Selincourt, *The Early Letters of William and Dorothy Wordsworth (1787-1805)* (Oxford: Oxford University Press, 1935), I, 66-67.

16. Helen Maria Williams, *Letters from France* (Delmar, N.Y.: Scholars' Facsimiles and Reprints, 1955), II, 52. This edition condenses eight volumes to two.

17. See Simon Schama, *Citizens: A Chronicle of the French Revolution* (New York: Vintage Books, 1989) for a fascinating and brief discussion of the flamboyant Mirabeau. Smith's and Williams's admiration for the man probably stems from his relative conservatism. He spoke in favor of a constitutional monarchy, but Schama (532-534) and other historians note that Mirabeau was in the pay of the king.

18. *The Analytical Review* 13 (August 1792), 428.

19. Williams, Smith, and others refer to Henry IV repeatedly as a model king, and they apparently got this perception from French reformers in the early stages of the Revolution, when many assumed that a constitutional monarchy might be the best model. Peter Burke reports that Good King Henry's name came up often in the *Cahiers* (letters from the provinces solicited by the Estates-General) as the sort of ruler the nation needed. See *Popular Culture in Early Modern Europe* (New York: NYU Press, 1978), 151.

20. James Boswell, *Life of Samuel Johnson* (New York: Heritage Press, 1963), I, Aetat 54: 317.

21. Jean-Jacques Rousseau, *The Social Contract and Discourses,* trans. G. D. H. Cole (New York: Everyman's Library, 1950), 311.

22. Cited in Goodwin, 539.

23. Jerome D. Wilson and William F. Ricketson, *Thomas Paine* (Boston: Twayne, 1989), 82.

24. Doyle, *The Oxford History of the French Revolution,* 130. The metaphor of the liberty tree manured with blood was probably a popular expression of the day. Thomas Jefferson's statement from a letter to W. S. Smith written in 1787, "The tree of liberty must be refreshed from time to time with the blood of patriots and tyrants. It is its natural manure," is another variation, although the earlier date is puzzling. See J. P. Foley, ed., *The Jefferson Cyclopedia* (New York: Russell and Russell, 1900), I, 499. Smith uses the metaphor again in *Marchmont,* when Althea comments on the death of a friend's husband who had gone "in search of a higher fortune . . . to those climates where the soil, manured with blood, seems to produce only disease and death" (III, 58). And a long footnote in *The Young Philosopher* details the sins of European kings, noting that "England . . . has seen its best blood manure its fields" in wars begun by tyrannical rulers (I, 88).

25. The asterisks are present in the text and result from a printer's error in this edition.

26. Allusions to the paintings of Salvator Rosa became *de rigueur* in gothic fiction.

27. In a curious letter at the end of the novel, Montfleuri declares his passion for Fanny in a letter to Desmond, which makes the sexuality of his response quite apparent, as opposed to Desmond's disinterested love for Geraldine. Montfleuri jokingly refers to Mrs. Waverley's concerns about his financial prospects and the danger to Fanny's soul in marrying a Catholic. He then affirms that her soul is not the object of his desire: "I shall not lead [her] out of the path that has been followed by the *souls of her ancestors,* or divert, from any other, it may like better to follow—*My* ambition lying quite in *another line.*" Later in the letter he writes, "My Fanni is a little angel, and I must have her—There is a good many chances of being reasonably happy with her, at least, for three or four years, and that is as much as any body has a right to expect" (III, 237-240). Perhaps Smith intended to contrast Montfleuri's carnal passion and clear-eyed realism about sexual attraction to Desmond's purer love, or perhaps she indulges in cultural stereotypes. But this "man talk" about women was unique in British sentimental fiction of the time, where sexual references were disguised by the language of sensibility.

28. Schama, 153.

29. Lefebvre, I, 241-242.

30. In a letter to Joseph Cooper Walker dated December 16, 1792, to an unnamed correspondent, Smith mentions "a Poem in two Books—which I am writing—about 1000 verses I think—& which will be sold

here in quarto at 4. and then printed in a small edition to make a second volume to the Sonnets and other poems already published" (Huntington).

31. Curran [*The Poems of Charlotte Smith*, ed. Stuart Curran (New York and Oxford: Oxford University Press, 1993)], 133-134. Since the poem is organized into two books, citations are to volume and line number in Curran's edition.

32. See Schama, 49 ff, for a discussion of the inequities of income between high officials of the church and lower clergy.

33. Smith's comment about the excesses of the masses in France is probably another republican commonplace. Mary Wollstonecraft suggests that the excesses of the mob in Paris stems from centuries of repression in her *Historical and Moral View of the Origin and Progress of the French Revolution* (1794).

34. In a letter to Joseph Cooper Walker dated January 20, 1794, she mentions having finished the first volume of "the Novel called 'The Exile'" (Huntington). Apparently she later changed the title to *The Banished Man*.

35. Reviewers had begun to note the number of errors in Smith's texts. She scolded William Davies in letters for sloppy work by his compositors, who, she writes, had "suffer'd many words to pass, which are not in English or any other language" in *The Banished Man* (August 29, 1794, Beinecke).

36. Du Fosse was the friend with whom Helen Maria Williams stayed in France. There seems no connection between him and Smith's turncoat aristocrat other than the fictional character's rejection of the ancien régime.

37. See R. R. Palmer, *The Age of the Democratic Revolution*, vol. 1 (New Brunswick, N.J.: Princeton University Press: 1959), 411-435, for a discussion of Polish Jacobinism.

38. *The British Critic* 4 (December 1794): 623. The early approval of *Desmond* soon changed, as evidenced by a letter from William Cowper to William Hayley written in 1793: "There goes a rumour likewise which I have with equal confidence gainsaid, that Mrs. Smith wrote her *Desmond* bribed to it by the democratic party, by whom they say she is now actually supported." Cowper also reports rumors that Hayley actually wrote *Desmond*. See *The Correspondence of William Cowper*, ed. Thomas Wright (New York: Haskell House, 1969), IV, 407-408.

Selected Bibliography

PRIMARY SOURCES

Curran, Stuart, ed. *The Poems of Charlotte Smith*. New York and Oxford: Oxford University Press, 1993. Contains nearly all the original poems published in the nine editions of *Elegiac Sonnets* during Smith's lifetime, as well as *The Emigrants, Beachy Head,* some of the children's poems, and the prologue to William Godwin's play *Antonio*. Also has an excellent introductory discussion of Smith's poems.

Smith, Charlotte. *The Banished Man*. 2d ed. 2 vols. London: Cadell, 1795. Cadell published the first edition in 1794.

———. *Beachy Head, with Other Poems*. London: Johnson, 1807.

———. *Beachy Head, with Other Poems*. New York: Scholars' Facsimiles and Reprints, 1993. Introduction by Terrence Hoagwood.

———. *Celestina, a Novel*. 3 vols. Dublin: Cadell, 1791.

———. *Conversations, Introducing Poetry; Chiefly on Subjects of Natural History for the Use of Children and Young Persons*. 2 vols. London: Johnson, 1804.

———. *Desmond, a Novel*. 3 vols. London: J. Robinson, 1792.

———. *Desmond, a Novel*. 3 vols. New York and London: Garland, 1974. Introduction by Gina Luria.

———. *Elegiac Sonnets*. London: Dodsley, 1784. Eight more editions would appear in Smith's lifetime.

———. *Emmeline, or The Orphan of the Castle*. Cadell: London, 1788.

———. *Emmeline, or The Orphan of the Castle*. London: Oxford English Novels, 1971. Introduction by Ann Ehrenpreis.

———. *Ethelinde, or The Recluse of the Lake*. 5 vols. London: Cadell, 1789.

———. *History of England, from the Earliest Records to the Peace of Amiens: In a Series of Letters to a Young Lady at School*. London: 1806. 3 vols. Vol. 1 and 2 by Smith; vol. 3 by Charlotte Mary Smith.

———. *Letters of a Solitary Wanderer, Containing Narratives of Various Descriptions*. 5 vols. London: Sampson Low, 1800.

———. *Marchmont, a Novel*. 4 vols. London: Low, 1796.

———. *Marchmont, a Novel*. 4 vols. in one. New York: Scholars' Facsimiles, 1989. Introduction by Mary Anne Schofield.

———. *Minor Morals, interspersed with sketches of natural history, historical anecdotes, and original stories*.

———. *Montalbert, a Novel*. 3 vols. London: Lowe, 1796.

———. *Montalbert, a Novel*. 3 vols. in one. New York: Scholars' Facsimiles, 1989. Introduction by Mary Ann Schofield.

———. *A Narrative of the Loss of the Catherine, Venus and Piedmont Transports, and the Thomas, Golden Grove and Aeolus Merchant Ships Near Weymouth*. London: Sampson Low, 1795.

———. *The Natural History of Birds, Intended Chiefly for Young Persons.* London: Johnson, 1807.

———. *The Old Manor House, a Novel.* London: J. Bell, 1793.

———. *The Old Manor House, a Novel.* Edited by Anne Henry Ehrenpreis. London: Oxford English Novels, 1969. Ehrenpreis includes an introduction.

———. *Rambles Farther: A Continuation of Rural Walks: In Dialogues Intended for the Use of Young Persons.* 2 vols. London: Cadell and Davies, 1796.

———. *The Romance of Real Life.* 2 vols. Dublin: 1787. A translation of *Les Causes Célèbres*.

———. *Rural Walks: In Dialogues Intended for the Use of Young Persons.* 2 vols. London: Cadell and Davies, 1795.

———. *The Wanderings of Warwick.* London: J. Bell, 1794.

———. *What Is She.* In *Modern Theatre.* Edited by Elizabeth Inchbald. 10 vols. London: Hurst Rees, Orme, and Brown, 1811. Attribution is uncertain.

———. *The Young Philosopher, A Novel.* London: Cadell and Davies, 1798.

———. *The Young Philosopher, a Novel.* 4 vols. New York: Garland, 1974. Introduction by Gina Luria.

Letters

Beinecke Library, Yale University. New Haven, Conn. Charlotte Smith's Letters.

Harvard Library. Cambridge, Mass. Charlotte Smith's Letters.

Huntington Library. San Merino, Calif. Charlotte Smith's Letters.

Princeton University Library. Princeton, N.J. Charlotte Smith's Letters.

Secondary Sources

Barbauld, Anna Laetitia. Introduction to *The Old Manor House.* London: F. C. and I. Rivington, 1820. Vol. 36 and 37 in Barbauld's British Novelists series.

Bowstead, Diana. "Charlotte Smith's *Desmond*: The Epistolary Novel as Ideological Argument." In *Fetter'd or Free? British Women Novelists, 1670-1815,* edited by Mary Anne Schofield and Cecilia Macheski. Athens: Ohio University Press, 1986. Bowstead finds that Smith used narrative voice in order to present a number of distinctive political positions. Brief mention of Smith's works appears in other essays of the collection.

Bray, Matthew. "Removing the Anglo-Saxon Yoke: The Francocentric Vision of Charlotte Smith's Later Work." *Wordsworth Circle* 43 (1993): 155-158. Bray argues that Smith's later works, including her children's books, demonstrate "a vision that went against the patriotic Anglo-Saxonism" current in England during the war with France.

Brydges, Samuel Egerton. *Censura Literaria.* Vol. 7. London, 1815. Brydges, a poet himself, was acquainted with Smith and defends her against those who disliked her political views.

Curran, Stuart. "The I Altered." In *Romanticism and Feminism,* edited by Anne K. Mellor. Bloomington: Indiana University Press, 1988. Curran places Smith in the context of other women poets of the late 18th century and the development of romanticism.

Dorset, Catherine Ann. "Charlotte Smith." In Sir Walter Scott. *The Lives of the Novelists.* London and New York: Everyman Library, n.d. Dorset, Smith's sister, wrote this biographical essay, which Scott included preceding his evaluation of the author's novels.

Foster, James R. "Charlotte Smith, Pre-Romantic Novelist." *PMLA* [*Publications of the Modern Language Association of America*], 43 (1928): 463-475.

———. *History of the Pre-Romantic Novel in England.* New York: *PMLA* [*Publications of the Modern Language Association*], 1949.

Fry, Carrol L. *Charlotte Smith: Popular Novelist.* New York: Arno, 1980.

Hilbish, Florence M. A. *Charlotte Smith: Poet and Novelist.* Philadelphia: University of Pennsylvania Press, 1941. An excellent biography with copious references to letters and other historical documents.

Kavanagh, Julia. "Charlotte Smith." In *English Women of Letters: Biographical Sketches,* Vol. 1. London: Hurst and Blackett, 1863.

Phillips, Richard. *British Public Characters of 1800-1801.* Vol. 3. London, 1798. The discussion is apparently based on an interview with Smith.

Rogers, Katherine M. "Inhibitions on Eighteenth-Century Women Novelists: Elizabeth Inchbald and Charlotte Smith." *Eighteenth-Century Studies* 11 (1988): 63-79.

———. *Feminism in Eighteenth-Century England.* Urbana: University of Illinois Press, 1982. A fine study of the work of women writers in this period, with insightful commentary on Smith's works.

Scott, Sir Walter. "Charlotte Smith." In *The Lives of the Novelists.* London and New York: Dent, n.d. Scott's discussion offers interesting insights into a more or less contemporary perspective on Smith's work.

Stanton, Judith. "Charlotte Smith's Literary Business: Income, Patronage, and Indigence." *The Age of Johnson: A Scholarly Annual* 6 (1987): 375-401. Stanton's study of Smith's correspondence offers interesting insights into the career of letters in the 1790s, as well as the author's life.

Tompkins, J. M. S. *The Popular Novel in England 1770-1800.* Lincoln: University of Nebraska Press, 1961. A thorough study of the British novel from 1770 to the early 1800s.

Zimmerman, Sarah. "Charlotte Smith's Letters and the Practice of Self-Presentation." *Princeton University Library Chronicle* 53 (1991): 50-77. Zimmerman uses Smith's letters to show the author's establishment of a public image.

Brent Raycroft (essay date 1998)

SOURCE: Raycroft, Brent. "From Charlotte Smith to Nehemiah Higginbottom: Revising the Genealogy of the Early Romantic Sonnet." *European Romantic Review* 9, no. 3 (summer 1998): 363-92.

[*In the following essay, Raycroft examines Smith's long absence from the literary canon and her recent reinstatement as one of the earliest Romantic poets.*]

I

This essay is primarily about writing Charlotte Smith back into the history of the early Romantic sonnet, but it is structured around a group of texts, critical and poetic, from the work of Samuel Taylor Coleridge. After sketching briefly the interconnected fame of Charlotte Smith and William Lisle Bowles, I introduce in this first section Coleridge's primary reference to Smith and a number of his more copious references to William Lisle Bowles, the latter constituting what I call the Coleridge-Bowles connection. Most of these citations are clustered in the mid-1790's, the main exception being Coleridge's discussion of Bowles's influence in the first chapter of the *Biographia Literaria,* published some twenty years later in 1817, a passage which has become a crux as well as a curiosity of Romantic literary history. In the third section of this essay my argument focusses on three parodic sonnets known as the Higginbottom sonnets, after their pseudonymous author "Nehemiah Higginbottom." These sonnets bridge the gap between the early and the later Coleridge: they were published first in the *Monthly Magazine* in 1797, but they appear again in the first chapter of the *Biographia Literaria,* just after the discussion of Bowles's poetry. In Coleridge's main text he "owns" the parodies and to some extent explicates them; the poems themselves are republished in a long footnote to the passage. In preparation for my reading of the Higginbottom sonnets, I devote the second section of this essay to a comparison of the sonnet-writing styles of Charlotte Smith and William Lisle Bowles, presenting a number of sonnets in their entirety. My overall purpose is to show that the recanonization of Charlotte Smith that has occurred in recent years opens up new ways of understanding the development of the early Romantic sonnet, and suspends some long-held and still functional certainties about the roles and the players in that development.

In *Poetic Form and British Romanticism* (1986), Stuart Curran observes that the "re-birth" of the sonnet in the late eighteenth century "coincides with the rise of a definable women's literary movement and with the beginnings of Romanticism. The palm in both cases should go to Charlotte Turner Smith" (30). With the appearance of Curran's landmark edition of the *Poems of Charlotte Smith* in 1993, this estimate of Smith's importance has been largely confirmed. In his introduction Curran opens with a claim that could not have been made ten years earlier, and which even now may surprise some readers: "Charlotte Smith was the first poet in England whom in retrospect we would call Romantic" (xix). Implicitly and explicitly, the present essay is in agreement. But I also want to show that this "retrospect," this retroactivity that Curran quietly inserts into his estimation of Smith as the "first" Romantic poet, measures a collective failure of criticism, not Smith's own failure to make a contemporary impact. Restoring her to her rightful place in the history of the sonnet will involve more than re-instatement and archaic "palms." Smith's long absence from the canon of Romantic poetry is a literary phenomenon worth examining in itself, and we find that it has as much to do with positive structures of exclusion as with simple neglect. One of these structures of exclusion is the Coleridge-Bowles connection, a central genealogical link in the history of the Romantic sonnet, constructed by Samuel Taylor Coleridge, celebrated by nineteenth-century literary historians, and reiterated in the twentieth century by influential critics such as W. K. Wimsatt and M. H. Abrams. Even Stuart Curran, Smith's most insightful and authoritative modern-day defender, has been swayed by the narrative implicit in the Coleridge-Bowles construct, at least in his earlier work. In a recent essay on Smith, Curran suggests that she is "the single most important voice that has been until quite recently suppressed from the historical record" ("Charlotte Smith and British Romanticism" 71). But in *Poetic Form and British Romanticism,* after awarding the palm of innovation to Smith, he evidences the "reborn" sonnet by printing, not one of hers, but one of William Lisle Bowles's.

Between their first publication in 1784 and the author's death in 1806, Charlotte Smith's *Elegiac Sonnets* were among the most popular and critically esteemed examples of the form. As early as 1786, a critic for the *Gentleman's Magazine* wrote that "[a] very trifling compliment is paid Mrs. Smith, when it is observed how much her Sonnets exceed those of *Shakespeare* and *Milton* . . ." (56:334). The *Critical Review* was only reiterating a prevailing opinion when it stated in 1802 that "[t]he sonnet has been revived by Charlotte Smith: her sonnets are assuredly the most popular in the language, and deservedly so" (34:393). Such estimates were not unanimous, of course. Anna Seward, a rival female sonneteer, wrote to a friend: "All the lines that are not the lines of others are weak and unimpressive; and these hedge-flowers to be preferred, by a critical dictator, to the roses and amaranths of the first poets the world has produced!!!—It makes me sick" (*Letters* 1:163).

The full title of W. L. Bowles's first, anonymous, edition of sonnets in 1789 was *Fourteen Sonnets. Elegiac and Descriptive,* employing a key word from Smith's title. His second edition of 1789 was retitled *Sonnets Written Chiefly in Picturesque Spots, during a tour* and was no longer anonymous. In fact, Bowles found it necessary to deny Smith's influence:

> It having been said that these Pieces were written in Imitation of the little Poems of Mrs *Smyth* [sic], the Author hopes he may be excused adding that *many* of them were written prior to Mrs Smyth's Publication. He is conscious of their great Inferiority to those beautiful and elegant compositions; but, such as they are, they were certainly written from his own feelings.
>
> [i]

Bowles's rather forced claim for linear priority plainly begs the question of whether the greater originality does not lie with Smith, and indeed her sonnets appeared in print five years before his. Bowles's sonnets, like Smith's, were very popular: nine editions of his 1789 volume (gradually augmented, also like Smith's) had been printed by 1805. Popularity worked against the literary reputations of both poets, however, as they were held responsible for the sustained vogue of melancholy sonnets in the late 1780s and early 1790s. By 1793 the *Monthly Review* was complaining that the sonnet had been "so much cultivated of late years . . . especially since Mr. Bowles and Mrs. Smith have gratified the public ear . . . that, to say the truth, we begin to be almost satiated with *sonnets*" (10:114). Note that the similarity of the two poets makes them interchangeable, so that by an innocuous sleight of hand Bowles's contribution can be listed first. Charles Lamb evinced even greater dislike for the fashion of melancholy sonnets when he made the following observation in a letter to Robert Lloyd in 1798:

> You may extract honey from everything; do not go a gathering after gall—the bees are wiser in their generation than the race of sonnet writers & complainers, Bowless & Charlotte Smiths, & all that tribe, who can see no joys but what are past, and fill peoples' heads with notions of the Unsatisfying nature of Earthly comforts. . . .
>
> (*Letters* 1:144)

Unlike Lamb and the *Monthly Review,* Coleridge at least puts Smith and Bowles in their right chronological order in his "Introduction to the Sonnets" of 1796. In the following year, Coleridge would protest in his own way the fashion of high melancholy in the sonnet by writing his Higginbottom parodies.

In Coleridge's "Introduction to the Sonnets" he makes the judgment that "Charlotte Smith and Bowles are they who first made the Sonnet popular among the present English; I am justified therefore . . . in deducing its laws from *their* compositions." The laws of this new sonnet, as Coleridge formulates them, are more thematic than technical. First of all, this new sonnet is "a small poem, in which some lonely feeling is developed." Formally it is based on the irregular tradition of Surrey and Shakespeare, rather than the stricter Petrarchan model, and the "most exquisite" are those "in which moral Sentiments, Affections, or Feelings, are deduced from, and associated with, the scenery of Nature" (*Poetical Works* 2:1139). In the small anthology that originally accompanied the "Introduction to the Sonnets," Smith appeared in the company not only of Bowles, but of Coleridge, Southey, and Lamb as well. The collection was never published in quantity, but Coleridge's "Introduction to the Sonnets" survived as an appendix to the second and several later editions of his *Poems.* Curiously enough, the year before Coleridge wrote his "Introduction," Charlotte Smith had herself placed Bowles's sonnets next to her own, in her first book for children, **Rural Walks** (1795). There is a scene where two students, Caroline and Elizabeth, recite sonnets they have memorized. Caroline's sonnet is one of Bowles's, a revised version "lately published" of his sonnet 4 "To the River Wenbeck." Elizabeth, "avowing her inferiority both in choice and manner," recites Smith's own **"Sonnet 4" "To the Moon"** (1:130-131).

Two powerful factors in the declining reputation of Smith's sonnets—and Bowles's as well—were the appearance of the sonnets of the major Romantics and a simultaneous shift in the canon of older poetry revalorizing the sonnets of Shakespeare and Milton. In the decades after Smith's death in 1806, the competition became very tough indeed. But there were other contributing factors. One that did not affect Bowles was the deep-set prejudice against admitting women into the mainstream of literary history. For many male critics it was scandalous enough that female writers should be enjoying *popular* success. Another factor was Smith's politics: unlike the conservative Bowles, Smith's position was somewhere between liberal and radical, and she staunchly supported the original intentions of the French Revolution even after England and France were at war. The contributing factor that I am most concerned with in this essay, though, is Coleridge's acknowledgement of debt to the poetry of William Lisle Bowles, both in his early writing and in the *Biographia Literaria.* Not only does Coleridge not mention Charlotte Smith in the *Biographia Literaria,* he praises Bowles in a way that doubly displaces her, contradicting his statements in the "Introduction to the Sonnets" and effectively undoing what he had done there to acknowledge her place in the development of the contemporary sonnet. Much more influential as literary criticism than the "Introduction to the Sonnets," which was out of print between 1803 and 1912, the *Biographia Literaria* continues to stand as an obstacle between Charlotte Smith's sonnets and her potential modern readers.

In his "Introduction to the Sonnets" Coleridge acknowledged Smith's role in the development of the contemporary sonnet as co-equal with, even prior to, the role played by Bowles. But in Coleridge's *personal* estimate, Bowles came first. Even in the "Introduction to the Sonnets" he is categorical: Bowles's sonnets possess a "marked superiority over all other sonnets." His reasons? "[T]hey domesticate with the heart and become part of our identity" (*Poetical Works* 2:1139). In *Poems on Various Subjects,* the first of the sonnets—or "Effusions" as they are called in the first edition—was a sonnet to Bowles:

> My heart has thank'd thee, Bowles! for those soft strains,
>   That on the still air floating, tremblingly
>   Wak'd in me Fancy, Love, and Sympathy . . .
>
>   . . . . .
>
>   And, when the *darker* day of life began,
>   And I did roam, a thought-bewilder'd man!
>   Thy kindred Lays an healing solace lent. . . .
>
> (*Poetical Works* 1:84)

The closing couplet recalls nothing less than the Creation, as Bowles's soothing influence on Coleridge is likened to "that great Spirit, who with plastic sweep / Mov'd on the darkness of the unformed deep."

With Coleridge's revision of this poem for his second edition of 1797, we have the first instance of what would become an insistent gender distinction. Coleridge again thanks Bowles for "those soft strains, / Whose sadness soothes me" but re-writes what follows, so that when

>   . . . the mightier throes of mind began,
> And drove me forth, a thought-bewildered man,
> Their mild and manliest melancholy lent
> A mingled charm, as the pang consigned
> To slumber. . . .
>
> (*Poetical Works* 1:12)

In the first edition of *Poems on Various Subjects,* Coleridge says that he calls his sonnets "Effusions" because "the title 'Sonnet' might have reminded my reader of the Poems of the Rev. W. L. Bowles—a comparison with whom would have sunk me below that mediocrity, on the surface of which I am at present enabled to float" (2:1137). But in the second edition of *Poems on Various Subjects* (1797), Coleridge dares the comparison he pretended to avoid earlier. The sonnet to Bowles continues to appear first, but the section is now entitled "Sonnets, / *Attempted in the Manner* / Of the Rev. W. L. Bowles" (2:1146). Coleridge's admiration of Bowles—"the bard of my idolatry," as he describes him in a letter to Thelwall in 1796 (*Letters* 1:259)—seems to have been partly an affectation from the beginning, genuine enough at some level, but strategically exaggerated.

As early as 1792 Coleridge had admitted to being "shocked" at the revisions Bowles was making in a new edition: "Every Omission and every alteration disgusts Taste & mangles Sensibility" (*Letters* 1:94). And by 1794 he was treating his penchant for Bowles with some levity, quoting himself in conversation with Thomas Holcroft: "Come—come—Mr Holcroft—as much unintelligible Metaphysics and as much bad Criticism as you please—but no *Blasphemy* against the divinity of *a Bowles!*" (*Letters* 1:139). In a letter of 1802 he complains of Bowles's "perpetual trick of *moralizing* every thing" (*Letters* 2:864). The comment turns immediately to a more general critique:

> never to see or describe any interesting appearance in nature, without connecting it by dim analogies with the moral world, proves faintness of Impression. . . . A Poet's *Heart and Intellect* should be *combined,* intimately combined & *unified,* with the great appearances in Nature—& not merely held in solution & loose mixture with them. . . . The truth is—Bowles has indeed the *sensibility* of a poet; but he has not the *Passion* of a great Poet."
>
> (*Letters* 2:864-5)

Coleridge may have outgrown his youthful devotion to Bowles's poetry, but the developmental significance of the lesson learned from it is emphasized again in 1817, in his discussion of Bowles's influence in the first chapter of the *Biographia Literaria.*

The opening topic of the *Biographia Literaria* is the effect of living authors on a young writer. From the outset, Coleridge describes his topic in a way that effectively and quietly excludes Charlotte Smith: "the writings of a contemporary . . . surrounded by the same circumstances, and disciplined by the same manners, possess a reality for him, and inspire an actual friendship as of a man for a man" (161).[1] Bowles's appeal is described as primarily stylistic, but with a profound psychological importance. In what amounts to a prose retelling of the early sonnet to Bowles, complete with the stress on gender, Coleridge portrays his youthful self as "bewildered . . . in metaphysics, and in theological controversy," (1:15) a state from which he was "auspiciously withdrawn . . . by the genial influence of a style of poetry, so tender, and yet so *manly,* so natural and real, and yet so dignified, and harmonious, as the sonnets, etc. of Mr Bowles!" (1:17 [italics added]). In the *Biographia Literaria* Coleridge takes a sober and distanced view of a fondness he had previously mocked, and the encounter with Bowles's poetry is thus written into his developmental autobiography as the first step toward psychic health. The personal significance is now also given a corresponding significance in the history of poetry, one with broader implications than the sonnet innovations Coleridge discussed in 1796: Bowles is given part credit for the very Romantic achievement of "combin[ing] natural thoughts with natural diction; [and] reconcil[ing] the heart with the head" (*Biographia Literaria* 1:24).

The decades of Charlotte Smith's greatest obscurity, between 1880 and 1920, were also the decades in which "British Romanticism" began to be formulated as a coherent period in academic discourse. *A Brief Handbook of English Authors* (1889), by Oscar Fay Adams, succinctly illustrates the occlusion of Charlotte Smith by the figure of Bowles during this period. The entry for Smith simply says "**Elegiac Sonnets** are her principal poems, and **The Old Manor House** is her best novel" (129); the entry for Bowles calls him "A graceful writer, to whom Wordsworth and Coleridge attributed their own poetic inspiration" (14). This, I think, is the earliest categorical statement of a stubborn misconception that would become more "factual" as it became less overstated: Bowles's influence on Wordsworth. C. H. Herford, in *The Age of Wordsworth* (1897), makes no mention of Charlotte Smith, but says that Bowles "will always be remembered as having fascinated both poets" (183). The *Harvard Classics* series of 1910 includes no poetry from Charlotte Smith, but Bowles's sonnet "Dover Cliffs" is printed immediately after the long selection of Wordsworth's poetry (41:697), like an endnote to a source.

Perhaps the most exorbitant positioning of Bowles's star in relation to his contemporaries is T. E. Casson's long essay "William Lisle Bowles" in *Eighteenth Century Literature: An Oxford Miscellany* (1909), reprinted as late as 1966:

> In the transition from the poetry of the eighteenth century to the poetry of the Romantic Movement, no critic has been able to put down his finger and say, 'Here the old ended, the new began'. . . . But no critic could deny the importance of the *Lyrical Ballads,* as the unmistakable manifesto of the later poetry. If, then, by his art a poet can be shown to have affected the two authors of that book, he may be reasonably regarded as having borne a share in the creation of the new forms.
>
> (151)

Casson reminds us that in Bowles's 1806 edition of Pope, he defended a poetics of Nature against Pope's poetics of Art, and raised the indignation of many readers, including Lord Byron. Thus "he may be said to have contributed, not only to the inception of another practice, but also to the erection of a new theory. Such a poet, and such a critic, was Bowles . . ." (151). Casson mentions Charlotte Smith only once, and it is not to credit her with any "inception" or "erection." Her name appears because he needs to quote the "Introduction to the Sonnets," where Coleridge "deduces" the laws of the melancholy sonnet from Smith and Bowles. Casson follows with, "legislation by such deductions would not satisfy the rigid historical critic" (160), implying that Coleridge was right about Bowles, but wrong about Charlotte Smith. As evidence that "Bowles was a definitively formative influence on Wordsworth" (167) Casson cites the following from Bowles's *Monody at Matlock* (1791):

> Nor may I, sweet dream!
> From thy wild banks and still retreats depart
> (Where now I meditate my casual theme)
> With out some mild improvement on my heart
> Poured sad, yet pleasing! so may I forget
> The crosses and the cares that sometimes fret
> Life's smoothest channel.

This, we are told, is "the very sentiment of the *Lines at Tintern Abbey*" (165).

The closest Wordsworth came to acknowledging an influence from Bowles was when he said to Samuel Rogers: "When Bowles's Sonnets first appeared,—a thin 4to [quarto] pamphlet, entitled *Fourteen Sonnets,*—I bought them in a walk through London with my dear brother, who was afterwards drowned at sea. I read them as we went along; and to the great annoyance of my brother, I stopped in a niche of London Bridge to finish the pamphlet" (*Recollections of the Table-Talk of Samuel Rogers* 261n).

Rogers's recollection has often been cited as evidence of Bowles's influence on the young Wordsworth. But as Jonathan Wordsworth observes in his introduction to the recent reprint of Bowles's *Fourteen Sonnets,* "The occasion seems to have been remembered more for John [Wordsworth's brother] . . . than for the poetry" ([I]). Though Jonathan Wordsworth is to this extent sceptical of the traditional reading of the anecdote, he follows custom by citing it without its deflating last sentence, which evidences no particular admiration on William Wordsworth's part: "Bowles' short pieces are his best: his long poems are rather *flaccid*" (Rogers 261n). In 1833 Wordsworth would use the contrast between himself and Bowles to qualify his appraisal of the poetry of a friend, the publisher Edward Moxon: "In the cadence and execution of your Sonnets, I seem to find more of the manner of Bowles' than my own, and this you must not think a disparagement, as Bowles in his sonnets has been very successful" (*Letters* 5:616). Despite such evidence, it became a commonplace of literary history in the late nineteenth and early twentieth century that an important influence was exerted on Wordsworth by W. L. Bowles.[2] Recently there has been some realignment. In the 1992 reprint of Smith's ***Elegiac Sonnets,*** Jonathan Wordsworth notes that "in her temperament she is as clearly Wordsworth's predecessor as Bowles is Coleridge's" ([iv]).[3] Even this generous division of labour stops short of acknowledging that Smith may have influenced Coleridge as well as Wordsworth, and earlier than either of them could have been influenced by Bowles.

II

An argument could be made that Smith's sonnets are simply better poems than Bowles's sonnets, and to some extent I make that argument in what follows. But it is just as important—especially for my reading of the Higginbottom parodies—to emphasize that Smith and Bowles were similar sonneteers, roughly equal in talent and in style. As Bowles sensed in his defensive advertisement to his second edition, it is their resemblance which establishes so decisively Smith's priority and originality. To rehearse the comparison in any detail may seem a trivial or even an unkind exercise, especially as Bowles has so often been used to provide a qualitative contrast with the major Romantics. But Bowles's privileged role in the received history of the Romantic sonnet is precisely what makes such a comparison illuminating.

I will begin by looking at the sonnet that Coleridge placed first in his early sonnet anthology,[4] a Bowles sonnet entitled "At Oxford, 1786":

> Bereave me not of Fancy's shadowy dreams,
>   Which won my heart, or when the gay career
>   Of life begun, or when at times a tear
> Sat sad on memory's cheek—though loftier themes
> Await the wakened mind to the high prize
>   Of wisdom, hardly earned with toil and pain,
>   Aspiring patient; yet on life's wide plain
> Left fatherless, where many a wanderer sighs

> Hourly, and oft our road is lone and long,
>   'Twere not a crime should we a while delay
>   Amid the sunny field; and happier they
> Who, as they journey, woo the charm of song,
> To cheer their way;—till they forget to weep,
> And the tired sense is hushed, and sinks to sleep.
>
>   (*Poetical Works* 1:23)

An appropriate sonnet for direct comparison (although not one that appeared in Coleridge's anthology) is Smith's **"Sonnet 47," "To Fancy,"** which addresses the same subject:

> Thee, Queen of Shadows!—shall I still invoke,
>   Still love the scene thy sportive pencil drew,
> When on mine eyes the early radiance broke
>   Which shew'd the beauteous rather than the true!
> Alas! long since those glowing tints are dead,
>   And now 'tis thine in darkest hues to dress
> The spot where pale Experience hangs her head
>   O'er the sad grave of murder'd Happiness!
> Thro' thy false medium, then, no longer view'd,
>   May fancied pain and fancied pleasure fly,
>   And I, as from me all thy dreams depart,
> Be to my wayward destiny subdued:
>   Nor seek perfection with a poet's eye,
>   Nor suffer anguish with a poet's heart!
>
>   (*Poems* 44)

Both sonnets are self-consciously melancholy, but Bowles's poem is less austere in sentiment and essentially optimistic in tone. Smith's sonnet is typically bleak and hyperbolic. In Bowles's poem the psychological process praised by the speaker—the indulging of Fancy's dreams—is legitimized by generalization to a "happier they" who also sing in the face of adversity. Smith's sonnet, despite its personifications and abstractions, remains particular, with a sustained focus on the poet's own "wayward destiny."

Each of these sonnets enacts a paradox of the age of sensibility: Smith's poem attempts to reject fancy's intensification of feelings, but at the same time is a creative indulgence in poetic language and the intensification of feeling. Bowles's optimistic stance, while attempting a defence of Fancy, verges on becoming an example of the "charm of song" that lulls a "happier they"—not quite the poet or the reader—to sleep. In this sense his poem is indeed soothing, if not soporific. At the same time, though, Bowles's lack of emotional focus permits him a greater discursive range, and he notes that "loftier themes await the awakened mind," an appeal to readers who, like Coleridge, aspired to the "high prize of wisdom" as well as fancy's consolations. Reflective distance between speaker and subject has little place in Charlotte Smith's sonnet. The "gay" and "sad" options that Bowles lists in his opening lines are for her irreversible phases of existence, and their narration occupies the rhetoric of the poem. If Fancy is "still invoke[d]", she is invoked in the service of an almost ruthlessly rational analysis. There is no room in Smith's plummeting iambs for Bowles's meditative "delay," which is enacted in his sonnet by halting metrical inversions and prosaic qualifications. If there is a distinguishing "manly" quality to this Bowles sonnet, it is significantly *not* high passion, but rather a paternal distance from the subject of suffering.

Coleridge had other criteria than manliness for excellence in the contemporary sonnet. One of these was the use of natural description in connection with moral sentiments. Of the three Bowles sonnets that Coleridge included in his early anthology, the most descriptive of natural phenomena is "At Dover, 1786":

> Thou, whose stern spirit loves the storm,
>   That, borne on Terror's desolating wings,
>   Shakes the high forest, or remorseless flings
> The shivering surge; when rising griefs deform
> Thy peaceful breast, hie to yon steep, and think,—
>   When thou dost mark the melancholy tide
>   Beneath thee, and the storm careering wide,—
> Tossed on the surge of life how many sink!
> And if thy cheek with one kind tear be wet,
>   And if thy heart be smitten, when the cry
>   Of danger and of death is heard more nigh,
> Oh, learn thy private sorrows to forget;
> Intent, when hardest beats the storm, to save
> One who, like thee, has suffered from the wave.
>
>   (*Poetical Works* 1:24)

This is the Bowles sonnet that Stuart Curran prints in his chapter on the sonnet in *Poetic Form and British Romanticism* (33). Having just conceded that Bowles's sonnets "are not sophisticated in subject or form" (31), Curran nonetheless finds in this exemplar "a truly remarkable rhetorical structure, one that continually folds in on itself and exhausts its alternatives in lightning shifts of perspective, denying the resolution it seems so forcefully to posit" (33).

A telling comparison here is with Smith's **"Sonnet 66," "Written in a tempestuous night, on the coast of Sussex,"** a poem which illustrates her descriptive powers and more:

> The night-flood rakes upon the stony shore;
>   Along the rugged cliffs and chalky caves
> Mourns the hoarse Ocean, seeming to deplore
>   All that are buried in his restless waves[.]—
> Mined by corrosive tides, the hollow rock
>   Falls prone, and rushing from its turfy height,
> Shakes the broad beach with long-resounding shock,
>   Loud thundering on the ear of sullen Night;
> Above the desolate and stormy deep,
>   Gleams the wan Moon, by floating mists opprest;
> Yet here while youth, and health, and labour sleep,
>   Alone I wander[.]—Calm untroubled rest,
> "Nature's soft nurse," deserts the sigh-swoln breast,
> And shuns the eyes, that only wake to weep!
>
>   (*Poems* 58)

Again we can see a marked difference, not only in the amount and vividness of natural description, but in the degree of dramatic immediacy and the emotional pitch. Given their contemporaneity and generic proximity, we could even say that there is a rhetorical or conversational relationship between these two poems. The addressee, the "Thou" of Bowles's sonnet is very like the speaker of a typical Charlotte Smith sonnet. "Hie to yon steep" from line 5 of Bowles's sonnet condenses a quasi-suicidal excursion and a poetic topos made conventional by Smith.[5] Smith's **"Sonnet 66"** was actually published later than Bowles "At Dover, 1786," but her style of melancholy had been popular since 1784. Indeed, in this particular comparison, we might say Smith is responding to Bowles as much as the reverse. Coleridge may have admired this Bowles sonnet and placed it first in his early anthology because he felt himself to be among its implied readers—felt an affinity, that is, with the "Thou" that the sonnet addresses. This would align Coleridge's bewildered, pre-Bowlesian self with the inconsolable sensibility of Charlotte Smith.

By "manly" Coleridge apparently did not mean passionate.[6] Perhaps, then, he meant "learned" or "intellectual:" But Bowles's sonnets are more learned than Smith's only in the sense that they are slightly more "regular," making more frequent use of a Petrarchan sestet. And they are more intellectual only in the sense that they grant consolatory power to reflective distance. If combining complexity with clarity can also be called a criterion of intellectual strength, then Smith's sonnets stand up well against Bowles's. And certainly hers are just as successful at associating sentiment with "the scenery of Nature," which was Coleridge's most exclusive criterion in his "Introduction to the Sonnets." Bowles's manliness does conform to a conventional gender distinction, of course, but one that was becoming antiquated in the Age of Sensibility: the dichotomy of the continent man and the incontinent woman, prevalent in the Renaissance. Bowles's sonnets are simply more reserved, more moderate. By the norms of the Age of Sensibility, though, when a man was permitted to be a Man of Feeling, moderation needed some special pleading, especially with a woman poet as a precursor. Bowles's manliness, then, lies not in his fulfilment of Coleridge's ideal for the contemporary sonnet, but simply in his mildness, in the very lack of passion for which Coleridge would later condemn him. Technically and thematically, the difference between the sonnets of Smith and Bowles is clear, if not great. But they did belong to what we call "opposite" sexes, and Coleridge's stress on Bowles's manliness can be interpreted as an attempt to make their difference absolute, and in the process separate a pair of poets whose names and poetic practices were in fact intimately associated.

Whatever Coleridge's root motive for preferring Bowles's sonnets to Smith's, he uses their gender difference to underwrite a perceived qualitative difference, evoking and enforcing the stereotypes of his time. Consider in this context Coleridge's epigram "On the Curious Circumstance that in the German Language the Sun is Feminine, and the Moon Masculine" (1802). The conclusion and punch line of the poem rework a German epigram explaining the gender differentiation: their wives are "common" as the sun and their husbands "horned" as the moon. Coleridge's original opening lines, however, show how the commonplace gender distinction of sun and moon in English usage could be understood in terms of contemporary poetry:

> Our English poets, bad and good, agree
> To make the Sun a male, the Moon a she.
> He drives *his* dazzling diligence on high,
> In verse, as constantly as in the sky;
> And cheap as blackberries our sonnets shew
> The Moon, Heaven's huntress, with *her* silver bow. . . .
>
> (*Poetical Works* 2:968)

The designation of sonnets as a "feminine" genre and sonnets to the Moon as the favourite theme of female sonneteers are each insights with a certain degree of truth. But the paradigm forces female poets into a scheme whereby they are the "bad" English poets, writing in a cheapened genre and limited by their gendered imaginations to variations on a single theme. Coleridge's stress on Bowles's manliness exempts him, as a sonneteer, from association with this paradigm of feminine inadequacy.

Charlotte Smith's sonnets do have a notorious monotony of theme. After reading them all one is struck by the number of exceptions and variations, of course, but it remains that there is not a single one that could be called happy, or even contented. Still, we should remind ourselves that variation on a single theme and a certain stubborn suffering are time-honoured traditions in the sonnet. Typically Smith's sonnets emphasize not the sorrows of love, but her own multiple misfortunes. Many of them attempt to convey the almost insupportable nature of the speaker's suffering, often dramatized by the failure of consolation, as in the sonnet **"To Fancy"** above. Smith cultivated an idiom in which hyperbole and sincerity are precariously blended. In her very first sonnet she complained of "the rugged path I'm doom'd to tread" (*Poems* 13); in **"Sonnet 4"** she numbers herself among the "sad children of Despair and Woe" (*Poems* 15); "pain and sorrow strike— how many ways" in **"Sonnet 10"** (*Poems* 19); **"Sonnet 34"** is "[d]ark with new clouds of evil yet to come" (*Poems* 37); in **"Sonnet 55,"** "—such evils in my lot combine, / As shut my languid sense—"(*Poems* 50); in **"Sonnet 84,"** the speaker is "[c]rush'd to the earth, by bitterest anguish prest" (*Poems* 73). Frequently, death is invoked as the only conceivable release. **"Sonnet 5"** concludes with the line "There's no oblivion—but in death alone" (*Poems* 16). The speaker never quite contemplates the act of suicide in Smith's sonnets, but those in the voice of Goethe's Werther (*Poems* 26-29) outnumber those translated from Petrarch (*Poems* 21-23). There are also frequent references to injustice: "Happiness," in the sonnet **"To Fancy"** above, is "murder'd"; "to deaf Pride, Misfortune pleads in vain!" in **"Sonnet 27"** (*Poems* 31), and in **"Sonnet 79"** the poet is "shrinking from the view / Of Violence and Fraud" (*Poems* 68). No such rhetoric of anguish or of moral indignation is to be found in Bowles.

Charlotte Smith's sorrows—the most pointed and recurrent of which was anxiety for her numerous children, culminating in grief for the death of an adult daughter in childbirth—were in large part gender-determined sorrows, and perhaps could not be expected to inspire a male poet to direct imitation. Even her poverty was the result of her legal non-entity and financial insecurity as a married woman with a debt-ridden husband. Bowles's fortune, by contrast, was one open only to men: he rose quickly in the Anglican church to vicar, and eventually became chaplain to the Prince Regent (not that he wrote of such matters in his sonnets).[7] Smith's grim insistence on adversity and her seldom varied tendency to move toward greater despair or to resolve on the note of death's release make her sonnets psychologically challenging, even daunting. Her language of complaint asks us to sympathize with a woman in sustained psychic pain, powerless except for her powers of expression. The only alternative is to reject the sonnets outright as over-wrought, exhibitionist, or insincere. I would suggest that Coleridge's manly compromise was to prefer the sonnets of a poet who was influenced by Charlotte Smith, but whose melancholy was closer to nostalgia than despair. In a *jeux d'esprit* of 1796 Coleridge praises "Such verse as Bowles, heart honour'd Poet sang, / That wakes the Tear, yet steals away the Pang" (*Poetical Works* 2.976). Bowles's melancholy was self-consoling. Charlotte Smith's was not.

In her dissertation of 1976, "The Sonnets of Charlotte Smith," Peggy Willard Gledhill observes that "[i]nasmuch as Coleridge forgot about Charlotte Smith, it is not surprising that many later critics have too" (95). Gledhill's main concern is with the structure of Smith's sonnets, but she is provoked at one point to make a more literary-historical comment when she takes M. H. Abrams to task for not exploring the origins of "the Greater Romantic Lyric" further than Gray's "Ode on a Distant Prospect of Eton College" (1747) and Coleridge's immediate indebtedness to Bowles. In Abrams's famous essay "Structure and Style in the Greater Romantic Lyric" no mention is made of Charlotte Smith, and the credit for "lyricizing" the local poem goes decisively and conventionally to Bowles. Abrams includes in his essay the text of "To the River Itchin, Near Winton" to "represent Bowles' procedure" (541). As Gledhill observes, without making a detailed argument, "everything he says about [the poem] could equally well apply to Smith's **"Sonnet 32"**" (94). In fact, Charlotte Smith wrote a number of sonnets inspired by the River Arun (**"5," "26," "30," "32," "33," "45"**), and several of them exhibit the qualities of the lyric local poem, if not the Greater Romantic Lyric, at least as well as Bowles's sonnet.

As a final illustration of the styles of these two poets, let's take Bowles's "To the River Itchin" and set it beside Smith's first river sonnet, her **"Sonnet 5," "To the South Downs."** I choose this sonnet by Smith rather than the one that prompted Gledhill's comment because it was published five years earlier than the Bowles sonnet, and because it possesses, in addition to lyric and loco-descriptive aspects, that special psychological feature that Abrams calls "a recollection of an earlier visit to the same location" (541). In Smith's **"To the South Downs"** we find her earliest apostrophe to the river Arun:

> Ah! hills belov'd!—where once a happy child,
>   Your beechen shades, "your turf, your flowers among,"[8]
> I wove your bluebells into garlands wild,
>   And woke your echoes with my artless song.
> Ah! hills belov'd!—your turf, your flowers remain;
>   But can they peace to this sad bosom restore;
> For one poor moment soothe the sense of pain,
>   And teach a breaking heart to throb no more?
> And you, Aruna!—in the vale below,
>   As to the sea your limpid waves you bear,
> Can you one kind Lethean cup bestow,
>   To drink a long oblivion to my care?
> Ah! no!—when all, e'en Hope's last ray is gone,
> There's no oblivion—but in death alone!
>
> (*Poems* 15-16)

Bowles's "To the River Itchin" was the eighth sonnet in his first edition:

> Itchin, when I behold thy banks again,
>   Thy crumbling margin, and thy silver breast,
>   On which the self-same tints still seem to rest,
> Why feels my heart the shiv'ring sense of pain?
>   Is it—that many a summer's day has past
> Since in life's morn, I carol'd on thy side?
> Is it—that oft, since then, my heart has sighed,
>   As Youth, and Hope's delusive dreams, flew fast?
> Is it—that those, who circled on thy shore,
> Companions of my youth, now meet no more?
>   Whate'er the cause, upon thy banks I bend
> Sorrowing, yet feel such solace at my heart,
>   As at the meeting of some long-lost friend,
>   From whom, in happier hours, we wept to part.
>
> (*Fourteen Sonnets* 9)

Abrams suggests in a note to his essay that "As late as 1806-20, in *The River Duddon*, Wordsworth adopted Bowles's design of a tour presented as a sequence of local-meditative sonnets"(558 n16). Charlotte Smith's sonnets to the Arun, although they were not published in sequence and do not comprise a volume or a "tour," are actually the first group of English sonnets inspired by a minor river. An earlier sonnet in the tradition is Thomas Warton Jr.'s "To the River Lodon" (1777), which in turn reworks the theme of a return to childhood haunts made popular by Gray's "Eton College" ode, where the Thames figures as an addressee. To pinpoint the beginning of the tradition of addressing sonnets to a river would be difficult; to suggest, as Abrams does, that Bowles was Wordsworth's model only foreshortens that tradition.

After providing the text of "To the River Itchin", Abrams is mildly deprecating: "Why Coleridge should have been moved to idolatry by so slender, if genuine, a talent as that of Bowles has been an enigma of literary history" ("Structure and Style" 541). He provides an answer to this enigma—effectively eliminating it as a critical problem—by locating the origins of the lyricized loco-descriptive poem in Bowles's early sonnets. It is easy to sympathize with Gledhill's wry puzzlement: "What seems equally enigmatic to me is the notion that Coleridge found 'Itchin' more poetic than 'Arun'" (94). And yet it is clear that he did. My point is only that we need not accept the chapter in literary history that has been extrapolated from Coleridge's preference.

Abrams states that "'To the River Itchin' . . . so impressed Coleridge that he emulated it in his sonnet 'To the River Otter'" (541). While this statement is probably correct, there is no record of Coleridge ever mentioning this particular Bowles sonnet. It was not one of the ones he included in his 1796 anthology *Sonnets from Various Authors,* nor one of the ones he later defended against Bowles's own revisions (*Letters* 1:318). Abrams, though he doesn't cite him, seems to have taken his cue from W. K. Wimsatt's 1954 essay "The Structure of Romantic Nature Imagery," in *The Verbal Icon.* As a "central exhibit" of this essay Wimsatt uses the same comparison: the similarity (and inevitable contrast) between Bowles's sonnet "To the River Itchin" and Coleridge's sonnet "To the River Otter." The latter, Wimsatt says, was "written in confessed imitation of Bowles" (105). This "confessed imitation" is evidenced in Wimsatt's footnote by nothing more than the sub-title from the 1797 *Poems on Various Subjects*: "Sonnets Attempted in the Manner of Rev. W. L. Bowles" (*Verbal Icon* 285 n3). This sub-title is more dedicatory than descriptive, and most of the sonnets printed under it are quite unlike Bowles's sonnets. A selection of them would later be more accurately titled by Coleridge as "Sonnets to Eminent Characters." "To the River Otter" resembles a W. L. Bowles sonnet more than a Charlotte Smith sonnet, to be sure, and it did appear as part of Coleridge's own contribution to *Sonnets From Various Authors.* But there was no "confessed imitation" of any particular sonnet by Bowles, who wrote several sonnets to river landscapes. The causal or genealogical connection between these two river sonnets has been inaccurately treated as authorized fact, when it is really just a credible critical construct. The point is slight in itself, and would not be worth stressing if this construct did not play such a crucial role in the narrative that has been told about the development of the Romantic sonnet and by extension about Romantic poetic practice as a whole.

As if he were aware of the tenuousness of the received narrative, Abrams provides a second reason for Coleridge's youthful admiration of Bowles, one that does not depend on his having lyricized the local poem and one that is more in accord with the explanation I have been making: it was Bowles's tone, the relative lightness of his melancholy, that appealed to Coleridge. Abrams quotes from Coleridge's letter to Southey (11 December 94): "my *Poetry* is crowded and sweats beneath a heavy burthen of Ideas and Imagery! It has seldom Ease." "This 'Ease'" says Abrams, "Coleridge had early discovered in Bowles" ("Structure and Style" 543). Even Charlotte Smith's defenders would not call her sonnets "easy", at least not in the complimentary sense. To explain the importance of this "ease", Abrams returns to the *Biographia Literaria* and Coleridge's claim that "of the then living poets Bowles and Cowper were, to the best of my knowledge, the first who combined natural thoughts with natural diction; the first who reconciled the heart with the head" (*Biographia Literaria* 1:24).

The influence of the *Biographia Literaria,* compounded by the influence of critical readings such as Abrams's, has elevated this last statement almost to the level of literary history. But we should remind ourselves that Coleridge is speaking primarily of his own development as a poet—he even lists the two authors in the order he read them, as he explains in a footnote (1:24). Bowles and Cowper reconciled the heart and the head "first" not so much for poetry in general as for Samuel Taylor Coleridge. Coleridge is fully aware of the incongruity of the major claim he makes for this minor poet, and he offers a theoretical proviso that for all its brilliance only obscures the matter: "it is peculiar to original genius to become less and less striking, in proportion to its success in improving the taste and judgement of its contemporaries" (1:24). Such logic is tempting. By this light I could claim Coleridge's very omission of Charlotte Smith's name in the *Biographia Literaria* as evidence that she was more original and more influential than Bowles and Cowper combined. What I will suggest, however, is a continuum between Coleridge's early pairing of Smith and Bowles in the "Introduction to the Sonnets" and his later pairing of Cowper and Bowles in the *Biographia Literaria,* a continuum between his early praise of sonnets that associated "Sentiments" with the "scenery of Nature" and his later desiderata, the combination of "natural thoughts with natural diction" and the reconciliation of "the heart with the head." Given how little else is said of Cowper in the *Biographia Literaria,* is there not a sense in which his more canonical name is simply replacing Smith beside Bowles? The *Biographia Literaria* doesn't simply *not mention* Charlotte Smith: it *misrepresents her as absent,* when in fact she was too strong a poetic presence to be left out of Coleridge's "Literary Life" entirely.

III

The absence of Charlotte Smith's name from the central texts of Romantic criticism is a significant absence, and often the gestures which exclude her constitute a kind of shadow presence on her part. One such gesture can be made graphically clear in Coleridge's Higginbottom parodies. In the first chapter of the *Biographia Literaria* we are advised that in order to understand the effect of Bowles's poetry on the author in his youth, "the reader must make himself acquainted with the general style of composition that was at that time deemed poetry" (1:24). Such an acquaintance would have included a knowledge of the sonnets of Charlotte Smith. I have cited enough of them by now, I think, that even readers who are new to her work will recognize her in the following, the first of the Higginbottom sonnets:

> Pensive at eve, on the *hard* world I mused,
> And *my poor* heart was sad; so at the Moon
> I gazed, and sighed, and sighed; for ah how soon
> Eve saddens into night! mine eyes perused
> With tearful vacancy the *dampy* grass
> That wept and glitter'd in the *paly* ray:
> And I *did pause me,* on my lonely way
> And *mused me,* on the *wretched ones* that pass
> O'er the bleak heath of sorrow. But alas!
> Most of *myself* I thought! When it befel,
> That the *soothe* spirit of the *breezy* wood
> Breath'd in mine ear: 'All this is very well,
> But much of ONE thing, is for NO thing good.'
> Oh *my poor heart's* INEXPLICABLE SWELL!
>
> (1:27n)

Coleridge explains in the *Biographia Literaria* that the Higginbottom sonnets were written to expose "the three sins of poetry, one or the other of which is the most likely to beset a young writer" (1:26). This first parody was designed to "excite a good-natured laugh at the spirit of doleful egotism, and at the recurrence of favourite phrases" (1:27).

If words like "dampy" and "paly" do not invoke Smith's idiom of favorite phrases, then "pensive," the repeated word "sighed," and the phrases "Eve saddens into night," "my lonely way" and "the wretched ones that pass / O'er the bleak heath of sorrow" certainly do. These are not exact citations from Smith, but the extremity of sorrow that the sonnet parodies is very much her characteristic tone, and the nocturnal meditation around which it is structured is very much her characteristic method. As for "doleful" egotism, Coleridge himself had used a similar phrase in the preface to the first edition of his own poems in 1796, where he defended his poetry against the anticipated charge of "querulous Egotism" (*Poetical Works* 2.1144). Charlotte Smith would use this same phrase in the preface to the second volume of her *Elegiac Sonnets and Other Poems,* published in 1797, acknowledging the charge of "'querulous egotism'" (*Poems* 10) as a typical complaint against *her* style. The admonition of the soothe spirit is on target as well, as the *unrelieved* quality of Smith's melancholy was something that even her most appreciative readers complained of. An appropriate comparison here would be with Smith's **"Sonnet 4," "To the Moon"**. Here we have one of the instantiating feminine moon sonnets that Coleridge would later generalize as being "cheap as blackberries":

> Queen of the silver bow! by thy pale beam,
>   Alone and pensive, I delight to stray
> And watch thy shadow trembling in the stream,
>   Or mark the floating clouds that cross thy way.
> And while I gaze, thy mild and placid light
>   Sheds a soft calm upon my troubled breast;
> And oft I think—fair planet of the night,
>   That in thy orb, the wretched may have rest:
> The sufferers of the earth perhaps may go,
>   Released by death—to thy benignant sphere;
> And the sad children of Despair and Woe
>   Forget, in thee, their cup of sorrow here.

> Oh! that I soon may reach thy world serene,
> Poor wearied pilgrim—in this toiling scene.
>
> (*Poems* 15)

The similarity between this sonnet and the first of the Higginbottom parodies is striking—in tone, structure and subject. That Charlotte Smith was the epitome of the sonneteer of "doleful egotism" may have been so obvious to Coleridge—and more importantly to his magazine readership—that it required no mention. In his detailed and definitive article, "Coleridge as Nehemiah Higginbottom," David Erdman traces resemblances between these three parodic sonnets and the sonnets of Lloyd, Lamb, Southey and others.[9] He concludes that the first Higginbottom sonnet is "a mockery, not primarily of anybody's sonnets, but of the intensely melancholy and nearly suicidal brooding recurrent in several of his own early poems, especially his *Chatterton* . . ." (575). But it was Charlotte Smith who established the contemporary precedent for this "nearly suicidal brooding" in sonnet form.[10]

The second of the Higginbottom sonnets is directed toward another sin of poetry, which Coleridge calls "low, creeping language and thoughts, under the pretense of simplicity" (*Biographia Literaria* 1:27), and it has a tone contrasting the first, a mildness that remind us of Bowles:

> Oh I do love thee meek SIMPLICITY!
> For of thy lays the lulling simpleness
> Goes to my heart, and soothes each small distress,
> Distress tho' small, yet haply great to me,
> Tis true on Lady Fortune's gentlest pad
> I amble on; and yet I know not why
> *So* sad I am, but should a friend and I
> Frown, pout and part, then I am *very* sad.
> And then with sonnets and with sympathy
> My dreamy bosom's mystic woes I pall;
> Now of my false friend plaining plaintively,
> Now raving at mankind in general;
> But whether sad or fierce, 'tis simple all,
> All very simple, meek SIMPLICITY!
>
> (1:27n)

Individual lines, as in the first Higginbottom sonnet, may point to colleagues of Coleridge or to himself, but the larger rhetorical and technical features of the sonnet—the vagueness of the melancholy, the ease of the consolation, even the hesitant, prosaic rhythm—are much like Bowles. According to Erdman, the second Higginbottom sonnet "is usually taken as a parody of Lamb, though Southey 'recognized' it as an attack upon his own style" (575). Erdman gives convincing evidence for Lloyd as the intended victim. I would argue that W. L. Bowles is being parodied as well, especially in the octave, which is where the sonnet actually attempts to imitate a style. We recall phrases from the sonnet "To the River Itchin": "Why feels my heart the shiv'ring sense of pain? . . . Whate'er the cause, upon thy banks I bend. . . . [S]ome long lost friend, / From whom, in happier hours, we wept to part." There is also a trace of the passage from the *Monody on Matlock* quoted above: "[t]he crosses and the cares that sometimes fret / Life's smoothest channel. . . ."

The in-joke targets of the Higginbottom parodies were no doubt the author and his own circle of friends. Coleridge says in a letter to Joseph Cottle that the sonnets were written "in ridicule of my own, & Charles Lloyd's, & Lamb's, & c & c" (*Letters* 1:357). And Lamb, Lloyd and Southey all seem to have taken offense (Erdman 575).[11] But the average reader of the *Monthly Magazine* may not have been able to make such determinations, nor the contributor to rely upon them: Lloyd and Lamb, even Coleridge, were not well known poets in 1797. As magazine satire, and as personal satire of friends as well, the sonnets would have worked best if the in-jokes were disguised beneath more widely recognizable references. The sequence of these first two Higginbottom sonnets, along with the fairly obvious tonal differences between them, suggests that they should be read in the light of Coleridge's own early definition of the contemporary sonnet as the innovation of Smith and Bowles. If he was indeed "justified . . . in deducing its laws from *their* compositions," his parodies of the contemporary sonnet may have had the same models.

In the *Biographia Literaria* Coleridge gives the Higginbottom sonnets some context, but he only links one to a specific writer. The third Higginbottom sonnet, designed to ridicule "the indiscriminate use of elaborate and swelling language," is ostensibly a self-parody, and it is nothing like the first two. Coleridge says its "phrases" were "borrowed entirely from my own poems" (1.27). Erdman, however, notes that a good deal of Coleridge's material in this sonnet is drawn not from his own writing, but from early verse manuscripts given to him by Wordsworth, the same source that Coleridge drew on for "Lewti" (Erdman 579). In the sentimental and archaic introduction of Jack and the forlorn maiden there is much that derives from Wordsworth's early style. In the prospect that closes the poem, however, Coleridge presents his own original "moon masculine":

> Still on his thighs their wonted brogues are worn,
> And thro' those brogues, still tattered and betorn,
> His hindward charms gleam an unearthly white,
> Ah! thus thro' broken clouds at night's high Noon
> Peeps in fair fragments forth the full-orb'd harvest-moon!
>
> (1:28)

In the company of this outrageous poem, the first two Higginbottom parodies can look very similar to one another. Perhaps this is part of Coleridge's joke. But sonnets 1 and 2 do have differences, and differences that illustrate symmetrical poetic errors: high egotism and low simplicity, the over-determination and under-determination of melancholy. In this stylistic contrast the first two Higginbottom sonnets resemble no pair of contemporary sonneteers more than Charlotte Smith and W. L. Bowles, whose names Coleridge had placed side by side just a year earlier in his "Introduction to the Sonnets."

In their triadic arrangement the Higginbottom sonnets could be said to parody a dialectic. The third Higginbottom sonnet may seem an inappropriate candidate for a synthesis, bypassing as it does the problem of melancholy by introducing the language and imagery of other genres, namely ballad and broad humour. Compositionally, though, the poem is a synthesis, or at least an aggregate—not of Smith and Bowles but of Wordsworth and Coleridge. In a way the third Higginbottom sonnet prefigures the more overt collaboration between these two poets that would soon produce the first edition of *Lyrical Ballads* (1798), a book notably devoid of sonnets. Perhaps this is too much to read into the text and sequence of three light-hearted parodies. But there is at least one link between the Higginbottom sonnets and the first *Lyrical Ballads,* if only by way of co-incidence: the month in which the Higginbottom parodies appeared in the *Monthly Magazine*—November 1797—is also the month in which we first have evidence of Coleridge and Wordsworth considering publication of their work in a single volume.[12]

The disproportionate role that Coleridge gives to Bowles in the *Biographia Literaria* has been interpreted in recent criticism as part of a larger rhetorical strategy concerning Coleridge's relationship with William Wordsworth. Donald H. Reiman observes in "Coleridge and the Art of Equivocation" that in the *Biographia Literaria* the author places his recounting of "youthful enthusiasms for Bowles's sonnets . . . between his declaration of the effect of Wordsworth's poetry on him and the full critique of Wordsworth's poems. . . ." This strategic move "not only frees Coleridge from the status of a blind worshipper of Wordsworth's genius, but partially negates the positive force of the declaration itself" (346-47). Raimonda Modiano has expanded upon the implications of Reiman's analysis in her essay "Coleridge and Wordsworth: The Ethics of Gift Exchange and Literary Ownership" (1989):

> Coleridge presents himself as a staunch Wordsworthian in artistic preferences but prior to and without any direct influence from Wordsworth. Moreover, while casting himself in the role of a Wordsworthian naturalist . . . Coleridge surreptitiously introduces a counter-model of natural style to the one adopted by Wordsworth, showing that Bowles achieved the combination of "natural thoughts with natural diction" by means of a "sustained and elevated style," and not by recourse to "the language of real men" or the choice of subjects from rural life.
>
> (113)

We do not need to decide where Charlotte Smith would stand in the aesthetic debates that were played out between Wordsworth and Coleridge to see that she was obscured by their alternately collaborative and adversarial attempts to write their own literary history.

I do not wish to conclude that Coleridge was heavily influenced by Charlotte Smith, only that he *could not* ignore her. Coleridge's melancholy sonnets were actually very few, and the most descriptive of them, the sonnet "To the River Otter," is squarely in the idiom of Bowles. Coleridge did, of course, write poems in the darker melancholy tradition, his "Dejection, An Ode" (1802) being the most obvious example. And in this ode, when he needs to describe his dejection in the fullness of its power, his imagery and tone approach Charlotte Smith's signature style. In particular the first half of the sixth strophe reminds us of Smith's extreme of misery, and her manner of expressing it:

> There was a time when, though my path was rough,
>   This joy within me dallied with distress,
> And all misfortunes were but as the stuff
>   Whence Fancy made me dreams of happiness:
> For hope grew round me, like the twining vine,
> And fruits, and foliage, not my own, seemed mine.
> But now afflictions bow me down to earth. . . .
>
> (76-82)

There are echoes of Wordsworth's "Immortality" ode here, and it has long been known that the two poems were written in a sort of conversation, as Coleridge and Wordsworth responded to each other's early drafts. Line 81 may even contain an acknowledgement of unfair poetic borrowing. But in such phrasings as "though my path was rough" and "But now afflictions bow me to earth" we can hear another idiom. We are reminded of the "rugged path" in Charlotte Smith's first sonnet, and from her **"Sonnet 84"** the description of the speaker "Crush'd to the earth, by bitterest anguish prest" (**Poems** 73). When Coleridge speaks of the failure of his "shaping spirit of Imagination" we could point to Smith's **"Sonnet 48"**: "Imagination now has lost her powers / To dress Affliction in a robe of flowers / . . . no more the bowers of Fancy bloom" (**Poems** 45).

The familiar and long-standing argument that the Romantic loco-descriptive lyric had its origin in the sonnets of William Lisle Bowles is valid only if we take Coleridge's poetry as paradigmatic of Romanticism, and his account of his own poetic development in the *Biographia Literaria* at face value. If we focus our attention just below the surface of the *Biographia Literaria,* at the level of the footnotes and beyond, we can read signs of Charlotte Smith's presence, and infer another configuration of influences. Bowles, the idol of Coleridge's youth and the straw man of his maturity is really a metonymic figure, masculinizing and "domesticating"—*to* Coleridge's heart and *for* literary history—"the general style of composition that was at that time deemed poetry." The overdetermination of the figure of Bowles obscured for a very long period a more populous scene of writing and a narrative of generic invention in which female poets played a large part. Particularly in the domain of the sonnet, it is a narrative in which Charlotte Smith had an inaugurating role, and in which Samuel Taylor Coleridge appeared more in the capacity of interested critic than exemplary poet. One of the ironies of this story is that after having taken such pains to place himself amongst and against contemporary authors of sonnets, Coleridge did not go on to become a major sonnet writer himself. Granted, close attention has been paid to Coleridge's "To The River Otter," and rightly so. But as David Erdman has pointed out, Coleridge was "guilty of" only three original sonnets in the twenty years following his early experiments in the form (571), experiments that effectively ended with the publication of his 1797 Higginbottom parodies.

A symmetrical irony is that Wordsworth, the most prolific of all the Romantic sonneteers, stayed entirely clear of sonnet production and the debates surrounding it in the 1790s. Even though his first published poem was a highly sentimental "Sonnet on Seeing Miss Helen Maria Williams Weep at a Tale of Distress" (1787), it was published pseudonymously, and never reprinted by the author. The total number of Wordsworth's sonnets before 1801 is less than ten, and most of these are from the juvenilia, that is, from before 1790. From 1801 to the end of his life, on the other hand, Wordsworth wrote and published literally hundreds of sonnets. Later in his life he would recall a moment of inspiration:

> one afternoon in 1801, my Sister read to me the sonnets of Milton. I had long been well acquainted with them, but I was particularly struck on that occasion by the dignified simplicity and majestic harmony that runs through most of them. . . . I took fire, if I may be allowed to say so, and produced three sonnets the same afternoon, the first I ever wrote except an irregular one at school. . . .
>
> (*Poetical Works* 3:417)

To examine or even to introduce properly the topic of Smith's influence on Wordsworth is beyond the scope of the present essay, but I will nonetheless close with another, more immediate record from this period of concentrated sonnet writing:

> 24 December 1802, Christmas Eve. William is now sitting by me at ½ past 10 o'clock. I have been beside him ever since tea running the heel of a stocking, repeating some of his sonnets to him, listening to his own repeating, reading some of Milton's and the Allegro and Penseroso. . . . [B]eloved William is turning over the leaves of Charlotte Smith's sonnets.
>
> (*Journals of Dorothy Wordsworth* 163-64)

Notes

1. Coleridge gave an erroneous impression to at least one correspondent, John Thelwall, by speaking about Bowles in these familiar terms: "You imagine that I know Bowles personally—I never *saw* him but once; & when I was a boy, & in Salisbury *market-place*" (Griggs, *Letters* [31 December 1796] 1.294). By 1797, Bowles and Coleridge had met. See Coleridge's letters to Bowles (*Letters* 1.317, 355). There is some evidence Coleridge knew Smith as well: on the 12th of February 1800, Coleridge adds as a postscript to a letter to Southey, "I pass this evening with Charlotte Smith at her house" (1:571). And a few months later, in a letter to Godwin, Coleridge writes "To Mrs Smith I am about to write a letter, with a book," and asks ". . . be so kind as to inform me of her direction" (1:589).

2. More recent attempts to present evidence for Bowles's influence on Wordsworth have been few

and distinctly modest. Duncan Wu notes Bowles's influence on two unpublished early sonnets by Wordsworth in "Wordsworth's Reading of Bowles," but his main point is to identify the edition mentioned by Wordsworth in the Rogers anecdote as the second edition rather than the first. Paul Bauschatz shows some points of similarity between Bowles's style and that of the early Wordsworth, and argues that an "implicit susceptibility to Bowles's voice" (34) can be traced in a variety of Wordsworth's very early poems. His argument focuses more on sound than sense, however, and he acknowledges that some of the best examples of Wordsworth showing Bowles's characteristic style (such as those mentioned in Wu's article) may well have been composed *before* Bowles's poetry had been published.

3. Bishop C. Hunt's "Charlotte Smith and William Wordsworth" (1970) is the first and thus far the most detailed study of Smith's influence on Wordsworth. Stuart Curran takes up the topic with authority in "The 'I' Altered" (1988), and again in his introduction to the *Poems of Charlotte Smith* (1993) and "Charlotte Smith and Early Romanticism" (1994).

4. The sonnets that Coleridge selected for this short anthology are listed by first line in the bibliography of the *Poetical Works* (2:1141), and reprinted in facsimile in Paul M. Zall's *Coleridge's "Sonnets from Various Authors"* (1968).

5. Beachy Head was Smith's favourite locale for such utterances. It is also a famous site for actual suicides. See Bernieres.

6. The term "manly" was no less vague in the 1790's than it is now. Generally it denoted any positive quality associated more with men than with women, for example physical courage or military prowess. At the same time, some authors were trying to restore it to its older sense of "human" or "humane." Thus Thelwall remarks: "by *manly* I mean *benevolent* and *peaceful*; for fury and devastation . . . are not the passions of human beings" *The Politics of English Jacobinism* 73.

7. See DeMontluzin 68-71.

8. Smith's note for this quotation refers to Gray's "Ode on A Distant Prospect of Eton College" line 8: "Whose turf, whose shades, whose flowers among."

9. A detail not in Erdman is that the phrase "pause me"—"And I did pause me on my lonely way"—from the first Higginbottom sonnet appears in Southey's sonnet 10 from his 1797 collection *Poems*: "I the while / Pause me in sadness" (Southey *Poems 1797* [Woodstock 1989] 116).

10. One of the most thorough treatments of Coleridge's early fascination with Chatterton and the late eighteenth-century vogue of the young genius-suicide is in George Dekker's *Coleridge and the Literature of Sensibility* (1978), in particular his chapter entitled "Blue Coat Boys." Charlotte Smith is not discussed.

11. The Engell and Bate *Biographia Literaria* has a detailed note on the reactions of Coleridge's friends to his parodies (1:278n2). The editors conclude that the three sonnets parody Lloyd, Southey, and Coleridge, respectively.

12. See W. J. B. Owen's introduction to his edition of *Lyrical Ballads 1798* (viii-xiv).

Works Cited

Abrams, M. H. "Structure and Style in the Greater Romantic Lyric." *From Sensibility to Romanticism.* Ed. F. W. Hilles and Harold Bloom. New York: Oxford UP, 1965, 527-60.

Adams, Oscar Fay. *A Brief Handbook of English Authors.* 5th ed. Boston: Houghton Mifflin, 1889.

Bauschatz, Paul. "Coleridge, Wordsworth, and Bowles." *Style* 27 (1993): 17-40.

Bowles, William Lisle. *Fourteen Sonnets 1789.* Intro. Jonathan Wordsworth. Oxford: Woodstock, 1991.

———. *Sonnets Written Chiefly in Picturesque Spots, during a tour.* 2nd ed. Bath: Cruttwell, 1789.

———. *The Poetical Works of William Lisle Bowles.* Ed. George Gilfillan. Edinburgh: Nichol, 1855.

Casson, T. E. "William Lisle Bowles." *Eighteenth-Century Literature: An Oxford Miscellany.* 1909. Freeport, NY: Books for Libraries, 1966. 151-183.

Coleridge, Samuel Taylor. *The Complete Poetical Works of Samuel Taylor Coleridge.* 2 vols. Ed. E. H. Coleridge. Oxford: Oxford UP, 1912.

———. *Samuel Taylor Coleridge.* The Oxford Authors. Ed. H. J. Jackson. Oxford: Oxford UP, 1985.

———. *Biographia Literaria.* 2 vols. James Engell and W. Jackson Bate, eds. Princeton: Princeton UP, 1983.

———. *Collected Letters of Samuel Taylor Coleridge.* Vol. 1. Ed. E. L. Griggs. Oxford: Clarendon, 1956.

Curran, Stuart. *Poetic Form and British Romanticism.* Oxford: Oxford UP, 1986.

———. "The 'I' Altered." *Romanticism and Feminism.* Ed. Anne K. Mellor. Bloomington: Indiana UP, 1988. 185-213.

———. ed. and intro. *The Poems of Charlotte Smith.* Women Writers in English 1350-1850. Oxford: Oxford UP, 1993.

———. "Charlotte Smith and British Romanticism." *South Central Review* 11 (1994): 64-78.

De Bernieres, Louis. "Legends of the Fall: The Short Way Down an English Cliff." *Harper's* Jan. 1996: 78-82.

De Montluzin, Emily Lorraine. *The Anti-Jacobins, 1798-1800: The Early Contributors to the* Anti-Jacobin Review. Basingstoke: Macmillan, 1988.

Dekker, George. *Coleridge and the Literature of Sensibility.* London: Vision, 1978.

Drake, Nathan. *Literary Hours, or Sketches Critical, Narrative, and Poetical.* 3 vols. 4th ed. London: Longman, 1820.

Erdman, David V. "Coleridge as Nehemiah Higginbottom." *Modern Language Notes* 73 (1958): 569-80.

Gledhill, Peggy Willard. "The Sonnets of Charlotte Smith." Diss. U of Oregon, 1976.

Herford, C. H. *The Age of Wordsworth.* 1897. London: G. Bell, 1960.

Hilbish, Florence May Anna. *Charlotte Smith, Poet and Novelist.* Philadelphia: U of Pennsylvania P, 1941.

Hunt, Bishop C. "Wordsworth and Charlotte Smith." *Wordsworth Circle* 1.3 (1970): 85-103.

Lamb, Charles and Mary. *The Letters of Charles and Mary Anne Lamb.* Vol. 1. *Letters of Charles Lamb, 1796-1801.* Ed. Edwin W. Marrs. Ithaca: Cornell UP, 1975.

Main, David M. *A Treasury of English Sonnets.* New York: Worthington, 1881.

Modiano, Raimonda. "Coleridge and Wordsworth: The Ethics of Gift Exchange and Literary Ownership." *Wordsworth Circle* 20 (1989): 113-20.

Pierce, Frederick E. *Currents and Eddies in the English Romantic Generation.* New Haven: Yale UP, 1918.

Ralston, Ramona Marie. "Wordsworth and the Feminized Sonnet: A Suppression of Eighteenth-Century Poetic Influence." Diss. University of Southern California, 1987.

Reiman, Donald H. "Coleridge and the Art of Equivocation." *Studies in Romanticism* 25 (1986): 325-349.

Seward, Anna. *Letters of Anna Seward.* 6 vols. Edinburgh: Constable, 1811.

Smith, Charlotte. *The Poems of Charlotte Smith.* Ed. Stuart Curran. Women Writers in English 1350-1850. Oxford: Oxford UP, 1993.

Southey, Robert. *Poems 1797.* Oxford: Woodstock, 1989.

Thelwall, John. *The Politics of English Jacobinism.* Ed. and intro. Gregory Claeys. University Park, Pennsylvania: Penn State UP, 1995.

Wimsatt, W. K. "The Structure of Romantic Nature Imagery." *The Verbal Icon.* Louisville: U of Kentucky P, 1954. 103-116.

Wordsworth, Dorothy. *The Journals of Dorothy Wordsworth.* Ed. Mary Moorman. Oxford: Oxford UP, 1971.

Wordsworth, William. *Poetical Works.* 5 vols. E. de Selincourt and Helen Darbishire, eds. Oxford: Clarendon P, 1958.

———. *Lyrical Ballads 1798.* Ed. and intro. W. J. B. Owen. Oxford: Oxford UP, 1969.

———. and Dorothy Wordsworth. *The Letters of William and Dorothy Wordsworth.* 5 vols. 2nd ed. Chester L. Shaver and Alan G. Hill, eds. Oxford: Clarendon, 1967-1979.

Wu, Duncan. "Wordsworth's Reading of Bowles." *Notes and Queries* 36 (1989): 166-67.

Zall, Paul M, ed. and intro. *Coleridge's "Sonnets from Various Authors"* bound with Rev. W. L. Bowles' *"Sonnets."* Glendale, CA: La Siesta P, 1968.

Diane Long Hoeveler (essay date 1998)

SOURCE: Hoeveler, Diane Long. "Gendering the Civilizing Process: The Case of Charlotte Smith's *Emmeline, the Orphan of the Castle.*" In *Gothic Feminism: The Professionalization of Gender from Charlotte Smith to the Brontës,* pp. 27-50. University Park: The Pennsylvania State University Press, 1998.

[*In the following excerpt, Hoeveler discusses* Emmeline *as an important text in the establishment of the female gothic novel tradition.*]

This desire of being always women, is the very consciousness that degrades the sex.

—Mary Wollstonecraft

I

In 1753, the British Parliament passed the Hardwicke Act, a law that was designed to prevent the clandestine or forced marriages of heiresses who were apparently believed to be so besieged by mercenary bourgeois suitors that the law had to step in to protect them. As Lawrence Stone has observed, the aristocracy at this time was so concerned with the fine points of passing on their property that they became incensed at "the ease with which penniless adventurers could entice or seduce their daughters and heiresses and irrevocably marry them without parental knowledge or consent." We can begin our examination of the female gothic novel by situating the texts that were written after the passage of this law as extended glosses on the motif of pursued and persecuted heiress-heroines. But in order to discuss the female gothic writer's impulse to civilize the process of marriage and by extension the newly emerging capitalist, let me briefly examine two works that attempt to explain the invention of the "civilizing process" that bourgeois women, of necessity, experienced: Norbert Elias's *The History of Manners* and Michel Bakhtin's *Rabelais and His World.*[1]

Elias's work traces the creation during the early modern period of what he calls *homo clausus,* an individual who will professionalize his gender and make total biological control of himself a private matter. Such an individual experiences the culturally imposed "standards of shame, delicacy, and self-control" and the "rising threshold of shame and embarrassment" about bodily functions as an endorsement of increasingly extreme forms of personal restraint, as the institution of "a wall, of something 'inside' man separating him from the outside world" (259). And it was, according to Elias, this newly created and controlled "public body" that was given validation by society, and which distinguished itself from the lower social classes by aping the courtly value of self-control, along with its acceptance of shame as the secret sin at its (bourgeois) heart. What Elias calls "manners," highly gendered customs, behavior, and fashions, now were diffused from the court to the upper class, and then to the next class down the social ladder until all classes were ultimately affected by the codes of conduct that were being advocated in the books of courtly behavior now saturating the newly literate population. According to Elias, it was through the imposition of such "manners" and the use of shame as a disciplinary tool that the modern state could come into existence. "Civilizing" the urban space meant that education and recreational activities were now controlled by "moral censorship," while the "new sensibilities" made physical violence, dueling, hunting, and public displays of bodily functions all abhorrent and grossly unacceptable behaviors (126-29).

Bakhtin's writings, on the other hand, privilege the "carnivalesque" body of the early modern period. This body enacts its essentially antibourgeois values through intense release of emotion, destroys authoritarian strictures, and challenges and inverts imposed political and religious systems. The lower classes and women, of course, were freest to indulge in such *charivari,* or communal dances, while the obverse of such "harmless" activity would be the carnage and mob violence of the French Revolution. The struggle between these two bodies—*homo clausus* and the carnivalesque—can be seen as one locus of meaning in the female gothic novel, although ironically the carnivalesque possibility is generally associated in these works not so much with lower-class women as with aristocratic practitioners of adultery, gossip, slander, and dueling or poisoning as the preferred means for settling scores. A woman like Radcliffe's Emily is advised by her father on the one hand to conform, to conceal, to privatize, while on the other hand the carnivalesque possibility is always open to her, luring her into sympathizing with and reenacting the history of the rampaging Bacchae Signora Laurentini, aka Sister Agnes. These two bodies, and the warfare between them, characterize the shifting personae of all the polarized women in Radcliffe's novels, or the struggle between the bodies of Jane and Bertha in *Jane Eyre* or Victoria and Lilla in Dacre's *Zofloya.*

Elias concludes that the middle class founded its status—its economic and political power—on the model of *homo clausus,* the retentive, controlled, concealed, and professionally gendered body. Such a body was usually coded as male and gained its power through the ability to distance others, to refuse engagement, and to mimic the scientific values of objectivity and rationality. The female body, on the other hand, was associated in this formula with diffuse energy, subjectivity, passion, and emotionality. As Gary Kelly has observed, the construction of both the sentimental and the reasonable "woman" during the late eighteenth century was part of a larger ideological project, the creation of a professional middle-class discourse system that would supplant the aristocracy at the same time it gained control over the lower classes. "Woman" in this cultural enterprise was crucial as a pawn in issues of property, children, and inheritance; and finally she constituted a certain technology of the self that we now recognize as "virtue" and "reason."[2]

In light of these theories, it becomes evident that the female gothic novel assisted in the bourgeois cultural revolution by helping to professionalize gender, by collaborating in the construction of the professionally middle-class woman and the professionally bourgeois paterfamilias. Women who did not conform to appropriately coded bourgeois norms—who reminded the reading audience of long discarded and disgraced aristocratic flaws like adultery, passion, gossip, slander, and physical violence—became themselves the targets of savage beatings throughout the works. Men who were coded as libidinous and aristocratic, like Rochester in *Jane Eyre* or Valancourt in *The Mysteries of Udolpho,* were allowed to survive and marry the heroine only after they had been subjected to a vicious beating or a series of shootings, and thereafter effectively renounced their flawed and anachronistic aristocratic tendencies.

Central to the ideological construction of gender during this period, as I have pointed out, was the emphasis on separate spheres for men and women, the public/private dichotomy that was played out in virtually every conduct book and quasi-religious tract published from the middle of the eighteenth century through at least the lifetimes of the Brontës. One of the best known of these tracts was Thomas Gisborne's *Enquiry into the Duties of the Female Sex* (1796), a companion volume to his *Enquiry into the Duties of Men in the Higher and Middle Classes of Society in Great Britain Resulting from Their Respective Situations, Positions, and Employments.* Gisborne claimed in the former text that men were particularly gifted in "the science of legislation, of jurisprudence, of political economy; the conduct of government in all its executive functions; the abstruse reaches of erudition, the inexhaustible depths of philosophy; the knowledge indispensable in the wide field of commercial enterprise; [and] the arts of defence and of attack." So while men were slashing and wounding each other in the public sphere, women were supposed to be content with ministering "to the comfort of husbands, of parents, of brothers and sisters, and of other relations, connections and friends, in the intercourse of domestic life." Further, Gisborne specifies that it is the responsibility of women to "form and improve the general manners, disposition, and conduct of the other sex, by society and example," while the final task of a woman for Gisborne was the "modelling [of] the human mind during the early stages of its growth, and fixing, while it is yet ductile, its growing principles of action."[3]

In the artificially constructed world of the conduct book scenario, men and women inhabited tightly demarcated spheres where duties, rights, and responsibilities were codified and thoroughly accepted by all parties. Such a worldview was seductive for an emerging bourgeoisie that wanted, nay needed, to believe that women were properly positioned as pawns in the broader masculine enterprise we call the patriarchy, that is, a codified system of inheritance and property transfer. But women did not quietly acquiesce to the conduct book construction of their nature and destiny. They wrote female gothic novels that proffered another, alternate fantasy, and in this version they emerged from the private domain with a vengeance. They mimed the mime, masqueraded as professionally feminine, and exploded the limited gender constructions that the masters like Gisborne were peddling.

When Ann Radcliffe's early villain the Marquis de Mazzini (in *A Sicilian Romance*) wants to insult his son, he can think of no greater crime than to accuse him of betraying "'the weak mind of a woman . . . Degenerate boy! Is it thus you reward my care? Do I live to see my son the sport of every idle tale a woman may repeat? Learn to trust reason and your senses, and you will then be worthy of my attention.'"[4] In gothic novels the sexes are arrayed along an axis of characteristics, with the extremes coded clearly as evil. Women who are excessively "masculine feminine"—sexual predators like the voracious gothic stepmother in *A Sicilian Romance* or the overly passionate women who find themselves confined to convents in *The Mysteries of Udolpho*—always die by the conclusion of the novel, leaving no heirs to carry on their character defects.

And, likewise, men who are excessively "masculine"—violent, aggressive, lustful, and adulterous, that is, men who refuse to be civilized and domesticated and professionally masculinized—also suffer a horrific punishment by the end of the novel. They invariably die guilt-wrecked deaths, usually by their own hands. Their sons and heirs, if there are any who are worthy of inheriting the always damaged estate, are considerably tamer creatures, having learned from their fathers that such extremely masculine characteristics do not bring happiness or longevity. The compulsion for both sexes formed under the machine of capitalism was to merge, to eliminate radical distinctions of gender and find some sort of moderate middle ground on which both could stand as equals. In the female gothic novel, the man left standing is invariably a man who has been stabbed or shot (usually twice, just for good measure), while the woman left standing is the one who has successfully navigated her way through labyrinthine corridors and out of towers and catacombs, bringing back into the light of day her long-lost mother. In both her first and last gothic novels, Radcliffe has her heroines find their mothers, thought in both cases to be long dead. Although the two middle novels play with variations on this theme, the daughter as savior of an earlier and gentler matriarchal tradition is clearly a key component to the ideology being promulgated here. The daughter as culture heroine marries the wounded son figure (one recalls Attis), and together they forge a new ideal couple, as moderate in its lineaments as the previous culture's idealized couple was Titan-like. We can observe that this ideology allows both hero and heroine to endure and survive that ultimate beating fantasy we call history.

According to the female gothic trajectory, the heroine, in her new and valorized masculinized role and identity as oedipal detective and reasonable, rational seeker of the family's buried secret, has become acceptable only because she has managed to abject/reject her "naturally" passionate feminine tendencies toward excess and emotion and cultivated in their place a rational and masculinely identified mind. Possessing the mind of a man means that women are first and foremost reasonable, calm, and easily able to control or better yet repress their emotions. "To think like a man" has for the past two hundred years been the highest praise that could be bestowed by the patriarchy on a woman. But what about men? Why would women seek to create a new masculine ideal that demanded that a man be wounded and vulnerable? To put it crudely, a wounded man is a castrated man is a safe (easily manipulated) man. A weak man, that is, a man who has been professionally gendered as "masculine" according to the bourgeois ideology, will not think he can tyrannize over his wife and children; this man will not attempt anything as foolish as adultery or its attendant sins; he will not chain his wife to rocks in a cave. The professionally gendered bourgeois man has had his dangerously masculine spirit tamed and put safely under the control of the professional girl-woman.

Critics of sensibility have long remarked on the enigma of the feminized hero, and most have placed him firmly within the traditions of sentimentality, originating as a Rousseauian creation or a Burkean spectacle of misplaced emotion. Claudia Johnson in her book *Equivocal Beings* has commented on Burke's hyperbolic reaction to Marie Antoinette's precarious state by noting that a man's need to cry out and moan over the fate of a threatened woman would appear to be yet another veiled sadistic scenario, displaced or elided by a fair amount of masochistic posturing by the sentimental male writing the narrative. The sadistic punishment of women, the trope of the besieged heroine, is for the male authors of the 1790s "not the unthinkable crime which chivalric sentimentality forestalls, but rather the one-thing-needful to solicit male tears and the virtues that supposedly flow with them, and the preposterousness of [the women writers'] work emerges from and engages this horrifying realization" (15).

For Johnson it was the female author of the 1790s who felt herself stripped of her traditional gender markings when the sentimental man assumed the characteristics that were formerly ascribed to the "female." As she asserts, the "sentimental man, having taken over once-feminine attributes, leaves to women only two choices: either the equivocal or the hyperfeminine. For if the man Werther is already the culture's paragon of feeling, then any feeling differentially attributed to women must be excessively delicate, morbidly *over*-sensitive" (12). Additionally, Johnson claims that under the sentimental dispensation "gender codes have not simply been reversed. They have been fundamentally disrupted. . . . [T]he conservative insistence upon the urgency of chivalric sentimentality fundamentally unsettled gender itself, leaving women without a distinct gender site. Under sentimentality, all women risk becoming equivocal beings" (11). As Johnson rightly argues, "under sentimentality the prestige of suffering belongs to men" (17), but what do you do about the spectacle of female suffering that marches across the pages of women's literature—particularly the female gothic—throughout the 1790s? Johnson chooses to read this suffering as an ambivalent gesture by women themselves to regain a sense of agency and subjectivity that had been denied to them by their culture. Johnson claims that "sentimentality upsets all markers of gender," while "female subjectivity itself is cast into doubt as culpable, histrionic, and grotesque" (16).[5]

The female gothic novel is certainly one site of gender confusion, one area in which women writers attempted to stake a claim for the power of professional femininity and victimization suffering. But this femininity had a vague political subtext, what we today would recognize as a species of proto-"feminism," in that women were advised in these novels not to trust to the goodwill of men but to manipulate or control those men—weakened by their own emotions—without those men actually being aware of it. The type of feminism that Wollstonecraft advocated was not perceived by her or her contemporaries as a social, political, or economic movement with a clear-cut agenda and principles. Despite her stated injunctions to women that their "first duty" was to themselves, Wollstonecraft initiated a pedagogical program detailing how best to prepare women to serve as loyal and devoted wives and raise judicious and sensible children. The issues that concerned Wollstonecraft and Radcliffe were fairly simple: they believed in access to education for women; they advocated the importance of the family presided over by intelligent and devoted parents and inhabited by dutiful children; and they understood the importance of marriage and the crucial nature of the choice of an appropriate spouse as a means of determining a woman's future status and opportunities.

What we have come to label one brand of "feminism" began in the fairly straightforward claims of women who were defined by their society as "orphans," that is, disinherited and worthless because the claims of the first-born son were seen as ever so much more significant. Female novelists like Hannah More and Maria Edgeworth may have practiced what Elizabeth Kowaleski-Wallace has labeled "patriarchal complicity," or an "equally strong longing for the father's sanction" in their writings. As popular purveyors of educational and religious tracts, they were complicit in creating the "myth of the benevolent patriarch" and the construction of what Kowaleski-Wallace has called "new-style patriarchy," promulgated by a "daughter whose attraction to her father compels her to seek his approval." But such a phenomenon is substantially problematized in the female gothic novel. Proving one's legitimacy, proving that one is not an "orphan," or fatherless, becomes a persistent refrain in female gothic novels. Why? Clearly, the answer one is forced finally to confront concerns the nature of the "patriarchy" as perceived by the very different white, middle-class women who were reading and writing gothic novels (as distinct from those who were attracted to the works of More and Edgeworth, for instance). To the female gothic consciousness, the patriarchy (or what we might more naively call "society") exists as a huge protection racket, a system of favors and exchanges according to which one's survival depends on having a powerful protector. As Jay Fliegelman has remarked with regard to the period, "neither Locke nor Rousseau believed that daughters should be encouraged to the same spirit of independence as their male counterparts. . . . [W]hereas sons were freed from parental dependence by the development of autonomous reason, daughters, whose virtue must always have a protector, were to find a similar liberation through marriage."[6] But when women were shut out of this system of protection, when their own names did not signal allegiance and ownership by a powerful patriarch, then they experienced life as a gothic chamber of horrors. Gothic heroines, if they were to survive, were then forced to seek protection from any surrogate protection agency they could find—the church, an educational institution, marriage to a chastened aristocrat, anything that would provide them a form of "cover," a means of protection that they did not possess in their own right.

II

Charlotte Smith's *Emmeline, the Orphan of the Castle* (1788) presents this ideology in pure undistilled form: women actually have been disinherited and hounded out of their rightful estates and properties by odious men who have found perverse pleasure in robbing and swindling them, and then like vultures have fattened themselves on the spoils of ill-gotten female wealth and goods. An intense fear of masculinity pervades *Emmeline,* while the threat of sexual violence—kidnapping, rape, or forced marriage—is always present for the heroine and other female characters unlucky enough to be without patriarchal protection. Scenarios of sexual violence as a theme have also recently been analyzed similarly by Daniel Watkins, who sees the phenomenon as a persistent and powerful leitmotif in canonical romantic poetry. For Watkins, "the romantic portrayal of gender necessarily depends first not upon language but rather upon the decline of feudal, or aristocratic, patriarchy and the emergence of capitalist, or bourgeois, patriarchy, and it therefore is bound up with historical acts of violence and oppression." Attempting to locate "the historically specific *logic* of gender stratification," Watkins explores acts of violence committed against female characters in the name of masculine privilege and out of the male fear of a new capitalistic economy that the poets (and their masculinist culture) felt threatened by. Thus the poets scapegoat women, doling out to them the violence that became one means by which the bourgeois poet could project onto another (helpless) object his own sense of historical displacement and redundancy.[7]

This same system of gender stratification, however, can be detected in the female gothic novel, in which the bourgeois woman writer punishes sexual women and castrates aristocratic men in the name of the civilizing process. Smith's Emmeline is plagued by her need to balance "sense" (her masculinist tendencies) and "sensibility" (her feminized romantic characteristics) in much the same way the heroines of Austen must a few years later. Both women writers present in their heroines the same diffuse anxiety, the same sense of powerlessness and dispossession, and always with the threat that real violence, real trauma could descend on the heroine who does not successfully navigate the treacherous gender straits. The female gothic heroine is a woman who has learned the lesson her author wants to teach to the general reading public: the patriarchy is a gigantic protection racket; there is no protection for women unless they too get a big stick behind them any way they can. If there is a system of "traffic in women," then sell yourself to the best (read: most controllable) bidder, the man with the most effective system of protection behind him. This may not be a comforting realization, but then the female gothic world was being constructed as an alternate female domain standing in contradistinction to the industrial and "realistic" world that male authors were codifying at the same time. If the male bildungsroman was a masculinist ideological project intended to depict the "patriarchy" as a benign force, the female gothic novel positioned the "patriarchy" as a duplicitous, inscrutable, good daddy/bad daddy. The ambivalence that saturates the female gothic novel can be traced precisely to this cynical and sometimes self-critical portrait of what a woman has to do in order to survive in a patriarchy. Smith, Radcliffe, and Austen's heroines may marry at the conclusion of their novels, but these marriages are less celebrations than they are quiet acceptances of their new keepers.

Just as Wollstonecraft was picking up her pen to attempt to write fiction, she was reading and reacting to the works of her contemporary, Charlotte Smith (1749-1806). And when Wollstonecraft was asked as one of her very first assignments to review Smith's first novel for the *Analytical Review* she did not find much to praise about it. It is significant that she particularly disliked the secondary story line, the adulterous and passionate romance between Lady Adelina and Fitz-Edward. She lashed out against the happy ending of their tortured love affair, condemning "the false expectations these wild scenes excite, [which] tend to debauch the mind, and throw an insipid kind of uniformity over the moderate and rational prospects of life, consequently adventures are sought for and created, when duties are neglected and content despised." But this reaction should not surprise us, because Wollstonecraft, who signed herself variously as "M," "W," or "T," became well known as a reviewer for her contempt for what she disparagingly called "feminine novels," or unnatural and affected productions. To be "feminine" in Wollstonecraft's lexicon was to be "ridiculous," "childish," full of "folly and improbability," and finally "stupid."[8] But there was nothing stupid about Charlotte Smith. She was a sentimentalist with a social and political agenda; she was an incipient gothic feminist.

From a privileged background, Smith married well and spent the first twenty years of her marriage to Benjamin Smith bearing twelve children, only six of whom would survive their mother. Smith squandered his paternal inheritance and found himself imprisoned for debt in 1784, and for a time Charlotte and the children joined him there; then they fled to France to escape creditors. Finally, she faced the inevitable and separated from her husband, knowing full well that the support of her surviving children would be her complete responsibility.[9] Smith did what she had to do: she wrote novels about women who marry fops, fools, or scoundrels and then try to deal heroically with the situations such incompetent men produce. Smith wrote ten novels, several translations, collections of poetry, and histories in order to support herself and her children over the next fifteen years. She has been largely ignored since the heyday of her popularity, although in the past five years she has enjoyed something of a critical renaissance. Her first novel, *Emmeline, the Orphan of the Castle,* clearly stands as the forgotten urtext for the female gothic novel tradition and deserves to be recognized as such. Read and admired by Radcliffe, the work was condemned by Wollstonecraft and satirized by Austen. So immediately popular that the first printing of 15,000 copies in 1788 sold out within six months, *Emmeline* was the rage of reading London and as such it served an important function in the transmission and transmutation of female-created ideologies.[10]

Emmeline is one of those novels that contains within it evidence of both the dominant prior discourse system and suggestions and hints of the next paradigm shift. *Emmeline,* in other words, is a sentimental novel with a gothic novel buried within it struggling to emerge as a full-blown genre in its own right. How can we characterize the sentimental residue found in *Emmeline*? Suffice it to say that Emmeline and the secondary female heroine, Lady Adelina, cry, weep, sob, or stifle a tear on virtually every occasion and at least once in every chapter of this long-winded novel. The sentimental code of conduct is implicit in the author's every judgment about what constitutes a "good" and what constitutes a "bad" character. We know that Emmeline's aunt, Lady Montreville, is evil when we are told that "her passions were as strong as her reason was feeble" (62). Emotions and displays of emotion are coded as dangerous throughout this text, while reason is lauded as the most valuable trait for human beings. The heroine, Emmeline or the "orphan" of the castle, struggles to prove her legitimacy and hence her rightful claim to her father's estate at the same time she attempts to avoid marrying her rich cousin, who stands in the position of aristocratic usurper of her own estate. We will not spoil too much of this plot by saying that Emmeline does prove her legitimacy. The papers she needed to do so were always in her own possession; she was simply too occupied fending off a variety of unpleasant suitors to read her parents' marriage license and her father's will.

The multiple suitor convention, brought to a fever pitch in sentimental literature by Richardson, is used here to suggest that the dominant and threateningly odious suitor has about him an incestuous air of familiarity. When Emmeline repulses her rich cousin Delamere as a possible husband, she is acting out the drama that Foucault has identified as characterizing the entire late eighteenth-century cultural enterprise. We will see the rejected incestuous suitor again in *Jane Eyre*'s St. John Rivers, *Wuthering Heights*'s Heathcliff, and *Mathilda*'s papa. Moving out of the family kinship clan and into an exogamous alliance, based on the property of one's body rather than one's blood, proved to be an enormously anxious and ambivalent activity for middle-class women and women writers. But Emmeline actually has three other unsuitable suitors in addition to Delamere. The first is a man who has served as the estate's caretaker and had in his possession the documents that proved Emmeline's rightful claim to the castle of Mowbray. This man appears to be motivated by simple greed: a blatant attempt to claim the castle of Mowbray as his own through marriage to the heiress. But Mr. Maloney (meant to be the object of suspicion by the fact of his Irish surname) is rejected by Emmeline as hopelessly beneath her in class, even though she thinks at this time that she is illegitimate and unworthy of any sort of marriage.

The second unsuitable catch snagged by poor Emmeline is a man named Mr. Rochely, an elderly and unpleasantly plump businessman. Rochely reveals a less than sentimental line of reasoning as he contemplates an engagement with the heroine: "He was determined to chuse beauty, but expected also fortune. He desired to marry a woman of family, yet feared the expensive turn of those brought up in high life; and [he] had a great veneration for wit and accomplishments, but dreaded, lest in marrying a woman who possessed them, he would be liable to be governed by superior abilities, or be despised for the mediocrity of his own understanding" (88). Suffice it to say that Emmeline has the good sense to despise him, even though her greedy and self-serving aunt and uncle desperately want to marry Emmeline off in order to get her out of the sight of their precious son and heir, Delamere. Again, even though the match would appear to provide a means of "erasing the blemish of her birth," Emmeline's innate dignity and pride cause her to reject Rochely.

Toward the conclusion of the novel, Emmeline also attracts as a suitor a French aristocrat, Bellozane, when she travels on the Continent with her friend and mother substitute Mrs. Stafford, who has been forced to flee creditors with her husband and children. Mr. and Mrs. Stafford's situation is a slightly veiled portrait of Smith's own financially desperate marriage to an improvident and foolish man. But Mrs. Stafford is the soul of discretion and common sense in this novel, a perfect chaperon and maternal guide to the young and beautiful Emmeline. Whereas Mrs. Stafford married badly, she is determined to see Emmeline married well, to a wise and good man, and she cannot abide the foppish French suitor anymore than she can stand Rochely. Emmeline's rejection of yet another passionate and unprincipled aristocrat at this point in the book is meant to suggest her increasing self-esteem. She knows that she is worthy of the best, and she is willing to wait no matter how many unpleasant suitors she has to reject.

It is this intense self-possession, this extreme sense of her own worth that puzzles bystanders of the gothic/sentimental heroine. How can a woman society has labeled "illegitimate" respect herself? In other words, how can a woman possess self-respect when the forces of the patriarchy have deemed her beneath their contempt and offered her no formal means of protection? The mystery of the gothic heroine's identity—her inwardness, her silence, her extreme control of her emotions in public, her sexual inviolability and purity—puzzles a social system that wants to believe that only it possesses the power to confer value. The villains of Smith's novel are not simply Emmeline's greedy aristocratic relatives, Lord and Lady Montreville, who want to disparage and patronize her. The more effectual villains in this novel are the upstart lawyers, the nouveau riche functionaries who attach themselves parasitically to the aristocrats and exploit whatever opening is presented to them: Richard Croft and his presumptuous son. The Crofts and their vicious allies commit the most unforgivable sin in the gothic/melodramatic universe: they slander the good name of a good woman.

It is in its subtle class distinctions, however, that ***Emmeline*** provides such an effective mirror of British society circa 1788. E. P. Thompson has noted that the translations of Voltaire, D'Holbach, and Volney into English made each of their "views appear more radical in English than in French." In particular, Volney's *Ruins of Empire* features a dialogue between the "useful labours that contribute to the support and maintenance of society" and the "valueless faction—priests, courtiers, public accountants, commanders of troops, in short, the civil, military, or religious agents of government." Thompson concludes that, "The notion of the parasitic aristocratic estate or order comes through as the more generalised 'class' of the wealthy and idle. From this the sociology of post-war Radicalism was to be derived, which divided society between the 'Useful' or 'Productive Classes' on the one hand, and courtiers, sinecurists, fund-holders, speculators and parasitic middlemen on the other." Croft and his son are meant to signify the ominous growth of the "parasitic middlemen," a new class of supposedly useful people who actually feed off a variety of vulnerable victims, namely, weary aristocrats or besieged women.

But as E. J. Clery has pointed out, political economy and civic humanism dominated Augustan political thought, valorizing the "real" wealth of land as opposed to finance capitalism, which was based on rumors and speculation and "encouraged the spread of a luxury—excessive consumption—which would corrupt individuals and destabilize the social order": "The attacks on novels and novel-reading in this period were part of the wider opposition to consumerism. In the case of supernatural fictions [or female gothic novels], the civic humanist objection to luxury commodities in general was supplemented by the enlightenment objection to a form of writing which perpetuated irrational ideas for the sake of affect. Within these complementary frameworks, supernatural fiction figures as the ultimate luxury commodity, produced by an 'unreal need' for unreal representations."[11] In order to conceal the "luxurious" or frivolous nature of novel reading, Smith cloaks her narrative in moral lessons of utility—maxims riddle the text—while she has her heroine and hero adhere to the strictest norms of civic humanism. Finally, in her validation of the values of Godolphin and his brother, she reinforces the hegemony of land-based wealth against all nouveau upstarts.

Repetitions or the threat of repetitions, the entropic power of history, characterize the plot of **Emmeline.** The secret marriage of Emmeline's parents is almost repeated years later in Emmeline's kidnapping and just-averted-in-the-nick-of-time forced marriage to Delamere. The adulterous affair of Adelina and Fitz-Edward, which produces another illegitimate child, a son, is used to slander Emmeline, who is accused by the upstart Crofts of being the unmarried mother of the child. The swirl of uncontrolled sexuality, fluid class status, and the naked power of the sword reverberates throughout this text in interesting and suggestive ways. The sword is always rattling in this novel, and the duel that is so feared finally does occur at the conclusion of the novel, thereby freeing Emmeline of the claims made on her by the passionate and violent Delamere. The repetitive structure, however, suggests that there are a limited number of scenarios permitted in this world for women. They can be wives, in which case they will either be the cause of disappointment or they will be disappointed. They can be mistresses, in which case the disappointment will be even more severe. Or they can be single and, therefore, sexual prey, in which case they will be kidnapped in the dead of night, slandered, and generally despised until they choose a protector-husband. And then the whole cycle will begin again.

To escape the sentimental impasse, the dead-end of emotions played out to their logical or illogical extreme, Smith presents a hero worthy of her heroine, Godolphin, who lives in a beautiful estate on the Isle of Wight—surely no coincidence, for the implication is that contact with society could only pollute him, and this is a man who has to be as highly principled and "good" as Emmeline in order to be worthy of her. Godolphin is tested when his sister has an adulterous affair with his best friend Fitz-Edward, runs away from her husband, and bears the resulting child in Bath, attended only by the generous and sympathetic Emmeline. Although she dreads her brother's wrath, Adelina and her son are saved when he decides to forgive her and offers her protection on his estate until her husband conveniently dies and she is free to marry Fitz-Edward. Godolphin loves Emmeline to distraction, but again he is "civilized" enough not to speak to her about his feelings until he is certain she does not love Delamere. Godolphin becomes *worthy* to be the hero of this text when he eschews "masculine" codes of conduct—epitomized in that very deadly masculine pastime of dueling—and empathizes instead with the "feminine" fates of his sister and Emmeline. Godolphin *becomes* a hero when he too feels his sister's disgrace so intensely that he sheds tears over her sexual downfall, and thereby proves that he is as "civilized" as the women who surround him.

Godolphin as a sentimental manly hero is contrasted throughout the work with Delamere, an antediluvian form of the hero, emotional, self-involved, passionate, prone to grabbing his sword or pistols and looking around for a duel to settle the score on his many grievances. We see the same sort of selfishly passionate man eradicated in Godwin's *Caleb Williams,* and in many ways Smith was as important an influence on Godwin as she was on Wollstonecraft. Delamere's emotions are sufficiently excessive to frighten Emmeline away from him and later cause him to become so ill with a fever that his life is thought to be in danger. The ideology of this tradition, however, is predicated on eliminating self-involved emotional men, eradicating them in favor of cool heads and benevolent and sentimental hearts like the one possessed by Godolphin. One is tempted to speculate that an emerging bourgeoisie locating its power in industrial capital and production found emotional and violent men to be anachronistic and embarrassing. Emotion in men was not a useful coin in the new capitalistic realm, at least not self-involved destructive emotions that produced the sort of undiffused energy that resulted in duels over issues like "honor."

Even Delamere's doting father, Emmeline's corrupt and usurping uncle, finds his son's excessive emotions a cause for concern. When Delamere tells his father that he will have nothing further to do with the Crofts, his father replies, "'Pooh, pooh! . . . you are always taking unreasonable aversions. Your blood is always boiling at some body or other. I tell you, the Crofts are good necessary, plodding people. Not too refined, perhaps, in points of honour, nor too strict in those of honesty; but excellent at the main chance, as you may see by what they have done for themselves'" (526). Several interesting shifts are revealed in this paternal homily. Lord Montreville senses that his son's "blood," his aristocratic heritage, has actually placed him at a disadvantage in the new social and economic world. People like the Crofts, capable of seizing the "main chance," have a control over themselves that the young aristocrat lacks. Further, in adhering to outdated notions of "honour," Delamere cripples himself and allows the Croft son to rise at his expense.

Indeed, it is a point of "honour" that dooms Delamere, precipitating the final duel that kills him. When his married sister decides to take a lover, she chooses one of Emmeline's spurned suitors, the French aristocrat Bellozane. After attending a play and seeing his sister openly flaunt her adulterous affair with the Frenchman, Delamere challenges him to a duel and he dies at Bellozane's hands. The death is gratuitous and had been foreshadowed since an earlier duel with another man who had the poor judgment to gossip about Emmeline and Delamere's relationship. The spiral here of adultery, dueling, "public scandal," and gossip, all coding behaviors that are strictly condemned by the civilizing sentimental tradition. In the new bourgeois order, very different values will be crucial: fidelity, monogamy, passivity, and decorum. To be sexually loose, violent, and prone to gossip is to be not only self-destructive but destructive of the social and economic fabric. In both codes, however, the issue is one of self-control. The older and aristocratic order, represented by the Montreville family, has lost control of itself, of their libidos as well as their tongues. The new order, represented by the chastened aristocrats, Emmeline and Godolphin, has learned the value of self-possession, restraint, bodily repression, and emotional control. Theirs are the genes that will reproduce and populate the future generation, whereas the violent and emotional genes of Delamere and his sister will be eradicated. The unlucky sister, we are pointedly told, ends her days in a French convent.

But the love stories that fill this text are almost ancillary to the real concerns of this work: inheritance, property ownership, social status, and class membership. This novel is also about how precarious it is for women to navigate and negotiate a social system that defines them always as appendages, dependents, ornaments, or incidental accoutrements to the "main chance," the patriarch. These characters find themselves drawn to France, ostensibly to escape creditors and live more cheaply, but they instead discover that they are led inexorably to retrace the final days of Emmeline's long-dead father. In a ramble through the French countryside, which would later influence Radcliffe's depictions of the landscape in *Udolpho*, Emmeline literally stumbles on her father's faithful servant Le Limosin, the only man alive who can testify to her parents' legitimate marriage in France. The human witness is as important in this culture as are the documents, the written records that testify to the marriage and the disposal of the estate. This is an important point and again reveals how decisively Smith captured the ideological strains of her culture. The older era—feudal, Catholic, and European based—relied on orality and human witnesses to verify truth. The new era—Protestant and technologically more sophisticated—relies instead on the veracity of written documents to prove claims and assert ownership of the estate. Emmeline's case was not complete without both modes, and these she was able to claim only by going back into the Old World of Europe and recovering, albeit vicariously, her father's history.

When Emmeline learns the truth, that she is the legal and legitimate heir to her father's estate, her first concern is that she has been deprived by her uncle of "education and affluence" (387). This statement is interesting for the priority it gives education in Emmeline's value system. By 1788 women understood the value of education in the social scheme of things. We know, of course, that Emmeline had largely educated herself by reading the moldy books left in her father's castle library: "Spenser and Milton, two or three volumes of the Spectator, an old edition of Shakespeare, and an odd volume or two of Pope" (7). We also know that Emmeline can play the harp, speak French, and sing very prettily, so we wonder exactly what sort of an education Emmeline thinks she has forfeited. It would appear that Emmeline is all too aware of not having the polish that either Mrs. Stafford or Lady Adelina possesses. And yet both of these women, raised with every advantage and educated in a way not allowed Emmeline, have married badly and lived to regret their choices. Smith's ideological purpose here appears to be subversive or at least ambivalent. On the one hand, she appears to advocate some form of formal education for women. On the other hand, even the best educations available to women of her day cannot and will not protect them from marrying foolish and improvident men (hence the necessity for the Hardwicke Act).

With an eyewitness in tow and papers that prove her parents were married not simply once but twice (by both Protestant and Catholic clergy), Emmeline descends on London and embarks on the most practical course she can imagine: she hires a lawyer and asks Godolphin's brother, Lord Westhaven, her rich and aristocratic future brother-in-law, to represent her claims against her uncle. This is interesting in itself, since Godolphin's brother has married Delamere's sister, Emmeline's cousin. The familial interconnections in this text come thick and fast; everyone it would appear is remotely related to everyone else, all of which makes the settlement of the estate a tricky business. In fact, at one point Emmeline exclaims that she thinks it best to drop the suit and conceal her growing love for Godolphin in the interest of family peace and harmony. Her words to Mrs. Stafford express the sense of powerlessness experienced by a woman in the grip of two generations of patriarchal power: "'I dread the mortified pride and furious jealousy of Lord Delamere on one hand; and on the other the authority of my uncle, who, 'till I am of age, will probably neither restore my fortune nor consent to my carrying it out of his family'" (452). Emmeline becomes acceptable in the eyes of the Montrevilles only when she possesses wealth and property in her own right. Only then will they consider her marriage to their son, but by then it is too late for this family to survive. Avarice, lust, greed, adultery, violence, and stupidity have doomed it. The Montrevilles have begun to resemble dodo birds, unable to evolve to the point of surviving a new, more reasonable, rational order.

When Emmeline produces the documents that prove her claims, the Montrevilles and their legal accomplices in crimes, the Crofts, are furious. The senior Mr. Croft had concealed the document in the first place, thinking his duplicity would never be discovered. And when it is, he is neither embarrassed nor contrite; he is furious. His psychology, the pathology of evil, is presented in some of the clearest lines of any female gothic text: "But as the aggressor never forgives, [Crofts] had conceived against Emmeline the most unmanly and malignant hatred, and had invariably opposed every tendency which he had observed in Lord Montreville to befriend and assist her, for no other reason but that he had already irreparably injured her" (455).

To be injured by someone places one in the position of being damaged goods in the eyes of the aggressor, and so women by their very status in such a society can only operate out of various positions of weakness. Emmeline cannot understand why the Crofts have constructed such a vicious slander campaign against her. Because she was seen holding Adelina's baby once by Delamere, she is vulnerable to being constructed by the Crofts as a fallen woman. Delamere believes the gossip on no evidence whatsoever, and from that mischief much misery ensues. But by the time Emmeline has learned about the gossip against her, she also has in her possession the documents that allow her to approach the patriarchy from a position of strength (read: money and land).

Emmeline is actually redeemed, however, not by the wills and eyewitnesses, but by her alliance with the aristocrat Lord Westhaven. It is his status as a reasonable and respected aristocrat that ensures the success of her claim. In Lord Westhaven, Emmeline knows that she has "found a protector too intelligent and too steady to be discouraged by evasion or chicanery—too powerful and too affluent to be thrown out of the pursuit, either by the enmity it might raise or the expense it might demand" (455). Lord Westhaven becomes the surrogate father Emmeline never had standing in the place of the missing phallic signifier; he becomes the stick, the "protector" she needs if she is to reclaim her rightful inheritance and the Castle of Mowbray. When she marries Westhaven's brother Godolphin, she closes the new and purged family circle around her. She and Godolphin move off the Isle of Wight and to Emmeline's remodeled family castle, where they live in blissful harmony with Mrs. Stafford and her children (sans husband) and Lady Adelina, her son, and the chastened Fitz-Edward.

Much was made at the time of its publication of the fact that Smith failed to punish Adelina and Fitz-Edward for their steamy adulterous affair (the one that Wollstonecraft condemned for "debauching the mind"). Living well appears to be the best revenge these characters are allowed, while the evil Crofts and the corrupt Montrevilles are punished by having to witness their children's blasted futures. Smith dealt finally in the coin of her sentimental realm, tears. Adelina and Fitz-Edward both shed their fair share of tears and are rewarded with a happy marriage—finally—to each other. Tears, the external indication of purified and purged emotion, appear to wash away all sins, including the most fearsome, adultery.

But tears actually stand as the reification of the new civilizing process that Elias has charted during the period. Tears signify one's membership in a new class of benevolent and tender-hearted bourgeoisie. Condemning a corrupt aristocracy was just one aspect of the larger social and cultural enterprise engaged in by women writers such as Smith. Violent outbursts of destructive emotion—dueling, adultery, gossip, and scandal mongering—were all characteristics of a flawed social and class system that no longer served the needs of a growing industrial economy. This crude and highly gendered social system coded dueling as masculinity run amok and gossip and adultery (verbal and sexual excess) as flamboyant femininity run rampant. In eradicating both extremes of behavior, the sentimental writer participated in her culture's attempts to write into existence a new gendered ideal: the womanly man and the manly woman. Godolphin cries and restrains himself as effectively as Emmeline cries and aggressively pursues the truth about her inheritance. He waits passively for her; she adventures until she is worthy enough to be his wife, because she has first been declared an heiress.

III

In this early female gothic work, the heroine sets the pattern that will be followed in the works of Radcliffe, satirized in Austen, hyperbolized in Dacre and Shelley, and finally canonized in the Brontës. The gothic feminist gains her property and bests the corrupt patriarchy, not alone but in allegiance with her accomplice: the feminized gothic hero and his patriarchal power base. *Emmeline* appears to present the "patriarchy" not as a monolithic power but instead as a contested space, with those contestants being first a corrupt aristocracy and the old, kin-based order it implies and second the rising bourgeoisie characterized by its commitment to exogamous marriages. Godolphin and his brother allow Emmeline to defeat her uncle, just as Rochester and a dead uncle allow Jane Eyre to have an estate and a properly chastised husband, "feminized" by his maiming and partial blinding. The wounds inflicted on the gothic hero are physical; the wounds inflicted on the gothic heroine are invariably emotional and psychological. But make no mistake: no one escapes unscathed in the gothic universe. To civilize a class and make a new social and cultural order requires ritual maiming, wounding, and testing. The construction of a "civilized" class of bourgeoisie required nothing less than the drastic purging and pruning of excessively gender-coded behaviors, characteristics, and emotions.

As we have seen in this text, dueling and physical violence are defined as extreme masculine behaviors, while the men who engage in such activities are eradicated by the end of the novel. And the appropriately masculine figure who emerges here as culture hero is a version of what I would call the sentimentally feminized man: Godolphin. But it is in the territory of the feminine that the real cultural work of this text occurs. *Emmeline* constructs a newly "feminine feminine" woman (in Irigaray's sense), a woman who has abjected out of her all "masculine feminine" tendencies, all excessively gender-coded behaviors like adultery, gossip, and diffuse libidinal energy. It would appear that the female gothic novel actually presents another version of the impulse that Kristeva has identified as operating primarily in male texts: intense abjection, a compulsive casting out of all those qualities that the social system defines as unclean. Kristeva defines the abject as that which "disturbs identity, system, order": "'subject' and 'object' push each other away, confront each other, collapse, and start again—inescapable, contaminated, condemned, at the boundary of what is assimilable, thinkable abject."[12] And the "boundary" that haunts the gothic is, I would claim, the amorphous construction of appropriately gendered behaviors. When a woman author holds female characters up to fictional scrutiny and then subjects them to literal and metaphorical beatings, she does so because she is operating out of a potent cultural force field, a coded system by which women warned other women how to behave and survive, how to masquerade as "feminine feminine" women in a man's world.

Irigaray builds on this notion when she defines masquerade as a form of male mimicry, a hysterical renunciation of authentic female desire because the woman can only know man's desire, not her own. That is, she can only become real in her own eyes by objectifying and positioning herself as an object of the obsessive male *gaze*. For Irigaray:

> Masquerade has to be understood as what women do in order to recuperate some element of desire, to participate in man's desire, but at the price of renouncing their own. In the masquerade, they submit to the dominant economy of desire in an attempt to remain 'on the market' in spite of everything. But they are there as objects for sexual enjoyment, as those who enjoy. What do I mean by masquerade? In particular . . . 'femininity' . . . a woman has to become a normal woman, that is, has to enter into the *masquerade of femininity* . . . [has to enter] into a system of values that is not hers, and in which she can "appear" and circulate only when enveloped in the needs/desires/fantasies of others, namely, men.[13]

Throughout the female gothic novel, woman paradoxically positions herself as the image of femininity in order to conceal that she has masculinized her subjectivity in a desperate bid to attract and hold the authenticating male gaze. The female gothic presents woman as spectacle rather than spectator precisely because the woman as author and reader has come to believe that she has no legitimate and independent existence in her own eyes; for the female gothic author and reader, woman's only reality can be found within the male signifying system she recognizes as the gothic, and in which she participates as both object and costume.

In the elaborately coded textual universe of the female gothic, professional femininity became very much a masquerade, and I use the term with not simply Irigaray's meaning in mind but also with Joan Rivière's seminal essay in view. For Rivière, "the mask of womanliness" and "authentic womanliness" are identical because femininity itself is an elaborate construction, a costume, a form of cover that shielded one from the blast furnace of the patriarchy. For Rivière, women who "wish for masculinity may put on a mask of womanliness to avert anxiety and the retribution feared from men." As Rivière observes, "Womanliness therefore could be assumed and worn as a mask, both to hide the possession of masculinity and to avert the reprisals expected if she was found to possess it—much as a thief will turn out his pockets and ask to be searched to prove that he has not the stolen goods. The reader may now ask how I define womanliness or where I draw the line between genuine womanliness and the 'masquerade.' My suggestion is not, however, that there is any such difference; whether radical or superficial, they are the same thing."[14] Rivière's thesis about femininity as an elaborately constructed and gendered masquerade has led to two alternate readings of the phenomenon: on the one hand the masquerade is seen as a "submission to dominant social codes," while on the other hand it has been read as a disruptive, subversive "resistance to patriarchal norms."[15] We are approaching once again the terrain of reading the conflicted female gothic text: is the genre socially subversive or does it actually encourage women to assume subject positions of acquiescence and passivity? As I will argue throughout, the female gothic, like masquerade as a guise of femininity, does both, and that bifurcated posture, ironically, has resulted in the very real basis of its continuing cultural power.

In an analogous manner I would contend that the British middle class built itself on the shorn backs of the aristocracy, taking wealth and property where they could and justifying the rout by exposing the emotional and spiritual inadequacies of the class they were replacing. It is no fluke that Emmeline is an aristocrat through her weak father and a member of the middle class through her beautiful mother. She is the embodiment of a society in transition, and thus unable to understand the rapid social and cultural changes occurring all around her. Her trip to France, a France on the verge of a violent revolution and political upheaval, suggests the political and social nature of her struggle to define herself. Just as the last residues of a strong feudal aristocracy were evaporating in France, so did Britain feel itself poised on the verge of cataclysmic transformation. The role and identity of women in this new social and political order were vague and amorphous at best. The fight to be a gothic heroine, to seize power and money and property in one's own right against the corrupt forces of an old regime, this was the central concern of the gothic feminist. To be a heroine in one's own right, however, led quickly to the realization that women finally could not act alone. They needed male allies; they needed a protection system behind them; they needed feminized husbands. But finding such a husband, a man who could be controlled, who could be trusted and safe, that was the challenge.

Notes

1. See Lawrence Stone, *Family, Sex, and Marriage in England, 1500-1800* (New York: Harper & Row, 1977), 35. Stone's controversial work charts the "growth of affective individualism" in eighteenth-century English bourgeois families as the expression

of "a new sensibility": "The Man of Feeling" embodying a "genuinely moral" movement, an "upsurge of new attitudes and emotions" (247, 238, chap. 6 passim). My emphasis is on how the woman of feeling gendered those moral movements through the topos of virtue in distress in the female gothic genre. On *homo clausus,* see Norbert Elias, *The Civilizing Process,* vol. 1, *The History of Manners,* trans. Edmund Jephcott (New York: Pantheon, 1978), 249-60; and the valuable discussion of "The Civilizing Process and British Commercial Capitalism" in G. J. Barker-Benfield, *The Culture of Sensibility: Sex and Society in Eighteenth-Century Britain* (Chicago. University of Chicago Press, 1992), 77-98. On the carnivalesque body, see Michel Bakhtin, *Rabelais and His World,* trans. Helena Iswolsky (Cambridge: MIT Press, 1968).

2. Gary Kelly, *Women, Writing, and Revolution: 1790-1827* (Oxford: Clarendon, 1993), 3-5. Markman Ellis provides a valuable overview of the relationship among sensibility, history, and the novel in his *Politics of Sensibility: Race, Gender, and Commerce in the Sentimental Novel* (Cambridge: Cambridge University Press, 1996), 5-48.

3. Thomas Gisborne, *An Enquiry into the Duties of the Female Sex* (London: 1797), 12-13.

4. Ann Radcliffe, *A Sicilian Romance,* ed. Alison Milbank (Oxford: Oxford University Press, 1993), 48-49.

5. See Claudia Johnson, *Equivocal Beings: Politics, Gender, and Sentimentality in the 1790s* (Chicago: University of Chicago Press, 1995).

6. See Elizabeth Kowaleski-Wallace, *Their Fathers' Daughters,* 9-20; and Jay Fliegelman, *Prodigals and Pilgrims: The American Revolution Against Patriarchal Authority* (New York: Cambridge University Press, 1982), 126. The nature of the "patriarchy" is, of course, a tremendously complicated and controversial subject, and I would claim that women are not by necessity its mindless and powerless victims. Recent contemporary feminists, such as Naomi Wolf and bell hooks, have asserted that women have developed a variety of enabling strategies that have allowed them to circumvent or undermine the patriarchy's power over them. For more detailed discussions of the theoretical and historical aspects of this question, see Gerda Lerner, *The Creation of the Patriarchy* (New York: Oxford University Press, 1986); and Susan Moll Okin, "Patriarchy and Married Women's Property in England," *ECS* [*Eighteenth Century Studies*] 17 (1983), 121-38.

7. Daniel Watkins, *Sexual Power in British Romantic Poetry* (Gainesville: University Press of Florida, 1996), 28, 30.

8. *Analytical Review* 1 (May-August 1788), 333. Wollstonecraft's reviews of Smith are discussed by Chris Jones, *Radical Sensibility: Literature and Ideas in the 1790s* (London: Routledge, 1993), 70-77. Also on the subject of Wollstonecraft as a reviewer, see Ralph Wardle, "Mary Wollstonecraft, Analytical Reviewer," *PMLA* [*Publications of the Modern Language Association of America*] 62 (1947), 1000-1007. Of interest, Wollstonecraft wrote a short but very positive review of Radcliffe's *Italian* (see her *Works,* ed. Janet Todd and Marilyn Butler, vol. 7 [London: Pickering, 1989], 484-85).

9. Carroll Lee Fry's *Charlotte Smith, Popular Novelist* (New York: Arno, 1980), 3-14, contains a biographical summary of Smith's life drawn from all the earlier sources.

10. Very little sustained critical commentary exists on *Emmeline*; however, the novel has recently been discussed as a paradigmatic work of sensibility by Janet Todd in her *Sensibility: An Introduction* (London: Metheun, 1986), 110-28. See also Katherine M. Rogers, "Inhibitions on Eighteenth-Century Women Novelists: Elizabeth Inchbald and Charlotte Smith," *ECS* 11 (1977), 63-76; Eva Figes, *Sex and Subterfuge: Women Novelists to 1850* (London: Macmillan, 1982), 56-68; Dale Spender, *Mothers of the Novel* (London: Pandora, 1986), 21-20; Mary Anne Schofield, *Masking and Unmasking the Female Mind: Disguising Romances in Feminine Fiction, 1713-1799* (Newark: University of Delaware Press, 1990); and Jane Spencer, *The Rise of the Woman Novelist* (Oxford: Blackwell, 1986). All quotations from Smith's *Emmeline, the Orphan of the Castle* are from the Pandora edition, ed. Zoe Fairbairns (London, 1988), with page numbers identified in parentheses in the text.

11. E. P. Thompson, *The Making of the English Working Class* (New York: Random House, 1964), 99; E. J. Clery, *The Rise of Supernatural Fiction, 1762-1800* (Cambridge: Cambridge University Press, 1995), 7.

12. Julia Kristeva, *Powers of Horror: An Essay on Abjection,* trans. Léon S. Roudiez (New York: Columbia University Press, 1982), 4, 18.

13. Luce Irigaray, *This Sex Which Is Not One,* 133-34. For a discussion of Irigaray's theories in relation to film, see Mary Ann Doane, "Film and Masquerade: Theorising the Female Spectator," *Screen* 23 (1982). 74-87: "For Rivière, as well as for Lacan and Irigaray who take up the concept within their work, masquerade specifies a norm of femininity—not a way out, a 'destabilization' of the image, as I argued. . . . But it is a curious norm, which indicates through its very contradictions the difficulty of *any* concept of femininity in a patriarchal society" (42-43). See also her "Masquerade Reconsidered: Further Thoughts on the Female Spectator," *Discourse* 11 (1988-89), 42-54.

14. Joan Rivière, "Womanliness as a Masquerade" (1929), reprinted in *Formations of Fantasy,* 35, 38.

15. Theories of femininity as masquerade, along with its association with gendered spectacles, spectatorship, exhibitionism, self-display, voyeurism, and woman as the object of an obsessive male *gaze*, have been crucial in redefining cinema theory as well as eighteenth-century literature. A useful overview of the issues here can be found in Catherine Craft-Fairchild, *Masquerade and Gender: Disguise and Female Identity in Eighteenth-Century Fictions by Women* (University Park: Penn State Press, 1993); and Terry Castle, *Masquerade and Civilization: The Carnivalesque in Eighteenth-Century English Culture and Fiction* (Stanford: Stanford University Press, 1986).

John M. Anderson (essay date 1998)

SOURCE: Anderson, John M. "In the Churchyard, Outside the Church: Personal Mysticism and Ecclesiastical Politics in Two Poems by Charlotte Smith." In *Seeing into the Life of Things: Essays on Literature and Religious Experience*, edited by John L. Mahoney, pp. 195-209. New York: Fordham University Press, 1998.

[*In the following essay, Anderson explores Smith's use of the conventional tropes associated with religious poetry to address social and political concerns.*]

Much of what we call great poetry, the poetry that stands most securely at the center of the canons of literature however much change may occur on its fringes, owes its stability to the fact that it is grounded in a foundation of shared narratives, genres, and tropes acquired in the course of a classical education. Writers who have been denied access to such an education (for reasons, most usually, of race, class, or gender) have often grounded their work in another, more broadly accessible tradition—that of the scriptures and of religious experience in general.[1] This tradition is, however, a hazardous source of raw materials because it partakes of revealed Truth; the very qualities which may make religious subjects attractive to "minor" poets—the certainty of its seriousness, the familiarity and at the same time the mystery of its imagery, and the strictly dogmatic conventions of religious expression (as opposed to the profound individuality which often characterizes individual religious experience)—may lead sophisticated readers to shy away from this poetry.[2] Such readers may give religious poetry superficial attention, may judge according to prejudice and thus never distinguish the valuable from the worthless. Thus, little magazines in *The Poets' Market* that receive floods of unsolicited submissions often seek to reduce the numbers by including in their advice to contributors the phrase "No Religious Poetry, Please." In the end, a canonical bias against religious poetry has necessarily contributed to the historical exclusion of important underprivileged poets, including women poets. The immense critical effort at present to restore to the canon important women poets of the past will necessarily involve re-reading, reconsidering, and perhaps appreciating for the first time much notable religious poetry.

A fine example is Charlotte Smith (1749-1806), who—besides being the author of a series of popular (often political) novels—often wrote poetry about religion. She never paraphrased the scriptures, as many of her contemporaries did, but the religious questions she addresses range from the social role of the church to psychological portraits of a woman's struggle between faith and despair. These are, of course, two quite different aspects of religion, and Smith addresses them in very different poetic forms—the one in an epic of powerful rhetoric and subtle political ideas, and the other in sonnets of psychological insight. We have remained too long unaware of the important social concerns, the complex ambiguities, the epic strength and lyrical passion of Charlotte Smith, who, as a religious poet, looks forward to George Eliot and Emily Dickinson.

These writers were not given to sweeping summary rejections like Shelley's "The Necessity of Atheism" or Keats's "Written in Disgust of Vulgar Superstition"; still less did they invent alternative mythologies in the manner of Blake. Their associations with established religion, as a social fact and as a source of language and imagery, went far too deep for such a response. Like Eliot and Dickinson, Smith underwent a complex struggle with the established church and defined a position for herself outside orthodoxy. Like Shelley's, Smith's reasons were certainly political, shaped by her support of the ideals of the French Revolution. Yet she places the most prominent explicit statement of her position—the ending of her epic *The Emigrants*—in the strongly apolitical imagery of an isolated soul finding completely sufficient communion with her God in nature.

The passage in question consists of only thirty-three lines, in a poem of nearly nine hundred. But the contemporary cultural significance of these lines is clear from the overwhelming critical response they received. Though other passages were more often quoted by critics—especially the action sequences which eventually made up the "fragment" that Smith later excerpted from her most ambitious poem—none received more critical comment. The reviewer for the *British Critic*, for example, expressed strong displeasure at considerable length:

> we lament that the gifted powers of imagination should be so grossly perverted, and we cannot but suspect that vanity (which absorbs all other considerations) predominates in the mind of a writer, who can court applause by the affectation of a criminal singularity. . . . This writer makes it her boast, that for her part she needs no exhortation to piety, since the works of creation serve her for that purpose. And, let us ask, what good heart do they *not* influence in the same manner? . . . Yet the genuine philosopher will not be content with silent meditation among hills and rocks: living, as he does, in social intercourse, he will join in social worship.
>
> (406)

This critic suggests ironically that Smith is affecting to avoid the crowd precisely in order to "court [its] applause." While the whole context of *The Emigrants* makes it clear that this "apolitical" passage does have political reverberations—that Smith has perhaps set herself apart from the crowd partly in order to address the crowd—the purpose is not to "court applause" but to commune with God. A rather more careful reading of the passage is clearly called for.

Though, like Wordsworth's nuns, she never fretted at working within the narrow room of the sonnet,[3] Smith, in her poetry, is rarely comfortable indoors. Like Dickinson, she rejoices in a free and solitary thought beyond the strictures and the censure of conventional society. But Dickinson would find this freedom and solitude in the confines of her room; Smith repeatedly finds it outdoors.[4] The church inspires in her a kind of moral claustrophobia.

Smith concludes her long poem with a kind of verse Last Will and Testament, and she thus reflects upon her own death, upon the reputation which will outlive her. She expects to be blamed, among other things, for her church attendance.

> And if, where regulated sanctity
> Pours her long orisons to Heaven, my voice
> Was seldom heard, . . . yet '*my prayer*' was made
> To him who hears even silence; not in domes
> Of human architecture, fill'd with crowds,
> But on these hills.
>
> (***Emigrants***, II.387-92)

Smith's conventional, female personification of "sanctity" here allows her to contrast this cool abstraction and her passionate self. The abstract regularity of "sanctity" is apparent in the structure of its "domes," so geometrical in comparison to the unpredictable, natural shapes of "these hills." ***The Emigrants*** is a political poem, and it is appropriately the church's exterior, political aspect that Smith objects to in these lines. She considers its interior, spiritual claims to mystical efficacy only by implication; these seem distorted by the oppressively regular forms that contain them.

She proceeds adroitly to a landscape imagery that is intricately designed to demonstrate that nothing essential is lost in moving beyond these forms.

> I made my prayer
> In unison with murmuring waves that now
> Swell with dark tempests, now are mild and blue,
> As the bright arch above; for all to me
> Declare omniscient goodness.
>
> (II.401-05)

The sea is the manifestation of God in these lines. Its atmospheric extremes are reconciled in the single concept of "omniscient goodness." Smith emphasizes that her escape to the wilderness has not, in the end, removed her so far from the "crowds," or from the conventions of church service. Like a preacher, she seems to have chosen a text, here from Psalm 65:7, which speaks of God stilling "the noise of the seas, the noise of their waves, and the tumult of the people." As the Psalmist's words point out, the fickle and "murmuring waves" are not much different from the crowds Smith has tried to leave behind. And Smith, exercising what her critic called "a criminal singularity" by praying outside the community, presents herself praying in quite orthodox "unison" with this crowd, away from any "dome," perhaps, but nevertheless beneath a church-like "arch."

The "bright arch above" to which Smith refers is a uniform blue and thus seems here to indicate the vault of the sky, though in architectural terms. The word "arch" is more appropriate to the rainbow—certainly an apt image, scriptural, in this context. But the rainbow, a prismatic analysis of pure white light, is an image fundamentally at odds with the "unison" upon which Smith insists.

The ironic contradictions of language and of the speaker's positioning of herself in relation to the community become more pronounced in the lines that follow:

> nor need I
> Declamatory essays to incite
> My wonder or my praise, when every leaf
> That Spring unfolds, and every simple bud,
> More forcibly impresses on my heart
> His power and wisdom.
>
> (II.405-10)

Pursuing a familiar argument against the corrupting intervention of language in favor of a pure direct experience of the Creation (an argument which has, despite its antiquity, come to sound so "Wordsworthian"), Smith continues to reject the community that shares the language in common, to champion instead the unspoken "impressions" made by Nature.

But like any such argument expressed in the very language it aspires to reject, this one cannot stand up to analysis. And Smith's speaker herself is less naïve than she may seem; she certainly chooses her examples shrewdly. Like the pure blue of the "bright arch," the single green that suffuses a natural "leaf" surely presents a clearer message than the artificial leaves of books with their eternally striving blacks and whites; yet the one like the other requires reading, though being "forcibly impresse[d]" sounds like a more passive process. And buds do come across as "simple" though each contains within it the potential for both fruit and seed—and for all the forked twigs of future trees. Still more suspiciously ingenuous is Smith's selection of "Spring" for her examples. It is stacking the deck in Nature's favor, surely, to make no mention of Winter.

But this manipulated imagery serves a rhetorical purpose of demonstrating the poet's generous willingness to give Providence the benefit of the doubt. She must establish that she has the best intentions, for she is about to venture into still more explosive territory. Still writing in a sympathetic, unimpassioned tone, Smith seeks to distinguish between the praiseworthy moral and emotional essence of religion and the destructiveness that occurs when this essence is corrupted.

> Saint-like Piety,
> Misled by Superstition, has destroy'd
> More than Ambition.
>
> (II.415-17)

The simplicity which finds its strength in purity, Smith suggests in an aphorism so filled with allegorical figures that it seems oracular, can easily become the simplicity of naïveté. This is an argument which seems unexceptionable when it is applied to any sect other than one's own, and Smith allows her readers to think here of the misled Catholics, rather than to apply the observation closer to home. Yet this depiction of over-zealous true-believers can be applied to excuse, or at least explain, the excesses of one's own community, religious or political. Smith erases the distinction:

> the sacred flame
> Of Liberty becomes a raging fire,
> When License and Confusion bid it blaze.
>
> (II.417-19)

With these lines, Smith returns to the explicitly political focus of *The Emigrants,* and indeed the remainder of the poem is wholly political, though it takes the form of a prayer.

Having examined the adroit political positioning which Charlotte Smith the epic poet achieves in an explicitly religious passage, it is the more enlightening to examine the subtle metaphysical explorations pursued by Charlotte Smith the writer of sonnets. Immediately before the passage I have quoted from *The Emigrants,* Smith gives a brief demonstration of the orthodox piety which she is about to bring into question; she paraphrases Thomas Gray's famous "Elegy Written in a Country Churchyard": "'I gave to misery all I had, my tears'" (II.386). One of her Elegiac Sonnets again recalls the Gray poem, but from the heightened remove of an almost Gothic context.

In comparison to *The Emigrants,* which remained out of print from its first publication in 1793 until Smith's collected poetry was published two hundred years later, Elegiac Sonnet XLIV, **"Written in the church-yard at Middleton in Sussex"** (which I shall refer to for the sake of brevity as the **"Middleton"** sonnet) has been reprinted rather often. It is one of the most prominent poems in recent anthologized selections of Charlotte Smith's work. Though it is not among the eight Smith poems selected by Dale Spender and Janet Todd for their 1989 anthology, it is one of the seven in Roger Lonsdale's landmark anthology of the same year, and Jennifer Breen includes it among the four Smith poems in her 1992 anthology.[5] Here is the text of the poem, including Smith's footnote.

> Press'd by the Moon, mute arbitress of tides,
>   While the loud equinox its power combines,
>   The sea no more its swelling surge confines,
> But o'er the shrinking land sublimely rides.
> The wild blast, rising from the Western cave,
>   Drives the huge billows from their heaving bed;
> Tears from their grassy tombs the village dead,[*]
> And breaks the silent sabbath of the grave!
> With shells and sea-weed mingled, on the shore
>   Lo! their bones whiten in the frequent wave;
>   But vain to them the winds and waters rave;
> *They* hear the warring elements no more:
> While I am doom'd—by life's long storm oppress't,
>   To gaze with envy on their gloomy rest.

[*]Middleton is a village on the margin of the sea, in Sussex, containing only two or three houses. There were formerly several acres of ground between its small church and the sea, which now, by its continual encroachments, approaches within a few feet of this half-ruined and humble edifice. The wall, which once surrounded the church-yard, is entirely swept away, many of the graves broken up, and the remains of bodies interred washed into the sea; whence human bones are found among the sand and shingles on the shore.[6]

A superficial reading of these lines might tempt us to dismiss them lightly as sentimental. They create perhaps a melancholy mood, a *frisson* of horror even—but little more than the fireworks of a minor poem. More considered re-readings lead to the recognition of something more profound. This is a considerable religious sonnet, worthy of the tradition of John Donne. The **"Middleton"** sonnet is a small masterpiece of compression, in which the poet has underscored her meanings with every resource available to her: the ambiguities and allusive reverberations of her language, the sound patterns created by that language, and the imagery it evokes. Ezra Pound would someday call these aspects of a poem *logopoeia, melopoeia,* and *phanopoeia,* respectively, but in favor of a simpler—though less precise—terminology, I will call them sense, sound effects, and imagery. Though these characteristics of the poet's art all function simultaneously, I will artificially untwist the strands in order to examine them each thoroughly.

The poem's most immediate impressions are probably visual. Smith has chosen a visually striking scene—the scattered bones of the churchyard, laid bare by the raging sea, lying white in the moonlight—made more striking by the juxtaposition of antithetical images. The "warring elements" of wind and water rage in stark contrast with the serenity of the moon above and the "grassy tombs" below. And the vastness of the sea and sky emphasizes the vulnerability of the little churchyard and its "village dead." This scene, which might have served as a subject for any number of Romantic painters—a Delacroix, say, or a Turner—is made still more Romantic by the addition of the melancholy figure of the speaker in the final couplet, whose whole life is epitomized as a "long storm." If this depiction of sublime nature has a religious significance, it is surely one of despair, a dark night of the soul. Yet this speaker is contemplative. A final striking contrast made visible by the picture Smith paints here is that between the insistent, intrusive physical world and the brooding, self-aware, interpreting mind that gazes "with envy on [the bones'] gloomy rest."

The imagery of this sonnet presents a moody study of contrasts, then, emphasizing the irreconcilable elements of the scene. The despair that these images convey arises from their striving, contradictory polarity. But this polarity is on the surface of the poem. Its sound effects, which work on a profounder and perhaps less conscious level, produce exactly the opposite effect. They weave these disparate elements together in intricate patterns which emphasize their unexpected similarities. Much of the religious power of the **"Middleton"** sonnet is the result of the subliminal workings of its unifying musical quality; to understand its religious depth, therefore, it is important first to examine in detail the sound effects by which Smith implies a divine order underlying and pervading the chaos of her visible world.

There is far more rhyming, far more sound effects of every kind, in the **"Middleton"** sonnet than the sonnet form requires. The poem begins, for instance, with a kind of ABBA form within the first line: *Press'd, Moon, mute, arbitress*. The painstaking brickwork of such patterning establishes a firm, resisting foundation—a consoling foundation of sounds which has little to do with rationality—within and upon which the poem's violent action and argument swirl. This patterning pervades the poem, from its first word, "Press'd," which rhymes with its last word, "rest." It must be noticed that these boundary-marking words rhyme, furthermore, in a particular way. The sound of *rest* is simply *Press'd* without its opening letter—an effect familiar from those "echo" poems in which the rhyming words diminish.[7] And the meanings of these two words are as nearly opposite as are their positions at the beginning and the end. The moon's pressing provides all the motion in the poem; the "rest" (a word which incidentally recalls the "remains"—all that is left—which Smith mentions in her footnote as well as "Rest in Peace") brings that motion to an end. It is a kind of musical "rest" as well, a silence. The moon is characterized as "mute"—an adjective which reflects audibly back on the noun with both alliteration and assonance. This silence characteristic of the governing moon is important in a poem of sound effects, where silence is a sign of both death and resurrection.

But before it reaches this final "rest," the poem is full of music. Smith employs both alliteration and assonance to great effect throughout. Consider the abundance of v's in lines 5-11. The rhyming nouns *cave* and *grave* (5, 8)—which "rhyme" in their sense as well as their sound—are rhymed again with *wave* and *rave* (10, 11)—and to this overflow is added *Drives, heaving, village,* and *vain*. And this v-sound returns in the final line—where it is used for the first time to describe an internal state, *envy*. This unusual, evocative, reverberating consonant provides a unifying note that vibrates quietly but insistently beneath the poem (and beneath the surface hiss of the equally insistent alliteration on the letter s). This musical constant softens the modulation when the sonnet shifts from the wide range and the wild noise of the octave to the hushed, reflective focus of the sestet.

Note the long-*i* sounds in the first five lines—all four of the rhyme words for the first quatrain—*tides, combines, confines, rides; while* and *sublimely, wild* and *rising*. With the first word of line 6, *Drives,* this sound suddenly ceases, to reappear only twice, as highlighting in the Rembrandt-gloom of lines 6-12: *silent* and *whiten*. In stark contrast, the sound appears three times in the penultimate line: *While, I,* and *life's*. Moreover, each of these words is essential. *While* marks the shift of meaning at the beginning of the couplet; *I* introduces the speaker for the first time; and *life's* explicitly expands the poem's specific imagery to a general application. A similar echo, again providing a darker contrast for the bright long-*i*, occurs when the interior rhyme of *doomed* and *gloomy* in the final couplet picks up the sound of the "moon, mute" in the opening.

The sounds and sights that the sonnet presents are emphatic, perhaps even verging on the melodramatic, but Smith creates all these effects in a nearly conversational tone which argues at last for an aesthetic of realism.[8] None of the images or sound effects seems unnatural or calls attention to itself in the manner of Smith's Della-Cruscan contemporaries. The same understated realism applies to the sense of the **"Middleton"** sonnet. Especially in her footnote Smith insists upon the "two or three houses" of the village, and its "small," "humble" church. This subdued presentation of the subject does nothing to diminish the poem's symbolic aspirations. It is appropriately set in a place called Middleton, beside a "half-ruined church," for it pivots quite thoroughly between a literal, materialistic, empirical expression of a melancholy longing for death on one hand, and on the other a metaphorical, allusive expression of hope in transformative resurrection.

Such ambiguities go to the heart of the poem. This sonnet is about the equinox, described as a powerful time of year—though an event of the solar, not the lunar calendar—but nowhere does it indicate which equinox is meant. The same word describes two quite different moments. Do we have here to do with the autumnal equinox, when all nature turns from light into darkness? Read with the right intonation, it is a spooky poem, and the traditional Christian holidays around the autumnal equinox, especially Halloween and All Souls' Day, fit it well. Or the vernal equinox, which marks the turning point from the death of winter's cold darkness toward the warm light of spring and life? The poem does not declare—it thus invites us to try each possibility. This equinox is not only powerful but "loud"—an odd adjective for the noun in any other poem than this.

Throughout the **"Middleton"** sonnet, the language revels in an almost Dickinsonian ambiguity. Let us take a single line (one which might have been written by Dickinson) as an example: "O'er the shrinking land sublimely rides." The word *shrinking* is both a literal description of the land which is being reduced in size by the action of the waves and also a personification of the land as a sentient creature which can draw back in fear. The word *sublimely* is a precise term for the kind of aesthetic effect the sea is producing, erasing boundaries, defying comprehension—but it is a deeply ambivalent effect, one which fascinates by horrifying. Finally, *rides* is very curiously employed here. Perhaps the word is used according to this OED definition: "(8) To float or move upon the water"—though Smith's line reverses the imagery and lets the water "move upon" the land. But other definitions may tell us at least as much: (9b), for instance, is "Of heavenly bodies: to appear to float in space," a definition which has much to recommend it, in a poem with such an explicitly sublunar setting (and the OED supports this definition with two citations from Milton about the moon). And the whole structure of the poem encourages support for (10) "To rest or turn *on* or *upon* something of the nature of a pivot." The pivoting that is the central motion of Smith's sonnet is made possible by such verbal ambiguities.

But she avails herself of ambiguities of structure as well. Take the opening image of the moon, for example. Seen only glancingly and never mentioned again, it is the only gendered figure in the poem; like "sanctity" in the *Emigrants* passage above, the moon is female (this is, in any case, a traditional Western conceit, from Artemis onward). We have seen already that this moon's pressing brings about all the action in the poem. She resembles the poet, and her abrupt disappearance is mirrored by the abrupt appearance of the speaker in the final couplet. In many of Smith's sonnets the moon plays an important role.⁹ And here the moon causes the sea to rave, like the "lunatic" of another important Smith sonnet, **"LXX," "On being cautioned against walking on an headland overlooking the sea, because it was frequented by a lunatic"** (Smith 61). That poem ends with Smith's speaker feeling the same "envy" for the lunatic as she feels here for the dead.

The *Elegiac Sonnets* as a whole provide one literary context for reading the **"Middleton"** sonnet—a context which emphasizes the tensions of its ambiguities. But for a religious understanding of the poem, there is clearly a still more important source, and not an unexpected one in a poem about a churchyard: the Bible. The Biblical story this poem most conspicuously recalls is a famous passage from Ezekiel, the allegory of the dry bones. "So I prophesied as I was commanded: and as I prophesied there was a noise, and behold a shaking, and the bones came together, bone to his bone" (37:7). It is a hopeful, resurrectional passage, in which God proceeds to promise "I will open your graves, and cause you to come up out of your graves, and bring you into the land of Israel" (37:12). But if Smith recalls this passage, she complicates her allusion by reversing important details: the bones Ezekiel is shown are most emphatically very dry; those that lie beneath Smith's gaze are very wet; Ezekiel speaks of a noise, Smith of silence. And most remarkably, Ezekiel presents his parable as a triumphant erasing of ambiguity, of difference, "And I will make them one nation in the land upon the mountains of Israel; and one king shall be king to them all; and they shall be no more two nations, neither shall they be divided into two kingdoms any more at all" (37:22). Smith seems to find a definitive explanation as well, but it is despair. The only hope available in the **"Middleton"** sonnet is the possibility of ambiguity. The "grassy" tombs of line 7 evoke a proverbial image of the brevity of human life—but it is clearly at the same time evidence of the triumph of life over death, as poets from King David to Whitman have implied.

There are a number of apocalyptic images in the poem—the sea rages beyond its limits, contrary to the promise God makes to Noah in Genesis 9:11. The dead leave their places of rest (see Matthew 27:52-53: "And the graves were opened; and many bodies of the saints which slept arose, And came out of the graves after his resurrection"), breaking the "silent sabbath of the grave!" The moon, which we learn in Genesis exists largely to mark holy days, is necessarily closely connected to the Sabbath. "Thus saith the Lord God: The gate of the inner court that looketh toward the east shall be shut the six working days; but on the sabbath it shall be opened, and in the day of the new moon it shall be opened" (Ezekiel 46:1). The Sabbath marks a boundary like the sea. "Or who shut up the sea with doors, when it brake forth, as if it had issued out of the womb. . . . And said, Hitherto shalt thou come, but no further: and here shall thy proud waves be stayed?" (Job 38:8, 11).

But of course Christ breaks the Sabbath repeatedly. And he justifies this behavior by referring to a higher reality, in much the same terms as Smith will use in *The Emigrants*. "Or have ye not read in the law how that on the sabbath days the priests in the temple profane the sabbath, and are blameless? But I say unto you, That in this place is one greater than the temple" (Matt. 12:5-6). The Resurrection itself is presented in the Gospels not as a breaking of the Sabbath, but as superseding it. "In the end of the sabbath as it began to dawn toward the first day of the week" (Matthew 28:1). A number of places in the Gospels which deal with this issue seem particularly relevant to the poem. Christ himself used the question of the Sabbath to explore polarities very like those in which Smith has positioned her poem. "Then said Jesus unto them, I will ask you one thing: Is it lawful on the sabbath day to do good, or to do evil? to save life, or to destroy it?" (Luke 6:9). These dichotomies are very much in accordance with the prophets; Ezekiel presents God bemoaning priests who "have put no difference between the holy and profane, neither have they shewed difference between the unclean and the clean, and have hid their eyes from my sabbaths, and I am profaned among them" (Ezek. 22:26). But the difficulty is the very ambiguity of the proof text. According to one interpretation it might be used to justify Christ's labors on the Sabbath; according to another it is the very passage to condemn them. In a fundamentally similar way, the same words which express the speaker's despair in the **"Middleton"** sonnet express her hope as well.

Charlotte Smith's religious opinions are impressively difficult to pin down in either of these poems. The subtly shifting rhetoric of her consideration of the church as a political entity is as ambivalent as the Negative Capability apparent in her psychological portrayal of religious experience. Her view from the inside out is as volatile and provocative as her view from the outside in. She never reaches the complacent or conventional stasis which we are too ready to expect of religious poetry. It is certainly time to expose the vivid bones of poetry long buried beneath such expectations; they may clatter unexpectedly together and take on new life.

Notes

1. Donna Landry characterizes the poems of one such group, eighteenth-century working-class women, as "a discourse elaborately coded and formalized: the same genres, modes, tropes, and preoccupations occur again and again, apparently without mutual recognition. . . . We can characterize this verse by the predominance of class-conscious georgic and pastoral poems, verse epistles to women, poems critical of marriage and of women's condition in general, poems in response to much-admired (usually male) poets, and versified narratives from the Scriptures" (13).

2. Roger Lonsdale writes, "The misrepresentation of the verse written by women in the eighteenth century of which I am most conscious is the limited space I have devoted to their efforts in the more ambitious or morally earnest genres, their pindaric odes, paraphrases of Scriptures, hymns" (xliv).

3. Wordsworth acknowledged that he read Smith's sonnets before composing his own.

4. Dickinson was never confined in her imagination, of course, and her poem "Some keep the Sabbath going to Church—," though it speaks of "staying at home," is similar to Smith's in its outdoor setting, among other things.

5. See Spender 294-99; Lonsdale 367-68; Breen 39-42.

6. Lonsdale excludes the footnote, Breen restores it.

7. A more famous religious poet than Smith—George Herbert—is perhaps the most remarkable practitioner of this technique. In his "Paradise," a poem in which the guiding metaphor is that of pruning, the rhyme words are themselves pruned: Grow, Row, Ow; Charm, Harm, Arm; and so on.

8. This aesthetic distinguishes the "Middleton" sonnet from such hypnotically "sounding" religious works as Gerard Manley Hopkins's "The Leaden Echo and the Golden Echo" which use very similar devices more extremely to achieve much the same effect of religious unity.

9. Beginning with Elegiac Sonnet IV, "To the moon" (Smith 15) and continuing through LXX, "To the invisible moon" (Smith 69).

Works Cited

Breen, Jennifer, ed. *Women Romantic Poets: 1785-1832: An Anthology*. London: Dent, 1992.

British Critic. 1 (1793): 406.

Landry, Donna. *The Muses of Resistance: Laboring-Class Women's Poetry in Britain, 1793-1796*. Cambridge: Cambridge UP, 1990.

Lonsdale, Roger, ed. *Eighteenth-Century Women Poets*. Oxford: Oxford UP, 1989.

Smith, Charlotte. *The Poems of Charlotte Smith*. Ed. Stuart Curran. Oxford: Oxford UP, 1993.

Spender, Dale, and Janet Todd, eds. *British Women Writers: An Anthology from the Fourteenth-Century to the Present*. New York: Bendrick, 1989.

Sarah M. Zimmerman (essay date 1999)

SOURCE: Zimmerman, Sarah M. "'Dost thou not know my voice?': Charlotte Smith and the Lyric's Audience." In *Romanticism, Lyricism, and History,* pp. 39-72. Albany: State University of New York Press, 1999.

[*In the following excerpt, Zimmerman explores Smith's strategy of appealing to the readers of her sonnets by developing a persona that is completely absorbed in private sorrow and oblivious to her audience.*]

> O! grief hath chang'd me since you saw me last,
> And careful hours with time's deformed hand
> Have written strange defeatures in my face:
> But tell me yet, dost thou not know my voice?
>
> —*The Comedy of Errors* (V.i.298-301)

No other grief that ever sighed has worn so much crape and bombazine.

—Viscount St. Cyres on Smith (1903)

Two poems addressed to Charlotte Smith appear in the August 1786 edition of the *European Magazine*, one submitted by "W. P.," another by a "constant Reader." The poems respond to the author of **Elegiac Sonnets,** a collection that had been "universally admired" (in Anna Letitia Barbauld's words) when it appeared two years earlier.[1] The poem by a "constant Reader," a sonnet, begins by admitting that propriety recommends against the intensely autobiographical quality of Smith's lyric poems: "'Tis said, and I myself have so believ'd / 'Fiction's the properest field for Poesy.'" Yet it is the suspect quality that arouses a response: "For sure than thine more sweet no strains can flow, / Than thine no tenderer plaints the heart can move, / More rouse the soul to sympathetic love; / And yet—sad source! they spring from REAL WOE."[2] Despite the reader's qualms, it is Smith's "REAL WOE" that is engaging. Many critics proved no more immune than this "constant Reader" to the spectacle of Smith's autobiographical speaker lamenting her plight in natural settings. And like this reader, they responded to the sonnets' forging of high emotion and believability. Readers and critics often reacted with "sympathy," their responses similarly personal in tone. According to Richard Phillips's *British Public Characters of 1800-1801,* "an elevation of sentiment, a refinement of taste, a feeling, and a delicacy, breathe through her productions, which by moving the affections and engaging the sympathy of the reader, excite in him a lively and permanent interest."³

Smith had practical reasons for needing to generate an "interest" both "lively" and lasting. *Elegiac Sonnets* was published for her family's support after her husband's imprisonment at the King's Bench for debt in December 1783. Smith had been born into far different circumstances: her father owned estates in Sussex and Surrey, and a townhouse in London. She experienced a social fall into economic instability only after a marriage at age fifteen proved emotionally and financially disastrous. The second son of Richard Smith, a West Indian merchant and a director of the East India Company, Benjamin Smith plunged the family into debt. Richard Smith's death might have alleviated the family's precarious situation, but their circumstances were actually worsened by his intricate will, which was, ironically, meant to protect Charlotte and the children from Benjamin's unreliability. When her husband was sent to debtor's prison, Smith turned to publication as a way to maintain the family's social standing until the estate was settled and her children could be educated as she desired. But the will generated legal entanglements that remained unresolved throughout her career; the Chancery suit was not finally settled until after her death. As a result, Smith's temporary venture into the literary marketplace lasted twenty-two years.

Elegiac Sonnets succeeded—both in providing financial respite and in establishing Smith as a popular poet who would earn her family's primary income after the couple separated in 1787. What follows is an account of how she found her audience with an unlikely vehicle: quiet, reflective sonnets featuring a solitary speaker lost in private sorrow. Rather than reaching out directly to the readers she needed so urgently, Smith turned away from them, performing the gesture that Northrop Frye describes as characteristic of the lyric poet, who "turns his back on his audience."⁴ Smith made an important discovery about the mode, which counters prevailing views of it: that a lyric speaker could win readers and hold their attention precisely by appearing to ignore them, by seeming absorbed in thought and oblivious to her surroundings. She became aware, in other words, of the impact that her poet could have on an audience on whom she turns her back in only the most literal sense. Smith's strong popular appeal illuminates the relationship between lyric poet and reading audiences as a dynamic exchange, a different account from predominant paradigms, which generally characterize the lyric's auditor as passive and silent. The availability of a wealth of contemporary responses to Smith's lyric poet by critics and readers illuminates a neglected aspect of the period's lyric poetry, for the mode's rhetorical capacities have been eclipsed by a conventional focus on psychological and emotional subtlety.

The discrepancy between Smith's immediate popularity and her virtual disappearance in the later arena of twentieth-century literary criticism recommends a return to her contemporaneous readers and critics. The contrast between their eager responses and her subsequent obscurity in literary history is telling. Qualities now generally deemed antithetical to the mode did not appear so to her readers: her sonnets combine self-consciousness with sincerity, introspection with rhetorical power. Popular success is not necessarily precluded in canonical models (although Byron's exclusion from M. H. Abrams's account of the "greater Romantic lyric" is suggestive), but a focus on the poet's subjectivity has discouraged consideration of readers' responses to lyric poems and lyric poems' responsiveness to their environments.⁵ Smith's example suggests a method for reading the period's lyric poems—within the specific circumstances of their production and consumption, and within the trajectories of poets' careers. Smith's own readers included those who have defined canonical Romanticism—William Wordsworth, Samuel Taylor Coleridge, Byron, Leigh Hunt, and John Keats. Together, Smith and her reading audiences bring into focus the mode's potential for a more dynamic relationship to its social contexts than we have come to expect.

Smith's sonnets are an important measure of how the Romantic canon was shaped according to one particular version of Romantic lyricism, a model based largely on the poems and critical prose of two of her successors, Coleridge and Wordsworth. Wordsworth's debts to Smith are political and poetic: he visited her in Brighton on his way to France in 1791, and he was given letters of introduction to her acquaintances, including Helen Maria Williams (who had left Orléans by the time he arrived). His literary debts to her begin at Hawkshead, where he read *Elegiac Sonnets,* and are formally acknowledged in a lavish 1835 explanatory note, expanded in 1837, to "Stanzas Suggested in a Steam-boat Off St. Bees' Heads."⁶ Wordsworth describes Smith as "a lady to whom English verse is under greater obligations than are likely to be either acknowledged or remembered": "She wrote little, and that little unambitiously, but with true feeling for rural nature, at a time when nature was not much regarded by English Poets; for in point of time her earlier writings preceded, I believe, those of Cowper and Burns."⁷ Coleridge's admiration of William Lisle Bowles has become a critical commonplace, and Bowles was, as Stuart Curran observes, one of Smith's "followers."⁸ Yet the connection between Coleridge and Smith is even more direct: in his "Introduction to the Sonnets" (1796), Coleridge cites Smith and Bowles as the poets who "first made the Sonnet popular among the present English," and he feels "justified" in "deducing its laws" from their works. According to their examples, the sonnet is a "small poem, in which some lonely feeling is developed," preferably "deduced from, and associated with, the Scenery of Nature."⁹

The qualities responsible for Smith's appeal to Wordsworth and Coleridge—solitariness, an attraction to natural scenes, and an emphasis on feeling—are recognizable in foundational accounts of Romantic lyricism, including Abrams's influential definition of the "greater Romantic lyric." Abrams bases his paradigm largely on Coleridge's and

Wordsworth's early poems, written in the period in which Smith's influence on them was keenest. It is not surprising, then, that the qualities that Coleridge and Wordsworth exclude in their laudatory portraits of Smith were also qualities subsequently deemed antithetical to canonical Romantic lyricism: a proven rhetorical ability that made her a popular poet. What was lost to canonical paradigms in Smith's example was an understanding of the mode's potential for engaging readers and responding to social concerns. Her poetry is especially provocative for the task of revising critical expectations of the period's lyric poems because her work resembles Wordsworthian poetics in important ways, and yet manifests marked differences, which cluster around the issue of her popular success. Thus, Smith helps to blur the lines between popular and canonical lyricism.

. . . . .

Smith's most important challenge to conventional assumptions about Romantic lyricism is her success in winning readers by seeming oblivious to them. Her example restores the significance of an overlooked corollary to Frye's famous description of the poet turning away from an audience: an acknowledgment that the audience, despite being ignored, remains on the scene. Smith knows that by seeming to forget her readers she gives them the pleasure of "overhearing." She employs the rhetorical allure of eavesdropping, making shrewd use of what is perhaps lyricism's most appealing quality, that of intimacy. Like Wordsworth, Smith finds in lyricism a vehicle for foregrounding the reflections and feelings of the poet. And like him, she drew charges of "egotism" for her intense introspection.[10] Yet Smith's sonnets disrupt an equation familiar to canonical accounts of the mode: that lyricism = disengagement. In her case, an intense autobiographical lyricism served a social function: it elicited responses that often matched her own in intensity.

Sir William Jones's comments on her sonnets exemplify the reaction that Smith desired. En route to India to assume a judgeship, Jones undertook a course of reading that included *Elegiac Sonnets*. In a letter, he thanks the friend who had given him "the tender strains of the unfortunate Charlotte, which have given us pleasure and pain." He reserves special praise for her most autobiographical poems: "[T]he sonnets which relate to herself are incomparably the best."[11] The *Gentleman's Magazine* concurs in its notice of the third edition (1786) of *Elegiac Sonnets,* judging that the "pieces . . . which are the genuine offspring of her own fancy, are by far the most interesting in her whole collection."[12] Although, from the first edition, the collection included both poems other than sonnets and translations of others' sonnets (Goethe, Petrarch, and Metastasio), the autobiographical sonnets that Jones admires established Smith's reputation.[13]

In her hands, an emphasis on interiority, which would also define the poetics of her canonical successors, turns a focus on the personal into a cult of personality. Smith's emphasis on the personal in *Elegiac Sonnets* is underlined by the collection's frontispiece portrait, which appeared in the first edition and in some subsequent editions. It is an engraving from a crayon drawing by George Romney, under which she places the first three lines cited in my epigraph, from *The Comedy of Errors* (lines that she slightly misquotes).[14] The lines from Shakespeare are printed in cursive, as if the poet had written them herself, and thereby taken personal possession of them. She omits the fourth line that I cite, but this is the line that, I would argue, underlies her poetic strategies: "But tell me yet, dost thou not know my voice?" Because Smith articulates private sorrows in the sonnets, readers came to feel as if they knew her, and so might respond to her as a familiar face in future volumes. A reviewer for the *British Critic,* quoting Smith, describes her appeal to readers: "So exquisite are the charms of Mrs. Smith's poetry, that it would indicate the utmost degree of insensibility not to be affected by her 'tale of tender woe, her sweet sorrow, her mournful melody.'"[15] Critics and readers not only associated the sonnet speaker with the poet herself, they also often addressed her as someone with whom they were personally acquainted, in reviews and in letters and poems submitted to periodicals (such as the sonnet by a "constant Reader").

The sonnets themselves aim to present the poet with the vividness of a portrait. In the poems, Smith allows readers ample opportunity to observe her, since she articulates her reflections and feelings while wandering through natural scenes. Readers respond because nothing, apparently, is demanded of them. **"To the moon" ("Sonnet IV")** is an especially apt example because it is accompanied, in some editions, by an engraving featuring a solitary female figure, one hand on her heart, the other extended before her as she gazes on the moon. The engraving visualizes, in the upward tilt of her head and the expressive position of her arms, the stylized verbal gestures of Smith's poetry, an unsurprising congruence given that she was closely involved with the production of her volumes and provided instructions for the plates commissioned for *Elegiac Sonnets*.[16] The first half of line one appears underneath the engraving:

> Queen of the silver bow!—by thy pale beam,
> Alone and pensive, I delight to stray,
> And watch thy shadow trembling in the stream,
> Or mark the floating clouds that cross thy way.
> And while I gaze, thy mild and placid light
> Sheds a soft calm upon my troubled breast;
> And oft I think—fair planet of the night,
> That in thy orb, the wretched may have rest:
> The sufferers of the earth perhaps may go,
> Released by death—to thy benignant sphere;
> And the sad children of Despair and Woe
> Forget, in thee, their cup of sorrow here.
> Oh! that I soon may reach thy world serene,
> Poor wearied pilgrim—in this toiling scene!

Smith's speaker is characteristically occupied in observing her natural surroundings and pursuing the thoughts they prompt, leaving the reader free to observe her. In poem and engraving, she looks away from an audience (in the portrait by Romney, Smith's gaze is also averted). Addressing her thoughts not to the reader, but to the moon, the speaker turns to the "fair planet" and imagines transcendence. Not only does she fail to notice auditors, she also envisions leaving the quotidian arena that she shares with them for another "benignant sphere." She wants to "forget," and she succeeds in losing sight of an audience and her environment. In the final couplet, the intensely personal nature of her meditations becomes apparent, with her confession that she is one of the "wretched" of whom she has spoken. The poem ends with a sharp focus on the speaker herself, as a "[p]oor wearied pilgrim."

Yet how do we account for the voyeuristic pleasure that Smith's sonnets provided a popular audience? What is the mechanism of this appeal? Michael Fried makes a relevant argument in his treatment of French painting in the second half of the eighteenth century. He describes the powerful effect on the viewer of watching a human figure who is absorbed, either in thought or in an event taking place. This air of distraction can create a "supreme fiction": that of the beholder's absence. The illusion of being ignored has an unexpected side effect—the beholder may experience the sensation of entering the picture, precisely because he or she is not made self-conscious in the act of watching, an awareness that can produce resistance. Smith's sonnets achieve a similar effect, via the poet's apparent obliviousness to an audience. What seems to be a desire on her part to turn away from social scenes as she wanders, "alone and pensive," proves captivating. Fried describes a "paradoxical relationship between painting and beholder": the painter seeks "to neutralize or negate the beholder's presence, to establish the fiction that no one is standing before the canvas." Yet "only if this is done can the beholder be stopped and held precisely there."[17] Fried's paradigm helps make explicit what is implicit in **Elegiac Sonnets**: just as on the stage, the social world is not excluded by the gesture of turning one's back to an audience. Like a member of a theater audience or the beholder of a painting, the reader of a lyric poem must lose the self-consciousness of spectatorship, must feel forgotten in order to forget himself or herself and make the necessary leap of identification.

Fried's argument is particularly relevant to Smith's sonnets because the poems resemble small tableaux in the collection's layout. There is one poem per page in most editions, and their intensely autobiographical quality renders them miniature, verbal self-portraits. Thus the reader is also a viewer, or spectator. The sonnets' copious natural images emphasize their pictorial quality, and the engravings that accompany several sonnets visualize the scenes that the poems describe, sometimes elaborately framing those scenes. An ornate border for the oval engraving of **"To the moon"** features thick foliage and an owl—presumably Athena's—atop a book. The speaker addresses Diana, whose unstrung bow and quiver frame the bird, as if the god has turned aside from the hunt to other topics. These emblems develop the portrait of the poet, who is thus associated with wisdom, purity, and female strength. The engraving significantly supplements the act of reading the poems, for readers can "see" the poet as they read her words. They can also "hear" her: working within the conventions of sensibility, Smith's liberal use of exclamations, sighs, and pauses strives to approximate the cadences of spoken language.

The emphasis on the visual in **Elegiac Sonnets** contributes to a theatrical dynamic that structures the poet's relationship to her audiences. It might seem that the dramatic cast of Smith's sorrows could alienate potentially distrustful readers. Early in her career, before she had made explicit the biographical sources of her elegiac tenor, a critic ventured to hope that her sorrows were fictitious: The *Gentleman's Magazine* reviewer cannot "forbear expressing a hope that the misfortunes she so often hints at, are all imaginary," since "[w]e must have perused her very tender and exquisite effusions with diminished pleasure, could we have supposed her sorrows to be real."[18] Yet as David Marshall explains, presenting oneself sympathetically, as Smith urgently needed to do, demands a measure of theatricality. Drawing on Adam Smith, Marshall argues that "since we cannot know the experience or sentiments of another person, we must represent in our imagination copies of the sentiments that we ourselves feel as we imagine ourselves in someone else's place and person." This means that "acts of sympathy are structured by theatrical dynamics that . . . depend on people's ability to represent themselves as tableaux, spectacles, and texts before others."

Smith uses all available verbal and visual means to represent vividly to readers the emotions her poet experiences. Her efforts to create a fullness of presence which might captivate readers are rendered explicit in the frontispiece portrait, which depicts Smith as a Shakespearean character. The sonnets demonstrate a theatrical dynamic in the lyric's often overlooked relationship between poet and auditor: her poems make clearer the implications of Frye's representation of the poet turning his back to an audience. What seems to be pure unself-consciousness on the poet's part, and passive reception by the reader, actually operates more dynamically: the poet presents herself in a particularly revealing way by expressing her reflections and emotions as in a soliloquy. The reader's ideal response is the going-out-of-oneself that Coleridge describes as readerly or sympathetic identification. Smith learned what Marshall, quoting Diderot, claims that good actors know: that it is "more important for the spectator to feel forgotten rather than literally be forgotten."[19]

In his account of the sonnet's "laws" derived from Smith and Bowles, Coleridge suggests that the reader's role involves an act of identification. He describes a mode of consumption which encourages a sense of intimacy: "Easily remembered from their briefness, and interesting alike to the eye and the affections, these are the poems which we can 'lay up in our heart and our soul,' and repeat them 'when we walk by the way, and when we lie down, and when we rise up.'" The reader identifies so strongly with the poet's "moral Sentiments, Affections, or Feelings" that they seem to be his or her own, and "hence they domesticate with the heart, and become, as it were, a part of our identity."[20] In a letter to Smith, William Cowper exemplifies the kind of response that Coleridge describes:

> I was much struck by an expression in your letter to Hayley, where you say that 'you will endeavor to take an interest in green leaves again.' This seems the sound of my own voice reflected to me from a distance, I have so often had the same thought and desire.[21]

Smith's poems and her letter to Hayley operate similarly: she succeeds in convincing others that they can understand her sorrows. In reading her words, Cowper mistakes her voice for his own and equates his thoughts and desires with hers. In Cowper's case, Smith wins not just sympathy but the practical assistance it inspires: he allowed her to dedicate **The Emigrants** (1793), her first long poem, to him. According to Marshall, when an act of sympathy is successful, the viewer may be moved to respond not just emotionally, but materially. He describes "the more specific response to a scene of tragedy, danger, or suffering that not only leaves one *affligé* but calls upon one to come to the assistance of someone in distress."[22] Thus Cowper reacts appropriately when he writes to William Hayley, who had himself aided Smith by accepting the dedication of **Elegiac Sonnets**: "I never want riches except when I hear of such distress."[23]

Accounts of Romantic lyricism have traditionally emphasized the poet's capacity for sympathetic identification with other persons or with beloved natural places; Smith's sonnets highlight another, less noticed structure of identification—between reader and poet. It is not that the reader has been entirely forgotten in paradigms of Romantic lyricism, but that figure is generally considered either tangential to the mode's main concerns—the identifications and understandings of the poet—or subordinate to them.[24] The intense identificatory relationship between reader and poet is, however, a primary site of the mode's rhetorical salience. The theatrical dynamic that informs Smith's lyric poems recommends a revision of paradigms that emphasize a standard of sincerity, without an attention to how this quality operates rhetorically. As the period's "poetic norm," the lyric has seemingly embodied its premium on sincerity, a quality traditionally associated with a naturalness of emotion and an emphasis on expressivity.[25] As a result, the theatrical dynamic established by the lyric scenario of "overhearing" articulated emotion has been neglected. Smith's sonnets foreground one of the mode's key complexities: the unexpected complementarity of sincerity and theatricality for contemporaneous readers, an issue to which I will return.

. . . . .

First, however, I want to address more specifically how **Elegiac Sonnets** won a popular audience. Smith's shrewd attention to the framing of her sonnets in the collection recommends a strategy for analyzing the rhetorical capacity of lyric poems: by reading them in the context of the volumes in which they appear. Smith is an excellent candidate for this kind of analysis because she reinforced the appealing self-portrait of the sonnets by carefully surrounding these poems with prefaces, explanatory notes, and engravings. The publication history of **Elegiac Sonnets** suggests that Smith keenly understood the nature of her readers' receptivity to her solitary poet. She took an active role in what Judith Phillips Stanton calls, quoting the poet, her "literary business," and this effort included crafting the collection to capitalize on the popularity of her melancholy speaker.[26] From the first edition, the collection's prose sections contributed to its success by enhancing the poems' portrait of the poet. In successive editions, Smith added new prefaces and expanded a section of explanatory notes that identifies literary allusions and the flowers, animals, and places mentioned in the poems. The prefaces and notes, with their conversational, quotidian prose, throw into bolder relief the poems' emphases on solitude, introspection, and a desire for transcendence. In a "memoir" published after Smith's death, the *Monthly Magazine* testifies to a contemporaneous association of her sonnets with an impulse toward transcendence. The critic speculates that Smith pursued her career after the sonnets' initial success because doing so "contributed to divert her thoughts, and to lead her mind into the visionary regions of fancy, rendering the sad realities she was suffering under, in some measure less poignant."[27]

In the sonnets themselves, Smith provides her audience with the pleasure of watching a poet removed from all that is mundane by the very language in which she spoke. Despite some experimentation with English and Italian forms, the poems follow strict rhyme schemes and use formal diction, a strategy that enhances a sense of the poet's detachment from daily experience. Thus, in addition to their strong focus on subjectivity, Smith's sonnets conform to another of the main ways in which lyricism is often assumed to distance itself from social contexts: a specialization of language that removes the poem from "the ordinary circuit of communication," in Jonathan Culler's terms.[28] In **"Written at the close of spring"** (**"Sonnet II"**), an explanatory note establishes the poem's linguistic difference from "ordinary" speech. The sonnet begins by describing how "[t]he garlands fade that Spring so lately wove, / Each simple flower which she had nursed in dew, / Anemonies, that spangled every grove, / The primrose wan, and harebell mildly blue." A brief explanatory note consists of two alternate names for the anemone: "*Anemony Nemeroso*" and "[t]he wood Anemony." Smith's gloss of "anemone" seems to translate from the rarefied language of poetry into the language of scientific classification and the vernacular. In the process the flower is transformed from poetic prop into an object from the reader's environment. In the poem, the anemone is significant only as a natural detail, which reminds the poet of her own lack of rejuvenation. In the explanatory note, the focus shifts to the flower as a natural object in the reader's environment, and the effect is to distinguish between poet's and readers' worlds.

A sense of the poet's remove from the ordinary is augmented by the establishment of a different temporality in the sonnets. Within the volume, the poet is held in a moment of perpetual sorrow that contrasts with a world of process in the prefaces and notes. **"Written at the close of spring"** thematizes the atemporality of the poet's world by juxtaposing the progress of the seasons with her unchanging state. The closing couplet asks, "Another May new buds and flowers shall bring; / Ah! why has happiness—no second Spring?" Thus the lyric, frequently associated with a desire for immortality and transcendence, seeks to wrest itself out of the cause and effect of social history, an impulse which prompted a new historical critique of the Romantic ideology. **"Written in the churchyard at Middleton in Sussex" ("Sonnet XLIV")** and its accompanying note exemplify how Smith's sonnets seem to register fleeting moments detached from their narrative contexts:

> Press'd by the Moon, mute arbitress of tides,
> While the loud equinox its power combines,
> The sea no more its swelling surge confines,
> But o'er the shrinking land sublimely rides.
> The wild blast, rising from the Western cave,
> Drives the huge billows from their heaving bed;
> Tears from their grassy tombs the village dead,
> And breaks the silent sabbath of the grave!
> With shells and sea-weed mingled, on the shore
> Lo! their bones whiten in the frequent wave;
> But vain to them the winds and waters rave;
> *They* hear the warring elements no more:
> While I am doom'd—by life's long storm opprest,
> To gaze with envy on their gloomy rest.

The sonnet records an almost gothic moment: the sea, driven by the moon, washes on shore in a wave that removes dirt from the village cemetery, uncovering the dead. By using the present tense, Smith emphasizes the transitoriness both of the poet's view of the white bones and of her flash of recognition that unlike herself, the dead can no longer be "opprest" by "life's long storm." Natural event and psychological revelation occur instantaneously. The reader who turns to the back of the volume to read the accompanying note finds, in contrast, a world of gradual but inexorable change:

> Middleton is a village on the margin of the sea, in Sussex, containing only two or three houses. There were formerly several acres of ground between its small church and the sea, which now, by its continual encroachments, approaches within a few feet of this half-ruined and humble edifice. The wall, which once surrounded the church-yard, is entirely swept away, many of the graves broken up, and the remains of bodies interred washed into the sea; whence human bones are found among the sand and shingles on the shore.

The note contains the prehistory and the aftermath of the sonnet's moment—its context. It reads as if the viewer has pulled back to a place from which the human and natural consequences of a transformative lyric instant could be surveyed. Smith's explanatory notes document a world of myriad change, embodied here in the erosion altering the landscape and the villagers' lives, while the speaker remains in an unalterable state of melancholy.

The sonnets' sense of timelessness is so pronounced that Smith eventually found it necessary publicly to defend her lingering sorrow. She addresses the issue in the preface to the sixth edition (1792) by reporting an exchange with a friend who had recommended that she try "'a more cheerful style of composition.'" The person who made what St. Cyres describes as this "highly unfortunate suggestion" receives in response a pointed justification: an account of continued misery. Recalling her early sonnets, she explains, "I wrote mournfully because I was unhappy—And I have unfortunately no reason yet, though nine years have since elapsed, to *change my tone*" (5). Smith's poet continues to hold her melancholy pose: it is as if she has been caught in one repeated moment of intense sorrow. Her sonnets seem to epitomize Sharon Cameron's description of how lyric poems "fight temporality with a vengeance," although Smith claims that her stasis is involuntary.[29] Yet St. Cyres cannily points to the rhetorical effect of this sense of lyric timelessness: "Having chosen to come forward as a Laureate of the Lachrymose, she thought herself bound in honour to live consistently up to her part, and treat whatever subject happened to engross her pen in terms of undiluted lachrymosity." Variety, she intuited, was not what her readers wanted. St. Cyres speculates that "quite an appreciable proportion of her tears was due to purely literary requirements," reminding us that she "was the servant of the public, and her many-headed master called for a melancholy tune."[30] His ironic commentary on Smith's career recognizes the rhetorical salience of a turn away from quotidian temporality and into an interior realm of the emotions, which have a chronology of their own.

I have been arguing that Smith's sonnets won readers by demonstrating her obliviousness to their presence, a pose enhanced by her formal language and what Cameron calls "lyric time." Yet her success depended equally upon her believability: the reader must have the sensation of witnessing "real woe" in order to respond with the sympathy and loyalty she required, publishing on average one work per year. The sonnets' success required both extreme emotions and a perception of their authenticity, a combination of exaggeration and actuality, theatricality and sincerity, which contemporary readers did not find contradictory. Leigh Hunt confirms her success at combining these qualities in her sonnets, testifying that several of them "are popular for their truth alone": "[E]verybody likes the sonnets because nobody doubts their being in earnest, and because they furnish a gentle voice to feelings that are universal."[31]

That most of Smith's readers seemed persuaded of the sonnets' truthfulness is especially remarkable given their self-consciously theatrical tenor. Moreover, as Adela Pinch points out, Smith's habitual use of literary allusions raises epistemological questions about the sources of her sorrow, since she borrows so many phrases to express it. How are her readers, or even the poet herself, to be sure that the despair she voices is hers?[32] Yet by the time that the first edition of the sonnets appeared in 1784, Smith's potential readers were well schooled in the conventions of sensibility, a tradition that collapsed the ostensible boundaries between life and art by presenting codes of behavior to be followed by poets, novel characters, and readers alike. As Janet Todd explains, "[i]n all forms of sentimental literature, there is an assumption that life and literature are directly linked, not through any notion of a mimetic depiction of reality but through the belief that the literary experience can intimately affect the living one."[33] Thus, Smith's readers would not necessarily question the authenticity of her poet's lamentations, even though her responses to loss were modeled on literary figures who had experienced a similar despair. The symbiotic relationship between art and life that sensibility prescribed would have encouraged Smith to borrow from other poets, even as her readers would feel encouraged to model their own expressions of grief on her poet—as contemporaneous sonnets addressed to or about Smith in periodicals suggest that many did.

In the preface to the first edition, Smith stakes her claim to the poems' sincerity by explaining their compositional origins: "Some very melancholy moments have been beguiled by expressing in verse the sensations those moments brought" (3). The explanatory notes support this claim to autobiographical veracity by grounding the poems in Smith's extensive reading and in her very public biography. A note to the poem, **"Written in Farm Wood, South Downs, in May 1784" ("Sonnet XXXI")**, glosses a reference to "Alpine flowers": "An infinite variety of plants are found on these hills, particularly about this spot: many sorts of Orchis and Cistus of singular beauty, with several others." The note contextualizes the poem autobiographically: the sonnet was written on walks in Smith's native Sussex, where "Alpine flowers" grew. Sir Walter Scott, who preferred her novels to her poetry, comments: "It may be remarked, that Mrs. Smith not only preserves in her landscapes the truth and precision of a painter, but that they sometimes evince marks of her own favourite pursuits and studies."[34] The notes' attention to natural historical detail lends an authenticity to the volume that in turn lends credence to her emotional claims: her poet's extreme sorrow is more believable because Smith situates her in a carefully documented environment. Thus, although Smith sets up a contrast between the self-consciously poetic natural imagery of the sonnets and the empirical and vernacular vocabulary of the notes, the notes serve to confirm the poems' truthfulness by showing that her descriptions—of her environment and, by implication, her emotions—are accurate.

John Clare testifies to the effectiveness of what might be termed a rhetoric of empirical evidence in the notes. In Clare's description of "[t]he Fern Owl or Goatsucker or Nightjar or nighthawk" in one of his unpublished Natural History Letters, he alludes to Smith's poem, **"Composed during a walk on the Downs, in November 1787" ("Sonnet XLII")**. He says of her poems, "I felt much pleasd with them because she wrote more from what she had seen of nature then from what she had read of it there fore those that read her poems find new images which they had not read of before tho they have often felt them & from those assosiations poetry derives the power of pleasing in the happiest manner."[35] Clare echoes Cowper's sense that reading Smith's sonnets is like finding one's own reactions recorded in them. For Clare, it is not emotions, but responses to natural scenes, that seem familiar, yet "new." He testifies to the pleasure of this experience as a reader and incorporates her example into his own poetics, especially his early, richly descriptive sonnets. What Clare learns from Smith is that a sense of the sincerity of the poet's responses to a natural environment could be compelling, a lesson he proves himself with his initial success in *Poems Descriptive of Rural Life and Scenery*. Thus the notes both verify the poet's sentiments and confirm the timelessness of her plight. They remove the poet from her readers' quotidian experience even as they render her more accessible to their understanding.

. . . . .

In the sonnets, Smith learns to exercise the rhetorical potential of the often overlooked relationship between the lyric poet and an audience; in her longer poems, *The Emigrants* and "Beachy Head," she most fully demonstrates that understanding, employing the capacity of lyricism for social ends. By turning her pen to specific causes, including but extending beyond her own financial relief, Smith pursues the implications of her discovery of the considerable appeal of an autobiographical lyric speaker lost in sorrowful reflections. In these poems, the implications of Smith's poetics for revisions of canonical models of Romantic lyricism are most fully evident.

These long poems represent not a departure from the sonnets but an extension of their poetic strategies. In *The Emigrants*, Smith makes a case for the émigrés arriving on British shores in 1793. Her rhetorical strategy remains lyric: she simply expands the sonnets' sharp focus on her autobiographical poet to include others whom she perceived as like her. Smith associates the émigrés with her already popular cultural figure, and thus attempts to lend to them some of the sympathy she had generated for herself. Stuart Curran describes the poem's "underlying metaphorical strategy," which is "to connect Charlotte Smith as center of perception to the exiles from France's Terror."[36] A strong sense of the poet's presence remains in the poem, even though the title figures are usually in the foreground. As the *European Magazine* observes, "we can discover" the poet "almost at the bottom of every page, as we may the portrait of some of the most renowned painters in the corner of their most favourite pictures." The critic recognizes the poem's lyric impetus by noting that "[t]he whole Poem may be considered as a soliloquy pronounced by the authoress."[37] Although much of the poem is devoted to describing the émigrés' circumstances, the speaker remains at its center, the filtering consciousness through which we view their wandering forms; their plight is seen through her melancholy lens.

Smith identifies herself with the émigrés by recalling her own experience of exile in Normandy, where the family fled from her husband's creditors, from fall 1784 to spring

1785. Smith seems to have accompanied her husband, with their children, because he could not speak French; she immediately returned to England in an effort to appease his creditors, but her failure prompted her return for the winter. She explains in the poem's dedication to Cowper that she was drawn to represent the plight of the émigrés because their figures "pressed upon an heart, that has learned, perhaps from its own sufferings, to feel with acute, though unavailing compassion, the calamity of others" (132). The émigrés were also attractive to Smith because their circumstances could easily be drawn into parallel with her own. Stanton points out that Smith emphasized her genteel origins in her works; she identified herself by her father's family estate in the first edition of **Elegiac Sonnets** by calling herself "Charlotte Smith, of Bignor Park, Sussex." In **The Emigrants,** she associates herself with French aristocrats, particularly a mother who sits disconsolate, surrounded by her children, on the Sussex shore. Smith features the clergy and nobility, whose falls from privilege made their histories resonate with her very public biography, although estimates of the social status of the émigrés have suggested that 25 percent were clergy, 17 percent nobility, and 51 percent from the Third Estate.[38]

Following Edmund Burke's *Reflections on the Revolution in France* and Thomas Paine's rebuttal in *The Rights of Man,* Smith enters the revolution debate with a poetics of sympathy pitched at middle- and upper-class readers. In the poem, she models for readers the kind of sympathetic response toward the émigrés that she wants them to imitate. **The Emigrants** is important to an understanding of the rhetorical salience of Smith's lyricism because it tests how successfully it could respond to social topics. Two facets of Smith's lyricism come into focus in **The Emigrants**: its potential for moving readers about others' causes, and the liabilities of this strategy for the poet. With **The Emigrants,** she learned that the strength of her poet's appeal could be turned against her, in that many critiques of the poem were highly personal in tone. Yet the negative responses that Smith received also testify to a contemporary understanding that lyric poetry could be an effective vehicle for addressing social events.

The poem appears in the same year as **The Old Manor House** Smith's fifth novel, and after the sixth edition of **Elegiac Sonnets,** (1792). It was published early in the summer of 1793, in the wake of the September massacres, the trial and execution of Louis XVI on 21 January 1793, and the outbreak, ten days later, of war between France and England. Smith's positive representation of revolution in France and reform in England in **Desmond** (1792) was followed by **The Emigrants** and **The Banished Man** (1794), a poem that promotes sympathy for the émigrés and a novel that features an émigré protagonist. These works are part of what Florence Hilbish calls Smith's "French period," which included works published from 1791 to 1793, written "out of the author's sympathy for those oppressed, whether politically, socially, or economically."[39] The publication of Smith's "French" works follows a trajectory similar to the autobiographical narrative that Wordsworth provides in *The Prelude,* detailing his change of heart after the declaration of war and the increasing violence of the revolution's aftermath. Smith intimates a similar conversion in the poem's dedication to Cowper. Yet although she laments the excesses of the revolution, she does not renounce radical ideals, as does Coleridge in "France: An Ode." In fact, Smith circumspectly defends her radical ideals in the dedication, arguing that "by confounding the original cause with the wretched catastrophes that have followed its ill management," the revolution itself has unfairly become tainted, and "the very name of Liberty" has "lost the charm it used to have in British ears." But Smith publicly distances herself from radical politics in defending the exiles of the ancien régime.

She joins instead a popular middle-class cause, promoted by conservative figures such as Hannah More, who published two pamphlets to raise money for the émigrés' support, one titled *An Elegant and Pathetic Address for the Ladies of Great Britain on behalf of the French Emigrants.* More's profits were contributed to a "Fund for the Relief of the Suffering Clergy of France in the British Dominions," begun by John Eardley Wilmot, son of the lord chief justice, in September 1792. Wilmot had advertised for a meeting to organize relief, one prominent enough to be reported in the *Gentleman's Magazine,* which had a solidly middle-class audience.[40] The meeting was attended by such prominent figures as Edmund Burke, William Wilberforce, and the bishops of London and Durham. Other groups were simultaneously being formed for similar purposes. In 1795 the duchess of York organized a committee specifically for "'female emigrants who were ill or *en couches.*'"[41] Thus when Smith represents an émigrée surrounded by her children in **The Emigrants,** she features a figure already prominent in the popular imagination.

The poem opens with an expansive description of the poet's view of the Sussex coast, a scene that prompts reflections on the contrast between its tranquility and human suffering. We recognize Smith's autobiographical poet "on the Cliffs to the Eastward of the Town of Brighthelmstone in Sussex" on "a Morning in November, 1792." She watches a group of exiles: several members of the Catholic clergy, a mother with children, and a nobleman who speaks to the woman. They are "Fortune's worthless favourites" (I.315) and, as such, Smith can align their circumstances with hers. Solitary sorrow gives way to shared misery as she exclaims, "Alas! how few the morning wakes to joy!" In the sonnets, the poet is usually the sole unhappy figure in the scenes she surveys, yet the emigrants are easily incorporated into the poet's contemplations. They are linked with the poet formally by repeated turns in thought, which join their plight with hers. After describing several members of the clergy wandering along the Sussex cliffs, the poet's reflections shift to her own sorrows:

> . . .—Still, as Men misled
> By early prejudice (so hard to break),
> I mourn your sorrows; for I too have known

> Involuntary exile; and while yet
> England had charms for me, have felt how sad
> It is to look across the dim cold sea,
> That melancholy rolls its refluent tides
> Between us and the dear regretted land
> We call our own—as now ye pensive wait
> On this bleak morning, gazing on the waves
> That seem to leave your shore . . .
>
> (I.153-63)

The passage begins with the poet observing "men misled" from a distance, but she quickly recognizes her affinity with them, practicing the sympathetic identification that she models for readers, as "I" becomes "us" and "we." She literally puts herself in their position: she recalls gazing "across the dim cold sea" toward home during her self-exile in France. In fact, meditation upon her own circumstances encourages the poet to detect signs of distress in others. She is drawn to the exiles because they resemble her; there is clearly a narcissistic impulse in her response to them. Yet that impulse also serves to keep her attention on their circumstances, and as a result she incorporates them into her meditations.

Like the poet of the sonnets, she observes her surroundings and then reflects upon what she sees. This turn inward is often assumed to mark the eclipse of the external world, yet here an internalizing impulse actually projects the poet into social scenes:

> Long wintry months are past; the Moon that now
> Lights her pale crescent even at noon, has made
> Four times her revolution; since with step,
> Mournful and slow, along the wave-worn cliff,
> Pensive I took my solitary way,
> Lost in despondence, while contemplating
> Not my own wayward destiny alone,
> (Hard as it is, and difficult to bear!)
> But in beholding the unhappy lot
> Of the lorn Exiles; who, amid the storms
> Of wild disastrous Anarchy, are thrown,
> Like shipwreck'd sufferers, on England's coast,
> To see, perhaps, no more their native land,
> Where Desolation riots: They, like me,
> From fairer hopes and happier prospects driven,
> Shrink from the future, and regret the past.
>
> (II.1-16)

The poet begins the passage "solitary" and "lost in despondence," but in the act of "contemplating" her "own wayward destiny," she begins to consider the "lorn Exiles." She demonstrates that the lyric's progress toward interiority need not lead to disengagement. The poem suggests that introspection should not be equated with solipsism, that a desire for transcendence can coexist with social feeling.

Moreover, the poem thematizes the poet's decision not to look away from what she sees. Near its opening, she confesses a desire for retreat, for the kind of detachment we expect of the lyric poet:

> How often do I half abjure Society,
> And sigh for some lone Cottage, deep embower'd
> In the green woods, that these steep chalky Hills
> Guard from the strong South West; where round their base
> The Beach wide flourishes, and the light Ash
> With slender leaf half hides the thymy turf!—
> There do I wish to hide me . . .
>
> (I.42-48)

The poet longs to be "embower'd" and alone, and thus seems to exemplify a desire that has characterized Romantic lyricism in canonical paradigms. She does not want to "witness" the suffering she describes, and imagines that turning away from it might bring relief of her own unhappiness: she "might better learn to bear" the "woes" that "injustice, and duplicity / And faithlessness and folly, fix on me" (I.57-60). She feels an impulse to forget "human woes," one she ignores only because she understands that no bower "Can shut out for an hour the spectre Care" (I.90). In Smith's account, the sharp self-consciousness of the lyric poet results in an inability to "shut out" others' sorrows, rather than the protection of a strictly interior realm.

In Smith's poem, memory exceeds the categories with which it is associated in canonical models of Romantic lyricism: it is not reduced to private consolation, nor does it serve the ideological work of obscuring traumatic historical scenes. In Abrams's account of the "greater Romantic lyric," recollection marks the moment in which the speaker turns away from a world of daily events to a personal past and to private emotions; much new historicist work concurs.[42] In *The Emigrants,* in contrast, the poet's memory becomes the vehicle for the émigrés' recollections. She "remembers" their social scenes: "Shuddering, I view the pictures they have drawn / Of desolated countries, where the ground, / Stripp'd of its unripe produce, was thick strewn / With various Death" (II.216-19). In Smith's poetry, the act of recollection need not distance the poet from others, nor is it inherently an isolating practice. The poet connects her own recollections of happier times with similar reflections by the exiles, whose thoughts she seems to overhear like the omniscient narrator of a novel.

Memory here is double-edged: it restores images of a blissful childhood even as it resuscitates a traumatic past. After rehearsing the emigrants' recollections, Smith turns to another set of memories for consolation. As Wordsworth will do in "Tintern Abbey," she reverts to childhood scenes for recovery from loss. But in *The Emigrants,* that loss is explicitly social:

> . . . Memory come!
> And from distracting cares, that now deprive
> Such scenes of all their beauty, kindly bear
> My fancy to those hours of simple joy,
> When, on the banks of Arun, which I see
> Makes its irriguous course thro' younder meads,
> I play'd; unconscious then of future ill!
>
> (II.328-34)

The "future ill" she refers to is the "chicane and fraud" that have prolonged the Chancery suit and necessitated her "never-ending toil" (II.355, 350). In an echo of Gray's "Eton Ode," the remembrance of former happiness involves reflection upon its dissolution. For Smith's poet, recollection provides both reassuring images of youthful vitality and a reliving of sorrows that, in *The Emigrants,* are decidedly social. Far from being the vehicle of her individual history alone, her memory cannot be distinguished from historical consciousness. Her memory does not excavate an isolated past, but rather brings with it traces of social history in the form of the contingent details associated with specific events.

Memory is social in Smith's poetry in another way—it strengthens the identificatory bond between poet and readers, and by extension, she hopes, between readers and émigrés. The faculty of memory is an intimate one, and it furthers Smith's efforts to make readers feel that they know her well enough to pity her and her subjects. As Walter Benjamin puts it, the "two elements of memory" are personal and social history: "Where there is experience in the strict sense of the word, certain contents of the individual past combine with material of the collective past."[43] Smith's poet shares with readers both her past and the émigrés' former lives. Memory plays a role in the sonnets—underlying their mournful tone is a quintessential phrase from **"Beachy Head"**—"I once was happy" (line 282). But in *The Emigrants,* her memories are allowed to develop. The effect is an enhancement of the intimacy between poet and readers fostered by the theatrical dynamic of "overhearing" private thoughts. The poet's disclosure of events in her past strengthens lyricism's autobiographical quality and lends emotional weight to the cult of personality generated by *Elegiac Sonnets.*

In considering how Smith develops the rhetorical uses of memory, I want to turn briefly to **"Beachy Head,"** unfinished at the time of her death, because in this poem she expands her repertoire of the historical uses to which her poet's memory may be put. **"Beachy Head"** features an antiquary who is Smith's alter ego in the poem, a figure who collects artifacts such as the "enormous bones" of the "huge unwieldy Elephant" (lines 412, 417), as the poet recalls the natural historical events such evidence indicates. Like *The Emigrants,* the poem opens with an embodiment of the lyric speaker's characteristic stance: she sits with her back toward us, on the "projecting headland" of Beachy Head, where she commands a vast perspective literally and figuratively. She begins, as in the sonnets and *The Emigrants,* by observing her natural surroundings: in the opening section, she follows a single day's passage, until she can see only a skiff "crossing on the moonbright line" before being "lost in shadow" (lines 115-17). After sweeping paragraphs of natural description comes the expected turn inward. The speaker compares herself to the familiar figure of "Contemplation," and the other primary figure associated with Romantic lyricism, "Memory." But here, the processes of reflection and recollection are the vehicles of both personal and social history. Repeated turns in thought link the Norman Conquest, the use of slave labor, theories of evolution, and her own past. As in *The Emigrants,* "Contemplation" raises social questions, and the evocation of "Memory" is followed by historical scenes:

> . . . Contemplation here,
> High on her throne of rock, aloof may sit,
> And bid recording Memory unfold
> Her scroll voluminous—bid her retrace
> The period, when from Neustria's hostile shore
> The Norman launch'd his galleys, and the bay
> O'er which that mass of ruin frowns even now
> In vain and sullen menace, then received
> The new invaders . . .
>
> (lines 117-25)

The speaker recalls, alternately, her own childhood and England's settlement; memory constructs a history of the ground on which she stands. The Sussex coast is both the site of her childhood and the setting for historical events. Memory's scroll is a historical record that documents the "growth," not only of a "poet's mind" but also of a nation. In **"Beachy Head,"** Smith aligns the lyric poet's practice of recollection with the historian's recovery of a social past.

In the poem, "Contemplation" and "Memory" facilitate social consciousness. The speaker begins her meditations by describing the scenes before her, the human and natural activity on the Channel, including "fishing vessels" and a "ship of commerce." Speculating on the ship's cargo leads the poet to reflect upon a political topic, namely, the use of slave labor for gathering pearls. Drawing on Robert Percival's *Account of the Island of Ceylon,* she imagines "the round pearl[s]" that the slave

> With perilous and breathless toil, tears off
> From the rough sea-rock, deep beneath the waves.
> These are the toys of Nature; and her sport
> Of little estimate in Reason's eye:
> And they who reason, with abhorrence see
> Man, for such gaudes and baubles, violate
> The sacred freedom of his fellow man—
> Erroneous estimate! . . .
>
> (lines 53-60)

These contemplations are especially pointed in a poem written before the abolition of the slave trade in 1807. This commentary is thoroughly integrated into wide-ranging speculations upon events past and present, human and natural, social and private. From these thoughts, the speaker turns her attention to the fishing boats returning home at evening and then to the Norman invasion, a brief account of which is incorporated into a description of the place. After narrating a setback to the British and Dutch forces in a 1690 naval battle against the French fought off Beachy Head, the speaker's "reflecting mind returns / To simple scenes of peace and industry" (lines 168-69).

Smith's success in gaining her primary end in *The Emigrants* is confirmed by critics who manifest the sympathy that she advocates.[44] The *Analytical Review* reports: "[S]he draws several interesting and affecting pictures of their misfortunes, and applauds that generous sympathy, which ministers relief to a brother in distress, without listening to the chilling remonstrance of national or political prejudice."[45] The *Monthly Review* also credits Smith with arousing readers' sympathy for the emigrants:

> Whatever is capable of exciting the generous emotions of sympathy is a proper subject of poetry, whose office is to afford pleasure by presenting interesting objects to the imagination. The sufferings of the French emigrants certainly furnish a subject of this kind; and poetry, like charity, will dwell only on such circumstances as are best fitted to excite its proper feelings. In the poem before us, Mrs. Smith has judiciously confined her attention to those particulars in the case of the emigrants, which have excited sympathy in the minds of the humane of all parties; and she describes their condition with that propriety and tenderness, which those who are acquainted with her former productions will be prepared to expect.[46]

Although Smith is praised here for choosing a "proper" subject and for treating it "with propriety and tenderness," these terms indicate the danger to Smith herself of her own poetic strategies: once she entered political debates, she submitted herself to critiques as a woman writer. In critical responses to *The Emigrants,* Smith discovered the risk to herself of turning her poet's personal appeal to political ends. Her poems' autobiographical focus made her particularly visible as a woman writer and thereby censurable along gendered lines.[47]

. . . . .

Smith's deft use of the lyric mode in *Elegiac Sonnets* made her a popular poet by drawing readers to her autobiographical lyric speaker. Yet Smith's prominence in her own works—in her poems' lyric speakers and her novels' autobiographical characters—had complex consequences for her career. In the early editions of the sonnets, Smith makes herself a sympathetic figure partly by presenting herself as reserved and solitary by nature. Adopting a familiar trope of modesty, she confides that she submits herself to public view only at others' urging: "Some of my friends, with partial indiscretion, have multiplied the copies they procured of several of these attempts, till they found their way into the prints of the day in a mutilated state; which, concurring with other circumstances, determined me to put them into their present form" (3). In the 1792 preface to the sixth edition, she assures readers, "I am well aware that for a woman—'The Post of Honor is a Private Station'" (6). But in the course of her career, it became clear that she continued to appear in public willingly, if under financial duress.

Smith risked gendered critiques even more directly when she eventually explained the biographical sources of her poet's habitual elegiac tenor. The sixth edition of *Elegiac Sonnets* marks a turning point in the volume's history: for the first time, Smith assigns a material cause to her unhappiness by referring to her legal battle with the trustees of her father-in-law's estate. Critics have noted that in her novels, her anger emerges in her villainization of lawyers, the judicial system, and extravagant and abusive husbands. Her rage also surfaces in her poems and prefaces. In 1792, she elaborates her story in the context of the conversation with the friend who suggested she might venture "a more cheerful style of composition":

> The time is indeed arrived, when I have been promised by 'the Honourable Men' who, nine years ago, undertook to see that my family obtained the provision their grandfather designed for them,—that 'all should be well, all should be settled.' But still I am condemned to feel the 'hope delayed that maketh the heart sick.'
>
> (5)

I turn now to the implications of Smith's eventual attribution of a precise source of agency to sorrows that in early editions seemed almost existential. For in making a more explicit call for sympathy from readers, as she does in this preface, Smith relinquished some of the indirection that had constituted the sonnets' appeal, and in doing so she discovered the rhetorical limits of her lyricism for a woman writer.

These restrictions were, however, not formal but social. An increasing ambivalence on the part of many of Smith's reviewers reflected not lyricism's rhetorical incapacity, but rather restrictions on what a woman poet with radical sympathies and a proven ability to move readers could say in a politically turbulent period. For Smith's new specificity about the sources of her sorrow gave her lamentations a political inflection that she increasingly employed not only to argue her own case in the court of public opinion but also to speak for others whom she considered fellow sufferers. Later editions of the *Sonnets* reflected this shift in Smith's public profile, when she added poems that alluded more explicitly both to the biographical sources of her poet's despair (such as **"Written at Bignor Park in Sussex, in August, 1799"** [**"Sonnet XCII"**]) and to social events (such as **"The Sea View"** [**"Sonnet LXXXIII"**], which expresses antiwar sentiments). More strikingly, in the same year that the preface to the sixth edition of the sonnets appeared, Smith published her fourth novel, ***Desmond,*** which features an English protagonist who travels to revolutionary France and is persuaded by its ideals.

Smith's increasing explicitness about the material conditions of her own melancholy was prompted by her frustration with the Chancery suit and the exhausting pace of her career. She established herself with the sonnets, but soon found it necessary to turn to a more remunerative genre, the novel. *Emmeline* appeared four years after the first edition of *Elegiac Sonnets,* which was then in its fourth edition. After the success of this novel, she published nine others between 1788 and 1798. She also entered the burgeoning marketplace for children's literature, beginning with ***Rural Walks*** (1795). Smith took several breaks from writing (in 1801, 1803, and 1805) in order to devote herself to her campaign to have Richard Smith's estate settled when it seemed that the Chancery suit might be resolved.[48] But persistent legal frustrations, and the continued financial needs of her family, kept her writing until her death in 1806; two works appeared posthumously: **Beachy Head, with Other Poems,** its title poem unfinished, and **The Natural History of Birds,** which also appeared in 1807. Smith also suffered the intermittent returns of her husband, who had legal rights to her earnings despite their separation. A book contract for **Desmond** named Benjamin, rather than Charlotte, as the legal party.[49]

In its notice of volume 2 of **Elegiac Sonnets** (1797), Joseph Johnson's politically liberal *Analytical Review* exemplifies the ideal response to her growing frankness. The reviewer advances Smith's bid for sympathy, and thus attempts to lend her the practical assistance that Cowper also wanted to provide: "We have chosen to extract these passages from the preface of our author, for the purpose of contributing, so far as lies in our power, to the notoriety of her injuries, and of exciting the public attention to the peculiar circumstances of aggravation which attend them." The critic anticipates that, not only would publicizing Smith's cause fan the flames of popular support, but it might also shame her adversaries in the Chancery suit into greater benevolence: "As to her oppressors, however they may be dead to honesty and humanity, we can scarcely believe it possible that they should have outlived all sensibility to shame: no man is not gratified with the smiles of the world, or is any one so completely hardened, that he would not feel mortified at one universal frown of contempt and indignation." Thus the critic becomes Smith's advocate, publicizing her cause and using the periodical's influence to pressure her "oppressors."[50]

Yet critics from both ends of the political spectrum—including the *Analytical Review*—were alarmed when it became clear that Smith understood her influence as a popular cultural figure, and that she was willing to use it to address social issues. They recognized that even Smith's habitual practices of self-promotion and self-defense were political gestures, for as Curran notes, many of her works reflect "her recognition that the law is a social code written by men for a male preserve, and that the principal function of women within its boundaries can only be to suffer consequences over which they have no control."[51] Critics have identified different moments as inaugurating a decline in Smith's popularity, and have attributed this decline to various causes, including her prolific output. Yet there is a persuasive consensus among Smith's latter-day critics that this decline begins sometime in the years in which her public figure became politicized, with the publication of the sixth edition of **Elegiac Sonnets, Desmond, The Old Manor House** (1793), **The Emigrants** (1793), and **The Banished Man** (1794).[52] In the two latter works, Smith renders sympathetic French émigrés from the nobility, aristocracy, and clergy in works that some critics read as a retraction of her support of revolution abroad and reform at home in **Desmond.**

Critical responses to **The Banished Man** by the *British Critic* and the *Analytical Review* testify to a keen contemporaneous recognition of the influence that Smith could exert in treating political topics. The *British Critic,* delighted with Smith's seeming change of heart about the revolution, deems that "she makes full atonement by the virtues of the Banished Man, for the errors of Desmond," and closes its review by "congratulating the lovers of their king and the constitution, in the acquisition of an associate like Mrs. Charlotte Smith." The critic concludes by declaring with evident satisfaction that "[s]uch a convert, gained by fair conviction, is a valuable prize to the commonwealth." The legitimacy of this boast is supported by the simultaneous lamentation of the *Analytical Review* for its perceived loss of Smith as an ally: "As commonly happens to new converts, she is beyond all measure vehement in her exclamations against the late proceedings of the french."[53]

Although critics such as these often directly assailed Smith's politics, others employed a more ingenious strategy, by censuring Smith's conduct as a woman writer. She was assailed for the very quality that had initiated her success—her works' intense autobiographical focus—when critics charged her with "egotism," a critique particularly damning for a woman whose literary success was greatly facilitated by her personal appeal. The *European Magazine* focuses on the autobiographical impulse of Smith's works in its review of **The Banished Man.** The critic explains that "the apology she makes for her frequent recurrence to family distresses will have its full weight with us," yet "we would have her rail like a gentlewoman always." Smith is warned that the strong language she uses for her enemies in the legal battle over her father-in-law's estate is reserved for men: "terms of abuse," she is told, have been "appropriated" by the "male sex," and their rights to them are not to be "invaded" by women, with one significant exception, "those resistless nymphs who deal out the scaly treasures of the ocean from a certain part of this metropolis."[54] Smith is publicly warned that her writings are taking her out of the company of respectable women and placing her in the company of the fishwives who populated Billingsgate Fishmarket, and whose colorful and unusually inventive obscenities have earned them a place to this day in encyclopedias of English culture and language.

In the course of her career, Smith discovered that she could only act indirectly, winning readers who might become advocates by turning away from them and asking for nothing. In the lyric, she found a mode in which she could render herself sympathetic by expressing her sorrows, ostensibly to herself, her solitary stance proof against charges that she had designs upon readers. Smith's averted gaze in the sonnets was both effective and necessary. Readers, including patrons and critics, were often glad to act for her, and Smith received generous assistance from publishers (especially her first publisher, Thomas Cadell Sr.), and from various patrons throughout her career. But she discovered that she was reliant upon their continued sympathy, and upon the sustained interest of her readers. She similarly lacked the ability to act for herself in the Chancery suit: she could not prod its resolution directly because women could not act as legal agents. The necessity of enlisting the help of others, including Sir George O'Brien Wyndham, third earl of Egremont, and continually urging them to act eventually cost her patrons, including Egremont and Hayley. In the sonnet **"To Dependence"** (**"Sonnet LVII"**), Smith's poet laments: "Dependence! heavy, heavy are thy chains." In the poem, Smith alludes to the Chancery suit in declaring her determination to devote herself to "the Mountain Nymph," (Milton's Liberty in "L'Allegro") even "tho' Pride combine / With Fraud to crush me."

In its final review of her poetry, published after her death, the *British Critic* provides a clear assessment of Smith's predicament. The review opens by acknowledging, "[w]e could not, indeed, always accord with her in sentiment." The critic chastises her in gendered terms: "With respect to some subjects beyond her line of experience, reading, and indeed talent, she was unfortunately wayward and preposterous; but her poetic feeling and ability have rarely been surpassed by any individual of her sex." Yet this censure is qualified by the review's close: "We take our leave of this author with unfeigned regret and sympathy." The critic explains why:

> Her life was embittered by sorrow and misfortune, [and] this gave an unavoidable tinge to her sentiments, which, from the gay and the vain, and the unfeeling, may excite a sneer of scorn and contempt; but in the bosoms of those who, like Charlotte Smith, with refined feelings, improved by thought and study, and reflection, have been compelled, like her, to tread the thorny paths of adversity, will prompt the generous wish, that fortune had favoured her with more complacency; and will induce the disposition to extenuate such portions of her productions, as sterner judgment is unable to approve.[55]

This eulogy of Smith, patronizing and "generous," censorious and admiring, testifies to her precarious position throughout her career: she could win sympathy but could not state her case bluntly without risking her income and her gentlewomanly reputation.

In the lyric, Smith found a formal vehicle of indirection and complexity: by appearing to be lost in mournful reflections, she won a popular audience; in presenting herself as a mother writing only to support her children, she gained a public position from which to pressure the trustees of her father-in-law's estate. Her career makes plain that for a woman writer dependent upon her earnings, the lyric offered the necessary guise of modesty, the proper stance of an averted gaze. Smith's pragmatic view of the form is highly instructive. By continuing to present her readers with more sonnets in the multiplying editions of **Elegiac Sonnets,** she proved herself wise enough to know that she had found in the sonnet's "small plot of ground" a rare and viable, yet sharply circumscribed, forum for a woman to make public the sorrows of dependence.

Notes

1. Anna Letitia Barbauld, introduction to *The Old Manor House,* by Charlotte Smith, in *The British Novelists* (London: F. C. and J. Rivington, 1810), 36:iii.

2. Unsigned "Sonnet to Mrs. Smith," *European Magazine* 10 (1786): 125.

3. Richard Phillips, *British Public Characters of 1800-1801* (London: Richard Phillips, 1801), 3:65.

4. Frye, *Anatomy of Criticism,* 271.

5. Abrams, "Structure and Style," 201-29.

6. Bishop C. Hunt Jr. describes a copy of the fifth edition (1789) owned by Wordsworth at Cambridge, which contains Wordsworth's marginalia. Hunt provides an extensive account of Smith's influence on Wordsworth in "Wordsworth and Charlotte Smith," *Wordsworth Circle* 1 (1970): 85-103.

7. William Wordsworth, *The Poetical Works of William Wordsworth,* ed. William Knight (London: Macmillan, 1896), 7:351. Kari Lokke explains that Wordsworth's citation of this poem is particularly significant, because the poem represents Smith's self-conscious statement of her poetic enterprise. See "Charlotte Smith and Literary History: 'Dark Forgetfulness' and the 'Intercession of Saint Monica,'" *Women's Studies* 27 (1998): 259-80.

8. Stuart Curran, *Poetic Form and British Romanticism* (New York: Oxford University Press, 1986), 32.

9. Coleridge, "Introduction to the Sonnets" (1796), in *The Complete Poetical and Dramatic Works of Samuel Taylor Coleridge,* ed. James Dykes Campbell (London: Macmillan, 1938), 543.

10. In her preface to *The Banished Man* (1794), Smith reports, "In the strictures on a late publication of mine, some Review (I do not now recollect which) objected to the too frequent allusion I made in it to my own circumstances." See *The Banished Man* (London: T. Cadell, Jr. and W. Davies, 1794), 1:viii. Other defenses against charges of egotism are found in the prefaces to *Marchmont* (1796) and to volume 2 of *Elegiac Sonnets* (1797).

11. William Jones to J. Shore, Esq. (16 August 1787), in *Memoirs of the Life, Writings and Correspondence of Sir William Jones,* by John Shore, Lord Teignmouth (London: John Hatchard, 1804), 2:139.

12. Unsigned notice of *Elegiac Sonnets, Gentleman's Magazine* 56 (1786): 334.

13. From the first edition, *Elegiac Sonnets* contains poems other than sonnets, but the sonnets continually outnumber them. These poems, like the sonnets, multiplied with expanding editions. "Metastasio" is Pietro Trapassi (1698-1782).

14. The lines Smith puts in her own mouth are Egeon's. Smith slightly misquotes him: "Oh! Time has Changed me since you saw me last, / And heavy Hours with Time's deforming Hand, / Have written strange Defeatures in my Face." Shakespeare's lines are quoted correctly in my epigraph.

15. Unsigned review of *The Emigrants, British Critic* 1 (1793): 403.

16. One of a group of Smith's letters housed by the Princeton University Library contains instructions for an engraver about altering the frontispiece portrait and one of the collection's engravings. I quote the letter at length in "Charlotte Smith's Letters and the Practice of Self-Presentation," *Princeton University Library Chronicle* 53 (1991): 50-77.

17. Michael Fried, *Absorption and Theatricality: Painting and Beholder in the Age of Diderot* (Chicago: University of Chicago Press, 1980), 108.

18. Unsigned notice of *Elegiac Sonnets, Gentleman's Magazine* 56 (1786): 333.

19. Marshall, *Surprising Effects of Sympathy*, 5, 107.

20. Coleridge, "Introductions to the Sonnets," 543.

21. William Cowper to Charlotte Smith (26 October 1793), in *The Correspondence of William Cowper*, ed. Thomas Wright (London: Hodder and Stoughton, 1904), 4:462.

22. Marshall, *Surprising Effects of Sympathy*, 128.

23. Cowper to William Hayley (29 January 1793), in *Correspondence of William Cowper*, 4:363.

24. Vendler and Bahti consider the role of the lyric's reader carefully, but each views that role as more passive and subordinate than I do. Vendler describes a lyric poem as "*a role offered to a reader.*" Her notion of the reader's identification with the poetic speaker is absolute: "[T]he reader is to be the voice speaking the poem" ("*Tintern Abbey*: Two Assaults," 184). Vendler's decisive account of the reader's capacity for sympathetic identification with the lyric speaker explains something important about that relationship: its potential for intensity. I view the relationship as more of a precarious exchange, however, and I would instead emphasize the potential for marked ambivalence by both parties. For Bahti's account of this relationship, see chapter 1, n. 70.

25. For Abrams's account of the significance of sincerity to Romantic poetry, see *Mirror and Lamp*, 317-19. For "the lyric as poetic norm," see ibid., 84-88. A number of critics have complicated Romantic accounts of sincerity. See Lionel Trilling, *Sincerity and Authenticity* (Cambridge: Harvard University Press, 1971) and Judith Pascoe, *Romantic Theatricality* (Ithaca: Cornell University Press, 1997).

26. Judith Phillips Stanton, "Charlotte Smith's 'Literary Business': Income, Patronage, and Indigence," in *The Age of Johnson*, ed. Paul J. Korshin (New York: AMS Press, 1987), 375-401.

27. This account of Smith's life appears in a section entitled "Memoirs of Eminent Persons," *Monthly Magazine* 22 (1807): 246.

28. Culler, *Structuralist Poetics*, 166. Culler follows Frye's claim that in the lyric "we turn away from our ordinary continuous experience in space or time, or rather from a verbal mimesis of it." According to Frye, this detachment requires a rejection of "the kind of language we use in coping with ordinary experience." Frye, "Approaching the Lyric," 31, 34.

29. Cameron, *Lyric Time*, 203.

30. Stafford Harry Northcote, Viscount St. Cyres, "The Sorrows of Mrs. Charlotte Smith," *Cornhill Magazine*, n.s., 15 (1903): 686-96.

31. Leigh Hunt, *The Book of the Sonnet*, ed. Leigh Hunt and S. Adams Lee (Boston: Roberts Brothers, 1867), 1:85.

32. Adela Pinch, *Strange Fits of Passion: Epistemologies of Emotion, from Hume to Austen* (Stanford, Calif.: Stanford University Press, 1996).

33. Todd, *Sensibility*, 4.

34. Sir Walter Scott, *The Miscellaneous Prose Works of Sir Walter Scott* (Edinburgh: Robert Cadell, 1849), 2:64.

35. John Clare, *The Natural History Prose Writings of John Clare*, ed. Margaret Grainger (Oxford: Clarendon Press, 1983), 34.

36. Curran, "The I Altered," 200.

37. Unsigned review of *The Emigrants, European Magazine* 24 (1793): 42.

38. Donald Greer, *The Incidence of the Emigration during the French Revolution* (Cambridge: Harvard University Press, 1951), 112.

39. Florence May Anna Hilbish, "Charlotte Smith, Poet and Novelist 1749-1806" (Ph.D. diss., University of Pennsylvania, 1941), 151.

40. The *Gentleman's Magazine* noticed and praised *Elegiac Sonnets* early in its publication history (in 1786). The periodical also published poems and letters from readers addressed to her. For its initial notice of the sonnets, see *Gentleman's Magazine* 56 (1786): 333-34.

41. Margery Weiner, *The French Exiles, 1789-1815* (London: John Murray, 1960), 103.

42. For instance, in Levinson's reading of "Tintern Abbey" in *Wordsworth's Great Period Poems*, memory obliterates an awareness of social history. Liu's definition of memory in Wordsworth's poetry as "the supervision of time by selfhood" similarly stresses the

subjugation of a social environment to subjectivity. See *Wordsworth*, 204.

43. Benjamin, "On Some Motifs in Baudelaire," 159. Pinch makes a relevant argument in her reading of Jane Austen's *Persuasion*: she defines lyricism in the novel as "a particular way of rendering consciousness' apprehension of the social." She too turns to Benjamin for aid in constructing a model of the lyric as social. See "Lost in a Book: Jane Austen's *Persuasion*," *Studies in Romanticism* 32 (1993): 99.

44. The *European Magazine* was less pleased, complaining that "no particular character, or even species of misfortune, is suffered to dwell long enough upon the mind to produce any very great and concentrated degree of anxiety and interest." The result is that "[w]e pity *all* too much to suffer acutely *any* one." Yet the critic concedes Smith's success in making readers aware of the ongoing violence across the Channel, worrying that "[t]here is but too much reason to fear, that this creature of her imagination has been many times realized in the course of the last two years, and that similar scenes are transacting at the very hour in which we are amusing ourselves with the contemplation of these fictitious sorrows!" Unsigned review of *The Emigrants*, *European Magazine* 24 (1793): 45.

45. Unsigned review of *The Emigrants*, *Analytical Review* 22 (1793): 91.

46. Review signed "E.," *Monthly Review* 12 (1793): 375.

47. As Mary Poovey has argued, women writers faced the necessity of remaining "proper ladies," and were chastened when they were judged to have lapsed from rigorous social codes. See *The Proper Lady and the Woman Writer* (Chicago: University of Chicago Press, 1984).

48. Stanton, "Charlotte Smith's 'Literary Business,'" 393.

49. Ibid., 376-77.

50. Unsigned review of vol. 2 of *Elegiac Sonnets*, *Analytical Review* 26 (1797): 158-59.

51. Curran, introduction to *Poems of Charlotte Smith*, xxi.

52. Stanton makes a cogent case that "after her first three conventional novels, Smith had begun [in *The Old Manor House*] to test the limits of what a woman might write." Derek Roper points out that, with the exception of the *Critical Review*, the major periodicals viewed this novel positively. He argues that Smith's decline in popularity began with her next novel, *The Banished Man*, since this and subsequent novels were "of less interest." See Stanton's introduction to *The Old Manor House*, ed. Anne Henry Ehrenpreis (Oxford: Oxford University Press, 1989), ix; and Roper, *Reviewing Before the "Edinburgh," 1788-1802* (London: Methuen, 1978), 130.

53. Unsigned review of *The Banished Man*, *British Critic* 4 (1794): 623. Unsigned review of *The Banished Man*, *Analytical Review* 20 (1794): 254.

54. Unsigned review of *The Banished Man*, *European Magazine* 26 (1794): 276. A reviewer for the *Critical Review* makes a related charge about *Letters of a Solitary Wanderer*. The critic suggests that "the story of the Hermit speaks to every one's bosom; and the affectionate sensibility of Frank Maynard is equally interesting and pathetic." Yet the critic goes on to suggest: "To similar tales of domestic life and domestic feelings perhaps Mrs. Smith might, with propriety, confine her exertions." Unsigned review of *Letters of a Solitary Wanderer*, *Critical Review* 32 (1801): 39.

55. Unsigned review of *Beachy Head, with other Poems*, *British Critic* 30 (1807): 170, 174.

Works Cited

Abrams, M. H. *The Mirror and the Lamp*. London: Oxford University Press, 1953.

———. "Structure and Style in the Greater Romantic Lyric." Reprinted in *Romanticism and Consciousness*, edited by Harold Bloom, 201-29. New York: Norton, 1970.

Bahti, Timothy. *Ends of the Lyric: Direction and Consequence in Western Poetry*. Baltimore: Johns Hopkins University Press, 1996.

Cameron, Sharon. *Lyric Time: Dickinson and the Limits of Genre*. Baltimore: Johns Hopkins University Press, 1979.

Cowper, William. *The Correspondence of William Cowper*. Edited by Thomas Wright. London: Hodder and Stoughton, 1904.

Culler, Jonathan. *Structuralist Poetics*. Ithaca: Cornell University Press, 1975.

Curran, Stuart. "The I Altered." In *Romanticism and Feminism*, edited by Anne K. Mellor, 185-207. Bloomington: Indiana University Press, 1988.

———. Introduction to *The Poems of Charlotte Smith*. Edited by Stuart Curran. New York: Oxford University Press, 1993.

Frye, Northrop. *Anatomy of Criticism*. Princeton: Princeton University Press, 1957.

———. "Approaching the Lyric." In *Lyric Poetry: Beyond New Criticism*, edited by Chaviva Hošek and Patricia Parker, 31-37. Ithaca: Cornell University Press, 1985.

Levinson, Marjorie. *Wordsworth's Great Period Poems*. Cambridge: Cambridge University Press, 1986.

Marshall, David. *The Surprising Effects of Sympathy: Marivaux, Diderot, Rousseau, and Mary Shelley*. Chicago: University of Chicago Press, 1988.

Roper, Derek. *Reviewing Before the Edinburgh, 1788-1802*. London: Methuen, 1978.

Stanton, Judith Phillips. "Charlotte Smith's 'Literary Business': Income, Patronage, and Indigence." In *The Age of Johnson,* edited by Paul J. Korshin, 375-401. New York: AMS Press, 1987.

———. Introduction to *The Old Manor House,* by Charlotte Smith, edited by Anne Henry Ehrenpreis. Oxford: Oxford University Press, 1989.

Todd, Janet. *Sensibility: An Introduction.* London: Methuen, 1986.

Vendler, Helen. "*Tintern Abbey*: Two Assaults." In *Wordsworth in Context,* edited by Pauline Fletcher and John Murphy, 173-90. Lewisburg, Pa.: Bucknell University Press, 1992.

Judith Hawley (essay date 1999)

SOURCE: Hawley, Judith. "Charlotte Smith's *Elegiac Sonnets*: Losses and Gains." In *Women's Poetry in the Enlightenment: The Making of a Canon, 1730-1820,* edited by Isobel Armstrong and Virginia Blain, pp. 184-98. Houndmills: Macmillan Press Ltd., 1999.

[*In the following essay, Hawley discusses Smith's role in the revival of the elegiac sonnet.*]

In Chapter 10 of the first volume of *Persuasion,* Jane Austen's favourite heroine, Anne Elliot, no longer in the spring of her life, finds herself musing on whether or not Captain Wentworth has transferred his affections from her to one of the Misses Musgrove. 'She occupied her mind as much as possible' by repeating to herself quotations from 'some few of the thousand poetical descriptions extant of autumn'.[1] When Wentworth gives a sign of his interest in Louisa Musgrove, Anne's equanimity is disturbed: she 'could not immediately fall into quotation again. The sweet scenes of Autumn were for a while put by—unless some tender sonnet, fraught with the apt analogy of the declining year, with declining happiness, and the images of youth and hope, and spring, all gone together, blessed her memory' (p. 83). This generic tender sonnet, which gives an insight into Miss Elliott's inner world and the sentimental vogue of the wider world, may be an allusion to the extremely popular *Elegiac Sonnets* of Charlotte Smith.[2] Smith's sonnets abound in comparisons between the recurrence of the seasons and the persistence of her loss. For example **"To melancholy"** begins conventionally enough, 'When latest Autumn spreads her evening veil . . .' (**"Sonnet XXXII,"** p. 34). One of her most popular sonnets, **"Written at the close of Spring"** ends: 'Another May new buds and flowers shall bring; / Ah! why has happiness—no second Spring?' (**"Sonnet II,"** p. 13) The association between loss and ritual return is fundamental to the move of consolation found in traditional elegies; yet consolation and renewal, as I will argue, are eschewed by Smith in her melancholy sonnets.

The poet and novelist, Charlotte Turner Smith, was a key figure both in the revival of the sonnet form at the end of the eighteenth century, and in the development of the woman's novel in the era of Romanticism and Revolution.[3] Born in 1749 into a wealthy family which had extensive estates in Sussex, Smith enjoyed all the educational privileges that a young girl of her class could hope for. When in 1765 she was pushed into marriage with Benjamin Smith, by her father, Nicholas Turner, whose remarriage after the death of Charlotte's mother seems to have made him keen to get his daughter off his hands, she was a talented and promising young lady, not quite 16. By the time she published the first edition of *Elegiac Sonnets* in 1784, a work which eventually filled two volumes and ran into numerous editions before her death in 1806, she was in severely reduced circumstances.[4] The profligacy of her husband, and his inability to manage his West Indian business, had driven them both into King's Bench debtors' prison.

Austen's allusion attests to the popularity of Smith's works into the nineteenth century, as well as to her amused fondness for them. The sense of lost promise is entirely appropriate for Anne Elliot at this point in the novel, but she is later to recover her love in a mature reflowering of her relationship with Captain Wentworth. Austen places this melancholy moment here as something that Anne will overcome (and perhaps outgrow); it is a period of painful uncertainty and self-denial which will be rewarded by the return of her lover.

The pattern we find in *Persuasion,* one of rewarded suffering, of a sacrificial offering which will be blessed and transformed, is close to the traditional structure and economy of the elegy. The formal elegy, alongside which Charlotte Smith's elegiac sonnets should be read, celebrates the dead by at once elevating and transcending them, finding a compensatory substitute for the loved one in the process. Peter Sacks, in his brilliantly subtle and richly suggestive interpretation of the genre, argues that elegies carry out the work of successful mourning:

> At the core of each procedure is the renunciatory experience of loss and the acceptance, not just of a substitute, but of the very means and practice of substitution. In each case such an acceptance is the price of survival; and in each case a successful resolution is not merely deprivatory, but offers a form of compensatory reward. The elegist's reward, especially, resembles or augments that of the child—both often involve inherited legacies and consoling identifications with symbolic, even immortal, figures of power.[5]

Sacks connects the poet's relation to the loved one to his relation to past poets, detecting an oedipal struggle for mastery and the right to inherit which is often played out in terms of a mastery over nature. This model of elegy, which equates a 'healthy' mourning with the renunciation of the dead, and is deeply entangled with masculine power struggles, has given poets and critics pause. Jahan Ramazani argues that modern poets such as Wilfred Owen and Sylvia Plath refuse to use the dead as stepping stones to power in this way.[6] Instead, by refusing to participate in the economy of 'healthy' mourning, certain modern poets occupy a critical position in their poetry which is akin to 'melancholia', the state which Freud designates the opposite of 'successful' mourning.[7] The oedipal model is also problematic when we come to consider gender. While Sacks is confident that a woman's subject position in relation to symbolic codes is 'not sufficiently different from those of the male to invalidate our discussion's relevance to both genders' (p. 12), Celeste Schenck disagrees, and argues that women write elegy differently because they relate to both the dead and the living differently.[8] Her assertion that women eschew competition and maintain a loving connectedness to the dead idealizes the gender, but her criticism of Freudian readings of elegy provides a necessary corrective.

Approaching Smith's elegiac sonnets with this discussion in mind, I think we need to ask about the object of her mourning: what has she lost? What does she hope to gain? The first question is raised in general terms by Freud's difficult question: What does a woman want?—a question which articulates a double (mis)understanding: what does she desire, and what does she lack? If women are culturally emplaced as the gender founded on want, on absence, how can they hope to recover something they never had? This lack relates to both kinds of inheritance discussed by Sacks: the transfer of property after death, and the inheritance of a cultural legacy or poetic voice. Having a weak claim to material ownership and to poetic power, women elegists do not have a direct route to the kinds of transcendence and consolation achieved by the best male elegists. These questions about losses and gains are raised more specifically by Charlotte Smith, because it is not always clear what or whose loss she is mourning. Some of her sonnets are elegies for individuals, for example Burns and Otway, and there are many in volume two which mourn the loss of her favourite daughter, Anna Augusta.[9] But overall her sonnets are pervaded by a sense of lament, of absence, 'the pain / Of knowing "such things were"—and are no more' (**Sonnet XC**, **"To oblivion"**, p. 77). (Anna Seward dubbed her sonnets 'everlasting lamentables'.[10]) So, what does Smith hope to gain, what substitute, what consolation can elegy provide for her?

Smith's elegies resolutely refuse consolation, and often seem to be trapped in the state of melancholia. There is something apparently pathological about her self-abnegation. In **"Sonnet LXVII"** she morbidly identifies herself with not just a graveyard but a ruined graveyard (p. 55). Repeatedly she mourns the death of her daughter Anna, and is quite unable to let her go. Furthermore, she denies herself any union with nature, or integration with society, or qualifications as a writer. Her rupture with nature, her alienation from society—'Alone I wander' (**"Sonnet LXVI"**, p. 58)—and her loss of identity as a mother, and her inadequacy as an artist are combined in 'Reflections on some drawings of plants', when she argues that, although she can draw pretty pictures of flowers, she cannot keep her favourite daughter, Anna alive in art (**"Sonnet XCI"**, pp. 77-8). In her botanical drawings she can capture in art a nature which might have some reference to herself and her daughter: 'These bells and golden eyes, embathed in dew' possibly recall her own eyes bathed in tears. The 'soft blush that warms the early Rose' may suggest in some way her young daughter, 'So early blighted'. But these figures are then repudiated because while Smith can in her painting 'arrest Spring's humid buds', she cannot arrest the force which arrested her budding daughter. These frozen living flowers, both artificial and natural, cannot represent her daughter because Smith pictures her to herself as 'that form adored, / That form, expressive of a soul divine', a form that hints at the supernatural, and perhaps supernatural because reflexively pictured—'adored'—by the mother. The correct frame and altar for this image-icon is the mother's 'bleeding breast' where she is enshrined by the 'too faithful' art of grief, an art which threatens to destroy the mother.

Smith's aesthetic could appear to be entirely negative. She modestly denies that she has any mastery of the sonnet form, 'shyly' insisting in the Preface to the first and second editions: 'The little Poems which are here called Sonnets, have, I believe, no very just claim that title: but they consist of fourteen lines' (p. 3). She often refuses closure: she ends her sonnet **"To oblivion"** (**"Sonnet XC"**, p. 77) with words borrowed from Thomas Warton's 'Ode I. To Sleep', reawakening his sense that closure is denied her: "'Death seems prepared to strike, yet still delays.'" By violating the genre of elegy with her refusal to accept an aesthetic consolation, she places herself outside systems of signification and of value.

Most often, Smith appears to be writing an elegy for herself, for her own lost promise. 'Not for me / Return those rosy hours which here I used to see!' she exclaims at the end of **"Sonnet XCII"**, **"Written at Bignor Park in Sussex, in August, 1799"** (p. 78), insisting that she is forever cast out from the home of her happy childhood. At the end of **"Sonnet LXXXIX"**, **"To the sun"**, she exclaims: 'nought thy rays illumine, *now* can charm / My misery, or to day convert my night!' (p. 76)

This state of abjection can be seen as symptomatic of the position of the woman/poet in this period. Stuart Curran considers her to be 'virtually an archetype of the female condition of the late eighteenth century'.[11] Her sensitivity to her alienation and dispossession are existential and typical. It was common in the eighteenth century for women writers to preface their works with humble apologies, insisting that they had no pretensions to literary greatness, they were merely trying to earn a crust for their children. Thus they negotiated entry into the public sphere of print by claiming that their writing was an extension of their maternal role. The role of the mourner (while in some contexts it can function as a protest, a refusal to behave in socially convenient ways) is also not untypical for a woman. In the nineteenth century at least the work of carrying the burden of mourning was performed more by women than by men.

Smith then appears to be a mother-martyr. Indeed the role she has been assigned in literary history—that of midwife to the Romantic sonnet, or even mother of Romanticism—

assumes that she laid herself down so that she could be transcended.[12] Poetry, said Wordsworth, owed her a debt which would not be repaid: she is 'a lady to whom English verse is under greater obligations than are likely to be either acknowledged or remembered'.[13] Perhaps she becomes the subject of elegy more traditionally conceived: she is the love-object whose literary death can be said to bring about a renewal of nature and the re-energizing of other poets' powers. Her loss is Romanticism's gain.

Yet Smith's perverse refusals also endow her with grace, strength and energy. While she wanders 'cheerless and unblest' (**"Sonnet LXII,"** p. 55) through the ruined landscape of her sonnets, she maintains a self-possession which comes from her dispossession; having lost so much, including the ties which bind her, she can speak in **"To dependence"** of her 'unfetter'd heart' (**"Sonnet LVII"**, p. 51). And while to argue that Smith's abjection is typical makes sense of some of Smith's inconsolable lamentations, it does not sufficiently acknowledge the specificities of her position. Here we need to consider Smith's biographical situation. The complexity of her lyric voice, a voice which can ventriloquize Shakespeare, Milton, Goethe and Petrarch, as I will later argue, alerts us that her sonnets are not merely autobiographical; nevertheless we need to attend to Smith's self-presentation, the public space she constructs for herself by manipulating aspects of her private life.

Although she wrote out of financial necessity—indeed when the first volume of **Elegiac Sonnets** was published she was in debtors' prison—she was not a labouring poet, like Ann Yearsley, petitioning to be admitted into the salons of the upper classes. She styled herself on her title page, 'Charlotte Smith of Bignor Park, in Sussex', not Charlotte Smith of King's Bench. The fact that she had fallen socially is of key importance. Moreover, for many years she hoped or expected to be restored; like Miss Flite in *Bleak House,* she expected a judgement on her case. She wrote out of a sense of entitlement. For her the economy of mourning was literally a financial matter. When her father-in-law, Richard Smith, a wealthy merchant, died in 1776, he bequeathed much of his estate to her children to prevent Benjamin Smith from squandering it. Because his will was far from clear, Smith spent the rest of her life involved in a complex legal battle with the trustees and executors, always desperate for money, and repeatedly straining the patience of her patrons.[14] The Preface to her second volume of **Sonnets** (1787) is outspoken in its exasperated resentment of the trustees who owed her money, and of the subscribers to her poems for whom she was obliged to write. She complains of the misfortunes she and her children have endured: the frustrated ambitions of her sons, the wounding of one of them, the death of her favourite daughter,

> The rest deprived of every advantage to which they are entitled; and the means of proper education for my youngest son denied me! while the money that their inhuman trustees have suffered yearly to be wasted, and what they keep possession of on false and frivolous pretences, would, if paid to those it belongs to, have saved me and them from all those now irremediable misfortunes.
>
> (pp. 7-8)

The Preface is a breaking into print of complaints Smith made in her letters. Her correspondence with Cadell and Davies, the London firm which published most of her poetical works, harps continually on the themes of loss and debt.[15] She used them as her personal bankers and agents, and behaved as if she considered her works as security for interim loans which she expected them to make her while she was waiting for her rightful inheritance. In 1788 she wrote to an unnamed correspondent: 'I have a Novel absolutely *pawned* to Cadell'.[16] Writing, she believed, was only an interim measure. When in February 1795 it seemed that the will was about to be settled, she wrote to Cadell and Davies: 'I hope therefore I shall no longer write for actual bread or appear in the mortifying character of a distrest Author'—but, she told him, as it would take a few weeks to sort out, in the meantime, 'if you have five Guineas of mine in your hands I shall be much oblig'd to you to send it down'.[17] The subscription for the second volume of sonnets was collected during a time of particular emotional and financial stress around the time of the death of Anna Augusta. A subscription edition is a charitable enterprise as well as a literary event; it felt to Smith like going cap in hand. In an undated letter to Cadell and Davies probably from around this time she angrily reminded them 'how little either from birth or education or connections I ought to turn beggar'. She was always conscious of her former status, and no more so than when she was restored to something like comfort when her sons' income and the partial success of her litigation produced benefits at the end of her life. When she offered her **Beachy Head** volume to Cadell and Davies in 1805 she re-estimated her worth and announced: 'The price I expect for it, is 300£. & a discharge of my debt to you'.[18]

Smith felt that her readers owed her pity just as she was owed money, security, status. Anna Seward complained of Smith's continual complaining that it was a 'perpetual dun on pity'.[19] Objecting to the fact that Smith was praised above Shakespeare and Milton by facile reviewers, Seward was critical of Smith's artistic ability, her characteristic mood and her relation to her predecessors. To Theophilus Smith she acidly wrote:

> I forget if I ever spoke to you about Mrs C. Smith's everlasting lamentables, which she calls sonnets, made up of hackneyed scraps of dismality, with which her memory furnished her from our various poets. Never were poetical whipt syllabubs, in black glasses, so eagerly swallowed by the odd taste of the public.[20]

Smith was troubled by accusations of plagiarism, and added notes identifying her 'book debts' from the third edition of her **Sonnets.** The conjunction of the charge of plagiarism and the characterization of her melancholy mood in Seward's criticism, although unsympathetic, points to a significant feature of Smith's poetics. By quoting and adapting the words of her predecessors she is at once retiring modestly behind them and assertively usurping them. (A similar double move of sympathetic identification and egoistical projection is made by Smith in her description and appropriation of the suffering of the French in her poem *The Emigrants*.) At the same time we should remember that the legacy Smith was pursuing was not for herself, but for her children. Simultaneously self-denying and usurping, Smith's sonnets are marked by melancholic self-abnegation, a kind of declaration of emotional bankruptcy.[21]

To work through the paradoxes contained in Smith's art of losing, what I want to do finally is to consider one sonnet in detail. (Smith's long footnote is given as an appendix to this article.)

"LXXIX": "To the goddess of botany"*

Of Folly weary, shrinking from the view
   Of Violence and Fraud, allow'd to take
   All peace from humble life; I would forsake
Their haunts for ever, and, sweet Nymph! with you
   Find shelter; where my tired, and tear-swoln eyes,
Among your silent shades of soothing hue,
   Your 'bells and florets of unnumber'd dyes'
   Might rest—And learn the bright varieties
That from your lovely hands are fed with dew;
   And every veined leaf, that trembling sighs
In mead or woodland; or in wilds remote,
   Or lurk with mosses in the humid caves,
Mantle the cliffs, on dimpling rivers float,
   Or stream from coral rocks beneath the Ocean waves.

The irregular form and the subject matter of this sonnet are interesting in several respects which are both unusual and characteristic of Smith. It is unnerving as an elegy. The poet is 'Of Folly weary, shrinking from the view / Of Violence and Fraud, allow'd to take / All peace from humble life . . .' What has been lost? Not a loved one but, I suppose, peace. A lower-case peace has been ravished by personified Folly, Violence and Fraud. Smith is veiling the occasion of this elegy and distancing it from her own life, though she alludes to the violence of her losses in her massive footnote.

In both sonnets and elegies we expect structural and psychological turns. In the case of elegy we might have several turns, from the loved one to nature, another turn to blame those who should have protected the dead, perhaps a turn outwards to criticize the world, and a move to detach oneself from the dead and to transcend them by describing how they have transcended their earthly life. Thus Milton in 'Lycidas' masterfully works through a series of deflections from the death of the shepherd, to the decline of the church, to the resurrection of a spiritualized Lycidas whose renewed fertility regenerates Milton's poetry. In doing so Milton leaves behind his dead friend and surpasses his own previous poetry. In the Italian sonnet we would expect a turn after the octave signalling some change of thought or feeling. In the English sonnet the turn is deferred until the final couplet, a structure which, as Paul Fussell says, 'invites images of balloons and pins'.[22]

Smith's form follows neither model: after a closed quatrain (abba), there is an unusual involved middle section of two tercets (cdccdc), finished with an interlaced quatrain (efef).[23] Here the turn is away from Folly and so on to Botany, and it occurs very early on in the poem in the move across the fourth to the fifth line. Perhaps there is a second half-turn when Smith says she will not just find shelter but will *learn* the bright varieties of flowers (l. 8), or the shelter is found in the learning process. But we do not at the end turn away from nature, transcending it, nor is the idea clinched in a neat final couplet. Rather, the sonnet opens up in a series of parallel possibilities: 'or in wilds remote . . .', 'Or lurk . . .', 'Or stream from coral rocks beneath the Ocean waves'. That last line seems both negative and positive. The image of streaming suggests directionality, progress; Peter Sacks notices the frequency with which images of springs or rivers occur in elegy. They may suggest inspiration, life force, the overcoming of a blockage, as opposed to images of the horizontal waste of the sea, a chaotic or negative force.[24] Smith's stream is buried under the sea, or rather stream is a verb and what we have is a surreal streaming out of bells and florets, and veined, trembling leaves from coral rocks beneath the ocean waves. It is not entirely clear what is the subject of the verb; do the leaves lurk, mantle and stream, or does Smith do so? Presumably the speaker 'might rest . . . Or lurk' while leaves sigh, but the syntax is so fluid that the speaker becomes lost in the imagined processes. Some of Smith's best sonnets situate the speaker on the sea shore on a perilous rocky cliff, contemplating the destructive forces of the sea. For example, in **"Written on the sea shore.—October, 1784"** (**"Sonnet XII"**, p. 20), she takes a solitary seat 'On some rude fragment of the rocky shore' and imagines herself shipwrecked and drowning with help arriving too late to save her. The ending of **"Sonnet LXXIX"** is much more ambiguous: the subject of the elegy which is, I would argue, Smith's own life, both streams with natural renewal and drowns.

Given special emphasis in the centre of the sonnet, clasped in the double tercet, is a line from Milton's 'Lycidas'. Poetry (in the form of a quotation) intervenes between the bad forces of human society (Folly, Violence and Fraud), and the comforts of nature (in the guise of Botany). Smith's 'bells and florets of unnumber'd dyes' actually misremembers Milton's 'Bells, and Flowrets of a thousand hues' (l. 135); 'hues' finds its way into the 'soothing hue' of the line above, and 'unnumber'd' might suggest that Smith has in mind flowers that are not numbered in verse. Her misquotation suggests gendered differences between their uses of nature and of elegy. Milton's 'bells and flowerets' appear in a section of 'Lycidas' in which he is calling for the return of a golden age:

             Return *Sicilian* Muse,
And call the Vales, and bid them hither cast
Their Bells, and Flowrets of a thousand hues.[25]

These lovely arcadian flowers, some described as artificial or endowed with human attributed ('quaint enameld eyes', l. 139), are to be plucked 'To strew the Laureat Herse where *Lycid* lies' (l. 151). In Smith's sonnet, on the other hand, these flowers do not inhabit a mythical realm; she claims that the haunts of Botany are readily accessible. Her language is more technical; the revision 'florets' suggests that 'varieties', 'humid' and 'mantle' also have the kind of scientific accuracy which, as Donald Davie has shown, is characteristic of Augustan poetic diction.[26] Botany in the late eighteenth century was considered a proper subject of study for women (but not exclusively a feminine preserve). The natural worlds of **"Sonnet LXXIX"** and of 'Lycidas' are not quite the same, and the poets behave differently in them. Unlike Milton, Smith will not pluck these flowers in a castrative and substitutive gesture, rather she wishes to learn how they sigh, and lurk, mantle and stream. Her gaze is not completely natural or neutral: she sees through the eyes of poetry and of science, eyes 'tear-swoln', but she wishes to observe nature, not to violate and transcend it.[27]

Charlotte Smith arrives at an ambiguous elegiac solution, for she does not find a detached token to substitute for the lost object. This ambiguity is echoed in her use of Milton, and thus in her sense of her relation to poetry. The fact that she includes Milton in inverted commas marks off his poetry as something that she wishes to associate herself with, but cannot surpass. Yet this poem is assertive as well as retiring. Smith adds a massive footnote which makes some pretty grand claims for her art, her right to enter the realm of poetry, and her social position, claims which are far from modest, though they pretend to appear so.[28] While describing a mood of complete abjection, Smith allies herself with Milton, Rousseau and Shakespeare by weaving her sorrows with theirs. She admits that she is 'without any pretensions to those talents which were in [Rousseau] so heavily taxed with that excessive irritability, too often if not always the attendant on genius', but because she asserts that she has the same sentiments as these great writers, and has suffered as the speakers she quotes have suffered, she also claims an entitlement to speak in their words. She says that, like Rousseau, 'I have been engaged in contending with persons whose cruelty has left so painful an impression on my mind, that I may well say, "Brillantes fleurs . . ."'. Finally she makes a strange approach at voicing Lear's tragic lament 'I am bound upon a wheel of fire . . .', by veiling her presumption first in the plural pronoun ('compels us') then in an imagined sufferer who 'feels like the wretched Lear'. Thus, slantwise, she appropriates these voices and advances on their genius.[29]

Smith writes strange elegies because, instead of being able to renounce what she has lost, or to say farewell to the dead, she feels that she is entitled to have what she has lost restored to her. What psychoanalysts refer to as 'the work of mourning' is for her partly a legal process of recovering an inheritance in the courts. That sense of entitlement is also there in her belief that because she has suffered like the great tragic figures, she has the right to voice her suffering in poetry. Nevertheless, her poetry is not haughtily presumptuous; it is marked by modest or self-cancelling gestures. After having been accused of plagiarism, she admitted her debts to her forebears by acknowledging them in footnotes and appendices. Furthermore she resists the traditional consolations of elegy, preferring to remain defeated and alienated, submerged beneath the ocean waves. I think it is also significant that the inheritance she was claiming was not for herself but for her children: she was still acting as mother-martyr. Nevertheless, although she does not achieve a 'successful' mourning, she does not succumb completely to melancholia because she does at least voice her lack, dunning the public for the pity she believes they owe her. Coleridge argued that elegy 'presents everything as lost and gone, or absent and future'.[30] Smith exists in a continual present of suffering, refusing nostalgic assimilation to a past imagined as whole, or an idealistic transcendence in the future; rather she makes an eternity of her present woe. In the end, given the complex exchange of energies in Smith's poetry, the debt does not run all one way; the binary opposition between losses and gains may not be an appropriate model when self-effacement can be so visible and so vivid.

APPENDIX

"Sonnet LXXIX": "To the goddess of botany"*

'Rightly to spell', as Milton wishes, in *Il Penseroso*, 'Of every herb that sips the dew' [ll. 170-2] seems to be a resource for the sick at heart—for those who from sorrow or disgust may without affectation say 'Society is nothing to one not sociable!' ['society is no comfort / To one not sociable'—Shakespeare, *Cymbeline*, IV.ii.12-13] and whose wearied eyes and languid spirits find relief and repose amidst the shades of vegetable nature.—I cannot now turn to any other pursuit that for a moment soothes my wounded mind.

'Je pris gout a cette récreation des yeux, qui dans l'infortune, repose, amuse, distrait l'esprit, et suspend le sentiment des peines' [I took a liking to this recreation of the eyes, which in misfortune rests, amuses, distracts the spirit and suspends the feelings of pain.] Thus speaks the singular, the unhappy Rousseau, when in his 'Promenades' [*Reveries du Promenade Solitaire*, Book 7] he enumerates the causes which drove him from the society of men, and occasioned his pursuing with renewed avidity the study of Botany. 'I was', says he, 'Forcé de m'abstenir de penser, de peur de penser a mes malheurs malgré moi; forcé de contenir les restes d'une imagination riante, mais languissante, que tant d'angoisses pourroient effaroucher a la fin—' ['I was forced to keep myself from thinking, to fear thinking about my misfortunes despite myself, was forced to repress the remnants of a cheerful but stagnant imagination which so much distress could startle to its end'].

Without any pretensions to those talents which were in him so heavily taxed with that excessive irritability, too often if not always attendant on genius, it has been my misfortune to have endured real calamities that have disqualified me for finding any enjoyment in the pleasures and pursuits which occupy the generality of the world. I have been engaged in contending with persons whose cruelty has left so painful an impression on my mind, that I may well say, 'Brillantes fleurs, émail des prés[,] ombrages frais, [ruisseaux,] bosquets, verdure, venez purifier mon imagination de tous [salie par tous] ces hideux objects!' ['Brilliant flowers, adornment of meadows, cool shades, [streams,] foliage, come purify my imagination sullied by all these hideous objects.']

Perhaps, if any situation is more pitiable than that which compels us to wish to escape from the common business and forms of life, it is that where the sentiment is forcibly felt, while it cannot be indulged; and where the sufferer, chained down to the discharge of duties from which the wearied spirit recoils, feels like the wretched Lear, when Shakespeare makes him exclaim 'Oh! I am bound upon a wheel of fire, / Which my own tears do scald like melted lead' (*King Lear,* IV.viii.47-8).[31]

Notes

1. Jane Austen, *Persuasion,* ed. John Davie (Oxford: Oxford University Press, 1980), p. 82.

2. Suggested by Anne Ehrenpreis in her introduction to *Emmeline* (Oxford: Oxford University Press, 1971), p. xiii, n. 1. Austen also alludes ironically to *Emmeline* (1788) in 'Catherine, or The Bower' (1792) and *Northanger Abbey* (1818). Quotations from Smith's poems are taken throughout from *The Poems of Charlotte Smith,* ed. Stuart Curran (New York and Oxford: Oxford University Press, 1993).

3. Aside from her *Sonnets,* Smith's publications include a long blank verse poem, *The Emigrants* (1793); several translations; ten novels written between 1788 and 1798; several volumes of mixed poetry and prose intended to introduce children to botany; and a volume of poetry left uncompleted at her death and published posthumously, *Beachy Head and Other Poems* (1807).

4. Later called *Elegiac Sonnets, and Other Poems, Elegiac Sonnets, and Other Essays by Charlotte Smith of Bignor Park, in Sussex* was first published by Dodsley in 1784; it was taken over by Cadell and Davies and expanded in subsequent editions. In 1789 a further expanded fifth edition, including poems from her novels, was published by subscription. A second volume was published by subscription in 1797; the two volumes were issued together in 1800, comprising the ninth edition of the first volume and the second edition of the second.

5. Peter M. Sacks, *The English Elegy: Studies in the Genre from Spencer to Yeats* (Baltimore and London: Johns Hopkins University Press, 1985), p. 8.

6. Jahan Ramazani, *Poetry of Mourning: The Modern Elegy from Hardy to Heaney* (Chicago and London: University of Chicago Press, 1994).

7. See Sigmund Freud, 'Mourning and Melancholia', trans. Joan Riviere, *General Psychoanalytical Theory,* ed. Philip Rieff (New York: Macmillan, 1963), pp. 164-79.

8. Celeste M. Schenck, 'Feminism and Deconstruction: Re-Constructing the Elegy', *Tulsa Studies in Women's Literature,* 5 (1986), pp. 13-27.

9. See, for example, sonnets XXVI, XXX, XXXII, LXXIV, LXXVIII, LXXXII, LXXXIX, XC, XCI in *The Poems of Charlotte Smith.*

10. *Letters of Anna Seward: Written between the Years 1784 and 1807,* 6 vols (Edinburgh and London, 1811), letter LXXI, to Theophilus Swift, 9 July 1789, vol. 2, p. 287.

11. Stuart Curran, 'Romantic Poetry: The I Altered', in Anne K. Mellor, (ed.), *Romanticism and Feminism* (Bloomington and Indianapolis: Indiana University Press, 1988), p. 200.

12. See, e.g. Curran's introduction to *The Poems of Charlotte Smith,* op. cit., p. xix.

13. *The Poetical Works of William Wordsworth,* ed. E. De Selincourt and Helen Darbishire (Oxford: Clarendon Press, 1970), vol. 4, p. 403.

14. In 1799 the principal issues of the will were resolved, but settlement was delayed. The will was finally resolved a few months before Smith's death in 1806, but it was not until 1813 that her four surviving children finally came into their inheritance. For details see Judith Phillips Stanton, 'Charlotte Smith's "Literary Business": Income, Patronage, and Indigence', in Paul J. Korshin (ed.), *The Age of Johnson: A Scholarly Annual,* vol. I (New York: AMS Press, 1987) pp. 375-401; and Curran's Introduction to *The Poems of Charlotte Smith,* esp. pp. xx-xxii.

15. Smith dealt initially with Thomas Cadell, Snr, with whom she came to a sympathetic arrangement; when he retired his successors, Thomas Cadell, Jr and William Davies, were less willing to give her such favourable terms for publishing her works, or to provide such frequent handouts. Her exchanges with them are frequently heated as she assumed they would publish whatever she chose to write. When they declined to accept her continuation of *Rural Walks,* she had her patron, the Duchess of Dorset, persuade them to do so (see her letters to Cadell and Davies, dated 20 February, 17 May, and 3 June 1795, in Beinecke Rare Book and Manuscript Library, Yale University, New Haven, CT).

16. Letter to [?], 10 February [1788?] (Beinecke).

17. Letter to Cadell and Davies, 20 February 1795 (Beinecke).

18. Letter to Cadell and Davies, 2 September 1805 (Beinecke). She had sold the copyright of the first volume of her sonnets to Cadell, Sr for £40 (see her

letter to Cadell, Sr, 8 September 1790 in the Houghton Library). Cadell and Davies refused and suggested, to her indignation, raising another subscription. She tried the scheme again in 1806, but the collection was eventually published by Johnson after her death.

19. Quoted in Curran, Introduction to *Poems of Charlotte Smith,* op. cit., p. xxv. See also *Letters of Anna Seward,* vol. VI, p. 43.

20. Letter LXXI, 9 July 1789, in *Letters,* vol. II, p. 287.

21. Considered in the light of Freud's 'Mourning and Melancholia', Smith might be seen as a depressive, punishing her husband for his inadequacies by assuming them herself.

22. Paul Fussell, *Poetic Meter and Poetic Form* (New York: Random House, 1965), p. 128.

23. Seward disapproved of Smith's formal experiments; in her discussions of the sonnet she dismissed Smith as inefficient (see *Letters,* vol. II, pp. 162-3, 222-24; vol. v, p. 58).

24. *The English Elegy,* p. 97.

25. 'Lycidas', in *Milton's Poems,* ed. B. A. Wright (London: J. M. Dent, 1969), ll.133-5, pp. 44-5.

26. Donald Davie, *The Language of Science and the Language of Literature, 1700-1740* (London: Sheed and Ward, 1963).

27. Judith Pascoe argues that Smith's botanical eye is truer to nature than the male Romantic gaze ('Female Botanists and the Poetry of Charlotte Smith', *Revisioning Romanticism: British Women Writers, 1776-1837,* ed. Carol Shiner Wilson and Joel Haefner (Philadelphia: University of Pennsylvania Press, 1994), pp. 193-209). Curran states that 'Beachy Head' testifies to an alternate Romanticism that seeks not to transcend or to absorb nature but to contemplate and honor its irreducible alterity' (Introduction, p. xxviii). Botany, however, has its troubling aspects; not only can it augment traditional symbolic identifications between the delicacy, transience and triviality of flowers and that of women, it imposes culturally specific systems of order on nature. The relationships between Smith, and nature, and romanticism need further study.

28. See Appendix, below.

29. She also ventriloquizes Petrarch and Werther, and in many of her sonnets she includes fragments of Shakespeare, always quoting from his plays, perhaps preferring to think in dramatic terms rather than contesting the immortal territory mapped out by the sonnets.

30. *The Table Talk and Omniana of Samuel Taylor Coleridge* (London, 1917), p. 281.

31. From *Poems of Charlotte Smith,* p. 68; translations by the editor.

Judith Stanton (essay date 2000)

SOURCE: Stanton, Judith. "Charlotte Smith and 'Mr. Monstroso': An Eighteenth-Century Marriage in Life and Fiction." *Women's Writing: The Elizabethan to Victorian Period* 7, no. 1 (2000): 7-22.

[*In the following essay, Stanton examines Smith's letters and concludes that her husband, Benjamin Smith, provided the model for many of the antagonists in her novels.*]

Benjamin Smith was rich, charming and handsome. Yet his miserable 41-year marriage to Charlotte Smith was an almost textbook case of the atrocities a man could legally inflict upon his wife and children in eighteenth-century England Her two most reliable biographers until recently[1] shed little light on what led the 37 year-old Charlotte Smith to leave her husband, taking her seven children with her. Catherine Ann Dorset, Charlotte's sister, was no doubt being discreet about her brother-in-law's outrages. F. M. A. Hilbish, writing in the 1930s, brings more serious charges against him, but only by shrewdly interpreting Charlotte's barely veiled fictional accounts of similar men and marriages.

Charlotte Smith's 430 letters, which I have edited, provide a great deal of information about Benjamin's degraded and ill-spent life. On the whole, the letters confirm Dorset's memories, substantiate Hilbish's surmises, and add to both. Even more interesting, new details in the letters permit us to identify Charlotte's many and varied uses of her husband as a model for antagonists in her fiction. The letters not only confirm facts from earlier accounts of her life but also reveal how very autobiographical her fiction is. In particular, they invite us to continue, as Hilbish did, to plunder Smith's fiction for her life story, especially where biographical information is scant.

Previous biographies, surviving estate papers, and especially the letters supply tantalizing glimpses of Charlotte and Benjamin's life. On 23 February 1765, 15 year-old Charlotte Turner was married to 24 year-old Benjamin Smith in an ill-considered but carefully orchestrated match (16 July 1804).[2] For two reasons, her father and the aunt who raised her thought the match to be advantageous, even necessary.

First, Charlotte may have been in the way at home. Her father, Nicholas Turner, "a gay man of the world" (Dorset, p. 25) whose properties once produced £4000 a year (2 July 1805), needed money. His bride-to-be, Miss Henrietta Meriton[3], came with a much-needed fortune of £20,000 (Hilbish, p. 36). Dorset speculates that Turner wanted to protect his much-loved daughter Charlotte from her new mother-in-law (pp. 24-25). Hilbish, drawing on pointedly autobiographical material from ***Letters of a Solitary Wanderer*** and ***Emmeline,*** extends Dorset's speculation and concludes that Charlotte and Miss Meriton disliked each other intensely (pp. 41-45). Whichever the reason, Smith later bitterly wrote that her father and aunt "sold [me] like a Southdown sheep" (4 February 1803).

Second, marriage to Benjamin promised Charlotte financial security. He was partner to his father Richard Smith, a respectable merchant from the West Indies and a director of the East India Company. In an interpolated story in *Celestina,* Charlotte depicts a husband burdened by gambling debts. The West Indian background of Elphinstone's family duplicates that of the Smiths. Like Benjamin's father Richard Smith, Elphinstone's father holds property in the West Indies (Antigua rather than Barbados) but returned to England with a wife, two sons, and three daughters, the exact composition of Benjamin's family. As with Benjamin, too, when Elphinstone's marriage to an innocent young woman is being arranged, his character is not scrutinized.

In any case, young Charlotte Turner was bright, beautiful, cheerful and accomplished: she read, drew, danced and acted, and had published her first poem. An elegant schooling in Kensington prepared her for the life of a gentleman's daughter and for a handsome and charming suitor. On their brief acquaintance[4], Benjamin probably appeared to be both. In later years, she took pride in their handsome children although she was preoccupied with the darker side of their resemblance to him: "Would to God none of the children partook of his nature" (3 March 1803), she wrote on one occasion. And again, "Would to God any one of them were not like him in some way or other" (26 April 1806).

Charlotte's aunt and other relatives set out only to ensure Charlotte's fortune by securing Benjamin's interest. Indeed, Charlotte may even have fallen in love—as a 14 year-old girl properly managed might do. Writing in 1803 to her patron, the Earl of Egremont, Charlotte was distressed to find that Benjamin was spreading a rumor that she had loved him. Yet several of her fictional self-portraits depict young women in love with debauchees in the making. Mrs Elphinstone, for one, admits to loving "*him*; he was the most cheerful and sanguine creature in the world" (*Celestina,* [London: T. Cadell, 1791], II, pp. 274-275).

Doubtless, Benjamin Smith had charm. However degenerate the characters modeled on him are, most of them are charming, from Mr Stafford and Delamere in *Emmeline* to Elphinstone and Vavasour in *Celestina* to Philip Somerive in *The Old Manor House.* Moreover, after the Smiths separated, while Benjamin lived in exile in Scotland, he successfully used his charm to convert Charlotte's supporters to his side. By 1803, the Earl of Egremont yielded to Benjamin's ingratiating qualities and turned against Charlotte. Inexplicably, and to Charlotte's great mortification, Egremont called her scapegrace husband "the best of the bunch" (5 March, 16 July and 13 August 1804). The best, he meant, of Richard Smith's heirs, a large, litigious family.

Whether Benjamin was educated or even literate is uncertain. In 1805, Charlotte complained that, among his other follies, he collected rare books, "tho he cannot write, even in his own language" (14 February 1805). Complete illiteracy seems unlikely on two accounts. First, two of her letters to him survive, written in terms that suggest he could read, as does the fact that he was a merchant. Second, one letter by him survives, written from his final residence, the Berwick jail (23 September 1805). Although the letter could have been written for him, the handwriting matches a signature of his from the 1770s and reproduced in Hilbish (p. 52). The truth is more likely what Hilbish surmises, drawing again on accounts in *Letters of a Solitary Wanderer.* Benjamin was probably typical of ill-educated rich boys from the West Indies, who were often placed in schools where they were abused, considered stupid, and paid other boys to do their lessons and take their floggings (pp. 46-47).

Charlotte Smith's depiction of the two Elphinstone brothers in *Celestina* only muddies the question. Like Benjamin and his only brother Richard, they were born and partially educated in the West Indies. The elder has "more money and less understanding than any boy of his age", is "tyrannical," and "as much hated for his overbearing temper as despised and laughed at for his ignorance and vanity" (II, p. 251). The younger, who figures in the novel, is "open, good humoured, and undesigning; too gay and careless to think, too quick to learn . . . [W]hen he neglected to do his business somebody or other was always willing to do it for him" (II, p. 251). The truth of Benjamin's character may lie between these two, with some part of him lending traits to each one. Certainly Smith's letters capture his mentality and intelligence: Benjamin Smith emerges from her correspondence as bright but ignorant, overbearing, and undisciplined.

Thus matched only in looks, extroverted temperament, and high expectations for fortune, the couple lived unhappily together for over 22 years. Catherine Dorset wrote that the marriage was still young when Charlotte Smith began to face "the mortifying conviction that she was subjected to one so infinitely her inferior". In what appears to be Smith's earliest surviving letter, she wrote a grim epigraph for her life:

> No disadvantage could equal those I sustained; the more my mind expanded, the more I became sensible of personal slavery; the more I improved and cultivated my understanding, the farther I was removed from those with whom I was condemned to pass my life; and the more clearly I saw by these newly-acquired lights the horror of the abyss into which I had unconsciously plunged.
>
> (p. 218)

In several stories of wives as ill-matched in marriage as she, Smith did not hesitate to re-create her experiences in this abyss. Each of these alter egos—Mrs Stafford, Mrs Elphinstone and Mrs Verney—has an improved and cultivated understanding and a sharp sense of being condemned for life to living with an inferior being. Smith describes the debasement and triumph of each woman in much the same language. Each morally inferior husband seeks out the town where he can practise his vices. Each condemned wife retreats to remote country locations. There the wives restore their own and their children's health and live modestly, adapting to reduced circumstances.

Details of Charlotte Smith's fictional bad marriages echo events and patterns of the 22 years she lived with her husband. During that time, Charlotte bore 12 children, nine of whom lived into adulthood. The Smiths moved several times, resorting early to moving to escape creditors, a frequent pattern of their later lives together and apart. From 1765 to 1768, they lived in London in a cramped, gloomy house. Southgate next provided a country location more congenial to Charlotte's health. In 1771, they returned to Tottenham near London, where Richard Smith hoped to rein in his son's spending. From 1774, they lived at Lys Farm in Hampshire until financial disaster struck in 1783. The 9 years in Hampshire may have held some happiness for both: Charlotte was always healthier and more comfortable in the country, and Benjamin achieved enough standing to be appointed sheriff in 1781.

Nevertheless, Charlotte's fate had long been sealed. Dorset and Hilbish give full, familiar accounts of the years of debt and desperation that led to the couple's separation (Dorset, pp. 26-48; Hilbish, pp. 57-101). In 1776, while the couple still lived at Lys Farm, Richard Smith's death opened the door for real misery. Spurning legal advice, he had written his own will. Complex and contradictory, it begged for litigation. Worse yet, he foolishly made Benjamin its executor, along with Charlotte and his wife Lucy.[5] The two women were powerless. No more suited to manage a trust than a company, Benjamin was charged in a *devastavit* by his brother-in-law, Thomas Dyer, for debts he had incurred against the estate (9 October 1793,? December 1802).[6] While he was at King's Bench Prison, until 2 July 1784, Charlotte dutifully spent much time with him and arranged to have her first volume of poems published to secure his release. By October, acting out of a sense of duty worthy of her most honorable heroines, she fled with him for a day to establish him in Dieppe, just ahead of creditors. After returning to England for the children, she joined him at a castle he had leased in Normandy. There the family spent a cold, harsh winter.

The imprisonment and flight to France deeply shook Charlotte's nerves and sense of security. As a novelist, she rehearsed some version of these events with each of the three couples modeled on her marriage. For Mrs Stafford, "nothing remained but to follow her husband to a prison, or prevail on him to go to the continent while she attempted anew to settle his affairs" (***Emmeline,*** [London: Oxford University Press, 1971], p. 301). After sending her husband ahead, Mrs Stafford takes out a mortgage on the estate and then embarks for Dieppe with her friend Emmeline (p. 302). The novel emphasizes "the fatigue of travelling with small children": Mrs Stafford traveled with three children younger than 5. Charlotte herself managed the journey with an infant, a toddler, two adolescents and no companion. Though Mr and Mrs Elphinstone in *Celestina* also travel with children, their trip to Antigua is not so desperate. Smith develops the most detailed and sinister flight to France in ***Desmond.***

In the spring of 1785, Charlotte returned to England with her husband and children to settle in Woolbeding in Sussex, still in such financial straits that she had no choice but to seek needed funds by publishing. The third and fourth editions of ***Elegiac Sonnets*** came out in 1786. A potentially more lucrative venture into publishing fiction failed, however, after Thomas Cadell withdrew her translation of *Manon Lescaut*. This loss of hoped-for funds no doubt hastened the end of an already shaky marriage.

On 15 April 1787, Charlotte Smith "quitted Mr Smith to avoid personal ill treatment on [the] one hand & an execution from Mr Silver [an unidentified creditor] on the other that would have stripped my family of the very beds they slept on" (? September 1802). Her biographers have shed little light on this event. Dorset criticizes Charlotte, however, for failing to make legal arrangements that would settle money on her and the children. This serious oversight meant that all the interest money on her three small fortunes of £2000, 2000 and 3000 legally belonged to Benjamin. She had no security but her wits. Similarly in ***Desmond,*** Geraldine Verney cannot get at her own small fortune because it was not properly settled on her during her lifetime, but on him ([London: G. G. J. & J. Robinson, 1792], III, p. 13). As to Benjamin's life after the separation, Charlotte's contemporary biographers are silent.

Smith's later letters paint a darker picture of Benjamin than one of mere financial irresponsibility. Imprudence, depravity, deceit, and abuse of others marked his entire life. During their London years, he regularly overspent his income of £2000 (the household costing £900 of that), a sum considerably greater than a mere competency. When funds dwindled, he enlisted his wife to beg more money from his father (10 February 1803). The harsh satire of Benjamin as Mr Stafford in *Emmeline* also depicts him as a foolish projector, which he was. Charlotte joked to friends that her husband would turn anything into a project. Destitute in 1804, Charlotte complained that he was "flourishing away at an handsome house & has sent for Guinea fowl, peacocks & a filtring stone" (13 August and 8 September 1804). He also begged for money for "*a collection of scarce* books, a new hobby horse of his" (14 February 1805).

Benjamin's fiscal transgressions, however, far exceeded the fictional Stafford's folly of trying to make money by fertilizing fields with discarded wigs. They more nearly resemble Philip Somerive's destruction of his family's estate under the watchful but powerless eye of his father in ***The Old Manor House.*** Mr Somerive, a gentle, ineffective father, suggests a portrait of Charlotte's father-in-law, who lent the couple great sums of money without inquiring too closely into their needs. In fact, the Somerives closely resemble Richard Smith and his children. Richard Smith even tried to effect Benjamin's reform by buying him houses—one in the country where Smith hoped to keep his son out of trouble, then one in town where he hoped to keep an eye on him. One of the two Somerive sons, Orlando, aspires to the priesthood, which Benjamin's older brother Richard attained. Both the real and fictional families have three daughters: the youngest Smith girl, a stepdaughter, was peripheral to family concerns; similarly, the eldest Somerive daughter is safely married and living in Ireland.

The most telling parallels lay in Philip's trespasses: gambling, wild spending, excessive drinking and violence. Benjamin squandered almost half of Richard Smith's estate, valued at £36,000 when his father died. Charlotte writes that Benjamin's executorship "consisted of dissipating about £16,000" (13 September 1802) or "in taking about seventeen thousand pounds *more* than could possibly belong to him" (? December 1802).[7] The loss, coupled with the estate's entanglement in litigation, drove three of Smith's five sons into the military for occupations suitable to their status, just as Philip's fiscal irresponsibility forced Orlando to join the army.

After Benjamin's separation from Charlotte, he lived primarily in Hamilton, Scotland, under an alias—Bryan, or Brian, Symmonds[8]—to escape prosecution for debt (14 April 1801). At Hamilton, he supported himself and a second family on money that he periodically recovered from his wife. A few years after the separation, Charlotte believed he had "another family by a cook who livd with him" (9 October 1793). This woman was doubtless "Mrs. Millar", whom Charlotte variously calls his "housekeeper", a Scotch cook (8 September 1804), his "bedmaker" (? August 1805) and "his femme de charge" (16 October 1803). It especially disgusted Charlotte that her husband supported his mistress with interest money from her own marriage portions:

> I am distressed for the means of paying for his family's food while he cocks his hat on one side, looks knowing & buckish & struts off with more than is left to any one of his children for his 'dear Mrs. Miller ("who had 300£ to her fortune & saved his life once.")'
>
> (14 October 1803)

Usually he traveled incognito to England to claim Charlotte's interest money and sometimes her book money. But when her payments arrived in July and January, he thought the weather was too severe for travel:

> he will not trust his invaluable life & most precious person while the weather is cold. Nor will he hazard the vernal equinox. He will only venture his butterfly form when the sun is in Taurus—or Gemini*.
>
> (10 February 1803), * i.e. in May or June

Charlotte recaps these unwelcome visits late in *The Old Manor House* with Benjamin in a cameo role. Monimia's unfeeling guardian consigns her to live with a Mrs Newill, a woman of sour temper and relaxed morals. When Mrs Newill's "brutal and extravagant husband" unexpectedly returns to town, those who had been "willing to promote her welfare, grew cold when they found their bounty served only to support the husband in drunkenness" ([London: Oxford University Press, 1989], p. 478). Interestingly, although several friends gave Charlotte money when asked, she never notes that Benjamin's presence cost her their support.

She does, however, remark upon Benjamin's "barbarous & unnatural conduct towards his children" (19 March 1802). Usually it manifested in his refusal to support them while claiming for himself money they needed desperately. Not only did he cost her children nearly half of their inheritance and impede the settlement of the estate by mismanaging it, but he also controlled her marriage portions. In 1801, he claimed most of the interest payments on one of the £2000 portions and would not allow her interest on the other due to her when her stepmother Mrs Chafys died (23 August 1801). He tied up the £3000 portion when he bought woodland from Sir James Lake (3 December 1802).

In *Desmond*, Charlotte draws on the debacle of her marriage portions to intensify her heroine's plight. Geraldine Verney owns that she would have given up her marriage portion to support her children, but could not: "'I have nothing during Mr. Verney's life, but a trifling allowance by way of pin-money, which *I* have never asked for, and *he* has never paid'" ([1792], III, p. 13).

Near the end of her life, Charlotte fought to ensure that her fortune would be settled on her three children born after Richard Smith died and so omitted from his will (25 January, 20 March, 1 June, 5 and 14 July 1804). In this one small matter, she ultimately succeeded. Nevertheless, it rankled that Benjamin provided for his mistress using the interest income from her marriage portions (25 January 1804). Never mind that it legally belonged to him. An honorable man, Charlotte believed, would never rob his children. Nor would he be petty. Much of Benjamin's financial high-handedness was on a grand scale, but some of it was niggling and mean-spirited: when she wrote him on business, he would return her letters unopened and unread to put her to extra expense (13 August 1804).

The children's maintenance money from the estate should have secured them modest support. But almost as soon as Charlotte separated from Benjamin, he learned to appropriate their money for his own use. In that year, he demanded and got £2520 for the care of his children in 1787, care which he did not provide (? September 1802). Elsewhere she claims that he received £2700 of their maintenance money and £700 more for trumped-up business expenses (? December 1802). In *Emmeline,* Lord Montreville's illegal appropriation of his niece's rightful estate shadows this practice.

What Charlotte called abuses and Benjamin claimed as a legal right continued throughout his life. From 1799 to 1803, he received £918 from the estate. Of all that, he gave £20 to George, £10 to Lionel, and *"one whole pound"* to his daughter Harriet, gravely ill from malaria. Despite that scant outlay for his children, he "got into Embarrassment again" (10 February 1803). In 1801, Charlotte tried but failed to compel him to support George for an ensigncy in the Army (31 July 1801). He did give his youngest son £20 (4 November 1801) but asked for it back (9 September 1802a). He returned to Scotland with £400 in all. In 1802, Lord Egremont urged Charlotte to send Benjamin £50 of medical bills incurred for Harriet's dangerous fevers, but he refused to pay even the first one for £13.8s. (11 August 1802). Egremont responded that "he did not consider him so honest a Man as an highwayman" (23 August 1802). In 1803, Benjamin received £744 in 6 months while Charlotte and the children received nothing (13 January 1804). During this time, she was nearly destitute.

Lucy Smith Newhouse, Charlotte and Benjamin's third daughter, was perhaps the neediest of all the Smith clan. Years after her father had left, Lucy married against her mother's wishes. The death of Lucy's husband, who had treated her brutally, left her with three young children. In spite of Charlotte's earlier opposition to the match, she took pains to provide for the hapless family. Benjamin took none. On one of his forays into England, as Charlotte recounted to Egremont, Lucy's "barbarous father with 500£ in his pocket pass'd her poor Cottage in a post chaise & pulld up the glass the moment he saw her who accidentally stood at the gate with those helpless Orphans" (14 and 15 October 1803). A year later, Charlotte quotes Benjamin as saying, "'if his daughter & her children were starving & perishing for want at his gate he would not give her a farthing to save their lives'" (13 August 1804).

Of all Smith's married antagonists, Verney in **Desmond** seems most clearly modeled on Benjamin's paternal practices. When Verney returns home unannounced after a 5-week absence with a dissolute companion, he runs his wife Geraldine out of the room in front of her guest, her kind friend Bethel. "'There, get ye along to the nusery [sic], that's the proper place for women and children'" (II, p. 36). Then, to Bethel, Verney claims the children are "'encumbrances'":

> "Poh," replied [Verney] carelessly, "I don't neglect her—but children—when one has a house full of them, as I think I am likely to have, pull confounded hard; and as to their promising I know nothing that they promise, but to grow up, to pull harder still, and find out that I am in their way before I have any mind to relinquish the enjoyments of this life".
>
> (II, p. 39)

In the letters, Charlotte supports her negative assessments of Benjamin by citing the opinions of two men of character who had dealt with him. William Augustus Bettesworth, "a very good Lawyer" in Hampshire and "much trusted as a Man of integrity and abilities," considered Benjamin Smith's conduct "Weak & extravagant" (3 December 1802). Mr Tayler, long involved with the trust settlement, concluded that Benjamin Smith was "quite incapable of governing or acting for himself" (4 November 1801). Their evaluations, along with Charlotte's many financial clashes with Benjamin, support her damning assertion that he was "as troublesome as some idea of power, extreme folly & total want of principal can make a Man" (15 March 1802).

Less frequently but with burning anger, Charlotte Smith wrote of physical abuse at the hands of her husband. He was "the wretch who has embitterd her life, insulted her, robbed her, struck her, attempted in the frantic jealousy of conscious unworthiness, to rob her of her character" (8 September 1804). Four accounts of incidents from their life together survive. She claimed to have witnesses good enough for court for two of them:

> once in his Coach going to dine at Lord Clanricardes he threw a large bunch of keys at me & hurt me on the breast, without any provocation but my saying we should make Lady Clanricarde wait & put her out of humour . . . another [witness], a relation of mine . . . has seen him strike & kick me, & once at table, throw a quartern loaf at my head without provocation at all but the phrenzy, for so it seemed at the moment.
>
> (25 January 1804)

Returning to Brighton in 1805, Smith recalls that years before she tried:

> to negociate [sic] with his Creditors for his return, & have watched at the window for Bailiffs, while he sat within, uttering curses against me, & while my *ten* children, one then at the breast, often clung round me in terror as his violence threatend my personal safety.
>
> (10 September 1805)

She first mentioned her danger in a 1793 letter to Joseph Cooper Walker: Benjamin's temper was "so capricious & often so cruel that my life was not safe" (9 October 1793). Not long after the separation, at the urging of friends, she agreed to see him again, thinking his visit would last only a few days. He stayed for 3 weeks. At first, he "treated me with more than his usual brutality—threatening to sell the furniture, the Books, and every necessary which I have twice saved from the rapacity of his creditors" (14 January 1788). Near the end of his stay, "a new fit of frenzy has seizd him; he has broke open all my drawers where my papers were". Then he left for London, planning to claim her earnings from Thomas Cadell, her publisher. This was the only account written during one of his "visits"; the rest are retrospective.

Remarkably, Smith depicts no such abuse in the novels, it being beyond the bounds of good taste in fiction, if not in life. I would argue, however, that she draws on her experience with her gin-soaked husband for much of the disrespectful, drunken and seductive behavior in her antagonists and minor characters. When Verney curses, his oaths suggest Charlotte's years of exposure to Benjamin Smith. Ignoring his wife, Verney greets Bethel:

> "Damme, Bethel, how long is it since I saw you last? I thought you were gone to kingdom come.—Here's Newminster and I, we came only last night from his

house in Norfolk,—Damme, we had to raise the wind together; for I have had the Philistines in my house and be cursed to them, who had laid violent hands on all my goods and chattels, except my wife and her brats, . . . I wish I could find out who is so damned generous, I'd try to touch them for the ready I want now".

(II, pp. 35-36)

After banishing Geraldine from the room, Verney tries to buy "'a hellish clever trotting mare'" from Bethel and swears "'by heaven'" his amazement that his mother-in-law has paid some of his large debts, for he thought "'she'd have seen me at the devil'" first (II, p. 38).

Finally, the letters give abundant examples of Benjamin's degraded life. Soon after they were separated, he admitted—or perhaps boasted—to Charlotte of his connections with people who indulged in "the desperation of gaming houses" (14 January 1788). She could not have been surprised. Benjamin certainly drank; she once described him as "this unhappy Man, who is drunk with Gin half his time & sleeps most of the rest" (5 December 1802). He may have eaten to excess: after one tormenting visit, Charlotte notes that he "waddled off to Hamilton" (14 October 1803). She first mentions his "infidelity, and with the most despicable objects" in 1793 (9 October). She knew that while married he "used to trespass with the kitchen staff", a practice she would have borne but for his violence. And of course, though the Smiths were never divorced, Benjamin managed to acquire a second family by living for many years with Mrs Miller in Scotland.

Apart from this anecdotal evidence, Charlotte gave few details about the nature of his gross debaucheries. Three of her revelations are suggestive. First, his relationship with his daughters is open to interpretation. While still at home, he committed "the most gross violations of decency and morality before his daughters" (5 November 1802). We can only speculate whether Charlotte considered these acts to be his usual drunkenness, his dallying with the female servants, or something worse, such as a sexual assault on one of the daughters. If he molested his daughters, it is unlikely that Charlotte would have been explicit. He was not above making sexual overtures, or worse, to women much younger than he. Once while passing through Petworth, he flirted with Harriet, his youngest daughter, perhaps not recognizing her as he batted "those amiable oglers of his" at her (30 July 1804). Second, already burdened with his Scottish family, he attempted bigamy by trying to take a second wife (5 December 1802):

a Miss Gordon—On whom he passd himself for a single Man, a person of fortune, under a temporary cloud—To this Woman, he actually lent my books, saying I was a relation of his familys!—& things went so far, that the *wedding presents* were bought.

(10 July 1804)

Worst of all, after he died at 63, Charlotte discovered that he had promised to marry an 18 year-old girl, "the niece of his old Concubine, with both of whom he lived in common!—and by the former, he has left a child which he desires his family to protect & bring up!" (26 April 1806). Thus, from the grave, he managed to mock his wife's moral sensibilities with a final lewd insult.

In the last 6 years of her life, Charlotte often describes her husband's trespasses specifically, mostly to the Earl of Egremont. Unfortunately, her candor turned Egremont against her and in Benjamin's favor. However debauched Benjamin was, Egremont found her reports of that debauchery unacceptably haranguing and indiscreet. Nor could she have helped her cause by constant complaints about Benjamin's failure to do his duty by the children. The Earl had six children by his long-time mistress, Elizabeth Iliffe. Though a man of his class would have considered himself far above a mere author's censure, his unhappy marriage to Iliffe in 1801 was surely untimely for Smith. Nor did he legitimize the children. The title passed to a cousin.

I suspect a further indiscretion in the sexual suggestiveness of Smith's many claims to being "degraded by belonging to such a monster" (3 March 1803). It disgusted her to be "yoke fellow with this idiotic brute" (23 August 1801). These allusions to the horror of her sexual bondage crystallized only once into an explicit statement. To her friend Sarah Rose, she laments that she was ever "sold, a *legal prostitute,* in my early youth, or what the law calls infancy" (15 June 1804).

Charlotte Smith had read widely in the melodramatic fiction of her day: gambling, debauchery, seduction and ruin were effective, routine plot devices. And yet the story of her life, as revealed by Dorset, Hilbish, and her own amazing letters, was scarcely superseded by anyone else's fiction. It is tempting to wonder just how far Benjamin Smith went. Smith's most degraded characters, Philip Somerive and Mr Verney, share too many factual points of similarity to Benjamin to dismiss their worst behavior as if it did not derive from his.

Near the end of **Desmond,** when Verney flees to France ahead of his wife Geraldine, he sends a friend back to get her. She is to leave the children behind, but she does not. The Duc de Romagnecourt "considered the sums he lost to Verney as a sort of passport to her favour" (III, p. 3). Bethel, Desmond, and Geraldine herself see this; in fact, Desmond agonizes that Verney has "sold her to him [the Duc]" (III, p. 42). The Duc attempts to seduce her and belittles her coldness, assured that she belongs to him. Geraldine leaves for France, "'myself a miserable slave, returning with trembling and reluctant steps, to put on the most dreadful of all fetters?—Fetters that would even destroy the freedom of my mind'" (III, p. 71).

No doubt Charlotte strongly identified with this heroine. Only the novelist Mrs Denzil is more autobiographical. Geraldine's image of the married woman as slave is also Smith's. She writes of her personal experience of enslavement in her letters as well as her novels, always in a cry of outrage and despair: She is worse off than "the veriest slave that ever drudged in a counting house" (7 July 1802) and "a wretched slave" (13 September 1802). Her life is "this weary pilgrimage, this worse than African bondage" (4 February 1803). While Geraldine's husband dies—surely a bit of authorial wishful thinking—Charlotte knew no release from bondage. Because true confessions were beyond the pale for a woman of Smith's class and sensibilities, she never would have admitted the depths of any degradation she might have experienced with her husband.

For again and again, the worst actions of Charlotte Smith's most despicable antagonists resemble Benjamin's known actions, as preserved in her letters, enough to lend credence to the many epithets she invented for him: "this ideotic [sic] brute" (23 August 1801), this "madman and a fool" (13 June 1802), this "biped" and "wretched monster" (1 November 1802), "this voracious unfeeling Monster" (9 January 1803), this "nauseous hypocrite" (8 September 1804), a "being, human only in form" (14 February 1805), "Mr. Monstroso" (16 July 1804). Even if Benjamin never sold his wife's favors, he must have been capable of anything. "Vicious animals", she wrote of him in 1802, "always become worse as they grow older" (5 November).

Hard documentary evidence of Benjamin Smith's shortcomings is limited. Estate papers confirm that sizeable amounts of money were awarded to him while he lived in exile in Scotland, and the address on one surviving note shows that he used an alias while there. His two prison terms for debt, the first in 1784 and the second from early 1804 until his death on 23 February 1806, confirm a lifelong pattern of fiscal irresponsibility. An article presenting Charlotte Smith's view of her husband is necessarily partisan. Her outrage will lead some, now as then, to blame her for not submitting to tradition and to law. Any money Benjamin secured from the Smith trust or his wife's marriage articles was his under the laws of his day.

Some might dismiss Charlotte's "Mr. Monstroso" as merely the construct of a wronged woman. Yet we must consider when, why, and for whom she constructed this portrait—not merely friends or even business associates but the Earl of Egremont. As her one-time patron and Trustee to the Smith estate, he was the one man who had the power to make or break her. In 1798, because he assumed the Trusteeship, she abandoned her lucrative novel writing, believing that her troubles were over. When Egremont repeatedly sided with Benjamin, she complained. When he exhorted her to be silent, she continued to confront him with the story of Benjamin Smith's dishonorable conduct toward his children and herself, insisting on her version of the truth. As a woman and as a wife in late eighteenth-century England, she had limited rights and little recourse to justice other than what she could obtain with her pen.

In 1802, Egremont suggested that if Charlotte and her children lived with Benjamin, the Trust income would be sufficient. Indignant, Charlotte explained her objections to the Earl's ill-considered proposal:

This idea I could easily convince you is erroneous, but it would be by an history of the former life and conduct of Mr B Smith which would be too long for you to read—If continual & unmeaning waste of money which he refusd to the absolute support of his children, if the most brutish & unmanly personal insults towards me so that my life was often in danger, if the most gross violations of decency and morality before his daughters, & if the entire annihilation of my faculties by terror of his frantic & furious passions on [sic] one hand, and on the other of Bailiffs that beseiged the doors, if all these circumstances would contribute to make the income do, then it might be a matter of prudence.

But I am sure your Lordship must see that the Man who is the horror of all his family, whose whole life has been a tissue of folly varied only by wickedness & without one virtue to redeem his bad qualities, who, whether as a Son, a brother, husband, father, or Guardian has invariably undone every one with whom he was connected as far as was in his power, & who now avails himself even of his vices to deprive his children of their support arising from my fortune after having spent all his own, & even that which ought to have been settled on me according to those very articles of which he now takes advantage: Your Lordship is too correct a judge of human nature not to be convinced that no good could possibly arise from my living with him.

(5 November 1802)

Moreover, she claims that she "can bring persons who will prove" that leaving him was "absolutely necessary", persons whose evidence would hold up in court. But she had never had the wherewithal to afford divorce proceedings. Within months, this stand cost her security, patronage, and what was left of her popularity and her career. Egremont, once her patron, was still in a position to be her strongest advocate. By insisting on telling him her version of the truth, she risked all and lost all. Even after Egremont forbade her to write to him, her outrage over the law's injustice and her husband's offenses against her and her hapless family echoes through the letters. Idealistically she believed in a code of honor and a cult of sensibility even after they failed her. Those beliefs compelled her to continue to anatomize her husband's offenses at any cost. The fact that she did so lends credibility to her story.

Notes

1. Dorset, "Charlotte Smith" in Sir Walter Scott, *Biographical Memoirs of Eminent Novelists* (Edinburgh, 1834); Florence May Anna Hilbish, *Charlotte Smith, Poet and Novelist (1749-1806)* (Philadelphia: University of Pennsylvania Press, 1941). Loraine Fletcher's *Charlotte Smith: A Critical Biography* (London: Macmillan, 1998) discusses the marriage throughout her study. Carrol Fry's *Charlotte Smith* (New York: Twayne, 1996) focuses on Smith's literary achievement.

2. Benjamin Smith was 3 years old in 1744 when he came to England from Barbados in the hold of a

cargo ship. For references to Charlotte Smith's letters, see the "List of Correspondence Cited".

3. Petworth House Archives 8204, West Sussex Records Office, Chichester.

4. A copy of an 18 August 1773 deed of settlement between Nicholas Turner, Charlotte's father, and Benjamin Smith mentions a deed between Turner and Miss Meriton from 24 and 25 August 1764. This suggests that only 6 months elapsed between Nicholas Turner's formal involvement with Miss Meriton and his success in marrying Charlotte off. Petworth House Archives, West Sussex Record Office, Chichester, UK, 8204.

5. Lucy Towers Smith, remarkably enough, was the maternal aunt who raised Charlotte and masterminded her marriage to Benjamin. She married Richard Smith on 15 May 1767, just over 2 years after Charlotte's wedding, and became a very wealthy woman.

6. In the two letters, Charlotte merely says the family brought the charges that sent Benjamin to King's Bench Prison. On a copy of Richard Smith's will with notes in her hand, she names Dyer (Petworth House Archives, West Sussex Record Office, Chichester, UK, 8202).

7. Dorset explicitly claims that £20,000 was lost "[b]esides what was expended in law, and what was wasted by improvidence" because Richard Smith let his solicitor persuade him to "lend that sum to a distressed baronet on mortgage" (p. 37).

8. The alias is given in two letters (13) June 1802 and 14 October 1803). A third letter, to Benjamin, preserves the alias and gives his Scottish address: "Bryan Symmonds, Esqre / Camberwell / Hamilton". Benjamin refused the note, putting her to the double expense of return postage. She sent the canceled noted to William Tyler, the Earl of Egremont's steward.

List of Charlotte Smith's Correspondence Cited

Letter to Thomas Cadell, Sr. 14 January 1788. Princeton University, Princeton, NJ.

Letter to Joseph Cooper Walker. 9 October 1793. Henry E. Huntington Library, San Marino, CA.

Letter to George Brian, the Earl of Egremont. 14 April 1801. Petworth House Archives, West Sussex Record Office, Chichester, UK.

Letter to George Brian, the Earl of Egremont. 31 July 1801. Petworth House Archives, West Sussex Record Office, Chichester, UK.

Letter to William Tyler. 23 August 1801. Petworth House Archives, West Sussex Record Office, Chichester, UK.

Letter to George Brian, the Earl of Egremont. 4 November 1801. Petworth House Archives, West Sussex Record Office, Chichester, UK.

Letter to William Tyler. 15 March 1802. Petworth House Archives, West Sussex Record Office, Chichester, UK.

Letter to William Tyler. 19 March 1802. Petworth House Archives, West Sussex Record Office, Chichester, UK.

Letter to William Tyler. 13 June 1802. Petworth House Archives, West Sussex Record Office, Chichester, UK.

Letter to William Tyler. 7 July 1802. Petworth House Archives, West Sussex Record Office, Chichester, UK.

Letter to George Brian, the Earl of Egremont. 11 August 1802. Petworth House Archives, West Sussex Record Office, Chichester, UK.

Letter to William Tyler. 23 August 1802. Petworth House Archives, West Sussex Record Office, Chichester, UK.

Letter to Samuel Rose. 9 September 1802. Mills Memorial Library. McMaster University, Hamilton, Ontario.

Letter to George Brian, the Earl of Egremont.? September 1802. Petworth House Archives, West Sussex Record Office, Chichester, UK.

Letter to William Tyler. 13 September 1802. Petworth House Archives, West Sussex Record Office, Chichester, UK.

Letter to William Tyler. 1 November 1802. Petworth House Archives, West Sussex Record Office, Chichester, UK.

Letter to George Brian, the Earl of Egremont. 5 November 1802. Petworth House Archives, West Sussex Record Office, Chichester, UK.

Letter to George Brian, the Earl of Egremont.? December 1802. Petworth House Archives, West Sussex Record Office, Chichester, UK.

Letter to George Brian, the Earl of Egremont. 3 December 1802. Petworth House Archives, West Sussex Record Office, Chichester, UK.

Letter to George Brian, the Earl of Egremont. 5 December 1802. Petworth House Archives, West Sussex Record Office, Chichester, UK.

Letter to George Brian, the Earl of Egremont. 9 January 1803. Petworth House Archives, West Sussex Record Office, Chichester, UK.

Letter to George Brian, the Earl of Egremont. 4 February 1803. Petworth House Archives, West Sussex Record Office, Chichester, UK.

Letter to George Brian, the Earl of Egremont. 10 February 1803. Petworth House Archives, West Sussex Record Office, Chichester, UK.

Letter to George Brian, the Earl of Egremont. 3 March 1803. Petworth House Archives, West Sussex Record Office, Chichester, UK.

Letter to George Brian, the Earl of Egremont. 14 October 1803. Petworth House Archives, West Sussex Record Office, Chichester, UK.

Letter to William Tyler. 16 October 1803. Petworth House Archives, West Sussex Record Office, Chichester, UK.

Letter to George Brian, the Earl of Egremont. 13 January 1804. Petworth House Archives, West Sussex Record Office, Chichester, UK.

Letter to George Brian, the Earl of Egremont. 25 January 1804. Petworth House Archives, West Sussex Record Office, Chichester, UK.

Letter to Sarah Rose. 5 March 1804. Henry E. Huntington Library, San Marino, CA.

Letter to George Brian, the Earl of Egremont. 20 March 1804. Petworth House Archives, West Sussex Record Office, Chichester, UK.

Letter to Thomas Cadell, Jr, and William Davies. 1 June 1804. Princeton University, Princeton, NJ.

Letter to Sarah Rose. 15 June 1804. Henry E. Huntington Library, San Marino, CA.

Letter to Benjamin Smith. 5 July 1804. Petworth House Archives, West Sussex Record Office, Chichester, UK.

Letter to George Brian, the Earl of Egremont. 10 July 1804. Petworth House Archives, West Sussex Record Office, Chichester, UK.

Letter to William Tyler. 14 July 1804. Petworth House Archives, West Sussex Record Office, Chichester, UK.

Letter to Sarah Rose. 16 July 1804. Houghton Library. Harvard University, Boston, MA.

Letter to Sarah Rose. 30 July 1804. Henry E. Huntington Library, San Marino, CA.

Letter to George Brian, the Earl of Egremont. 13 August 1804. Petworth House Archives, West Sussex Record Office, Chichester, UK.

Letter to George Brian, the Earl of Egremont. 8 September 1804. Petworth House Archives, West Sussex Record Office, Chichester, UK.

Letter to Sarah Rose. 14 February 1805. Henry E. Huntington Library, San Marino, CA.

Letter to Sarah Rose. 2 July 1805. Beinecke Rare Book and Manuscript Library, Osborne Collection. Yale University, New Haven, CT.

Letter to Sarah Rose. 10 September 1805. Houghton Library. Harvard University, Boston, MA.

Letter to Sarah Rose. 26 April 1806. Henry E. Huntington Library, San Marino, CA.; The John Comyn Collection.

FURTHER READING

Biographies

Hilbish, Florence May Anna. *Charlotte Smith, Poet and Novelist (1749-1806)*. Philadelphia: University of Pennsylvania, 1941, 603 p.
Comprehensive biography and critical estimate of Smith's poetry and prose.

Stanton, Judith Phillips. "Charlotte Smith's 'Literary Business': Income, Patronage, and Indigence." *The Age of Johnson: A Scholarly Annual* 1 (1987): 375-401.
Details Smith's financial obligations as the impetus for much of her writing.

Criticism

Cook, Kay K. "The Aesthetics of Loss: Charlotte Smith's *The Emigrants* and *Beachy Head*." In *Approaches to Teaching British Women Poets of the Romantic Period*, edited by Stephen C. Behrendt and Harriet Kramer Linkin, pp. 97-128. New York: The Modern Language Association of America, 1997.
Discusses the influence of the French Revolution on Smith's poetry.

Ehrenpreis, Anne Henry. "*Northanger Abbey*: Jane Austen and Charlotte Smith." *Nineteenth-Century Fiction* 25, no. 3 (December 1970): 343-48.
Examines similarities in the characterization of Clarinthia Ludford in Smith's *Ethelinde*, Camilla Stanley in Austen's *Catharine*, and Isabella Thorpe in Austen's *Northanger Abbey*.

Ford, Susan Allen. "Tales of the Times: Family and Nation in Charlotte Smith and Jane West." In *Family Matters in the British and American Novel*, edited by Andrea O'Reilly Herrera, Elizabeth Mahn Nollen, and Sheila Reitzel Foor, pp. 15-29. Bowling Green: Bowling Green State University Popular Press, 1997.
Compares Smith's *Desmond* with Jane West's *A Tale of the Times*, examining the manner in which each novel makes use of the family as the grounds for the profound changes in culture and society brought on by the age of revolution.

Harries, Elizabeth W. "'Out in Left Field': Charlotte Smith's Prefaces, Bourdieu's Categories, and the Public Sphere." *Modern Language Quarterly* 58, no. 4 (December 1997): 457-73.
Discusses Smith's ability to enter the cultural field of late eighteenth-century England despite the limitations placed on women writers at that time.

Hunt, Bishop C., Jr. "Wordsworth and Charlotte Smith." *The Wordsworth Circle* 1, no. 3 (summer 1970): 85-103.
Explores Smith's influence on the young William Wordsworth.

Labbe, Jacqueline M. "Selling One's Sorrows: Charlotte Smith, Mary Robinson, and the Marketing of Poetry." *The Wordsworth Circle* 25, no. 2 (spring 1994): 68-71.

>Studies the successful strategy whereby Smith and Robinson used their personal hardships to their advantage in marketing their poetry.

Labbe, Jacqueline M. "Every Poet Her Own Drawing Master: Charlotte Smith, Anna Seward and *ut pictura poesis*." In *Early Romantics: Perspectives in British Poetry from Pope to Wordsworth,* edited by Thomas Woodman, pp. 200-14. Houndmills: The Macmillan Press Ltd., 1998.

>Discusses the manner in which both Smith and Seward diverged from the conventions of romantic poetry inspired by paintings.

Magee, William H. "The Happy Marriage: The Influence of Charlotte Smith on Jane Austen." *Studies in the Novel* 7, no. 1 (spring 1975): 120-32.

>Traces Smith's influence on Austen's *Juvenilia* and later novels.

Robinson, Daniel. "Reviving the Sonnet: Women Romantic Poets and the Sonnet Claim." *European Romantic Review* 6, no. 1 (summer 1995): 98-127.

>Examines the role of women poets, Smith among them, in reviving the sonnet form in the late eighteenth century and adapting it to better suit the mood of the times.

Whiting, George W. "Charlotte Smith, Keats, and the Nightingale." *Keats-Shelley Journal* 12 (winter 1963): 4-8.

>Compares Smith's sonnet *"Farewell to the Nightingale"* to Keats's *"Ode to a Nightingale,"* suggesting that the former influenced the latter.

Wikborg, Eleanor. "Political Discourse versus Sentimental Romance: Ideology and Genre in Charlotte Smith's *Desmond* (1792)." *English Studies* 78, no. 6 (November 1997): 522-31.

>Discusses the conflicting elements of Smith's novel involving tone, ideology, genre conventions, and the expectations associated with gender.

Additional coverage of Smith's life and career is contained in the following sources published by the Gale Group: *Dictionary of Literary Biography,* **Vols. 39 and 109.**

In Memoriam

Alfred, Lord Tennyson

The following entry presents criticism of Tennyson's poem *In Memoriam* (1850). For information on Tennyson's complete career, see *NCLC*, Volumes 30 and 65.

INTRODUCTION

One of the most influential Victorian poems, Alfred Lord Tennyson's *In Memoriam* (1850) is actually 133 poetic fragments or sections that differ in theme, tone, and presentation, but are all unified by the poetic persona's grief, doubt, and search for faith. The composition of *In Memoriam* was initiated by Tennyson's deep suffering at the loss of his brilliant young friend, the promising poet and scholar Arthur Henry Hallam, who died suddenly in 1833 at the age of twenty-two. Although many of the sections were written in the three years following Hallam's death, when Tennyson's grief was most acute, he continued adding to and rearranging his long poem as science and religion shook traditional beliefs in God and Christianity. Finally, in 1850, Tennyson published his lyrical elegy. Immediately well-received, it brought Tennyson considerable fame and was undoubtedly influential in the decision to appoint Tennyson as William Wordsworth's successor as British poet laureate.

PLOT AND MAJOR CHARACTERS

Although the 133 individual sections of *In Memoriam* present varying stages of doubt, faith, and consolation, they are all unified by the *abba* stanza form. Originally, Tennyson intended to call the poem "Fragments of an Elegy," and later often referred to his work as "The Way of the Soul." The actual title, however, was suggested by Emily Sellwood, Tennyson's future wife. *In Memoriam* has been argued by some critics to be deeply autobiographical, while others contend that it is foremost artistic and fictional; Tennyson himself claimed that the poem is actually the voice of all humanity, and not his own. The style and form of the emotional verse preclude conclusive identification of more than a few characters. There may also be no definitive answer to the question of genre, as its interior struggle is both highly personal and universal. The poem expresses deeply personal emotions and questions of faith, often directly resulting from the loss of Hallam. Contradictions abound, however, and with each assertion of doubt in God, Tennyson complicates the emotion by offering verses, or even single images or words, of hope and renewal. This culminates in section 95 when the poetic voice is reunited with the spirit of Hallam through a mystical experience. Finally, while closure is never truly found, the poem ends with a sense of consolation. Loss is accepted, faith is affirmed, and the presentation of a marriage leaves the reader with a measure of hope.

MAJOR THEMES

Most critics agree that *In Memoriam* can readily be divided into four sections marked by the three Christmas celebrations following Hallam's death. The mood progresses from despair, longing, doubt, and sorrow to hope, inner-peace, and faith. The poem considers death and the stages of bereavement as the narrator experiences intense grief, nostalgia, and disconsolation, as well as the contemplation of immortality with the desire for a future reunion with the dead. The eventual outcome of this renewed faith is tempered with knowledge of scientific advancement and is necessarily compatible with it. *In Memoriam* seeks to represent man's journey to understand suffering, love, and his own purpose.

CRITICAL RECEPTION

Criticism of *In Memoriam* has been rich and varied. During Tennyson's lifetime, his poem enjoyed universal acclaim. The Victorian reader shared his own spiritual doubt with the narrative voice of the poem and found solace. After Tennyson's death, his poem and his reputation alike suffered critical backlash. Many twentieth-century readers found the dramatic melancholy and the questioning of faith to be dated and naïve. The early twentieth-century vogue for dismissing Tennyson, and likewise *In Memoriam*, has largely passed, and critics since the 1960s have been greatly interested in the poem. Many scholars, including K.W. Gransden, consider *In Memoriam* to be an elegy. Gransden finds Tennyson's approach too tentative and exploratory as it seeks to adequately convey the poetic vision. Other critics have explored the influence of nineteenth-century scientific discovery on both Tennyson as a thinker and writer and on Victorian religious beliefs. One critic, Robert Dilligan, turned to computer analysis to help unravel the syntax and prosody of *In Memoriam*. The vehemence with which Tennyson's poem longs for the lost Hallam has led some critics, including Christopher Craft, to examine the homoerotic underpinnings of the poem and to question whether the obvious passages of male love are simply written with a sensibility unique to its time or are indicative of a different level of comfort with homosexuality. Likewise, analyses of the poem's linguistic structure, poetics, language, symbolism, and structure abound. *In Memoriam* remains an important work for critical examination as its themes of grief, doubt, loss, and longing are universal to humankind.

PRINCIPAL WORKS

Poems by Two Brothers [with Frederick and Charles Tennyson] (poetry) 1827
"Timbuctoo" (poem) 1827
Poems, Chiefly Lyrical (poetry) 1830
Poems (poetry) 1832
Poems 2 vols. (poetry) 1842
The Princess: A Medley (poem) 1847
In Memoriam (poem) 1850
"Ode on the Death of the Duke of Wellington" (poem) 1852
Maud, and Other Poems (poetry) 1855
Idylls of the King (poetry) 1859; enlarged edition, 1874
Enoch Arden, Etc. (poetry) 1864
The Holy Grail, and Other Poems (poetry) 1869
Gareth and Lynette, Etc. (poetry) 1872
Queen Mary: A Drama (drama) 1875
Harold: A Drama (drama) 1876
Ballads and Other Poems (poetry) 1880
Becket (drama) 1884
The Cup and The Falcon (drama) 1884
Tiresias, and Other Poems (poetry) 1885
Locksley Hall Sixty Years After, Etc. (poetry) 1886
Demeter, and Other Poems (poetry) 1889
The Death of Oenone, Akbar's Dream, and Other Poems (poetry) 1892
The Foresters, Robin Hood and Maid Marian (drama) 1892

CRITICISM

A. C. Bradley (essay date 1910)

SOURCE: Bradley, A. C. "The 'Way of the Soul.'" In *A Commentary on Tennyson's* In Memoriam, pp. 36-48. Hamden, CT: Archon Books, 1966.

[*In the following excerpt, originally published in 1910, Bradley provides an explication of Tennyson's work and explains its appeal to readers as the expression of a shared and common experience.*]

THE 'WAY OF THE SOUL.'

It is a fashion at present to ascribe the great popularity of **In Memoriam** entirely to the 'teaching' contained in it, and to declare that its peculiar position among English elegies has nothing to do with its poetic qualities. This is equivalent to an assertion that, if the so-called substance of the poem had been presented in common prose,[1] the work would have gained the same hold upon the mass of educated readers that is now possessed by the poem itself. Such an assertion no one would make or consciously imply. The ordinary reader does not indeed attempt to separate the poetic qualities of a work from some other quality that appeals to him; much less does he read the work in terror of being affected by the latter; but imagination and diction and even versification can influence him much as they influence the people who talk about them, and he would never have taken **In Memoriam** to his heart if its consoling or uplifting thoughts had not also touched his fancy and sung in his ears. It is true, however, that he dwells upon these thoughts, and that the poem is often valued by him for its bearing upon his own life; and true again that this is one reason why he cares for it far more than for elegies certainly not inferior to it as poems. And perhaps here also many devotees of poetry may resemble him more than they suppose.

This peculiar position of **In Memoriam** seems to be connected with two facts. In the first place, it alone among the most famous English elegies is a poem inspired by deep personal feelings. Arthur Hallam was a youth of extraordinary promise, but he was also 'dear as the mother to the son.' The elegy on his death, therefore, unlike those on Edward King or Keats or Clough, bears the marks of a passionate grief and affection; and the poet's victory over sorrow, like his faith in immortality, is felt to be won in a struggle which has shaken the centre of his being. And then, as has been observed already, the grief and the struggle are portrayed in all their stages and phases throughout months and years; and each is depicted, not as it may have appeared when the victory was won, but as it was experienced then and there. In other elegies for example, scarcely anything is to be found resembling the earlier sections, which describe with such vividness and truth the varied feelings of a new grief; scarcely anything, again, like the night-poems (LXVII. ff.), or the poem of the second anniversary (XCIX.), or those of the third springtime (CXV., CXVI.). Stanzas like these come home to readers who never cared for a poem before, and were never conscious of feeling poetically till sorrow opened their souls. Thus much of **In Memoriam** is nearer to ordinary life than most elegies can be, and many such readers have found in it an expression of their own feelings, or have looked to the experience which it embodies as a guide to a possible conquest over their own loss. 'This,' they say to themselves as they read, 'is what I dumbly feel. This man, so much greater than I, has suffered like me and has told me how he won his way to peace. Like me, he has been forced by his own disaster to meditate on "the riddle of the painful earth," and to ask whether the world can really be governed by a law of love, and is not rather the work of blind forces, indifferent to the value of all that they produce and destroy.'

A brief review, first of the experience recorded in *In Memoriam*, and then of the leading ideas employed in it, may be of interest to such readers, and even to others, as it may further the understanding of the poem from one point of view, although it has to break up for the time that unity of substance and form which is the essence of poetry.

The early sections portray a soul in the first anguish of loss. Its whole interest is fixed on one thing in the world; and, as this thing is taken away, the whole world is darkened. In the main, the description is one of a common experience, and the poem shows the issue of this experience in a particular case.

Such sorrow is often healed by forgetfulness. The soul, flinching from the pain of loss, or apprehensive of its danger, turns away, at first with difficulty, and afterwards with increasing ease, from the thought of the beloved dead. 'Time,' or the incessant stream of new impressions, helps it to forget. Its sorrow gradually perishes, and with its sorrow its love; and at last 'all it was is overworn,' and it stands whole and sound. It is not cynical to say that this is a frequent history, and that the ideas repelled in section XC. are not seldom true.

Sometimes, again, the wound remains unhealed, although its pain is dulled. Here love neither dies nor changes its form; it remains a painful longing for something gone, nor would anything really satisfy it but the entire restoration of that which is gone. All the deeper life of the soul is absorbed in this love, which from its exclusively personal character is unable to coalesce with other interests and prevents their growth.

In neither of these extreme cases is there that victory of which the poet thinks even in the first shock of loss, when he remembers how it has been said

> That men may rise on stepping-stones
> Of their dead selves to higher things.

In the first case there is victory of a kind, but it is a victory which in the poet's eyes is defeat; the soul may be said to conquer its sorrow, but it does so by losing its love; it is a slave in the triumph of Time. In the second case, the 'self' refuses to die and conquers time, but for that very reason it is bound to the past and unable to rise to higher things. The experience portrayed in *In Memoriam* corresponds with neither case, but it resembles each in one particular. Sorrow is healed, but it is not healed by the loss of love: for the beloved dead is the object of continual thought, and when regret has passed away love is found to be not less but greater than before. On the other hand regret does pass away, and love does not merely look forward to reunion with its object but unites freely with other interests. It is evident that the possibility of this victory depends upon the fact that, while love does not die, there is something in the soul which does die. The self 'rises' only on the basis of a 'dead self.' In other words, love changes though it does not perish or fade; and with the change in it there is a corresponding change in the idea of its object. The poem exhibits this process of two-fold change.

At the beginning love desires simply that which was, the presence and companionship of the lost friend; and this it desires unchanged and in its entirety. It longs for the sight of the face, the sound of the voice, the pressure of the hand. These doubtless are desired as tokens of the soul; but as yet they are tokens essential to love, and that for which it pines is the soul as known and loved through them. If the mourner attempts to think of the dead apart from them, his heart remains cold, or he recoils: he finds that he is thinking of a phantom; 'an awful thought' instead of 'the human-hearted man he loved'; 'a spirit, not a breathing voice.' This he does not and cannot love. It is an object of awe, not of affection; the mere dead body is a thousand-fold dearer than this,—naturally, for this is not really a spirit, a thinking and loving soul, but a ghost. As then he is unable to think of the object of his love except as 'the hand, the lips, the eyes,' and 'the meeting of the morrow,' he feels that what he loves is simply gone and lost, and he finds his one relief in allowing fancy to play about the thought of the tokens that remain (see the poems to the ship).

The process of change consists largely in the conquest of the soul over its bondage to sense. So long as this bondage remains, its desire is fixed on that which really is dead, and it cannot advance. But gradually it resigns this longing, and turns more and more to that which is not dead. The first step in its advance is the perception that love itself is of infinite value and may survive the removal of the sensible presence of its object. But no sooner has this conviction been reached and embraced (XXVII.) than suddenly the mourner is found to have transferred his interest from the sensible presence to the soul itself, while, on the other hand, the soul is no longer thought of as a mere awful phantom, but has become what the living friend had been, something both beloved and loving (XXX.). This conquest is, indeed, achieved first in a moment of exaltation which cannot be maintained; but its result is never lost, and gradually strengthens. The feeling that the soul of the dead is something shadowy and awful departs for ever, and step by step the haunting desire for the bodily presence retires. Thought is concentrated on that which lives, the beauty of the beloved soul, seen in its remembered life on earth, and doubtless shown more fully elsewhere in a life that can be dimly imagined. At last the pining for what is gone dies completely away, but love is found to be but stronger for its death, and to be no longer a source of pain. It has grown to the dimensions of its object, and this object is not only distant and desired, but also present and possessed. And more—the past (which is not wholly past, since it lives and acts in the soul of the mourner) has lost its pang and retained its loveliness and power: 'the days that are no more' become a life in death instead of a 'death in life'; and even the light of the face, the sound of the voice, and the pressure of the hand, now that the absorbing desire for them is still, return in the quiet inward world.

Another aspect of this change is to be noticed. So long as the mourner's sorrow and desire are fixed on that which dies they withdraw his interest from all other things. His world seems to depend for its light on that which has passed away, and he cries, 'All is dark where thou art not.' But as his love and its object change and grow, this exclusiveness lessens and its shadow shrinks. His heart opens itself to other friendships; the sweetness of the spring returns; and the 'mighty hopes' for man's future which the friend had shared, live again as the dead friend ceases to be a silent voice and becomes a living soul. Nor do the reviving activities simply flourish side by side with love for this soul, and still less do they compete with it. Rather they are one with it. The dead man lives in the living, and 'moves him on to nobler ends.' It is at the bidding of the dead that he seeks a friendship for the years to come. His vision of the ideal man that is to be is a memory of the man that trod this planet with him in his youth. He had cried, 'All is dark where thou art not,' and now he cries,

> Thy voice is on the rolling air;
> I hear thee where the waters run;
> Thou standest in the rising sun,
> And in the setting thou art fair.

For the sake of clearness little has been so far said of the thoughts of the mourner regarding the life beyond death. These thoughts touch two main subjects, the hope of reunion, and the desire that the dead friend should think of the living and should even communicate with him. The recurrent speculations on the state of the dead spring from this hope and this desire. They recur less frequently as the soul advances in its victory. This does not mean that the hope of reunion diminishes or ceases to be essential to the mourner's peace and faith; but speculation on the nature both of this reunion and of the present life of the dead is renounced, and at last even abruptly dismissed (CVII., CVIII.). The singer is content to be ignorant and to wait in faith.

It is not quite so with the desire that the dead friend should now remember the living, and should even communicate with him. True, this desire is at one moment put aside without unhappiness (LXV.), and it ceases to be an urgent and disturbing force. But long after the pining for the bodily presence has been overcome, it remains and brings with it pain and even resentment. It seems to change from a hope of 'speech' or 'converse' to a wish that the dead should in some way be 'near' to or 'touch' the living; and thus it suggests the important group of sections XC.-XCV. Here the poet even wishes at first for a vision; and although he at once reflects that neither this nor any other appeal to sense could convince him that the dead was really with him,[2] he does not surrender either here or later (CXXII.) the idea of some more immediate contact of souls.[3] On the other hand, he is not sure that the idea is realised, nor does his uncertainty disturb his peace. What he desires while he remains on earth is contact with 'that which is,' the reality which is half revealed and half concealed by nature and man's earthly life, and which, by its contact, convinces him of the reason and love that rule the world; and, as now he thinks of his friend as 'living in God,' he neither knows nor seeks to know whether that which touches him is to be called the soul of his friend or by some higher name.

It appears then that the victory over sorrow portrayed in the poem is dependent upon a change in the love felt by the living for the dead, and upon a corresponding change in the idea of the dead. And some readers may even be inclined to think that the change is so great that at last the dead friend has really ceased to be to the living an individual person. He is, they will say, in some dim fashion 'mixed with God and Nature,' and as completely lost in 'the general soul' as is Adonais in Shelley's pantheistic poem: and so the poet's love for him has not merely changed, it has perished, and its place has been taken by a feeling as vaguely general and as little personal as the object to which it is directed. As my purpose is neither to criticise nor to defend the poet's ideas, but simply to represent them, I will confine myself to pointing out that the poem itself flatly denies the charge thus brought against it, and by implication denies the validity of the antitheses on which the charge rests. It is quite true that, as the poet advances, he abandons all attempts to define the life beyond death, and to form an image of his friend, 'whate'er he be.' It is quite true also that he is conscious that his friend, at once human and divine, known and unknown, far and near, has become something 'strange,' and is 'darklier understood' than in the old days of earthly life. But it is equally clear that to the poet his friend is not a whit less himself because he is 'mixed with God and Nature,' and that he is only 'deeplier loved' as he becomes 'darklier understood.' And if the hope of reunion is less frequently expressed as the sense of present possession gains in strength, there is nothing in the poem to imply that it becomes less firm as the image of reunion becomes less definite. The reader may declare that it ought to do so; he may apply to the experience here portrayed his customary notions of human and divine, personal and impersonal, individual and general; and he may argue that whatever falls under one of these heads cannot fall under the other. But whether his ideas and his argument are true or false, the fact is certain that for the experience portrayed in *In Memoriam* (and, it may be added, in *Adonais* also) they do not hold. For the poets the soul of the dead, in being mingled with nature, does not lose its personality; in living in God it remains human and itself; it is still the object of a love as 'personal' as that which was given to

> the touch of a vanished hand,
> And the sound of a voice that is still.

Notes

1. This, in strictness, is an impossible supposition. Anything that could be so presented would not be really the substance of the poem.

2. His reflections on the difficulty or impossibility of any such proof are expressed in XCII. with a concise-

ness which is characteristic of Tennyson and conceals from many readers the full force and bearing of his thoughts.

3. This idea is not confined to *In Memoriam*. Tennyson, we are told, thought 'that there might be a more intimate communion than we could dream of between the living and the dead, at all events for a time' (*Memoir* [Hallam Lord Tennyson, *Alfred Lord Tennyson: A Memoir*, 2 vols. (New York, 1897)], 1. 320).

J. M. Cohen (essay date 1949)

SOURCE: Cohen, J. M. "'In Memoriam': a Hundred Years After." *Cornhill Magazine* 164, no. 980 (autumn 1949): 151-64.

[*In the following essay, Cohen states that Tennyson's* In Memoriam *is the record of the author's own experience following the death of contemporary poet and friend, Arthur Hallam.*]

'Answer for me that I have given my belief in **"In Memoriam,"**' Tennyson would instruct his son Hallam when dealing with one of those numerous correspondents who questioned his Christian belief. To whom could a doubting reader turn with more assurance than to the Laureate for confirmation of his wavering faith? The answer in the passage to which Tennyson referred his troubled applicant was unequivocal:

> And so the Word had breath, and wrought
> With human hands the creed of creeds
> In loveliness of perfect deeds,
> More strong than all poetic thought.

Had his convictions and his poetry remained throughout on this pedestrian level, had the Sunday school piety of this quatrain faithfully expressed the nature and intensity of his religious thought, the poem would not bear this re-examination a hundred years after its completion. **'In Memoriam,'** however, is the record of a profound and deeply individual experience, the central experience of Alfred Tennyson's life. Before it was written, all the best of his work was coloured by melancholy and apprehension. By following Arthur Hallam down to the grave and facing with him the stark fact of death Tennyson, at least partially, conquered the fear and weakness of his own nature, and won a certain spiritual security, which enabled him to envisage the perils and uncertainties of life with greater calm. 'He that is near Me is near the fire,' is a traditional saying of Christ's which the poet frequently quoted. 'The fire was the fire of inspiration,' his son explains. 'For in **"In Memoriam"** the soul, after grappling with anguish and darkness, doubt and death, emerges with the inspiration of a strong and steadfast faith.' He fails to comment, however, on the strange confusion throughout the poem between the figures of Christ and of his father's dead friend. But it is this revealing and seemingly unconscious identification that gave **'In Memoriam'** its especial strength. Before it was written the emotion in Tennyson's poems was monotonous and dilute; the poet seemed to be the inchoate servant of his own not very profound sadness. After 1850 come the good Farringford years; he is a happier man and makes his long postponed marriage; but the later poems to which we return with any pleasure are very few. The **'Idylls of the King'** treat a great theme with the encaustic piety of a knighted architect restoring a mediaeval church. In contrast **'The Ring and the Book'** is a secular building, erected in a contemporary style to suit a human and contemporary need. After **'In Memoriam'** Tennyson was a great figure but seldom a good poet; before it he was sometimes a good poet, but certainly no great figure: only into **'In Memoriam'** did all his virtues flow.

The poem was sixteen years in the making. The twenty-four-year-old Tennyson who pencilled its first lines on a stray sheet had a few months before published his 1833 volume and established himself for all posterity with **'The Lotos Eaters'** and **'Oenone'**; his 'lost Arthur,' whose body was at that moment travelling home from 'the Italian shore,' had been a year his junior. On 'the elegy's' anonymous publication Tennyson was forty, and Arthur Hallam, had he lived, would have been thirty-nine. In the interval the poem had been composed, section by section, in the 'long butcher-ledger-like book' which so narrowly escaped loss upon its completion; 'some in Lincolnshire, some in London, Essex, Gloucestershire, Wales, anywhere I happened to be,' the poet tells us; and during all those years, which saw as well the writing of much of the 1842 volume—of **'Morte d'Arthur,' 'Ulysses'** and **'St. Agnes Eve'**—and of **'The Princess,'** the central theme of the poet's life was, beyond all question, his mourning for his Cambridge friend.

A great number of his contemporaries testify to Arthur Hallam's outstanding promise. 'A man of wonderful mind and knowledge on all subjects, hardly credible at his age,' wrote Alford, later Dean of Canterbury. 'When most bereavements will be forgotten, he will still be remembered,' testified Gladstone, a truer prophet than he knew. For a future bishop, Thirlwall, he was 'the only man of my own standing before whom I bow in conscious inferiority in everything.' But for Tennyson he was more, a close friend and future brother-in-law: Hallam had fallen in love with Emily Tennyson at the age of eighteen or nineteen, and spent long weeks of his vacations at Somersby Vicarage, the Tennysons' home. And yet one more firm bond united the two men: Hallam's belief in Tennyson's poetry, and the support he gave him in the face of 'the captious and unintelligent criticism' of **'Blackwood'** and the **'Quarterly,'** which considerably rattled the over-sensitive poet. But deeply though Tennyson treasured their many-sided intimacy the relationship between them was by no means exclusive; they were both members of a wide and brotherly intellectual circle. But long before his death Arthur Hallam had achieved an outstanding place in the poet's affections.

Alfred, Lord Tennyson, 1809-1892.

For the sixteen years of the poem's writing Tennyson's mourning for Hallam had a significance in his life comparable only to Flaubert's death cult for his dead friends, which was his lifelong religion. But the losses which the Frenchman celebrated in the inner graveyard of his heart were many; that of Alfred le Poittevin, the intellectual companion to whom he was bound by more exclusive ties than was Tennyson to Hallam, was only the first. For Flaubert death followed death; for Tennyson there was but one. Each successive loss plunged Flaubert deeper into a melancholy isolation from which only remorseless work could temporarily relieve him; to Tennyson the death of Hallam brought a secret strength, confirming him ultimately in a deeply personal faith hammered out during the years of '**In Memoriam**''s composition.

His thoughts, however, immediately upon his friend's death, turned to suicide, against which course he forthwith argued in '**The Two Voices**' with a dogmatism which is both dull and unconvincing. He succeeded in forcing upon himself a theoretical consolation, however, that it took him in practice sixteen years to achieve. How much more compelling is the 'still small voice' tempting him to self-destruction than the 'little whisper silver-clear, A murmur, "Be of better cheer,"' with which he finds solace. For the tempter speaks in lines of authentic strength:

> Then comes the check, the change, the fall,
> Pain rises up, old pleasures pall.
> There is one remedy for all.
>
> Yet hadst thou, thro' enduring pain,
> Link'd month to month with such a chain
> Of knitted purport, all were vain.
>
> Thou had'st not between death and birth
> Dissolved the riddle of the earth.
> So were thy labour little-worth . . .

The despair is more genuine than the comfort. If the best of Tennyson's poetry had hitherto always a dying fall, the death of Arthur Hallam served only to reinforce that underlying sense of fatality, most directly expressed in '**The Vision of Sin**,' but implicit also in the weak cadences of '**The Lotos Eaters**.' The younger Tennyson had been only too ready to foresee and accept defeat, awarding himself the dubious comfort of a ready-made and moralising faith. '**In Memoriam**' marks the stages by which loss was turned to gain, and it is not by chance that the sequence, opening with Emily Tennyson's loss of her lover, closes with her sister Cecilia's marriage to another of Tennyson's friends, Edmund Lushington; the publication of the poem was immediately followed by his own marriage to Emily Sellwood.

It is in this symbolic plan rather than in the buoyantly orthodox introductory verses that we must read the true nature of Tennyson's hard-won faith. 'I rejoiced in the Introduction,' wrote Bishop Westcott, 'which appeared to me to be the mature summing up, after an interval, of the many strains of thought in the "**Elegies**" . . . his splendid faith . . . seems to me to express a lesson of the Gospel which the circumstances of all time encourage us to master.' Certainly the Bishop could quote lines to support his case:

> Our little systems have their day;
>   They have their day and cease to be:
>   They are but broken lights of thee,
> And thou, O Lord, art more than they.

Yet such passages are as unconvincing as the forced moral of the '**The Two Voices**.' Tennyson's acceptance did not go so far, and indeed the Bishop's hearty encomium stresses a familiar aspect of the prevalent Victorian misconception concerning the Laureate. Again in his praise of 'honest doubt,' Tennyson laid himself open to claims of kinship from the scientific agnostics. In reality, however, most of his more public and deliberately broadminded pronouncements were based on a minor personality which, a shy man, he readily assumed when he felt that a statement was expected of him. In contrast to Hallam, the Tennysons had been enthusiastic for the Reform Bill, and I think that it was with the family voice that the poet welcomed the forward march of Victorian progress, which in private caused him considerable alarm. From Hallam he took over a hatred of tyranny, and from his Cambridge circle a rather cloudy political optimism, that had no very deep roots in his nature. With Hallam he had made a dangerous journey to the Spanish frontier bearing funds for a democratic, constitutional and anti-clerical insurrection; and it was from John Sterling, perhaps, that he caught his enthusiasm for large-scale and high-principled progress— 'the Parliament of man, the Federation of the world.' His own judgments were apt to be narrower and more subjective, as witness his celebration of the ennobling effects of war—in this case the Crimean War—at the conclusion of **'Maud.'** His public attitude to the niceties of religious dogma, too, was Hallam's, for whom 'the essential feelings of religion subsist in the utmost diversity of forms.' Tennyson's were no doctrinal doubts, however; they were a far more fundamental questioning of his own significance in a universe whose tremendous laws were even now being laid bare by his scientific contemporaries. It did not help him to disown his qualms by labelling them the **'Supposed Confessions of a Second-rate Sensitive Mind not in unity with itself.'** It was with his own voice that he prayed:

> . . . Oh teach me yet
> Somewhat before the heavy clod
> Weighs on me, and the busy fret
> Of that sharp-headed worm begins
> In the gross blackness underneath.

Death was terrible to him, and the fear of annihilation beyond the grave most real and present. But the teaching he asked for was not to be found in Hallam's liberal Christianity. A refuge in aestheticism, 'a lordly pleasure-house' erected by many artists from Flaubert to our own contemporaries, he rejected in **'The Palace of Art,'** though with the final hope that 'Perchance I may return with others there When I have purged my guilt.' It would be easy to enlarge on this word 'guilt' and attribute to Tennyson a profound neurosis. If there was some self-frustrating sense of sin and inadequacy in the poet before the writing of **'In Memoriam,'** it was largely dispelled in that poem. He had never known the inhibiting isolation from experience of Clough nor, despite the evidence of **'The Two Voices'** and the mad monologue in **'Maud,'** had he more than momentarily wandered the hallucinatory streets of the City of Dreadful Night. Only in **'Maud'** do we find a suggestion of Thomson's insomniac despair:

> . . . my heart is a handful of dust,
> And the wheels go over my head,
> And my bones are shaken with pain
> For into a shallow grave they are thrust,
> Only a yard beneath the street,
> And the hoofs of the horses beat, beat,
> The hoofs of the horses beat,
> Beat into my scalp and my brain.

But though 'one of the best-known doctors for the insane wrote that it was the most faithful representation of madness since Shakespeare,' it is in fact no more than melancholic. Tennyson had no touch of that majestic schizophrenia which we have of late years come to confuse with genius.

This frustrating melancholy, which finds expression in his too ready confusion of dream with reality, remained constant to him throughout his early life: his most familiar landscape is of autumn, of ripe fruit dropping to decay, of weariness and sleep. The CORNHILL reader could have been in no doubt as to the authorship of one of his greatest poems, which he found in his February number in 1860; the opening lines of **'Tithonus'** are in themselves a signature:

> The woods decay, the woods decay and fall,
> The vapours weep their burthen to the ground,
> Man comes and tills the field and lies beneath,
> And after many a summer dies the swan.

This consciousness of the transience, unreality and corruption of the worldly scene was rooted, in part, in his dreamy and melancholic languor, but it was reinforced in no uncertain way by a recurrent and other-worldly experience with which Tennyson was frequently visited. He describes it, rather unexpectedly, in one of his least successful poems, **'The Princess.'** The 'blue-eyed Prince,' its faintly Arthurian hero, is introducing some supernatural trappings, which appear highly significant yet play no further part in the development of that ill-assorted Girtonian idyll.

> Myself too had weird seizures, Heaven knows what:
> On a sudden in the midst of men and day,
> And while I walk'd and talk'd as heretofore,
> I seemed to move amongst a world of ghosts,
> And feel myself the shadow of a dream.

This state of dissociation must have been very frequent with the younger Tennyson, and one can often view his most detailed and myopic descriptions as a very deliberate effort to re-attach himself to the outward scene, or as evidence of a heightened sharpness of vision associated with an increased spiritual awareness. Despite the evidence of his extreme short sight, and the consequently greater clarity to him of nearby objects, I think it significant that it is often things seen at a considerable distance that he notes most minutely, 'The leaves that tremble round the nightingale,' for instance, or 'the twinkling laurel scattering silver lights;' there must have been moments when his vision at a distance was extraordinarily acute.

It is possible that these 'weird seizures' were sometimes most alarming. 'If God were to withdraw himself for one single instant from this Universe,' he would frequently say, 'everything would vanish into nothingness.' This statement throws some light, I think, on the strangely detached state described in the lines quoted, and on the shimmering emptiness of his earliest poetry. There were moments for him in which God—or his consciousness—did withdraw from the Universe, leaving no distinction between dream and reality. This, however, was only a partial and negative aspect of a more complete and positive experience, which he several times described in notes or in conversation.

'A kind of waking trance I have frequently had,' he wrote, 'quite up from boyhood, when I have been all alone. This has generally come upon me thro' repeating my own name two or three times to myself silently, till all at once, as it were out of the intensity of the consciousness of individuality, the individuality itself seemed to dissolve and fade away into boundless being, and this not a confused state, but the clearest of the clearest, the surest of the surest, the weirdest of the weirdest, utterly beyond words, where death was an almost laughable impossibility, the loss of personality (if so it were) seeming no extinction but the only true life. This might be the state which St. Paul describes, "Whether in the body I cannot tell, or whether out of the body I cannot tell."'—'It is no nebulous ecstasy,' he said on another occasion, 'but a state of transcendent wonder, associated with absolute clearness of mind.'

Now this rapt state so readily called up by the mere repetition of his name—one is reminded of the Hindu's use of the syllable OM—left the poet weary and melancholy on its passing. Extinction, which seemed laughably impossible at one moment, was a very haunting fear at the next. He did not use the word 'mystical' to describe his state—for him that word had the sense of 'delusive'—but in claiming kinship with St. Paul, and in another place with Plotinus, he did confuse an almost involuntary fluctuation in consciousness with something greater and even more mysterious. The chief significance of these states for Tennyson was undoubtedly the certainty which they momentarily gave him of the spirit's survival after death, or of its existence in a state outside the bounds of Time. For the fear of extinction, of man's transient insignificance in a Universe subject to mindless laws, was Tennyson's abiding nightmare.

His readiest associations with death were the family's departure from Somersby Vicarage some years after his father's passing and his loss of Arthur Hallam. So much is clear from section cii. of **'In Memoriam'**—section ciii. of the later editions:

> On that last night before we went
>   From out the doors where I was bred,
>   I dreamed a vision of the dead
> Which left my after-morn content.

'The dead' is Hallam. Yet from the association with Somersby Vicarage we know that it is also the poet's father. In his dream Tennyson dwells in a hall where maidens serve a veiled statue which he knows as Hallam's. But soon he is himself summoned to go down to a shore, where everything assumes a vaster significance. He is facing the prospect of his own death, while the maidens, chanting 'the history of that great race, which is to be' and 'the shaping of a star,' stress the theme of his own insignificance—which does not distress him here. For before him he sees 'A great ship lift her shining sides.'

> The man we loved was there on deck,
>   But thrice as large as man he bent
>   To greet us. Up the side I went,
> And fell in silence on his neck.
>
> Whereat those maidens with one mind
>   Bewailed their lot; I did them wrong:

> 'We served thee here,' they said, 'so long,
> And wilt thou leave us now behind?'
>
> So rapt I was, they could not win
>   An answer from my lips, but he
>   Replying, 'Enter likewise ye
> And go with us?' they entered in.

This, by no means the finest section of the poem, reveals an aspect of its meaning which on a fresh reading throws up corresponding facets in many other places. 'The man we loved,' who has passed beyond the sea of death and whose cult is practised in the dream-like hall of the living, can on that last shore, which is the moment of death, save not only the poet, but the maidens, who stand for the beauty and creativeness of this world. It is no mere accident that the next section opens with the name of Christ. Hallam stands, subsuming perhaps the figure of Tennyson's father, for the dead Redeemer, returning from the further shore to rescue the poet from the ever present fear of death, to save him from the suspicion that the Priestess Sorrow is not lying when

> 'The stars,' she whispers, 'blindly run;
>   A web is wov'n across the sky;
>   From out waste places comes a cry,—
> And murmurs from the dying sun.'

A mechanist's universe, that will deny the validity of Tennyson's 'weird seizures,' is the counterpart of death, from which he can be saved only by a visitor bearing witness from beyond the grave. 'It is possible,' he once claimed when discussing his supernormal states, 'that there may be a more intimate communion than we could dream of between the living and the dead, at all events for a time.' The same thought finds expression in verse:

> The Ghost in man, the Ghost that once was Man,
> But cannot wholly free itself from Man,
> Are calling to each other thro' a dawn
> Stranger than earth has ever seen; the veil
> Is rending, and the Voices of the day
> Are heard across the Voices of the dark.

The debt of these lines to crude spiritualism is obvious, but Tennyson's claim to communion with his dead friend was not generally based on so materialistic a hypothesis.

The plan of the poem is a loose one and falls into place around the three Christmas Eve sections; the lyrics were not written with a view to their assembly in a single poem, or even for publication. 'The different moods of sorrow,' in Tennyson's own words, 'as in a drama are dramatically given,' and most dramatic is his opening acceptance of his loss as he follows Hallam to his burial beneath the churchyard yew, the symbol of death itself:

> And gazing on thee, sullen tree,
>   Sick for thy stubborn hardihood,
>   I seem to fail from out my blood
> And grow incorporate with thee.

But this acceptance, this assumption of death in the midst of life, yields only too soon to that familiar apathy in which even Sorrow is unreal.

> To sleep I give my powers away;
>   My will is bondsman to the dark;
>   I sit within a helmless bark . . .

The image of the ship of death stays with Tennyson to the end. In the last section of **'In Memoriam'** the figure of Hallam is at the prow; in his final **'Crossing the Bar,'** however, the helmsman is no longer his dead friend, but 'my Pilot,' the Saviour Himself. The flux and reflux of emotion in these opening sections persist throughout the poem. The fourth section ends on a note of resolution: 'Thou shalt not be the fool of loss'; but in the seventh he is standing desolate once more outside the dark house in which he and Hallam used to meet, while 'On the bald street breaks the blank day.'

Then, having traced the ship bearing his friend's body from the Italian shore to the lonely churchyard beside the Bristol Channel, where he was buried, he once more prays for his grief to be made more real to him:

> Come Time, and teach me, many years,
>   I do not suffer in a dream;
>   For now so strange do these things seem,
> Mine eyes have leisure for my tears; . . .

Yet only two sections later he welcomes this sense of unreality as some palliative for the terror that strikes him with the rising storm:

> And but for fancies, which aver
>   That all thy motions gently pass
>   Athwart a plane of molten glass,
> I scarce could brook the strain and stir
>
> That makes the barren branches loud;—

Then, doubting the reality of his detachment, he is plunged back from 'calm despair' into 'wild unrest.' Again he doubts; this time it is the fluctuations of sorrow and his own sanity that he calls into question: the only abiding reality is that 'ritual of the dead' celebrated beneath the churchyard yew. Again, in the twenty-first section, he calls the validity of his feelings into question and their relevance in the contemporary world:

>   . . . Is this an hour
>   For private sorrow's barren song,
>   When more and more the people throng
> The chairs and thrones of civil power.

And again he is confronted with the Shadow that, having wrapped Hallam in the fold of his mantle, now sits and waits for the poet himself. The whole first part of the poem is riddled with doubts and self distrust; not only does Tennyson question the strength and durability of his own feelings, but he calls into question as well the purpose of his writing and even the value of poetry in a scientific age. The second part opens, however, with the motive of resurrection:

> The time draws near the birth of Christ:
>   The moon is hid; the night is still;
>   The Christmas bells from hill to hill
> Answer each other in the mist.

And even the memory of the absent Christmas guest, himself now identified with the 'mute Shadow,' does not outweigh the seasonal good news that Hope is born. The Christmas poems were among the first sections of **'In Memoriam'** to be written; It was in fact from the simple germ of death, sailing 'the placid ocean plains,' and rebirth, rung out on the Christmas bells, that the poem was elaborated; a rebirth that was not only stated with carol-like simplicity in the last section quoted, but re-stated, with all the solemnity of a Bach bass aria, by the theme of Lazarus and the mystery of death.

> Behold a man raised up by Christ!
>   The rest remaineth unrevealed;
>   He told it not; or something sealed
> The lips of that Evangelist.

Late in the poem Tennyson summons his friend likewise to return from the dead 'in thine after form And like a finer light in light,' but such a conclusive reassurance is impossible. Therefore he can only call on Hallam to be near him at the moment of his own death, in a lyric that recalls the terror-stricken accents of Dunbar's 'Timor mortis conturbatme,' and then, conscious of his own 'inner vileness,' questions whether he dare face 'the clear eye' of his returning friend; he can only accept the scientist's picture of the universe, and then, frightened by its dwarfing scale, clamour yet again for some promise of man's immortality, without which 'Twere best at once to sink to peace.' If he concludes on a note of faith, it is certainly not the unequivocal and unwavering faith of the Introduction. 'Faith must give the last word,' wrote Professor Sidgwick, a sympathetic but more sceptical questioner on religious matters, 'but the last word is not the whole utterance of the truth: the whole truth is that assurance and doubt must alternate in the moral world in which we at present live, somewhat as night and day alternate in the physical world.' He could not have interpreted more faithfully the changing moods of **'In Memoriam.'** The poem contains Tennyson's finest writing, because in it he confronted his own doubts, no longer dismissing them as the **'Confessions of a Second rate Sensitive Mind,'** and because his love of Hallam brought into play far deeper emotions than did the more literary subjects of his early poems. Many of the lyrics, in fact, are so deeply felt, and draw on such a range of individual yet familiar imagery—without ever descending to the commonplace—that they seem the uncontrived and natural expression of feelings that could be expressed in no other way; the music of the words and the overall impression, moreover, carry the reader past any lines whose exact meaning and syntax are doubtful. Here the poem stands with Shakespeare and the Gospels, in which much that is extremely difficult to comprehend passes almost unnoticed, so compelling and universal is the central theme, so deeply bedded in man's common thought the images.

Paradoxically, it was the spectre of Hallam—which lent such majesty to his own memorial verses—that conferred that dead quality which we find in most of Tennyson's later poetry. For if the memory of his dead friend gave him a renewed confidence in life, blest his marriage and freed him from the worst of his melancholy fears, it also inspired those most deliberately 'great' utterances of his later years. Hallam stood to Tennyson for a high seriousness that demanded mighty themes; to be worthy of his friend, he undertook to recount the great Arthurian legend, over which Hallam had presided in bright unworldly mock-mediaeval armour from the first, 'like a modern gentleman of stateliest port;' it was but natural that the completed Idylls should be dedicated to the nation's Hallam, the dead Prince Albert.

But there was another Tennyson, who was too often crowded out by the Laureate's majestic presence, the Lincolnshire man with a fine eye for natural detail and a sensitive ear for the rhythms of country speech; it was the heir to Crabbe's 'gift of a hard pathos'—Tennyson's own words—that was thrust aside, the man who can challenge Barnes or Hawker as a poet of crisply drawn local scenery. We do not look to this man for pronouncements on war, science, and evolution; these are the utterances of a mere laurel crowned mask. What is permanent in Tennyson is not all charged with the deep emotion of '**In Memoriam**,' nor even with the more transient feelings of the songs from '**the Princess**,' '**Ulysses**' or '**Tithonus**'; there is a quality of wit in such poems as '**Audley End**' and '**Walking to the Mail**,' a power of observation and even a sense of character, which make the earlier half of the collected works a quarry for the lover of descriptive poetry. What could be better drawn in the Dutch school of still life than the pasty in '**Audley End**':

> . . . a pasty costly made,
> Where quail and pigeon, lark and leveret lay,
> Like fossils of the rocks, with golden yolks
> Imbedded and injellied . . . ?

And how exactly recorded are the lines with which he ends '**The Golden Year**':

> and, high above, I heard them blast
> The steep slate-quarry, and the great echo flap
> And buffet round the hills from bluff to bluff.

Even '**the Princess**' is rich in such observations, noted, I feel, on sundry occasions and packed into the poem of the moment without great care for their relevance:

> Walter warp'd his mouth at this
> To something so mock-solemn, that I laugh'd
> And Lilia woke with sudden shrilling mirth
> An echo like a ghostly woodpecker,
> Hid in the ruins.

Trivial perhaps beside the great theme of female education and the sex war, such lines have a Frithlike matter-of-factness much more appealing than the large G. F. Watts canvases that the later Tennyson felt himself called upon to fill. Then again we catch him in an ironic narrative mood in '**Walking to the Mail**,' whose conversational tones look forward to the flat delicacy of Robert Frost:

> . . . his house, for so they say,
> Was haunted with a jolly ghost, that shook
> The curtains, whined in lobbies, tapt at doors
> And rummaged like a rat; no servant stayed:
> The farmer vext packs up his beds and chairs,
> And all his household stuff; and with his boy
> Betwixt his knees, his wife upon the tilt,
> Sets out, and meets a friend, who hails him, 'What! You're flitting!'—'Yes, we're flitting,' says the ghost
> (For they had packed the thing among the beds),
> 'Oh well,' says he, 'you flitting with us too—
> Jack, turn the horses' heads and home again.'

The dialect poems, too, have their own slow-witted rustic humour, though their sentimentality would look a little naïve translated into Southern English. There was, in fact, a certain tough provinciality about Alfred Tennyson that did not survive in the Laureate, a quality of minute observation that we miss once he devoted himself to universal themes. It is a quality that we value—and perhaps overvalue—today, lacking as we do contemporary poetry on great themes.

'I have written what I have felt and known,' said Tennyson of '**In Memoriam**,' 'and I will never write anything else.' It is true that he wrote very little else on that level, for only during its writing was he 'carrying a bit of Chaos about him, which he was manufacturing into Cosmos.' Yet for ever afterwards he bore in his heart the deified figure of his dead friend, whose approval on his far shore he sought to win and keep. Can it have been Hallam, then, from whom he pleaded for release in the character of the aged '**Tithonus**'?

> Can thy love,
> Thy beauty, make amends, tho' even now,
> Close over us, the silver star, thy guide,
> Shines in those tremulous eyes that fill with tears
> To hear me? Let me go: take back thy gift:
> Why should a man desire in any way
> To vary from the kindly race of men,
> Or pass beyond the goal of ordinance
> Where all should pause, as is most meet for all?

For if '**In Memoriam**' left him with a faith that survived the pillar shatterings of the scientific Sampsons, it saddled him also with an ideal of righteousness and high-mindedness that it was very hard to live up to and, thumbing through the correctly laidout wastes of the last six hundred pages of his Works, in search of the occasional oasis of the lines to Fitzgerald or to Virgil, one regrets with Tithonus that

'The Gods themselves cannot recall their gifts.'

James G. Taaffe (essay date 1963)

SOURCE: Taaffe, James G. "Circle Imagery in Tennyson's *In Memoriam*." *Victorian Poetry* 1, no. 2 (April 1963): 123-31.

[*In the following essay, Taaffe offers a close reading of* In Memoriam, *focusing on its circle imagery and connecting the poem to Dante's* Divina Commedia.]

In Memoriam, Tennyson tells us, "was meant to be a kind of *Divina Commedia*, ending with happiness." The poem, beginning with the burial of Arthur Henry Hallam, he says, "concludes with the marriage of my youngest sister Cecilia."[1] This statement has been generally believed to indicate the movement of the poem from a Tennysonian *Inferno* to a Victorian *Paradiso*: from a "wasteland" to a "mystical vision . . . assuredly the sanction of his faith."[2] In an article entitled "The Symbolic Imagination" Allen Tate has perceptively discussed the central symbol and image of Dante's *Divina Commedia*; it is the circle which both defines and creates Dante's cosmos. From its first appearance in Canto III of the *Inferno* until its conception in the triune circles, the circle is the primary architectural and thematic device in the poem.[3] Probably Tennyson was aware of the centrality of this image in Dante's poem, for he chose the circle for one of the primary images of his elegy for the promising young Dante scholar.[4] But whether this choice was actually motivated by an admiration of Dante's poem one, of course, cannot say. We do know, however, that Tennyson's "knowledge of astronomy was most remarkable, and the accuracy of his talk about the stars surprised more than one of the great astronomers. Of late the spectrum analysis of light, and the photographs which reveal starlight in the interstellar spaces where stars were hitherto undreamt of, and the idea of the all-pervading luminiferous aether, particularly interested him" (*Memoir,* II, 408, n. 1). Surely his knowledge of this field and its language of "cycles" and "orbits" was the chief source of Tennyson's circle imagery; his own suggestion of his poem, however, as a *Divina Commedia* allows us to explain the image in the Dantean connection.

Critics have yet to investigate the various ambiguities and rich suggestiveness of the poem's circle imagery. In *A Commentary on Tennyson's* **"In Memoriam"** A. C. Bradley remarks that "from the first Tennyson's poems show a special fondness for circular or spherical appearances in landscape."[5] Apart from recognizing the recurrence and discussing individual ambiguities, Bradley does little to explain Tennyson's fondness for such images in the elegy. Jerome Buckley, one of Tennyson's more recent critics, has considered that the architecture of the poem is "stylistic . . . it depends above all on the recurrence of an imagery to which Tennyson's sensibility both consciously and unconsciously attaches particular meaning." Buckley further discusses what he thinks the four basic images of the poem: "the dark (or night), the day (or light), the rain (or water), and the hand" (*Tennyson,* pp. 112-113). To Buckley's list I would add images of circles. Such imagery was attractive to Tennyson because it offered him, in appropriate terms, convenient metaphors for his concept of moral evolution. The motion and direction of each individual, as well as his moral development, are frequently indicated in terms of circles and spheres. In a poem as diffuse as *In Memoriam* no one would expect to find every circle reference thematically significant, but the references that are rich and allusive do directly reveal some of the poem's major concerns; their repetition acts as well as a structural device.

Poems IX through XVII, a "group connected by reference to the ship that brings the body of the dead from 'the Italian shore' to England" (Bradley, p. 90), introduce three significant examples of the circle imagery of *In Memoriam*.[6] In Poem XII (preceded by the lyric of calm despair, "Calm is the morn without a sound") the poet's state of increased ecstasy finds its metaphoric expression in the "wild pulsation" of a dove's wings who "springs / To bear thro' Heaven a tale of woe."[7] His soul must "haste away / O'er ocean-mirrors rounded large" in search of the ship bearing his friend's body. The calmness of the sea causes its reflective quality, and to the winging soul the ocean beneath appears an ever-expanding but ever-circular mirror. No matter where the soul flies or in what position, it remains at the imaginary center of a circular sea beneath it. As the lyric concludes, the speaker is acutely aware of the loss he has suffered and of the present fact that there is no relief available. The friend is dead, the ecstasy at his "return" is crushed, and after the soul "circle[s] moaning in the air: / 'Is this the end? Is this the end?'" it returns to where the "body sits," having been only "an hour away." The arrival of Hallam's body is not the end of the poet's personal suffering, and it is precisely this sense of personal suffering, this "tale of woe," which must always be reflected on those "ocean-mirrors rounded large" from whose center the poet cannot now escape. Tennyson's own sense of personal loss is so great that flight from self in imagination (even for an hour's duration) provides only intensification of the present emotional condition. The poem will move, however, to a final "statement": flights of the imagination propelled by love and a firm belief in immortality—not viewed as anodynes for personal suffering—can be the poet's greatest personal joy. The conditions are not, however, ready as yet for the revelation, and the poet must run his "widow'd race" (IX, 18) without the aid of a Virgil to explain what is to come.

Poem XVII (the final lyric in the section on the ship) repeats significantly the circle images of XII. The poet had long awaited the ship; in his imagination, when he had left this "mortal ark" (XII, 6), this "weight of nerves" (XII, 7), he saw the spirit of Hallam "move / Thro' circles of the bounding sky" (XVII, 5-6). Positions are reversed from what they were in XII. There is as yet no overt suggestion that the circles through which the soul moves act as metaphors for the world that soul inhabits, but it is true they represent a world accessible to Tennyson only in spirit and only temporarily. Into this world his prayers and his imagination project him, but he and Hallam remain separate entities. The central accomplishment of *In Memoriam* is, of course, the poet's final firm conviction that the "circle" of Hallam in the world of the dead is actually part of a larger circle, or cycle, of all existence. Tennyson grieves now, for Hallam has physically left the circle of life, and the poet's blessing stands separate, "like a line of light" (XVII, 10) to guard Hallam home. Connections between the two seem impossible now, but the poet, struggling in his dark ways, will eventually raise himself to Hallam through the power of love. He will not rise vertically, but spirally, falling back periodically as he moves on "stepping-stones . . . to higher things" (I, 3-4). Eventually faith will conquer doubt, and the circle image functions to indicate a spiritual direction, thus contributing in its way to the spiritual cosmology of *In Memoriam.*

"The idea of the continued life of the beloved dead now emerges, and in various forms becomes the principal subject of this Second Part."[8] Poem XXX, a lyric describing the first Christmas Eve without Hallam, illustrates Bradley's general statement and echoes the circle imagery of Part I. Part of the poet's world, his family, "in a circle hand-in-hand" (XXX, 11) attempts to celebrate the occasion with "A merry song we sang with him / Last year" (XXX, 15-16). The attempt at frivolity becomes impetuous, then ceases. A second song, with "a higher range" (XXX, 21) is begun; the song introduces ideas of future existence. Men do not die, but pierce the highest flame of spiritual existence. The body, unchanged in essence but strengthened, moves higher in different worlds until it reaches that of the seraph in the realm of immutability. The living, then, represent only one of the "circles" of existence; bound now by "the fickle and the frail" (XXX, 25), each of us is dominated by time and space. Appropriately, the final image of XXX, concerned with the birth of Christ, evokes the joy and happiness which accompany thoughts of immortality.

At present, the poet, whose own life is lived upon "this round of green" and under "this orb of flame" (XXXIV, 4), can only speculate upon the stages of existence; he decides, however, that even in various stages individuals retain their separate and unique identities by which we knew them.[9] He knows there may be traceable connections between levels of existence, but he has "lost the links that bound / Thy changes" (XLI, 6-7). He does, however, in XLV, contemplate the process of becoming separate which each individual experiences; the poem is worth citing:

> The baby new to earth and sky,
>   What time his tender palm is prest
>   Against the circle of the breast,
> Has never thought that 'this is I':
>
> But as he grows he gathers much,
>   And learns the use of 'I' and 'me,'
>   And finds 'I am not what I see,
> And other than the things I touch.'
>
> So rounds he to a separate mind
>   From whence clear memory may begin,
>   As thro' the frame that binds him in
> His isolation grows defined.
>
> This use may lie in blood and breath,
>   Which else were fruitless of their due,
>   Had man to learn himself anew
> Beyond the second birth of Death.

The verb for the process of growing awareness is, significantly, "rounds." The developing consciousness becomes a separate and whole circular unit whose movements towards separateness—so "rounds" implies—have been regular, measured, evenly spaced, and perhaps then, *natural*. The individual, whose source is cloudy and unclear, begins the long process, through various manifestations, towards perfection by first defining himself. First we are associated with the "round of green," an earth whose shape is orderly and whose movements are cyclic; on the earth's surface the seasons return every year, and in the earth's orbit "the same stars wheeled in their courses; the flowers and trees blossomed and the birds sang yearly in their appointed months" (*Memoir,* I, 312-313). From this circular earth each individual separates and becomes a circle of its own, capable of further development through the power of love.[10]

These significant images of circular movement are carried over into XLVII:

> That each, who seems a separate whole,
>   Should move his rounds, and fusing all
>   The skirts of self again, should fall
> Remerging in the general Soul,
>
> Is faith as vague as all unsweet.
>   Eternal form shall still divide
>   The eternal soul from all beside;
> And I shall know him when we meet.
>
> (ll. 1-8)

The interesting phrase again involves a circle image, "move his rounds," by which Tennyson seems to indicate movement within an orbit of which the individual consciousness is the center. The phrase also has the larger and more general sense of "live one's life," but its terms specify exactly how one does "live his life" (cf. the phrase, "move his course," in CXVIII, 19). He does it literally by "moving his rounds." The theory, central to *In Memoriam,* which Tennyson describes, is this: man retains his individual essence throughout eternity (his circle is never violated) and his movements are viewed metaphorically as expansions to a higher quality of existence. One seeks naturally some "landing place" (XLVII, 15) upon the "last and sharpest height" (XLVII, 13). It seems obvious, then, that human existence travels an expanding orbit, and that direction along that path represents a betterment of the individual orb without denying it its individuality. "What vaster dream," Tennyson asks, "can hit the mood / Of Love on earth?" (XLVII, 11-12). It is precisely this dream that sustains his faith in immortality and which rests at the basis of his faith in love.

Tennyson is not arguing that man's spiritual progress is an automatic movement, but he is assuming the existence of an inherent moral consciousness which aids one in pursuit of moral perfection. The emphasis on individual development in particular, and the later exhortation

> Arise and fly
> The reeling Faun, the sensual feast;
> Move upward, working out the beast,
> And let the ape and tiger die.
>
> (CXVIII, 25-28)

indicate the compatibility of Tennyson's moral outlook with contemporary scientific theory. The "reeling Faun" is obviously one moving in circles, but "reeling" suggests sterile movement upon the same plane (i.e., always upon a self-indulgent and animal level). The spiralling imagery of the poem skillfully suggests Tennyson's hope that man himself will evolve spiritually, "working out the beast" in his move towards immortality. Man's duty was to evolve, and Tennyson expresses the way of this evolution in terms of circles and orbs.[11]

At his death, then, Hallam had progressed to a phase of existence apart from Tennyson's, and the poet's continued references to Hallam "mixing with his proper sphere" have, as in LX, a much more than superficial significance within the broader context of *In Memoriam.* Hallam is, indeed, "with all the circle of the wise" (LXI, 3); his orbit and his sphere are far from the reach of mortals on earth. The entire planet metaphor is carried through Poems LX and LXI by suggestion and recapitulated and enlarged in LXIII. Here, as the poet contends, his own sympathy for beings "lower" (and thus lesser) than himself does not retard his "heart / In its assumptions up to heaven" (LXIII, 3-4). Likewise, he hopes, Hallam may act toward him, while

> unto vaster motions bound,
> The circuits of thine orbit round
> A higher height, a deeper deep.
>
> (ll. 10-12)

Seen as a planet, Hallam has his own path, and as he climbs higher and higher he looks deeper and deeper onto the stationary locus of Tennyson's orbit. The central power of cosmic proportions with the potential to link us to other levels of existence is love.

Through the suggestive ambiguities of circle images in Part Two, Tennyson has postulated the fact of his separation from Hallam, his "lost" friend's continued existence, and sought consolation in thoughts of a future meeting through the power of love. The image is less suggestive of metaphoric interpretation in Part Three (LXXVIII-CIII), which contains a greater number of occasional poems and casual references to the circle. The reason for this is probably, as Bradley suggests, that "the centre of interest is shifted to the present life of the poet enriched by love for the dead" (pp. 170-171). Hallam, whose shortened stay on earth is likened to the crescent segment which, if given time, would have grown to a full glow (LXXXIV, 4),[12] is now received in circular company by

> The great Intelligences fair
> That range above our mortal state,
> In circle round the blessed gate.
>
> (LXXXV, 21-23)[13]

The magnificent recapitulation of Poem CIII which sees Hallam as the center of an ideal race of humanity already existing in another world yet to come in this one is testament of Tennyson's faith in spiritual as well as "physical" evolution.[14]

While in Parts Two and Three Tennyson indicates his sustaining faith in love, in Part Four (CIV-CXXXI) he makes some attempt, in terms of circle imagery, to show that art or poetry can also be an essential part of the poet's faith and that creative effort can also bring about some relationship between this world and the one in which Hallam "lives." The key lyric of Part Four is Poem CXXII: Elizabeth Chapman has an excellent summary of the poem:

> As the poet has felt aforetime the soul of Arthur transfuse his own, and been rapt above the night of loss and gloom into a burst of creative energy and unfettered play of high imagination, so now again he craves that inspiring presence. Again there are strong stirrings of poetic fancy within which long to slip the thoughts of life and death and play freely round things bright and glad and beautiful. The spirit of his friend will quicken these with joyous sympathy.[15]

Bradley has speculated (pp. 219-226) about two of the central questions of Poem CXXII: what are the two occasions referred to and can they be traced to biographical events or do they have their counterparts in the elegy as a whole? Although these are not irrelevant questions, it is more to the point of this article to examine the specific imagery of CXXII to show that Tennyson has employed circle imagery to describe part of the poetic process; he illustrates how the imaginative act is, per se, entrance or how it offers connection to other worlds. The very act of creation, stimulated by a yearning to "burst the folded gloom, / To bare the eternal Heavens again" (ll. 3-4) and powered by a "strong imagination," results in the *rolling* of "A sphere of stars about my soul, / In all her motion one with law" (ll. 7-8). Tennyson is implying that the creative act (the writing of *In Memoriam* itself) brings to man the sensation (which he receives in "placid awe") of increasing the circumference of his individual orbit and of rolling and moving in some concentricity with a sphere of stars. That is to say, the imaginative act raises man into an area where he is to experience visions of future happiness. Experiencing such visions now intensifies the present existence ("every dewdrop paints a bow, / The wizard lightnings deeply glow" [ll. 18-19]). At the moment of this ecstasy, "all the breeze of Fancy blows," the poet's vision intensifies, his world increases, and he escapes from "the thoughts of life and death" (l. 16). As with Dante, Tennyson is not rewarded immediately with his vision of oneness and concentricity. First Tennyson is convinced of the fact of personal immortality and divine love; the periods of doubt have been endured, and faith and art have raised the poet to sensations of concentric movement with heavenly circles.

The "aesthetics" of *In Memoriam* are not those of art for art's sake, "truest lord of Hell" for Tennyson. Poetry, the imaginative experience, the "breeze of Fancy," has a significant mission among men; it intensifies and enriches common experience. Not to be valued solely for its own sake, poetry—or specifically, the writing of poetry—was for man a way of penetrating other circles of existence, a "stepping stone" to "higher things." Its mission is, for the poet, cosmic. The reader, brought to share this experience, should be convinced of poetry's power. The result of the creative attempt is expressed in Poem CXXX, where the "connection" made between the worlds of Tennyson and Hallam is seen in terms of the circle:

> Far off thou art, but ever nigh,
>   I have thee still, and I rejoice;
>   I prosper, circled with thy voice;
> I shall not lose thee tho' I die.
>
> (ll. 13-16)

The poem has achieved what it set out to do; Tennyson and Hallam are spiritually reunited, and the statement of faith,

> I see in part
> That all, as in some piece of art,
> Is toil coöperant to an end.
>
> (CXXVIII, 22-24)

with its juxtaposition of "all" and "art" implies, in the light of my discussion, that the end of both is the same. It is that end, envisioned or experienced, which in both *In Memoriam* and the *Divina Commedia* is seen in terms of the circle imagery.

Tennyson's use of the circle as a major image is certainly not unique, nor does it indicate a direct borrowing from Dante. If a debt exists, it is to a tradition of the circle in poetry, a tradition where from the Renaissance to the nineteenth century (and beyond), "le cercle est la figure de la perfection de l'être."[16]

Notes

1. Hallam Tennyson, *Alfred Lord Tennyson: A Memoir* (London, 1897), I, 304—hereafter cited as *Memoir*.

2. Jerome H. Buckley, *Tennyson: The Growth of a Poet* (Cambridge, Mass., 1960), pp. 122, 124.

3. [Allen Tate, "The Symbolic Imagination: The Mirrors of Dante,"] *KR* [*The Kenyon Review*], XIV (1952), 256-277.

4. Among *The Writings of Arthur Henry Hallam,* ed. T. H. Vail Motter (New York, 1943), are translations from Dante's *Vita Nuova,* and two essays, "The Influence of Italian upon English Literature," and "On Gabriele Rossetti's Dante Theories."

5. (London, 1920), p. 94.

6. I have not attempted to deal with all instances of circle imagery in the poem but have concentrated only on those which seem to be significant thematically.

7. All citations in my text from *In Memoriam* are to *The Poetical Works of Alfred Tennyson* (Cambridge, Mass., 1881).

8. Bradley, pp. 107-108. For the sake of convenience, I have followed Bradley's divisions of the poem: Part I: I-XXVII; Part II: XXVIII-LXXVII; Part III: LXXVIII-CIII; Part IV: CIV-CXXXI.

9. "If the absorption into the divine in the after-life be the creed of some," wrote Tennyson in Poem XLVII, "let them at all events allow us many existences of individuality before this absorption; since this short-lived individuality seems to be but too short a preparation for so mighty a union" (*Memoir,* I, 319).

10. One is tempted here to cite the final lines of Dante's poem as an example of the circle as an image of faultless activity:

> ma già volgeva il mio disiro e il velle.
> sì come rota ch' egualmente è mossa.
> l'amor che move il sole e l'altre stelle.

Through the power of love the individual sphere moves in concentricity with the Primum Mobile. Interestingly also, CXVIII informs us that man himself may have been under the power of "cyclic storms" which had to do with his own evolution to human kind. The scientific language of this lyric is the subject of an article by Walker Gibson, "Behind the Veil: A Distinction Between Poetic and Scientific Language in Tennyson, Lyell, and Darwin," *VS* [*Victorian Studies*] II. (September, 1958), 60-68.

11. The ultimate connection between human and divine was one to which man would evolve through the expression of his free will. To Tennyson "man's Free-will is but a bird in a cage; he can stop at the lower perch, or he can mount to a higher. Then that which is and knows will enlarge his cage, give him a higher and a higher perch, and at last break off the top of his cage, and let him out to be one with the Free-will of the universe" (*Memoir,* I, 318-319).

12. The suggestiveness of the word "crescent" should be obvious; it is usually applied to a phase of the moon, a separate orb, whose light is received from a greater source. One does not have to carry the analogy far to see Hallam as a "crescent" whose glory was only partial but who now basks in the full light of deity.

13. One can hardly escape at this point the obvious reference to Dante (*Paradiso,* xxviii), specifically to the Intelligences or orders of spirits who are the movers of the various concentric circles of light. This is the one specific reference to that poem, but its presence indicates that the debt may be deep.

14. See the suggestive article by John D. Rosenberg, "The Two Kingdoms of *In Memoriam,*" JEGP [*Journal of English and Germanic Philology*], LVIII (April, 1959), 228-240.

15. *A Companion to "In Memoriam"* (London, 1888), p. 66.

16. Georges Poulet, *Les Metamorphoses du Cercle* (Plon, 1961), p. 518.

Carlisle Moore (essay date 1963)

SOURCE: Moore, Carlisle. "Faith, Doubt, and Mystical Experience in *In Memoriam.*" *Victorian Studies* 7, no. 2 (December 1963): 155-69.

[*In the following essay, Moore discusses Tennyson's* In Memoriam, *focusing on the author's struggle with questions of faith and his search for mystical reunion with the deceased Arthur Henry Hallam.*]

We are still wont to think that Tennyson must abide our question because he confused personal confession and public prophecy. **In Memoriam** especially, with its wavering progression from a deeply-felt religious doubt to the proclamation of a universal faith, has been dismissed as a typical instance of Victorian rationalization which no longer speaks to us. Yet with all the commentaries, analyses, and keys which have appeared since 1850 the poem still eludes consensus. In its own time readers generally accepted it as a poem of faith and rejoiced with Kingsley to find "in the science and history of the nineteenth century new and living fulfillments of the words which we learnt at our mothers' knee."[1] But the praise was not unanimous. Some critics thought the doubt which they saw there made the faith less than "honest," and objected to Tennyson's admitting it even into the concluding sections.[2] Nevertheless, for half a century **In Memoriam** brought solace to worried and struggling believers, many of whom did not perceive and were therefore not troubled by its ambiguities, while those readers who did perceive them were comforted by the commentaries which, like A. C. Bradley's, charted the triumphal journey from doubt to faith.[3]

The critical reaction came when religion began to lose its hold on the individual conscience. Carlyle's loss of the traditional faith in which he had been reared produced what William James called "the sick shudder of the frustrated religious demand."[4] Leslie Stephen, writing about his own similar loss a generation later, confessed, "I did not feel that the solid ground was giving way beneath my feet, but rather that I was being relieved of a cumbrous burden. I was not discovering that my creed was false, but that I had never really believed it."[5] As the need for spiritual support diminished, or was satisfied by other supports, religion as an institution began to lose its social value. Separated from ethics it did not have to be regarded as the indispensable basis of all moral conduct. One could be both happy and good, apparently, without benefit of faith. **In Memoriam,** therefore, with its intense spiritual struggles seemed to an agnostic to be a somewhat foolish and misguided poem, the faith attained therein meaningless or insincere. It is not without irony that Tennyson was rescued from the neglect in which most Victorians languished during the early decades of this century when it was discovered that those struggles had produced some of his best poetry. It mattered little that in the hands of Sir Harold Nicolson the rescue involved splitting Tennyson in two and throwing away the worser half: the "prosperous Isle-of-Wight Victorian" wrote pontifical verse lacking both inspiration and sincerity, but elsewhere, in the lines of the "lonely, frightened spirit crouched broodingly over thoughts of death . . . the mystical genius of Tennyson comes upon one in a flash, and there can be no question of the reality of his emotion and his impulse."[6] Later T. S. Eliot's critical authority made it more than ever impossible to read **In Memoriam** as a poem of faith, though he did defend it against the charge of insincerity.[7] All that remained to be said in behalf of Tennyson's long struggle for faith was that he had fought a good fight and remained a good doubter.

The critical wheel had thus turned full circle. From being hailed as a noble poem of faith despite its admixture of doubt, **In Memoriam** came to be defended as a moving poem of doubt despite its unconvincing faith. In both cases large portions of the whole were ignored or ruled out of consideration. Each judgment reflected special views of its age: post-Darwinian and post-Freudian. But it may be asked whether such partial readings of the poem can be said to do it justice. Having discovered the genuineness of the doubt, perhaps we should re-examine the faith, should ask whether in the light of that "mystical genius" of Tennyson's which Nicolson recognized both are not admissible and, indeed, wholly reconcilable, when the poem is seen in relation to the phenomenon of religious conversion.

In its external, formal aspect **In Memoriam** is a public utterance, a conspicuous attempt to reconcile opposing tendencies which seemed to Tennyson and his contemporaries to be threatening the foundations of English society. Viewed thus it is fundamentally an effort to save religion from science by adducing a Coleridgean philosophy of religious experience against the demonstration of God from nature, or by reconciling the nineteenth-century belief in the progress of the species with the Christian concept of salvation.[8] Beneath this great argument lies Tennyson's intimate response to Hallam's death cast into language which expresses his shifting thoughts and moods over a period of seventeen years. Though he employed many of the familiar terms and concepts of his time he also, in a remarkable way, conveyed the mystical quality of his own vision and experience. T. S. Eliot remarks that Tennyson's "surface" (by which he means technical skill) "is intimate with his depths." But for Eliot, Tennyson's depths are depths of sorrow; Tennyson is "the saddest of all English poets" (p. 203). It is strange that the poet of "the moment in the rose-garden" should have taken no notice of Tennyson's similar moment in the garden at Somersby. The trance-like experience of Section XCV marks the climax of the poet's efforts to commune with the spirit of Hallam; it provides a nexus between the disparate elements of doubt and faith; and it tends to draw the poem away from the tradition of the pastoral elegy, in which the turning point, "He is not dead, he lives!," is so often merely a rhetorical device, and associates the poem with another kind of tradition altogether, that of religious conversion. Jerome H. Buckley pointed out in 1951 that "Though loosely organised as an aesthetic whole, *In Memoriam* closely followed the general pattern of nineteenth-century conversion" in the way it "traced the soul's growth from unshadowed hope through the denial of life itself towards the final conquest of doubt and despair."[9] But he did not explore the work from this point of view except to demonstrate that in it and similar works the pattern of conversion often found expression in certain recurring images of fire and water, of which Teufelsdroeckh's "Baphometic Fire-Baptism" in *Sartor Resartus* is probably the clearest example.

As the stock-in-trade of Methodism, conversion became immensely popular in the late eighteenth and early nineteenth centuries. Against a background of philosophic skepticism on the one hand and of the hard Calvinist creed of damnation on the other, there developed a widespread feeling that a saving faith was attainable by everyone, whatever his status, through a sudden electrifying emotional and spiritual crisis, and thousands were "reborn" in a quick and easy way that sensitive minds distrusted. Herr Teufelsdroeckh observed sardonically that such conversions represented "a new-attained progress in the Moral Development of man; hereby has the Highest come home to the bosoms of the most Limited; what to Plato was but a hallucination, and to Socrates a Chimera, is now clear and certain to your Zinzendorfs, your Wesleys, and the poorest of their Pietists and Methodists."[10] Teufelsdroeckh's own conversion belongs to a different order, for it was not primarily an acceptance of Christ nor was it induced by a heavy burden of sin, but rather by a fear that God did not love the world. With some romantic dramatization, Teufelsdroeckh repeats in its main outlines Carlyle's own spiritual crisis experienced on Leith Walk in 1821.[11] Not a doctrinal conversion, like Newman's adoption of a creed and submission to authority, this was rather, like Mill's reading of Marmontel, a spontaneous awakening, an intellectual and emotional discovery of new truths which though not self-induced answered a personal need and, in Carlyle's case, was strongly mystical. Moreover, it was attended by the two conditions which seem to characterize the intellectual species of conversion. The first of these conditions is a state of mind which for reasons known or unknown has become unbearable and is rationally irremediable. The occasion may be a fear for one's own security, or virtue, or a broader concern for the spiritual welfare of society or the cosmos. The second is the occurrence of a climactic experience during which a power greater than oneself is felt to be taking control and directing one towards a solution.[12] Often this does not complete the conversion but only begins it. Sometimes it is followed by a prolonged period of doubt which delays and modifies the faith ultimately attained. Sometimes there are repetitions of the original experience. Even John Wesley's conversion, which he dated precisely at a quarter of nine, 24 May 1738, was followed by fears and agonizing doubts.

Both of these conditions are to be found in *In Memoriam*. The grief and "wild despair" which are now so much admired cannot be endured indefinitely. Hallam's death, the "soul-shaking event" in his otherwise undramatic life, had exacerbated Tennyson's already brooding and hypersensitive temperament to a state of depression which no mere passage of time can remedy. Domestic and personal troubles before 1833 had prepared the way: the death of his father in 1831, the mental breakdown of his younger brother Edward and the opium-addiction of Charles in 1832, and Croker's harsh treatment of his 1832 *Poems* in the *Quarterly Review*. After 1833 the burden of family business fell on his shoulders when Frederick left on a pleasure trip to Italy. He was concerned for his mother, for his sister Emily who had been engaged to Hallam, and for Septimus who was also, for a time, threatened with a mental breakdown. The unfriendly reception of his poems continued to worry him, and kept him from venturing to publish another volume. There was little money to support the large family, and when his grandfather died in 1835 the Somersby Tennysons were, as always, slighted.[13] Upon these depressing circumstances the loss of Hallam came like the jolt which turns already sub-freezing water to ice: "Break, thou deep vase of chilling tears, / That grief hath shaken into frost!"[14] Preoccupied already with the bearing of science on religion, he could not fail to find in this personal loss a demonstration of the finality of death and the remoteness of God.

It is significant that there is no sense of sin, or sinfulness, in Tennyson's unhappiness. He fears divine neglect, not divine punishment (LII), and grieves because he has been left desolate, "widowed," and alone, with no sure prospect of reunion with the one in whom he had found not only affection but support in a world growing increasingly harsh and alien. With Hallam gone even Christ seemed distant. During that first Christmas of 1833 he thought of Christ only in connection with the miracle of Lazarus which occurred long ago (XXXI), and the second Christmas did not banish his sense of loss.[15] There is some tendency to identify Hallam and Christ in spirit, to think longingly of Christ as a human savior (XXXII, XXXVI) who, as he saved

Lazarus and inspired Mary's perfect faith, may with "mortal sympathy" and love save Hallam in the other world; but this develops slowly. Meanwhile, God is remoter still. Although His existence seems sure, His goodness and love cannot be seen in His creation of nature "red in tooth and claw" (XXXIV, LV, LVI). However self-centered his despair, Tennyson's concern for the immortality of all souls is real: "Else earth is darkness at the core, / And dust and ashes all that is" (XXXIV). The threat of current evolutionary ideas to the doctrine of immortality was equally real, and the more disturbing because it did not help, as Lionel Stevenson remarks, to read into these ideas a spiritual principle of successively higher incarnations of the soul. For he had still to persuade himself (and others) in a more than purely rational and logical way that man's "inward sense of immortality is stronger and truer than the inconsistent physical forms of the universe."[16] Even after the intellect was satisfied the heart still felt the loneliness and grief of personal loss: "We cannot hear each other speak" (LXXXII). It remained for an intuitive conviction of immortality to be achieved through an actual, possibly a mystical, contact with the spirit of the lost one.

This brings us to the second necessary condition of conversion. "Tennyson was at heart a mystic," wrote Sir Charles Tennyson, "with a capacity for true mystical experience."[17] Many evidences of this may be found in his poems, from among the earliest (**"Armageddon,"** 1823-24) to the latest (**"The Ring,"** 1889). *In Memoriam* contains many signs of it, and in an important group of sections, from XC through XCIV, there is a plea for a vision of Hallam which is answered with the trance-like experience which ultimately gives him the assurance he has sought.

Everything had led up to this episode. The opening sections, with their mood of enforced calm expressing the poet's loss and initial shock, the subsequent despair and confusion, nevertheless constitute a developing (if not orderly) series of lucid pictures of the past (the yew tree, the house on Wimpole Street) and the imagined present (the ship returning, anticipations of its arrival, the burial) which are threaded with his increasing anguish. As efforts to control it, or divert it, or reason it away, fail, the larger significance of Hallam's death becomes clearer, creating fresh fears, and Tennyson comes to feel the need of some sort of contact with Hallam's spirit to revive his belief in man's immortal spirit and in love as the universal law (XLII).

In response to this need, but also as a direct expression of Tennyson's sensibility, there are mystical intimations throughout the poem, from the earliest sections, in which he hopes that he may "reach a hand thro' time to catch / The far-off interest of tears"; and in the presence of the old yew tree he feels himself disembodied: "I seem to fail from out my blood / And grow incorporate into thee." In Section XII he again describes himself as leaving his own body, "I leave this mortal ark behind, / A weight of nerves without a mind," and hasting over seas to the ship which brings the dead Hallam home he can only "circle moaning in the air" and return "to where the body sits, and learn / That I have been an hour away." This half-dream, half-trance leads to the fear, in Section XVI, that his grief has unbalanced his mind, "made me that delirious man / Whose fancy fuses old and new, / And flashes into false and true." When with the oscillating movement of the poem calm returns, and the first Christmas brings a degree of resignation ("'Tis better to have loved and lost . . ."), he begins to search for convincing evidence of immortality in man's life ("My own dim life should teach me this, / That life shall live for evermore" [XXXIV]), or in the "tale" of the life and resurrection of Christ (XXXVI), or, hopefully, within his own consciousness. Truths lie "Deep-seated in our mystic frame," but "darkly-joined." Perhaps in the same way that there existed the Wordsworthian possibility of receiving intimations of our life before our birth, in "A little flash, a mystic hint," so there is the possibility of communication between souls in the afterlife and here.

> If such a dreamy touch should fall,
>   O turn thee round, resolve the doubt;
>   My guardian angel will speak out,
> In that high place and tell thee all.
>
> (XLIV)

This seems to anticipate, though as yet without much hope, a communion with the spirit of Hallam in some sort of trance or vision, and it is clear that Tennyson attaches immense importance to such experiential evidence in the resolution of his doubts. Soon he gives more direct expression to his desire to be made aware of Hallam's accrual presence: "Be near me when my light is low . . . Be near me when the sensuous frame / Is rack'd with pangs that conquer trust . . . when my faith is dry . . . when I fade away" (L); then more generally:

> Be near us when we climb or fall:
>   Ye watch, like God, the rolling hours
>   With larger other eyes than ours,
> To make allowance for us all.
>
> (LI)

If Hallam remains distant it is not, Tennyson believes, because of his own human shortcomings, the despair, the sensuous nature, the spiritual dryness, of which he is humbly aware, for he is confident his love for Hallam will redeem him (LII).

Meanwhile rational consolation ("Oh yet we trust that somehow good / Will be the final goal of ill" [LIV]) yields inevitably to rational depression: "O for thy voice to soothe and bless! / What hope of answer, or redress? / Behind the veil, behind the veil" (LVI). The next large group of sections (LVII-LXXXIX) dwells on wavering moods of resignation and despair, while the anniversary of Hallam's death (LXXII), the second Christmas (LXXVIII), and the New Year (LXXXIII), pass him by without much helping or hurting. He did dream of a "mystic glory" shining on Hallam's grave (LXVII), but in this dream ("kinsman thou to death and trance") his efforts to see Hallam's features are frustrated and confused,

> Till all at once beyond the will
> I hear a wizard music roll,
> And thro' a lattice on the soul
> Looks thy fair face and makes it still.
>
> (LXX)

Still, there is no communion or sign of recognition in such dreams or fancies, and the poet reaches a state of emotional equilibrium (LXXXII, LXXXIII) in which, blaming no person or thing ("I wage not any feud with Death"), he seem resigned to his "low beginnings of content" (LXXXIV), and grateful at least for the memory and friendship of Hallam. It is in such a state of resignation that, according to James,[18] religious conversions are likely to occur. It is the turning point both of the poem and of the poet's hopes. At the very bottom of his fortunes he realizes that there is "in my grief a strength reserved." There are "mighty hopes that make us men." And though "in dear words of human speech / We two communicate no more," he has a premonition that "I shall prove / A meeting somewhere, love with love" (LXXXV). Still sad, he now thinks less about himself, more about Hallam's days at Cambridge (LXXXVII) and at Somersby (LXXXIX), and this leads directly into a group of sections (XC-CVI) in which Tennyson invokes the spirit of Hallam: "Come, beauteous in thine after form, / And like a finer light in light" (XCI), culminating in the unmistakable awareness of his spirit in Section XCV.

The trance occurs in a large group of sections in which Tennyson describes the circumstances leading up to his mystical experience and records its immediate consequences. In Section XC he begins to think about what he desires so much, namely the return of Hallam. But the subject is, at this stage, general and hypothetical. If men could return from death they might not be welcomed back either by their wives, now "in other hands," or by their sons, jealous of their inheritance; but these wives and sons have not felt love. Tennyson, who has, can only cry to Hallam, "Come thou back to me!," and in the next section (XCI) he asks Hallam to appear either in body or in visible spirit. Ever prone to doubt, Tennyson now fears that he might distrust such a vision (XCII) as a "canker of the brain," and might discredit the phantom's spoken prophecies as mere presentiments. "I shall not see thee," he writes in the next section (XCIII). Therefore, he begs Hallam to "Descend, and touch, and enter" so that he may feel his presence. Yet, this may be impossible, since (XCIV) one needs a peaceful and serene spirit to hold communion with the dead.

It is clear that up to this point Tennyson has been preparing both himself and us for the climactic experience which is told in Section XCV. Providing an effective change of pace and tone, this section is the richly descriptive narrative of one summer evening at Somersby (1835), spent singing old songs with the members of his family and watching the approach of night, when, after the others had gone to bed and he was alone, he reread Hallam's letters, and suddenly felt a presence.

> So word by word, and line by line,
> The dead man touched me from the past,
> And all at once it seem'd at last
> The living soul was flashed on mine.
>
> And mine in this was wound, and whirl'd
> About empyreal heights of thought,
> And came on that which is, and caught
> The deep pulsations of the world.
>
> (XCV)

It is well known that until 1878 the phrases "The living soul" and "mine in this" read "His living soul" and "mine in his." For twenty-eight years this section of the poem described a personal contact with Hallam's spirit, a contact which by itself could indeed resolve all doubts and restore one's faith in immortality. It was a record of genuine mystical experience, a clear sign from a beloved spirit in the next world which, because it effected, or seemed to effect, the dispelling of all religious doubts, had all the earmarks of a conversion comparable in its way with St. Paul's.

Among critics Section XCV has occasioned both perplexity and indignation. Why, if he wanted to record a conversion, did Tennyson make emendations which removed the personal element, and throw the whole thing into doubt? And why did he wait so long to make them? John D. Rosenberg writes, "If 'The living soul' is not Hallam's, the lines are without meaning"; for Paull F. Baum they cause the whole section and with it the whole poem to fail as a clear and honest work of art.[19] It is certainly true that the earlier version is the clearer. We may well ask why it did not satisfy Tennyson. Certainly the bereaved poet desired an intimate, even a physical contact. But we have seen that he has already rejected this possibility (XCII, XCIII) in favor of a vaguer if no less real spiritual one. We have no way of knowing whether the contact described in the earlier version is what he thought he had felt, or what he wanted to think he had felt. In time he was convinced that it suggested a more personal contact than the trance justified. There is, indeed, ample meaning in the amended version if it is understood that Hallam's spirit is not in a state of isolation but exists as an all but indistinguishable part of the universal spirit of the Deity. The poet, reading Hallam's letters, feels in his trance the touch of this spirit, which conveys a comforting sense of the closeness of his friend and convinces him for the moment that they have touched. It is this necessary ambiguity that the final version seems meant to convey: the contact suggested both Hallam and the Deity. The poem cannot be called dishonest unless its maker is here compromising his belief or distorting his actual experience. Tennyson seems to have tried, rather, to correct the record. To James Knowles he said later that what he felt was "perchance the Deity . . . my conscience was troubled by 'his'. I've often had a strange feeling of being bound and wrapped in the Great Soul" (Knowles, p. 186). Nor does it seem just to commit the poem to clarity, if it deals with an experience that by its very nature is beyond clarity, and if its parts are consistent with the whole. The idea of Hallam merged in the Deity is no afterthought but finds grateful expression in many of the later sections (e.g., XCVII, CXXII, CXXIV, CXXX):

> To feel thee some diffusive power,
> I do not therefore love thee less . . .
>
> Tho' mix'd with God and Nature thou,
> I seem to love thee more and more.
>
> (CXXX)

Though at the expense of clarity, the emendations enlarge and universalize the whole experience of the trance. They also introduce an admixture of doubt into the very middle of the newly-awakened faith which, religiously and psychologically, is not unprecedented. The faith of the saints was made arduous by doubt. Quite apart from the emendations, however, Tennyson's trance was followed immediately by doubt: "At length my trance / Was cancell'd, stricken through with doubt."[20] It is not surprising that its end should have been sudden, the return to reality a shock. "Sometimes," he told Knowles, "I get carried away out of sense and body, and rapt into mere existence, till the accidental touch or movement of one of my own fingers is like a great shock and blow and brings the body back with a terrible start" (Knowles, p. 169). It is the nature, not the actual occurrence of the experience that the poet doubts. Tennyson is not, in fact, so worried as his critics are by the uncertainty of his trance-contact, but seems content not to know whether it was Hallam or "some higher name" he has touched, or both. The last four stanzas of this section, which Bradley calls "one of the most wonderful descriptive passages in all poetry" (p. 192), express a mood of exalted calm.

That the experience belonged to the phenomenon of conversion is clear from what follows. Through it his doubts have been scotched, his faith has become stronger. He thinks now of another, perhaps Hallam, who fought against doubt to a stronger faith (XCVI); he reflects that honest faith in these times does not exclude doubt, that even the strongest faith "Dwells not in the light alone / But in the darkness and the cloud, / As over Sinai's peaks." His own faith was intuitive, based not only on "the unreality of the material and the reality of the spiritual world but on the mystic's power of spiritual communion and the capacity of the human mind to transcend the material and in some sense apprehend infinity" (*Six Tennyson Essays,* pp. 110-111). Rational argument had failed as the basis for religious evidence, but there was the appeal to experience, the same appeal which is found in Coleridge, Carlyle, and Maurice, and earlier in Kant and Schleiermacher: "the heart / Stood up and answer'd 'I have felt'" (CXXIV). The "Ring out wild bells" passage (CVI) celebrates his victory, and he resolves to cease his introspective grief and, after Goethe and Carlyle, accept sorrow as a strengthener of the soul. In Section CXX he compares his struggles with St. Paul's; he recalls the climactic trance of Section XCV, repeating his uncertainty about its precise nature ("Oh, wast thou with me, dearest, then, / Whilst I rose up against my doom"), and asks Hallam to return ("be with me now, / And enter in at breast and brow") in another mystical experience

> As in the former flash of joy,
> I slip the thoughts of life and death;
>
> And all the breeze of fancy blows,
> And every dewdrop paints a bow,
> The wizard lightnings deeply glow,
> And every thought breaks out a rose.
>
> (CXXII)

No second trance occurs, but Tennyson is not despondent on this occasion either, for his memory of the first has enabled him to accept the ordinary state of human ignorance. Having transcended this state once, in a "flash of joy," he is strong enough to withstand all rational doubts and natural terrors:

> And all is well, tho' faith and form
> Be sunder'd in the night of fear;
> Well roars the storm to those that hear
> A deeper voice across the storm.
>
> (CXXVII)

Natural terrors will remain, though deprived of their old effect because of the "deeper voice" which came to him from a divine source "across" (not in, or through) the storm.

Yet the repeated "all is well" of Sections CXXVI and CXXVII, mentioned along with war, social injustices, and dying aeons, conveys a profound sense of sadness that so much evil should be prerequisite to eventual good. The triumph is muted. Such faith as he has won leaves great questions unanswered: Why so much evil? Why is our vision so limited? Like religious skeptics of all ages, he "would see a sign." He had felt one, and he was grateful for the evidence which despite "The freezing reason's colder part" enabled him to believe that "all is well." The attitude is not very different from T. S. Eliot's in "Little Gidding": "Sin is Behovely, but / All shall be well, and / All manner of thing shall be well." Beginning with doubt and fear, Tennyson ends with doubt and hope. It should not be giving him too much the benefit of his doubts to say that this attitude is not dated, but will have relevance for as long as man separates faith and reason.[21]

It is at this point that we can see why **In Memoriam** is neither a poem wholly of faith nor one wholly of doubt. Its faith admits an ignorance of the whole truth and leaves room for doubt; its doubt, having made room for itself after Hallam's death, had to make room for faith after the trance of Section XCV. Love and hope are the bonds. For if religious faith is necessarily incomplete, so is science. A faith which is at once intuitive and intellectual will not be attainable until faith and knowledge meet. Tennyson hoped that with evolutionary progress man would ultimately find that religion and science reveal one and the same truth.[22]

Meanwhile, one of the strengths of the Christian religion, as Sir Thomas Browne had observed, is its absence of logical proof. If miraculous visions occurred daily we should depreciate or ignore them, like the Israelites who "made their gods of gold, / Altho' the trumpet blew so loud" (XCVI). Not that doubt is to be nurtured; it is to be endured, like a hairshirt, as a chastener of one's faith. Far from falling back on the standard affirmations of his day,[23] Tennyson chose a limited faith which required courage to sustain. The position taken in the concluding sections and the Prologue was his final position. That he never went beyond it has been lamented and deplored, but considering its dependence on the progress of the species, it is a position which hardly admits of much advancement in a lifetime.

When all is said, *In Memoriam* remains one of the most egoistic of elegies. The selfless sorrow felt for Hallam's premature death is soon obscured by Tennyson's tragic bereavement, by his anguished desire for sensible contact with Hallam, and by his prolonged efforts to establish the idea of a loving deity. The poem would be more autobiography than elegy if Tennyson had not contrived so well to work his experience into the traditional elegiac form. It was, I think, the trance that enabled him to use the elegiac turning-point, "He is not dead, he lives!," with conviction, to combine the pattern of elegy with the pattern of conversion. Yet he departs more from that of elegy. As Bradley observed, the turning point is not so clearly marked as in *Lycidas* and *Adonais*. Indeed it is hard to locate at all (p. 30). But this is because Tennyson is following his own experience rather than poetic tradition. The announcement that "he lives!," accordingly, had to be delayed until after the period of uncertainty and doubt that succeeded the trance, and as with Carlyle, whose "Everlasting Yea" had to follow the long "Centre of Indifference," his faith evolved slowly.

But if *In Memoriam* is not pure elegy, neither is it a straight record of experience. Tennyson arranged the elegies to lead from the moment of mystical contact through a slow recovery to a faith that stopped short of completion, at least in the Wesleyan sense. Brought up in the evangelical tradition, he came naturally by his knowledge of conversion and its various stages. For his final construction of the whole it was his own much less dramatic conversion that supplied the pattern, but even this was modified to admit discourses and arguments that had little to do with that experience. The result is a form which, like the envelope-quatrain, he made uniquely his own. His success, considering the difficulties he encountered, is almost without precedent. Few long poems achieve such a synthesis of disparate parts. During the long period of its composition Tennyson gained not only artistic development[24] but religious and emotional maturity. We have seen that along with the many strands of thought and feeling that run through it—reflections on science, on nature, on society, on the relationships between this life and the next, on the Christmases and the anniversaries, and on his concern for his relatives and friends—there is the clear strand of mystical experience leading up to and beyond the gentle but significant trance in the garden at Somersby which enabled him to recover his faith, determined the peculiar leaven of doubt in that faith, and, finally, enriched the inner character of the poem itself.

Notes

1. Edgar F. Shannon, *Tennyson and the Reviewers* (Cambridge, Mass., 1952), p. 149.

2. Strongest objections to Tennyson's theological doubts came from the High Church *English Review* which scolded him for having no faith at all, and from the Thunderer's *Times* which denounced "the enormous exaggeration of the grief," and the tone of "amatory tenderness"; further recognition of the serious doubt in the poem can be seen where it is recommended as spiritual therapy for the bereaved, e.g., by Lewes writing in the *Leader*: "All who have sorrowed will listen with delight to the chastened strains here poured forth in *In Memoriam*" (Shannon, pp. 142, 149-157).

3. *A Commentary on Tennyson's In Memoriam,* 3rd ed. (London, 1936), pp. 36-43. Among the many which preceded Bradley's (originally published in 1901) were F. W. Robertson, *Analysis of Mr. Tennyson's "In Memoriam"* (London, 1862); Alfred Gatty, *A Key to Tennyson's "In Memoriam"* (London, 1881); John F. Genung, *Tennyson's "In Memoriam": Its Purpose and Structure* (London, 1881); and Elizabeth R. Chapman, *A Companion to "In Memoriam"* (London, 1888). For a recent analytical and structural study of the poem see Eleanor B. Mattes, *In Memoriam: the Way of a Soul* (New York, 1951).

4. *Will to Believe and Other Essays* (New York, 1927), p. 42.

5. *Some Early Impressions* (London, 1924), p. 70.

6. *Tennyson* (London, 1923), pp. 14, 27.

7. Eliot, in *Essays Ancient and Modern* (London, 1936), favored discarding the faith which "is a poor thing" and keeping the doubt which "is a very intense experience"; but he insisted that to be adequately understood the poem must be read entire (pp. 182-188). Following Eliot, Samuel C. Burchell, in "Tennyson's Dark Night," *South Atlantic Quarterly,* LIV (1955), thinks the twentieth century first to appreciate *In Memoriam* as an expression of anguish and doubt: "There is a concreteness in the pessimism and despair of Tennyson and *In Memoriam,* and it is something for which we can have great sympathy . . . after a period of being a schoolboy's medicine and a clergyman's platitude, *In Memoriam* now finally merits the serious attention of modern critics" (p. 81).

8. See Graham Hough, "The Natural Theology of *In Memoriam*," *Review of English Studies,* XXIII (1948), 244-256; and John D. Rosenberg, "The Two Kingdoms of *In Memoriam*," *Journal of English and German Philology,* LVIII (1959), 228-240.

9. *The Victorian Temper* (Cambridge, Mass., 1951), p. 87.

10. *Sartor Resartus,* ed. C. F. Harrold (New York, 1937), p. 198.

11. See my "*Sartor Resartus* and the Problem of Carlyle's Conversion," *PMLA* [*Publications of the Modern Language Association*], LXX (1955), 662-681.

12. For more detailed analysis of conversion see William James, *Varieties of Religious Experience* (London, 1902), pp. 189-258; A. D. Nock, *Conversion* (Oxford, 1933), pp. 1-16, 254-271; and Robert H. Thouless, *The Psychology of Religion* (Cambridge, 1923), pp. 187-224. Among the class of spontaneous, or involuntary, conversions, James distinguishes the moral conversion, involving little or no intellectual readjustment, from the fuller, spiritual one which involves far-reaching intellectual and emotional changes. These vary in three main respects: the state of consciousness out of which they arise, the nature of the crisis itself, and the effects of the crisis. The inductors may be a feeling of personal sinfulness, weariness of self (accidie), or the fear of a godless world. (For Carlyle, Mill, and Tennyson, the crux was not a burden of sin, or even the loss of belief in God, but the lack of moral, rational meaning in the universe and human life.) Though sometimes gradual the crisis is more often instantaneous, attended by trance or vision: and the effects are a feeling of peace and harmony, a perception of truths not known before, and an enhanced view of the objective world (pp. 248 ff.). There is an interesting discussion of "The Metaphysics of Conversion" by R. H. Hutton in his *Contemporary Thought and Thinking* (London, 1894), I, 369-376.

13. Charles Tennyson, *Alfred Tennyson* (New York, 1949), pp. 105-154. See also R. W. Rader's "Tennyson in the Year of Hallam's Death," *PMLA,* LXXVII (1962), 419-424, for a study, using fresh materials, of Tennyson's inner grief and outer behavior in 1834.

14. Sec. IV; see Thomas Bayne, "Carlyle and Tennyson," *N & Q* [*Notes and Queries*], 7th ser., XI (1891), 204.

15. Sec. LXXVIII. Though few readers doubt the depth of his grief, some have wondered whether it was quite healthy for a man to grieve so long for another man, as if there were a decent maximum as well as a decent minimum for mourning. Paull F. Baum's view, in *Tennyson Sixty Years After* (Chapel Hill, 1948), is that "the composition of these elegies [became] a kind of habit and the death of Hallam a kind of convenience to the muse" (p. 116), but this deliberately ignores the early and lasting association in Tennyson's mind of Hallam's death with the distressing problem of man's ultimate destiny.

16. Lionel Stevenson, *Darwin Among the Poets* (Chicago, 1932), p. 89.

17. *Six Tennyson Essays* (London, 1954), p. 96. See also James Knowles, "Aspects of Tennyson," *Nineteenth Century,* XXXIII (1893), 169, 186. According to Sir Charles, Tennyson was not a complete mystic but "possessed in some degree the power mystics have claimed through the centuries, to establish immediate communication . . . between the spirit of man, entangled among material things, and . . . God" (p. 71). Tennyson believed that he possessed this power and told both Tyndall and Knowles how he could induce trance-states by concentrating on his own name (*Alfred Lord Tennyson, A Memoir, by His Son* [London, 1897], II, 473-474). He described it also in "The Ancient Sage." This has led some critics, e.g., Robert Preyer, "Tennyson as an Oracular Poet," *Modern Philology,* LV (1958), 250, to dismiss his mystical experience as self-hypnosis. That it is larger than this, and unforced, seems evident from its presence throughout his poetry. The experience described in *In Memoriam,* as we shall see, is spontaneous. He distrusted the current cult of spiritualism, and was self-conscious about his own modest capacity, protesting to Tyndall: "By God Almighty, there is no delusion in the matter! It is no nebulous ecstasy, but a state of transcendent wonder, associated with absolute clearness of mind" (*A Memoir,* II, 473-474).

18. James cites the apathy and exhaustion of Teufelsdroeckh on the Rue de l'Enfer. Tennyson's mood of resignation and acceptance, bringing a certain relief, invites the mystical contact: "So long as the egoistic worry of the sick soul guards the door, the expansive confidence of the soul of faith gains no presence. But let the former faint away, even but for a moment, and the latter can profit by the opportunity" (p. 212).

19. Rosenberg, p. 234n; Baum, pp. 307-308. While granting beauty in many of the lyrics Baum accuses Tennyson of "perverting" his poem; he should not have attempted to "arrange" them at all. Further, his glossing of "The living soul" as "The Deity, maybe" betrays a "weakness inherent in Tennyson's character . . . we have a right to expect some sort of clear statement: either it *was* the Deity—for the purposes of the poem, of course—or it was not" (p. 307).

20. Sec. XCV. I take it that "cancell'd" does not mean repudiated but, rather, brought so suddenly to an end that Tennyson could not be sure of either the nature or the identity of the spirit whose presence he had felt. Bradley concludes: "Probably at the moment of the experience he did think his friend's soul was present, but thereafter never felt any certainty on the subject" (p. 191n). But this uncertainty did not "cancel" the growing certainty, stemming from this experience, that his plea for contact with Hallam had somehow been granted.

21. In his *Tennyson, the Growth of a Poet* (Cambridge, Mass., 1960), Jerome H. Buckley also sees the trance as effecting Tennyson's recovery of faith: "his experience has given him the certitude that 'science' could not establish and therefore could not destroy. Though unable to sustain his vision, the 'I' of the poem finds

his mystical insight the surest warrant for spiritual recovery." After comparing Tennyson's faith with Pascal's ("who likewise trusted the reasons of the heart which reason could not know") and with Kierkegaard's existentialism ("which similarly balances the demands of the inner life against the claims of nineteenth-century 'knowledge'"), he concludes that it had genuine relevance and importance in a Victorian England which was finding all dogmatic positions increasingly vulnerable. Jonathan Bishop, in "The Unity of 'In Memoriam'" (*Victorian Newsletter,* No. 21 [Spring 1962], p. 13, n. 7) agrees.

22. Sec. CXXVIII, and the Prologue; also *A Memoir,* I, 323.

23. This indictment still persists. See Jacob Korg, "The Pattern of Fatality in Tennyson's Poetry," *VNL,* [*Victorian Newsletter*] No. 14, (Fall 1958), pp. 8-11.

24. For an excellent study of the maturing of Tennyson's conception and mastery of his poetic art during these years, see E. D. H. Johnson, "*In Memoriam*: The Way of the Poet," *VS* [*Victorian Studies*], II (1958), 139-148.

K. W. Gransden (essay date 1964)

SOURCE: Gransden, K. W. "The Poem." In *Tennyson: In Memoriam,* pp. 42-60. London: Edward Arnold (Publishers) LTD., 1964.

[*In the following excerpt, Gransden examines* In Memoriam *as an elegy, noting that Tennyson's approach is tentative and exploratory, resulting in a poem that documents his trial and error as he attempted to translate his vision into words.*]

Tennyson at one time thought of calling **In Memoriam** 'Fragments of an Elegy', a title which overstresses the intermittent nature of the poem at the expense of its underlying unity and development. A better pointer is his subtitle 'The Way of the Soul', and his remark, quoted in the *Memoir,* that the poem is a kind of divine comedy beginning with a death and ending with a marriage. The poem moves from the darkness of loss towards the light of hope and future gain: we shall see that both meanings of 'loss', as the opposite of finding and the opposite of gain, are important. Another parallel suggested by the subtitle is with Donne's second anniversary (*The Progresse of the Soule*) which also carries the required domestic note: that is, in Donne's case, a poem primarily intended for the attention and solace of a particular household, and in Tennyson's, a poem primarily intended as an act of autobiography and autotherapy and secondarily as an account of experience which the poet hoped might be of wider service.

The poem, like **'Locksley Hall'** and **Maud,** aroused, inevitably, speculation as to the nature and extent of its autobiographical element. One problem was that of chronology. How far does the poem's time-sequence correspond to that of actual events? (One of the chief features of any transmutation of life into art is that the needs of art generally dictate a new tempo.) We know that the poems were not written in the order in which Tennyson, after seventeen years' work, finally arranged them for publication. Three Christmases elapse in the poem but these cannot actually be the first three Christmases after Hallam's death (1833, 1834 and 1835) since the third Christmas is also apparently Tennyson's first after leaving Somersby in 1837.

Another problem (to which Bradley devotes several pages) was Tennyson's supposed borrowings from earlier poets, particularly Herbert (who is echoed several times in the introductory stanzas). A modern reader, familiar with *The Waste Land,* will not find this surprising and will not feel any need to reconcile any such borrowings with the originality of the new poem. More interesting, perhaps, is the way in which Tennyson's reading of Herbert may have taught him something of the technique of dramatising one's difficulties in verse, of conducting spiritual argument. The crude dialogue form of **'The Two Voices'** becomes in **In Memoriam** something much more subtle and flexible.

> 'So careful of the type?' but no.
>   From scarped cliff and quarried stone
>   She cries, 'A thousand types are gone:
> I care for nothing, all shall go.'

Nor does it detract from the originality of the poem to suggest that it may to some extent be read as a poet's commonplace book, a *journal in time* in which the entries are separated by time and silence; the working up into a unified whole of material some of which is quite new to English poetry but some of which is so familiar that even in Tennyson's hands its expression hardly rises above the level of the embroidered text:

> Behold, we know not anything;
>   I can but trust that good shall fall
>   At last—far off—at last, to all,
> And every winter change to spring.

In its new context, such a stanza may be enriched by everything else the poet has to say about the future: it is perhaps not too far-fetched to say that the word 'but' in the second line is the most significant word in the stanza, the 'placing' qualificatory key-word by which a commonplace may open into a whole philosophy of experience.

At the other extreme are those sections of the poem in which Tennyson is trying out difficult scientific or metaphysical hypotheses: and here, his anxiety to be accurate and fair, and at the same time to give his own feelings their full weight, produces obscurities of a kind not normally associated with Victorian verse. The once-notorious obscurities of Browning are of a different kind, for Browning will usually be found to be wrapping up quite simple ideas in layers of verbal cotton wool, multiplying examples or analogies and repeating the same idea in different ways, thereby spoiling even his more lyrical poems. In 'Two in the Campagna', this annoying procedure lies open to the reader and even forms the subject of the poem. The thread of a perfectly familiar proposition is compared to a spider's web and the idea is only 'tantalising' because Browning deliberately makes it so; by playing with an idea he reduces its claim on our serious attention.

The difficulties of **In Memoriam** arise, not from elaboration but from compression; not from word-play but from Tennyson's own genuine struggle with difficult ideas and strong emotions. In getting these ideas and emotions under the control of a strict lyric stanza, Tennyson produces a kind of opaqueness—that is, we think we see to the bottom, but find the logic occluded by the very gnomic quality of the utterance. I do not want to imply that Tennyson is cheating—the very reverse is the case. His approach is, *au fond,* tentative and exploratory, but the highly finished form of the stanzas, their technical assurance, seems to imply a corresponding intellectual assurance which Tennyson is far from claiming. He is always in complete control of his imagery, but underneath ideas are being offered and withdrawn, hypotheses are tested and rejected. Tennyson's achievement is that he has left all the evidence of this hard work in the poem without detracting from the poem's authority.

One example of the process I am thinking of is to be seen in Tennyson's use of the word 'and' at the beginning of lines or sentences. I have counted over three hundred instances of this use, in which 'and' carries the emotional force of one of the stronger Greek enclitics, rather than the sequential force of the conjunction; it often introduces a proposition which does not follow logically from its predecessor but which, inevitably, we want to read as if it did. Thus an emotional formula appears disguised as an intellectual argument: it has to do this because no satisfactory argument has been found, because—indeed—the attempt to find such an argument is the subject of the poem. There are some good examples in the introductory stanzas:

(1) He thinks he was not made to die;
And thou hast made him; thou art just.
(2) They are but broken lights of thee;
And thou, O Lord, art more than they,
(3) For knowledge is of things we see;
And yet we trust it comes from thee.

In (1) it does not follow that man is immortal because (like the rest of creation) he is of divine origin and God is just: but emotionally it is central to the poem that this argument should work. Much, therefore, must be understood in that 'and': something like 'for after all, it is thou who hast made man and it would not be fair if thou hadst given him the power to believe himself immortal if in fact he is not'. In (2) the choice of 'and' as the linking word (rather than 'for' or 'since') helps to disguise the vagueness of the emotive line 'they are but broken lights of thee': the lines mean that man is fragmentary, God is wholeness, and a whole must be more than a part. A hypothesis is framed as a gnomic utterance. In (3) 'and yet' conceals some such argument as 'knowledge is of things we see, and our trouble is with the unseen; but God is unseen, and is the source of all knowledge, so why should he not send more knowledge and, ultimately, knowledge of the unseen too?' Tennyson is here offering a favourite speculation: that there is no reason why the causes of man's present despair should not one day be removed.

Such uses of 'and' can be seen as intensified emotive repetitions of a position reached in a previous proposition, carrying with them the force of a new step forward. Moreover, in many lines beginning with 'and' there is a suppressed verb which has to be understood from a previous line: the omission of these verbs contributes to the gnomic and opaque quality of many of the stanzas. Examples are 'and vacant chaff well meant for grain' (VI, 4), 'and those wild eyes that watch the wave' (XXXVI, 15), 'and such refraction of events as often rises ere they rise' (XCII, 16).

Thus the compressed, gnomic quality of so much of **In Memoriam** is often the result of syntactical ellipsis, or apposition, telescoping argument, as in the lines at the end of CVIII:

'Tis held that sorrow makes us wise,
Whatever wisdom sleeps in thee.

'Whatever' suggests that Tennyson does not know what kind of wisdom sleeps in Hallam, though elsewhere in the poem (e.g. in CXIII) there are attempts to define it. The vague generalised adjective combines with the negative verb 'sleeps' to produce a turning away from precision, a gesture towards the hopelessness of defining this important unknown. The two lines must of course be taken with what precedes them, where Tennyson says that all his attempts to scrutinise the mystery of things are 'barren faith' and 'vacant yearnings' and that he'll

rather take what fruit may be
Of sorrow under human skies:

but this does not help as much as it seems to. For if the poet would rather learn from his own grief than from Hallam's death ('the second state sublime'), why then should such store be set by Hallam's death? Several thoughts seem to be present at once: (1) a straight eighteenth-century type of antithesis, viz. '*we* can only be made wise by sorrow, but Hallam's wisdom (whatever its nature, and whether or not it be active), is achieved without sorrow'; (2) 'I don't know what kind of wisdom Hallam has, but in any case it is dormant, no use to me'; (3) (connecting up with the return of the same idea in CIX and CXIII) 'if I did not profit by Hallam's wisdom while he lived I cannot expect to do so now he is dead'; and (4) 'if Hallam had lived his wisdom would have helped not only me but the whole age; but now that wisdom is dormant so I can only hope it is true (as they say) that sorrow makes us wise, since this seems to be the only source of wisdom left to me'.

Elsewhere (in LXI) Tennyson does try to pursue Hallam's newly acquired wisdom, but the attempt falters:

> Tho' following with an upward mind
>   The wonders that have come to thee,
>   Thro' all the secular to-be,
> But evermore a life behind.

This suggests that Hallam's wisdom, far from being dormant, still sets the pace for the living. (The word 'secular' is used, as in LXXVI, in its nineteenth-century sense, of the long processes of change, and not in the older sense of 'age-long' given by Bradley—Tennyson would have come across the usage in Lyell's *Principles of Geology* from which an example is quoted in the *N.E.D.*). And the lines in LXXXII

> Eternal process moving on,
>   From state to state the spirit walks

again suggest the dead as active in wisdom and progress. We are told that they achieve insight into the processes of creation not yet fully revealed in time but one day to be revealed; meanwhile the dead can say

> I triumph in conclusive bliss
> And that serene result of all.

But in the first part of *In Memoriam* the partial insight of the living is more real to Tennyson than any speculation about the total insight of the dead. The pessimism of grief can be seen in that curious, baffled 'evermore' in 'evermore a life behind'. Tennyson feels Hallam is always going to have the advantage of his early death, he will always be the one who got there first; he has skipped the years of uncertainty to which Tennyson is condemned. One may dismiss this as simply another example of the humanist fallacy, an inability and a refusal to separate in the mind the two processes of time and eternity; but the confusion is a source of the very real emotional speculations in the first half of the poem, the sense of having been abandoned.

'Whatever' (in the lines just discussed) is one of the large number of negative qualifying words to be found in the early part of *In Memoriam,* where the vocabulary should be compared with that of 'The Two Voices'. They demonstrate the workings of a mind rather than its conclusions:

> I sometimes hold it half a sin
>   To put in words the grief I feel;
>   For words, like Nature, half reveal
> And half conceal the Soul within.

Where a modern poet might admit to a technical difficulty in expressing 'just what I mean'—

> Words strain,
> Crack and sometimes break under the burden

—Tennyson finds a moral and psychological difficulty. He is not even sure that so personal a grief ought to be expressed at all.

We must also distinguish between a genuine doubt as to the propriety of articulation where a profound personal feeling is concerned, and the conventional inarticulateness of the elegist working on commission. Donne for instance:

> Language thou art too narrow, and too weake
> To ease us now: great sorrow cannot speake.

And Tennyson himself, in some lines written to James Spedding on the death of his brother, had said

> Words weaker than your grief would make
> Grief more.

Although *In Memoriam* finishes by being a public poem Tennyson makes it clear that it started as a private one; he says it was begun, not to 'part and prove', not to close 'grave doubts and answers here proposed', but to express, so far as was possible, his own feelings and to find, in the mechanics of versified articulation (which by the mere fact of its *being* versified, necessarily carries with it a suggestion of feelings being arranged, like flowers in a vase) some relief from sorrow. Thus characteristically he anticipates, and deals with as part of the poem itself, any objections that may be raised as to its consistency or its finality. Rather, the poem is a door opening on to a sequence of vistas. It is the poem's therapeutic quality which is first emphasised: it is the end product of compulsive activity:

> But for the unquiet heart and brain
>   A use in measured language lies;
>   The sad mechanic exercise,
> Like dull narcotics, numbing pain.

(Thus 'I pipe but as the linnet sings' does not mean that the poem is naïve and artless but that he could not help writing it.)

Tennyson further stresses that beneath all our intellectual show we are essentially inarticulate, unable to find words (other than formulas of doubtful value) to express our deepest feelings. And when he speaks in the first part of the poem of trusting 'what I feel is Lord of all' it is the word 'feel' which asks to be stressed; and when he says 'I can but trust that good shall fall', in a stanza already discussed, he at once comments:

> So runs my dream: but what am I?
>   An infant crying in the night:
>   An infant crying for the light:
> And with no language but a cry.

The 'dream', the ultimate vision of reality, cannot be precisely articulated: the frightened child, like the 'man in wrath' who (in CXXIV) opposes his feelings to materialist theories, is inarticulate because he cannot help it. (And compare 'they called me fool, they called me child', in the crown of thorns poem.) Yet the child's cry and the angry man's claim that his feelings are not to be explained away by science, are both valid responses to experience.

In XIX Tennyson expands the earlier statement (in V) that words may afford some covering (both protective and definitive) to the nakedness of grief; here grief is compared to the tidal movements which affect the River Wye. As the deeper waters of the Severn flood into the Wye, the smaller river becomes silent, absorbed in the larger; at the ebb, the noises of the Wye itself are heard again. This double movement of waters is finely used to express the imperfect articulation of 'the deepest grief of all'. The tears that cannot fall are the real tears. As the poem proceeds, submerged feelings rise towards the surface, they 'rise in the heart' (see 'Tears, idle tears', in **The Princess**). The whole emphasis of the early part of the sequence is on the secretness of inner feeling, while later, this feeling gradually merges (and emerges) into a new view of experience.

This intense grief with which the poem begins seemed real to Tennyson but he clearly felt others might not find it justifiable. So the prayer in XIII

> Come, Time, and teach me, many years,
>   I do not suffer in a dream

is precise, and is precisely answered. What times teaches in the poem is not just that 'loss is common to the race' (a lesson which Tennyson rejects early in the sequence as irrelevant) but that it is a part of experience which, though it seemed to exist as a dream in a brain disordered by grief, is in fact something each man must master, assimilate and accept as part of the total pattern of human experience. Thus the poem is addressed both to the reader who comes to doubt but stays to understand, and to the poet himself, and one can see passages in which the one or the other audience is uppermost in the poet's mind. The poem's popularity shows that the Victorians felt Tennyson had not only done something for himself, turned loss into gain, which would have appealed to their practical sense, but had also done something for humanity at large. Individual experiences of loss are not weakened by repetition but intensified. The clamour of the indifferent, the false attempts to use scientific theory to discredit human hopes, only emphasise the importance of Tennyson's undertaking. And the final dismissal of theory by personal feeling in

> And like a man in wrath the heart
> Stood up and answer'd 'I have felt',

is significant because it is not *my* heart but the heart of man; so, too, in the closing poems of the cycle Tennyson changes from 'I' (I shall not lose thee tho' I die) to 'we': the pooling of experience increases the stature of man.

The poem has three time values. There is the present—grief and suffering—to which we must add that the poem's present is itself offered to the reader as a grief past and overcome. This is emphasised by the introductory stanzas, written in 1849, the year before the poem was published and sixteen years after it was begun: so that the words

> Forgive my grief for one remov'd . . .
> Forgive these wild and wandering cries

are among the first we read. Though addressed to 'the strong Son of God, immortal Love' they seem equally to be addressed to the reader, a characteristic attempt to forestall criticism.

The second time value is the past: memories of Hallam, arousing the nostalgia with which the poem is commonly associated ('thinking of the days that are no more'). There is finally the future: speculation as to Hallam's new state, the relation between the living and the dead, and a possible connection between man's gradual evolution on earth as a race and his instant evolution in heaven as an individual (see CXVIII discussed in Chapter 1).

The present is the felt and recorded desire to surrender to despair and the moral struggle not to (see for instance IV in which darkness and sleep, a 'type' of death, temporarily conquer the will). The past is places where Tennyson and Hallam were together, e.g. the Cambridge poem LXXXVII. The future is opaque, the battleground of faith and doubt, the realm of speculation which at first seems useless because irresoluble and is only gradually worked out into an acceptable pattern. It is here that Tennyson has to work hardest to reconcile personal feelings with, intellectual hypothesis. He feels it to be the poet's duty to do this, to set his personal feelings into the context of the whole of human experience, however distasteful (at first) or difficult the process seems. Thus, in XXXIV, he says that if there were no immortality the poet could set aside moral considerations and concentrate on aesthetic ones. The need to believe in a moral purpose in man's creation requires a corresponding sense of moral purpose in the poet. Death, and the grief it brings to the living, is at first noted as an intolerable evil, a black mark against the universe. In LV death is seen as part of the natural process and the wish to believe man an exception, an 'evil dream'. The poem's triumph is that it converts this evil dream into a dream of good, and finally into the total reality of man's experience.

> O yet we trust that somehow good
>   Shall be the final goal of ill

'O yet', that is, despite evidence to the contrary; 'somehow', that is, in ways of which science is still ignorant. Yet the imperative 'shall' observes that any other conclusion is intolerable, and points away from the tentative half-hearted faith of the opening poems (expressed in words like 'failing', 'faltering', 'grope', etc.) towards the triply repeated formula of acceptance, 'all is well', with which the poem ends and which recalls the words of Dame Julian of Norwich quoted at the end of T. S. Eliot's *Four Quartets*: 'and all shall be well'.

Thus **In Memoriam** is a journey from doubt and despair to acceptance, a journey through time and experience, in which past, present and future co-exist, and in which different modes of experience (memory, speculation, vision) all find a place. As T. S. Eliot says in *Burnt Norton* 'only through time time is conquered'; and again in *The Dry Salvages*:

> Here the impossible union
> Or spheres of existence is actual
> Here the past and future
> Are conquered and reconciled

At the start of the poem Tennyson wants to remain fixed in grief, in the total absorption of loss; he resists the processes of time by which grief may (and as time itself will show, must) be conquered. But he is not immediately prepared to

> reach a hand thro' time to catch
> The far-off interest of tears.

The idea of loss is central to the poem: financial imagery occurs in several places, e.g. gain, credit, influence-rich all occur in LXXX. Here, present loss may be eventual profit but Tennyson does not yet want to be comforted by borrowing on the doubtful security of this future dividend. Grief is his only immediate asset and he is not yet ready to risk it on a theory he has not yet tested. He repulses the 'victor hours' (the effects of time) and in the yew tree poem (II) seems ready to identify himself with the tree, as a symbol of unchanging gloom. One notices the word 'fail' at this point: the sense is that of the poet's life-processes running down in sympathy with Hallam's: there is a strong desire to 'cease'. So too in L, the prayer of the sinking soul, in which Tennyson anticipates his own death. In this poem, again, there is the feeling (helped by the monosyllables) of time being halted, natural processes being slowed down almost to a stop:

> Be near me when my light is low,
>   When the blood creeps and the nerves prick
>   And tingle; and the heart is sick,
> And all the wheels of Being slow . . .

This mood persists even after the return of Hallam's body to England and the burial. In XXVI, however, time begins to show its strength and the poet must struggle to keep his grief perpetually present. Can love survive time and separation? The desire (and the need) to prove that it can begins: the victor hours are already showing their hand:

> Still onward winds the dreary way;
>   I with it; for I long to prove
>   No lapse of moons can canker Love,
> Whatever fickle tongues may say.

In the early part of the sequence love is still identified with grief, grief seen as the only true evidence of enduring love: 'let love clasp grief lest both be drowned' in the victor hours poem precisely formulates the poet's early need: he 'still would grieve on'. But already in that characteristic 'I long to prove' the first doubt as to time's power to change one's feelings is, half apprehensively, admitted. Later in the same poem (XXVI) he says that if love does turn to indifference and there is no immortality, then he would despise his grief and wish for death. This idea is taken up again in XXXV, a subtler version of **'The Two Voices'**. The argument here is (1) even if all things die, it is still worth loving for love's own sake:

> Might I not say? 'Yet even here,
>   But for one hour, O Love, I strive
>   To keep so sweet a thing alive:'

But (2) the objection to this comes from love itself; the very nature of love would be altered if there were no immortality: love would be 'half dead to know that it would die'. And (3) the nineteenth-century evolutionists put in their warning:

> But I should turn mine ears and hear
>
> The moanings of the homeless sea,
>   The sound of streams that swift or slow
>   Draw down Aeonian hills and sow
> The dust of continents to be;

The known, reachable, comfortable limits of human life are contrasted with the formless and homeless sea, outside the control of *homo domesticus*. (One thinks of 'the unplumb'd salt estranging sea' in Arnold's 'Marguerite' and the desolation of his 'Dover Beach'.) The processes of creation seem to be on the wrong side. But (4) the poet rejects the fruitless hypothesis:

> If Death were seen
> At first as Death, Love had not been,
> Or been in narrowest working shut . . .

Tennyson here adduces his own experience of love as evidence for immortality. While paying lip-service to scientific formulas, he insists that man may be an exception to whatever rules these seem to prove. Otherwise, human love could never have been experienced. Here we must bear in mind Tennyson's deep sense of waste: so much love concentrated into so few years must somehow be made to go on being valuable; in the same way, the whole splendour of human achievement through history becomes pointless if man is a doomed race (see LVI). Throughout the poem Tennyson links the immortality of the individual with that of the race. Like the seventeenth-century elegists, he has to come to terms with a divine law which can cut good men off in their prime: will the same law, one day, cut off the whole race? The seventeenth century could draw a theological moral from premature death and even, with a little ingenuity, find in it a positive gain; but Tennyson, far more involved in Hallam than was Jonson in Salomon Pavy or Donne in Lord Harrington, finds it harder to take refuge in neat and pious formulas. Of course ***In Memoriam*** is not really about Hallam at all, but about Tennyson after Hallam's death. Thus it is his own intense feelings that at first prevent him from seeing Hallam's death (as Donne saw Harrington's) as some kind of triumphant achievement on Hallam's part. The triumph, when it comes, is Tennyson's rather than Hallam's. Donne used the elegy, as the patron would have required him to do, to praise the dead man; Tennyson specifically refuses to use ***In Memoriam*** to praise Hallam (see LXXV), partly because his achievement was less than his potential (a seventeenth-century elegist would have been expected to use all his literary skill to get round this, but Tennyson knew that the Victorian world

which credits what is done
Is cold to all that might have been);

and partly because he is unable to convey Hallam's qualities to those who did not know him (see XII). People must deduce those qualities from the strength of the poet's grief and love. It is not until near the end of the sequence, in the rather uninteresting poems CIX-CXI, that any attempt is made to describe Hallam. We then learn that he was a good critic, logical, moral, not ascetic, freedom-loving, beautiful, a good influence on others, and a gentleman. But the picture that emerges is too idealised, and comes too late in the poem, to be significant.

Tennyson makes it clear that while Hallam lived no thought of time's destroying their friendship entered his mind. In LXXXIV he supposes that, if Hallam had lived to old age and they had both died at roughly the same time, there would have been no problem: Christ would have taken them 'as a single soul'. But now the link is broken:

But thou art turn'd to something strange,
And I have lost the links that bound
Thy changes;

The words used here (in XLI) imply, as they must be intended to, the interruption of a happy and well-tried domestic routine which can never be resumed. In the longest poem in the sequence (LXXXV), in which Tennyson, with characteristic honesty and conscientiousness, excuses himself for again thinking of other, earthly friendships, the point is stressed that, however Hallam's new state is to be conjectured, nevertheless

in dear words of human speech
We two communicate no more.

From the grief of the living left behind Tennyson turns, in XLIV and some later poems, to the conjectured state of the dead. Perhaps after all the link may not be quite broken: the dead may retain images of their former life as well as their new knowledge. Tennyson suggests that these intimations of mortality may be comparable to the intimations received by the living either of a previous existence (but this primitive idea of reincarnation, though found in **'The Two Voices',** is dropped in *In Memoriam*) or of the earliest, forgotten days of life. During our first year after birth we have no conscious processes; then we begin to be self-conscious. Individualisation is a mental process. This is most interestingly stated in XLV:

The baby new to earth and sky,
    What time his tender palm is prest
    Against the circle of the breast,
Has never thought that 'this is I'.

But as he grows he gathers much,
    And learns the use of 'I' and 'me',
    And finds 'I am not what I see,
And other than the things I touch'.

So rounds he to a separate mind
    From whence clear memory may begin,
    As thro' the frame that binds him in
His isolation grows defined.

In these fine lines the word 'isolation' carries undertones of a sadness not strictly required, since its primary meaning here is purely technical (bio-physical). But Tennyson is also thinking of another kind of isolation. Love is the coming together of two isolates: thought-processes can only operate through language. In the last verse of this poem Tennyson draws a speculative conclusion:

This use may lie in blood and breath,
    Which else were fruitless of their due,
    Had man to learn himself anew
Beyond the second birth of Death.

This ties up with the feeling of waste which prompted the argument for immortality deduced from the preciousness of love; but the lines have a further implication: that if we never grew up on earth we should have to go through the process in heaven. Death must be an advance on life, not a mere repetition of it. Self-knowledge must be carried over and incorporated into the new knowledge, the 'conclusive bliss' and insight into 'that serene result of all' offered by death. But the use of 'may' suggests that Tennyson is not entirely happy about his hypothesis, though Shaw would not have found it absurd. Life involves considerable effort, and Tennyson does not want to feel that this effort is wasted: but it would not be wasted if (1) there were a 'second birth of death'; and (2) man carried over into this the habits formed in life. Man would be in a better position to concentrate on the new knowledge made available after death if he did not at the same time have to try to re-establish his own identity. In the preface to his evolutionary play *Back to Methuselah*, in which he seeks to replace Darwinism with the earlier theories of Lamarck (who believed that the life force, the will, not the blind force of natural selection, was the cause of evolution) Shaw writes 'the moment we form a habit we want to get rid of the consciousness of it so as to economise our consciousness for fresh conquests of life'. Like Shaw, Tennyson is constantly trying to put back into evolutionary theory the spiritual element which Darwinism, it seemed, was about to discard; like Shaw, too, he felt that the greatest stumbling-block to man's moral progress was the shortness of his life and the inevitability of his death. Only by getting over this obstacle could he see a way out of the mechanistic heresy; and he got over it by positing death as a development in the individual paralleling the development of the race on earth, rather as the embryo's nine months in the womb takes it through ages of natural selection from primitive cell to highly developed organism, yet still leaves it only at the beginning. So in **'The Ancient Sage'** he speculates:

Who knows? or whether this earth-narrow life
Be yet but yolk, and forming in the shell?

Like Shaw, Tennyson felt that human life must somehow be prolonged if it is not to be cruel and pointless, and this would have seemed particularly important when a man died young as Hallam did; he needed to feel that its unused potential ('the force that would have forged a name') was retained for some new activity:

> I know transplanted human worth
> Will bloom to profit otherwhere;

and again, in LXXV, he is thinking of the waste which, without an evolutionary immortality, Hallam's death must have been:

> But somewhere, out of human view,
>   What'er thy hands are set to do
> Is wrought with tumult of acclaim.

Tennyson cannot relinquish the idea of Gray's 'applause of list'ning senates to command', the

> Hands, that the rod of empire might have sway'd
> Or wak'd to ecstasy the living lyre.

Although Gray's dead missed high achievement by leading a quiet life not a short one, Hallam does become a village Hampden, a Cromwell guiltless of his country's blood; this is clear from LXIV, from which I quoted at the beginning of Chapter 1. In that poem Hallam, looking back from eternity upon his life on earth, is compared to a man of humble origins who has risen to high place while Tennyson, left behind on earth, becomes the boyhood friend who

> in the furrow musing stands:
> 'Does my old friend remember me?'

And in LX and XCVII Tennyson again casts himself in an inferior role and looks up to Hallam. All these poems emphasise the way in which Tennyson tries to think of Hallam's death as a success story, a kind of promotion. By advancing in heaven and not on earth Hallam finds achievement without its concomitant disappointments and misunderstandings. Like Adonais

> From the contagion of the world's slow stain
> He is secure.

But besides positing for Hallam the triumphs he missed on earth, Tennyson wants him also to remember the happy life they shared on earth, memories of which he himself still retains. Again, this is part of the feeling that nothing must be lost, that there must be continuity; what seems to have been lost must be seen as gain. Time lost is time wasted and the poem is a protest against that proposition. The link which seemed in the first time of grief to have been broken is replaced by 'some strong bond which is to be'.

I have said that it is wrong to think of Tennyson as a crude meliorist. He accepts the evidence of the evolutionists, but transferred to human history this requires (as scientists themselves saw) modification. The roar of traffic is not necessarily an improvement on the stillness of the central sea, but man must evolve to ever nobler ends since any other kind of change would be a counsel of despair. This cannot be proved, though man's previous record may be an argument in its favour, and attempts to prove it are gradually abandoned in favour of gestures towards the 'larger hope' and other vague and distant ends 'to which the whole creation moves'. Knowledge being concerned only with the phenomenal cannot help here, but wisdom can; and by this, as we have seen, Tennyson meant insight into moral law gained through experience, or, as he said in **'Oenone',** 'self-reverence, self-knowledge, self-control' (the last term recurs in the last stanza of *In Memoriam*). Thus we learn a kind of stretching out of human dignity beyond the present limits of science and what T. S. Eliot called 'the lifetime of one man only'.

The importance of love, which has directed the whole poem, is that it can make such leaps into the dark seem both intelligible and valuable. So the introductory stanzas are addressed to the 'Strong Son of God, immortal Love'. When Tennyson personifies God it is usually as Christ and usually periphrastically, as 'He that died in Holy Land' (compare *Lycidas,* 'Him who walked the waves').

Moreover, love is not a vague emotion but a powerful specific. In CXXVIII, Tennyson says that his love for Hallam is related to, but is greater than, faith in man's moral evolution—the second pillar upon which the poem's structure is built. He argues that if time is a mere process of change and decay it would offer man no hope: the so-called evolutionary process, instead of being a progress to ever nobler ends, would merely be the blind mutations of chance. Love, having been tested by experience, is stronger than faith in the related, but unverifiable, concept of spiritual evolution. Tennyson's love for Hallam has defied time and death: it is

> The love that rose on stronger wings,
> Unpalsied when he met with Death

And the line, stated twice in CXXVI, 'Love is and was my Lord and King', underlines the central significance of love, both as personal experience tested through time, and as a principle operating in the universe through Christ. What is to be admired in the poem is the way it reconciles a traditional renaissance individualism with the contemporary emphasis on the species: the close view and the long view.

Thus *In Memoriam* is itself an example of the process of moral evolution which it describes. Its value as a record of experience on the two levels of personal suffering and intellectual speculation, lies in the fact that it demonstrates how man can progress from despair both about the 'type' and about the 'single life' to a position in which both may be secured against destruction. In CXVII, another poem addressed to conquered time—the 'days and hours' which had at the beginning of the cycle seemed enemies of love—Tennyson again stresses his acceptance of his role in time. His ultimate meeting with Hallam, of which he is by now sure, will be 'fuller gain' (after the repeated use of the word 'loss' at the beginning of the cycle the use of 'gain' is significant)

> For every grain of sand that runs,
>   And every span of shade that steals,
>   And every kiss of toothed wheels
> And all the courses of the suns.

The stanza emphasises the poet's time-consciousness. He knows now that life has to be lived through moment by moment and that, until his life's end, he will be subject to the processes of time. But his 'proper place' is with Hallam: he reverts to the feeling of a broken link which must be renewed if his love is to have any meaning. He is prepared to be isolated from Hallam through time, but only because he believes that his love will be resumed beyond time.

Thus Tennyson reconciles two attitudes to the dead Hallam: his feeling, while he himself is still alive, that Hallam's presence can be felt by him as part of the universe; and his belief that, after his own death, 'I shall know him when we meet'. Hallam's metamorphosis, then, is itself subordinate to Tennyson's timebound state; it exists only in his mind as a means of turning grief into acceptance. When Tennyson himself quits time, he will no longer need to imagine Hallam as 'standing in the rising sun'. Thus (as is stated in CXXIX) Hallam is at once far off and near; part of a 'dream of good' and an immortal recognisable being waiting for Tennyson to follow him out of time. This I take to be the significance of the words

> Strange friend, past, present and to be;
> Loved deeplier, darklier understood.

Hallam is 'strange' because he now has a double existence: as part of Tennyson's timebound philosophy and as an eternal being existing outside time. Again, T. S. Eliot in the *Four Quartets* comes nearest of any later poet to expressing the complex idea resolved in *In Memoriam,* when he says

> See, now they vanish,
> The faces and places, with the self which, as it could,
>   loved them,
> To become renewed, transfigured, in another pattern.

Eugene R. August (essay date 1969)

SOURCE: August, Eugene R. "Tennyson and Teilhard: The Faith of *In Memoriam.*" *PMLA* 84, no. 2 (March 1969): 217-26.

[*In the following essay, August discusses Tennyson's depiction of faith in terms of nineteenth-century scientist Pierre Teilhard de Chardin's* The Phenomenon of Man, *concluding that while some critics condemn* In Memoriam *for failing to adequately portray faith, Tennyson is actually offering a radically modern depiction of it.*]

"*In Memoriam* can, I think, justly be called a religious poem . . . because of the quality of its doubt. Its faith is a poor thing, but its doubt is a very intense experience."[1] Thus, in the early years of this century did T. S. Eliot state the case for reading *In Memoriam* as a poem of doubt veneered by an inadequate faith. By calling the poem's faith "a poor thing," Eliot apparently meant two things. First, the faith was not deeply professed by Tennyson himself: "Tennyson's contemporaries . . . may have been taken in by it," Eliot says, "but I don't think that Tennyson himself was, quite: his feelings were more honest than his mind" (p. 187). And, second, the faith was poor because serious-thinking men today could see through its contradictions. "The hope of immortality," Eliot argues, "is confused (typically of the period) with the hope of the gradual and steady improvement of this world" (p. 186). Eliot's two points are related: the poem's faith is a poor thing because Tennyson was half aware that he had compromised his religious beliefs with the Philistine doctrine of material progress.

In one form or another these objections to the poem's faith have been leveled at *In Memoriam* since its publication. As early as the 1850's Matthew Arnold was reading it as a poem of doubt. In "The Scholar-Gipsy" (ll. 182-186), he drew a gloomy portrait of the author of *In Memoriam*:

> . . . and amongst us one,
> Who most has suffered, takes dejectedly
> His seat upon the intellectual throne;
> And all his store of sad experience he
>   Lays bare of wretched days.[2]

For Arnold, the poem's faith was too poor a thing to cure the strange disease of modern life.

In the twentieth century, Harold Nicolson argued that the real *In Memoriam* was to be found in the original, heart-wrung elegies lamenting Hallam's death, and not in "the theological treatise on the conflict between faith and doubt, religion and dogma, belief and science."[3] Hoping to make Tennyson palatable to a recalcitrant generation, Nicolson directed attention away from the "outdated" faith to the poignant lament for Hallam. He urged the reader to "forget the delicate Laureate of a cautious age; the shallow thought, the vacant compromise. . . . Let us recall only the low booming of the North Sea upon the dunes; . . . the cold, the half-light, and the gloom" (p. 306).

Later critics have not been kinder to the poem's faith.[4] E. D. H. Johnson feels that Tennyson's alienated vision is falsified by *In Memoriam*'s triumphant conclusion. Only half aware of the inadequate compromise he had effected, Tennyson "chooses to believe," according to Johnson, that he has "brought his poetry into tune with the spirit of the age."[5] Robin Mayhead, hostile to Tennyson as an artist, apparently regards it as a historical curiosity that anyone took the poem's faith seriously.[6] Even a sympathetic critic like Valerie Pitt winces over "Tennyson's half-comprehending and totally unconvincing reconciliation of the religious and the scientific conceptions of the universe."[7] Summing up the case against the poem's faith, George O. Marshall in the recent *Tennyson Handbook* states that *In Memoriam* no longer serves its purpose "of bolstering faith in the meaning of life."⁸ Quoting Eliot on the quality of the poem's doubt, Marshall concludes: "And so it seems to the twentieth century, which regards Tennyson as much more pessimistic than his contemporaries thought him to be" (p. 124). In short, the poem's faith is a poor thing.

This alleged inadequacy in the poem should be faced squarely. Tennyson intended the poem to portray a convincing resolution of doubt by faith. He called *In Memoriam* "the way of a soul," which was supposed to portray not only "the different moods of sorrow" but also "my conviction that fear, doubts, and suffering will find answer and relief only through Faith in a God of Love."⁹ If the poem's faith is a poor thing, then *In Memoriam* is badly flawed because it does not achieve the resolution that it is so obviously trying for. Moreover, its worth is diminished if present-day readers can discover nothing but antiquarian value in its faith. The faiths embodied in *The Divine Comedy* and *Paradise Lost* have relevance to modern man (as Dorothy L. Sayers and C. S. Lewis have so ably demonstrated),¹⁰ and clearly their value to us is thereby enhanced. About *In Memoriam*, therefore, the question should be honestly raised: can twentieth-century men who have lived through two world wars, Auschwitz and Hiroshima, Korea and Vietnam, still take seriously Tennyson's belief in progress and his hope of immortality? The question is not whether all men can share Tennyson's faith (for that is clearly impossible), but whether liberally minded men can accord it respect. Or, must modern readers reject the faith of *In Memoriam* as a poor thing, a shabby compromise between traditional religion and a belief in material progress?

This article proposes that the faith of *In Memoriam* is anything but a Victorian curiosity. On the contrary, it foreshadows a recent and dynamic strand of twentieth-century religious thought, perhaps best expounded by the priest-paleontologist Pierre Teilhard de Chardin. Linking Tennyson's name with Teilhard's will no doubt seem ludicrous to many. What can "the stupidest of English poets" have in common with "the Aquinas of the Atomic Age"? And yet, just as surely as Tennyson anticipated the religious doubt that Charles Darwin was to precipitate upon the Victorian era, so also did he anticipate the shape of the faith that Teilhard was to forge in the twentieth century from his synthesis of religion and science. Moreover, the way in which Tennyson prepares the reader to accept the poem's faith is similar to that used by Teilhard in his masterwork *The Phenomenon of Man*. In both thought and strategy, then, there is a bond between the two men.¹¹

Viewed in the light of Teilhard's work, the faith of *In Memoriam* can be seen more clearly for what it is—a faith so radically modern that many critics, thinking in more conventional terms, have mistakenly dismissed it as a poor thing.

II

Putting *In Memoriam* side by side with *The Phenomenon of Man* reveals their agreement on three crucial points: the importance of seeing the human phenomenon in the light of recent scientific knowledge, the nature of doubt that afflicts modern man, and the shape that belief must take if man is to survive. Often, what Tennyson as poet portrays in particular and personal terms is what Teilhard as scientist discusses in general ones. Finally, both works attempt in a similar way to awaken the reader's assent to their new vision of man.

In Memoriam is one of the few poems in which an attempt is made to see man as a biological phenomenon with a past, present, and future. Teilhard, at the start of *The Phenomenon of Man,* stresses the need for men to base their thought on the realities of the human phenomenon; either man will see, Teilhard says, or he will perish.¹² Tennyson, studying works like the *Principles of Geology*, the *Vestiges of Creation*, and the *Preliminary Discourse on the Study of Natural Philosophy*, was making this effort to see the phenomenon of man as contemporary science revealed it. In *In Memoriam* he is acutely aware that man's biological past stretches backward into the dim origins of life, that this planet is but a tiny globe spinning through an immeasurable universe, and that time and space are not comfortably tailored to man's measure:

> They say,
> The solid earth whereon we tread
>
> In tracts of fluent heat began,
>   And grew to seeming-random forms,
>   The seeming prey of cyclic storms,
> Till at the last arose the man.¹³

Tennyson, of course, does not have Teilhard's more advanced, firsthand scientific knowledge. Like most Victorians, he "thinks of science as entirely inductive and empirical; he has no inkling of the extent to which later science will be deductive and conceptual."¹⁴ He is uncertain, moreover, how the different species originated (Darwin's famous study was not published until nine years after the poem was), and he holds a somewhat confused concept of embryonic development.¹⁵ These vagaries, however, never eclipse the essential accuracy of his scientific view. Tennyson, as A. C. Bradley noted in 1929, is the only poet "to whose habitual way of seeing, imagining, or thinking, it makes any real difference that Laplace, or for that matter Copernicus, ever lived."¹⁶ When Tennyson asks us in *In Memoriam* to "contemplate all this work of Time" (CXVII.1), he is urging only what he himself has done throughout the poem.

The immediate result of this effort to see is a paralyzing doubt about the meaning of human existence. This doubt, recorded so vividly in *In Memoriam,* is the same malady described in *The Phenomenon of Man*. Teilhard points out that anxiety is the price modern man pays for seeing the world anew: "For our mind to adjust itself to lines and horizons enlarged beyond measure, it must renounce the comfort of familiar narrowness" (p. 225). To his credit, Tennyson had renounced the familiar narrowness of conventional concepts of the universe. But the result of this daring is evident in *In Memoriam*'s terrifying fear that man is an insignificant event in a purposeless universe. Teilhard calls this fear "the malady of space-time." "The whole psychology of modern disquiet," he says, "is linked with the sudden confrontation with space-time. . . . In the first and most widespread degree, the 'malady of space-time' manifests itself as a rule by a feeling of futility, of being crushed by the enormities of the cosmos" (pp. 225-226). There could be no better description of the doubt pervading *In Memoriam,* especially Sections LV and LVI where Tennyson desperately wonders: "Are God and Nature then at strife, / That Nature lends such evil dreams?" (LV.5-6).[17] So careless of the individual life, Nature implies that a man's individual existence is negligible. Worse, Nature has wiped out "a thousand types," implying that the whole human species is a foredoomed joke. In this absurd world, man—who can perceive the awful absurdity—is an evolutionary monstrosity:

> Dragons of the prime,
> That tare each other in their slime,
> Were mellow music match'd with him.
>
> (LVI.22-24)

Faced with such a horror, Tennyson can only exclaim: "O life as futile, then, as frail!" (LVI.25).

It is a mistake to argue that "despite numerous references to scientific ideas, despite [Tennyson's] anxiety to keep up to date with scientific progress, science has little or nothing to do with his best and most characteristic poetry."[18] On the contrary, the much-admired quality of doubt in *In Memoriam* has everything to do with science. Tennyson's doubt springs directly from "living" a boundless universe. "Which of us," Teilhard asks, "has ever in his life really had the courage to look squarely at and try to 'live' a universe formed of galaxies whose distance apart runs into hundreds of thousands of light years? Which of us, having tried, has not emerged from the ordeal shaken in one or other of his beliefs?" (p. 226). Tennyson tried to live the kind of universe Teilhard describes. Once, responding to his brother's fears about attending a dinner party, Tennyson remarked, "Fred, think of Herschel's great star-patches, and you will soon get over all that" (*Memoriam*, I, 20). In **"The Two Voices,"** Tennyson's small, still voice of Despair constantly alludes to man's insignificance in a boundless universe.[19] Early in *In Memoriam,* Sorrow voices the worst fear of the space-time malady when she whispers that the stars "blindly run" (III.5). Clearly "one or other" of Tennyson's beliefs had been badly shaken. The gloom of the lonely Lincolnshire poet, so rightly admired by Nicolson and others, stems partly from Tennyson's attempt to look squarely at and live Herschel's great star-patches.

The doubt of *In Memoriam,* of course, had particular as well as cosmic origins, and here again there is a parallel with Teilhard's experience. Arthur Hallam's apparently senseless death precipitated Tennyson's spiritual crisis by painfully straining the poet's belief in spiritual evolution. How could Nature be aiming at the evolution of finer men like Hallam when it wantonly destroyed the living Hallam in his youth? *In Memoriam* is largely the way of a soul trying to cope with the meaning of this death. This kind of experience was well known to Teilhard, and his work is at least partly a response to death's challenge to faith. When his friend Davidson Black died suddenly in 1934, Teilhard wrote:

> Today I am deeply aware of the call to rescue the world from the blackness of its materialism. You already know that Dr Black has died. The apparent absurdity of that untimely end, the noble but blind acceptance of this tragedy by his friends here, the complete absence of "light" on the poor body lying in that cold room at the Peiping Union Medical College—all these lent a leaden quality to my sadness, and revolted my spirit.
>
> Either there is an escape from death—somewhere—for an individual's thought, for his self-consciousness, or else the world is a hideous mistake. And if it is, then there is no use in our going on. But, since the uselessness of going on is an idea intolerable to everyone, the alternative must be to *believe.* To awaken this belief shall be, now more than ever, my task. I swear it. I have sworn it on the mortal remains of Davy, that more than brother of mine.[20]

In another letter, the priest wrote: "I miss Black very much. Missing him is like a shadow, or an emptiness that I carry wherever I go."[21] The similarity to the sorrow of *In Memoriam* should be obvious, for Tennyson also was aware that if there was not some escape from death, then the world is a hideous mistake.

Both Tennyson and Teilhard agree that if men cannot believe in survival after death, then human life, activity, and the entire evolutionary process will grind to a halt. If there is no chance that "life shall live for evermore," Tennyson says, then "earth is darkness at the core, / And dust and ashes all that is" (XXXIV.3-4). Teilhard argues that "the radical defect in all forms of belief in progress, as they are expressed in positivist credos, is that they do not definitely eliminate death" (pp. 269-270). Attacking those "positivist and critical" thinkers who say "that the new generation, less ingenuous than their elders, no longer believes in a future and in a perfecting of the world," Teilhard asks: "Has it even occurred to those who write and repeat these things that, if they were right, all spiritual movement on earth would be virtually brought to a stop? . . . Even on stacks of material energy, even under the spur of immediate fear or desire, *without the taste for life,* mankind would soon stop inventing and constructing for a work it knew to be doomed in advance" (pp. 230-231). As a basic wage for human effort, man needs to know, first, that there can be a "suitable outcome" to evolution and, second, that "there is for us, in the future, under some form or another, at least collective, not only continuation but also *survival*" (pp. 232-233). Without such a belief in progress and survival, man is doomed. "If progress is a myth," Teilhard writes, "that is to say, if faced by the work involved we can say: 'What's the good of it all?' our efforts will flag. With that the whole of evolution will come to a halt—because we are evolution" (p. 231).

This paralysis of human effort is exactly what afflicts Tennyson in *In Memoriam*. As usual, the poet depicts in personal terms what the scientist has discussed in general ones. The very first poem of *In Memoriam* presents this paralysis:

> I held it truth, with him who sings
>   To one clear harp in divers tones,
>   That men may rise on stepping-stones
> Of their dead selves to higher things.
>
> But who shall so forecast the years
>   And find in loss a gain to match?
>   Or reach a hand thro' time to catch
> The far-off interest of tears?

The preterite "held" indicates that Tennyson can no longer share Goethe's belief in spiritual progress and survival.[22] Who can forecast the years and see whether evolution will have a suitable outcome? Who can honestly affirm that a man can evolve spiritually in this life and the next, catching the far-off interest of his tears and rising thereby to higher things? Or, even if there is material progress, if there is no survival, what comfort is it to the man living now to know that the yet-unborn will find a gain in his loss? Under such conditions, Tennyson can only give himself over to the calm despair and wild unrest that live in woe (XI, XV, XVI). His whole life becomes virtually paralyzed, with only "the sad mechanic exercise" of verse-making to numb his pain (V).

The belief that there is no human survival is portrayed by both Tennyson and Teilhard as a disabling fear that death may be stronger than love. Again, Tennyson expresses this fear at the very outset of *In Memoriam*: in the latter half of the first poem, he says:

> Let Love clasp Grief lest both be drown'd,
>   Let darkness keep her raven gloss.
>   Ah, sweeter to be drunk with loss,
> To dance with Death, to beat the ground,
>
> Than that the victor Hours should scorn
>   The long result of love, and boast,
>   'Behold the man that loved and lost,
> But all he was is overworn.'

With the passage of time, Tennyson guesses that his love for Hallam will ebb away and that the dead man will not survive even in the poet's affections. Love, Teilhard says, "becomes impoverished with remoteness in space—and still more, much more, with difference in time. For love to be possible there must be co-existence" (p. 269). But precisely because Tennyson cannot at first conceive that the dead Hallam is coexistent, he is appalled at the prospect of love's impoverishment as time draws the two men farther apart. Teilhard speaks of love as spiritual energy, but if this energy is perpetually diminished by time, man will suffer what Teilhard calls the "sickness of the dead end—the anguish of feeling shut in" (p. 228). Once more, man will sense that the "earth is darkness at the core, / And dust and ashes all that is."

The cure for this sickness lies in faith. But faith in what? Certainly not popular Christianity, with its literal reading of Genesis, its antiquated theologies, and its fierce sectarianism. That kind of Christianity cannot cure the space-time malady because (among other reasons) it refuses to see the phenomenon of man squarely. But neither Tennyson nor Teilhard rejects Christianity because some forms of it are too narrow. Instead, both men grope toward a renewed understanding of Christianity: they search for what Newman calls legitimate developments of Christian doctrine. In both Tennyson and Teilhard the shape of these developments is strikingly similar.

For one thing, both men believe in progress. So too do many other people. The important thing, however, is that Tennyson and Teilhard mean much the same thing by progress, namely spiritual growth or what Teilhard calls "hominisation"—which he defines as "the progressive phyletic spiritualisation in human civilisation of all the forces contained in the animal world" (p. 180). Too often Tennyson is regarded as the Lord Macaulay of Victorian verse, hymning the imminent brave new world of technological prosperity. But for Tennyson progress means primarily something else:

> Let knowledge grow from more to more,
>   But more of reverence in us dwell;
>   That mind and soul, according well,
> May make one music as before,
>
> But vaster.
>
>   (Prologue, ll. 25-29)

Tennyson does not disparage material progress, and he does want knowledge to grow from more to more. But he introduces another, more important concept of progress: the growth of reverence for some ideal manhood—in this case, the "Strong Son of God" of the Prologue. In short, Tennyson looks toward the spiritual perfection of man's humanity: "the valiant man and free, / The larger heart, the kindlier hand" (CVI.29-30).[23] Teilhard's concept of progress is similar. He too wants knowledge to grow from more to more; in fact, the increase of knowledge is one of the prerequisites of human progress (pp. 248-250). But he also believes that knowledge must contribute to increased *hominisation*. To Teilhard, progress also means increased reverence for the highest, holiest manhood. As man learns to direct his own evolution, Teilhard says, he must choose to grow into what he worships (pp. 283-285). For Teilhard, as for Tennyson, this ideal manhood is found in Christ.

Thus, both Tennyson and Teilhard believe that evolution has shifted from a biological natural selection to a spiritual growth which is partly man-controlled. In man, evolution has become conscious of itself, Teilhard says, and "for an elementary part *we hold it in our hands,* responsible for its past to its future" (p. 225). It is up to men to perfect the process of *hominisation*. This belief is precisely what Tennyson has in mind in passages like this:

>   Arise and fly
>   The reeling Faun, the sensual feast;
>   Move upward, working out the beast,
>   And let the ape and tiger die.[24]
>
>   (CXVIII.25-28)

To both Tennyson and Teilhard, then, progress means *hominisation,* that is, men rising on stepping stones of their dead selves to higher things.

Both agree that man's spiritual growth cannot take place in isolation. As **In Memoriam** progresses, Tennyson comes to realize that sorrowing in solitude cuts him off from the life of the world: he learns he must escape the Palace of Sorrow just as surely as the artist's soul must escape the Palace of Art. When, after much struggle, he finally declares in Poem CVIII.1-3,

>   I will not shut me from my kind,
>   And, lest I stiffen into stone,
>   I will not eat my heart alone,

he has made an important decision to return to life with others here on earth. For Teilhard, isolation is a blind alley to be avoided: "No evolutionary future awaits man except in association with all other men" (p. 246).[25] He condemns ideas of egocentric, racial, or national survival and exalts the concept of mega-synthesis, "the 'super-arrangement' to which *all* the thinking elements of the earth find themselves . . . subject" (p. 244; italics mine).

Both men recognize that spiritual progress will suffer setbacks and will take a long, long time. Both men feel that discouragement at the slow rate of improvement is, in Teilhard's words, "a feeling to be overcome" (p. 254). Contrary to what some critics have written, Tennyson does not believe that Utopia is just around the corner:

>   No doubt vast eddies in the flood
>   Of onward time shall yet be made.
>
>   (CXXVIII.5-6)

The consummation of the earth is a *far-off,* divine event.[26] Teilhard also recognizes that man has a long way to go, and he warns against feeling discouraged because of this: "After all half a million years, perhaps even a million, were required for life to pass from the pre-hominids to modern man. Should we now start wringing our hands because, less than two centuries after glimpsing a higher state, modern man is still at loggerheads with himself?" (p. 255). For Tennyson also, discouragement is a feeling to be overcome. By refusing to shut himself from his kind, he takes a step to free himself from the anxiety that comes of realizing that "mankind is as yet on one of the lowest rungs of the ladder" (*Memoir,* I, 324). In Poem CXXVII.1-4, he has achieved the overview that banishes discouragement:

>   And all is well, tho' faith and form
>   Be sunder'd in the night of fear;

>   Well roars the storm to those that hear
>   A deeper voice across the storm.

Both men are concerned with the problem of finding a faith for the here-and-now. Despite their attention to the goal of evolution, neither forgets that faith is valid only if it works *in the present* to nourish living men in their endeavors for the future. Once men believe that evolution can have a suitable outcome, then they can begin to work toward that outcome. With his new-found faith, Tennyson finds that he can turn from writing elegies in solitude and can move on (like the "rude swain" of Milton's *Lycidas*) to "fresh Woods and Pastures new."[27] In Poem CVI.19-20, Tennyson calls upon the New Year bells to "Ring out, ring out my mournful rhymes, / But ring the fuller minstrel in." Similarly, Teilhard realizes that without a particular kind of faith mankind will "go on strike," refusing the effort needed to move evolution forward (p. 305). His concern is that men should see the necessity for striving in the present, and his work is dedicated to curing the paralysis of will caused by the space-time malady. Tennyson makes the same point in Poem CXXVIII: if the changes wrought by time are merely deceptions posing as progress, then man could only scorn the whole evolutionary process. But because Tennyson can see that all is "toil cöoperant to an end" (l. 24), he can return confidently to fruitful activity.

There are, then, profound similarities between the faiths of Tennyson and Teilhard. They both believe that progress must now be spiritual, that man is at least partly responsible for the direction evolution will take, that man must grow in conjunction with all other men, that the process of *hominisation* has only begun, and that discouragement at this thought must be overcome for man to work fruitfully in the present.

We are now in a position to recognize one of the fundamental misunderstandings that led T. S. Eliot to judge the faith of **In Memoriam** as a poor thing. Tennyson, Eliot believes, tried to effect a compromise between "the religious attitude" and the Philistine belief that a materialistic Utopia was near at hand.[28] But, Eliot continues, Tennyson sensed that God and Mammon could not both be served and was not quite taken in by the very compromise he tried to effect. Eliot writes: "There is evidence elsewhere—even in an early poem, **Locksley Hall,** for example—that Tennyson by no means regarded with complacency all the changes that were going on about him in the progress of industrialism and the rise of the mercantile and manufacturing and banking classes. . . . Temperamentally, he was opposed to the doctrine that he was moved to accept and to praise."[29]

Clearly, Eliot has misjudged Tennyson's concept of progress. Tennyson never connected human perfectibility with "the progress of industrialism and the rise of the mercantile and manufacturing and banking classes." Nor did he ever believe that an imminent Utopia was taking shape in "all the changes that were going on about him." Poem CVI ("Ring out, wild bells") is almost a summary of Tennyson's idea of progress, and it is hardly a celebration of industrialism and the rise of the Philistines. Eliot has failed to distinguish between the Philistine "doctrine" of materialistic progress which Tennyson opposed and the "doctrine" of spiritual progress that he accepted and praised. This failure to distinguish between the two concepts of progress undermines Eliot's conclusion about the quality of faith in *In Memoriam.*

But to return to Tennyson and Teilhard. As persons, both men share significant characteristics. Both have a strong dash of the mystic, both have a lifelong interest in science, and both see the world from this double perspective. Both men renounce "systems" of thought. Tennyson's famous statement in the Prologue (ll. 17-18), "Our little systems have their day; / They have their day and cease to be," is paralleled by Teilhard's disclaimer in the Foreword to *The Phenomenon of Man*: "So please do not expect a final explanation of things here, nor a metaphysical system" (p. 35). Later he says, "Besides, I know the danger of trying to construct a lasting edifice with hypotheses which are only expected to last for a day, even in the minds of those who originate them" (p. 39).[30] Both men are acutely aware that knowledge grows from more to more. In both men, however, this relativity is balanced by faith in an Absolute. Both look to the future and see man evolving toward a "crowning race . . . No longer half-akin to brute" (Epilogue, ll. 128-133), or—to use Teilhard's words—toward the "hyper-personal" at Point Omega.

Both *In Memoriam* and *The Phenomenon of Man* are concerned with a faith beyond the forms of faith. Neither work seems overtly permeated by Christianity, but both are (in the authors' opinions) valid developments of it. Both men believe in a cosmic Christianity and a Christ beyond the merely sectarian Christs. Throughout *The Phenomenon of Man* Teilhard speaks primarily as a religiously neutral sage, naming the evolutionary goal as the "hyperpersonal" or "Omega." Only in the Epilogue does he equate Omega with a Christ who is both the historical Jesus and the cosmic Person toward whom the whole creation moves. Tennyson sometimes speaks of the evolutionary goal in Christian terms, such as, "the Christ that is to be" (CVI.32), but more often he too uses religiously neutral terms, such as, "the Power in darkness whom we guess" (CXXIV.4). The Prologue to *In Memoriam,* written last, is the most openly Christian part of the poem, yet it too shies away from sectarian Christianity and points instead to a Christ who is both personal and cosmic. Tennyson's Prologue, however, is no more an inconsistency or an afterthought than Teilhard's Epilogue.

The Prologue to *In Memoriam* has especially puzzled many readers, but an understanding of Tennyson's cosmic Christianity helps to clarify some of its difficulties. Critics have objected to the Prologue for frequently contradictory reasons. For some, like Henry Sidgwick, "Faith, in the introduction, is too completely triumphant" (*Memoir,* I, 304). For others, it is not nearly triumphant enough, particularly in lines like: "Thou madest man, he knows not why, / He *thinks* he was not made to die" (ll. 10-11; italics mine). To some critics, the Prologue is too Christian: "There is nothing especially Christian in [the Epilogue's] creed of a dimly defined Deity and the progress of the universe toward some remote goal He purposes," writes Eleanor Mattes, "whereas the Prologue is in the form of a prayer to Christ, 'Strong Son of God, immortal Love,' the Word who was God's agent in the Creation."[31] To others, the Prologue is not Christian enough, especially when Tennyson apparently hesitates to affirm Christ's dual nature: "Thou *seemest* human and divine" (l. 13; italics mine). Dissatisfaction with the Prologue has caused some critics to dismiss it as an afterthought or as a muddled attempt to quiet Emily Sellwood's fears about Tennyson's religious beliefs.

But is there such confusion in the Prologue? And is there really such a discrepancy between its Christianity and the faith expressed in the rest of the poem? Not if we recognize that Tennyson is praying to a cosmic Christ—and not to the sectarian Christs preached by the churches of his day. Tennyson's Christ-that-is-to-be is a Christ to be found "when Christianity without bigotry will triumph, when the controversies of creeds shall have vanished" (*Memoir,* I, 326). Tennyson's Christ is larger than the "little systems" of nineteenth-century sectarianism can picture.

The paradox remains, however: even while affirming Christ's dual nature in the Prologue (Christ is both the "Strong Son of God" and "the highest, holiest manhood"), Tennyson avoids a clear-cut assertion of the doctrine by saying that Christ *seems* human and divine. The contradiction is partly resolved when we see that Tennyson's hesitancy reflects his abhorrence of theological squabbling, especially about the Incarnation. "He disliked discussion on the Nature of Christ," Tennyson's son reports, "'seeing that such discussion was mostly unprofitable, for none knoweth the Son but the Father'" (*Memoir,* I, 326). Furthermore, Tennyson was aware, as Newman was, that Christian doctrine would develop through the centuries. He knew that men might come to understand the Incarnation differently than most nineteenth-century Christians did. For Tennyson, "the forms of Christian religion would alter; but . . . the spirit of Christ would still grow from more to more 'in the roll of the ages'" (*Memoir,* I, 326).[32] The Prologue is the prayer of a man who poises belief with an awareness that his form of belief is not the last word on the subject.[33]

To say this, however, is not to say that Tennyson is hopelessly muddled in his belief. T. S. Eliot, who holds this view, writes that Tennyson "was desperately anxious to hold the faith of the believer, without being very clear about what he wanted to believe: he was capable of illumination which he was incapable of understanding. The 'Strong Son of God, immortal Love', with an invocation of whom the poem opens, has only a hazy connexion with the Logos, or the Incarnate God."[34] Examined closely, Eliot's complaint is basically that Tennyson's belief is not defined in familiar, first-century terms and is therefore vague.

But Tennyson was aware that first-century definitions of faith were sometimes derived from outmoded concepts of the world and needed to be re-expressed in modern terms for modern man. Teilhard explains the situation in this way:

> During the first century of the Church, Christianity made its decisive entry into human thought, boldly assimilating the Jesus of the Gospels to the Logos of Alexandria. We cannot fail to see the logical sequel to this gesture and the prelude to a similar success in the instinct which is today impelling the faithful, two thousand years later, to adopt the same tactics—not, this time, with the ordering principle of the static Greek kosmos, but with the neo-Logos of modern philosophy—the evolutionary principle of a universe in movement.[35]

Tennyson in *In Memoriam* is following that instinct to assimilate the historical Jesus with the neo-Logos of an evolving universe. The "hazy connexion" between the Christ of Tennyson's Prologue and the first-century Logos is Eliot's misunderstanding of the direction in which Tennyson's belief is tending: like Teilhard, Tennyson is trying to transpose belief out of "a field of thought that most modern people have left behind them."[36]

The Prologue, and indeed the whole of *In Memoriam*, indicates that Tennyson could have assented more readily to Teilhard's cosmic Christ than to the Christs preached by nineteenth-century clergymen unaware of or hostile to the world-view opened up by science. In Tennyson's day, little attention was devoted to the cosmic aspects of Pauline and Johannine teaching, and few—if any—theologians attempted to synthesize this cosmic Christianity with the recent scientific discoveries.[37] The result was, of course, that the nineteenth century produced no Aquinas to whom Tennyson could play Dante. *In Memoriam* was intended to be "a kind of *Divina Commedia*" (*Memoir*, I, 304), but Tennyson was well aware that no Angelic Doctor had appeared to reconcile "faith and form . . . sunder'd in the night of fear" (CXXVII.1-2).

Ultimately, Tennyson and Teilhard see the universe in a process of *Christogenesis,* that is, an attempt to give birth to Christ again by evolving *AfterChrists*—to borrow Hopkins' word. There is little doubt that the three Christmases which serve as crucial landmarks in *In Memoriam* form a leitmotif emphasizing the new birth of Christ with which the universe is in labor. Like St. Paul in Romans viii.18-27, Tennyson and Teilhard see Nature suffering birth pangs, trying to give birth to a Christ-that-is-to-be, a "Jesus, the centre towards whom all moves."[38]

Both Tennyson and Teilhard see love as the spiritual energy that moves creation toward its new birth. Teilhard argues that love has a long evolutionary history: "If there were no internal propensity to unite, even at a prodigiously rudimentary level—indeed in the molecule itself—it would be physically impossible for love to appear higher up, with us, in 'hominised' form" (p. 264). Teilhard sees love as the sign of successful "involution" in the universe: love is "the more or less direct trace marked on the heart of the element by the psychical convergence of the universe upon itself" (p. 265). Thus, human love—in all its varied forms—is the highest evolutionary manifestation of the energy that drives creation toward universal convergence and is itself the sign of that movement.

Again, what the scientist speaks of in general terms, the poet portrays in personal ones. When Tennyson speaks of love, he usually means his own love for Hallam: this is the love that he fears in Poem I will be drowned unless it clings to grief. But as Tennyson becomes increasingly aware in *In Memoriam* that the dead Hallam is (to use Teilhard's term) "co-existent" with himself, he discovers that love is stronger than death. His love has not been impoverished by remoteness in space or difference in time, as the experience of Poem XCV demonstrates. With this awareness, Tennyson can again believe in a cosmic love that can bring about a suitable outcome to evolution:

> The love that rose on stronger wings,
> Unpalsied when he met with Death,
> Is comrade of the lesser faith
> That sees the course of human things.
>
> (CXVIII.1-4)

Tennyson has come to recognize that his own love for Hallam is a particular, direct trace of the universal psychical convergence. If his love for Hallam can survive death and can grow into "vaster passion," then there is hope that the larger, cosmic pattern of convergence can be fulfilled: "Behold, I dream a dream of good, / And mingle all the world with thee" (CXXIX.11-12).

It is no "semantic sleight-of-hand" when Tennyson, in the Prologue, identifies "immortal Love" with Christ.[39] Just as Dante sees in his love for Beatrice a reflection of and a participation in the Love that moves the sun and other stars, so also Tennyson comes to see in his love for Hallam a reflection of and a participation in the immortal Love toward whom the whole creation moves. For Tennyson, love is ultimately a Person—Christ in the Prologue, God in the Epilogue. And here again he agrees with Teilhard. For Teilhard, Omega is in the final analysis a "supremely attractive" Person, whom he names God-Omega (p. 287) and Christ (p. 297).

The identification of Love with Christ in the Prologue of *In Memoriam* should awaken us to hints that appear in the body of the poem: if we read carefully, we can see Tennyson working toward this identification within the poem. (The process resembles that in Newman's *Apologia*: at the outset, we know that Newman is going to identify truth with Roman Catholic doctrine, and as we read, we watch him working toward that identification.) Throughout *In Memoriam* itself, Tennyson focuses on Hallam, but the figure of Christ is always present in the background.[40] Hallam, Tennyson comes to recognize, is "a noble type" of the ideal man, an *AfterChrist* or *BeforeOmega*, who awakens Tennyson to "the highest, holiest manhood" found in

Christ. It is fitting, therefore, that Hallam's birthday be celebrated as another Christmas, as it indeed is in Poem CVII. As *AfterChrist,* Hallam shares the human-divine nature (CXXIX.5); as *BeforeOmega,* he reconciles God and Nature, thereby indicating in his own self that evolution can have both a suitable outcome and a focus (CXXX). The dead Hallam thus shows forth the divine love to Tennyson just as the dead Beatrice did to Dante. Like the just man in Hopkins' sonnet, Hallam "acts in God's eye what in God's eye he is— / Christ."[41] Teilhard explains the process this way: in order for man to love Omega, this supremely attractive Prime Mover Ahead must somehow be present to man now. Space and time impoverish love, Teilhard says; therefore, "to be supremely attractive, Omega must be supremely present" (p. 269). In **In Memoriam** Tennyson discovers that Christ-Omega is supremely present in Hallam. Thus, to both Tennyson and Teilhard, the focus of evolution is at times in sight even now, and this vision of the end, present even now, enables men to continue striving toward the one far-off divine event at Point Omega.

III

In addition to the similarity of vision shared by Tennyson and Teilhard, there is also a similarity of technique. Neither man attempts merely to argue the reader into assent. Both are aware, with Newman, that "the whole man" is involved in Real Assent. Rational or logical arguments can win National Assent, that is, agreement to intellectual propositions. To win Real Assent, the whole man must be engaged and must share the same vision as the writer. This is what both Tennyson and Teilhard attempt to do. **In Memoriam** has its "structure" of sorts, *The Phenomenon of Man* has its "rational" framework, but both works recreate experiences which the reader shares. By living through the same experiences as the writer, the reader is slowly led to accept the same conclusions that the writer was forced to accept. There is nothing deceptive about this persuasive technique: the writer uses art to revivify the experience which led him to his faith; the reader, by reading the work, is put through a similar experience and is led to assent (if he can) to the writer's beliefs.

Teilhard is not just a philosopher whose thought can be epitomized. Rather, he is a sage with a vision to communicate. In the Foreword to *The Phenomenon of Man* he says that his work "may be summed up as an attempt *to see* and *to show* what happens to man, and what conclusions are forced upon us, when he is placed fairly and squarely within the framework of phenomenon and appearance" (p. 31). Like the Victorian sages discussed by John Holloway, Teilhard's "main task is to quicken his reader's perceptiveness; and he does this by making a far wider appeal than the exclusively rational appeal.... He gives expression to his outlook imaginatively."[42] In Teilhard's book, the reader is given an overview of the phenomenon of man, from its primitive origins in the "stuff of the universe," to its present spiritual crisis, to its future evolution. This survey, however, is more than just a scientific treatise; it is an artistically constructed narrative told by a skillfully created persona. When, for example, Teilhard concludes a section of his book with the solemn words, "Thought is born" (p. 160), this brief dramatic sentence is a carefully prepared-for climax, designed to awaken in the reader a sense of the awesomeness of what has happened. Images are used to clarify and actualize abstract concepts; some images, like "the great spiral of life," form leitmotifs. Words are used connotatively as well as denotatively. For example, discussing the "noosphere," the envelope of thought and culture that man lives in, Teilhard concludes:

> With that [awareness of the noosphere] it bursts upon us how utterly warped is every classification of the living world . . . in which man only figures logically as a *genus* or a new family. This is an error of perspective which deforms and uncrowns the whole phenomenon of the universe. To give man his true place in nature it is not enough to find one more pigeon-hole in the edifice of our systemisation or even an additional order or branch. With hominisation, in spite of the insignificance of the anatomical leap, we have the beginning of a new age. The earth 'gets a new skin.' Better still, it finds its soul.
>
> (p. 182)

Even in translation, the passage bristles with emotion evoked to a great extent by skillful word choices. This is hardly the place for an extended study of the art of *The Phenomenon of Man,* but any account of the book must recognize that art is a fundamental part of its effort to win the reader's assent.

Similarly, Tennyson uses art to reconstruct his own experiences after Hallam's death. With Tennyson—or, more accurately, with the speaker in the poem—the reader relives the shock of loss, the collapse of faith, the struggle to achieve emotional balance, the slowly dawning awareness of hope and faith, the mystical intuitions, and the final release of returning joy. Tennyson also uses art to show man placed squarely within the framework of phenomenon and appearance. Like Teilhard, he attempts to make us *see* the work of time. When the poem has been experienced, the reader can understand at least how the speaker has achieved his final faith. But perhaps the reader will also recognize the inherent rightness of that faith. If the poet's vision is valid, if his art is skillful, and if the reader's mind and heart are right, then there is a good chance that poet and reader will be in accord when the poem reaches its conclusion.

In any event, it is time to re-evaluate the quality of faith in **In Memoriam.** If Teilhard's "work gives our generation the comprehensive view it sorely needs," as Arnold J. Toynbee says, then the faith of **In Memoriam**—with its many resemblances to Teilhard's vision—cannot be dismissed as a poor thing.

Notes

1. T. S. Eliot, "In Memoriam," *Essays Ancient and Modern* (London, 1936), p. 187.

2. *The Poems of Matthew Arnold,* ed. Kenneth Allott (New York, 1965), p. 341. See Allott's note to ll. 182-190 identifying Tennyson as the poet referred to in these lines.

3. *Tennyson: Aspects of His Life, Character, and Poetry,* rev. ed. (Garden City, N. Y., 1962), p. 299. This book was originally published in 1923.

4. Some notable exceptions: Basil Willey, "Tennyson," *More Nineteenth Century Studies: A Group of Honest Doubters* (New York, 1966); Jerome Hamilton Buckley, *Tennyson: The Growth of a Poet* (Boston, 1965); and Carlisle Moore, "Faith, Doubt, and Mystical Experience in *In Memoriam,*" VS [*Victorian Studies*], VII (1963), 155-169.

5. *The Alien Vision of Victorian Poetry* (Hamden, Conn., 1963), p. 21.

6. "The Poetry of Tennyson," *From Dickens to Hardy,* ed. Boris Ford (Harmondsworth, Middlesex, 1958), pp. 243-244, n. 13.

7. *Tennyson Laureate* (Toronto, 1963), p. 101.

8. New York, 1963, p. 122.

9. Quoted in Hallam Lord Tennyson, *Alfred Lord Tennyson: A Memoir,* I (New York, 1897), 304-305—hereafter cited as *Memoir.*

10. See especially Dorothy L. Sayers' introductions and notes to *The Comedy of Dante Alighieri the Florentine,* trans. Dorothy L. Sayers and Barbara Reynolds, 3 vols. (Baltimore, 1949-62); and C. S. Lewis, *Preface to* Paradise Lost (New York, 1961).

11. There is no question of "influence" here: Tennyson did not influence Teilhard any more than he influenced Darwin. On Tennyson's anticipating Darwin, see Willey, "Tennyson," *More Studies,* p. 87, and Buckley, *Tennyson,* p. 121.

12. Pierre Teilhard de Chardin, *The Phenomenon of Man,* tr. Bernard Wall (New York, 1961), p. 31. Unless otherwise noted, all references to Teilhard's writing are to this text.

13. *In Memoriam* CXVIII.7-12. All quotations from Tennyson's poetry are taken from *Works,* ed. Hallam Lord Tennyson, 6 vols. (New York, 1908).

14. Buckley, *Tennyson,* p. 276, n. 16.

15. Willey, "Tennyson," *More Studies,* pp. 83-84.

16. *A Miscellany* (London, 1929), p. 31.

17. Throughout the paper Tennyson is referred to as the speaker in the poem. An absolute identification of author and speaker is questionable, however, because the poem is not strictly autobiographical. See *Memoir,* I, 304.

18. Mayhead, "Tennyson," *From Dickens to Hardy,* p. 239.

19. See, e.g., ll. 22-30.

20. Quoted in Claude Cuénot, *Teilhard de Chardin,* tr. Vincent Colimore (Baltimore, 1965), p. 158.

21. Quoted in Cuénot, p. 158.

22. For the identification of "him who sings," see *Memoir,* II, 391 and n. With the reading of Poem I given here, cf. Lore Metzger, "The Eternal Process: Some Parallels Between Goethe's *Faust* and Tennyson's *In Memoriam,*" *Victorian Poetry,* I (1963), 189-196.

23. Cf. *Locksley Hall Sixty Years After,* l. 276: "Forward, till you see the highest Human Nature is divine."

24. Valerie Pitt objects to this passage: "The modern mind can scarce endure this; moral endeavor is not its ideal, and it recognises that the energies of the ape and tiger are not without their place in the higher life of man" (*Tennyson Laureate,* pp. 113-114). It is difficult to quarrel with generalizations about "the modern mind," but Basil Willey apparently disagrees with Miss Pitt about it: "We have rightly learned from the nineteenth century that man must make himself, and be the changer as well as the product of his own environment. But we must also learn that if man makes himself wholly in his own image, he may find that like Frankenstein he has created his own destroyer" ("Origins and Development of the Idea of Progress," *Ideas and Beliefs of the Victorians,* New York, 1966, p. 39).

Also, has Miss Pitt confused Tennyson's tiger with Blake's? To Tennyson, the ape and tiger in *In Memoriam* represent only unreflecting animalism. Is it accurate to see in them energies that have their place in the higher life of man? Do they not function much as Dante's leopard, lion, and she-wolf do in Canto i of Hell, that is, as symbols of what obstructs man in his efforts to climb higher?

With Tennyson's idea, cf. Teilhard's statement: "See how the animals behave (monkeys, for example, or even certain insects): we see them doing things that are materially culpable, and only need the emergence of a fuller consciousness to become fully reprehensible." Quoted in Henri de Lubac, *Teilhard de Chardin: The Man and His Meaning,* tr. René Hague (New York, 1967), p. 101, n. 16.

25. Cf. a canceled section of *In Memoriam* (originally CXXVII) in which Tennyson calls upon the "Victor Hours" to "fuse the peoples into one" (*Memoir,* I, 307).

26. *The Idylls of the King,* describing the deterioration of King Arthur's civilization, is devoted primarily to depicting one such eddy in the flood. In *Locksley Hall Sixty Years After,* the old man says (ll. 235-236):

> Forward then, but still remember how the course of Time
>   will swerve,
> Crook and turn upon itself in many a backward streaming
>   curve.

27. Cf. Joseph Sendry, "*In Memoriam* and *Lycidas*," *PMLA,* LXXXII (Oct. 1967), 437-443.

28. "In Memoriam," *Essays,* p. 187.

29. "In Memoriam," *Essays,* p. 187.

30. Cf. de Lubac, *Teilhard,* p. 97: "Moreover, [Teilhard] never achieved a definitive formulation of his thought, nor did he ever claim to provide a complete theological or dogmatic exposition."

31. *In Memoriam: The Way of a Soul* (New York, 1951), p. 91. It is interesting to note that while Mrs. Mattes immediately identifies the "Strong Son of God" with the Word of God, or the Logos, T. S. Eliot finds only a "hazy connexion" between the two. See below in text.

32. Cf. Teilhard's "O Christ, ever greater!" See de Lubac, *Teilhard,* pp. 45-54.

33. Cf. *Memoir,* I, 309-312, where Tennyson's "reverent impatience of formal dogma" is discussed. Note that Tennyson's attitude is different from poising belief with unbelief, as exemplified in the famous prayer: "O God, if there is a God, save my soul, if I have a soul."

34. Eliot, "In Memoriam," *Essays,* pp. 184-185.

35. Quoted in de Lubac, *Teilhard,* p. 38.

36. Teilhard de Chardin, quoted in de Lubac, *Teilhard,* p. 116.

37. See de Lubac, *Teilhard,* p. 44.

38. Quoted in de Lubac, *Teilhard,* p. 44.

39. See Pitt, *Tennyson Laureate,* p. 115.

40. See, e.g., the three Christmases in XXVIII, XXIX, XXX, LXXVIII, CIV, and CV; as well as XXXI, XXXII, XXXVI, LXIX, and CVI.

41. *Poems of Gerard Manley Hopkins,* ed. W. H. Gardner and N. H. MacKenzie, 4th ed. (London, 1967), p. 90.

42. *The Victorian Sage* (New York, 1965), p. 10.

Joanne P. Zuckermann (essay date 1971)

SOURCE: Zuckermann, Joanne P. "Tennyson's *In Memoriam* as Love Poetry." *Dalhousie Review* 51, no. 2 (summer 1971): 202-17.

[*In the following essay, Zuckermann depicts* In Memoriam *as a series of love poems influenced by Shakespeare's sonnets.*]

Most of the few modern explanations of **In Memoriam** have, like E. B. Mattes' **In Memoriam**: *The Way of a Soul*[1] and Graham Hough's "Natural Theology in **In Memoriam**",[2] concerned themselves principally with the source and precise meaning of the poem's intellectual speculations. While inevitably admitting Tennyson's ultimate subjectivism, critics have concerned themselves little with the nature of the subjective experiences underlying the poem or the literary conventions governing their presentation.

In Memoriam is indeed in one sense a philosophical poem: it must have been amongst the works which prompted Jowett to say to Tennyson, just before the latter's death: "Your poetry has an element of philosophy more to be considered than any regular philosophy in England".[3] But its philosophy is based not on the premise *Cogito, ergo sum,* but on the premise *Amo, ergo sumus,* and its relationship to a tradition of speculative or philosophical love poetry is clear. It is, in fact, one of the greatest series of love poems in the English language, and it seems to me that it can be most fruitfully approached by considering it as such, and by examining the literary conventions, the diction and the imagery through which the experiences of love and loss are presented and directed in the poem. This article is intended as the beginning of such an approach.

In Memoriam is both a traditional love poem and an evidently Victorian love poem. Interwoven with the depiction of the love of Tennyson and Hallam, which is sometimes presented in terms of an older and more obviously timeless tradition, are dozens of references to and vignettes of domestic love—of marriage, of parents and children, of brothers and sisters, of the widowed, and of the simple, rural love-tragedies which play such an important part in Victorian literature and popular writing. My aim in this article is to explore the way in which these conventions are blended, and to show how Tennyson builds up his philosophy not on the external intellectual supports which provide its flourishes and decorations and sometimes its tools, but on the simple, self-validating experience of human love. I wish, that is, to examine the poem on the kind of basis which Tennyson himself suggests in lyric XLIX, in which he indicates that it utilizes 'random influences', 'From art, from nature and the schools', but makes it clear that these are only the masks and tools of a personal emotional experience.

The poem in its final form is, of course, both personal and universal in its interest, and Tennyson said firmly that it was to be viewed as "a poem, *not* an actual biography", and that the "I" of the poem was sometimes to be regarded not as the poet, but as "the voice of the human race speaking through him".[4] He conceived of it as a "kind of *Divina Comedia,* leading from despair to happiness".[5] This latter description clearly refers not only to the structural outline of the poem and the fact that it is a carefully shaped whole rather than a mere diary of experience, but also to the role of a dead human beloved in leading the poet to a perception of universal truth and love; as Beatrice is to Dante, so Hallam is to Tennyson.

A sense of what one might almost call the poem's archaism, of its contact with older traditions of love poetry, was early noted by Sara Coleridge. In contrasting the essential modernism of *The Prelude* (which she recognised even in the 1850 version, published in the same year as **In Memoriam**) with the less fundamentally original quality of **In Memoriam,** she commented on the "Petrarchanism" of the latter work.⁶ This is indeed one of many examples of a Victorian poet's reaching back to older traditions of love poetry. The Rossettis, of course, were under a special family influence: but one thinks too of the influence of Donne upon Browning, the greatest of the Victorian love-poets, and the allusions to Dante in "One Word More"; or one recalls Coventry Patmore, writing the best lyrics of *The Angel in the House* under the influence of the Metaphysicals. But the love poem which most pervasively influenced **In Memoriam,** which we know that Tennyson read with special attention during the period of its composition, and which may even have helped to suggest its form, are undoubtedly Shakespeare's Sonnets.

Both the Sonnets and **In Memoriam** are series of lyric poems in a continuously used metrical form, in which a story is discerned through the lyric utterances rather than related in narrative form. In creating such a series, Tennyson has, as it were, accidentally stumbled upon an ideal solution to the problem of devising an appropriate form for a long poem, in an age which, if anything, rather overvalued the spontaneity of the brief lyric outburst. It has been frequently recognized that this was one of the problems confronting Victorian poets, and that the characteristic solution was to build up a longer poem out of shorter units. One sees this type of poetic form in such poems as **Maud, The Idylls of the King** and **The Ring and the Book,** and it is in some sense perpetuated in Yeats's rather Wordsworthian insistence that his total poetic output should be placed in a certain order and regarded as a single major work. Tennyson, however, has achieved perhaps the most perfect compromise between lyric spontaneity and major constructive art in **In Memoriam,** by taking a large group of highly personal poems, commenced without any view to publication, and arranging them in a series which must be read as a carefully structured whole. One of the few models which could really have helped to suggest such a solution is that of the sonnet sequence.

The resemblances between **In Memoriam** and Shakespeare's Sonnets are evident—the many meditative poems, the occasional poems referring to or commemorating an external event or an anniversary, the groups of lyrics on related themes which form smaller units within the larger work—but of course Tennyson has gone much further towards ordering his series than Shakespeare. His obvious model for the poem's larger structure is the major elegy, as represented by *Lycidas* (to which there are many resemblances and allusions) and *Adonais* (which Hallam has been the first to bring back to England in printed form). The models afforded by the sonnet sequence and the elegy fuse easily, since Shakespeare's sequence is so pervaded by the sense of time, transience and loss as to be almost anticipatorily elegiac. Sonnets like "Not marble nor the gilded monuments" (55), "Since brass nor stone, nor earth, nor boundless sea", (65) and "To me fair friend you never can be old" (104) seem almost predestined models for elegiac poetry. One wonders too, in an idle and tentative way, if Shakespeare's reference to a three years' friendship in the last-mentioned sonnet might have suggested Tennyson's time-scheme of a three years' mourning, which does not, of course, correspond to the actual span of time covered by the poem. At all events, the completed **In Memoriam** combines much of the generalising bent of the classical, public elegy, which was usually written for a person not well known to the poet, with a much greater degree of the poignantly personal quality of the Sonnets.

Not that Shakespeare's Sonnets lack generalisation and universal validity: few works seem to speak so personally for every reader, or so convincingly of general truth. But their universality springs, paradoxically, from their very intimacy. By addressing them directly to the Friend and the Dark Lady, like letters, Shakespeare has reduced to a minimum the need for description and narrative, aimed at the unknowing and potentially unsympathetic world, which would particularise and restrict them: of the beauty which he promises so often to immortalise, he actually describes not so much as the colour of eyes and hair. What we hear is the voice of the basic emotion itself, expressing itself through universally recognised patterns of imagery. In the same way Tennyson, whilst giving poignancy by the occasional reference to hand or eye, offers no description of Hallam, and withholds even the most generalised account of his character and activities until late in the sequence. His lyrics are addressed to various friends, to God, to himself, to a number of personifications, and in some of the most crucial instances, to Hallam himself. Both sequences, Shakespeare's and Tennyson's are "overheard" poetry, and derive many of their most distinctive features from this fact.

The resemblance of **In Memoriam** to the Sonnets is particularly apparent in lyrics LX-LXV, and an examination of this group throws much light on the way in which the techniques of love poetry are made to serve Tennyson's special ends. In LX Tennyson compares himself, deserted by the dead Hallam, to:

> . . . some poor girl whose heart is set
> On one whose rank exceeds her own.

The beloved moves on to his proper sphere, and she is left to find "the baseness of her lot", and "envying all who meet him there". In LXII Hallam is again likened to one who has outgrown a childhood sweetheart, although this time a girl below him in moral stature rather than mere social position. In LXIII Hallam's possible pitying memories of Tennyson are compared to the poet's love for his dog or horse, whilst in LXIV Hallam is seen as a great public figure, whose boyhood friend, left behind in their simple home, still wistfully broods on him and wonders if he remembers their relationship. The spirit throughout the group is one of the utmost humility and self-abnegation. The highborn lover, the public man, and the poet bestowing a little spare affection on his dog or horse, are all images of a higher being, moving in his "proper sphere" and wholly right in his attitude to those so far below him. The deserted girl in LX cries "How should he love a thing so low?" and Tennyson begins LXII by a direct renunciatory address to Hallam:

> Though if an eye that's downward cast
> Could make thee somewhat blench or fail,
> Then be my love an idle tale
> And fading legend of the past.

Yet throughout the section one feels, as one always does feel with this type of love poetry, that a tendency to blame the beloved or to demand more assertively some return of affection, has been overcome by strength of love, exercise of will, and magnanimity.

None of this is literally appropriate to Tennyson's situation. Hallam has not "deserted" him, however justifiably and properly: he has been snatched away by death. Unlike the highborn lover and the public man, he had no opportunity to make the false but romantically generous choice and count the world well lost for love. But an exclamation at the end of lyric LXI makes us recognise, early in the group, the provenance and nature of these emotions, and recall the situation in which they were literally appropriate:

> I loved thee, Spirit, and love, nor can
> The soul of Shakespeare love thee more.

It is almost as though Tennyson wishes at this point to render absolutely overt a resemblance which is present throughout the section in tone, emotional quality and increased archaism of diction, but is not elsewhere thrust upon our attention by close verbal parallels or direct allusions. Thus alerted, we remark the similarity of the deserted girl of LX, all humility, yet still "Half jealous of she knows not what / And envying all who meet him there", to the Shakespeare of Sonnets 57 and 58, who dare not chide the beloved for his voluntary absences, but must "Like a sad slave stay, and think of naught / Save where you are how happy you make those". Similarly Tennyson in LXII, exonerating the beloved from even thinking about him if it would be a source of pain or trouble, echoes, although with an exact reversal of roles, the Shakespeare of 72:

> No longer think of me when I am dead
> . . . . .
> for I love you so,
> That I in your sweet thoughts would be forgot,
> If thinking on me then should make you woe.

Lyric LXV deserves quoting in full, both as the climax of this section, and for the key it provides to Tennyson's method and achievement throughout *In Memoriam*. Here again the archaism of diction is unusually marked, and one notes the characteristically Shakespearean initial epithet, 'sweet', and the Shakespearean sound-patterns of a line like the second in the last stanza:

> Sweet soul, do with me as thou wilt;
> I lull a fancy trouble-tost
> With 'Love's too precious to be lost,
> A little grain shall not be spilt.'
>
> And in that solace can I sing,
> Till out of painful phrases wrought
> There flutters up a happy thought,
> Self-balance on a lightsome wing;
>
> Since we deserved the name of friends,
> And thine effect so lives in me,
> A part of mine may live in thee
> And move thee on to nobler ends.

By treating love cut off by death in terms and images appropriate to love slighted or rejected, Tennyson has eventually come, in this lyric, to a sense of a continuing and mutual relationship, in which both he and Hallam can still give and receive. What reassures him, here and throughout the poem, is his sense that Hallam has survived in such a way that he can still make human claims upon him and humanly generous concessions to him. And this sense is expressed through, makes its impression upon the reader by means of, and is to some extent actually generated in Tennyson by, the diction and techniques of love poetry. Hallam is constantly addressed throughout the poem as though he were the living recipient of conventional love poetry, and this perhaps does more than anything else to establish the conviction of his survival. He is both addressed and spoken of in the third person in the language of such love poetry: "My Arthur", "Dearest", "My Love", "The man I held as half divine", "A little while from his embrace", "Mine, mine, for ever, ever mine",—such epithets and phrases ring throughout the poem. Even the more neutral "friend" in such lines as "Since we deserved the name of friends", and "Unto me no second friend", takes on the power of love-language once the Shakespearean context is established. In the lyric just quoted in full, the nature of Tennyson's conviction is made particularly clear. It is self-validating and self-sustaining—"Self-balanced on a lightsome wing"; and it is not merely recorded in poetry, it is generated in part by the act of writing poetry; the poet creates it by singing, and it is wrought out of "phrases".

The group of lyrics we have been examining follows closely upon one of the poem's most serious and best-known outbreaks of doubt and questioning. In lyric LV the prodigal bounty of Nature has led Tennyson to reflect that "So careful of the type she seems, so careless of the single life", whilst in LVI geological evidence has pressed upon him the thought that not only is the individual doomed to die fruitlessly, but the race itself is heading for extinction. No speculative reply is attempted, no external counter-evidences are adduced: after a brief interlude, Tennyson produces, by way of answer to his doubts, the group of Shakespearean love-lyrics. Not that he wishes to suggest too great a certainty: he deliberately belittles his own achievement by the use of such words as "sing", "flutters", "fancy", "lightsome", in the concluding lyric of the section. But ultimately, of course, he did believe that the testimony of the imagination and the emotions was more valid than that of the reason, and in those lyrics in which he distinguishes between knowledge and wisdom, or shows us the heart leaping up "like a man in wrath" to answer the claims of the "freezing reason", he makes explicit his views. If *In Memoriam* were to be given a Shakespearean epigraph, it would come after all not from the Sonnets but from "The Phoenix and the Turtle": "Love hath reason, reason none". In later life his only anxiety about *In Memoriam* was that it suggested too much *speculative* certainty: he would almost have liked to add another section, which, by reopening the poem's intellectual doubt, would "throw man back to the more primitive impulses and feelings".[7]

T. S. Eliot felt that Tennyson had gone further than he thus acknowledged, not merely suggesting too much purely speculative certainty, but essentially falsifying the record of his feelings. He called it a poem of religious despair, and commented that "Its faith is a poor thing".[8] But the real key to Eliot's dislike of Tennyson's faith comes, I believe, earlier in his essay, and involves less a judgment of the strength or reality of that faith, or the effectiveness of its artistic expression, than a criticism of its nature and foundations. He writes: "Yet the renewal craved for seems at best but a continuance, or a substitute for the joys of friendship upon earth. His desire for immortality is never quite the desire for Eternal Life: his concern is for the loss of man rather than for the gain of God".[9] This is a fair and perceptive comment on the poem, but not necessarily, as Eliot clearly intends it to be, a serious indictment of it. We are being offered not a literary assessment of the poem's value, but the statement of a conflict of opinion between an ascetic poet of renunciation, and a very different poet, who approaches a variety of religious experience not by renouncing, but by clinging to human love. It is, indeed, difficult to see what is, in Eliot's terms, "religious" about the poem's despair: in its despair and faith alike, it is a poem of human love before it is anything else.

Certainly the tendency which Eliot disapproves of is not peculiar to Tennyson: it is characteristic of the Victorian era. Writers as diverse as Elizabeth Barrett Browning, Robert Browning, Coventry Patmore, Christina Rossetti, Dante Gabriel Rossetti, Charles Kingsley and Charles Reade image the resumption in Heaven of human relationships severed by death, or treat romantic love as a guarantee of personal immortality.[10] Even George Gissing bears negative testimony to the strength of the tradition, when he makes one of the characters in *New Grub Street* remark: "The days of romantic love are gone by. The scientific spirit has put an end to that kind of self-deception. Romantic love was inextricably blended with all sorts of superstitions—belief in personal immortality, in superior beings, in—in all the rest of it.'"[11]

Walter Houghton, in *The Victorian Frame of Mind,* deals very briefly, at the end of his section on "Love", with the profound significance of idealized romantic love in Victorian literature.[12] He points out that it could serve as a kind of substitute religion for some of the agnostics of the period, whilst men clinging to faith but troubled by doubts could use human love as a prop to their religion, treating it as a foretaste and guarantee of Heaven. But in such a general and wide-ranging survey of the period, Houghton is not able to investigate and develop the topic as fully as its importance merits. One might almost say that what the solitary, in his various guises of wanderer, seeker, outcast and hermit, was to the Romantic imagination, the pair, involved in a profound human relationship, was to the Victorian mind.

"Romantic love" implies an extreme idealization of human love, and an extreme insistence on fidelity and permanence, which is essentially "monogamous" even where the love is, as often in the medieval tradition, extra-marital. Thus defined it is not a prominent theme in Romantic poetry. It seems a gross over simplification, but not a total distortion, to suggest that the Romantic quest for permanence was carried on mainly in relation to nature, and that as science cut the ground from under the nature worshipper's feet, attention was transferred to romantic fidelity in love. It may be too facile to compare Wordsworth in "A slumber did my spirit steal" consigning the beloved to the custody of "rocks and stones and trees", with Tennyson in *In Memoriam* perceiving that "The hills are shadows and they flow / From form to form and nothing stands", and clinging to the individual human personality: but it indicates something of what was taking place.

Houghton, in discussing the interaction of religious impulses and romantic love, does not mention *In Memoriam.* In a sense this is scarcely surprising, since love-poetry is generally thought of as dealing with a romantic and physical attachment between a man and a woman. One perhaps invites misapprehension by linking *In Memoriam* with Shakespeare's Sonnets and discussing it as love poetry. After all, Tennyson does use a sexual relationship as a metaphor for his own relationship with Hallam on many occasions. Occasionally he takes on the male identity, but he casts himself as the female, the wife or the deserted girl, often enough to explain the delicious absurdity of one of the earliest reviews which commented: "These touching lines evidently come from the full heart of the widow of a military man".[13] To suggest that there was anything consciously or overtly homosexual about the relationship is obviously absurd, and to speculate about its latent or suppressed tendencies is largely irrelevant to a consideration of *In Memoriam* as poetry: but nevertheless the fact that it celebrates a supreme love between men is of some importance in considering its scope and techniques.

Here, as in the matter of the poem's form, Tennyson seems to have had ready made for him a situation which other Victorian writers went out of their way to construct. He is celebrating a love relationship which both is and is not an ordinary romantic one. One might compare Browning's use of the relationship between Pompilia and Caponsacchi in *The Ring and the Book,* which borrows and transforms many motifs and conventions of romantic and chivalric poetry to present a special type of non-physical relationship. Or one might cite the minor example of *The Cloister and The Hearth,* in which a married man, believing his wife to be dead, takes the vows of a celibate priesthood, and must establish a special type of relationship with her when he rediscovers her. Both Browning and Reade show their lovers passing beyond death, looking to other than an earthly fruition of their love.

Most of the best love literature deals with unhappy or frustrated love, of course, because in such situations love becomes its own reward, and the writer is impelled to deal with the nature of the emotion and its profounder implications, rather than the mundane details of the relationship's consummation and continuation. But in relationships in which consummation and the daily trivia of shared existence are not merely denied but in some way out of the question, this effect is heightened. Browning and Reade deal with situations in which the straightforward living out of the relationship in commonplace domesticity is tabooed in a special way, and by taking priests as their heroes force us to place the romantic relationships in an explicitly religious context. But Tennyson had experienced a relationship with a similar value for poetry, and such a one as no Victorian writer would ever have created as a fiction: and he had the Shakespearean precedent for presenting this relationship through the conventions of romantic love poetry. *In Memoriam* is what it is, an exploration of human love in a religious context and against a background of loss and deprivation, not only because Hallam died, but because of the intrinsic nature of the relationship between the two, and the literary conventions available for its presentation.

Yet Tennyson does use, in abundance, the realistic and mundane domestic imagery which his theme removes from the central position in the poem. Perhaps its most prevalent images are the domestic ones of various kinds. The poem thus looks in two directions: towards the romantic, the ideal and unknowable through its theme of sublime love and premature death, and towards the practical business of living, the duties and domesticities of daily life, through its dominant imagery and many of its incidents. This is the familiar Tennysonian dichotomy—Ulysses and Telemachus raising their critic-branded heads—but the two strains are unusually well fused in this poem, since the domestic imagery accommodates both an exceedingly romantic view of marital love and fidelity, and an exceedingly practical view of marital and domestic duty.

A really full exploration of the domestic imagery of *In Memoriam* is certainly needed, but I wish to conclude this article with a brief examination of two examples of this aspect of the poem, the section in which personal immortality is first mentioned, and a few of the lyrics which deal directly with marriage.

It is very noticeable that the first intimations of faith and hope in *In Memoriam* arise in a domestic context. In lyric XVIII, when Hallam's body is finally brought home and buried, the stress is entirely on a purely pagan sense of homecoming:

> 'Tis well; 'tis something; we may stand
> Where he in English earth is laid,
> And from his ashes may be made
> The violet of his native land.

Tennyson was admittedly not present at Hallam's funeral, and so is unlikely to write about it in any detail, but the total absence of all religious reference, at a point where the lost beloved is being buried in a churchyard with Christian rites, is still striking. It is indeed necessary to the poem, which derives faith from love and loss, that the purely human experience of total grief should be established first.

The earliest explicitly religious references occur in the section dealing with the poem's first Christmas, beginning with lyric XXVIII. But the bells of this lyric, although they ring out the traditional message of "Peace and goodwill, goodwill and peace", call the poet's attention less to these words than to the fact that they are the bells of "four hamlets round". Their associations are local and biographical, and they bring Tennyson a measure of stability not because of their religious message, but because "they controlled me when a boy". In the last line he refers to them as "The merry, merry bells of Yule", giving the festival its pagan name.

In the next lyric the only mention of the church is a passing reference to "the cold baptismal font", from which the poet shrinks away to make a wreath for the home. The next lyric begins with a domestic celebration of Christmas, its centre not the altar but the hearth. The family try in vain to pretend merriment, and eventually, sitting hand in hand in a circle, they are moved to tears by a song which they sang the year before with Hallam. Then "a gentler feeling" comes upon them, and they are able to see death as peace and rest. Finally, after silence and tears:

> Our voices took a higher range;
> Once more we sang, 'They do not die
> Nor lose their mortal sympathy,
> Nor change to us, although they change.
>
> Rapt from the fickle and the frail
> With gather'd power, yet the same,
> Pierces the keen seraphic flame
> From orb to orb, from veil to veil.'

And then, and then only is Tennyson ready to conclude the lyric with a prayerful and explicitly Christian welcome to Christmas morning. Two things are noticeable here. Firstly, the family, like Tennyson in lyric XVI, *sing* their way to faith and solace, and at the climax of their experience, Tennyson invents the words of their song. Through the fusion of the family's song with the poet's lyric utterance, the singing of a domestic Christmas becomes a metaphor for what the poet himself is experiencing—the attainment of faith not through speculative reasoning but through surrender to artistic and emotional impulse. Secondly, the poet has selected an occasion ideally suited to his purpose, a major religious festival which was becoming, in Victorian England, very much the festival of the secular home and family, and has worked toward its religious meaning through its domestic celebration, in explicit isolation from the Church.

In the next two lyrics, XXXI and XXXII, the particularly rationally incredible miracle of the raising of Lazarus is simply accepted without comment and used as a basis for reflection, the domestic context being maintained by a focussing of attention on the relationship between Lazarus and his sister. After the interestingly ambiguous XXXIII, Tennyson attains a note of personal affirmation in lyric XXXIV:

> My own dim life should teach me this,
> That life shall live for evermore,
> Or earth is darkness at the core,
> And dust and ashes all that is.

This confident note will not be consistently maintained: even here the affirmation has the passion of despair, and soon the new-found faith will be probed and tested. But from this point onwards the notion of Hallam's personal survival is never long absent from the poem, and soon belief in it will begin to be strengthened by poems directly addressed to him.

Throughout the poem religious experience arises from, or is carefully related to a domestic context: one of the most striking examples is lyric XCV, in which the poet's visionary experience is carefully prepared for by an account of the preceding family scene on the lawn, with such concrete realistic details as "the fluttering urn". Domestic imagery is also frequently used metaphorically, most interestingly in those lyrics in which Hallam and Tennyson are compared to a married couple, in which it would, I think, be possible to show a steady and consistent development in the use of the image. In lyric XCVII the "marriage" of Hallam and Tennyson persists, unbroken by death, at once binding the poet to the remote but ever near ideal, and enabling him to carry on contentedly in his own lower sphere:

> Two partners of a married life—
> I look'd on these and thought of thee
> In vastness and in mystery,
> And of my spirit as of a wife.

The husband of this marriage is no longer the young man of their early days: he is rapt in deep thought, and despite their continuing union seems to have moved away from his wife—"He seems so near and yet so far", whilst "the faithless people" even say that he no longer loves her. But she treasures the withered violet he gave her years ago, and maintains a blind but unshakeable faith in his love. This is, of course, a purely human faith in the emotional constancy of a human being, but it is described in terms which inevitably suggest religious faith. Indeed, when the wife is contrasted with "the faithless people", one almost sees her as the Church as the Bride of Christ. In the strength of her faith, she is able to carry on a life of simple grace and usefulness, which is still somehow linked to and animated by her husband's larger sphere:

> For him she plays, to him she sings,
> Of early faith and plighted vows;
> She knows but matters of the house,
> And he, he knows a thousand things.

Again a domestic song becomes a metaphor for Tennyson's activity as poet, and reminds us of the crucial role this plays in sustaining his faith.

This lyric is full of the same humility and restrained self-abnegation as the Shakespearean group which we examined earlier. Tennyson is not, after all, in ordinary human terms, as confined, meek and ignorant as the wife of the poem, whatever he may be in relation to a beautiful spirit, and his placing himself on her level shows the willed humility of romantic love. And the wife in the lyric partially wills her belief: she sings "of plighted vows" rather than of purely spontaneous emotions, and she resolutely refuses to listen to "faithless people".

Indeed, *In Memoriam* as a whole does not simply depict spontaneous and irresistible emotion triumphing over the "freezing reason"; it is also, to some extent, a triumph of the will. The spontaneous instinct, the love which can sometimes leap intuitively across the barrier of death, is there; but it is confirmed and strengthened into a creed by the exercise of the will—at once the religious will to believe, the romantic will to remain faithful in love, and the artistic will to create. Certainly one can hardly help sensing, in reading the poem, that Tennyson believed in part because he wanted to believe, and it is this aspect of the poem which has disturbed most modern readers and critics, leading them to feel it valueless for them as a religious and philosophical document, and falsified as an emotional record.

But the view that faith is not merely a supernatural gift but a virtue, and loss of faith not merely a deprivation but a wilful sin, that faith depends in part on the will, is perfectly orthodox and traditional. This view became particularly important in the nineteenth century: we might recall the Pope's reflections in *The Ring and the Book,* or Bishop Blougram's willed choice between "a life of doubt diversified by faith" and "a life of faith diversified / by doubt". Or we may remember Coleridge arguing, in the *Biographia Literaria,* that religion, as the source of morality, must have a moral origin, and that "the evidence of its doctrines could not, like the truths of abstract science, be wholly independent of the will".[14]

The same considerations apply to human "faith" or fidelity in love: one "falls in love", but the maintenance of the bond depends in part upon the will, and the "faithless one" has been traditionally regarded as reprehensible, as much under the code which governed "false Cressida" and "true Troilus" as under religiously and socially sanctioned attitudes toward marriage like those prevailing in Victorian England. The exercise of the will in *In Memoriam* seems to me fundamentally of this kind: not the self-blinding of a stupid, cowardly or philosophically anti-rational man trampling on his own legitimate doubts, but the will of a romantic or chivalric lover, often imaged as a married lover, spurning temptations to infidelity. For this reason it seems not a means of falsification, but an essential part of the poem, of the emotions involved, and of the tradition to which the poem belongs.

The elegy ends with an epithalamium for Cecilia Tennyson and Edmund Lushington. Earlier in the poem Tennyson has avoided mention of orthodox religion in his treatment of Hallam's funeral, has not entered the church for the celebration of a festival so mysterious as Christmas, and has found the baptismal font, the source of a purely supernatural life, "cold". But now, when human love and domesticity move into the church in triumphal procession, for the celebration of a natural sacrament, ratified but not conferred by the Church, Tennyson can join the crowd and take part in the ceremonies. Cecilia, "Her feet, my darling, on the dead" and her ear to "the most living word of life", forms an almost physical link between past and future, death and life, human sorrow and divine consolation. But the words of the marriage ceremony actually quoted are lacking in all reference to the supernatural:

> The 'Wilt thou?' answer'd, and again
> The 'Wilt thou?' asked, till out of twain
> Her sweet 'I will' has made you one.

What has created the mysterious and indissoluble union, which the whole poem is now seen as leading up to, is not the supernatural activity of the Church, but the assent and resolve of the human will, ratifying and rendering permanent the romantic passion which was an essential accompaniment to this act of the will, but which could not have stood alone. Insofar as Cecilia and Edmund are symbolic equivalents of Hallam and Tennyson, Cecilia evidently stands for Tennyson, since she is his blood relative, and since he has most often depicted himself as the wife: and it should be noticed that it is Cecilia's "I will", in one sense dependent and responsive, but in another final and conclusive, which actually rivets the unbreakable link. And by then the poem has become Tennyson's "I will".

The writing of it had been an exercise both of art and of autotherapy, and in hitting upon its form, an elegy composed of a series of love-lyrics, Tennyson took a major step towards the solution of both his artistic and his personal problems. The faith and solace which he found, he found in part through singing of them: he learned to feel Hallam's presence by addressing him; and by addressing him in both the language of traditional love-poetry and the imagery of Victorian domestic fiction, he was able to give the fullest possible expression to his feelings, and to take in the widest possible range of interest. One of the major principles of the poem's unity is its inter-weaving of different modes and images of human love.

A fuller examination of **In Memoriam** as love poetry is obviously necessary. More attention needs to be given to the development of particular strands of imagery, to the distribution of archaic diction, to the shifts between "I" as the poet and "I" as "the voice of the human race speaking through him", and to the shifts between poems nominally addressed to different listeners, in particular the distribution and immediate context of the poems addressed directly to Hallam. But I hope that I have succeeded in indicating some of the lines of enquiry for such an approach to the poem.

Notes

1. E. B. Mattes, *In Memoriam: The Way of a Soul* (New York, 1951).

2. *R. E. S.* [Review of English Studies], XXIII (1947).

3. Charles Tennyson, *Alfred Tennyson* (London, 1949), p. 531.

4. Hallam Lord Tennyson, *Tennyson: A Memoir* (London, 1897), I, 305.

5. *Ibid.*, p. 304.

6. *Memoir and Letters of Sara Coleridge. Edited by her daughter* Edith Coleridge, 2nd edn. (London, 1873), II, 345.

7. *Tennyson: Student's Cambridge Edition* (New York, Houghton Mifflin Co., N. D.), p. 832.

8. *Essays Ancient and Modern* (London, 1936), p. 187.

9. *Ibid.*, p. 185.

10. See, for example, EBB's "A Child's Grave in Florence": Patmore's *The Angel in the House,* especially Canto XI, Prelude 2, and his "Tristitia": the discussion Kingsley's *Yeast* (*The Life and Works of Charles Kingsley*), XV (London, of the text: 'In Heaven they neither marry nor are given in marriage' in Macmillan and Co., 1902), 94-6: Christina Rossetti's 'House and Home': and Dante Gabriel Rossetti's 'The Blessed Damozel'.

11. *World's Classics* edn. (London, 1958), p. 323.

12. *The Victorian Frame of Mind,* 1830-1870 (New Haven, 1957), pp. 389-393.

13. Hallam Lord Tennyson, *Tennyson: A Memoir* (London, 1897).

14. 2nd edn. (London, 1847), Vol. I, pt. II, pp. 206-7.

Francis P. Devlin (essay date 1972)

SOURCE: Devlin, Francis P. "Dramatic Irony in the Early Sections of Tennyson's *In Memoriam.*" *Papers on Language and Literature* 8, no. 2 (spring 1972): 172-83.

[*In the following essay, Devlin explores dramatic irony as it appears in five conventional images from the first twenty lyrics of* In Memoriam, *theorizing that this device serves to unify the poem and draw distinctions between the poet and the narrative voice.*]

Speaking of *In Memoriam,* Tennyson wrote in an 1883 letter that "the different moods of sorrow as in a drama are dramatically given. . . ."[1] This brief remark suggests a view of Tennyson's elegy as a kind of drama, with the narrator as protagonist and his struggles to reintegrate his sensibility and achieve psychic balance as the nexus of action. That *In Memoriam* benefits from such an approach is evidenced by the increasing number of critical studies which identify the shifting consciousness of the narrator as the dramatic center of the poem.[2] So far, however, the dramatic irony in *In Memoriam,* an understanding of which promotes a sharper awareness of the psychological focus of the poem and reveals more fully the force of the poet's shattered world and his struggles toward eventual harmony, has received little attention.

Images of commonplace realities which because of their natural or conventional associations come equipped with familiar intellectual and emotional overtones form the basis of the dramatic irony in *In Memoriam.* These "societal symbols," as Elizabeth Waterson terms them, are a staple of Tennyson's poetic craft (the seasonal motif in *Idylls of the King,* the flower imagery in *Maud,* the sea symbolism in "Ulysses" and "The Lotos-Eaters"), and much of the commentary on *In Memoriam* explores this phase of the poem.[3] For Jerome Buckley and R. A. Foakes, it is precisely Tennyson's manipulation of such conventional images that gives the poem its basic unity.[4] And in a recent article on the seasonal imagery in *In Memoriam,* Marvel Shmiefsky details the archetypal significance of some of these images.[5] Nevertheless, the role of conventional imagery as an agent of dramatic irony in *In Memoriam,* an irony traditionally inhering in the contrast between a speaker's intended meaning and the additional significance his words and actions hold for the reader, has not yet been discussed. Essentially, the narrator in the first part of Tennyson's elegy continually expresses his obsession with death and separation through imagery connoting rebirth and renewal—connotations which he either ignores or slights—and this disparity forms the center of the dramatic irony in the poem.

An examination of five of these conventional images, taken from the first twenty lyrics of the poem, illuminates the effect of dramatic irony on significant aspects of *In Memoriam*: the reader's role as direct witness to, rather than auditor of, the developing action of the poem; his degree of involvement in the narrator's plight; the essential design of the poem as shaped by the speaker's evolving consciousness; and the fundamental distinction between narrator and author. The precise manner in which the ironies emerge varies considerably; often the ironic reversal of value is sudden and total, at other times more gradual and less absolute. Still, each has as its common denominator the narrator's unconscious use of traditional signs of renewal as ironic emblems of grief and finality.

The value given the violet in lyric 18 typifies the ironic treatment of symbols of rebirth early in the poem. The narrator describes the burial of Hallam following the return of his body to England.

'Tis well; 'tis something; we may stand
 Where he in English earth is laid,
 And from his ashes may be made
The violet of his native land.

'Tis little; but it looks in truth
 As if the quiet bones were blest
 Among familiar names to rest
And in the places of his youth.[6]

The violet, as a perennial spring flower, traditionally suggests rebirth and rejuvenation as well as cyclic permanence. These values, moreover, are reinforced by the implicit parallel between the violet's growing from Hallam's remains and spring's annual emergence from the death of winter. The narrator's unwitting denial of these symbolic possibilities involves both the explicit bestowal of new value on the image and the simultaneous and, in this case, direct diminution of its traditional overtones.

The first of these patterns is the more obvious. Although the speaker finds some consolation in knowing that Hallam is buried in English soil and that "from his ashes may be made / The violet of his native land," he sees the flower simply as a memorial to his dead friend. Convinced of his irreconcilable separation from Hallam, he looks to the violet merely as a floral grave marker, suggestive perhaps of the past attractiveness and value of his buried companion and obviously representing to the narrator here the only tangible good emerging from Hallam's death. Although the flower as memorial has some traditional sanction and precedent (as in the Narcissus myth), the narrator's concomitant failure to exploit the flower's inherent associations of rebirth (as in the myths of Attis, Adonis, and Hyacinthus) points up his fixation with grief and his inability to derive from the tragedy permanent consolation.[7]

The second pattern, that of direct diminution, is more complex, involving as it does a relatively ordered reduction of the violet's potential as an emblem of emerging life. The affirmation of the initial clause, "'Tis well," which suggests a break in the narrator's preoccupation with loss, is immediately qualified and narrowed by the words "'tis something"; and the opening clause in line 5, "'Tis little," further diminishes the force of the image as a symbol for a sustaining vision. This reductive effect is heightened by the narrator's increasingly particularized description of Hallam's burial site. Although the linking of Hallam's ashes with the fertility of a flower-bearing earth implies future growth and perhaps the idea that death is a necessary prelude to new life, these overtones are undercut by the narrator's tendency to localize and particularize the scene: the epithet "English earth" instantly restricts the universality of the image; the change to "his native land" further reduces the focus to the place of one's birth, both in the sense of country and a particular locale; and the additional shift to "the places of his youth" explicitly limits the scene to a familiar setting. By reducing the perspective to an identifiable burial place, the narrator reveals his instinctive desire to concentrate on the physical, to emphasize Hallam's mortality and at the same time to deny unconsciously the possibilities for new life implicit in his basic image.

The Phosphor or morning-star image in lyric 9 is also treated ironically. Here the narrator prays that nature will grant safe passage to the ship bearing Hallam's body back to England.

> Fair ship, that from the Italian shore
>   Sailest the placid ocean-plains
>   With my lost Arthur's loved remains,
> Spread thy full wings, and waft him o'er.
>
> So draw him home to those that mourn
>   In vain; a favorable speed
>   Ruffle thy mirrored mast, and lead
> Through prosperous floods his holy urn.
>
> All night no ruder air perplex
>   Thy sliding keel, till Phosphor, bright
>   As our pure love, through early light
> Shall glimmer on the dewy decks.

Traditionally, Phosphor has a dual significance; as the morning star it suggests the coming of dawn and new life, and as Venus, the power of love. The description itself also evokes these values: night passes to Phosphor and glimmering light, and the morning star shines "bright / As our pure love." Ironically, however, the narrator turns the symbol into an image of intense loss. Much of the diction points to separation and finality. Hallam, whether on the continent or in England, is the speaker's "lost" Arthur, and the mourners who await the body weep "in vain." The final stanza, a poignant expression of total estrangement, intensifies this sensation of loss.

> My Arthur, whom I shall not see
>   Till all my widowed race be run;
>   Dear as the mother to the son,
> More than my brothers are to me.

As in the violet passage, this lyric focuses on the physical. The speaker looks not to Hallam's spirit but to his "loved remains" and his "holy urn." His sole consolation is the anticipated return of Hallam's body. Seen in this context, the morning star points not to the future but to the past, to the friend who is irretrievably gone. By denying the force of the image as a symbol of light in darkness and new life, the narrator also lessens its value as a symbol of love. At this point the speaker's love simply heightens his sense of loss; in no way is it a revitalizing emotion, affirming Hallam's entrance into a "second state sublime."

A more submerged irony arises in the narrator's graceful analogy between the fluctuations of tidal water in the River Wye and his alternating expressions of sorrow (lyric 19).

> The Danube to the Severn gave
>   The darkened heart that beat no more;
>   They laid him by the pleasant shore,
> And in the hearing of the wave.
>
> There twice a day the Severn fills;
>   The salt sea-water passes by,
>   And hushes half the babbling Wye,
> And makes a silence in the hills.
>
> The Wye is hushed nor moved along,
>   And hushed my deepest grief of all,
>   When filled with tears that cannot fall,
> I brim with sorrow drowning song.
>
> The tide flows down, the wave again
>   Is vocal in its wooded walls;
>   My deeper anguish also falls,
> And I can speak a little then.

As a continuing pattern, the diurnal rise and fall of the tides naturally suggests an abiding permanence that transcends temporal change. The narrator's concern with the entire cycle (from ebb to flow and back again) and his insistence on its repetitiveness ("There twice a day the Severn fills") strongly evoke these associations of an enduring order. Again, however, the speaker's tendency to localize the symbol converts it into an ironic image of grief and isolation. In the first stanza the speaker immediately links the Severn with the corruption and finality of the grave—"The Danube to the Severn gave / The darkened heart that beat no more"—which in turn prompts him to see in the tidal process a mirror of personal grief rather than an image of immutability.

Also rich in dramatic irony is the narrator's development of the dove image in lyric 12. Anxious for the arrival of his dead friend, the speaker compares his spirit to a dove darting fitfully about the approaching vessel.

> Lo, as a dove when up she springs
>   To bear through heaven a tale of woe,
>   Some dolorous message knit below
> The wild pulsations of her wings;
>
> Like her I go, I cannot stay;
>   I leave this mortal ark behind,
>   A weight of nerves without a mind,
> And leave the cliffs, and haste away
>
> O'er ocean-mirrors rounded large,
>   And reach the glow of southern skies,
>   And see the sails at distance rise,
> And linger weeping on the marge,
>
> And saying, "Comes he thus, my friend?
>   Is this the end of all my care,"
>   And circle moaning in the air,
> "Is this the end? Is this the end?"

The bird departing the narrator's "mortal ark" is an ironic counterpart to the biblical dove returning to Noah with a welcomed sign of life (Genesis 8:11). Instead of hope, the dove bears a "dolorous message" and brings only continued sorrow. Even its frantic and uncertain motion neutralizes its traditional value. Beyond its biblical echoes, the dove-ark combination provides another level of irony.

Leaving the speaker's "mortal ark," the bird actualizes its value as a conventional symbol for man's spirit, but both the implications of the symbol and the logic of his description are missed by the speaker. Obsessed by death, he fails to see that Hallam, like himself, has a spirit separable from his "mortal ark" and that the dove-ark image itself answers negatively the query, "Is this [Hallam's death] the end? Is this the end?"

The famous "Dark House" lyric (7) involves another ironic treatment of a well-known biblical image. Here the religious parallel is recalled through a biblical analogue with values vastly different from those expressed in the lyric. This short, three-stanza description of the narrator's return to the house once occupied by Hallam is filled with keen anguish and despair.

> Dark house, by which once more I stand
>   Here in the long unlovely street,
>   Doors, where my heart was used to beat
> So quickly, waiting for a hand,
>
> A hand that can be clasped no more—
>   Behold me, for I cannot sleep,
>   And like a guilty thing I creep
> At earliest morning to the door.
>
> He is not here; but far away
>   The noise of life begins again,
>   And ghastly through the drizzling rain
> On the bald street breaks the blank day.

The opening epithet, "Dark house," a common metaphor for the grave, immediately defines the narrator's mood as he stands before the silent doors, pained by the thought of "a hand that can be clasped no more." Ironically, however, the very words with which he confronts again the fact of Hallam's death—"He is not here"—are also the words of the angel announcing before the empty tomb of Christ that the Lord has risen (Matthew 28:6).[8] The sharp contrast between the angel's joyful message of rebirth and the narrator's pained concentration on Hallam's death intensifies the feeling of desolation overwhelming the lyric.

These five images, with their disparate levels of meaning, reveal the fabric of dramatic irony in the first part of *In Memoriam*. Crucial to this dramatic irony is the speaker's failure to acknowledge the contrary values of his images. That he is not being consciously ironic here is underscored by his normally explicit and perceptive appraisal of his limited vision. Evidence of this perspicacity is clear and abundant: in lyric 3 he confirms the distorted perspective created by sorrow; in lyric 4 he acknowledges his loss of will in the face of grief; and in other instances he explicitly gauges the distance between his feelings and the moods embodied by his surroundings (lyrics 11, 15, 38). Moreover, the speaker is consistently direct and uninhibited, and his emotional limitations are honestly and straight-forwardly admitted. Thus it would be out of character for the narrator consciously to evoke contrary meanings without directly indicating their significance in terms of his own distress.

Common to each image are, also, ancillary details heightening its conventional meaning and increasing the force of the dramatic irony. In the "Dark House" lyric, for instance, the irony derives not merely from the narrator's unconscious repetition of the angel's words but also from additional echoes of the biblical scene. Hallam's house resembles an empty tomb; the speaker approaches like an anguished disciple; even the hour—"earliest morning"—recalls the biblical setting. Similar details surround each of the images: the violet springs from Hallam's ashes; Phosphor is linked explicitly to the narrator's love; the tidal rhythm is constant and unchanging; and the dove flies from the speaker's "mortal ark." Though the context in each lyric works most strongly to support the narrator's perspective, a secondary pattern reinforcing opposite values also informs the poetry and strengthens the ironic tension.

Most important, however, is the effect of dramatic irony on fundamental aspects of *In Memoriam*. In the first place the dramatic irony reinforces the reader's role as direct witness to the developing action of the poem, a role dictated by the general form of *In Memoriam*—which, in T. S. Eliot's phrase, resembles a "concentrated diary of a man confessing himself."[9] Despite the prologue, where the narrator confidently describes the sustaining faith which has emerged from his tortuous and often terrifying emotional journey, the poem itself is told from the perspective of someone who has not yet overcome his doubts but is in the very process of achieving psychic balance. That is to say, the poem is given a form which "is not imposed by the poet in conclusion . . . [but] embodies the poet's dialogue with himself and his winning through to conclusions."[10] The reader thus assumes the position of witness rather than auditor as he becomes not a listener for whom an emotional crisis is being recounted but a spectator who observes directly and immediately the narrator's psychological struggles. This relationship between reader and narrator, so essential to maintaining the dramatic quality of the poem, is considerably strengthened by the manner in which Tennyson sets up the dual levels of awareness necessary for the dramatic irony. In place of an omniscient narrator pointing directly to the ironic overtones in the speaker's language, Tennyson places the burden for perceiving the irony squarely on the reader. In lyric 18, for instance, there is no second voice reminding the reader of the violet's value as a symbol of rebirth; instead, he is confronted merely with the narrator's vision of the flower as grave marker. To perceive the ironic limitations of this vision requires, therefore, that the reader himself recognize the natural and mythic and even the conventionally Victorian associations of the violet and attend closely to the narrator's description which ironically reinforces the overtones of renewal. Thus by operating without the assistance of an omniscient narrator, the dramatic irony underscores the reader's role as direct witness to the speaker's emotional conflicts.

The dramatic irony also affects the reader's involvement in the action of the poem. While doing so, it performs two ostensibly divergent roles: it acts as a distancing agent to prevent the reader's total absorption in the narrator's plight, and at the same time it serves to deepen the reader's awareness of the narrator's intense disorientation. Irony of any sort, but particularly dramatic irony, demands that the reader attend to a secondary context as well as to an immediate subject.[11] No matter how forcefully the reader feels the suffering of Oedipus, for example, the dramatic irony in the play directs part of his attention away from Oedipus's immediate torment and toward the inexorable chain of prophecies which Oedipus in his struggles to circumvent fate unknowingly fulfills. Accordingly, one effect of the dramatic irony in *In Memoriam* is to establish a certain distance between reader and speaker. However strongly the reader may react to the narrator's anxiety in lyric 12, his awareness of the larger meanings of the dove image both effects and requires detachment from the narrator's perspective and demands that his attention be partly directed toward the values missed by the speaker. Simultaneous with this distancing effect, the dramatic irony also increases the reader's insight into the obsessive nature of the narrator's grief. The speaker's inability to see in the development of the dove image a remedy for his distress deepens the reader's awareness of the narrator's fragmented vision and draws him into closer sympathy with the speaker's anguish.

The dramatic irony can simultaneously distance the reader from the narrator and heighten his compassion for the narrator's plight, since the speaker, despite his ironic insensibility, is not a "victim" of the irony, at least not in the sense in which this term is usually understood. Dramatic irony commonly operates at the expense of a character or group of characters, pointing up their pride, foolishness, or similar shortcomings. In other words, such irony often acts as an agent of criticism, however gentle or sharp. In *In Memoriam,* however, the effect of the dramatic irony is quite different, although the speaker in the poem, like the usual victim of irony, employs language which conveys meanings contrary from those he intends. The reason for this difference is both obvious and important. Normally, the levels of meaning ignored by the speaker serve in some way either to compromise his own sense of self-importance or to undermine his prospects for success. In *In Memoriam* just the reverse occurs as the values missed by the speaker foreshadow his eventual triumph over the psychological torment clouding his vision and paralyzing his sensibility in the first part of the poem. The suggestions of permanency and order implicit in the tidal cycle (lyric 19) but overlooked by the narrator, for instance, adumbrate his later intuition of the "deep pulsations of the world," that abiding pattern transcending "the shocks of Chance— / The blows of Death" (95).

This last point suggests the role played by dramatic irony in shaping and directing the general design of *In Memoriam,* which Tennyson saw as a "kind of *Divina Commedia,* ending in happiness."[12] Although in the initial stage of the poem the despondent narrator seems far removed from the revitalized figure who later speaks glowingly of a God of Love and of the future progress of humanity, his emotional journey from its very inception involves an inner movement which leads in the direction of his eventual recovery. These suggestions of renewal occur most clearly in the narrator's intermittent refusals to succumb completely to sorrow (see, for example, lyrics 3 and 4) and in his acknowledgment in the very first lyric that out of man's tragedy might emerge a deepened spirituality and knowledge of self. Along with these overt signs of recovery appear various image clusters (like the light in lyric 4 and the calm in lyric 11) which tend to undercut the darkness and gloom of the early sections.[13] The dramatic irony in *In Memoriam* provides another means of heightening this impulse toward renewed hope. For one thing, the connotations of new life which ironically inform the narrator's utterances of grief subvert the finality which the speaker initially sees in Hallam's tragedy. And secondly, the very fact that the dramatic irony here, like all irony, involves a discrepancy between appearance and reality helps to neutralize the hopelessness of the initial lyrics by suggesting that the narrator's vision of a universe without purpose inaccurately represents the real nature of things.

Moreover, the eventual disappearance of dramatic irony as an operative principle in *In Memoriam* reinforces the fundamental movement of the elegy. As the narrator emerges from grief, his sensitivity to beauty and life, in both nature and human society, correspondingly increases. A consequence of this expanded sensitivity is the speaker's perception of positive values in imagery formerly used to express his sorrow. For instance, the rebirth symbolism of the violet, ignored by the narrator in lyric 18, directly controls the flower's role in lyric 115.

> . . . and in my breast
>   Spring wakens too; and my regret
>   Becomes an April violet,
> And buds and blossoms like the rest.

(The speaker's somewhat ambiguous use of the term *regret* is clarified in the following lyric where he defines his feeling as "Less yearning for the friendship fled / Than some strong bond which is to be"). Similarly, Phosphor in lyric 121, surrounded by images of awakening life, finally actualizes its potential as a symbol of rebirth.

> Bright Phosphor, fresher for the night,
>   By thee the world's great work is heard
>   Beginning, and the wakeful bird;
> Behind thee comes the greater light:
>
> The market boat is on the stream,
>   The voices hail it from the brink;
>   Thou hear'st the village hammer clink,
> And see'st the moving of the team.

No longer bound to the past, as in lyric 9, the speaker can now find in Phosphor, the precursor of dawn, a powerful image of his renewed spirit. Moreover, the value of Phosphor as a symbol of love is fully realized in the final stanza.

> Sweet Hesper-Phosphor, double name
>   For what is one, the first, the last,

> Thou, like my present and my past,
> Thy place is changed; thou art the same.

By uniting Hesper and Phosphor (the dual phases of Venus, planet of love), the speaker sees in his enduring affection for his dead friend a potent affirmation of Hallam's continued existence. Love here becomes a basis for spiritual faith rather than a stimulant for grief (as it had been in lyric 9). Once the narrator objectifies his emotional rejuvenation through these traditional images of renewal, the dramatic irony disappears, since the disparity between the reader's perspective and the narrator's no longer exists. Thus the speaker's assumption of an angle of vision formerly accessible only to the reader clearly gauges the extent of his recovery and highlights the fundamental design and rhythm of the poem.

Finally, the dramatic irony reaffirms the very basic and essential distinction between the author Tennyson and the narrator of the lyrics. In order to duplicate accurately the experience of his grief, Tennyson has given his narrator a limited awareness, a capacity to say more than he understands. Although it is clear that the narrator's struggles are Tennyson's own and that the author has cast himself in the role of protagonist, it is equally clear that as author Tennyson is constantly alert to various ways of heightening the reader's awareness of the narrator's plight. These devices reveal a poet carefully orchestrating the expressions of his personal sorrow and demonstrate that for all its effect of spontaneous emotion, **In Memoriam** remains the work of an author who, here as elsewhere, is justly noted for scrupulous revision and control.[14] And persuasive evidence of this skill is the operation of dramatic irony in the first section of the poem, a technique which compels the reader to experience the narrator's anguish more fully and at the same time reveals the masterful control with which Tennyson communicates his own deep and genuine grief.

Notes

1. Hallam Lord Tennyson, *Alfred Lord Tennyson: A Memoir,* 2 vols. (New York, 1897), 1: 304.
2. See, for instance, Jerome H. Buckley, *Tennyson: The Growth of a Poet* (Boston, 1960), p. 110; Valerie Pitt, *Tennyson Laureate* (London, 1962), p. 101; and J. C. C. Mays, "'In Memoriam': An Aspect of Form," *University of Toronto Quarterly* 35 (October 1965): 26.
3. See Elizabeth Waterson, "Symbolism in Tennyson's Minor Poems," in *Critical Essays on the Poetry of Tennyson,* ed. John Killham (London, 1960), p. 113.
4. Buckley, pp. 112-14, and [R. A. Foakes,] *The Romantic Assertion* (New Haven, Conn., 1958), pp. 124-34.
5. "'In Memoriam': Its Seasonal Imagery Reconsidered," *Studies in English Literature 1500-1900* 7 (1967): 721-39.
6. Christopher Ricks, ed., *The Poems of Tennyson* (London, 1969), p. 880. All citations of the poem are from this edition.
7. See Frazer's comment on the rebirth value of spring flowers like the violet: "The hyacinth sprang from the blood of the hapless youth [Hyacinthus], as anemones and roses from the blood of Adonis, and violets from the blood of Attis; like these vernal flowers it heralded the advent of another spring and gladdened the hearts of men with the promise of a joyful resurrection" (Sir James George Frazer, *The New Golden Bough,* ed. Theodore H. Gaster [New York, 1959], p. 320). Moreover, nineteenth-century studies of flower symbolism frequently point to the notions of rebirth popularly associated with the planting of flowers on graves, especially spring flowers like the violet. See, for example, H. G. Adams, *The Language and Poetry of Flowers* (New York, 1860), p. 141, and Hilderic Friend, *Flowers and Flower Lore,* 2 vols. (London, 1883), 2: 561-62.
8. John D. Rosenberg mentions the contrast between the meaning of the New Testament allusion and its functions in lyric 7, although he does not see it as part of an ironic pattern ("The Two Kingdoms of *In Memoriam,*" *Journal of English and Germanic Philology* 58 [1959]: 230).
9. "In Memoriam," in *Critical Essays on the Poetry of Tennyson,* p. 212.
10. Mays, p. 35.
11. On this and other general aspects of irony see D. C. Muecke, *Irony* (London, 1970).
12. *Memoir,* 1: 304.
13. Foakes, p. 125.
14. See Pitt's discussion of the manuscripts of *In Memoriam,* in her *Tennyson Laureate,* pp. 277-80.

Susan Gliserman (essay date 1975)

SOURCE: Gliserman, Susan. "Early Victorian Science Writers and Tennyson's *In Memoriam*: A Study in Cultural Exchange." *Victorian Studies* 18, nos. 3 and 4 (March and June 1975): 437-59.

[*In the following excerpt, Gliserman looks at the works of nineteenth-century scientists Peter Mark Roget, William Whewell, and Charles Lyell as representative of the science writers read by Tennyson and explores the ways in which* In Memoriam *uses scientific language in reference to scientific discovery and as a literary style.*]

* * *

A number of commentators, most recently Milton Millhauser, have identified passages in [Tennyson's] poetry as reflecting awareness of specific scientific issues.[1] References of this kind are often straightforward and incontestable. For example, in **"The Palace of Art,"** the Soul uses recent descriptions of the stages of embryonic development in the human fetus: "From change to change four times within the womb / The brain is moulded." John Killham has identified these lines as referring to Frederich Tiedemann's discovery that the human fetal brain took on structures during the stages of its development resembling the characteristics of each of the four major classes of animals.[2] Again, in *In Memoriam* critics agree that the speaker's exclamation of "O, Earth what changes hast thou seen" is a direct reference to recent geological descriptions of the history of the earth. Accord is not always so easily reached, however. Tennyson's language is frequently not specific enough to make definite judgments about the theory or data to which he is referring. George Potter argues that many of the passages in which Stevenson found references to the idea of evolution could just as easily refer to eighteenth-century concepts of development, or to the idea of the Great Chain of Being, as they could to Darwinian evolution. Killham has in turn reversed many of Potter's decisions (*Tennyson and "The Princess,"* pp. 230-266).

It does seem, however, that after one reads the kind of science that Tennyson was reading, some of the scholarly quibbles over exact identification are misplaced. The science writers' language is frequently as inexact as Tennyson's. In trying to convey meaning they use the language available to their audiences. This kind of inexactness seems most apparent to me in the astronomer John Nichol's imprecise, impressionistic, and metaphoric descriptions of astronomical systems. When Nichol writes in *Thoughts of a System of a World* of the "circuits of these orbits . . . carrying along with them every one, joy, sorrow, life and death" or of the heavens "containing within their still and silent majesty even those stupendous and correspondingly prolific cycles," his language is very close to Tennyson's.[3] In *In Memoriam* Hallam is addressed as one who is "unto vaster motions bound, / The circuits of thine orbit round / A higher height, a deeper deep," (Lyric LXIII) and as having seen "All knowledge that the sons of flesh / Shall gather in the cycled times" (Lyric LXXXV). It is necessary, then, to enlarge one's sense of "science" if one is to judge the impact of this writing on Tennyson and on his poems. Science writers often use language and phrases drawn from other contexts to make their audiences aware of the emotional meanings of what appears to be neutral information. And these contexts are very likely to be eighteenth-century concepts, Biblical phrases, or commonly shared imprecise ways of talking about issues. This shared body of language frequently becomes extremely important to Tennyson in his own effort to communicate his response to the affective meanings of the science he read.

The extent to which this language is shared, even to the point of being contemporary cliché, is not often realized. Walker Gibson in an essay defining the differences between poetic and scientific language argues that for the scientists the data is observed, recorded and speculated on, but for the poet it is experienced. In discussing Lyrics LV and LVI of *In Memoriam,* which end with "What hope of answer, or redress? / Behind the veil, behind the veil," he notes: "In the poem, we are taken right up to the veil, we almost see it; no scientist, I suppose, would want to claim that there is any such thing as a 'veil.'"[4] This may, in fact, be true about early Victorian scientists when they are writing as scientific observers and recorders. But when they were writing the kind of book which was intended to mediate between the results of scientific observation and the wish of a general audience to understand scientific information and theories in certain ways, they are free to experience their data and to use such metaphors as the "veil." The word occurs with great frequency in science writing in exactly the same way that Tennyson uses it. Nichol's use of the word is again most striking. In fact, one could read Lyric LVI of *In Memoriam* as Tennyson's response to Nichol's positive vision:

> The glories I have described, cannot be ALL:—Shrouded by the veil of day, they would, had the Earth, like the sluggish Moon, turned on its axis only as it revolves in its orbit, have been hidden hopelessly and forever, by the garish beams of the Sun . . . Is it not possible, then, that through other conditions of being engirt by other Universes which though at present veiled—thinly, it may be—are yet real and vast as the World of Stars: What are those dream-like and inscrutable thoughts which start up in moments of stillness, apparently as from the deeps—like the movement of the leaves during a silent night, in prognostic of the breeze that has yet scarce come—if not the rustlings of Schemes and order of Existences, near but unseen?
>
> (*Thoughts on a System of the World,* pp. 73-74)

But the idea of a "veil" is also used in a very hackneyed way when Nichol says that an analogy is "wanting to remove the veil from the mind of Astronomers," or when Neil Arnott, a physician who wrote frequently about science, describes the laws of science as "a major power which unveils the face of the universe," and again when Roget remarks that Nature has "thrown a dense veil over the interior machinery of life."[5] Science is commonly conceived as a process of uncovering the order of the universe, and Nichol as well as Tennyson is using these associations when he describes his intensely felt perceptions of the universe.

More significant are imprecise but emotionally charged descriptions which become the focal point for important scientific controversies. Important examples of this charged language are the numerous verbal strategies used to make "Nature" a conscious, protective force. These strategies had become such a pervasive and persuasive way to talk about function and purpose in biology that Geoffroy St. Hilaire found it necessary to counteract the language as well as the concept:

> I ascribe no intention to God, for I mistrust the feeble powers of my reason. I observe facts merely, and go no further. I only pretend to the character of the historian of *what is.* I cannot make nature an intelligent being who does nothing in vain, who acts by the shortest mode, who does all for the best.[6]

Both Roget and Whewell in their reaction against St. Hilaire focus on his rejection of the language of beneficent purpose. Whewell even quotes Kant to substantiate his contention that the idea of purpose is necessary to biological investigation. He chooses Kant, in part, I think, because Kant uses this language:

> It is well known that the anatomizers of plant and animal, in order to investigate their structure, and to obtain an insight into the grounds why and to what end such parts, and exactly such an internal form, come before them, assume, as indispensably necessary, this maxim, that in such a creation *nothing is in vain,* and proceed upon it in the same way in which in general natural philosophy we proceed upon the principle that *nothing happens by chance.* . . .
>
> (*History,* III, 513)

Both Roget and Whewell accept St. Hilaire's discoveries but not the organizing philosophy behind them. It is important to realize, however, that the philosophical question is not simply belief or unbelief in God. It is, rather, a very complex scientific issue about how the concepts of purpose and function should be used to interpret biological structures. Part of Darwin's solution to the puzzle of development depended on establishing in what sense "purpose" was a useful concept. When Tennyson uses this language in *In Memoriam,* Lyrics LIV-LVI, he is placing himself in relation to this dispute:

> O yet we trust . . .
>
> That nothing walks with aimless feet;
>   That not one life shall be destroy'd,
>   Or cast as rubbish to the void,
> When God hath made the pile complete;
>
> That not a worm is cloven in vain;
>   That not a moth with vain desire
>   Is shrivell'd in a fruitless fire,
> Or but subserves another's gain.
>
> (LIV)

Tennyson here and in the two lyrics following is testing the concept of "Nature's" caring. In the next two lyrics the reference to science is clear—geological evidence reveals that species have died out. These stanzas seem on the surface to be concerned only with the problem of individual faith and trust. At the most they seem to voice the threat that science held for a religious conception of the world. Yet, in fact, the controversy is not between religion and science but between different scientific viewpoints. If Whewell, Roget, and others had not described the meaning of St. Hilaire's position, Tennyson would not have been able to use the language of trust and caring with those complex emotional and intellectual resonances which place his poem of personal grief and religious conflict among public and relatively precise scientific discourses.

In sum, "science" as I use the word is manifested in Tennyson's poetry both in specific, clear references to scientific discoveries and in those more generally phrased descriptions used by the science writers and Tennyson alike. Indeed, the latter are often the more important appropriations of science writing in Tennyson's poems in that it is often through these "non-scientific" verbal strategies that the science writers are conveying their most strongly felt convictions about their profession and its findings. When Tennyson includes these phrases in his poems, they are likely to have a strong resonance both for him and his audience, a resonance which connects specific scientific information and theory with the affective meanings many scientists, poets, and their readers in Tennyson's generation may be presumed to share as they tried to assimilate the matter of science to the other parts of their intellectual and emotional lives.

I

Tennyson uses science in *In Memoriam* in two generally significant ways. First, he uses the science writer's landscapes to create experiential environments for the speaker. These environments focus the emotional tensions associated with science. On the one hand, feelings of insignificance, loss of identity, and even of an identity with the aggressive forces of the external environment are experienced and expressed in landscapes like those Lyell presents in his *Principles of Geology.* Balancing this world of uncontained change are landscapes of a caring, sustaining environment similar to those created by Roget and Whewell in their Bridgewater treatises. Second, Tennyson associates with the figure of Hallam many of the ordering and nurturing energies of creation which writers like Roget and Whewell attributed to God. Tennyson also often adopts perspectives and strategies like those of Lyell to argue against his speaker's subjective wish to see a world which cares for him. Because Hallam is a powerful figure in Tennyson's personal life, when he invokes him as a principle of purpose and caring in the same manner as that used by Roget and Whewell, his arguments often reflect his own desire to be with Hallam as well as to participate in the scientific controversy about purpose. Similarly, when the data and explanations of science seem to stand in the way of the speaker's wish to join Hallam, his distress is as much a sign of Tennyson's personal state as it is a stage in a scientific argument. The point is that by associating the arguments of scientists with Hallam and with certain crises in the speaker's feelings, Tennyson depended on a vocabulary and rhetoric already made public in science and scientific disputes. By this means he presumably expected readers to understand and share the conflicts he felt and resolved in his sorrow for a dead friend.

To organize the nurturing cosmos of *In Memoriam,* Tennyson frequently draws on his reading in astronomy; to organize the landscapes of a hostile and aggressive environment, he draws on his reading in geology. The speaker's relationship to each of these landscapes is different. To adapt a distinction of Roman Jakobson and Morris Halle,[7] the speaker experiences the nurturing world as a metaphor of himself, while he feels himself to be a metonymy of the hostile landscape. The latter threatens to impose an identity on him; the former enables him to find himself in a world which seems to be an enlargement of his capacity for love and a realization of his wish for beneficent order.

When in Lyric XCV, for example, the speaker is finally united with Hallam and the universe, the union is described in words drawn indiscriminately from Biblical and astronomical cosmographies—orbs, orbiting, orbing, spheres, cycling, rolling, blaze, light—which create a cosmos of order and glory in which Hallam now resides as a being who knows, cares for, is identified with, and even touches the speaker. On the other hand, in crises of self-esteem like that of Lyrics LV and LVI the speaker looks at a landscape organized around geological evidence of the extinction of species and of the violent forces which have shaped the physical world. Such landscapes are quite consciously defined in the poem against a background of assurances by other science writers that the universe is caring and sustaining. But a part of the experience of these lyrics is that of being reduced to only one more object in an historical or spatial set, one term in a dehumanizing geological or biological sequence. In the sense that an ability to assimilate science to the needs of the self is an analogue of the creation of poetry itself, passages like that describing the union with Hallam also contain overtones of personal strength and control. Passages like that of Lyrics LV and LVI, in which Nature at least temporarily denies the speaker's wish to survive as an individual, carry overtones of a loss of control as the data of science block his effort to make a universe fit to his subjective need.

The attributes which Tennyson gives to Hallam in the poem are unmistakably connected to arguments like those of Whewell and Roget. Part of Hallam's value is that he becomes the person who gives the speaker back a desirable image of himself. By imagining Hallam, the speaker begins to reconstruct his own identity. The recurring concern in the poem—whether and how Hallam "sees," "watches," or "does not see" the speaker—reflects the speaker's need to be seen in order objectively to see himself whole. Like Whewell's parent-god, Hallam also energizes the universe and makes it personally responsive. In the passages placing Hallam in the cosmic landscapes of astronomy we see primarily his separateness, his expanded understanding, and his god-like care: "Be near us when we climb or fall; / Ye watch, like God, the rolling hours / With larger other eyes than ours, / To make allowance for us all" (LI); "so mayst thou watch me where I weep, / As, unto vaster motions bound, / The circuits of thine orbit round / A higher height, a deeper deep" (LXIII). Hallam's responsiveness is clear; he can "be near," "watch," and "make allowance for." Yet he is separate, his motions are part of the cosmic universe and he, like God, can perceive the entire expanse of time. When Hallam is not presented as part of the cosmic world he is the more familiar parent and adviser. In Lyric IX he is described as "Dear as the mother to the son"; in other lyrics Tennyson creates imaginary conversations with Hallam to gain solace and understanding. Hallam, then, is both an environment—the magical, subjective, value-laden, cosmic world—and the personal parental force within this world. In the poem Hallam is analogous to both Whewell's ordering, caring personality and to the supportive fabric of organic relationships found in Roget.

The image of himself the speaker receives from the landscapes Tennyson made from the data of geology may be said to be like those the strategies of Lyell in his *Principles of Geology* must have created in the minds of many contemporary readers. For Lyell it was necessary to remove human projections from the world in order to observe it objectively. He set about frustrating his readers' ability to make these projections. The speaker of *In Memoriam* takes on Lyell's ability to place subjective perceptions in a logical context and, thereby, to place the self in an historical and spatial position. This positioning of the self is done in a way which denies anything more than the status of an object to the individual.

> Might I not say? "Yet even here,
>   But for one hour, O Love, I strive
>   To keep so sweet a thing alive."
> But I should turn mine ears and hear
>
> The moanings of the homeless sea,
>   The sound of streams that swift or slow
>   Draw down Aeonian hills, and sow
> The dust of continents to be.
>
> (XXXV)

Here the geological evidence of expansive and destructive time sequences negates the tentative subjective assertion of human love. Lyell's landscapes are also often animated by violent, apparently purposeless energies. So are some of the landscapes of *In Memoriam,* and Tennyson sometimes adds to this animation by personifications of time, science, and nature, which in the crisis of Lyrics L and LV-LVI become terrible energies of destruction and extinction. In Lyric L time is "a maniac scattering dust, / And Life, a Fury slinging flame"; and the well-known personification of Nature in LV and LVI ("So careful of the type she seems, / So careless of the single life") ends in the near extinction of the speaker ("The spirit does but mean the breath: / I know no more").

There are unquestionably personal sources, experiences of an intense confusion of the boundaries of the self, wound into these passages in which the speaker sometimes perceives himself as an object with little vitality, and sometimes through his identification with Hallam infuses the external world with his own vitality. In the entire poem, however, the movements into the geological landscape and into Hallam's cosmos take on parallel structures and serve a common end beyond their expression of Tennyson's different emotional states. Both states are necessary stages in the process of clarifying the speaker's relationship to his environment. In that clarification Tennyson gives a meaning to the affective meanings of the science books he has read, and in effect his poem tells others how to read these books, how, literally, to take the science of their culture.

II

The interplay between the two kinds of landscape and the use of science to characterize Hallam and to describe the speaker's moods of doubt constitute one of the narrative patterns of the poem. These patterns, and the linear progression from doubt to faith in the poem, have been described by a number of critics and with a variety of terms and emphases.[8] It is questionable whether they need restatement. In this section I will consider not the pattern of the entire poem, but the pattern of the speaker's relationship with the two landscapes Tennyson makes from science. Concerning the pattern of the entire poem, it is enough to say that, in the terms in which I am discussing the poem, the speaker first attempts to make metaphoric identities between himself and external reality, attempts which fail. He moves downward into a confusion of self and an environment which is now felt as asserting its meanings on him. He then recreates himself through a union with a universe ordered by the meaning of the glorified Hallam. The speaker can no more stay in this nurturing cosmic landscape than he can in the hostile geological one, however, because its tendency toward perfection, completion, and stasis also means a loss of vitality and autonomous identity.[9] The speaker of the poem must finally understand moments of continuity, love, and assurance as the experience of a separate self in a vital universe. After sorting and clarifying his own identity, that of the external world, and the relationship between them, the speaker again at the end of the poem asserts the value of the self through the evidence of evolution.

It is worth nothing that Tennyson's use of evolution in the poem seems not to be consistently based in Tennyson's personal experience and its tensions. When the speaker counsels in one of the final lyrics,

> Arise and fly
> The reeling Faun, the sensual feast;
> Move upward, working out the beast,
> And let the ape and tiger die.
>
> (CXVIII)

the self-acceptance which is the major gain of the poem seems to be denied. The speaker is not moving into a new conception of his relationship as a mortal human with the environment. He is rather using a resolution of some science writers to look beyond himself and to leave behind rather than to express the meaning of his own experience. It is perhaps because Tennyson's use of evolution in the poem seems often to be incompletely assimilated to its emotional and intellectual structure that it is easily recognizable as a separate, "scientific" system of explanation. Tennyson's use of astronomy and geology is so bound up in the emotional states which are expressed in their language that critics often do not acknowledge that his use of astronomy is "science," just as they sometimes see his use of geology not as science but as a response to the challenge of science to a religious view of the creation. The value of recalling the ways in which writers like Roget, Whewell, and Lyell presented the matter which Tennyson took into his poem is that it can then be recognized how closely and fully Tennyson was drawing on his reading in science when he made and counterposed landscapes which complete or threaten personal need and identity.

Apart from the final lyrics in which the idea of evolution is used, the sequence of relationships between the speaker and an environment described in the language and ideas of science usually begins with the speaker in a perspective isolated from these environments. He projects himself into and imagines these worlds through hypothetical imaginings—"would that it were" or "if it were, what then." The climaxes of these imaginings are marked by a breaking down (in the case of the world geology gives him) or a breaking through (the union with Hallam) of the language of speculation. The speaker does not only imagine, he becomes each of these environments. If he is not to lose his sense of autonomous identity, he must then return to his human perspective, to his own body and the sensory data it gives him, and after his experience try again to stabilize and understand his relationship with external reality.

The stages marking the speaker's movement to a union with Hallam's nurturing world can be defined by fluctuations in his ability to imagine this world. From the first Christmas lyric to the negative vision of the geological world in Lyrics LV and LVI, the self's sense of isolation from the value-laden cosmos is overwhelming. The subjective, hypothetical syntax indicates the speaker's extreme tenuousness in conceiving an imaginative connection between himself and Hallam's cosmic existence. This tenuousness reflects an increasing lack of trust in the external world and is the prelude to the breakdown of inner trust. In Lyric XLI the wish "Deep folly! / yet that this could be— / That I could wing my will with might / To leap the grades of life and light, / And flash at once, my friend, to thee" is a product of the speaker's fear that he will never be united with Hallam. The "inner trouble," "the spectral doubt," keeps him from imaginatively participating in this world. In Lyric XLVII the speaker expresses his fear that though they may be united at last, both their identities, "The skirts of self," would be fused and then fall "Re-emerging in the general soul." He argues that this would be unbearable, but his affirmation is extremely tentative: "He seeks at least / Upon the last and sharpest height, / Before the spirits fade away, / Some landing-place to clasp and say, / 'Farewell! We lose ourselves in light.'" The lowest point is in Lyric LI, which immediately precedes the vision of the geological world. Here the speaker no longer thinks of himself united with Hallam but sees Hallam as separate and god-like. Both the fragmentation of inner wholeness and the fear of inner evil keep the speaker from imagining a possible union: "Do we indeed desire the dead / Should still be near us at our side? / Is there no baseness we would hide? / No inner vileness that we dread?"

As the speaker begins to rely on memory and dreams to connect himself to Hallam, he is able to imagine Hallam's world positively and to avoid the painful aspects of the separation. He becomes willing to allow movement and change in the cosmic landscape as opposed to his earlier efforts to seek out a protective stasis. In Lyrics LXXIII and LXXXII the willingness to accept the separation from Hallam is conveyed through images of a changing universe organized by meaningful laws—"So many worlds, so much to do, / So little done, such things to be, / How know I what had need of thee"; and again "Eternal process moving on, / From state to state the spirit walks; / And these are but the shatter'd stalks, / Or ruin'd chrysalis of one." In Lyric XCIII the speaker calls to Hallam to come to him from his cosmic universe of "tenfold-complicated change":

> Descend, and touch, and enter; hear
>   The wish too strong for words to name,
>   That in this blindness of the frame
> My Ghost may feel that thine is near.

The universe into which the speaker is finally taken when "the dead man touch'd me from the past" in Lyric XCV is not a static one: there is a balance of active movement and contained process. The verbs "wound," "whirled," "come on," and "caught" suggest a dynamic world within a predictable rhythm implied in phrases describing the "deep pulsations of the world" and the "Aeonian music measuring out / The steps of Time—the shocks of Chance— / The blows of Death." But the experience itself is a passive one. The speaker is taken up into Hallam's soul, Hallam's cosmos—"And mine in this was wound, and whirl'd." He has been given value by being incorporated in the larger identity of Hallam and the universe Hallam now is.

This loss of personal identity and the incorporation of the self into a non-human perspective creates an imbalance which must be restored. The speaker, in a sense, then reverses the roles, becomes active and gives back to Hallam the care that was given to him. The first stanza of Lyric CXXII portrays the vision not as a gift from Hallam to a passive being, but as an active assertion of identity on the part of the speaker: "O, wast thou with me, dearest, then, / While I rose up against my doom, / And yearn'd to burst the folded gloom, / To bare the eternal heavens again." The second stanza makes the cosmic union metaphoric rather than an actual amalgamation with the universe: "To feel once more, in placid awe, / The strong imagination roll / A sphere of stars about my soul, / In all her motion one with law." The experience is seen as occurring within the self, the language of the cosmic universe stands for an inner psychic reality. The image of resolution is again that of a central self within a cycling sphere. The self, thereby, re-experiences the vision symbolically without losing his individuality to it. The lyric continues in a gesture of mutuality. Instead of the speaker being taken into Hallam's spirit, Hallam is asked to enter him:

> If thou wert with me, and the grave
>   Divide us not, be with me now,
>   And enter in at breast and brow
> Till all my blood, a fuller wave,
>
> Be quicken'd with a livelier breath.
>
> (CXXII)

The structure of the speaker's relationship with the second scientific landscape of the poem, that made from the evidence and theories of geology, is the mirror image of his relationship with Hallam's cosmos. Just as he strives to overcome the separation between his and Hallam's world, so he also strives, at first futilely, to maintain a distance between himself and the chaotic, aggressive object world of Lyell's scientific perspective. In the early lyrics the scientific perspectives are presented by dramatized personae outside the speaker. In Lyric III "Sorrow" creates the possibility of a chaotic, distressed universe, and in Lyric XXI it is a bystander who proposes that the ability of science to transgress against the external world should affect him more than personal sorrow. In both lyrics a dramatic situation is created for the speaker; should he accept these perspectives as a way to define himself? In Lyrics XXXIV and XXXV the negative perspectives have become part of the speaker's own perceptions. He has internalized the logic of this negative world to the extent that he can speculate on the consequences of seeing the world in these terms. The lyrics themselves are set in a hypothetic, subjunctive frame. The speaker does not yet believe the world to be this way; he is simply imagining what it would be like if there were no possibility that the world could sustain subjective interpretations, if there were no possibility of immortality or of eternal love:

> My own dim life should teach me this,
>   That life shall live for evermore,
>   Else earth is darkness at the core,
> And dust and ashes all that is.
>
> (XXXIV)

Yet within this assertion of the necessity of personal immortality, we find the speaker creating the scientific landscape with all its chaos and aggression. In Lyric XXXIV the possibility that the universe has no meaning makes the speaker feel that his own subjective vitality is obscured. The solar system without God, however, is not simply an abstract system, but is conceived as a manifestation of chaos:

> This round of green, this orb of flame,
>   Fantastic beauty; such as lurks
>   In some wild Poet, when he works
> Without a conscience or an aim.
>
> (XXXIV)

In this chaos "'Twere best at once to sink to peace, / Like birds the charming serpent draws, / To drop head-foremost in the jaws / Of vacant darkness and to cease." The wish to die, "to sink to peace," is the negative reflection of the wish for the completed processes of Hallam's world. Here the speaker is aware of the dangers of stasis imagined as a death which is both a sinking to peace and an annihilation in the "vacant darkness" of a serpent's jaws. Other tensions are also kept in play in these two lyrics. The earth is dark at the core and possessed of a "fantastic beauty" of color and light. In the sentence which argues that "life shall live for evermore" the speaker's "dim life" is associated through alliteration with "darkness" and "dust." A pattern of "s" alliteration is established in which images of rest are associated with death and a loss of vitality: "sink to peace" and "cease"; "dust," "ashes," "serpent draws," "darkness"; and finally, in lines which combine the association of "s" and "d" sounds with listlessness and death:

> And Love would answer with a sigh,
> "The sound of that forgetful shore
> Will change my sweetness more and more,
> Half-dead to know that I shall die."
>
> (XXXV)

The various tensions in these lyrics make the speaker's arguments finally inconclusive. In the logic of the argument the geological evidence should support the original condition that "life shall live for evermore." But instead the evidence becomes an adjunct to the argument and eventually to the wish for personal death as the speaker muses on three separate conceptions of the world. First, the world is empty, darkness at the core, so that one can give in to death as an ultimate withdrawal. Second, the world is not controlled by any human or divine law and is threatening and aggressive. Third, the universe must be good and sustaining, or how could one live.

In Lyric L, the scientific perspective begins no longer to be contained within speculative musings. Momentarily the logic of its landscape is an experienced reality, and it frustrates the speaker's ability to assimilate the external world in positive ways. The litany form of Lyric L, "Be near me," is the speaker's last attempt in this sequence to place Hallam between himself and a vision of Time as a maniac and of man as "the flies of latter spring, / That lay their eggs, and sting and sing / And weave their petty cells and die." The intellectual hypothesizing of the early stanzas is now a physical reality: "the sensuous frame / Is rack'd with pangs that conquer trust" (L).

In Lyrics LIV-LVI the loss of trust is expressed as a loss of order and care in the universe. The speaker recalls arguments ("That nothing walks with aimless feet" [LIV]) like those in which Roget and Whewell proposed a responsive, caring personality to guard against their increasing awareness of the implications of a universe running by its own mechanics of cycle and change. But the speaker's trust in a fabric of caring is without support: "O, yet we trust that somehow good"; "Behold, we know not anything; / I can but trust" (LIV). He attempts to assert, in the form of a question, that the "wish" that the universe have meaning and purpose is proof of "God within the soul" (LV). Confronted with evidence that types but not individuals survive, he seizes upon that suggestion of a plan and falls upon "the great world's altar-stairs, / That slope thro' darkness up to God" (LV). The scientific data, however, argue a Nature which cares neither for the "single life" nor for the type: "From scarped cliff and quarried stone / She cries, 'A thousand types are gone; / I care for nothing, all shall go'" (LVI). Nature is now actively hostile, "red in tooth and claw," attacking man's faith. Man, who once thought himself to be meaningfully involved in his world—"who roll'd the psalm," "who built," "who trusted God was love," "who loved," "who suffer'd," "who battled"—is now perceived as a passive object to "Be blown about the desert dust, / Or seal'd within the iron hills" (LVI). This last realization negates the speaker's earlier hope that after death personal identity will be preserved in a "still garden of the souls" (XLII). He has now fully perceived Lyell's insistence that "such is *not the plan of nature*" to preserve "an unbroken series of monuments to commemorate the vicissitudes of the organic creation." Man is left open to the random, obliterating forces of the universe.[10]

The argument of Lyrics LIV-LVI leads the speaker to a perception not only of man's eventual annihilation but also of his identity with the brutal violence of his world. Man is "A monster then, a dream, / A discord. Dragons of the prime, / That tare each other in their slime, / Were mellow music match'd with him" (LVI). In earlier lyrics the speaker's speculations on the meaning of similar scientific data had ended in his speculative conclusion that if he believed man was only matter, then he would have experienced love only "in his coarsest Satyr-shape" which "bruised the herb and crush'd the grape / And bask'd and battenen'd in the woods" (XXXV). The speaker had also feared that there may be some "inner vileness," "some hidden shame" (LI) which would keep Hallam from comforting him. This association of man's animal nature and the speaker's self-blaming sense of his inferiority and imperfection emerges with this emotional logic: universe and Nature are not responsive and caring because I am violent, aggressive in wanting love, and bestial. It is this guilt which must be confronted and which Hallam must absolve before the speaker can begin to clarify his relationship to Lyell's geological landscape. The speaker's query at the end of Lyric LVI—"O for thy voice to soothe and bless! / What hope of answer, or redress? / Behind the veil, behind the veil"—is doubly significant. He is asking both if there is hope that the brutalities of the physical world are redeemed and if there is hope that he himself (to the extent that he is identified with this world) can gain absolution.

After the speaker's union with Hallam in Lyric XCV, and while he is redefining that experience to resume his own identity in Hallam's cosmos, he also redefines his relationship to the geological landscape. He now describes this landscape differently. It is no longer aggressive and distressful. In Lyric CXXIII the hills are "shadows," "mist," and "clouds"; they "flow / From form to form," "They melt like mist"; "Like clouds they shape themselves and go." As the reflexive verbs imply, the harmony and integrity of this world exist neither in stasis nor in open-ended change, but in an organic system which regulates and closes itself. Just as the earth can contain the "stillness of the central sea" within a present actuality where "the long street roars" (CXXIII), so the speaker can himself exist within this external, changing world which is not him: "But in my spirit will I dwell, / And dream my dream, and hold it true" (CXXIII). In a sense he holds the perspective of Lyell in balance with those of Roget and Whewell, neither compromising the other.

> I found Him not in world or sun,
>   Or eagle's wing, or insect's eye,
>   Nor thro' the questions men may try,
> The petty cobwebs we have spun.
>
>   (CXXIV)

It may be said that the final outcome of Tennyson's confrontation with Lyell's world is an ability to disentangle the confusion of subjective and objective realities which the Bridgewater treatises and similar scientific writings had encouraged. As Roget and Whewell had recognized, the world of caring and trust could be maintained as an explanation not by selecting from scientific data but only by granting their own integrity and logic to the observations and explanations of contemporary science. The last stanza of Lyric CXXIV captures this sense of redefined relationships: "And what I am beheld again / What is."

In these final lyrics the poem reaches an equilibrium in which each encounter with an intensified vision of the self, in its union with Hallam and in its negative image when it is associated with the perspectives of geology, has been understood and redefined. There is an element of this resolution, however, which threatens the equilibrium. The union with Hallam does not seem to be enough to eradicate permanently the fear of an animal, aggressive identity which will alienate the responsive universe. In the final lyrics, therefore, the speaker literally cannot bear his perception of his animalistic nature, and he projects negative human traits onto the theories of social revolutionaries and "scientists." Social progress is described as a vaguely sexual "boldness" which becomes, "when the time has birth, / A lever to uplift the earth" (CXIII); or it is a kind of earthquake:

> They tremble, the sustaining crags;
>   The spires of ice are toppled down,
>
> And molten up, and roar in flood;
>   The fortress crashes from on high,
>   The brute earth lightens to the sky,
> And the great Aeon sinks in blood.
>
>   (CXXVII)

It is scientists who seem to license these visions of aggression and upheaval by saying that men are "magnetic mockeries," "cunning casts in clay," and "the greater ape" (CXX); or by proposing that the world began "In tracts of fluent heat" and "cyclic storms" and man rose from the "reeling Faun, the sensual feast," "the ape and tiger" (CXVIII). The speaker, for his part, dissociates himself from views that men are animals or clay: "Let Science prove we are, and then / What matters Science unto men, / At least to me?" (CXX).

This projection is an interesting reversal of roles. All the science writers Tennyson read were very much concerned to avoid precisely this implication of their own work. Even Lyell was careful not to endanger religious faith by his presentation of the geological evidence. In *In Memoriam* we see Tennyson finally using the name of science to call up conflicts and ambivalences which the science writers he read had tried to resolve. Lyell had already set man in his moral state apart from the material creation; Tennyson uses the perspectives of Lyell's geological world to accomplish his own dissociation from science as well as from physical reality. When Whewell allows his reader to experience the negative emotional possibilities in the construction of the universe, the strategy is used to establish control over chaos and a functional dependency on God. Tennyson uses the strategy but fully explores the ambivalences associated with such a dependent state as well as with the helpless, aggressive, or insignificant states which propel men to this dependency. What Tennyson adds to the dynamic of scientific controversy, in short, is the energy from his own feelings about his participation in a world of matter and his wishes for dependency and fusion in a metaphysical cosmos. To a great extent, Tennyson comes to terms with these ambivalences, although as I have suggested, his use of the idea of evolution at the end of the poem seems to me to be a rescue from and not an engagement with the emotional tensions he has confronted earlier in the poem. But the intention of this study has not been to describe and assess the structure of the poem. It has been to consider it as an agent in a cultural exchange of ideas and feelings about science. From that point of view the interest of the poem is that its sustained concentration on the affective and personal, on how it feels to exist within the reassuring or threatening perspectives of other writers on science, gives it a character and status different from those of the books of the science writers whose data and strategies Tennyson took into his poem, and from whose writings he seems to distinguish his poem in its last passages.

III

A thorough explanation of how *In Memoriam* functioned in its culture as a poem which used science would require, first of all, an intensive examination of the biographies of Tennyson and the science writers he read during the years he was writing the poem. Tennyson's biographers and critics have delineated the conflicting concerns of his life and poetry in those years: his wish to withdraw and to continue his career, his fear of stasis and of chaos, his depressions and those moments when his identity seemed joined to a higher force, the entire question of his separate identity and his relatedness to others.[11] These concerns helped to determine not only how he wrote *In Memoriam,* but also what he found in and took from the books and reviews on science he read. Many of these books and reviews were themselves mediating texts intended to express and affect attitudes toward their data and theories. It may be presumed, therefore, that they bear a relationship to the biographies of their writers like that of *In Memoriam* to Tennyson's biography. The experience of reading Roget, as I have noted, is different from that of reading Whewell, and Lyell's book is yet more different from these Bridgewater treatises in its strategies and their implications. One reason for this difference is surely that each book comes from a different personality and defends, to recall Norman Holland's argument, a different psychic configuration of conviction, desire, and need.

Biographical investigations, by identifying and accounting for what is singular in each of these books, would also help to determine what the science writers and Tennyson had in common, the intellectual and especially the affective structures they shared. The question then is the representativeness of these writers and their common structures of idea and feeling. Who else in early Victorian England shared them? To answer this question one would try to connect affective patterns to social structures, for example, to class, the content and organization of education, to family structures, and to ways of bringing up children. One would also have to know as much as possible about the audiences of the science writers, the audience of Tennyson's poems, and how far the audiences overlapped. Whom did these writings affect? To what degree did they provide new affective meanings for their readers, and to what degree may it be assumed that readers and writers who lived in the same social structures of class, education, and family already shared structures of feeling?

The final term of the cultural exchange, the uses and function of Tennyson's poem in his culture, must always be guessed at, for readers leave fewer records than writers. Yet here some suggestions can be made. Reading *In Memoriam* in terms of some of the science writers Tennyson read has provided a way to describe Tennyson's individual perception as a reader of certain conflicts and solutions in those scientific books. Tennyson's own needs not only led him to combine strategies and landscapes he found in Roget, Whewell, Lyell, and others in a personally satisfying way, but also forced him to add perceptions of his own. Thus Whewell's sense of God as omnipotent parent is neglected in *In Memoriam* in favor of the more feminine, responsive Hallam. Here, as elsewhere in the poem, Tennyson borrowed a strategy for maintaining a belief in the supportive universe and altered it to suit his own needs. In a quite different way Tennyson's ability to perceive and to experience the dangers inherent in a fusion of self and environment allowed him to clarify the ways in which the science writers' use of subjectivity and animism confused the issues.

But taken this way, Tennyson's reformulations in his writing of the data and meanings of science are only one more personal creation to be added to a wide-ranging debate. For the purposes of this study I have considered the literary structure of the science writing as no different from that of Tennyson's poems. The basic assumption has been that any attempt to give affective meaning to science, and especially to do this in order to persuade a general audience, would result in the authors' recreation of both individual and shared tensions, ambivalences, and conflicts. The usefulness of treating discursive prose as a kind of self-dramatization and a construction of imagined worlds has been demonstrated by critics like John Holloway, George Levine, and William Madden.[12] Both Stanley Hyman and Walter F. Cannon have similarly found that affective and cognitive problems in Darwin's life are recreated in the language and structure of his prose.[13] This method of treating prose is analogous in some ways to the analyst's assumption that patterns of meaning will emerge in patients' descriptions of how they see events and people. It is unlikely, however, that Victorian audiences would so freely do away with the distinctions between a book on science and a poem using science. The transformation of the data and strategies of science into poems is likely to have been a significant event in the Victorians' assimilation of science.

To define exactly how that transformation affected people's perceptions of science is more difficult. Victorian readers must have made distinctions among different kinds of science writing. The textbook presentation of Lyell's *Elements of Geology* indicates that it is to be taken as a faithful recording of the physical world, or at least of the methods and activities of scientists investigating the physical world. The Bridgewater treatises, on the other hand, are well marked as works in which the writer's purpose is to give subjective meaning to the data and to provide a restructuring of a shared world view. It would be possible to order the books Tennyson knew on a continuum from those which propose themselves as records of objective observation to those which present themselves as individual resolutions to problems of meaning. It seems that these quite different stances toward the information would be understood by both reader and author to contain different proportions of subjective shaping. On a scale such as this Nichol's *Architecture of the Heavens* and Whewell's *Animal and Vegetable Physiology* would be much closer to Tennyson's *In Memoriam* than they would be to Lyell's textbook, *Elements of Geology*.

The final move into poetry, into a world acknowledged to be primarily "fictional," personal, and symbolic, would seem to demand a corresponding attitude and behavior from the reader. Some evidence which suggests this shift in expectation and response can be found in the way each kind of work was criticized. Even the most emotion-laden scientific arguments were defended and attacked in a form which implied intellectual judgment and logic. For example, Whewell criticizes atheistical scientists like St. Hilaire with scientific or logical arguments. He protects his belief in an unknown, divinely originated life-force by pointing to the fact that scientists cannot account for the way digestive processes change food into living matter. On the other hand, Henry Sidgwick, in remembering his response to *In Memoriam,* stresses that his intellectual criticisms of Tennyson's ideas were subordinate to his emotional experience of the poem: "I remember feeling that Clough *represented* my individual habits of thought and sentiment more than [Tennyson], although as a poet he *moved* me less."[14]

A description of what the fictional and personal nature of the poem allowed reader and author to do which the science writings did not involves one in the broad question of the function of literary forms and in the specific problem of the function of literature for Victorians. Hypothesizing from the example of Tennyson's poems, it would seem that the poem provided meanings in a form which sufficiently distanced them from the immediate realities of the conflicts. It is significant that the negative meanings in the discoveries of the scientists are always presented as part of the dramatic action of the poems and in such a way that the reader must experience them. The symbolic, "fictional" aspect of the poems and the fact that they record an individual perception seem to provide an insulation for the reader so that negative possibilities can be confronted directly.

In the science writing these negative possibilities—that the world may not be morally and compassionately organized, that man may be both the ultimate destroyer and physically linked to lower animals, that extended time and space perspectives imply a diminished human nature and the end to the human species—inform the argumentative strategies. However, the reader must often consciously experience only the defensive maneuvers and not the possibilities themselves. The negative meanings appear in an author's use of metaphoric language, as in Lyell's description of wilfully aggressive forces. Or they are often fully expressed as arguments to be rejected, as Lyell, Roget, and Whewell each fully described the meaning of the arguments of Lamarck and St. Hilaire in order to put them aside. The very form in which these negative meanings occur allows and indeed instructs the reader not to acknowledge them. Occasionally Whewell in his *Astronomy and General Physics,* and Lyell more frequently in the *Principles of Geology,* come close to making the reader experience a non-human cosmos and earth. Yet the emergence of this experience is in some sense inadvertent. It occurs because the explanation Whewell gives for the implications of the ether theory, and the emphasis Lyell places on the unique moral status of man, are simply not equal to the experience of emotional disequilibrium their arguments and perspectives have created. In Tennyson's poem the conflicts of the inner world, the emotional contradictions and needs, become central and are experienced and resolved in their own terms. The experience can be lived through, transformed, and resolved. In the poem the scientific issues themselves have a tendency to become symbolic representations of the inner conflict. But for Whewell to dramatize the eventual destruction of the cosmos, and for Lyell to point to the destructive aspects of man (and especially European man), is to make a subjective perception of disintegration or of inner evil appear as a "scientific truth."

In some sense this insulation from external reality which the poem provides is likely to be a common element in all experience of literary works. The imagined world of the poem, because it is free from the pressure to refer to the external world directly, allows the author and the reader creatively to re-imagine conflicts which when argued in the science of objective fact would be very difficult to manage. However, judging from the way that scientists treated Tennyson after the publication of *In Memoriam,* it would appear that the Victorian reader expected more from the poet, and certainly more from the Poet Laureate. The many scientists who sent Tennyson copies of their work seem to be yielding to Tennyson the function of making social meanings for their discoveries. Even men like Tyndall and Huxley, who were themselves actively engaged in creating these social meanings, deferred to Tennyson as one who had a special sort of knowledge not open to them. Tennyson as sage would seem to have had to protect the unknown and unknowable in each individual not only from the logic of the external discoveries, but from the logic of inner awareness as well. Tennyson is seen as the guardian of the sacred, while the science writers are conceived of as dealing with the secular reality. Weston La Barre notes that,

> The secular is the realm of mundane workaday technology, or ego control, and of constantly evolving adaptation to the environment. The secular is a realm of relatively low emotional charge. By contrast, the sacred is a realm of adaptation to anxieties, to crises both social and personal, and to common unsolved problems like death. The sacred is a realm of high emotional potential.[15]

To determine how Tennyson's poems were used in conjunction with other writings on science, one must know the extent to which Tennyson was conceived to be not simply a poet whose work had value as a symbolic resolution of conflict, but as a special kind of person who had a special knowledge of the sacred world.

A study of cultural exchange, then, must also consider the form in which meanings were created and exchanged and the social roles of, in the example I have studied in this essay, science writers and poets. Science writing for early Victorian readers could and did express varying degrees of subjective response and interpretation. But one supposes that this writing was always treated differently from a poem. In reading a poem one knew one was supposed to "hear" emotional conflicts and a personal voice. Moreover, Tennyson became a special case. Partly through his own definition of his role as a poet who spoke on public as well as private matters, partly through his attraction to those questions concerning existence which also seemed to be troubling many of his contemporaries, and later through his socially defined role as Laureate, Tennyson became one of the sages who could establish the emotional truth of scientific discoveries. Readers of *In Memoriam* are likely to have expected their innermost conflicts to be expressed in the poem, to have wished for them to be resolved there, and therefore to have believed in the resolutions which issue from the affective meanings Tennyson gave to science in his poem.

Notes

1. Milton Millhauser, *Fire and Ice: The Influence of Science on Tennyson's Poetry,* Tennyson Society Monographs, No. 4 (Lincoln: The Tennyson Society, 1971). See also George Potter, "Tennyson and the

Theory of Evolution," *Essays and Studies,* XXVI (1940), 7-29; E. A. Mooney, "A Note on Astronomy in Tennyson's *The Princess,*" *Modern Language Notes,* LXIV (1949), 98-102; Graham Hough, "The Natural Theology of *In Memoriam,*" *Review of English Studies,* XXIII (1947), 244-256; Norman Lockyer, *Tennyson as a Scientist and Poet of Nature* (London: Macmillan, 1910); Lionel Stevenson, *Darwin Among the Poets* (Chicago: University of Chicago Press, 1932); and Georg Roppen, *Evolution and Poetic Belief: A Study in Some Victorian and Modern Writers* (Oslo: Oslo University Press, 1956).

2. John Killham, *Tennyson and "The Princess"* (London: Athlone Press, 1958), pp. 234-240.

3. John Nichol, *Thoughts on Some Important Points Relating to the System of the World* (Boston: J. Munroe, 1848), p. 130. Originally published in Edinburgh in 1846.

4. Walker Gibson, "Behind the Veil: A Distinction Between Poetic and Scientific Language in Tennyson, Lyell, and Darwin," *Victorian Studies,* II (1958), 60-68.

5. John Nichol, *Views of The Architecture of the Heavens* (New York: H. A. Chapin, 1840), p. 74. Originally published in Edinburgh in 1837. Neil Arnott, *Elements of Physics* (Philadelphia: Carey, Lea, and Carey, 1829), p. xxxiii. Originally published in London in 1827. Peter Mark Roget, *Animal and Vegetable Physiology,* 3rd edition (London: William Pickering, 1840), I, 14. First edition published 1834.

6. Quoted in William Whewell's *History of the Inductive Sciences,* 2nd edition (London: John W. Parker, 1847), III, 512. Originally published in 1837. Roget discusses St. Hilaire in *Animal and Vegetable Physiology,* I, 354-362.

7. Roman Jakobson and Morris Halle, *Fundamentals of Language* ('S-Gravenhage: Mouton, 1956), Part II, pp. 76-82. W. David Shaw uses this distinction in "The Transcendentalist Problem in Tennyson's Poetry of Debate," *Philological Quarterly,* XLVI (1967), 79-94. However, while Shaw is looking for linguistic uses of metaphor and metonomy, I am using the terms to describe psychological states in which the speaker of the poem feels himself to be in different relationships with external reality.

8. A. C. Bradley's description of the movement of the poem based on the three Christmases is standard: see *A Commentary on Tennyson's "In Memoriam,"* 2nd edition (London: Macmillan, 1902). See also Jerome Buckley's remarks on the poem in Chapter V of *The Victorian Temper* (Cambridge, Mass.: Harvard University Press, 1951); Carlisle Moore, "Faith, Doubt, and Mystical Experience, in *In Memoriam,*" *VS* [*Victorian Studies*], VII (1963), 155-169; John D. Rosenberg, "The Two Kingdoms of *In Memoriam,*" *Journal of English and Germanic Philology,* LVIII (1959), 228-240; Jonathan Bishop, "The Unity of *In Memoriam,*" *Victorian Newsletter,* No. 21 (1962), pp. 9-14; J. C. Mays, "*In Memoriam*: An Aspect of Form," *University of Toronto Quarterly,* XXXV (1965), 22-46; E. D. H. Johnson, "*In Memoriam*: The Way of a Poet," *VS,* II (1958), 139-148; and Graham Hough's previously cited "The Natural Theology of *In Memoriam.*"

9. See G. Robert Stange, "Tennyson's Garden of Art: A Study of 'The Hesperides,'" *PMLA* [*Publications of the Modern Language Association*], LXVII (1952), 732-743; Robert J. Preyer, "Alfred Tennyson: The Poetry and Politics of Conservative Vision," *VS,* IX (1966), 325-352; and Arthur J. Carr, "Tennyson as a Modern Poet," *UTQ* [*University of Toronto Quarterly*], XIX (1950), 361-382.

10. Charles Lyell, *Principles of Geology* (London: John Murray, 1830-33), III, 34.

11. See the biographies by Hallam Tennyson, *Alfred Lord Tennyson: A Memoir* (London: Macmillan, 1897) and Charles Tennyson, *Alfred Tennyson* (New York: Macmillan, 1949). See also Christopher Ricks, *Tennyson* (New York: Collier Books, 1972); Ralph Rader, *Tennyson's "Maud": The Biographical Genesis* (Berkeley: University of California Press, 1963); and W. D. Paden, *Tennyson in Egypt: A Study of the Imagery of the Earlier Work* (Lawrence: University of Kansas Press, 1942).

12. John Holloway, *The Victorian Sage* (New York: Macmillan, 1953); George Levine, *The Boundaries of Fiction* (Princeton, N.J.: Princeton University Press, 1968); *The Art of Victorian Prose,* edited by George Levine and William Madden (London: Oxford University Press, 1968).

13. Stanley Edgar Hyman, *The Tangled Bank: Darwin, Marx, Fraser, and Freud as Imaginative Writers* (New York: Atheneum, 1962); Walter F. Cannon, "Darwin's Vision in *On the Origin of Species,*" in *The Art of Victorian Prose,* pp. 154-176.

14. Arthur Sidgwick and E. M. Sidgwick, *Henry Sidgwick, A Memoir* (London: Macmillan, 1906), I, 301.

15. Weston La Barre, *The Ghost Dance: Origins of Religion* (New York: Doubleday, 1970), p. 44.

John D. Boyd (essay date 1976)

SOURCE: Boyd, John D. "The Principles of Analogy and the Immortality Question in Tennyson's *In Memoriam.*" *University of Toronto Quarterly* 45, no. 2 (winter 1976): 123-38.

[*In the following essay, Boyd focuses on the congruence of different conceptions of immortality in Tennyson's poem. The critic also discusses Tennyson's predisposition to analogy.*]

Since metaphor and simile are special kinds of analogies, there is a sense in which all poetry, at its very roots, exemplifies analogical thinking. Beyond this, however, some poets show a special predisposition toward the imaginative exploration of analogies. Tennyson is one of these. Speaking in the context of intellectual history, one might remark that Tennyson's mind, while thoroughly absorbing the dominant nineteenth-century paradigm of Reality-as-Process, also seems to have retained the analogical way of apprehending truth so characteristic of the Medieval, Renaissance, and Enlightenment outlooks. All of Tennyson's more philosophical poems reveal the importance which analogy had in his serious speculative efforts,[1] and *In Memoriam,* his masterpiece in this class of poetry, is particularly saturated with the analogical mode of thinking and feeling. I should like to suggest some of the disparate levels of the poem at which the principle of analogy is vital.

The clearest evidence, perhaps, is to be found in those relatively rare portions of the poem in which the speaker's musings may be called argument in the narrow sense; in which abstractions, logical inferences, and even approaches to formal syllogism appear. Such argument constitutes no more than about twenty of the 132 sections, less than a sixth of the whole. For that reason it is easy to isolate the passages in question from their lyrical or dramatic context, and to examine their methods of operation.

A convenient example is sections XL to XLVII, where the speaker tries to discover what basis there might be for believing that his dead friend remembers him (a condition presumably necessary if present communication is to occur). These poems are built upon examination of a series of analogies: the speaker considers various familiar natural conditions which one might suppose analogous to the state of the soul after death, and various earthly relationships (family to new bride, low-born maiden to admired man of higher class, man to his horse, etc.) which might be analogous to the relationship between a living and a deceased friend. One feels tempted to say that Tennyson's formal arguments, of which these poems are typical, always involve a strenuous effort of the speaker to believe in certain constructive analogies, to take his own metaphors literally. The often quoted conclusion to section CXXIV (sometimes misleadingly regarded as the only real argument in the work)[2] is another instructive example:

> And like a man in wrath the heart
> Stood up and answer'd, "I have felt."
>
> No, like a child in doubt and fear;
> But that blind clamour made me wise;
> Then was I as a child that cries,
> But, crying, knows his father near . . .

These lines are typically Tennysonian, in that what may at first appear to be mere illustrative analogy turns out to be the very crux of an important argument toward a desired conclusion. Line 17 suggests that the speaker is being admirably cautious, not wishing to claim too much for his heart's urgent promptings. But what looks at first like caution instantly becomes a quiet, more oblique boldness: as soon as the speaker can feel himself a clamouring child, further details of that convenient analogy compel the very assurance he needs. A crying child implies a comforting father, and so a modest (and on Tennyson's part, perhaps unconscious) sleight-of-hand with the use of analogy—in this case, in the form of simile—leads on to the most assured victory over the cosmic *Angst* with which the speaker had begun this line of thought. The victory is expressed thus:

> And what I am behold again
> What is, and no man understands;
> And out of darkness came the hands
> That reach thro' nature, moulding men.

The same process, through-obstacles-to-reassurance-by-casual-analogy, can be seen at many points where feelingful meditation (the predominant mode of *In Memoriam*) gives way to declamation or to argument in the strictest sense. A more muted instance occurs in section LIV:

> O, yet we trust that somehow good
> Will be the final goal of ill,
> To pangs of nature, sins of will,
> Defects of doubt, and taints of blood;
>
> That nothing walks with aimless feet;
> That not one life shall be destroyed . . .
>
> Behold, we know not anything;
> I can but trust that good shall fall
> At last—far off—at last, to all,
> And every winter change to spring . . .

The last line I have quoted is the interesting one here. Although the main point of this section, ostensibly, is to insist upon the limits of human knowledge, the need to rely on blind trust since proof is not available—still, the seasonal analogy does its work surreptitiously. The reader may well wonder whether good is always the final goal of ill, but he is unlikely to doubt that every winter does indeed change to spring (in the literal sense). And the result of this reference, apparently a mere suggestive illustration among all the other natural examples in the preceding stanza, is to give a half-conscious but decisive weight of inevitability to the happy conclusion so fervently sought.[3]

These hidden turns by analogy in the argument are easily overlooked, because of their superficial resemblance to mere decorative examples. But the close reader may distinguish among several recurrent devices: (a) Analogy (usually from nature) used as illustrative embellishment, often in the form of simile or metaphor: 'I do but sing because I must, / And pipe but as the linnet sings . . .' (b) extended formal analogy, a kind of shortened Homeric simile, where parallels between some natural phenomenon and the speaker's state of mind are explored: the comparison in section IV between deep unexpressed grief, and 'a vase of chilling tears, / That grief hath shaken into frost!'; or in section XIX, between the speaker's alternating moods of expressible and inexpressible sorrow, and the action of the tide upon the Severn and the Wye rivers. (c) explicit argument by the successive consideration of hypothetical analogies: sections XL to XLVII (already mentioned) on the question of what the dead may remember of this life; or sections LXIII and LXIV, dealing with the same question (d) those subtle cases, which I have just been examining, peculiarly intermediate between casual illustration of some argumentative assertion, and a compressed argument by analogy in support of that assertion.

The pattern of analogy manifests itself, secondly, in the many verbal cross-references and recurrent images and phrases throughout the poem: light and dark, water, the hand, pastoral imagery, the deserted house, Hallam as Christ, the tension of opposites, the path of life, dream visions, etc. The point to be made here is the way in which Tennyson uses these familiar devices (which might collectively be called leitmotifs) not merely to create a vague, pervasive unity, but to suggest the persistent organic development, in the depths of the speaker's psyche, of major problems. Thus the claims of artistic unity and of psychological continuity alike are satisfied.

Both David Shaw and Robert Langbaum have alluded to thematic foreshadowing in *In Memoriam*: Shaw speaks of the circularity of the typical Confession form, noting that 'The final resolutions of the author's problems are usually evident, at least by analogy (or in embryonic and symbolic ways), at a very early stage of the confession.' He illustrates this by showing the importance of the 'revelation-and-concealment' pattern in the poem, citing section V, and examining section LXVII (where the speaker dreams of the silver light stealing across Hallam's tomb), as notable embodiments of this pattern. Langbaum, generalizing less, sees the nightingale poem (LXXXVIII) as an embryonic preparation for the vision of XCV.[4] Neither critic goes as far as he might in suggesting the frequency and range of thematic foreshadowing in the poem, the ubiquity of strings of analogical variants on certain themes. Even if we look only at the motifs named by Shaw and Langbaum, we will discover that the sections they highlight (LXVII and LXXXVIII) are no more prominent than many other passages serving the same anticipatory function. To name only two: the mention of a possible gain to arise from loss, in the work's first lyric, might be regarded as a suggestion of the revelation-and-concealment theme; and the first Christmas poem, XXVIII (where the bells bring 'sorrow touch'd with joy') surely anticipates the nightingale of section LXXXVIII, and thus the vision of XCV, as do at least half a dozen other lyrics.

Or one might cite the important concept of Progress, evolution upward toward a higher goal. This idea is not only frequently and explicitly mentioned (most emphatically in the latter sections), but is also omnipresent at the level of imagery, phraseology, and casual allusion. Its presence in section I,

> I held it truth, with him who sings
> To one clear harp in divers tones,
> That men may rise on stepping-stones
> Of their dead selves to higher things . . .

has been anticipated twice in the prologue, and there are at least thirty such unobtrusive instances in the poem proper, perhaps as many more in the epilogue. Generally the reader may select any important concept in the poem's argument, and find the same pattern of emphasis and development through reiteration at different levels of meaning. The method is far more intricate than mere 'elegant variation,' and might better be termed continuous thematic metamorphosis. (It has its musical counterpart in such contemporaries of the poet as Liszt and Wagner.)

The main crisis with which the *In Memoriam* speaker is confronted is, of course, death: the death of a friend, and the Principle of Death in all its many forms, personal, social, and cosmic. As in *Lycidas,* the premature death of a good and promising young man becomes the occasion, rather gradually in Tennyson's poem, for anguished questionings into the meaning of man and the design of the cosmos. Accordingly, the main positive thrust of the work is the speaker's effort to achieve faith in some kind of compensation not only for his personal loss, but for the evil and sufferings inflicted upon all of living creation. The form that compensation takes for the speaker (who presents himself as spokesman for a Christian community) is of course some kind of afterlife, a 'deep dawn behind the tomb.'[5] And the central argument of the poem, to which all other discernible arguments are subsidiary, is the argument for immortality.

I should speak of 'arguments,' for the speaker ultimately achieves faith in *three* varieties of immortality, which form a kind of analogical triad.[6] We might describe them as follows: I Immortality through memory: the persistence of a living image of the deceased loved one, and the sustenance and intensification of the love felt for him. This continued life-through-memory may of course subsist in the minds of many of the dead person's acquaintances; in Tennyson's poem it is dramatized in but one consciousness, that of the lyric speaker and only real 'character.' II Immortality in the ordinary Christian sense: survival of a man's spirit and personal identity after death. (Tennyson's concept of heaven may be in some respects unorthodox, in accordance with his very Broad Church Christianity, but this is of little importance in understanding *In Memoriam.*) One might also list under this heading, or perhaps under number I, the dead man's memory of his earthly life; it is an important subsidiary problem in the poem, because it seems a necessary precondition for any communication with the dead that might occur while the speaker yet lives, a communication much longed for and apparently achieved before the poem's serene conclusion. This remembrance by the dead of their past life is in one sense the complementary opposite of immortality of the first type, but it may also be seen as a corollary of immortality type II (because speculation about it helps the speaker imagine the *nature* of an afterlife). III Immortality in the racial sense: survival not of the individual but of mankind as a species, which will at once survive and become a new species as it transcends its present limitations. The speaker suggests that this will come about through a process which is not merely biological, but also a spiritual-social-political betterment effected partly by divine directives, partly by human effort and will.

All three senses of immortality have of course been noted by readers of the poem; there is nothing covert about the presence of any of them. What seems not to have been investigated with care is the relations established in the poem *among* the three members of this analogy. When the problem comes up in critical discussion at all, the assumption is usually that there *is* no convincingly established relation; that the second and third, in particular, have the status of *a priori* assertions, smuggled illegitimately into what preposterously claims itself to be an argument. Consequently, their unassimilated presence is often said to reflect the author's ineptness as a philosophical thinker. Thus T.S. Eliot:

> The hope of immortality is confused (typically of the period) with the hope of the gradual and steady improvement of this world.

Or Paull F. Baum:

> the illogical conclusion, the happy ending wherein the immortality of mankind through evolution is substituted for the immortality of the individual soul . . .[7]

There is this much truth in these claims: the interrelations among the three senses are never declared in the poem with the stark explicitness Tennyson generally uses, in addition to more oblique means, to underscore his most important assertions. Nor can I find evidence in other poems, or in statements recorded in his son's memoir,[8] to prove that he understood these interrelations with conscious articulateness. One need not deny, however, that an intelligible relation exists among them in the poem. I hope to show that they are indeed related in patterns psychologically coherent, if not logically systematic.

One succinct way to clarify the poem's emotive-perceptual 'argument' for immortality, is by a series of propositions followed, where necessary, with supporting examples: (1) Certain patterns of distribution may be observed, as the relative prominence of the members of the immortality triad varies during different parts of the poem. If we use Bradley's useful scheme of dividing the work into four main parts (I-XXVII; XXVIII-LXXVII; LXXVIII-CIII; and CIV-epilogue),[9] we can quickly describe the distribution pattern. Part I of the poem stresses our first type of immortality (love-and-memory); its main concern is about the nature and persistence of the speaker's love for his dead friend. Here there is no mention of the other two types. Part II is densest in speculations about immortality; it stresses mostly the second type (personal survival after death), the question of memories which the dead may retain of the living, and the related problem of a possible reunion before the speaker dies. Part III is again preoccupied with a possible reunion, and an actual occurrence of it is dramatized in the climactic section XCV, then recapitulated in the dream of section CIII. Part IV, the poem's extended coda, comes back to the first type, rising to levels of confidence far beyond the tentative affirmations which closed the poem's first part. The question of racial immortality becomes most emphatic here, and it is mostly asserted and eulogized, not reasoned about, as the other immortality types had been earlier. (One notable exception is in section CXVIII: '. . . Nor dream of human love and truth, / As dying Nature's earth and lime . . .'). By this phase of the poem the second type (personal immortality) has receded in prominence; its reality is taken for granted, and further details about it no longer claim the speaker's attention.

(2) The three types of immortality, although terms of a kind of analogy, are related not logically but by an emotive bond. What the poem's affective argument entails, in brief, is a persistent process in which the speaker's feelings of confidence (or of insecurity) about one term of the triad transfer by an associational link (unrecognized by the conscious reason) to one or both other members of the triad. This process will be examined below.

(3) Most important, immortality type I is the pre-eminent member of the triad in several distinct ways. First and most obvious, the experience of love and memory is the very *raison d'être* for the entire work. The speaker is concerned about the question of immortality not with the philosopher's disinterested curiosity, but only because he feels he must reach affirmative conclusions about it if his noblest experience in life, that of love, is to be vindicated. Without the initial experiential facts of love and death the speaker would not care about immortality, nor, perhaps, would anyone.

Not surprisingly, then, the first type is alluded to in more of the poem's 132 sections than either of the other two; it is present almost continually, at least by implication, throughout. It is the subject of discussion at the outset:

> Let Love clasp Grief lest both be drown'd,
>   Let darkness keep her raven gloss.
>   Ah, sweeter to be drunk with loss,
> To dance with Death, to beat the ground,
>
> Than that the victor Hours should scorn
>   The long result of love, and boast,
>   "Behold the man that loved and lost,
> But all he was is overworn."

and it is prominent throughout both the opening and the closing groups of poems.

The first immortality type, moreover, is central in all the retrospective, stock-taking poems, such as XXVII ('Tis better to have loved and lost . . .'), LXXXV (which repeats these phrases, and speaks of 'I, the divided half of such / A friendship as had master'd Time; / Which masters Time indeed, and is / Eternal, separate from fears . . .'), and

CXXI (Hesper-Phosphor). These, like section CXXVI and other passages explicitly *about* love (or its divine analogue, 'immortal Love'), reveal that the psychological process the speaker is above all concerned with is that of his love.

Finally, as our preliminary summary has asserted, the first member of the triad is a kind of 'prime mover' in the course of the speaker's reflections about immortality in any or all senses. Again and again he begins a new line of thought with some expression of the present condition of his memory and continuing love for his friend, and then suddenly shifts, in an emotive thrust which is logically a non sequitur, to one or the other of the remaining immortality types. I have found twenty or more instances of this pattern, but a few will suffice as representative examples. Sometimes the emotive shift takes place very rapidly, within a single section or even stanza—as when, in the first Christmas section, XXX, the sad holiday celebrants' brooding over Hallam, whose absence is paradoxically felt as a tragic Presence ('. . . an awful sense / Of one mute Shadow watching all . . .') gives way suddenly and dramatically to the work's first explicit assertion of our second immortality type (hence, shift from type I to type II):

> Our voices took a higher range;
>   Once more we sang: "They do not die
>   Nor lose their mortal sympathy,
> Nor change to us, although they change;
>
> "Rapt from the fickle and the frail
>   With gather'd power, yet the same,
>   Pierces the keen seraphic flame
> From orb to orb, from veil to veil."[10]

An even clearer instance of this kind of rapid shift occurs in the famous section XCV, where a reading of the friend's letters, written long ago, activates first the emotionally charged memory (immortality type I) and then, without warning, the sensation of the dead friend reaching out in spirit from his present heavenly dwelling place (type II):

> So word by word, and line by line,
>   The dead man touch'd me from the past,
>   And all at once it seem'd at last
> The living soul was flash'd on mine . . .[11]

At other times the transition from one member of the triad to another takes place not suddenly but gradually, over a series of several sections; the essential pattern is still recognizably the same. The Sleep and Dreams sequence, for example, sections LXVII to LXXI, moves from an obvious variant of our first immortality type (dreams of the dead friend), to some confident assertions of immortality type II:

> O hollow wraith of dying fame,
>   Fade wholly, while the soul exults,
>   And self-infolds the large results
> Of force that would have forged a name.
>
>   (LXXIII)
>
> So here shall silence guard thy fame;
>   But somewhere, out of human view,
>   Whate'er thy hands are set to do
> Is wrought with tumult of acclaim.
>
>   (LXXV)

The opening of part III of the work, sections LXXVIII to LXXX, consists of retrospective assessments of Hallam's character. These lyrics are suffused both with love and the softened remnants of grief. They lead into section LXXXII, a credo celebrating immortality type II:

> Eternal process moving on,
>   From state to state the spirit walks;
>   And these are but the shatter'd stalks,
> Or ruin'd chrysalis of one.
>
> Nor blame I Death, because he bare
>   The use of virtue out of earth;
>   I know transplanted human worth
> Will bloom to profit, otherwhere.

Many further examples could be noted. Sections XCIX to CII (retrospective, nostalgic poems about Hallam, occasioned by the speaker's move away from Somersby with his family) culminate in the dream of CIII, an allegorical vision of reunion with Hallam, in which we encounter the first clear mention of immortality type III: 'And one would chant the history / Of that great race which is to be . . .' (ll. 34-5). Or there are sections CXXI to CXXIV, where we observe a casual meditative movement from one to another of our three immortality types.

What these shifts reveal is that the speaker's feelings about his dead friend, as experienced in vivid memories and in moments when the sense of an ongoing love for him is especially poignant, form a potent core within the psyche which radiates outward to the level of both thoughts and sensory perceptions. Thus they largely determine at any given moment what the speaker thinks about the philosophical problems he confronts, and the way the world looks and feels to him.

Alternatively, regarding Tennyson's meditation as a kind of argument, we could say that the speaker's emotional assent toward the first kind of immortality (the continuing life of his love-and-memory), tends to compel his thinking about the other two. Typically but not invariably, moods of exaltation and confidence often associated with the experience of love-and-memory can hold the members of the immortality triad together or, more precisely perhaps, can blur the distinctions among them. At times we can localize this blurring effect. In CIII, for example, the dreamer's vision of Hallam's living presence, promising reunion, provokes an almost casual assertion about 'that great race which is to be,' an assertion which bears no apparent logical relation to the experience which seems to trigger it. Again in the famous section CVI ('Ring out, wild bells . . .') the mood of uplift objectified in the festive Christmas bells calls forth a psalm-like utterance in which the poet's emotional recovery from trauma is linked in the most matter-of-fact way with the progress of the human race:

> Ring out the grief that saps the mind,
>   For those that here we see no more;
>   Ring out the feud of rich and poor,
> Ring in redress to all mankind.

Section CXVIII shows, more clearly than any other, how a mood of sanguine affirmation originating in the speaker's memories of Hallam (as dramatized in the preceding sections CXVI and CXVII) may lead to an assertion which illustrates the affective linking of immortality types:

> Contemplate all this work of Time,
>   The giant laboring in his youth;
>   Nor dream of human love and truth
> As dying Nature's earth and lime;
>
> But trust that those we call the dead
>   Are breathers of an ampler day
>   For ever nobler ends. They say,
> The solid earth whereon we tread
>
> In tracts of fluent heat began,
>   And grew to seeming-random forms,
>   The seeming prey of cyclic storms,
> Till at the last arose the man;
>
> Who throve and branch'd from clime to clime,
>   The herald of a higher race,
>   And of himself in higher place,
> If so he type this work of time
>
> Within himself, from more to more;
>   Or, crown'd with attributes of woe
>   Like glories, move his course, and show
> That life is not as idle ore,
>
> But iron dug from central gloom,
>   And heated hot with burning fears,
>   And dipt in baths of hissing tears,
> And batter'd with the shocks of doom
>
> To shape and use. Arise and fly
>   The reeling faun, the sensual feast;
>   Move upward, working out the beast,
> And let the ape and tiger die.

This poem not only merges two members of the triad, but in fact sets up an implicit analogy among at least five sorts of progress: (1) the evolution of the natural world from 'tracts of fluent heat' to Man; (2) the progress of each man from his earthly life to 'an ampler day' in heaven (immortality II); (3) the evolution of mankind into a 'higher race' (immortality III); (4) the evolution of the speaker's own state of mind from doubt to faith, through the purgation of suffering;[12] (5) the advancement of effort and achievement, only vaguely suggested, which occurs even *after* one has reached the 'ampler day' of heaven ('. . . breathers of an ampler day / *For ever nobler ends*'; emphasis mine). This poem suggests that Tennyson, like many of his contemporaries, was so enthusiastic about the notion of Progress that given the right emotional impetus, he tended to use whatever confidence he could muster about any one instance of it, as *prima facie* evidence for believing in all other instances.

I mentioned earlier that the emotive transfer of confidence from the first type to the others was typical but not invariable in the poem. Sometimes the current runs in another direction: feelings of despair about either personal or racial immortality evoke a compensatory, reassuring movement of the speaker's feelings toward immortality type I. This is further evidence that the first type functions as a 'home base' from which the speaker can venture out to build hopeful conclusions about other problematic issues, or where, when momentarily overcome with doubts, he can settle comfortably until the heavy mood lifts. We see this process at work, for example, just after the terrifying pessimism about both individual and racial immortality in sections LIV to LVI. The speculations about man's doubtful future break off abruptly in LVII:

> Peace; come away: the song of woe
>   Is after all an earthly song.
>   Peace; come away: we do him wrong
> To sing so wildly: let us go . . .

The speaker then reaches a tentative emotional equilibrium, before taking a new direction, with a sad yet reassuring contemplation of the dead friend (immortality I):

> Yet in these ears, till hearing dies,
>   One set slow bell will seem to tell
>   The passing of the sweetest soul
> That ever look'd with human eyes.
>
> I hear it now, and o'er and o'er,
>   Eternal greetings to the dead;
>   And "Ave, Ave, Ave" said,
> "Adieu, adieu," for evermore.

It is hardly a mystery that the love-and-memory experience should be the controlling member of the immortality triad. It is the only mode of immortality in relation to which direct and certain knowledge is possible; the truth and importance of its promptings are felt intuitively, and it is a self-validating experience. The reality of the other kinds of immortality, however, is always uncertain, problematic, and must therefore be certified either by reasoning and empirical 'evidence,' or by a sort of benign contagion from this first Centre of Certainty, love-and-memory. Neither is the emotive transference between types I and II particularly surprising. From one perspective, they are related as subject and object of a single psychic entity: it seems natural that a feeling of indubitable certainty about one's love as a durable subjective experience, might lead to a similar feeling about the continuing life of its object. Immortality III, however, is much more distantly related to the other two than they are to each other, and so the affective leaps by which the speaker accepts it are more readily perceived as logical non sequiturs, however intelligible they may be psychologically.

As was stated earlier, there is no good reason to believe that Tennyson understood the workings of the psychological processes we have been observing at work in his poem, not fully and consciously at least. And yet, as if by design, the importance of the immortality triad in the poem is underscored by one further pattern. That is a series of three analogous confessional poems (widely spaced) which express a single thought in relation, successively, to each of the three immortality types. (The thought is one which H. N. Fairchild terms 'emotional pragmatism.')[13] I shall quote each of these three sections, and paraphrase to bring out the relation of analogy. There is section XXVI:

> And if that eye which watches guilt
>   And goodness, and hath power to see
>   Within the green the moulder'd tree,
> And towers fallen as soon as built—
>
> Or if indeed that eye foresee
>   Or see—in Him is no before—
>   In more of life true life no more
> And Love the indifference to be,
>
> Then might I find, ere yet the morn
>   Breaks hither over Indian seas,
>   That shadow waiting with the keys,
> To shroud me from my proper scorn.

'If I could look far ahead in time from this moment, and see that my love will eventually have extinguished itself, I would as soon die now.' (Focus on love-and-memory, immortality I).

Section XXXIV:

> My own dim life should teach me this,
>   That life shall live for evermore,
>   Else earth is darkness at the core,
> And dust and ashes all that is;
>
> This round of green, this orb of flame
>   Fantastic beauty; such as lurks
>   In some wild poet, when he works
> Without a conscience or an aim.
>
> What then were God to such as I?
>   'T were hardly worth my while to choose
>   Of things all mortal, or to use
> A little patience ere I die;
>
> 'T were best at once to sink to peace,
>   Like birds the charming serpent draws,
>   To drop head-foremost in the jaws
> Of vacant darkness and to cease.

'My own experience should teach me that either life shall, in all its forms, live forever—or else this life would hardly be worth the living; I would as soon die now.' (Focus on immortality in the sense of an afterlife, immortality II).

Section LVI:

> And he, shall he,
>
> Man, her last work, who seem'd so fair,
>   Such splendid purpose in his eyes,
>   Who roll'd the psalm to wintry skies,
> Who built him fanes of fruitless prayer,
>
> Who trusted God was love indeed
>   And love Creation's final law—
>   Tho' Nature, red in tooth and claw
> With ravine, shriek'd against his creed—
>
> Who loved, who suffer'd countless ills,
>   Who battled for the True, the Just,
>   Be blown about the desert dust,
> Or seal'd within the iron hills?
>
> No more? A monster then, a dream,
>   A discord. Dragons of the prime,
>   That tare each other in their slime,
> Were mellow music match'd with him.
>
> O life as futile, then, as frail!
>   O for thy voice to soothe and bless!
>   What hope of answer, or redress?
> Behind the veil, behind the veil.

'Shall man, the latest and noblest work of nature, merely perish like all his lower predecessors? If so, man is a monstrous internal contradiction, life futile and frail. (The wish for immediate death, in such a case, is unexpressed but implicit.)' (Focus on species evolution, immortality III). The argument is in each case the same, and certain common imagery in reference to death ('That Shadow waiting with the keys . . .'; the bird and serpent, death as a drop 'in the jaws / Of vacant darkness . . .'; monstrous dragons of the prime) seem designed to signal the parallelism.

Both the various patterns of analogy and the poem's musings on immortality come to fruition in the much maligned and little discussed epilogue to the poem.[14] However forced its reference to Hallam as the link between man and the 'Christ that is to be' may seem, however anticlimactic its domestic wedding tableau, the poem deserves examination for the care with which it gathers up all the central motifs, which have undergone extensive development-through-analogies throughout, and sounds them with a final flourish. The musical metaphor is suggestive: the epilogue is a full orchestra recapitulation of the symphonic poem it brings to a close. It restates the themes of immortality I (lines 9-24), immortality II (85-8, 140), and immortality III (127-39)—taken up in the order in which they were developed in the work as a whole. Moreover, like section CXXI (Hesper-Phosphor), the epilogue is full of specific muted allusions to earlier experiences of the speaker, occasions and arguments which have already been encountered in the poem proper.[15] Most salient, perhaps, the epilogue sounds the full diapason of analogous references to the motif of Progress—from a hope for the bridal couple's future growth in happiness (65-6), to the closing 'one far-off divine event, / To which the whole creation moves.' And these Progress allusions are sounded in a sequence which, like **In Memoriam** as a whole, moves from the individual toward the universal, from past to present to near future to distant future. At the same time there is a perceptible feeling of gradual, infinite expansion in space (consider stanzas 2, 7-27, 28-31, and 35-6). Finally and appropriately, the poem closes with the mention of God's love, thus reinforcing once more the analogy between individual human love, and the Love which is 'Creation's final law,' and so ending with a reminder of that force which has been shown throughout to govern both the way of one man's soul, and, by inference, the evolution of the universe.

Notes

1. I know of no general discussions of this matter. For a good illustrative study, see Thomas J. Assad, 'Analogy in Tennyson's "Crossing the Bar"' *Tulane Studies in English,* 8, 153-63.

2. See, for example, H. N. Fairchild's discussion of *In Memoriam: Religious Trends in English Poetry* IV (1830-80) (New York 1957) 114.

3. Tennyson uses much the same argumentative pattern in these lines from 'The Ancient Sage' (1885):

   Cleave ever to the sunnier side of doubt,
   And cling to Faith beyond the forms of Faith! . . .

   She sees the best that glimmers thro' the worst,
   She feels the sun is hid but for a night,
   She spies the summer thro' the winter bud,
   She tastes the fruit before the blossom falls,
   She hears the lark within the songless egg,
   She finds the fountain where they wail'd 'Mirage!'

   [68-9, 72-7]

   In this example, one may note the way in which Tennyson has used repetition, metrical and grammatical parallelism to reinforce the analogy. This is more subtle than mere emphasis by repetition: everywhere in nature that we look, the Sage seems to imply, we find another case which extends and supports our analogy. And the repeated pattern in nature is echoed by the repeated pattern in verse.

4. W. David Shaw, '*In Memoriam* and the Rhetoric of Confession,' *ELH,* XXXVIII (March 1971) 82, 91-4; Robert Langbaum, 'The Dynamic Unity of *In Memoriam,*' in *The Modern Spirit* (New York 1970) 65-8

5. *In Memoriam* XLVI

6. Certain insights about the mechanism of emotive transference as a mode by which Tennyson moves from one kind of immortality to another, I owe in part to a former student, Mr Gilbert Allen.

7. T. S. Eliot, *Selected Essays* (London 1953 edition) 186; Paull F. Baum, *Tennyson Sixty Years After* (Chapel Hill 1948) 123

8. Hallam, Lord Tennyson, *Alfred Lord Tennyson: A Memoir* (New York 1897) two volumes

9. A. C. Bradley, *A Commentary on Tennyson's 'In Memoriam'* (London 1901; third edition 1920) 20-35

10. This assertion of a doctrine of personal immortality is unusual in some ways: it is one of the two or three occasions in the poem where the speaker seems, somewhat cryptically, to commit himself to the non-Christian belief in metempsychosis, or reincarnation. And there is an hysterical ring to it, as if it provided necessary relief from the despondent mood just preceding, but carried no real confidence (an example of what Kenneth Burke would call 'qualitative progression'). The affirmation expressed by the words is under-cut somewhat, in short, by the tonal context. As a serious claim for personal immortality it is preliminary, merely anticipatory of later confident reassertions, such as LXXV, LXXXV, or CXXVII. Nevertheless it illustrates neatly the process of emotive transference from one member of the triad to another.

11. We may observe, in this climactic group of poems (XC-XCV) one of the few instances of what is virtually an *explicit* recognition by the speaker of the role of love-and-memory as a trigger for psychic experiences which (at least momentarily) seem to constitute a direct, intuitive intimation of immortality in my second sense. For in XCII the speaker worries lest, even if he should experience the direct communion he hopes for, he might be forced to regard it as a mere trick of memory:

    I might count in vain
    As but the canker of the brain;
    Yea, tho' it spake and made appeal

    To chances where our lots were cast
    Together in the days behind,
    I might but say, I hear a wind
    Of memory murmuring the past.

    This fear may possibly be confirmed in XCV, as the trance-like contact of two souls is immediately 'cancell'd, stricken thro' with doubt . . . ,' probably the same doubt referred to in the passage just quoted. This impression is strengthened by the suddenly rising wind which ends the lyric: is this a 'correspondent breeze' of the sort M. H. Abrams has examined, or precisely that 'wind / Of memory' the speaker was so ready to be suspicious of? The tantalizing ambiguity about such a critical matter is, of course, characteristic of Tennyson's religious poems.

12. This process is not explicitly mentioned, but seems to be (as the burning fears and hissing tears suggest) the analogical pattern which gives the speaker a kind of warrant for assuming—lines 18-25—that man's future progress will involve struggle and suffering.

13. Fairchild, *Religious Trends in English Poetry* 119

14. There *is* a good brief discussion of the epilogue (one having little in common with my perspective here) in John D. Rosenberg, 'The Two Kingdoms of *In Memoriam,*' *JEGP* [*Journal of English and Germanic Philology*] LVIII (1959) 228-40.

15. The careful student or teacher of *In Memoriam* may wish, for example, to check out the following sug-

gested parallels or allusions: lines 2-4: cf. XIX, 10-12; lines 15-16: cf. CIII, 11-15 and 41-4; lines 19-20: cf. I, 1-4; lines 57-9: cf. LXXVII, 8-12; lines 61-2: cf. CVI; lines 71-3: cf. LXVII, 1-8; lines 77-8: cf. XIII, 16-20, XVII, 5-12, and LXXXVI, 11-16; lines 85-7: cf. XXX, 7-9; lines 93-6 and 101-2: a general reminder of death and past sorrows, which lends special poignancy to present joys; lines 102-5: cf. LXXXVII, 18-20; lines 109-12 and 117: cf. LXVII; line 122: cf. CIII, 5-6 and CI, 11-12; lines 123-4: cf. XLV; line 141: cf. Prologue, 1; lines 143-4: cf. LIV, 1-16.

James Kilroy (essay date 1977)

SOURCE: Kilroy, James. "The Chiastic Structure of *In Memoriam, A. H. H.*" *Philological Quarterly* 56, no. 3 (summer 1977): 358-73.

[*In the following essay, Kilroy looks at the use of chiasmus, or inversion of the second of two parallel phrases, throughout* In Memoriam, *with particular focus on several stanzas at the center of the work.*]

One of the recurrent challenges to critics of Victorian poetry has been the attempt to describe the structure of Tennyson's greatest poem, *In Memoriam, A. H. H.* Few deny its unity, but explanations of how its one hundred thirty-three separate poems are organized into an artistic whole have ranged from Eliot's description of it as "the concentrated diary of a man confessing himself" to the much more elaborate schemes proposed by A. C. Bradley and Valerie Pitt.[1] Despite the knowledge that Tennyson added two sections after the trial edition and that he once considered entitling it *Fragments of an Elegy,* readers report a single, coherent effect and an impression of careful architectonics. There are, of course, unifying features such as the references to the passing of seasons, recurring Christmas celebrations and anniversaries of Arthur Hallam's death. But claims of thematic unity have put unjustified importance on a single section, the mystical vision reported in Section XCV. And the structural importance of the central group of poems, the most discomforting episodes which compromise the middle of the "nine natural groups," has been overlooked.

The stanzaic scheme, quatrains rhyming abba, has been recognized as absolutely appropriate to the dramatic nature of the poem. Christopher Ricks notes that it would be "utterly unsuitable for sustained argument," but allows its "exquisite aptness" for a poem in which moods, ideas and theories circle and hover, or advance but only to recede.[2] Tennyson's own description of the verses as "short swallow-flights of song, that dip / Their wings in tears, and skim away" suggests a similar symmetrical pattern, in which a single exciting fall is framed before and after by parallel structures. The stanza constitutes a *chiasmus,* reinforced by thought and syntax, and such a chiastic pattern is found in the entire poem as well.[3]

In the smallest unit, the quatrain, a chiastic structure dominates. The repeated rhymes of first and last lines adapt themselves well either to reiteration of the same sentiment or to balance of opposed claims in the polar lines. In between the rhymed couplet achieves graver weight and often constitutes a single statement framed by the opening and closing lines. Of course such absolute symmetry does not occur in every quatrain, but the rhyme scheme encourages the major thought or deepest feeling to gravitate toward the middle. Just as the center of gravity can be seen in individual quatrains, the larger units of the poem's structure reveal a similar chiastic plan. Each of the poem's one hundred thirty-three sections is made up of a series of quatrains arranged so as to constitute a discrete episode. For, as Tennyson himself indicated, the poem is a dramatic work, in which "the different moods of sorrow as in a drama are dramatically given."[4] But within each of the numbered episodes, and the prologue and epilogue as well, there is only rarely a logical structure which assumes progress; more typical is a circular reiteration at the end of the opening statement, with amplification or emphasis often occurring at the end. Even when thought is moved along within the section, it is by carefully balanced dialectic.

The entire poem exhibits a similar chiastic pattern of sections. In defending one or another theory of the poem's structure, previous critics have often over-simplified. From A. C. Bradley's claim, itself based on the poet's own comment, that the poem is divided by the three Christmas observances (Sections XXVIII, LXXVIII, and CIV), through Valerie Pitt's cogent arguments that the two anniversaries (LXXII and XCIX) provide more likely points of division, the most basic observation about *In Memoriam* is too easily slighted: that is that the critical number is not four, nor three, nor even nine, but one hundred thirty-one. Each of the sections is a distinct expression, with an independent subject and form. The arrangement of sections, however, does reveal a pattern: a movement from initial grief downward to near despair and a concomitant choking of expression, and then upward to acceptance and articulation. That pattern is clearly exposed if we consider the poem as composed of the "nine natural groups" which Tennyson mentioned in a letter to his friend James Knowles.[5] It should not be surprising that the groups are of unequal length, nor that they cover unequal periods of time, for human experience is never so symmetrically neat. What matters is that they serve as roughly equivalent thematic units arranged, like the quatrain, to invest the greatest weight in the center of the poem. Thus the middle group, the fifth of nine such, is the low point, while around it framing groups symmetrically advance and then retreat. Of course something happens, and the chiastic structure does not require return to exactly the starting point. But the poem's greatest intensity occurs in the middle, not at the conclusion; the parallel elements of framing sections form a chiasmus, reflecting the structure of individual lyrics and quatrains. Thus, the dramatic progress of the poem does not lead to putting greatest weight on Section XCV, nor on dividing action at Christmases or anniversaries either, but rather on that group of sections which record the nadir of the speaker's experience.[6] Consideration of the poem as centering on the middle of the nine "natural groups" also reinforces the major themes of the poem, its consideration of the nature and force of love and the difficulty of faith, especially in face of contemporary scientific discoveries. Even the subject of the difficulty of verbal expression, so nicely analyzed by E. D. H. Johnson, is most fully revealed by considering the poem as having a chiastic structure centering on Section L through LVIII.[7]

The nine groups are so arranged as to form a chiasmus whose central unit presents the very nadir of the speaker's experience and the central thematic statements. To reveal that pattern it will be necessary to discuss the nine groups as four pairs of parallel units, noting the ways in which they direct attention toward the central passages. The chiastic structure formed in the stanzaic unit is amplified in the arrangement of these larger units, as well as in the patterns within sections or groups of sections with the prologue and epilogue, the outermost statements of the poem, completing the overall pattern.

The first of the nine groups consists of Sections I through VIII, and as a structural unit it establishes the poem's main concerns. In the very first section, most of the entire poem's content is made evident. The speaker relates his belief in progress, connecting evolution with personal immortality in the very first stanza: "That men may rise on stepping-stones / Of their dead selves to higher things." John D. Rosenberg convincingly argues that these two elements with their related aspects, scientific fact and religious faith respectively, are the main components of the synthesis which the poem achieves.[8] To that should be added the subject of love, emphasized in the rest of the poem as a third major theme and mentioned in this opening section. The shift from past to future to present tense has the effect of relegating a belief in progress to the past. At the poem's opening, then, the speaker stands between a past now lost and a future untenable consolation and he sees no alternative to turning away, to indulging in grief. Section V introduces the theme of poetic composition, when the question is raised of whether or not it is even proper to express grief. Standard arguments follow: the deception and ambiguities of expression versus the consolation to the poet found in even such a "dull, mechanic exercise." Rather than being a subordinate theme, as it has sometimes been regarded, it is clearly integrated into the dramatic situation and made equal to the other themes. The positive reasons offered are really unhealthy: poetry as therapy might be recommended but the imagery makes it clear that in this speaker's view, it would be only a narcotic. Expression of grief is reduced to mere wallowing in it. Of course at this point in the poem such a view of poetry is appropriate; later his struggle out of despair will find a correlation in a more healthy and productive view of poetry as well. The changing situation of the speaker, his place in the emerging drama, also accounts for the deliberately cloying and sentimental statements of some of these early sections. The groups of scenes of domestic bliss are products of self-pity, a stage not unexpected in such a situation. In Section VII the depressed state of the speaker darkens the scenes he relates; he admits this in Section VIII, again resorting to sentimental images of a happy lover whose hopeful perspectives are shattered at the absence of his beloved. The section ends with rather maudlin and self-deprecating comments on his poetry. The closing lines of Section VIII clearly indicate the closure of one act, albeit a preliminary one. In a series of eight episodes the central themes are established—as is the nature of the poem's organization—which shift in time as the speaker questions, evades, rationalizes, but again and again submits to intellectual analysis of his own evasions. Like so many of Tennyson's early poems this group succeeds better in posing questions than in providing answers. Its focus is on dramatic apprehension rather than logical discourse, and the method is appropriate to revelation of characters and situation in such detail as to make the reader share in the emotion and even participate in intellectual analysis of the situation. Irony is too vague a term to describe the relation of reader to narrator in such a case. "Sympathy," the term favored by Tennyson's contemporaries, comes closer if it is seen as including emotional empathy along with participating in the logical analysis. Such is the tone of the closing lines of this unit: the echoes of Ben Jonson's song, "To Celia," provide an appropriate final comment: the hopes that his tribute of poetry may live, or at least close the matter.

The last group, Section CIV through CXXXI, closes by exhorting others to join in a song which will endure, "a cry above the conquered years," thus ending with confidence by proclaiming the efficacy of poetic expression. The other themes raised in the first group are similarly concluded. The last group begins with a repetition of the opening lines of the fourth group, "The time draws near the birth of Christ," but with contrasting accounts of Christmas traditions observed. More important are the parallels to the first group. By CV his belief in progress is asserted, as the speaker looks toward a better future not just for himself but for mankind as well. In this context, the "Ring out wild bells" section is not simply the set piece of jubilation it appears to be when extracted and set in an anthology; it is a dramatic utterance, revealing the conscious struggle to overcome grief and seek hope. By now Time, whose changes have proven to be inexorable, is accepted instead of regretted. And so, with a fierce energy the speaker exhorts Time to work its way toward progress and the aid of mankind. Here the movement from personal grief to public good is clearly expressed; personal sorrow is associated with materialism and sectarian strife. Yet the last group should not be misread as a statement of placid assurance, for the struggle which appeared throughout earlier sections continues to the end. In living through another anniversary of his friend's birth, or resolving not to shut himself from others, he continues to resist the self-pity which characterized much of the opening expression. The challenges raised by recent scientific theories of change, most positively termed either progress or evolution are, in the end, faced and accepted. Sections CXV through CXVIII, are not one long piece of logical dialectic, but a series of episodes in which are presented the problem, his hope to settle it, and finally, in CXVIII, the most full reconciliation of his personal need for hope and contemporary theories of evolution. Appropriately, he uses the first person plural form to express his confident conclusions regarding the nebular hypothesis and the moral progress compatible with evolution. This set of authoritative, confident exhortations contrasts sharply with the illogical, self-serving evasions uttered in the opening sections.

Marking the enormous progress achieved over the series of statements, Section CXIX serves as a companion to VII. Now the speaker can remember the past, face the dawn and, finally, clasp the hand of his friend—if only in imagination. It is that touch, that union with the departed which he had sought in VII and throughout later episodes. Most striking is the contrast of his final self-assurance with the self-doubt of the opening. In Section CXX, to the objections of scientific materialism he replies not with logical arguments but with faith in his own worth: "I was *born* to other things." Concurrent with the restoration of hope and the renewal of his own personality is the revival of confidence in his love for the lost friend, so that by Section CXXIII such love provides stability and assurance in the face of all fears.

In terms of dramatic development, that is as far as the speaker progresses, and in the concluding eight sections he summarizes his final position. Section CXXIV is the most comprehensive of these; in it he attempts to express how he reached the stage of confidence and peace. It was not through rational investigation, nor from natural evidence but through intuition. He tries to express this, first saying that in defense against despair or destruction by freezing intellect his heart "stood up and answered 'I have felt.'" But immediately, as if that account is insufficient, he returns to the simile offered before at the low point of his experience when in Section LIV he called himself a child crying for light. The addition of the last two stanzas to Section CXXIV provides needed elaboration of his recovery. But equally important, those stanzas make it clear that it is an act of expression which is given credit for turning him to recovery:

> Then was I as a child that cries,
> But, crying, knows his father near.

It is not certain that had he not cried, the child in the simile would not have felt reassurance. But it is likely to be so, so that the vocal expression itself serves a therapeutic, consoling function. And in the case of this speaker, there is no doubt that expression, *via* the poem itself, leads to consolation. The conclusion he finally reaches is not adaptable to familiar discourse:

> And what I am beheld again
> What is, and no man understands.

But that should not be dismissed or even discounted as evasive, for he has reached a point where logical discourse is impossible. He has apprehended some higher reality; he has even apprehended himself ("what I am"); but he does not claim to have comprehended either. In the last several sections other concerns raised in the opening sections reappear, all transformed by the experiences which have transpired. Love, the loss of which the speaker had feared in Section VII, is confidently proclaimed as victor over all forces of change and loss. Evolutionary change, the force specified in the first three sections as antithetical to belief in man's dignity and some sense of order, is accepted and even exalted in the last sections. Clearly religious faith is restored, and the voice of Sorrow which haunted him in Sections I and III is replaced by a "deeper voice" proclaiming social truth and finally by the voice of his friend Hallam. In the last section appears the final resolution of all themes and the final polar element in the carefully balanced structure. It consists of a single sentence, addressed to free will, employing a tone of extreme confidence and eloquence. A metaphor of earthquakes is established in the first lines:

> O living will that shalt endure
> When all that seems shall suffer shock.

Free will is set against earthly things as exempt from change and deterioration, and as palpable also: it is "living," while reality is only that which "seems." This full reversal of values is called attention to by the deliberately slow pace set by the language: the second line is a tongue-twister which requires equal emphasis on each of the last four words. The will is exhorted to rise out of the rock, so that we, the speaker now taking on the authority of mankind, may

> . . . lift from out of the dust
> A voice as unto him that hears,
> A cry above the conquered years. . . .

This confident statement represents the ultimate development of the theme of expression which pervades the poem; at the end he has a voice, and knows that it can be heard, and even speaks for more than himself. Faith in God, hope for the future, and most of all, love—the speaker ends proclaiming the most confident belief in the unity of all things. The Christian overtones are undeniable and remarkable in a poem which has not employed many explicit Christian symbols or echoed the Gospel language very clearly. Just as each of the Gospels ends with references to spreading the word, this poem ends with the proclamation of faith in expression and constitutes that confident voice as well.

The second (IX-XIX) and penultimate (LCIX-CIII) groups are largely transitional. But important parallels establish their function in filling in parts of the chiasmus. The second group is concerned with the disposal of the body of the dead Hallam. Although the tone is lighter and less self-pitying, the series of episodes advances the main themes, adding special weight to the theme of poetic expression of grief. But now there is added complexity as an inner dialogue begins—not of the present self with an earlier one, but of two aspects of the mourner's character. He comments on his own concern for the safe and calm transport of the corpse, seeing it objectively for a moment. The passion is still there, however, for the section ends with more defiant or hopeless imaginings. In Section XII he dreams of leaving his mortal body and flying like a dove out to the ship bearing Hallam's corpse, but reaches only a question, "Is this the end?" So too in Section XIII, he knows that his inability to comprehend what has happened is giving rise to imaginings and excessive grief; he knows it, but he goes on imagining as though torturing himself with the thoughts of Hallam alive. So overtaxed are his powers to construct consoling fictions that in XV he questions whether the shock has unhinged his reason making him unable to distinguish fact from fiction or to express the difference. This is an essential question, related not only to his experience of shock at this point of the narrative but to the whole theme of poetic expression. Can I report facts with accuracy and my responses without distortion? he asks. In fact that issue is the central subject, at least on one level, of the entire poem; and it is a question with no simple answer except the poem itself. Of course the theme of achieving ordered expression relates to that of discerning some cosmic order as well, but by Section XVI that possibility is not raised. This early in the poem he has not faced that possibility and failing to see order he recognizes only delirium. But by the last of the sections in this group, the scenes of the ship's arrival and the burial, the speaker has achieved a surer grip of reality. The "firmer mind" begins to form, and he recognizes the finality of Hallam's death. And once having faced the hard fact of death, "My deeper anguish . . . falls / And I can speak a little then" (XIX, ll. 15-16). Still he is careful to add that it is only the "lesser griefs that may be said," while the most profound, heartfelt ones remain unspoken.

The penultimate, shortest group of sections, XCIX through CIII, reveals parallel changes. The speaker, revisiting places of youthful happiness, realizes the independent existence of familiar scenes of nature. It is actuality, not imagined things, which sustains him at this point. Recalling his friend's death is no less painful, but there now is no self-pity nor resentment. Even the acknowledgment that the scenes he now views will change is expressed as a mature judgment, not as a plea or cry. But more important in the chiastic structure of the poem is the parallel contained in the motif of voyage. Whereas the earlier group dealt with the journey home of the body of Hallam, this group centers on a voyage away as the family prepares to move from its home. A culmination comes in Section CIII in a vision of the dead. A dove, paralleling that in XII, summons the speaker to a voyage out to sea, which becomes a mystical voyage out of the self. But whereas in the second group he was unable to achieve communion, but only asked "Is this the end?" he is successful in this eighth group, and achieves communion and inspiration as well. More important yet, he achieves confidence in his craft, his ability to speak and write this poem.

The closer to the central group of sections, the more contorted is expression for the speaker. Thus both the third and seventh groups are less explicit than sections nearer the extreme ends of the chiasmus. In Sections XX-XXVII the speaker can with ease write about various peripheral matters, but the closer he comes to the most painful recognition of the loss of his friend, the more he evades, rationalizes or feels choked from expression. At this point in his bereavement it is natural for the speaker to distort his view of the past, but with regularity he questions the accuracy of his own descriptions and conclusions. Such admission of his own unreliability might be claimed to preclude the reader's involvement in the emotional situation; but, on the contrary, in making the reader aware of the contrivance and distortion of the character's statements, a tension between opposite forces adds to the dramatic intensity. It is as though the speaker is fighting against himself and all the while being sucked deeper into despondency. In the same way his repeated attempts to define just what he is trying to achieve by expressing his grief or writing this poem functions as a potent dramatic situation. In Section XXVI he expresses his intention in an even more defensive way:

> . . . I long to prove
>   No lapse of moons can canker Love,
> Whatever fickle tongues may say.

Similarly his comments on God are tentative, nearly hypothetical, so that the reader senses his longing to believe, to trust, to rely on God; but even as palpable are his uncertainty, confusion and even fear. This group of sections ends with an assertion, as though the speaker needs to stake out at least some matters as certain. Almost ironically it is love he cites as the single sure value. And its eminence is determined by intuition:

> I hold it true, whate'er befall;
>   I feel it, when I sorrow most;
>   'Tis better to have loved and lost
> Than never to have loved at all.

Whatever the limitations of language, some conclusions are tenable, at least as derived from feelings. And his intuition is reliable, as it turns out; the value of love, and the continuing effect of it, form the subject of the discourse to follow.

Conversely, the seventh group, LXXII through XCVIII, marks a stage of recovery and resolution of certain problems raised in the earlier section. His struggle to explain why he is writing this poem progresses toward a conclusion as his relationship to his dead friend slowly improves or becomes clearer. Even within the first section of this group, there is some recovery from anger and depression into acceptance and consolation. By now he has progressed to the point of reentering the world convinced that if he cannot rise above suffering, at least he cannot be hurt any deeper. The grounds of his earlier resentment fall away, not because some logical argument has dispelled them, but just because having gone through the depths of misery he is purged of resentment and susceptible to belief again. In the next section, LXXIV, he is able to see his friend's face—the very act of imagination he had struggled earlier to perform. But still he adds there is more that he now sees which must be left unsaid. Yet the extent to which he has recovered from depression and the change in his attitude toward his own literary composition are most clearly seen in Section LXXVII which concludes the discussion of the merit of his verses. By this point he has achieved distance from his own experience and activities; he knows that his efforts to write his reactions and thoughts will emanate in nothing more substantial than pages that tell "a grief, then changed to something else, / Sung by a long-forgotten mind," and yet he persists, stating his intentions as being two-fold: "to breathe my loss" and "to utter love." Comparison with the group in the parallel position of the chiasmus, Sections XX-XXVII, reveals how changed his attitudes toward poetic composition are. The return of his confidence in human relations is signalled by the sections on the second Christmas and the section addressed to his brother Charles. There remains some strain; evidence of the effort at recovery he is making is seen in the curious section, LXXX, in which he imagines what might have happened had he died and his friend lived. The imagery of this section is the most telling indicator of how he is forcing himself to optimism. Unlike the other sections it employs the language of commerce; words such as "gain," "credit," "influence," and "save" make us associate this section either with Shakespeare's Sonnets 30 or 38 which also achieve ironic effects through commercial references, or with Tennyson's **"Ulysses"** where similar terms are employed for ironic effect. The chiastic structure is supported by another repetition, the opening lines of LXXXV, which repeat those famous lines of XXVII. It is no late realization that it is better to have loved and lost, but one which he felt even when he suffered most. This section serves as the very center of the seventh group, summarizing his progress to this point and dispassionately stating his position at this time. What is new is an utterly transformed view of the power and function of expression. The section is itself a gift of words, addressed to Edmund Lushington as Hallam Tennyson's note indicates, and as such it constitutes proof that he has begun to recover, to regain speech. Furthermore it is about words: it starts with a recollection of the words of consolation which it took him time to understand. The nightingale of Section LXXXVIII parallels the linnets of Sections XXI and XXVII, now singing of "fierce extremes." But gradually the speaker comes closer to what he had longed for: some sort of communion and reunion with his dead friend. From Section XC to the most analyzed episode, XCV, the wish to rejoin his friend grows, suspense is built, and the setting for the big scene is established.

The chiastic structure of the poem, reinforced by symmetrical placing of parallel statements and stages of thought places the greatest emphasis at the very center of the poem, in the fifth of nine groups. Therefore, Section XCV, sometimes claimed to be the climax of the poem, is not that. But it is undeniably important as a capsule statement of the progress of the poem to this point, as well as a distinct experience in itself. Like the big scenes of his other dramatic poems, it is recorded in the past tense, not the present, despite the fact that the episodes leading up to it and those that follow are in the present tense, and it is effectively presented in dramatic form as a vivid experience. Although a detailed examination of the dramatic structure of this section is not necessary to this paper, it should be noted that the effect of the trance or vision involves a revival of the speaker's power of expression: he becomes able to "read" of the past, and hear "silent-speaking words." The counter-attack of faith takes the form of language, "word by word, line by line." And although he cannot find adequate words to recapture or report the experience, a fact which he regrets, he does make an effort in the form of this section itself. The closing sections of the group, XCVI through XCVIII, elaborate upon the growth of faith he experiences, the revival of love and the restoration of his power of expression, culminating in the last section, explicit proof in the form of a balanced and yet feeling letter to an unnamed friend. Thus it closes as a strong contrast to the way in which the parallel group opened: the expression he had earlier despaired of is achieved.

The fourth and sixth of the "natural groups," XXVII-XLIX and LIX-LXXI, serve as the immediate frame of the central crucial movement of the poem, and so in these two groups parallel thematic elements are quite clearly stated. From his consideration of the Lazarus story on, the speaker is troubled by the question of what occurs after death. The possibility of immortality, the comparison of death to sleep, are most clearly stated in XLIII and the following several sections. But by the contrasting poems in the sixth group, LXVIII through LXXI, a transformed tone dominates. If the matter is not settled, at least it is viewed from a different perspective. Even more striking are the parallel uses of domestic imagery when in Sections XL and LX the speaker describes a bride on her wedding day. Whereas in the earlier section it is feelings of the family she is leaving which provide a metaphor for the speaker's grief, in the later section he is able to enter the more complex but mature psychology of the bride herself. In both groups the subject of poetic composition is prominent, with XLVIII providing the fullest, most accurate description of his intention in the entire poem.

The group of sections L-LVIII, the very middle one of the nine groups, constitutes the low point for the speaker, the thematic crux, the place at which each of the strands is interlinked and most fully developed. His struggle against despair has become gradually weaker, and the evasions and distractions which he posed have become transparent. In earlier sections he had avoided referring to his present position and he had hidden behind references to mankind or transferred his private doubts to hypothetical questions. But in this group of sections the defenses fall; in a series of dramatic utterances breaking forth he reaches the nadir of his experience. Although he opens the group by appealing to friends for help, aid is not forthcoming and very quickly he sinks to despair and even a longing for death. The difference in tone from earlier sections is striking: he is speaking without guile or self-evasion. Letting forth his grief after so long stifling it is not done without worries that he is doing wrong. In LI he questions whether he really does want help and whether he should reveal his "inner vileness." Once again this is couched in terms of mankind—"we" instead of "one"—although in the two central stanzas he slips into the first person. The fear that his submission is sinful or sacrilegious is restated, more clearly now because he reveals his fear that love is betrayed in the process. In succeeding sections the gravitational pull of despair intensifies, and although he attempts consolation in LIII it is inadequate to counter the dizzying, drowning forces that oppress him.

Finally, in Section LIV and continuing for the next few sections, the nadir is reached. When the speaker attempts to define "the good," he is reduced to basic claims and an intensified awareness of the inadequacy of his own speech. It begins in the abstract: "we trust" but it becomes painfully personal by the end. The first three stanzas list things hoped for, the bare requirements for any hopeful view of life. But they are followed with the admission "Behold, we know not anything." He shifts to the first person and admits that all he has is some slim hope; but even that he reduces by stressing how far off the beneficial results are likely to be. Then the last stanza undercuts even the bare hope that preceded by referring to it as only a dream:

> So runs my dream: but what am I?
> An infant crying in the night:
> An infant crying for the light:
> And with no language but a cry.

At the very depth of his experience the speaker's concern is with his inability to express himself. The general observations now have been reduced to focus on his personal misery; the comments on expression and poetry have likewise come to bear only on his inability to say anything; the speaker has been dragged down to the hard facts of his own confusion. Thus stripped of defenses, he proceeds to admit his personal need for a belief in immortality. The theory entertained in the first stanza of LV is not, then, another piece of abstract theorizing intended to distract the speaker by raising his attention from actual suffering to a higher and hopefully benevolent plan. It is simpler and more painful than that. The opening sentence is more a challenge than a question: "Does it not?" rather than "Does it?" And what it states, not in any confident manner, is the central, necessary challenge which the speaker has avoided facing, the minimum irreducible fact necessary to make life bearable: the immortality of man, particularly both his friend and himself. The insistence on this is not based on reason but on instinct—instinct backed into a corner at that. Something "likest God," some minor identity, paraphrasable perhaps as soul, gives out the wish for immortality. Admittedly the logical order is weak and the underlying emotion is most strong, but this entire statement of need results from his immediate anxiety. No matter how broken, how confused, and close to despair he is, the belief in God is not sacrificed. He still pleads to God: not with firm knowledge of the efficacy of his prayers but with "lame hands of faith" and faint trust. The emphasis is still on his call to God, even though that is only a faint cry. Section LVI culminates the most depressed set of episodes, relating theories of evolution, religious belief in a divine order, and man's need to love in a single desolate view. It is clear that he still is struggling against despair and in desperation asks if man is no more than the deceived but corrupted product of an indifferent physical force. Of course no answer comes; and he even fears no answer ever will come. But at this lowest point he forsakes speech for hearing: if speech is inadequate maybe there remains a chance for hearing a voice which can console.

It is to that which he turns in Section LVII, and begins the climb upward. The speaker responds to a voice urging him to come away. He has no inflated confidence in his poem; he even admits he thinks it will fail. But his sense of hearing is strong, and in some mysterious way it becomes clear that the crisis has passed. The group of sections closes with LVIII, which extends the metaphors of hearing, but from an echoing distance, both of time and place. He hears and accepts the advice of the high muse to wait, desist from expressions of grief, and listen for consolation.

The prologue and epilogue may be considered as separate from the body of the poem. Of course they reiterate the central concerns of the poem; in their internal structures, reflect the chiastic pattern of the whole poem. In the prologue the opening confident proclamation of Christ as "immortal Love" is gradually replaced by more and more personal admissions of uncertainty and prayers of humility. Conversely the epilogue moves from the personal to greater and greater confidence, culminating in a paean in praise of God who unifies all and gives significance to everything.

Closer analysis of individual quatrains would reveal frequent use of the chiastic pattern, paralleling the structure of the whole poem, and it could even be argued that certain pairs of images reinforce such a symmetrical balance. However it is sufficient to note the importance of the calculated balance of the nine "natural groups" one against the other on either side of the focal, middle group; for by noting that structure the dramatic nature of the poem is most clearly discerned. The subjects described as major themes and other subsidiary ones as well, all receive fullest expression in the central group, not as a result of discursive analysis, but as measured by the intensity of expression. Finally it is expression itself, hearing as well as speaking, which leads to the resolution of the poem. Thus at the very center of the chiasmus, the middle section of the middle group, LIV, appears the most painful and honest admission of man's inability to be more than "an infant crying for the light." But that admission, futile though it seems at the time, is the germ of eventual salvation.

Notes

1. T. S. Eliot, "In Memoriam," *Essays Ancient and Modern* (New York: Harcourt Brace, 1936), p. 196; A. C. Bradley, *Commentary on Tennyson's In Memo-*

riam (London: Macmillan, 1907); Valerie Pitt, *Tennyson Laureate* (London: Barrie & Rockliff, 1962).

2. Christopher Ricks, *Tennyson* (New York: Macmillan, 1972), pp. 228-30.

3. The rhetorical term "chiasmus" describes a sentence pattern in which parallel units are set in reversed order (e.g., "John rode to the city; to the country rode Mary.") In describing the structure of larger units such as stories, parables and entire works, Biblical scholars have long used the term "chiastic" to describe a structure such as is suggested by the Greek letter *chi* (X), with parallel rhetorical or plot units in reversed order. Although the term is not frequently used in literary criticism of modern languages, it is well accepted among Biblical scholars. See Nils Wilhelm Lund, *Chiasmus in the New Testament* (U. of North Carolina, 1942) and John Bligh, *Galatians in Greek* (U. of Detroit, 1966) for discussion and applications.

4. Hallam Lord Tennyson, *Alfred Lord Tennyson: A Memoir* (London: Macmillan, 1897), i, 304-305.

5. This scheme is admirably discussed in Martin Svaglic, "A Framework for Tennyson's *In Memoriam*," *JEGP* [*Journal of English and Germanic Philology*], 61 (1962), 810-25. However, he does not discuss the poem's chiastic arrangement nor the way in which the theme of poetic expression is integrated into the poem's dramatic structure.

6. James R. Kincaid describes the poem as balancing on a pivotal section, LVI, so that its two halves balance ironic against comic visions: *Tennyson's Major Poems* (New Haven: Yale U. Press, 1975), pp. 80-109.

7. E. D. H. Johnson, "*In Memoriam*: The Way of the Poet, "*Victorian Studies,* 2 (1958), 139-48.

8. John D. Rosenberg, "The Two Kingdoms of *In Memoriam*," *JEGP,* 63 (1959), 228-40.

Gerald L. Bruns (essay date 1978)

SOURCE: Bruns, Gerald L. "'The Lesser Faith': Hope and Reversal in Tennyson's *In Memoriam*." *Journal of English and Germanic Philology* 77 (1978): 247-64.

[*In the following essay, Bruns examines the organization of* In Memoriam, *asserting that the poem's reversals of hope and faith need to be critically explored and understood rather than resolved, as some critics contend.*]

For me, the most credible readings of *In Memoriam* are those that have been concerned less with the unity or totality of the poem than with its variable or heterogeneous nature.[1] In this paper I want to engage this variability once more, not in order to resolve it into an ideal form, but simply to understand its meaning. Although my title predicts a thesis, or a conclusion, my intention is not a tendentious one; rather, it is to think through the peculiar reversals that Tennyson's lyrics force us to undergo at the end of his poem, when our expectations of some kind of generic repose, whether elegiac or comic or whatever, seem less than adequately or conventionally fulfilled. At the same time, however, I want to resist the notion that these reversals are simply instances of the "vacillating state" that was Tennyson's enduring mental or psychological condition. This perception of Tennyson's awkward mental life may be accurate and even interesting, but it can also be a critical nuisance, especially when it combines with our habit of regarding *In Memoriam* in terms of an imperious ideal of unity. Such an ideal tends to persuade us that the poet's inability (or reluctance) to locate a certain or discernible center in the midst of disorder is a form of aesthetic failure; or, conversely (and worse), it may compel us to break up our experience of reading the poem into explanations of the poem's "hidden" or "unnoticed" or "complex" wholeness.

I begin instead with the assumption that there is nothing wrong with Tennyson's poem or with Tennyson's mind. *In Memoriam* is admittedly a poem of divergent parts, but I regard this as a phenomenon to be understood, not a problem to be solved or regretted. Tennyson perhaps did not disguise his waywardness as well as other writers might have, but it may also be that the Victorians generally were less anxious about composing heterogeneous works than we are about reading them. *In Memoriam* has, after all, something of the fugitive character of Ruskin's *Modern Painters,* or of those loose and baggy monsters of Victorian fiction, or of famous discrete essays gathered into a deceptively single volume. A corollary of this assumption is that we should not conceive of *In Memoriam* according to the model of a problem-solving mechanism whose operation will either yield or fail to yield a solution, or resolution, or summary intellectual relief. Literary critics seem quietly addicted to this model, which is a short and easy method for describing how the human mind shows its power of reason, and thus they are inclined to think of *In Memoriam* as a work of emotional or psychological grandeur, rich enough in ideas, but haphazardly so: not a particularly intelligent poem. Yet each lyric is an act of thinking that generates a series or array of meanings, and if it is difficult to find for these meanings a uniform interpretive arrangement, this does not mean that the poem is intellectually flaccid or inadequate to its themes. One could say that the poem proceeds according to a principle of adjacency rather than consistency, but perhaps even the notion of "process" should be left out of account, if only to forestall the expectation that the poem conforms to some complicated principle of development.

I

No doubt *In Memoriam* was meant (at some point during the composition of its parts) to conform to such a principle. One of Tennyson's "official" responses to his poem was to say it "begins with a funeral and ends with a marriage—begins in death and ends in promise of a new life—a sort of Divine Comedy, cheerful at the close."[2] Tennyson was perhaps no better a commentator than any of us, but one may still appreciate his thesis: in rough approximation to a sublime or sacred comedy, *In Memoriam* begins in chaos and ends with the evocation of a new cosmos, a newly felt order of creation predicated upon the active unity of God and Nature. In the death of Hallam the poet had suffered the shattering of a world once ennobled by the presence of human excellence and harmonized by personal affection, by a sense of belonging or of being at home, but he speaks in the end of a world restored through the inauguration of a love that is no less real or personal for having been diffused throughout a cosmic and impersonal space:

> My love involves the love before;
> My love is vaster passion now;
> Though mixed with God and Nature thou,
> I seem to love thee more and more.
>
> Far off thou art, but ever nigh;
> I have thee still, and I rejoice;
> I prosper, circled with thy voice;
> I shall not lose thee though I die.[3]
>
> (CXXX, 9-16)

The categories of absence and presence, infinite distance and proximity of feeling, are traversed by the energies of love, and on this basis the poet is moved to affirm not only Hallam's immortality and man's but, as "comrade" to this higher faith, God's presence in the world—his presence, less as a personal incarnation within human time than as an immanent and creative power that drives history forward toward a point of coherence and repose: as the famous lines tell us, "all, as in some piece of art, / Is toil cöoperant to an end" (CXXVIII, 23-24). To be sure, this end—the spiritualization of man within the temporal order, his eventual entry into an earthly City of God—is figured mainly as a synecdoche of desire, but this is so because Tennyson's thinking is sanctioned by love. Its content is the theme of hope (a theme we shall be in a position to characterize more precisely later on), in the sense that the poet "sees the course of human things" (CXXVIII, 4), but not from the theoretical standpoint of a philosophy of history, nor from the transcendental standpoint of a Romantic or Yeatsian revelation—totalist visions, as we shall see, that are rich and terrifying in their complications. Instead, he sees "in part" (CXXVIII, 22), as one enlightened by mystery.[4] For him, the emptiness of profane time is filled with the presence of a sacred meaning, and for the time being—the time of one's life or in real human time—merely to sense this presence is ground enough for hope.

He sees "as one enlightened by mystery": yet what sort of seeing is this? The idea of mystery is rarely a useful critical concept, because it presupposes an unspeakable distance between experience and interpretation. This distance, however, is precisely what is characteristic of *In Memoriam,* the more so because Tennyson assumes the sagelike responsibility of constructing a version of what he cannot know: the nature of time and the course of human history. *In Memoriam* expresses a discontinuity between the poet's response to time and his interpretation of it; or, better, it expresses a difference between lived experience and reasoned sight or transcendent vision. Time is filled with the presence of a sacred meaning, but a presence only, not a product or content of understanding. Its distinctive feature is its irreducibility before the power of explanation. But if time incorporates a dimension that cannot be comprehended in its totality, the poet nevertheless claims to know the pressure of its reality (even as he grows conscious of Hallam's presence), and accordingly he is moved to bear witness, as one filled with hope, to its *formal* difference from the dimension of ordinary experience. In Tennyson's poem the experience of time is regularly figured as an experience of circularity:[5] time is the ancient adversary who carries man through the cycle of birth, growth, decay or violence, and death: he is, in Tennyson's striking metaphor, "a maniac scattering dust" (L, 7). It is in part to counter this adversary that Tennyson takes recourse to the model of comedy, which (soberly, as with elegiac restraint) superimposes upon the circularity of temporal experience the saving and mythic patterns of recurrence and renewal, as in the last Christmas sequence:

> Be neither song, nor game, nor feast;
> Nor harp be touched, nor flute be blown;
> No dance, no motion, save alone
> What lightens in the lucid east
>
> Of rising worlds by yonder wood.
> Long sleeps the summer in the seed;
> Run out your measured arcs, and lead
> The closing cycle rich in good.
>
> (CV, 21-28)

But despite this virtue of renewal—despite the repose that the model of comedy might have conferred upon the poet and his poem's ending—Tennyson's desire is to break through the cycle. For him, the hidden form of time is its *linearity*: in its deepest recesses (in its sacred meaning) time is not repetition but emergence and development, not merely the ceaseless making and undoing of random forms (CXXIII) but formation according to providential design (CXXIV). Interestingly, the one is not cancelled by the other: circularity is not so much opposed to providential design as different from it—adjacent, as though of a different order, but not contradictory. Or, again, Tennyson seeks to interpret time from the standpoint of its end, not in terms of a repetition or a version of the past. Time in this sense is history—the gradual emergence of a meaning that is present in time but impossible to fully grasp, even as the meaning of a narrative informs and secretly compels a course of events, but becomes accessible to understanding only by virtue of the narrative's completion.[6] Thus one may know the presence of meaning in history without knowing how that meaning is to be spoken. The best that one can do is to construct for history an intelligible *form*: insofar as history is providential, the linearity of time may be figured vertically rather than horizontally.

It is an ascension in and through time as through successive orders of nature:

> Arise and fly
> The reeling Faun, the sensual feast;
> Move upward, working out the beast,
> And let the ape and tiger die.
>
> (CXVIII, 25-28)

II

It is necessary, however, to balance this schematic or formalized account of the poet's "lesser faith" (CXXVIII, 3)—his movement, so to speak, from nature to history, or from the circularity of temporal experience to a developmental construction of time—by a critical and more searching account of how this faith is actually engaged by the poet's imagination. Love opens the poet to the mystery of things and so makes possible the act of hope that implicates both the poet (CXVII) and mankind (CXVIII) in a benevolent future, but the hard fact is that this act of hope does not possess comedy's magic power of transformation—the power, for example, of conjuring a golden world where.

> all the breeze of Fancy blows,
> And every dew-drop paints a bow,
> The wizard lightnings deeply glow,
> And every thought breaks out a rose.
>
> (CXXII, 17-20)

It is important to accept this work of Fancy as a real event in the poet's experience, but it remains an event only, part of the enthusiasm with which in this lyric he invokes the spirit of Hallam, not a state or privileged domain. It cannot be used to signal "the course of human things," especially because it is itself an episode in what becomes a perplexing (because discontinuous) turn of events. For not long after, at precisely that moment when the poet is illuminated by the tidings of love's "sentinel" (CXXVI, 9) and is in turn moved to affirm time's sacred meaning, he imagines most powerfully the terrible ordeal of time's destructiveness:

> And all is well, though faith and form
>   Be sundered in a night of fear;
>   Well roars the storm to those that hear
> A deeper voice across the storm,
>
> Proclaiming social truth shall spread,
>   And justice, even though thrice again
>   The red fool-fury of the Seine
> Should pile her barricades with dead.
>
> But ill for him that wears a crown,
>   And him, the lazar, in his rags:
>   They tremble, the sustaining crags;
> The spires of ice are toppled down,
>
> And molten up, and roar in flood;
>   The fortress crashes from on high,
>   The brute earth lightens to the sky,
> And the great æon sinks in blood,
>
> And compassed by the fires of Hell;
>   While thou, dear spirit, happy star,
>   O'erlook'st the tumult from afar,
> And smilest, knowing all is well.
>
> (CXXVII)

"And all is well": this, Tennyson would later say, "'is the keynote of the whole.'"[7] But the hope that time's hidden movement is guided by a God of Love does not preserve the poet from a terrifying vision of the world's annihilation; it does not free him from the imagination of disaster. It is possible, of course, to explain away such a vision, whose terror can be made a matter of one's point of view.[8] Tennyson, after all, is the great poet of adjusted perspectives, as when in 1892 he drove out one of his recurrent episodes of melancholy by asserting defiantly, "God *is* love, transcendent, all-pervading! We do not get *this* faith from Nature or the world. If we look at Nature alone, she tells us that God is disease, murder and rapine. We get this faith from ourselves, from what is highest in us.'"[9] By this same token, if we interpret history too strictly from the standpoint of our experience in time, we see only what Mircea Eliade has called "the terror of history": catastrophes that are nothing less than demonic when suffered in the immediacy of the present, and that traditionally have compelled man to nullify such experience by withdrawing to a point outside of time, as to the imagination of such cosmic distance as Hallam achieves, or to such interior distance as the world of the spirit appears to provide the poet (CXXIII).[10]

We should note in passing, however, that such distancing is a two-edged sword, for its effect is to devalue historical reality, as when Yeats, in "The Gyres," responds to bloody cataclysm by laughing in "tragic joy," thus asserting over and against the destruction of all temporal things the judgment of transcendence: "What matter?"[11] For in the cosmic view of things events in and of themselves do not matter; what matter are the patterns that they execute—the forms of eternal recurrence or, if we are thinking of Tennyson's poem, of linearity and development. The difficulty is that when such saving judgment is achieved ("What matter?" "all is well") the immediacy of individual life is not therefore deprived of its reality, but continues to assert its claim upon human feeling. This is why Hallam's smile is likely to strike us as being overdistanced—rather like the smile of those Lucretian gods who, in **"The Lotos-Eaters,"** take such cruel delight in the misery of human events. More to the point, Hallam seems profoundly careless of "the single life" that forms the most vital portion of historical reality, and thus he appears to countermand the poet himself, who has made the value of "the single life" one of his poem's most compelling affirmations (LIV).

Can one value history and still remain a part of it, or can it be valued only from a safe distance? One needs to pose this question fairly. I do not mean to undervalue the power of explanation that we may bring to bear upon "And all is well." The spirit of Hallam, after all, does *not* dwell in any Lucretian or Yeatsian universe but has come to exist as part of the dynamics or economy of human destiny. He is "mixed with God and Nature," and it is, in effect, under his aegis that even now the catastrophes of time are being redeemed by the deeper movement of the "historical process." Moreover, the catastrophe upon which Hallam smiles is rhetorically as well as cosmically distanced, in the sense that "And all is well" is bounded (one could say: "buttressed") on both sides by firm enunciations of love as a power that confers upon the single life in time the strength to endure history's eruptions. Hallam knows that "the course of human things" must be referred for its meaning and value to this higher principle of love. Man's temporal experience may not be illusory; indeed, the cycles and their cataclysmic endings are real—part of

> The deep pulsations of the world,
>
> æonian music measuring out
> The steps of Time—the shocks of Chance—
> The blows of Death.
>
> (XCV, 40-43)

But taken by itself such experience is incomplete and will remain only an experience of terror if it is not informed at the same time by the saving experience of love—saving, or mitigating, because it is only through love that one acquires the sense of an ending, that is, the intimation that history's changes are determined by a sacred final cause: that "one far-off divine event, / To which the whole creation moves" (Epilogue, l. 144)

Nevertheless, having fairly considered this explanation (which surely brings us close to Tennyson's meaning), we must in equal fairness consider how it bears upon (and is complicated by) our experience of reading Tennyson's poem. The peculiarity of "And all is well" is that it confounds this explanation, and (like mystery) sets interpretation at defiance. For "And all is well" turns upon a rupture that isolates the keynote from the imagination that carries the poem forward, as though the poem were motivated as much by a principle of terror as by the principle of love. To be sure, the lyric begins safely enough as a distanced affirmation of the benevolence of time despite isolated moments of terror:

> Well roars the storm to those that hear
> A deeper voice across the storm.
>
> (CXXVII, 3-4)

We have already learned that man is only the "seeming prey of cyclic storms" (CXVIII, 11), and that through faith, or through the emulation of types (like Hallam) that herald a "higher race" (CXVIII, 14), he can, at least in spirit, transcend catastrophe, even as the poet can transcend the flow of material things by reposing among things of a different, less vulnerable order (CXXIII). But "And all is well" develops as though in forgetfulness of this meaning. Suddenly, the whole temper of the poem, which is to say its fundamental point of view and the emotion that such a viewpoint generates, undergoes a sharp reversal:

> But ill for him that wears a crown,
> And him, the lazar, in his rags:
> They tremble, the sustaining crags;
> The spires of ice are toppled down,
>
> And molten up, and roar in flood;
> The fortress crashes from on high.
>
> (CXXVII, 9-14)

Why this amplification of disaster? For it is clear that the attitude toward catastrophe in these lines is no longer controlled by the transcending power of love; instead, the tone becomes consonant with terror. The decorum of the keynote is broken by a sharp appeal to fear and trembling, quite as though the God of Love who otherwise dominates the concluding sections of *In Memoriam* had suddenly been displaced by the fierce Jahweh of the Old Testament, who regularly visited catastrophes upon his faithless people in order to recall them to the Covenant. The poet thus falls perceptibly out of character, becoming a prophet not of new life but of divine wrath—divine wrath, moreover, that appears to know no bounds. Our expectations are, perhaps, that "all is well," but not for all: not for those who presumably fail to hear "the deeper voice across the storm." But in defiance of these expectations the opposition of king and beggar forms a social rather than moral category: it incorporates the whole of mankind—and, just so, in retrospect we can see that the movement of "And all is well" obliterates the saving distinction between the faithful and the damned, because it is a movement from the particular to the general, from local, momentary events—a "night of fear," recurrent (and therefore temporary) reigns of political terror—to the consummation of all earthly and temporal life:

> The brute earth lightens to the sky,
> And the great æon sinks in blood,
> And compassed by the fires of Hell. . . .
>
> (CXXVII, 15-17)

Doubtless (we can only hope) this bloodly conflagration is merely one of the "vast eddies in the flood / Of onward Time" (CXXVIII, 5-6), a lapse of history into cyclic endings, but the poet's language resists the thinking that would make it so, because the language derives its energy from what amounts to a new category of time: the supernatural dimension of Apocalypse. Notice that the limits that these lines place upon destruction are limits that define both totality and finality, as in an eschatological vision. It is as though Hallam were smiling upon the annihilation of all that is not transcendent, as though the "great æon" were human history itself. Hallam's smile is thus made all the more inscrutable, as in an augury of a fearful Second Coming, a vision of a divine holocaust that destroys not only temporal things but time itself—a prophecy, in other words, not of new and everlasting life fashioned out of love, nor even life born of something like a Carlylean "Fire-Baptism," but simply of that dread Day of Wrath when both king and beggar will be called equally to account.[12]

This dire Apocalypse—this foreshadowing, not of Paradise, but of Inferno—is a metaphor that turns back our expectations of time and history: it disrupts the sense of an ending that, at least since Section CXVIII, Tennyson appears to have been fashioning for his poem. The ideas with which he has fleshed out his sense of mankind's future have been roughly those of an early nineteenth-century historicist (a Liberal Anglican, perhaps), for whom the categories of linearity and development serve as a way of implicating the intelligibility and, ultimately, the sacredness of human events.[13] We have been asked to "Contemplate all this work of Time" (CXVIII, 1) according to an explanatory model of evolution, thus to place our trust in a historical vision that distributes mankind along a progressive continuum. Even in "And all is well" we have been asked to look forward to a time within time when "social truth" and "justice" shall prevail as in a new golden age—but suddenly the fulfillment of this historical design is figured negatively as a consummation of man's world by "the fires of Hell." Hallam continues intrepidly to smile, knowing (somehow) that "all is well," but on the poet's part the categories of historicism that would have been consonant with such a smile are abandoned for those of Apocalypse—and a darkly foreshortened Apocalypse at that. "Love is and was my Lord and King" (CXXVI, 1), the poet has assured us, but the anticipated Kingdom of God is displaced by a Vision of Judgment purely and simply. In the end, time is imagined to repose, not in the plentitude of comedy, but in the desolation of eternal damnation.

III

What is the reason for this rupture of imagination and idea? Part of the answer, certainly, may be derived from the formal nature of *In Memoriam* itself. Those critics are in the main correct who find that the parts of the poem have not been organized into a system of interdependent and mutually determining lyrics: conventional exegesis, whereby one lyric is used to interpret another, carries us only a very little way: one poem will light up another, as the saying goes, but only to darken others. Each lyric represents, not a relation within a systematic discourse, but an instance of mental activity whose progress is marked by contingency.[14] Or, alternatively, we may say that the poem is well known to be reflexive or inward-looking, a monument of subjectivity. Its expressions of doubt attend less to doubtful propositions of belief than to doubt's travail, even as its expressions of belief are generated less by a coherent body of faith than by the dynamics of faithfulness, as though the poet were concerned to improvise a sort of phenomenology of the spirit that brackets the content of belief in order to disclose the manifold and conflicting conditions of experience in which faith is forced to make its appearance. As a recent commentator has suggested, "What Tennyson believes is not particularly important. Much more important is the way his mind and his poem work."[15]

Yet certainly it is an odd and complacent thing to say that what Tennyson believes isn't important. Why isn't it? As true as these decidedly formalist views of the poem may be, they remain incomplete, and they make *In Memoriam* seem less urgent (and surely less thoughtful) than it appears to be in the experience of reading it. Better to argue, I believe, that the peculiar breach of imagination and idea that troubles "And all is well" is not an accident of composition but a necessary component of Tennyson's "lesser faith"—that is, of his relation to time and history.[16] For the radical shift of feeling from a rhetoric of hope that announces "all is well" to the rhetoric of fear that appropriates the metaphor of Apocalypse is rather a kind of dialectical reversal—not a reversion to an earlier state of doubt when time in its natural destructiveness seemed entirely the mortal enemy of man, but a return of Tennyson upon his own thinking, or upon his own impulse toward explanation and wish-fulfillment—an impulse that would reduce time to a pure idea of history, and so substitute for the reality of man's temporal life a merely conceptual alternative or reward. Time is irreducible, and its terror helps to make it so, because terror is a reality that cannot be humanly contained within the restraints of explanation. Apocalyptic terror heightens this point, and becomes thereby a decisive metaphor, because least among all forms of terror does Apocalypse belong to the realm of explanation—to natural or philosophical history; rather, it belongs to the realm of sacred literature, in which human history passes human understanding, and in which terror is not a problem, but a mystery.[17]

Admittedly, to argue thus is simply to adduce one explanation the more; it is not to resolve the elemental conflict that appears to abide within Tennyson's "lesser faith"—the conflict between universal design and individual value, or between history as it is conceived and history as it is lived. This conflict is of special interest, not simply because it is another instance of Victorian distrust of transcendental paper-visions, but because it constitutes the form in which Tennyson confronts the characteristic dilemma of historicism: namely, as Eliade puts the question, "How can the 'terror of history' be tolerated from the view point of historicism?"[18] How can we affirm the reality of history against the cyclicism that generates myths of destruction and renewal—how can we affirm this reality, and invest it with human (not to mention sacred) value, when history leaves man so vulnerable to catastrophe? Tennyson's position seems to be that the mere historicist cannot tolerate this dilemma; he cannot accept the mystery of terror, which forever maintains its presence in the world in defiance of all valuations of history, and which forces the man of faith into a posture of defiance all his own: "And all is well, though faith and form / Be sundered in the night of fear"—as though terror had the power to deprive belief of its positive explanations, but not of its meaning. It is the drama of this impasse between meaning and explanation that makes "And all is well" (or, for that matter, *In Memoriam* itself) such a persistently compelling poem, and which leads us to acknowledge once more that time for Tennyson is not homogeneous but is breached by opposition: there is the time of history that is sacred because it is shaped by God toward some perfect end, but over and against this millennial tract of time there is the time of experience—a cyclical time insofar as its daily theme is the destruction of all temporal things, their inescapable and reeling return to the aboriginal chaos whence they came. It is worth noting that in Section CXVIII Tennyson momentarily adumbrates the model of the Catastrophism, with its idea of development through violent transformation, as a way of suggesting how these two orders of time might be related:

>   . . . life is not as idle ore,
>
> But iron dug from central gloom,
>   And heated hot with burning fears,
>   And dipt in baths of hissing tears,
> And battered with the shocks of doom
>
> To shape and use.
>
>   (ll. 20-25)

The metaphor of life as iron helps to obscure the human issue, but not to abolish it: even more than most explanations (how can one predicate life of iron?), this one leaves entirely unguarded the single life of man as a creature of the present whose subjection to "the shocks of doom" weighs heavily upon the valuation of history.

This weight, however, is nothing less than the traditional oppression of mystery, wherein meaning abides without explanation. For the point is that terror is present in Tennyson's poem—is present, moreover, at the end, when theme and feeling ought to be converging toward repose—as something more than a problem to be solved by explanation. Terror cannot be distanced or forgotten or imagined away, because it is part of the mystery of time, part of the hiddenness of time's sacred meaning, and therefore part of the exigency of hope. This is what Reinhold Niebuhr has in mind when he says that the "basic message of Christianity is a message of hope in tragedy," by which he means a hope that is born, almost absurdly, of despair (the sense of being utterly forsaken and forsakable).[19] It is what Paul Ricoeur means when he writes, in "Christianity and the Meaning of History," that "it is essential that hope always remain in direct contact with the dramatic, disquieting aspect of history. It is precisely when hope is no longer the hidden meaning of an apparent nonsense, when it has freed itself from all ambiguity, that it comes back to rational and reassuring progress and heads toward stagnant abstractions."[20] Tennyson seems to have understood this point very well, that ambiguity or irreducible doubleness is the environment of hope, that hope freed from its contraries—from the imagination of disaster and the "terror of history"—is deprived of its occasion, and therefore of its reason and its life. For hope is the cry of its occasion: uprooted from man's lived experience, it becomes mere fantasy, or (worse) an abstract and mildly credible possibility among other possibilities equally remote, equally arbitrary: a conventional optimism, a vague Utopianism. The metaphor of Apocalypse, whose foreshadowing of Inferno betrays optimism by confounding the reasons that optimism needs, is in this sense a necessary correlative to the keynote of "all is well": it suggests that the genesis of Tennyson's hope is not part of an abstraction or escape from time, a leap into transcendence, but part of a movement through the reality of history, even as the movement of "And all is well" is not a movement away from terror but an unrestrained imagination of it.

IV

This matter of the doubleness of hope seems to receive a second rendering in the lyric that immediately follows "And all is well":

> The love that rose on stronger wings,
>   Unpalsied when he met with Death,
>   Is comrade to the lesser faith
> That sees the course of human things.
>
> No doubt vast eddies in the flood
>   Of onward time shall yet be made,
>   And thronèd races may degrade;
> Yet O ye mysteries of good,
>
> Wild Hours that fly with Hope and Fear,
>   If all your office had to do
>   With old results that look like new;
> If this were all your mission here,
>
> To draw, to sheathe a useless sword,
>   To fool the crowd with glorious lies,
>   To cleave a creed in sects and cries,
> To change the bearing of a word,
>
> To shift an arbitrary power,
>   To cramp the student at his desk,
>   To make old bareness picturesque
> And tuft with grass a feudal tower;
>
> Why then my scorn might well descend
>   On you and yours. I see in part
>   That all, as in some piece of art,
> Is toil cöoperant to an end.
>
>   (CXXVIII)

The critical task here, as in the case of "And all is well," is to read the poem's opening and closing affirmations without forgetting the utterances that connect them. Tennyson here testifies to his faith in providential history by apostrophizing those "mysteries of good" that drive time forward to its sacred end, but characteristically he does so with the mysteries of evil (including evil's banalities) in the foreground of his imagination. For the apostrophe is part of a dramatic reversal ("*Yet* O ye mysteries"): the poet proceeds by heaping up a catalogue of events that belong not to a world made Utopian by love but to a world of melancholy and all-too-human experience. The movement of the lyric, in other words, resembles a dialectic, the turning of Tennyson upon his own thinking, thus affirming the sacred meaning of history without abstracting that meaning from history itself. The "mysteries of good" are addressed not in the purity of their transcendence, but as mysteries: they are conjured by opposition, in a movement through an inventory that names the backwardness of time—discloses, in Ricoeur's word, the "ambiguity" of oved" (CXXXI, 10) is also that which makes affirmation [a] difficult and perhaps impossible thing to fix in a formu[la]tion: freedom from any sort of closure. More than any[thi]ng else, it is this freedom that proves so exasperating to [ou]r efforts of hard interpretation, the more so as we con[tin]ue to make the coherence of many meanings into one a [pri]vileged feature of mental activity. Accordingly, the [te]mptation will always remain to think of Tennyson's faith [an]d particularly his "lesser faith'") as insubstantial: so [ma]ny watery or unmastered aspirations toward the Un[kn]own—a groundless array of religious feelings intensi[fie]d by love but finally less credible than the turmoil of [th]e poet's doubt. But this sense of the poem's impoverish[m]ent disappears when we understand that the poet's faith [is] inseparable not only from love but from hope. The poet [dr]eams "a dream of good" (CXIX, 11)—admittedly a pri[va]te and subjective phenomenon—but this dreaming can[no]t be explained as the musing of an abstract or closeted [so]ul. It is not reducible to an imaginary wish-fulfilment [th]at abolishes the terrifying features of human life. On the [co]ntrary, what is striking about the poet's subjectivity is [its] openness to the world and to visions of terror that only [th]e world can occasion. This openness contrasts sharply [wi]th what I take to be the closure of doubt, which is to [sa]y the skepticism toward "double meanings" and "oppo[sit]e and inseparable truths" that earlier had closed up the [po]et's spirit in an amplification of grief.

Notes

1. Numerous studies have tried to describe the unity of *In Memoriam* according to a diversity of forms or models (structural, organic, symbolic, developmental, musical, etc.). Some of these are quite compelling—see, e. g., Robert Langbaum's "The Dynamic Unity of *In Memoriam*," in *The Modern Spirit: Essays on the Continuity of Nineteenth- and Twentieth-Century Literature* (New York: Oxford Univ. Press, 1970), pp. 51-75. I have no doubt that we will continue to find new and impressive ways of discussing the poem's organization, and of discovering patterns and coherences that render the poem accessible to interpretation. Yet it remains true that the starting point of any such enterprise is the experience of the poem's discontinuities, which are not to be explained away. A good example of how this experience informs and strengthens a critical study of the poem is James R. Kincaid's discussion in *Tennyson's Major Poems: The Comic and Ironic Patterns* (New Haven: Yale Univ. Press, 1975), pp. 80-109.

2. From Tennyson's conversation with James Knowles, in *Nineteenth-Century*, 33 (1893), 182.

3. The edition that I have used is *The Poems of Tennyson*, ed. Christopher Ricks (London: Longmans, Green, and Co., 1969).

4. I have used the term "mystery" with Reinhold Niebuhr's statement in mind: "Mystery does not annul meaning but enriches it. It prevents the realm of meaning from being reduced too simply to rational intelligibility" (*Faith and History: A Comparison of Christian and Modern Views of History* [New York: Charles Scribner's Sons, 1949], p. 103). Tennyson would have felt a great kinship with Niebuhr, whose conviction it was that "Perplexities, too simply solved, produce despair" (*Faith and History*, p. 233).

5. See James G. Taaffe, "Circle Imagery in Tennyson's *In Memoriam*," in *Victorian Poetry*, 1 (1963), 123-31.

6. As in Wilhelm Dilthey's conception that the "category of meaning" that we bring to bear upon history "designates the relation, rooted in life itself, of parts to whole." But this "is a relation which is never complete. One would have to wait for the end of a life and, in the hour of death, survey the whole to ascertain the relation between the whole and its parts. One would have to wait for the end of history to have all the material necessary to determine its meaning" (*Gesammelte Schriften* [Stuttgart: B. G. Teubner, 1938], VII, p. 233). The translation is H. P. Rickman's, from *Meaning in History: Wilhelm Dilthey's Thoughts on History and Society* (London: George Allen & Unwin, 1961), p. 106. See also J. Hills Miller, "Narrative and History," in *ELH*, 41 (1974), 460-61.

7. Quoted by Hallam Tennyson in *Alfred Lord Tennyson: A Memoir* (London: Macmillan, 1897), I, 298.

8. Thus most commentators attend only to the opening and closing stanzas of "And all is well." John D. Rosenberg, "The Two Kingdoms of *In Memoriam*," in *Journal of English and Germanic Philology*, 58 (1959), is virtually alone in considering the poem in its troubling totality: "Hallam, witness to this incandescent holocaust, 'smil[eth], knowing all is well.' The line is very nearly incredible. The smile is diabolic or divine, expressing either pyromaniacal joy or sublime content in the knowledge that the flaming of the earth is prelude to a finer order and a higher race" (p. 237).

9. *Alfred Lord Tennyson: A Memoir*, I, 314.

10. Eliade's famous distinction between cosmos and history in relation to historical catastrophe is particularly pertinent to *In Memoriam*. See Mircea Eliade, *The Myth of Eternal Return*, trans. Willard Trask (New York: Bollingen, 1954), pp. 146-52.

11. *Collected Poems of W. B. Yeats* (New York: Macmillan, 1956), p. 291.

12. See John D. Rosenberg's discussion of cyclic and apocalyptic time in *The Fall of Camelot: A Study of Tennyson's "Idylls of the King"* ([Cambridge, Mass.: Harvard Univ. Press, 1973], esp. pp. 34-37). Rosenberg remarks that "In *In Memoriam* Hallam is the 'herald of a higher race,' a 'noble type' of perfected man . . . ; in the *Idylls*, through a cataclysmic reversal of evolution, men 'reel back into the beast.' Evolution has been tinged with Apocalypse." Evolution

hope. Nor is this ambiguity merely an ironic turn of thought, for what is dramatized in this lyric is the poet's felt relation to his theme, which is to say his own historicity, even his own doubleness as a being whose time is breached, who casts his eyes toward an invisible and even unspeakable end, all the while imagining those baleful circumstances that would otherwise (were he a merely positive thinker) finally compel his scorn of history and history's God.

This helps to explain the curiously negative formulation of Tennyson's "lesser faith," for what is finally affirmed in "The Love that rose on stronger wings" is the belief that history's disquieting aspects are not a sum total, but parts and consequences of the temporality and therefore of the incompleteness of God's design. One cannot help thinking here of Arthur's lament in the midst of his own catastrophe in the *Idylls of the King*:

> O me! for why is all around us here
> As if some lesser god had made the world,
> But had not force to shape it as he would . . . ?[21]

History cannot be experienced from within as a plenum or a system but only in its changes as a world that has not yet been brought fully into being—a half-created work. It is as though the poet of *In Memoriam,* like Arthur, recognized himself as a creature of the present caught up in the shaping of recalcitrant material—in a process of "toil" or becoming whose diverse antagonisms disclose a basic opposition between the brute stuff of creation and the ideality of its formal cause. Here indeed is what history looks like from the standpoint of the single life; yet the single life is not closed. To move from matter to form, as from part to whole or from experience to idea, requires nothing less than a dialectical reversal: the movement of a mind that can contemplate, by turns or adjacently, the negativity of history as a time of suffering and death and history's sacred meaning as a continuation in time of God's creative act.

Contradictions, of course, may be unthinkingly held, but I use the term "dialectic" to emphasize that Tennyson is not an unthinking agent in his poem. To be sure, the term will be misleading if it merely implies a grammar of self-regulating procedures by which the mind obtains from variable and contradictory meanings a set of systematic results. Were this the whole of the case, I would seem to be doing no more than reverting to the old illusion that beneath the irregular surface of *In Memoriam* there is at work some law of internal necessity that, once discovered and described, will enable us to make sense of the poem in all of its heterogeneous details. But I find the term "dialectic" useful because it does not refer simply to a method of resolving logical difficulties but, on the contrary, describes a form of meditation whose distinctive feature is its concreteness or historicity. "Dialectic," Merleau-Ponty writes, "is not the idea of reciprocal action, nor that of the solidarity of opposites and their sublation [into some higher synthesis]." It is not an abstract, self-correcting op-

eration of thought but an activity carrie doubleness of being and thinking. Dialecti not predictable in its results. It does not d ordered relationships, like the binary oppo turalism, or Marxist super- and infrastruc Merleau-Ponty says, "these relationships a osities, paradoxes"—moments of terror, f erupt within the tidings of love. "They when one grasps them in . . . experience," perience is there "room, without contradic magic, for relationships with double mea site and inseparable truths, for sublation genesis, for a plurality of levels or order look for other words to describe Tennys this poem, but for my part I cannot find characterize the habit of mind that gives li *riam* than to borrow Merleau-Ponty's wor

At the very least these words do not misre and expansive nature of Tennyson's min have felt that any act of thinking would be simply if it were left unfinished or indecis anything out of account. There is no reso at *In Memoriam*'s end, because what ma poet's affirmation of those "truths that is clearly "tinged with Apocalypse" in *In Memoriam* as well—as Rosenberg suggested earlier in "The Two Kingdoms of *In Memoriam*" (p. 237).

13. See Duncan Forbes, *The Liberal Anglican Idea of History* (Cambridge: Cambridge Univ. Press, 1952), pp. 63-86. Tennyson had no "philosophy" of history, but it is possible to reconstruct his reflections into a fairly coherent exposition. See Henry Kozicki, "Philosophy of History in Tennyson's Poetry to the 1842 Volume," *ELH*, 42 (1975), 88-106. This matter has also been discussed by Ward Hellstrom, *On the Poems of Tennyson* (Gainsville: Univ. of Florida Press, 1972), pp. 26-36; and John Killman, *Tennyson and 'The Princess': Reflections of an Age* (London: Athlone Press, 1958), pp. 243-66. Also useful in this context is Susan Gliserman, "Early Victorian Science Writers and Tennyson's *In Memoriam*," *Victorian Studies*, 18 (1974), 277-308; 437-459. For my part I regard Tennyson as a historicist in Maurice Mandelbaum's sense of the term in *History, Man, and Reason: A Study in Nineteenth-Century Thought* (Baltimore: Johns Hopkins Univ. Press, 1971), p. 42: "Historicism is the belief that an adequate understanding of the nature of any phenomenon and an adequate assessment of its value are to be gained through considering it in terms of the place which it occupied and the role which it played within a process of development."

14. See Henry Puckett, "The Subjunctive Imagination in *In Memoriam*," *Victorian Poetry*, 12 (1974), 97-124.

15. Puckett, p. 107.

16. It is worth noting in this connection that Tennyson substituted "And all is well" for a much less ambiguous lyric. The original Section CXXVII is published in *Alfred Lord Tennyson: A Memoir*, I, 307:

> Are those the far-famed Victor Hours
>   That ride to death the griefs of men?
>   I fear not; if I fear'd them, then
> Is this blind flight the winged Powers.
>
> Behold, ye cannot bring but good,
>   And see, ye dare not touch the truth,
>   Nor Sorrow beauteous in her youth,
> Nor Love that holds a constant mood.
>
> Yet must be wiser than your looks,
>   Or wise yourselves, or wisdom-led,
>   Else this wild whisper round my head
> Were idler than a flight of rooks.
>
> Go forward! crumble down a throne,
>   Dissolve a world, condense a star,
>   Unsocket all the joints of war,
> And fuse the peoples into one.

17. As in Gabriel Marcel's distinction between problem and mystery in *Being and Having* (trans. Katherine Farrer [New York: Harper & Row, 1965], pp. 117-18): "A problem is something which I meet, which I find complete before me, but which I can therefore lay siege to and reduce. But a mystery is something in which I am myself involved, and it can therefore only be thought of as a sphere where the distinction between what is in me and what is before me loses its meaning and initial validity. A genuine problem is subject to appropriate technique by the exercise of which it is defined: whereas, a mystery, by definition, transcends every conceivable technique. It is, no doubt, always possible (logically and psychologically) to degrade a mystery so as to turn it into a problem. But this is a fundamentally vicious proceeding, whose springs might perhaps be discovered in a kind of corruption of intelligence" (p. 117).

18. Eliade, p. 150.

19. Reinhold Niebuhr, *Beyond Tragedy: Essays on the Christian Interpretation of History* (New York: Charles Scribner's Sons, 1937), p. 19.

20. Paul Ricoeur, *History and Truth*, trans. Charles A. Kelbley (Evanston: Northwestern Univ. Press, 1965), pp. 96-97. See also p. 95: "Hope tells me that there is a meaning [in history] and that I should seek it. But it also tells me that this meaning is hidden; after having encountered the absurd, it now faces system. Christianity has an instinctive distrust of systematic philosophies of history which would like to provide us with the key to intelligibility. One has to choose system or mystery."

21. *Poems of Tennyson*, pp. 1742-43.

22. [Maurice] Merleau-Ponty, *Adventures of the Dialectic*, trans. Joseph Bien (Evanston: Northwestern Univ. Press, 1973), pp. 203-204.

Joseph Sendry (essay date 1980)

SOURCE: Sendry, Joseph. "*In Memoriam*: Twentieth-Century Criticism." *Victorian Poetry* 18, no. 2 (summer 1980): 105-18.

[*In the following essay, Sendry provides a comprehensive overview of twentieth-century criticism on* In Memoriam.]

Twentieth-Century criticism of **In Memoriam** begins, conceptually as well as chronologically, with A. C. Bradley's *A Commentary on Tennyson's "In Memoriam,"* first published in 1901. Bradley offered exegesis and informative annotation of the entire poem along with richly concise biographical, bibliographical, and literary background. What he claimed not to offer was "aesthetic criticism," investigation of what Christopher Ricks (in *Tennyson*, 1972) calls "the most important critical question about **In Memoriam** . . . the first and most obvious one: in what sense do the 133 separate sections ranging in length from 12 lines to 144 lines, constitute a whole, a poetic unity, a poem?" In fact, Bradley had his doubts, which he expressed in an unregarded footnote to his 1914 lecture on "The Reaction against Tennyson" (published in *Miscellanies*, 1929). Admitting its greatness, Bradley still found **In Memoriam** "very defective as an 'organism'." Doubts and disavowal notwithstanding, Bradley did touch on the question of unity when in the *Commentary* he examined "the bearing of the sections on one another." He posited three ways in which they are related: through an "internal chronology," marked chiefly by three Christmases; through thematic groupings, each several sections in length, involving over 100 of the 131 units in the poem; and through "the Way of the Soul," Tennyson's phrase for what Bradley calls "the experience recorded in the poem." The first and third items have furnished a veritable program for subsequent "aesthetic criticism" of **In Memoriam.**

During the "reaction against Tennyson," which Bradley diagnosed so acutely, a new orthodoxy was enunciated by Sir Harold Nicolson, whose *Tennyson: Aspects of His Life, Character, and Poetry* appeared in 1923. In attempting to rehabilitate his subject Nicolson postulated his now familiar dichotomy between the melancholy romantic lyricist, who was worth preserving, and the moralistic spokesman for Victorianism, who was not. **In Memoriam** belonged to the first of these Tennysons, and the last words in the book were reserved for it. But the **In Memoriam** that Nicolson valued comprised individual lyrics, "plangent elegies . . . scribbled in the old account book . . . from 1833 to 1840" and not (an implicit reference to Bradley) "that artificially constructed synthesis which appeared in 1850 . . . with its three arbitrary divisions of Despair, Regret, and Hope."

Romantic melancholy scarcely provided the best ground for defending an unfashionable poem the year after *Ulysses* and *The Waste Land* were published, especially since the definitive modernist verdict that Tennyson was a poet of dissociated sensibility had already been pronounced by T. S. Eliot in 1921. The opening of Eliot's 1936 essay, "In Memoriam" (*Essays, Ancient and Modern*), promised a more sympathetic hearing: "Tennyson is a great poet, for reasons that are perfectly clear." As the essay proceeded, however, Eliot seemed to take his cues from Nicolson. Much of the canon is discarded, the work of the laureate years *en bloc*. **In Memoriam** is still accorded a place of honor, now singled out for its doubt as well as for its melancholy. As if in rebuttal to Nicolson's selective pruning, Eliot declared that "**In Memoriam** is the whole poem . . . a long poem made by putting together lyrics, which have only the unity and continuity of a diary . . . a diary of which we have to read every word." But a diary has a low degree of order, and a mandate to read every word is no guide to analysis. Having declared **In Memoriam** "the most unapproachable" of Tennyson's poems, Eliot gave little help in approaching it.

Eliot, however, approved of **In Memoriam** and so did W. H. Auden in 1944, when in his introduction to *A Selection of the Poems of Alfred, Lord Tennyson* he called Tennyson "the stupidest English poet" but acknowledged the poem "his masterpiece." In that introduction Auden cited Nicolson's view of the poet's career; in the anthology following he tacitly endorsed the critic's view of the poem by placing it in the virtually exclusive company of lyrics and shorter pieces of a melancholy cast. It was left to Paull F. Baum to assault the poem directly. In *Tennyson: Sixty Years After* (1948), the first book-length study after Nicolson's, Baum posed questions of unity that his predecessors had skirted and gave emphatically negative answers. The poem, as he saw it, was hastily and arbitrarily assembled from materials that are incompatible in genre (the personal elegy and the philosophical poem) and style. "Parts of the poem will live," he predicted, "but as a single poem it has had its day and ceased to be."

Baum's willingness to write off **In Memoriam** as a poem was shared by the few critics who expressed themselves on the matter (Humphry House in *All in Due Time* [1955] was one). But the small volume of scholarship published from the mid-thirties to the mid-fifties tended to treat **In Memoriam** as a document in the history of ideas. Much of the best work on the scientific and religious background comes from this period: George R. Potter's "Tennyson and the Biological Theory of the Mutability of Species" (*PQ* [*Philological Quarterly*], 16 [1937], 321-343), William R. Rutland's "Tennyson and the Theory of Evolution" (*E & S* [*Essays and Studies by Members of the English Association*], 26 [1940], 7-29), and Graham Hough's "The Natural Theology of **In Memoriam**" (*RES* [*Review of English Studies*], 23 [1947], 244-256). The ideas underlying the work also figure in the chapters on Tennyson in Basil Willey's *More Nineteenth-Century Studies* and Georg Roppen's *Evolution and Poetic Belief* (both 1956). Eleanor Bustin Mattes' **In Memoriam**: *The Way of A Soul* (1951), the first book devoted exclusively to the elegy since Bradley's a half-century earlier, was the most ambitious undertaking of this kind. Besides assigning sources for certain ideas (Wordsworth, Hallam, Isaac Taylor, Carlyle, Lyell, Herschel, and Chambers), Mattes attempted to date the composition of each section. In the first *MLA Guide to Research* on the Victorian poets (1956) Baum praised the book as "just what needed to be done." From the perspective of 1980 its usefulness is considerably diminished: what Mattes describes as sources are sometimes only parallels, and her largely conjectural dating has been rendered obsolete by manuscripts now available.

By the late 1950's the critical fortunes of **In Memoriam** had undergone a reversal: a new inclination to accept the work as poetry was coupled with a dramatic increase in the number of scholars who were working on it. Several developments contributed to this change. The bias nurtured by the New Criticism against long poems and poems seemingly lacking in irony, paradox, and ambiguity lost force as the prestige of that movement began to wane. The Victorian label, an onus that Tennyson and his elegy have had to bear throughout this century, became less burdensome as scholars began to detect continuity rather than conflict between the Victorians and the moderns. By 1964 a reviewer in the *TLS* [*Times Literary Supplement*] (for January 23) could describe a book as having "an archaic air" because it used the word "Victorian" in a pejorative sense. The founding in 1957 of the interdisciplinary journal *Victorian Studies* and of *Victorian Poetry* in 1963 insured Tennyson scholars, and prospective scholars, regular outlets for publication. The major contribution of the latter is indicated by its subtitle, "A *Critical* Journal of Victorian Literature." Finally, assumptions about the improvised construction of *In Memoriam* itself had to be reexamined in light of the notebooks and loose papers that Sir Charles Tennyson sold to Harvard in 1954, the major manuscript of the elegy that Lord Tennyson put on loan at Lincoln in 1959, and the eventual release in 1968 of what had long been thought the only major MS, the one given to Trinity College, Cambridge in 1897.

Arthur J. Carr's perceptive and sympathetic treatment of *In Memoriam* in "Tennyson as a Modern Poet," published in 1950 (*UTQ* [*University of Toronto Quarterly*], 19, 361-382), put him ahead of an advance guard that arrived at the end of the decade with the publication of three studies. In an essay appearing in the second volume of *Victorian Studies*, "*In Memoriam*: The Way of the Poet" (1958, 139-148), E. D. H. Johnson, starting with Bradley's "Way of the Soul" through stages defined by the three Christmases, went on to describe a parallel, subsidiary structure in the poet-speaker's developing sense of his own art. In "The Two Kingdoms of *In Memoriam*" (*JEGP* [*Journal of English and Germanic Philology*], 58 [1959], 228-240), John D. Rosenberg focused on two concepts, evolutionary progress and the religious belief in the coming Kingdom of God on earth, not for their significance in the history of ideas but as they give shape to the poem. And in *The Romantic Assertion* (1958) R. A. Foakes proposed a method of considering precisely the kind of poetry that eluded the New Critics. His chapter on *In Memoriam* examines the symbolic importance that certain largely traditional imagery accumulates within a long poem directed toward the affirmation of basic values.

If a single turning point in the reorientation of twentieth-century Tennyson criticism exists, the date would be 1960 and the event the publication of Jerome H. Buckley's *Tennyson: The Growth of A Poet*. Buckley's was the first major study in this century to appraise the entire Tennyson corpus without belaboring him for his Victorianism. The chapter on *In Memoriam* defines the unity of that poem as "stylistic," based on the recurrence of key images, rather than "architectonic." Besides imagery Buckley took up such matters as the speaker's recovery of assent—which he finds analogous to that in *The Prelude*—and the relation of *In Memoriam* to literary tradition, especially to the pastoral. The practice of addressing several aspects of a work in a single discussion—understandable in dealing with one as elusive and complex as *In Memoriam*—is observed by most scholars who produced general studies after Buckley's (most notably Pitt, 1962; Ryals, 1964; Hellstrom, 1972; Ricks, 1972; Priestley, 1973; Kincaid, 1975; Shaw, 1976; Culler, 1977; Kozicki, 1979) and by authors of many articles. These discussions reenact in small what has been taking place at large in the *In Memoriam* criticism of the past two decades: many different matters have been addressed at the same time and often in the same place. In this survey, therefore, it will be convenient to shift from a chronological to a topical order to distinguish better the current issues in *In Memoriam* criticism.

On the central issue, the relation of the many parts to one whole, no clear consensus has emerged. Attempts at formulation tend to gravitate toward one of two poles: *In Memoriam* as a record of experience (Tennyson's **"Way of the Soul"** and Eliot's "diary of a man confessing himself" fit here) or as a literary artifice. Various terms have been used to designate the opposition: "process" versus "product" by A. Dwight Culler in *The Poetry of Tennyson* (1977), or "developmental" versus "architectural" by James R. Kincaid (*Tennyson's Major Poems: the Comic and Ironic Patterns*, 1975). Alan Sinfield, who has applied this dichotomy most systematically and fruitfully in *The Language of Tennyson's* **"In Memoriam"** (1971), entitled one of his chapters **"In Memoriam:"** The Linnet and the Artifact"—the linnet representing romantic impulses, individual and expressive, and the artifact, "Enlightenment" or classical qualities such as objectivity, impersonality, and generality. As the "and" in the chapter heading suggests, the two orientations need not be mutually exclusive, and they have in fact been applied by Sinfield and others at the same time to different aspects of the poem.

Commentators have been generally more articulate in describing the poem as process than as artifact. "Process" here refers to the evolution of the speaker's consciousness, the successive stages of which are represented by various sections. In this process advances are cumulative, but detours, setbacks, and failures of understanding occur along the way. (A distinct advantage of examining the poem as "process" is that it provides a way of accommodating such discontinuities.) With different emphases this view has been most effectively expounded by J. C. C. Mays ("*In Memoriam*: An Aspect of Form," *UTQ*, 35 [1965], 22-46); by Robert Langbaum in *The Modern Spirit* (1970), where the title of the relevant essay, "The Dynamic Unity of *In Memoriam*," is itself revealing; by Alan Sinfield (1971), when he says "The . . . structure embodies a kind of rhythm of experience . . . difficult to define further"; by John D. Boyd ("*In Memoriam* and the 'Logic of Feeling'," *VP* [*Victorian Poetry*], 10 [1972], 95-110); and by Harry Puckett ("Subjunctive Imagination in *In Memoriam*," *VP*, 12 [1974], 97-124).

The more thoroughgoing statements of the "process" position highlight the sense of autobiographical immediacy that the poem often conveys. As Mays has put it, "The most important means to unity in *In Memoriam* is the feeling that all the time Tennyson is there beside us, talking." At least three critics, however, have offered interpretations that modify this aspect of the "process" approach in the direction of artifice: Ward Hellstrom in *On the Poems of Tennyson* (1972); Francis P. Delvin in "Dramatic Irony in the Early Sections of Tennyson's *In Memoriam*" (*PLL* [*Papers on Language and Literature*], 8 [1972], 172-

183); and Michael Mason in "*In Memoriam*: The Dramatization of Sorrow" (*VP*, 10 [1972], 161-177). Like the "process" critics this group describes the unity of the poem in terms of the speaker's developing consciousness. Their distinctive note is the dramatization of the speaker. Hellstrom pointedly refers to this figure as "the persona" in "a work of art rather than conventional autobiography." In Mason he gains an identity independent of his author because by the end of the poem the reader is aware of recurrent distortions in the way he represents the world. For Delvin dramatic irony begins to operate in the first twenty sections, as the putative reader catches in five specified images optimistic overtones of which the speaker is unaware.

In speaking of *In Memoriam* as an artifact, the critics have been noticeably more reticent. Exceptions would be E. D. H. Johnson, who states (1958) that Bradley "has demonstrated the organic unity of the elegy," and more recently Joanne P. Zuckermann (in "Tennyson's *In Memoriam* as Love Poetry," *DR* [*Dalhousie Review*], 51 [1971], 202-217), who argues that the poem is "a carefully shaped whole." Sinfield, whose analysis gives the classical "artifact" equal place with the romantic "linnet," has located the first in the appeal of the poem to public or general experience and in the stylization of its language rather than in the arrangement of its parts within a whole. The critic who addressed this question in the most explicitly aesthetic terms is probably Valerie Pitt in *Tennyson Laureate* (1962). The first to use the major manuscripts for critical purposes, Pitt argued, from revisions and rearrangements during composition and departures from autobiographical fact, that Tennyson was assembling his elegy according to an artistic plan. The same issues are treated in a few compact pages (pp. 119-123) by F. E. L. Priestley in *Language and Structure in Tennyson's Poetry* (1973).

A major theme in discussions of *In Memoriam* as the product of conscious construction has been A. C. Bradley's "internal chronology," a scheme based on Tennyson's comments in the *Memoir* and the Eversley Edition, whereby the three Christmases divide the poem into four segments. Critics of the last generation such as Baum, House, and Willey followed Nicolson in labelling this arrangement "artificial," in their view an ill-advised, last-minute attempt to impose an appearance of unity on essentially disparate material. Converting "artifice" to a term of approval, Pitt introduced a new element into the debate by proposing the poet's alternate scheme, relayed by James Knowles in *The Nineteenth Century* for January, 1893. As Pitt interprets the Knowles scheme, divisions are marked by anniversaries of Hallam's death instead of by Christmases. It is worth noting that Knowles's is a nine-part division in which breaks occur not only at the two anniversaries but also at two of the Christmases. It could even be taken as a modified, more highly differentiated version of Bradley's. Each system has found scholarly adherents, and each has been used to organize scholarly work. Bradley's, for example, underlies E. D. H. Johnson's article of 1958 and the chapter on *In Memoriam* in Clyde de L. Ryals' *Theme and Symbol in Tennyson's Poems to 1850* (1964); Knowles's was adopted by Martin J. Svaglic in "A Framework for Tennyson's *In Memoriam*" (*JEGP*, 61 [1962], 810-825); by James Kilroy in "The Chiastic Structure of *In Memoriam, A. H. H.*" (*PQ* [*Philological Quarterly*], 56 [1977], 358-373); and by Culler in his 1977 book.

Some commentators have dismissed both schemes. Mays considers them irreconcilable, concoctions by the aged Tennyson to obscure a youthful visionary outlook that he no longer found congenial. Kincaid thinks that any division of the poem into "integral parts" misses the point, that *In Memoriam* mirrors a world without structure. The attention devoted to these schemes has not been wholly salutary, for it has tended to reduce highly complex questions of structure to relatively simple matters of grouping the sections or of internal chronology. It is safe to say that no claim for poetic wholeness can be either established or overthrown by an analysis that fails to go well beyond these preliminaries. The test of any scheme lies in its usefulness for disclosing more comprehensive patterns—whether thematic, symbolic, stylistic, or generic—that could constitute evidence of aesthetic order.

A fairly large number of critics have chosen to differentiate among parts of the elegy by identifying climaxes or turning points. Most of that number would name as the pivotal section XCV, where through a trance the poet experiences a longed-for if indescribable union with his friend, accompanied by a profound intuition of meaning in things. Majority opinion holds that the encounter produces a fundamental reorientation of the poet's outlook and of the direction of the poem, the exact nature of which depends on the interpretation being offered. Robert Langbaum's formulation is probably the most representative: "In a mystical trance the poet has the epiphany that transforms and transcends all the problems of the poem." Jonathan Bishop's (in "The Unity of *In Memoriam*," *VN* [*Victorian Newsletter*], 21 [1962], 9-14) is the most unusual. For him the poet's contact with the dead was achieved by reading Hallam's letters; in a similar way, the unity of the poem is to be realized through Tennyson's words in the reader's mind.

The significance of XCV, and of turning points generally, was confronted directly in an exchange between Harry Puckett and Alan Sinfield in 1976 in the pages of this journal. The immediate issue was whether the subjunctive is the dominant grammatical mood throughout the poem, as Puckett argued in 1974, or whether it is supplanted by the indicative after XCV, as Sinfield contended in 1976 ("'That Which Is': The Platonic Indicative in *In Memoriam* XCV," 14, 247-252. For Puckett's rejoinder see 14, 340). Beyond the grammatical issue, however, lies a fundamental difference concerning the interpretation and function of XCV. For Sinfield the section refers to an encounter with ultimate reality and brings about a shift not only in grammar but in the orientation of the entire work as well. For Puckett the experience recorded in XCV is as provisional as the role of the section: "What Tennyson believes is not particularly important. Much more important is the way his mind and poem work. The process is far more important than any particular outcome at any particular point."

Beyond the interpretation of XCV, a yet more fundamental question is involved in the exchange. As an extreme statement of the "process" position, Puckett's serves to move to the foreground some key implications of that position for the structure of the poem. If we think of aesthetic order as rhythmic in nature, encompassing the alternation of more and less prominent elements within a system, it becomes clear that Puckett's formulation allows relatively little scope for aesthetic analysis. Sinfield's, which clearly distinguishes between more and less dominant elements and envisages the subordination of one to another within the whole, allows proportionately more room for treating the poem as an artistic entity. (By the same token, an approach to *In Memoriam* through its climaxes or turning points is likely to give a better vantage from which to discern its structure than the Bradley and Knowles schemes, neither of which considers the relative significance of the divisions it proposes. Once *In Memoriam* is conceived as an internally differentiated structure, a structure that includes a principle—or principles—of grouping as well as principles of subordination, it becomes, if not clear, at least clearer, how the poem may be dealt with as an aesthetic whole.

Some critics who take XCV as a climax have further differentiated their analysis by relating that section to other visionary peaks. Carr, for example, adds the dream of CIII. Mays and K. W. Grandsen (the latter in *Tennyson*: *In Memoriam,* 1964) also include one or more of the earlier dream sections (LXVIII-LXXI). Shaw's adaptation of this general approach in *Tennyson's Style* suggests the refinement of which it is capable. He postulates what are in effect two systems operating concurrently. One, centering on "catharsis" or emotional relief, has as its high points the three visionary passages just mentioned. In the second system the intellectual despair adumbrated in the "scientific" sections (e.g. XXXV and LVI) is resolved in CXXIII and CXXX, where the soul realizes its own imaginative power and achieves "consolation."

Two minority reports on the function of XCV within the structure of *In Memoriam* should be mentioned. Kincaid has probably argued more strongly than any other critic for a "planned center" of *In Memoriam* other than XCV. In his reading the poem starts over, so to speak, at LVII, when comedy (roughly, affirmation) becomes disengaged from its previously close interplay with irony (negation), to go its single, finally unpersuasive, way. And though Henry Kozicki's interpretation resists any neat classification, it shares a good deal with "process" views, especially that of Puckett. In the interests of maintaining an open-ended stance Kozicki (in "'Meaning' in Tennyson's *In Memoriam,*" *SEL* [*Studies in English Literature*], 17 [1977], 673-694, represented in *Tennyson and Clio,* 1979) rejects all readings that give XCV climactic importance, and without naming specific turning points, claims that the development of the persona (taken as "collective mind") proceeds in convulsive stages through the will's activity in the world. No doubt a good many other studies could be subsumed within the framework of climactic and subordinate structures, but one general observation must suffice. Basic questions concerning the structure of *In Memoriam* remain unresolved. In attempting to answer these questions, twentieth-century critics should depart from Bradley's example and bring "aesthetic criticism"—artifact no less than process—within their range of concern.

For many poems, help in resolving such questions might well be found by locating the work within its genre. But as Priestley has shown, the very notion of genre that Tennyson received from the Romantics was no longer a stable model to be imitated but a repertory of effects to be combined in changing ways. Thus *In Memoriam* he pronounces "entirely *sui generis,*" and W. David Shaw, elaborating on Priestley's premises, urges that its "chief generic innovation is a fusion of disparate features." Complexities such as these have prevented neither scholar (nor, it appears, anyone else) from pursuing inquiries into the genre of *In Memoriam,* but they do suggest the orientation that such inquiries consistently take. Unable to offer a genre that will adequately contain this poem, scholars define its peculiar character by the ways in which it stymies, modifies, or reverses generic expectations as often as by the ways in which it fulfills them.

This tension between participation in and opposition to a given genre is well illustrated in studies concerning the literary type with which *In Memoriam* is most often aligned, the pastoral elegy. Since they also recapitulate a large tension between process and artifact, these studies assume a pattern among themselves congruent with the one discernible among discussions of structure. For Priestley, Sinfield, and Carr pastoral elegy implies "artifact" or "formal structure" and association through literary tradition with the general experience of mankind. The characteristic pattern of feeling is, in Priestley's terms, from "wild questioning grief to acceptance," though he sees the clarity of this pattern opposed by the waywardness of an extended chronology not found in the traditional elegy. When similar elements (an extended elegiac pattern playing against moments of feeling) are scrutinized by Andrew Fichter ("Ode and Elegy: Idea and Form in Tennyson's Early Poetry," *ELH,* 40 [1973], 398-427), they produce a different result: Tennyson's use of pastoral is "a process rather than a design."

Similarly, the issues involved in the exchange between Sinfield and Puckett on XCV as turning point are replicated in discussions of the pastoral. Kerry McSweeney (in "The Pattern of Natural Consolation in *In Memoriam,*" *VP,* 11 [1973], 87-99) takes XCV as the equivalent of the peripeteia of the traditional elegy (the sudden turn from "he is dead" to "he is not dead"), and interprets the reversal in purely naturalistic terms as the speaker's reconciliation with the external world and through memory with his own past. Carlisle Moore's interpretation is antithetical to

McSweeney's, and so, correspondingly, is his outlook on genre ("Faith, Doubt, and Mystical Experience in *In Memoriam*," VS [*Victorian Studies*], 7 [1963], 155-169). Though Moore also takes XCV as a peripeteia, he believes that the experience presented there is so deeply felt as to dislodge the work from pastoral, where the turn is a matter of literary convention, and to relocate it within the poetry of conversion. Culler takes the next logical step by affirming that, although it incorporates various pastoral elements, *In Memoriam* lies outside pastoral tradition: since its outlook is gradualist, based on degrees of change, it lacks the peripeteia that is (to him) the essential feature of the genre.

The pastoral conventions used by Tennyson are described succinctly by Buckley and diffusely by Eric Smith in his chapter on *In Memoriam* in *By Mourning Tongues: Studies in English Elegy* (1977). I have argued in "*In Memoriam* and *Lycidas*" (*PMLA*, 82 [1967], 437-443) for the specific influence of Milton's elegy, which is probably most significant in the way Tennyson apologizes for intrusions of weighty metaphysical and theological matters into pastoral song, only to reverse himself at the end of the poem (CIII) as he celebrates his subject's apotheosis. Ian H. C. Kennedy's enumeration of conventional elements ("*In Memoriam* and the Tradition of Pastoral Elegy," *VP*, 15 [1977], 351-366) is largely a survey of their transformations. (For example, he locates the turn in the poet's gradual admission that "he *is* dead"—a necessary prelude to his own recovery.)

The next most important genre—or perhaps better, generic field—into which *In Memoriam* has been placed by recent critics is the literature of confession or conversion. Eliot's characterization of the poem in 1936 as the "diary of a man confessing himself" had become well enough established in the next decade that Graham Hough could observe (unapprovingly) that "it is now commonly assumed that its virtues are entirely those of personal confession." Carlisle Moore compares Tennyson's encounter with spirit in XCV to St. Paul's on the road to Damascus. In *The Victorian Temper* (1951) Jerome Buckley begins the chapter entitled "The Pattern of Conversion" (on a type of autobiographical narrative common among Tennyson's contemporaries) with an examination of that phenomenon in *In Memoriam*. The most systematic and original contribution in this vein is W. David Shaw's "*In Memoriam* and the Rhetoric of Confession" (*ELH*, 38 [1971], 80-103, condensed on pp. 133-138 of *Tennyson's Style*). Shaw sees the confession-conversion narrative extending back through Bunyan's *Grace Abounding* to St. Augustine and laterally to Carlyle's *Sartor*, Mill's *Autobiography*, and Newman's *Apologia*. The conversion experience is only one of nine features that Shaw ascribes of this genre, but he clearly considers it to have climatic status. Those critics of the "process" persuasion who stress the gradual or intermittent character of the speaker's development would naturally look for models elsewhere than on the road to Damascus: Culler in the aphoristic and miscellaneous meditations of the Broad Church movement (starting with Coleridge's *Aids to Reflection*) and Mays in *Piers Plowman*, for the way it enacts its protagonist's fluctuating struggle to achieve understanding.

Though neither a genre nor a tradition, the poetry of Dante has been proposed as a model for *In Memoriam*, frequently enough to merit notice here. Comparisons of *In Memoriam* to the *Divine Comedy* (even Tennyson's own: "it begins with a funeral and ends with a marriage") and *La Vita Nuova* (which Hallam translated), though often suggestive, have been able to accommodate only limited features of the elegy. James G. Taaffe thinks that the image specified in his title, "Circle Imagery in Tennyson's *In Memoriam* (*VP*, 1 [1963], 123-131) was inspired by Dante. Sinfield (1971) finds *Paradiso* XII informing the climactic vision of *In Memoriam* XCV. Hellstrom makes Hallam a Beatrice figure, leading the poet to a vision of cosmic love. Kincaid has argued that just as the *Inferno* is structured to imply the *Paradiso*, the opening of *In Memoriam* forecasts its optimistic conclusion. Most recently Carl Dawson in his chapter on *In Memoriam* in *Victorian Noon* (1979) cites Dante as a significant example in showing mid-nineteenth-century English poets how to fashion an "epos" from private experience. The most ambitious attempt to record Dantesque parallels, Gordon Hirsch's "Tennyson's *Commedia*" (*VP*, 8 [1970], 93-106), returns us to the standard pattern of genre studies by concluding that, despite notable similarities, *In Memoriam* departs fundamentally from the proposed model, here in its lack of Dante's confidently sustained vision.

The more highly developed the conventions of a literary type, the more possibilities it promises for comparative analysis. The sonnet sequence (like the diary) has few formal conventions and so can offer few avenues into a structure as complex as that of *In Memoriam*. Thus Ricks, who designates the relation of parts to whole by the term "congeries," uses the sonnet sequence to illustrate that viewpoint in his 1971 book. Holding a contrary view, Joanne Zuckermann must supplement her discussion of the sonnet sequence with a treatment of the ways in which *In Memoriam* participates in Victorian literary modes of idealizing love other than those in sonnets. On the other hand, Sinfield's association of Tennyson with the Symbolists successfully exploits several aspects of that complex movement to clarify important features of *In Memoriam*. The Symbolist emphasis on immediacy of experience that led Verlaine to observe that even the finest long poem is but a series of short poems linked by prose makes more intelligible *In Memoriam*'s succession of short lyrics. And the preference of this movement for the mystical or supernatural, conveyed through symbol, highlights distinctive qualities of Tennysonian experience and expression.

The points at which literary traditions merge with broader traditions in the history of ideas are not always sharply delineated—as the *In Memoriam* criticism of the last two decades illustrates. Whereas critics before 1960 tended to treat intellectual influences apart from their poetic context, the direction of recent scholarship has been to assimilate discussion of ideas into more inclusive analyses. The trend is well illustrated by the new critical uses to which Tennyson's reading in the geologist Charles Lyell have been put. Instead of setting forth Lyell's ideas, Culler analogizes his doctrine of uniformitarianism in geology (replacing catastrophism in that science) with the gradual change of feeling in *In Memoriam* (replacing the abrupt turn of the pastoral elegy). For Susan Gliserman ("Early Victorian Science Writers and Tennyson's *In Memoriam*: A Study in Cultural Exchange," VS, 18 [1975], 277-308, 437-459) Lyell's prose and that of two scientific confreres, Whewell and Roget, served Tennyson as models of rhetorical strategy in dealing with man's relation to the physical universe. Walker Gibson, on the other hand, emphasizes how Tennyson's rhetoric and especially his grammar differ from those of Lyell, now joined by Darwin (VS, 2 [1958], 60-68). In an ingenious application of intellectual history to literary criticism, Ward Hellstrom presses the Liberal Anglican historians of the 1820's and 1830's into service to define the theme of Tennyson's elegy: the speaker's discovery of divine unity in terrestrial diversity, paralleling the Anglicans' view of historical process. Clyde de L. Ryals draws on Carlyle's call for a "new Mythus" to replace Christianity to explain the apotheosis of Hallam, as the replacement for Christ, at the end of the poem ("'The Heavenly Friend': The 'New Mythus' of *In Memoriam*," *Personalist*, 43 [1962], 383-402).

Though pairing Tennyson with one of our contemporaries instead of one of his own, Eugene R. August in "Tennyson and Teilhard: The Faith of *In Memoriam*" (*PMLA*, 84 [1969], 217-226) comes closer to the older history-of-ideas approach as he demonstrates the similarity of Tennyson's views to those of a twentieth-century believer in a creation moving toward one far-off divine event. The more usual way of bringing Tennyson together with modern thinkers has been to reinterpret his elegy according to their categories—sometimes in ways that would surprise the poet. Critics who practice this method include William B. Brashear in *The Living Will: A Study of Tennyson and Nineteenth-Century Subjectivism* (1969), who invokes Nietzsche; Henry Kozicki, who uses concepts from the philosophy of history, especially those of Hegel; and Gerald L. Bruns, who in "'The Lesser Faith': Hope and Reversal in Tennyson's *In Memoriam*" (*JEGP*, 77 [1978], 247-264) gives Merleau-Ponty's idea of "dialectical reversal" a central role.

While many questions remain unsettled concerning the structure of *In Memoriam*, unmistakable progress has been made, mostly during the last decade, in describing its texture. The stylistic showpieces (e.g. VII, LXXXVI, XCV, CXXI) have never suffered total neglect, and so it must suffice here to mention one study, John D. Boyd's "*In Memoriam* and the 'Logic of Feeling'" (*VP*, 10 [1972], 95-110) that uses analysis of such tours de force—mostly landscapes, so vibrantly presented, the critic argues, as to "induce us to share empathically the speaker's experience"—to arrive at a larger formulation on the structure of the poem. Another direction from which stylistic approaches have regularly been made is through figures of thought or speech. In "The Principle of Analogy and the Immortality Question in Tennyson's *In Memoriam*" (*UTQ*, 45 [1976], 123-138), Boyd describes ways in which the figure of thought named in the title works to integrate the elegy. Imagery, however, has most consistently and successfully provided the point of entry into this labyrinthine poem. Analysis of image patterns (e.g. light-darkness, water, family life, circles, the human hand) plays a key role in many studies of a more general nature (e.g. those of Foakes, Buckley, Ryals, Sinfield, Devlin, Hellstrom, Mason). Probably the most distinctive treatment of imagery as such is Marvel Shmiefsky's "*In Memoriam*: Its Seasonal Imagery Reconsidered" (*SEL*, 7 [1967], 721-739), an archetypal approach, which, more than most of its kind, stays in touch with the text as it traces motifs such as rebirth and the descent into hell.

The major achievements in the stylistic study of *In Memoriam* are the relevant chapters in the books of Priestley (1973) and Shaw (1976) and—above all and in toto—Sinfield's *The Language of Tennyson's "In Memoriam"* (1971). Priestley, though he deals expertly with passages of text, operates much of the time on a higher level of generalization: Tennyson's experiments with genre, his strategies of indirection, and his sense of the inherent limits of language. The categories that organize Shaw's analysis (which draws significantly on traditional grammar, rhetoric, and logic—and, with due acknowledgment, on Priestley) are the major themes that make up his interpretation of the poem. For example, under the rubric of "catharsis," Shaw explains several stylistic means that the poet uses to enact the conquest of his grief. Sinfield, making profitable use of linguistics, defines his concern more strictly as "the poetically significant uses of language." His linguistic orientation manifests itself in the categories used to organize the chapters: diction, syntax, sound, rhythm. The method permits him to highlight the stylistic cameos as well as to survey the less adorned verse in the background. At the same time Sinfield extends his range to include the "manifold relationships of language with other aspects of the poem," a privilege that he uses with restraint and to good advantage.

This survey began with A. C. Bradley and so should any list of recommended readings on *In Memoriam*. Bradley did his work so responsibly that on most points he can still be considered reliable. Jonathan Bishop called him "unsupersedable." If he has been superseded, it would be by Christopher Ricks, whose introductory material in the 1968 Longmans Edition of *The Poems of Tennyson* has a pellucid pithiness approaching Bradley's, but now supplemented by information diligently culled from recently available documents. At this writing Ricks's is the most authoritative edition of the poem, distinguished by annotation that includes abundant, if not complete, manuscript readings. A new critical edition of *In Memoriam*, prepared by Susan Shatto and Marion Shaw for publication by Oxford University Press, can be expected to contain bibliographical description of all the manuscripts and an inclusive listing of variants. Though it would be unwise to look to the manuscripts for a key to all remaining mysteries, they contain enough evidence to lay to rest the old assumption that *In Memoriam* was assembled without a plan. My article "*In Memoriam*: The Minor Manuscripts" (*HLB* [*Harvard Library Bulletin*], 27 [1979], 36-64) has the fullest account now available of how the manuscripts were used in composition.

To the non-specialist wishing to gain a foothold in the criticism of *In Memoriam,* I suggest the following selection from the items discussed above. On the intellectual background Graham Hough's 1947 article offers the most in the least space: discussion of both scientific and religious influences along with careful scholarship. The chapter in Buckley's 1960 book gives a balanced, well-informed critical overview; Priestley's 1973 study combines cogent general commentary with penetrating discussion of specific aspects of Tennyson's language and thought. Both avoid the tedious paraphrase that continues to plague *In Memoriam* scholarship, and neither finds clear, direct expression an obstacle to communicating significant ideas. Pitt's chapter from *Tennyson Laureate* and Puckett's 1974 article merit attention as clear articulations of opposite positions on the structure of the elegy. If I were to recommend a single piece of criticism, it would be Alan Sinfield's book *The Language of Tennyson's* "*In Memoriam.*" Sinfield's skill in stylistic analysis is such that what begins as close reading of texts opens out, quite legitimately, into vistas on most major aspects of the poem.

Robert Dilligan (essay date 1980)

SOURCE: Dilligan, Robert. "Computers and Style: The Prosody of *In Memoriam.*" *Victorian Poetry* 18, no. 2 (summer 1980): 179-96.

[*In the following essay, Dilligan provides a computer-aided analysis of* In Memoriam *that enlightens the connection between grammar and prosody, The critic also provides a detailed discussion of the poem's syntax.*]

I

One way of understanding how a critic may use a computer is to make an analogy between a computer and a piano. From a logical point of view, a piano is a binary machine with eighty-eight switches of which, because of the limitations of its operators, only about ten can be depressed at any given time. Thought of in this way, a piano seems a rather useless machine. But we are not accustomed to think of a piano as a binary machine; rather, we think of it as an instrument used to interpret a kind of human experience—music. Whether the piano will be used to play sonatas or "Chopsticks" is the decision of the player; the piano makes either possible. Similarly, a critic who has learned to use a computer has opened up a way of exploring a kind of human experience—his own reading of a text. Of course music is written for the piano, and poems are not written for the computer. But the distinction between a machine—so easily seen as something inhuman and threatening—and an instrument—usually seen as an extension of human capacities—is crucial to a proper conception of the role of the computer in literary criticism and scholarship. It should be regarded as an instrument or enabling device that opens up a whole range of possibilities for the critic trained in its use. Despite its seeming strangeness, reading with the aid of a computer system is no more subversive to the spirit of literary inquiry than is reading with notecard and pen at hand.

In this essay, I shall describe the way in which Tennyson plays his language against the limits of his metrical form in *In Memoriam.* My purpose is to illustrate the way in which computer-assisted methodology can help us understand the unity of the poem. For the sake of clarity I will first discuss stylistic features of the poem independently of any interpretation. But I wish to make clear from the outset that I regard stylistic description as inseparable from interpretation. The test of any stylistic description is whether it helps us to read with greater comprehension, and in selecting the features for description one is making an inescapable judgment about their importance in interpretation. What I hope to show, then, is that by using a computer-assisted methodology one may arrive at a description of the style of the poem which will be useful to any critic's interpretive endeavor.[1]

The stylistic analysis in this essay is based on the connection between grammar and prosody pointed out by Paul Kiparsky[2] in his response to what he sees as the failure of Morris Halle and Samuel Keyser to take syntax into account in their description of traditional English prosody.[3] While my approach to prosody in this essay derives from the work of these three scholars, it is different in at least one of its concerns. Where they have addressed themselves to the general question of metrical competence—what constitutes a metrical line?—I have tried to deal with a specific question of performance—how do I read *In Memoriam*?

In order to answer this question by means of the computer, I had to supply the machine with very explicit information and instructions. Not only did the text of the poem have to be typed into the computer but also a complete set of grammatical and prosodic rules had to be programmed. The linguistic formalism of Kiparsky, Halle, and Keyser simplified the programming in many ways as did the work of Donald Ross and David Rasche in developing parsing programs suitable for literary analysis.[4] But the work of the computer was far from automatic. The grammatical programs parse with about 75 percent accuracy and so their results had to be corrected. Since I was exploring my own reading of the poem, I had to mark the text to indicate pauses and stresses not inferable from general grammatical or phonetic rules. The computer was also supplied with a pronouncing dictionary of British received pronunciation so that lexical stress and vowel patterning could be discussed in terms of a British rather than an American audience.[5]

A computer can do no more than record, rearrange, and then reproduce anything it is supplied with. It has no imagination or understanding in a Coleridgean or any other sense and since it "has no other counters to play with, but fixities and definities," I suppose one might regard it as fanciful. In this case, the computer rearranged the text according to grammatical categories (noun, verb, subject, predicate, etc.) and prosodic features (caesura, assonance, alliteration, elision, etc.). The resulting rearrangements were then classified according to four major categories: diction, line structure, verse period structure, and stanzaic structure. Within such categories as these, the computer enables the critic to pay thorough and systematic attention to the details of style.

The contribution of the computer to this discussion of the prosody of *In Memoriam* is both essential and secondary. It is essential in that I would not have attempted so detailed an inquiry into the syntax and phonology of the poem without its aid; but there is no reason beyond this pragmatic one for employing it. None of the results I present here are such that, given more time and patience than I possess, I could not have arrived at them without the computer. Understanding the details of how the computer was programmed, then, is not crucial to an understanding of the results presented here.[6] The prosodic analysis I offer is that of my own reading of the poem and it must stand or fall, like any other reading, on its own merits. The only claim I make is that it is more detailed and explicit than such readings usually are and therefore perhaps more open both to understanding and to refutation.[7] I will focus my discussion of the prosody of *In Memoriam* on the syntax of the line and touch only in passing on phonology, diction, and stanzaic organization. But within this focus I hope to show how helpful the computer can be in understanding the prosodic unity of the poem.

II

The Prologue of *In Memoriam,* as one might expect, sets the stylistic as well as the thematic perspective for the poem. Written just before publication, it directs the reader's attention back over the experience of grief and the experience of writing about it ("Forgive these wild and wandering cries") much as the Epilogue of the poem directs the reader's attention forward to "one far-off divine event." The formal, liturgical tone of the Prologue is established by a rhetoric dominated by the traditional schemes of repetition. Not only is anaphora ("Thou madest Life . . . Thou madest Death," "Our wills are ours . . . Our wills are ours," "Forgive what seemed . . . Forgive my grief . . . forgive these wild and wandering cries . . . forgive them where they fail in truth") a major element of the syntactic structure of the Prologue, but also such schemes as polyptoton ("And in thy wisdom make me wise"), epistrophe ("Our little systems have their day; / They have their day"), chiasmus ("They are but broken lights of thee, / And thou, O Lord, art more than they"), epanalepsis ("Thou seemest human and divine, / The highest, holiest manhood, thou"), and anadiplosis ("let it grow. / Let knowledge grow") are so pervasive that the Prologue could serve as a textbook example of the use of repetitive schemes. The incantatory effect of such language, we are told in section V, is closely connected with the poet's attempt to cope with his grief at Hallam's death:

> But, for the unquiet heart and brain,
>   A use in measured language lies;
>   The sad mechanic exercise,
> Like dull narcotics, numbing paid.

But these repetitions do more than produce numbness. They are so pervasive a part of the style of the poem as to establish a pattern of expectation and gratification of the sort that Kenneth Burke regards as fundamental to any experience of literary form.[8] To understand their pervasiveness is, I would argue, to understand the stylistic manner of the poem.

To a surprising extent, the meter of *In Memoriam* affects not only the position of stress within a line but also the position of grammatical form classes. Many of us who have learned Latin have had the experience, after gaining some proficiency in translating Virgil, of being utterly stumped on first trying Horace. Clearly Horace's metrical innovations ("princeps Aeolium carmen ad Italos / deduxisse modos," *Odes* III. 30) have syntactic consequences which the beginning Latinist can appreciate only too well. The syntax of *In Memoriam,* though not so complex as that of Horace's odes, is certainly as much determined by its meter. The distribution and placement of adjectives, nouns, and verbs—in fact, of all major form classes—show patterns affected by the meter of the poem.

The pattern of gratification and expectation established by the syntax of the poem is perhaps most explicitly felt in lines which in some way break the pattern. One such line is the concluding line of section VII, a line that Eliot singles out for praise and that every reader must pause over: "On the bald street breaks the blank day." The force of this line can hardly be explained by the rather commonplace poeticism of its inverted subject or by its alliterative pattern. LXVII. 6 has both these features but is pale by comparison: "As slowly steals a silver flame." It is rather the unusual placement of the verb and adjectives in metrically weak positions, underscored by the alliterative pattern, which counterpoints—indeed springs—the rhythm of the line and catches the reader's attention.[9] Only ten lines in the poem have a main verb in position five; in fact, of 2731 main verbs in the poem, only 381 occur in odd-numbered positions, and of these 381, 218 are unstressed copulative verbs. This leaves only 163 stressed verbs in odd-numbered positions in the poem. The adjectives in the line, "bald" and "blank," both monosyllabic and in odd-numbered positions, violate two well established expectations. There are twice as many polysyllabic adjectives in the poem as monosyllabic ones (1135 vs. 554) and seven times as many adjectives in even-numbered positions as there are in odd-numbered positions (1476 vs. 203).

In Memoriam has an overall pattern of syntactic regularity to which the reader should be attentive. Major grammatical form classes fall into odd-numbered or even-numbered positions. Adjectives, adverbs, nouns, particles, and verbs occur predominantly in even-numbered positions. Auxiliary verbs, conjunctions, determiners, pronouns, and "to" introducing an infinitive occur predominantly in odd-numbered positions. Of the major form classes, only prepositions and copulative verbs do not show a consistent preference for odd or even positions.[10] The expectation of repetition established in the Prologue is gratified throughout the poem by this regularity, which is so well defined that it exerts a powerful influence even when the reader is not explicitly conscious of it. What this suggests is that a careful reader of *In Memoriam* will pay particular attention to those lines which violate the usual expectations for the positioning of syntactic classes. And a consideration of lines in which nouns or verbs are displaced from even-numbered positions reveals that for these form classes such displacements are an important stylistic device.

The most striking example of the use of displaced nouns for emphasis occurs in section XI, as part of a general repetition of the word "calm" in a series of grammatically ambiguous lines in which it hovers between being a noun or an adjective:

> Calm is the morn without a sound,
> . . . . .
> Calm and deep peace on this high wold,
> . . . . .
> Calm and still light on yon great plain
> . . . . .
> Calm and deep peace in this wide air.

(One should also note the displaced adjectives in these lines.) These lines are followed by two lines in which the repetition of "calm" is again grammatically ambiguous and then grammatically and metrically unexceptional: "And in my heart, if calm at all, / If any calm, a calm despair." The anxiety underlying the calm the poem ostensibly describes is rendered here by the grammatical ambiguity combined with the unusual placement of the word "calm"—whether read as noun or adjective—in an odd-numbered position. (The fact that the word is capitalized because of its initial position gives a hint, unrealized as it turns out, of a personification.) The reader who thinks, after stanza four, that he is on to Tennyson's game and decides to read each stanza as beginning with an adjective, is immediately brought up short by the opening of stanza five: "Calm on the seas, and silver sleep." That the "calm" described is not a reconciliation of grief but rather a heightening of it is driven home by another repetition of "calm" as a noun in an odd-numbered position: "And dead calm in that noble breast / Which heaves but with the heaving deep."

Section XI is admittedly an extreme case of the use of repetitive displacement of a form class, though not so extreme if we bear in mind the rhetoric of the Prologue. In a number of other sections, the displacement of nouns produces similar effects. This displacement can be found in 65 lines of the poem. Among the striking examples are

> Silence, till I be silent too.
>
> (XIII. 8)
>
> The wild unrest that lives in woe
>
> (XV. 15)
>
> Peace and goodwill, goodwill and peace,
>
> (XXVIII. 11)
>
> Man dies: nor is there hope in dust:
>
> (XXXV. 4)
>
> When the blood creeps, and the nerves prick
>
> (L. 2)
>
> Sleep, Death's twin-brother, times my breath;
>
> (LXVIII. 2)
>
> The hard heir strides about their lands.
>
> (XC. 15)
>
> The dead man touched me from the past,
>
> (XCV. 34)
>
> The brute earth lightens to the sky,
>
> (CXXXVII. 15)

These lines also illustrate the way Tennyson generally restricts his displaced nouns to the first position of a line and/ or precedes or follows them with another stressed syllable to avoid an unmetrical line. (In fact, the only unmetrical line in the poem contains a displaced noun: "Is it, then, regret for buried time," CXVI. 1). Section XCV, the apotheosis section, contains four lines with displaced nouns which illustrate their use:

> The white kine glimmered, and the trees
>
> (ll. 15, 51)
>
> And in the house light after light
>
> (l. 19)
>
> The dead man touched me from the past,
>
> (l. 34)
>
> The large leaves of the sycamore,
>
> (l. 55)

The successive stresses in these lines, combined with the displacement, produce a dramatic slowing of pace in the development of the section. Given the rarity of nouns whose stressed syllable falls in an odd-numbered position (65 out of 4270), it is safe to say that wherever they occur they call attention to the lines in a way the reader should take into account in any interpretation of the poem.[11]

At first glance, there would appear to be far more displaced verbs than displaced nouns in *In Memoriam*. As was mentioned above, 381 of 2731 main verbs occur in odd-numbered positions. But the majority of these, as we have already observed, are unstressed copulative verbs. This leaves only 163 stressed verbs in odd positions. Still, there are more than twice as many displaced verbs in the poem as there are displaced nouns. While only about 1.5 percent of all nouns are displaced, 6 percent of all verbs are stressed verbs in odd positions. An examination of how Tennyson uses these verbs reveals not only that he is much more systematic in his placement of them than he is with displaced nouns but also that he uses them for structuring entire poems.

Of the 163 displaced verbs, 126 occur in position 1, 21 occur in position 3, 10 occur in position 5, and 6 occur in position 7. It is most unusual, then, for these verbs to occur anywhere but in position 1.[12] To understand the ramifications of this pattern we must consider how it is realized with different grammatical categories of verbs. The few displaced copulative verbs in position 1 are either the first word in a question or a contraction ("'tis" or "'twas"). Where a displaced imperative does not occur in position 1, it is usually accompanied by another imperative in position 1, as in

    Ring out, ring out my mournful rhymes,

                                          (CVI. 19)

    Rise, happy morn, rise, holy morn,

                                          (XXX. 29)

    Ring out the old, ring in the new,

                                          (CVI. 5)

    Divide us not, be with me now,

                                          (CXXII. 10)

The two exceptions, one halfway through the poem, the other in the Epilogue, come at moments when the poet turns from his obsession with the past to his hope for the future. The first occurs at the opening of section LXV: "Sweet soul, do with me as thou wilt" (l. 1). In this section, the memory of their friendship is seen as a pledge of immortality for both, as the concluding stanza of the section makes clear:

    Since we deserved the name of friends,
        And thine effect so lives in me,
        A part of mine may live in thee
    And move thee on to noble ends.

The other such use of an imperative occurs at the turning point of the Epilogue: "But now set out: the noon is near" (l. 41). This unusual use of the imperative marks the beginning of the final movement of the poem which will direct the reader's attention forward in time through the wedding day and the departure on the wedding trip to the hoped-for conception and birth of a child, to the crowning race, and ultimately to "one far-off divine event."

The subjunctives in position 1 are all instances of the use of "Let": "Let knowledge grow from more to more" (Prologue, l. 25); "Let Love clasp Grief lest both be drowned" (I. 9). I. 9 is the only instance in the poem in which both elements of the periphrastic subjunctive are displaced: the clash of four strong stresses against the usual metrical smoothness of the poem is one measure of the anguish with which the poem opens.[13]

The 41 displaced predicate verbs in position 1 are related to the way Tennyson uses enjambment.[14] The displaced verbs in position 3 are generally followed by a particle, an adverb, or a stressed double preposition:

    The cheeks drop in; the body bows;

                                          (XXXV. 3)

    The tide flows down, the wave again

                                          (XIX. 13)

    And bats went round in fragrant skies

                                          (XCV. 9)

The one exception occurs in the Epilogue, where the shadow of Hallam's death falls upon the poet for the last time: "A shade falls on us like the dark" (l. 93).

There are two strikingly effective uses of displaced verbs in position 5. The first has already been noted: "On the bald street breaks the blank day" (VII. 12). The second is ominously spondaic: "When the dark hand struck down through time" (LXXII. 19). The other three displaced predicate verbs in position 5 (XXI. 7, CIII. 15, and CXXII. 20) are not particularly distinguished. Likewise, the displaced verbs in position 7 are of no particular interest and resemble those in position 3 which are followed by particles or adverbs. These occur at IX. 15, XVII. 7, XLIV. 15, LX. 14, and Epilogue, l. 89.

But displaced verbs in position 1 are also used as structural elements for entire poems as well as for effects in particular lines. In two sections, L ("Be near me when my light is low") and CVI ("Ring out, wild bells, to the wild sky"), displaced verbs in position 1 are the single most distinctive stylistic feature. In both, Tennyson explores the metrical effect of displacement as a structural device for an entire poem. In section XCI ("When rosy plumelets tuft the larch"), he uses displaced verbs to begin the main clauses of the two sentences that make up the poem: "When rosy plumelets tuft the larch. . . . Come, wear the form. . . . When summer's hourly-mellowing change / May breathe . . . come: not in watches of the night . . . Come, beauteous in thine after form." Given the preponderately systematic use of displaced verbs in the poem, one must conclude, as with displaced nouns, that where they occur they must be taken into account in interpretation as one would a more widely recognized scheme of repetition such as polyptoton or anthimeria.

The final aspect of the relationship of line position to syntax that I wish to consider is rhyme. My reason for discussing it last is that it leads logically into a discussion of the syntactic structure of the entire line. As we shall see, the ***In Memoriam*** line is characterized syntactically by increasing regularity in the last four positions. The single most massive element in this stability is the restriction of form / function classes used in rhyme position. Five form / function classes account for 2189 out of the 2896 rhyme words in the poem. Nouns in prepositional phrases account for 1121 rhyme words, predicate verbs for 560, noun objects for 267, noun subjects for 134, and predicate adverbs for 107. While this restriction is in itself quite striking, its full implications can be understood only when we consider the way in which these form / function classes occur throughout the poem.[15] The only form / function class which shows a real affinity for the rhyme position is the noun in prepositional phrases. Among the others, the most unusual is the use of the noun subject as a rhyme word, since subjects occur most typically at the beginning of the line.

A consideration of the syntax of the lines in ***In Memoriam*** brings us much closer to the nature of the "measured language" of the poem. We have already described a pervasive patterning of form classes within the line. The way in which these classes are arranged within the line is, for me at least, the essence of the style of the poem: the way lines seem to have a deep resonance echoing through the poem like a series of melodies.

The simplest way this effect is achieved is through the verbatim or almost verbatim repetition of lines:

> Doors, where my heart was used to beat
>
> (VII. 3, CXIX. 1)

> Old Yew, which graspest at the stones
>
> (II. 1)

> Dark yew, that graspest at the stones
>
> (XXXIX. 4)

> Till all my widowed race be run;
>
> (IX. 18, XVII. 20)

> What whispers from thy lying lip?
>
> (III. 4)

> What whispered from her lying lips?
>
> (XXXIX. 10)

> And in thy wisdom make me wise.
>
> (Prologue, l. 44)

> Nor let thy wisdom make me wise.
>
> (CIX. 24)

> The white kine glimmered, and the trees
>
> (XCV. 15, 51)

The effect of such repetitions (the above is by no means a complete list) is to reinforce one's experience of typological unity in the poem where, as in Herbert, "This verse marks that, and both doe make a motion / Unto a third, that ten leaves off doth ly" ("The H. Scriptures II").

This "marking" of one verse by another is also achieved in a number of poems in which lines of identical syntactical and metrical structure are played off against each other. This is most noticeable in consecutive lines:

> The seeming-wanton ripple break,
> The tender-pencilled shadow play
>
> (XLIX. 11-12)

> And Time, a maniac scattering dust,
> And Life, a Fury slinging flame.
>
> (L. 7-8)

> An infant crying in the night:
> An infant crying for the light:
>
> (LIV. 18-19)

> A distant dearness in the hill,
> A secret sweetness in the stream.
>
> (LXIV. 19-20)

> The cataract flashing from the bridge,
> The breaker breaking on the beach.
>
> (LXXI. 15-16)

The same effect is produced in separated lines, as in the opening lines of stanzas two, three, and four of section XCIX, the second anniversary poem:

> Who tremblest through thy darkling red
>
> (l. 5)

> Who murmurest in the foliaged eaves
>
> (l. 9)

> Who wakenest with thy balmy breath
>
> (l. 13)

These contiguous metrical and syntactical pairings, striking as they are in themselves, also tend to sensitize the ear to wider echoes. Section CVI ("Ring out, wild bells") is, of course, the *locus classicus* for the effect. And I would point to similar pairing between lines I. 2 and 4, XI. 5 and 13, XLIX. 5 and 7, LXVI. 6 and 11, CXXVIII. 16 and 18.

Such repetitions of lines and syntactic pairings of lines within poems are, for me, among the clearest signals of a pervasive stylization of line syntax in the poem. I would, in fact, argue that their effect is to establish the typological unity of the poem on and through its metrical level. Consider, for example, the following lines:

> The chalice of the grapes of God;
>
> (X. 16)

> His license in the field of time,
>
> (XXVII. 6)

> The bases of my life in tears.
> (XLIX. 16)
>
> Thy kindred with the great of old.
> (LXXIV. 8)
>
> Her shadow on the blaze of kings:
> (XCVIII. 19)

or the lines:

> The violet of his native land.
> (XVIII. 4)
>
> The primrose of the later year,
> (LXXXV. 119)
>
> The herald of a higher race,
> (CXVIII. 14)
>
> The stillness of the central sea.
> (CXXIII. 4)

or the lines:

> Her early Heaven, her happy views;
> (XXXIII. 6)
>
> A little flash, a mystic hint;
> (XLIV. 8)
>
> A higher height, a deeper deep.
> (LXIII. 12)
>
> The larger heart, the kindlier hand;
> (CVI. 30)
>
> The reeling Faun, the sensual feast;
> (CXVIII. 26)
>
> The white-faced halls, the glancing rills,
> (Epilogue, l. 113)

While these lines do not echo thematically or semantically as do the closer pairings, they nevertheless create a kind of *déjà vu* quality which deepens and complicates the experience of reading the poem. It is not that these repetitions are linked to any theme or help render or repeat any particular emotion. Rather, the repetitions enable us to experience the language of the poem in a primitive, incantatory way. Such language seems to come from what Eliot has termed the "auditory imagination . . . the feeling for syllable and rhythm, penetrating far below the conscious levels of thought and feeling, invigorating every word; sinking to the most primitive and forgotten, returning to the original and bringing something back, seeking the beginning and the end."[16] It is in instances like these that I find meaning in the notion that poetry is language conscious of itself.

The extent of this echoing of lines in the poem is fairly large. 2050 lines in the poem are syntactically unique. This leaves 846 lines as possible candidates for such echoing, and of these I find well over half (510) to echo directly with at least one other line.[17] But what makes this echoing extremely pervasive is the extent to which concluding phrases of lines are metrically repetitive in a way that is reminiscent of oral formulaic technique.

We have already noted the high frequency of nouns in prepositional phrases as rhyme words. Tennyson is in the habit of ending lines with prepositional phrases like "of a wasted youth," "with the dawning soul," "in the flowery walk," and "by the growing hour." This is the most frequently used of a number of prepositional structures for line endings. There are 138 lines in the poem which end with this syntactical and metrical pattern, and 20 more in which the pattern is varied only by the use of a bisyllabic preposition, as in "beneath the clover sod" and "about the dappled pools." Another such "formula" is of the form

PREPOSITION + NOUN + COORDINATOR + NOUN

usually combined with alliteration or antithesis: "of light and shade" (Prologue, l. 5), "in man and brute" (Prologue, l. 6), "on tower and tree" (XV. 7), "of life and light" (XLI. 11), "to earth and sky" (XLV. 1), "in blood and breath" (XLV. 13), "of beam and shade" (LXXII. 15), "with God and man" (LXXX. 8), "on form and face" (LXXXII. 2), "of wind and wave" (LXXXV. 73), "of light or gloom" (LXXXV. 74), "with dusk and bright" (LXXXIX. 2), "like life and death" (XCV. 63), "in creek and cove" (CI. 16), "of sheet and shroud" (CIII. 54), "with mask and mime" (CV. 10), "of rich and poor" (CVI. 11), "on lawn and lea" (CXV. 9), "at breast and brow" (CXXII. 11), "of life and death" (CXXII. 16), "in world or sun" (CXXIV. 5), "with Hope and Fear" (CXXVIII. 9), "in woe and weal" (CXXIX. 2), "in star and flower" (CXXX. 6). Another such formula extends over the last six positions of the line:

DETERMINER / OBJ + NOUN / OBJ + PREPOSITION + NOUN

(With a slight variation in that either the noun object or the preposition may be bisyllabic): "the firstling to the flock" (II. 6), "the noise about thy keel" (X. 1) "the ritual of the dead" (XVIII. 12), "a desert in the mind" (LXVI. 6), "the glory of a hand" (LXIX. 17), "the splendour of the sun" (LXXII. 8), "a picture in the brain" (LXXX. 9), "the sorrow in my blood" (LXXXIII. 14), "the canker of the brain" (XCII. 3), "the spectres of the mind" (XCVI. 15), "the labyrinth of the mind" (XCVII. 21), "the shaping of a star" (CIII. 36), "the spirit of the song" (CXXV. 10).[18] These prepositional phrases seem to be singled out by Tennyson as formulaic in the sense that the traditional schemes of repetition are formulaic: they represent language consciously manipulated by the craft of the poet in a way that could serve as a model for imitation by other poets.

We may gain some perspective on the extent to which the last part of the line in *In Memoriam* is formulaic through the following statistics. There are thirty-seven structures that occur ten or more times in the last four words of a line and that account for 1008 lines. Of these, 28 structures accounting for 791 lines end in nouns that are the objects of prepositions. If we consider the last three words of the line, 326 lines end with the structure PREPOSITION + DETERMINER + NOUN and 206 with the structure DETERMINER + ADJECTIVE + NOUN in a prepositional phrase. If we consider the last two words of each line, 320 lines end with the structure PREPOSITION + NOUN. The degree of repetition of form classes and structures in the first four words of the line is not nearly as high as this.[19] The five most frequent form and function classes in position 1 of the line account for 1540 lines as contrasted with the five most frequent rhyme classes which account for 2189 lines. The most frequent line opener, a clausal coordinator, occurs 457 times and the second most frequent one, the preposition, occurs 335 times. (As noted above, prepositions are fairly evenly distributed throughout the line.) This contrasts with the prepositional noun which occurs 1121 times and the predicate verb which occurs 560 times. Thus the two most frequent rhyme classes account for more lines (1671) than do the five most frequent line openers (1540).

The structures at the beginnings of lines are simply those we would expect at the beginning of clauses and sentences, and given the amount of endstopping in the poem (74 percent in my reading), line and sentence or clause opening tend to coincide. Thus the two most frequent structures for the first two words are PRONOUN / SUBJECT + VERB / PREDICATE (190 lines) and DETERMINER / SUBJECT + NOUN / SUBJECT (181 lines). For the first three words, the most frequent structure is DETERMINER / SUBJECT + ADJECTIVE / SUBJECT + NOUN / SUBJECT (79 lines) and for the first four words, the most frequent structure is a kernel sentence: PRONOUN / SUBJECT + VERB / PREDICATE + DETERMINER / OBJECT + NOUN / OBJECT (51 lines). In cases where there is a high frequency phrase structure at the beginning of the line which is not a subject, as for example a phrase of the structure PREPOSITION + NOUN, what we find is that this is much less likely to occur at the beginning (118 times) than at the end of a line (320 times). It is, then, only as the last phrase in a line that prepositional phrases take on a formulaic character in *In Memoriam,* but that they do become formulaic there is a key feature of the stylistic manner of the poem. It would be much too ingenious to claim that this movement in the direction of syntactic stability as the line progresses in some way parallels the general movement in the poem from uncertainty to certainty. Nor would I claim, as Wilde might, that this movement is "self-conscious and deliberate" on Tennyson's part. I am much more comfortable, in fact, with the subconscious elements of Eliot's "auditory imagination" as an explanation of the source of this patterning.[20] But if the poet may bring back such patterns from the depths of his subconscious, we may also, with the aid of a computer, bring back the recognition of these patterns in our reading; and as we gather information about how we read a poem, we may also acquire insight into how we ought to read it.

III

The commingling in *In Memoriam* of elegiac occasion and autobiographical impulse with epic scope and lyric form has baffled and intrigued readers since its publication. It would take far more space than this essay to rehearse the endless debates over the unity and meaning of the poem. But the extensive knowledge of the stylistic manner of the poem revealed through computational analysis can help us understand the kind of response the poem evokes. The strikingly pervasive patterning of its metrical and syntactic features surely must explain why, despite its disparate, conflicting, and often obscure thematic and narrative development, so many readers experience the poem as a unified whole. If, as Robert Langbaum has observed, the poem has "a dynamic unity of thought and feeling dependent on a dialectical principle of growth of a single consciousness,"[21] a primary means of enabling the reader to experience this unity must be sought in Tennyson's prosodic consistency, which is the linguistic means through which the center of consciousness of the poem is presented.

Without attempting a complete explication of the poem, I would like to suggest how an understanding of its stylistic manner would relate to its interpretation. The interpretations of the poem that seem to me most cogent are those like Langbaum's which stress its dialectical nature.[22] Critics who see the poem as a pattern of opposing intellectual, emotional, linguistic, and thematic concerns are, I believe, able to do justice to the poem in ways that critics who deny or evade this perspective cannot. In fact, I would argue that an understanding of the stylistic manner of the poem leads to an understanding of the dialectic contraries that underlie the poem.

In section V of the poem, Tennyson writes that "words, like Nature, half reveal / And half conceal the Soul within"; and the question of how words are like nature ("red in tooth and claw") is crucial in the poem. To answer it in the light of the stylistic manner of the poem one must see the poem as an exploration of the possibilities and limitations of its own style. A structuralist description of the conventional elegiac situation might present an elegy as two pairs of binary opposites: the first pair are psychological, grief and consolation; the second pair are intellectual, language and nature. The problem for the elegist is to transform the despair of grief into the hope of consolation; to do this he must express grief in a special kind of language ("measured language") which bears a privileged, magical relationship to nature. What this language signifies is not a sign but nature itself. When put in this language, the fact of death is perceived as part of the recurrent natural pattern of life and death to which all things are subject and in which consolation follows grief as spring follows winter. What Tennyson shows in *In Memoriam* is the inadequacy of the assumptions about nature and language that lie behind this model.[23]

When he tries to work within the classical elegiac conventions, Tennyson discovers that he cannot use them to transform his grief to consolation. At best he finds that his language is merely palliative, "like dull narcotics"; at worst, his attempts short-circuit, and instead of offering catharsis for his suffering, his language so intensifies his grief that it deprives him of his power of speech:

> So runs my dream: but what am I?
>   An infant crying in the night:
>   An infant crying for the light:
> And with no language but a cry.
>
> (LIV. 17-20)

The repetition here is not "parnassian." "Infant" derives from the Latin *infandum*—tongue-tied. It is one of a series of etymological puns in the poem—"the *secular* to be," "The *spirit* does but mean the breath," "grow *incorporate* into thee" (my italics)—which enrich its diction. To recover his power of speech, Tennyson must abandon the naive elegiac model and explore a much more complicated and general one whose binary terms are those of sign and signified and stimulus and response. It is the failure of "measured language," I would argue, that provides the motive for the transcendence of the traditional elegiac model which makes the poem a success.[24]

A reading of the poem along these lines brings into sharp focus the connection between those sections that deal with the development of the poet and those that deal with nature. The "fragments of an elegy" embedded in the poem also take on formal as well as thematic importance. The failure of the apotheosis, for example, when the poet's vision is "cancelled, stricken through with doubt" (XCV. 44) is seen as the last and greatest of the failures of the elegiac convention. Immediately after this failure, the poet must face the second anniversary of Hallam's death and the removal from Somersby. But despite these failures and crises, the search for a "voice to soothe and bless" continues as it has from the beginning of the poem. It is not merely that the poet's "love has talked with rocks and trees," but that the rocks and trees answer him, and their answers help him make his own voice into the voice he seeks, the one which will pronounce the benediction with which the poem ends. Who or what speaks and to whom are also important as the various speakers contribute to the final voice of the poem (which we hear for the first time, as I have pointed out, in the Prologue). The most important rhetorical figures in the poem after the schemes of repetition are apostrophe and prosopopoeia, which by their nature call attention to a voice which either comes from an unusual subject or is directed to an unusual object.

But besides helping us understand the internal organization of a poem, computer-assisted stylistic analysis also helps us see individual poems in a broader and more precise context. Assertions about literature by their nature are mythic and metaphysical. Like myths, they confer on us the marvelous ability to deal with aspects of our experience that we can see "through a glass, darkly" if at all. But like metaphysical systems, what from one point of view is their strength is from another their weakness. As Bergson, Wittgenstein, Ayer, Russell, and other modern philosophers have pointed out, the problem with them is not that they account for our world but that they account for any conceivable world. No set of circumstances or experiences could raise any doubt about their truth. This has led some, following Wittgenstein, to attempt to reduce metaphysics to the level of literal "nonsense." But as Karl Popper has argued, the attempt to banish metaphysics even from physics appears impossible and as long as we keep our theories in touch with the experiences from which they arise, metaphysical statements about anything, even literature, have at least a pragmatic usefulness and may lead in the direction of testable theories.[25] Most obviously, critics interested in questions of stylistic development of individual writers and of period and genre related styles might test and sharpen their hunches by means of the computer.

The logical status of the assertions about stylistics made with the aid of the computer is a question worth considering. It seems to me that with the computer it is much easier to make what Popper would call refutable conjectures. The stylistic features of *In Memoriam* we have discussed here offer an illustration of how this may be a possibility. Are the repetitions of form classes and formulas in the poem unique to it, or to Tennyson's verse generally, or to a particular historical period of style? What are the connections between metrical and syntactical choice in poetic language? The ease with which a computer can test answers to these questions provides a motive for stylisticians to make their assertions as formalizable as possible. In adopting such formalism, they would by implication be making a stronger claim for the scientific nature of stylistics than is usually made. Rather than being scientific in Arnold's sense of being systematically laid out and followed up,[26] refutable stylistic assertions would be scientific in an explicitly empirical way. No amount of data could ever establish them as true but they could be framed in a way that would enable them to be proven false. For example, to those who would ask me how I know that what I point to in *In Memoriam* is not common to all poems in the same meter, I would answer that I have not read any other poems in the same way as I have read *In Memoriam,* and that the only way to answer their question is to do so.

Notes

1. Two recent books on Tennyson discuss various aspects of his style: W. David Shaw, *Tennyson's Style* (Cornell Univ. Press, 1976), and Alan Sinfield, *The Language of Tennyson's "In Memoriam"* (New York, 1971). Neither of these studies deals with the syntax and phonology of the poem in the same way or with the same amount of detail as this essay. Two recent essays, Harry Puckett's "Subjunctive Imagination in *In Memoriam,*" VP [*Victorian Poetry*], 12 (1974), 97-124, and Alan Sinfield's rejoinder, "'That Which Is': The Platonic Indicative in *In Memoriam* XCV,"

1. *VP*, 14 (1976), 247-252, have pointed to the formal significance of grammatical mood in the poem. This essay deals in a systematic way with a much wider range of syntactical features than mood.

2. "Stress, Syntax, and Meter," *Language*, 51 (1975), 576-616.

3. Morris Halle and Samuel Jay Keyser, *English Stress: Its Form, Its Growth, and Its Role in Verse* (New York, 1971).

4. For a non-technical description of Ross and Rasche's system and its algorithms, see D. Ross, "Beyond the Concordance: Algorithms for Description of English Clauses and Phrases," in *The Computer and Literary Studies,* ed. A. J. Aitken, R. W. Bailey, and N. Hamilton-Smith (Univ. of Edinburgh Press, 1973), pp. 85-99.

5. Daniel Jones, *An English Pronouncing Dictionary* (New York, 1924).

6. All the programs for this investigation were written in PL/I and run on IBM 370/158 and 370/168 computers under the MVS and VM operating systems. I wish to thank Professor Antonio Zampolli, Head of the Linguistics Division of the Centro Nazionale Universitario dello Calculo Elettronico of the University of Pisa, and the Humanities Division of the University of Southern California for providing computer facilities for this study.

7. In the discussion that follows I will give a number of frequency counts and percentages derived from computer assisted analysis of the poem. To the best of my knowledge, these are accurate to within 1 percent. I offer no formal statistical analysis of them because they require none. The analysis I offer here is empirical but not statistical. One does not need the binomial theorem to demonstrate that an odd-even distribution of 65 to 4270 is unusually skewed.

8. *Counter-Statement* (Univ. of California Press, 1968), p. 122.

9. I use the term "position" here as Halle and Keyser define it: a phonological sequence consisting of a single syllable or a sonorant sequence incorporating at most two vowels immediately adjoining or separated by a sonorant consonant (Halle and Keyser, p. 169). The position of a stressed polysyllabic word is determined by the location of its primary stress. Thus, "immortal" in line 1 of the poem is regarded as being in position 6. The term "rhyme position" is used to refer to the last word of a line, no matter what its metrical position.

10. Among form classes that favor even-numbered positions the distributions for odd versus even positions are: adjectives, 203 to 1486; adverbs, 154 to 596; nouns, 65 to 4205; particles, 5 to 270; verbs, 381 to 2350. Among form classes that favor odd-numbered positions the distributions of odd to even positions are: auxiliary verbs, 402 to 138; conjunctions, 1101 to 103; determiners, 2276 to 357; infinitive marker ("to"), 197 to 17. Both prepositions and verb complements tend slightly toward odd-numbered positions but not so markedly as these; the distribution for prepositions is 1279 to 831; for verb-complements, 228 to 150.

11. The following list gives the location of lines in which displaced nouns occur by position. Position 1: VII. 7, XI. 17, XIII. 1, XIII. 8, XVII. 14, XIX. 6, XXVIII. 11, XXVIII. 12, XXXV. 4, XLIV. 4, XLVI. 11, LVI. 9, LVII. 1, LVII. 3, LXVIII. 2, LXX. 5, LXXI. 1, LXXII. 5, LXXII. 18, LXXXI. 5, LXXXIX. 1, XCIII. 8, XCIX. 4, XCIX. 15, CIX. 1, CXV. 18, CXIX. 1, CXXVI. 1, CXXVI. 5; Position 3: XI. 9, XV. 5, XXIX. 11, L. 2, LVIII. 8, LXXIX. 20, LXXXIII. 2, LXXXIII. 13, LXXXV. 32, LXXXV. 98, XC. 15, XCV. 34, XCV. 51, XCV. 55, CII. 11, CIII. 40, CVII. 20, CXXVII. 7, CXXVII. 15, Epilogue, l. 63, Epilogue, l. 64; Position 5: XXXIV. 19, LXVII. 15, LXXVIII. 7, XCV. 19, CXIV. 8, CXIV. 25, CXVI. 1, CXIX. 6, CXXI. 3, CXXII. 4, CXXIII. 3, CXXIV. 22; Position 7: XL. 22, L. 2, LXXIII. 9.

12. The following table, which divides these verbs by their function class, reveals several distinct subcategories within this general pattern.

POSITION	1	3	5	7
COPULATIVE	11	8	1	1
IMPERATIVE	63	2	4	0
PREDICATE	42	10	5	5
SUBJUNCTIVE	10	0	0	0
TOTAL	126	21	10	6

13. If the poem were "perfectly" regular, it would contain 11,584 stresses, 2,896 (25%) in each even-numbered position. In my reading of the poem, I find 10,703 stresses distributed as follows: 439 (4.09%) in position 1; 2,375 (22.18%) in position 2; 279 (2.60%) in position 3; 2,389 (22.31%) in position 4; 108 (1.00%) in position 5; 2,238 (20.90%) in position 6; 94 (.87%) in position 7; 2,781 (25.97%) in position 8. Positions 2, 4, and 6 are virtually indistinguishable with respect to frequency of stress; position 8 is affected by the demands of rhyme. Only 8 percent of the stresses occur in odd-numbered positions. Weak endings (the vast majority of these are auxiliary verbs and pronouns) seem to be avoided assiduously. Initial inversions seem to me to be far fewer than in pentameter. The most frequently occurring stress pattern, the regular 2, 4, 6, 8, occurs 1,030 times as contrasted with the second most frequent, 2, 4, 8, which occurs 377 times. If anything, all this shows the phonological regularity of the poem to be obsessive.

14. The 41 lines with predicate verbs in position 1 are: II. 8, VI. 16, VIII. 6, IX. 2, IX. 7, XIV. 7, XVII. 16, XXIII. 16, XXIII. 20, XXVI. 14, XXVIII. 4, XXVIII. 7, XXX. 12, XXX. 27, XXXII. 7, XXXV. 11,

XL. 8, XLIII. 16, XLIV. 7, LI. 7, LXX. 16, LXXII. 1, LXXVII. 12, LXXXIV. 15, LXXXVIII. 2, XCI. 4, XCV. 16, XCV. 20, XCV. 52, XCV. 58, XCV. 93, XCVIII. 17, XCIX. 1, CI. 6, CVII. 8, CXI. 19, CXII. 4, CXII. 10, CXVI. 7, CXXIV. 16, CXXXII. 11, CXXXII. 53.

15. The following table gives their distributions:

POSITION	1	2	3	4	5	6	7	8
NOUN PREP	0	143	2	413	4	335	0	1089
VERB PRED	47	553	13	412	6	309	6	560
NOUN OBJ	2	145	2	297	2	176	1	267
NOUN SUBJ	19	322	24	296	7	234	6	134
ADVERB PRED	47	131	27	87	11	78	15	107

16. T. S. Eliot, *The Use of Poetry and the Use of Criticism* (Harvard Univ. Press, 1933), p. 112.

17. Among other lines that echo, the reader might consider XV. 18, XLVIII. 10, LV. 20, XCI. 2; XCIV. 13 and CXXV. 9; XII. 10, XVI. 7, LXIV. 6, LXXII. 24, LXXXIV. 3; XIX. 8, XXII. 16, LXIV. 26, LXVI. 12, LXXII. 8, LXXXI. 11, LXXXVII. 4, LXXXIX. 35, CIX. 20, CXXI. 16; II. 6, XX. 6, CIII. 16; XXV. 4, LV. 10, LXIV. 19-20, LXXI. 3, LXXII. 12, LXXXV. 14, LXXXV. 75, LXXXV. 86, LXXXIX. 24, XCV. 40, XCIX. 12, C. 4, CIV. 7, CVI. 18, CXXVII. 4, CXXXII. 116.

18. The formula also occurs in X. 4, X. 5, XIII. 9, XVI. 9, XIX. 8, XX.6, XXI. 3, XXII. 16, XXIX. 12, XXXVI. 3, XLIV. 4, LX. 6, LXIII. 3, LXIV. 26, LXVI. 11, LXVI. 12, LXVIII. 10, LXIX. 14, LXXII. 8, LXXX. 11, LXXXI. 11, LXXXVII. 4, LXXXIX. 35, XC. 14, XCIV. 9, XCVII.22, C. 16, CIII. 3, CIII. 16, CVI. 31, CIX. 20, CXIX. 4, CXXI. 16.

19. Lines of 5 or more words account for 2,836 of 2,896 lines in the poem. There are 512 lines with 8 words, 1,132 lines with 7 words, 907 lines with 6 words, 235 lines with 5 words, 55 lines with 4 words, 3 lines with 3 words, and 2 lines with 2 words. There is, then, some overlap in comparing the first four words of the line with the last four but considerably less with the first three as compared with the last three.

20. As Peter Gillett has observed in his essay "Tennyson's Mind at the Work of Creation," *VP*, 15 (1977), 321, "if one may roughly divide all poets into two great classes, the conscious and the preconscious, then Tennyson belongs to the latter and more intriguing class." See also Irving Edgar, "The Psychological Sources of Poetic Creative Experience and Tennyson's *In Memoriam*," in *Essays in English Literature and History* (New York, 1972), pp. 1-14.

21. "The Dynamic Unity of *In Memoriam*," in *The Modern Spirit* (Oxford Univ. Press, 1970), p. 60.

22. The seminal essay for this view, not only of *In Memoriam* but of Tennyson's poetry in general, is Allan Danzig's "The Contraries: A Central Concept in Tennyson's Poetry," *PMLA* [*Publications of the Modern Language Association*], 77 (1962), 577-585.

23. For an account of Tennyson's use of elegiac conventions see Joseph Sendry, "*In Memoriam* and *Lycidas*," *PMLA*, 82 (1967), 437-443 and Ian Kennedy, "*In Memoriam* and the Tradition of Pastoral Elegy," *VP*, 15 (1977), 351-366.

24. I would maintain, then, that Kerry McSweeney's argument in "The Pattern of Natural Consolation in *In Memoriam*," *VP*, 11 (1973), 87-99 is misleading in its assertion of the similarity between the poem and traditional pastoral elegy. From my perspective, it is the failure of the traditional elegiac stance that makes the poem so rich.

25. Popper, *Conjectures and Refutations: The Growth of Scientific Knowledge*, 3rd ed. (London, 1969), pp. 34-39.

26. "Literature and Science," in *Philistinism in England and America*, Vol. X of *The Complete Prose Works of Matthew Arnold*, ed. R. H. Super (Univ. of Michigan Press, 1974), p. 57.

Arthur Pollard (essay date 1981)

SOURCE: Pollard, Arthur. "*In Memoriam* as a Personal Poem." *Tennyson Research Bulletin* 3, no. 5 (November 1981): 175-84.

[*In the following essay, originally delivered as a lecture to the Tennyson Society in 1981, Pollard describes* In Memoriam *as a personal poem with universal application as the author relates his own experience of loss and bereavement.*]

First of all, I should like to express my thanks and also my sense of humility at the honour you have conferred upon me in asking me to deliver the Tennyson lecture this year. The year just past saw great activity and success in securing the vast bulk of the Tennyson material and particularly the rightly-named Lincoln manuscript of **In Memoriam** for permanent deposit at the Research Centre (and I should like to pay my own personal tribute to all those, and not least the Lincolnshire County Council—most enlightened action for a local authority—who did so much and in the end succeeded so well). In the light of the events of 1980 it seemed to me appropriate, indeed almost obligatory, that your lecturer this year should devote his attention to **In Memoriam.**

I have, however, special reasons for my choice, and particularly for treating it in the way I propose. Some ten years ago I gave a talk about *In Memoriam* at Horncastle. Sir Charles Tennyson was in the audience. That was the first occasion on which I had met him, altogether too late in his life, alas, for me. In the discussion which followed he paid me the kind of gracious tribute which was so in keeping with his own character and generosity, whilst at the same time he picked up for comment several points with that incisiveness that we all knew so well. In the course of his complimentary remarks he was kind enough to say that he felt that I had appreciated the poem with such tenderness because I must be a poet myself. In that he was wrong; but if he was right to detect tenderness in my understanding of the poem, I think it may have derived from the private circumstances in which I composed my lecture.

Like Hallam, my own wife had died only a few months before; like him, suddenly struck down and by the same cause, cerebral haemorrhage. What therefore Sir Charles attributed to the poet in me came, if it came at all, more likely from my own bereft condition and the extent to which *In Memoriam* therefore spoke with especial directness and peculiar poignancy to me at that time.

It was my recollection of this event together specifically with some remarks by P. F. Baum in his *Tennyson Sixty Years After* that led me to the choice of my subject for this paper. Lest, however, any of you may fear that I shall embarrass you by too blatantly baring my soul or my emotions, let me hasten to add that I am aware of this danger and that after-events have done much to place my personal bereavement in perspective, an experience again that finds parallel and enlightenment by comparison with Tennyson's own.

There will nonetheless be an element of subjectivity in what I have to say. That may be no bad thing, for surely one element in our own century's failure properly to appreciate certain nineteenth-century poems and poets has been our fear of expressing our feelings. Professor Philip Collins in his fine paper on *The Victorians and Tears* has shown that, excessive as some of their displays of pathos may appear to us, there was in them a directness in the display of emotion that it is not altogether to our credit that we seem so embarrassed to regard. This restraint, to put it no worse, once made us suspicious, and even slighting, of Dickens, and it still confines our response to death. I think it was Geoffrey Gorer who said that we in our day are as reticent and even ashamed about death as the Victorians were about sex.

I have indicated what directed me to my topic, but equally I might have been guided to it by some words of Tennyson himself, a sentence which out of context seems paradoxical, if not contradictory: "It is a very impersonal poem as well as personal." That is part of what Knowles reported the poet as saying in the passage that contains the more famous, but for our purposes only equally relevant, comment that *In Memoriam* "is rather the cry of the whole human race than mine. In the poem altogether private grief swells out into thought of, and hope for, the whole world. It begins with a funeral and ends with a marriage—begins with death and ends with promise of a new life—a sort of Divine Comedy, cheerful at the close" (*Nineteenth Century,* XXXIII, 1893, p. 182).

Later in that same remark Tennyson added: "It's too hopeful, this poem, more than I am myself." From that T. S. Eliot may have derived a clue for his judgement that the doubt is more convincing than the faith. Eliot's sentence, however, seems to me to be more concerned with the way in which Tennyson was affected by and reacted to some public issues of his day, particularly the assault on traditional religious belief by new scientific theories. Eliot however may be the child of his and our time. Evolutionary optimism, like other aspects of Victorian doctrines of progress, seems hard to accept in our disillusioned century. That matter is a public issue and will not concern me. I want to concentrate on Tennyson's reaction to his private grief and the way in which we may read *In Memoriam* as a personal poem.

How, if it is in his own words, "rather the cry of the whole human race than mine," is it possible for that to be done? I should like to suggest that the private grief does swell out, but not just into thought of, and hope for, the whole human race in terms of doctrinal and intellectual acceptance and modification of theories which puzzled and afflicted the public of his time. If it is true in Dryden's words that the poet ideally should possess a more comprehensive soul or in Keats' that a poem should be a wording of the reader's own highest thoughts, then *In Memoriam* should embody and express an experience into which Tennyson can lead us and to which those who have found themselves in a comparable situation may respond with particular recognition.

In Memoriam is the cry of the whole human race because it confronts us with the universal phenomenon of and response to bereavement. What gives it its power and importance is that it is the report of a poet, of one more acutely endowed to respond than the rest of us ordinary men. It is time therefore to make some distinctions. The character I am just now attributing to the poem is its universality. At the other extreme is its privateness, the way in which what happened to Tennyson when Hallam died happened to him alone. I want to differentiate the private and the personal. In so far as the poem records the private only (if it ever does that only), we intrude and may well feel embarrassed. In so far as it records the private as a recognisable relationship and which thus takes on something of the universal experience of mankind, it is describing what I prefer to define as personal. After all, what happens to us all and all the time is what in the sociologists' horrible jargon is called interpersonal relationships. It is with that kind of experience, with which in however pallid a fashion we may be able to compare our own, that I am principally concerned in examining *In Memoriam* as a personal poem.

It is at this point that I must return to Baum if only to show how my differences with him helped to set off and to crystallise my own thoughts about the personal character of the poem. He states, rightly in my view, that "the subject of *In Memoriam* is twofold," namely, Tennyson's grief and his doubt and adds: "*In Memoriam* is therefore both an elegy and a philosophical poem; and each aspect, sorrow and consolation, has a double meaning, the personal and the impersonal" (*Tennyson Sixty Years After*, 1948, p. 119). Baum goes on to claim that the form of the verse may suit elegy but not a philosophic poem and that the autobiographic and the speculative sit ill side by side. I have already said that I am deliberately eschewing any consideration of *In Memoriam* as a public or philosophical poem, but you may well be wondering why I did not choose Baum's word for my title and set out to consider the poem as elegy. Here too I was deliberate in my choice, for though elegy ranges wide, it often, indeed usually, has within it a degree of the formal and sometimes indeed a lack of the personal that made me feel it not quite the appropriate description of the way in which I look at *In Memoriam*. Nor was 'lament' sufficient, for that too is limiting, even though it emphasises the personal response: it connotes too exclusively the emotional and the depressive reaction.

It might seem from what I have already said of Baum that his main quarrel is with *In Memoriam* in its philosophical and speculative character, but though this, I think, would be true, he is not uncritical of its personal emphases. He can and does recognise the power of Tennyson's experience, but it is always with qualified comment (and I italicise the reservations):

> We . . . witness his sufferings in many intimate details; he confides to us the shadows and gleams of light as they came to him, the moments which to him seemed important then *though to us they may appear inconsequent because they are not ours and because he has not fused them into a true whole.* We are thus permitted to observe Tennyson's mind through many of the stages of his experience, even when his thoughts are unworthy and the tone confessional . . . we are permitted to see him now yearning for comfort, now distracted by trivial incidents, now seeking ecstatic communion with the dead, now agreeably at home with the living.
>
> (p.127)

The comment concludes somewhat condescendingly: "Read in this sense *In Memoriam* is a remarkably frank and disarming revelation." Christopher Ricks showed better grasp and greater economy when he said that it was at once "anonymous but confessional, private but naked" (*Tennyson*, 1978, p. 221).

I believe that Baum is very characteristic of a certain type of twentieth-century reader. He shows it in the way in which he distances himself from Tennyson. Thus: "Although there is never any doubt, biographically, of Tennyson's sincerity, there is a question whether he has made his personal suffering interesting, sufficiently real to the reader and therefore worthy of such protracted mourning. It is a question if parts of the poem are not too personal and intimate" (p. 120). Indeed, it seems to me that he confesses his own disqualification when he writes:

> If . . . our minds are not naturally sympathetic to a story of this sort, if we do not readily share the kind of personal suffering which was Tennyson's, if the kind of religious doubt which he felt is foreign to us, if our hearts do not passionately yearn for direct communion with those who are separated from us by death, and if our minds can be satisfied without a belief in the everlasting survival of the individual self, then, in spite of the biographic interest in *In Memoriam* the poem will not awaken a quick response in us . . . and we will look for that literary art, that dramatic power by which all great poetry enlists our affections and stirs our emotions and creates a sense of common human experience even when the immediate grounds for it are not always there. . . . And this quality we shall not always find, for *In Memoriam* as a whole does not possess it.
>
> (pp. 128-9)

I think that what I. A. Richards might have called doctrinal irrelevances got in the way for Baum. There is certainly no trace of any willing suspension of disbelief being exercised in Tennyson's favour here.

That obstinate refusal of imaginative empathy meets its countervailing reply in the perhaps over-lyrical, over-rhetorical but certainly more sympathetic sentences of A. C. Benson, writing with the poet's own century still in sight:

> Tennyson's *In Memoriam* is probably the noblest monument ever raised by the human spirit to the memory of a lost and unforgotten friend. . . . It is the story of an overwhelming loss, when a soul is confronted by the fact that a kindred spirit, to whose touch all the chords of the survivor's being had vibrated, is suddenly swept, without a shadow of warning, a hint of doom, into the unseen; and the bereaved stretches feeble hands into the darkness, and finds no answer there; such a loss freezes the heart at its very source; very gradually the cloud lifts; the healing influence of time asserts itself; and the grieving spirit rises out of the shadow into a firm belief in immortality and into an absolute trust in the great purpose of God.
>
> (*Tennyson*, 1904; 1912 reprint, p. 169)

Even parts of that comment, however, emphasise rather what *In Memoriam* has to say about Hallam and about the poet's faith rather than his grief. Tennyson himself said: "Let Love clasp Grief lest both be drown'd," and yet he knew that sense of self-betrayal which expressing grief conveyed. It was too sacred a thing and therefore

> I sometimes hold it half a sin
> To put in words the grief I feel.
>
> (5. 1-2)

J. B. Steane appropriately recalls Rickie's remarks to Agnes about her fiancé's death in Forster's *The Longest Journey*:

> It's the worst thing that can ever happen to you in all your life and you've got to mind it—you've got to mind it. They'll come saying, 'Bear up—trust to time'—No, no; they're wrong. Mind it.
>
> (q. *Tennyson*, 1966, p. 77)

In Memoriam is about just that, about giving full and honest recognition to grief, about minding it.

How then did Tennyson mind it? For the most part, by what Baum describes as "frank and disarming revelation." Tennyson begins with exactly the situation that Rickie said Agnes would find herself in, coping with and having to reject all those well-meaning but quite ineffectual comforters:

> One writes, that 'Other friends remain,'
>   That 'Loss is common to the race'—
>   And common is the commonplace,
> And vacant chaff well meant for grain.
>
> (6. 1-4)

The opening sections of the poem are dominated by the old yew (2) and the dark house (7), the one the unageing, unfeeling, detached symbolic guardian of the churchyard, the other the once inviting but now cheerless and unopening entrance to the Hallam home. Tennyson contemplates the severe finality of "A hand that can be clasp'd no more" (and they recall, of course, those other plangent lines:

> O for the touch of a vanish'd hand
> And the sound of a voice that is still).

The sentence "He is not here" has mocking overtones in the context of its earlier usage in the accounts of our Lord's Resurrection. Sections 11-15 chart the fluctuations between "calm despair and wild unrest" (16), states of feeling that are reflected in the moods of nature which are described, but again with ironic parallels as between the "calm and deep peace on this high wold" and "in my heart, if calm at all, / If any calm, a calm despair" (ll. 5, 14-15). It would be tedious, and it is unnecessary, to attempt to trace in detail the progress of Tennyson's emotions. Numbed grief, ineffectual fury against death, resignation to everlasting farewell, these are but some of the moods before the poem begins to move out of mourning and into something more like confidence and faith.

I am interested not so much in generalised transient states of feeling but rather in more exact and specific representations of the experience of bereavement. These are all of them facets of time—past, present and future; actual, possible and merely fanciful.

It is with an aspect of this last, the fanciful, that I want to begin. I refer to Tennyson's awareness of the place that dreams usurp in the type of situation that he is exploring. It may be the dream of deception like that of

> the widower, when he sees
> A late-lost form that sleep reveals
> And moves his doubtful arms, and feels
> Her place is empty
>
> (13. 1-4)

or perhaps it is the nightmare terror in which

> I find a trouble in thine eye,
>   Which makes me sad I know not why,
>   Nor can my dream resolve the doubt;
>
> But ere the lark hath left the lea
>   I wake, and I discern the truth;

> It is the trouble of my youth
> That foolish sleep transfers to thee
>
> (68. 10-16)

or, more happily, in the later calmer phase it can be the vision which represents Hallam much in the terms of "The Passing of Arthur" (103).

If such are some manifestations of the unconscious response, the conscious is, as one might expect, associated particularly with the memory of places and occasions. There is the passing reference to the London house already mentioned; there is the visit to Cambridge with its "reverend walls . . . high-built organs . . . the measured pulse of racing oars . . . long walk of limes" and then "the rooms in which he dwelt. / Another name was on the door." (87); there is even the irrational but quite understandable hatred of the place where Hallam died:

> I have not seen, I will not see
> Vienna; rather dream that there,
> A treble darkness, Evil haunts.
>
> (98.11-13)

It is, however, the place with which the most tender of Hallam's associations with the Tennyson family were linked that evokes the poet's most tender reminiscences, not least because Tennyson's own connections with it had come to a sorrowful end. I refer, of course, to Somersby, where

> Witch-elms that counterchange the floor
>   Of this flat lawn with dusk and bright;
>   And thou, with all thy breadth and height
> Of foliage, towering sycamore;
>
> How often, hither wandering down,
>   My Arthur found your shadows fair.
>
> (89. 1-6)

It is such details of remembered comradeship that remain in the memory and give added poignancy to recollection of the places with which they are associated, a poignancy itself reinforcing the sadness of removal from familiar places:

> No gray old grange, or lonely fold,
>   Or low morass and whispering reed,
>   Or simple stile from mead to mead,
> Or sheepwalk up the windy wold . . .
>
> But each has pleased a kindred eye,
>   And each reflects a kindlier day;
>   And, leaving these, to pass away,
> I think once more he seems to die.
>
> (100.5-8, 17-20)

That first Christmas after Hallam's death Tennyson "slept and woke with pain, [and] almost wish'd no more to wake," but at least he was able to hear those familiar "four voices of four hamlets round" (28), and together then the family wove "the holly round the Christmas hearth" (30).

After the departure from Somersby there was only "A single peal of bells below, / [and] these are not the bells I know" (104); and "To-night ungather'd let us leave / This laurel, let this holly stand" (105).

The first group of Christmas poems was, we know, amongst the earliest written after the death of Hallam. They remind us how powerfully and how vividly his presence impressed itself upon the Tennysons from the time of his first visit to Somersby at Christmas 1829. How marvellous it must have been to have had Hallam there and, sad though it is to have to say it, to have him there and the father, Dr Tennyson, gloomy, alcoholic and half-mad, away! Hallam's capacity to give to experience a heightened significance is reflected in the passage I quoted above from section 100. There in Tennyson's detailed and precise catalogue of the several features of the landscape is all the familiarity and love of the place he knew. To it he adds, after Hallam's death, a new emotion by which, though the happiness of the past is not obliterated, it is now suffused by a pervasive and ineluctable sadness from those very associations which gave birth to the original happiness— "each reflects a kindlier day [by which] once more he seems to die."

Alongside the past beyond recall except in plangent memory Tennyson is also left to envisage an unrealised future, the might-have-been had Hallam still been there. This is delineated in several perspectives of time, each determined by the distance from the date of Hallam's death. There is, for instance, section 14 in which Tennyson portrays that experience of early bereavement in which somehow, neither quite deliberately nor quite spontaneously, the relict is at times quite unable to believe in the reality of the loved one's death:

> If one should bring me this report,
>   That thou hadst touched the land to-day
> And I went down unto the quay
> And found thee lying in the port . . .
>
> And I perceived no touch of change,
>   No hint of death in all his frame,
>   But found him all in all the same
> I should not feel it to be strange.
>
> (ll. 1-4, 17-20)

Tennyson accurately sets that experience in the context of the desire not just for continued company but also within the bereaved's need for the consolation and support in his loss that he knew the loved one had possessed the strength to provide:

> And I should tell him all my pain,
>   And how my life had drooped of late,
>   And he should sorrow o'er my state
> And marvel what possessed my brain.
>
> (ll. 13-16)

At greater distance from the event Tennyson seeks strength by comparing his own feelings at the loss of Hallam with what he thinks those of Hallam would have been, had the situation been reversed. This is obviously a more self-conscious version of the might-have-been, and Tennyson's language acknowledges it as such. With his sensitive, profound and comprehensive appreciation of Hallam's character (and I shall not have time to examine those sections, 109-114, which deal with this) he recognises that Hallam's would have been

> A grief as deep as life or thought,
> But stayed in peace with God and man
>
> (80. 7-8)

but he then deliberately considers his own position and posits the contrast with the way in which Hallam would have reacted:

> I make a picture in the brain;
>   I hear the sentence that he speaks;
>   He bears the burthen of the weeks
> But turns his burthen into gain . . .
>
> (80. 9-12)

The final stage of the might-have-been is that vision, at once happy in what it imagines and sad that it will never be, of Hallam and Emily married and with children, and "boys of thine / Had babbled 'Uncle' on my knee" (84. 12-13), of whom he could passingly persuade himself:

> I seem to meet their least desire
>   To clap their cheeks, to call them mine.
>
> (ll. 17-18)

That is the happiness, even though it is but seeming. The next two lines with their negatives constitute the sadness:

> I see their unborn faces shine
> Beside the never-lighted fire.
>
> (ll. 19-20)

But this is not to say that the association of Tennyson and Hallam must now be all fancy and unreality. The poet finds and enjoys a very real continuing "commerce with the dead" (85. 93), one, however, which requires preparation of heart and mind so that the "spirit is at peace with all" (94. 8). Then, with the world shut out, "The spirits from their golden day . . . [can] haunt the silence of the breast" (94. 6, 9). Earlier it had been merely the belief that "in the songs [he] love[d] to sing / A doubtful gleam of solace live[d]" (38. 7-8), by which

> If any care for what is here
>   Survive in spirits rendered free,
>   Then are these songs I sing of thee
> Not all ungrateful to thine ear.
>
> (38. 9-12)

From this belief that what he sang might please Hallam, Tennyson moves through the thought of his possible unworthiness, of his shame if Hallam were to see—

> Do we indeed desire the dead
>   Should still be near us at our side?
>   Is there no baseness we would hide?
> No inner vileness that we dread?
>
>   (51. 1-4)

—by way of his faith in possible communion with Hallam that I have noted above through to the experience of actual communion described in the dialogue of section 85. Even that, however, is but prelude to the climax, the visionary communication, as

> word by word, and line by line,
>   The dead man touched me from the past,
>   And all at once it seemed at last
> The living soul was flash'd on mine.
>
>   (95. 33-6)

It happened, as all who have read about and appreciated the friendship of Hallam and Tennyson recognise, when and where it had to happen—

> By night we linger'd on the lawn,
>   For underfoot the herb was dry
>   And genial warmth; and o'er the sky
> The silvery haze of summer drawn
>
>   (95. 1-4)

—in a setting redolent of associations with Hallam, in a late evening of high midsummer—at Somersby.

Looking backward, say, to section 41 it is possible to see how far Tennyson had travelled in his experience and understanding of his separation from Hallam. There he had feared that it was permanent:

> Yet oft when sundown skirts the moor
>   An inner trouble I behold,
>   A spectral doubt which makes me cold
> That I shall be thy mate no more.
>
>   (41. 17-20)

Now he knows the reality of present communion and it enables him to look forward with renewed

> trust that those we call the dead
> Are breathers of an ampler day
> For ever nobler ends.
>
>   (118. 5-7)

Ironically, it is this ampler vision that is less convincing, because, as I believe, it goes beyond Tennyson's relations with Hallam himself which are the originating and consistently sustaining source of the poem's inspiration.

Tennyson's argument is never as convincing as his experience. Even in his deepest uncomprehending sorrow his subjective personal certainty is never wholly extinguished. Love, he never doubts, cannot die—"If Death were seen / At first as Death, Love had not been" (35. 18-19). But that is an unfulfilled and unfulfillable condition; death is never total because it cannot destroy love. That being so, there is nothing either illogical or stridently superficial in his claim:

> If e'er when faith had fallen asleep,
>   I heard a voice, 'believe no more' . . .
>
> A warmth within my breast would melt
>   The freezing reason's colder part,
>   And like a man in wrath the heart
> Stood up and answer'd, 'I have felt.'
>
>   (124. 9-10, 13-16)

That assertion leads on quite naturally to the hymn-like celebration of section 126—"Love is and was my lord and king."

It is possible therefore—and again an accurate reflection of one mourning another, himself both much loved and selflessly loving—that Tennyson can imagine Hallam's spirit urging him to

> 'Arise and get thee forth and seek
> A friendship for the years to come.'
>
>   (85. 79-80)

In the same spirit Tennyson himself can paradoxically yet without contradiction acknowledge his continuing and undismissible desire for Hallam—

> Whatever change the years have wrought,
>   I find not yet one lonely thought
> That cries against my wish for thee
>
>   (90. 21-4)

—and at the same time accept Hallam's spirit's advice:

> My heart, tho' widow'd, may not rest
>   Quite in the love of what is gone,
>   But seeks to beat in time with one
> That warms another living breast.
>
>   (85. 113-16)

It is impossible to pretend to love those who are gone without being able and wanting to love someone who lives.

I return to Tennyson's remark to Knowles that the poem "begins with a funeral and ends with a marriage—begins with death and ends with promise of new life—a sort of Divine Comedy, cheerful at the close" and, of course, he explicitly states in the Epilogue that he has not

> felt so much of bliss
> Since first he told me that he loved
>   A daughter of our house; nor proved
> Since that dark day a day like this.
>
>   (5-8)

He goes on:

> Regret is dead, but love is more
>   Than in the summers that are flown

> For I myself with these have grown
> To something greater than before.
>
> (17-20)

That for me is the real significance of the Epilogue; not its celebration of Cecilia's marriage, not its anticipation of the "one far-off divine event," but the testimony it gives of the way Tennyson emerged from the long-drawn-out experience of Hallam's death and his own sorrow; no question of being cheerful at the close, no question of "private grief swell[ing] out into thought of and hope for the whole world," but of the poet himself as individual being spiritually stronger, fuller and more developed, perfected through suffering.

From the first numbed moments of trying simply to comprehend that the loved one is dead, through the months and years of sorrow and despair, by mingled recollection and anticipation, on to communion here and now and the expectation of communion to be, in the understanding of death and bereavement by means of all-embracing love—thus did Tennyson provide in *In Memoriam* the most comprehensive and perceptive account and explanation of human loss and separation that any poet has ever written. Thus did he nobly succeed in the aim, as he attributed it to his own Melpomene,

> To lull with song an aching heart
> And render human love his dues.
>
> (37. 15-16)

It is not surprising that the most distinguished mourner of the poet's own generation could say of her own bereavement: "Next to the Bible, *In Memoriam* is my comfort."

Peter Hinchcliffe (essay date 1983)

SOURCE: Hinchcliffe, Peter. "Elegy and Epithalamium in *In Memoriam*." *University of Toronto Quarterly* 52, no. 3 (spring 1983): 241-62.

[*In the following essay, Hinchcliffe considers whether* In Memoriam *is a complete poem or an anthology and asserts that Tennyson specifically organized the individual poems comprising it to form an elegy.*]

I

If literature is a map, then scholars and critics are surveyors and cartographers. Our task is to take new bearings and to draw new contours, not just to complete the work of our predecessors, but to determine where we have moved from those predecessors in relation to the landmarks that we study. As literary works recede into the past, some perspectives—immediacy of response and personal recollection, for example—become closed to us, but new perspectives open out. Critical studies of *In Memoriam* written during the last twenty-five years show us a poem more complex and serious than readers of the two previous generations would have been willing to accept, and a different kind of poem from the one that Tennyson's Victorian readers acclaimed. Yet despite the increasing sophistication of our map-making skills *In Memoriam* remains stubbornly puzzling, and the questions that puzzle its readers can be reduced to two: 'Is it possible to apprehend the *In Memoriam* sequence as a whole poem?' and 'What kind of poem is it?' In other words, the central issues are structural and generic, and if we could give assured answers to those two questions, we would know better how to read *In Memoriam.*

The difficulties of apprehending the structure of *In Memoriam* are obvious and formidable. The 133 individual poems were written from time to time over seventeen years, and not in continuous order. Though scholars have been able to date the composition of many sections, we know very little about Tennyson's act of arranging or how he made his final choice of inclusion. (Not all the sections that Tennyson wrote made their way into the final version of *In Memoriam*. See Appendix A to Christopher Ricks's *Poems of Tennyson*.) Within the published text we find an encyclopedic variety of subject-matter and many different signs of organization—recurring anniversaries, repeated metaphors, patterns of syntax, etc—yet each of these signs just misses becoming definitive. The ending of *In Memoriam* is problematic in a way that some readers find gravely disturbing. Tennyson's own comments about the structure of *In Memoriam* are tantalizing gems of reticence and indirection, worthy of the Ancient Sage or of Merlin himself. The common element in all these difficulties is that author and poem are always saying both too much and too little, but Tennyson seems to have found this a necessary condition of writing *In Memoriam*: 'words, like Nature, half reveal / And half conceal the Soul within' (5.3-4). Finally, of all the long poems in English, *In Memoriam* insists most strongly on the singularity of its parts. Sorrow

> holds it sin and shame to draw
> The deepest measure from the chords:
>
> Nor dare she trust a larger lay,
>   But rather loosens from the lip
> Short swallow-flights of song, that dip
>   Their wings in tears, and skim away.
>
> (48.11-16)

When we consider the genre of *In Memoriam*, we encounter again this same difficulty of too much and too little. *In Memoriam* appears too long to be read with assurance as an elegy, too short to be taken for anything else. Several recent critics have been troubled by what seems to be its displacement or rejection of the pastoral motifs that are conventional in elegy. Others, aware that the use of traditional genres by nineteenth-century English writers has itself become a critical problem, look to other forms than elegy to explain what kind of poem it is. As it does with its indications of structure, *In Memoriam* provides the reader with a bewildering variety of generic signals. Epic, drama, novel, confessional autobiography, sonnet sequence, collection of aphorisms—all have been claimed as formal models for *In Memoriam,* and epic and sonnet sequence, at least, are hinted at by Tennyson himself. These generic claims are competing, not complementary; I do not see how any poetic sequence could fulfil more than a couple of them. Moreover, just to list the possible genres is to realize that my two initial questions are inextricably related. The judgment that any reader makes about the wholeness of the poem will affect his or her perceptions of genre, and vice versa.

Fortunately, some of these difficulties resolve themselves in the reading. Despite the self-deprecating insistence upon singularity that recurs throughout the sequence, most people who reach the end of *In Memoriam* believe that they have read a complete poem and not an anthology—though many do not seem to have read the same poem. Similarly, as we read we do not juggle all the generic possibilities but choose one as our dominant assumption and read in the light of that.

What happens, I believe, as we read *In Memoriam* is this. The whole sequence is coherent (at this point I will not say 'unified'), and its coherence is rhetorical rather than argumentative or thematic. Tennyson made an initial choice of stanza and metre, and as he wrote he developed patterns of trope and syntax, such as sustained comparisons of higher and lower, and the repeated subjunctive and optative verbs that make so many of the *In Memoriam* lyrics hypothetical. Devices like these gave Tennyson the shape and proportions with which he worked, and they help to create the intuitive sense of coherence that most readers feel.[1]

However, rhetoric does not determine the contents of the poem or their order. After many years of reading and teaching *In Memoriam* I can find no single argument that unites all the sections, yet I would call none of it random. My understanding is of separate patterns of argument and image that are related to each other in ways that enable us to speak of a plurality where all the parts are homologous. Moreover, although the order of the particular sections is not inevitable, their placing is guided by a powerful sense of direction which is provided, I believe, by Tennyson's acceptance of the requirements of elegy—for that is *my* dominant assumption.

To illustrate and clarify these statements I propose to write a discussion of genre in *In Memoriam* in which I shall concentrate upon the trope of the bride leaving home as a metaphor for the death of Arthur Hallam. This trope is introduced in section 40, and it undergoes expansions and changes in the rest of the sequence until it reappears in its original form in the Epilogue. By itself the bride-leaving-home trope constitutes a minor pattern in the whole poem, but it is related to larger actions. Specifically, it forms a necessary part of defining the elegiac consolation that Tennyson hopes to achieve. This achievement of consolation is only partial, in my view, and I contend that because Tennyson is completely faithful to his genre he reaches an impasse at the end of *In Memoriam.* Elegy requires the apotheosis of Arthur Hallam and his transformation into a type; but Tennyson wants to retain Hallam as his personal and private friend. Tennyson's attempts to be true to both these demands result in what Barbara Herrnstein Smith has called 'failures of closure' at the end of the sequence.[2] Tennyson retrieves his failures as best he can in the Epilogue, which replaces elegy by its complementary genre, epithalamium.

The necessary prelude to this argument is a brief poetics of elegy and epithalamium, and to that we now turn.

II

From its first appearance in our culture, in the Greek eclogues of Alexandria, the elegy has exhibited an extraordinary variety and flexibility of subject-matter, conventions, and poetic action. However, one can abstract a typical poetic action that is performed by elegies written in English, at least since the seventeenth century. This typical action involves acknowledging an absence. The absence may consist of a lost time or place, as in elegies whose subject is exile. It may even take the form of an anticipated presence, as in erotic elegies like John Donne's Elegy XIX 'To His Mistress, Going to Bed.' Most poems that we call elegy, however, acknowledge an absence caused by the death of a beloved person. In the related forms of dirge and complaint, acknowledging an absence and lamenting it are the whole action of the poem. Elegy differs from these simpler forms in moving beyond lament to some recovery of what has been lost. The exile can create a new homeland in his place of banishment; the lover in Donne's elegy can anticipate the pleasures of sexual union; the mourner can assert that his beloved has transcended death: 'Weep no more, woeful shepherds, weep no more, / For Lycidas your sorrow is not dead.'

This achievement requires a double ritual action, which is both fast and slow. Elegies move as swiftly as they can to the announcement that death has been transcended, a catastrophic change from woe to joy, as Dwight Culler calls it in his book on Tennyson.[3] Yet the advance to this joyful catastrophe is delayed by another action, a meditative probing of alternatives that appear to lead the elegist towards dead ends—false consolations and false endings—from which he must retreat and begin his journey again (e.g., the 'Fame is the spur' passage and St Peter's speech in 'Lycidas,' or the Lost Angel in 'Adonais,' who mistakes her own tear for one of his). The meditative aspect of elegy is not simply a delaying tactic. Meditation is necessary to provide a context in which the catastrophic change can be accepted as valid, for part of the elegist's task is to construct a new emotional and moral order that will replace the chaos of his initial experience of grief, an order in which the beloved's death can be regarded as purposeful and necessary. This act of reconstruction is unavoidably slow and difficult, but when it is complete the elegy achieves an anagnorisis, Aristotle's term in the *Poetics* for recognition or discovery. And, as Aristotle tells us, the most effective anagnorisis is one in which the poet realizes the truth of something that he knew all along.

The joyful catastrophe of elegy manifests itself in some combination of the following actions: the beloved undergoes an apotheosis, like Lycidas 'sunk low, but mounted high,' or the soul of Adonais transformed into a star. Simultaneously with this apotheosis, the beloved returns to earth and is absorbed into the natural cycle—so Lycidas returns as 'Genius of the shore' at the same time as he is being entertained by the saints above, and Adonais 'is made one with Nature . . . / . . . a portion of the loveliness / Which once he made more lovely' (lines 370, 379-80). Finally the beloved is assigned an exemplary or tutelary role that he can fulfil only in death—Genius of the shore or the star beaconing from the abode of the immortals. This new role may be combined either with the apotheosis or with the return to earth, and it is an essential part of the consolation because it goes beyond asserting that the beloved has transcended death to accept this death and to justify it. In other words, when the ritual of elegy is complete, apotheosis and anagnorisis become one.

What is involved in all these different forms of consoling vision is a transformation of the beloved from an individual person into a type. This transformation seems to be a necessary characteristic of elegy. Think, for example, of Gray's poet replaced by his own epitaph at the end of 'Elegy Written in a Country Churchyard,' or of Abraham Lincoln become a type for all the dead of the Civil War in 'When Lilacs Last in the Dooryard Bloom'd,' and of these dead in turn subsumed into 'Lilac and star and bird' (line 205). Even erotic elegies of anticipation tend to transform the beloved into a type: 'O my America! my new-found-land' (Elegy XIX.27).

Any description of elegy must consider its relations to pastoral, especially when one is preparing to discuss *In Memoriam*, for it has been maintained that Tennyson's poem uses pastoral motifs so sparsely and in such unorthodox ways that *In Memoriam* cannot be called an elegy at all.[4] Such statements appear to confuse a pattern of action—loss and recovery—with one conventional way of depicting loss, which is the function of pastoral imagery. The main sources of pastoral images in our culture, Greek and Latin lyric poetry and the Bible, associate pastoral life with a state of lost innocence. Since the time of Bion and Moschus elegies have drawn upon pastoral imagery for their depiction of loss, and with the assimilation of biblical pastoral into secular poetry during the Middle Ages and the Renaissance a tradition of great richness has developed. The connection between elegy and pastoral is unbreakably intimate, yet it is not necessarily definitive. As an analogy one might consider the hero's death at the end of a tragedy. Certainly this death is one of the identifying conventions of the genre, yet this particular depiction of loss and defeat is not required by any definition of tragedy, and no one denies that *Œdipus Rex* is tragic. Furthermore, we do not identify every literary death as tragic, nor is every use of pastoral elegiac. Pastoral appears in idyll and in satire, genres which also require recognizable images of innocence, but which have different patterns of action.

In Memoriam uses pastoral conventions less obviously than most earlier elegies, or even later ones like 'Thyrsis.' Yet the traditional pastoral motifs are all there: a mourning shepherd playing on his pipes (section 21), Melpomene, the pastoral muse of Spenser's *Shepherd's Calendar* (section 37), idyllic memories of the past (e.g., sections 23, 71, and especially 89), a flower passage (section 83), and, many times throughout the sequence, the cycle of the seasons. That the presence of these motifs is not obvious is due, first, to the comparatively great length of *In Memoriam*, which dilutes the effects that other elegies concentrate. Second, it is due to Tennyson's exploiting the less than definitive nature of pastoral conventions, as he does with all the other organizing signs in the sequence. We shall examine this later, with particular attention to section 89.

One more general remark about elegy is necessary before we examine *In Memoriam* itself: elegies are anxious poems. They reach their resolution through justifying the beloved's death, deifying him and asserting that he serves as an example for the poet to follow. This is indeed consoling, yet it points to an inescapable difficulty. No matter how hopeful a poet's personal belief in immortality or how strong the dynamics of elegy, there is something factitious in denying what everyone who has experienced bereavement knows, that we apprehend a beloved person's death as a final and irrevocable separation. Elegy makes this denial, but at the cost of generating anxiety. Successful tragedy reaches an ending in which all the potential energy of the plot has been discharged. Elegy, by comparison, seems to be an inherently unstable form. The suicidal hyperbole with which Shelley concludes 'Adonais' is an eminent example of this instability. Even when an elegy succeeds in resolving its action, as I think 'Lycidas' does, a lingering feeling may remain that the elegist has put something over on his readers.

The characteristics that make elegy a dangerous form for some poets are in fact particularly congenial to Tennyson's imagination, which thrives on anxiety. From early poems like **'The Lady of Shalott'** and **'The Palace of Art'** to late poems like **'Lucretius'** and **'Balin and Balan'** anxiety is one of the main sources of his imaginative energy.[5] The anxious poems are the more authentic ones; rarely do we find in Tennyson's serene poems a complete and unforced resolution. **'Audley Court'** is a fine example of such a poem, but it is exceptional. More common is a poem like **'The Ancient Sage,'** which, to me at least, gives the impression of an anxious poet trying to sound serene against all his instincts and better judgment. Yet if anxiety is to be a source of poetry and not of imaginative paralysis, it must be directed and controlled, for even a poet for whom anxiety is the natural mood can go too far. At the end of *In Memoriam* Tennyson attempts to control anxiety by shifting from elegy to epithalamium. This shift is not arbitrary because their attitude towards anxiety forms one of the main links between the two genres.

If one is willing to accept any hierarchical ranking of genres, then elegy is a minor one, related to the major genre of tragedy as epithalamium is related to the major genre of comedy.[6] Tragedy ends, if not always with death, certainly with loss—loss of power, virtue, and the hero's place in the social order. Comedy usually ends with a marriage, which signifies the re-integration of an order that has been threatened with chaos. Where tragedy and comedy end, elegy and epithalamium begin. They are both retrospective genres, looking back to a prior event, and introspective as well, for the protagonist in these two forms laments someone else's death or celebrates someone else's marriage, then reflects upon its significance for his own life. One could almost relate the four genres in a proportional equation:

tragedy/elegy = comedy/epithalamium

Not quite, however. Marriage (ideally, at least) is a self-justifying event; death is not. We have already seen how elegy's attempt to justify death generates anxiety which can provide most of the emotional energy of the poem. An epithalamium, by contrast, is a poem of stable serenity. Despite its subject-matter, epithalamium is less erotic than its counterpart, because there is no frustrated personal desire in the poet's celebration of the sexual union of bride and groom. As an example, compare Tennyson's address to Hallam in an elegiac lyric like section 129, 'Dear friend, far off, my lost desire,' with the chaste description of his sister's wedding night in the Epilogue.

III

In Memoriam enacts with great fidelity the elegiac patterns that I have traced. The poem begins with meditations upon the loss that Arthur Hallam's death has occasioned for the poet who speaks throughout the sequence. What he has lost is Hallam's personal presence and the significance of present and future time. Present time is a blank, and a real future is unimaginable (though the first two-thirds of *In Memoriam* abounds in hypothetical futures); only the irrecoverable past has meaning. The poet, then, has a double task: he must regain a sense of Hallam's presence, and he must learn how to justify the ways of time to men.

The recovery of Hallam's presence is achieved in a triple apotheosis of dream and vision which culminates in sections 71, 95, and 103. This apotheosis is followed by Hallam's return to the earth, most obviously in section 130, 'Thy voice is on the rolling air,' but implicitly in many others of the last thirty-five sections; and by Hallam's transformation into an exemplary type of public virtue in sections 109-14. The public career that Hallam lost through his death becomes a model for everyone who reads the poem. We readers can realize the unfulfilled possibilities, and so the hypothetical future becomes a real one. These actions constitute *In Memoriam*'s joyful catastrophe, a prolonged one, to be sure, but given the size of the whole poem I do not think that it is too prolonged. The visions and transformations can still strike the reader as sudden.

In Memoriam's anagnorisis, the construction of a new imaginative order in which time's ways are justified, takes longer to achieve, and the approach to it is necessarily in-direct. Throughout most of *In Memoriam* the poet perceives time as an adversary, senseless, 'a maniac scattering dust' (50.1), and cruel, 'that remorseless iron hour' (84.14). Section 1 is a meditation upon strategies for outwitting this adversary:

> But who shall so forecast the years
>   And find in loss a gain to match?
>   Or reach a hand through time to catch
> The far-off interest of tears?
>
> Let Love clasp Grief lest both be drowned,
>   Let darkness keep her raven gloss:
>   Ah, sweeter to be drunk with loss,
> To dance with death, to beat the ground,
>
> Than that the victor Hours should scorn
>   The long result of love, and boast,
>   'Behold the man that loved and lost,
> But all he was is overworn.'
>
> (Lines 5-16)

In subsequent sections this adversarial relation is sustained, as the poet tries to coerce random time into teleology. As late as section 85 (two-thirds of the way through *In Memoriam*, though the lines I quote were written by 1834,)[7] the poet celebrates a small victory over his enemy:

> I, the divided half of such
> A friendship as had mastered Time;
>
> Which masters Time indeed, and is
>   Eternal, separate from fears:
>   The all-assuming months and years
> Can take no part away from this:
>
> (Lines 63-8)

Only after the threefold apotheosis is complete, and after the poet has announced the new stage of his life that began with the Tennyson family's move from Somersby to Epping (section 108), can he disengage himself from this unresolvable conflict. Tentatively at first, then with increasing certitude, the poet accepts that time has work to do. Time's duration and delays are necessary if the love of Hallam and the poet is to reach its due fulfilment, and if the human race is to attain its full moral growth (sections 117 and 118). In section 123, 'There rolls the deep where grew the tree,' the poet accepts geological change without fear. He no longer perceives this change as a threat to human love because it too is part of the work of time. Finally, in section 128, the poet, who has laboured so long to erect a monument to his friend, recognizes that time is also an artist, and in time's extended works he can find the reflection of his own achievement: 'I see in part / That all, as in some piece of art, / Is toil cöoperant to an end' (lines 22-4).

Yet this recognition that time is teleological has already been implied in the transformation of Hallam into a type whose future can be fulfilled by the poem's readers, and in the three dreams and visions with their celebration of past, present, and future. The poet's first dream about Hallam in section 71 recovers the past and brings it to life again:

> Sleep, kinsman thou to death and trance
> And madness, thou has forged at last
> A night-long Present of the Past
> In which we went through summer France.
>
> (Lines 1-4)

The mystic vision of section 95 restores not just the presence of Hallam but also present time. As Hallam's 'living soul was flashed' on the poet's, the united friends 'came on that which is, and caught / The deep pulsations of the world, / Æonian music measuring out / The steps of Time—the shocks of Chance— / The blows of Death' (lines 36, 39-43). The dream vision of 103, like 'Morte D'Arthur,' which it so much resembles, looks from a dying present to a future of hope. Apotheosis and anagnorisis come together, and the elegiac paradigm that I sketched above is complete.

Here is a more ample version of this account, showing how Tennyson uses metaphor to flesh out the formal paradigm. The earliest sections of *In Memoriam* form a complaint; they recount the loss that the poet must express before the poetic action of recovery can begin. By the time the sequence has reached the stopping-point of the first Christmas, the poet knows that his consolation will be found in enduring the passage of time and asserting the permanence of love:

> Still onwards winds the dreary way;
> I with it; for I long to prove
> No lapse of moons can canker Love,
> Whatever fickle tongues may say.
>
> (26.1-4)

His next task is to find a vehicle that will articulate this consolation. In sections 31-6 the poet attempts to construct a theodicy based upon the raising of Lazarus, but no sooner has he stated his argument than Urania intervenes to chide Melpomene, the poet's muse. Melpomene's art is not expounding revelation but 'render[ing] human love his dues' (37.16), and—reluctantly—she turns from divine argument to domestic metaphor.[8]

Section 40 begins with a comparison of 'Spirits breathed away' to a bride who leaves her parents' home to begin her married life:

> parting with a long embrace
> She enters other realms of love;
>
> Her office there to rear, to teach,
> Becoming as is meet and fit
> A link among the days, to knit
> The generations each with each;
>
> And, doubtless, unto thee [Hallam's spirit] is given
> A life that bears immortal fruit
> In those great offices that suit
> The full-grown energies of heaven.
>
> (Lines 11-20)

A comparison of marriage with death is one of Tennyson's master-metaphors, used in many ways throughout the whole of his career. (Tennyson's earliest extant poem is a translation of part of Claudian's **'Rape of Proserpine'**; **'The Death of Œnone'** was completed in 1890.) Here the point of the comparison is that the dead friend, like a bride, is entrusted with the mediating office of linking past and future. It has been pointed out before, but it bears repeating, that the speaker in *In Memoriam* never seriously doubts the immortality of the soul, but he fears the nature of that immortality.[9] In particular, he fears that continued friendship between the dead and the living may not be possible, and section 40 throws this fear into high relief. A bride links past and future by sending news and visiting her old home, but this is precisely what the dead cannot do.

Section 41 voices a further fear, that the poet will be permanently separated from his friend because of the different times of their deaths:

> Yet oft when sundown skirts the moor
> An inner trouble I behold,
> A spectral doubt which makes me cold,
> That I shall be thy mate no more,
>
> Though following with an upward mind
> The wonders that have come to thee,
> Through all the secular to-be,
> But evermore a life behind.
>
> (Lines 17-24)

Baldly put, this is an eccentric scruple, yet it is the true basis of all the poet's doubts. To counter them he constructs a new argument in sections 42-7 which can be paraphrased as follows: Time is teleological because life after death is a more mature version of earthly life, as adulthood is a mature version of infancy. If the buried memories of infancy can influence the course of adult life, then the memories of earthly life may do the same to life after death. Therefore the influence of the poet on Arthur Hallam may continue, at least to the point of mutual recognition after the poet's own death.[10]

In composing this argument Tennyson drew extensively upon the ideas of his age about physiology, natural science—especially astronomy—and philosophical theology to devise what Dwight Culler has called 'a science of immortality.'[11] Yet this argument is a false consolation, like the theodicy before it. No sooner has the poet recounted his version of reunion, 'And we shall sit at endless feast, / Enjoying each the other's good' (47.9-10), than the assurance begins to fade. What if this reunion should be only a moment of farewell? This section is followed by two self-deprecating lyrics where the poet questions again the value of his own words. Then come the 'evolution poems' (50-8) which end the first half of *In Memoriam*.

In these poems the consoling formula, already shaky, is subjected to a test of experience, and the analogical argument of sections 40-7 collapses. In section 53, 'How many a father have I seen,' the poet confronts a scandalous paradox. The wages of sin may be virtue; there is no predictable link among the days of an individual human life.

When he considers the 'secret meaning' of Nature's deeds (55.10), the only sign of purpose that he finds is prodigal abundance to counterbalance reckless waste. The fossils in 'scarpèd cliff and quarried stone' (56.2) record that this prodigality extends through the whole of history. In the face of such evidence the poet can no longer maintain his assertion that time is teleological, and this realization leads to another, unbearable analogy which is implied throughout this group of poems: 'If time is without significance, then so is my love.' This dismay is compounded by a failure of presence. 'Be near me when my light is low' is the poet's prayer to Hallam in the first line of section 50, but the desired presence never manifests itself. The voice of Nature in section 56 is also a disavowal of presence: 'Thou makest thine appeal to me: / I bring to life, I bring to death: / The spirit does but mean the breath: / I know no more' (lines 5-8). The poet's last cry to Hallam's spirit is a lament for his unanswered prayer, 'O for thy voice to soothe and bless!' (56.26), but Hallam's voice is silent.

After all this there would appear to be nothing left to say, and in section 57 it sounds as though *In Memoriam* were in fact concluding. But in elegies, as well as a convention of false consolations, there is also a convention of false endings, as I pointed out above. Recall again St Peter's speech in 'Lycidas,' or the warning to the philosopher-child in Wordsworth's 'Intimations Ode,' which is close enough to elegy to provide a pertinent example. Both appear to be speeches of dreadful finality, yet those poems are able to renew themselves and move on to true consolation. Something similar happens at this point in *In Memoriam*. Urania, the high Muse, intervenes a second time to chide Melpomene: 'Wherefore grieve / Thy brethren with a fruitless tear? / Abide a little longer here, / And thou shalt take a nobler leave' (57.9-12). The reason for Urania's second rebuke is essentially the same as in section 37. Melpomene has attempted another argument beyond her art, and again the remedy is for her to 'Go down beside thy native rill' (37.5) and meditate on the immediacy of personal experience.

Section 59 sends us back to *In Memoriam*'s beginnings, but not to the beginning of the sequence, and in this respect the address to Sorrow is misleading. The path that the poet and his muse retrace is the one that led from section 40 to section 47, and the argument of the next group of poems, 60-5, requires another version of the bride-leaving-home metaphor as its vehicle. The pattern of this trope is the same as the previous one. Hallam's spirit is the blessed and favoured person who leaves home, and the poet identifies himself with those who remain behind; but there is a change of roles, a change of direction in the link among the days, and—most important—a change in the kind of assurance that the poet seeks.

Instead of a bride, feminine and passive, Hallam's spirit now takes the role of one whose death is compared to the emergence of a gifted man from domestic and rural obscurity to public, civic brilliance. The poet is feminine in two of these poems, passive in all of them, and entirely at the mercy of Hallam, who can maintain the ties of friendship or break them, as he pleases. In section 60 the poet is 'Like some poor girl whose heart is set / On one whose rank exceeds her own' (lines 3-4). In section 62 the poet is 'some unworthy heart' (line 7), the old flame of a virtuous man who perhaps looks back upon his youthful folly with condescension. Two other poems in this group concentrate upon Hallam's exalted state. In section 61 the poet imagines Hallam consorting in heaven with Shakespeare and others in 'the circle of the wise' (line 3). The poet sees himself as 'slight,' 'dwarfed,' and 'blanched with darkness' by comparison. Finally, in section 64, Hallam is depicted as a man of great abilities but 'low estate' who has broken through the barrier of social class to embrace a career as a statesman. The poet is his childhood friend, now a humble country labourer. In all of these lyrics Hallam's spirit moves in an atmosphere of confidence, but the poet resides in doubt. 'How should he love a thing so low?' the poor girl of section 60 asks herself (line 16), and the country labourer muses, 'Does my old friend remember me?' (line 28).

All of these comparisons sound as though they should provoke complicated anxieties that will take a long time to resolve themselves, but this is not the case. In only twelve lines section 65 transforms all the poet's fears into a serene assurance that mutual friendship between the dead and the living may indeed continue. This sudden change comes about because, either directly or by implication, the poet is able to solve the problems that were so intractable in the previous attempt at consolation. In sections 55 and 56 the poet had been appalled at the random prodigality of Nature, 'finding that of fifty seeds / She often brings but one to bear' (55.11-12). The answer to that fear is in section 65, in the economy of love that wastes nothing: '"Love's too precious to be lost, / A little grain shall not be spilt"' (lines 3-4). The link among the days that the poet asserts here is not the joining of a dead past with an unimaginably distant future, as it was before. Now the link is one of easy reciprocity, joining present with present:

> Since we deserved the name of friends,
>   And thine effect so lives in me,
>   A part of mine may live in thee
> And move thee on to noble ends.
>
> (Lines 9-12)

Finally, there is an implication throughout this group of poems that leads to assurance. The questions in the poems demand answers, and the answers depend upon the poet's judgment of Arthur Hallam's character. Is Hallam the kind of man who would jilt his lover or cut his friend just because he has advanced in the social world? No, he is too much of a gentleman. Like other implications in *In Memoriam* this one appears both eccentric and a bit banal when we spell it out—very Victorian, we could say. Yet it is the true response to the equally eccentric fear of section 40, that the poet would find himself 'evermore a life behind' his dead friend. To overcome that fear the poet tried to work out the 'science of immortality' which failed him when he tested it. Now he has replaced that unworkable attempt at consolation with one that depends upon personal trust rather than scientific or philosophical demonstration.

In the previous movement of *In Memoriam* the poet had expressed a need to overtake a friend who kept advancing beyond his reach. After the act of acceptance in section 65 the poet abandons his strenuous attempts at pursuit. Instead, he waits for Hallam's spirit to reveal itself to him, and this opens the way for the true consolation of the visionary apotheoses. The dream of sections 68-71, the trance of section 95, and the second dream in section 103 all occur at Hallam's initiative, after the poet has relaxed his own efforts to conjure up his friend's spirit. The poet's assurance that these experiences are valid depends upon personal trust in Arthur Hallam's benevolence and power rather than upon any scientific demonstration.

The trope of the bride leaving home plays no direct part in these lyrics of apotheosis, but the 'divinely gifted man' of section 64 is revived and amplified for the group of poems that present Hallam as the exemplary type of public virtue (sections 109-14). As in the group that we have just examined, roles change again, and so does the nature of the link among the days. In those earlier poems Hallam's public status pointed back to the poet himself and his private anxiety: 'Does my old friend remember me?' The implied answer to the poet's question must be yes, and the reason for this affirmation must be Hallam's possession of exactly the kinds of virtue that are spelled out in sections 109-11. To all who knew him Hallam was the fount of 'heart-affluence,' of intelligent judgment, of trustworthiness, together with power to impress those qualities upon his companions: 'And thus he bore without abuse / The grand old name of gentleman' (111.21-2). Like the gentleman in John Henry Newman's celebrated definition, 'he is one who never inflicts pain.'

However, Hallam as he appears in these later poems is more than what he was in life. The poet is also concerned with the public role that would certainly have been Hallam's if he had lived:

> A life in civic action warm,
>   A soul on highest mission sent,
>   A potent voice of Parliament,
> A pillar steadfast in the storm,
>
> Should licensed boldness gather force,
>   Becoming, when the time has birth,
>   A lever to uplift the earth
> And roll it in another course.
>
> (113.9-16)

In section 64 Hallam was described as 'The pillar of a people's hope, / The centre of a world's desire' (lines 15-16). Here he is again a pillar, but a pillar of refuge in revolutionary times and an exemplar of moral perfection that the whole world can aspire to. Thus the link among the days changes once again, as *In Memoriam* directs its readers to an immediate future where their responsibility is to live out Hallam's unfulfilled career.

The poet's role also changes in this group from the friend left behind to a companion who 'felt thy triumph was as mine' (110.14), and who is able to impute his own 'imitative will' (line 20) to the whole world:

> I would the great world grew like thee,
>   Who grewest not alone in power
>   And knowledge, but by year and hour
> In reverence and in charity.
>
> (114.25-8)

This last quotation also signifies a consolidation of the earlier turning away from science towards personal trust as the authority for a consoling order. In section 114 Knowledge is praised for her beauty and power but relegated to a position inferior to Wisdom and the affective virtues: 'Let her know her place; / She is the second, not the first' (lines 15-16). The higher qualities, of course, are the ones characteristic of Arthur Hallam. This does not constitute a repudiation of science. It is quite compatible with the poet's maintaining a keen interest in scientific phenomena. Indeed, the number and range of scientific references increase in the last sections of *In Memoriam,* but the poet no longer accepts scientific knowledge as an authority that can direct his will. Trust and affection have that office.

Finally we come to the group of poems that provide the justification of the works of time—not a theodicy but a 'chronodicy.' I have already traced this pattern, culminating in the poet's recognition that time is an artist like himself. The bride/friend-leaving-home-trope has no place here, but just as it lies behind the visions of apotheosis, so the attitudes of trust and affection that have been established through this trope lie behind *In Memoriam*'s chronodicy. There is one final hint of connection, in section 128.10. Like the bride and the dead friend of the previous groups, time has a mediating 'office' that goes beyond appearances.

So far, so good.

What I have written is, I believe, a valid account of how *In Memoriam* functions as an elegy. This account does not interpret the whole poem, of course. In particular, it ignores the encyclopedic discussion that is such a striking feature of *In Memoriam,* and it gives little indication of the part played in the sequence by the constant expression of changing feelings. However, I do not intend my generic description to be exclusive. Cultural concerns and personal feeling in *In Memoriam* can be related to the poem's elegiac action because all are dealt with as aspects of time with which the poet must come to terms, but they point in the direction of other genres as well. For me, they point mostly towards epic, and it is instructive to compare *In Memoriam* with Wordsworth's *Prelude,* the other great English poem of 1850. The two works are reciprocals of each other, for *The Prelude* is a heroic poem whose main action is an account of loss and recovery, 'Imagination and Taste, How Impaired and Restored,' thus pointing the whole work in the direction of elegy. Yet the presence of an elegiac action does not prevent our apprehending *The Prelude* as a poem in which Wordsworth has solved the problem of how to write a post-Miltonic epic by taking his own life as his subject and internalizing the heroic action. Similarly, I can see **In Memoriam** as a poem that leans heavily in the direction of the same kind of Romantic epic as *The Prelude*—in its encyclopedic treatment of early Victorian culture and in its account of the poet's heroic endurance—yet to acknowledge this does not destroy my apprehension of the poem as an elegy.

A more serious objection to my paradigmatic reading of **In Memoriam** is that the sequence does not end at the point where I have located the completion of its elegiac action; it continues through four more sections and 184 more lines. Indeed, section 128 itself is in some measure an afterthought, being absent from the privately printed trial edition and incomplete in two extant manuscripts (see Ricks's textual notes, *Poems of Tennyson*, p 978).

This brings us to a real crux in our reading of **In Memoriam**: can any systematic explanation adequately and consistently account for the ending of the sequence? Certainly some readers of **In Memoriam** find the ending eminently satisfying. Others find that it makes them uneasy, though few can say precisely how or why. My own responses lie with the uneasy readers, and one purpose of this essay is to suggest some formal and structural reasons for our sense of dissatisfaction with the ending of the poem.

In a book that I have already mentioned, Barbara Herrnstein Smith's *Poetic Closure,* the author explains in general terms how poems achieve their endings:

> Closure occurs when the concluding portion of a poem creates in the reader a sense of appropriate cessation. It announces and justifies the absence of further development; it reinforces the feeling of finality, completion, and composure which we value in all works of art; and it gives ultimate unity and coherence to the reader's experience of the poem by providing a point from which all the preceding elements may be viewed comprehensively and their relations grasped as part of a significant design.[12]

This summary describes an ideal poem. Actual poems have closures that are relatively strong or weak, and a further remark of Professor Smith's is useful in understanding how readers can react so differently to the ending of **In Memoriam**:

> The reader's experience of closure both depends upon and affects his interpretation of the poem—not his critical exegesis, but his general impression of, in both senses, its *design*: its intention (tones and motives) and its pattern (most significant generating principles). Again, when closural effects are fairly strong, readers with more or less different interpretations of a poem are likely to agree about the adequacy of its conclusion. But when the effects are weak, the reader's interpretation may become crucial in his experience of closure.[13]

In Memoriam's closural effects are weak ones, I believe. After the lyrics that present Arthur Hallam as a type of civic virtue, the sequence begins its final movement with the last change of seasons, 'Now fades the last long streak of snow' (section 115). I have already abstracted from this movement the justification of time, which culminates in section 128. That is one possible closure for **In Memoriam,** but there are others in this same movement. Section 121, the Hesper-Phosphor poem, also sounds as though it could be an ending; so does the next section; so does section 127. Yet all these possible conclusions move the reader in different directions. Section 128 is the conclusion of an extended argument. Section 121 is a metonymic poem in which the morning and evening star stands as a 'double name' for the poet's experience persisting through all change. Section 122 is a reprise of the vision in section 95, and it ends with an epiphany of Hallam's presence in the poet, 'enter[ing] in at breast and brow' (line 11), an epiphany that is expressed in striking metaphors of compression and expansion:

> And all the breeze of Fancy blows,
>   And every dew-drop paints a bow,
>   The wizard lightnings deeply glow,
> And every thought breaks out a rose.
>
> (Lines 17-20)

Section 127 is an apocalyptic justification of Hallam's role as a type of civic virtue, and a final apotheosis as well: 'While thou, dear spirit, happy star, / O'erlook'st the tumult from afar, / And smilest, knowing all is well' (lines 18-20). Finally, each of the last three numbered sections is a peroration, yet there seems to be no natural climactic order among them, as is shown by Tennyson's transposing sections 129 and 130 in the trial edition.

Readers who can find complete satisfaction in the ending of the **In Memoriam** sequence are fortunate, their experience is valid, and in a different frame of mind I could share it, but this experience seems to depend upon a heavily thematic reading of the poem.[14] Those readers who emphasize the doctrinal elements in **In Memoriam**— whether those doctrines are theological or scientific—are most likely to find that the ending provides 'a sense of appropriate cessation.' But readers who approach **In Memoriam** in formal terms are apt to find that the rhetorical ambiguity of the final lyrics renders the conclusion less than adequate. In the introduction to this paper I have already suggested my own explanation for the inadequacies of the ending. In developing **In Memoriam** as an elegy Tennyson has transformed Hallam into a type, as the genre demands. Yet surely this is not what Tennyson really wants. He wants Hallam as his personal friend, and he wants his poem to celebrate the retention of friendship. To some extent the final lyrics of **In Memoriam** are assertions of friendship retained, but can we (or the poet) really believe those assertions?

> Dear friend, far off, my lost desire,
>   So far, so near in woe and weal;
>   O loved the most, when most I feel
> There is a lower and a higher;
>
> Known and unknown; human, divine;
>   Sweet human hand and lips and eye;
>   Dear heavenly friend that canst not die,
> Mine, mine, for ever, ever mine.
>
> (129.1-8)

Can Arthur Hallam really be type and friend at the same time? Is the last line that I have quoted an expression of certitude or of desperation? Answers to these questions will differ, and they will depend upon each reader's interpretation, the general impression of design that Barbara Smith sees as crucial to our experience of closure. My own answer is that the poet cannot have it both ways, and that all his assertions to the contrary lead him to an impasse of anxiety because the formal requirements of elegy compel him to say both more and less than he means. ('It's too hopeful, this poem, more than I am myself,' Tennyson confessed to James Knowles some twenty years after *In Memoriam* was published.[15]) The Epilogue, with its generic change from elegy to epithalamium, provides the poet with a chance of escaping from his impasse and achieving closure.[16]

IV

The Epilogue employs the trope of the bride leaving home in the same form as its first appearance in section 40. Again the figure of the bride mediates between the dead and the living, standing on the graves that form the floor of the church while 'the most living words of life' of the marriage service are recited. This bride is also destined to be a link among the days, joining the present stage of human development to a future of perfection. The Epilogue ends with the poet imagining the conception of his sister's child, 'a closer link / Betwixt us and the crowning race / Of those that, eye to eye, shall look / On knowledge' (lines 127-30).

However, the strength of the Epilogue lies less in its continuation of the main themes of *In Memoriam* than in the ways it can take the subsidiary anxieties of the sequence and close them off, one by one. Its tactics is diversion.[17] To begin with, the Epilogue is a palinode. The monument of love is complete, 'like a statue solid-set, / And moulded in colossal calm' (lines 15-16), and the poet proclaims the changes in his own body and spirit that make him a different person from the one who 'embalm[ed] / in dying songs a dead regret' (lines 13-14). Thus the Epilogue justifies bringing *In Memoriam* to publication. The marriage of Edmund Lushington and Cecilia Tennyson is a surrogate for the cancelled marriage of Arthur Hallam and Emily Tennyson that was lamented in section 84. The October wedding responds to the autumn funeral procession with which *In Memoriam* began. By giving away the bride, the poet (we might as well call him Tennyson by this point) takes on the role of his own father, thereby overcoming the conflicting feelings about the death of his father, as well as Hallam's death, that animate sections 100-3 and 105. The signing of the parish register, 'your names, which shall be read, / Mute symbols of a joyful morn, / By village eyes as yet unborn' (lines 57-9), is Tennyson's answer to his own previous doubts about the lasting efficacy of the written word (see especially section 77). Finally, just as Tennyson enacts his father's role at the wedding, so in the final night-piece that concludes the epithalamium he takes on the role of Arthur Hallam himself. The panorama of landscape and cosmos is seen from the same perspective as Hallam's in his final apotheosis as the 'dear spirit, happy star' of section 127.

The Epilogue is a wonderful display of poetic dexterity, but it does not resolve the central anxiety of *In Memoriam*. None of its stratagems, not Tennyson's 'conjecture' of Hallam as an invisible guest at the marriage feast, not the marvellous *tour de force* of the last sentence, eleven stanzas long in the *Eversley Edition*, not even that sentence's approving use of 'link' (line 127) and 'type' (line 138), can finally divert us from the emptiness of heart with which *In Memoriam* ends. For Arthur Hallam has not been recovered and retained. If Hallam's personal presence is to be discovered anywhere in *In Memoriam,* it is back in section 89, the poem in which Tennyson recalls his joy at Hallam's visits to Somersby. This lyric is a concentrated summary of the whole pastoral tradition, with its Theocritan format of feasting and song, its Virgilian concern with public affairs, and, in the final couplet, the biblical promised land flowing with milk and honey. Section 89 is unique among the *In Memoriam* poems in being an idyll, not an elegy, perfectly resolved and stable, with no hint of anxiety in its joy. It is unique also in being the only place in *In Memoriam* where we actually hear Arthur Hallam speak. What Hallam says is a warning against accepting types in place of individual persons: 'For "ground in yonder social mill / We rub each other's angles down, / "And merge" he said "in form and gloss / The picturesque of man and man"' (89.39-42). But this version of pastoral is not definitive for the whole sequence, and Hallam's warning slips by unheeded.

Several recent commentators have dealt with the ending of *In Memoriam* by describing the whole work as a poem in process, reaching out beyond its final lines to a fulfilment that transcends biography and history.[18] I do not see *In Memoriam* as transcendent in that way. The poem really does end at its last line, but I would draw a distinction between closing a poem and concluding it. The change of genre from elegy to epithalamium enabled Tennyson to close the sequence that he had written, but I doubt if he ever finished it. Outcroppings of its continuation appear in **'De Profundis,' 'In the Valley of Cauteretz,' 'In the Garden at Swainston,'** and **'Vastness'**; groundswells move through *Maud* and *Idylls of the King.*

In Memoriam has been compared in the pages of this journal to *Piers Plowman* and to *Ulysses*.[19] I would like to reach my own closure with another comparison, to D.H.

Lawrence's *Women in Love*. The action of *Women in Love* is a mirror-image of *In Memoriam*: it begins with a marriage and ends with a death—in Austria—and an English funeral. Like *In Memoriam*, *Women in Love* is eschatological without being transcendent, and it closes without really concluding. Furthermore, there is evidence that *In Memoriam* was somewhere in Lawrence's mind as he worked on *Women in Love*.[20]

When I try to imagine how Tennyson lived with *In Memoriam* after he had closed it, I am drawn to the final dialogue between Rupert and Ursula in Lawrence's novel. This would not be the conversation of Alfred Tennyson and Emily Sellwood, of course; but it might be the silent-speaking words of 'the poet' (for one last time) talking with his spirit as with a wife (cf section 97):

'Aren't I enough for you?' she asked.

'No,' he said. 'You are enough for me, as far as a woman is concerned. You are all women to me. But I wanted a man friend, as eternal as you and I are eternal. . . .

'Having you, I can live all my life without anybody else, any other sheer intimacy. But to make it complete, really happy, I wanted eternal union with a man too: another kind of love,' he said.

'I don't believe it,' she said. 'It's an obstinacy, a theory, a perversity.'

'Well—' he said.

'You can't have two kinds of love. Why should you!'

'It seems as if I can't,' he said. 'Yet I wanted it.'

'You can't have it, because it's false, impossible,' she said.

'I don't believe that,' he answered.[21]

Better yet, let us give Tennyson himself the last word, the closing lines of **'Vastness,'** which he published in 1885, more than fifty years after Arthur Hallam had died:

> Peace, let it be! for I loved him, and love him for
> ever: the dead are not dead but
> alive.

Notes

1. This assertion needs to be argued in detail, and other people have done this better than I could do, though in piecemeal fashion. See Alan Sinfield, *The Language of In Memoriam* (Oxford: Blackwell 1971), and the pertinent chapters of F. E. L. Priestley, *Language and Structure in Tennyson's Poetry* (London: André Deutsch 1973), W. David Shaw, *Tennyson's Style* (Ithaca: Cornell University Press 1976), and Robert Pattison, *Tennyson and Tradition* (Cambridge, Mass.: Harvard University Press 1979). For the most recent survey of critical writing on *In Memoriam* the reader is directed to Joseph Sendry, '*In Memoriam*: Twentieth-Century Criticism,' *Victorian Poetry*, 18 (1980), 105-18.

2. Barbara Herrnstein Smith, *Poetic Closure: A Study of How Poems End* (Chicago: University of Chicago Press 1968), pp 210-34.

3. A. Dwight Culler, *The Poetry of Tennyson* (New Haven: Yale University Press 1976), p 150. Culler denies that *In Memoriam* is generically an elegy because he sees the poem's 'gradualist' action as precluding catastrophe.

4. E.g. Robert Langbaum, 'The Dynamic Unity of *In Memoriam*' in *The Modern Spirit* (New York: Oxford University Press 1970), pp 51-75; Kerry McSweeney, 'The Pattern of Natural Consolation in *In Memoriam*,' *Victorian Poetry*, 11 (1973), 87-99; Ian H. C. Kennedy, '*In Memoriam* and the Tradition of Pastoral Elegy,' *Victorian Poetry*, 15 (1977), 351-66. All three of these studies suggest that Tennyson uses pastoral conventions to subvert the elegiac pattern of loss and recovery, thereby transforming *In Memoriam* from a ritual poem to a poem of experience.

5. There is a room for a full study of Tennyson's 'anxiety of influence,' especially towards Keats (Harold Bloom's chapter in *Poetry and Repression* is only a beginning). However, what I have in mind here is anxiety in its ordinary sense, an intense feeling of distress and expectancy that often has no definite object. The plight of the Lady of Shalott is the most concise example of anxiety in Tennyson's poetry: 'She has heard a whisper say, / A curse is on her if she stay / To look down to Camelot. / She knows not what the curse may be.'

6. Recent discussions of nineteenth-century elegy emphasize its affinities with 'public' genres like ode and prophecy. Later in this paper I offer some remarks on *In Memoriam* and epic, but elegy is flexible enough to move to the minor key as well. See Andrew Fichter, 'Ode and Elegy: Idea and Form in Tennyson's Early Poetry,' *ELH*, 40 (1973), 398-427; Michael Cooke, 'Elegy, Prophecy and Satire in the Romantic Order,' in *Acts of Inclusion* (New Haven: Yale University Press 1979), pp 1-54.

7. The earliest MS versions of section 85 have recently been redated (from 1833) by Joseph Sendry. See his '*In Memoriam*: The Minor Manuscripts,' *Harvard Library Bulletin*, 27 (1979), 45 and n.

8. A full account of why this theodicy is rejected would require another essay, but here are the main reasons. First, the raising of the dead, even through a divine miracle, is a frightening and repugnant notion to Tennyson (cf section 90—despite its brave disclaimer—'The Lotos Eaters,' and especially 'Enoch Arden'). I think that this is so because Tennyson can only imagine such a resurrection as reversing the forward direction of time, and in Tennyson's poetry reversals of direction are always disastrous. Second, in

section 36 the poet boasts that the Bible is written in plain language, but throughout *In Memoriam* scriptural language shares this characteristic with the language of poetry, that its real power lies in its reticence.

9. See Christopher Ricks's introductory note to 'Tithonus' in *Poems of Tennyson* (London: Longmans 1969), p 1113, and Culler, *Poetry of Tennyson*, pp 174-5.

10. Sections 41, 42, 44, and 45 are among the poems that appear in the fragmentary Huntington MS, which Joseph Sendry dates as 1837-9: '*In Memoriam*: The Minor Manuscripts,' pp 49-51. This almost certainly means that section 40, which first appears in the later Trinity MS, was composed afterwards as a way of focussing an inchoate argument.

11. Culler, *Poetry of Tennyson*, p 175.

12. Smith, *Poetic Closure*, p 36.

13. Ibid, p 212.

14. For example, a study of the Christology of *In Memoriam* would require that the concept of 'type' be treated much more favourably than I treat it here, and surely that would be the proper way to approach *In Memoriam* from that perspective. How right Tennyson was to talk about 'weaving' the sections together.

15. James Knowles, 'Aspects of Tennyson II: A Personal Reminiscence,' *Nineteenth Century*, 33 (January 1893), p 182.

16. Between the printing of the trial edition in March 1850 and the publication of the first regular edition on 1 June Tennyson added four new sections to the final movement: 119, 120, 121, 128. Section 124 was expanded by three stanzas, and sections 129 and 130 were transposed. See Ricks's textual notes to these sections, or the more detailed remarks by Susan Shatto and Marion Shaw in the commentary to their edition of *In Memoriam* (Oxford: Clarendon 1982), pp 285ff. No other part of *In Memoriam* underwent so many last-minute adjustments; nowhere else do Tennyson's revisions have such little effect.

17. Pattison, approaching in *In Memoriam* with the dominant assumption that idyll is Tennyson's major form, finds the Epilogue a formally satisfying completion of the elegy that precedes it. See *Tennyson and Tradition*, pp 111, 127.

18. E.g.: J. C. C. Mays, '*In Memoriam*: An Aspect of Form' *UTQ*, 35 (1965), 22-46; Henry Kozicki, *Tennyson and Clio: History in the Major Poems* (Baltimore: Johns Hopkins University Press 1979). The phrase 'poem in process' is from Culler, *Poetry of Tennyson*, p 217.

19. Mays, '*In Memoriam*: An Aspect of Form,' p 33, and Arthur J. Carr, 'Tennyson as a Modern Poet,' *UTQ*, 19 (1950), p 361.

20. In 'The Crown,' a group of essays that stands behind the final version of *Women in Love* as 'Study of Thomas Hardy' stands behind *The Rainbow*, Lawrence twice uses Tennyson's phrase 'the infant crying in the night' to describe and condemn a state of emotional immaturity that renders its victims incapable of fruitful struggle for the crown of love. The infant crying in the night finds its way into the text of *Women in Love* as part of Gudrun's railing against Gerald Crich in chapter 30. 'The Crown' also contains a reference to 'the delicate blue speedwells of childhood,' which sounds like Lawrence remembering 'The little speedwell's darling blue' of *In Memoriam* 83.10. See 'The Crown' in *Phoenix II*, ed Warren Roberts and Harry T. Moore (London: Heinemann 1968), pp 366, 414, 396.

21. D. H. Lawrence, *Women in Love* (Harmondsworth: Penguin 1960), p 541.

Rob Johnson (essay date 1987)

SOURCE: Johnson, Rob. "Strategies of Containment: Tennyson's *In Memoriam*." In *Post-Structuralist Readings of English Poetry*, edited by Richard Machin and Christopher Norris, pp. 308-31. Cambridge, NY: Cambridge University Press, 1987.

[*In the following essay, Johnson examine Tennyson's deliberately ambiguous rhetoric whereby faith and doubt are explored through various alternative presentations in* In Memoriam.]

In defending his commentary on ***In Memoriam*** against readers of Tennyson who doubted the necessity or value of such an enterprise, A. C. Bradley declared: "We read for the most part half-asleep, but a poet writes wide-awake."[1] This remark sounds across eight decades with a curiously contemporary ring, closely paralleling Paul de Man's defence of deconstructionist reading against the charge that it is a gratuitous addition to the text: "by reading the text as we did we were only trying to come closer to being as rigorous a reader as the author had to be to write the sentence in the first place".[2]

The complex play of utterance that Bradley recognized in ***In Memoriam*** is often the result of a studiedly ambiguous rhetoric that may, for instance, deliberately exploit the element of difference in language, evoking significations of word or image incongruous with those ostensibly demanded by the argument. Or the syntax may distribute emphasis in ways that, while not destroying the ostensible meaning, make it appear more problematical than any prose paraphrase would suggest. Or the dividing line between elements of similarity and difference in a simile may be so blurred as to leave its interpretation more or less speculative. Or the speaker of the poem, constituted by rhetoric, may also be fragmented by it; so that "I" no longer signifies a unified subject but either of two "I"s, one of which regards the other's reactions with wonder, incredulity or dismay. All such play of utterance serves to dramatize a consciousness initially disoriented and dispersed by grief and at the end—taking its final state to be represented in the Prologue—still resorting to stratagem to assert one element of itself (faith) against another (doubt) that cannot be totally expelled but can only be confronted and contained.

The poem has not, indeed, always been read in this way. An eminently intelligent Victorian, the philosopher Henry Sidgwick, commented, for instance, that, in the Prologue, "Faith . . . is too completely triumphant . . . Faith must give the last word: but the last word is not the whole utterance of the truth: the whole truth is that assurance and doubt must alternate in the moral world in which we at present live, somewhat as night and day alternate in the physical world."[3] It is arguable, however, that Sidgwick's "whole truth" comes close to a fair summing-up of the situation actually presented in the Prologue—if, that is, the Prologue is read with due attention to its rhetorical emphases and setting-out. So read, the Prologue is an instance of how "difference"—used here in a very general sense to cover any discrepant and potentially disruptive element in personal consciousness, in society at large and in current perceptions of the cosmos—is contained but cannot be eradicated. What follows is an examination of **In Memoriam**'s rhetorical dramatization of difference—and of the stratagems by which the speaker of the poem seeks to contain it.

The opening stanza of the Prologue voices an ostensibly confident faith and strongly echoes the New Testament:

> Strong Son of God, immortal Love,
>   Whom we, that have not seen thy face,
>   By faith, and faith alone, embrace,
> Believing where we cannot prove.

There are several possible references here. The one mentioned by Tennyson himself[4] is 1 John 4:12: "No man hath seen God at any time. If we love one another God dwelleth in us." Another is the remark of the risen Christ to doubting Thomas: "Blessed are they who have not seen and have believed" (John 20:29). Yet another is 1 Peter 1:7,8: "Jesus Christ: whom having not seen ye love; in whom, though now ye see him not, yet believing, ye rejoice." All these are obviously relevant to the conjuncture in the Prologue of seeing and not seeing, believing (and, by implication, doubting) and loving. A more pointed comparison, however, is with another passage that expressly states what the others leave implicit—John 1:18: "No man hath seen God at any time; the only begotten Son . . . he hath declared him."

God has not been seen but the Son has. To some extent, therefore, the mystery of the Father has been dispelled by the Son in whose love God is manifest; but the odd thing about the being addressed in the Prologue as "Strong Son of God, immortal Love" is that, so far from dispelling the mystery of the Father, he seems fully to partake of it:

> Thine are these orbs of light and shade;
>   Thou madest Life in man and brute;
>   Thou madest Death; and lo, thy foot
> Is on the skull which thou hast made.
>
> Thou wilt not leave us in the dust:
>   Thou madest man, he knows not why,
>   He thinks he was not made to die;
> And thou hast made him: thou art just.
> Thou seemest human and divine,
>   The highest, holiest manhood, thou:
>   Our wills are ours, we know not how;
> Our wills are ours, to make them thine.

Though hailed as "immortal Love", the Son is addressed first as the author of an ambiguous creation, responsible both for life and death, paralleled in the (literal and symbolic) "orbs of light and shade". The Son has his foot on the skull, traditionally a symbol of his triumph over death. But quite apart from the point that a skull, whatever its literary or graphic context, is inevitably a *memento mori,* the symbolism is slanted into ambiguity. The rather inexplicit "and lo", leading on from "Thou madest death", might convey that the placing of the Son's foot is a confirmation of what has just been said. Is this a triumph over death or over the dead? Is the Son only the triumphant New Testament redeemer? Does he not also suggest the enigmatic deity of Job? "The Lord gave and the Lord hath taken away". Certainly, in contrast with the New Testament passages, the Son's "declaration" of the Father seems to add remarkably little to what the Father has already, somewhat cryptically and ominously, declared on his own behalf. The text of creation, so far from being elucidated, seems to remain as the Father had left it.

We do gather in stanza four that the Son of God is to be identified with the incarnate Christ though the identification is oddly tentative. "Seemest" in "Thou seemest human and divine" (as if said by somebody encountering Christ—or the idea of Christ—for the first time) is, however, characteristic of **In Memoriam.** In this stanza we are confronted with two mysteries of faith: the combination of humanity and divinity in the Son and of free will and creaturely dependence ("Thou madest man") in ourselves. "Our wills are ours" but how can they be when we are "thine" through and through? The scope of free will is in any case limited. "To make them thine", echoing the three times repeated "thou madest", points a contrast as well as a parallel between the Son as maker of all things, including man, and man as (within limits) "maker" of himself. It is soon apparent, indeed, that the strength attributed to the Son of God in the opening line implies a proportionate weakness in the speaker. The repetition of "thine" and "thou", built up over twelve lines and locked, with the aid of a purely emphatic "thou", into the rhyme-scheme in the last four, brings home the Son's dominance of his creation and the consequent creaturely dependence of the speaker in common with all human beings. (And yet we have no assurance of the Son's strength other than "faith alone"—

and what is the faith of such a weak creature worth?) This recognition of dependence is later explicitly extended to Hallam: "Forgive my grief for one removed, / Thy creature."

This is not the idealized Hallam in the later stanzas of the poem; though the Prologue, printed with the date 1849, is presumably delivered with retrospective awareness and with the force of the speaker's spiritual gains behind it. This reference is the first mention of the occasion for the poem and for much of the Prologue the speaker does not even use the first person singular. He shifts from "we", associating himself, presumably, with human beings in general, to "he", as if arrogating the stance of a detached, superior—even rather derisive—observer:

> Thou madest man, he knows not why,
>   He thinks he was not made to die;
> And thou hast made him; thou art just.

There is a perfectly good argument here, if we waive the point that its premises are a matter of "faith alone". "God has made man. Man believes he has an immortal soul. God is just. God, being just, would not make a being that believed itself to have an immortal soul when in fact it did not. Therefore man has an immortal soul." There is a disparity, however, between the structure of the argument and its rhetorical setting-out that obscures its force and makes the conviction of immortality seem distinctly precarious. As in the symbol of Christ with his foot on the skull, connections are omitted or blurred. The metrical emphasis on "thinks", coming close on "he knows not why", makes the conviction seem, *not* what the argument requires it to be—some sort of innate idea of immortality proper to man as man—but merely what a manifestly fallible and ignorant creature "thinks". In the context, "thinks", like "feels" elsewhere in *In Memoriam,* carries a subversive implicit contrast with other expressions such as "knows" or "has good reason to believe" and a strong suggestion of its colloquial connotation: "but little does he know". Such suggestions could be carried further into an ironic reading of "thou art just" or a rueful unspoken parenthesis: "thou hadst better be!"

The intention in these remarks, as in previous remarks about Christ and the skull, is not simply to subvert the conventional reading. The passage "means" what the paraphrase of its argument represents it as meaning. But the setting out does suggest another and less reassuring perspective and at least an incipient alternative reading that cannot, once entertained, be dismissed. Hence the overtone of grimness and anxiety in what is, logically speaking, a positive argument. The effect resembles a version of *Hamlet* in which the Prince commands centre stage but Claudius is also always present, reminding the audience of another possible construction of events. It would obviously be perverse to deny the speaker's commitment to a belief in man's immortal soul; but it would equally obviously be naive to read that commitment as serenely untroubled.

To dismiss these two unlikely hypothetical readings is not, however, necessarily to point to any assured middle ground between them. Given that there is an interplay of faith and doubt in the Prologue, how are we to describe it? Faith desperately battling against a doubt that, in spite of all its efforts, keeps breaking through? Faith nobly confronting doubt and emerging from the struggle with head bloody but unbowed? Both these hypothetical readings could be supported by reference to the play of signifiers that constitutes "the text". Each might be described, in deconstructionist rhetoric, as a "misreading" in the sense that each is subject to correction by the other or by some further alternative reading that would still not be definitive. The Prologue presents faith and doubt as coexisting. But how do we describe that coexistence? Interplay? (As above.) Conflict? Challenge and response? Tremulous balance? Mutual deconstruction? The position taken here is not that the play of signifiers is simply "free". Within the limits set by "the text", different readings—different constructions of how faith and doubt interrelate—are, however, possible and any reading for which we settle will be haunted by our awareness of others.

Through his consciousness of other possible readings the reader constructs the haunted consciousness of the speaker in the Prologue. Arrived at a position of faith that reconciles him to his physical separation from the deceased, the speaker is still haunted by the earlier readings of himself and the world that form the substance of the narrative that follows. In the earliest phase of the poem[5] he was too disoriented by grief to be capable of reading himself at all. Bradley's citation of St Augustine in the *Confessions,* describing his state of mind after the death of a friend, is apt: "I became a great puzzle to myself, and asked my soul why she was so sad and why she so exceedingly disquieted me, but she knew not what to answer to me."[6] The analogy with *In Memoriam* is close, extending to the rhetoric, the subject being divided between the "I" that is puzzled and the "I" that puzzles, the self that interrogates and the soul that is unable to answer:

> O heart, how fares it with thee now,
>   That thou shouldst fail from thy desire,
>   Who scarcely darest to inquire,
> "What is it makes me beat so low?"

(IV)

The Speaker projects his grief as a feminized Sorrow:

> O Sorrow, cruel fellowship,
>   O Priestess in the vaults of Death,
>   O sweet and bitter in a breath,
> What whispers from thy lying lip?

(III)

What Sorrow whispers is that "the stars . . . blindly run", anticipating a later reading of the experience of bereavement: that the world-process does not favour the individual life, in which alone value resides, and is therefore "meaningless". As a priestess, Sorrow is perverting her office, promoting not faith but faithlessness; so she presents a double aspect—holy but deceptive. She is "cruel" but to renounce her would be to renounce "fellowship" with the deceased. In his confusion, the speaker is unable to confront the reading of life that Sorrow seems to be proposing and dismisses her as simply lying. It is clear, however, that this is merely an instance of one constituent of the "I" refusing to acknowledge another. Apostrophe (the address to a personified component of consciousness or to an external object such as a house, a yew-tree, the ship which is bringing back Hallam's body) is a device by which the reader overhears the dialogue of the speaker's mind with itself. *In Memoriam* is thus, in a sense, "confessional" poetry—but only at an obvious rhetorical remove.

Tennyson himself made the salutary point that in **In Memoriam**, "'I' is not always the author speaking of himself."[7] In the first phase of **In Memoriam** the "I" is not even a coherent fictive presence. This difference of the "I" from itself is strikingly dramatized in the fantasy of Lyric XIV, in which the ship bearing Hallam's corpse arrives and a living Hallam steps down the plank:

> And if along with these should come
>   The man I held as half-divine;
>   Should strike a sudden hand in mine,
> And ask a thousand things of home;
>
> And I should tell him all my pain,
>   And how my life had drooped of late,
>   And he should sorrow o'er my state
> And marvel what possessed my brain;
>
> And I perceived no touch of change,
>   No hint of death in all his frame,
>   But found him all in all the same,
> I should not feel it to be strange.

The effect lies in the build-up to the last line in which the "I" of the preceding narrative is scrutinized by an implicit other "I" who finds it strange that the first "I" finds nothing strange. The "I" is divided in Antony Easthope's terms,[8] between the subject of the enunciation (the previously concealed "I" in the final line) and the subject of the enounced (the "I" of the preceding narrative.) The speaker of these early lyrics is a stranger to himself, baffled by his own behaviour and the feelings that prompt it:

> What words are these have fallen from me?
>   Can calm despair and wild unrest
>   Be tenants of a single breast,
> Or sorrow such a changeling be?
>
>   (XVI)

Here the speaker confronts two pervasive, ambivalent and troubling aspects of the world: difference and change. His own consciousness is as much a confusing prospect of shifting light and shade as external nature is. He raises the possibility that Sorrow, in her "deep self", is no "changeling" (XVI). But her "deep self" is perhaps unable to communicate: his words are "only words" and move "upon the topmost froth of thought" (LII). He elsewhere refers to Sorrow as sporting with words (XLVIII) and to grief as playing with "symbols" (LXXXV); and he is quite clear that his "brief lays" are not to be read as offering answers to serious philosophical questions:

> If these brief lays, of Sorrow born,
>   Were taken to be such as closed
>   Grave doubts and answers here proposed,
> Then these were such as men might scorn.
>
>   (XLVIII)

Rather, Sorrow "sports with words" and

>   loosens from the lip
>   Short swallow-flights of song, that dip
>   Their wings in tears, and skim away.

This quality of sportiveness—"sportiveness" being arguably a feature of all poetic utterance—is evident in the poem that alludes to it. Is not "closed / Grave doubts", for instance, as much a play on words as "I shall not murder / The mankind of her going with a grave truth" in Dylan Thomas's "A Refusal to Mourn"? It may be supposed, since he says as much, that the various forms of verbal play offer the speaker at least "a doubtful gleam of solace" (XXXVIII)—an escape, even, into a world where, as for Yeats's Happy Shepherd, "words alone are certain good". But elsewhere words present him with a play of difference that accentuates life's uncertainties and apparent contradictions. Any solace the speaker could derive from such verbal play might well be "doubtful"—at most, perhaps, the solace of imposing poetic form on the constant slippage of meaning that words undergo in response to the fissile and volatile nature of consciousness, as in this echo of *Hamlet* I.ii ("Ay, madam, it is common"):

> One writes, that "Other friends remain",
>   That "Loss is common to the race"—
>   And common is the commonplace,
> And vacant chaff well meant for grain.
>
> That loss is common would not make
>   My own less bitter, rather more:
>   Too common! Never morning wore
> To evening, but some heart did break.
>
>   (VI)

"Common" slips, between the consoler and the inconsolable, from "common to the race—therefore you are not alone" through "commonplace—therefore not worth saying and, in the circumstances, merely offensive" to "too common—therefore suggesting a pessimistic view of the nature of things". The consoler thus merely reinforces the bereaved in his philosophical and religious anxieties. Also, the transitions from one implication of "common" to another and the derisory repetition of the word invite us to recall another sense: "common—and therefore not worth much". The speaker feels that Hallam and his grief at Hallam's death are being devalued.

Another instance is worth quoting in full:

Calm is the morn without a sound,
   Calm as to suit a calmer grief,
   And only thro' the faded leaf
The chestnut pattering to the ground:

Calm and deep peace on this high wold,
   And on these dews that drench the furze,
   And all the silvery gossamers
That twinkle into green and gold:

Calm and still light on yon great plain
   That sweeps with all its autumn bowers,
   And crowded farms and lessening towers,
To mingle with the bounding main:

Calm and deep peace in this wide air,
   These leaves that redden to the fall;
   And in my heart, if calm at all,
If any calm, a calm despair:

Calm on the seas, and silver sleep,
   And waves that sway themselves in rest,
   And dead calm in that noble breast
Which heaves but with the heaving deep.

                           (XI)

This lyric is the third in a series of nine in which the speaker follows in imagination the return of Hallam's body by sea. The maritime connotations of "calm" are thus strong, through not foregrounded until the sardonic last two lines. The lyric draws on pastoral and elegiac tradition but subverts the traditional expectations. Gray's "Elegy Written in a Country Churchyard" proceeds from "All the air a solemn stillness holds" to a correspondingly calm and solemn meditation on life. In Tennyson's poem we encounter a speaker who, far from being capable of general reflections on life, is not even wise to himself (and knows it). The suggestion of a correspondence between calm in nature and calm in the speaker's mind is evoked to be ironically dismissed. In any case, calm is no more a constant factor in human consciousness than is calm at sea, where it may be calm after or before a storm, calm that assists a ship's passage or that becalms it. It may be "calm of mind, all passion spent", philosophical calm or, explicitly here, the calm of somebody drained by despair. There is no precise and necessary link between "calm" and anything it signifies—nor between pastoral—elegiac signals and the sort of message they traditionally convey. The crucial element of difference is hinted at in the second line: not only is "calmer grief" ambiguous, as Bradley points out[9] ("calmer grief than mine" or "a grief grown calmer"?) but "as to suit" (as against "that suits") leaves it quite uncertain whether there is any reference to the speaker's actual state of mind or not. By the fourth stanza, he is in any case explicitly and emphatically uncertain about his own feelings: "if calm at all, / If any calm". The traditional "pathetic fallacy" is parodied in a parallel—that is also a contrast—between the "calm and deep peace" of the autumnal landscape and the speaker's (no more than possible) "calm despair". The speaker's calm ("if any calm") signifies difference from the calm of nature, not affinity with it. The notion of a spiritual affinity with nature is further parodied in another studiedly incongruous comparison between the calm (in motion) of the sea and the "dead calm" in the corpse's breast "which heaves but with the heaving deep". A similar effect of parody occurs at the end of the previous lyric where the speaker recoils from the thought that "hands so often clasped in mine, / Should toss with tangle and with shells". "Toss" and "heaves", both parodies of living movement, confront us with the brute physical reality in which alone, perhaps, our difference from the rest of the world will end. The conclusion is described by Bradley as "a transition of wonderful dignity and pathos".[10] It could also be read as overwrought feeling finding relief in something approaching black humour. "There may be a question whether I'm calm or not—but there's certainly no question in Arthur's case!" Is the "dead calm" of the corpse the only calm that is constant, unqualified and invulnerable?

The speaker of *In Memoriam* first confronts us as dismayed by the volatility and strangeness of his reactions: he wonders if his suffering is a dream (XIII) and his consciousness has the incoherence of delirium (XVI). He later sees a prospect of escape from this state of fragmented self-perception in an experience of apparent mystical communion in which, he believes, "what I am behold again / What is, and no man understands" (CXXIV). What is constant in himself relates to a transcendental constant. For the present, however, the speaker can hope only that this volatility and seeming multiplicity of the self may offer the possibility of spiritual progress—

   That men may rise on stepping-stones
     Of their dead selves to higher things.

                           (I)

Foreshadowed here is the ambivalent attitude to change (which erodes values but may also consolidate and enrich them) and difference (which estranges but which is also the condition of fruitful relationship).

As consciousness is fluid, so are the terms in which we attempt to capture it. Faith, for instance, is not presented as a theological virtue, capable of clear definition. "Faith", as signifier, has no consistent and precise reference. It may signify faint trust (LV) defiant assertion (CXXIV) fearful, childlike dependence (ibid.) traditional "simple faith" (XXXII, XXXIII, XCVI) a rarefied, possibly pantheistic belief that "has centre everywhere" (XXXIII) a sheer determination to behave "as if" the object of faith existed—

   That we may raise from out of dust
     A voice as unto him that hears.

                          (CXXXI)

One phase of faith may rapidly pass into another (CXXIV). And faith may differ so much from one person to another—even when the object of faith is at least ostensibly the same—as to become unrecognizable. The faith that lies in "honest doubt"—and is thus defined in terms of what is commonly supposed to be its opposite—is unlikely to be recognized by the simple believer for whom "doubt is Devil-born" and whose faith is defined in terms of love: "I cannot understand; I love" (XCVII). It is the concept of love—identified with God and "Creation's finest law" (LVI)—that comes closest to being a constant in **In Memoriam** and a constant object of faith; though at one point even love is seen as capable of degenerating into unattractive forms that are none the less still forms of love—into "mere fellowship of sluggish moods" or, further, into "his coarsest Satyr-shape" (XXXV). The poem's settled concern is, however, with the threats to human love posed by death, the changes and chances of this mortal life and of the speculative hereafter and—with implicit reference to the speaker and Hallam—the necessary but hazardous element of difference between the parties.

The importance of "difference" in **In Memoriam** and in Tennyson's poetry generally can be brought home by the following, wrenched from its context in a much later poem, **"The Ancient Sage"**:

> For Knowledge is the swallow on the lake
> That sees and stirs the surface-shadow there
> But never yet hath dipt into the abysm,
> The Abysm of all Abysms, beneath, within
> The blue of sky and sea, the green of earth,
> And in the million-millionth of a grain
> Which cleft and cleft again for evermore,
> And ever vanishing, never vanishes.

The infinite divisibility of matter was invoked by Tennyson, according to his son, as an argument against materialism: "Look at the mystery of a grain of sand; you can divide it for ever and ever. You cannot conceive anything material of which you cannot conceive the half."[11] ("Half", as K. W. Gransden has pointed out,[12] is a recurring word in Tennyson.) In **"The Ancient Sage"**, as in **In Memoriam** decades earlier, "the Nameless", whatever transcends all change and division, is to be found not in external nature—

> I found Him not in world or sun
>   Or eagle's wing or insect's eye—
>
> (CXXIV)

but within the self. The defect of nature emphasized in the later poem is not, however, the amorality and random destructiveness of natural processes but nature's incorrigible plurality. A phenomenal world that differentiates itself *ad infinitum* provides no possible access to that which transcends all difference, the "One" towards which the speaker of **In Memoriam** gropes:

> He, They, One, All; within, without;
> The Power in darkness whom we guess.
>
> (ibid.)

At the close of **In Memoriam** "one" is dominant:

> One God, one law, one element,
> And one far-off divine event,
> To which the whole creation moves.
>
> (CXXXI [Epilogue])

Difference is cancelled, at least in prospect, and change contained as progress. Relationship (however conceived) to the "One" demands a "oneness" of the individual soul; but this unity of the self is frustrated by the diversity of the world and of our responses to it.

> O, tell me where the senses mix,
> O tell me where the passions meet,
>
> Whence radiate.
>
> (LXXXVIII)

At such moments we are conscious of Tennyson's affinity with the French Symbolists and, at home, with Walter Pater in his quest for "the focus where the greatest number of vital forces unite in their purest energy".[13] Pater seeks to maintain this focus strictly within a world of flux in which forces are constantly being dispersed—hence, presumably, his paradoxical metaphor of the "hard gemlike flame". Tennyson's epiphanies have more in common with Eliot's "moment in and out of time", though he links his transcendentalism with a Victorian progressivist orientation towards the future: the "one far-off divine event". Progress thus becomes a collective movement in time towards what is eternally present but revealed to us now only in privileged moments that, however convincing at the time, are always vulnerable to retrospective doubt. Such a moment, towards the close of the poem, is the vision of Hallam "mix'd with God and Nature" (CXXX), hence eternal and omnipresent though still inexplicably an individual, the object of personal love. This vision, if only it could be maintained, would be a mystical union not only of two friends but of "Oneness" and difference.

Such a union would end the division by which the self is constituted in the first place. Self is initially defined by difference:

> The baby new to earth and sky,
>   What time his tender palm is prest
>   Against the circle of the breast,
> Has never thought that "this is I":
>
> But as he grows he gathers much,
>   And learns the use of "I", and "me",
>   And finds "I am not what I see,
> And other than the things I touch."
>
> So rounds he to a separate mind
>   From whence clear memory may begin,
>   As through the frame that binds him in
> His isolation grows defined.
>
> This use may lie in blood and breath,
>   Which else were fruitless of their due,
>   Had man to learn himself anew
> Beyond the second birth of Death.
>
> (XLV)

The child's progress is dramatized through a shift in signification from a circle enclosing the world (the infantile world of which he, not yet distinguished from the mother, is the circumference) to a circle whose circumference excludes him from a world now perceived as separate. It is a progress that involves losses as well as gains: he "grows", "gathers", "learns", "finds" but is in a sense dispossessed of what he "sees" and "touches". He "rounds"—becomes complete in himself—but is "separated" and "bound" (through a "frame" that constricts as well as giving shape). The process that defines the self also defines its isolation. (Compare Arnold's "Yes, in the sea of life enisled".) So ambiguous is the process that its only conceivable use could be to ensure our spiritual progress beyond the grave.

Under stress of grief, the speaker has a heightened sense of the difference by which self is constituted. It is arguably as a stratagem to escape this sense of estrangement that he pursues similarity in difference, devising similes for himself and his situation out of the world from which he feels himself excluded. He is like a happy lover who finds his beloved is not at home (VIII); a bereaved husband (IX, XIII); the parents of a young girl on her wedding day (XL); a poor girl hopelessly in love with a man of superior rank (LX); the humble childhood friend of a great statesman (LXIV); the wife in an intellectually unequal marriage (XCVII). In all these similes, of course, Hallam plays the complementary role. Most of them present the attentive reader with a question: just how "apt" is this simile supposed to be? In one instance—the simile of the intellectually unequal marriage—the reader is virtually warned off from pressing it too far: we are told that the speaker's love, personified as the subject of the enounced, perceives similarities that, like the spectre of the Brocken, are a hallucinatory projection of itself:

> My love has talk'd with rocks and trees;
>   He finds on misty mountain-ground
>   His own vast shadow glory-crown'd;
> He sees himself in all he sees.
>
> (XCVII)

This mental process recalls the one described by Coleridge in "Frost at Midnight": "the idling Spirit . . . everywhere / Echo or mirror seeking of itself". In another instance the potentially consoling simile of the young girl leaving home on her marriage is elaborated, with highly explicit reference to Hallam, only to be immediately subverted:

> Ay me, the difference I discern!
>   How often shall her old fireside
>   Be cheered with tidings of the bride,
> How often she herself return.
>
> (XL)

The speaker's simile-hunting could be seen, in one aspect, as regressive behaviour: his adult self-concept in disarray, he reverts, in Lacanian terms, to the "mirror-stage" in which the child, growing towards a sense of separate identity, begins to find an image of himself in the "mirror" of other persons and objects. Regressiveness is, after all, something that the speaker—"an infant crying in the night" (LIV)—virtually attributes to himself.

When we come to particular similes, it is often very much up to the reader to determine their precise rhetorical force. What, in a given instance, is the proportionate importance of similarity and of difference? Thus the speaker's comparison of himself to "some poor girl" in love with a man hopelessly beyond her reach (LX) occurs in the first of a series of poems which, Bradley remarks, "are criticised by some readers on the ground that they are written in a tone of excessive and unnatural humility"[14]—as perhaps in the conclusion of this poem:

> At night she weeps, "How vain am I!
> How should he love a thing so low?"
>
> (LX)

Much depends on how closely we assimilate "she" to the speaker. Clearly, if the comparison is to have any point, he must see himself as sharing some of the girl's abjectness. But the effect is also to differentiate him from her; his ability to see himself as "some poor girl" implies a degree of detachment. He is not wallowing in the abjectness of his grief: it might be truer to say that he is wondering at it. He is, to recall the passage from St Augustine, a puzzle to himself. Taken aback by his grief—and perhaps feeling himself unmanned by it—he projects it, in feminine form, as other.

The same sort of question is presented by a later simile in which the departed Hallam is compared to "some divinely gifted man" of humble birth who rises to become "the pillar of a people's hope" and the speaker to a childhood friend

> Who ploughs with pain his native lea
>   And reaps the labour of his hands,
>   Or in the furrow musing stands:
> "Does my old friend remember me?"
>
> (LXIV)

This simile does more than underline the speculative question: supposing that personality does survive death, how can we be sure that the departed will remember the people they knew in this life? It could be read as conveying the sense of desertion that is a common component of grief. The speaker is less obviously distant from the humble childhood friend than from the "poor girl" in the earlier lyric. Any disparity is rather between Hallam, passively elevated by death, and the upwardly mobile politician, born "on a simple village green",

> Who breaks his birth's invidious bar,
>   And grasps the skirts of happy chance,
>   And breasts the blows of circumstance,
> And grapples with his evil star;
>
> Who makes by force his merit known
>   And lives to clutch the golden keys,
>   To mould a mighty state's decrees,
> And shape the whisper of the throne;
>
> And moving up from high to higher,
>   Becomes on Fortune's crowning slope

> The pillar of a people's hope,
> The centre of a world's desire.
>
> (LXIV)

Such aggressive and insidious energy, evoked particularly in the verbs, might suggest, among other possible literary precedents, Marlowe's Tamburlaine or at least Dryden's Achitophel. If we seriously press the analogy between Hallam and this lively exponent of the career open to the talents, we may begin to ask what sort of Hallam we are seeing. The answer could be a less innocuous figure than the Hallam that the speaker seems generally concerned to promote. Does the simile open up a further dimension of ambiguity in the speaker's feelings? It admits a variety of readings, all defensible and none definitive.

Both the similes just considered postulate difference between the speaker and the departed Hallam; but difference also characterized their relationship in life. It was indeed the enabling condition of their friendship: "his unlikeness fitted mine" (LXXIX). Not much is ever said of this unlikeness, though it has been hinted at earlier:

> So many worlds, so much to do,
>   So little done, such things to be,
>   How know I what had need of thee,
> For thou wert strong as thou wert true?
>
> (LXXIII)

Hallam's death occurred because his strength was needed elsewhere in a universe imagined as containing many inhabited worlds. "Strong"—like "Strong Son of God" in the Prologue—might also imply a contrast with the speaker. "We are both 'true' but you are 'strong' as well—which is why you are gone elsewhere and I sit lingering here." But Hallam's strength could also conceivably have separated him from the speaker in this world. "Strong" and "true" do not denote incompatible qualities; but there is a suggestion that in practice these qualities could pull in different directions, an intimation of something volatile and uncertain in the relationship. "Unlikeness" between persons, like other forms of difference, has both positive and negative aspects.

It is therefore important that difference should be contained so that it may enrich, not disrupt, a relationship. The value of "unlikeness" is explained in a lyric addressed to Charles Tennyson, that opens by echoing a much earlier one (IX) in which there is a stark opposition between the speaker's love of the deceased and his love for his brothers:

> "More than my brothers are to me,"—
>   Let this not vex thee, noble heart!
>   I know thee of what force thou art
> To hold the costliest love in fee.
>
> But thou and I are one in kind,
>   As moulded like in Nature's mint;
>   And hill and wood and field did print
> The same sweet forms in either mind.

> For us the same cold streamlet curled
>   Through all his eddying coves, the same
>   All winds that roam the twilight came
> In whispers of the beauteous world.
>
> At one dear knee we proffered vows,
>   One lesson from one book we learned,
>   Ere childhood's flaxen ringlet turned
> To black and brown on kindred brows.
>
> And so my wealth resembles thine,
>   But he was rich where I was poor,
>   And he supplied my want the more
> As his unlikeness fitted mine.
>
> (LXXIX)

The monetary imagery is appropriate to the quite matter-of-fact appraisal of the two relationships. The speaker and his brother belong to the same currency, "printed" off the same plate, the common experience of natural sights and sounds and of family life. Hallam, however, provided something else that the speaker had come to need: not more of the same but foreign exchange. The fact that this explanation is now possible confirms what the preceding lyric, describing the second Christmas in the narrative sequence, had already indicated: difference, the disruptive element, has been contained.

The second Christmas lyric follows a series of lyrics (LXXIII-LXXVII) which dwell on the destructiveness of change and the ephemerality of fame, particularly poetic fame. The speaker eventually arrives at an implied assurance that, whatever else may yield to change, his love and grief are constant. Or are they? Can there be a last state of grief that is worse than the first?

> O sorrow, then can sorrow wane?
> O grief, can grief be changed to less?
>
> O last regret, regret can die!
>
> (LXXVIII)

This fear—that he may lose his hold even on the grief with which he has come to identify himself—is prompted by the contrast with the first Christmas following Hallam's death which had been dominated by "an awful sense / Of one mute Shadow watching all" (XXX). This earlier Christmas is described as an occasion of cruel irony: "The time draws near the birth of Christ" (XXVIII) but Christ, it seems, is stillborn:

> Yet go, and while the holly boughs
>   Entwine the cold baptismal font,
>   Make one wreath more for Use and Wont,
> That guard the portals of the house;
>
> Old sisters of a day gone by,
>   Gray nurses, loving nothing new;
>   Why should they miss their yearly due
> Before their time? They too will die.
>
> (XXIX)

These two quasi-mythological figures, for all their grimness, are guardians of the household, conservative presences that will let nothing threaten its continuity and stability—including the inhibiting effect of Hallam's memory ("How dare we keep our Christmas Eve?"). Under their influence, the family simulates enough Christmas cheer to raise a song proclaiming the faith that the dead do not "lose their mortal sympathy, / Nor change to us, although they change" (XXX). The song is less an expression of faith than a foreshadowing of a faith that will be achieved later. The speaker himself can raise only hope—or, more precisely, a prayer that hope may be possible:

> O Father, touch the east, and light
> The light that shone when Hope was born.
>
> (XXX)

A year later the situation has changed. There are no overt signs of grief and this suggests a new source of grief: the death of grief. But the speaker quickly reassures himself:

> O last regret, regret can die!
> No—mixt with all this mystic frame,
> Her deep relations are the same,
> But with long use her tears are dry.
>
> (LXXVIII)

It is quite appropriate that the reassuring address to the speaker's brother should immediately follow this realization. Hallam has now been assimilated into "the mystic frame", the structuring of the self, the pattern of personal thought and feeling as moulded, in part at least, by experience—much of it, in this instance, the experience of family and countryside that the two brothers have shared. "The mystic frame", as its previous use indicates, is also the level of spiritual perception where "truths . . . darkly join" (XXXVI). In the present context it could also be taken to mean the framework of religious custom to which the family conforms, especially at Christmas, and with which the memory of Hallam is now intimately linked. The self is not now seen as structured independently of others and of the (structured) experience it shares with them; so that "the mystic frame" is not limited by the individual's conscious "isolation" (XLV). Or as Tennyson once engagingly put it: "every human being is a vanful of human beings, of those who have gone before him, and of those who form part of his life".[15]

The speaker can now acknowledge to his brother the value of Hallam's "unlikeness" because it is no longer seen as a threat. Difference has been contained. The point is brought out quite explicitly later when the speaker, about to lose his childhood home, is split between "two spirits of a diverse love"—love for the home of his childhood and love for the same place as associated with Hallam. These two loves are both so deeply incorporated into the mystic frame that they "will not yield each other way". As he leaves, however, "They mix in one another's arms / To one pure image of regret" (CII). Hallam has been domesticated—received into the mystic frame as he was received into the family, when alive, as a house guest. Indeed Hallam is constantly a visitor, whether alive or dead, physical or spiritual, actual or imagined—right up to the Epilogue where he is a conjectured "stiller guest" at the wedding. He is recalled as a "welcome guest" at the Christmas before his death (XXIX); he is a shadowy and disturbing guest at the Christmas following (XXX). He is recalled later as coming down as a visitor from London, on which occasion

> He brought an eye for all he saw;
> He mixt in all our simple sports.
>
> (LXXXIX)

And why not? we may ask. But this participation by Hallam, now a sophisticated visitor from the city, is significant as (presumably needed) evidence that he is still one of "us". The awaited arrival of Hallam's corpse is a parody of his visits in life. The role of visitor is also at times assumed by the speaker. Creeping "like a guilty thing" to the door of Hallam's old home, he is virtually a visitor turned away (VII). He imagines himself as "an honoured guest" in the household of a Hallam still alive and married into the family (LXXXIV). His later mystical (or imagined) encounters with the departed (XCV and CXXX) are still visits—or visitations—by Hallam.

The most distinguished visitor in the poem is, however, Christ in the house of Mary after the raising of Lazarus (XXXII). Mary's eyes on this occasion are "homes of silent prayer", a domestic metaphor paralleled in "household fountains never dry" (CIX) for the inner sources of Hallam's conversation, and, less unusually, "the household jar within" (XCIV) for emotional disturbance. Such images exemplify the status of domesticity in *In Memoriam.* Visits are important because the household is important. It is important that Hallam's body be brought home to England if only because it "flatters . . . home-bred fancies" (X). In contrast is the homelessness of the dead sailor whose "heavy-shotted hammock-shroud / Drops in his vast and wandering grave" (VI). The value of home is evident in the address to Charles Tennyson, as it is—negatively—in the third Christmas lyric when the family has moved from the home of the speaker's childhood and of Hallam's visits to "new unhallowed ground" (CIV). Home, by implication, is consecrated ground and virtually becomes so in the Christmas lyrics. Christ can be seen as the archetypal visitor, and the Incarnation as the domestication of divinity itself.

"Oneness", in this poem, begins, humanly speaking, at home. Home is the locus of value within the social order and, for humanity in its present state, within the cosmic order. The political standpoint of *In Memoriam* derives, directly or not, from Edmund Burke, the Burke of *Reflections on the Revolution in France* (1790). For Burke continuity and stability are assured by an entrenched landed aristocracy and gentry. Tennyson's social perspective has shifted into a lower key: in *In Memoriam,* it is the ordinary household, rather than the large country seat, that ensures the unity and continuity of the national life. The perspective is middle-class and domestic. The preoccupations, however, are very much the same as Burke's. When the newly wedded girl leaves her parents' home

> She enters other realms of love;
>
> Her office there to rear, to teach,
>   Becoming as is meet and fit
>   A link among the days, to knit
> The generations each with each.
>
> (XL)

Denied public distinction, the wife and mother—"the angel in the house"—has nevertheless a crucial role in the body politic: to foster the continuity that, amid the spectacular transformations overtaking modern England, was so much the concern of writers and political thinkers from Scott and Burke onwards. Continuity—"oneness" as it embraces the generations—also begins at home.

The restraining and stabilizing influence of domesticity, institutionalized in marriage, is assumed in a metaphorical address to Sorrow:

> O Sorrow, wilt thou live with me
>   No casual mistress, but a wife,
>   My bosom-friend and half of life;
> As I confess it needs must be?
>
> O Sorrow, wilt thou rule my blood,
>   Be sometimes lovely like a bride,
>   And put thy harsher moods aside,
> If thou wilt have me wise and good?
>
> My centred passion cannot move,
>   Nor will it lessen from to-day;
>   But I'll have leave at times to play
> As with the creature of my love;
>
> And set thee forth, for thou art mine,
>   With so much hope for years to come,
>   That, howsoe'er I know thee, some
> Could hardly tell what name were thine.
>
> (LIX)

The analogy is here quite close and detailed. The "wife", as her part in a stratagem for keeping the husband "wise and good", is clearly meant to have some of the attributes of the mistress from whom she is distinguished. The stratagem by which the speaker hopes to come to terms with his grief is analogous to marriage as a stratagem for containing male sexuality. And grief is analogous to sexual appetite in so far as grief is a potentially subversive and destructive emotion. The metaphor can be read as very pointedly sustained in the last stanza: "I shall lavish so much adornment on you that people will wonder if you are a respectable married woman at all." Here, as elsewhere, the "I" rhetorically confronts, as other, a divisive element within itself in the hope of containing it.

The speaker's most ambitious stratagem for containing difference and achieving "oneness" is attained in lyric CXXX:

> Thy voice is on the rolling air;
>   I hear thee where the waters run;
>   Thou standest in the rising sun,
> And in the setting thou art fair.
>
> What art thou then? I cannot guess;
>   But tho' I seem in star and flower
>   To feel thee some diffusive power,
> I do not therefore love thee less:
>
> My love involves the love before;
>   My love is vaster passion now;
>   Tho' mix'd with God and Nature thou,
> I seem to love thee more and more.
>
> Far off thou art, but ever nigh;
>   I have thee still, and I rejoice;
>   I prosper, circled with thy voice;
> I shall not lose thee though I die.
>
> (CXXX)

The cosmic perspective is assimilated. Hallam stands, like a figure from Revelation,[16] in the rising sun. Love and "vastness" are coextensive. Though Hallam is differentiated from nothing—not even clearly from the speaker who feels him as a "diffusive power"—he is none the less still conceived as a distinct object of love. Though he no longer has an individual body, he is none the less "heard" and "felt". The stratagem is highly effective—at least if we suppose the speaker to be entirely convinced of its validity. Difference is banished. Since Hallam is not differentiated from anything, nothing can estrange the speaker from Hallam; equally, Hallam cannot estrange the speaker from anything else. "Oneness" prevails; but relationship (implying difference) somehow remains possible. The speaker, apparently, has it all ways. How much we concern ourselves with the credibility—or intelligibility—of this mystical perspective may depend on how far the text seems to invite us to consider it as the final outcome of the speaker's struggles. If the speaker's final state is not here at all but in the Prologue, then there is no reason to suppose that the experience described is any more a permanent and comprehensive answer to life's problems than are most Romantic epiphanies. This vision of the cosmic Hallam is introduced at the end of the previous lyric:

> Behold, I dream a dream of good,
> And mingle all the world with thee.
>
> (CXXIX)

"A dream of good" may be contrasted with another sort of dream:

> Are God and Nature then at strife,
>   That Nature lends such evil dreams?—
>
> (LV)

"Nature" here being a rather feverish construction of Lyall's *Principles of Geology* and Chambers's *Vestiges of Creation*. The implication could be that since we have no certain knowledge of the nature of things but only "dreams", it is wise to settle for "good" dreams as against "evil" ones. Again, it is the dreamer, the subject of the verb, who mingles Hallam and the world—they do not mingle of their own accord. "Behold, I dream" has the force of "See what I'm doing." Faith is not here a gift of God passively received but an act of will, of that "living will that shalt endure" (CXXXI). To put it in Romantic literary terms, faith here has less in common with Wordsworthian "wise passiveness" than with active Coleridgean imagination, "the shaping spirit".

The actual existence of the object of faith is by no means unhesitatingly maintained, for all the speaker's visionary fervour. The characteristic "seem" occurs in two crucial places. And in the following lyric the "living will" is invoked

> That we may lift from out of dust
>   A voice as unto him that hears—
>
> (CXXXI)

a turn of phrase ("*as* unto") by no means indicating total intellectual confidence that there is indeed "one who hears". Faith is a matter of will, of still trusting, even though less "faintly" than before, the larger hope. The nearest the speaker ever comes to a passive, unsolicited encounter with an independently existing spiritual presence is in the earlier experience when he reads the dead man's letters in the garden at night:

> So word by word and line by line,
>   The dead man touched me from the past,
>   And all at once it seemed at last
> The living soul was flashed on mine.
>
> (XCV)

There is nothing particularly mystical about the initial effect of reading the letters: the dead man "touches" the living through the material signs that trigger memories of his former presence. "Flashed" is certainly a metaphor for some sort of immediate non-physical contact; but it is characteristically qualified by "seemed" and a few lines later we read: "At length my trance / Was cancelled, stricken through with doubt." Furthermore, although it is the speaker who is "touched" and "flashed on", his experience is not entirely passive: it is invited by his act of reading the letters, an act motivated by his "hunger" for the dead man's presence. So even here there is an element of purposive action; and in the end there is no assurance that the invited response, though forthcoming and in excess of what was anticipated, is anything more than an echo of the invitation itself. The experience (*as* experience) is not open to question; its significance, in retrospect, is. Are we to suppose that the "dream" of the cosmic Hallam—rhetorically, far more overtly staged and perhaps far more consciously and deliberately induced—is any less open to retrospective questioning? Not if the Prologue is to be taken, as presumably it is, as evidence of the speaker's final standpoint. There Hallam is no longer a "diffusive power", scarcely distinguishable from Christ as omnipresent Logos. He is unambiguously restored to creaturely status. "He lives in thee" may recall the subsequently described but chronologically earlier vision; but it has quite different implications. Hallam is no longer omnipresent—that is, always "here", always heard, seen and felt throughout nature: he is now "there"—"and there / I find him worthier to be loved". Hallam is still loved but safely distanced—a new stratagem and one perhaps easier to maintain in the teeth of experience and adverse criticism.

The speaker never escapes from "the dialogue of the mind with itself".[17] Difference is never conclusively banished. No "dream of good" is more than one alternative, haunted by the possibility of other dreams. The "living will"—described by Tennyson elsewhere as "that which we know as Free-will, the higher and enduring part of man"[18]—would have no *raison d'être* at all, except in a world of difference where alternatives constantly confront us and rejected alternatives stubbornly refuse to quit the field. In the Prologue faith asserts itself in an indefinitely continuing confrontation with doubt and through a rhetoric that dramatizes the confrontation. It is an act of will that involves an act of the imagination, a choice of "dreams". But imagination remains susceptible to the dream that faith rejects.

Notes

1. A. C. Bradley, *A Commentary on Tennyson's In Memoriam,* 3rd ed. (London: Macmillan, 1910), p. xii.

2. Paul de Man, *Allegories of Reading: figural language in Rousseau, Nietzche, Rilke and Proust* (New Haven and London: Yale University Press, 1979), p. 17.

3. Hallam Tennyson, *Alfred Lord Tennyson, A Memoir,* 2 vols. (London: Macmillan, 1897), vol. 1, p. 304. All subsequent references to the *Memoir* are to the first volume.

4. Hallam Tennyson, *Tennyson,* p. 312n.

5. That is, up to and including lyric XXVII. (Corresponding to Part I in Bradley's division of the poem. See Bradley, *In Memoriam,* p. 30.)

6. Augustine, *Confessions,* IV, 4. Quoted Bradley, *In Memoriam,* p. 86.

7. Hallam Tennyson, *Tennyson,* p. 305.

8. Anthony Easthope, *Poetry and Discourse* (London: Methuen [New Accents], 1983) pp. 42-3.

9. Bradley, *In Memoriam,* p. 93.

10. Ibid.

11. Hallam Tennyson, *Tennyson,* p. 319n.

12. K. W. Gransden, *Tennyson: In Memoriam,* Studies in English Literature No. 22 (London: Edward Arnold, 1964), p. 25.

13. Walter Pater, *The Renaissance* (New York: New American Library, 1959), Conclusion.

14. Bradley, *In Memoriam*, p. 157.

15. Hallam Tennyson, *Tennyson*, p. 323n.

16. Revelation 19:17. See *The Poems of Tennyson,* ed. Christopher Ricks, Longmans' Annotated English Poets (London, 1969), p. 979n.

17. Matthew Arnold, Preface to the first Edition of *Poems,* 1853.

18. Hallam Tennyson, *Tennyson*, p. 319.

A. A. Markley (essay date 1993)

SOURCE: Markley, A. A. "The Foot Upon the Skull: *In Memoriam* and the Tradition of Roman Love Elegy." *Tennyson Research Bulletin* 6, no. 2 (November 1993): 112-21.

[*In the following essay, Markley asserts that Tennyson's allusions to Roman love elegy are an attempt to heighten the expression of experience and emotion throughout* In Memoriam.]

Tennyson opens his prologue to **In Memoriam** with an invocation to the 'Strong Son of God, immortal Love'. The Victorian reader would immediately recognize the identification of Christ here; moreover there is an echo of George Herbert's 'Love', which begins with the invocation 'Immortal Love' (Hill 1971, 119). Nevertheless, this address to a deified 'Love' sets up an immediate association with the genre of Latin love elegy popular in the late Roman Republic and the early Roman Empire. Tennyson's first line echoes not only Herbert, but also Propertius I.1, in which the narrator speaks of his first encounter with oppressive 'Amor' upon meeting his lover Cynthia:

> Cynthia prima suis miserum me cepit ocellis,
>   contactum nullis ante cupidinibus.
> tum mihi constantis deiecit lumina fastus
>   et caput impositis pressit Amor pedibus
>
>   (I.1.1-4)

> *It was Cynthia who first captured miserable me*
> *with her eyes,*
> *Me, never before touched by desire.*
> *Then Love forced me to cast down my eyes*
> *of steady haughtiness,*
> *and stepped on my head with his foot.*

Tennyson's second stanza cements the association with Propertius:

> Thine are these orbs of light and shade;
>   Thou madest Life in man and brute;
>   Thou madest Death; and lo, thy foot
> Is on the skull which thou hast made.

While Tennyson's stanza obviously refers to the victory of Christ over Death, and even brings to mind references to Christ's heel bruising the head of Satan in Genesis and in Milton (*Paradise Lost* X.181, XII.430), it is likewise important to note that the poet has very skillfully infused Christian and Classical elements here in the image of the foot upon the skull. It is also significant that Tennyson's narrator introduces his grief in this poem and explains it as having been caused by a 'fair creature'. In doing so he grounds his poem from the very beginning within the Roman elegiac tradition.

The study of classical literature was one of Tennyson's lifelong pursuits, and the influence of classical verse on the technical aspects of his poetry has long been acknowledged. George Clayton Tennyson taught Greek and Latin to his children, and made them memorize long passages of Latin, including the odes of Horace. Tennyson's library contained numerous volumes of Latin poetry, including several editions of the complete works of Horace and Ovid, and several collections of the works of Catullus, Tibullus, and Propertius. Indeed, the poet asked that a volume of Horace's *Opera* and one containing collected works of Catullus, Tibullus and Propertius be brought to him just days before he died (Campbell 1971, 39, 59).

In **In Memoriam** Tennyson employs a wide range of traditional situations which the Roman elegists used repeatedly to invoke complex relationships and intense emotional states. His chief reason for doing so is certainly that the posture of the tormented lover and the depth of passion and longing that Propertius and the other elegists achieved in the persona of that lover provided a rich starting point for Tennyson in his attempt to express the profound loss that he experienced upon his friend's death. By alluding to Roman elegy throughout **In Memoriam,** the poet invites the reader into that context and within it experiments with ways to express his own emotional state and his psychological progression through grief.

As he does with his opening invocation in the Prologue, the narrator of **In Memoriam** frequently refers to and addresses a personified Love. While referring to Christ on one level, these addresses also continue to remind the reader of the frequent addresses to 'Love' in Roman elegy. In section 35, for example, Tennyson sets up a dialogue with the persona of Love concerning the erosions of time. Section 126 proclaims Love as 'my lord and king', placing him in a position of command—a treatment of Love very much in the elegiac tradition, in which Love is often addressed as a military commander. Here the narrator speaks of himself as in attendance at the court of Love, waiting to hear the news that couriers bring, and sleeping at court 'Encompassed by his faithful guard' (126.8) conscious upon hearing the pacing sentinel that all is well in the 'deep night'. A passage in Ovid's *Amores* also describes Amor as a military figure:

> Militat omnis amans, et habet sua castra Cupido;
>   Attice, crede mihi, militat omnis amans.
>
>   (I.9.1-2)

> *All lovers are soldiers, and Cupid has his own camp*;
> *Atticus, believe me, all lovers are soldiers.*

Tennyson draws a portrait of Love that is different from that of the elegiac poets, yet he does so in the context of similar metaphors and situations.

As in his repeated addresses to Love, Tennyson also evokes the conventions of Roman elegy in his invocations to 'Sorrow', whom the speaker addresses much as the Roman elegist did his mistress. In section 3 the narrator first mentions Sorrow, characterizing her as a sibyl-like priestess in the 'vaults of Death'. In section 16 he speaks of the varying emotions which reveal themselves through his poems and he attributes the cause of his mutable emotional state to Sorrow. This characterization of Sorrow and the narrator's subjugation to her resembles the Roman elegist's descriptions of his subjugation to his mistress. The degree of passion and emotion that the narrator feels is provided by the elegiac conventions, although the replacement of the mistress with Sorrow locates the reader in the specific context of **In Memoriam**.

Sorrow's role as the addressed 'lover' is taken furthest in 59, in which the speaker proposes marriage to her. Like the anguished elegiac lover, he invites Sorrow to 'rule my blood', and to 'put thy harsher moods aside'—a reference that particularly recalls the personality of the typical *domina* in elegiac poetry. Although marriage proposals are not usual in the repartee between the classical elegist and his mistress—indeed often the lady is already married to someone else—the proposal here demonstrates the degree of the speaker's devotion and dedication to the object of his love, a stance common in the tradition of love elegy.

Tennyson again evokes the conventions of Roman love elegy in his consideration of the eternal nature of the love that exists between the speaker and his friend. Sections 129 and 130 are a pair of addresses to the friend, before the poet closes **In Memoriam** with the prayer to the 'living will' of section 131. Section 129 contains the speaker's testament of his all-encompassing love for his friend, and 130 a valediction expressing his assurance that his friend has become a part of the living world around him, 'mix'd with God and Nature' (130.11). Here the speaker also expresses his faith that he will never lose his friend through death. This certainty on the part of the narrator recalls the Roman lover's assurances of the infinite limits of his love for his mistress. Propertius, in poem I.19, speaks of his eternal love for Cynthia in the context of his own death:

> illic quidquid ero, semper tua dicar imago:
> traicit et fati litora magnus amor.
>
> (I.19.11-12)

> *There, whatever I may be, may I always be called your*
> *shade: Great Love penetrates the shores of fate.*

In **In Memoriam** an earlier expression of the narrator's eternal love for his friend occurs in the first stanza of 26, in the poet's statement that 'No lapse of time can canker Love, / Whatever fickle tongues may say', (26.3-4), a passage which echoes Catullus's similar sentiment concerning disapproving onlookers in poems 5 and 7. In poem 5 Catullus writes that he will exchange so many kisses with Lesbia that the numbers will be thrown all into confusion, so that no malcontent will be able to cast an 'evil eye' on the lovers when he sees their kisses to be so many. Similarly, in poem 7, Catullus writes of innumerable kisses that 'an evil tongue' will not be able to curse.

Yet another characteristic of Roman elegy which Tennyson builds upon is the hyperbolic listing of the mistress's idealized virtues. Propertius lists Cynthia's beauty, her gait, and her graceful mannerisms in II.1; in II.2 he compares her physical virtues to those of the goddesses. In II.3 Propertius denies that he loves Cynthia for her physical features, and glorifies her accomplishments as a dancer and as a composer and singer of lyric poems.

Ovid likewise sings the virtues of Corinna in *Amores* I.5, in which he catalogues the specific charms of his lover's body in a description of a sexual encounter with her. In II.15 he again speaks of her ideal physical features in an expression of envy for a ring that will be touched and worn by her.

Tennyson produces an encomium in section 109, in which his narrator catalogues his friend's virtues, albeit virtues that are less superficial and not associated with the physical qualities usually enumerated by the Roman elegists. The narrator lists such features as his friend's 'critic clearness', 'seraphic intellect', pure passion and love of freedom; he characterizes his friend as an ideal human being, embodying a manhood 'fused with female grace', and possessed of extraordinary wisdom. In the epilogue to **In Memoriam** this characterization culminates in the suggestion that Hallam manifested on earth a nobler type of human being that is to come, the 'crowning race' of the future, 'Appearing ere the times were ripe' (139).

Tennyson also draws on the emotional content and situation of Roman elegy in his exploration of his narrator's grief at being separated from his beloved friend. The Roman elegist was very often preoccupied by his despair at being separated from his mistress by such physical barriers as the night and the barred doors of his lover's home, or by the greater barriers of geographical distance occasioned by travel. This is the 'paraclausithyron' theme and Propertius I.16 provides a perfect example of this sub-genre of Roman elegy. Here the door itself repeats the typical speech of the excluded lover, a long, doleful address to the door which he calls 'more inwardly unfeeling' than his mistress herself ('Ianua vel domina penitus crudelior ipsa' I.16.17). The lover asks of the door:

> cur numquam reserata meos admittis amores,
> nescia furtivas reddere mota preces?
>
> (I.16.19-20)

> *Why do you never, unbolted, admit my desires,*
> *knowing nothing of emotions, nor how to answer my*
> *secret requests?*

Similarly, in Tibullus I.1, the narrator describes himself as sitting as a 'janitor', or door-keeper, before his mistress's 'harsh doors'. In I.2, Tibullus's speaker wishes the bolted door of his mistress would suffer the harshness of rain and lightning bolts, and begs it to yield to him and open quietly to allow him to slip inside, remembering the many times when the poet serenaded the door and bedecked its posts with garlands (I.2.7-14).

Ovid's speaker in *Amores* I.6 comparably addresses the porter of Corinna's home and begs him to open the door. In poem II.1 the lover trusts that his songs will eventually succeed in making Corinna's doors give way, and in III.11 he speaks of his weariness in putting up with Corinna's rejection and refers to his long hours of lying in vigil before her locked-up house, watching in anguish as other men slip out from meetings with her at night.

In their edition of **In Memoriam,** Susan Shatto and Marion Shaw have identified Tennyson's use of the paraclausithyron tradition in sections 7 and 119 of the poem (Shatto and Shaw, 1982, 26); in both sections the speaker addresses the doors of his friend's former home with the lines:

> Doors where my heart was used to beat
> So quickly . . .
>
> (7.3-4 and 119.1-2)

In both sections the narrator has come to the house while the rest of the world sleeps, and in both he reflects on times spent with his friend. A definite progression in his psychological state can be perceived as having taken place between the composition of 7 and 119. In section 7 he stands in the 'unlovely' street, waiting for his friend's hand; then, realizing that he can no longer clasp that hand, he creeps away as the 'blank day' breaks. In 119, however, though standing in the street he smells the meadow and hears birds singing, he sees the glimmer of a more promising dawn, and in a vivid memory he takes his friend's hand. The doors remain closed, but, unlike the elegiac lovers who experience ultimate rejection, Tennyson's speaker has at last found a means to get beyond the doors.

Tennyson again writes of the situation of the excluded lover in section 94, when he speaks of the purity of heart necessary for a communion with the dead:

> But when the heart is full of din,
>   And doubt beside the portal waits,
>   They can but listen at the gates,
> And hear the household jar within.
>
> (94.13-16)

Here again the poet has appropriated Roman elegiac tradition in order to convey the emotional pain of exclusion and separation.

In addition to experimenting with the convention of the paraclausithyron, Tennyson also evokes the despair of separation from the beloved in ways that reflect other aspects of this theme in Roman poetry, particularly the common situation of the elegist's laments at being separated from his lover by geographical distance. In Propertius's ode I.8 the speaker expresses his horror at Cynthia's decision to travel to Illyria:

> Tune igitur demens, nec te mea cura moratur?
>
> (I.8.1)

I say, are you out of your mind? Does your love for me not detain you?

In II.16 Ovid finds himself in Sulmo, far away from his lover, and he curses those who first made roads upon the earth. He continues his lamentation:

> Ulmus amat vitem, vitis non deserit ulmum;
>   separor a domina cur ego saepe mea?
> at mihi te comitem iuraras usque futuram—
>   per me perque oculos, sidera nostra, tuos!
>
> (II.16.41-44)

The elm loves the vine, the vine does not desert the elm;
Why then am I so often separated from my lady? But you
swore that you would accompany me—You swore by me
and by those eyes, my stars, of yours!

A section of **In Memoriam** which Tennyson developed out of this theme of despair at travel and separation is the cycle of sections that concerns the arrival of the ship bearing Hallam's body (poems 9-17). In these sections the poet's obsession with the loss of his friend causes him to fear for the safe passage of his friend's body. The theme of separation is also at work in **In Memoriam** in section 67, in which the narrator speculates on the distance between himself and his friend's sepulchre as he lies down to sleep in the moonlight, which shines on both places at once. The speaker also concentrates on the distance between him and his friend in section 117, an address to the 'days and hours' that separate him from his friend's embrace. While the elegist frequently prays for the quick passage of the time that he must endure before seeing his mistress again, Tennyson's narrator recognizes the function of this time to 'hold me from my proper place . . . For fuller gain of after bliss' (117.4).

In section 117, the speaker's expression of the delight that will accrue 'a hundredfold', especially following the reference to his friend's embrace, recalls Catullus's estimation of the hundreds and thousands of kisses that he desires from Lesbia in poem 5. Likewise, the image of innumerable grains of sand in line 9 of 117 and the reference to the 'kiss' of toothed wheels in line 12 recalls Catullus 7, which compares the speaker's numbering of desired kisses to the number of grains of sand on the beach of Cyrene. The 'courses of the suns', invoked here as a unit of measuring the time of one's life, is another poetic convention used by Catullus in poem 5, and may recall Andrew Marvell's 'To His Coy Mistress', which also owes a debt to Catullus: 'Thus though we cannot make our Sun stand still / Yet we will make him run,' (45-46).

In section 98 Tennyson's narrator expresses his hatred for Vienna, the city in which his friend died, another emotional situation that conventionally grows out of the elegist's obsession with his separation from his beloved. Here the speaker vows that he will never see Vienna, and with the hyperbolic tendency of the elegist, he characterizes it as a place haunted by evil in which friends are often parted, fathers bend 'above more graves', and sadness darkens the 'blaze of kings'. The last three stanzas of the section detail the aspects of Vienna that the speaker's friend admired and enjoyed, and this attention to the attractive features that the city held for his friend compounds the reader's perception of the speaker's bitterness. The Roman elegist's bitterness toward the places that take his mistress away from him lie in the same vein; examples are Propertius's views of 'frigid Illyria' in I.8 and of 'corrupt Baiae' in I.11 as well as Tibullus's 'harsh grain field' in poem II.3.

Throughout *In Memoriam* Tennyson experiments with the weaving together of traditions—strands of Christian symbolism, and a wide range of traditional conventions common to the genre of Latin love elegy. In fusing these traditions, the poet evokes a sense of the intense emotional states of the characteristic elegiac lover and shapes this familiar stance in the development of a more modern, Christian narrative persona. The depth of passion and longing that Latin elegy lends to the Victorian Christian framework of the poem provides the reader with a very graphic and powerful expression of human experience and emotion.

Works Cited

Barber, E. A., 1987, *Sexti Properti: Carmina.* Oxford: Oxford University Press.

Campbell, Nancie, 1971, *Tennyson in Lincoln: A Catalogue of the Collections in the Research Centre,* volume I. Lincoln: The Tennyson Society.

Fordyce, John, 1961, *Catullus.* Oxford: Oxford University Press.

Hill, Robert W., 1971, *Tennyson's Poetry.* New York: Norton.

Kenney, E. J., 1986, *Ovid Nasonis: Amores, Medicamina Faciei Femineae, Ars Amatoria, Remedia Amoris.* Oxford: Oxford University Press.

Postgate, J. P., 1987, *Tibulli: Aliorumque Carminum Libri Tres.* Oxford: Oxford University Press.

Ricks, Christopher, 1987, *The Poems of Tennyson.* Essex: Longman.

Shatto and Shaw, 1982, Susan Shatto and Marion Shaw, *Tennyson: In Memoriam.* Oxford: Oxford University Press.

Patrick Scott (essay date 1996)

SOURCE: Scott, Patrick. "Tennyson, Lincolnshire, and Provinciality: The Topographical Narrative of *In Memoriam.*" *Victorian Poetry* 34, no. 1 (spring 1996): 39-51.

[*In the following essay, Scott portrays* In Memoriam *as a topographical narrative and argues that Tennyson wrote it with a sense of "provincial self-consciousness."*]

Tennyson writes to Emily Sellwood, perhaps some time in 1838:

> I have dim mystic sympathies with tree and hill reaching far back into childhood. A known landskip is to me an old friend, that continually talks to me of my youth and half-forgotten things, and does more for me than many a friend that I know.[1]

This is a remarkable passage in many ways, not least in its timing and audience. In 1838, Tennyson had recently left, after twenty-eight years of almost continuous residence, the "known landskip" of his Somersby childhood, and as things turned out had left it more or less permanently. The original recipient of the letter was the old friend he would marry, and as time passed she would become almost the sole remaining voice to talk to him of his Lincolnshire youth. And the mystic significance of "tree and hill" reverberates through so many lines of *In Memoriam* that this letter's privileging of landscape over friendship, and its linking of landscape with the amnesiac insecurities of a migratory adulthood, might make one reread Tennyson's poem as elegizing not a person, Arthur Hallam, but a place, Lincolnshire, or rather as elegizing what place itself had come to represent for Tennyson and his early Victorian contemporaries. We can best tease out this broader theme of local rootedness and uprootedness in Tennyson's writing and generation by reexamining the treatment of geographical dislocation in *In Memoriam* itself.[2]

The question of place in poetry has long been intellectually embarrassing. Few topics in literary history so readily evoke, on the one hand, chauvinist, tourist-board sentimentality or, on the other, a deracinated superciliousness. And few topics leave literary criticism so complacently inconsistent, operating on a kind of theoretical double-standard—now praising Burns or Wordsworth or Hardy for reliance on their local culture (as against a false metropolitan hegemony), now concurring in George Eliot's portrayal or Matthew Arnold's critique of local culture as narrowminded provincialism.[3] The Victorians themselves recognized this conflict, and it is tellingly enacted at the end of Arnold's second term as Oxford's professor of poetry, when his successor Francis Doyle immediately lectured on Virgil and Tennyson under the fighting title "Provincial Poetry."[4] But current critical practice should surely call into question both these extreme reactions. The Romantic attempt to root inner spiritual truth in a specific geographical origin now seems the last bastion of a futile essentialism, while at the same time the metropolitan center no longer holds. Our decentering of critical authority should, in principle, allow the revaluation of literary locale. Seamus Heaney has puckishly asserted that such literal decentering should be a main plank of the postmodern creative agenda: "A literary scene, in which the provinces revolve around the center is demonstrably a Copernican one, [but] the task of talent is to reverse things to a Ptolemaic condition."[5] Heaney's revalorization of localism is surely too simple, and is indeed belied by the subtlety of his own discussion later in the same essay. Yet more theoretical discussions have not taken us much further. Marxians have often seemed more comfortable with the contingencies of time rather than of place. Edward de Soja has recently argued in his bravely titled *Postmodern Geographies* that late nineteenth-century historicism "successfully occluded, devalued, and depoliticized space as an object of critical discourse," and that renewed geographical interest should help us break from the "carceral historicism" of conventional critical theory.[6] Yet there is little sign of this theoretical breakout really happening. As David Simpson has shown in his essay on the literary ethnographer Clifford Geertz, contemporary celebrations of particularity or localism have in practice often functioned as strategies to fudge ethical or analytical difficulties.[7]

Certainly, Heaney's neo-Ptolemaicism is too simple for the discussion of Tennyson, because Tennyson came, not from a glamorous place—from Scotland or the Lakes or Wessex or Derry—but from Lincolnshire, the kind of county even its own tourist board keeps touting as undiscovered. There is something touchingly absurd about the many late Victorian attempts to make Tennyson's Lincolnshire a place of literary pilgrimage, until one realizes that none of the turn-of-the-century Tennyson-and-Lincolnshire books could have expected that readers would actually go there—the sites and villages they describe were miles from the nearest railway, and depended in the nineteenth century on weekly or twice-weekly carriers' carts for their link to the smallest market town.[8] In the tiny village of Somersby itself, the Birthplace, Somersby Rectory, has never been open to visitors on a regular basis; a pilgrimage to Tennyson country has long been foredoomed never to find its shrine. Today, in mid-Lincolnshire, driving a car, the unwary literary pilgrim feels trapped in an endless maze or network of tiny non-villages, each a mile or so from the next one, each little more than a road-intersection, though how evocative the place-names—Hagworthingham, Bag Enderby, Ashby Puerorum—will have looked in prospect on one's tourist map.

Tennyson himself must have sensed something of this absurdity. When in 1890 he had to acknowledge a presentation copy of John Cuming Walters' new book *In Tennyson Land being a Brief Account of the Home and Early Surroundings of the Poet Laureate and an Attempt to Identify the Scenes and trace the Influences of Lincolnshire in His Works,* the thank-you note seems distinctly ungrateful:

> My father thanks you for your book [Tennyson had his son Hallam write the unlucky author]. He thinks that however pleasant your volume you have ridden your hobby to death. **The Ode to Memory** and *In Memoriam* alone . . . contain any reference to Somersby. All the poems which you quote . . . **The Brook, Mariana, Lady of Shallott,** etc. have nothing of Lincolnshire about them and are purely imaginative inventions.

The coup de grace of this extraordinary thank-you letter came in its final quotation from Shakespeare's *Midsummer Night's Dream,* where the "imagination bodies forth / The form of things unknown," and the poet's pen "gives to airy nothing a local habitation and a name."[9]

Tennyson married a Lincolnshire woman he had known since before Hallam's death. Their servants after marriage came from Lincolnshire.[10] He retained a Lincolnshire accent all his life. But after the family left Somersby in 1837, he never went back for any extended period. He looked for a married home in the Lake District, Malvern, Sussex, Kent, almost anywhere except Lincolnshire.[11] Late in life he passed up the opportunity to buy the Somersby estate for his son Hallam. Even his peerage was gazetted to not one, but two, locations in counties other than Lincolnshire.[12] As Philip Collins has commented, it is striking that Tennyson, the poet of Lincolnshire, never cites any specific Lincolnshire placename in his writings, outside the comically disowned dialect poetry (p. 6). Indeed, already by the 1840s, Tennyson was being criticized by Lincolnshire friends for neglecting them, and wrote defensively to T. H. Rawnsley: "However appearances are against me I *have* a love for old Lincolnshire faces and things."[13] Nonetheless, he excused himself from a visit and quoted Burns in dialect, no less, on the inevitable changes that time brings. In an interesting letter also to his uncle Tennyson asserts that his brother Septimus will never regain mental health unless he gets away from Lincolnshire immediately.[14] Tennyson experienced and internalized a radical cultural disjunction or dislocation, symbolized by his attitude to Somersby, a dislocation that late Victorian fans like Walters or Napier or the Rawnsleys were trying to reverse or deny.

Now the study of place in Tennyson is significant because his experience of place and displacement, rootedness and uprootedness, was paradigmatic for a whole generation, and indeed became culturally normative for generations afterwards. The shifting nineteenth-century vocabulary of place—origin, locality, region, provinciality, cosmopolitanism, and so on—marks the cultural shifts and insecurities of the period, quite as much as those idealist high-cultural vocabularies that effaced poetic topography. And there are sound historical reasons why Tennyson's own geographical uprooting resonated so strongly with his contemporaries. The nineteenth century saw an enormous increase, not just in emigration overseas, but in internal migration, as changed agricultural practices, urban expansion, and improved inland transportation made physical and social uprooting the normative experience for the majority of Britons. Tennyson scholars have too often assimilated his treatment of place, like other aspects of his poetry, to a modified or elegized Romanticism; his late Victorian fans were assimilating him to a kind of sentimentalized and unthreateningly marginal regionalism; but the central Victorian experience that his poetry embodies is the uncomfortable recognition of one's own provinciality, the discovery that the mystic sympathies of one's own half-forgotten cultural origin carry no abstract or transcendent cultural authority even for one's later self.

What we may call the topographical narrative of *In Memoriam* may be easily surveyed, but it is more subtly inflected than, under Romantic influence, we have commonly assumed. The opening segment of the poem is set firmly in Lincolnshire, dealing with a loss elsewhere; it covertly takes for granted that Tennyson knows where he is, that the "real life" threatened by Hallam's death-in-absence is being lived in a known landskip. The first churchyard section (section 2) is patently not about Hallam's grave but about Tennyson finding *his* identity lying, not within himself, but in the familiarities of near-pagan village fatalism. His impatient dialogue with the commonplace "cultured" responses to Hallam's death is a response to correspondents living elsewhere (section 6), or to passing travellers, the classical *viator* or wayfarer (section 21). The reality of Tennyson's bereavement is articulated locally, within the rectory family, in consciousness of the younger sister who now must foresee perpetual maidenhood. It is no accident that *In Memoriam*'s first set-piece landscape section is also one of the great anthology-sections for Tennyson's Lincolnshire fans:

> Calm and deep peace on this high wold,
>   And on these dews that drench the furze,
>   And all the silvery gossamers
> That twinkle into green and gold:
>
> Calm and still light on yon great plain
>   That sweeps with all its autumn bowers,
>   And crowded farms and lessening towers,
> To mingle with the bounding main.
>
> (11.5-12)[15]

It is also surely not coincidental that the vowel-qualities of this section should rely so heavily on just those diphthongs that are distinctively divocalic in mid-Lincolnshire dialect—the autumn bowers, great plain—as well as on distinctively local word choice—yon, world.[16] The perspective is looking out from the south edge of the wolds across the wide, wild, waste, enormous marsh of southeast Lincolnshire, to the North Sea, yet the linguistic grounding remains in the wold village. There is an endearing, perhaps deliberate and self-mocking, parochialism in referring to anywhere in Lincolnshire as a *high* wold (nowhere in the Tennyson area is over 250 feet above sea level), and the juxtaposition of Tennyson's birthplace culture with a world beyond, where churches lessen and even farm people are crowds, suggests the cultural insecurities that underwrite Tennyson's assertion of "calm despair." Moreover, in this first *In Memoriam* segment, Tennyson's metaphors of his bereavement seem disproportionately drawn from the experiences of his own Lincolnshire life. The household servants left placeless after their master dies in section 20, for instance, recall not Hallam's but Tennyson's father's death in 1831. The "happy lover" who goes courting to a nearby manor house only to find (in section 8) that the girl is "gone and far from home" surely recalls the story of Tennyson's own Rosa Baring, **"Locksley Hall,"** and *Maud*.[17]

This initial taken-for-granted topographical footing gives way to a poem that is all over the place, yet Somersby provides one of the continuing benchmarks for the poem's progression—the succession of family Christmases. These Christmases delineate Tennyson's emerging sense of his experience as ambiguous, limiting, provincial, rather than as the valorized local origin of his Romantic predecessors, and his regionalist successors. (One of the differences between Wordsworth's sense of place and Tennyson's is that Wordsworth, at least in *The Prelude,* does not have a family to relate to or move away from.) *In Memoriam*'s first Christmas is the most deeply conflicted, symbolized in the punning status of the wreaths the family weaves for house and church, at once funereal and mockingly festive, a "vain pretence of gladness." It is a conflict with a very localized setting, in the close village network of the south wolds. The Christmas bells that answer each other are "four voices of four hamlets round / From far and near, or mead and moor," and Tennyson resents how much these "merry merry bells of Yule" still rule his "troubled spirit," "for they controlled me when a boy" (section 28). Provincial origins, like family responsibilities, are here, at the end of *In Memoriam*'s first segment, both coercive and in some degree resented; the Christmas games are "vain pretence of gladness" (section 30).

By the second Christmas, more briefly narrated, the family has repressed its grief, but Tennyson himself stands half outside the process of regional recuperation. He now sees the revival of "our ancient games" as perhaps saving fictions. The "mimic pictures" of the tableaux are valued because the actors are alive and not the statues they pretend; the central synedoche is a game of blindman's bluff, or, as Tennyson threateningly calls it, "hoodman's [i.e., hangman's] blind," where a seeing subject willingly makes himself unable to see for the sake of familial cohesion, but still stands ready to strike or make captive unpredictably (section 78).[18]

And with the third Christmas, the poem's decentering from Lincolnshire and family origin has become literalized, with the Tennysons' move from Somersby to High Beech. Now a single unfamiliar Essex church replaces the four close wold hamlets; "these are not the bells I know":

> Like strangers' voices here they sound
>   In lands where not a memory strays
>   Nor landmark breathes of other days
> But all is new unhallowed ground.
>
> (104.8-12).

The father's grave is left behind, the laurels and holly are left unwreathed, and as for family Christmas games, "change of place, like growth of time, / Has broke the bond of dying use" (105.11-12). "Use," "bond," and "dying" are all uncomfortable puns—Tennyson's relocation has broken not just a link but a restriction, which is of declining utility as well being a vanishing folk custom, even though the games had served well enough in previous years to help the family cope with dying. The Christmas dawn that comes this third year brings not a ritually regenerated family circle, but "rising worlds" (105.24-25), the end of Ptolemaic localism, and the wild unfamiliar bells of the famous new year ring in not just a Maurice-an-Christian Socialist millennium, but quite explicitly "ring out false pride in *place* and blood" (106.21; my italics).

The *locus classicus* for **In Memoriam** as an elegy of place must, of course, be the three-canto sequence about leaving Somersby, sections 100-102:

> I climb the hill: from end to end
> Of all the landscape underneath,
> I find no place that does not breathe
> Some gracious memory of my friend;
>
> No gray old grange, or lonely fold,
> Or low morass and whispering reed,
> Or simple stile from mead to mead,
> Or sheepwalk up the windy wold;
>
> . . . . .
>
> But each has pleased a kindred eye,
> And each reflects a kindlier day;
> And, leaving these, to pass away,
> I think once more he seems to die
>
> (100.1-20).

What is striking in light of this theme is the duality of Tennyson's parting—is it Somersby and Lincolnshire that is to pass away, become uncared for and forgotten with the Tennysons' departure, or is it Tennyson who passes away, in some sense dies, as "year by year the landscape grow[s] / Familiar to the stranger's child," and "year by year our memory fades / From all the circle of the hills" (101.19-20, 23-24)?

This basic narrative of displacement is straightforward enough, but it tends to be misinterpreted by assimilation to either Romantic or Arnoldian views of geographical origin. Romantics would have Tennyson internalize Lincolnshire, Arnoldians transcend it, but he does neither. The simple reading is, of course, to treat Somersby as symbol and surrogate for Hallam himself, and to see the departure from local attachment, the shift of perspective to an astronomical or geological breadth of vista, as a kind of philosophical distance or acceptance of Hallam's death, the relinquishing of individualized affections, rather like Wordsworth's mixed sense of loss in "Tintern Abbey" or the Immortality Ode. Another way of reading **In Memoriam** is to see the displacement theme as Tennyson's personal inscription of the fundamental nineteenth-century Carlylean or sociological shift, from *gemeinschaft* to *gesellschaft,* from the close nexus of the rural community to the alienated individualism of the Victorian city, as for instance in the two Wimpole Street cantos, sections 7 and 119, as Tennyson comes to accept that dawn returns even in a Hallamless London, not just in the nostalgic gloaming of a Lincolnshire garden (section 95). Or, thirdly, one might read the poem not primarily in terms of loss at all, but as the ultimately triumphant affirmation of poetry's capacity to transcend the merely temporal or contingent, to hear "a chirp of birds" and "smell the meadow" in a city street (section 119), to hold Hallam and Somersby and God harmless from nineteenth-century erosions, present forever in the poet's dream, in effect turning Lincolnshire, like Hardy's Wessex, into a country of the mind.

All these readings yield much from the poem, yet they seem to me to iron out too many of its provincial awkwardnesses. **In Memoriam**'s basic narrative of displacement is complicated by the way in which Somersby and Lincolnshire intertwine for Tennyson with at least two other aspects of provinciality—on the one hand the self-identification of social class and on the other the social enmeshment of courtship and marriage. Part of Tennyson's love-hate relation with Lincolnshire in the poem is his feeling of social—that is class—marginality everywhere else; not only did the Somersby Tennysons often feel disinherited, excluded, within Lincolnshire society by the wealth and aristocratic pretensions of the Tennyson D'Eyncourts of Bayons, but, with the exception of the Etonian Frederick, when they went up to Cambridge, they were in fact provincial, untutored, in clothing and behavior and ideas.[19] Part of Tennyson's investment in Hallam stemmed from Hallam's unchallengeable status as a gentleman, his acceptance of Tennyson as an equal, and his willingness to marry into Tennyson's family. With others even of his literary Cambridge friends, Tennyson felt out of place or as he once wrote self-mockingly to Monckton Milnes, "a barndoor fowl, among peacocks" (*Letters,* 1:146). The Cambridge cantos of **In Memoriam** glamorize Hallam only to express more clearly Tennyson's sense of subsequent awkwardness where he had once been accepted, for when he revisits Hallam's neo-Gothic college rooms, "another name was on the door" (section 87), and the young barbarians within are holding a wine party, not discussing Dante or the latest theological development. When Tennyson walks around London in the 1840s, and fantasizes on the feelings of "some divinely gifted man" who makes it all the way from humble village birth to ultimate political control, as "the centre of a world's desire" (section 64), his thoughts switch awkwardly back to the rejection felt by his surrogate's former village friends who still "plow with pain his native lea." If Romanticism was for both authors and readers a kind of erasure of social rank, an imaginative self-ennoblement, Tennyson was a rather fearful, partial Romantic, who, even when he gained literal lordliness, sat on the crossbenches without serious involvement in power. From leaving Lincolnshire till his gazetting as Laureate, Tennyson's class identity was uncertain, unpredictable, almost as changeable as his myriad temporary addresses through the 1840s, in rented rooms or as a self-invited guest with friends.

The other complication to *In Memoriam*'s basic displacement narrative is marriage or kinship. Lincolnshire is associated for Tennyson with courtship. In marrying Emily Sellwood, the lawyer's daughter from the local market town of Horncastle, Tennyson "married back" into the provincial society he had left, marrying indeed his brother Charles's sister-in-law. A Lincolnshire historian, Christopher Sturman, has recently been documenting from local newspapers the extent of Tennyson's Lincolnshire dance-going in the 1830s, and his other known flirtations of the period—Rosa Baring, Sophy Rawnsley—were both Lincolnshire girls.[20] Hallam had been going to marry into this Lincolnshire society, not just into Tennyson's family. Engagement to Emily Tennyson gave Hallam a place to shake off the dust and steam of town.

The poem's movement is not only toward a transcendent spiritual idealism, but toward marriage, from elegy to epithalamium, and this movement complicates Tennyson's account of having to leave Lincolnshire, the nexus of family. There are, in fact, two marriages in the poem, but neither of them is set at Somersby, and neither supplants the initial bereavement by providing either Emily Tennyson or Tennyson himself with a Hallam-substitute.[21] The first marriage section (97-98) reacts to Charles and Louise Tennyson-Turner's honeymoon trip up the Rhine and to Vienna, where Arthur Hallam died. The very name provokes Tennyson to provincial denunciation of the evils of continental immorality:

> I have not seen, I will not see
>   Vienna; rather dream that there,
>   A treble darkness, Evil haunts
> The birth, the bridal.
>
> (98.11-14)

One might compare this with Tennyson's Podsnappish comments on French or Irish politics, the "red fool-fury of the Seine" or the "blind hysterics of the Celt" (127.7; 109.15). He falls back into dialect for the denunciation; in Vienna, he says "a thousand wants *gnarr* at the heels of men." One of his separations from Hallam is his wondering rejection here of Hallam's own expressed preference for Viennese society over that of any other "mother town" (98.16-17, 20-32).

The second major marriage section, the Epilogue, makes the point most clearly. Many readings of *In Memoriam* center the poem in the visionary experience of section 95, a healing and transforming mystical escape from Somersby into a spirit world. *In Memoriam* ends quite differently if we confront the entire conclusion, the epithalamium for Edmund Lushington's marriage to Cecilia Tennyson in 1842; from a Lincolnshire perspective, or as a resolution of the poem's bereavements, this epilogue is a marriage of the wrong sister to the wrong man, neither Hallam nor Tennyson, in the wrong church, treading on the wrong graves. As Timothy Peltason points out, the epilogue introduces a calculated gap in the time scheme of the poem—following the basic three-year sequence, we are now told it is three-times-three years since Hallam's death.[22] One might add that this same phrase three-times-three is dissociated from Hallam's death to signify the cheers at the wedding breakfast, and Tennyson must now accept not the reconciling communion chalice of Somersby church but the alien farming grape of Eastern France, champagne. The marriage theme in the poem, from beginning to end, leaves bereavement unresolved, with Tennyson always the groomsman and never the groom. The epilogue's final elegiac moonclad landscape is not in Lincolnshire but geographically indistinct, with towers and friths and mountains, and it resolves nothing. At the final marriage breakfast, Tennyson is an awkward outsider to other people's recentering of their lives. His final thought of place is of displacement; even the whole creation "moves" and its destination is far off.

What I have been trying to suggest through this rereading of *In Memoriam* is that Tennyson's greatness is in some way related to his self-consciousness in the 1830s and 1840s of provinciality, the post-Ptolemaic consciousness that one's own origin or center of values is not equally central to others. Of course, Tennyson's literal transmutation of the Romantic valorization of poetic place stands for me as a metaphor of other poetic elements where the quarrel between Romantic essentialism and post-structuralist subversion has, I think, been too one-sided. Significantly, the leading postmodern Tennyson critic, Alan Sinfield, has to reread Tennyson's poem of the early 1830s about staying in the provinces, in Lincolnshire, rather than following his brother and the Romantic poets to Italy: "You ask me why, though ill at ease, / Within this region I subsist" (*Poems,* 1:531). In its origins, this is a defensively provincial poem about resisting the cultural centripetalism of classical tradition, but Sinfield reads the poem instead as Tennyson's privileging of metropolitan, imperialist British culture over the marginalized exoticism of the third world (p. 39). Tennyson's geographic center, like his personal centering, was always more problematic than that; the dissemination of value from the known landscapes of his youth to the dispersed sites of his adult experience left him not with a new idealist confidence or modernist cosmopolitanism, but awkwardly self-conscious about the roots of his adult identity.

What is grossly and literally evident about the Tennysonian topographical displacement is also true metaphorically about more malleable aspects of his poetry—its cultural and literary rootings, its political instincts, its religious grounding. Tennyson's rueful, awkward, self-conscious provinciality set up a continuing paradigm for much that is best in later British poetry—in Hardy, and Larkin, and Heaney. It is a paradigm that other traditionally privileged cultures might do well to examine as their Romantic-idealist national identities are called into question by the dislocations of world economics, and by new consciousness of competing cultural values. In a sense, we are all provincials now, but Tennyson was one of the first to write provincial self-consciousness into the literary canon.

Notes

1. *Letters of Alfred Lord Tennyson,* ed. Cecil Y. Lang and Edgar F. Shannon, Jr., 3 vols. (Cambridge: Belknap Press of Harvard Univ. Press, 1980-87), 1:166 (hereafter *Letters*). Research for this essay was supported by a summer fellowship from the National Endowment for the Humanities.

2. The best general treatment of Tennyson's Lincolnshire background is Philip Collins' lecture, *Tennyson, Poet of Lincolnshire* (Lincoln: Tennyson Society, 1984); cf. also Sir Charles Tennyson, *Alfred Tennyson and Somersby* (Lincoln: Tennyson Society, 1962; rev. ed., 1974), and note 8 below.

3. See Robin Gilmour, "Regional and Provincial in Victorian Literature," in R. P. Draper, ed., *The Literature of Region and Nation* (New York: St. Martin's Press, 1989), pp. 51-60; Ronald Blythe, "An Inherited Perspective," in his *Characters and their Landscapes* (San Diego: Harcourt Brace Jovanovich, 1984), pp. 1-13; Gillian Tindall, *Countries of the Mind: The Meaning of Place to Writers* (London: Hogarth Press, 1991); Jeremy Hooker, *The Poetry of Place* (Manchester: Carcanet, 1982).

4. Sir Francis Doyle, "Provincial Poetry," in his *Lectures delivered before the University of Oxford, 1868* (London, 1869).

5. Seamus Heaney, "The Regional Forecast," in Draper, p. 13.

6. Edward de Soja, *Postmodern Geographies: The Reassertion of Space in Critical Social Theory* (London: Verso, 1989), pp. 4, 2, 1.

7. David Simpson, "Being There?: Literary Criticism, Localism, and Local Knowledge," *CritQ* [*Critical Quarterly*] 35, no. 3 (1993): 3-17, discussing Clifford Geertz, *Local Knowledge* (New York: Basic Books, 1983). For an historian's critique of localism, see Michael O'Brien, "On Transcending the Mollusc: Cosmopolitanism and Historical Discourse," *Gettysburg Review*, 1, no. 3 (1988): 457-468. Simpson draws attention to two interesting literary explanations of the locality-history parallel: Vincent P. Pecora, "The Limits of Local Knowledge," in H. Aram Veeser, ed., *The New Historicism* (London: Routledge, 1989), pp. 243-276, and Leah S. Marcus, *Puzzling Shakespeare: Local Reading and its Discontents* (Berkeley: Univ. of California Press, 1988).

8. William White, *History Gazeteer and Directory of Lincolnshire* (Sheffield: Independent Office, 1856), pp. 724-733, shows no carriers to Somersby or Bag Enderby, carriers twice weekly to Salmonby and Hagworthingham, three times for Ormsby, and daily from Tetford. For traditional topographical comment, see, for example, William Howitt, "Alfred Tennyson," in his *Homes and Haunts of the Most Eminent British Poets* (London: Richard Bentley, 1847), 2:452-470; Drummond Rawnsley, "Lincolnshire Scenery and Character as Illustrated by Mr. Tennyson," *Macmillan's Magazine* 29 (December 1873): 140-144, repr. in Hardwicke D. Rawnsley, *Memories of the Tennysons* (Glasgow: James MacLehose, 1900), pp. 185-200; J. Cuming Walters, *In Tennyson Land* (London: George Redway, 1890); Alfred J. Church, *The Laureate's Country: A Description of Places Connected with the Life of Alfred Lord Tennyson* (London: Seeley, 1891); G. G. Napier, *The Homes and Haunts of Alfred Lord Tennyson, Poet Laureate* (Glasgow: James MacLehose, 1892); Helen Allingham and Arthur Paterson, *The Homes of Tennyson* (London: Adam and Charles Black, 1905); Willingham F. Rawnsley, "Tennyson and Lincolnshire," in Hallam, Lord Tennyson, ed., *Tennyson and his Friends* (London: Macmillan, 1911), pp. 8-32, and the same author's "Somersby and the Tennysons," in his *Highways and Byways in Lincolnshire* (London: Macmillan, 1914), pp. 341-357; and Oliver Huckel, *Through England with Tennyson: A Pilgrimage to Places Associated with the Great Laureate* (New York: Crowell, 1913). Recent examples include *A Guide to Tennyson's Lincolnshire* (Skegness: C. H. Major, 1973); *Tennyson's Lincolnshire: An Illustrated Guide* (n.p.: Manpower Services Commission for the Tennyson Society, 1985); and Prisca Furlong, *Aesthetic East Lindsey Treasured by Tennyson and Modern Man* (Louth: Imp-Art Publications, 1989). For a recent academic visitor's experience, see Patrick J. McCarthy, "Tennyson Country: The Past Present," *VIJ* [*Victorians Institute Journal*] 21 (1993): 143-153.

9. *Letters,* 3:410; *Midsummer Night's Dream,* 5.1.14-17; cf. *Letters,* 3:432 ("you follow a blind guide in 'Tennyson Land'"). See also Hallam Tennyson's protest against "The Localizing Craze," *Athenaeum*, February 15, 1890, p. 214 (and *Letters,* 3:412-413, and Tennyson's own earlier complaint that "one localises it here and then another localises it there, and they pin me down to this spot and this meaning, till they make me almost sorry I had written at all," quoted by Collins, p. 11, from Rawnsley, *Memories of the Tennysons*, pp. 112-113.

10. P. E. Hall, *Tennyson Research Bulletin*, 1, no. 1 (1967), item C3.

11. Charles Tennyson, *Alfred Tennyson* (London: Macmillan, 1949; reissued 1968), pp. 259-261; *Letters*, 2:340, 343, 345.

12. Baron Tennyson, of Aldworth, in the county of Sussex, and of Freshwater, in the Isle of Wight (*Letters*, 3:278 n. 1).

13. *Letters*, 1:246; see similar refusal in 1850 to Sophy Rawnsley Elmhirst, *Letters*, 2:346.

14. On Septimus Tennyson's need to leave Somersby, see *Letters*, 1:106, quoted in Sir Charles Tennyson and Hope Dyson, *The Tennysons: Background to Ge-

nius (London: Macmillan, 1974), p. 80; see also Alfred's comment on Edward Tennyson, in *Letters,* 1:59-60.

15. *The Poems of Tennyson,* ed. Christopher Ricks, 3 vols. (Berkeley: Univ. of California Press, 1987), 2:330 (hereafter *Poems*).

16. The most convenient treatments are probably G. Edward Campion, *Lincolnshire Dialects* (Boston: Richard Kay, 1976), and the same author's *A Tennyson Dialect Glossary* (Lincoln: The Lincolnshire Association, 1969), but see also Jabez Good, *A Glossary or Collection of Words . . . current in East Lincolnshire,* 3rd ed. (Long Sutton: H. Pulford, n.d.; repr. Skegness: C. H. Major, 1973); Tennyson's own accent is described by Charles Tennyson, "On Reading Tennyson," in his *Six Tennyson Essays* (London: Cassell, 1954), pp. 188-197, and Donald S. Hair, *Tennyson's Language* (Toronto: Univ. of Toronto Press, 1991), pp. 64-66.

17. For the servants leaving Somersby, see *Letters,* 1:61 (May 18, 1831); on Rosa Baring, Ralph Wilson Rader, *Tennyson's Maud: The Biographical Genesis* (Berkeley: Univ. of California Press, 1963).

18. This domestic game should not be confused with the Lincolnshire variant of street football, the "Haxey Hood Game"; see Mrs. Gutch and Mabel Peacock, *Examples of Printed Folk-Lore Concerning Lincolnshire* (London: David Nutt for the Folk-Lore Society, 1908), pp. 267-274; or Ethel Rudkin, *Lincolnshire Folklore* (Gainsborough: Belton, 1936), pp. 90-97.

19. On Tennyson in Cambridge, see Robert Bernard Martin, *Tennyson: The Unquiet Heart* (Oxford: Clarendon Press, 1980), pp. 52-54. For a less sympathetic account of class in *In Memoriam,* see Alan Sinfield, *Alfred Tennyson* (Oxford: Blackwell, 1986), esp. pp. 117-122, 149-150.

20. Christopher Sturman, "Arthur Eden and Harrington Hall," *TRB* [*Tennyson Research Bulletin*] 5, no. 3 (1989): 130-143, and also Martin, *Tennyson,* pp. 210-228.

21. On the marriage theme, see Christopher Ricks, *Tennyson* (Berkeley: Univ. of California Press, 1989), p. 206.

22. Timothy Peltason, *Reading* In Memoriam (Princeton: Princeton Univ. Press, 1985), p. 164.

Gerhard Joseph (essay date 1998)

SOURCE: Joseph, Gerhard. "Producing the 'Far-Off Interest of Tears': Tennyson, Freud, and the Economics of Mourning." *Victorian Poetry* 36, no. 2 (summer 1998): 123-33.

[*In the following essay, Joseph examines loss in* In Memoriam *through a Freudian lens, focusing on several sections in which the critic illustrates Tennyson's use of economic terminology to express grief.*]

I live, live intensely, and am fed by life, and my value, whatever it might be, is my own kind of expression of that. Art makes life, makes interest, makes importance.

Henry James, to H. G. Wells

Art makes interest; it is a way of investing something that might be called life or experience—that is a species of risk.

Adam Phillips, *The Beast in the Nursery*[1]

Like Alice's Humpty Dumpty with his self-interested definition of "glory," when I make a word do a lot of work, but especially when that work is double if not downright duplicitous, I try to pay it extra.[2] My coinage for such interesting—to me, at any rate—labor may be thought of as a species of interest I am willing to pay because, to adapt the Henry James of my first epigraph, I have been fed by life in a transformative fashion.[3]

Such a reiteration of "interest" in its various senses is by way of prologue to an argument that will eventually belabor and put a rather fierce pressure[4] upon the phrase "far-off interest of tears," both within and without its Tennysonian context in the opening of **In Memoriam.** Let me therefore pay and say a few more words about my consuming—and thus consumerist—interest in the production of interest. Here again and in Humpty-Dumpty fashion, I conflate the terms consumption and production as a literary critic's ludic response to the economic theorist's penchant for keeping the two terms or at least their referents apart. For I want to allude—or rather say that a poet like Tennyson can allude—simultaneously to the concept of interest in its productive financial and its consumptionist affective sense.[5]

By the productive financial sense, I of course mean the economic mechanism by which a debt or a loss may over time produce new money or value; and by the consumptionist affective sense, I mean the emotional appeal through which the death of a friend may or may not sustain the long-term attention or interest of a poet, an extended literary text like **In Memoriam** hold the interest of the individual reader—or for that matter sustain the interest of an interpretive community far-removed in time from its moments of authorial invention.[6]

Historically (or rather pocket historically), the rise in social value of the two kinds of interest, the financial and the affective, roughly parallel each other. For just as the charging of interest in the financial sense moved from being sinfully usurious, at least in most instances, during the Middle Ages to emerge as a normative means for the production of new capital under Renaissance capitalism,[7] so in what Albert O. Hirschman in *The Passions and the Interests: Political Arguments for Capitalism Before its Triumph* has called a late Renaissance Kuhnian paradigm shift, with Machiavelli as a seminal figure, interest and self-interest as affect displaced the passions and reason as the mainspring of all human behavior, including the creation of and response to aesthetic objects.[8] From such a perspective, an apparently opposed Victorian "interestedness" (or earnestness) and Arnoldian "disinterestedness" would merely express this newer affective dispensation in different registers.

In light of the foregoing, I would want the reader to understand that whenever I pun, or suggest that Tennyson puns, by invoking financial and affective interest simultaneously, I have the above twin meliorizations in mind as etymological and thus historical contexts for Victorian usage. For "etymologies," as Jonathan Culler has rightly said, "give us respectable puns, endowing pun-like effects with the authority of science and even of truth."[9]

After his wife's death in 1825, George Tennyson asked his grandson Alfred, the sixteen-year-old would-be poet, to write an elegy for his grandmother—and rewarded him with ten shillings, along with the prediction, "There, that is the first money you will have earned by your poetry, and, take my word for it, it will be the last."[10] In recounting the well-known incident, Robert Bernard Martin, Tennyson's most authoritative recent biographer, comments that while the elegy, if it was ever written, has disappeared, "that is less to be regretted than the loss of Alfred's reply" (p. 44). Martin is of course right as to specifics, but the point of the anecdote is that Tennyson's entire career constitutes a reply to his grandfather's sneer at the impracticality of a poetic vocation and what it might "earn." For as the shrewd bargainer with a series of largely compliant publishers,[11] as the master of the imposing estates of Aldworth and Farringford, as the cherished friend of the titled and the well-to-do, the laureate and eventually ennobled Alfred Lord Tennyson managed to amass the kind of material fortune from his craft that no poet before or since has been able to match.

Such a lifelong accumulation of money and property is no doubt tied to Tennyson's sense of early deprivation, a thesis confirmed by Martin's index with its unusually large number of page entries under "financial matters and fear of poverty" (p. 636). To summarize a familiar story, the situation at the Somersby rectory during Tennyson's youth was quite desperate, with his father, George Clayton Tennyson, having to provide for a family of eleven children on a rural minister's salary. The sense of dire need was intensified both by the grandfather's disinheritance of the family in favor of the father's younger brother Charles and by the father's subsequent early death, events that further deepened Alfred's financial insecurity. That radical feeling of dispossession led to the break of the engagement with Emily Sellwood and to a virtually homeless, nomadic existence between 1832 and 1850. In that latter *annus mirabilis* of Tennyson's life the publication of ***In Memoriam*** and the achievement of the laureateship rescued him from actual deprivation and thus also made marriage to Emily financially viable. But even later in life when there was every ostensible reason to feel comfortable, Tennyson would continue to plead, if not quite poverty, at least an unusual monetary anxiety, for he sincerely believed that his monetary demands were largely incomprehensible to outsiders, and that he was perpetually on the brink of financial ruin. Indeed, one of the least attractive qualities of this "best-paid literary man in England" (Martin, p. 377) was his continuing willingness to take large sums of charity from others, Edward FitzGerald and his Aunt Russell for instance, and his keeping until his death in 1892 the annual government pension of 200 pounds originally bestowed in 1845 and intended for relief from financial misery to struggling artists (Martin, pp. 292-293, 376-377).

As many of us might well testify from our own lives, anxiety about money is often the outward sign of a more deep-seated existential dread. And I would suggest that this is especially the case with the "blackblooded" Tennyson, the poet whose recurring poetic subject is a free-floating melancholia of which the material concerns are biographical expressions. In W. H. Auden's famous slur, Tennyson is the "stupidest" of the English poets because he is so thoroughly fixated on the one plangent thing: "There was little about melancholia that he didn't know," says Auden. "There was little else that he did."[12] As Douglas Bush's more sympathetically phrased version of the critical truism goes, Tennyson is the most Virgilian of the English poets, the one who most persistently gives us the *lacrimae rerum*, the *Aeneid*'s tears for passing things.[13] For it is not merely the depth of Tennyson's mining of what in **"Tears, Idle Tears"** he calls "divine despair" that makes him (rather than Matthew Arnold, his only male competitor for the title) the Victorian poet of loss and abandonment, but also the wide range of losses that he mourns in a coverage that is all but systematic—from private to public to metaphysical loss, from erotic to political and military failure, from the death of a son or a beloved friend or a national hero like Wellington to, as the terrible voices of Sorrow and Nature in ***In Memoriam*** would have it, the coming death of the human species, the earth and its very sun.

As a sign of such an all-consuming groundswell of doom, the metaphor of monetary loss and gain, of cash-nexus exchange, might on the face of it seem reductive and materially squalid, a prosaic entry from the accountant's ledger. And yet Tennyson's poetry frequently confronts the issue of all-pervasive loss in precisely such crass financial terms, nowhere more so than in his masterpiece on the subject of universal loss and possible recompense, ***In Memoriam***. Such an economic framing of the matter occurs at the very opening of the poem, in Section 1:

> I held it truth, with him who sings
>   To one clear harp in divers tones,
>   That men may rise on stepping-stones
> Of their dead selves to higher things.
>
> But who shall so forecast the years
>   And find in loss a gain to match?
>   Or reach a hand through time to catch
> The far-off interest of tears?[14]

If one is looking for a microcosmic moment (or Diltheyan "impression-point") to forecast the rambling, well-nigh interminable structure of ***In Memoriam*** as a whole, this will do as well as any other, especially since Hallam finally does "touch" (l. 34) the speaker at the poem's emotional climax, the mystical vision of Section 95. While there are other allusions along the way, Tennyson most directly picks up the economic theme in Sections 80 to 84: as over against an "aristocratic preserve of silence" with which he had enshrouded Hallam in Section 75 and elsewhere, he now speaks the "language of [capitalist] finance and manufacture," the reserve of his other, his "industrial and entrepreneurial constituency," exchanging the "living death of aristocratic silence" for the "burgeoning recovery of [bourgeois] capital," in Herbert Tucker's words.[15] In the first of these economic Sections (80), the speaker, summoning forth Arthur Hallam,

> make[s] a picture in the brain;
> I hear the sentence that he speaks;
> He bears the burthen of the weeks
> But turns his burthen into gain.
>
> His credit thus shall set me free;
> And, influence-rich to soothe and save,
> Unused example from the grave
> Reach out dead hands to comfort me.

That is, imagining how Hallam would have reacted if he, the speaker, had died first, he learns from Hallam, an "unused example from the grave," how the emotional economy by which loss is turned into gain works. By what Tucker so felicitously terms a "miracle of emotional capitalism" (p. 392) the speculating mourner is thus able to tap the unused credit of the dead Hallam for his own gain, "unused" because Hallam's life had not accumulated its acturially normal span of days.

But while we can say with a certain confidence how money accrues short- or long-term interest and how credit may facilitate the process of turning loss into gain (no need for talk of an economic "miracle" here), within mourning the transcendence of loss in order to make room for a new object of desire is deeply mysterious. Or so Sigmund Freud, another nineteenth-century representative poet in his wholesale reliance upon the economic metaphor, assures us. As Freud says in a great passage from the essay "Mourning and Melancholia," when the loved object no longer exists,

> people never willingly abandon a libidinal position, not even, indeed, when a substitute is already beckoning to them. This opposition can be so intense that a turning away from reality takes place and a clinging to the object through the medium of hallucinatory wishful psychosis. Normally, respect for reality gains the day. Nevertheless its orders cannot be obeyed at once. They are carried out bit by bit, at great expense of time and cathectic energy, and in the meantime the existence of the lost object is psychically prolonged. Each single one of the memories and expectations in which the libido is bound to the object is brought up and hypercathected, and detachment of the libido is accomplished in respect of it. *Why this compromise by which the command of reality is carried out piecemeal should be so extraordinarily painful is not at all easy to explain in terms of economics.* (Italics added)[16]

That is, the compromising work of mourning involves a highly duplicitous act of memorialization as the alternative impulses of remembering and forgetting ensue over time: I say "duplicitous" because the ego, in its desire for self-preservation, remembers, according to Freud, in order to forget, prolongs the attachment in order to detach. "The lost object," says Christopher Craft in a wonderful application of the passage to the homoerotics of *In Memoriam,* "thus suffers a thousand posthumous deaths at the now murderous hands of the mourner" who, however stealthily, prepares to bind himself to a new object in the chain of recuperative substitutions we call life.[17] No wonder *In Memoriam* is shot through with shame at abandoning the object, is written by the creeping "guilty thing" of Section 7.

But the sentence I would like to single out for emphasis is the climactic one in which Freud expresses puzzlement about the process: "Why this compromise by which the command of reality is carried out piecemeal should be so extraordinarily painful is not at all easy to explain in terms of economics." Why should Freud insist upon explaining the gradual conquest of the mourner's pain "in terms of economics"? Whatever the answer to that question (and I'm not sure I have one), it is no doubt the case that from *The Interpretation of Dreams* onward, Freud tended to define psychic processes as an elaborate economic system—and one particularly capitalist in nature: as he says in the *Interpretation,* "A daytime thought may very well play the part of *entrepreneur* for a dream, but the *entrepreneur,* who, as people say, has the idea and initiative to carry it out, can do nothing without capital; he needs a *capitalist* who can afford the outlay, and the capitalist who provides the psychical outlay for the dream is invariably and indisputably, whatever may be the thoughts of the previous day, *a wish from the unconscious*" (*Interpretation of Dreams,* 5:561; italics in original). Freud would go on to define all mental operations but especially the operation of the unconscious as a balance of payments, of capitalist loss and gain, within a psychic marketplace. He thus sees the relationship between the sexual instincts and the instincts of self-preservation as "one of those considerations which deserve to be described as *economic,*" and, of the sources of symptom formation, he insists that "a merely *dynamic* view of mental processes is insufficient; an *economic* line of approach is also needed" ("Some Thoughts on Development and Regression—Aetiology," *Standard Edition* 16:356; "The Paths to the Formation of Symptoms," 16:374). It thus makes sense that in "Mourning and Melancholia" he should wish to express the gradual process of object substitution within mourning in economic terms—and be puzzled by the gap between the experience of intense pain and the positivist language of political economy, that most "dismal" of nineteenth-century sciences.[18]

I thus find a prefiguration of that puzzlement in the mourner of *In Memoriam*'s opening question about whether he can find an interest that will accrue from Hallam's loss, since there is a parallel to be drawn between the interest-bearing work of mourning and that of the elegiac poem: the transformation of loss into gain in some interesting elegiac poems is, one might say, based upon the principle of short-term interest while in others the interest is "far-off": the initial meaninglessness of the weeper's tears in **"Tears, Idle Tears,"** for instance, generates a meaning, the epiphanic recognition of the abstract idea or *Sondergott*,[19] Death in Life, in the lyric's closing line. But how "idle" or meaningless can those tears have been if it takes only four short stanzas to explicate their meaning fully? Their "interest" is thus comparatively short-term—and in a rather literal-minded sense, the interest of tears can only be short term since a mourner's tear ducts can generate only a limited number of tears at a given outburst of a sense of grief. Conversely, the very temporal/spatial length of **In Memoriam** and of the implied experience behind it is arguably the most important thing about that elegy: the fact that the mourner goes through so many permutations of remembering and forgetting, gets so many non-Hallam related issues involved in his rambling structure, and demonstrates that the loss cannot be easily overcome—all of these matters argue that the loss-into-gain economics depends upon the expenditure of a good deal of time and psychic energy before a *"far-off* interest" may be available to the writer—and presumably to the reader who will, if he so chooses, maintain his imaginative investment in the poem until its very end. If the mourner's work doesn't make interest in the reader come alive, he just won't read on; he'll withdraw his investment and cut his loss of time.[20] But there is a pretty good chance that the reader will stay interested, since of all the affects interest is the one that is the most readily sustainable because it doesn't require the intensity and therefore undergo the immediate eclipse to which, say, fear or disgust or joy are prone (as Keats reminds us with respect to a joy "whose hand is ever at his lips / Bidding adieu" in the "Ode on Melancholy").[21]

At any rate, in the elegiac poem as in the mourning upon which it is based, the fact that mourning (and not merely instinctive immediate tears) is indeed what's at work depends upon the evidence of elaborate staying power, the generation of far-off rather than merely short-term interest: for in his *Three Essays on the Theory of Sexuality* Freud proposed that the object was merely "soldered" on to the instinct, that our primary commitment was to our desire and not to its target, and thus the ego had a great potential for promiscuous mobility, moving from object to object with relative ease. Freud thus, according to Adam Phillips, embraced the perseverance of mourning with great relief, since it seemed to suggest that the ego was wedded to its relationship with loved (and hated) others in a deeply conservative way. "Mourning," says Phillips, "is immensely reassuring because it convinces us of something we might otherwise easily doubt: our attachment to others. The protracted painfulness of mourning confirms something that psychoanalysis had put into question: how intransigently devoted we are to people we love and hate. Despite the evidence of our dreams, our capacity for infinite substitution, [for merely short-term interest, that is] is meagre,"[22] or so the prolonged act of mourning assures us. And part of the appeal of **In Memoriam** is its demonstration that this is indeed the case—that the parade of mourning's pain can go on virtually without end (or at any rate for 131 meandering cantos and for at least three Christmases) and thus generate a far-off interest for a Tennyson, whose favorite expression, incidentally, was "far, far away." To be sure, that expression is usually associated with his "passion of the past" rather than with the distanced future he imagines in **In Memoriam,** but the long perspectives of retrospect and prolepsis clearly touch each other within his melancholic imagination.

Still, for both Freud and Tennyson the process of painful, piecemeal transformation is something of a mystery: for all his theoretical insight, Freud remains puzzled about how to find a foundational language for the experience of mourning, about whether or not his systemic economic metaphor is the appropriate one—and, if not, to what alternative figural system he might go. What, furthermore, is the evolutionary value of mourning? Likewise, as I've quoted Tucker as having said, Tennyson's metamorphosis of the debt burden of "loss" into far-off "gain" is a *"miracle"* of emotional capitalism, that is, is not to be explained in the matter-moulded forms of speech, whose epistemological efficacy **In Memoriam** at various points throws into doubt. In a "capitalization of the unconscious" that unites nineteenth-century literature and psychology,[23] both Tennyson and Freud may thus employ a language that seems to ground a deeply mysterious mourning in something as relatively solid, worldly, and familiar as the political economy of their day: the artist and the analyst are not thus far from what we might call the Victorian "materialist."

To summarize then, Freud tries to explain the pain of mourning "in terms of economics," in terms of a coherent system, to return to my key sentence from "Mourning and Melancholia"; the no-nonsense nineteenth-century positivist in him believes that his "system" is grounded in the experiential real. But, of course, the closet poet in him, as distinct from the self-advertised would-be scientist, knows that the unconscious has no systemic language, "economic" or otherwise, and that the laying out of a comprehensive pattern for the unconscious is always something of a hubristic absurdity. Thus a poet as such, like Tennyson, is more consistently in touch with the ungrounded, recursively metaphorical nature of what he thinks and says. The poet knows that if he uses a given trope, it is one of many, a contingent thing that will soon give way . . . to another trope, as **In Memoriam** demonstrates in its accumulative complexity. He more explicitly than the scientist or social scientist betrays the ever-receding "as if" remainder (itself a mathematico-economic trope) of what he half reveals and half conceals in pursuit of affect—in pursuit of the heartfelt, tearful loss that he—and we—follow like a sinking star beyond the utmost bound of human interest.

Notes

1. The first epigraph comes from James's *Letters* (1984), as quoted by Adam Phillips, *The Beast in the*

Nursery: On Curiosity and Other Appetites (New York: Pantheon Books, 1998), p. 3; the second comes from pp. 5-6 of Phillips' book, a study of how the psychoanalyst "aims to restore the artist in the patient, the part of the person that makes interest despite, or whatever, the early environment" (p. 4).

2. Lewis Carroll, "Through the Looking Glass and What Alice Found There," in *Alice in Wonderland*, ed. Donald J. Gray (New York: Norton, 1971), p. 164.

3. James's notion of being fed by a life that he can transform into art is the jumping off point to the opening chapter, "The Interested Party," of Adam Phillips, *The Beast in the Nursery*. While the artist can make something especially interesting and interest-bearing of his life in his art, we ordinary people are generally also blessed with his ability to transform, "to mak[e] something of what we are given, even when we are merely making do" (p. 3). One of the reasons people go to psychoanalysis, according to Phillips, is that they are feeling undernourished, that they thus cannot generate interest in themselves and others, that everything feels flat, stale, and unprofitable.

4. The application of such pressure on a single phrase by which to read a work as long and complex as *In Memoriam* would be my version, for the purposes of this essay, of elaborating upon Wilhelm Dilthey's "impression-point" (*gefühlter Eindruckspunkt*), the single part of the whole gestalt around which the work of art articulates itself. (*Gesammelte Schriften* [Stuttgart, 1913-58], vols. V, VI [*Die geistige Welt*]). Frank Kermode, in *The Genesis of Secrecy* (New York: Harvard Univ. Press, 1979), uses the temporal "moment of interpretation" for the critic's, as over against Dilthey's artist's, spatial impression-point—and adds that a given work may have as many such moments or points as it has interpreters (p. 16).

5. This essay was originally given as a paper at a conference organized by the Society for Critical Exchange at the University of Exeter, July 23-26, 1998, on the interface of Literature and Economics. My point was thus a comparative one in the context of that disciplinary exchange: economic historians and theorists tend to separate production and consumption, at least diachronically, arguing that the classical political economists from Adam Smith to Marx emphasized production in their theories of value while Keynsians and post-Keynsians up to Baudrillard shifted that focus to consumption (although Regenia Gagnier, in "Culture and Economics," *Victorian Literature and Culture* 26 [1998]: 478, argues that the shift began to occur as early as 1871). Through the use of puns and other figural devices, poets like Tennyson, on the other hand, can conflate the terms and the referents behind them.

6. In a recent book entitled *Literary Interest* (Cambridge: Harvard Univ. Press, 1993) Steven Knapp tries to define what is unique to an "interest" that is idiosyncratically literary. He argues that literary interpretation is of necessity and always at odds with authorial intention, strictly speaking (sometimes radically so, as with his extended example of the Romantic reading of *Paradise Lost*). And it is this dialectic between the assumed authorial "inner" and the articulated interpretive "outer" that for Knapp generates the interest that is specifically literary. Thus, the "far-off interest" that Tennyson seems manifestly to have in mind, roughly speaking (which is the only way we can speak of authorial intention), is to affirm and solidify for himself and his readers a Hallam-affiliated Strong Son of God and belief in the immortality of the soul. But the interpretive long-term interest of *In Memoriam* over the years has of necessity been more various and of other orders—has been, say, in how the affirmed "trust" of the speaker is "faint" indeed, in how the poem's doubt, as T. S. Eliot suggested some time ago, is considerably stronger and more interesting than its faith.

7. See J. T. Noonan, *The Scholastic Analysis of Usury* (Cambridge: Harvard Univ. Press, 1957).

8. Albert O. Hirschman, *The Passions and the Interests: Political Arguments for Capitalism before its Triumph* (Princeton: Princeton Univ. Press, 1977): "As happens frequently with concepts that are suddenly thrust to the center of the stage . . . interest appeared so self-evident a notion that nobody bothered to define it precisely. Nor did anyone explain the place it occupied in relation to the two categories that had dominated the analysis of human motivation since Plato, namely, the passions on the one hand, and reason on the other. But it is precisely against the backdrop of this traditional dichotomy that the emergence of a third category in the late sixteenth and early seventeenth century can be understood. Once passion was deemed destructive and reason ineffectual, the view that human action could be exhaustively described by attribution to either one or the other meant an exceedingly somber outlook for humanity. A message of hope was therefore conveyed by the wedging of interest in between the two traditional categories of human motivation. Interest was seen to partake in effect of the better nature of each, as the passion of self-love upgraded and contained by reason, and as reason given direction and force by passion. The resulting hybrid form of human action was considered exempt from both the destructiveness of passion and the ineffectuality of reason" (pp. 43-44).

For a more strictly economic consideration of self-interest as "the soul of modern economic man" (p. 2), see Milton L. Myers, *The Soul of Modern Economic Man: Ideas of Self-Interest—Thomas Hobbes to Adam Smith* (Chicago: Univ. of Chicago Press, 1983).

9. "The Call of the Phoneme," in *On Puns: The Foundation of Letters,* ed. Jonathan Culler (London: Blackwell, 1988), pp. 2-3.

10. Anne Ritchie, *Records of Tennyson, Browning, and Ruskin,* 1892; as cited in Robert Bernard Martin, *Tennyson: The Unquiet Heart* (Oxford: Clarendon Press, 1980), p. 44.

11. See June Steffenson Hagen, *Tennyson and His Publishers* (University Park: Pennsylvania State Univ. Press, 1979).

12. W. H. Auden, *Selections from the Poems of Alfred Tennyson* (New York: Doubleday, 1944), p. x.

13. Douglas Bush, *Mythology and the Romantic Tradition in English Literature* (Cambridge: Harvard Univ. Press, 1937), pp. 227-228.

14. All citations of Tennyson's Poetry are from *The Poems of Tennyson,* ed. Christopher Ricks, 3 vols. (Berkeley: Univ. of California Press, 1987). Tracing the economic "far-off interest" back through an early line in the juvenilian *The Devil and the Lady,* Edward Young's *Night Thoughts,* and Shakespeare's *Rape of Lucrece* and *Richard the Third,* Ricks argues that Tennysonian allusion is itself an "interest which accures" to a wealth that has been bestowed upon him by past poets (and self-borrowing), "a various poetic inheritance with which he confronted our human inheritance: our inheriting the earth, and its being a dying earth" ("Tennyson Inheriting the Earth," in *Studies in Tennyson,* ed. Hallam Tennyson [London: Macmillan, 1981], p. 104).

15. Herbert F. Tucker, *Tennyson and the Doom of Romanticism* (Cambridge: Harvard Univ. Press, 1988), p. 391.

16. *Standard Edition of the Complete Psychological Works of Sigmund Freud,* ed. James Strachey (London: Hogarth Press and the Institute of Psychoanalysis, 1953-72). 14: 244-245.

17. Christopher Craft, "'Descend, and Touch, and Enter': Tennyson's Strange Manner of Address," in *Critical Essays on Alfred Lord Tennyson,* ed. Herbert F. Tucker (New York: G. K. Hall, 1993), p. 166.

18. For a work that seeks "to reaffirm the fundamental economic principle of psychoanalysis, and *that* in its most radical form" (p. 85) with respect to the problematics of sexuality, the ego, and the death drive, see Jean Laplanche, *Life and Death in Psychoanalysis,* trans. Jeffrey Mehlman (Baltimore: Johns Hopkins Univ. Press, 1976).

19. Leo Spitzer so calls the "particular god" in "'Tears, Idle Tears' Again," in *Critical Essays on the Poetry of Tennyson,* ed. John Killham (London: Routledge and Kegan Paul, 1960), p. 192.

20. Adam Phillips, *The Beast in the Nursery*: "Something is transformed—work is done on [the artist's experience]—in the service of making interest, sustaining curiosity, keeping one's appetite alive. . . . The writer's appetite has to incite the reader's appetite" (p. 6).

21. This point is made in *Affect, Imagery, Consciousness,* 4 vols. (New York: Springer, 1962-92) by Silvan Tomkins, a sociologist whose work has recently had a theoretical impact in literary studies because of Eve Kosofsky Sedgwick and Adam Frank's anthologizing and proselytizing in *Shame and Its Sisters: A Silvan Tomkins Reader* (Durham: Duke Univ. Press, 1995). Comparing interest-excitement to eight other affects he distinguishes (enjoyment-joy, surprise-startle, distress-anguish, fear-terror, shame-humiliation, contempt-disgust, and anger-rage), Tomkins argues that the relatively low intensity of interest makes it the most sustainable of the affects in the presence of complex objects (like the manifold implications of Arthur Hallam's death over several years) and accounts for its frequent, but also its sometimes intermittent, staying power. The section on interest appears on pp. 75-80 of *Shame and Its Sisters.*

22. Adam Phillips, *Terrors and Experts* (Cambridge: Harvard Univ. Press, 1996), p. 78.

23. Ronald Thomas, "Capitalizing the Unconscious: Nineteenth-Century Fictional Autobiography," *Dreams of Authority: Freud and the Fictions of the Unconscious* (Ithaca: Cornell Univ. Press, 1990), pp. 137-191.

Robert Bernard Hass (essay date 1998)

SOURCE: Hass, Robert Bernard. "The Mutable *Locus Amoenus* and Consolation in Tennyson's *In Memoriam,*" *SEL* 38, no. 4 (autumn 1998): 669-87.

[*In the following essay, Hass depicts* In Memoriam *as a pastoral elegy and focuses on Tennyson's use of* locus amoenus *to control his grief and find consolation.*]

If literary criticism judges the success of an elegy by the amount of consolation it can offer, then it is not surprising that Alfred Lord Tennyson's **In Memoriam** has been read in this century with a cautious skepticism. Although Tennyson's contemporaries praised the poem as a fine representation of Victorian confidence and religious faith,[1] most modern readers have had difficulty accepting the poem's "retreat" into Christian theology as well as Tennyson's belief that evolutionary forces impel all organic life toward higher, perfected types. Perhaps the most damaging assessments of **In Memoriam** came surprisingly from poets rather than critics. T. S. Eliot responded to Tennyson's masterpiece with a backhanded compliment, suggesting that the greatness of **In Memoriam** lay not in its consolation but in the "quality of its doubt."[2] W. H. Auden, too, was ambivalent about the poem, and although he praised **In Memoriam**'s melancholia, he considered Tennyson the "'stupidest of English poets.'"[3] What is perhaps most interesting about these assessments is that their authors were not so much reacting to Tennyson's poetry as they were to his stature as the supreme representative of an outdated, "genteel" tradition. In fact, in their efforts to revitalize language and "make it new," most twentieth-century poets failed to recognize that Tennyson's search for consolation shared affinities with their own later attempts to reconcile religious faith and twentieth-century pessimism.

Several commentators have amply demonstrated that *In Memoriam* exploits many conventions of the pastoral elegy.[4] Though the poem does not adhere strictly to the genre's traditional form, it does share the elegy's overall movement from lamentation to consolation and employs several of the genre's recurrent motifs, including the invocation to the muse, the memory of the deceased poet, the questioning of divine powers, and the *anagnorisis* and *apotheosis* that traditionally characterize the elegy's form.[5] Such generic distinctions have proven highly useful in studying *In Memoriam,* and, as my title suggests, I wish to extend those studies by exploring a distinct motif within the pastoral elegy—the *locus amoenus,* the pleasant or happy place—and show that Tennyson's appropriation of several different *loci* leads him to a startling epiphany: the knowledge that the production of new, imaginative conventions can lessen the threat of the harsh natural world and confer upon the poet a small measure of control in the face of natural determinism. By demonstrating that Tennyson continually shifts his poetic gaze to find or construct a new *locus amoenus,* I will argue that the consolation of *In Memoriam* depends not so much upon Tennyson's affirmations of the afterlife and perfected types, but rather upon the imaginative, pragmatic processes that make those affirmations possible.[6]

I

Although most scholars have referred to the *locus amoenus* as if it were a stable concept, the cultural assumptions informing it have dictated the elements it contains, and its emphases have changed significantly over the years. As Peter Sacks has argued, the origins of pastoral elegy can be traced historically to book 1 of Ovid's *Metamorphoses.*[7] In retelling the Greek myth of Pan and Syrinx, Ovid poses the fundamental question that all subsequent pastoral elegy attempts to answer: to what extent can art adequately compensate for the loss of someone dear? Ovid's account closely mirrors most Greek versions, but instead of focusing on the myth's obvious sexual imagery, Ovid concentrates on Pan's grief and how he alleviates it by preserving Syrinx's memory through art and music. Strategically placing the story next to the Apollo and Daphne episode, Ovid tells the story of how Pan rapaciously pursues the wood nymph, Syrinx, who is completely repulsed by the potential union. Refusing Pan's advances, Syrinx flees to the banks of Ladon and prays to the gods for help so that she does not have to drown herself. Just at the moment of union, Zeus answers Syrinx by transforming her into a musical instrument made of reeds:

> so, when Pan had caught her
> And thought he held a nymph, it was only reeds
> That yielded in his arms, and while he sighed,
> The soft air stirring in the reeds made also
> The echo of a sigh. Touched by this marvel,
> Charmed by the sweetness of the tone, he murmured
> *This much I have!* and took the reeds, and bound them
> With wax, a tall and shorter one together,
> And called them Syrinx still.[8]

As is the case with all poetic revisions, the most striking aspect of this passage is that Ovid uses tradition, as does Tennyson, not only as a source for subject material but also as a *locus* for poetic invention. In departing from most versions of the myth, Ovid transforms Pan from a sexually insatiable, languorous god of the woods into an artist filled with melancholy and longing. In conceiving of Pan as mourner instead of predator, Ovid thus equips him with an instrument whose music will continually remind him of the peaceful place where he first found his beloved. The initial moments of solace are fleeting, however, and by the end of the passage, Pan returns to his normal duties as the keeper of his herds, flocks, and beehives. But now, however, he possesses a tool—the reed pipe—which evokes a pleasant memory of both Syrinx and the peaceful river and allows him to deflect his thwarted love toward a tangible object in the natural world.

Without extending the current disagreements over how the idyllic moment functions in verse,[9] we should recognize that the durability of pastoral elegy as a generic form can in part be attributed to the changes in the *locus amoenus* as it responds to the needs of culture. By the Renaissance, certainly, the *locus amoenus* had transformed significantly, reflecting the theological conditions that informed a predominately Christian culture. Departing from Virgil's version of the *locus amoenus* as rural haven from political strife, several poets, most notably Radbert and Petrarch, began to depict the *locus amoenus* as a sensuous and permanent heavenly paradise.[10] Given the biblical account of Eden as a place of perfection and harmony, such a transformation was almost inevitable, and while it is impossible in the scope of this essay to list all the mutations that led to this transformation, it is possible to highlight the most significant change: the gradual shift in the *locus amoenus* away from natural consolation and toward divine providence.

Perhaps John Milton's "Lycidas" best exemplifies the merging traditions, for here we find both classical and Christian *loci* operating simultaneously within the poem. Although Milton contends that heaven offers one the highest form of consolation, he nevertheless acknowledges the value of the classical *locus amoenus*:

> return, Sicilian Muse,
> And call the vales, and bid them hither cast
> Their bells and flow'rets of a thousand hues.
> Ye valleys low where the mild whispers use
> Of shades and wanton winds and gushing brooks,
> On whose fresh lap the swart star sparely looks,
> Throw hither all your quaint enameled eyes,

> That on the green turf suck the honied show'rs
> And purple all the ground with vernal flow'rs.[11]

Although Milton's *locus amoenus* retains pastoral's essential ingredients—the grove, brook, shade, and song—what is most obviously different is that he has created a happy place that does not collapse beneath despair and doubt. For Milton, the *locus amoenus* is not merely a poetic convention, but a real place that can be earned through a virtuous life and death. Accordingly, it exists beyond the limits of human rationality, and because it cannot be validated by either empirical test or by language, it remains an eternal, idyllic spot whose contemplation affords the poet the highest possible form of consolation.

While Milton's *locus amoenus* was acceptable to those who swore devotion to Christian theology, to most post-Enlightenment poets the concept of heaven had become a quaint relic from the past. As advances in science began to erode the Christian assumptions that Milton had taken for granted, several Romantic writers responded with their own new version of the *locus amoenus* and divided the cosmos into two worlds—the world of change and appearance (the earthly realm) and the world of eternal forms which were accessible only through intuition. Highly indebted to Plato, Percy Bysshe Shelley's *locus amoenus* in "Adonais," for example, is not the idyllic, heavenly grove of Christian verse but rather an abstract concept, imperfectly defined as the "One." Shelley does not mention God, nor does he suggest that John Keats's soul has entered the realm of the angels:

> The One remains, the many change and pass;
> Heaven's light forever shines, Earth's shadows fly;
> Life, like a dome of many-coloured glass,
> Stains the white radiance of Eternity,
> Until Death tramples it to fragments.[12]

Though Shelley uses terms such as "Heaven," "light," and "benediction" to designate his ideal realm, he is careful not to let imaginative knowledge congeal into constricting absolutes. Instead, he concerns himself most with keeping his poetic imagination flexible enough so that he can explore new possibilities for hope and redemption. Emphasizing process over product and recognizing the dangers of letting the mind become a slave to dogma, Shelley actually contradicts himself, becoming pantheistic instead of transcendental:

> He is made one with Nature: there is heard
> His voice in all her music, from the moan
> Of thunder, to the song of night's sweet bird;
> He is a presence to be felt and known
> In darkness and in light, from herb and stone,
> Spreading itself where'er that Power may move
> Which has withdrawn his being to its own.[13]

Clearly, Shelley identifies Adonais with a mythological nature spirit whose fate represents the death of the spring vegetation (an event that the earliest Greek pastorals often lamented). For one who had declared himself an atheist at the age of eighteen, it seems as if Shelley's only recourse was to fuse neoplatonic idealism with Romanticism—for him, an acceptable solution to the metaphysical problems of the age. Though his *locus amoenus* cannot be defined precisely, its very ambiguity keeps open the possibility of continually new imaginative structures which enable the poet to locate several consolations simultaneously.

As these preceding examples demonstrate, throughout the history of poetry the *locus amoenus* has appeared in many forms, each of which has responded to major shifts in cultural and philosophical paradigms. Despite the changes in the classical, Christian, and Romantic versions of the motif, however, two stable themes emerge. First, the *locus amoenus* is always an imagined, poetic activity that allows the poet to create some version of an ideal realm that is far removed from the painful difficulties of the real world. By imaginatively creating the landscape of one's desires, the poet, in effect, controls nature and transforms its wildness into a realm that is suitable for human harmony and habitation. Second, the *locus amoenus* offers an ideal that remains unattainable because it exists only in language. As soon as real history and time enter the poet's consciousness, the imaginative activity ceases, and the poet's characters leave their distant artificial realm and enter one that reflects the actual world of the present day. Such is the case with Tennyson's ***In Memoriam***, and, as I hope to make clear, this process of creation and collapse, of desire and inaccessibility, makes ***In Memoriam*** an exemplar of the elegiac tradition.

II

Though ***In Memoriam*** does not compile pastoral elegy's usual concentration of motifs, the poem nevertheless attains literary excellence even as it departs from a unified elegiac form. ***In Memoriam*** might instead be classified as a meditation or, perhaps more appropriately, a poetic struggle to repair the disruption of the cosmic order caused by Arthur Henry Hallam's untimely death. If Tennyson made a number of false turns in finding that consolation, he was equally aware of the degrees and types of real consolation that his imagination could conjure. And, typically, the available consolation he finds often arises out of his manipulation of the *locus amoenus*. By appropriating the classical, Christian, and Romantic versions of the idyllic spot, he discovers that the imagination, while being partially determined by the laws of nature, can also alleviate their harsh realities by creating a self-enclosed, protective world that reflects one's desires.

As most commentators on ***In Memoriam*** have noted, Tennyson's need to find consolation was necessitated, in part, by his acquisition of scientific knowledge. Well schooled in most of the major scientific developments of his day, Tennyson read with great interest the works of Sir Charles Lyell, Robert Chambers, and Charles Darwin, as well as the works of many other scientists, including John Tyndall, Sir Richard Owen, Sir Joseph Dalton Hooker, and Sir Norman Lockyer.[14] Primarily disconcerting to him at the time of ***In Memoriam***'s composition was Lyell's *Prin-*

ciples of Geology, a controversial work that shattered biblical interpretations of the earth's age by displaying irrefutable geological evidence for Uniformitarianism. This evidence, coupled with new astronomical theories, began to erode traditional forms of religion, and, as new ethical systems arose, it became clear to many Victorians that people would have to find happiness and goodness without the benefit of religious faith.

For Tennyson, however, the question of the soul became increasingly problematic in the face of the new science. Nature, which Enlightenment scientists had once perceived as a window to the divine, was now perceived by many to be hostile and indifferent to the species for whom it was supposedly created. With such opposing views operating upon Tennyson's imagination, his vacillation between doubt and faith was almost inevitable. On one hand, Tennyson perceived nature as a harmonious place where humans and animals lived out their lives in a providentially designed cosmos. On the other, however, he viewed nature as a destructive force. Such a contrast corresponds well to Tennyson's production of different *loci amoeni*. Beset by doubt about nature and the immortality of Hallam's soul, Tennyson creates ideal, harmonious places that help alleviate his suffering. The imaginative visions are temporary, however, and as soon as history and scientific rationality break down his imaginative constructs, the process comes full circle, and he is once again beset by doubt. Not until Tennyson realizes the power of his imagination to offset his vision of a hostile nature does he find the lasting consolation that forces psychological recovery.

From the start of the poem, Tennyson exploits both visions of nature and transforms them in response to his shifting moods. Although we cannot be sure of the composition dates of each individual lyric, it is clear that early in the poem Tennyson commits his thought to the "friendly" view of nature. After he describes his initial grief and the hope that the "fair ship" will return Hallam's body safely to England, Tennyson offers several sections of retrospective, classical pastoral in which he gives us the first glimpse of the *locus amoenus*. In section 11, Tennyson yearns for the calm "morn without a sound" (line 1), and later, in section 21, he assumes the role of the shepherd and summons a happy memory of the past as an idyllic place that is suitable for a communion with a loved one:

> I sing to him that rests below,
>   And since the grasses round me wave
>   I take the grasses of the grave,
> And make them pipes whereon to blow.[15]

Because Tennyson's grief is so severe early in the poem, contemplation of present time and future time is almost inconceivable, making it necessary for him to call up Hallam's presence by invoking a pastoral artifice which gives him if not a real glimpse of the past, then at least an imagined view of the past that will suffice. Section 21 serves as the prelude to the real imaginative connection, for here we see the traditional pastoral image of the shepherd, who plays his pipe by Hallam's grave. Not until section 22, however, does Tennyson achieve a real communion with Hallam in an idyllic landscape that shares affinities with the classical *locus*:

> The path by which we twain did go,
>   Which led by tracts that pleased us well,
>   Thro four sweet years arose and fell,
> From flower to flower, from snow to snow;
>
> And we with singing cheer'd the way
>   And crown'd with all the season lent,
>   From April on to April went,
> And glad at heart from May to May.
>
>   (lines 1-8)

The singing that "cheers the way" functions as a metaphor for the poetic process that continues throughout the natural growth and development of a friendship. This growth corresponds to the passing of time and the seasons, and life, like an artistic friendship, is portrayed as a "path" through the natural world. There is no mention of threatening forces beyond the landscape; there is no hint of natural decay. He ignores the harsh inevitability of seasonal change and essentially suspends time, creating an unstable landscape where change and eternal youth are both present, yet antithetical to each other. Later, in section 23, he describes the landscape itself as a romantic panorama where the hills and fields "hum the murmur of a happy Pan" (line 12) and offer the young shepherds an expansive place large enough for them to exercise their imaginations:

> And all we met was fair and good,
>   And all was good that Time could bring,
>   And all the secret of the Spring
> Moved in the chambers of the blood;
>
> And many an old philosophy
>   On Argive heights divinely sang,
>   And round us all the thicket sang
> To many a flute of Arcady.
>
>   (lines 17-24)

The "old philosoph[ies]" that Tennyson happily refers to are those that formerly allowed one to contemplate a teleological view of the universe. Even time itself is beneficial, as all participants of the thicket harmonize with the poets' imagined songs. Tennyson's happiness, however, is short-lived, for even though the old philosophies are capable of stimulating imaginative reverie, they are incapable of providing lasting comfort in the face of the new science, which Tennyson, by this point in the poem, has accepted as truth. In the very next section (24), the shift toward despair is signified by Tennyson's description of sunspots (discovered by Galileo in 1611), which have "dash'd" the "very source and font of day" (lines 3-4), the platonic metaphor for God. Recognizing the "old philosoph[ies']" deficiencies, Tennyson then questions his own subjectivity, suggesting that his fantasies about nature and immortality are nothing but the dreams of a child, who, like twentieth-century existential heroes, cries out to the diminished "light" that cannot answer:

> So runs my dream: but what am I?
>   An infant crying in the night:
>   An infant crying for the light:
> And with no language but a cry.
>
>   (section 54, lines 17-20)

Language, too, he asserts, cannot sustain the *locus amoenus,* and his verse, once described in section 5 as a "sad mechanic exercise" (line 7) that could "numb" sorrow's pain, is now ineffective, even when a personified "Sorrow" attempts to sing (section 48, line 1). Verse (and by implication all art) breaks down and leaves the speaker with nothing, not even an echo to signify some lasting presence of the deceased:

> Nor dare she trust a larger lay
>   But rather loosens from the lip
>   Short swallow-flights of song, that dip
> Their wings in tears, and skim away.
>
>   (section 48, lines 13-6)

Finally, as the images of a pastoral landscape deteriorate into doubt, Tennyson replaces his nostalgic view of nature with one that anticipates twentieth-century naturalism. Here nature appears as an evolutionary force that is indifferent to human emotional needs. She is "red in tooth and claw" (section 56, line 15), unconcerned about the individual's fate, and, in Tennyson's most desperate moments, extremely hostile. In many ways, the hostile nature Tennyson conjures is as much an imaginative construct as the *locus amoenus.* Although scientific knowledge surely informs us about the nature of the physical world, Tennyson's interpretation of that knowledge is so extreme that one might be tempted to call this alternative view the *locus lacrimosus.* For Tennyson, this version is embedded with evil and represents a projected fear that humans are inconsequential and acted upon as easily as those species that have been fossilized in stone:

> "So careful of the type?" but no.
>   From scarped cliff and quarried stone
>   She cries, "A thousand types are gone;
> I care for nothing, all shall go."
>
>   (section 56, lines 1-4)

Tennyson then magnifies his fears by suggesting that his life's endeavors have been foolish. In the following stanzas, he questions why nature is ambivalent even though he has been a dutiful servant who has "suffer'd countless ills" (line 17). He also suggests that poets, those who more than others have praised divine law, should be offered some sort of divine protection. Lamenting the fact that neither he nor Hallam has been offered divine favors, Tennyson reaches the nadir of the poem, and his concern shifts from Hallam's life toward his own:

> O life as futile, then as frail!
>   O for thy voice to soothe and bless!
>   What hope of answer, or redress?
> Behind the veil, behind the veil.
>
>   (section 56, lines 25-8)

Raising such a bleak cry of despair, Tennyson poignantly feels the need to resurrect hope, and in the process, he comes to one of the poem's most startling insights:

> Peace; come away: the song of woe
>   Is after all an earthly song.
>   Peace; come away: we do him wrong
> To sing so wildly: let us go.
>
>   (section 57, lines 1-4)

Surely, if the classical *locus amoenus* with its saving and congenial landscapes is merely inconsequential artifice, then, by the same logic, the *locus lacrimosus,* with its hostile and destructive landscapes, must be perceived as artifice from the opposite perspective. The startling realization that the harsh view of nature is also an "earthly song," constructed into many different forms by subjective perception, ultimately becomes for Tennyson his rationale for diminishing the importance of scientific knowledge. Science, like poetry, is merely another conventional guide through the flux of nature and, as such, cannot possibly uncover the deepest secrets of reality. Despair and joy are merely two different versions of a singular subjectivity, neither of which can be validated as being absolutely true or false.

The idea of a shaping subjectivity becomes more prominent in sections 59-71, where Tennyson embarks upon a series of English idylls that share affinities with the Romantic impulse toward reverie. Like so many of his earlier poems, Tennyson's gaze now shifts to a distant imaginative vision, and, as always, the surrounding landscape plays an important role.[16] Throughout these sections, images of darkness, moonlight, and winter dominate the setting with Dantean glooms, leading the poet back into his depression:

> The mystic glory swims away,
>   From off my bed, the moonlight dies;
>   And closing eaves of wearied eyes
> I sleep till dusk is dipt in gray;
>
> And then I know the mist is drawn
>   A lucid veil from coast to coast,
>   And in the dark church, like a ghost,
> Thy tablet glimmers to the dawn.
>
>   (section 67, lines 9-16)

Because the setting is once again infused with sorrow and the memory of Hallam's grave, Tennyson finds it necessary to sing:

> Till out of painful phrases wrought
>   There flutters up a happy thought
>   Self-balanced on a lightsome wing.
>
>   (section 65, lines 6-8)

Of course Tennyson invokes another state of consciousness which serves as an alternative to the world that has rejected him. In a moment of mystical union, Tennyson enters a trancelike reverie, fusing the classical *locus amoe-*

nus and the Romantic *locus amoenus* to offset both the remoteness of God and his fear that the universe has lost all sense of rational purpose. At first, the images of his reverie are not clear:

> I cannot see the features right,
>   When on the gloom I strive to paint
>   The face I know; the hues are faint
> And mix with hollow masks of light.
>
> (section 70, lines 1-4)

Significantly, the reverie is a gradual event that depends on the mind's ability to sharpen its focus, to "paint" the memory of Hallam, until the real world, with all of its woeful elements, disappears momentarily into the background of the poem. Suddenly, Hallam's image comes into focus, and Tennyson rejoices in the power of his spontaneous communion:

> Till all at once beyond the will
>   I hear a wizard music roll
>   And thro' a lattice on the soul
> Looks thy fair face and makes it still.
>
> (section 70, lines 13-6)

Finally, in section 71, Tennyson resurrects the classical *locus amoenus*, which characterized the retrospective pastoral of the early sections. Writing in present tense, Tennyson seeks to convey the immediacy of this mystical union and suggests that humans *can* communicate with the dead. The two poets speak in peaceful settings that are conducive to contemplation, companionship, and, for Tennyson, psychological recovery:

> While now we talk as once we talk'd
>   Of men and minds, the dust of change,
>   The days that grow to something strange,
> In walking as of old we walk'd
>
> Beside the river's wooded reach,
>   The fortress, and the mountain ridge,
>   The cataract flashing from the bridge,
> The breaker breaking on the beach.
>
> (section 71, lines 9-16)

Although the *locus amoenus* is an imaginative construct that lies between a past ideal and some future perfection that represents a return to that lost ideal, Tennyson is momentarily content to remain in past time. Alternating between classical Arcadia and Romantic reverie for several more sections, Tennyson uses memory and a series of visionary travels to sustain Hallam's presence. Often this strategy breaks down; despite these failures, however, Tennyson does not concern himself with locating the *locus amoenus* in regard to a future paradise. Because his grief is still quite severe at this point in the poem, Tennyson seems reluctant to abandon what little solace he finds at a given moment, as if relinquishing even the slightest consolation might throw him back into the severe depression of the opening stanzas. By repeating the same method of constructing an idyll and then letting it decay, Tennyson's verse, in fact, assumes the characteristics of a bipolar personality. As soon as the hard realities of external history begin to creep into his idyllic construct, mystical assurance turns to doubt, joy turns into complaint, and proffered expressions of love turn into a solipsistic yearning for death and escape.

Fortunately, Tennyson himself seems to have realized the false consolation of past time. After the second Christmas, a section which many critics have marked as the turning point in the poem, the pastoral sections begin to take on a different character. Instead of concentrating upon "universal" images to create the *locus amoenus,* Tennyson now begins to infuse objects from the English landscape and explore the nature of present time and how it can inform the future. The passing of time seems to ameliorate the constant reminders of Hallam's absence; hence, the pastoral images that inform the later idylls are not accompanied by the same anxiety or doubt. Section 86, with its beautiful pastoral flourish, seems to me the best example of a shift from the pure artifice of the earlier *loci*. Here, the three versions of the *locus amoenus,* the classical, with its emphasis upon leisure; the Romantic, with its emphasis upon sustained reverie; and the Christian, with its emphasis upon eternal paradise, fuse in a moment of clear and concentrated repose that is in no way threatened by the external world. The accumulation of the tradition's changing motifs amalgamate and form the first moment of stable consolation in the poem:

> Sweet after showers, ambrosial air,
>   That rollest from the gorgeous gloom
>   Of evening over brake and bloom
> And meadow, slowly breathing bare
>
> The round of space, and rapt below
>   Thro' all the dewy tassell'd wood
>   And shadowing down the horned flood
> In ripples, fan my brows and blow
>
> The fever from my cheek, and sigh
>   The full new life that feeds thy breath
>   Throughout my frame, till Doubt and Death,
> Ill brethren, let the fancy fly
>
> From belt to belt of crimson seas
>   On leagues of odor streaming far,
>   To where in yonder orient star
> A hundred spirits whisper "Peace."
>
> (section 86, lines 1-16)

The final lines of this section signify an abrupt shift away from the earlier Christian doubt of section 56 and suggest that Tennyson has come to a different conclusion about the nature of science. Though science is still an integral part of human knowledge, it does not have enough authority to deny the stellafication of human souls. The hostile view of nature, which once dominated Tennyson's psyche, has now been transformed into a consoling wind, a vehicle that can transport human beings toward intuitive contemplation of future paradise. Section 89 corroborates this reading. These lyrics suggest that science can control the will only if one isolates the self from a nature that can heal. Significantly, these assertions come from the voice of Hallam, who, appearing for the first and only time in the poem, speaks the authoritative argument about the dangers of scientific advances:

> But if I praised the busy town,
>   He loved to rail against it still,
>   For "ground in yonder social mill
> We rub each other's angles down,
>
> "And merge," he said "in form and gloss
>   The picturesque of man and man."
>   We talked: the stream beneath us ran,
> The wine-flask lying couch'd in moss,
>
> Or cool'd within the glooming wave;
>   And last, returning from afar,
>   Before the crimson-circled star
> Had fallen into her father's grave,
>
> And brushing ankle-deep in flowers,
>   We heard behind the woodbine veil
>   The milk that bubbled in the pail
> And buzzings of the honeyed hours.
>
> (section 89, lines 37-52)

Clearly, Hallam's spoken words convey the dehumanization of individuals at the hands of industrial technology, and while Tennyson himself may have found some redeeming value in industrial progress, Hallam, it appears, can never accept modern society's intervention between humans and the natural world. Here, society is portrayed as a "mill," and what is ground is not the physical body, but the properties of individual genius that enable one to contemplate ethereal things.

Tennyson, however, refuses to succumb to this pessimistic vision. Significantly, by channeling his imagination in a more positive direction, Tennyson once again evokes the classical and Christian traditions to counter the perceived dangers of the Industrial Age. Each accumulated image lends itself easily to the next, and the result, as in "Lycidas," is a movement away from the idyllic spot toward the land of "milk and honey"—the future paradise promised to the Hebrews in the book of Exodus. All of the elements of the *locus amoenus* conspire to form an acceptable consolation: the communion with the dead soul, the freedom to pursue leisure, the dialogue among poets, the contemplation of an ethereal world, the attempted return to Eden and the Golden Age, and the brief but sustained reverie that allows the moment to take shape. Each element contributes to the stability of the lyric, and the accumulated strength of the three traditions gives the lyric a final and plausible sincerity.

III

The question of sincerity is, in fact, one problem of *In Memoriam* that most twentieth-century commentators have tended to belabor. Especially disconcerting to some are Tennyson's notions of a final paradise, his insistence that Hallam's soul is still present among the living, and his belief that nature impels itself toward higher states of perfection. While there is some credibility to these objections, I would argue that the brief moments of hope that Tennyson settles upon are necessary for the poem to be successful. In short, what Tennyson has learned by employing the various forms of the *locus amoenus* is that he can actively engage imaginative language to control, manage, transform, and, finally, end the frightening dangers of a hostile environment. In the face of a deterministic world, he carves out small niches of alternative realities that meet the demands of his personal desires. By the end of the poem, Tennyson is so adept at constructing new imaginative forms that he ultimately instills redemptive value and spiritual meaning into the world.

Section 107 illustrates this point well. By this late stage in the poem's composition, Tennyson is able to transform a hostile landscape simply by shifting his imagination toward more optimistic perspectives. I am quoting the whole lyric here, as I believe it is central to Tennyson's method for finding consolation:

> It is the day when he was born.
>   A bitter day that early sank
>   Behind a purple-frosty bank
> Of Vapor, leaving night forlorn.
>
> The time admits not flowers or leaves
>   To deck the banquet. Fiercely flies
>   The blast of North and East, and ice
> Makes daggers at the sharpened eaves,
>
> And bristles all the brakes and thorns
>   To yon hard crescent, as she hangs
>   Above the wood which grides and clangs
> Its leafless ribs and iron horns
>
> Together, in the drifts that pass
>   To darken on the rolling brine
>   That breaks the coast. But fetch the wine,
> Arrange the board and brim the glass;
>
> Bring in great logs and let them lie,
>   To make a solid core of heat;
>   Be cheerful minded, talk and treat
> Of all things even as he were by;
>
> We keep the day. With festal cheer,
>   With books and music, surely we
>   Will drink to him, whate'er he be,
> And sing the songs he loved to hear.
>
> (section 107, lines 1-24)

Real consolation, it appears, rests in one's knowledge that the mind can erect the necessary boundaries that will save the psyche from the destructive forces of mechanistic decay. While nature certainly exists as a real and bitterly cold force, the mind protects itself from those forces by its freely willed capacity to exert mental control over the physical environment. This movement of mind is precisely the impulse that informs the third Christmas lyric. Looking out the window, the speaker concentrates upon the brutally hostile forces that threaten the house's inhabitants. In the first half of the poem, winter is portrayed as "bitter" (section 107, line 2). The icicles hanging upon the eaves are characterized as "daggers," and the trees, sheathed in that ice, grind together, competing with one another and clashing their "iron horns" (section 107, lines 8, 12).

Had the lyric ended at this point, it would be clear that Tennyson had learned little during the poem's composition. This is certainly not the case, however, for in a characteristic reversal signified by the word "[b]ut" (section 107, line 15), Tennyson engages the imagination, shifts his perspective and begins to sculpt and transform those very threatening elements. He imaginatively turns the bitter cold into "a core of heat" (section 107, line 18). The "daggers" of ice melt into a glass of wine, and the bristling woods turn into harmless logs that become the source of a new warmth. Particularly poignant is the solace Tennyson now finds in community. Instead of remaining immersed in a solipsistic fear, he is now aided by family members and friends who collaborate with him to thwart the bleak scene outside.

Such saving acts of mind continually recur throughout the final lyrics of **In Memoriam.** In the last sections of the poem, for example, Tennyson ultimately contemplates the existence of heaven—the final imagined *locus amoenus* of the poem. Because the human mind, with its limited organizing structures, can neither adequately verify nor falsify the existence of God, Tennyson chooses to believe in the more optimistic proposition, thus sustaining a modest faith in the mind's capacity to imagine such affirmation. Moving beyond his personal struggle with the destructive forces of nature, Tennyson ultimately believes that poetry is a useful medium that can show people how to cope with a world whose religious certainties have been shattered by nineteenth-century materialism. For Tennyson, the discovery that imaginative activity is a saving medium that can be shared by others is finally the best and most acceptable resolution to **In Memoriam.** At the heart of his work is an enduring belief that material reality and imaginative reality function together in the mediation between abstraction and experience. Such a flexible, reciprocal system opens the doors for all sorts of redemptive possibilities—including those of the *locus amoenus,* in whose imaginative construction he found the pragmatic method to satisfy his need for hope in the modern world.[17]

Notes

1. For a good summary of the Victorian response, see John Dixon Hunt, introduction to *In Memoriam: A Casebook,* ed. Hunt (London: Macmillan, 1970), pp. 13-5.

2. T. S. Eliot, "In Memoriam," in *Selected Essays, 1917-32* (New York: Harcourt, Brace, 1950), p. 294.

3. W. H. Auden, quoted in Hunt, p. 18.

4. Several scholars have discussed Tennyson and the tradition of the pastoral elegy, the most important of which are Joseph Sendry ("In Memoriam and Lycidas," PMLA [Publications of the Modern Language Association] 82, 5 [October 1967]: 437-43); Robert Langbaum ("The Dynamic Unity of *In Memoriam,*" in *The Modern Spirit: Essays on the Continuity of Nineteenth-and Twentieth-Century Literature* [New York: Oxford Univ. Press, 1970], pp. 51-75); Kerry McSweeney ("The Pattern of Natural Consolation in *In Memoriam,*" VP [Victorian Poetry] 11, 2 [Summer 1973]: 87-99); Ian H. C. Kennedy ("In Memoriam and the Tradition of Pastoral Elegy," VP 15, 4 [Winter 1977]: 351-66); and Peter Hinchcliffe ("Elegy and Epithalamium in *In Memoriam,*" UTQ [University of Toronto Quarterly] 52, 3 [Spring 1983]: 241-62). For a general introduction to classical sources in Tennyson, see Robert Pattison's excellent *Tennyson and Tradition* (Cambridge MA: Harvard Univ. Press, 1979).

5. McSweeney, p. 88.

6. Several commentators have discussed Tennyson's imagined moments of peaceful repose, wherein he finds some solace from grief. Christopher Ricks, for example, has suggested that the sections of the poem that have a "Horatian elegiac serenity" do not "constitute . . . the poem's faith, but its hope" and that Tennyson "accommodate[s]" psychological crises in "a world of imagined peace" (*Tennyson* [New York: Macmillan, 1972], p. 225). Timothy Peltason, on the other hand, while sharing some of Ricks's views, is not as firmly convinced that Tennyson finds adequate consolation. Though he admits that Tennyson "must practice again and again the turn away from unhappiness," he also suggests that "the last lyrics of the poem" only "imperfectly suppress" Tennyson's "continuing uncertainties . . . about the course of the human future and about the precise terms of his own undoubted joy" (*Reading "In Memoriam"* [Princeton: Princeton Univ. Press, 1985], p. 121). Finally, Isobel Armstrong argues along with Peltason that while Tennyson "resolve[s]" some of his grief in sections 55 and 59, which "assum[e] an ultimate transcendence," the poem's "intrinsic scepticism" "qualifies" the success of "such events" (*Victorian Poetry: Poetry, Poetics, and Politics* [London: Routledge, 1993], p. 268).

7. For an excellent discussion of classical pastoral elegy, see Peter M. Sacks's *The English Elegy: Studies in the Genre from Spenser to Yeats* (Baltimore: Johns Hopkins Univ. Press, 1985), pp. 5-8.

8. Ovid, "Jove and Io," in *Ovid: Metamorphoses,* trans. Rolfe Humphries (Bloomington: Indiana Univ. Press, 1967), pp. 21-7, 24-5, lines 130-8.

9. Most recent discussions of pastoral elegy have focused on the *locus amoenus* as a site for political subversion. A good postmodern introduction to the politics of pastoral is Annabel Patterson's *Pastoral and Ideology* (Berkeley: Univ. of California Press, 1987).

10. Thomas P. Harrison, ed., *The Pastoral Elegy: An Anthology* (1939; rprt. New York: Octagon Books, 1968), pp. 6-8, 6.

11. John Milton, "Lycidas," in *The Complete Poetical Works of John Milton,* ed. Douglas Bush (Boston: Houghton Mifflin, 1965), pp. 141-7, lines 133-41.

12. Percy Bysshe Shelley, "Adonais," in *The Norton Anthology of English Literature,* gen. ed. M. H. Abrams, 4th edn., vol. 2 (New York: W. W. Norton, 1979), pp. 746-59, lines 460-4.

13. Shelley, lines 370-6.

14. Howard W. Fulweiler, "Tennyson's *In Memoriam* and the Scientific Imagination," *Thought* 59, 234 (September 1984): 283-302, 297-9.

15. Tennyson, *In Memoriam A. H. H.,* in *The Poems of Tennyson,* ed. Christopher Ricks (London: Longmans, Green and Co., 1969), pp. 853-988, section 21, lines 1-4. All further references to the poem will be to this edition and occur parenthetically in the text.

16. Pauline Fletcher argues that Tennyson's landscapes in *In Memoriam* are bleakest when Hallam's presence cannot be evoked (*Gardens and Grim Ravines: The Language of Landscape in Victorian Poetry* [Princeton: Princeton Univ. Press, 1983], p. 24.

17. I would like to thank Christopher Clausen, Robin Schulze, Matthew Kinservik, Andrew Furman, and the readers at *SEL* [*Studies in English Literature*], all of whom gave me valuable advice during the composition of this essay.

Julian Lamb (essay date 1999)

SOURCE: Lamb, Julian. "*In Memoriam* as Biography." *Critical Review* 39 (1999): 20-28.

[*In the following essay, Lamb considers* In Memoriam *as an act of self discovery on par with the poet's cognitive and emotional experience, thus serving as a biographical record of the poet's "secondary life experience."*]

It is not sufficiently recognized that Keats' 'Ode to a Nightingale' is a dramatic poem. The drama or action of the poem does not come from the nightingale itself. The bird does little more than sing and, eventually, fly away. Most of the drama comes from the poet's asserting faith and doubt in a number of different areas; this is the drama of emotion and cognition. However, there is another drama taking place which is so pervasive that we barely notice it: the drama of the poet writing the poem. The link between the second last and last stanzas serves to bring this out:

> The same that oft-times hath
> Charm'd magic casements, opening on the foam
> Of perilous seas, in faery lands forlorn.

> Forlorn! the very word is like a bell
> To toll me back from thee to my sole self!

The dramatic change of mood that the poet undergoes hinges on the use of the word 'forlorn'. In this moment we can see how the writing of the poem is itself part of the emotional drama of the poet's own life. This is an intrinsic part of the poem's power. The phrase 'My heart aches' gains much of its impact from our willingness to believe that the writing of the line happens simultaneously with the aching of the heart. The conventional wisdom of more expressive theories of poetry claims that the latter is responsible for the former: the poetry is the expression of the emotion. However, through the example above, we see that a single word is responsible for changing the poet's emotional state. The same process occurs in Tennyson's ***In Memoriam.*** Here the experience of doubt moving into faith runs concurrently with the experience of increasing optimism about the directive powers of poetry and the imagination. As in 'Ode to a Nightingale' the drama is in this coincidence.

The influence of expressive theories of poetry is evident in a conception of literary biography which treats poetic experience as a type of secondary experience. The orthodox approach to biography would be to ask the question, 'what influence did a particular life experience have on the writing of a particular poem?' This question places poetry in a subordinate position to life, perhaps even outside it. Wordsworth's conception of poetry as emotion recollected in tranquillity implies the *a priori* existence of the emotion, the life experience before the poem. Certainly, the life experience has a determining bearing on the poetry, but is not the reverse also true: that the writing of poetry can have a determining bearing on life? An expressive theory of poetry cannot adequately conceptualize this. The notion of poetry as discovery, which conceives of the poetic experience running concurrent with the emotional and cognitive experience of the poet, on the other hand, is always open to the possibility that the writing of the poem can affect the poet. Far from being simply an expression of life—of a type of once-removed, secondary reality—the poetic experience becomes, at least potentially, a pivotal point in a poet's life. This is the conceptual lens through which I would like to look at ***In Memoriam.***

In his article, '*In Memoriam*: the Way of the Poet', E. D. H. Johnson extends A. C. Bradley's quadripartite arrangement of the poems in ***In Memoriam*** by linking the stages of the poet's growth from despair to faith with the poem's aesthetic growth:

> Part One: Despair (ungoverned sense)
> Part Two: Doubt (mind governing sense, i.e. despair)
> Part Three: Hope (spirit governing mind, i.e. doubt)
> Part Four: Faith (spirit harmonizing sense and mind)

These emotional changes in the poet allow for the aesthetic changes in the poem:

> Part One: Poetry as a release from emotion
> Part Two: Poetry as escape from thought

Part Three: Poetry as self-realization
Part Four: Poetry as mission

Johnson observes that 'the demands which Tennyson made on his art in each of the four parts were directly responsive to the psychological needs of the phase through which he was passing.'[1] But Johnson's observations, although astute, are limited because they cannot conceive of the poet's spiritual growth being in any significant way responsive to his aesthetic growth. The poetic experience always lags behind the emotional and cognitive. The unity of the poems in *In Memoriam*, according to Johnson, lies simply in their being products of the poet's spiritual journey. A far more dynamic unity can be discerned, however, if we view the poetic act as running concurrently with the emotional and cognitive process, the aesthetic running simultaneously with the spiritual.

One might compare Pope's *Essay on Man* with *In Memoriam* because both poems respond to the scientific knowledge of the day and try to relate it to questions of religion and moral judgement. Where Pope is optimistic, however, Tennyson is pessimistic—at least for the bulk of his poem. 'The difference,' writes Robert Langbaum, 'is that for the Victorians, scientific knowledge was antithetical to, rather than productive of, a religious and ethical position.'[2] In composing *In Memoriam* after Hallam's death, Tennyson was faced with profound theological and philosophical questions. Ancient faiths both in the benevolent life of nature and in a Christian God had been devalued and rendered obsolete. In section 55 the poet asks:

> Are God and Nature then at strife,
> That Nature lends such evil dreams?
> So careful of the type she seems,
> So careless of the single life,

only to respond in the next section with the hard scientific voice of the geologist looking at fossils:

> 'So careful of the type?' but no.
> From scarped cliff and quarried stone
> She cries, A thousand types are gone;
> I care for nothing, all shall go.

In Memoriam leads Tennyson into attempting to reconcile science with religion. This attempted reconciliation, however, does not manifest itself as a logical argument. As John D. Boyd has suggested, 'The movement of the speaker's development with respect to [the question of individual immortality] is from confidence to anxiety, to precarious satisfaction, back to confidence, to doubt, to ecstatic certainty, and back to confidence broken by a moment of doubt, quickly dispelled.'[3] In 'The Prologue', moreover, Tennyson describes the following lyrics as 'wild and wandering cries'. The poet suggests that they are taking him to various places and states; there is a sense that he himself does not know where they will lead. There is also a pervading impression that the poetic experience shapes, moulds, and creatively discovers the emotional and cognitive. This is not a rational argument for faith, but the struggle of a wandering mind, the drama of an evolving soul searching for meaning.

The search for meaning in the universe seems, at first, hopeless (section 34):

> My own dim life should teach me this,
> That life shall live for evermore,
> Else earth is darkness at the core,
> And dust and ashes all that is;
>
> This round of green, this orb of flame,
> Fantastic beauty; such as lurks
> In some wild poet, when he works
> Without a conscience or an aim.
>
> What then were God to such as I?
> 'T were hardly worth my while to choose
> Of things all mortal, or to use
> A little patience ere I die.
>
> 'T were best at once to sink to peace,
> Like birds the charming serpent draws,
> To drop head-foremost in the jaws
> Of vacant darkness and to cease.

What makes this section of vital importance is the central metaphor upon which it turns. The meaningless world—'earth is darkness at the core, / And dust and ashes all that is'—is compared to the 'wild poet, when he works / Without a conscience or an aim'. The non-teleological world and the non-teleological poem are dynamically and inextricably linked. This becomes manifest in the use of the word 'peace' in the final stanza, to evoke either death or the end of writing (the poem having been described as a 'cry' many times). This connection establishes a relationship in which the poetic experience runs concurrently with and simultaneously to the emotional and cognitive experience. The search for teleology in the poem is the search for teleology in the world and, of course, vice-versa: the poet's search for faith is also a search for poetic form and unity. The concurrence between the aimlessness of the world and that of the poem is evident in section 16, where the poet asks:

> What words are these have fallen from me?
> Can calm despair and wild unrest
> Be tenants of a single breast,
> Or Sorrow such a changeling be?
>
> Or doth she only seem to take
> The touch of change in calm or storm,
> But knows no more of transient form
> In her deep self, than some dead lake
>
> That holds that shadow of a lark
> Hung in that shadow of a heaven? . . .
>
> And made me that delirious man
> Whose fancy fuses old and new,
> And flashes into false and true,
> And mingles all without a plan?

The important point here is that the transience and disparity of the poetry is described in natural terms, implying that the universe, too, 'mingles all without a plan'. The non-teleological universe gives Tennyson the vocabulary to discuss his formless, wandering poem. We have a situation in which words are not expressive of an *a priori* faith and doubt but are in a process of articulating each other: of discovering each other through themselves. The poetic act, therefore, is not temporally or existentially secondary to Tennyson's moods or emotions. On the contrary, it is concurrent and simultaneous with them.

The rampant pessimism in most of the poem engages with the countervailing current of the poet's struggle against it. The very existence of the struggle implies a type of instinctive but unstated faith.[4] The central struggle of the poem is the poet's attempt to apply that faith to the universe around him. The 'lame hands of faith' in section 55 gather only 'dust and chaff'. The same seems to happen in section 35:

> Yet if some voice that man could trust
> Should murmur from the narrow house,
> 'The cheeks drop in, the body bows;
> Man dies, nor is there hope in dust;'
>
> Might I not say? 'Yet even here,
> But for one hour, O Love, I strive
> To keep so sweet a thing alive.'
> But I should turn mine eyes and hear
>
> The moanings of the homeless sea,
> The sound of streams that swift or slow
> Draw down aeonian hills, and sow
> The dust of continents to be.

This doubt as to an inherent teleology in the universe is repeated in sections 54, 55, and 56; a stanza from section 56 is representative:

> O life as futile, then, as frail!
> O for thy voice to soothe and bless!
> What hope of answer, or redress?
> Behind the veil, behind the veil.

What is not so obvious, however, is that running alongside this drama is that of the poet attempting to apply his faith to the creation of poetic forms. This is no easy task, since he believes in the essential formlessness of faith (section 33):

> O thou that after toil and storm
> Mayst seem to have reach'd a purer air,
> Whose faith has centre everywhere,
> Nor cares to fix itself to form.

As J. C. C. Mays points out, 'Tennyson's attitude towards form as a regrettable necessity, the notion that only through form can faith express itself for men and yet imperfectly, is one whose working-out is a central theme of ***In Memoriam.***'[5] The 'regrettable necessity' of giving form to faith even though the latter is restricted in the process is, according to Mays, a common subject of many of Tennyson's poems. 'He urged men "to cling to faith beyond the forms of faith"', but he also said that 'I dread the losing hold of forms.'[6] Section 5 illustrates a similar ambivalence:

> I sometimes hold it half a sin
> To put in words the grief I feel;
> For words, like Nature, half reveal
> And half conceal the soul within.
>
> But, for the unquiet heart and brain,
> A use in measured language lies;
> The sad mechanic exercise,
> Like dull narcotics numbing pain.
>
> In words, like weeds, I'll wrap me o'er,
> Like coarsest clothes against the cold:
> But the large grief which these enfold
> Is given in outline and no more.

The tension between faith and the scientific view of the universe is paralleled by that between faith and poetic form. The reciprocal relationship is illustrated above in the likening of words to natural phenomena; they 'half reveal / And half conceal the soul within'. Nature half reveals God, words half reveal the poet. The likening of words to weeds in the final stanza emphasizes the parallel and sets the conceptual scene for the remainder of the poem. In much the same way that the poet can begin to discern a teleology in natural phenomena which so far have appeared to him as seen through the lens of science, he can also find faith in the poetic form which so far has hampered his attempts to articulate that faith. The use of the metaphor in section 88 further emphasizes the connection between the two:

> Wild bird, whose warble, liquid sweet,
> Rings Eden thro' the budded quicks,
> O, tell me where the senses mix,
> O, tell me where the passions meet,
>
> Whence radiate: fierce extremes employ
> Thy spirits in the darkening leaf,
> And in the midmost heart of grief
> Thy passion clasps a secret joy.

Just as the bird's answer to grief is beyond its own understanding, so the poet suggests that even if his harp begins in woe, some force beyond his understanding will take him elsewhere:

> And I—my harp would preclude woe—
> I cannot all command the strings;
> The glory of the sum of things
> Will flash along the chords and go.

Significantly, this claim is represented through the use of birdsong—a natural phenomenon. The poet's hope is not that he find adequate expression of a faith in teleology, but that he will find that faith itself: 'The glory of the sum of things / Will flash along the chords and go.' This fulfils the promise of the muse in section 58: 'Abide a little longer here, / And thou shalt take a nobler leave'.

The wildness of the earlier sections of ***In Memoriam*** comprises a confused oscillation of moods and emotions; the poetry 'mingles all without a plan.' This oscillation is associated with formlessness. As the poem progresses the oscillations become less extreme, until the final thirty or so sections, in which there is no oscillation at all. The question is this: is the progress towards form a result of the poet's spiritual growth, or is the poet's spiritual growth a result of a progress to form? Most critics of *In Memoriam*—E. D. H. Johnson is one example—would argue the former, often unknowingly. But as I have tried to show the relationship between the poet's search for unity in his poem runs concurrently with his search for unity in the universe. The concurrence is so precise that one has to dispose of the language of cause and effect, of one being responsible for the other. Instead we must allow ourselves conceptual leeway within which to imagine that they are both responsible for and responsive to each other.

The hint of optimism in section 88 is representative of an increasing inclination to trust the directive power of poetry and the poetic experience. The reflective section 85 looks back on more turbulent times: 'so shall grief with symbols play / And pining life be fancy-fed'. Indeed, artistic endeavour is seen as an assimilating and unifying force:

> Likewise the imaginative woe,
> That loved to handle spiritual strife,
> Diffused the shock thro' all my life,
> But in the present broke the blow.

The cry, which at first seemed aimless, seems to have had a directive power. The spiritual wandering and poetic formlessness of the earlier sections are simultaneously resolving themselves. Johnson, like many others, can only conceive of this change in terms of its being a direct result of the poet's mood: 'it would appear that the demands which Tennyson made on his art in each of the four parts were directly responsive to the psychological needs of the phase through which he was passing.'[7] But is it not also a case of the poetic experience speaking back to the poet? Through the act of writing the poem, the poet is not expressing but discovering his spiritual growth. In section 96 Hallam's search for religious certitude is presented with artistic connotations:

> I know not: one indeed I knew
> In many a subtle question versed,
> Who touch'd a jarring lyre at first,
> But ever strove to make it true;
>
> Perplext in faith, but pure in deeds,
> At last he beat his music out.

Hallam's search ends only when he 'beats his music out'. The creative act is not only expressive but, at least partly, constitutive of the faith.

Section 123 of the poem shows that the poet is no longer troubled by the science of the day. He looks on nature with a faith which he finds compatible with the world around him. It is not even disturbed by the turbulence of natural change:

> There rolls the deep where grew the tree.
> O earth, what changes hast thou seen!
> There where the long street roars hath been
> The stillness of the central sea.
>
> The hills are shadows, and they flow
> From form to form, and nothing stands;
> They melt like mist, the solid lands,
> Like clouds they shape themselves and go.
>
> But in my spirit will I dwell,
> And dream my dream, and hold it true;
> For tho' my lips may breathe adieu,
> I cannot think the thing farewell.

The poetic experience is here presented as a basis for Tennyson's religious faith. When looking back on his struggle, the process of artistic creation becomes the figure which encompasses the organic totality of his experience: 'I see in part / That all, as in some piece of art, / Is toil coöperant to an end' (127). The important point here is that both the poet's emotional and cognitive experience and his poetic experience have gained a teleology. Moreover, they seem to have done this together. In casting a glance back over his spiritual pilgrimage, the poet empathizes with each aesthetic movement (125):

> Whatever I have said or sung,
> Some bitter notes my harp would give,
> Yea, tho' there often seem'd to live
> A contradiction on the tongue,
>
> Yet Hope had never lost her youth,
> She did but look through dimmer eyes;
> Or Love but play'd with gracious lies,
> Because he felt so fix't in truth;
>
> And if the song were full of care,
> He breathed the spirit of the song;
> And if the words were sweet and strong
> He set his royal signet there;
>
> Abiding with me till I sail
> To seek thee on the mystic deeps,
> And this electric force, that keeps
> A thousand pulses dancing, fail.

The poem keeps alive the struggle (section 124) so that

> A warmth within the breast would melt
> The freezing reason's colder part,
> And like a man in wrath the heart
> Stood up and answer'd, 'I have felt.'
>
> No, like a child in doubt and fear:
> But that blind clamour made me wise;
> Then was I as a child that cries,
> But, crying, knows his father near,
>
> And what I am beheld again,
> What is, and no man understands;
> And out of darkness came the hands
> That reach thro' nature, moulding men.

The cry makes real that thing that is cried for.[8] The formless cry of the poem makes real its own form through the very crying for it. The poet's ability to perceive 'the hands / That reach thro' nature' is the result of the lamentation for such formative forces.

All this suggests that Tennyson believed in faith not as something to be achieved but as something to be experienced. Robert Langbaum writes that 'Tennyson's faith informs the new ecumenical spirit which recognizes all creeds as possible responses to an ultimate reality that can be experienced but not known.'[9] To use Ulysses' words, it is the striving, the seeking and the finding without ever really arriving. To arrive is to stop and, since we 'cannot rest from travel', we 'will drink / Life to the lees'. In this light, *In Memoriam* can be seen as a poem about the way in which faith experiences poetry and poetry experiences faith though the mutual act of discovery. Indeed, this is the terrain that I have tried to map; in doing so I have also tried to reflect on the biographical importance of the poem. By seeing the poem not so much as a thing but as an action—an act of discovery—we become aware of its vital biographical importance.

A brief digression may serve to clarify what I mean. Plato would view a picture of a tree as a second rate tree: it is once (in Plato's case more than once) removed from reality, and relies on the existence of a tree to make its existence possible. Aristotle, on the other hand, would view it as a picture: as part of reality. *In Memoriam* is not an expression of doubt and faith which is once removed from the actual experience of them. *In Memoriam* is a poem. The poetic experience runs concurrent and simultaneous with the experience of doubt and faith. The former does not occur once removed from the latter. Far from it: they occur together, informing and responding to each other. The poetic act is, therefore, biographically significant in that it has the potential to change what a poet thinks and feels; it is Keats' use of the word 'forlorn' on a large scale. Indeed, viewing poetry as not so much a thing but an act (act and actor are inseparable), makes it biographically indispensable.

A final observation as to the relationship between biography and the poem's form and unity: the biographical significance of the poem demands that we see the poetic experience running concurrent with the emotional and cognitive experience. And, of course, vice-versa. This is a case of life feeding poetry, and poetry feeding life: 'So long as men can breathe or eyes can see, / So long lives this, and this gives life to thee.'

Notes

1. E. D. H. Johnson, '*In Memoriam*: the Way of the Poet', *Victorian Studies*, 2: 2 (Dec. 1958), 148.

2. Robert Langbaum, *The Modern Spirit: Essays on the Continuity of Nineteenth- and Twentieth-Century Literature* (London: Chatto and Windus, 1970), 51.

3. John D. Boyd, '*In Memoriam* and the "Logic of Feeling"', *Victorian Poetry*, 10 (1972), 100.

4. See Langbaum, *The Modern Spirit*, 63 and 70.

5. J. C. C. Mays, '*In Memoriam*: An Aspect of Form', *University of Toronto Quarterly*, 35: 1 (Oct. 1965), 24.

6. Ibid.

7. Johnson, '*In Memoriam*', 148.

8. Langbaum, *The Modern Spirit*, 72.

9. Ibid. 75.

FURTHER READING

Criticism

Armstrong, Isobel. "Tennyson in the 1850s: From Geology to Pathology—*In Memoriam* (1850) to *Maud* (1855)." In *Tennyson: Seven Essays,* edited by Philip Collins, pp. 102-40. New York: St. Martin's Press, 1992.

　　Examines the radical historical changes that took place between the composition of *In Memoriam* and *Maud*, influencing Tennyson's poetic perspective.

Battaglia, Francis Joseph. "The Use of Contradiction in *In Memoriam*." *English Language Notes* 4, no. 1 (September 1966): 41-46.

　　Explores contradictions and counter-statements in *In Memoriam* as modern in their expression of dramatic change.

Brantley, Richard. "Evangelical Principles of Tennyson's *In Memoriam*." In *English Romanticism Preludes and Postludes: Essays in Honor of Edwin Graves Wilson,* edited by Donald Schoonmaker and John A. Alford, pp. 115-26. East Lansing, MI: Colleagues Press, 1993.

　　Focuses on the way Methodism and experimental-Edwardsean evangelicalism of the eighteenth-century appears in specific sections of *In Memoriam.*

Craft, Christopher. "'Descend, and Touch, and Enter': Tennyson's Strange Manner of Address." *Genders* 1 (spring 1988): 83-101.

　　Explores male love and homoeroticism in *In Memoriam.*

Dale, Peter Allan. "'Gracious Lies': The Meaning of Metaphor in *In Memoriam*." *Victorian Poetry* 18, no. 2 (summer 1980): 147-67.

　　Examines Tennyson's use of metaphors to communicate complex emotions in *In Memoriam.*

Gates, Sarah. "Poetics, Metaphysics, Genre: The Stanza Form of *In Memoriam*." *Victorian Poetry* 37, no. 4 (winter 1999): 507-19.

Asserts that the *abba* stanza form as the only constant in the "extraordinarily self-contradictory, fluidly granulated" *In Memoriam*.

Hair, Donald S. "Soul and Spirit in *In Memoriam*." *Victorian Poetry* 34, no. 2 (summer 1996): 175-91.

Compares the concepts of "soul" and "spirit" from *In Memoriam* with St. Paul's first letter to the Corinthians, wherein the natural body and the spiritual body are differentiated.

Halliday, M. A. K. "Poetry as Scientific Discourse: The Nuclear Sections of Tennyson's *In Memoriam*." In *Functions of Style*, edited by David Birch and Michael O'Toole, pp. 31-44. London: Pinter Publishers, 1988.

Identifies sections of *In Memoriam* as attempting to come to terms with nineteenth-century scientific ideology.

Hirsh, Elizabeth A. "'No Record of Reply': *In Memoriam* and Victorian Language Theory." *ELH* 55, no. 1 (spring 1988): 233-57.

Examines Victorian language theory as Tennyson knew it and compares *In Memoriam* with John Donaldson's *The New Cratylus* (1839).

Kolb, Jack. "Gladstone and Tennyson's *In Memoriam*." *Victorian Poetry* 23, no. 2 (summer 1985): 196-99.

Discusses the supposed rivalry between Tennyson and William Ewart Gladstone—which may have resulted from jealousy over mutual friendship with Arthur Henry Hallam.

Kozicki, Henry. "'Meaning' in Tennyson's *In Memoriam*." *Studies in English Literature 1500-1900* 17, no. 4 (autumn 1977): 673-94.

Suggests that *In Memoriam* presents the narrative persona as moving from grief to happiness through a developing consciousness, a "willed construction of meaning," and faith in God.

Manning, Sylvia. "Death and Sex from Tennyson's Early Poetry to *In Memoriam*." In *Sex and Death in Victorian Literature*, edited by Regina Barreca, pp. 194-210. London: Macmillan, 1990.

Reviews Tennyson's portrayal of death and sex from his early poetry through *In Memoriam*, demonstrating how this portrayal changes once death actually touches the poet.

Mays, J. C. C. "*In Memoriam*: An Aspect of Form." *University of Toronto Quarterly* 35, no. 1 (October 1965): 22-46.

Examines the form of *In Memoriam* by means of the use of the word "form" throughout the poem.

McGhee, Richard D. "*In Memoriam*: The Ways of an Artist." *Studia Neophilologica* 47 (1975): 333-52.

Discusses the consciously artificial structure of *In Memoriam* and argues that while the content is personal, the poem is nevertheless the creation of an artist, not merely a grieving man's autobiography.

Nunokawa, Jeff. "*In Memoriam* and the Extinction of the Homosexual." *ELH* 58, no. 2 (summer 1991): 427-38.

Explores *In Memoriam* for its homosexual content, arguing that boyhood love gives way to heterosexuality.

Shaw, Marion. "*In Memoriam* and Popular Religious Poetry." *Victorian Poetry* 15, no. 1 (spring 1977): 1-8.

Discusses the manner in which *In Memoriam* follows the familiar nineteenth-century tradition of hymn poetry, which along with Biblical imagery would have been familiar and comforting to readers.

Shaw, W. David. "Consolation and Catharsis in *In Memoriam*." *Modern Language Quarterly* 37, no. 1 (March 1976): 47-67.

Considers *In Memoriam* from the narrator's perspective, defining his experience as an expression of grief leading to catharsis and followed by consolation, which renders the poem an introverted, intellectual autobiography.

Waller, John O. "Francis Turner Palgrave's Criticisms of Tennyson's *In Memoriam*." *Victorian Newsletter* no. 52 (fall 1977): 13-17.

Discusses Victorian poetry editor and Tennyson friend Francis Turner Palgrave's notes to his edition of *In Memoriam*.

Additional coverage of Tennyson's life and career is contained in the following sources published by the Gale Group: *Concise Dictionary of British Literary Biography 1832-1890*; *DISCovering Authors*; *DISCovering Authors: British*; *DISCovering Authors: Canadian*; *DISCovering Authors Modules: Most Studied Authors and Poets*; *DISCovering Authors 3.0*; *Dictionary of Literary Biography*, Vol. 32; and *World Literature Criticism*.

How to Use This Index

The main references

> **Calvino, Italo**
> 1923-1985 .... CLC 5, 8, 11, 22, 33, 39,
> 73; SSC 3

list all author entries in the following Gale Literary Criticism series:

   BLC = *Black Literature Criticism*
   CLC = *Contemporary Literary Criticism*
   CLR = *Children's Literature Review*
   CMLC = *Classical and Medieval Literature Criticism*
   DA = *DISCovering Authors*
   DAB = *DISCovering Authors: British*
   DAC = *DISCovering Authors: Canadian*
   DAM = *DISCovering Authors: Modules*
       DRAM: *Dramatists Module;* **MST:** *Most-Studied Authors Module;*
       MULT: *Multicultural Authors Module;* **NOV:** *Novelists Module;*
       POET: *Poets Module;* **POP:** *Popular Fiction and Genre Authors Module*
   DC = *Drama Criticism*
   HLC = *Hispanic Literature Criticism*
   LC = *Literature Criticism from 1400 to 1800*
   NCLC = *Nineteenth-Century Literature Criticism*
   NNAL = *Native North American Literature*
   PC = *Poetry Criticism*
   SSC = *Short Story Criticism*
   TCLC = *Twentieth-Century Literary Criticism*
   WLC = *World Literature Criticism, 1500 to the Present*

The cross-references

> See also CANR 23; CA 85-88;
> obituary CA116

list all author entries in the following Gale biographical and literary sources:

   AAYA = *Authors & Artists for Young Adults*
   AITN = *Authors in the News*
   BEST = *Bestsellers*
   BW = *Black Writers*
   CA = *Contemporary Authors*
   CAAS = *Contemporary Authors Autobiography Series*
   CABS = *Contemporary Authors Bibliographical Series*
   CANR = *Contemporary Authors New Revision Series*
   CAP = *Contemporary Authors Permanent Series*
   CDALB = *Concise Dictionary of American Literary Biography*
   CDBLB = *Concise Dictionary of British Literary Biography*
   DLB = *Dictionary of Literary Biography*
   DLBD = *Dictionary of Literary Biography Documentary Series*
   DLBY = *Dictionary of Literary Biography Yearbook*
   HW = *Hispanic Writers*
   JRDA = *Junior DISCovering Authors*
   MAICYA = *Major Authors and Illustrators for Children and Young Adults*
   MTCW = *Major 20th-Century Writers*
   SAAS = *Something about the Author Autobiography Series*
   SATA = *Something about the Author*
   YABC = *Yesterday's Authors of Books for Children*

Literary Criticism Series
Cumulative Author Index

20/1631
See Upward, Allen
A/C Cross
See Lawrence, T(homas) E(dward)
Abasiyanik, Sait Faik 1906-1954
See Sait Faik
See also CA 123
Abbey, Edward 1927-1989 .... **CLC 36, 59**
See also ANW; CA 45-48; 128; CANR 2, 41; DA3; DLB 256; MTCW 2; TCWW 2
Abbott, Lee K(ittredge) 1947- .... **CLC 48**
See also CA 124; CANR 51, 101; DLB 130
Abe, Kobo 1924-1993 .... **CLC 8, 22, 53, 81**
See also CA 65-68; 140; CANR 24, 60; DAM NOV; DFS 14; DLB 182; MJW; MTCW 1, 2; SFW 4; TCLC 121
Abe Kobo
See Abe, Kobo
Abelard, Peter c. 1079-c. 1142 ...... **CMLC 11**
See also DLB 115, 208
Abell, Kjeld 1901-1961 .... **CLC 15**
See also CA 191; 111; DLB 214
Abish, Walter 1931- .... **CLC 22; SSC 44**
See also CA 101; CANR 37; CN 7; DLB 130, 227
Abrahams, Peter (Henry) 1919- .... **CLC 4**
See also AFW; BW 1; CA 57-60; CANR 26; CDWLB 3; CN 7; DLB 117, 225; MTCW 1, 2; RGEL 2; WLIT 2
Abrams, M(eyer) H(oward) 1912- ... **CLC 24**
See also CA 57-60; CANR 13, 33; DLB 67
Abse, Dannie 1923- .... **CLC 7, 29; PC 41**
See also CA 53-56; CAAS 1; CANR 4, 46, 74; CBD; CP 7; DAB; DAM POET; DLB 27, 245; MTCW 1
Abutsu 1222(?)-1283 .... **CMLC 46**
See also Abutsu-ni
Abutsu-ni
See Abutsu
See also DLB 203
Achebe, (Albert) Chinua(lumogu)
1930- ...... **CLC 1, 3, 5, 7, 11, 26, 51, 75, 127, 152; BLC 1; WLC**
See also AAYA 15; AFW; BPFB 1; BW 2, 3; CA 1-4R; CANR 6, 26, 47; CDWLB 3; CLR 20; CN 7; CP 7; CWRI 5; DA; DA3; DAB; DAC; DAM MST, MULT, NOV; DLB 117; DNFS 1; EXPN; EXPS; LAIT 2; MAICYA 1, 2; MTCW 1, 2; NFS 2; RGEL 2; RGSF 2; SATA 38, 40; SATA-Brief 38; SSFS 3, 13; WLIT 2
Acker, Kathy 1948-1997 .... **CLC 45, 111**
See also CA 117; 122; 162; CANR 55; CN 7
Ackroyd, Peter 1949- .... **CLC 34, 52, 140**
See also BRWS 6; CA 123; 127; CANR 51, 74, 99; CN 7; DLB 155, 231; HGG; INT 127; MTCW 1; RHW

Acorn, Milton 1923-1986 .... **CLC 15**
See also CA 103; CCA 1; DAC; DLB 53; INT 103
Adamov, Arthur 1908-1970 .... **CLC 4, 25**
See also CA 17-18; 25-28R; CAP 2; DAM DRAM; GFL 1789 to the Present; MTCW 1; RGWL 2
Adams, Alice (Boyd) 1926-1999 .. **CLC 6, 13, 46; SSC 24**
See also CA 81-84; 179; CANR 26, 53, 75, 88; CN 7; CSW; DLB 234; DLBY 1986; INT CANR-26; MTCW 1, 2; SSFS 14
Adams, Andy 1859-1935 .... **TCLC 56**
See also TCWW 2; YABC 1
Adams, Brooks 1848-1927 .... **TCLC 80**
See also CA 123; DLB 47
Adams, Douglas (Noel) 1952-2001 .. **CLC 27, 60**
See also AAYA 4, 33; BEST 89:3; BYA 14; CA 106; 197; CANR 34, 64; CPW; DA3; DAM POP; DLB 261; DLBY 1983; JRDA; MTCW 1; NFS 7; SATA 116; SATA-Obit 128; SFW 4
Adams, Francis 1862-1893 .... **NCLC 33**
Adams, Henry (Brooks)
1838-1918 .... **TCLC 4, 52**
See also AMW; CA 104; 133; CANR 77; DA; DAB; DAC; DAM MST; DLB 12, 47, 189; MTCW 1; NCFS 1
Adams, John 1735-1826 .... **NCLC 106**
See also DLB 31, 183
Adams, Richard (George) 1920- ... **CLC 4, 5, 18**
See also AAYA 16; AITN 1, 2; BPFB 1; BYA 5; CA 49-52; CANR 3, 35; CLR 20; CN 7; DAM NOV; DLB 261; FANT; JRDA; LAIT 5; MAICYA 1, 2; MTCW 1, 2; NFS 11; SATA 7, 69; YAW
Adamson, Joy(-Friederike Victoria)
1910-1980 .... **CLC 17**
See also CA 69-72; 93-96; CANR 22; MTCW 1; SATA 11; SATA-Obit 22
Adcock, Fleur 1934- .... **CLC 41**
See also CA 25-28R, 182; CAAE 182; CAAS 23; CANR 11, 34, 69, 101; CP 7; CWP; DLB 40; FW
Addams, Charles (Samuel)
1912-1988 .... **CLC 30**
See also CA 61-64; 126; CANR 12, 79
Addams, Jane 1860-1945 .... **TCLC 76**
See also AMWS 1; FW
Addison, Joseph 1672-1719 .... **LC 18**
See also BRW 3; CDBLB 1660-1789; DLB 101; RGEL 2; WLIT 3
Adler, Alfred (F.) 1870-1937 .... **TCLC 61**
See also CA 119; 159

Adler, C(arole) S(chwerdtfeger)
1932- .... **CLC 35**
See also AAYA 4, 41; CA 89-92; CANR 19, 40, 101; CLR 78; JRDA; MAICYA 1, 2; SAAS 15; SATA 26, 63, 102, 126; YAW
Adler, Renata 1938- .... **CLC 8, 31**
See also CA 49-52; CANR 95; CN 7; MTCW 1
Adorno, Theodor W(iesengrund)
1903-1969 .... **TCLC 111**
See also CA 89-92; 25-28R; CANR 89; DLB 242
Ady, Endre 1877-1919 .... **TCLC 11**
See also CA 107; CDWLB 4; DLB 215; EW 9
A.E. .... **TCLC 3, 10**
See also Russell, George William
See also DLB 19
Aelfric c. 955-c. 1010 .... **CMLC 46**
See also DLB 146
Aeschines c. 390B.C.-c. 320B.C. ..... **CMLC 47**
See also DLB 176
Aeschylus 525(?)B.C.-456(?)B.C. .. **CMLC 11, 51; DC 8; WLCS**
See also AW 1; CDWLB 1; DA; DAB; DAC; DAM DRAM, MST; DFS 5, 10; DLB 176; RGWL 2
Aesop 620(?)B.C.-560(?)B.C. .... **CMLC 24**
See also CLR 14; MAICYA 1, 2; SATA 64
Affable Hawk
See MacCarthy, Sir (Charles Otto) Desmond
Africa, Ben
See Bosman, Herman Charles
Afton, Effie
See Harper, Frances Ellen Watkins
Agapida, Fray Antonio
See Irving, Washington
Agee, James (Rufus) 1909-1955 ...... **TCLC 1, 19**
See also AITN 1; AMW; CA 108; 148; CDALB 1941-1968; DAM NOV; DLB 2, 26, 152; DLBY 1989; LAIT 3; MTCW 1; RGAL 4
Aghill, Gordon
See Silverberg, Robert
Agnon, S(hmuel) Y(osef Halevi)
1888-1970 .... **CLC 4, 8, 14; SSC 30**
See also CA 17-18; 25-28R; CANR 60, 102; CAP 2; MTCW 1, 2; RGSF 2; RGWL 2
Agrippa von Nettesheim, Henry Cornelius
1486-1535 .... **LC 27**
Aguilera Malta, Demetrio 1909-1981
See also CA 111; 124; CANR 87; DAM MULT, NOV; DLB 145; HLCS 1; HW 1
Agustini, Delmira 1886-1914
See also CA 166; HLCS 1; HW 1, 2; LAW

383

Aherne, Owen
See Cassill, R(onald) V(erlin)
Ai 1947- .... **CLC 4, 14, 69**
See also CA 85-88; CAAS 13; CANR 70; DLB 120
Aickman, Robert (Fordyce)
1914-1981 .... **CLC 57**
See also CA 5-8R; CANR 3, 72, 100; DLB 261; HGG; SUFW
Aiken, Conrad (Potter) 1889-1973 .... **CLC 1, 3, 5, 10, 52; PC 26; SSC 9**
See also AMW; CA 5-8R; 45-48; CANR 4, 60; CDALB 1929-1941; DAM NOV, POET; DLB 9, 45, 102; EXPS; HGG; MTCW 1, 2; RGAL 4; RGSF 2; SATA 3, 30; SSFS 8
Aiken, Joan (Delano) 1924- .... **CLC 35**
See also AAYA 1, 25; CA 9-12R, 182; CAAE 182; CANR 4, 23, 34, 64; CLR 1, 19; DLB 161; FANT; HGG; JRDA; MAICYA 1, 2; MTCW 1; RHW; SAAS 1; SATA 2, 30, 73; SATA-Essay 109; WYA; YAW
Ainsworth, William Harrison
1805-1882 .... **NCLC 13**
See also DLB 21; HGG; RGEL 2; SATA 24; SUFW
Aitmatov, Chingiz (Torekulovich)
1928- .... **CLC 71**
See also CA 103; CANR 38; MTCW 1; RGSF 2; SATA 56
Akers, Floyd
See Baum, L(yman) Frank
Akhmadulina, Bella Akhatovna
1937- .... **CLC 53**
See also CA 65-68; CWP; CWW 2; DAM POET
Akhmatova, Anna 1888-1966 ..... **CLC 11, 25, 64, 126; PC 2**
See also CA 19-20; 25-28R; CANR 35; CAP 1; DA3; DAM POET; EW 10; MTCW 1, 2; RGWL 2
Aksakov, Sergei Timofeyvich
1791-1859 .... **NCLC 2**
See also DLB 198
Aksenov, Vassily
See Aksyonov, Vassily (Pavlovich)
Akst, Daniel 1956- .... **CLC 109**
See also CA 161
Aksyonov, Vassily (Pavlovich)
1932- .... **CLC 22, 37, 101**
See also CA 53-56; CANR 12, 48, 77; CWW 2
Akutagawa Ryunosuke
1892-1927 .... **TCLC 16; SSC 44**
See also CA 117; 154; DLB 180; MJW; RGSF 2; RGWL 2
Alain 1868-1951 .... **TCLC 41**
See also CA 163; GFL 1789 to the Present
Alain de Lille c. 1116-c. 1203 .... **CMLC 53**
See also DLB 208
Alain-Fournier .... **TCLC 6**
See also Fournier, Henri Alban
See also DLB 65; GFL 1789 to the Present; RGWL 2
Alanus de Insluis
See Alain de Lille
Alarcon, Pedro Antonio de
1833-1891 .... **NCLC 1**
Alas (y Urena), Leopoldo (Enrique Garcia)
1852-1901 .... **TCLC 29**
See also CA 113; 131; HW 1; RGSF 2
Albee, Edward (Franklin III) 1928- . **CLC 1, 2, 3, 5, 9, 11, 13, 25, 53, 86, 113; DC 11; WLC**
See also AITN 1; AMW; CA 5-8R; CABS 3; CAD; CANR 8, 54, 74; CD 5; CDALB 1941-1968; DA; DA3; DAB; DAC; DAM DRAM, MST; DFS 2, 3, 8, 10, 13, 14; DLB 7; INT CANR-8; LAIT 2; MTCW 1, 2; RGAL 4; TUS

Alberti, Rafael 1902-1999 .... **CLC 7**
See also CA 85-88; 185; CANR 81; DLB 108; HW 2; RGWL 2
Albert the Great 1193(?)-1280 ...... **CMLC 16**
See also DLB 115
Alcala-Galiano, Juan Valera y
See Valera y Alcala-Galiano, Juan
Alcayaga, Lucila Godoy
See Godoy Alcayaga, Lucila
Alcott, Amos Bronson 1799-1888 .... **NCLC 1**
See also DLB 1, 223
Alcott, Louisa May 1832-1888 . **NCLC 6, 58, 83; SSC 27; WLC**
See also AAYA 20; AMWS 1; BPFB 1; BYA 2; CDALB 1865-1917; CLR 1, 38; DA; DA3; DAB; DAC; DAM MST, NOV; DLB 1, 42, 79, 223, 239, 242; DLBD 14; FW; JRDA; LAIT 2; MAICYA 1, 2; NFS 12; RGAL 4; SATA 100; WCH; WYA; YABC 1; YAW
Aldanov, M. A.
See Aldanov, Mark (Alexandrovich)
Aldanov, Mark (Alexandrovich)
1886(?)-1957 .... **TCLC 23**
See also CA 118; 181
Aldington, Richard 1892-1962 .... **CLC 49**
See also CA 85-88; CANR 45; DLB 20, 36, 100, 149; RGEL 2
Aldiss, Brian W(ilson) 1925- . **CLC 5, 14, 40; SSC 36**
See also AAYA 42; CA 5-8R; CAAE 190; CAAS 2; CANR 5, 28, 64; CN 7; DAM NOV; DLB 14, 261; MTCW 1, 2; SATA 34; SFW 4
Alegria, Claribel 1924- .... **CLC 75; HLCS 1; PC 26**
See also CA 131; CAAS 15; CANR 66, 94; CWW 2; DAM MULT; DLB 145; HW 1; MTCW 1
Alegria, Fernando 1918- .... **CLC 57**
See also CA 9-12R; CANR 5, 32, 72; HW 1, 2
Aleichem, Sholom .... **TCLC 1, 35; SSC 33**
See also Rabinovitch, Sholem
Aleixandre, Vicente 1898-1984 ... **TCLC 113; HLCS 1**
See also CANR 81; DLB 108; HW 2; RGWL 2
Alencon, Marguerite d'
See de Navarre, Marguerite
Alepoudelis, Odysseus
See Elytis, Odysseus
See also CWW 2
Aleshkovsky, Joseph 1929-
See Aleshkovsky, Yuz
See also CA 121; 128
Aleshkovsky, Yuz .... **CLC 44**
See also Aleshkovsky, Joseph
Alexander, Lloyd (Chudley) 1924- ... **CLC 35**
See also AAYA 1, 27; BPFB 1; BYA 5, 6, 7, 9, 10, 11; CA 1-4R; CANR 1, 24, 38, 55; CLR 1, 5, 48; CWRI 5; DLB 52; FANT; JRDA; MAICYA 1, 2; MAICYAS 1; MTCW 1; SAAS 19; SATA 3, 49, 81, 129; SUFW; WYA; YAW
Alexander, Meena 1951- .... **CLC 121**
See also CA 115; CANR 38, 70; CP 7; CWP; FW
Alexander, Samuel 1859-1938 .... **TCLC 77**
Alexie, Sherman (Joseph, Jr.)
1966- .... **CLC 96, 154**
See also AAYA 28; CA 138; CANR 95; DA3; DAM MULT; DLB 175, 206; MTCW 1; NNAL
Alfau, Felipe 1902-1999 .... **CLC 66**
See also CA 137
Alfieri, Vittorio 1749-1803 .... **NCLC 101**
See also EW 4; RGWL 2

Alfred, Jean Gaston
See Ponge, Francis
Alger, Horatio, Jr. 1832-1899 .... **NCLC 8, 83**
See also DLB 42; LAIT 2; RGAL 4; SATA 16; TUS
Al-Ghazali, Muhammad ibn Muhammad
1058-1111 .... **CMLC 50**
See also DLB 115
Algren, Nelson 1909-1981 ..... **CLC 4, 10, 33; SSC 33**
See also AMWS 9; BPFB 1; CA 13-16R; 103; CANR 20, 61; CDALB 1941-1968; DLB 9; DLBY 1981, 1982, 2000; MTCW 1, 2; RGAL 4; RGSF 2
Ali, Ahmed 1908-1998 .... **CLC 69**
See also CA 25-28R; CANR 15, 34
Alighieri, Dante
See Dante
Allan, John B.
See Westlake, Donald E(dwin)
Allan, Sidney
See Hartmann, Sadakichi
Allan, Sydney
See Hartmann, Sadakichi
Allard, Janet .... **CLC 59**
Allen, Edward 1948- .... **CLC 59**
Allen, Fred 1894-1956 .... **TCLC 87**
Allen, Paula Gunn 1939- .... **CLC 84**
See also AMWS 4; CA 112; 143; CANR 63; CWP; DA3; DAM MULT; DLB 175; FW; MTCW 1; NNAL; RGAL 4
Allen, Roland
See Ayckbourn, Alan
Allen, Sarah A.
See Hopkins, Pauline Elizabeth
Allen, Sidney H.
See Hartmann, Sadakichi
Allen, Woody 1935- .... **CLC 16, 52**
See also AAYA 10; CA 33-36R; CANR 27, 38, 63; DAM POP; DLB 44; MTCW 1
Allende, Isabel 1942- . **CLC 39, 57, 97; HLC 1; WLCS**
See also AAYA 18; CA 125; 130; CANR 51, 74; CDWLB 3; CWW 2; DA3; DAM MULT, NOV; DLB 145; DNFS 1; FW; HW 1, 2; INT CA-130; LAIT 5; LAWS 1; MTCW 1, 2; NCFS 1; NFS 6; RGSF 2; SSFS 11; WLIT 1
Alleyn, Ellen
See Rossetti, Christina (Georgina)
Alleyne, Carla D. .... **CLC 65**
Allingham, Margery (Louise)
1904-1966 .... **CLC 19**
See also CA 5-8R; 25-28R; CANR 4, 58; CMW 4; DLB 77; MSW; MTCW 1, 2
Allingham, William 1824-1889 .... **NCLC 25**
See also DLB 35; RGEL 2
Allison, Dorothy E. 1949- .... **CLC 78, 153**
See also CA 140; CANR 66, 107; CSW; DA3; FW; MTCW 1; NFS 11; RGAL 4
Alloula, Malek .... **CLC 65**
Allston, Washington 1779-1843 .... **NCLC 2**
See also DLB 1, 235
Almedingen, E. M. .... **CLC 12**
See also Almedingen, Martha Edith von
See also SATA 3
Almedingen, Martha Edith von 1898-1971
See Almedingen, E. M.
See also CA 1-4R; CANR 1
Almodovar, Pedro 1949(?)- .... **CLC 114; HLCS 1**
See also CA 133; CANR 72; HW 2
Almqvist, Carl Jonas Love
1793-1866 .... **NCLC 42**
Alonso, Damaso 1898-1990 .... **CLC 14**
See also CA 110; 131; 130; CANR 72; DLB 108; HW 1, 2**

Alov
See Gogol, Nikolai (Vasilyevich)

Alta 1942- .... **CLC 19**
See also CA 57-60

Alter, Robert B(ernard) 1935- .... **CLC 34**
See also CA 49-52; CANR 1, 47, 100

Alther, Lisa 1944- .... **CLC 7, 41**
See also BPFB 1; CA 65-68; CAAS 30; CANR 12, 30, 51; CN 7; CSW; GLL 2; MTCW 1

Althusser, L.
See Althusser, Louis

Althusser, Louis 1918-1990 .... **CLC 106**
See also CA 131; 132; CANR 102; DLB 242

Altman, Robert 1925- .... **CLC 16, 116**
See also CA 73-76; CANR 43

Alurista
See Urista, Alberto H.
See also DLB 82; HLCS 1

Alvarez, A(lfred) 1929- .... **CLC 5, 13**
See also CA 1-4R; CANR 3, 33, 63, 101; CN 7; CP 7; DLB 14, 40

Alvarez, Alejandro Rodriguez 1903-1965
See Casona, Alejandro
See also CA 131; 93-96; HW 1

Alvarez, Julia 1950- .... **CLC 93; HLCS 1**
See also AAYA 25; AMWS 7; CA 147; CANR 69, 101; DA3; MTCW 1; NFS 5, 9; SATA 129; WLIT 1

Alvaro, Corrado 1896-1956 .... **TCLC 60**
See also CA 163

Amado, Jorge 1912-2001 ... **CLC 13, 40, 106; HLC 1**
See also CA 77-80; 201; CANR 35, 74; DAM MULT, NOV; DLB 113; HW 2; LAW; LAWS 1; MTCW 1, 2; RGWL 2; WLIT 1

Ambler, Eric 1909-1998 .... **CLC 4, 6, 9**
See also BRWS 2; CA 9-12R; 171; CANR 7, 38, 74; CMW 4; CN 7; DLB 77; MSW; MTCW 1, 2

Ambrose, Stephen E(dward)
1936- .... **CLC 145**
See also CA 1-4R; CANR 3, 43, 57, 83, 105; NCFS 2; SATA 40

Amichai, Yehuda 1924-2000 .. **CLC 9, 22, 57, 116; PC 38**
See also CA 85-88; 189; CANR 46, 60, 99; CWW 2; MTCW 1

Amichai, Yehudah
See Amichai, Yehuda

Amiel, Henri Frederic 1821-1881 .... **NCLC 4**
See also DLB 217

Amis, Kingsley (William)
1922-1995 ...... **CLC 1, 2, 3, 5, 8, 13, 40, 44, 129**
See also AITN 2; BPFB 1; BRWS 2; CA 9-12R; 150; CANR 8, 28, 54; CDBLB 1945-1960; CN 7; CP 7; DA; DA3; DAB; DAC; DAM MST, NOV; DLB 15, 27, 100, 139; DLBY 1996; HGG; INT CANR-8; MTCW 1, 2; RGEL 2; RGSF 2; SFW 4

Amis, Martin (Louis) 1949- .... **CLC 4, 9, 38, 62, 101**
See also BEST 90:3; BRWS 4; CA 65-68; CANR 8, 27, 54, 73, 95; CN 7; DA3; DLB 14, 194; INT CANR-27; MTCW 1

Ammons, A(rchie) R(andolph)
1926-2001 .... **CLC 2, 3, 5, 8, 9, 25, 57, 108; PC 16**
See also AITN 1; AMWS 7; CA 9-12R; 193; CANR 6, 36, 51, 73, 107; CP 7; CSW; DAM POET; DLB 5, 165; MTCW 1, 2; RGAL 4

Amo, Tauraatua i
See Adams, Henry (Brooks)

Amory, Thomas 1691(?)-1788 .... **LC 48**
See also DLB 39

Anand, Mulk Raj 1905- .... **CLC 23, 93**
See also CA 65-68; CANR 32, 64; CN 7; DAM NOV; MTCW 1, 2; RGSF 2

Anatol
See Schnitzler, Arthur

Anaximander c. 611B.C.-c. 546B.C. .... **CMLC 22**

Anaya, Rudolfo A(lfonso) 1937- ...... **CLC 23, 148; HLC 1**
See also AAYA 20; BYA 13; CA 45-48; CAAS 4; CANR 1, 32, 51; CN 7; DAM MULT, NOV; DLB 82, 206; HW 1; LAIT 4; MTCW 1, 2; NFS 12; RGAL 4; RGSF 2; WLIT 1

Andersen, Hans Christian
1805-1875 ... **NCLC 7, 79; SSC 6; WLC**
See also CLR 6; DA; DA3; DAB; DAC; DAM MST, POP; EW 6; MAICYA 1, 2; RGSF 2; RGWL 2; SATA 100; WCH; YABC 1

Anderson, C. Farley
See Mencken, H(enry) L(ouis); Nathan, George Jean

Anderson, Jessica (Margaret) Queale
1916- .... **CLC 37**
See also CA 9-12R; CANR 4, 62; CN 7

Anderson, Jon (Victor) 1940- .... **CLC 9**
See also CA 25-28R; CANR 20; DAM POET

Anderson, Lindsay (Gordon)
1923-1994 .... **CLC 20**
See also CA 125; 128; 146; CANR 77

Anderson, Maxwell 1888-1959 .... **TCLC 2**
See also CA 105; 152; DAM DRAM; DLB 7, 228; MTCW 2; RGAL 4

Anderson, Poul (William)
1926-2001 .... **CLC 15**
See also AAYA 5, 34; BPFB 1; BYA 6, 8, 9; CA 1-4R; 181; 199; CAAE 181; CAAS 2; CANR 2, 15, 34, 64; CLR 58; DLB 8; FANT; INT CANR-15; MTCW 1, 2; SATA 90; SATA-Brief 39; SATA-Essay 106; SCFW 2; SFW 4; SUFW

Anderson, Robert (Woodruff)
1917- .... **CLC 23**
See also AITN 1; CA 21-24R; CANR 32; DAM DRAM; DLB 7; LAIT 5

Anderson, Roberta Joan
See Mitchell, Joni

Anderson, Sherwood 1876-1941 ..... **TCLC 1, 10, 24, 123; SSC 1, 46; WLC**
See also AAYA 30; AMW; BPFB 1; CA 104; 121; CANR 61; CDALB 1917-1929; DA; DA3; DAB; DAC; DAM MST, NOV; DLB 4, 9, 86; DLBD 1; EXPS; GLL 2; MTCW 1, 2; NFS 4; RGAL 4; RGSF 2; SSFS 4, 10, 11

Andier, Pierre
See Desnos, Robert

Andouard
See Giraudoux, Jean(-Hippolyte)

Andrade, Carlos Drummond de ..... **CLC 18**
See also Drummond de Andrade, Carlos
See also RGWL 2

Andrade, Mario de .... **TCLC 43**
See also de Andrade, Mario
See also LAW; RGWL 2; WLIT 1

Andreae, Johann V(alentin)
1586-1654 .... **LC 32**
See also DLB 164

Andreas Capellanus fl. c. 1185- .... **CMLC 45**
See also DLB 208

Andreas-Salome, Lou 1861-1937 ... **TCLC 56**
See also CA 178; DLB 66

Andress, Lesley
See Sanders, Lawrence

Andrewes, Lancelot 1555-1626 .... **LC 5**
See also DLB 151, 172

Andrews, Cicily Fairfield
See West, Rebecca

Andrews, Elton V.
See Pohl, Frederik

Andreyev, Leonid (Nikolaevich)
1871-1919 .... **TCLC 3**
See also CA 104; 185

Andric, Ivo 1892-1975 .... **CLC 8; SSC 36**
See also CA 81-84; 57-60; CANR 43, 60; CDWLB 4; DLB 147; EW 11; MTCW 1; RGSF 2; RGWL 2

Androvar
See Prado (Calvo), Pedro

Angelique, Pierre
See Bataille, Georges

Angell, Roger 1920- .... **CLC 26**
See also CA 57-60; CANR 13, 44, 70; DLB 171, 185

Angelou, Maya 1928- ..... **CLC 12, 35, 64, 77, 155; BLC 1; PC 32; WLCS**
See also AAYA 7, 20; AMWS 4; BPFB 1; BW 2, 3; BYA 2; CA 65-68; CANR 19, 42, 65; CDALBS; CLR 53; CP 7; CPW; CSW; CWP; DA; DA3; DAB; DAC; DAM MST, MULT, POP; DLB 38; EXPN; EXPP; LAIT 4; MAICYA 2; MAICYAS 1; MAWW; MTCW 1, 2; NCFS 2; NFS 2; PFS 2, 3; RGAL 4; SATA 49; WYA; YAW

Angouleme, Marguerite d'
See de Navarre, Marguerite

Anna Comnena 1083-1153 .... **CMLC 25**

Annensky, Innokenty (Fyodorovich)
1856-1909 .... **TCLC 14**
See also CA 110; 155

Annunzio, Gabriele d'
See D'Annunzio, Gabriele

Anodos
See Coleridge, Mary E(lizabeth)

Anon, Charles Robert
See Pessoa, Fernando (Antonio Nogueira)

Anouilh, Jean (Marie Lucien Pierre)
1910-1987 . **CLC 1, 3, 8, 13, 40, 50; DC 8**
See also CA 17-20R; 123; CANR 32; DAM DRAM; DFS 9, 10; EW 13; GFL 1789 to the Present; MTCW 1, 2; RGWL 2

Anthony, Florence
See Ai

Anthony, John
See Ciardi, John (Anthony)

Anthony, Peter
See Shaffer, Anthony (Joshua); Shaffer, Peter (Levin)

Anthony, Piers 1934- .... **CLC 35**
See also AAYA 11; BYA 7; CA 21-24R; CAAE 200; CANR 28, 56, 73, 102; CPW; DAM POP; DLB 8; FANT; MAICYA 2; MAICYAS 1; MTCW 1, 2; SAAS 22; SATA 84; SATA-Essay 129; SFW 4; SUFW; YAW

Anthony, Susan B(rownell)
1820-1906 .... **TCLC 84**
See also FW

Antoine, Marc
See Proust, (Valentin-Louis-George-Eugene-)Marcel

Antoninus, Brother
See Everson, William (Oliver)

Antonioni, Michelangelo 1912- .... **CLC 20, 144**
See also CA 73-76; CANR 45, 77

Antschel, Paul 1920-1970
See Celan, Paul
See also CA 85-88; CANR 33, 61; MTCW 1

Anwar, Chairil 1922-1949 .... **TCLC 22**
See also CA 121

Anzaldua, Gloria (Evanjelina) 1942-
See also CA 175; CSW; CWP; DLB 122; FW; HLCS 1; RGAL 4

Apess, William 1798-1839(?) .... **NCLC 73**
See also DAM MULT; DLB 175, 243; NNAL

Apollinaire, Guillaume 1880-1918 .. **TCLC 3, 8, 51; PC 7**
See also Kostrowitzki, Wilhelm Apollinaris de
See also CA 152; DAM POET; DLB 258; EW 9; GFL 1789 to the Present; MTCW 1; RGWL 2; TWA; WP

Apollonius of Rhodes
See Apollonius Rhodius
See also AW 1; RGWL 2

Apollonius Rhodius c. 300B.C.-c. 220B.C. .... **CMLC 28**
See also Apollonius of Rhodes
See also DLB 176

Appelfeld, Aharon 1932- ... **CLC 23, 47; SSC 42**
See also CA 112; 133; CANR 86; CWW 2; RGSF 2

Apple, Max (Isaac) 1941- .... **CLC 9, 33; SSC 50**
See also CA 81-84; CANR 19, 54; DLB 130

Appleman, Philip (Dean) 1926- .... **CLC 51**
See also CA 13-16R; CAAS 18; CANR 6, 29, 56

Appleton, Lawrence
See Lovecraft, H(oward) P(hillips)

Apteryx
See Eliot, T(homas) S(tearns)

Apuleius, (Lucius Madaurensis) 125(?)-175(?) .... **CMLC 1**
See also AW 2; CDWLB 1; DLB 211; RGWL 2; SUFW

Aquin, Hubert 1929-1977 .... **CLC 15**
See also CA 105; DLB 53

Aquinas, Thomas 1224(?)-1274 ..... **CMLC 33**
See also DLB 115; EW 1

Aragon, Louis 1897-1982 .... **CLC 3, 22**
See also CA 69-72; 108; CANR 28, 71; DAM NOV, POET; DLB 72, 258; EW 11; GFL 1789 to the Present; GLL 2; MTCW 1, 2; RGWL 2; TCLC 123

Arany, Janos 1817-1882 .... **NCLC 34**

Aranyos, Kakay 1847-1910
See Mikszath, Kalman

Arbuthnot, John 1667-1735 .... **LC 1**
See also DLB 101

Archer, Herbert Winslow
See Mencken, H(enry) L(ouis)

Archer, Jeffrey (Howard) 1940- .... **CLC 28**
See also AAYA 16; BEST 89:3; BPFB 1; CA 77-80; CANR 22, 52, 95; CPW; DA3; DAM POP; INT CANR-22

Archer, Jules 1915- .... **CLC 12**
See also CA 9-12R; CANR 6, 69; SAAS 5; SATA 4, 85

Archer, Lee
See Ellison, Harlan (Jay)

Archilochus c. 7th cent. B.C.- .... **CMLC 44**
See also DLB 176

Arden, John 1930- .... **CLC 6, 13, 15**
See also BRWS 2; CA 13-16R; CAAS 4; CANR 31, 65, 67; CBD; CD 5; DAM DRAM; DFS 9; DLB 13, 245; MTCW 1

Arenas, Reinaldo 1943-1990 .. **CLC 41; HLC 1**
See also CA 124; 128; 133; CANR 73, 106; DAM MULT; DLB 145; GLL 2; HW 1; LAW; LAWS 1; MTCW 1; RGSF 2; WLIT 1

Arendt, Hannah 1906-1975 .... **CLC 66, 98**
See also CA 17-20R; 61-64; CANR 26, 60; DLB 242; MTCW 1, 2

Aretino, Pietro 1492-1556 .... **LC 12**
See also RGWL 2

Arghezi, Tudor -1967 .... **CLC 80**
See also Theodorescu, Ion N.
See also CA 167; CDWLB 4; DLB 220

Arguedas, Jose Maria 1911-1969 .... **CLC 10, 18; HLCS 1**
See also CA 89-92; CANR 73; DLB 113; HW 1; LAW; RGWL 2; WLIT 1

Argueta, Manlio 1936- .... **CLC 31**
See also CA 131; CANR 73; CWW 2; DLB 145; HW 1

Arias, Ron(ald Francis) 1941-
See also CA 131; CANR 81; DAM MULT; DLB 82; HLC 1; HW 1, 2; MTCW 2

Ariosto, Ludovico 1474-1533 .... **LC 6**
See also EW 2; RGWL 2

Aristides
See Epstein, Joseph

Aristophanes 450B.C.-385B.C. .... **CMLC 4, 51; DC 2; WLCS**
See also AW 1; CDWLB 1; DA; DA3; DAB; DAC; DAM DRAM, MST; DFS 10; DLB 176; RGWL 2

Aristotle 384B.C.-322B.C. .... **CMLC 31; WLCS**
See also AW 1; CDWLB 1; DA; DA3; DAB; DAC; DAM MST; DLB 176; RGEL 2; TWA

Arlt, Roberto (Godofredo Christophersen) 1900-1942 .... **TCLC 29; HLC 1**
See also CA 123; 131; CANR 67; DAM MULT; HW 1, 2; LAW

Armah, Ayi Kwei 1939- .... **CLC 5, 33, 136; BLC 1**
See also AFW; BW 1; CA 61-64; CANR 21, 64; CDWLB 3; CN 7; DAM MULT, POET; DLB 117; MTCW 1; WLIT 2

Armatrading, Joan 1950- .... **CLC 17**
See also CA 114; 186

Armitage, Frank
See Carpenter, John (Howard)

Arnette, Robert
See Silverberg, Robert

Arnim, Achim von (Ludwig Joachim von Arnim) 1781-1831 ..... **NCLC 5; SSC 29**
See also DLB 90

Arnim, Bettina von 1785-1859 .... **NCLC 38**
See also DLB 90; RGWL 2

Arnold, Matthew 1822-1888 ..... **NCLC 6, 29, 89; PC 5; WLC**
See also BRW 5; CDBLB 1832-1890; DA; DAB; DAC; DAM MST, POET; DLB 32, 57; EXPP; PAB; PFS 2; WP

Arnold, Thomas 1795-1842 .... **NCLC 18**
See also DLB 55

Arnow, Harriette (Louisa) Simpson 1908-1986 .... **CLC 2, 7, 18**
See also BPFB 1; CA 9-12R; 118; CANR 14; DLB 6; FW; MTCW 1, 2; RHW; SATA 42; SATA-Obit 47

Arouet, Francois-Marie
See Voltaire

Arp, Hans
See Arp, Jean

Arp, Jean 1887-1966 .... **CLC 5**
See also CA 81-84; 25-28R; CANR 42, 77; EW 10; TCLC 115

Arrabal
See Arrabal, Fernando

Arrabal, Fernando 1932- ... **CLC 2, 9, 18, 58**
See also CA 9-12R; CANR 15

Arreola, Juan Jose 1918-2001 ...... **CLC 147; HLC 1; SSC 38**
See also CA 113; 131; 200; CANR 81; DAM MULT; DLB 113; DNFS 2; HW 1, 2; LAW; RGSF 2

Arrian c. 89(?)-c. 155(?) .... **CMLC 43**
See also DLB 176

Arrick, Fran .... **CLC 30**
See also Gaberman, Judie Angell
See also BYA 6

Artaud, Antonin (Marie Joseph) 1896-1948 .... **TCLC 3, 36; DC 14**
See also CA 104; 149; DA3; DAM DRAM; DLB 258; EW 11; GFL 1789 to the Present; MTCW 1; RGWL 2

Arthur, Ruth M(abel) 1905-1979 ..... **CLC 12**
See also CA 9-12R; 85-88; CANR 4; CWRI 5; SATA 7, 26

Artsybashev, Mikhail (Petrovich) 1878-1927 .... **TCLC 31**
See also CA 170

Arundel, Honor (Morfydd) 1919-1973 .... **CLC 17**
See also CA 21-22; 41-44R; CAP 2; CLR 35; CWRI 5; SATA 4; SATA-Obit 24

Arzner, Dorothy 1900-1979 .... **CLC 98**

Asch, Sholem 1880-1957 .... **TCLC 3**
See also CA 105; GLL 2

Ash, Shalom
See Asch, Sholem

Ashbery, John (Lawrence) 1927- .. **CLC 2, 3, 4, 6, 9, 13, 15, 25, 41, 77, 125; PC 26**
See also Berry, Jonas
See also AMWS 3; CA 5-8R; CANR 9, 37, 66, 102; CP 7; DA3; DAM POET; DLB 5, 165; DLBY 1981; INT CANR-9; MTCW 1, 2; PAB; PFS 11; RGAL 4; WP

Ashdown, Clifford
See Freeman, R(ichard) Austin

Ashe, Gordon
See Creasey, John

Ashton-Warner, Sylvia (Constance) 1908-1984 .... **CLC 19**
See also CA 69-72; 112; CANR 29; MTCW 1, 2

Asimov, Isaac 1920-1992 ..... **CLC 1, 3, 9, 19, 26, 76, 92**
See also AAYA 13; BEST 90:2; BPFB 1; BYA 4, 6, 7, 9; CA 1-4R; 137; CANR 2, 19, 36, 60; CLR 12, 79; CMW 4; CPW; DA3; DAM POP; DLB 8; DLBY 1992; INT CANR-19; JRDA; LAIT 5; MAICYA 1, 2; MTCW 1, 2; RGAL 4; SATA 1, 26, 74; SCFW 2; SFW 4; YAW

Assis, Joaquim Maria Machado de
See Machado de Assis, Joaquim Maria

Astell, Mary 1666-1731 .... **LC 68**
See also DLB 252; FW

Astley, Thea (Beatrice May) 1925- .. **CLC 41**
See also CA 65-68; CANR 11, 43, 78; CN 7

Astley, William 1855-1911
See Warung, Price

Aston, James
See White, T(erence) H(anbury)

Asturias, Miguel Angel 1899-1974 .... **CLC 3, 8, 13; HLC 1**
See also CA 25-28; 49-52; CANR 32; CAP 2; CDWLB 3; DA3; DAM MULT, NOV; DLB 113; HW 1; LAW; MTCW 1, 2; RGWL 2; WLIT 1

Atares, Carlos Saura
See Saura (Atares), Carlos

Athanasius c. 295-c. 373 .... **CMLC 48**

Atheling, William
See Pound, Ezra (Weston Loomis)

Atheling, William, Jr.
See Blish, James (Benjamin)

Atherton, Gertrude (Franklin Horn)
1857-1948 .... **TCLC 2**
See also CA 104; 155; DLB 9, 78, 186; HGG; RGAL 4; SUFW; TCWW 2

Atherton, Lucius
See Masters, Edgar Lee

Atkins, Jack
See Harris, Mark

Atkinson, Kate .... **CLC 99**
See also CA 166; CANR 101

Attaway, William (Alexander)
1911-1986 .... **CLC 92; BLC 1**
See also BW 2, 3; CA 143; CANR 82; DAM MULT; DLB 76

Atticus
See Fleming, Ian (Lancaster); Wilson, (Thomas) Woodrow

Atwood, Margaret (Eleanor) 1939- ... **CLC 2, 3, 4, 8, 13, 15, 25, 44, 84, 135; PC 8; SSC 2, 46; WLC**
See also AAYA 12; BEST 89:2; BPFB 1; CA 49-52; CANR 3, 24, 33, 59, 95; CN 7; CP 7; CPW; CWP; DA; DA3; DAB; DAC; DAM MST, NOV, POET; DLB 53, 251; EXPN; FW; INT CANR-24; LAIT 5; MTCW 1, 2; NFS 4, 12, 13, 14; PFS 7; RGSF 2; SATA 50; SSFS 3, 13; YAW

Aubigny, Pierre d'
See Mencken, H(enry) L(ouis)

Aubin, Penelope 1685-1731(?) .... **LC 9**
See also DLB 39

Auchincloss, Louis (Stanton) 1917- .. **CLC 4, 6, 9, 18, 45; SSC 22**
See also AMWS 4; CA 1-4R; CANR 6, 29, 55, 87; CN 7; DAM NOV; DLB 2, 244; DLBY 1980; INT CANR-29; MTCW 1; RGAL 4

Auden, W(ystan) H(ugh) 1907-1973 . **CLC 1, 2, 3, 4, 6, 9, 11, 14, 43, 123; PC 1; WLC**
See also AAYA 18; AMWS 2; BRW 7; BRWR 1; CA 9-12R; 45-48; CANR 5, 61, 105; CDBLB 1914-1945; DA; DA3; DAB; DAC; DAM DRAM, MST, POET; DLB 10, 20; EXPP; MTCW 1, 2; PAB; PFS 1, 3, 4, 10; WP

Audiberti, Jacques 1900-1965 .... **CLC 38**
See also CA 25-28R; DAM DRAM

Audubon, John James 1785-1851 . **NCLC 47**
See also ANW; DLB 248

Auel, Jean M(arie) 1936- .... **CLC 31, 107**
See also AAYA 7; BEST 90:4; BPFB 1; CA 103; CANR 21, 64; CPW; DA3; DAM POP; INT CANR-21; NFS 11; RHW; SATA 91

Auerbach, Erich 1892-1957 .... **TCLC 43**
See also CA 118; 155

Augier, Emile 1820-1889 .... **NCLC 31**
See also DLB 192; GFL 1789 to the Present

August, John
See De Voto, Bernard (Augustine)

Augustine, St. 354-430 .... **CMLC 6; WLCS**
See also DA; DA3; DAB; DAC; DAM MST; DLB 115; EW 1; RGWL 2

Aunt Belinda
See Braddon, Mary Elizabeth

Aunt Weedy
See Alcott, Louisa May

Aurelius
See Bourne, Randolph S(illiman)

Aurelius, Marcus 121-180 .... **CMLC 45**
See also Marcus Aurelius
See also RGWL 2

Aurobindo, Sri
See Ghose, Aurabinda

Austen, Jane 1775-1817 ...... **NCLC 1, 13, 19, 33, 51, 81, 95; WLC**
See also AAYA 19; BRW 4; BRWR 2; BYA 3; CDBLB 1789-1832; DA; DA3; DAB; DAC; DAM MST, NOV; DLB 116; EXPN; LAIT 2; NFS 1, 14; WLIT 3; WYAS 1

Auster, Paul 1947- .... **CLC 47, 131**
See also CA 69-72; CANR 23, 52, 75; CMW 4; CN 7; DA3; DLB 227; MTCW 1

Austin, Frank
See Faust, Frederick (Schiller)
See also TCWW 2

Austin, Mary (Hunter) 1868-1934 . **TCLC 25**
See also Stairs, Gordon
See also ANW; CA 109; 178; DLB 9, 78, 206, 221; FW; TCWW 2

Averroes 1126-1198 .... **CMLC 7**
See also DLB 115

Avicenna 980-1037 .... **CMLC 16**
See also DLB 115

Avison, Margaret 1918- .... **CLC 2, 4, 97**
See also CA 17-20R; CP 7; DAC; DAM POET; DLB 53; MTCW 1

Axton, David
See Koontz, Dean R(ay)

Ayckbourn, Alan 1939- ...... **CLC 5, 8, 18, 33, 74; DC 13**
See also BRWS 5; CA 21-24R; CANR 31, 59; CBD; CD 5; DAB; DAM DRAM; DFS 7; DLB 13, 245; MTCW 1, 2

Aydy, Catherine
See Tennant, Emma (Christina)

Ayme, Marcel (Andre) 1902-1967 ... **CLC 11; SSC 41**
See also CA 89-92; CANR 67; CLR 25; DLB 72; EW 12; GFL 1789 to the Present; RGSF 2; RGWL 2; SATA 91

Ayrton, Michael 1921-1975 .... **CLC 7**
See also CA 5-8R; 61-64; CANR 9, 21

Azorin .... **CLC 11**
See also Martinez Ruiz, Jose
See also EW 9

Azuela, Mariano 1873-1952 .. **TCLC 3; HLC 1**
See also CA 104; 131; CANR 81; DAM MULT; HW 1, 2; LAW; MTCW 1, 2

Baastad, Babbis Friis
See Friis-Baastad, Babbis Ellinor

Bab
See Gilbert, W(illiam) S(chwenck)

Babbis, Eleanor
See Friis-Baastad, Babbis Ellinor

Babel, Isaac
See Babel, Isaak (Emmanuilovich)
See also EW 11; SSFS 10

Babel, Isaak (Emmanuilovich)
1894-1941(?) .... **TCLC 2, 13; SSC 16**
See also Babel, Isaac
See also CA 104; 155; MTCW 1; RGSF 2; RGWL 2

Babits, Mihaly 1883-1941 .... **TCLC 14**
See also CA 114; CDWLB 4; DLB 215

Babur 1483-1530 .... **LC 18**

Babylas 1898-1962
See Ghelderode, Michel de

Baca, Jimmy Santiago 1952- .... **PC 41**
See also CA 131; CANR 81, 90; CP 7; DAM MULT; DLB 122; HLC 1; HW 1, 2

Baca, Jose Santiago
See Baca, Jimmy Santiago

Bacchelli, Riccardo 1891-1985 .... **CLC 19**
See also CA 29-32R; 117

Bach, Richard (David) 1936- .... **CLC 14**
See also AITN 1; BEST 89:2; BPFB 1; BYA 5; CA 9-12R; CANR 18, 93; CPW; DAM NOV, POP; FANT; MTCW 1; SATA 13

Bache, Benjamin Franklin
1769-1798 .... **LC 74**
See also DLB 43

Bachman, Richard
See King, Stephen (Edwin)

Bachmann, Ingeborg 1926-1973 .... **CLC 69**
See also CA 93-96; 45-48; CANR 69; DLB 85; RGWL 2

Bacon, Francis 1561-1626 .... **LC 18, 32**
See also BRW 1; CDBLB Before 1660; DLB 151, 236, 252; RGEL 2

Bacon, Roger 1214(?)-1294 .... **CMLC 14**
See also DLB 115

Bacovia, George 1881-1957 .... **TCLC 24**
See also Vasiliu, Gheorghe
See also CDWLB 4; DLB 220

Badanes, Jerome 1937- .... **CLC 59**

Bagehot, Walter 1826-1877 .... **NCLC 10**
See also DLB 55

Bagnold, Enid 1889-1981 .... **CLC 25**
See also BYA 2; CA 5-8R; 103; CANR 5, 40; CBD; CWD; CWRI 5; DAM DRAM; DLB 13, 160, 191, 245; FW; MAICYA 1, 2; RGEL 2; SATA 1, 25

Bagritsky, Eduard 1895-1934 .... **TCLC 60**

Bagrjana, Elisaveta
See Belcheva, Elisaveta Lyubomirova

Bagryana, Elisaveta -1991 .... **CLC 10**
See also Belcheva, Elisaveta Lyubomirova
See also CA 178; CDWLB 4; DLB 147

Bailey, Paul 1937- .... **CLC 45**
See also CA 21-24R; CANR 16, 62; CN 7; DLB 14; GLL 2

Baillie, Joanna 1762-1851 .... **NCLC 71**
See also DLB 93; RGEL 2

Bainbridge, Beryl (Margaret) 1934- . **CLC 4, 5, 8, 10, 14, 18, 22, 62, 130**
See also BRWS 6; CA 21-24R; CANR 24, 55, 75, 88; CN 7; DAM NOV; DLB 14, 231; MTCW 1, 2

Baker, Carlos (Heard)
1909-1987 .... **TCLC 119**
See also CA 5-8R; 122; CANR 3, 63; DLB 103

Baker, Elliott 1922- .... **CLC 8**
See also CA 45-48; CANR 2, 63; CN 7

Baker, Jean H. .... **TCLC 3, 10**
See also Russell, George William

Baker, Nicholson 1957- .... **CLC 61**
See also CA 135; CANR 63; CN 7; CPW; DA3; DAM POP; DLB 227

Baker, Ray Stannard 1870-1946 .... **TCLC 47**
See also CA 118

Baker, Russell (Wayne) 1925- .... **CLC 31**
See also BEST 89:4; CA 57-60; CANR 11, 41, 59; MTCW 1, 2

Bakhtin, M.
See Bakhtin, Mikhail Mikhailovich

Bakhtin, M. M.
See Bakhtin, Mikhail Mikhailovich

Bakhtin, Mikhail
See Bakhtin, Mikhail Mikhailovich

Bakhtin, Mikhail Mikhailovich
1895-1975 .... **CLC 83**
See also CA 128; 113; DLB 242

Bakshi, Ralph 1938(?)- .... **CLC 26**
See also CA 112; 138; IDFW 3

Bakunin, Mikhail (Alexandrovich)
1814-1876 .... **NCLC 25, 58**

Baldwin, James (Arthur) 1924-1987 . **CLC 1, 2, 3, 4, 5, 8, 13, 15, 17, 42, 50, 67, 90, 127; BLC 1; DC 1; SSC 10, 33; WLC**
See also AAYA 4, 34; AFAW 1, 2; AMWS 1; BW 1; CA 1-4R; 124; CABS 1; CAD; CANR 3, 24; CDALB 1941-1968; CPW; DA; DA3; DAB; DAC; DAM MST, MULT, NOV, POP; DFS 15; DLB 2, 7,

33, 249; DLBY 1987; EXPS; LAIT 5; MTCW 1, 2; NFS 4; RGAL 4; RGSF 2; SATA 9; SATA-Obit 54; SSFS 2

Bale, John 1495-1563 .... **LC 62**
See also DLB 132; RGEL 2

Ball, Hugo 1886-1927 .... **TCLC 104**

Ballard, J(ames) G(raham) 1930- . **CLC 3, 6, 14, 36, 137; SSC 1, 53**
See also AAYA 3; BRWS 5; CA 5-8R; CANR 15, 39, 65, 107; CN 7; DA3; DAM NOV, POP; DLB 14, 207, 261; HGG; MTCW 1, 2; NFS 8; RGEL 2; RGSF 2; SATA 93; SFW 4

Balmont, Konstantin (Dmitriyevich) 1867-1943 .... **TCLC 11**
See also CA 109; 155

Baltausis, Vincas 1847-1910
See Mikszath, Kalman

Balzac, Honore de 1799-1850 ... **NCLC 5, 35, 53; SSC 5; WLC**
See also DA; DA3; DAB; DAC; DAM MST, NOV; DLB 119; EW 5; GFL 1789 to the Present; RGSF 2; RGWL 2; SSFS 10; SUFW

Bambara, Toni Cade 1939-1995 ...... **CLC 19, 88; BLC 1; SSC 35; WLCS**
See also AAYA 5; AFAW 2; BW 2, 3; BYA 12, 14; CA 29-32R; 150; CANR 24, 49, 81; CDALBS; DA; DA3; DAC; DAM MST, MULT; DLB 38, 218; EXPS; MTCW 1, 2; RGAL 4; RGSF 2; SATA 112; SSFS 4, 7, 12; TCLC 116

Bamdad, A.
See Shamlu, Ahmad

Banat, D. R.
See Bradbury, Ray (Douglas)

Bancroft, Laura
See Baum, L(yman) Frank

Banim, John 1798-1842 .... **NCLC 13**
See also DLB 116, 158, 159; RGEL 2

Banim, Michael 1796-1874 .... **NCLC 13**
See also DLB 158, 159

Banjo, The
See Paterson, A(ndrew) B(arton)

Banks, Iain
See Banks, Iain M(enzies)

Banks, Iain M(enzies) 1954- .... **CLC 34**
See also CA 123; 128; CANR 61, 106; DLB 194, 261; HGG; INT 128; SFW 4

Banks, Lynne Reid .... **CLC 23**
See also Reid Banks, Lynne
See also AAYA 6; BYA 7

Banks, Russell 1940- .... **CLC 37, 72; SSC 42**
See also AMWS 5; CA 65-68; CAAS 15; CANR 19, 52, 73; CN 7; DLB 130; NFS 13

Banville, John 1945- .... **CLC 46, 118**
See also CA 117; 128; CANR 104; CN 7; DLB 14; INT 128

Banville, Theodore (Faullain) de 1832-1891 .... **NCLC 9**
See also DLB 217; GFL 1789 to the Present

Baraka, Amiri 1934- . **CLC 1, 2, 3, 5, 10, 14, 33, 115; BLC 1; DC 6; PC 4; WLCS**
See also Jones, LeRoi
See also AFAW 1, 2; AMWS 2; BW 2, 3; CA 21-24R; CABS 3; CAD; CANR 27, 38, 61; CD 5; CDALB 1941-1968; CP 7; CPW; DA; DA3; DAC; DAM MST, MULT, POET, POP; DFS 3, 11; DLB 5, 7, 16, 38; DLBD 8; MTCW 1, 2; PFS 9; RGAL 4; WP

Baratynsky, Evgenii Abramovich 1800-1844 .... **NCLC 103**
See also DLB 205

Barbauld, Anna Laetitia 1743-1825 .... **NCLC 50**
See also DLB 107, 109, 142, 158; RGEL 2

Barbellion, W. N. P. .... **TCLC 24**
See also Cummings, Bruce F(rederick)

Barber, Benjamin R. 1939- .... **CLC 141**
See also CA 29-32R; CANR 12, 32, 64

Barbera, Jack (Vincent) 1945- .... **CLC 44**
See also CA 110; CANR 45

Barbey d'Aurevilly, Jules-Amedee 1808-1889 .... **NCLC 1; SSC 17**
See also DLB 119; GFL 1789 to the Present

Barbour, John c. 1316-1395 .... **CMLC 33**
See also DLB 146

Barbusse, Henri 1873-1935 .... **TCLC 5**
See also CA 105; 154; DLB 65; RGWL 2

Barclay, Bill
See Moorcock, Michael (John)

Barclay, William Ewert
See Moorcock, Michael (John)

Barea, Arturo 1897-1957 .... **TCLC 14**
See also CA 111; 201

Barfoot, Joan 1946- .... **CLC 18**
See also CA 105

Barham, Richard Harris 1788-1845 .... **NCLC 77**
See also DLB 159

Baring, Maurice 1874-1945 .... **TCLC 8**
See also CA 105; 168; DLB 34; HGG

Baring-Gould, Sabine 1834-1924 ... **TCLC 88**
See also DLB 156, 190

Barker, Clive 1952- .... **CLC 52; SSC 53**
See also AAYA 10; BEST 90:3; BPFB 1; CA 121; 129; CANR 71; CPW; DA3; DAM POP; DLB 261; HGG; INT 129; MTCW 1, 2

Barker, George Granville 1913-1991 .... **CLC 8, 48**
See also CA 9-12R; 135; CANR 7, 38; DAM POET; DLB 20; MTCW 1

Barker, Harley Granville
See Granville-Barker, Harley
See also DLB 10

Barker, Howard 1946- .... **CLC 37**
See also CA 102; CBD; CD 5; DLB 13, 233

Barker, Jane 1652-1732 .... **LC 42**
See also DLB 39, 131

Barker, Pat(ricia) 1943- .... **CLC 32, 94, 146**
See BRWS 4; CA 117; 122; CANR 50, 101; CN 7; INT 122

Barlach, Ernst (Heinrich) 1870-1938 .... **TCLC 84**
See also CA 178; DLB 56, 118

Barlow, Joel 1754-1812 .... **NCLC 23**
See also AMWS 2; DLB 37; RGAL 4

Barnard, Mary (Ethel) 1909- .... **CLC 48**
See also CA 21-22; CAP 2

Barnes, Djuna 1892-1982 .... **CLC 3, 4, 8, 11, 29, 127; SSC 3**
See also Steptoe, Lydia
See also AMWS 3; CA 9-12R; 107; CAD; CANR 16, 55; CWD; DLB 4, 9, 45; GLL 1; MTCW 1, 2; RGAL 4; TUS

Barnes, Julian (Patrick) 1946- . **CLC 42, 141**
See also BRWS 4; CA 102; CANR 19, 54; CN 7; DAB; DLB 194; DLBY 1993; MTCW 1

Barnes, Peter 1931- .... **CLC 5, 56**
See also CA 65-68; CAAS 12; CANR 33, 34, 64; CBD; CD 5; DFS 6; DLB 13, 233; MTCW 1

Barnes, William 1801-1886 .... **NCLC 75**
See also DLB 32

Baroja (y Nessi), Pio 1872-1956 ..... **TCLC 8; HLC 1**
See also CA 104; EW 9

Baron, David
See Pinter, Harold

Baron Corvo
See Rolfe, Frederick (William Serafino Austin Lewis Mary)

Barondess, Sue K(aufman) 1926-1977 .... **CLC 8**
See also Kaufman, Sue
See also CA 1-4R; 69-72; CANR 1

Baron de Teive
See Pessoa, Fernando (Antonio Nogueira)

Baroness Von S.
See Zangwill, Israel

Barres, (Auguste-)Maurice 1862-1923 .... **TCLC 47**
See also CA 164; DLB 123; GFL 1789 to the Present

Barreto, Afonso Henrique de Lima
See Lima Barreto, Afonso Henrique de

Barrett, Andrea 1954- .... **CLC 150**
See also CA 156; CANR 92

Barrett, Michele .... **CLC 65**

Barrett, (Roger) Syd 1946- .... **CLC 35**

Barrett, William (Christopher) 1913-1992 .... **CLC 27**
See also CA 13-16R; 139; CANR 11, 67; INT CANR-11

Barrie, J(ames) M(atthew) 1860-1937 .... **TCLC 2**
See also BRWS 3; BYA 4, 5; CA 104; 136; CANR 77; CDBLB 1890-1914; CLR 16; CWRI 5; DA3; DAB; DAM DRAM; DFS 7; DLB 10, 141, 156; FANT; MAICYA 1, 2; MTCW 1; SATA 100; SUFW; WCH; WLIT 4; YABC 1

Barrington, Michael
See Moorcock, Michael (John)

Barrol, Grady
See Bograd, Larry

Barry, Mike
See Malzberg, Barry N(athaniel)

Barry, Philip 1896-1949 .... **TCLC 11**
See also CA 109; 199; DFS 9; DLB 7, 228; RGAL 4

Bart, Andre Schwarz
See Schwarz-Bart, Andre

Barth, John (Simmons) 1930- ... **CLC 1, 2, 3, 5, 7, 9, 10, 14, 27, 51, 89; SSC 10**
See also AITN 1, 2; AMW; BPFB 1; CA 1-4R; CABS 1; CANR 5, 23, 49, 64; CN 7; DAM NOV; DLB 2, 227; FANT; MTCW 1; RGAL 4; RGSF 2; RHW; SSFS 6

Barthelme, Donald 1931-1989 ... **CLC 1, 2, 3, 5, 6, 8, 13, 23, 46, 59, 115; SSC 2**
See also AMWS 4; BPFB 1; CA 21-24R; 129; CANR 20, 58; DA3; DAM NOV; DLB 2, 234; DLBY 1980, 1989; FANT; MTCW 1, 2; RGAL 4; RGSF 2; SATA 7; SATA-Obit 62; SSFS 3

Barthelme, Frederick 1943- ...... **CLC 36, 117**
See also CA 114; 122; CANR 77; CN 7; CSW; DLB 244; DLBY 1985; INT CA-122

Barthes, Roland (Gerard) 1915-1980 .... **CLC 24, 83**
See also CA 130; 97-100; CANR 66; EW 13; GFL 1789 to the Present; MTCW 1, 2

Barzun, Jacques (Martin) 1907- ..... **CLC 51, 145**
See also CA 61-64; CANR 22, 95

Bashevis, Isaac
See Singer, Isaac Bashevis

Bashkirtseff, Marie 1859-1884 .... **NCLC 27**

Basho, Matsuo
See Matsuo Basho
See also RGWL 2; WP

Basil of Caesaria c. 330-379 .... **CMLC 35**

Bass, Kingsley B., Jr.
See Bullins, Ed

Bass, Rick 1958- .... **CLC 79, 143**
See also ANW; CA 126; CANR 53, 93; CSW; DLB 212

Bassani, Giorgio 1916-2000 .... **CLC 9**
See also CA 65-68; 190; CANR 33; CWW 2; DLB 128, 177; MTCW 1; RGWL 2

Bastian, Ann .... **CLC 70**

Bastos, Augusto (Antonio) Roa
See Roa Bastos, Augusto (Antonio)

Bataille, Georges 1897-1962 .... **CLC 29**
See also CA 101; 89-92

Bates, H(erbert) E(rnest)
1905-1974 .... **CLC 46; SSC 10**
See also CA 93-96; 45-48; CANR 34; DA3; DAB; DAM POP; DLB 162, 191; EXPS; MTCW 1, 2; RGSF 2; SSFS 7

Bauchart
See Camus, Albert

Baudelaire, Charles 1821-1867 . **NCLC 6, 29, 55; PC 1; SSC 18; WLC**
See also DA; DA3; DAB; DAC; DAM MST, POET; DLB 217; EW 7; GFL 1789 to the Present; RGWL 2

Baudouin, Marcel
See Peguy, Charles (Pierre)

Baudouin, Pierre
See Peguy, Charles (Pierre)

Baudrillard, Jean 1929- .... **CLC 60**

Baum, L(yman) Frank 1856-1919 ... **TCLC 7**
See also CA 108; 133; CLR 15; CWRI 5; DLB 22; FANT; JRDA; MAICYA 1, 2; MTCW 1, 2; NFS 13; RGAL 4; SATA 18, 100; WCH

Baum, Louis F.
See Baum, L(yman) Frank

Baumbach, Jonathan 1933- .... **CLC 6, 23**
See also CA 13-16R; CAAS 5; CANR 12, 66; CN 7; DLBY 1980; INT CANR-12; MTCW 1

Bausch, Richard (Carl) 1945- .... **CLC 51**
See also AMWS 7; CA 101; CAAS 14; CANR 43, 61, 87; CSW; DLB 130

Baxter, Charles (Morley) 1947- . **CLC 45, 78**
See also CA 57-60; CANR 40, 64, 104; CPW; DAM POP; DLB 130; MTCW 2

Baxter, George Owen
See Faust, Frederick (Schiller)

Baxter, James K(eir) 1926-1972 .... **CLC 14**
See also CA 77-80

Baxter, John
See Hunt, E(verette) Howard, (Jr.)

Bayer, Sylvia
See Glassco, John

Baynton, Barbara 1857-1929 .... **TCLC 57**
See also DLB 230; RGSF 2

Beagle, Peter S(oyer) 1939- .... **CLC 7, 104**
See also BPFB 1; BYA 9, 10; CA 9-12R; CANR 4, 51, 73; DA3; DLBY 1980; FANT; INT CANR-4; MTCW 1; SATA 60, 130; SUFW; YAW

Bean, Normal
See Burroughs, Edgar Rice

Beard, Charles A(ustin)
1874-1948 .... **TCLC 15**
See also CA 115; 189; DLB 17; SATA 18

Beardsley, Aubrey 1872-1898 .... **NCLC 6**

Beattie, Ann 1947- ..... **CLC 8, 13, 18, 40, 63, 146; SSC 11**
See also AMWS 5; BEST 90:2; BPFB 1; CA 81-84; CANR 53, 73; CN 7; DA3; DAM NOV, POP; DLB 218; DLBY 1982; MTCW 1, 2; RGAL 4; RGSF 2; SSFS 9

Beattie, James 1735-1803 .... **NCLC 25**
See also DLB 109

Beauchamp, Kathleen Mansfield 1888-1923
See Mansfield, Katherine
See also CA 104; 134; DA; DA3; DAC; DAM MST; MTCW 2; TEA

Beaumarchais, Pierre-Augustin Caron de
1732-1799 .... **LC 61; DC 4**
See also DAM DRAM; DFS 14; EW 4; GFL Beginnings to 1789; RGWL 2

Beaumont, Francis 1584(?)-1616 .... **LC 33; DC 6**
See also BRW 2; CDBLB Before 1660; DLB 58

Beauvoir, Simone (Lucie Ernestine Marie Bertrand) de 1908-1986 .... **CLC 1, 2, 4, 8, 14, 31, 44, 50, 71, 124; SSC 35; WLC**
See also BPFB 1; CA 9-12R; 118; CANR 28, 61; DA; DA3; DAB; DAC; DAM MST, NOV; DLB 72; DLBY 1986; EW 12; FW; GFL 1789 to the Present; MTCW 1, 2; RGSF 2; RGWL 2

Becker, Carl (Lotus) 1873-1945 ..... **TCLC 63**
See also CA 157; DLB 17

Becker, Jurek 1937-1997 .... **CLC 7, 19**
See also CA 85-88; 157; CANR 60; CWW 2; DLB 75

Becker, Walter 1950- .... **CLC 26**

Beckett, Samuel (Barclay)
1906-1989 .. **CLC 1, 2, 3, 4, 6, 9, 10, 11, 14, 18, 29, 57, 59, 83; SSC 16; WLC**
See also BRWR 1; BRWS 1; CA 5-8R; 130; CANR 33, 61; CBD; CDBLB 1945-1960; DA; DA3; DAB; DAC; DAM DRAM, MST, NOV; DFS 2, 7; DLB 13, 15, 233; DLBY 1990; GFL 1789 to the Present; MTCW 1, 2; RGSF 2; RGWL 2; SSFS 15; WLIT 4

Beckford, William 1760-1844 .... **NCLC 16**
See also BRW 3; DLB 39, 213; HGG; SUFW

Beckman, Gunnel 1910- .... **CLC 26**
See also CA 33-36R; CANR 15; CLR 25; MAICYA 1, 2; SAAS 9; SATA 6

Becque, Henri 1837-1899 .... **NCLC 3**
See also DLB 192; GFL 1789 to the Present

Becquer, Gustavo Adolfo
1836-1870 .... **NCLC 106; HLCS 1**
See also DAM MULT

Beddoes, Thomas Lovell
1803-1849 .... **NCLC 3; DC 15**
See also DLB 96

Bede c. 673-735 .... **CMLC 20**
See also DLB 146

Bedford, Donald F.
See Fearing, Kenneth (Flexner)

Beecher, Catharine Esther
1800-1878 .... **NCLC 30**
See also DLB 1, 243

Beecher, John 1904-1980 .... **CLC 6**
See also AITN 1; CA 5-8R; 105; CANR 8

Beer, Johann 1655-1700 .... **LC 5**
See also DLB 168

Beer, Patricia 1924- .... **CLC 58**
See also CA 61-64; 183; CANR 13, 46; CP 7; CWP; DLB 40; FW

Beerbohm, Max
See Beerbohm, (Henry) Max(imilian)

Beerbohm, (Henry) Max(imilian)
1872-1956 .... **TCLC 1, 24**
See also BRWS 2; CA 104; 154; CANR 79; DLB 34, 100; FANT

Beer-Hofmann, Richard
1866-1945 .... **TCLC 60**
See also CA 160; DLB 81

Beg, Shemus
See Stephens, James

Begiebing, Robert J(ohn) 1946- .... **CLC 70**
See also CA 122; CANR 40, 88

Behan, Brendan 1923-1964 ...... **CLC 1, 8, 11, 15, 79**
See also BRWS 2; CA 73-76; CANR 33; CBD; CDBLB 1945-1960; DAM DRAM; DFS 7; DLB 13, 233; MTCW 1, 2

Behn, Aphra 1640(?)-1689 .... **LC 1, 30, 42; DC 4; PC 13; WLC**
See also BRWS 3; DA; DA3; DAB; DAC; DAM DRAM, MST, NOV, POET; DLB 39, 80, 131; FW; WLIT 3

Behrman, S(amuel) N(athaniel)
1893-1973 .... **CLC 40**
See also CA 13-16; 45-48; CAD; CAP 1; DLB 7, 44; IDFW 3; RGAL 4

Belasco, David 1853-1931 .... **TCLC 3**
See also CA 104; 168; DLB 7; RGAL 4

Belcheva, Elisaveta Lyubomirova
1893-1991 .... **CLC 10**
See also Bagryana, Elisaveta

Beldone, Phil "Cheech"
See Ellison, Harlan (Jay)

Beleno
See Azuela, Mariano

Belinski, Vissarion Grigoryevich
1811-1848 .... **NCLC 5**
See also DLB 198

Belitt, Ben 1911- .... **CLC 22**
See also CA 13-16R; CAAS 4; CANR 7, 77; CP 7; DLB 5

Bell, Gertrude (Margaret Lowthian)
1868-1926 .... **TCLC 67**
See also CA 167; DLB 174

Bell, J. Freeman
See Zangwill, Israel

Bell, James Madison 1826-1902 ... **TCLC 43; BLC 1**
See also BW 1; CA 122; 124; DAM MULT; DLB 50

Bell, Madison Smartt 1957- .... **CLC 41, 102**
See also AMWS 10; BPFB 1; CA 111, 183; CAAE 183; CANR 28, 54, 73; CN 7; CSW; DLB 218; MTCW 1

Bell, Marvin (Hartley) 1937- .... **CLC 8, 31**
See also CA 21-24R; CAAS 14; CANR 59, 102; CP 7; DAM POET; DLB 5; MTCW 1

Bell, W. L. D.
See Mencken, H(enry) L(ouis)

Bellamy, Atwood C.
See Mencken, H(enry) L(ouis)

Bellamy, Edward 1850-1898 ...... **NCLC 4, 86**
See also DLB 12; NFS 15; RGAL 4; SFW 4

Belli, Gioconda 1949-
See also CA 152; CWW 2; HLCS 1

Bellin, Edward J.
See Kuttner, Henry

Belloc, (Joseph) Hilaire (Pierre Sebastien Rene Swanton) 1870-1953 ...... **TCLC 7, 18; PC 24**
See also CA 106; 152; CWRI 5; DAM POET; DLB 19, 100, 141, 174; MTCW 1; SATA 112; WCH; YABC 1

Belloc, Joseph Peter Rene Hilaire
See Belloc, (Joseph) Hilaire (Pierre Sebastien Rene Swanton)

Belloc, Joseph Pierre Hilaire
See Belloc, (Joseph) Hilaire (Pierre Sebastien Rene Swanton)

Belloc, M. A.
See Lowndes, Marie Adelaide (Belloc)

Bellow, Saul 1915- . **CLC 1, 2, 3, 6, 8, 10, 13, 15, 25, 33, 34, 63, 79; SSC 14; WLC**
See also AITN 2; AMW; BEST 89:3; BPFB 1; CA 5-8R; CABS 1; CANR 29, 53, 95; CDALB 1941-1968; CN 7; DA; DA3; DAB; DAC; DAM MST, NOV, POP; DLB 2, 28; DLBD 3; DLBY 1982; MTCW 1, 2; NFS 4, 14; RGAL 4; RGSF 2; SSFS 12

Belser, Reimond Karel Maria de 1929-
See Ruyslinck, Ward
See also CA 152

Bely, Andrey .... **TCLC 7; PC 11**
See also Bugayev, Boris Nikolayevich
See also EW 9; MTCW 1

Belyi, Andrei
See Bugayev, Boris Nikolayevich
See also RGWL 2

Bembo, Pietro 1470-1547 .... **LC 79**
See also RGWL 2

Benary, Margot
See Benary-Isbert, Margot

Benary-Isbert, Margot 1889-1979 .... **CLC 12**
See also CA 5-8R; 89-92; CANR 4, 72; CLR 12; MAICYA 1, 2; SATA 2; SATA-Obit 21

Benavente (y Martinez), Jacinto
1866-1954 .... **TCLC 3; HLCS 1**
See also CA 106; 131; CANR 81; DAM DRAM, MULT; GLL 2; HW 1, 2; MTCW 1, 2

Benchley, Peter (Bradford) 1940- .. **CLC 4, 8**
See also AAYA 14; AITN 2; BPFB 1; CA 17-20R; CANR 12, 35, 66; CPW; DAM NOV, POP; HGG; MTCW 1, 2; SATA 3, 89

Benchley, Robert (Charles)
1889-1945 .... **TCLC 1, 55**
See also CA 105; 153; DLB 11; RGAL 4

Benda, Julien 1867-1956 .... **TCLC 60**
See also CA 120; 154; GFL 1789 to the Present

Benedict, Ruth (Fulton)
1887-1948 .... **TCLC 60**
See also CA 158; DLB 246

Benedikt, Michael 1935- .... **CLC 4, 14**
See also CA 13-16R; CANR 7; CP 7; DLB 5

Benet, Juan 1927-1993 .... **CLC 28**
See also CA 143

Benet, Stephen Vincent 1898-1943 . **TCLC 7; SSC 10**
See also CA 104; 152; DA3; DAM POET; DLB 4, 48, 102, 249; DLBY 1997; HGG; MTCW 1; RGAL 4; RGSF 2; SUFW; WP; YABC 1

Benet, William Rose 1886-1950 ..... **TCLC 28**
See also CA 118; 152; DAM POET; DLB 45; RGAL 4

Benford, Gregory (Albert) 1941- .... **CLC 52**
See also BPFB 1; CA 69-72, 175; CAAE 175; CAAS 27; CANR 12, 24, 49, 95; CSW; DLBY 1982; SCFW 2; SFW 4

Bengtsson, Frans (Gunnar)
1894-1954 .... **TCLC 48**
See also CA 170

Benjamin, David
See Slavitt, David R(ytman)

Benjamin, Lois
See Gould, Lois

Benjamin, Walter 1892-1940 .... **TCLC 39**
See also CA 164; DLB 242; EW 11

Benn, Gottfried 1886-1956 ..... **TCLC 3; PC 35**
See also CA 106; 153; DLB 56; RGWL 2

Bennett, Alan 1934- .... **CLC 45, 77**
See also CA 103; CANR 35, 55, 106; CBD; CD 5; DAB; DAM MST; MTCW 1, 2

Bennett, (Enoch) Arnold
1867-1931 .... **TCLC 5, 20**
See also BRW 6; CA 106; 155; CDBLB 1890-1914; DLB 10, 34, 98, 135; MTCW 2

Bennett, Elizabeth
See Mitchell, Margaret (Munnerlyn)

Bennett, George Harold 1930-
See Bennett, Hal
See also BW 1; CA 97-100; CANR 87

Bennett, Hal .... **CLC 5**
See also Bennett, George Harold
See also DLB 33

Bennett, Jay 1912- .... **CLC 35**
See also AAYA 10; CA 69-72; CANR 11, 42, 79; JRDA; SAAS 4; SATA 41, 87; SATA-Brief 27; WYA; YAW

Bennett, Louise (Simone) 1919- ...... **CLC 28; BLC 1**
See also BW 2, 3; CA 151; CDWLB 3; CP 7; DAM MULT; DLB 117

Benson, E(dward) F(rederic)
1867-1940 .... **TCLC 27**
See also CA 114; 157; DLB 135, 153; HGG; SUFW

Benson, Jackson J. 1930- .... **CLC 34**
See also CA 25-28R; DLB 111

Benson, Sally 1900-1972 .... **CLC 17**
See also CA 19-20; 37-40R; CAP 1; SATA 1, 35; SATA-Obit 27

Benson, Stella 1892-1933 .... **TCLC 17**
See also CA 117; 155; DLB 36, 162; FANT

Bentham, Jeremy 1748-1832 .... **NCLC 38**
See also DLB 107, 158, 252

Bentley, E(dmund) C(lerihew)
1875-1956 .... **TCLC 12**
See also CA 108; DLB 70; MSW

Bentley, Eric (Russell) 1916- .... **CLC 24**
See also CA 5-8R; CAD; CANR 6, 67; CBD; CD 5; INT CANR-6

Beranger, Pierre Jean de
1780-1857 .... **NCLC 34**

Berdyaev, Nicolas
See Berdyaev, Nikolai (Aleksandrovich)

Berdyaev, Nikolai (Aleksandrovich)
1874-1948 .... **TCLC 67**
See also CA 120; 157

Berdyayev, Nikolai (Aleksandrovich)
See Berdyaev, Nikolai (Aleksandrovich)

Berendt, John (Lawrence) 1939- ...... **CLC 86**
See also CA 146; CANR 75, 93; DA3; MTCW 1

Beresford, J(ohn) D(avys)
1873-1947 .... **TCLC 81**
See also CA 112; 155; DLB 162, 178, 197; SFW 4; SUFW

Bergelson, David 1884-1952 .... **TCLC 81**

Berger, Colonel
See Malraux, (Georges-)Andre

Berger, John (Peter) 1926- .... **CLC 2, 19**
See also BRWS 4; CA 81-84; CANR 51, 78; CN 7; DLB 14, 207

Berger, Melvin H. 1927- .... **CLC 12**
See also CA 5-8R; CANR 4; CLR 32; SAAS 2; SATA 5, 88; SATA-Essay 124

Berger, Thomas (Louis) 1924- .. **CLC 3, 5, 8, 11, 18, 38**
See also BPFB 1; CA 1-4R; CANR 5, 28, 51; CN 7; DAM NOV; DLB 2; DLBY 1980; FANT; INT CANR-28; MTCW 1, 2; RHW; TCWW 2

Bergman, (Ernst) Ingmar 1918- ...... **CLC 16, 72**
See also CA 81-84; CANR 33, 70; DLB 257; MTCW 2

Bergson, Henri(-Louis) 1859-1941 . **TCLC 32**
See also CA 164; EW 8; GFL 1789 to the Present

Bergstein, Eleanor 1938- .... **CLC 4**
See also CA 53-56; CANR 5

Berkeley, George 1685-1753 .... **LC 65**
See also DLB 101, 252

Berkoff, Steven 1937- .... **CLC 56**
See also CA 104; CANR 72; CBD; CD 5

Berlin, Isaiah 1909-1997 .... **TCLC 105**
See also CA 85-88; 162

Berman, Chaim (Icyk) 1929-1998 ... **CLC 40**
See also CA 57-60; CANR 6, 31, 57, 105; CN 7

Bern, Victoria
See Fisher, M(ary) F(rances) K(ennedy)

Bernanos, (Paul Louis) Georges
1888-1948 .... **TCLC 3**
See also CA 104; 130; CANR 94; DLB 72; GFL 1789 to the Present; RGWL 2

Bernard, April 1956- .... **CLC 59**
See also CA 131

Berne, Victoria
See Fisher, M(ary) F(rances) K(ennedy)

Bernhard, Thomas 1931-1989 ..... **CLC 3, 32, 61; DC 14**
See also CA 85-88; 127; CANR 32, 57; CDWLB 2; DLB 85, 124; MTCW 1; RGWL 2

Bernhardt, Sarah (Henriette Rosine)
1844-1923 .... **TCLC 75**
See also CA 157

Bernstein, Charles 1950- .... **CLC 142**
See also CA 129; CAAS 24; CANR 90; CP 7; DLB 169

Berriault, Gina 1926-1999 .... **CLC 54, 109; SSC 30**
See also CA 116; 129; 185; CANR 66; DLB 130; SSFS 7,11

Berrigan, Daniel 1921- .... **CLC 4**
See also CA 33-36R; CAAS 1; CANR 11, 43, 78; CP 7; DLB 5

Berrigan, Edmund Joseph Michael, Jr.
1934-1983
See Berrigan, Ted
See also CA 61-64; 110; CANR 14, 102

Berrigan, Ted .... **CLC 37**
See also Berrigan, Edmund Joseph Michael, Jr.
See also DLB 5, 169; WP

Berry, Charles Edward Anderson 1931-
See Berry, Chuck
See also CA 115

Berry, Chuck .... **CLC 17**
See also Berry, Charles Edward Anderson

Berry, Jonas
See Ashbery, John (Lawrence)
See also GLL 1

Berry, Wendell (Erdman) 1934- ... **CLC 4, 6, 8, 27, 46; PC 28**
See also AITN 1; AMWS 10; ANW; CA 73-76; CANR 50, 73, 101; CP 7; CSW; DAM POET; DLB 5, 6, 234; MTCW 1

Berryman, John 1914-1972 ... **CLC 1, 2, 3, 4, 6, 8, 10, 13, 25, 62**
See also AMW; CA 13-16; 33-36R; CABS 2; CANR 35; CAP 1; CDALB 1941-1968; DAM POET; DLB 48; MTCW 1, 2; PAB; RGAL 4; WP

Bertolucci, Bernardo 1940- ...... **CLC 16, 157**
See also CA 106

Berton, Pierre (Francis Demarigny)
1920- .... **CLC 104**
See also CA 1-4R; CANR 2, 56; CPW; DLB 68; SATA 99

Bertrand, Aloysius 1807-1841 .... **NCLC 31**
See also Bertrand, Louis oAloysiusc

Bertrand, Louis oAloysiusc
See Bertrand, Aloysius
See also DLB 217

Bertran de Born c. 1140-1215 .... **CMLC 5**

Besant, Annie (Wood) 1847-1933 ..... **TCLC 9**
See also CA 105; 185

Bessie, Alvah 1904-1985 .... **CLC 23**
See also CA 5-8R; 116; CANR 2, 80; DLB 26

Bethlen, T. D.
See Silverberg, Robert

Beti, Mongo .... **CLC 27; BLC 1**
See also Biyidi, Alexandre
See also AFW; CANR 79; DAM MULT; WLIT 2

Betjeman, John 1906-1984 ...... **CLC 2, 6, 10, 34, 43**
See also BRW 7; CA 9-12R; 112; CANR 33, 56; CDBLB 1945-1960; DA3; DAB; DAM MST, POET; DLB 20; DLBY 1984; MTCW 1, 2

Bettelheim, Bruno 1903-1990 .... **CLC 79**
See also CA 81-84; 131; CANR 23, 61; DA3; MTCW 1, 2

Betti, Ugo 1892-1953 .... **TCLC 5**
See also CA 104; 155; RGWL 2

Betts, Doris (Waugh) 1932- ..... **CLC 3, 6, 28; SSC 45**
See also CA 13-16R; CANR 9, 66, 77; CN 7; CSW; DLB 218; DLBY 1982; INT CANR-9; RGAL 4

Bevan, Alistair
See Roberts, Keith (John Kingston)

Bey, Pilaff
See Douglas, (George) Norman

Bialik, Chaim Nachman 1873-1934 .... **TCLC 25**
See also CA 170

Bickerstaff, Isaac
See Swift, Jonathan

Bidart, Frank 1939- .... **CLC 33**
See also CA 140; CANR 106; CP 7

Bienek, Horst 1930- .... **CLC 7, 11**
See also CA 73-76; DLB 75

Bierce, Ambrose (Gwinett) 1842-1914(?) ..... **TCLC 1, 7, 44; SSC 9; WLC**
See also AMW; BYA 11; CA 104; 139; CANR 78; CDALB 1865-1917; DA; DA3; DAC; DAM MST; DLB 11, 12, 23, 71, 74, 186; EXPS; HGG; LAIT 2; RGAL 4; RGSF 2; SSFS 9; SUFW

Biggers, Earl Derr 1884-1933 .... **TCLC 65**
See also CA 108; 153

Billings, Josh
See Shaw, Henry Wheeler

Billington, (Lady) Rachel (Mary) 1942- .... **CLC 43**
See also AITN 2; CA 33-36R; CANR 44; CN 7

Binchy, Maeve 1940- .... **CLC 153**
See also BEST 90:1; BPFB 1; CA 127; 134; CANR 50, 96; CN 7; CPW; DA3; DAM POP; INT CA-134; MTCW 1; RHW

Binyon, T(imothy) J(ohn) 1936- .... **CLC 34**
See also CA 111; CANR 28

Bion 335B.C.-245B.C. .... **CMLC 39**

Bioy Casares, Adolfo 1914-1999 ... **CLC 4, 8, 13, 88; HLC 1; SSC 17**
See also Casares, Adolfo Bioy; Miranda, Javier; Sacastru, Martin
See also CA 29-32R; 177; CANR 19, 43, 66; DAM MULT; DLB 113; HW 1, 2; LAW; MTCW 1, 2

Birch, Allison .... **CLC 65**

Bird, Cordwainer
See Ellison, Harlan (Jay)

Bird, Robert Montgomery 1806-1854 .... **NCLC 1**
See also DLB 202; RGAL 4

Birkerts, Sven 1951- .... **CLC 116**
See also CA 128; 133; 176; CAAE 176; CAAS 29; INT 133

Birney, (Alfred) Earle 1904-1995 .. **CLC 1, 4, 6, 11**
See also CA 1-4R; CANR 5, 20; CP 7; DAC; DAM MST, POET; DLB 88; MTCW 1; PFS 8; RGEL 2

Biruni, al 973-1048(?) .... **CMLC 28**

Bishop, Elizabeth 1911-1979 ..... **CLC 1, 4, 9, 13, 15, 32; PC 3, 34**
See also AMWS 1; CA 5-8R; 89-92; CABS 2; CANR 26, 61, 108; CDALB 1968-1988; DA; DA3; DAC; DAM MST, POET; DLB 5, 169; GLL 2; MAWW; MTCW 1, 2; PAB; PFS 6, 12; RGAL 4; SATA-Obit 24; TCLC 121; WP

Bishop, John 1935- .... **CLC 10**
See also CA 105

Bishop, John Peale 1892-1944 ..... **TCLC 103**
See also CA 107; 155; DLB 4, 9, 45; RGAL 4

Bissett, Bill 1939- .... **CLC 18; PC 14**
See also CA 69-72; CAAS 19; CANR 15; CCA 1; CP 7; DLB 53; MTCW 1

Bissoondath, Neil (Devindra) 1955- .... **CLC 120**
See also CA 136; CN 7; DAC

Bitov, Andrei (Georgievich) 1937- ... **CLC 57**
See also CA 142

Biyidi, Alexandre 1932-
See Beti, Mongo
See also BW 1, 3; CA 114; 124; CANR 81; DA3; MTCW 1, 2

Bjarme, Brynjolf
See Ibsen, Henrik (Johan)

Bjoernson, Bjoernstjerne (Martinius) 1832-1910 .... **TCLC 7, 37**
See also CA 104

Black, Robert
See Holdstock, Robert P.

Blackburn, Paul 1926-1971 .... **CLC 9, 43**
See also CA 81-84; 33-36R; CANR 34; DLB 16; DLBY 1981

Black Elk 1863-1950 .... **TCLC 33**
See also CA 144; DAM MULT; MTCW 1; NNAL; WP

Black Hobart
See Sanders, (James) Ed(ward)

Blacklin, Malcolm
See Chambers, Aidan

Blackmore, R(ichard) D(oddridge) 1825-1900 .... **TCLC 27**
See also CA 120; DLB 18; RGEL 2

Blackmur, R(ichard) P(almer) 1904-1965 .... **CLC 2, 24**
See also AMWS 2; CA 11-12; 25-28R; CANR 71; CAP 1; DLB 63

Black Tarantula
See Acker, Kathy

Blackwood, Algernon (Henry) 1869-1951 .... **TCLC 5**
See also CA 105; 150; DLB 153, 156, 178; HGG; SUFW

Blackwood, Caroline 1931-1996 .... **CLC 6, 9, 100**
See also CA 85-88; 151; CANR 32, 61, 65; CN 7; DLB 14, 207; HGG; MTCW 1

Blade, Alexander
See Hamilton, Edmond; Silverberg, Robert

Blaga, Lucian 1895-1961 .... **CLC 75**
See also CA 157; DLB 220

Blair, Eric (Arthur) 1903-1950 .... **TCLC 123**
See also Orwell, George
See also CA 104; 132; DA; DA3; DAB; DAC; DAM MST, NOV; MTCW 1, 2; SATA 29

Blair, Hugh 1718-1800 .... **NCLC 75**

Blais, Marie-Claire 1939- .... **CLC 2, 4, 6, 13, 22**
See also CA 21-24R; CAAS 4; CANR 38, 75, 93; DAC; DAM MST; DLB 53; FW; MTCW 1, 2

Blaise, Clark 1940- .... **CLC 29**
See also AITN 2; CA 53-56; CAAS 3; CANR 5, 66, 106; CN 7; DLB 53; RGSF 2

Blake, Fairley
See De Voto, Bernard (Augustine)

Blake, Nicholas
See Day Lewis, C(ecil)
See also DLB 77; MSW

Blake, William 1757-1827 .... **NCLC 13, 37, 57; PC 12; WLC**
See also BRW 3; BRWR 1; CDBLB 1789-1832; CLR 52; DA; DA3; DAB; DAC; DAM MST, POET; DLB 93, 163; EXPP; MAICYA 1, 2; PAB; PFS 2, 12; SATA 30; WCH; WLIT 3; WP

Blanchot, Maurice 1907- .... **CLC 135**
See also CA 117; 144; DLB 72

Blasco Ibanez, Vicente 1867-1928 . **TCLC 12**
See also BPFB 1; CA 110; 131; CANR 81; DA3; DAM NOV; EW 8; HW 1, 2; MTCW 1

Blatty, William Peter 1928- .... **CLC 2**
See also CA 5-8R; CANR 9; DAM POP; HGG

Bleeck, Oliver
See Thomas, Ross (Elmore)

Blessing, Lee 1949- .... **CLC 54**
See also CAD; CD 5

Blight, Rose
See Greer, Germaine

Blish, James (Benjamin) 1921-1975 . **CLC 14**
See also BPFB 1; CA 1-4R; 57-60; CANR 3; DLB 8; MTCW 1; SATA 66; SCFW 2; SFW 4

Bliss, Reginald
See Wells, H(erbert) G(eorge)

Blixen, Karen (Christentze Dinesen) 1885-1962
See Dinesen, Isak
See also CA 25-28; CANR 22, 50; CAP 2; DA3; DLB 214; MTCW 1, 2; SATA 44

Bloch, Robert (Albert) 1917-1994 .... **CLC 33**
See also AAYA 29; CA 5-8R; 179; 146; CAAE 179; CAAS 20; CANR 5, 78; DA3; DLB 44; HGG; INT CANR-5; MTCW 1; SATA 12; SATA-Obit 82; SFW 4; SUFW

Blok, Alexander (Alexandrovich) 1880-1921 .... **TCLC 5; PC 21**
See also CA 104; 183; EW 9; RGWL 2

Blom, Jan
See Breytenbach, Breyten

Bloom, Harold 1930- .... **CLC 24, 103**
See also CA 13-16R; CANR 39, 75, 92; DLB 67; MTCW 1; RGAL 4

Bloomfield, Aurelius
See Bourne, Randolph S(illiman)

Blount, Roy (Alton), Jr. 1941- .... **CLC 38**
See also CA 53-56; CANR 10, 28, 61; CSW; INT CANR-28; MTCW 1, 2

Bloy, Leon 1846-1917 .... **TCLC 22**
See also CA 121; 183; DLB 123; GFL 1789 to the Present

Bluggage, Oranthy
See Alcott, Louisa May

Blume, Judy (Sussman) 1938- .... **CLC 12, 30**
See also AAYA 3, 26; BYA 1, 8, 12; CA 29-32R; CANR 13, 37, 66; CLR 2, 15, 69; CPW; DA3; DAM NOV, POP; DLB 52; JRDA; MAICYA 1, 2; MAICYAS 1; MTCW 1, 2; SATA 2, 31, 79; WYA; YAW

Blunden, Edmund (Charles) 1896-1974 .... **CLC 2, 56**
See also BRW 6; CA 17-18; 45-48; CANR 54; CAP 2; DLB 20, 100, 155; MTCW 1; PAB

Bly, Robert (Elwood) 1926- .... **CLC 1, 2, 5, 10, 15, 38, 128; PC 39**
See also AMWS 4; CA 5-8R; CANR 41, 73; CP 7; DA3; DAM POET; DLB 5; MTCW 1, 2; RGAL 4

Boas, Franz 1858-1942 .... **TCLC 56**
See also CA 115; 181

Bobette
See Simenon, Georges (Jacques Christian)

Boccaccio, Giovanni 1313-1375 ... **CMLC 13; SSC 10**
See also EW 2; RGSF 2; RGWL 2
Bochco, Steven 1943- .... **CLC 35**
See also AAYA 11; CA 124; 138
Bode, Sigmund
See O'Doherty, Brian
Bodel, Jean 1167(?)-1210 .... **CMLC 28**
Bodenheim, Maxwell 1892-1954 .... **TCLC 44**
See also CA 110; 187; DLB 9, 45; RGAL 4
Bodker, Cecil 1927- .... **CLC 21**
See also CA 73-76; CANR 13, 44; CLR 23; MAICYA 1, 2; SATA 14, 133
Bodker, Cecil 1927-
See Bodker, Cecil
Boell, Heinrich (Theodor)
1917-1985 ..... **CLC 2, 3, 6, 9, 11, 15, 27, 32, 72; SSC 23; WLC**
See also Boll, Heinrich
See also CA 21-24R; 116; CANR 24; DA; DA3; DAB; DAC; DAM MST, NOV; DLB 69; DLBY 1985; MTCW 1, 2
Boerne, Alfred
See Doeblin, Alfred
Boethius c. 480-c. 524 .... **CMLC 15**
See also DLB 115; RGWL 2
Boff, Leonardo (Genezio Darci)
1938- .... **CLC 70; HLC 1**
See also CA 150; DAM MULT; HW 2
Bogan, Louise 1897-1970 ...... **CLC 4, 39, 46, 93; PC 12**
See also AMWS 3; CA 73-76; 25-28R; CANR 33, 82; DAM POET; DLB 45, 169; MAWW; MTCW 1, 2; RGAL 4
Bogarde, Dirk
See Van Den Bogarde, Derek Jules Gaspard Ulric Niven
See also DLB 14
Bogosian, Eric 1953- .... **CLC 45, 141**
See also CA 138; CAD; CANR 102; CD 5
Bograd, Larry 1953- .... **CLC 35**
See also CA 93-96; CANR 57; SAAS 21; SATA 33, 89; WYA
Boiardo, Matteo Maria 1441-1494 .... **LC 6**
Boileau-Despreaux, Nicolas 1636-1711 . **LC 3**
See also EW 3; GFL Beginnings to 1789; RGWL 2
Bojer, Johan 1872-1959 .... **TCLC 64**
See also CA 189
Bok, Edward W. 1863-1930 .... **TCLC 101**
See also DLB 91; DLBD 16
Boland, Eavan (Aisling) 1944- .. **CLC 40, 67, 113**
See also BRWS 5; CA 143; CANR 61; CP 7; CWP; DAM POET; DLB 40; FW; MTCW 2; PFS 12
Boll, Heinrich
See Boell, Heinrich (Theodor)
See also BPFB 1; CDWLB 2; EW 13; RGSF 2; RGWL 2
Bolt, Lee
See Faust, Frederick (Schiller)
Bolt, Robert (Oxton) 1924-1995 .... **CLC 14**
See also CA 17-20R; 147; CANR 35, 67; CBD; DAM DRAM; DFS 2; DLB 13, 233; LAIT 1; MTCW 1
Bombal, Maria Luisa 1910-1980 ...... **SSC 37; HLCS 1**
See also CA 127; CANR 72; HW 1; LAW; RGSF 2
Bombet, Louis-Alexandre-Cesar
See Stendhal
Bomkauf
See Kaufman, Bob (Garnell)
Bonaventura .... **NCLC 35**
See also DLB 90

Bond, Edward 1934- .... **CLC 4, 6, 13, 23**
See also BRWS 1; CA 25-28R; CANR 38, 67, 106; CBD; CD 5; DAM DRAM; DFS 3,8; DLB 13; MTCW 1
Bonham, Frank 1914-1989 .... **CLC 12**
See also AAYA 1; BYA 1, 3; CA 9-12R; CANR 4, 36; JRDA; MAICYA 1, 2; SAAS 3; SATA 1, 49; SATA-Obit 62; TCWW 2; YAW
Bonnefoy, Yves 1923- .... **CLC 9, 15, 58**
See also CA 85-88; CANR 33, 75, 97; CWW 2; DAM MST, POET; DLB 258; GFL 1789 to the Present; MTCW 1, 2
Bontemps, Arna(ud Wendell)
1902-1973 .... **CLC 1, 18; BLC 1**
See also BW 1; CA 1-4R; 41-44R; CANR 4, 35; CLR 6; CWRI 5; DA3; DAM MULT, NOV, POET; DLB 48, 51; JRDA; MAICYA 1, 2; MTCW 1, 2; SATA 2, 44; SATA-Obit 24; WCH; WP
Booth, Martin 1944- .... **CLC 13**
See also CA 93-96; CAAE 188; CAAS 2; CANR 92
Booth, Philip 1925- .... **CLC 23**
See also CA 5-8R; CANR 5, 88; CP 7; DLBY 1982
Booth, Wayne C(layson) 1921- .... **CLC 24**
See also CA 1-4R; CAAS 5; CANR 3, 43; DLB 67
Borchert, Wolfgang 1921-1947 .... **TCLC 5**
See also CA 104; 188; DLB 69, 124
Borel, Petrus 1809-1859 .... **NCLC 41**
See also DLB 119; GFL 1789 to the Present
Borges, Jorge Luis 1899-1986 ... **CLC 1, 2, 3, 4, 6, 8, 9, 10, 13, 19, 44, 48, 83; HLC 1; PC 22, 32; SSC 4, 41; WLC**
See also AAYA 26; BPFB 1; CA 21-24R; CANR 19, 33, 75, 105; CDWLB 3; DA; DA3; DAB; DAC; DAM MST, MULT; DLB 113; DLBY 1986; DNFS 1, 2; HW 1, 2; LAW; MSW; MTCW 1, 2; RGSF 2; RGWL 2; SFW 4; SSFS 4, 9; TCLC 109; WLIT 1
Borowski, Tadeusz 1922-1951 .... **TCLC 9; SSC 48**
See also CA 106; 154; CDWLB 4, 4; DLB 215; RGSF 2; SSFS 13
Borrow, George (Henry)
1803-1881 .... **NCLC 9**
See also DLB 21, 55, 166
Bosch (Gavino), Juan 1909-2001
See also CA 151; DAM MST, MULT; DLB 145; HLCS 1; HW 1, 2
Bosman, Herman Charles
1905-1951 .... **TCLC 49**
See also Malan, Herman
See also CA 160; DLB 225; RGSF 2
Bosschere, Jean de 1878(?)-1953 ... **TCLC 19**
See also CA 115; 186
Boswell, James 1740-1795 ... **LC 4, 50; WLC**
See also BRW 3; CDBLB 1660-1789; DA; DAB; DAC; DAM MST; DLB 104, 142; WLIT 3
Bottomley, Gordon 1874-1948 ..... **TCLC 107**
See also CA 120; 192; DLB 10
Bottoms, David 1949- .... **CLC 53**
See also CA 105; CANR 22; CSW; DLB 120; DLBY 1983
Boucicault, Dion 1820-1890 .... **NCLC 41**
Boucolon, Maryse
See Conde, Maryse
Bourget, Paul (Charles Joseph)
1852-1935 .... **TCLC 12**
See also CA 107; 196; DLB 123; GFL 1789 to the Present
Bourjaily, Vance (Nye) 1922- .... **CLC 8, 62**
See also CA 1-4R; CAAS 1; CANR 2, 72; CN 7; DLB 2, 143

Bourne, Randolph S(illiman)
1886-1918 .... **TCLC 16**
See also AMW; CA 117; 155; DLB 63
Bova, Ben(jamin William) 1932- ...... **CLC 45**
See also AAYA 16; CA 5-8R; CAAS 18; CANR 11, 56, 94; CLR 3; DLBY 1981; INT CANR-11; MAICYA 1, 2; MTCW 1; SATA 6, 68, 133; SFW 4
Bowen, Elizabeth (Dorothea Cole)
1899-1973 . **CLC 1, 3, 6, 11, 15, 22, 118; SSC 3, 28**
See also BRWS 2; CA 17-18; 41-44R; CANR 35, 105; CAP 2; CDBLB 1945-1960; DA3; DAM NOV; DLB 15, 162; EXPS; FW; HGG; MTCW 1, 2; NFS 13; RGSF 2; SSFS 5; SUFW; WLIT 4
Bowering, George 1935- .... **CLC 15, 47**
See also CA 21-24R; CAAS 16; CANR 10; CP 7; DLB 53
Bowering, Marilyn R(uthe) 1949- .... **CLC 32**
See also CA 101; CANR 49; CP 7; CWP
Bowers, Edgar 1924-2000 .... **CLC 9**
See also CA 5-8R; 188; CANR 24; CP 7; CSW; DLB 5
Bowie, David .... **CLC 17**
See also Jones, David Robert
Bowles, Jane (Sydney) 1917-1973 ..... **CLC 3, 68**
See also CA 19-20; 41-44R; CAP 2
Bowles, Paul (Frederick) 1910-1999 . **CLC 1, 2, 19, 53; SSC 3**
See also AMWS 4; CA 1-4R; 186; CAAS 1; CANR 1, 19, 50, 75; CN 7; DA3; DLB 5, 6, 218; MTCW 1, 2; RGAL 4
Bowles, William Lisle 1762-1850 . **NCLC 103**
See also DLB 93
Box, Edgar
See Vidal, Gore
See also GLL 1
Boyd, James 1888-1944 .... **TCLC 115**
See also CA 186; DLB 9; DLBD 16; RGAL 4; RHW
Boyd, Nancy
See Millay, Edna St. Vincent
See also GLL 1
Boyd, Thomas (Alexander)
1898-1935 .... **TCLC 111**
See also CA 111; 183; DLB 9; DLBD 16
Boyd, William 1952- .... **CLC 28, 53, 70**
See also CA 114; 120; CANR 51, 71; CN 7; DLB 231
Boyle, Kay 1902-1992 .... **CLC 1, 5, 19, 58, 121; SSC 5**
See also CA 13-16R; 140; CAAS 1; CANR 29, 61; DLB 4, 9, 48, 86; DLBY 1993; MTCW 1, 2; RGAL 4; RGSF 2; SSFS 10, 13, 14
Boyle, Mark
See Kienzle, William X(avier)
Boyle, Patrick 1905-1982 .... **CLC 19**
See also CA 127
Boyle, T. C.
See Boyle, T(homas) Coraghessan
See also AMWS 8
Boyle, T(homas) Coraghessan
1948- .... **CLC 36, 55, 90; SSC 16**
See also Boyle, T. C.
See also BEST 90:4; BPFB 1; CA 120; CANR 44, 76, 89; CN 7; CPW; DA3; DAM POP; DLB 218; DLBY 1986; MTCW 2; SSFS 13
Boz
See Dickens, Charles (John Huffam)
Brackenridge, Hugh Henry
1748-1816 .... **NCLC 7**
See also DLB 11, 37; RGAL 4
Bradbury, Edward P.
See Moorcock, Michael (John)
See also MTCW 2

Bradbury, Malcolm (Stanley)
1932-2000 .... **CLC 32, 61**
See also CA 1-4R; CANR 1, 33, 91, 98; CN 7; DA3; DAM NOV; DLB 14, 207; MTCW 1, 2

Bradbury, Ray (Douglas) 1920- .... **CLC 1, 3, 10, 15, 42, 98; SSC 29, 53; WLC**
See also AAYA 15; AITN 1, 2; AMWS 4; BPFB 1; BYA 4, 5, 11; CA 1-4R; CANR 2, 30, 75; CDALB 1968-1988; CN 7; CPW; DA; DA3; DAB; DAC; DAM MST, NOV, POP; DLB 2, 8; EXPN; EXPS; HGG; LAIT 3, 5; MTCW 1, 2; NFS 1; RGAL 4; RGSF 2; SATA 11, 64, 123; SCFW 2; SFW 4; SSFS 1; SUFW; YAW

Braddon, Mary Elizabeth
1837-1915 .... **TCLC 111**
See also Aunt Belinda
See also CA 108; 179; CMW 4; DLB 18, 70, 156; HGG

Bradford, Gamaliel 1863-1932 .... **TCLC 36**
See also CA 160; DLB 17

Bradford, William 1590-1657 .... **LC 64**
See also DLB 24, 30; RGAL 4

Bradley, David (Henry), Jr. 1950- ... **CLC 23, 118; BLC 1**
See also BW 1, 3; CA 104; CANR 26, 81; CN 7; DAM MULT; DLB 33

Bradley, John Ed(mund, Jr.) 1958- . **CLC 55**
See also CA 139; CANR 99; CN 7; CSW

Bradley, Marion Zimmer
1930-1999 .... **CLC 30**
See also Chapman, Lee; Dexter, John; Gardner, Miriam; Ives, Morgan; Rivers, Elfrida
See also AAYA 40; BPFB 1; CA 57-60; 185; CAAS 10; CANR 7, 31, 51, 75, 107; CPW; DA3; DAM POP; DLB 8; FANT; FW; MTCW 1, 2; SATA 90; SATA-Obit 116; SFW 4; YAW

Bradshaw, John 1933- .... **CLC 70**
See also CA 138; CANR 61

Bradstreet, Anne 1612(?)-1672 .... **LC 4, 30; PC 10**
See also AMWS 1; CDALB 1640-1865; DA; DA3; DAC; DAM MST, POET; DLB 24; EXPP; FW; PFS 6; RGAL 4; WP

Brady, Joan 1939- .... **CLC 86**
See also CA 141

Bragg, Melvyn 1939- .... **CLC 10**
See also BEST 89:3; CA 57-60; CANR 10, 48, 89; CN 7; DLB 14; RHW

Brahe, Tycho 1546-1601 .... **LC 45**

Braine, John (Gerard) 1922-1986 . **CLC 1, 3, 41**
See also CA 1-4R; 120; CANR 1, 33; CDBLB 1945-1960; DLB 15; DLBY 1986; MTCW 1

Bramah, Ernest 1868-1942 .... **TCLC 72**
See also CA 156; CMW 4; DLB 70; FANT

Brammer, William 1930(?)-1978 .... **CLC 31**
See also CA 77-80

Brancati, Vitaliano 1907-1954 .... **TCLC 12**
See also CA 109

Brancato, Robin F(idler) 1936- .... **CLC 35**
See also AAYA 9; BYA 6; CA 69-72; CANR 11, 45; CLR 32; JRDA; MAICYA 2; MAICYAS 1; SAAS 9; SATA 97; WYA; YAW

Brand, Max
See Faust, Frederick (Schiller)
See also BPFB 1; TCWW 2

Brand, Millen 1906-1980 .... **CLC 7**
See also CA 21-24R; 97-100; CANR 72

Branden, Barbara .... **CLC 44**
See also CA 148

Brandes, Georg (Morris Cohen)
1842-1927 .... **TCLC 10**
See also CA 105; 189

Brandys, Kazimierz 1916-2000 .... **CLC 62**

Branley, Franklyn M(ansfield)
1915- .... **CLC 21**
See also CA 33-36R; CANR 14, 39; CLR 13; MAICYA 1, 2; SAAS 16; SATA 4, 68

Brathwaite, Edward Kamau 1930- . **CLC 11; BLCS**
See also BW 2, 3; CA 25-28R; CANR 11, 26, 47, 107; CDWLB 3; CP 7; DAM POET; DLB 125

Brathwaite, Kamau
See Brathwaite, Edward Kamau

Brautigan, Richard (Gary)
1935-1984 ..... **CLC 1, 3, 5, 9, 12, 34, 42**
See also BPFB 1; CA 53-56; 113; CANR 34; DA3; DAM NOV; DLB 2, 5, 206; DLBY 1980, 1984; FANT; MTCW 1; RGAL 4; SATA 56

Brave Bird, Mary
See Crow Dog, Mary (Ellen)
See also NNAL

Braverman, Kate 1950- .... **CLC 67**
See also CA 89-92

Brecht, (Eugen) Bertolt (Friedrich)
1898-1956 ..... **TCLC 1, 6, 13, 35; DC 3; WLC**
See also CA 104; 133; CANR 62; CDWLB 2; DA; DA3; DAB; DAC; DAM DRAM, MST; DFS 4, 5, 9; DLB 56, 124; EW 11; IDTP; MTCW 1, 2; RGWL 2

Brecht, Eugen Berthold Friedrich
See Brecht, (Eugen) Bertolt (Friedrich)

Bremer, Fredrika 1801-1865 .... **NCLC 11**
See also DLB 254

Brennan, Christopher John
1870-1932 .... **TCLC 17**
See also CA 117; 188; DLB 230

Brennan, Maeve 1917-1993 ... **CLC 5; TCLC 124**
See also CA 81-84; CANR 72, 100

Brent, Linda
See Jacobs, Harriet A(nn)

Brentano, Clemens (Maria)
1778-1842 .... **NCLC 1**
See also DLB 90; RGWL 2

Brent of Bin Bin
See Franklin, (Stella Maria Sarah) Miles (Lampe)

Brenton, Howard 1942- .... **CLC 31**
See also CA 69-72; CANR 33, 67; CBD; CD 5; DLB 13; MTCW 1

Breslin, James 1930-
See Breslin, Jimmy
See also CA 73-76; CANR 31, 75; DAM NOV; MTCW 1, 2

Breslin, Jimmy .... **CLC 4, 43**
See also Breslin, James
See also AITN 1; DLB 185; MTCW 2

Bresson, Robert 1901(?)-1999 .... **CLC 16**
See also CA 110; 187; CANR 49

Breton, Andre 1896-1966 .. **CLC 2, 9, 15, 54; PC 15**
See also CA 19-20; 25-28R; CANR 40, 60; CAP 2; DLB 65, 258; EW 11; GFL 1789 to the Present; MTCW 1, 2; RGWL 2; WP

Breytenbach, Breyten 1939(?)- .. **CLC 23, 37, 126**
See also CA 113; 129; CANR 61; CWW 2; DAM POET; DLB 225

Bridgers, Sue Ellen 1942- .... **CLC 26**
See also AAYA 8; BYA 7, 8; CA 65-68; CANR 11, 36; CLR 18; DLB 52; JRDA; MAICYA 1, 2; SAAS 1; SATA 22, 90; SATA-Essay 109; WYA; YAW

Bridges, Robert (Seymour)
1844-1930 .... **TCLC 1; PC 28**
See also BRW 6; CA 104; 152; CDBLB 1890-1914; DAM POET; DLB 19, 98

Bridie, James .... **TCLC 3**
See also Mavor, Osborne Henry
See also DLB 10

Brin, David 1950- .... **CLC 34**
See also AAYA 21; CA 102; CANR 24, 70; INT CANR-24; SATA 65; SCFW 2; SFW 4

Brink, Andre (Philippus) 1935- . **CLC 18, 36, 106**
See also AFW; BRWS 6; CA 104; CANR 39, 62, 109; CN 7; DLB 225; INT CA-103; MTCW 1, 2; WLIT 2

Brinsmead, H. F(ay)
See Brinsmead, H(esba) F(ay)

Brinsmead, H. F.
See Brinsmead, H(esba) F(ay)

Brinsmead, H(esba) F(ay) 1922- ...... **CLC 21**
See also CA 21-24R; CANR 10; CLR 47; CWRI 5; MAICYA 1, 2; SAAS 5; SATA 18, 78

Brittain, Vera (Mary) 1893(?)-1970 . **CLC 23**
See also CA 13-16; 25-28R; CANR 58; CAP 1; DLB 191; FW; MTCW 1, 2

Broch, Hermann 1886-1951 .... **TCLC 20**
See also CA 117; CDWLB 2; DLB 85, 124; EW 10; RGWL 2

Brock, Rose
See Hansen, Joseph
See also GLL 1

Brod, Max 1884-1968 .... **TCLC 115**
See also CA 5-8R; 25-28R; CANR 7; DLB 81

Brodkey, Harold (Roy) 1930-1996 ... **CLC 56**
See also CA 111; 151; CANR 71; CN 7; DLB 130; TCLC 123

Brodskii, Iosif
See Brodsky, Joseph
See also RGWL 2

Brodsky, Iosif Alexandrovich 1940-1996
See Brodsky, Joseph
See also AITN 1; CA 41-44R; 151; CANR 37, 106; DA3; DAM POET; MTCW 1, 2

Brodsky, Joseph . **CLC 4, 6, 13, 36, 100; PC 9**
See also Brodsky, Iosif Alexandrovich
See also AMWS 8; CWW 2; MTCW 1

Brodsky, Michael (Mark) 1948- .... **CLC 19**
See also CA 102; CANR 18, 41, 58; DLB 244

Brodzki, Bella ed. .... **CLC 65**

Brome, Richard 1590(?)-1652 .... **LC 61**
See also DLB 58

Bromell, Henry 1947- .... **CLC 5**
See also CA 53-56; CANR 9

Bromfield, Louis (Brucker)
1896-1956 .... **TCLC 11**
See also CA 107; 155; DLB 4, 9, 86; RGAL 4; RHW

Broner, E(sther) M(asserman)
1930- .... **CLC 19**
See also CA 17-20R; CANR 8, 25, 72; CN 7; DLB 28

Bronk, William (M.) 1918-1999 .... **CLC 10**
See also CA 89-92; 177; CANR 23; CP 7; DLB 165

Bronstein, Lev Davidovich
See Trotsky, Leon

Bronte, Anne 1820-1849 ..... **NCLC 4, 71, 102**
See also BRW 5; BRWR 1; DA3; DLB 21, 199

Bronte, (Patrick) Branwell
1817-1848 .... **NCLC 109**

Bronte, Charlotte 1816-1855 ...... **NCLC 3, 8, 33, 58, 105; WLC**
See also AAYA 17; BRW 5; BRWR 1; BYA 2; CDBLB 1832-1890; DA; DA3; DAB; DAC; DAM MST, NOV; DLB 21, 159, 199; EXPN; LAIT 2; NFS 4; WLIT 4

Bronte, Emily (Jane) 1818-1848 ... **NCLC 16, 35; PC 8; WLC**
See also AAYA 17; BPFB 1; BRW 5; BRWR 1; BYA 3; CDBLB 1832-1890; DA; DA3; DAB; DAC; DAM MST, NOV, POET; DLB 21, 32, 199; EXPN; LAIT 1; WLIT 3

Brontes
See Bronte, Anne; Bronte, Charlotte; Bronte, Emily (Jane)

Brooke, Frances 1724-1789 .... **LC 6, 48**
See also DLB 39, 99

Brooke, Henry 1703(?)-1783 .... **LC 1**
See also DLB 39

Brooke, Rupert (Chawner)
1887-1915 ..... **TCLC 2, 7; PC 24; WLC**
See also BRWS 3; CA 104; 132; CANR 61; CDBLB 1914-1945; DA; DAB; DAC; DAM MST, POET; DLB 19, 216; EXPP; GLL 2; MTCW 1, 2; PFS 7

Brooke-Haven, P.
See Wodehouse, P(elham) G(renville)

Brooke-Rose, Christine 1926(?)- ...... **CLC 40**
See also BRWS 4; CA 13-16R; CANR 58; CN 7; DLB 14, 231; SFW 4

Brookner, Anita 1928- .. **CLC 32, 34, 51, 136**
See also BRWS 4; CA 114; 120; CANR 37, 56, 87; CN 7; CPW; DA3; DAB; DAM POP; DLB 194; DLBY 1987; MTCW 1, 2

Brooks, Cleanth 1906-1994 . **CLC 24, 86, 110**
See also CA 17-20R; 145; CANR 33, 35; CSW; DLB 63; DLBY 1994; INT CANR-35; MTCW 1, 2

Brooks, George
See Baum, L(yman) Frank

Brooks, Gwendolyn (Elizabeth)
1917-2000 .. **CLC 1, 2, 4, 5, 15, 49, 125; BLC 1; PC 7; WLC**
See also AAYA 20; AFAW 1, 2; AITN 1; AMWS 3; BW 2, 3; CA 1-4R; 190; CANR 1, 27, 52, 75; CDALB 1941-1968; CLR 27; CP 7; CWP; DA; DA3; DAC; DAM MST, MULT, POET; DLB 5, 76, 165; EXPP; MAWW; MTCW 1, 2; PFS 1, 2, 4, 6; RGAL 4; SATA 6; SATA-Obit 123; WP

Brooks, Mel .... **CLC 12**
See also Kaminsky, Melvin
See also AAYA 13; DLB 26

Brooks, Peter (Preston) 1938- .... **CLC 34**
See also CA 45-48; CANR 1, 107

Brooks, Van Wyck 1886-1963 .... **CLC 29**
See also AMW; CA 1-4R; CANR 6; DLB 45, 63, 103

Brophy, Brigid (Antonia)
1929-1995 .... **CLC 6, 11, 29, 105**
See also CA 5-8R; 149; CAAS 4; CANR 25, 53; CBD; CN 7; CWD; DA3; DLB 14; MTCW 1, 2

Brosman, Catharine Savage 1934- ..... **CLC 9**
See also CA 61-64; CANR 21, 46

Brossard, Nicole 1943- .... **CLC 115**
See also CA 122; CAAS 16; CCA 1; CWP; CWW 2; DLB 53; FW; GLL 2

Brother Antoninus
See Everson, William (Oliver)

The Brothers Quay
See Quay, Stephen; Quay, Timothy

Broughton, T(homas) Alan 1936- ..... **CLC 19**
See also CA 45-48; CANR 2, 23, 48

Broumas, Olga 1949- .... **CLC 10, 73**
See also CA 85-88; CANR 20, 69; CP 7; CWP; GLL 2

Broun, Heywood 1888-1939 .... **TCLC 104**
See also DLB 29, 171

Brown, Alan 1950- .... **CLC 99**
See also CA 156

Brown, Charles Brockden
1771-1810 .... **NCLC 22, 74**
See also AMWS 1; CDALB 1640-1865; DLB 37, 59, 73; FW; HGG; RGAL 4

Brown, Christy 1932-1981 .... **CLC 63**
See also BYA 13; CA 105; 104; CANR 72; DLB 14

Brown, Claude 1937-2002 ... **CLC 30; BLC 1**
See also AAYA 7; BW 1, 3; CA 73-76; CANR 81; DAM MULT

Brown, Dee (Alexander) 1908- ... **CLC 18, 47**
See also AAYA 30; CA 13-16R; CAAS 6; CANR 11, 45, 60; CPW; CSW; DA3; DAM POP; DLBY 1980; LAIT 2; MTCW 1, 2; SATA 5, 110; TCWW 2

Brown, George
See Wertmueller, Lina

Brown, George Douglas
1869-1902 .... **TCLC 28**
See also Douglas, George
See also CA 162

Brown, George Mackay 1921-1996 ... **CLC 5, 48, 100**
See also BRWS 6; CA 21-24R; 151; CAAS 6; CANR 12, 37, 67; CN 7; CP 7; DLB 14, 27, 139; MTCW 1; RGSF 2; SATA 35

Brown, (William) Larry 1951- .... **CLC 73**
See also CA 130; 134; CSW; DLB 234; INT 133

Brown, Moses
See Barrett, William (Christopher)

Brown, Rita Mae 1944- .... **CLC 18, 43, 79**
See also BPFB 1; CA 45-48; CANR 2, 11, 35, 62, 95; CN 7; CPW; CSW; DA3; DAM NOV, POP; FW; INT CANR-11; MTCW 1, 2; NFS 9; RGAL 4

Brown, Roderick (Langmere) Haig-
See Haig-Brown, Roderick (Langmere)

Brown, Rosellen 1939- .... **CLC 32**
See also CA 77-80; CAAS 10; CANR 14, 44, 98; CN 7

Brown, Sterling Allen 1901-1989 ...... **CLC 1, 23, 59; BLC 1**
See also AFAW 1, 2; BW 1, 3; CA 85-88; 127; CANR 26; DA3; DAM MULT, POET; DLB 48, 51, 63; MTCW 1, 2; RGAL 4; WP

Brown, Will
See Ainsworth, William Harrison

Brown, William Wells 1815-1884 ... **NCLC 2, 89; BLC 1; DC 1**
See also DAM MULT; DLB 3, 50, 183, 248; RGAL 4

Browne, (Clyde) Jackson 1948(?)- ... **CLC 21**
See also CA 120

Browning, Elizabeth Barrett
1806-1861 ... **NCLC 1, 16, 61, 66; PC 6; WLC**
See also BRW 4; CDBLB 1832-1890; DA; DA3; DAB; DAC; DAM MST, POET; DLB 32, 199; EXPP; PAB; PFS 2; TEA; WLIT 4; WP

Browning, Robert 1812-1889 . **NCLC 19, 79; PC 2; WLCS**
See also BRW 4; BRWR 2; CDBLB 1832-1890; DA; DA3; DAB; DAC; DAM MST, POET; DLB 32, 163; EXPP; PAB; PFS 1, 15; RGEL 2; TEA; WLIT 4; WP; YABC 1

Browning, Tod 1882-1962 .... **CLC 16**
See also CA 141; 117

Brownmiller, Susan 1935- .... **CLC 159**
See also CA 103; CANR 35, 75; DAM NOV; FW; MTCW 1, 2

Brownson, Orestes Augustus
1803-1876 .... **NCLC 50**
See also DLB 1, 59, 73, 243

Bruccoli, Matthew J(oseph) 1931- ... **CLC 34**
See also CA 9-12R; CANR 7, 87; DLB 103

Bruce, Lenny .... **CLC 21**
See also Schneider, Leonard Alfred

Bruin, John
See Brutus, Dennis

Brulard, Henri
See Stendhal

Brulls, Christian
See Simenon, Georges (Jacques Christian)

Brunner, John (Kilian Houston)
1934-1995 .... **CLC 8, 10**
See also CA 1-4R; 149; CAAS 8; CANR 2, 37; CPW; DAM POP; DLB 261; MTCW 1, 2; SCFW 2; SFW 4

Bruno, Giordano 1548-1600 .... **LC 27**
See also RGWL 2

Brutus, Dennis 1924- ... **CLC 43; BLC 1; PC 24**
See also AFW; BW 2, 3; CA 49-52; CAAS 14; CANR 2, 27, 42, 81; CDWLB 3; CP 7; DAM MULT, POET; DLB 117, 225

Bryan, C(ourtlandt) D(ixon) B(arnes)
1936- .... **CLC 29**
See also CA 73-76; CANR 13, 68; DLB 185; INT CANR-13

Bryan, Michael
See Moore, Brian
See also CCA 1

Bryan, William Jennings
1860-1925 .... **TCLC 99**

Bryant, William Cullen 1794-1878 . **NCLC 6, 46; PC 20**
See also AMWS 1; CDALB 1640-1865; DA; DAB; DAC; DAM MST, POET; DLB 3, 43, 59, 189, 250; EXPP; PAB; RGAL 4

Bryusov, Valery Yakovlevich
1873-1924 .... **TCLC 10**
See also CA 107; 155; SFW 4

Buchan, John 1875-1940 .... **TCLC 41**
See also CA 108; 145; CMW 4; DAB; DAM POP; DLB 34, 70, 156; HGG; MSW; MTCW 1; RGEL 2; RHW; YABC 2

Buchanan, George 1506-1582 .... **LC 4**
See also DLB 132

Buchanan, Robert 1841-1901 .... **TCLC 107**
See also CA 179; DLB 18, 35

Buchheim, Lothar-Guenther 1918- .... **CLC 6**
See also CA 85-88

Buchner, (Karl) Georg 1813-1837 . **NCLC 26**
See also CDWLB 2; DLB 133; EW 6; RGSF 2; RGWL 2

Buchwald, Art(hur) 1925- .... **CLC 33**
See also AITN 1; CA 5-8R; CANR 21, 67, 107; MTCW 1, 2; SATA 10

Buck, Pearl S(ydenstricker)
1892-1973 .... **CLC 7, 11, 18, 127**
See also AAYA 42; AITN 1; AMWS 2; BPFB 1; CA 1-4R; 41-44R; CANR 1, 34; CDALBS; DA; DA3; DAB; DAC; DAM MST, NOV; DLB 9, 102; LAIT 3; MTCW 1, 2; RGAL 4; RHW; SATA 1, 25

Buckler, Ernest 1908-1984 .... **CLC 13**
See also CA 11-12; 114; CAP 1; CCA 1; DAC; DAM MST; DLB 68; SATA 47

Buckley, Vincent (Thomas)
1925-1988 .... **CLC 57**
See also CA 101

Buckley, William F(rank), Jr. 1925- . **CLC 7, 18, 37**
See also AITN 1; BPFB 1; CA 1-4R; CANR 1, 24, 53, 93; CMW 4; CPW; DA3; DAM POP; DLB 137; DLBY 1980; INT CANR-24; MTCW 1, 2; TUS

Buechner, (Carl) Frederick 1926- . **CLC 2, 4, 6, 9**
See also BPFB 1; CA 13-16R; CANR 11, 39, 64; CN 7; DAM NOV; DLBY 1980; INT CANR-11; MTCW 1, 2

Buell, John (Edward) 1927- .... **CLC 10**
See also CA 1-4R; CANR 71; DLB 53

Buero Vallejo, Antonio 1916-2000 ... **CLC 15, 46, 139; DC 18**
See also CA 106; 189; CANR 24, 49, 75; DFS 11; HW 1; MTCW 1, 2

Bufalino, Gesualdo 1920(?)-1990 ...... **CLC 74**
See also CWW 2; DLB 196

Bugayev, Boris Nikolayevich 1880-1934 .... **TCLC 7; PC 11**
See also Bely, Andrey; Belyi, Andrei
See also CA 104; 165; MTCW 1

Bukowski, Charles 1920-1994 ... **CLC 2, 5, 9, 41, 82, 108; PC 18; SSC 45**
See also CA 17-20R; 144; CANR 40, 62, 105; CPW; DA3; DAM NOV, POET; DLB 5, 130, 169; MTCW 1, 2

Bulgakov, Mikhail (Afanas'evich) 1891-1940 .... **TCLC 2, 16; SSC 18**
See also BPFB 1; CA 105; 152; DAM DRAM, NOV; NFS 8; RGSF 2; RGWL 2; SFW 4

Bulgya, Alexander Alexandrovich 1901-1956 .... **TCLC 53**
See also Fadeyev, Alexander
See also CA 117; 181

Bullins, Ed 1935- ... **CLC 1, 5, 7; BLC 1; DC 6**
See also BW 2, 3; CA 49-52; CAAS 16; CAD; CANR 24, 46, 73; CD 5; DAM DRAM, MULT; DLB 7, 38, 249; MTCW 1, 2; RGAL 4

Bulwer-Lytton, Edward (George Earle Lytton) 1803-1873 .... **NCLC 1, 45**
See also DLB 21; RGEL 2; SFW 4; SUFW

Bunin, Ivan Alexeyevich 1870-1953 .... **TCLC 6; SSC 5**
See also CA 104; RGSF 2; RGWL 2

Bunting, Basil 1900-1985 ...... **CLC 10, 39, 47**
See also BRWS 7; CA 53-56; 115; CANR 7; DAM POET; DLB 20; RGEL 2

Bunuel, Luis 1900-1983 ... **CLC 16, 80; HLC 1**
See also CA 101; 110; CANR 32, 77; DAM MULT; HW 1

Bunyan, John 1628-1688 ..... **LC 4, 69; WLC**
See also BRW 2; BYA 5; CDBLB 1660-1789; DA; DAB; DAC; DAM MST; DLB 39; RGEL 2; WCH; WLIT 3

Buravsky, Alexandr .... **CLC 59**

Burckhardt, Jacob (Christoph) 1818-1897 .... **NCLC 49**
See also EW 6

Burford, Eleanor
See Hibbert, Eleanor Alice Burford

Burgess, Anthony . **CLC 1, 2, 4, 5, 8, 10, 13, 15, 22, 40, 62, 81, 94**
See also Wilson, John (Anthony) Burgess
See also AAYA 25; AITN 1; BRWS 1; CDBLB 1960 to Present; DAB; DLB 14, 194, 261; DLBY 1998; MTCW 1; RGEL 2; RHW; SFW 4; YAW

Burke, Edmund 1729(?)-1797 .... **LC 7, 36; WLC**
See also BRW 3; DA; DA3; DAB; DAC; DAM MST; DLB 104, 252; RGEL 2

Burke, Kenneth (Duva) 1897-1993 ... **CLC 2, 24**
See also AMW; CA 5-8R; 143; CANR 39, 74; DLB 45, 63; MTCW 1, 2; RGAL 4

Burke, Leda
See Garnett, David

Burke, Ralph
See Silverberg, Robert

Burke, Thomas 1886-1945 .... **TCLC 63**
See also CA 113; 155; CMW 4; DLB 197

Burney, Fanny 1752-1840 .... **NCLC 12, 54, 107**
See also BRWS 3; DLB 39; RGEL 2

Burney, Frances
See Burney, Fanny

Burns, Robert 1759-1796 ... **LC 3, 29, 40; PC 6; WLC**
See also BRW 3; CDBLB 1789-1832; DA; DA3; DAB; DAC; DAM MST, POET; DLB 109; EXPP; PAB; RGEL 2; WP

Burns, Tex
See L'Amour, Louis (Dearborn)
See also TCWW 2

Burnshaw, Stanley 1906- .... **CLC 3, 13, 44**
See also CA 9-12R; CP 7; DLB 48; DLBY 1997

Burr, Anne 1937- .... **CLC 6**
See also CA 25-28R

Burroughs, Edgar Rice 1875-1950 . **TCLC 2, 32**
See also AAYA 11; BPFB 1; BYA 4, 9; CA 104; 132; DA3; DAM NOV; DLB 8; FANT; MTCW 1, 2; RGAL 4; SATA 41; SCFW 2; SFW 4; YAW

Burroughs, William S(eward) 1914-1997 .. **CLC 1, 2, 5, 15, 22, 42, 75, 109; WLC**
See also Lee, William; Lee, Willy
See also AITN 2; AMWS 3; BPFB 1; CA 9-12R; 160; CANR 20, 52, 104; CN 7; CPW; DA; DA3; DAB; DAC; DAM MST, NOV, POP; DLB 2, 8, 16, 152, 237; DLBY 1981, 1997; HGG; MTCW 1, 2; RGAL 4; SFW 4; TCLC 121

Burton, Sir Richard F(rancis) 1821-1890 .... **NCLC 42**
See also DLB 55, 166, 184

Burton, Robert 1577-1640 .... **LC 74**
See also DLB 151; RGEL 2

Busch, Frederick 1941- ..... **CLC 7, 10, 18, 47**
See also CA 33-36R; CAAS 1; CANR 45, 73, 92; CN 7; DLB 6, 218

Bush, Ronald 1946- .... **CLC 34**
See also CA 136

Bustos, F(rancisco)
See Borges, Jorge Luis

Bustos Domecq, H(onorio)
See Bioy Casares, Adolfo; Borges, Jorge Luis

Butler, Octavia E(stelle) 1947- .... **CLC 38, 121; BLCS**
See also AAYA 18; AFAW 2; BPFB 1; BW 2, 3; CA 73-76; CANR 12, 24, 38, 73; CLR 65; CPW; DA3; DAM MULT, POP; DLB 33; MTCW 1, 2; NFS 8; SATA 84; SCFW 2; SFW 4; SSFS 6; YAW

Butler, Robert Olen, (Jr.) 1945- .... **CLC 81**
See also BPFB 1; CA 112; CANR 66; CSW; DAM POP; DLB 173; INT CA-112; MTCW 1; SSFS 11

Butler, Samuel 1612-1680 .... **LC 16, 43**
See also DLB 101, 126; RGEL 2

Butler, Samuel 1835-1902 .... **TCLC 1, 33; WLC**
See also BRWS 2; CA 143; CDBLB 1890-1914; DA; DA3; DAB; DAC; DAM MST, NOV; DLB 18, 57, 174; RGEL 2; SFW 4; TEA

Butler, Walter C.
See Faust, Frederick (Schiller)

Butor, Michel (Marie Francois) 1926- .... **CLC 1, 3, 8, 11, 15, 161**
See also CA 9-12R; CANR 33, 66; DLB 83; EW 13; GFL 1789 to the Present; MTCW 1, 2

Butts, Mary 1890(?)-1937 .... **TCLC 77**
See also CA 148; DLB 240

Buxton, Ralph
See Silverstein, Alvin; Silverstein, Virginia B(arbara Opshelor)

Buzo, Alexander (John) 1944- .... **CLC 61**
See also CA 97-100; CANR 17, 39, 69; CD 5

Buzzati, Dino 1906-1972 .... **CLC 36**
See also CA 160; 33-36R; DLB 177; RGWL 2; SFW 4

Byars, Betsy (Cromer) 1928- .... **CLC 35**
See also AAYA 19; BYA 3; CA 33-36R, 183; CAAE 183; CANR 18, 36, 57, 102; CLR 1, 16, 72; DLB 52; INT CANR-18; JRDA; MAICYA 1, 2; MAICYAS 1; MTCW 1; SAAS 1; SATA 4, 46, 80; SATA-Essay 108; WYA; YAW

Byatt, A(ntonia) S(usan Drabble) 1936- .... **CLC 19, 65, 136**
See also BPFB 1; BRWS 4; CA 13-16R; CANR 13, 33, 50, 75, 96; DA3; DAM NOV, POP; DLB 14, 194; MTCW 1, 2; RGSF 2; RHW

Byrne, David 1952- .... **CLC 26**
See also CA 127

Byrne, John Keyes 1926-
See Leonard, Hugh
See also CA 102; CANR 78; INT CA-102

Byron, George Gordon (Noel) 1788-1824 ..... **NCLC 2, 12, 109; PC 16; WLC**
See also BRW 4; CDBLB 1789-1832; DA; DA3; DAB; DAC; DAM MST, POET; DLB 96, 110; EXPP; PAB; PFS 1, 14; RGEL 2; WLIT 3; WP

Byron, Robert 1905-1941 .... **TCLC 67**
See also CA 160; DLB 195

C. 3. 3.
See Wilde, Oscar (Fingal O'Flahertie Wills)

Caballero, Fernan 1796-1877 .... **NCLC 10**

Cabell, Branch
See Cabell, James Branch

Cabell, James Branch 1879-1958 .... **TCLC 6**
See also CA 105; 152; DLB 9, 78; FANT; MTCW 1; RGAL 4; SUFW

Cabeza de Vaca, Alvar Nunez 1490-1557(?) .... **LC 61**

Cable, George Washington 1844-1925 .... **TCLC 4; SSC 4**
See also CA 104; 155; DLB 12, 74; DLBD 13; RGAL 4

Cabral de Melo Neto, Joao 1920-1999 .... **CLC 76**
See also CA 151; DAM MULT; LAW; LAWS 1

Cabrera Infante, G(uillermo) 1929- . **CLC 5, 25, 45, 120; HLC 1; SSC 39**
See also CA 85-88; CANR 29, 65; CDWLB 3; DA3; DAM MULT; DLB 113; HW 1, 2; LAW; LAWS 1; MTCW 1, 2; RGSF 2; WLIT 1

Cade, Toni
See Bambara, Toni Cade

Cadmus and Harmonia
See Buchan, John

Caedmon fl. 658-680 .... **CMLC 7**
See also DLB 146

Caeiro, Alberto
See Pessoa, Fernando (Antonio Nogueira)

Caesar, Julius .... **CMLC 47**
See also Julius Caesar
See also AW 1; RGWL 2

Cage, John (Milton, Jr.) 1912-1992 . **CLC 41**
See also CA 13-16R; 169; CANR 9, 78; DLB 193; INT CANR-9

Cahan, Abraham 1860-1951 .... **TCLC 71**
See also CA 108; 154; DLB 9, 25, 28; RGAL 4

Cain, G.
See Cabrera Infante, G(uillermo)

Cain, Guillermo
See Cabrera Infante, G(uillermo)

Cain, James M(allahan) 1892-1977 .. CLC 3, 11, 28
See also AITN 1; BPFB 1; CA 17-20R; 73-76; CANR 8, 34, 61; CMW 4; DLB 226; MSW; MTCW 1; RGAL 4

Caine, Hall 1853-1931 .... TCLC 97
See also RHW

Caine, Mark
See Raphael, Frederic (Michael)

Calasso, Roberto 1941- .... CLC 81
See also CA 143; CANR 89

Calderon de la Barca, Pedro 1600-1681 .... LC 23; DC 3; HLCS 1
See also EW 2; RGWL 2

Caldwell, Erskine (Preston) 1903-1987 .... CLC 1, 8, 14, 50, 60; SSC 19
See also AITN 1; AMW; BPFB 1; CA 1-4R; 121; CAAS 1; CANR 2, 33; DA3; DAM NOV; DLB 9, 86; MTCW 1, 2; RGAL 4; RGSF 2; TCLC 117

Caldwell, (Janet Miriam) Taylor (Holland) 1900-1985 .... CLC 2, 28, 39
See also BPFB 1; CA 5-8R; CANR 5; DA3; DAM NOV, POP; DLBD 17; RHW

Calhoun, John Caldwell 1782-1850 .... NCLC 15
See also DLB 3, 248

Calisher, Hortense 1911- ..... CLC 2, 4, 8, 38, 134; SSC 15
See also CA 1-4R; CANR 1, 22, 67; CN 7; DA3; DAM NOV; DLB 2, 218; INT CANR-22; MTCW 1, 2; RGAL 4; RGSF 2

Callaghan, Morley Edward 1903-1990 .... CLC 3, 14, 41, 65
See also CA 9-12R; 132; CANR 33, 73; DAC; DAM MST; DLB 68; MTCW 1, 2; RGEL 2; RGSF 2

Callimachus c. 305B.C.-c. 240B.C. .... CMLC 18
See also AW 1; DLB 176; RGWL 2

Calvin, Jean
See Calvin, John
See also GFL Beginnings to 1789

Calvin, John 1509-1564 .... LC 37
See also Calvin, Jean

Calvino, Italo 1923-1985 .... CLC 5, 8, 11, 22, 33, 39, 73; SSC 3, 48
See also CA 85-88; 116; CANR 23, 61; DAM NOV; DLB 196; EW 13; MTCW 1, 2; RGSF 2; RGWL 2; SFW 4; SSFS 12

Camden, William 1551-1623 .... LC 77
See also DLB 172

Cameron, Carey 1952- .... CLC 59
See also CA 135

Cameron, Peter 1959- .... CLC 44
See also CA 125; CANR 50; DLB 234; GLL 2

Camoens, Luis Vaz de 1524(?)-1580
See also EW 2; HLCS 1

Camoes, Luis de 1524(?)-1580 .... LC 62; HLCS 1; PC 31
See also RGWL 2

Campana, Dino 1885-1932 .... TCLC 20
See also CA 117; DLB 114

Campanella, Tommaso 1568-1639 .... LC 32
See also RGWL 2

Campbell, John W(ood, Jr.) 1910-1971 .... CLC 32
See also CA 21-22; 29-32R; CANR 34; CAP 2; DLB 8; MTCW 1; SCFW; SFW 4

Campbell, Joseph 1904-1987 .... CLC 69
See also AAYA 3; BEST 89:2; CA 1-4R; 124; CANR 3, 28, 61, 107; DA3; MTCW 1, 2

Campbell, Maria 1940- .... CLC 85
See also CA 102; CANR 54; CCA 1; DAC; NNAL

Campbell, Paul N. 1923-
See hooks, bell
See also CA 21-24R

Campbell, (John) Ramsey 1946- ..... CLC 42; SSC 19
See also CA 57-60; CANR 7, 102; HGG; INT CANR-7; SUFW

Campbell, (Ignatius) Roy (Dunnachie) 1901-1957 .... TCLC 5
See also AFW; CA 104; 155; DLB 20, 225; MTCW 2; RGEL 2

Campbell, Thomas 1777-1844 .... NCLC 19
See also DLB 93, 144; RGEL 2

Campbell, Wilfred .... TCLC 9
See also Campbell, William

Campbell, William 1858(?)-1918
See Campbell, Wilfred
See also CA 106; DLB 92

Campion, Jane .... CLC 95
See also AAYA 33; CA 138; CANR 87

Campion, Thomas 1567-1620 .... LC 78
See also CDBLB Before 1660; DAM POET; DLB 58, 172; RGEL 2

Camus, Albert 1913-1960 ...... CLC 1, 2, 4, 9, 11, 14, 32, 63, 69, 124; DC 2; SSC 9; WLC
See also AAYA 36; AFW; BPFB 1; CA 89-92; DA; DA3; DAB; DAC; DAM DRAM, MST, NOV; DLB 72; EW 13; EXPN; EXPS; GFL 1789 to the Present; MTCW 1, 2; NFS 6; RGSF 2; RGWL 2; SSFS 4

Canby, Vincent 1924-2000 .... CLC 13
See also CA 81-84; 191

Cancale
See Desnos, Robert

Canetti, Elias 1905-1994 .. CLC 3, 14, 25, 75, 86
See also CA 21-24R; 146; CANR 23, 61, 79; CDWLB 2; CWW 2; DA3; DLB 85, 124; EW 12; MTCW 1, 2; RGWL 2

Canfield, Dorothea F.
See Fisher, Dorothy (Frances) Canfield

Canfield, Dorothea Frances
See Fisher, Dorothy (Frances) Canfield

Canfield, Dorothy
See Fisher, Dorothy (Frances) Canfield

Canin, Ethan 1960- .... CLC 55
See also CA 131; 135

Cankar, Ivan 1876-1918 .... TCLC 105
See also CDWLB 4; DLB 147

Cannon, Curt
See Hunter, Evan

Cao, Lan 1961- .... CLC 109
See also CA 165

Cape, Judith
See Page, P(atricia) K(athleen)
See also CCA 1

Capek, Karel 1890-1938 .... TCLC 6, 37; DC 1; SSC 36; WLC
See also CA 104; 140; CDWLB 4; DA; DA3; DAB; DAC; DAM DRAM, MST, NOV; DFS 7, 11 !**; DLB 215; EW 10; MTCW 1; RGSF 2; RGWL 2; SCFW 2; SFW 4

Capote, Truman 1924-1984 . CLC 1, 3, 8, 13, 19, 34, 38, 58; SSC 2, 47; WLC
See also AMWS 3; BPFB 1; CA 5-8R; 113; CANR 18, 62; CDALB 1941-1968; CPW; DA; DA3; DAB; DAC; DAM MST, NOV, POP; DLB 2, 185, 227; DLBY 1980, 1984; EXPS; GLL 1; LAIT 3; MTCW 1, 2; NCFS 2; RGAL 4; RGSF 2; SATA 91; SSFS 2

Capra, Frank 1897-1991 .... CLC 16
See also CA 61-64; 135

Caputo, Philip 1941- .... CLC 32
See also CA 73-76; CANR 40; YAW

Caragiale, Ion Luca 1852-1912 ...... TCLC 76
See also CA 157

Card, Orson Scott 1951- .... CLC 44, 47, 50
See also AAYA 11, 42; BPFB 1; BYA 5, 8; CA 102; CANR 27, 47, 73, 102, 106; CPW; DA3; DAM POP; FANT; INT CANR-27; MTCW 1, 2; NFS 5; SATA 83, 127; SCFW 2; SFW 4; YAW

Cardenal, Ernesto 1925- .... CLC 31, 161; HLC 1; PC 22
See also CA 49-52; CANR 2, 32, 66; CWW 2; DAM MULT, POET; HW 1, 2; LAWS 1; MTCW 1, 2; RGWL 2

Cardozo, Benjamin N(athan) 1870-1938 .... TCLC 65
See also CA 117; 164

Carducci, Giosue (Alessandro Giuseppe) 1835-1907 .... TCLC 32
See also CA 163; EW 7; RGWL 2

Carew, Thomas 1595(?)-1640 . LC 13; PC 29
See also BRW 2; DLB 126; PAB; RGEL 2

Carey, Ernestine Gilbreth 1908- ...... CLC 17
See also CA 5-8R; CANR 71; SATA 2

Carey, Peter 1943- .... CLC 40, 55, 96
See also CA 123; 127; CANR 53, 76; CN 7; INT CA-127; MTCW 1, 2; RGSF 2; SATA 94

Carleton, William 1794-1869 .... NCLC 3
See also DLB 159; RGEL 2; RGSF 2

Carlisle, Henry (Coffin) 1926- .... CLC 33
See also CA 13-16R; CANR 15, 85

Carlsen, Chris
See Holdstock, Robert P.

Carlson, Ron(ald F.) 1947- .... CLC 54
See also CA 105; CAAE 189; CANR 27; DLB 244

Carlyle, Thomas 1795-1881 ...... NCLC 22, 70
See also BRW 4; CDBLB 1789-1832; DA; DAB; DAC; DAM MST; DLB 55, 144, 254; RGEL 2

Carman, (William) Bliss 1861-1929 .... TCLC 7; PC 34
See also CA 104; 152; DAC; DLB 92; RGEL 2

Carnegie, Dale 1888-1955 .... TCLC 53

Carossa, Hans 1878-1956 .... TCLC 48
See also CA 170; DLB 66

Carpenter, Don(ald Richard) 1931-1995 .... CLC 41
See also CA 45-48; 149; CANR 1, 71

Carpenter, Edward 1844-1929 .... TCLC 88
See also CA 163; GLL 1

Carpenter, John (Howard) 1948- ... CLC 161
See also AAYA 2; CA 134; SATA 58

Carpentier (y Valmont), Alejo 1904-1980 . CLC 8, 11, 38, 110; HLC 1; SSC 35
See also CA 65-68; 97-100; CANR 11, 70; CDWLB 3; DAM MULT; DLB 113; HW 1, 2; LAW; RGSF 2; RGWL 2; WLIT 1

Carr, Caleb 1955(?)- .... CLC 86
See also CA 147; CANR 73; DA3

Carr, Emily 1871-1945 .... TCLC 32
See also CA 159; DLB 68; FW; GLL 2

Carr, John Dickson 1906-1977 .... CLC 3
See also Fairbairn, Roger
See also CA 49-52; 69-72; CANR 3, 33, 60; CMW 4; MSW; MTCW 1, 2

Carr, Philippa
See Hibbert, Eleanor Alice Burford

Carr, Virginia Spencer 1929- .... CLC 34
See also CA 61-64; DLB 111

Carrere, Emmanuel 1957- .... CLC 89
See also CA 200

Carrier, Roch 1937- .... CLC 13, 78
See also CA 130; CANR 61; CCA 1; DAC; DAM MST; DLB 53; SATA 105

Carroll, James P. 1943(?)- .... CLC 38
See also CA 81-84; CANR 73; MTCW 1

Carroll, Jim 1951- .... CLC 35, 143
See also AAYA 17; CA 45-48; CANR 42

Carroll, Lewis ... **NCLC 2, 53; PC 18; WLC**
See also Dodgson, Charles L(utwidge)
See also AAYA 39; BRW 5; BYA 5, 13; CDBLB 1832-1890; CLR 2, 18; DLB 18, 163, 178; DLBY 1998; EXPN; EXPP; FANT; JRDA; LAIT 1; NFS 7; PFS 11; RGEL 2; SUFW; WCH

Carroll, Paul Vincent 1900-1968 ...... **CLC 10**
See also CA 9-12R; 25-28R; DLB 10; RGEL 2

Carruth, Hayden 1921- ..... **CLC 4, 7, 10, 18, 84; PC 10**
See also CA 9-12R; CANR 4, 38, 59; CP 7; DLB 5, 165; INT CANR-4; MTCW 1, 2; SATA 47

Carson, Rachel Louise 1907-1964 .... **CLC 71**
See also AMWS 9; ANW; CA 77-80; CANR 35; DA3; DAM POP; FW; LAIT 4; MTCW 1, 2; NCFS 1; SATA 23

Carter, Angela (Olive) 1940-1992 ...... **CLC 5, 41, 76; SSC 13**
See also BRWS 3; CA 53-56; 136; CANR 12, 36, 61, 106; DA3; DLB 14, 207, 261; EXPS; FANT; FW; MTCW 1, 2; RGSF 2; SATA 66; SATA-Obit 70; SFW 4; SSFS 4, 12; WLIT 4

Carter, Nick
See Smith, Martin Cruz

Carver, Raymond 1938-1988 ..... **CLC 22, 36, 53, 55, 126; SSC 8, 51**
See also AMWS 3; BPFB 1; CA 33-36R; 126; CANR 17, 34, 61, 103; CPW; DA3; DAM NOV; DLB 130; DLBY 1984, 1988; MTCW 1, 2; RGAL 4; RGSF 2; SSFS 3, 6, 12, 13; TCWW 2

Cary, Elizabeth, Lady Falkland 1585-1639 .... **LC 30**

Cary, (Arthur) Joyce (Lunel) 1888-1957 .... **TCLC 1, 29**
See also BRW 7; CA 104; 164; CDBLB 1914-1945; DLB 15, 100; MTCW 2; RGEL 2

Casanova de Seingalt, Giovanni Jacopo 1725-1798 .... **LC 13**

Casares, Adolfo Bioy
See Bioy Casares, Adolfo
See also RGSF 2

Casas, Bartolome de las 1474-1566
See Las Casas, Bartolome de
See also WLIT 1

Casely-Hayford, J(oseph) E(phraim) 1866-1903 .... **TCLC 24; BLC 1**
See also BW 2; CA 123; 152; DAM MULT

Casey, John (Dudley) 1939- .... **CLC 59**
See also BEST 90:2; CA 69-72; CANR 23, 100

Casey, Michael 1947- .... **CLC 2**
See also CA 65-68; CANR 109; DLB 5

Casey, Patrick
See Thurman, Wallace (Henry)

Casey, Warren (Peter) 1935-1988 .... **CLC 12**
See also CA 101; 127; INT 101

Casona, Alejandro .... **CLC 49**
See also Alvarez, Alejandro Rodriguez

Cassavetes, John 1929-1989 .... **CLC 20**
See also CA 85-88; 127; CANR 82

Cassian, Nina 1924- .... **PC 17**
See also CWP; CWW 2

Cassill, R(onald) V(erlin) 1919- ... **CLC 4, 23**
See also CA 9-12R; CAAS 1; CANR 7, 45; CN 7; DLB 6, 218

Cassiodorus, Flavius Magnus c. 490(?)-c. 583(?) .... **CMLC 43**

Cassirer, Ernst 1874-1945 .... **TCLC 61**
See also CA 157

Cassity, (Allen) Turner 1929- .... **CLC 6, 42**
See also CA 17-20R; CAAS 8; CANR 11; CSW; DLB 105

Castaneda, Carlos (Cesar Aranha) 1931(?)-1998 .... **CLC 12, 119**
See also CA 25-28R; CANR 32, 66, 105; DNFS 1; HW 1; MTCW 1

Castedo, Elena 1937- .... **CLC 65**
See also CA 132

Castedo-Ellerman, Elena
See Castedo, Elena

Castellanos, Rosario 1925-1974 .... **CLC 66; HLC 1; SSC 39**
See also CA 131; 53-56; CANR 58; CDWLB 3; DAM MULT; DLB 113; FW; HW 1; LAW; MTCW 1; RGSF 2; RGWL 2

Castelvetro, Lodovico 1505-1571 .... **LC 12**

Castiglione, Baldassare 1478-1529 ...... **LC 12**
See also Castiglione, Baldesar
See also RGWL 2

Castiglione, Baldesar
See Castiglione, Baldassare
See also EW 2

Castillo, Ana (Hernandez Del) 1953- .... **CLC 151**
See also AAYA 42; CA 131; CANR 51, 86; CWP; DLB 122, 227; DNFS 2; FW; HW 1

Castle, Robert
See Hamilton, Edmond

Castro (Ruz), Fidel 1926(?)-
See also CA 110; 129; CANR 81; DAM MULT; HLC 1; HW 2

Castro, Guillen de 1569-1631 .... **LC 19**

Castro, Rosalia de 1837-1885 ... **NCLC 3, 78; PC 41**
See also DAM MULT

Cather, Willa (Sibert) 1873-1947 .... **TCLC 1, 11, 31, 99; SSC 2, 50; WLC**
See also AAYA 24; AMW; AMWR 1; BPFB 1; CA 104; 128; CDALB 1865-1917; DA; DA3; DAB; DAC; DAM MST, NOV; DLB 9, 54, 78, 256; DLBD 1; EXPN; EXPS; LAIT 3; MAWW; MTCW 1, 2; NFS 2, 19; RGAL 4; RGSF 2; RHW; SATA 30; SSFS 2, 7; TCWW 2

Catherine II
See Catherine the Great
See also DLB 150

Catherine the Great 1729-1796 .... **LC 69**
See also Catherine II

Cato, Marcus Porcius 234B.C.-149B.C. .... **CMLC 21**
See also Cato the Elder

Cato the Elder
See Cato, Marcus Porcius
See also DLB 211

Catton, (Charles) Bruce 1899-1978 . **CLC 35**
See also AITN 1; CA 5-8R; 81-84; CANR 7, 74; DLB 17; SATA 2; SATA-Obit 24

Catullus c. 84B.C.-54B.C. .... **CMLC 18**
See also AW 2; CDWLB 1; DLB 211; RGWL 2

Cauldwell, Frank
See King, Francis (Henry)

Caunitz, William J. 1933-1996 .... **CLC 34**
See also BEST 89:3; CA 125; 130; 152; CANR 73; INT 130

Causley, Charles (Stanley) 1917- .... **CLC 7**
See also CA 9-12R; CANR 5, 35, 94; CLR 30; CWRI 5; DLB 27; MTCW 1; SATA 3, 66

Caute, (John) David 1936- .... **CLC 29**
See also CA 1-4R; CAAS 4; CANR 1, 33, 64; CBD; CD 5; CN 7; DAM NOV; DLB 14, 231

Cavafy, C(onstantine) P(eter) ... **TCLC 2, 7; PC 36**
See also Kavafis, Konstantinos Petrou
See also CA 148; DA3; DAM POET; EW 8; MTCW 1; RGWL 2; WP

Cavallo, Evelyn
See Spark, Muriel (Sarah)

Cavanna, Betty .... **CLC 12**
See also Harrison, Elizabeth (Allen) Cavanna
See also JRDA; MAICYA 1; SAAS 4; SATA 1, 30

Cavendish, Margaret Lucas 1623-1673 .... **LC 30**
See also DLB 131, 252; RGEL 2

Caxton, William 1421(?)-1491(?) .... **LC 17**
See also DLB 170

Cayer, D. M.
See Duffy, Maureen

Cayrol, Jean 1911- .... **CLC 11**
See also CA 89-92; DLB 83

Cela, Camilo Jose 1916-2002 .... **CLC 4, 13, 59, 122; HLC 1**
See also BEST 90:2; CA 21-24R; CAAS 10; CANR 21, 32, 76; DAM MULT; DLBY 1989; EW 13; HW 1; MTCW 1, 2; RGSF 2; RGWL 2

Celan, Paul -1970 .... **CLC 10, 19, 53, 82; PC 10**
See also Antschel, Paul
See also CDWLB 2; DLB 69; RGWL 2

Celine, Louis-Ferdinand .. **CLC 1, 3, 4, 7, 9, 15, 47, 124**
See also Destouches, Louis-Ferdinand
See also DLB 72; EW 11; GFL 1789 to the Present; RGWL 2

Cellini, Benvenuto 1500-1571 .... **LC 7**

Cendrars, Blaise .... **CLC 18, 106**
See also Sauser-Hall, Frederic
See also DLB 258; GFL 1789 to the Present; RGWL 2; WP

Centlivre, Susanna 1669(?)-1723 .... **LC 65**
See also DLB 84; RGEL 2

Cernuda (y Bidon), Luis 1902-1963 . **CLC 54**
See also CA 131; 89-92; DAM POET; DLB 134; GLL 1; HW 1; RGWL 2

Cervantes, Lorna Dee 1954- .... **PC 35**
See also CA 131; CANR 80; CWP; DLB 82; EXPP; HLCS 1; HW 1

Cervantes (Saavedra), Miguel de 1547-1616 .... **LC 6, 23; HLCS; SSC 12; WLC**
See also BYA 1, 14; DA; DAB; DAC; DAM MST, NOV; EW 2; LAIT 1; NFS 8; RGSF 2; RGWL 2

Cesaire, Aime (Fernand) 1913- . **CLC 19, 32, 112; BLC 1; PC 25**
See also BW 2, 3; CA 65-68; CANR 24, 43, 81; DA3; DAM MULT, POET; GFL 1789 to the Present; MTCW 1, 2; WP

Chabon, Michael 1963- .... **CLC 55, 149**
See also CA 139; CANR 57, 96

Chabrol, Claude 1930- .... **CLC 16**
See also CA 110

Challans, Mary 1905-1983
See Renault, Mary
See also CA 81-84; 111; CANR 74; DA3; MTCW 2; SATA 23; SATA-Obit 36

Challis, George
See Faust, Frederick (Schiller)
See also TCWW 2

Chambers, Aidan 1934- .... **CLC 35**
See also AAYA 27; CA 25-28R; CANR 12, 31, 58; JRDA; MAICYA 1, 2; SAAS 12; SATA 1, 69, 108; WYA; YAW

Chambers, James 1948-
See Cliff, Jimmy
See also CA 124

Chambers, Jessie
See Lawrence, D(avid) H(erbert Richards)
See also GLL 1

Chambers, Robert W(illiam)
1865-1933 .... **TCLC 41**
See also CA 165; DLB 202; HGG; SATA 107; SUFW

Chamisso, Adelbert von
1781-1838 .... **NCLC 82**
See also DLB 90; RGWL 2; SUFW

Chance, John T.
See Carpenter, John (Howard)

Chandler, Raymond (Thornton)
1888-1959 .... **TCLC 1, 7; SSC 23**
See also AAYA 25; AMWS 4; BPFB 1; CA 104; 129; CANR 60, 107; CDALB 1929-1941; CMW 4; DA3; DLB 226, 253; DLBD 6; MSW; MTCW 1, 2; RGAL 4

Chang, Eileen 1921-1995 .... **SSC 28**
See also CA 166; CWW 2

Chang, Jung 1952- .... **CLC 71**
See also CA 142

Chang Ai-Ling
See Chang, Eileen

Channing, William Ellery
1780-1842 .... **NCLC 17**
See also DLB 1, 59, 235; RGAL 4

Chao, Patricia 1955- .... **CLC 119**
See also CA 163

Chaplin, Charles Spencer
1889-1977 .... **CLC 16**
See also Chaplin, Charlie
See also CA 81-84; 73-76

Chaplin, Charlie
See Chaplin, Charles Spencer
See also DLB 44

Chapman, George 1559(?)-1634 .... **LC 22**
See also BRW 1; DAM DRAM; DLB 62, 121; RGEL 2

Chapman, Graham 1941-1989 .... **CLC 21**
See also Monty Python
See also CA 116; 129; CANR 35, 95

Chapman, John Jay 1862-1933 .... **TCLC 7**
See also CA 104; 191

Chapman, Lee
See Bradley, Marion Zimmer
See also GLL 1

Chapman, Walker
See Silverberg, Robert

Chappell, Fred (Davis) 1936- ..... **CLC 40, 78**
See also CA 5-8R; CAAE 198; CAAS 4; CANR 8, 33, 67; CN 7; CP 7; CSW; DLB 6, 105; HGG

Char, Rene(-Emile) 1907-1988 .... **CLC 9, 11, 14, 55**
See also CA 13-16R; 124; CANR 32; DAM POET; DLB 258; GFL 1789 to the Present; MTCW 1, 2; RGWL 2

Charby, Jay
See Ellison, Harlan (Jay)

Chardin, Pierre Teilhard de
See Teilhard de Chardin, (Marie Joseph) Pierre

Chariton fl. 1st cent. (?)- .... **CMLC 49**

Charlemagne 742-814 .... **CMLC 37**

Charles I 1600-1649 .... **LC 13**

Charriere, Isabelle de 1740-1805 .. **NCLC 66**

Chartier, Emile-Auguste
See Alain

Charyn, Jerome 1937- .... **CLC 5, 8, 18**
See also CA 5-8R; CAAS 1; CANR 7, 61, 101; CMW 4; CN 7; DLBY 1983; MTCW 1

Chase, Adam
See Marlowe, Stephen

Chase, Mary (Coyle) 1907-1981 .... **DC 1**
See also CA 77-80; 105; CAD; CWD; DFS 11; DLB 228; SATA 17; SATA-Obit 29

Chase, Mary Ellen 1887-1973 .... **CLC 2; TCLC 124**
See also CA 13-16; 41-44R; CAP 1; SATA 10

Chase, Nicholas
See Hyde, Anthony
See also CCA 1

Chateaubriand, Francois Rene de
1768-1848 .... **NCLC 3**
See also DLB 119; EW 5; GFL 1789 to the Present; RGWL 2

Chatterje, Sarat Chandra 1876-1936(?)
See Chatterji, Saratchandra
See also CA 109

Chatterji, Bankim Chandra
1838-1894 .... **NCLC 19**

Chatterji, Saratchandra .... **TCLC 13**
See also Chatterje, Sarat Chandra
See also CA 186

Chatterton, Thomas 1752-1770 .... **LC 3, 54**
See also DAM POET; DLB 109; RGEL 2

Chatwin, (Charles) Bruce
1940-1989 .... **CLC 28, 57, 59**
See also AAYA 4; BEST 90:1; BRWS 4; CA 85-88; 127; CPW; DAM POP; DLB 194, 204

Chaucer, Daniel
See Ford, Ford Madox
See also RHW

Chaucer, Geoffrey 1340(?)-1400 .. **LC 17, 56; PC 19; WLCS**
See also BRW 1; BRWR 2; CDBLB Before 1660; DA; DA3; DAB; DAC; DAM MST, POET; DLB 146; LAIT 1; PAB; PFS 14; RGEL 2; WLIT 3; WP

Chavez, Denise (Elia) 1948-
See also CA 131; CANR 56, 81; DAM MULT; DLB 122; FW; HLC 1; HW 1, 2; MTCW 2

Chaviaras, Strates 1935-
See Haviaras, Stratis
See also CA 105

Chayefsky, Paddy .... **CLC 23**
See also Chayefsky, Sidney
See also CAD; DLB 7, 44; DLBY 1981; RGAL 4

Chayefsky, Sidney 1923-1981
See Chayefsky, Paddy
See also CA 9-12R; 104; CANR 18; DAM DRAM

Chedid, Andree 1920- .... **CLC 47**
See also CA 145; CANR 95

Cheever, John 1912-1982 ..... **CLC 3, 7, 8, 11, 15, 25, 64; SSC 1, 38; WLC**
See also AMWS 1; BPFB 1; CA 5-8R; 106; CABS 1; CANR 5, 27, 76; CDALB 1941-1968; CPW; DA; DA3; DAB; DAC; DAM MST, NOV, POP; DLB 2, 102, 227; DLBY 1980, 1982; EXPS; INT CANR-5; MTCW 1, 2; RGAL 4; RGSF 2; SSFS 2, 14

Cheever, Susan 1943- .... **CLC 18, 48**
See also CA 103; CANR 27, 51, 92; DLBY 1982; INT CANR-27

Chekhonte, Antosha
See Chekhov, Anton (Pavlovich)

Chekhov, Anton (Pavlovich)
1860-1904 . **TCLC 3, 10, 31, 55, 96; DC 9; SSC 2, 28, 41, 51; WLC**
See also BYA 14; CA 104; 124; DA; DA3; DAB; DAC; DAM DRAM, MST; DFS 1, 5, 10, 12; EW 7; EXPS; LAIT 3; RGSF 2; RGWL 2; SATA 90; SSFS 5, 13, 14

Cheney, Lynne V. 1941- .... **CLC 70**
See also CA 89-92; CANR 58

Chernyshevsky, Nikolai Gavrilovich
See Chernyshevsky, Nikolay Gavrilovich
See also DLB 238

Chernyshevsky, Nikolay Gavrilovich
1828-1889 .... **NCLC 1**
See also Chernyshevsky, Nikolai Gavrilovich

Cherry, Carolyn Janice 1942-
See Cherryh, C. J.
See also CA 65-68; CANR 10

Cherryh, C. J. .... **CLC 35**
See also Cherry, Carolyn Janice
See also AAYA 24; BPFB 1; DLBY 1980; FANT; SATA 93; SCFW 2; SFW 4; YAW

Chesnutt, Charles W(addell)
1858-1932 .... **TCLC 5, 39; BLC 1; SSC 7, 54**
See also AFAW 1, 2; BW 1, 3; CA 106; 125; CANR 76; DAM MULT; DLB 12, 50, 78; MTCW 1, 2; RGAL 4; RGSF 2; SSFS 11

Chester, Alfred 1929(?)-1971 .... **CLC 49**
See also CA 196; 33-36R; DLB 130

Chesterton, G(ilbert) K(eith)
1874-1936 . **TCLC 1, 6, 64; PC 28; SSC 1, 46**
See also BRW 6; CA 104; 132; CANR 73; CDBLB 1914-1945; CMW 4; DAM NOV, POET; DLB 10, 19, 34, 70, 98, 149, 178; FANT; MSW; MTCW 1, 2; RGEL 2; RGSF 2; SATA 27; SUFW

Chiang, Pin-chin 1904-1986
See Ding Ling
See also CA 118

Ch'ien, Chung-shu 1910-1998 .... **CLC 22**
See also CA 130; CANR 73; MTCW 1, 2

Chikamatsu Monzaemon 1653-1724 ... **LC 66**
See also RGWL 2

Child, L. Maria
See Child, Lydia Maria

Child, Lydia Maria 1802-1880 .. **NCLC 6, 73**
See also DLB 1, 74, 243; RGAL 4; SATA 67

Child, Mrs.
See Child, Lydia Maria

Child, Philip 1898-1978 .... **CLC 19, 68**
See also CA 13-14; CAP 1; DLB 68; RHW; SATA 47

Childers, (Robert) Erskine
1870-1922 .... **TCLC 65**
See also CA 113; 153; DLB 70

Childress, Alice 1920-1994 .. **CLC 12, 15, 86, 96; BLC 1; DC 4**
See also AAYA 8; BW 2, 3; BYA 2; CA 45-48; 146; CAD; CANR 3, 27, 50, 74; CLR 14; CWD; DA3; DAM DRAM, MULT, NOV; DFS 2, 8, 14; DLB 7, 38, 249; JRDA; LAIT 5; MAICYA 1, 2; MAICYAS 1; MTCW 1, 2; RGAL 4; SATA 7, 48, 81; TCLC 116; WYA; YAW

Chin, Frank (Chew, Jr.) 1940- ...... **CLC 135; DC 7**
See also CA 33-36R; CANR 71; CD 5; DAM MULT; DLB 206; LAIT 5; RGAL 4

Chin, Marilyn (Mei Ling) 1955- .... **PC 40**
See also CA 129; CANR 70; CWP

Chislett, (Margaret) Anne 1943- ...... **CLC 34**
See also CA 151

Chitty, Thomas Willes 1926- .... **CLC 11**
See also Hinde, Thomas
See also CA 5-8R; CN 7

Chivers, Thomas Holley
1809-1858 .... **NCLC 49**
See also DLB 3, 248; RGAL 4

Choi, Susan .... **CLC 119**

Chomette, Rene Lucien 1898-1981
See Clair, Rene
See also CA 103

Chomsky, (Avram) Noam 1928- ..... **CLC 132**
See also CA 17-20R; CANR 28, 62; DA3; DLB 246; MTCW 1, 2

Chopin, Kate .. **TCLC 5, 14; SSC 8; WLCS**
See also Chopin, Katherine
See also AAYA 33; AMWS 1; CDALB 1865-1917; DA; DAB; DLB 12, 78; EXPN; EXPS; FW; LAIT 3; MAWW; NFS 3; RGAL 4; RGSF 2; SSFS 2, 13

Chopin, Katherine 1851-1904
See Chopin, Kate
See also CA 104; 122; DA3; DAC; DAM MST, NOV

Chretien de Troyes c. 12th cent. - . **CMLC 10**
See also DLB 208; EW 1; RGWL 2

Christie
See Ichikawa, Kon

Christie, Agatha (Mary Clarissa) 1890-1976 .. **CLC 1, 6, 8, 12, 39, 48, 110**
See also AAYA 9; AITN 1, 2; BPFB 1; BRWS 2; CA 17-20R; 61-64; CANR 10, 37, 108; CBD; CDBLB 1914-1945; CMW 4; CPW; CWD; DA3; DAB; DAC; DAM NOV; DFS 2; DLB 13, 77, 245; MSW; MTCW 1, 2; NFS 8; RGEL 2; RHW; SATA 36; YAW

Christie, Philippa .... **CLC 21**
See also Pearce, Philippa
See also BYA 5; CANR 109; CLR 9; DLB 161; MAICYA 1; SATA 1, 67, 129

Christine de Pizan 1365(?)-1431(?) .... **LC 9**
See also DLB 208; RGWL 2

Chubb, Elmer
See Masters, Edgar Lee

Chulkov, Mikhail Dmitrievich 1743-1792 .... **LC 2**
See also DLB 150

Churchill, Caryl 1938- .... **CLC 31, 55, 157; DC 5**
See also BRWS 4; CA 102; CANR 22, 46, 108; CBD; CWD; DFS 12; DLB 13; FW; MTCW 1; RGEL 2

Churchill, Charles 1731-1764 .... **LC 3**
See also DLB 109; RGEL 2

Churchill, Sir Winston (Leonard Spencer) 1874-1965 .... **TCLC 113**
See also BRW 6; CA 97-100; CDBLB 1890-1914; DA3; DLB 100; DLBD 16; LAIT 4; MTCW 1, 2

Chute, Carolyn 1947- .... **CLC 39**
See also CA 123

Ciardi, John (Anthony) 1916-1986 . **CLC 10, 40, 44, 129**
See also CA 5-8R; 118; CAAS 2; CANR 5, 33; CLR 19; CWRI 5; DAM POET; DLB 5; DLBY 1986; INT CANR-5; MAICYA 1, 2; MTCW 1, 2; RGAL 4; SAAS 26; SATA 1, 65; SATA-Obit 46

Cibber, Colley 1671-1757 .... **LC 66**
See also DLB 84; RGEL 2

Cicero, Marcus Tullius 106B.C.-43B.C. .... **CMLC 3**
See also AW 1; CDWLB 1; DLB 211; RGWL 2

Cimino, Michael 1943- .... **CLC 16**
See also CA 105

Cioran, E(mil) M. 1911-1995 .... **CLC 64**
See also CA 25-28R; 149; CANR 91; DLB 220

Cisneros, Sandra 1954- .. **CLC 69, 118; HLC 1; SSC 32**
See also AAYA 9; AMWS 7; CA 131; CANR 64; CWP; DA3; DAM MULT; DLB 122, 152; EXPN; FW; HW 1, 2; LAIT 5; MAICYA 2; MTCW 2; NFS 2; RGAL 4; RGSF 2; SSFS 3, 13; WLIT 1; YAW

Cixous, Helene 1937- .... **CLC 92**
See also CA 126; CANR 55; CWW 2; DLB 83, 242; FW; GLL 2; MTCW 1, 2

Clair, Rene .... **CLC 20**
See also Chomette, Rene Lucien

Clampitt, Amy 1920-1994 .... **CLC 32; PC 19**
See also AMWS 9; CA 110; 146; CANR 29, 79; DLB 105

Clancy, Thomas L., Jr. 1947-
See Clancy, Tom
See also CA 125; 131; CANR 62, 105; DA3; INT CA-131; MTCW 1, 2

Clancy, Tom .... **CLC 45, 112**
See also Clancy, Thomas L., Jr.
See also AAYA 9; BEST 89:1, 90:1; BPFB 1; BYA 10, 11; CMW 4; CPW; DAM NOV, POP; DLB 227

Clare, John 1793-1864 .. **NCLC 9, 86; PC 23**
See also DAB; DAM POET; DLB 55, 96; RGEL 2

Clarin
See Alas (y Urena), Leopoldo (Enrique Garcia)

Clark, Al C.
See Goines, Donald

Clark, (Robert) Brian 1932- .... **CLC 29**
See also CA 41-44R; CANR 67; CBD; CD 5

Clark, Curt
See Westlake, Donald E(dwin)

Clark, Eleanor 1913-1996 .... **CLC 5, 19**
See also CA 9-12R; 151; CANR 41; CN 7; DLB 6

Clark, J. P.
See Clark Bekederemo, J(ohnson) P(epper)
See also CDWLB 3; DLB 117

Clark, John Pepper
See Clark Bekederemo, J(ohnson) P(epper)
See also AFW; CD 5; CP 7; RGEL 2

Clark, M. R.
See Clark, Mavis Thorpe

Clark, Mavis Thorpe 1909-1999 ...... **CLC 12**
See also CA 57-60; CANR 8, 37, 107; CLR 30; CWRI 5; MAICYA 1, 2; SAAS 5; SATA 8, 74

Clark, Walter Van Tilburg 1909-1971 .... **CLC 28**
See also CA 9-12R; 33-36R; CANR 63; DLB 9, 206; LAIT 2; RGAL 4; SATA 8

Clark Bekederemo, J(ohnson) P(epper) 1935- .... **CLC 38; BLC 1; DC 5**
See also Clark, J. P.; Clark, John Pepper
See also BW 1; CA 65-68; CANR 16, 72; DAM DRAM, MULT; DFS 13; MTCW 1

Clarke, Arthur C(harles) 1917- .... **CLC 1, 4, 13, 18, 35, 136; SSC 3**
See also AAYA 4, 33; BPFB 1; BYA 13; CA 1-4R; CANR 2, 28, 55, 74; CN 7; CPW; DA3; DAM POP; DLB 261; JRDA; LAIT 5; MAICYA 1, 2; MTCW 1, 2; SATA 13, 70, 115; SCFW; SFW 4; SSFS 4; YAW

Clarke, Austin 1896-1974 .... **CLC 6, 9**
See also CA 29-32; 49-52; CAP 2; DAM POET; DLB 10, 20; RGEL 2

Clarke, Austin C(hesterfield) 1934- .. **CLC 8, 53; BLC 1; SSC 45**
See also BW 1; CA 25-28R; CAAS 16; CANR 14, 32, 68; CN 7; DAC; DAM MULT; DLB 53, 125; DNFS 2; RGSF 2

Clarke, Gillian 1937- .... **CLC 61**
See also CA 106; CP 7; CWP; DLB 40

Clarke, Marcus (Andrew Hislop) 1846-1881 .... **NCLC 19**
See also DLB 230; RGEL 2; RGSF 2

Clarke, Shirley 1925-1997 .... **CLC 16**
See also CA 189

Clash, The
See Headon, (Nicky) Topper; Jones, Mick; Simonon, Paul; Strummer, Joe

Claudel, Paul (Louis Charles Marie) 1868-1955 .... **TCLC 2, 10**
See also CA 104; 165; DLB 192, 258; EW 8; GFL 1789 to the Present; RGWL 2

Claudian 370(?)-404(?) .... **CMLC 46**
See also RGWL 2

Claudius, Matthias 1740-1815 .... **NCLC 75**
See also DLB 97

Clavell, James (duMaresq) 1925-1994 .... **CLC 6, 25, 87**
See also BPFB 1; CA 25-28R; 146; CANR 26, 48; CPW; DA3; DAM NOV, POP; MTCW 1, 2; NFS 10; RHW

Clayman, Gregory .... **CLC 65**

Cleaver, (Leroy) Eldridge 1935-1998 .... **CLC 30, 119; BLC 1**
See also BW 1, 3; CA 21-24R; 167; CANR 16, 75; DA3; DAM MULT; MTCW 2; YAW

Cleese, John (Marwood) 1939- .... **CLC 21**
See also Monty Python
See also CA 112; 116; CANR 35; MTCW 1

Cleishbotham, Jebediah
See Scott, Sir Walter

Cleland, John 1710-1789 .... **LC 2, 48**
See also DLB 39; RGEL 2

Clemens, Samuel Langhorne 1835-1910
See Twain, Mark
See also CA 104; 135; CDALB 1865-1917; DA; DA3; DAB; DAC; DAM MST, NOV; DLB 12, 23, 64, 74, 186, 189; JRDA; MAICYA 1, 2; SATA 100; YABC 2

Clement of Alexandria 150(?)-215(?) .... **CMLC 41**

Cleophil
See Congreve, William

Clerihew, E.
See Bentley, E(dmund) C(lerihew)

Clerk, N. W.
See Lewis, C(live) S(taples)

Cliff, Jimmy .... **CLC 21**
See also Chambers, James
See also CA 193

Cliff, Michelle 1946- .... **CLC 120; BLCS**
See also BW 2; CA 116; CANR 39, 72; CD-WLB 3; DLB 157; FW; GLL 2

Clifford, Lady Anne 1590-1676 .... **LC 76**
See also DLB 151

Clifton, (Thelma) Lucille 1936- .... **CLC 19, 66; BLC 1; PC 17**
See also AFAW 2; BW 2, 3; CA 49-52; CANR 2, 24, 42, 76, 97; CLR 5; CP 7; CSW; CWP; CWRI 5; DA3; DAM MULT, POET; DLB 5, 41; EXPP; MAICYA 1, 2; MTCW 1, 2; PFS 1, 14; SATA 20, 69, 128; WP

Clinton, Dirk
See Silverberg, Robert

Clough, Arthur Hugh 1819-1861 ... **NCLC 27**
See also BRW 5; DLB 32; RGEL 2

Clutha, Janet Paterson Frame 1924-
See Frame, Janet
See also CA 1-4R; CANR 2, 36, 76; MTCW 1, 2; SATA 119

Clyne, Terence
See Blatty, William Peter

Cobalt, Martin
See Mayne, William (James Carter)

Cobb, Irvin S(hrewsbury) 1876-1944 .... **TCLC 77**
See also CA 175; DLB 11, 25, 86

Cobbett, William 1763-1835 .... **NCLC 49**
See also DLB 43, 107, 158; RGEL 2

Coburn, D(onald) L(ee) 1938- .... **CLC 10**
See also CA 89-92

Cocteau, Jean (Maurice Eugene Clement) 1889-1963 ...... **CLC 1, 8, 15, 16, 43; DC 17; WLC**
See also CA 25-28; CANR 40; CAP 2; DA; DA3; DAB; DAC; DAM DRAM, MST, NOV; DLB 65, 258; EW 10; GFL 1789 to the Present; MTCW 1, 2; RGWL 2; TCLC 119

Codrescu, Andrei 1946- .... **CLC 46, 121**
See also CA 33-36R; CAAS 19; CANR 13, 34, 53, 76; DA3; DAM POET; MTCW 2

Coe, Max
See Bourne, Randolph S(illiman)

Coe, Tucker
See Westlake, Donald E(dwin)

Coen, Ethan 1958- .... **CLC 108**
See also CA 126; CANR 85

Coen, Joel 1955- .... **CLC 108**
See also CA 126

The Coen Brothers
See Coen, Ethan; Coen, Joel

Coetzee, J(ohn) M(ichael) 1940- ...... **CLC 23, 33, 66, 117, 161**
See also AAYA 37; AFW; BRWS 6; CA 77-80; CANR 41, 54, 74; CN 7; DA3; DAM NOV; DLB 225; MTCW 1, 2; WLIT 2

Coffey, Brian
See Koontz, Dean R(ay)

Coffin, Robert P(eter) Tristram
1892-1955 .... **TCLC 95**
See also CA 123; 169; DLB 45

Cohan, George M(ichael)
1878-1942 .... **TCLC 60**
See also CA 157; DLB 249; RGAL 4

Cohen, Arthur A(llen) 1928-1986 ...... **CLC 7, 31**
See also CA 1-4R; 120; CANR 1, 17, 42; DLB 28

Cohen, Leonard (Norman) 1934- ...... **CLC 3, 38**
See also CA 21-24R; CANR 14, 69; CN 7; CP 7; DAC; DAM MST; DLB 53; MTCW 1

Cohen, Matt(hew) 1942-1999 .... **CLC 19**
See also CA 61-64; 187; CAAS 18; CANR 40; CN 7; DAC; DLB 53

Cohen-Solal, Annie 19(?)- .... **CLC 50**

Colegate, Isabel 1931- .... **CLC 36**
See also CA 17-20R; CANR 8, 22, 74; CN 7; DLB 14, 231; INT CANR-22; MTCW 1

Coleman, Emmett
See Reed, Ishmael

Coleridge, Hartley 1796-1849 .... **NCLC 90**
See also DLB 96

Coleridge, M. E.
See Coleridge, Mary E(lizabeth)

Coleridge, Mary E(lizabeth)
1861-1907 .... **TCLC 73**
See also CA 116; 166; DLB 19, 98

Coleridge, Samuel Taylor
1772-1834 ...... **NCLC 9, 54, 99, 111; PC 11, 39; WLC**
See also BRW 4; BRWR 2; BYA 4; CDBLB 1789-1832; DA; DA3; DAB; DAC; DAM MST, POET; DLB 93, 107; EXPP; PAB; PFS 4, 5; RGEL 2; WLIT 3; WP

Coleridge, Sara 1802-1852 .... **NCLC 31**
See also DLB 199

Coles, Don 1928- .... **CLC 46**
See also CA 115; CANR 38; CP 7

Coles, Robert (Martin) 1929- .... **CLC 108**
See also CA 45-48; CANR 3, 32, 66, 70; INT CANR-32; SATA 23

Colette, (Sidonie-Gabrielle)
1873-1954 .... **TCLC 1, 5, 16; SSC 10**
See also Willy, Colette
See also CA 104; 131; DA3; DAM NOV; DLB 65; EW 9; GFL 1789 to the Present; MTCW 1, 2; RGWL 2

Collett, (Jacobine) Camilla (Wergeland)
1813-1895 .... **NCLC 22**

Collier, Christopher 1930- .... **CLC 30**
See also AAYA 13; BYA 2; CA 33-36R; CANR 13, 33, 102; JRDA; MAICYA 1, 2; SATA 16, 70; WYA; YAW 1

Collier, James Lincoln 1928- .... **CLC 30**
See also AAYA 13; BYA 2; CA 9-12R; CANR 4, 33, 60, 102; CLR 3; DAM POP; JRDA; MAICYA 1, 2; SAAS 21; SATA 8, 70; WYA; YAW 1

Collier, Jeremy 1650-1726 .... **LC 6**

Collier, John 1901-1980 .... **SSC 19**
See also CA 65-68; 97-100; CANR 10; DLB 77, 255; FANT; SUFW

Collingwood, R(obin) G(eorge)
1889(?)-1943 .... **TCLC 67**
See also CA 117; 155; DLB 262

Collins, Hunt
See Hunter, Evan

Collins, Linda 1931- .... **CLC 44**
See also CA 125

Collins, (William) Wilkie
1824-1889 .... **NCLC 1, 18, 93**
See also BRWS 6; CDBLB 1832-1890; CMW 4; DLB 18, 70, 159; MSW; RGEL 2; RGSF 2; SUFW; WLIT 4

Collins, William 1721-1759 .... **LC 4, 40**
See also BRW 3; DAM POET; DLB 109; RGEL 2

Collodi, Carlo .... **NCLC 54**
See also Lorenzini, Carlo
See also CLR 5; WCH

Colman, George
See Glassco, John

Colonna, Vittoria 1492-1547 .... **LC 71**
See also RGWL 2

Colt, Winchester Remington
See Hubbard, L(afayette) Ron(ald)

Colter, Cyrus 1910-2002 .... **CLC 58**
See also BW 1; CA 65-68; CANR 10, 66; CN 7; DLB 33

Colton, James
See Hansen, Joseph
See also GLL 1

Colum, Padraic 1881-1972 .... **CLC 28**
See also BYA 4; CA 73-76; 33-36R; CANR 35; CLR 36; CWRI 5; DLB 19; MAICYA 1, 2; MTCW 1; RGEL 2; SATA 15; WCH

Colvin, James
See Moorcock, Michael (John)

Colwin, Laurie (E.) 1944-1992 .... **CLC 5, 13, 23, 84**
See also CA 89-92; 139; CANR 20, 46; DLB 218; DLBY 1980; MTCW 1

Comfort, Alex(ander) 1920-2000 .... **CLC 7**
See also CA 1-4R; 190; CANR 1, 45; CP 7; DAM POP; MTCW 1

Comfort, Montgomery
See Campbell, (John) Ramsey

Compton-Burnett, I(vy)
1892(?)-1969 .... **CLC 1, 3, 10, 15, 34**
See also BRW 7; CA 1-4R; 25-28R; CANR 4; DAM NOV; DLB 36; MTCW 1; RGEL 2

Comstock, Anthony 1844-1915 ...... **TCLC 13**
See also CA 110; 169

Comte, Auguste 1798-1857 .... **NCLC 54**

Conan Doyle, Arthur
See Doyle, Sir Arthur Conan
See also BPFB 1; BYA 4, 5, 11

Conde (Abellan), Carmen 1901-1996
See also CA 177; DLB 108; HLCS 1; HW 2

Conde, Maryse 1937- ..... **CLC 52, 92; BLCS**
See also BW 2, 3; CA 110; CAAE 190; CANR 30, 53, 76; CWW 2; DAM MULT; MTCW 1

Condillac, Etienne Bonnot de
1714-1780 .... **LC 26**

Condon, Richard (Thomas)
1915-1996 .... **CLC 4, 6, 8, 10, 45, 100**
See also BEST 90:3; BPFB 1; CA 1-4R; 151; CAAS 1; CANR 2, 23; CMW 4; CN 7; DAM NOV; INT CANR-23; MTCW 1, 2

Confucius 551B.C.-479B.C. .... **CMLC 19; WLCS**
See also DA; DA3; DAB; DAC; DAM MST

Congreve, William 1670-1729 . **LC 5, 21; DC 2; WLC**
See also BRW 2; CDBLB 1660-1789; DA; DAB; DAC; DAM DRAM, MST, POET; DFS 15; DLB 39, 84; RGEL 2; WLIT 3

Connell, Evan S(helby), Jr. 1924- . **CLC 4, 6, 45**
See also AAYA 7; CA 1-4R; CAAS 2; CANR 2, 39, 76, 97; CN 7; DAM NOV; DLB 2; DLBY 1981; MTCW 1, 2

Connelly, Marc(us Cook) 1890-1980 . **CLC 7**
See also CA 85-88; 102; CANR 30; DFS 12; DLB 7; DLBY 1980; RGAL 4; SATA-Obit 25

Connor, Ralph .... **TCLC 31**
See also Gordon, Charles William
See also DLB 92; TCWW 2

Conrad, Joseph 1857-1924 .... **TCLC 1, 6, 13, 25, 43, 57; SSC 9; WLC**
See also AAYA 26; BPFB 1; BRW 6; BRWR 2; BYA 2; CA 104; 131; CANR 60; CDBLB 1890-1914; DA; DA3; DAB; DAC; DAM MST, NOV; DLB 10, 34, 98, 156; EXPN; EXPS; LAIT 2; MTCW 1, 2; NFS 2; RGEL 2; RGSF 2; SATA 27; SSFS 1, 12; WLIT 4

Conrad, Robert Arnold
See Hart, Moss

Conroy, (Donald) Pat(rick) 1945- ... **CLC 30, 74**
See also AAYA 8; AITN 1; BPFB 1; CA 85-88; CANR 24, 53; CPW; CSW; DA3; DAM NOV, POP; DLB 6; LAIT 5; MTCW 1, 2

Constant (de Rebecque), (Henri) Benjamin
1767-1830 .... **NCLC 6**
See also DLB 119; EW 4; GFL 1789 to the Present

Conway, Jill K(er) 1934- .... **CLC 152**
See also CA 130; CANR 94

Conybeare, Charles Augustus
See Eliot, T(homas) S(tearns)

Cook, Michael 1933-1994 .... **CLC 58**
See also CA 93-96; CANR 68; DLB 53

Cook, Robin 1940- .... **CLC 14**
See also AAYA 32; BEST 90:2; BPFB 1; CA 108; 111; CANR 41, 90, 109; CPW; DA3; DAM POP; HGG; INT CA-111

Cook, Roy
See Silverberg, Robert

Cooke, Elizabeth 1948- .... **CLC 55**
See also CA 129

Cooke, John Esten 1830-1886 .... **NCLC 5**
See also DLB 3, 248; RGAL 4

Cooke, John Estes
See Baum, L(yman) Frank

Cooke, M. E.
See Creasey, John

Cooke, Margaret
See Creasey, John

Cooke, Rose Terry 1827-1892 .... **NCLC 110**
See also DLB 12, 74

Cook-Lynn, Elizabeth 1930- .... **CLC 93**
See also CA 133; DAM MULT; DLB 175; NNAL

Cooney, Ray .... **CLC 62**
See also CBD

Cooper, Douglas 1960- .... **CLC 86**

Cooper, Henry St. John
See Creasey, John

Cooper, J(oan) California (?)- .... **CLC 56**
See also AAYA 12; BW 1; CA 125; CANR 55; DAM MULT; DLB 212

Cooper, James Fenimore
1789-1851 .... **NCLC 1, 27, 54**
See also AAYA 22; AMW; BPFB 1; CDALB 1640-1865; DA3; DLB 3, 183, 250, 254; LAIT 1; NFS 9; RGAL 4; SATA 19; WCH

Coover, Robert (Lowell) 1932- ...... **CLC 3, 7, 15, 32, 46, 87, 161; SSC 15**
See also AMWS 5; BPFB 1; CA 45-48; CANR 3, 37, 58; CN 7; DAM NOV; DLB 2, 227; DLBY 1981; MTCW 1, 2; RGAL 4; RGSF 2

Copeland, Stewart (Armstrong)
1952- .... **CLC 26**

Copernicus, Nicolaus 1473-1543 .... **LC 45**

Coppard, A(lfred) E(dgar)
1878-1957 .... **TCLC 5; SSC 21**
See also CA 114; 167; DLB 162; HGG; RGEL 2; RGSF 2; SUFW; YABC 1

Coppee, Francois 1842-1908 .... **TCLC 25**
See also CA 170; DLB 217

Coppola, Francis Ford 1939- ... **CLC 16, 126**
See also AAYA 39; CA 77-80; CANR 40, 78; DLB 44

Corbiere, Tristan 1845-1875 .... **NCLC 43**
See also DLB 217; GFL 1789 to the Present

Corcoran, Barbara (Asenath)
1911- .... **CLC 17**
See also AAYA 14; CA 21-24R; CAAE 191; CAAS 2; CANR 11, 28, 48; CLR 50; DLB 52; JRDA; MAICYA 2; MAICYAS 1; RHW; SAAS 20; SATA 3, 77, 125

Cordelier, Maurice
See Giraudoux, Jean(-Hippolyte)

Corelli, Marie .... **TCLC 51**
See also Mackay, Mary
See also DLB 34, 156; RGEL 2; SUFW

Corman, Cid .... **CLC 9**
See also Corman, Sidney
See also CAAS 2; DLB 5, 193

Corman, Sidney 1924-
See Corman, Cid
See also CA 85-88; CANR 44; CP 7; DAM POET

Cormier, Robert (Edmund)
1925-2000 .... **CLC 12, 30**
See also AAYA 3, 19; BYA 1, 2, 6, 8, 9; CA 1-4R; CANR 5, 23, 76, 93; CDALB 1968-1988; CLR 12, 55; DA; DAC; DAM MST, NOV; DLB 52; EXPN; INT CANR-23; JRDA; LAIT 5; MAICYA 1, 2; MTCW 1, 2; NFS 2; SATA 10, 45, 83; SATA-Obit 122; WYA; YAW

Corn, Alfred (DeWitt III) 1943- .... **CLC 33**
See also CA 179; CAAE 179; CAAS 25; CANR 44; CP 7; CSW; DLB 120; DLBY 1980

Corneille, Pierre 1606-1684 .... **LC 28**
See also DAB; DAM MST; EW 3; GFL Beginnings to 1789; RGWL 2

Cornwell, David (John Moore)
1931- .... **CLC 9, 15**
See also le Carre, John
See also CA 5-8R; CANR 13, 33, 59, 107; DA3; DAM POP; MTCW 1, 2

Cornwell, Patricia (Daniels) 1956- . **CLC 155**
See also AAYA 16; BPFB 1; CA 134; CANR 53; CMW 4; CPW; CSW; DAM POP; MSW; MTCW 1

Corso, (Nunzio) Gregory 1930-2001 . **CLC 1, 11; PC 33**
See also CA 5-8R; 193; CANR 41, 76; CP 7; DA3; DLB 5, 16, 237; MTCW 1, 2; WP

Cortazar, Julio 1914-1984 ... **CLC 2, 3, 5, 10, 13, 15, 33, 34, 92; HLC 1; SSC 7**
See also BPFB 1; CA 21-24R; CANR 12, 32, 81; CDWLB 3; DA3; DAM MULT, NOV; DLB 113; EXPS; HW 1, 2; LAW; MTCW 1, 2; RGSF 2; RGWL 2; SSFS 3; WLIT 1

Cortes, Hernan 1485-1547 .... **LC 31**

Corvinus, Jakob
See Raabe, Wilhelm (Karl)

Corvo, Baron
See Rolfe, Frederick (William Serafino Austin Lewis Mary)
See also GLL 1; RGEL 2

Corwin, Cecil
See Kornbluth, C(yril) M.

Cosic, Dobrica 1921- .... **CLC 14**
See also CA 122; 138; CDWLB 4; CWW 2; DLB 181

Costain, Thomas B(ertram)
1885-1965 .... **CLC 30**
See also BYA 3; CA 5-8R; 25-28R; DLB 9; RHW

Costantini, Humberto 1924(?)-1987 . **CLC 49**
See also CA 131; 122; HW 1

Costello, Elvis 1955- .... **CLC 21**

Costenoble, Philostene 1898-1962
See Ghelderode, Michel de

Costenoble, Philostene 1898-1962
See Ghelderode, Michel de

Cotes, Cecil V.
See Duncan, Sara Jeannette

Cotter, Joseph Seamon Sr.
1861-1949 .... **TCLC 28; BLC 1**
See also BW 1; CA 124; DAM MULT; DLB 50

Couch, Arthur Thomas Quiller
See Quiller-Couch, Sir Arthur (Thomas)

Coulton, James
See Hansen, Joseph

Couperus, Louis (Marie Anne)
1863-1923 .... **TCLC 15**
See also CA 115; RGWL 2

Coupland, Douglas 1961- .... **CLC 85, 133**
See also AAYA 34; CA 142; CANR 57, 90; CCA 1; CPW; DAC; DAM POP

Court, Wesli
See Turco, Lewis (Putnam)

Courtenay, Bryce 1933- .... **CLC 59**
See also CA 138; CPW

Courtney, Robert
See Ellison, Harlan (Jay)

Cousteau, Jacques-Yves 1910-1997 .. **CLC 30**
See also CA 65-68; 159; CANR 15, 67; MTCW 1; SATA 38, 98

Coventry, Francis 1725-1754 .... **LC 46**

Coverdale, Miles c. 1487-1569 .... **LC 77**
See also DLB 167

Cowan, Peter (Walkinshaw) 1914- ..... **SSC 28**
See also CA 21-24R; CANR 9, 25, 50, 83; CN 7; DLB 260; RGSF 2

Coward, Noel (Peirce) 1899-1973 . **CLC 1, 9, 29, 51**
See also AITN 1; BRWS 2; CA 17-18; 41-44R; CANR 35; CAP 2; CDBLB 1914-1945; DA3; DAM DRAM; DFS 3, 6; DLB 10, 245; IDFW 3, 4; MTCW 1, 2; RGEL 2

Cowley, Abraham 1618-1667 .... **LC 43**
See also BRW 2; DLB 131, 151; PAB; RGEL 2

Cowley, Malcolm 1898-1989 .... **CLC 39**
See also AMWS 2; CA 5-8R; 128; CANR 3, 55; DLB 4, 48; DLBY 1981, 1989; MTCW 1, 2

Cowper, William 1731-1800 ...... **NCLC 8, 94; PC 40**
See also BRW 3; DA3; DAM POET; DLB 104, 109; RGEL 2

Cox, William Trevor 1928-
See Trevor, William
See also CA 9-12R; CANR 4, 37, 55, 76, 102; DAM NOV; INT CANR-37; MTCW 1, 2

Coyne, P. J.
See Masters, Hilary

Cozzens, James Gould 1903-1978 . **CLC 1, 4, 11, 92**
See also AMW; BPFB 1; CA 9-12R; 81-84; CANR 19; CDALB 1941-1968; DLB 9; DLBD 2; DLBY 1984, 1997; MTCW 1, 2; RGAL 4

Crabbe, George 1754-1832 .... **NCLC 26**
See also BRW 3; DLB 93; RGEL 2

Crace, Jim 1946- .... **CLC 157**
See also CA 128; 135; CANR 55, 70; CN 7; DLB 231; INT CA-135

Craddock, Charles Egbert
See Murfree, Mary Noailles

Craig, A. A.
See Anderson, Poul (William)

Craik, Mrs.
See Craik, Dinah Maria (Mulock)
See also RGEL 2

Craik, Dinah Maria (Mulock)
1826-1887 .... **NCLC 38**
See also Craik, Mrs.; Mulock, Dinah Maria
See also DLB 35, 163; MAICYA 1, 2; SATA 34

Cram, Ralph Adams 1863-1942 ..... **TCLC 45**
See also CA 160

Cranch, Christopher Pearse
1813-1892 .... **NCLC 115**
See also DLB 1, 42, 243

Crane, (Harold) Hart 1899-1932 .... **TCLC 2, 5, 80; PC 3; WLC**
See also AMW; CA 104; 127; CDALB 1917-1929; DA; DA3; DAB; DAC; DAM MST, POET; DLB 4, 48; MTCW 1, 2; RGAL 4

Crane, R(onald) S(almon)
1886-1967 .... **CLC 27**
See also CA 85-88; DLB 63

Crane, Stephen (Townley)
1871-1900 ...... **TCLC 11, 17, 32; SSC 7; WLC**
See also AAYA 21; AMW; BPFB 1; BYA 3; CA 109; 140; CANR 84; CDALB 1865-1917; DA; DA3; DAB; DAC; DAM MST, NOV, POET; DLB 12, 54, 78; EXPN; EXPS; LAIT 2; NFS 4; PFS 9; RGAL 4; RGSF 2; SSFS 4; WYA; YABC 2

Cranshaw, Stanley
See Fisher, Dorothy (Frances) Canfield

Crase, Douglas 1944- .... **CLC 58**
See also CA 106

Crashaw, Richard 1612(?)-1649 .... **LC 24**
See also BRW 2; DLB 126; PAB; RGEL 2

Craven, Margaret 1901-1980 .... **CLC 17**
See also BYA 2; CA 103; CCA 1; DAC; LAIT 5

Crawford, F(rancis) Marion
1854-1909 .... **TCLC 10**
See also CA 107; 168; DLB 71; HGG; RGAL 4; SUFW

Crawford, Isabella Valancy
1850-1887 .... **NCLC 12**
See also DLB 92; RGEL 2

Crayon, Geoffrey
See Irving, Washington

Creasey, John 1908-1973 .... **CLC 11**
See also Marric, J. J.
See also CA 5-8R; 41-44R; CANR 8, 59; CMW 4; DLB 77; MTCW 1

Crebillon, Claude Prosper Jolyot de (fils)
1707-1777 .... **LC 1, 28**
See also GFL Beginnings to 1789

Credo
See Creasey, John

Credo, Alvaro J. de
See Prado (Calvo), Pedro

Creeley, Robert (White) 1926- .. **CLC 1, 2, 4, 8, 11, 15, 36, 78**
See also AMWS 4; CA 1-4R; CAAS 10; CANR 23, 43, 89; CP 7; DA3; DAM POET; DLB 5, 16, 169; DLBD 17; MTCW 1, 2; RGAL 4; WP

Crevecoeur, Hector St. John de
See Crevecoeur, Michel Guillaume Jean de
See also ANW

Crevecoeur, Michel Guillaume Jean de 1735-1813 .... **NCLC 105**
See also Crevecoeur, Hector St. John de
See also AMWS 1; DLB 37

Crevel, Rene 1900-1935 .... **TCLC 112**
See also GLL 2

Crews, Harry (Eugene) 1935- ..... **CLC 6, 23, 49**
See also AITN 1; BPFB 1; CA 25-28R; CANR 20, 57; CN 7; CSW; DA3; DLB 6, 143, 185; MTCW 1, 2; RGAL 4

Crichton, (John) Michael 1942- .... **CLC 2, 6, 54, 90**
See also AAYA 10; AITN 2; BPFB 1; CA 25-28R; CANR 13, 40, 54, 76; CMW 4; CN 7; CPW; DA3; DAM NOV, POP; DLBY 1981; INT CANR-13; JRDA; MTCW 1, 2; SATA 9, 88; SFW 4; YAW

Crispin, Edmund .... **CLC 22**
See Montgomery, (Robert) Bruce
See also DLB 87; MSW

Cristofer, Michael 1945(?)- .... **CLC 28**
See also CA 110; 152; CAD; CD 5; DAM DRAM; DFS 15; DLB 7

Croce, Benedetto 1866-1952 .... **TCLC 37**
See also CA 120; 155; EW 8

Crockett, David 1786-1836 .... **NCLC 8**
See also DLB 3, 11, 183, 248

Crockett, Davy
See Crockett, David

Crofts, Freeman Wills 1879-1957 .. **TCLC 55**
See also CA 115; 195; CMW 4; DLB 77; MSW

Croker, John Wilson 1780-1857 .... **NCLC 10**
See also DLB 110

Crommelynck, Fernand 1885-1970 .. **CLC 75**
See also CA 189; 89-92

Cromwell, Oliver 1599-1658 .... **LC 43**

Cronenberg, David 1943- .... **CLC 143**
See also CA 138; CCA 1

Cronin, A(rchibald) J(oseph) 1896-1981 .... **CLC 32**
See also BPFB 1; CA 1-4R; 102; CANR 5; DLB 191; SATA 47; SATA-Obit 25

Cross, Amanda
See Heilbrun, Carolyn G(old)
See also BPFB 1; CMW; CPW; MSW

Crothers, Rachel 1878-1958 .... **TCLC 19**
See also CA 113; 194; CAD; CWD; DLB 7; RGAL 4

Croves, Hal
See Traven, B.

Crow Dog, Mary (Ellen) (?)- .... **CLC 93**
See also Brave Bird, Mary
See also CA 154

Crowfield, Christopher
See Stowe, Harriet (Elizabeth) Beecher

Crowley, Aleister .... **TCLC 7**
See also Crowley, Edward Alexander
See also GLL 1

Crowley, Edward Alexander 1875-1947
See Crowley, Aleister
See also CA 104; HGG

Crowley, John 1942- .... **CLC 57**
See also BPFB 1; CA 61-64; CANR 43, 98; DLBY 1982; SATA 65; SFW 4

Crud
See Crumb, R(obert)

Crumarums
See Crumb, R(obert)

Crumb, R(obert) 1943- .... **CLC 17**
See also CA 106; CANR 107

Crumbum
See Crumb, R(obert)

Crumski
See Crumb, R(obert)

Crum the Bum
See Crumb, R(obert)

Crunk
See Crumb, R(obert)

Crustt
See Crumb, R(obert)

Crutchfield, Les
See Trumbo, Dalton

Cruz, Victor Hernandez 1949- .... **PC 37**
See also BW 2; CA 65-68; CAAS 17; CANR 14, 32, 74; CP 7; DAM MULT, POET; DLB 41; DNFS 1; EXPP; HLC 1; HW 1, 2; MTCW 1; WP

Cryer, Gretchen (Kiger) 1935- .... **CLC 21**
See also CA 114; 123

Csath, Geza 1887-1919 .... **TCLC 13**
See also CA 111

Cudlip, David R(ockwell) 1933- .... **CLC 34**
See also CA 177

Cullen, Countee 1903-1946 .... **TCLC 4, 37; BLC 1; PC 20; WLCS**
See also AFAW 2; AMWS 4; BW 1; CA 108; 124; CDALB 1917-1929; DA; DA3; DAC; DAM MST, MULT, POET; DLB 4, 48, 51; EXPP; MTCW 1, 2; PFS 3; RGAL 4; SATA 18; WP

Cum, R.
See Crumb, R(obert)

Cummings, Bruce F(rederick) 1889-1919
See Barbellion, W. N. P.
See also CA 123

Cummings, E(dward) E(stlin) 1894-1962 .. **CLC 1, 3, 8, 12, 15, 68; PC 5; WLC**
See also AAYA 41; AMW; CA 73-76; CANR 31; CDALB 1929-1941; DA; DA3; DAB; DAC; DAM MST, POET; DLB 4, 48; EXPP; MTCW 1, 2; PAB; PFS 1, 3, 12, 13; RGAL 4; WP

Cunha, Euclides (Rodrigues Pimenta) da 1866-1909 .... **TCLC 24**
See also CA 123; LAW; WLIT 1

Cunningham, E. V.
See Fast, Howard (Melvin)

Cunningham, J(ames) V(incent) 1911-1985 .... **CLC 3, 31**
See also CA 1-4R; 115; CANR 1, 72; DLB 5

Cunningham, Julia (Woolfolk) 1916- .... **CLC 12**
See also CA 9-12R; CANR 4, 19, 36; CWRI 5; JRDA; MAICYA 1, 2; SAAS 2; SATA 1, 26, 132

Cunningham, Michael 1952- .... **CLC 34**
See also CA 136; CANR 96; GLL 2

Cunninghame Graham, R. B.
See Cunninghame Graham, Robert (Gallnigad) Bontine

Cunninghame Graham, Robert (Gallnigad) Bontine 1852-1936 .... **TCLC 19**
See also Graham, R(obert) B(ontine) Cunninghame
See also CA 119; 184

Currie, Ellen 19(?)- .... **CLC 44**

Curtin, Philip
See Lowndes, Marie Adelaide (Belloc)

Curtis, Price
See Ellison, Harlan (Jay)

Cutrate, Joe
See Spiegelman, Art

Cynewulf c. 770- .... **CMLC 23**
See also DLB 146; RGEL 2

Cyrano de Bergerac, Savinien de 1619-1655 .... **LC 65**
See also GFL Beginnings to 1789; RGWL 2

Czaczkes, Shmuel Yosef Halevi
See Agnon, S(hmuel) Y(osef Halevi)

Dabrowska, Maria (Szumska) 1889-1965 .... **CLC 15**
See also CA 106; CDWLB 4; DLB 215

Dabydeen, David 1955- .... **CLC 34**
See also BW 1; CA 125; CANR 56, 92; CN 7; CP 7

Dacey, Philip 1939- .... **CLC 51**
See also CA 37-40R; CAAS 17; CANR 14, 32, 64; CP 7; DLB 105

Dagerman, Stig (Halvard) 1923-1954 .... **TCLC 17**
See also CA 117; 155; DLB 259

D'Aguiar, Fred 1960- .... **CLC 145**
See also CA 148; CANR 83, 101; CP 7; DLB 157

Dahl, Roald 1916-1990 .... **CLC 1, 6, 18, 79**
See also AAYA 15; BPFB 1; BRWS 4; BYA 5; CA 1-4R; 133; CANR 6, 32, 37, 62; CLR 1, 7, 41; CPW; CWRI 5; DA3; DAB; DAC; DAM MST, NOV, POP; DLB 139, 255; HGG; JRDA; MAICYA 1, 2; MTCW 1, 2; RGSF 2; SATA 1, 26, 73; SATA-Obit 65; SSFS 4; YAW

Dahlberg, Edward 1900-1977 .. **CLC 1, 7, 14**
See also CA 9-12R; 69-72; CANR 31, 62; DLB 48; MTCW 1; RGAL 4

Daitch, Susan 1954- .... **CLC 103**
See also CA 161

Dale, Colin .... **TCLC 18**
See also Lawrence, T(homas) E(dward)

Dale, George E.
See Asimov, Isaac

Dalton, Roque 1935-1975(?) .... **PC 36**
See also CA 176; HLCS 1; HW 2

Daly, Elizabeth 1878-1967 .... **CLC 52**
See also CA 23-24; 25-28R; CANR 60; CAP 2; CMW 4

Daly, Maureen 1921- .... **CLC 17**
See also AAYA 5; BYA 6; CANR 37, 83, 108; JRDA; MAICYA 1, 2; SAAS 1; SATA 2, 129; WYA; YAW

Damas, Leon-Gontran 1912-1978 .... **CLC 84**
See also BW 1; CA 125; 73-76

Dana, Richard Henry Sr. 1787-1879 .... **NCLC 53**

Daniel, Samuel 1562(?)-1619 .... **LC 24**
See also DLB 62; RGEL 2

Daniels, Brett
See Adler, Renata

Dannay, Frederic 1905-1982 .... **CLC 11**
See also CA 1-4R; 107; CANR 1, 39; CMW 4; DAM POP; DLB 137; MTCW 1

D'Annunzio, Gabriele 1863-1938 ... **TCLC 6, 40**
See also CA 104; 155; EW 8; RGWL 2

Danois, N. le
See Gourmont, Remy(-Marie-Charles) de

Dante 1265-1321 .... **CMLC 3, 18, 39; PC 21; WLCS**
See also DA; DA3; DAB; DAC; DAM MST, POET; EFS 1; EW 1; LAIT 1; RGWL 2; WP

d'Antibes, Germain
See Simenon, Georges (Jacques Christian)

Danticat, Edwidge 1969- .... **CLC 94, 139**
See also AAYA 29; CA 152; CAAE 192; CANR 73; DNFS 1; EXPS; MTCW 1; SSFS 1; YAW

Danvers, Dennis 1947- .... **CLC 70**

Danziger, Paula 1944- .... **CLC 21**
See also AAYA 4, 36; BYA 6, 7, 14; CA 112; 115; CANR 37; CLR 20; JRDA; MAICYA 1, 2; SATA 36, 63, 102; SATA-Brief 30; WYA; YAW

Da Ponte, Lorenzo 1749-1838 .... **NCLC 50**

Dario, Ruben 1867-1916 ... **TCLC 4; HLC 1; PC 15**
See also CA 131; CANR 81; DAM MULT; HW 1, 2; LAW; MTCW 1, 2; RGWL 2

Darley, George 1795-1846 .... **NCLC 2**
See also DLB 96; RGEL 2

Darrow, Clarence (Seward) 1857-1938 .... **TCLC 81**
See also CA 164

Darwin, Charles 1809-1882 .... **NCLC 57**
See also BRWS 7; DLB 57, 166; RGEL 2; WLIT 4

Darwin, Erasmus 1731-1802 .... **NCLC 106**
See also DLB 93; RGEL 2

Daryush, Elizabeth 1887-1977 ...... **CLC 6, 19**
See also CA 49-52; CANR 3, 81; DLB 20

Dasgupta, Surendranath 1887-1952 .... **TCLC 81**
See also CA 157

Dashwood, Edmee Elizabeth Monica de la Pasture 1890-1943
See Delafield, E. M.
See also CA 119; 154

da Silva, Antonio Jose 1705-1739 .... **NCLC 114**
See also Silva, Jose Asuncion

Daudet, (Louis Marie) Alphonse 1840-1897 .... **NCLC 1**
See also DLB 123; GFL 1789 to the Present; RGSF 2

Daumal, Rene 1908-1944 .... **TCLC 14**
See also CA 114

Davenant, William 1606-1668 .... **LC 13**
See also DLB 58, 126; RGEL 2

Davenport, Guy (Mattison, Jr.) 1927- .... **CLC 6, 14, 38; SSC 16**
See also CA 33-36R; CANR 23, 73; CN 7; CSW; DLB 130

David, Robert
See Nezval, Vitezslav

Davidson, Avram (James) 1923-1993
See Queen, Ellery
See also CA 101; 171; CANR 26; DLB 8; FANT; SFW 4; SUFW

Davidson, Donald (Grady) 1893-1968 .... **CLC 2, 13, 19**
See also CA 5-8R; 25-28R; CANR 4, 84; DLB 45

Davidson, Hugh
See Hamilton, Edmond

Davidson, John 1857-1909 .... **TCLC 24**
See also CA 118; DLB 19; RGEL 2

Davidson, Sara 1943- .... **CLC 9**
See also CA 81-84; CANR 44, 68; DLB 185

Davie, Donald (Alfred) 1922-1995 .... **CLC 5, 8, 10, 31; PC 29**
See also BRWS 6; CA 1-4R; 149; CAAS 3; CANR 1, 44; CP 7; DLB 27; MTCW 1; RGEL 2

Davie, Elspeth 1919-1995 .... **SSC 52**
See also CA 120; 126; 150; DLB 139

Davies, Ray(mond Douglas) 1944- ... **CLC 21**
See also CA 116; 146; CANR 92

Davies, Rhys 1901-1978 .... **CLC 23**
See also CA 9-12R; 81-84; CANR 4; DLB 139, 191

Davies, (William) Robertson 1913-1995 .... **CLC 2, 7, 13, 25, 42, 75, 91; WLC**
See also Marchbanks, Samuel
See also BEST 89:2; BPFB 1; CA 33-36R; 150; CANR 17, 42, 103; CN 7; CPW; DA; DA3; DAB; DAC; DAM MST, NOV, POP; DLB 68; HGG; INT CANR-17; MTCW 1, 2; RGEL 2

Davies, Walter C.
See Kornbluth, C(yril) M.

Davies, William Henry 1871-1940 ... **TCLC 5**
See also CA 104; 179; DLB 19, 174; RGEL 2

Da Vinci, Leonardo 1452-1519 ..... **LC 12, 57, 60**
See also AAYA 40

Davis, Angela (Yvonne) 1944- .... **CLC 77**
See also BW 2, 3; CA 57-60; CANR 10, 81; CSW; DA3; DAM MULT; FW

Davis, B. Lynch
See Bioy Casares, Adolfo; Borges, Jorge Luis

Davis, Gordon
See Hunt, E(verette) Howard, (Jr.)

Davis, H(arold) L(enoir) 1896-1960 . **CLC 49**
See also ANW; CA 178; 89-92; DLB 9, 206; SATA 114

Davis, Rebecca (Blaine) Harding 1831-1910 .... **TCLC 6; SSC 38**
See also CA 104; 179; DLB 74, 239; FW; NFS 14; RGAL 4

Davis, Richard Harding 1864-1916 .... **TCLC 24**
See also CA 114; 179; DLB 12, 23, 78, 79, 189; DLBD 13; RGAL 4

Davison, Frank Dalby 1893-1970 ..... **CLC 15**
See also CA 116; DLB 260

Davison, Lawrence H.
See Lawrence, D(avid) H(erbert Richards)

Davison, Peter (Hubert) 1928- .... **CLC 28**
See also CA 9-12R; CAAS 4; CANR 3, 43, 84; CP 7; DLB 5

Davys, Mary 1674-1732 .... **LC 1, 46**
See also DLB 39

Dawson, Fielding 1930-2002 .... **CLC 6**
See also CA 85-88; CANR 108; DLB 130

Dawson, Peter
See Faust, Frederick (Schiller)
See also TCWW 2, 2

Day, Clarence (Shepard, Jr.) 1874-1935 .... **TCLC 25**
See also CA 108; DLB 11

Day, John 1574(?)-1640(?) .... **LC 70**
See also DLB 62, 170; RGEL 2

Day, Thomas 1748-1789 .... **LC 1**
See also DLB 39; YABC 1

Day Lewis, C(ecil) 1904-1972 . **CLC 1, 6, 10; PC 11**
See also Blake, Nicholas
See also BRWS 3; CA 13-16; 33-36R; CANR 34; CAP 1; CWRI 5; DAM POET; DLB 15, 20; MTCW 1, 2; RGEL 2

Dazai Osamu .... **TCLC 11; SSC 41**
See also Tsushima, Shuji
See also CA 164; DLB 182; MJW; RGSF 2; RGWL 2

de Andrade, Carlos Drummond
See Drummond de Andrade, Carlos

de Andrade, Mario 1892-1945
See Andrade, Mario de
See also CA 178; HW 2

Deane, Norman
See Creasey, John

Deane, Seamus (Francis) 1940- ...... **CLC 122**
See also CA 118; CANR 42

de Beauvoir, Simone (Lucie Ernestine Marie Bertrand)
See Beauvoir, Simone (Lucie Ernestine Marie Bertrand) de

de Beer, P.
See Bosman, Herman Charles

de Brissac, Malcolm
See Dickinson, Peter (Malcolm)

de Campos, Alvaro
See Pessoa, Fernando (Antonio Nogueira)

de Chardin, Pierre Teilhard
See Teilhard de Chardin, (Marie Joseph) Pierre

Dee, John 1527-1608 .... **LC 20**
See also DLB 136, 213

Deer, Sandra 1940- .... **CLC 45**
See also CA 186

De Ferrari, Gabriella 1941- .... **CLC 65**
See also CA 146

Defoe, Daniel 1660(?)-1731 .. **LC 1, 42; WLC**
See also AAYA 27; BRW 3; BRWR 1; BYA 4; CDBLB 1660-1789; CLR 61; DA; DA3; DAB; DAC; DAM MST, NOV; DLB 39, 95, 101; JRDA; LAIT 1; MAICYA 1, 2; NFS 9, 13; RGEL 2; SATA 22; WCH; WLIT 3

de Gourmont, Remy(-Marie-Charles)
See Gourmont, Remy(-Marie-Charles) de

de Hartog, Jan 1914- .... **CLC 19**
See also CA 1-4R; CANR 1; DFS 12

de Hostos, E. M.
See Hostos (y Bonilla), Eugenio Maria de

de Hostos, Eugenio M.
See Hostos (y Bonilla), Eugenio Maria de

Deighton, Len .... **CLC 4, 7, 22, 46**
See also Deighton, Leonard Cyril
See also AAYA 6; BEST 89:2; BPFB 1; CDBLB 1960 to Present; CMW 4; CN 7; CPW; DLB 87

Deighton, Leonard Cyril 1929-
See Deighton, Len
See also CA 9-12R; CANR 19, 33, 68; DA3; DAM NOV, POP; MTCW 1, 2

Dekker, Thomas 1572(?)-1632 ..... **LC 22; DC 12**
See also CDBLB Before 1660; DAM DRAM; DLB 62, 172; RGEL 2

Delafield, E. M. .... **TCLC 61**
See also Dashwood, Edmee Elizabeth Monica de la Pasture
See also DLB 34; RHW

de la Mare, Walter (John) 1873-1956 . **TCLC 4, 53; SSC 14; WLC**
See also CA 163; CDBLB 1914-1945; CLR 23; CWRI 5; DA3; DAB; DAC; DAM MST, POET; DLB 19, 153, 162, 255; EXPP; HGG; MAICYA 1, 2; MTCW 1; RGEL 2; RGSF 2; SATA 16; SUFW; WCH

Delaney, Franey
See O'Hara, John (Henry)

Delaney, Shelagh 1939- .... **CLC 29**
See also CA 17-20R; CANR 30, 67; CBD; CD 5; CDBLB 1960 to Present; CWD; DAM DRAM; DFS 7; DLB 13; MTCW 1

Delany, Martin Robison 1812-1885 .... **NCLC 93**
See also DLB 50; RGAL 4

Delany, Mary (Granville Pendarves) 1700-1788 .... **LC 12**

Delany, Samuel R(ay), Jr. 1942- . **CLC 8, 14, 38, 141; BLC 1**
See also AAYA 24; AFAW 2; BPFB 1; BW 2, 3; CA 81-84; CANR 27, 43; DAM MULT; DLB 8, 33; MTCW 1, 2; RGAL 4; SCFW

De La Ramee, (Marie) Louise 1839-1908
See Ouida
See also SATA 20

de la Roche, Mazo 1879-1961 .... **CLC 14**
See also CA 85-88; CANR 30; DLB 68; RGEL 2; RHW; SATA 64

De La Salle, Innocent
See Hartmann, Sadakichi

Delbanco, Nicholas (Franklin)
1942- .... **CLC 6, 13**
See also CA 17-20R; CAAE 189; CAAS 2; CANR 29, 55; DLB 6, 234

del Castillo, Michel 1933- .... **CLC 38**
See also CA 109; CANR 77

Deledda, Grazia (Cosima)
1875(?)-1936 .... **TCLC 23**
See also CA 123; RGWL 2

Deleuze, Gilles 1925-1995 .... **TCLC 116**

Delgado, Abelardo (Lalo) B(arrientos) 1930-
See also CA 131; CAAS 15; CANR 90; DAM MST, MULT; DLB 82; HLC 1; HW 1, 2

Delibes, Miguel .... **CLC 8, 18**
See also Delibes Setien, Miguel

Delibes Setien, Miguel 1920-
See Delibes, Miguel
See also CA 45-48; CANR 1, 32; HW 1; MTCW 1

DeLillo, Don 1936- ..... **CLC 8, 10, 13, 27, 39, 54, 76, 143**
See also AMWS 6; BEST 89:1; BPFB 1; CA 81-84; CANR 21, 76, 92; CN 7; CPW; DA3; DAM NOV, POP; DLB 6, 173; MTCW 1, 2; RGAL 4

de Lisser, H. G.
See De Lisser, H(erbert) G(eorge)
See also DLB 117

De Lisser, H(erbert) G(eorge)
1878-1944 .... **TCLC 12**
See also de Lisser, H. G.
See also BW 2; CA 109; 152

Deloire, Pierre
See Peguy, Charles (Pierre)

Deloney, Thomas 1543(?)-1600 .... **LC 41**
See also DLB 167; RGEL 2

Deloria, Vine (Victor), Jr. 1933- ...... **CLC 21, 122**
See also CA 53-56; CANR 5, 20, 48, 98; DAM MULT; DLB 175; MTCW 1; NNAL; SATA 21

Del Vecchio, John M(ichael) 1947- .. **CLC 29**
See also CA 110; DLBD 9

de Man, Paul (Adolph Michel)
1919-1983 .... **CLC 55**
See also CA 128; 111; CANR 61; DLB 67; MTCW 1, 2

DeMarinis, Rick 1934- .... **CLC 54**
See also CA 57-60, 184; CAAE 184; CAAS 24; CANR 9, 25, 50; DLB 218

Dembry, R. Emmet
See Murfree, Mary Noailles

Demby, William 1922- .... **CLC 53; BLC 1**
See also BW 1, 3; CA 81-84; CANR 81; DAM MULT; DLB 33

de Menton, Francisco
See Chin, Frank (Chew, Jr.)

Demetrius of Phalerum c.
307B.C.- .... **CMLC 34**

Demijohn, Thom
See Disch, Thomas M(ichael)

Deming, Richard 1915-1983
See Queen, Ellery
See also CA 9-12R; CANR 3, 94; SATA 24

Democritus c. 460B.C.-c. 370B.C. ... **CMLC 47**

de Montherlant, Henry (Milon)
See Montherlant, Henry (Milon) de

Demosthenes 384B.C.-322B.C. ...... **CMLC 13**
See also AW 1; DLB 176; RGWL 2

de Natale, Francine
See Malzberg, Barry N(athaniel)

de Navarre, Marguerite 1492-1549 ..... **LC 61**
See also Marguerite d'Angouleme; Marguerite de Navarre

Denby, Edwin (Orr) 1903-1983 .... **CLC 48**
See also CA 138; 110

Denham, John 1615-1669 .... **LC 73**
See also DLB 58, 126; RGEL 2

Denis, Julio
See Cortazar, Julio

Denmark, Harrison
See Zelazny, Roger (Joseph)

Dennis, John 1658-1734 .... **LC 11**
See also DLB 101; RGEL 2

Dennis, Nigel (Forbes) 1912-1989 ...... **CLC 8**
See also CA 25-28R; 129; DLB 13, 15, 233; MTCW 1

Dent, Lester 1904(?)-1959 .... **TCLC 72**
See also CA 112; 161; CMW 4; SFW 4

De Palma, Brian (Russell) 1940- ...... **CLC 20**
See also CA 109

De Quincey, Thomas 1785-1859 ..... **NCLC 4, 87**
See also BRW 4; CDBLB 1789-1832; DLB 110, 144; RGEL 2

Deren, Eleanora 1908(?)-1961
See Deren, Maya
See also CA 192; 111

Deren, Maya .... **CLC 16, 102**
See also Deren, Eleanora

Derleth, August (William)
1909-1971 .... **CLC 31**
See also BPFB 1; BYA 9, 10; CA 1-4R; 29-32R; CANR 4; CMW 4; DLB 9; DLBD 17; HGG; SATA 5; SUFW

Der Nister 1884-1950 .... **TCLC 56**

de Routisie, Albert
See Aragon, Louis

Derrida, Jacques 1930- .... **CLC 24, 87**
See also CA 124; 127; CANR 76, 98; DLB 242; MTCW 1

Derry Down Derry
See Lear, Edward

Dersonnes, Jacques
See Simenon, Georges (Jacques Christian)

Desai, Anita 1937- .... **CLC 19, 37, 97**
See also BRWS 5; CA 81-84; CANR 33, 53, 95; CN 7; CWRI 5; DA3; DAB; DAM NOV; DNFS 2; FW; MTCW 1, 2; SATA 63, 126

Desai, Kiran 1971- .... **CLC 119**
See also CA 171

de Saint-Luc, Jean
See Glassco, John

de Saint Roman, Arnaud
See Aragon, Louis

Desbordes-Valmore, Marceline
1786-1859 .... **NCLC 97**
See also DLB 217

Descartes, Rene 1596-1650 .... **LC 20, 35**
See also EW 3; GFL Beginnings to 1789

De Sica, Vittorio 1901(?)-1974 .... **CLC 20**
See also CA 117

Desnos, Robert 1900-1945 .... **TCLC 22**
See also CA 121; 151; CANR 107; DLB 258

Destouches, Louis-Ferdinand
1894-1961 .... **CLC 9, 15**
See also Celine, Louis-Ferdinand
See also CA 85-88; CANR 28; MTCW 1

de Tolignac, Gaston
See Griffith, D(avid Lewelyn) W(ark)

Deutsch, Babette 1895-1982 .... **CLC 18**
See also BYA 3; CA 1-4R; 108; CANR 4, 79; DLB 45; SATA 1; SATA-Obit 33

Devenant, William 1606-1649 .... **LC 13**

Devkota, Laxmiprasad 1909-1959 . **TCLC 23**
See also CA 123

De Voto, Bernard (Augustine)
1897-1955 .... **TCLC 29**
See also CA 113; 160; DLB 9, 256

De Vries, Peter 1910-1993 ..... **CLC 1, 2, 3, 7, 10, 28, 46**
See also CA 17-20R; 142; CANR 41; DAM NOV; DLB 6; DLBY 1982; MTCW 1, 2

Dewey, John 1859-1952 .... **TCLC 95**
See also CA 114; 170; DLB 246; RGAL 4

Dexter, John
See Bradley, Marion Zimmer
See also GLL 1

Dexter, Martin
See Faust, Frederick (Schiller)
See also TCWW 2

Dexter, Pete 1943- .... **CLC 34, 55**
See also BEST 89:2; CA 127; 131; CPW; DAM POP; INT 131; MTCW 1

Diamano, Silmang
See Senghor, Leopold Sedar

Diamond, Neil 1941- .... **CLC 30**
See also CA 108

Diaz del Castillo, Bernal 1496-1584 .. **LC 31; HLCS 1**
See also LAW

di Bassetto, Corno
See Shaw, George Bernard

Dick, Philip K(indred) 1928-1982 ... **CLC 10, 30, 72**
See also AAYA 24; BPFB 1; BYA 11; CA 49-52; 106; CANR 2, 16; CPW; DA3; DAM NOV, POP; DLB 8; MTCW 1, 2; NFS 5; SCFW; SFW 4

Dickens, Charles (John Huffam)
1812-1870 .... **NCLC 3, 8, 18, 26, 37, 50, 86, 105, 113; SSC 17, 49; WLC**
See also AAYA 23; BRW 5; BYA 1, 2, 3, 13, 14; CDBLB 1832-1890; CMW 4; DA; DA3; DAB; DAC; DAM MST, NOV; DLB 21, 55, 70, 159, 166; EXPN; HGG; JRDA; LAIT 1, 2; MAICYA 1, 2; NFS 4, 5, 10, 14; RGEL 2; RGSF 2; SATA 15; SUFW; TEA; WCH; WLIT 4; WYA

Dickey, James (Lafayette)
1923-1997 .... **CLC 1, 2, 4, 7, 10, 15, 47, 109; PC 40**
See also AITN 1, 2; AMWS 4; BPFB 1; CA 9-12R; 156; CABS 2; CANR 10, 48, 61, 105; CDALB 1968-1988; CP 7; CPW; CSW; DA3; DAM NOV, POET, POP; DLB 5, 193; DLBD 7; DLBY 1982, 1993, 1996, 1997, 1998; INT CANR-10; MTCW 1, 2; NFS 9; PFS 6, 11; RGAL 4

Dickey, William 1928-1994 .... **CLC 3, 28**
See also CA 9-12R; 145; CANR 24, 79; DLB 5

Dickinson, Charles 1951- .... **CLC 49**
See also CA 128

Dickinson, Emily (Elizabeth)
1830-1886 ... **NCLC 21, 77; PC 1; WLC**
See also AAYA 22; AMW; AMWR 1; CDALB 1865-1917; DA; DA3; DAB; DAC; DAM MST, POET; DLB 1, 243; EXPP; MAWW; PAB; PFS 1, 2, 3, 4, 5, 6, 8, 10, 11, 13; RGAL 4; SATA 29; WP; WYA

Dickinson, Mrs. Herbert Ward
See Phelps, Elizabeth Stuart

Dickinson, Peter (Malcolm) 1927- .. **CLC 12, 35**
See also AAYA 9; BYA 5; CA 41-44R; CANR 31, 58, 88; CLR 29; CMW 4; DLB 87, 161; JRDA; MAICYA 1, 2; SATA 5, 62, 95; SFW 4; WYA; YAW

Dickson, Carr
See Carr, John Dickson

Dickson, Carter
See Carr, John Dickson

Diderot, Denis 1713-1784 .... LC 26
See also EW 4; GFL Beginnings to 1789; RGWL 2

Didion, Joan 1934- . CLC 1, 3, 8, 14, 32, 129
See also AITN 1; AMWS 4; CA 5-8R; CANR 14, 52, 76; CDALB 1968-1988; CN 7; DA3; DAM NOV; DLB 2, 173, 185; DLBY 1981, 1986; MAWW; MTCW 1, 2; NFS 3; RGAL 4; TCWW 2

Dietrich, Robert
See Hunt, E(verette) Howard, (Jr.)

Difusa, Pati
See Almodovar, Pedro

Dillard, Annie 1945- .... CLC 9, 60, 115
See also AAYA 6, 43; AMWS 6; ANW; CA 49-52; CANR 3, 43, 62, 90; DA3; DAM NOV; DLBY 1980; LAIT 4, 5; MTCW 1, 2; NCFS 1; RGAL 4; SATA 10

Dillard, R(ichard) H(enry) W(ilde)
1937- .... CLC 5
See also CA 21-24R; CAAS 7; CANR 10; CP 7; CSW; DLB 5, 244

Dillon, Eilis 1920-1994 .... CLC 17
See also CA 9-12R, 182; 147; CAAE 182; CAAS 3; CANR 4, 38, 78; CLR 26; MAICYA 1, 2; MAICYAS 1; SATA 2, 74; SATA-Essay 105; SATA-Obit 83; YAW

Dimont, Penelope
See Mortimer, Penelope (Ruth)

Dinesen, Isak .... CLC 10, 29, 95; SSC 7
See also Blixen, Karen (Christentze Dinesen)
See also EW 10; EXPS; FW; HGG; LAIT 3; MTCW 1; NCFS; NFS 9; RGSF 2; RGWL 2; SSFS 3, 6, 13; WLIT 2

Ding Ling .... CLC 68
See also Chiang, Pin-chin

Diphusa, Patty
See Almodovar, Pedro

Disch, Thomas M(ichael) 1940- ... CLC 7, 36
See also AAYA 17; BPFB 1; CA 21-24R; CAAS 4; CANR 17, 36, 54, 89; CLR 18; CP 7; DA3; DLB 8; HGG; MAICYA 1, 2; MTCW 1, 2; SAAS 15; SATA 92; SCFW 4; SFW 4

Disch, Tom
See Disch, Thomas M(ichael)

d'Isly, Georges
See Simenon, Georges (Jacques Christian)

Disraeli, Benjamin 1804-1881 ... NCLC 2, 39, 79
See also BRW 4; DLB 21, 55; RGEL 2

Ditcum, Steve
See Crumb, R(obert)

Dixon, Paige
See Corcoran, Barbara (Asenath)

Dixon, Stephen 1936- .... CLC 52; SSC 16
See also CA 89-92; CANR 17, 40, 54, 91; CN 7; DLB 130

Doak, Annie
See Dillard, Annie

Dobell, Sydney Thompson
1824-1874 .... NCLC 43
See also DLB 32; RGEL 2

Doblin, Alfred .... TCLC 13
See also Doeblin, Alfred
See also CDWLB 2; RGWL 2

Dobrolyubov, Nikolai Alexandrovich
1836-1861 .... NCLC 5

Dobson, Austin 1840-1921 .... TCLC 79
See also DLB 35, 144

Dobyns, Stephen 1941- .... CLC 37
See also CA 45-48; CANR 2, 18, 99; CMW 4; CP 7

Doctorow, E(dgar) L(aurence)
1931- .... CLC 6, 11, 15, 18, 37, 44, 65, 113
See also AAYA 22; AITN 2; AMWS 4; BEST 89:3; BPFB 1; CA 45-48; CANR 2, 33, 51, 76, 97; CDALB 1968-1988; CN 7; CPW; DA3; DAM NOV, POP; DLB 2, 28, 173; DLBY 1980; LAIT 3; MTCW 1, 2; NFS 6; RGAL 4; RHW

Dodgson, Charles L(utwidge) 1832-1898
See Carroll, Lewis
See also CLR 2; DA; DA3; DAB; DAC; DAM MST, NOV, POET; MAICYA 1, 2; SATA 100; YABC 2

Dodson, Owen (Vincent)
1914-1983 .... CLC 79; BLC 1
See also BW 1; CA 65-68; 110; CANR 24; DAM MULT; DLB 76

Doeblin, Alfred 1878-1957 .... TCLC 13
See also Doblin, Alfred
See also CA 110; 141; DLB 66

Doerr, Harriet 1910- .... CLC 34
See also CA 117; 122; CANR 47; INT 122

Domecq, H(onorio Bustos)
See Bioy Casares, Adolfo

Domecq, H(onorio) Bustos
See Bioy Casares, Adolfo; Borges, Jorge Luis

Domini, Rey
See Lorde, Audre (Geraldine)
See also GLL 1

Dominique
See Proust, (Valentin-Louis-George-Eugene-)Marcel

Don, A
See Stephen, Sir Leslie

Donaldson, Stephen R(eeder)
1947- .... CLC 46, 138
See also AAYA 36; BPFB 1; CA 89-92; CANR 13, 55, 99; CPW; DAM POP; FANT; INT CANR-13; SATA 121; SFW 4; SUFW

Donleavy, J(ames) P(atrick) 1926- .... CLC 1, 4, 6, 10, 45
See also AITN 2; BPFB 1; CA 9-12R; CANR 24, 49, 62, 80; CBD; CD 5; CN 7; DLB 6, 173; INT CANR-24; MTCW 1, 2; RGAL 4

Donne, John 1572-1631 ..... LC 10, 24; PC 1; WLC
See also BRW 1; BRWR 2; CDBLB Before 1660; DA; DAB; DAC; DAM MST, POET; DLB 121, 151; EXPP; PAB; PFS 2, 11; RGEL 2; WLIT 3; WP

Donnell, David 1939(?)- .... CLC 34
See also CA 197

Donoghue, P. S.
See Hunt, E(verette) Howard, (Jr.)

Donoso (Yanez), Jose 1924-1996 ... CLC 4, 8, 11, 32, 99; HLC 1; SSC 34
See also CA 81-84; 155; CANR 32, 73; CDWLB 3; DAM MULT; DLB 113; HW 1, 2; LAW; LAWS 1; MTCW 1, 2; RGSF 2; WLIT 1

Donovan, John 1928-1992 .... CLC 35
See also AAYA 20; CA 97-100; 137; CLR 3; MAICYA 1, 2; SATA 72; SATA-Brief 29; YAW

Don Roberto
See Cunninghame Graham, Robert (Gallnigad) Bontine

Doolittle, Hilda 1886-1961 . CLC 3, 8, 14, 31, 34, 73; PC 5; WLC
See also H. D.
See also AMWS 1; CA 97-100; CANR 35; DA; DAC; DAM MST, POET; DLB 4, 45; FW; GLL 1; MAWW; MTCW 1, 2; PFS 6; RGAL 4

Doppo, Kunikida .... TCLC 99
See also Kunikida Doppo

Dorfman, Ariel 1942- .... CLC 48, 77; HLC 1
See also CA 124; 130; CANR 67, 70; CWW 2; DAM MULT; DFS 4; HW 1, 2; INT CA-130; WLIT 1

Dorn, Edward (Merton)
1929-1999 .... CLC 10, 18
See also CA 93-96; 187; CANR 42, 79; CP 7; DLB 5; INT 93-96; WP

Dor-Ner, Zvi .... CLC 70

Dorris, Michael (Anthony)
1945-1997 .... CLC 109
See also AAYA 20; BEST 90:1; BYA 12; CA 102; 157; CANR 19, 46, 75; CLR 58; DA3; DAM MULT; DLB 175; LAIT 5; MTCW 2; NFS 3; NNAL; RGAL 4; SATA 75; SATA-Obit 94; TCWW 2; YAW

Dorris, Michael A.
See Dorris, Michael (Anthony)

Dorsan, Luc
See Simenon, Georges (Jacques Christian)

Dorsange, Jean
See Simenon, Georges (Jacques Christian)

Dos Passos, John (Roderigo)
1896-1970 ... CLC 1, 4, 8, 11, 15, 25, 34, 82; WLC
See also AMW; BPFB 1; CA 1-4R; 29-32R; CANR 3; CDALB 1929-1941; DA; DA3; DAB; DAC; DAM MST, NOV; DLB 4, 9; DLBD 1, 15; DLBY 1996; MTCW 1, 2; NFS 14; RGAL 4

Dossage, Jean
See Simenon, Georges (Jacques Christian)

Dostoevsky, Fedor Mikhailovich
1821-1881 . NCLC 2, 7, 21, 33, 43; SSC 2, 33, 44; WLC
See also Dostoevsky, Fyodor
See also AAYA 40; DA; DA3; DAB; DAC; DAM MST, NOV; EW 7; EXPN; NFS 3, 8; RGSF 2; RGWL 2; SSFS 8

Dostoevsky, Fyodor
See Dostoevsky, Fedor Mikhailovich
See also DLB 238

Doughty, Charles M(ontagu)
1843-1926 .... TCLC 27
See also CA 115; 178; DLB 19, 57, 174

Douglas, Ellen .... CLC 73
See also Haxton, Josephine Ayres; Williamson, Ellen Douglas
See also CN 7; CSW

Douglas, Gavin 1475(?)-1522 .... LC 20
See also DLB 132; RGEL 2

Douglas, George
See Brown, George Douglas
See also RGEL 2

Douglas, Keith (Castellain)
1920-1944 .... TCLC 40
See also BRW 7; CA 160; DLB 27; PAB; RGEL 2

Douglas, Leonard
See Bradbury, Ray (Douglas)

Douglas, Michael
See Crichton, (John) Michael

Douglas, (George) Norman
1868-1952 .... TCLC 68
See also BRW 6; CA 119; 157; DLB 34, 195; RGEL 2

Douglas, William
See Brown, George Douglas

Douglass, Frederick 1817(?)-1895 .. NCLC 7, 55; BLC 1; WLC
See also AFAW 1, 2; AMWS 3; CDALB 1640-1865; DA; DA3; DAC; DAM MST, MULT; DLB 1, 43, 50, 79, 243; FW; LAIT 2; NCFS 2; RGAL 4; SATA 29

Dourado, (Waldomiro Freitas) Autran
1926- .... CLC 23, 60
See also CA 25-28R, 179; CANR 34, 81; DLB 145; HW 2

Dourado, Waldomiro Autran
See Dourado, (Waldomiro Freitas) Autran
See also CA 179

Dove, Rita (Frances) 1952- .... **CLC 50, 81; BLCS; PC 6**
See also AMWS 4; BW 2; CA 109; CAAS 19; CANR 27, 42, 68, 76, 97; CDALBS; CP 7; CSW; CWP; DA3; DAM MULT, POET; DLB 120; EXPP; MTCW 1; PFS 1, 15; RGAL 4

Doveglion
See Villa, Jose Garcia

Dowell, Coleman 1925-1985 .... **CLC 60**
See also CA 25-28R; 117; CANR 10; DLB 130; GLL 2

Dowson, Ernest (Christopher)
1867-1900 .... **TCLC 4**
See also CA 105; 150; DLB 19, 135; RGEL 2

Doyle, A. Conan
See Doyle, Sir Arthur Conan

Doyle, Sir Arthur Conan
1859-1930 .... **TCLC 7; SSC 12; WLC**
See also Conan Doyle, Arthur
See also AAYA 14; BRWS 2; CA 104; 122; CDBLB 1890-1914; CMW 4; DA; DA3; DAB; DAC; DAM MST, NOV; DLB 18, 70, 156, 178; EXPS; HGG; LAIT 2; MSW; MTCW 1, 2; RGEL 2; RGSF 2; RHW; SATA 24; SCFW 2; SFW 4; SSFS 2; WCH; WLIT 4; WYA; YAW

Doyle, Conan
See Doyle, Sir Arthur Conan

Doyle, John
See Graves, Robert (von Ranke)

Doyle, Roddy 1958(?)- .... **CLC 81**
See also AAYA 14; BRWS 5; CA 143; CANR 73; CN 7; DA3; DLB 194

Doyle, Sir A. Conan
See Doyle, Sir Arthur Conan

Dr. A
See Asimov, Isaac; Silverstein, Alvin; Silverstein, Virginia B(arbara Opshelor)

Drabble, Margaret 1939- ...... **CLC 2, 3, 5, 8, 10, 22, 53, 129**
See also BRWS 4; CA 13-16R; CANR 18, 35, 63; CDBLB 1960 to Present; CN 7; CPW; DA3; DAB; DAC; DAM MST, NOV, POP; DLB 14, 155, 231; FW; MTCW 1, 2; RGEL 2; SATA 48

Drapier, M. B.
See Swift, Jonathan

Drayham, James
See Mencken, H(enry) L(ouis)

Drayton, Michael 1563-1631 .... **LC 8**
See also DAM POET; DLB 121; RGEL 2

Dreadstone, Carl
See Campbell, (John) Ramsey

Dreiser, Theodore (Herman Albert)
1871-1945 .... **TCLC 10, 18, 35, 83; SSC 30; WLC**
See also AMW; CA 106; 132; CDALB 1865-1917; DA; DA3; DAC; DAM MST, NOV; DLB 9, 12, 102, 137; DLBD 1; LAIT 2; MTCW 1, 2; NFS 8; RGAL 4

Drexler, Rosalyn 1926- .... **CLC 2, 6**
See also CA 81-84; CAD; CANR 68; CD 5; CWD

Dreyer, Carl Theodor 1889-1968 ...... **CLC 16**
See also CA 116

Drieu la Rochelle, Pierre(-Eugene)
1893-1945 .... **TCLC 21**
See also CA 117; DLB 72; GFL 1789 to the Present

Drinkwater, John 1882-1937 .... **TCLC 57**
See also CA 109; 149; DLB 10, 19, 149; RGEL 2

Drop Shot
See Cable, George Washington

Droste-Hulshoff, Annette Freiin von
1797-1848 .... **NCLC 3**
See also CDWLB 2; DLB 133; RGSF 2; RGWL 2

Drummond, Walter
See Silverberg, Robert

Drummond, William Henry
1854-1907 .... **TCLC 25**
See also CA 160; DLB 92

Drummond de Andrade, Carlos
1902-1987 .... **CLC 18**
See also Andrade, Carlos Drummond de
See also CA 132; 123; LAW

Drury, Allen (Stuart) 1918-1998 .... **CLC 37**
See also CA 57-60; 170; CANR 18, 52; CN 7; INT CANR-18

Dryden, John 1631-1700 ..... **LC 3, 21; DC 3; PC 25; WLC**
See also BRW 2; CDBLB 1660-1789; DA; DAB; DAC; DAM DRAM, MST, POET; DLB 80, 101, 131; EXPP; IDTP; RGEL 2; TEA; WLIT 3

Duberman, Martin (Bauml) 1930- ..... **CLC 8**
See also CA 1-4R; CAD; CANR 2, 63; CD 5

Dubie, Norman (Evans) 1945- .... **CLC 36**
See also CA 69-72; CANR 12; CP 7; DLB 120; PFS 12

Du Bois, W(illiam) E(dward) B(urghardt)
1868-1963 ... **CLC 1, 2, 13, 64, 96; BLC 1; WLC**
See also AAYA 40; AFAW 1, 2; AMWS 2; BW 1, 3; CA 85-88; CANR 34, 82; CDALB 1865-1917; DA; DA3; DAC; DAM MST, MULT, NOV; DLB 47, 50, 91, 246; EXPP; LAIT 2; MTCW 1, 2; NCFS 1; PFS 13; RGAL 4; SATA 42

Dubus, Andre 1936-1999 ..... **CLC 13, 36, 97; SSC 15**
See also AMWS 7; CA 21-24R; 177; CANR 17; CN 7; CSW; DLB 130; INT CANR-17; RGAL 4; SSFS 10

Duca Minimo
See D'Annunzio, Gabriele

Ducharme, Rejean 1941- .... **CLC 74**
See also CA 165; DLB 60

Duchen, Claire .... **CLC 65**

Duclos, Charles Pinot- 1704-1772 .... **LC 1**
See also GFL Beginnings to 1789

Dudek, Louis 1918- .... **CLC 11, 19**
See also CA 45-48; CAAS 14; CANR 1; CP 7; DLB 88

Duerrenmatt, Friedrich 1921-1990 ... **CLC 1, 4, 8, 11, 15, 43, 102**
See also Durrenmatt, Friedrich
See also CA 17-20R; CANR 33; CMW 4; DAM DRAM; DLB 69, 124; MTCW 1, 2

Duffy, Bruce 1953(?)- .... **CLC 50**
See also CA 172

Duffy, Maureen 1933- .... **CLC 37**
See also CA 25-28R; CANR 33, 68; CBD; CN 7; CP 7; CWD; CWP; DFS 15; DLB 14; FW; MTCW 1

Du Fu
See Tu Fu
See also RGWL 2

Dugan, Alan 1923- .... **CLC 2, 6**
See also CA 81-84; CP 7; DLB 5; PFS 10

du Gard, Roger Martin
See Martin du Gard, Roger

Duhamel, Georges 1884-1966 .... **CLC 8**
See also CA 81-84; CANR 35; DLB 65; GFL 1789 to the Present; MTCW 1

Dujardin, Edouard (Emile Louis)
1861-1949 .... **TCLC 13**
See also CA 109; DLB 123

Dulles, John Foster 1888-1959 .... **TCLC 72**
See also CA 115; 149

Dumas, Alexandre (pere)
1802-1870 .... **NCLC 11, 71; WLC**
See also AAYA 22; BYA 3; DA; DA3; DAB; DAC; DAM MST, NOV; DLB 119, 192; EW 6; GFL 1789 to the Present; LAIT 1, 2; NFS 14; RGWL 2; SATA 18; WCH

Dumas, Alexandre (fils)
1824-1895 .... **NCLC 9; DC 1**
See also DLB 192; GFL 1789 to the Present; RGWL 2

Dumas, Claudine
See Malzberg, Barry N(athaniel)

Dumas, Henry L. 1934-1968 .... **CLC 6, 62**
See also BW 1; CA 85-88; DLB 41; RGAL 4

du Maurier, Daphne 1907-1989 .. **CLC 6, 11, 59; SSC 18**
See also AAYA 37; BPFB 1; BRWS 3; CA 5-8R; 128; CANR 6, 55; CMW 4; CPW; DA3; DAB; DAC; DAM MST, POP; DLB 191; HGG; LAIT 3; MSW; MTCW 1, 2; NFS 12; RGEL 2; RGSF 2; RHW; SATA 27; SATA-Obit 60; SSFS 14

Du Maurier, George 1834-1896 ..... **NCLC 86**
See also DLB 153, 178; RGEL 2

Dunbar, Paul Laurence 1872-1906 . **TCLC 2, 12; BLC 1; PC 5; SSC 8; WLC**
See also AFAW 1, 2; AMWS 2; BW 1, 3; CA 104; 124; CANR 79; CDALB 1865-1917; DA; DA3; DAC; DAM MST, MULT, POET; DLB 50, 54, 78; EXPP; RGAL 4; SATA 34

Dunbar, William 1460(?)-1520(?) .... **LC 20**
See also DLB 132, 146; RGEL 2

Duncan, Dora Angela
See Duncan, Isadora

Duncan, Isadora 1877(?)-1927 .... **TCLC 68**
See also CA 118; 149

Duncan, Lois 1934- .... **CLC 26**
See also AAYA 4, 34; BYA 6, 8; CA 1-4R; CANR 2, 23, 36; CLR 29; JRDA; MAICYA 1, 2; MAICYAS 1; SAAS 2; SATA 1, 36, 75, 133; WYA; YAW

Duncan, Robert (Edward)
1919-1988 .... **CLC 1, 2, 4, 7, 15, 41, 55; PC 2**
See also CA 9-12R; 124; CANR 28, 62; DAM POET; DLB 5, 16, 193; MTCW 1, 2; PFS 13; RGAL 4; WP

Duncan, Sara Jeannette
1861-1922 .... **TCLC 60**
See also CA 157; DLB 92

Dunlap, William 1766-1839 .... **NCLC 2**
See also DLB 30, 37, 59; RGAL 4

Dunn, Douglas (Eaglesham) 1942- .... **CLC 6, 40**
See also CA 45-48; CANR 2, 33; CP 7; DLB 40; MTCW 1

Dunn, Katherine (Karen) 1945- .... **CLC 71**
See also CA 33-36R; CANR 72; HGG; MTCW 1

Dunn, Stephen (Elliott) 1939- .... **CLC 36**
See also CA 33-36R; CANR 12, 48, 53, 105; CP 7; DLB 105

Dunne, Finley Peter 1867-1936 ...... **TCLC 28**
See also CA 108; 178; DLB 11, 23; RGAL 4

Dunne, John Gregory 1932- .... **CLC 28**
See also CA 25-28R; CANR 14, 50; CN 7; DLBY 1980

Dunsany, Lord .... **TCLC 2, 59**
See also Dunsany, Edward John Moreton Drax Plunkett
See also DLB 77, 153, 156, 255; FANT; IDTP; RGEL 2; SFW 4; SUFW

Dunsany, Edward John Moreton Drax Plunkett 1878-1957
See Dunsany, Lord
See also CA 104; 148; DLB 10; MTCW 1

du Perry, Jean
See Simenon, Georges (Jacques Christian)
Durang, Christopher (Ferdinand)
1949- .... **CLC 27, 38**
See also CA 105; CAD; CANR 50, 76; CD 5; MTCW 1
Duras, Marguerite 1914-1996 . **CLC 3, 6, 11, 20, 34, 40, 68, 100; SSC 40**
See also BPFB 1; CA 25-28R; 151; CANR 50; CWW 2; DLB 83; GFL 1789 to the Present; IDFW 4; MTCW 1, 2; RGWL 2
Durban, (Rosa) Pam 1947- .... **CLC 39**
See also CA 123; CANR 98; CSW
Durcan, Paul 1944- .... **CLC 43, 70**
See also CA 134; CP 7; DAM POET
Durkheim, Emile 1858-1917 .... **TCLC 55**
Durrell, Lawrence (George)
1912-1990 ..... **CLC 1, 4, 6, 8, 13, 27, 41**
See also BPFB 1; BRWS 1; CA 9-12R; 132; CANR 40, 77; CDBLB 1945-1960; DAM NOV; DLB 15, 27, 204; DLBY 1990; MTCW 1, 2; RGEL 2; SFW 4
Durrenmatt, Friedrich
See Duerrenmatt, Friedrich
See also CDWLB 2; EW 13; RGWL 2
Dutt, Toru 1856-1877 .... **NCLC 29**
See also DLB 240
Dwight, Timothy 1752-1817 .... **NCLC 13**
See also DLB 37; RGAL 4
Dworkin, Andrea 1946- .... **CLC 43, 123**
See also CA 77-80; CAAS 21; CANR 16, 39, 76, 96; FW; GLL 1; INT CANR-16; MTCW 1, 2
Dwyer, Deanna
See Koontz, Dean R(ay)
Dwyer, K. R.
See Koontz, Dean R(ay)
Dwyer, Thomas A. 1923- .... **CLC 114**
See also CA 115
Dybek, Stuart 1942- .... **CLC 114**
See also CA 97-100; CANR 39; DLB 130
Dye, Richard
See De Voto, Bernard (Augustine)
Dyer, Geoff 1958- .... **CLC 149**
See also CA 125; CANR 88
Dylan, Bob 1941- .... **CLC 3, 4, 6, 12, 77; PC 37**
See also CA 41-44R; CANR 108; CP 7; DLB 16
Dyson, John 1943- .... **CLC 70**
See also CA 144
E. V. L.
See Lucas, E(dward) V(errall)
Eagleton, Terence (Francis) 1943- .. **CLC 63, 132**
See also CA 57-60; CANR 7, 23, 68; DLB 242; MTCW 1, 2
Eagleton, Terry
See Eagleton, Terence (Francis)
Early, Jack
See Scoppettone, Sandra
See also GLL 1
East, Michael
See West, Morris L(anglo)
Eastaway, Edward
See Thomas, (Philip) Edward
Eastlake, William (Derry)
1917-1997 .... **CLC 8**
See also CA 5-8R; 158; CAAS 1; CANR 5, 63; CN 7; DLB 6, 206; INT CANR-5; TCWW 2
Eastman, Charles A(lexander)
1858-1939 .... **TCLC 55**
See also CA 179; CANR 91; DAM MULT; DLB 175; NNAL; YABC 1

Eberhart, Richard (Ghormley)
1904- .... **CLC 3, 11, 19, 56**
See also AMW; CA 1-4R; CANR 2; CDALB 1941-1968; CP 7; DAM POET; DLB 48; MTCW 1; RGAL 4
Eberstadt, Fernanda 1960- .... **CLC 39**
See also CA 136; CANR 69
Echegaray (y Eizaguirre), Jose (Maria Waldo) 1832-1916 .... **TCLC 4; HLCS 1**
See also CA 104; CANR 32; HW 1; MTCW 1
Echeverria, (Jose) Esteban (Antonino)
1805-1851 .... **NCLC 18**
See also LAW
Echo
See Proust, (Valentin-Louis-George-Eugene-)Marcel
Eckert, Allan W. 1931- .... **CLC 17**
See also AAYA 18; BYA 2; CA 13-16R; CANR 14, 45; INT CANR-14; MAICYA 2; MAICYAS 1; SAAS 21; SATA 29, 91; SATA-Brief 27
Eckhart, Meister 1260(?)-1327(?) ... **CMLC 9**
See also DLB 115
Eckmar, F. R.
See de Hartog, Jan
Eco, Umberto 1932- .... **CLC 28, 60, 142**
See also BEST 90:1; BPFB 1; CA 77-80; CANR 12, 33, 55; CPW; CWW 2; DA3; DAM NOV, POP; DLB 196, 242; MSW; MTCW 1, 2
Eddison, E(ric) R(ucker)
1882-1945 .... **TCLC 15**
See also CA 109; 156; DLB 255; FANT; SFW 4; SUFW
Eddy, Mary (Ann Morse) Baker
1821-1910 .... **TCLC 71**
See also CA 113; 174
Edel, (Joseph) Leon 1907-1997 .. **CLC 29, 34**
See also CA 1-4R; 161; CANR 1, 22; DLB 103; INT CANR-22
Eden, Emily 1797-1869 .... **NCLC 10**
Edgar, David 1948- .... **CLC 42**
See also CA 57-60; CANR 12, 61; CBD; CD 5; DAM DRAM; DFS 15; DLB 13, 233; MTCW 1
Edgerton, Clyde (Carlyle) 1944- ...... **CLC 39**
See also AAYA 17; CA 118; 134; CANR 64; CSW; INT 134; YAW
Edgeworth, Maria 1768-1849 .... **NCLC 1, 51**
See also BRWS 3; DLB 116, 159, 163; FW; RGEL 2; SATA 21; WLIT 3
Edmonds, Paul
See Kuttner, Henry
Edmonds, Walter D(umaux)
1903-1998 .... **CLC 35**
See also BYA 2; CA 5-8R; CANR 2; CWRI 5; DLB 9; LAIT 1; MAICYA 1, 2; RHW; SAAS 4; SATA 1, 27; SATA-Obit 99
Edmondson, Wallace
See Ellison, Harlan (Jay)
Edson, Russell 1935- .... **CLC 13**
See also CA 33-36R; DLB 244; WP
Edwards, Bronwen Elizabeth
See Rose, Wendy
Edwards, G(erald) B(asil)
1899-1976 .... **CLC 25**
See also CA 201; 110
Edwards, Gus 1939- .... **CLC 43**
See also CA 108; INT 108
Edwards, Jonathan 1703-1758 .... **LC 7, 54**
See also AMW; DA; DAC; DAM MST; DLB 24; RGAL 4
Efron, Marina Ivanovna Tsvetaeva
See Tsvetaeva (Efron), Marina (Ivanovna)
Egoyan, Atom 1960- .... **CLC 151**
See also CA 157
Ehle, John (Marsden, Jr.) 1925- ...... **CLC 27**
See also CA 9-12R; CSW

Ehrenbourg, Ilya (Grigoryevich)
See Ehrenburg, Ilya (Grigoryevich)
Ehrenburg, Ilya (Grigoryevich)
1891-1967 .... **CLC 18, 34, 62**
See also CA 102; 25-28R
Ehrenburg, Ilyo (Grigoryevich)
See Ehrenburg, Ilya (Grigoryevich)
Ehrenreich, Barbara 1941- .... **CLC 110**
See also BEST 90:4; CA 73-76; CANR 16, 37, 62; DLB 246; FW; MTCW 1, 2
Eich, Guenter 1907-1972 .... **CLC 15**
See also Eich, Gunter
See also CA 111; 93-96; DLB 69, 124
Eich, Gunter
See Eich, Guenter
See also RGWL 2
Eichendorff, Joseph 1788-1857 .... **NCLC 8**
See also DLB 90; RGWL 2
Eigner, Larry .... **CLC 9**
See also Eigner, Laurence (Joel)
See also CAAS 23; DLB 5; WP
Eigner, Laurence (Joel) 1927-1996
See Eigner, Larry
See also CA 9-12R; 151; CANR 6, 84; CP 7; DLB 193
Einhard c. 770-840 .... **CMLC 50**
See also DLB 148
Einstein, Albert 1879-1955 .... **TCLC 65**
See also CA 121; 133; MTCW 1, 2
Eiseley, Loren Corey 1907-1977 .... **CLC 7**
See also AAYA 5; ANW; CA 1-4R; 73-76; CANR 6; DLBD 17
Eisenstadt, Jill 1963- .... **CLC 50**
See also CA 140
Eisenstein, Sergei (Mikhailovich)
1898-1948 .... **TCLC 57**
See also CA 114; 149
Eisner, Simon
See Kornbluth, C(yril) M.
Ekeloef, (Bengt) Gunnar
1907-1968 .... **CLC 27; PC 23**
See also Ekelof, (Bengt) Gunnar
See also CA 123; 25-28R; DAM POET
Ekelof, (Bengt) Gunnar 1907-1968
See Ekeloef, (Bengt) Gunnar
See also DLB 259; EW 12
Ekelund, Vilhelm 1880-1949 .... **TCLC 75**
See also CA 189
Ekwensi, C. O. D.
See Ekwensi, Cyprian (Odiatu Duaka)
Ekwensi, Cyprian (Odiatu Duaka)
1921- .... **CLC 4; BLC 1**
See also AFW; BW 2, 3; CA 29-32R; CANR 18, 42, 74; CDWLB 3; CN 7; CWRI 5; DAM MULT; DLB 117; MTCW 1, 2; RGEL 2; SATA 66; WLIT 2
Elaine .... **TCLC 18**
See also Leverson, Ada
El Crummo
See Crumb, R(obert)
Elder, Lonne III 1931-1996 .... **DC 8**
See also BLC 1; BW 1, 3; CA 81-84; 152; CAD; CANR 25; DAM MULT; DLB 7, 38, 44
Eleanor of Aquitaine 1122-1204 ... **CMLC 39**
Elia
See Lamb, Charles
Eliade, Mircea 1907-1986 .... **CLC 19**
See also CA 65-68; 119; CANR 30, 62; CDWLB 4; DLB 220; MTCW 1; SFW 4
Eliot, A. D.
See Jewett, (Theodora) Sarah Orne
Eliot, Alice
See Jewett, (Theodora) Sarah Orne
Eliot, Dan
See Silverberg, Robert

Eliot, George 1819-1880 ...... **NCLC 4, 13, 23, 41, 49, 89; PC 20; WLC**
See also BRW 5; BRWR 2; CDBLB 1832-1890; CN 7; CPW; DA; DA3; DAB; DAC; DAM MST, NOV; DLB 21, 35, 55; RGEL 2; RGSF 2; SSFS 8; WLIT 3

Eliot, John 1604-1690 .... **LC 5**
See also DLB 24

Eliot, T(homas) S(tearns) 1888-1965 ...... **CLC 1, 2, 3, 6, 9, 10, 13, 15, 24, 34, 41, 55, 57, 113; PC 5, 31; WLC**
See also AAYA 28; AMW; AMWR 1; BRW 7; BRWR 2; CA 5-8R; 25-28R; CANR 41; CDALB 1929-1941; DA; DA3; DAB; DAC; DAM DRAM, MST, POET; DFS 4, 13; DLB 7, 10, 45, 63, 245; DLBY 1988; EXPP; LAIT 3; MTCW 1, 2; PAB; PFS 1, 7; RGAL 4; RGEL 2; WLIT 4; WP

Elizabeth 1866-1941 .... **TCLC 41**

Elkin, Stanley L(awrence) 1930-1995 .. **CLC 4, 6, 9, 14, 27, 51, 91; SSC 12**
See also AMWS 6; BPFB 1; CA 9-12R; 148; CANR 8, 46; CN 7; CPW; DAM NOV, POP; DLB 2, 28, 218; DLBY 1980; INT CANR-8; MTCW 1, 2; RGAL 4

Elledge, Scott .... **CLC 34**

Elliot, Don
See Silverberg, Robert

Elliott, Don
See Silverberg, Robert

Elliott, George P(aul) 1918-1980 .... **CLC 2**
See also CA 1-4R; 97-100; CANR 2; DLB 244

Elliott, Janice 1931-1995 .... **CLC 47**
See also CA 13-16R; CANR 8, 29, 84; CN 7; DLB 14; SATA 119

Elliott, Sumner Locke 1917-1991 ..... **CLC 38**
See also CA 5-8R; 134; CANR 2, 21

Elliott, William
See Bradbury, Ray (Douglas)

Ellis, A. E. .... **CLC 7**

Ellis, Alice Thomas .... **CLC 40**
See Haycraft, Anna (Margaret)
See also DLB 194; MTCW 1

Ellis, Bret Easton 1964- ...... **CLC 39, 71, 117**
See also AAYA 2, 43; CA 118; 123; CANR 51, 74; CN 7; CPW; DA3; DAM POP; HGG; INT CA-123; MTCW 1; NFS 11

Ellis, (Henry) Havelock 1859-1939 .... **TCLC 14**
See also CA 109; 169; DLB 190

Ellis, Landon
See Ellison, Harlan (Jay)

Ellis, Trey 1962- .... **CLC 55**
See also CA 146; CANR 92

Ellison, Harlan (Jay) 1934- ... **CLC 1, 13, 42, 139; SSC 14**
See also AAYA 29; BPFB 1; BYA 14; CA 5-8R; CANR 5, 46; CPW; DAM POP; DLB 8; HGG; INT CANR-5; MTCW 1, 2; SCFW 2; SFW 4; SSFS 13, 14, 15; SUFW

Ellison, Ralph (Waldo) 1914-1994 .... **CLC 1, 3, 11, 54, 86, 114; BLC 1; SSC 26; WLC**
See also AAYA 19; AFAW 1, 2; AMWS 2; BPFB 1; BW 1, 3; BYA 2; CA 9-12R; 145; CANR 24, 53; CDALB 1941-1968; CSW; DA; DA3; DAB; DAC; DAM MST, MULT, NOV; DLB 2, 76, 227; DLBY 1994; EXPN; EXPS; LAIT 4; MTCW 1, 2; NCFS 3; NFS 2; RGAL 4; RGSF 2; SSFS 1, 11; YAW

Ellmann, Lucy (Elizabeth) 1956- ..... **CLC 61**
See also CA 128

Ellmann, Richard (David) 1918-1987 .... **CLC 50**
See also BEST 89:2; CA 1-4R; 122; CANR 2, 28, 61; DLB 103; DLBY 1987; MTCW 1, 2

Elman, Richard (Martin) 1934-1997 .... **CLC 19**
See also CA 17-20R; 163; CAAS 3; CANR 47

Elron
See Hubbard, L(afayette) Ron(ald)

Eluard, Paul .... **TCLC 7, 41; PC 38**
See also Grindel, Eugene
See also GFL 1789 to the Present; RGWL 2

Elyot, Thomas 1490(?)-1546 .... **LC 11**
See also DLB 136; RGEL 2

Elytis, Odysseus 1911-1996 .... **CLC 15, 49, 100; PC 21**
See also Alepoudelis, Odysseus
See also CA 102; 151; CANR 94; CWW 2; DAM POET; EW 13; MTCW 1, 2; RGWL 2

Emecheta, (Florence Onye) Buchi 1944- .... **CLC 14, 48, 128; BLC 2**
See also AFW; BW 2, 3; CA 81-84; CANR 27, 81; CDWLB 3; CN 7; CWRI 5; DA3; DAM MULT; DLB 117; FW; MTCW 1, 2; NFS 12, 14; SATA 66; WLIT 2

Emerson, Mary Moody 1774-1863 .... **NCLC 66**

Emerson, Ralph Waldo 1803-1882 . **NCLC 1, 38, 98; PC 18; WLC**
See also AMW; ANW; CDALB 1640-1865; DA; DA3; DAB; DAC; DAM MST, POET; DLB 1, 59, 73, 183, 223; EXPP; LAIT 2; NCFS 3; PFS 4; RGAL 4; WP

Eminescu, Mihail 1850-1889 .... **NCLC 33**

Empedocles 5th cent. B.C.- .... **CMLC 50**
See also DLB 176

Empson, William 1906-1984 ... **CLC 3, 8, 19, 33, 34**
See also BRWS 2; CA 17-20R; 112; CANR 31, 61; DLB 20; MTCW 1, 2; RGEL 2

Enchi, Fumiko (Ueda) 1905-1986 ..... **CLC 31**
See also Enchi Fumiko
See also CA 129; 121; FW; MJW

Enchi Fumiko
See Enchi, Fumiko (Ueda)
See also DLB 182

Ende, Michael (Andreas Helmuth) 1929-1995 .... **CLC 31**
See also BYA 5; CA 118; 124; 149; CANR 36; CLR 14; DLB 75; MAICYA 1, 2; MAICYAS 1; SATA 61, 130; SATA-Brief 42; SATA-Obit 86

Endo, Shusaku 1923-1996 ..... **CLC 7, 14, 19, 54, 99; SSC 48**
See also Endo Shusaku
See also CA 29-32R; 153; CANR 21, 54; DA3; DAM NOV; MTCW 1, 2; RGSF 2; RGWL 2

Endo Shusaku
See Endo, Shusaku
See also DLB 182

Engel, Marian 1933-1985 .... **CLC 36**
See also CA 25-28R; CANR 12; DLB 53; FW; INT CANR-12

Engelhardt, Frederick
See Hubbard, L(afayette) Ron(ald)

Engels, Friedrich 1820-1895 .. **NCLC 85, 114**
See also DLB 129

Enright, D(ennis) J(oseph) 1920- .. **CLC 4, 8, 31**
See also CA 1-4R; CANR 1, 42, 83; CP 7; DLB 27; SATA 25

Enzensberger, Hans Magnus 1929- .... **CLC 43; PC 28**
See also CA 116; 119; CANR 103

Ephron, Nora 1941- .... **CLC 17, 31**
See also AAYA 35; AITN 2; CA 65-68; CANR 12, 39, 83

Epicurus 341B.C.-270B.C. .... **CMLC 21**
See also DLB 176

Epsilon
See Betjeman, John

Epstein, Daniel Mark 1948- .... **CLC 7**
See also CA 49-52; CANR 2, 53, 90

Epstein, Jacob 1956- .... **CLC 19**
See also CA 114

Epstein, Jean 1897-1953 .... **TCLC 92**

Epstein, Joseph 1937- .... **CLC 39**
See also CA 112; 119; CANR 50, 65

Epstein, Leslie 1938- .... **CLC 27**
See also CA 73-76; CAAS 12; CANR 23, 69

Equiano, Olaudah 1745(?)-1797 .... **LC 16; BLC 2**
See also AFAW 1, 2; CDWLB 3; DAM MULT; DLB 37, 50; WLIT 2

Erasmus, Desiderius 1469(?)-1536 ...... **LC 16**
See also DLB 136; EW 2; RGWL 2

Erdman, Paul E(mil) 1932- .... **CLC 25**
See also AITN 1; CA 61-64; CANR 13, 43, 84

Erdrich, Louise 1954- .... **CLC 39, 54, 120**
See also AAYA 10; AMWS 4; BEST 89:1; BPFB 1; CA 114; CANR 41, 62; CDALBS; CN 7; CP 7; CPW; CWP; DA3; DAM MULT, NOV, POP; DLB 152, 175, 206; EXPP; LAIT 5; MTCW 1; NFS 5; NNAL; PFS 14; RGAL 4; SATA 94; SSFS 14; TCWW 2

Erenburg, Ilya (Grigoryevich)
See Ehrenburg, Ilya (Grigoryevich)

Erickson, Stephen Michael 1950-
See Erickson, Steve
See also CA 129; SFW 4

Erickson, Steve .... **CLC 64**
See also Erickson, Stephen Michael
See also CANR 60, 68

Ericson, Walter
See Fast, Howard (Melvin)

Eriksson, Buntel
See Bergman, (Ernst) Ingmar

Ernaux, Annie 1940- .... **CLC 88**
See also CA 147; CANR 93; NCFS 3

Erskine, John 1879-1951 .... **TCLC 84**
See also CA 112; 159; DLB 9, 102; FANT

Eschenbach, Wolfram von
See Wolfram von Eschenbach

Eseki, Bruno
See Mphahlele, Ezekiel

Esenin, Sergei (Alexandrovich) 1895-1925 .... **TCLC 4**
See also CA 104; RGWL 2

Eshleman, Clayton 1935- .... **CLC 7**
See also CA 33-36R; CAAS 6; CANR 93; CP 7; DLB 5

Espriella, Don Manuel Alvarez
See Southey, Robert

Espriu, Salvador 1913-1985 .... **CLC 9**
See also CA 154; 115; DLB 134

Espronceda, Jose de 1808-1842 ..... **NCLC 39**

Esquivel, Laura 1951(?)- ... **CLC 141; HLCS 1**
See also AAYA 29; CA 143; CANR 68; DA3; DNFS 2; LAIT 3; MTCW 1; NFS 5; WLIT 1

Esse, James
See Stephens, James

Esterbrook, Tom
See Hubbard, L(afayette) Ron(ald)

Estleman, Loren D. 1952- .... **CLC 48**
See also AAYA 27; CA 85-88; CANR 27, 74; CMW 4; CPW; DA3; DAM NOV, POP; DLB 226; INT CANR-27; MTCW 1, 2

Etherege, Sir George 1636-1692 .... **LC 78**
See also BRW 2; DAM DRAM; DLB 80; PAB; RGEL 2

Euclid 306B.C.-283B.C. .... **CMLC 25**

Eugenides, Jeffrey 1960(?)- .... **CLC 81**
See also CA 144

Euripides c. 484B.C.-406B.C. .... **CMLC 23, 51; DC 4; WLCS**
See also AW 1; CDWLB 1; DA; DA3; DAB; DAC; DAM DRAM, MST; DFS 1, 4, 6; DLB 176; LAIT 1; RGWL 2

Evan, Evin
See Faust, Frederick (Schiller)

Evans, Caradoc 1878-1945 ... **TCLC 85; SSC 43**
See also DLB 162

Evans, Evan
See Faust, Frederick (Schiller)
See also TCWW 2

Evans, Marian
See Eliot, George

Evans, Mary Ann
See Eliot, George

Evarts, Esther
See Benson, Sally

Everett, Percival
See Everett, Percival L.
See also CSW

Everett, Percival L. 1956- .... **CLC 57**
See also Everett, Percival
See also BW 2; CA 129; CANR 94

Everson, R(onald) G(ilmour) 1903-1992 .... **CLC 27**
See also CA 17-20R; DLB 88

Everson, William (Oliver) 1912-1994 .... **CLC 1, 5, 14**
See also CA 9-12R; 145; CANR 20; DLB 5, 16, 212; MTCW 1

Evtushenko, Evgenii Aleksandrovich
See Yevtushenko, Yevgeny (Alexandrovich)
See also RGWL 2

Ewart, Gavin (Buchanan) 1916-1995 .... **CLC 13, 46**
See also BRWS 7; CA 89-92; 150; CANR 17, 46; CP 7; DLB 40; MTCW 1

Ewers, Hanns Heinz 1871-1943 ..... **TCLC 12**
See also CA 109; 149

Ewing, Frederick R.
See Sturgeon, Theodore (Hamilton)

Exley, Frederick (Earl) 1929-1992 .... **CLC 6, 11**
See also AITN 2; BPFB 1; CA 81-84; 138; DLB 143; DLBY 1981

Eynhardt, Guillermo
See Quiroga, Horacio (Sylvestre)

Ezekiel, Nissim 1924- .... **CLC 61**
See also CA 61-64; CP 7

Ezekiel, Tish O'Dowd 1943- .... **CLC 34**
See also CA 129

Fadeyev, A.
See Bulgya, Alexander Alexandrovich

Fadeyev, Alexander .... **TCLC 53**
See also Bulgya, Alexander Alexandrovich

Fagen, Donald 1948- .... **CLC 26**

Fainzilberg, Ilya Arnoldovich 1897-1937
See Ilf, Ilya
See also CA 120; 165

Fair, Ronald L. 1932- .... **CLC 18**
See also BW 1; CA 69-72; CANR 25; DLB 33

Fairbairn, Roger
See Carr, John Dickson

Fairbairns, Zoe (Ann) 1948- .... **CLC 32**
See also CA 103; CANR 21, 85; CN 7

Fairfield, Flora
See Alcott, Louisa May

Fairman, Paul W. 1916-1977
See Queen, Ellery
See also CA 114; SFW 4

Falco, Gian
See Papini, Giovanni

Falconer, James
See Kirkup, James

Falconer, Kenneth
See Kornbluth, C(yril) M.

Falkland, Samuel
See Heijermans, Herman

Fallaci, Oriana 1930- .... **CLC 11, 110**
See also CA 77-80; CANR 15, 58; FW; MTCW 1

Faludi, Susan 1959- .... **CLC 140**
See also CA 138; FW; MTCW 1; NCFS 3

Faludy, George 1913- .... **CLC 42**
See also CA 21-24R

Faludy, Gyoergy
See Faludy, George

Fanon, Frantz 1925-1961 .... **CLC 74; BLC 2**
See also BW 1; CA 116; 89-92; DAM MULT; WLIT 2

Fanshawe, Ann 1625-1680 .... **LC 11**

Fante, John (Thomas) 1911-1983 ..... **CLC 60**
See also CA 69-72; 109; CANR 23, 104; DLB 130; DLBY 1983

Farah, Nuruddin 1945- .. **CLC 53, 137; BLC 2**
See also AFW; BW 2, 3; CA 106; CANR 81; CDWLB 3; CN 7; DAM MULT; DLB 125; WLIT 2

Fargue, Leon-Paul 1876(?)-1947 .... **TCLC 11**
See also CA 109; CANR 107; DLB 258

Farigoule, Louis
See Romains, Jules

Farina, Richard 1936(?)-1966 .... **CLC 9**
See also CA 81-84; 25-28R

Farley, Walter (Lorimer) 1915-1989 .... **CLC 17**
See also BYA 14; CA 17-20R; CANR 8, 29, 84; DLB 22; JRDA; MAICYA 1, 2; SATA 2, 43, 132; YAW

Farmer, Philip Jose 1918- .... **CLC 1, 19**
See also AAYA 28; BPFB 1; CA 1-4R; CANR 4, 35; DLB 8; MTCW 1; SATA 93; SCFW 2; SFW 4

Farquhar, George 1677-1707 .... **LC 21**
See also BRW 2; DAM DRAM; DLB 84; RGEL 2

Farrell, J(ames) G(ordon) 1935-1979 .... **CLC 6**
See also CA 73-76; 89-92; CANR 36; DLB 14; MTCW 1; RGEL 2; RHW; WLIT 4

Farrell, James T(homas) 1904-1979 . **CLC 1, 4, 8, 11, 66; SSC 28**
See also AMW; BPFB 1; CA 5-8R; 89-92; CANR 9, 61; DLB 4, 9, 86; DLBD 2; MTCW 1, 2; RGAL 4

Farrell, Warren (Thomas) 1943- ...... **CLC 70**
See also CA 146

Farren, Richard J.
See Betjeman, John

Farren, Richard M.
See Betjeman, John

Fassbinder, Rainer Werner 1946-1982 .... **CLC 20**
See also CA 93-96; 106; CANR 31

Fast, Howard (Melvin) 1914- ... **CLC 23, 131**
See also AAYA 16; BPFB 1; CA 1-4R, 181; CAAE 181; CAAS 18; CANR 1, 33, 54, 75, 98; CMW 4; CN 7; CPW; DAM NOV; DLB 9; INT CANR-33; MTCW 1; RHW; SATA 7; SATA-Essay 107; TCWW 2; YAW

Faulcon, Robert
See Holdstock, Robert P.

Faulkner, William (Cuthbert) 1897-1962 .... **CLC 1, 3, 6, 8, 9, 11, 14, 18, 28, 52, 68; SSC 1, 35, 42; WLC**
See also AAYA 7; AMW; AMWR 1; BPFB 1; BYA 5; CA 81-84; CANR 33; CDALB 1929-1941; DA; DA3; DAB; DAC; DAM MST, NOV; DLB 9, 11, 44, 102; DLBD 2; DLBY 1986, 1997; EXPN; EXPS; LAIT 2; MTCW 1, 2; NFS 4, 8, 13; RGAL 4; RGSF 2; SSFS 2, 5, 6, 12

Fauset, Jessie Redmon 1882(?)-1961 .... **CLC 19, 54; BLC 2**
See also AFAW 2; BW 1; CA 109; CANR 83; DAM MULT; DLB 51; FW; MAWW

Faust, Frederick (Schiller) 1892-1944(?) .... **TCLC 49**
See also Austin, Frank; Brand, Max; Challis, George; Dawson, Peter; Dexter, Martin; Evans, Evan; Frederick, John; Frost, Frederick; Manning, David; Silver, Nicholas
See also CA 108; 152; DAM POP; DLB 256

Fawkes, Guy
See Benchley, Robert (Charles)

Fearing, Kenneth (Flexner) 1902-1961 .... **CLC 51**
See also CA 93-96; CANR 59; CMW 4; DLB 9; RGAL 4

Fecamps, Elise
See Creasey, John

Federman, Raymond 1928- .... **CLC 6, 47**
See also CA 17-20R; CAAS 8; CANR 10, 43, 83, 108; CN 7; DLBY 1980

Federspiel, J(uerg) F. 1931- .... **CLC 42**
See also CA 146

Feiffer, Jules (Ralph) 1929- ...... **CLC 2, 8, 64**
See also AAYA 3; CA 17-20R; CAD; CANR 30, 59; CD 5; DAM DRAM; DLB 7, 44; INT CANR-30; MTCW 1; SATA 8, 61, 111

Feige, Hermann Albert Otto Maximilian
See Traven, B.

Feinberg, David B. 1956-1994 .... **CLC 59**
See also CA 135; 147

Feinstein, Elaine 1930- .... **CLC 36**
See also CA 69-72; CAAS 1; CANR 31, 68; CN 7; CP 7; CWP; DLB 14, 40; MTCW 1

Feke, Gilbert David .... **CLC 65**

Feldman, Irving (Mordecai) 1928- ...... **CLC 7**
See also CA 1-4R; CANR 1; CP 7; DLB 169

Felix-Tchicaya, Gerald
See Tchicaya, Gerald Felix

Fellini, Federico 1920-1993 .... **CLC 16, 85**
See also CA 65-68; 143; CANR 33

Felsen, Henry Gregor 1916-1995 ..... **CLC 17**
See also CA 1-4R; 180; CANR 1; SAAS 2; SATA 1

Felski, Rita .... **CLC 65**

Fenno, Jack
See Calisher, Hortense

Fenollosa, Ernest (Francisco) 1853-1908 .... **TCLC 91**

Fenton, James Martin 1949- .... **CLC 32**
See also CA 102; CANR 108; CP 7; DLB 40; PFS 11

Ferber, Edna 1887-1968 .... **CLC 18, 93**
See also AITN 1; CA 5-8R; 25-28R; CANR 68, 105; DLB 9, 28, 86; MTCW 1, 2; RGAL 4; RHW; SATA 7; TCWW 2

Ferdowsi, Abu'l Qasem 940-1020 . **CMLC 43**
See also RGWL 2

Ferguson, Helen
See Kavan, Anna

Ferguson, Niall 1964- .... **CLC 134**
See also CA 190

Ferguson, Samuel 1810-1886 .... **NCLC 33**
See also DLB 32; RGEL 2

Fergusson, Robert 1750-1774 .... **LC 29**
See also DLB 109; RGEL 2

Ferling, Lawrence
See Ferlinghetti, Lawrence (Monsanto)

Ferlinghetti, Lawrence (Monsanto)
1919(?)- ..... **CLC 2, 6, 10, 27, 111; PC 1**
See also CA 5-8R; CANR 3, 41, 73; CDALB 1941-1968; CP 7; DA3; DAM POET; DLB 5, 16; MTCW 1, 2; RGAL 4; WP

Fern, Fanny
See Parton, Sara Payson Willis

Fernandez, Vicente Garcia Huidobro
See Huidobro Fernandez, Vicente Garcia

Fernandez-Armesto, Felipe .... **CLC 70**

Fernandez de Lizardi, Jose Joaquin
See Lizardi, Jose Joaquin Fernandez de

Ferre, Rosario 1942- ...... **CLC 139; HLCS 1; SSC 36**
See also CA 131; CANR 55, 81; CWW 2; DLB 145; HW 1, 2; LAWS 1; MTCW 1; WLIT 1

Ferrer, Gabriel (Francisco Victor) Miro
See Miro (Ferrer), Gabriel (Francisco Victor)

Ferrier, Susan (Edmonstone)
1782-1854 .... **NCLC 8**
See also DLB 116; RGEL 2

Ferrigno, Robert 1948(?)- .... **CLC 65**
See also CA 140

Ferron, Jacques 1921-1985 .... **CLC 94**
See also CA 117; 129; CCA 1; DAC; DLB 60

Feuchtwanger, Lion 1884-1958 .... **TCLC 3**
See also CA 104; 187; DLB 66

Feuillet, Octave 1821-1890 .... **NCLC 45**
See also DLB 192

Feydeau, Georges (Leon Jules Marie)
1862-1921 .... **TCLC 22**
See also CA 113; 152; CANR 84; DAM DRAM; DLB 192; GFL 1789 to the Present; RGWL 2

Fichte, Johann Gottlieb
1762-1814 .... **NCLC 62**
See also DLB 90

Ficino, Marsilio 1433-1499 .... **LC 12**

Fiedeler, Hans
See Doeblin, Alfred

Fiedler, Leslie A(aron) 1917- .. **CLC 4, 13, 24**
See also CA 9-12R; CANR 7, 63; CN 7; DLB 28, 67; MTCW 1, 2; RGAL 4

Field, Andrew 1938- .... **CLC 44**
See also CA 97-100; CANR 25

Field, Eugene 1850-1895 .... **NCLC 3**
See also DLB 23, 42, 140; DLBD 13; MAICYA 1, 2; RGAL 4; SATA 16

Field, Gans T.
See Wellman, Manly Wade

Field, Michael 1915-1971 .... **TCLC 43**
See also CA 29-32R

Field, Peter
See Hobson, Laura Z(ametkin)
See also TCWW 2

Fielding, Helen 1959(?)- .... **CLC 146**
See also CA 172; DLB 231

Fielding, Henry 1707-1754 .. **LC 1, 46; WLC**
See also BRW 3; BRWR 1; CDBLB 1660-1789; DA; DAB; DAC; DAM DRAM, MST, NOV; DLB 39, 84, 101; RGEL 2; WLIT 3

Fielding, Sarah 1710-1768 .... **LC 1, 44**
See also DLB 39; RGEL 2

Fields, W. C. 1880-1946 .... **TCLC 80**
See also DLB 44

Fierstein, Harvey (Forbes) 1954- ..... **CLC 33**
See also CA 123; 129; CAD; CD 5; CPW; DA3; DAM DRAM, POP; DFS 6; GLL 1

Figes, Eva 1932- .... **CLC 31**
See also CA 53-56; CANR 4, 44, 83; CN 7; DLB 14; FW

Finch, Anne 1661-1720 .... **LC 3; PC 21**
See also DLB 95

Finch, Robert (Duer Claydon)
1900-1995 .... **CLC 18**
See also CA 57-60; CANR 9, 24, 49; CP 7; DLB 88

Findley, Timothy 1930- .... **CLC 27, 102**
See also CA 25-28R; CANR 12, 42, 69, 109; CCA 1; CN 7; DAC; DAM MST; DLB 53; FANT; RHW

Fink, William
See Mencken, H(enry) L(ouis)

Firbank, Louis 1942-
See Reed, Lou
See also CA 117

Firbank, (Arthur Annesley) Ronald
1886-1926 .... **TCLC 1**
See also BRWS 2; CA 104; 177; DLB 36; RGEL 2

Fish, Stanley
See Fish, Stanley Eugene

Fish, Stanley E.
See Fish, Stanley Eugene

Fish, Stanley Eugene 1938- .... **CLC 142**
See also CA 112; 132; CANR 90; DLB 67

Fisher, Dorothy (Frances) Canfield
1879-1958 .... **TCLC 87**
See also CA 114; 136; CANR 80; CLR 71,; CWRI 5; DLB 9, 102; MAICYA 1, 2; YABC 1

Fisher, M(ary) F(rances) K(ennedy)
1908-1992 .... **CLC 76, 87**
See also CA 77-80; 138; CANR 44; MTCW 1

Fisher, Roy 1930- .... **CLC 25**
See also CA 81-84; CAAS 10; CANR 16; CP 7; DLB 40

Fisher, Rudolph 1897-1934 .. **TCLC 11; BLC 2; SSC 25**
See also BW 1, 3; CA 107; 124; CANR 80; DAM MULT; DLB 51, 102

Fisher, Vardis (Alvero) 1895-1968 ...... **CLC 7**
See also CA 5-8R; 25-28R; CANR 68; DLB 9, 206; RGAL 4; TCWW 2

Fiske, Tarleton
See Bloch, Robert (Albert)

Fitch, Clarke
See Sinclair, Upton (Beall)

Fitch, John IV
See Cormier, Robert (Edmund)

Fitzgerald, Captain Hugh
See Baum, L(yman) Frank

FitzGerald, Edward 1809-1883 .... **NCLC 9**
See also BRW 4; DLB 32; RGEL 2

Fitzgerald, F(rancis) Scott (Key)
1896-1940 . **TCLC 1, 6, 14, 28, 55; SSC 6, 31; WLC**
See also AAYA 24; AITN 1; AMW; AMWR 1; BPFB 1; CA 110; 123; CDALB 1917-1929; DA; DA3; DAB; DAC; DAM MST, NOV; DLB 4, 9, 86, 219; DLBD 1, 15, 16; DLBY 1981, 1996; EXPN; EXPS; LAIT 3; MTCW 1, 2; NFS 2; RGAL 4; RGSF 2; SSFS 4, 15

Fitzgerald, Penelope 1916-2000 . **CLC 19, 51, 61, 143**
See also BRWS 5; CA 85-88; 190; CAAS 10; CANR 56, 86; CN 7; DLB 14, 194; MTCW 2

Fitzgerald, Robert (Stuart)
1910-1985 .... **CLC 39**
See also CA 1-4R; 114; CANR 1; DLBY 1980

FitzGerald, Robert D(avid)
1902-1987 .... **CLC 19**
See also CA 17-20R; DLB 260; RGEL 2

Fitzgerald, Zelda (Sayre)
1900-1948 .... **TCLC 52**
See also AMWS 9; CA 117; 126; DLBY 1984

Flanagan, Thomas (James Bonner)
1923- .... **CLC 25, 52**
See also CA 108; CANR 55; CN 7; DLBY 1980; INT 108; MTCW 1; RHW

Flaubert, Gustave 1821-1880 .... **NCLC 2, 10, 19, 62, 66; SSC 11; WLC**
See also DA; DA3; DAB; DAC; DAM MST, NOV; DLB 119; EW 7; EXPS; GFL 1789 to the Present; LAIT 2; NFS 14; RGSF 2; RGWL 2; SSFS 6

Flavius Josephus
See Josephus, Flavius

Flecker, Herman Elroy
See Flecker, (Herman) James Elroy

Flecker, (Herman) James Elroy
1884-1915 .... **TCLC 43**
See also CA 109; 150; DLB 10, 19; RGEL 2

Fleming, Ian (Lancaster) 1908-1964 . **CLC 3, 30**
See also AAYA 26; BPFB 1; CA 5-8R; CANR 59; CDBLB 1945-1960; CMW 4; CPW; DA3; DAM POP; DLB 87, 201; MSW; MTCW 1, 2; RGEL 2; SATA 9; YAW

Fleming, Thomas (James) 1927- ...... **CLC 37**
See also CA 5-8R; CANR 10, 102; INT CANR-10; SATA 8

Fletcher, John 1579-1625 .... **LC 33; DC 6**
See also BRW 2; CDBLB Before 1660; DLB 58; RGEL 2

Fletcher, John Gould 1886-1950 .... **TCLC 35**
See also CA 107; 167; DLB 4, 45; RGAL 4

Fleur, Paul
See Pohl, Frederik

Flooglebuckle, Al
See Spiegelman, Art

Flora, Fletcher 1914-1969
See Queen, Ellery
See also CA 1-4R; CANR 3, 85

Flying Officer X
See Bates, H(erbert) E(rnest)

Fo, Dario 1926- .... **CLC 32, 109; DC 10**
See also CA 116; 128; CANR 68; CWW 2; DA3; DAM DRAM; DLBY 1997; MTCW 1, 2

Fogarty, Jonathan Titulescu Esq.
See Farrell, James T(homas)

Follett, Ken(neth Martin) 1949- .... **CLC 18**
See also AAYA 6; BEST 89:4; BPFB 1; CA 81-84; CANR 13, 33, 54, 102; CMW 4; CPW; DA3; DAM NOV, POP; DLB 87; DLBY 1981; INT CANR-33; MTCW 1

Fontane, Theodor 1819-1898 .... **NCLC 26**
See also CDWLB 2; DLB 129; EW 6; RGWL 2

Fontenot, Chester .... **CLC 65**

Foote, Horton 1916- .... **CLC 51, 91**
See also CA 73-76; CAD; CANR 34, 51; CD 5; CSW; DA3; DAM DRAM; DLB 26; INT CANR-34

Foote, Mary Hallock 1847-1938 .. **TCLC 108**
See also DLB 186, 188, 202, 221

Foote, Shelby 1916- .... **CLC 75**
See also AAYA 40; CA 5-8R; CANR 3, 45, 74; CN 7; CPW; CSW; DA3; DAM NOV, POP; DLB 2, 17; MTCW 2; RHW

Forbes, Cosmo
See Lewton, Val

Forbes, Esther 1891-1967 .... **CLC 12**
See also AAYA 17; BYA 2; CA 13-14; 25-28R; CAP 1; CLR 27; DLB 22; JRDA; MAICYA 1, 2; RHW; SATA 2, 100; YAW

Forche, Carolyn (Louise) 1950- .... **CLC 25, 83, 86; PC 10**
See also CA 109; 117; CANR 50, 74; CP 7; CWP; DA3; DAM POET; DLB 5, 193; INT CA-117; MTCW 1; RGAL 4

Ford, Elbur
See Hibbert, Eleanor Alice Burford

Ford, Ford Madox 1873-1939 ... **TCLC 1, 15, 39, 57**
See also Chaucer, Daniel
See also BRW 6; CA 104; 132; CANR 74; CDBLB 1914-1945; DA3; DAM NOV; DLB 34, 98, 162; MTCW 1, 2; RGEL 2

Ford, Henry 1863-1947 .... **TCLC 73**
See also CA 115; 148

Ford, John 1586-1639 .... **LC 68; DC 8**
See also BRW 2; CDBLB Before 1660; DA3; DAM DRAM; DFS 7; DLB 58; IDTP; RGEL 2

Ford, John 1895-1973 .... **CLC 16**
See also CA 187; 45-48

Ford, Richard 1944- .... **CLC 46, 99**
See also AMWS 5; CA 69-72; CANR 11, 47, 86; CN 7; CSW; DLB 227; MTCW 1; RGAL 4; RGSF 2

Ford, Webster
See Masters, Edgar Lee

Foreman, Richard 1937- .... **CLC 50**
See also CA 65-68; CAD; CANR 32, 63; CD 5

Forester, C(ecil) S(cott) 1899-1966 ... **CLC 35**
See also CA 73-76; 25-28R; CANR 83; DLB 191; RGEL 2; RHW; SATA 13

Forez
See Mauriac, Francois (Charles)

Forman, James
See Forman, James D(ouglas)

Forman, James D(ouglas) 1932- .... **CLC 21**
See also AAYA 17; CA 9-12R; CANR 4, 19, 42; JRDA; MAICYA 1, 2; SATA 8, 70; YAW

Fornes, Maria Irene 1930- . **CLC 39, 61; DC 10; HLCS 1**
See also CA 25-28R; CAD; CANR 28, 81; CD 5; CWD; DLB 7; HW 1, 2; INT CANR-28; MTCW 1; RGAL 4

Forrest, Leon (Richard) 1937-1997 .. **CLC 4; BLCS**
See also AFAW 2; BW 2; CA 89-92; 162; CAAS 7; CANR 25, 52, 87; CN 7; DLB 33

Forster, E(dward) M(organ) 1879-1970 ...... **CLC 1, 2, 3, 4, 9, 10, 13, 15, 22, 45, 77; SSC 27; WLC**
See also AAYA 2, 37; BRW 6; BRWR 2; CA 13-14; 25-28R; CANR 45; CAP 1; CDBLB 1914-1945; DA; DA3; DAB; DAC; DAM MST, NOV; DLB 34, 98, 162, 178, 195; DLBD 10; EXPN; LAIT 3; MTCW 1, 2; NCFS 1; NFS 3, 10, 11; RGEL 2; RGSF 2; SATA 57; SUFW; WLIT 4

Forster, John 1812-1876 .... **NCLC 11**
See also DLB 144, 184

Forster, Margaret 1938- .... **CLC 149**
See also CA 133; CANR 62; CN 7; DLB 155

Forsyth, Frederick 1938- .... **CLC 2, 5, 36**
See also BEST 89:4; CA 85-88; CANR 38, 62; CMW 4; CN 7; CPW; DAM NOV, POP; DLB 87; MTCW 1, 2

Forten, Charlotte L. 1837-1914 .... **TCLC 16; BLC 2**
See also Grimke, Charlotte L(ottie) Forten
See also DLB 50, 239

Foscolo, Ugo 1778-1827 .... **NCLC 8, 97**
See also EW 5

Fosse, Bob .... **CLC 20**
See also Fosse, Robert Louis

Fosse, Robert Louis 1927-1987
See Fosse, Bob
See also CA 110; 123

Foster, Hannah Webster 1758-1840 .... **NCLC 99**
See also DLB 37, 200; RGAL 4

Foster, Stephen Collins 1826-1864 .... **NCLC 26**
See also RGAL 4

Foucault, Michel 1926-1984 . **CLC 31, 34, 69**
See also CA 105; 113; CANR 34; DLB 242; EW 13; GFL 1789 to the Present; GLL 1; MTCW 1, 2

Fouque, Friedrich (Heinrich Karl) de la Motte 1777-1843 .... **NCLC 2**
See also DLB 90; RGWL 2; SUFW

Fourier, Charles 1772-1837 .... **NCLC 51**

Fournier, Henri Alban 1886-1914
See Alain-Fournier
See also CA 104; 179

Fournier, Pierre 1916- .... **CLC 11**
See Gascar, Pierre
See also CA 89-92; CANR 16, 40

Fowles, John (Robert) 1926- . **CLC 1, 2, 3, 4, 6, 9, 10, 15, 33, 87; SSC 33**
See also BPFB 1; BRWS 1; CA 5-8R; CANR 25, 71, 103; CDBLB 1960 to Present; CN 7; DA3; DAB; DAC; DAM MST; DLB 14, 139, 207; HGG; MTCW 1, 2; RGEL 2; RHW; SATA 22; WLIT 4

Fox, Paula 1923- .... **CLC 2, 8, 121**
See also AAYA 3, 37; BYA 3, 8; CA 73-76; CANR 20, 36, 62, 105; CLR 1, 44; DLB 52; JRDA; MAICYA 1, 2; MTCW 1; NFS 12; SATA 17, 60, 120; WYA; YAW

Fox, William Price (Jr.) 1926- .... **CLC 22**
See also CA 17-20R; CAAS 19; CANR 11; CSW; DLB 2; DLBY 1981

Foxe, John 1517(?)-1587 .... **LC 14**
See also DLB 132

Frame, Janet .. **CLC 2, 3, 6, 22, 66, 96; SSC 29**
See also Clutha, Janet Paterson Frame
See also CN 7; CWP; RGEL 2; RGSF 2

France, Anatole .... **TCLC 9**
See also Thibault, Jacques Anatole Francois
See also DLB 123; GFL 1789 to the Present; MTCW 1; RGWL 2; SUFW

Francis, Claude .... **CLC 50**
See also CA 192

Francis, Dick 1920- .... **CLC 2, 22, 42, 102**
See also AAYA 5, 21; BEST 89:3; BPFB 1; CA 5-8R; CANR 9, 42, 68, 100; CDBLB 1960 to Present; CMW 4; CN 7; DA3; DAM POP; DLB 87; INT CANR-9; MSW; MTCW 1, 2

Francis, Robert (Churchill) 1901-1987 .... **CLC 15; PC 34**
See also AMWS 9; CA 1-4R; 123; CANR 1; EXPP; PFS 12

Francis, Lord Jeffrey
See Jeffrey, Francis
See also DLB 107

Frank, Anne(lies Marie) 1929-1945 .... **TCLC 17; WLC**
See also AAYA 12; BYA 1; CA 113; 133; CANR 68; DA; DA3; DAB; DAC; DAM MST; LAIT 4; MAICYA 1; MAICYAS 1; MTCW 1, 2; NCFS 2; SATA 87; SATA-Brief 42; WYA; YAW

Frank, Bruno 1887-1945 .... **TCLC 81**
See also CA 189; DLB 118

Frank, Elizabeth 1945- .... **CLC 39**
See also CA 121; 126; CANR 78; INT 126

Frankl, Viktor E(mil) 1905-1997 ...... **CLC 93**
See also CA 65-68; 161

Franklin, Benjamin
See Hasek, Jaroslav (Matej Frantisek)

Franklin, Benjamin 1706-1790 .... **LC 25; WLCS**
See also AMW; CDALB 1640-1865; DA; DA3; DAB; DAC; DAM MST; DLB 24, 43, 73, 183; LAIT 1; RGAL 4; TUS

Franklin, (Stella Maria Sarah) Miles (Lampe) 1879-1954 .... **TCLC 7**
See also CA 104; 164; DLB 230; FW; MTCW 2; RGEL 2; TWA

Fraser, George MacDonald 1925- ...... **CLC 7**
See also CA 45-48; 180; CAAE 180; CANR 2, 48, 74; MTCW 1; RHW

Fraser, Sylvia 1935- .... **CLC 64**
See also CA 45-48; CANR 1, 16, 60; CCA 1

Frayn, Michael 1933- .... **CLC 3, 7, 31, 47**
See also BRWS 7; CA 5-8R; CANR 30, 69; CBD; CD 5; CN 7; DAM DRAM, NOV; DLB 13, 14, 194, 245; FANT; MTCW 1, 2; SFW 4

Fraze, Candida (Merrill) 1945- .... **CLC 50**
See also CA 126

Frazer, Andrew
See Marlowe, Stephen

Frazer, J(ames) G(eorge) 1854-1941 .... **TCLC 32**
See also BRWS 3; CA 118

Frazer, Robert Caine
See Creasey, John

Frazer, Sir James George
See Frazer, J(ames) G(eorge)

Frazier, Charles 1950- .... **CLC 109**
See also AAYA 34; CA 161; CSW

Frazier, Ian 1951- .... **CLC 46**
See also CA 130; CANR 54, 93

Frederic, Harold 1856-1898 .... **NCLC 10**
See also AMW; DLB 12, 23; DLBD 13; RGAL 4

Frederick, John
See Faust, Frederick (Schiller)
See also TCWW 2

Frederick the Great 1712-1786 .... **LC 14**

Fredro, Aleksander 1793-1876 .... **NCLC 8**

Freeling, Nicolas 1927- .... **CLC 38**
See also CA 49-52; CAAS 12; CANR 1, 17, 50, 84; CMW 4; CN 7; DLB 87

Freeman, Douglas Southall 1886-1953 .... **TCLC 11**
See also CA 109; 195; DLB 17; DLBD 17

Freeman, Judith 1946- .... **CLC 55**
See also CA 148; DLB 256

Freeman, Mary E(leanor) Wilkins 1852-1930 .... **TCLC 9; SSC 1, 47**
See also CA 106; 177; DLB 12, 78, 221; EXPS; FW; HGG; MAWW; RGAL 4; RGSF 2; SSFS 4, 8; SUFW; TUS

Freeman, R(ichard) Austin 1862-1943 .... **TCLC 21**
See also CA 113; CANR 84; CMW 4; DLB 70

French, Albert 1943- .... **CLC 86**
See also BW 3; CA 167

French, Marilyn 1929- .... **CLC 10, 18, 60**
See also BPFB 1; CA 69-72; CANR 3, 31; CN 7; CPW; DAM DRAM, NOV, POP; FW; INT CANR-31; MTCW 1, 2

French, Paul
See Asimov, Isaac

Freneau, Philip Morin 1752-1832 .. **NCLC 1, 111**
See also AMWS 2; DLB 37, 43; RGAL 4

Freud, Sigmund 1856-1939 .... **TCLC 52**
See also CA 115; 133; CANR 69; EW 8; MTCW 1, 2; NCFS 3

Freytag, Gustav 1816-1895 .... **NCLC 109**
See also DLB 129
Friedan, Betty (Naomi) 1921- .... **CLC 74**
See also CA 65-68; CANR 18, 45, 74; DLB 246; FW; MTCW 1, 2
Friedlander, Saul 1932- .... **CLC 90**
See also CA 117; 130; CANR 72
Friedman, B(ernard) H(arper)
1926- .... **CLC 7**
See also CA 1-4R; CANR 3, 48
Friedman, Bruce Jay 1930- ...... **CLC 3, 5, 56**
See also CA 9-12R; CAD; CANR 25, 52, 101; CD 5; CN 7; DLB 2, 28, 244; INT CANR-25
Friel, Brian 1929- .... **CLC 5, 42, 59, 115; DC 8**
See also BRWS 5; CA 21-24R; CANR 33, 69; CBD; CD 5; DFS 11; DLB 13; MTCW 1; RGEL 2
Friis-Baastad, Babbis Ellinor
1921-1970 .... **CLC 12**
See also CA 17-20R; 134; SATA 7
Frisch, Max (Rudolf) 1911-1991 ... **CLC 3, 9, 14, 18, 32, 44**
See also CA 85-88; 134; CANR 32, 74; CDWLB 2; DAM DRAM, NOV; DLB 69, 124; EW 13; MTCW 1, 2; RGWL 2; TCLC 121
Fromentin, Eugene (Samuel Auguste)
1820-1876 .... **NCLC 10**
See also DLB 123; GFL 1789 to the Present
Frost, Frederick
See Faust, Frederick (Schiller)
See also TCWW 2
Frost, Robert (Lee) 1874-1963 .. **CLC 1, 3, 4, 9, 10, 13, 15, 26, 34, 44; PC 1, 39; WLC**
See also AAYA 21; AMW; AMWR 1; CA 89-92; CANR 33; CDALB 1917-1929; CLR 67; DA; DA3; DAB; DAC; DAM MST, POET; DLB 54; DLBD 7; EXPP; MTCW 1, 2; PAB; PFS 1, 2, 3, 4, 5, 6, 7, 10, 13; RGAL 4; SATA 14; WP; WYA
Froude, James Anthony
1818-1894 .... **NCLC 43**
See also DLB 18, 57, 144
Froy, Herald
See Waterhouse, Keith (Spencer)
Fry, Christopher 1907- .... **CLC 2, 10, 14**
See also BRWS 3; CA 17-20R; CAAS 23; CANR 9, 30, 74; CBD; CD 5; CP 7; DAM DRAM; DLB 13; MTCW 1, 2; RGEL 2; SATA 66
Frye, (Herman) Northrop
1912-1991 .... **CLC 24, 70**
See also CA 5-8R; 133; CANR 8, 37; DLB 67, 68, 246; MTCW 1, 2; RGAL 4
Fuchs, Daniel 1909-1993 .... **CLC 8, 22**
See also CA 81-84; 142; CAAS 5; CANR 40; DLB 9, 26, 28; DLBY 1993
Fuchs, Daniel 1934- .... **CLC 34**
See also CA 37-40R; CANR 14, 48
Fuentes, Carlos 1928- ... **CLC 3, 8, 10, 13, 22, 41, 60, 113; HLC 1; SSC 24; WLC**
See also AAYA 4; AITN 2; BPFB 1; CA 69-72; CANR 10, 32, 68, 104; CDWLB 3; CWW 2; DA; DA3; DAB; DAC; DAM MST, MULT, NOV; DLB 113; DNFS 2; HW 1, 2; LAIT 3; LAW; LAWS 1; MTCW 1, 2; NFS 8; RGSF 2; RGWL 2; WLIT 1
Fuentes, Gregorio Lopez y
See Lopez y Fuentes, Gregorio
Fuertes, Gloria 1918-1998 .... **PC 27**
See also CA 178, 180; DLB 108; HW 2; SATA 115

Fugard, (Harold) Athol 1932- . **CLC 5, 9, 14, 25, 40, 80; DC 3**
See also AAYA 17; AFW; CA 85-88; CANR 32, 54; CD 5; DAM DRAM; DFS 3, 6, 10; DLB 225; DNFS 1, 2; MTCW 1; RGEL 2; WLIT 2
Fugard, Sheila 1932- .... **CLC 48**
See also CA 125
Fukuyama, Francis 1952- .... **CLC 131**
See also CA 140; CANR 72
Fuller, Charles (H., Jr.) 1939- .... **CLC 25; BLC 2; DC 1**
See also BW 2; CA 108; 112; CAD; CANR 87; CD 5; DAM DRAM, MULT; DFS 8; DLB 38; INT CA-112; MTCW 1
Fuller, Henry Blake 1857-1929 .... **TCLC 103**
See also CA 108; 177; DLB 12; RGAL 4
Fuller, John (Leopold) 1937- .... **CLC 62**
See also CA 21-24R; CANR 9, 44; CP 7; DLB 40
Fuller, Margaret
See Ossoli, Sarah Margaret (Fuller)
See also AMWS 2; DLB 183, 223, 239
Fuller, Roy (Broadbent) 1912-1991 ... **CLC 4, 28**
See also BRWS 7; CA 5-8R; 135; CAAS 10; CANR 53, 83; CWRI 5; DLB 15, 20; RGEL 2; SATA 87
Fuller, Sarah Margaret
See Ossoli, Sarah Margaret (Fuller)
Fuller, Sarah Margaret
See Ossoli, Sarah Margaret (Fuller)
See also DLB 1, 59, 73
Fulton, Alice 1952- .... **CLC 52**
See also CA 116; CANR 57, 88; CP 7; CWP; DLB 193
Furphy, Joseph 1843-1912 .... **TCLC 25**
See also CA 163; DLB 230; RGEL 2
Fuson, Robert H(enderson) 1927- ..... **CLC 70**
See also CA 89-92; CANR 103
Fussell, Paul 1924- .... **CLC 74**
See also BEST 90:1; CA 17-20R; CANR 8, 21, 35, 69; INT CANR-21; MTCW 1, 2
Futabatei, Shimei 1864-1909 .... **TCLC 44**
See also Futabatei Shimei
See also CA 162; MJW
Futabatei Shimei
See Futabatei, Shimei
See also DLB 180
Futrelle, Jacques 1875-1912 .... **TCLC 19**
See also CA 113; 155; CMW 4
Gaboriau, Emile 1835-1873 .... **NCLC 14**
See also CMW 4; MSW
Gadda, Carlo Emilio 1893-1973 .... **CLC 11**
See also CA 89-92; DLB 177
Gaddis, William 1922-1998 ... **CLC 1, 3, 6, 8, 10, 19, 43, 86**
See also AMWS 4; BPFB 1; CA 17-20R; 172; CANR 21, 48; CN 7; DLB 2; MTCW 1, 2; RGAL 4
Gaelique, Moruen le
See Jacob, (Cyprien-)Max
Gage, Walter
See Inge, William (Motter)
Gaines, Ernest J(ames) 1933- ...... **CLC 3, 11, 18, 86; BLC 2**
See also AAYA 18; AFAW 1, 2; AITN 1; BPFB 1; BW 2, 3; BYA 6; CA 9-12R; CANR 6, 24, 42, 75; CDALB 1968-1988; CLR 62; CN 7; CSW; DA3; DAM MULT; DLB 2, 33, 152; DLBY 1980; EXPN; LAIT 5; MTCW 1, 2; NFS 5, 7; RGAL 4; RGSF 2; RHW; SATA 86; SSFS 5; YAW
Gaitskill, Mary 1954- .... **CLC 69**
See also CA 128; CANR 61; DLB 244
Galdos, Benito Perez
See Perez Galdos, Benito
See also EW 7

Gale, Zona 1874-1938 .... **TCLC 7**
See also CA 105; 153; CANR 84; DAM DRAM; DLB 9, 78, 228; RGAL 4
Galeano, Eduardo (Hughes) 1940- . **CLC 72; HLCS 1**
See also CA 29-32R; CANR 13, 32, 100; HW 1
Galiano, Juan Valera y Alcala
See Valera y Alcala-Galiano, Juan
Galilei, Galileo 1564-1642 .... **LC 45**
Gallagher, Tess 1943- ...... **CLC 18, 63; PC 9**
See also CA 106; CP 7; CWP; DAM POET; DLB 120, 212, 244
Gallant, Mavis 1922- . **CLC 7, 18, 38; SSC 5**
See also CA 69-72; CANR 29, 69; CCA 1; CN 7; DAC; DAM MST; DLB 53; MTCW 1, 2; RGEL 2; RGSF 2
Gallant, Roy A(rthur) 1924- .... **CLC 17**
See also CA 5-8R; CANR 4, 29, 54; CLR 30; MAICYA 1, 2; SATA 4, 68, 110
Gallico, Paul (William) 1897-1976 ..... **CLC 2**
See also AITN 1; CA 5-8R; 69-72; CANR 23; DLB 9, 171; FANT; MAICYA 1, 2; SATA 13
Gallo, Max Louis 1932- .... **CLC 95**
See also CA 85-88
Gallois, Lucien
See Desnos, Robert
Gallup, Ralph
See Whitemore, Hugh (John)
Galsworthy, John 1867-1933 .... **TCLC 1, 45; SSC 22; WLC**
See also BRW 6; CA 104; 141; CANR 75; CDBLB 1890-1914; DA; DA3; DAB; DAC; DAM DRAM, MST, NOV; DLB 10, 34, 98, 162; DLBD 16; MTCW 1; RGEL 2; SSFS 3
Galt, John 1779-1839 .... **NCLC 1, 110**
See also DLB 99, 116, 159; RGEL 2; RGSF 2
Galvin, James 1951- .... **CLC 38**
See also CA 108; CANR 26
Gamboa, Federico 1864-1939 .... **TCLC 36**
See also CA 167; HW 2; LAW
Gandhi, M. K.
See Gandhi, Mohandas Karamchand
Gandhi, Mahatma
See Gandhi, Mohandas Karamchand
Gandhi, Mohandas Karamchand
1869-1948 .... **TCLC 59**
See also CA 121; 132; DA3; DAM MULT; MTCW 1, 2
Gann, Ernest Kellogg 1910-1991 ..... **CLC 23**
See also AITN 1; BPFB 2; CA 1-4R; 136; CANR 1, 83; RHW
Garber, Eric 1943(?)-
See Holleran, Andrew
See also CANR 89
Garcia, Cristina 1958- .... **CLC 76**
See also CA 141; CANR 73; DNFS 1; HW 2
Garcia Lorca, Federico 1898-1936 . **TCLC 1, 7, 49; DC 2; HLC 2; PC 3; WLC**
See also Lorca, Federico Garcia
See also CA 104; 131; CANR 81; DA; DA3; DAB; DAC; DAM DRAM, MST, MULT, POET; DFS 10; DLB 108; HW 1, 2; MTCW 1, 2
Garcia Marquez, Gabriel (Jose)
1928- ... **CLC 2, 3, 8, 10, 15, 27, 47, 55, 68; HLC 1; SSC 8; WLC**
See also AAYA 3, 33; BEST 89:1, 90:4; BPFB 2; BYA 12; CA 33-36R; CANR 10, 28, 50, 75, 82; CDWLB 3; CPW; DA; DA3; DAB; DAC; DAM MST, MULT, NOV, POP; DLB 113; DNFS 1, 2; EXPN; EXPS; HW 1, 2; LAIT 2; LAW; LAWS 1; MTCW 1, 2; NCFS 3; NFS 1, 5, 10; RGSF 2; RGWL 2; SSFS 1, 6; WLIT 1

Garcilaso de la Vega, El Inca 1503-1536
See also HLCS 1; LAW

Gard, Janice
See Latham, Jean Lee

Gard, Roger Martin du
See Martin du Gard, Roger

Gardam, Jane (Mary) 1928- .... **CLC 43**
See also CA 49-52; CANR 2, 18, 33, 54, 106; CLR 12; DLB 14, 161, 231; MAICYA 1, 2; MTCW 1; SAAS 9; SATA 39, 76, 130; SATA-Brief 28; YAW

Gardner, Herb(ert) 1934- .... **CLC 44**
See also CA 149; CAD; CD 5

Gardner, John (Champlin), Jr.
1933-1982 ...... **CLC 2, 3, 5, 7, 8, 10, 18, 28, 34; SSC 7**
See also AITN 1; AMWS 6; BPFB 2; CA 65-68; 107; CANR 33, 73; CDALBS; CPW; DA3; DAM NOV, POP; DLB 2; DLBY 1982; FANT; MTCW 1; NFS 3; RGAL 4; RGSF 2; SATA 40; SATA-Obit 31; SSFS 8

Gardner, John (Edmund) 1926- .... **CLC 30**
See also CA 103; CANR 15, 69; CMW 4; CPW; DAM POP; MTCW 1

Gardner, Miriam
See Bradley, Marion Zimmer
See also GLL 1

Gardner, Noel
See Kuttner, Henry

Gardons, S. S.
See Snodgrass, W(illiam) D(e Witt)

Garfield, Leon 1921-1996 .... **CLC 12**
See also AAYA 8; BYA 1, 3; CA 17-20R; 152; CANR 38, 41, 78; CLR 21; DLB 161; JRDA; MAICYA 1, 2; MAICYAS 1; SATA 1, 32, 76; SATA-Obit 90; WYA; YAW

Garland, (Hannibal) Hamlin
1860-1940 .... **TCLC 3; SSC 18**
See also CA 104; DLB 12, 71, 78, 186; RGAL 4; RGSF 2; TCWW 2

Garneau, (Hector de) Saint-Denys
1912-1943 .... **TCLC 13**
See also CA 111; DLB 88

Garner, Alan 1934- .... **CLC 17**
See also AAYA 18; BYA 3, 5; CA 73-76, 178; CAAE 178; CANR 15, 64; CLR 20; CPW; DAB; DAM POP; DLB 161, 261; FANT; MAICYA 1, 2; MTCW 1, 2; SATA 18, 69; SATA-Essay 108; SUFW; YAW

Garner, Hugh 1913-1979 .... **CLC 13**
See also Warwick, Jarvis
See also CA 69-72; CANR 31; CCA 1; DLB 68

Garnett, David 1892-1981 .... **CLC 3**
See also CA 5-8R; 103; CANR 17, 79; DLB 34; FANT; MTCW 2; RGEL 2; SFW 4; SUFW

Garos, Stephanie
See Katz, Steve

Garrett, George (Palmer) 1929- .. **CLC 3, 11, 51; SSC 30**
See also AMWS 7; BPFB 2; CA 1-4R; CAAE 202; CAAS 5; CANR 1, 42, 67, 109; CN 7; CP 7; CSW; DLB 2, 5, 130, 152; DLBY 1983

Garrick, David 1717-1779 .... **LC 15**
See also DAM DRAM; DLB 84, 213; RGEL 2

Garrigue, Jean 1914-1972 .... **CLC 2, 8**
See also CA 5-8R; 37-40R; CANR 20

Garrison, Frederick
See Sinclair, Upton (Beall)

Garro, Elena 1920(?)-1998
See also CA 131; 169; CWW 2; DLB 145; HLCS 1; HW 1; LAWS 1; WLIT 1

Garth, Will
See Hamilton, Edmond; Kuttner, Henry

Garvey, Marcus (Moziah, Jr.)
1887-1940 .... **TCLC 41; BLC 2**
See also BW 1; CA 120; 124; CANR 79; DAM MULT

Gary, Romain .... **CLC 25**
See also Kacew, Romain
See also DLB 83

Gascar, Pierre .... **CLC 11**
See also Fournier, Pierre

Gascoyne, David (Emery)
1916-2001 .... **CLC 45**
See also CA 65-68; 200; CANR 10, 28, 54; CP 7; DLB 20; MTCW 1; RGEL 2

Gaskell, Elizabeth Cleghorn
1810-1865 .... **NCLC 5, 70, 97; SSC 25**
See also BRW 5; CDBLB 1832-1890; DAB; DAM MST; DLB 21, 144, 159; RGEL 2; RGSF 2

Gass, William H(oward) 1924- . **CLC 1, 2, 8, 11, 15, 39, 132; SSC 12**
See also AMWS 6; CA 17-20R; CANR 30, 71, 100; CN 7; DLB 2, 227; MTCW 1, 2; RGAL 4

Gassendi, Pierre 1592-1655 .... **LC 54**
See also GFL Beginnings to 1789

Gasset, Jose Ortega y
See Ortega y Gasset, Jose

Gates, Henry Louis, Jr. 1950- .... **CLC 65; BLCS**
See also BW 2, 3; CA 109; CANR 25, 53, 75; CSW; DA3; DAM MULT; DLB 67; MTCW 1; RGAL 4

Gautier, Theophile 1811-1872 .. **NCLC 1, 59; PC 18; SSC 20**
See also DAM POET; DLB 119; EW 6; GFL 1789 to the Present; RGWL 2; SUFW

Gawsworth, John
See Bates, H(erbert) E(rnest)

Gay, John 1685-1732 .... **LC 49**
See also BRW 3; DAM DRAM; DLB 84, 95; RGEL 2; WLIT 3

Gay, Oliver
See Gogarty, Oliver St. John

Gay, Peter (Jack) 1923- .... **CLC 158**
See also CA 13-16R; CANR 18, 41, 77; INT CANR-18

Gaye, Marvin (Pentz, Jr.)
1939-1984 .... **CLC 26**
See also CA 195; 112

Gebler, Carlo (Ernest) 1954- .... **CLC 39**
See also CA 119; 133; CANR 96

Gee, Maggie (Mary) 1948- .... **CLC 57**
See also CA 130; CN 7; DLB 207

Gee, Maurice (Gough) 1931- .... **CLC 29**
See also AAYA 42; CA 97-100; CANR 67; CLR 56; CN 7; CWRI 5; MAICYA 2; RGSF 2; SATA 46, 101

Gelbart, Larry (Simon) 1928- .... **CLC 21, 61**
See also Gelbart, Larry
See also CA 73-76; CANR 45, 94

Gelbart, Larry 1928-
See Gelbart, Larry (Simon)
See also CAD; CD 5

Gelber, Jack 1932- .... **CLC 1, 6, 14, 79**
See also CA 1-4R; CAD; CANR 2; DLB 7, 228

Gellhorn, Martha (Ellis)
1908-1998 .... **CLC 14, 60**
See also CA 77-80; 164; CANR 44; CN 7; DLBY 1982, 1998

Genet, Jean 1910-1986 .. **CLC 1, 2, 5, 10, 14, 44, 46**
See also CA 13-16R; CANR 18; DA3; DAM DRAM; DFS 10; DLB 72; DLBY 1986; EW 13; GFL 1789 to the Present; GLL 1; MTCW 1, 2; RGWL 2

Gent, Peter 1942- .... **CLC 29**
See also AITN 1; CA 89-92; DLBY 1982

Gentile, Giovanni 1875-1944 .... **TCLC 96**
See also CA 119

Gentlewoman in New England, A
See Bradstreet, Anne

Gentlewoman in Those Parts, A
See Bradstreet, Anne

Geoffrey of Monmouth c.
1100-1155 .... **CMLC 44**
See also DLB 146

George, Jean
See George, Jean Craighead

George, Jean Craighead 1919- .... **CLC 35**
See also AAYA 8; BYA 2, 4; CA 5-8R; CANR 25; CLR 1; 80; DLB 52; JRDA; MAICYA 1, 2; SATA 2, 68, 124; WYA; YAW

George, Stefan (Anton) 1868-1933 . **TCLC 2, 14**
See also CA 104; 193; EW 8

Georges, Georges Martin
See Simenon, Georges (Jacques Christian)

Gerhardi, William Alexander
See Gerhardie, William Alexander

Gerhardie, William Alexander
1895-1977 .... **CLC 5**
See also CA 25-28R; 73-76; CANR 18; DLB 36; RGEL 2

Gerson, Jean 1363-1429 .... **LC 77**
See also DLB 208

Gersonides 1288-1344 .... **CMLC 49**
See also DLB 115

Gerstler, Amy 1956- .... **CLC 70**
See also CA 146; CANR 99

Gertler, T. .... **CLC 134**
See also CA 116; 121

Ghalib .... **NCLC 39, 78**
See also Ghalib, Asadullah Khan

Ghalib, Asadullah Khan 1797-1869
See Ghalib
See also DAM POET; RGWL 2

Ghelderode, Michel de 1898-1962 ..... **CLC 6, 11; DC 15**
See also CA 85-88; CANR 40, 77; DAM DRAM; EW 11

Ghiselin, Brewster 1903-2001 .... **CLC 23**
See also CA 13-16R; CAAS 10; CANR 13; CP 7

Ghose, Aurabinda 1872-1950 .... **TCLC 63**
See also CA 163

Ghose, Zulfikar 1935- .... **CLC 42**
See also CA 65-68; CANR 67; CN 7; CP 7

Ghosh, Amitav 1956- .... **CLC 44, 153**
See also CA 147; CANR 80; CN 7

Giacosa, Giuseppe 1847-1906 .... **TCLC 7**
See also CA 104

Gibb, Lee
See Waterhouse, Keith (Spencer)

Gibbon, Lewis Grassic .... **TCLC 4**
See also Mitchell, James Leslie
See also RGEL 2

Gibbons, Kaye 1960- .... **CLC 50, 88, 145**
See also AAYA 34; AMWS 10; CA 151; CANR 75; CSW; DA3; DAM POP; MTCW 1; NFS 3; RGAL 4; SATA 117

Gibran, Kahlil 1883-1931 . **TCLC 1, 9; PC 9**
See also CA 104; 150; DA3; DAM POET, POP; MTCW 2

Gibran, Khalil
See Gibran, Kahlil

Gibson, William 1914- .... **CLC 23**
See also CA 9-12R; CAD; CANR 9, 42, 75; CD 5; DA; DAB; DAC; DAM DRAM, MST; DFS 2; DLB 7; LAIT 2; MTCW 2; SATA 66; YAW

Gibson, William (Ford) 1948- ... **CLC 39, 63; SSC 52**
See also AAYA 12; BPFB 2; CA 126; 133; CANR 52, 90, 106; CN 7; CPW; DA3; DAM POP; DLB 251; MTCW 2; SCFW 2; SFW 4

Gide, Andre (Paul Guillaume) 1869-1951 ..... **TCLC 5, 12, 36; SSC 13; WLC**
See also CA 104; 124; DA; DA3; DAB; DAC; DAM MST, NOV; DLB 65; EW 8; GFL 1789 to the Present; MTCW 1, 2; RGSF 2; RGWL 2

Gifford, Barry (Colby) 1946- .... **CLC 34**
See also CA 65-68; CANR 9, 30, 40, 90

Gilbert, Frank
See De Voto, Bernard (Augustine)

Gilbert, W(illiam) S(chwenck) 1836-1911 .... **TCLC 3**
See also CA 104; 173; DAM DRAM, POET; RGEL 2; SATA 36

Gilbreth, Frank B(unker), Jr. 1911-2001 .... **CLC 17**
See also CA 9-12R; SATA 2

Gilchrist, Ellen (Louise) 1935- .. **CLC 34, 48, 143; SSC 14**
See also BPFB 2; CA 113; 116; CANR 41, 61, 104; CN 7; CPW; CSW; DAM POP; DLB 130; EXPS; MTCW 1, 2; RGAL 4; RGSF 2; SSFS 9

Giles, Molly 1942- .... **CLC 39**
See also CA 126; CANR 98

Gill, Eric 1882-1940 .... **TCLC 85**

Gill, Patrick
See Creasey, John

Gillette, Douglas .... **CLC 70**

Gilliam, Terry (Vance) 1940- .... **CLC 21, 141**
See also Monty Python
See also AAYA 19; CA 108; 113; CANR 35; INT 113

Gillian, Jerry
See Gilliam, Terry (Vance)

Gilliatt, Penelope (Ann Douglass) 1932-1993 .... **CLC 2, 10, 13, 53**
See also AITN 2; CA 13-16R; 141; CANR 49; DLB 14

Gilman, Charlotte (Anna) Perkins (Stetson) 1860-1935 ..... **TCLC 9, 37, 117; SSC 13**
See also BYA 11; CA 106; 150; DLB 221; EXPS; FW; HGG; LAIT 2; MAWW; MTCW 1; RGAL 4; RGSF 2; SFW 4; SSFS 1

Gilmour, David 1946- .... **CLC 35**

Gilpin, William 1724-1804 .... **NCLC 30**

Gilray, J. D.
See Mencken, H(enry) L(ouis)

Gilroy, Frank D(aniel) 1925- .... **CLC 2**
See also CA 81-84; CAD; CANR 32, 64, 86; CD 5; DLB 7

Gilstrap, John 1957(?)- .... **CLC 99**
See also CA 160; CANR 101

Ginsberg, Allen 1926-1997 .... **CLC 1, 2, 3, 4, 6, 13, 36, 69, 109; PC 4; WLC**
See also AAYA 33; AITN 1; AMWS 2; CA 1-4R; 157; CANR 2, 41, 63, 95; CDALB 1941-1968; CP 7; DA; DA3; DAB; DAC; DAM MST, POET; DLB 5, 16, 169, 237; GLL 1; MTCW 1, 2; PAB; PFS 5; RGAL 4; TCLC 120; WP

Ginzburg, Eugenia .... **CLC 59**

Ginzburg, Natalia 1916-1991 .... **CLC 5, 11, 54, 70**
See also CA 85-88; 135; CANR 33; DFS 14; DLB 177; EW 13; MTCW 1, 2; RGWL 2

Giono, Jean 1895-1970 .... **CLC 4, 11; TCLC 124**
See also CA 45-48; 29-32R; CANR 2, 35; DLB 72; GFL 1789 to the Present; MTCW 1; RGWL 2

Giovanni, Nikki 1943- .... **CLC 2, 4, 19, 64, 117; BLC 2; PC 19; WLCS**
See also AAYA 22; AITN 1; BW 2, 3; CA 29-32R; CAAS 6; CANR 18, 41, 60, 91; CDALBS; CLR 6, 73; CP 7; CSW; CWP; CWRI 5; DA; DA3; DAB; DAC; DAM MST, MULT, POET; DLB 5, 41; EXPP; INT CANR-18; MAICYA 1, 2; MTCW 1, 2; RGAL 4; SATA 24, 107; YAW

Giovene, Andrea 1904-1998 .... **CLC 7**
See also CA 85-88

Gippius, Zinaida (Nikolayevna) 1869-1945
See Hippius, Zinaida
See also CA 106

Giraudoux, Jean(-Hippolyte) 1882-1944 .... **TCLC 2, 7**
See also CA 104; 196; DAM DRAM; DLB 65; EW 9; GFL 1789 to the Present; RGWL 2

Gironella, Jose Maria 1917-1991 ..... **CLC 11**
See also CA 101; RGWL 2

Gissing, George (Robert) 1857-1903 .... **TCLC 3, 24, 47; SSC 37**
See also BRW 5; CA 105; 167; DLB 18, 135, 184; RGEL 2

Giurlani, Aldo
See Palazzeschi, Aldo

Gladkov, Fyodor (Vasilyevich) 1883-1958 .... **TCLC 27**
See also CA 170

Glanville, Brian (Lester) 1931- .... **CLC 6**
See also CA 5-8R; CAAS 9; CANR 3, 70; CN 7; DLB 15, 139; SATA 42

Glasgow, Ellen (Anderson Gholson) 1873-1945 .... **TCLC 2, 7; SSC 34**
See also AMW; CA 104; 164; DLB 9, 12; MAWW; MTCW 2; RGAL 4; RHW; SSFS 9

Glaspell, Susan 1882(?)-1948 . **TCLC 55; DC 10; SSC 41**
See also AMWS 3; CA 110; 154; DFS 8; DLB 7, 9, 78, 228; MAWW; RGAL 4; SSFS 3; TCWW 2; YABC 2

Glassco, John 1909-1981 .... **CLC 9**
See also CA 13-16R; 102; CANR 15; DLB 68

Glasscock, Amnesia
See Steinbeck, John (Ernst)

Glasser, Ronald J. 1940(?)- .... **CLC 37**

Glassman, Joyce
See Johnson, Joyce

Gleick, James (W.) 1954- .... **CLC 147**
See also CA 131; 137; CANR 97; INT CA-137

Glendinning, Victoria 1937- .... **CLC 50**
See also CA 120; 127; CANR 59, 89; DLB 155

Glissant, Edouard 1928- .... **CLC 10, 68**
See also CA 153; CWW 2; DAM MULT

Gloag, Julian 1930- .... **CLC 40**
See also AITN 1; CA 65-68; CANR 10, 70; CN 7

Glowacki, Aleksander
See Prus, Boleslaw

Gluck, Louise (Elisabeth) 1943- .. **CLC 7, 22, 44, 81, 160; PC 16**
See also AMWS 5; CA 33-36R; CANR 40, 69, 108; CP 7; CWP; DA3; DAM POET; DLB 5; MTCW 2; PFS 5, 15; RGAL 4

Glyn, Elinor 1864-1943 .... **TCLC 72**
See also DLB 153; RHW

Gobineau, Joseph-Arthur 1816-1882 .... **NCLC 17**
See also DLB 123; GFL 1789 to the Present

Godard, Jean-Luc 1930- .... **CLC 20**
See also CA 93-96

Godden, (Margaret) Rumer 1907-1998 .... **CLC 53**
See also AAYA 6; BPFB 2; BYA 2, 5; CA 5-8R; 172; CANR 4, 27, 36, 55, 80; CLR 20; CN 7; CWRI 5; DLB 161; MAICYA 1, 2; RHW; SAAS 12; SATA 3, 36; SATA-Obit 109

Godoy Alcayaga, Lucila 1899-1957 .... **TCLC 2; HLC 2; PC 32**
See also Mistral, Gabriela
See also BW 2; CA 104; 131; CANR 81; DAM MULT; DNFS; HW 1, 2; MTCW 1, 2

Godwin, Gail (Kathleen) 1937- ..... **CLC 5, 8, 22, 31, 69, 125**
See also BPFB 2; CA 29-32R; CANR 15, 43, 69; CN 7; CPW; CSW; DA3; DAM POP; DLB 6, 234; INT CANR-15; MTCW 1, 2

Godwin, William 1756-1836 .... **NCLC 14**
See also CDBLB 1789-1832; CMW 4; DLB 39, 104, 142, 158, 163, 262; HGG; RGEL 2

Goebbels, Josef
See Goebbels, (Paul) Joseph

Goebbels, (Paul) Joseph 1897-1945 .... **TCLC 68**
See also CA 115; 148

Goebbels, Joseph Paul
See Goebbels, (Paul) Joseph

Goethe, Johann Wolfgang von 1749-1832 ... **NCLC 4, 22, 34, 90; PC 5; SSC 38; WLC**
See also CDWLB 2; DA; DA3; DAB; DAC; DAM DRAM, MST, POET; DLB 94; EW 5; RGWL 2

Gogarty, Oliver St. John 1878-1957 .... **TCLC 15**
See also CA 109; 150; DLB 15, 19; RGEL 2

Gogol, Nikolai (Vasilyevich) 1809-1852 .... **NCLC 5, 15, 31; DC 1; SSC 4, 29, 52; WLC**
See also DA; DAB; DAC; DAM DRAM, MST; DFS 12; DLB 198; EW 6; EXPS; RGSF 2; RGWL 2; SSFS 7

Goines, Donald 1937(?)-1974 . **CLC 80; BLC 2**
See also AITN 1; BW 1, 3; CA 124; 114; CANR 82; CMW 4; DA3; DAM MULT, POP; DLB 33

Gold, Herbert 1924- ... **CLC 4, 7, 14, 42, 152**
See also CA 9-12R; CANR 17, 45; CN 7; DLB 2; DLBY 1981

Goldbarth, Albert 1948- .... **CLC 5, 38**
See also CA 53-56; CANR 6, 40; CP 7; DLB 120

Goldberg, Anatol 1910-1982 .... **CLC 34**
See also CA 131; 117

Goldemberg, Isaac 1945- .... **CLC 52**
See also CA 69-72; CAAS 12; CANR 11, 32; HW 1; WLIT 1

Golding, William (Gerald) 1911-1993 ..... **CLC 1, 2, 3, 8, 10, 17, 27, 58, 81; WLC**
See also AAYA 5; BPFB 2; BRWR 1; BRWS 1; BYA 2; CA 5-8R; 141; CANR 13, 33, 54; CDBLB 1945-1960; DA; DA3; DAB; DAC; DAM MST, NOV; DLB 15, 100, 255; EXPN; HGG; LAIT 4; MTCW 1, 2; NFS 2; RGEL 2; RHW; SFW 4; WLIT 4; YAW

Goldman, Emma 1869-1940 .... **TCLC 13**
See also CA 110; 150; DLB 221; FW; RGAL 4

Goldman, Francisco 1954- .... **CLC 76**
See also CA 162

Goldman, William (W.) 1931- ...... **CLC 1, 48**
See also BPFB 2; CA 9-12R; CANR 29, 69, 106; CN 7; DLB 44; FANT; IDFW 3, 4

Goldmann, Lucien 1913-1970 .... **CLC 24**
See also CA 25-28; CAP 2

Goldoni, Carlo 1707-1793 .... **LC 4**
See also DAM DRAM; EW 4; RGWL 2

Goldsberry, Steven 1949- .... **CLC 34**
See also CA 131

Goldsmith, Oliver 1730-1774 .. **LC 2, 48; DC 8; WLC**
See also BRW 3; CDBLB 1660-1789; DA; DAB; DAC; DAM DRAM, MST, NOV, POET; DFS 1; DLB 39, 89, 104, 109, 142; IDTP; RGEL 2; SATA 26; TEA; WLIT 3

Goldsmith, Peter
See Priestley, J(ohn) B(oynton)

Gombrowicz, Witold 1904-1969 .... **CLC 4, 7, 11, 49**
See also CA 19-20; 25-28R; CANR 105; CAP 2; CDWLB 4; DAM DRAM; DLB 215; EW 12; RGWL 2

Gomez de Avellaneda, Gertrudis
1814-1873 .... **NCLC 111**
See also LAW

Gomez de la Serna, Ramon
1888-1963 .... **CLC 9**
See also CA 153; 116; CANR 79; HW 1, 2

Goncharov, Ivan Alexandrovich
1812-1891 .... **NCLC 1, 63**
See also DLB 238; EW 6; RGWL 2

Goncourt, Edmond (Louis Antoine Huot) de
1822-1896 .... **NCLC 7**
See also DLB 123; EW 7; GFL 1789 to the Present; RGWL 2

Goncourt, Jules (Alfred Huot) de
1830-1870 .... **NCLC 7**
See also DLB 123; EW 7; GFL 1789 to the Present; RGWL 2

Gongora (y Argote), Luis de
1561-1627 .... **LC 72**
See also RGWL 2

Gontier, Fernande 19(?)- .... **CLC 50**

Gonzalez Martinez, Enrique
1871-1952 .... **TCLC 72**
See also CA 166; CANR 81; HW 1, 2

Goodison, Lorna 1947- .... **PC 36**
See also CA 142; CANR 88; CP 7; CWP; DLB 157

Goodman, Paul 1911-1972 ..... **CLC 1, 2, 4, 7**
See also CA 19-20; 37-40R; CAD; CANR 34; CAP 2; DLB 130, 246; MTCW 1; RGAL 4

Gordimer, Nadine 1923- ...... **CLC 3, 5, 7, 10, 18, 33, 51, 70, 123, 160, 161; SSC 17; WLCS**
See also AAYA 39; AFW; BRWS 2; CA 5-8R; CANR 3, 28, 56, 88; CN 7; DA; DA3; DAB; DAC; DAM MST, NOV; DLB 225; EXPS; INT CANR-28; MTCW 1, 2; NFS 4; RGEL 2; RGSF 2; SSFS 2, 14; WLIT 2; YAW

Gordon, Adam Lindsay
1833-1870 .... **NCLC 21**
See also DLB 230

Gordon, Caroline 1895-1981 . **CLC 6, 13, 29, 83; SSC 15**
See also AMW; CA 11-12; 103; CANR 36; CAP 1; DLB 4, 9, 102; DLBD 17; DLBY 1981; MTCW 1, 2; RGAL 4; RGSF 2

Gordon, Charles William 1860-1937
See Connor, Ralph
See also CA 109

Gordon, Mary (Catherine) 1949- .... **CLC 13, 22, 128**
See also AMWS 4; BPFB 2; CA 102; CANR 44, 92; CN 7; DLB 6; DLBY 1981; FW; INT CA-102; MTCW 1

Gordon, N. J.
See Bosman, Herman Charles

Gordon, Sol 1923- .... **CLC 26**
See also CA 53-56; CANR 4; SATA 11

Gordone, Charles 1925-1995 .. **CLC 1, 4; DC 8**
See also BW 1, 3; CA 93-96, 180; 150; CAAE 180; CAD; CANR 55; DAM DRAM; DLB 7; INT 93-96; MTCW 1

Gore, Catherine 1800-1861 .... **NCLC 65**
See also DLB 116; RGEL 2

Gorenko, Anna Andreevna
See Akhmatova, Anna

Gorky, Maxim .... **TCLC 8; SSC 28; WLC**
See also Peshkov, Alexei Maximovich
See also DAB; DFS 9; EW 8; MTCW 2

Goryan, Sirak
See Saroyan, William

Gosse, Edmund (William)
1849-1928 .... **TCLC 28**
See also CA 117; DLB 57, 144, 184; RGEL 2

Gotlieb, Phyllis Fay (Bloom) 1926- .. **CLC 18**
See also CA 13-16R; CANR 7; DLB 88, 251; SFW 4

Gottesman, S. D.
See Kornbluth, C(yril) M.; Pohl, Frederik

Gottfried von Strassburg fl. c.
1170-1215 .... **CMLC 10**
See also CDWLB 2; DLB 138; EW 1; RGWL 2

Gould, Lois 1932(?)-2002 .... **CLC 4, 10**
See also CA 77-80; CANR 29; MTCW 1

Gourmont, Remy(-Marie-Charles) de
1858-1915 .... **TCLC 17**
See also CA 109; 150; GFL 1789 to the Present; MTCW 2

Govier, Katherine 1948- .... **CLC 51**
See also CA 101; CANR 18, 40; CCA 1

Gower, John c. 1330-1408 .... **LC 76**
See also BRW 1; DLB 146; RGEL 2

Goyen, (Charles) William
1915-1983 .... **CLC 5, 8, 14, 40**
See also AITN 2; CA 5-8R; 110; CANR 6, 71; DLB 2, 218; DLBY 1983; INT CANR-6

Goytisolo, Juan 1931- .... **CLC 5, 10, 23, 133; HLC 1**
See also CA 85-88; CANR 32, 61; CWW 2; DAM MULT; GLL 2; HW 1, 2; MTCW 1, 2

Gozzano, Guido 1883-1916 .... **PC 10**
See also CA 154; DLB 114

Gozzi, (Conte) Carlo 1720-1806 .... **NCLC 23**

Grabbe, Christian Dietrich
1801-1836 .... **NCLC 2**
See also DLB 133; RGWL 2

Grace, Patricia Frances 1937- .... **CLC 56**
See also CA 176; CN 7; RGSF 2

Gracian y Morales, Baltasar
1601-1658 .... **LC 15**

Gracq, Julien .... **CLC 11, 48**
See also Poirier, Louis
See also CWW 2; DLB 83; GFL 1789 to the Present

Grade, Chaim 1910-1982 .... **CLC 10**
See also CA 93-96; 107

Graduate of Oxford, A
See Ruskin, John

Grafton, Garth
See Duncan, Sara Jeannette

Graham, John
See Phillips, David Graham

Graham, Jorie 1951- .... **CLC 48, 118**
See also CA 111; CANR 63; CP 7; CWP; DLB 120; PFS 10

Graham, R(obert) B(ontine) Cunninghame
See Cunninghame Graham, Robert (Gallnigad) Bontine
See also DLB 98, 135, 174; RGEL 2; RGSF 2

Graham, Robert
See Haldeman, Joe (William)

Graham, Tom
See Lewis, (Harry) Sinclair

Graham, W(illiam) S(idney)
1918-1986 .... **CLC 29**
See also BRWS 7; CA 73-76; 118; DLB 20; RGEL 2

Graham, Winston (Mawdsley)
1910- .... **CLC 23**
See also CA 49-52; CANR 2, 22, 45, 66; CMW 4; CN 7; DLB 77; RHW

Grahame, Kenneth 1859-1932 .... **TCLC 64**
See also BYA 5; CA 108; 136; CANR 80; CLR 5; CWRI 5; DA3; DAB; DLB 34, 141, 178; FANT; MAICYA 1, 2; MTCW 2; RGEL 2; SATA 100; WCH; YABC 1

Granger, Darius John
See Marlowe, Stephen

Granin, Daniil .... **CLC 59**

Granovsky, Timofei Nikolaevich
1813-1855 .... **NCLC 75**
See also DLB 198

Grant, Skeeter
See Spiegelman, Art

Granville-Barker, Harley
1877-1946 .... **TCLC 2**
See also Barker, Harley Granville
See also CA 104; DAM DRAM; RGEL 2

Granzotto, Gianni
See Granzotto, Giovanni Battista

Granzotto, Giovanni Battista
1914-1985 .... **CLC 70**
See also CA 166

Grass, Guenter (Wilhelm) 1927- ... **CLC 1, 2, 4, 6, 11, 15, 22, 32, 49, 88; WLC**
See also BPFB 2; CA 13-16R; CANR 20, 75, 93; CDWLB 2; DA; DA3; DAB; DAC; DAM MST, NOV; DLB 75, 124; EW 13; MTCW 1, 2; RGWL 2

Gratton, Thomas
See Hulme, T(homas) E(rnest)

Grau, Shirley Ann 1929- .... **CLC 4, 9, 146; SSC 15**
See also CA 89-92; CANR 22, 69; CN 7; CSW; DLB 2, 218; INT CA-89-92, CANR-22; MTCW 1

Gravel, Fern
See Hall, James Norman

Graver, Elizabeth 1964- .... **CLC 70**
See also CA 135; CANR 71

Graves, Richard Perceval
1895-1985 .... **CLC 44**
See also CA 65-68; CANR 9, 26, 51

Graves, Robert (von Ranke)
1895-1985 .. **CLC 1, 2, 6, 11, 39, 44, 45; PC 6**
See also BPFB 2; BRW 7; BYA 4; CA 5-8R; 117; CANR 5, 36; CDBLB 1914-1945; DA3; DAB; DAC; DAM MST, POET; DLB 20, 100, 191; DLBD 18; DLBY 1985; MTCW 1, 2; NCFS 2; RGEL 2; RHW; SATA 45

Graves, Valerie
See Bradley, Marion Zimmer

Gray, Alasdair (James) 1934- .... **CLC 41**
See also CA 126; CANR 47, 69, 106; CN 7; DLB 194, 261; HGG; INT CA-126; MTCW 1, 2; RGSF 2

Gray, Amlin 1946- .... **CLC 29**
See also CA 138

Gray, Francine du Plessix 1930- ..... **CLC 22, 153**
See also BEST 90:3; CA 61-64; CAAS 2; CANR 11, 33, 75, 81; DAM NOV; INT CANR-11; MTCW 1, 2

Gray, John (Henry) 1866-1934 ...... **TCLC 19**
See also CA 119; 162; RGEL 2

Gray, Simon (James Holliday) 1936- ..... **CLC 9, 14, 36**
See also AITN 1; CA 21-24R; CAAS 3; CANR 32, 69; CD 5; DLB 13; MTCW 1; RGEL 2

Gray, Spalding 1941- ..... **CLC 49, 112; DC 7**
See also CA 128; CAD; CANR 74; CD 5; CPW; DAM POP; MTCW 2

Gray, Thomas 1716-1771 .... **LC 4, 40; PC 2; WLC**
See also BRW 3; CDBLB 1660-1789; DA; DA3; DAB; DAC; DAM MST; DLB 109; EXPP; PAB; PFS 9; RGEL 2; WP

Grayson, David
See Baker, Ray Stannard

Grayson, Richard (A.) 1951- .... **CLC 38**
See also CA 85-88; CANR 14, 31, 57; DLB 234

Greeley, Andrew M(oran) 1928- ...... **CLC 28**
See also BPFB 2; CA 5-8R; CAAS 7; CANR 7, 43, 69, 104; CMW 4; CPW; DA3; DAM POP; MTCW 1, 2

Green, Anna Katharine 1846-1935 .... **TCLC 63**
See also CA 112; 159; CMW 4; DLB 202, 221; MSW

Green, Brian
See Card, Orson Scott

Green, Hannah
See Greenberg, Joanne (Goldenberg)

Green, Hannah 1927(?)-1996 .... **CLC 3**
See also CA 73-76; CANR 59, 93; NFS 10

Green, Henry .... **CLC 2, 13, 97**
See also Yorke, Henry Vincent
See also BRWS 2; CA 175; DLB 15; RGEL 2

Green, Julian (Hartridge) 1900-1998
See Green, Julien
See also CA 21-24R; 169; CANR 33, 87; DLB 4, 72; MTCW 1

Green, Julien .... **CLC 3, 11, 77**
See also Green, Julian (Hartridge)
See also GFL 1789 to the Present; MTCW 2

Green, Paul (Eliot) 1894-1981 .... **CLC 25**
See also AITN 1; CA 5-8R; 103; CANR 3; DAM DRAM; DLB 7, 9, 249; DLBY 1981; RGAL 4

Greenaway, Peter 1942- .... **CLC 159**
See also CA 127

Greenberg, Ivan 1908-1973
See Rahv, Philip
See also CA 85-88

Greenberg, Joanne (Goldenberg) 1932- .... **CLC 7, 30**
See also AAYA 12; CA 5-8R; CANR 14, 32, 69; CN 7; SATA 25; YAW

Greenberg, Richard 1959(?)- .... **CLC 57**
See also CA 138; CAD; CD 5

Greenblatt, Stephen J(ay) 1943- .... **CLC 70**
See also CA 49-52

Greene, Bette 1934- .... **CLC 30**
See also AAYA 7; BYA 3; CA 53-56; CANR 4; CLR 2; CWRI 5; JRDA; LAIT 4; MAICYA 1, 2; NFS 10; SAAS 16; SATA 8, 102; WYA; YAW

Greene, Gael .... **CLC 8**
See also CA 13-16R; CANR 10

Greene, Graham (Henry) 1904-1991 .... **CLC 1, 3, 6, 9, 14, 18, 27, 37, 70, 72, 125; SSC 29; WLC**
See also AITN 2; BPFB 2; BRWR 2; BRWS 1; BYA 3; CA 13-16R; 133; CANR 35, 61; CBD; CDBLB 1945-1960; CMW 4; DA; DA3; DAB; DAC; DAM MST, NOV; DLB 13, 15, 77, 100, 162, 201, 204; DLBY 1991; MSW; MTCW 1, 2; RGEL 2; SATA 20; SSFS 14; WLIT 4

Greene, Robert 1558-1592 .... **LC 41**
See also DLB 62, 167; IDTP; RGEL 2; TEA

Greer, Germaine 1939- .... **CLC 131**
See also AITN 1; CA 81-84; CANR 33, 70; FW; MTCW 1, 2

Greer, Richard
See Silverberg, Robert

Gregor, Arthur 1923- .... **CLC 9**
See also CA 25-28R; CAAS 10; CANR 11; CP 7; SATA 36

Gregor, Lee
See Pohl, Frederik

Gregory, Lady Isabella Augusta (Persse) 1852-1932 .... **TCLC 1**
See also BRW 6; CA 104; 184; DLB 10; IDTP; RGEL 2

Gregory, J. Dennis
See Williams, John A(lfred)

Grekova, I. .... **CLC 59**

Grendon, Stephen
See Derleth, August (William)

Grenville, Kate 1950- .... **CLC 61**
See also CA 118; CANR 53, 93

Grenville, Pelham
See Wodehouse, P(elham) G(renville)

Greve, Felix Paul (Berthold Friedrich) 1879-1948
See Grove, Frederick Philip
See also CA 104; 141, 175; CANR 79; DAC; DAM MST

Greville, Fulke 1554-1628 .... **LC 79**
See also DLB 62, 172; RGEL 2

Grey, Zane 1872-1939 .... **TCLC 6**
See also BPFB 2; CA 104; 132; DA3; DAM POP; DLB 9, 212; MTCW 1, 2; RGAL 4; TCWW 2

Grieg, (Johan) Nordahl (Brun) 1902-1943 .... **TCLC 10**
See also CA 107; 189

Grieve, C(hristopher) M(urray) 1892-1978 .... **CLC 11, 19**
See also MacDiarmid, Hugh; Pteleon
See also CA 5-8R; 85-88; CANR 33, 107; DAM POET; MTCW 1; RGEL 2

Griffin, Gerald 1803-1840 .... **NCLC 7**
See also DLB 159; RGEL 2

Griffin, John Howard 1920-1980 ..... **CLC 68**
See also AITN 1; CA 1-4R; 101; CANR 2

Griffin, Peter 1942- .... **CLC 39**
See also CA 136

Griffith, D(avid Lewelyn) W(ark) 1875(?)-1948 .... **TCLC 68**
See also CA 119; 150; CANR 80

Griffith, Lawrence
See Griffith, D(avid Lewelyn) W(ark)

Griffiths, Trevor 1935- .... **CLC 13, 52**
See also CA 97-100; CANR 45; CBD; CD 5; DLB 13, 245

Griggs, Sutton (Elbert) 1872-1930 .... **TCLC 77**
See also CA 123; 186; DLB 50

Grigson, Geoffrey (Edward Harvey) 1905-1985 .... **CLC 7, 39**
See also CA 25-28R; 118; CANR 20, 33; DLB 27; MTCW 1, 2

Grillparzer, Franz 1791-1872 . **NCLC 1, 102; DC 14; SSC 37**
See also CDWLB 2; DLB 133; EW 5; RGWL 2

Grimble, Reverend Charles James
See Eliot, T(homas) S(tearns)

Grimke, Charlotte L(ottie) Forten 1837(?)-1914
See Forten, Charlotte L.
See also BW 1; CA 117; 124; DAM MULT, POET

Grimm, Jacob Ludwig Karl 1785-1863 .... **NCLC 3, 77; SSC 36**
See also DLB 90; MAICYA 1, 2; RGSF 2; RGWL 2; SATA 22; WCH

Grimm, Wilhelm Karl 1786-1859 .. **NCLC 3, 77; SSC 36**
See also CDWLB 2; DLB 90; MAICYA 1, 2; RGSF 2; RGWL 2; SATA 22; WCH

Grimmelshausen, Hans Jakob Christoffel von
See Grimmelshausen, Johann Jakob Christoffel von
See also RGWL 2

Grimmelshausen, Johann Jakob Christoffel von 1621-1676 .... **LC 6**
See also Grimmelshausen, Hans Jakob Christoffel von
See also CDWLB 2; DLB 168

Grindel, Eugene 1895-1952
See Eluard, Paul
See also CA 104; 193

Grisham, John 1955- .... **CLC 84**
See also AAYA 14; BPFB 2; CA 138; CANR 47, 69; CMW 4; CN 7; CPW; CSW; DA3; DAM POP; MSW; MTCW 2

Grossman, David 1954- .... **CLC 67**
See also CA 138; CWW 2

Grossman, Vasily (Semenovich) 1905-1964 .... **CLC 41**
See also CA 124; 130; MTCW 1

Grove, Frederick Philip .... **TCLC 4**
See also Greve, Felix Paul (Berthold Friedrich)
See also DLB 92; RGEL 2

Grubb
See Crumb, R(obert)

Grumbach, Doris (Isaac) 1918- . **CLC 13, 22, 64**
See also CA 5-8R; CAAS 2; CANR 9, 42, 70; CN 7; INT CANR-9; MTCW 2

Grundtvig, Nicolai Frederik Severin 1783-1872 .... **NCLC 1**

Grunge
See Crumb, R(obert)

Grunwald, Lisa 1959- .... **CLC 44**
See also CA 120

Guare, John 1938- .... **CLC 8, 14, 29, 67**
See also CA 73-76; CAD; CANR 21, 69; CD 5; DAM DRAM; DFS 8, 13; DLB 7, 249; MTCW 1, 2; RGAL 4

Gubar, Susan (David) 1944- .... **CLC 145**
See also CA 108; CANR 45, 70; FW; MTCW 1; RGAL 4

Gudjonsson, Halldor Kiljan 1902-1998
See Laxness, Halldor
See also CA 103; 164; CWW 2

Guenter, Erich
See Eich, Guenter

Guest, Barbara 1920- .... **CLC 34**
See also CA 25-28R; CANR 11, 44, 84; CP 7; CWP; DLB 5, 193

Guest, Edgar A(lbert) 1881-1959 ... **TCLC 95**
See also CA 112; 168

Guest, Judith (Ann) 1936- .... **CLC 8, 30**
See also AAYA 7; CA 77-80; CANR 15, 75; DA3; DAM NOV, POP; EXPN; INT CANR-15; LAIT 5; MTCW 1, 2; NFS 1

Guevara, Che .... **CLC 87; HLC 1**
See also Guevara (Serna), Ernesto

Guevara (Serna), Ernesto
1928-1967 .... **CLC 87; HLC 1**
See also Guevara, Che
See also CA 127; 111; CANR 56; DAM MULT; HW 1

Guicciardini, Francesco 1483-1540 ..... **LC 49**

Guild, Nicholas M. 1944- .... **CLC 33**
See also CA 93-96

Guillemin, Jacques
See Sartre, Jean-Paul

Guillen, Jorge 1893-1984 . **CLC 11; HLCS 1; PC 35**
See also CA 89-92; 112; DAM MULT, POET; DLB 108; HW 1; RGWL 2

Guillen, Nicolas (Cristobal)
1902-1989 .... **CLC 48, 79; BLC 2; HLC 1; PC 23**
See also BW 2; CA 116; 125; 129; CANR 84; DAM MST, MULT, POET; HW 1; LAW; RGWL 2; WP

Guillen y Alavarez, Jorge
See Guillen, Jorge

Guillevic, (Eugene) 1907-1997 .... **CLC 33**
See also CA 93-96; CWW 2

Guillois
See Desnos, Robert

Guillois, Valentin
See Desnos, Robert

Guimaraes Rosa, Joao
See Rosa, Joao Guimaraes
See also LAW

Guimaraes Rosa, Joao 1908-1967
See also CA 175; HLCS 2; LAW; RGSF 2; RGWL 2

Guiney, Louise Imogen
1861-1920 .... **TCLC 41**
See also CA 160; DLB 54; RGAL 4

Guinizelli, Guido c. 1230-1276 ...... **CMLC 49**

Guiraldes, Ricardo (Guillermo)
1886-1927 .... **TCLC 39**
See also CA 131; HW 1; LAW; MTCW 1

Gumilev, Nikolai (Stepanovich)
1886-1921 .... **TCLC 60**
See also CA 165

Gunesekera, Romesh 1954- .... **CLC 91**
See also CA 159; CN 7

Gunn, Bill .... **CLC 5**
See also Gunn, William Harrison
See also DLB 38

Gunn, Thom(son William) 1929- .. **CLC 3, 6, 18, 32, 81; PC 26**
See also BRWS 4; CA 17-20R; CANR 9, 33; CDBLB 1960 to Present; CP 7; DAM POET; DLB 27; INT CANR-33; MTCW 1; PFS 9; RGEL 2

Gunn, William Harrison 1934(?)-1989
See Gunn, Bill
See also AITN 1; BW 1, 3; CA 13-16R; 128; CANR 12, 25, 76

Gunn Allen, Paula
See Allen, Paula Gunn

Gunnars, Kristjana 1948- .... **CLC 69**
See also CA 113; CCA 1; CP 7; CWP; DLB 60

Gurdjieff, G(eorgei) I(vanovich)
1877(?)-1949 .... **TCLC 71**
See also CA 157

Gurganus, Allan 1947- .... **CLC 70**
See also BEST 90:1; CA 135; CN 7; CPW; CSW; DAM POP; GLL 1

Gurney, A(lbert) R(amsdell), Jr.
1930- .... **CLC 32, 50, 54**
See also AMWS 5; CA 77-80; CAD; CANR 32, 64; CD 5; DAM DRAM

Gurney, Ivor (Bertie) 1890-1937 ... **TCLC 33**
See also BRW 6; CA 167; PAB; RGEL 2

Gurney, Peter
See Gurney, A(lbert) R(amsdell), Jr.

Guro, Elena 1877-1913 .... **TCLC 56**

Gustafson, James M(oody) 1925- ... **CLC 100**
See also CA 25-28R; CANR 37

Gustafson, Ralph (Barker)
1909-1995 .... **CLC 36**
See also CA 21-24R; CANR 8, 45, 84; CP 7; DLB 88; RGEL 2

Gut, Gom
See Simenon, Georges (Jacques Christian)

Guterson, David 1956- .... **CLC 91**
See also CA 132; CANR 73; MTCW 2; NFS 13

Guthrie, A(lfred) B(ertram), Jr.
1901-1991 .... **CLC 23**
See also CA 57-60; 134; CANR 24; DLB 6, 212; SATA 62; SATA-Obit 67

Guthrie, Isobel
See Grieve, C(hristopher) M(urray)

Guthrie, Woodrow Wilson 1912-1967
See Guthrie, Woody
See also CA 113; 93-96

Guthrie, Woody .... **CLC 35**
See also Guthrie, Woodrow Wilson
See also LAIT 3

Gutierrez Najera, Manuel 1859-1895
See also HLCS 2; LAW

Guy, Rosa (Cuthbert) 1925- .... **CLC 26**
See also AAYA 4, 37; BW 2; CA 17-20R; CANR 14, 34, 83; CLR 13; DLB 33; DNFS 1; JRDA; MAICYA 1, 2; SATA 14, 62, 122; YAW

Gwendolyn
See Bennett, (Enoch) Arnold

H. D. .... **CLC 3, 8, 14, 31, 34, 73; PC 5**
See also Doolittle, Hilda

H. de V.
See Buchan, John

Haavikko, Paavo Juhani 1931- .. **CLC 18, 34**
See also CA 106

Habbema, Koos
See Heijermans, Herman

Habermas, Juergen 1929- .... **CLC 104**
See also CA 109; CANR 85; DLB 242

Habermas, Jurgen
See Habermas, Juergen

Hacker, Marilyn 1942- . **CLC 5, 9, 23, 72, 91**
See also CA 77-80; CANR 68; CP 7; CWP; DAM POET; DLB 120; FW; GLL 2

Hadrian 76-138 .... **CMLC 52**

Haeckel, Ernst Heinrich (Philipp August)
1834-1919 .... **TCLC 83**
See also CA 157

Hafiz c. 1326-1389(?) .... **CMLC 34**
See also RGWL 2

Haggard, H(enry) Rider
1856-1925 .... **TCLC 11**
See also BRWS 3; BYA 4, 5; CA 108; 148; DLB 70, 156, 174, 178; FANT; MTCW 2; RGEL 2; RHW; SATA 16; SCFW; SFW 4; SUFW; WLIT 4

Hagiosy, L.
See Larbaud, Valery (Nicolas)

Hagiwara, Sakutaro 1886-1942 .... **TCLC 60; PC 18**
See also CA 154

Haig, Fenil
See Ford, Ford Madox

Haig-Brown, Roderick (Langmere)
1908-1976 .... **CLC 21**
See also CA 5-8R; 69-72; CANR 4, 38, 83; CLR 31; CWRI 5; DLB 88; MAICYA 1, 2; SATA 12

Hailey, Arthur 1920- .... **CLC 5**
See also AITN 2; BEST 90:3; BPFB 2; CA 1-4R; CANR 2, 36, 75; CCA 1; CN 7; CPW; DAM NOV, POP; DLB 88; DLBY 1982; MTCW 1, 2

Hailey, Elizabeth Forsythe 1938- ..... **CLC 40**
See also CA 93-96; CAAE 188; CAAS 1; CANR 15, 48; INT CANR-15

Haines, John (Meade) 1924- .... **CLC 58**
See also CA 17-20R; CANR 13, 34; CSW; DLB 5, 212

Hakluyt, Richard 1552-1616 .... **LC 31**
See also DLB 136; RGEL 2

Haldeman, Joe (William) 1943- .... **CLC 61**
See also Graham, Robert
See also AAYA 38; CA 53-56, 179; CAAE 179; CAAS 25; CANR 6, 70, 72; DLB 8; INT CANR-6; SCFW 2; SFW 4

Hale, Sarah Josepha (Buell)
1788-1879 .... **NCLC 75**
See also DLB 1, 42, 73, 243

Halevy, Elie 1870-1937 .... **TCLC 104**

Haley, Alex(ander Murray Palmer)
1921-1992 .... **CLC 8, 12, 76; BLC 2**
See also AAYA 26; BPFB 2; BW 2, 3; CA 77-80; 136; CANR 61; CDALBS; CPW; CSW; DA; DA3; DAB; DAC; DAM MST, MULT, POP; DLB 38; LAIT 5; MTCW 1, 2; NFS 9

Haliburton, Thomas Chandler
1796-1865 .... **NCLC 15**
See also DLB 11, 99; RGEL 2; RGSF 2

Hall, Donald (Andrew, Jr.) 1928- .... **CLC 1, 13, 37, 59, 151**
See also CA 5-8R; CAAS 7; CANR 2, 44, 64, 106; CP 7; DAM POET; DLB 5; MTCW 1; RGAL 4; SATA 23, 97

Hall, Frederic Sauser
See Sauser-Hall, Frederic

Hall, James
See Kuttner, Henry

Hall, James Norman 1887-1951 ..... **TCLC 23**
See also CA 123; 173; LAIT 1; RHW 1; SATA 21

Hall, (Marguerite) Radclyffe
1880-1943 .... **TCLC 12**
See also BRWS 6; CA 110; 150; CANR 83; DLB 191; MTCW 2; RGEL 2; RHW

Hall, Rodney 1935- .... **CLC 51**
See also CA 109; CANR 69; CN 7; CP 7

Hallam, Arthur Henry
1811-1833 .... **NCLC 110**
See also DLB 32

Halleck, Fitz-Greene 1790-1867 .... **NCLC 47**
See also DLB 3, 250; RGAL 4

Halliday, Michael
See Creasey, John

Halpern, Daniel 1945- .... **CLC 14**
See also CA 33-36R; CANR 93; CP 7

Hamburger, Michael (Peter Leopold)
1924- .... **CLC 5, 14**
See also CA 5-8R; CAAE 196; CAAS 4; CANR 2, 47; CP 7; DLB 27

Hamill, Pete 1935- .... **CLC 10**
See also CA 25-28R; CANR 18, 71

Hamilton, Alexander
1755(?)-1804 .... **NCLC 49**
See also DLB 37

Hamilton, Clive
See Lewis, C(live) S(taples)

Hamilton, Edmond 1904-1977 .... **CLC 1**
See also CA 1-4R; CANR 3, 84; DLB 8; SATA 118; SFW 4

Hamilton, Eugene (Jacob) Lee
See Lee-Hamilton, Eugene (Jacob)

Hamilton, Franklin
See Silverberg, Robert

Hamilton, Gail
See Corcoran, Barbara (Asenath)

Hamilton, Mollie
See Kaye, M(ary) M(argaret)

Hamilton, (Anthony Walter) Patrick
1904-1962 .... **CLC 51**
See also CA 176; 113; DLB 10, 191

Hamilton, Virginia (Esther)
1936-2002 .... **CLC 26**
See also AAYA 2, 21; BW 2, 3; BYA 1, 2, 8; CA 25-28R; CANR 20, 37, 73; CLR 1, 11, 40; DAM MULT; DLB 33, 52; DLBY 01; INT CANR-20; JRDA; LAIT 5; MAICYA 1, 2; MAICYAS 1; MTCW 1, 2; SATA 4, 56, 79, 123; SATA-Obit 132; WYA; YAW

Hammett, (Samuel) Dashiell
1894-1961 .... **CLC 3, 5, 10, 19, 47; SSC 17**
See also AITN 1; AMWS 4; BPFB 2; CA 81-84; CANR 42; CDALB 1929-1941; CMW 4; DA3; DLB 226; DLBD 6; DLBY 1996; LAIT 3; MSW; MTCW 1, 2; RGAL 4; RGSF 2

Hammon, Jupiter 1720(?)-1800(?) . **NCLC 5; BLC 2; PC 16**
See also DAM MULT, POET; DLB 31, 50

Hammond, Keith
See Kuttner, Henry

Hamner, Earl (Henry), Jr. 1923- ..... **CLC 12**
See also AITN 2; CA 73-76; DLB 6

Hampton, Christopher (James)
1946- .... **CLC 4**
See also CA 25-28R; CD 5; DLB 13; MTCW 1

Hamsun, Knut .... **TCLC 2, 14, 49**
See also Pedersen, Knut
See also EW 8; RGWL 2

Handke, Peter 1942- .... **CLC 5, 8, 10, 15, 38, 134; DC 17**
See also CA 77-80; CANR 33, 75, 104; CWW 2; DAM DRAM, NOV; DLB 85, 124; MTCW 1, 2

Handy, W(illiam) C(hristopher)
1873-1958 .... **TCLC 97**
See also BW 3; CA 121; 167

Hanley, James 1901-1985 ...... **CLC 3, 5, 8, 13**
See also CA 73-76; 117; CANR 36; CBD; DLB 191; MTCW 1; RGEL 2

Hannah, Barry 1942- .... **CLC 23, 38, 90**
See also BPFB 2; CA 108; 110; CANR 43, 68; CN 7; CSW; DLB 6, 234; INT CA-110; MTCW 1; RGSF 2

Hannon, Ezra
See Hunter, Evan

Hansberry, Lorraine (Vivian)
1930-1965 ... **CLC 17, 62; BLC 2; DC 2**
See also AAYA 25; AFAW 1, 2; AMWS 4; BW 1, 3; CA 109; 25-28R; CABS 3; CANR 58; CDALB 1941-1968; DA; DA3; DAB; DAC; DAM DRAM, MST, MULT; DFS 2; DLB 7, 38; FW; LAIT 4; MTCW 1, 2; RGAL 4

Hansen, Joseph 1923- .... **CLC 38**
See also Brock, Rose; Colton, James
See also BPFB 2; CA 29-32R; CAAS 17; CANR 16, 44, 66; CMW 4; DLB 226; GLL 1; INT CANR-16

Hansen, Martin A(lfred)
1909-1955 .... **TCLC 32**
See also CA 167; DLB 214

Hansen and Philipson eds. .... **CLC 65**

Hanson, Kenneth O(stlin) 1922- ...... **CLC 13**
See also CA 53-56; CANR 7

Hardwick, Elizabeth (Bruce) 1916- . **CLC 13**
See also AMWS 3; CA 5-8R; CANR 3, 32, 70, 100; CN 7; CSW; DA3; DAM NOV; DLB 6; MAWW; MTCW 1, 2

Hardy, Thomas 1840-1928 .. **TCLC 4, 10, 18, 32, 48, 53, 72; PC 8; SSC 2; WLC**
See also BRW 6; BRWR 1; CA 104; 123; CDBLB 1890-1914; DA; DA3; DAB; DAC; DAM MST, NOV, POET; DLB 18, 19, 135; EXPN; EXPP; LAIT 2; MTCW 1, 2; NFS 3, 11, 15; PFS 3, 4; RGEL 2; RGSF 2; WLIT 4

Hare, David 1947- .... **CLC 29, 58, 136**
See also BRWS 4; CA 97-100; CANR 39, 91; CBD; CD 5; DFS 4, 7; DLB 13; MTCW 1

Harewood, John
See Van Druten, John (William)

Harford, Henry
See Hudson, W(illiam) H(enry)

Hargrave, Leonie
See Disch, Thomas M(ichael)

Harjo, Joy 1951- .... **CLC 83; PC 27**
See also CA 114; CANR 35, 67, 91; CP 7; CWP; DAM MULT; DLB 120, 175; MTCW 2; NNAL; PFS 15; RGAL 4

Harlan, Louis R(udolph) 1922- .... **CLC 34**
See also CA 21-24R; CANR 25, 55, 80

Harling, Robert 1951(?)- .... **CLC 53**
See also CA 147

Harmon, William (Ruth) 1938- .... **CLC 38**
See also CA 33-36R; CANR 14, 32, 35; SATA 65

Harper, F. E. W.
See Harper, Frances Ellen Watkins

Harper, Frances E. W.
See Harper, Frances Ellen Watkins

Harper, Frances E. Watkins
See Harper, Frances Ellen Watkins

Harper, Frances Ellen
See Harper, Frances Ellen Watkins

Harper, Frances Ellen Watkins
1825-1911 ..... **TCLC 14; BLC 2; PC 21**
See also AFAW 1, 2; BW 1, 3; CA 111; 125; CANR 79; DAM MULT, POET; DLB 50, 221; MAWW; RGAL 4

Harper, Michael S(teven) 1938- ... **CLC 7, 22**
See also AFAW 2; BW 1; CA 33-36R; CANR 24, 108; CP 7; DLB 41; RGAL 4

Harper, Mrs. F. E. W.
See Harper, Frances Ellen Watkins

Harpur, Charles 1813-1868 .... **NCLC 114**
See also DLB 230; RGEL 2

Harris, Christie (Lucy) Irwin
1907-2002 .... **CLC 12**
See also CA 5-8R; CANR 6, 83; CLR 47; DLB 88; JRDA; MAICYA 1, 2; SAAS 10; SATA 6, 74; SATA-Essay 116

Harris, Frank 1856-1931 .... **TCLC 24**
See also CA 109; 150; CANR 80; DLB 156, 197; RGEL 2

Harris, George Washington
1814-1869 .... **NCLC 23**
See also DLB 3, 11, 248; RGAL 4

Harris, Joel Chandler 1848-1908 ... **TCLC 2; SSC 19**
See also CA 104; 137; CANR 80; CLR 49; DLB 11, 23, 42, 78, 91; LAIT 2; MAICYA 1, 2; RGSF 2; SATA 100; WCH; YABC 1

Harris, John (Wyndham Parkes Lucas) Beynon 1903-1969
See Wyndham, John
See also CA 102; 89-92; CANR 84; SATA 118; SFW 4

Harris, MacDonald .... **CLC 9**
See also Heiney, Donald (William)

Harris, Mark 1922- .... **CLC 19**
See also CA 5-8R; CAAS 3; CANR 2, 55, 83; CN 7; DLB 2; DLBY 1980

Harris, Norman .... **CLC 65**

Harris, (Theodore) Wilson 1921- .... **CLC 25, 159**
See also BRWS 5; BW 2, 3; CA 65-68; CAAS 16; CANR 11, 27, 69; CDWLB 3; CN 7; CP 7; DLB 117; MTCW 1; RGEL 2

Harrison, Barbara Grizzuti 1934- . **CLC 144**
See also CA 77-80; CANR 15, 48; INT CANR-15

Harrison, Elizabeth (Allen) Cavanna
1909-2001
See Cavanna, Betty
See also CA 9-12R; 200; CANR 6, 27, 85, 104; MAICYA 2; YAW

Harrison, Harry (Max) 1925- .... **CLC 42**
See also CA 1-4R; CANR 5, 21, 84; DLB 8; SATA 4; SCFW 2; SFW 4

Harrison, James (Thomas) 1937- ...... **CLC 6, 14, 33, 66, 143; SSC 19**
See also Harrison, Jim
See also CA 13-16R; CANR 8, 51, 79; CN 7; CP 7; DLBY 1982; INT CANR-8

Harrison, Jim
See Harrison, James (Thomas)
See also AMWS 8; RGAL 4; TCWW 2

Harrison, Kathryn 1961- .... **CLC 70, 151**
See also CA 144; CANR 68

Harrison, Tony 1937- .... **CLC 43, 129**
See also BRWS 5; CA 65-68; CANR 44, 98; CBD; CD 5; CP 7; DLB 40, 245; MTCW 1; RGEL 2

Harriss, Will(ard Irvin) 1922- .... **CLC 34**
See also CA 111

Harson, Sley
See Ellison, Harlan (Jay)

Hart, Ellis
See Ellison, Harlan (Jay)

Hart, Josephine 1942(?)- .... **CLC 70**
See also CA 138; CANR 70; CPW; DAM POP

Hart, Moss 1904-1961 .... **CLC 66**
See also CA 109; 89-92; CANR 84; DAM DRAM; DFS 1; DLB 7; RGAL 4

Harte, (Francis) Bret(t)
1836(?)-1902 .... **TCLC 1, 25; SSC 8; WLC**
See also AMWS 2; CA 104; 140; CANR 80; CDALB 1865-1917; DA; DA3; DAC; DAM MST; DLB 12, 64, 74, 79, 186; EXPS; LAIT 2; RGAL 4; RGSF 2; SATA 26; SSFS 3

Hartley, L(eslie) P(oles) 1895-1972 ... **CLC 2, 22**
See also BRWS 7; CA 45-48; 37-40R; CANR 33; DLB 15, 139; HGG; MTCW 1, 2; RGEL 2; RGSF 2; SUFW

Hartman, Geoffrey H. 1929- .... **CLC 27**
See also CA 117; 125; CANR 79; DLB 67

Hartmann, Sadakichi 1869-1944 ... **TCLC 73**
See also CA 157; DLB 54

Hartmann von Aue c. 1170-c. 1210 .... **CMLC 15**
See also CDWLB 2; DLB 138; RGWL 2

Hartog, Jan de
See de Hartog, Jan

Haruf, Kent 1943- .... **CLC 34**
See also CA 149; CANR 91

Harwood, Ronald 1934- .... **CLC 32**
See also CA 1-4R; CANR 4, 55; CBD; CD 5; DAM DRAM, MST; DLB 13

Hasegawa Tatsunosuke
See Futabatei, Shimei

Hasek, Jaroslav (Matej Frantisek)
1883-1923 .... **TCLC 4**
See also CA 104; 129; CDWLB 4; DLB 215; EW 9; MTCW 1, 2; RGSF 2; RGWL 2

Hass, Robert 1941- ... **CLC 18, 39, 99; PC 16**
See also AMWS 6; CA 111; CANR 30, 50, 71; CP 7; DLB 105, 206; RGAL 4; SATA 94

Hastings, Hudson
See Kuttner, Henry

Hastings, Selina .... **CLC 44**

Hathorne, John 1641-1717 .... **LC 38**

Hatteras, Amelia
See Mencken, H(enry) L(ouis)

Hatteras, Owen .... **TCLC 18**
See also Mencken, H(enry) L(ouis); Nathan, George Jean

Hauptmann, Gerhart (Johann Robert)
1862-1946 .... **TCLC 4; SSC 37**
See also CA 104; 153; CDWLB 2; DAM DRAM; DLB 66, 118; EW 8; RGSF 2; RGWL 2

Havel, Vaclav 1936- ..... **CLC 25, 58, 65, 123; DC 6**
See also CA 104; CANR 36, 63; CDWLB 4; CWW 2; DA3; DAM DRAM; DFS 10; DLB 232; MTCW 1, 2

Haviaras, Stratis .... **CLC 33**
See also Chaviaras, Strates

Hawes, Stephen 1475(?)-1529(?) .... **LC 17**
See also DLB 132; RGEL 2

Hawkes, John (Clendennin Burne, Jr.)
1925-1998 .. **CLC 1, 2, 3, 4, 7, 9, 14, 15, 27, 49**
See also BPFB 2; CA 1-4R; 167; CANR 2, 47, 64; CN 7; DLB 2, 7, 227; DLBY 1980, 1998; MTCW 1, 2; RGAL 4

Hawking, S. W.
See Hawking, Stephen W(illiam)

Hawking, Stephen W(illiam) 1942- . **CLC 63, 105**
See also AAYA 13; BEST 89:1; CA 126; 129; CANR 48; CPW; DA3; MTCW 2

Hawkins, Anthony Hope
See Hope, Anthony

Hawthorne, Julian 1846-1934 .... **TCLC 25**
See also CA 165; HGG

Hawthorne, Nathaniel 1804-1864 ... **NCLC 2, 10, 17, 23, 39, 79, 95; SSC 3, 29, 39; WLC**
See also AAYA 18; AMW; AMWR 1; BPFB 2; BYA 3; CDALB 1640-1865; DA; DA3; DAB; DAC; DAM MST, NOV; DLB 1, 74, 183, 223; EXPN; EXPS; HGG; LAIT 1; NFS 1; RGAL 4; RGSF 2; SSFS 1, 7, 11, 15; SUFW; WCH; YABC 2

Haxton, Josephine Ayres 1921-
See Douglas, Ellen
See also CA 115; CANR 41, 83

Hayaseca y Eizaguirre, Jorge
See Echegaray (y Eizaguirre), Jose (Maria Waldo)

Hayashi, Fumiko 1904-1951 .... **TCLC 27**
See also Hayashi Fumiko
See also CA 161

Hayashi Fumiko
See Hayashi, Fumiko
See also DLB 180

Haycraft, Anna (Margaret) 1932-
See Ellis, Alice Thomas
See also CA 122; CANR 85, 90; MTCW 2

Hayden, Robert E(arl) 1913-1980 . **CLC 5, 9, 14, 37; BLC 2; PC 6**
See also AFAW 1, 2; AMWS 2; BW 1, 3; CA 69-72; 97-100; CABS 2; CANR 24, 75, 82; CDALB 1941-1968; DA; DAC; DAM MST, MULT, POET; DLB 5, 76; EXPP; MTCW 1, 2; PFS 1; RGAL 4; SATA 19; SATA-Obit 26; WP

Hayek, F(riedrich) A(ugust von)
1899-1992 .... **TCLC 109**
See also CA 93-96; 137; CANR 20; MTCW 1, 2

Hayford, J(oseph) E(phraim) Casely
See Casely-Hayford, J(oseph) E(phraim)

Hayman, Ronald 1932- .... **CLC 44**
See also CA 25-28R; CANR 18, 50, 88; CD 5; DLB 155

Hayne, Paul Hamilton 1830-1886 . **NCLC 94**
See also DLB 3, 64, 79, 248; RGAL 4

Hays, Mary 1760-1843 .... **NCLC 114**
See also DLB 142, 158; RGEL 2

Haywood, Eliza (Fowler)
1693(?)-1756 .... **LC 1, 44**
See also DLB 39; RGEL 2

Hazlitt, William 1778-1830 ...... **NCLC 29, 82**
See also BRW 4; DLB 110, 158; RGEL 2

Hazzard, Shirley 1931- .... **CLC 18**
See also CA 9-12R; CANR 4, 70; CN 7; DLBY 1982; MTCW 1

Head, Bessie 1937-1986 .... **CLC 25, 67; BLC 2; SSC 52**
See also AFW; BW 2, 3; CA 29-32R; 119; CANR 25, 82; CDWLB 3; DA3; DAM MULT; DLB 117, 225; EXPS; FW; MTCW 1, 2; RGSF 2; SSFS 5, 13; WLIT 2

Headon, (Nicky) Topper 1956(?)- ..... **CLC 30**

Heaney, Seamus (Justin) 1939- ..... **CLC 5, 7, 14, 25, 37, 74, 91; PC 18; WLCS**
See also BRWR 1; BRWS 2; CA 85-88; CANR 25, 48, 75, 91; CDBLB 1960 to Present; CP 7; DA3; DAB; DAM POET; DLB 40; DLBY 1995; EXPP; MTCW 1, 2; PAB; PFS 2, 5, 8; RGEL 2; WLIT 4

Hearn, (Patricio) Lafcadio (Tessima Carlos)
1850-1904 .... **TCLC 9**
See also CA 105; 166; DLB 12, 78, 189; HGG; RGAL 4

Hearne, Vicki 1946-2001 .... **CLC 56**
See also CA 139; 201

Hearon, Shelby 1931- .... **CLC 63**
See also AITN 2; AMWS 8; CA 25-28R; CANR 18, 48, 103; CSW

Heat-Moon, William Least .... **CLC 29**
See also Trogdon, William (Lewis)
See also AAYA 9

Hebbel, Friedrich 1813-1863 .... **NCLC 43**
See also CDWLB 2; DAM DRAM; DLB 129; EW 6; RGWL 2

Hebert, Anne 1916-2000 .... **CLC 4, 13, 29**
See also CA 85-88; 187; CANR 69; CCA 1; CWP; CWW 2; DA3; DAC; DAM MST, POET; DLB 68; GFL 1789 to the Present; MTCW 1, 2

Hecht, Anthony (Evan) 1923- ...... **CLC 8, 13, 19**
See also AMWS 10; CA 9-12R; CANR 6, 108; CP 7; DAM POET; DLB 5, 169; PFS 6; WP

Hecht, Ben 1894-1964 .... **CLC 8**
See also CA 85-88; DFS 9; DLB 7, 9, 25, 26, 28, 86; FANT; IDFW 3, 4; RGAL 4; TCLC 101

Hedayat, Sadeq 1903-1951 .... **TCLC 21**
See also CA 120; RGSF 2

Hegel, Georg Wilhelm Friedrich
1770-1831 .... **NCLC 46**
See also DLB 90

Heidegger, Martin 1889-1976 .... **CLC 24**
See also CA 81-84; 65-68; CANR 34; MTCW 1, 2

Heidenstam, (Carl Gustaf) Verner von
1859-1940 .... **TCLC 5**
See also CA 104

Heifner, Jack 1946- .... **CLC 11**
See also CA 105; CANR 47

Heijermans, Herman 1864-1924 .... **TCLC 24**
See also CA 123

Heilbrun, Carolyn G(old) 1926- .... **CLC 25**
See also Cross, Amanda
See also CA 45-48; CANR 1, 28, 58, 94; FW

Hein, Christoph 1944- .... **CLC 154**
See also CA 158; CANR 108; CDWLB 2; CWW 2; DLB 124

Heine, Heinrich 1797-1856 .... **NCLC 4, 54; PC 25**
See also CDWLB 2; DLB 90; EW 5; RGWL 2

Heinemann, Larry (Curtiss) 1944- .. **CLC 50**
See also CA 110; CAAS 21; CANR 31, 81; DLBD 9; INT CANR-31

Heiney, Donald (William) 1921-1993
See Harris, MacDonald
See also CA 1-4R; 142; CANR 3, 58; FANT

Heinlein, Robert A(nson) 1907-1988 . **CLC 1, 3, 8, 14, 26, 55**
See also AAYA 17; BPFB 2; BYA 4, 13; CA 1-4R; 125; CANR 1, 20, 53; CLR 75; CPW; DA3; DAM POP; DLB 8; EXPS; JRDA; LAIT 5; MAICYA 1, 2; MTCW 1, 2; RGAL 4; SATA 9, 69; SATA-Obit 56; SCFW 4; SFW 4; SSFS 7; YAW

Helforth, John
See Doolittle, Hilda

Heliodorus fl. 3rd cent. - .... **CMLC 52**

Hellenhofferu, Vojtech Kapristian z
See Hasek, Jaroslav (Matej Frantisek)

Heller, Joseph 1923-1999 . **CLC 1, 3, 5, 8, 11, 36, 63; WLC**
See also AAYA 24; AITN 1; AMWS 4; BPFB 2; BYA 1; CA 5-8R; 187; CABS 1; CANR 8, 42, 66; CN 7; CPW; DA; DA3; DAB; DAC; DAM MST, NOV, POP; DLB 2, 28, 227; DLBY 1980; EXPN; INT CANR-8; LAIT 4; MTCW 1, 2; NFS 1; RGAL 4; YAW

Hellman, Lillian (Florence)
1906-1984 .. **CLC 2, 4, 8, 14, 18, 34, 44, 52; DC 1**
See also AITN 1, 2; AMWS 1; CA 13-16R; 112; CAD; CANR 33; CWD; DA3; DAM DRAM; DFS 1, 3, 14; DLB 7, 228; DLBY 1984; FW; LAIT 3; MAWW; MTCW 1, 2; RGAL 4; TCLC 119

Helprin, Mark 1947- .... **CLC 7, 10, 22, 32**
See also CA 81-84; CANR 47, 64; CDALBS; CPW; DA3; DAM NOV, POP; DLBY 1985; FANT; MTCW 1, 2

Helvetius, Claude-Adrien 1715-1771 .. **LC 26**

Helyar, Jane Penelope Josephine 1933-
See Poole, Josephine
See also CA 21-24R; CANR 10, 26; CWRI 5; SATA 82

Hemans, Felicia 1793-1835 ...... **NCLC 29, 71**
See also DLB 96; RGEL 2

Hemingway, Ernest (Miller)
1899-1961 .... **CLC 1, 3, 6, 8, 10, 13, 19, 30, 34, 39, 41, 44, 50, 61, 80; SSC 1, 25, 36, 40; WLC**
See also AAYA 19; AMW; AMWR 1; BPFB 2; BYA 2, 3, 13; CA 77-80; CANR 34; CDALB 1917-1929; DA; DA3; DAB; DAC; DAM MST, NOV; DLB 4, 9, 102, 210; DLBD 1, 15, 16; DLBY 1981, 1987, 1996, 1998; EXPN; EXPS; LAIT 3, 4; MTCW 1, 2; NFS 1, 5, 6, 14; RGAL 4; RGSF 2; SSFS 1, 6, 8, 9, 11; TCLC 115; WYA

Hempel, Amy 1951- .... **CLC 39**
See also CA 118; 137; CANR 70; DA3; DLB 218; EXPS; MTCW 2; SSFS 2

Henderson, F. C.
See Mencken, H(enry) L(ouis)

Henderson, Sylvia
See Ashton-Warner, Sylvia (Constance)

Henderson, Zenna (Chlarson)
1917-1983 .... **SSC 29**
See also CA 1-4R; 133; CANR 1, 84; DLB 8; SATA 5; SFW 4

Henkin, Joshua .... **CLC 119**
See also CA 161

Henley, Beth .... **CLC 23; DC 6, 14**
See also Henley, Elizabeth Becker
See also CABS 3; CAD; CD 5; CSW; CWD; DFS 2; DLBY 1986; FW

Henley, Elizabeth Becker 1952-
See Henley, Beth
See also CA 107; CANR 32, 73; DA3; DAM DRAM, MST; MTCW 1, 2

Henley, William Ernest 1849-1903 .. **TCLC 8**
See also CA 105; DLB 19; RGEL 2

Hennissart, Martha
See Lathen, Emma
See also CA 85-88; CANR 64

Henry VIII 1491-1547 .... **LC 10**
See also DLB 132

Henry, O. .... **TCLC 1, 19; SSC 5, 49; WLC**
See Porter, William Sydney
See also AAYA 41; AMWS 2; EXPS; RGAL 4; RGSF 2; SSFS 2

Henry, Patrick 1736-1799 .... **LC 25**
See also LAIT 1

Henryson, Robert 1430(?)-1506(?) ...... **LC 20**
See also BRWS 7; DLB 146; RGEL 2

Henschke, Alfred
See Klabund

Hentoff, Nat(han Irving) 1925- .... **CLC 26**
See also AAYA 4, 42; BYA 6; CA 1-4R; CAAS 6; CANR 5, 25, 77; CLR 1, 52; INT CANR-25; JRDA; MAICYA 1, 2; SATA 42, 69, 133; SATA-Brief 27; WYA; YAW

Heppenstall, (John) Rayner
1911-1981 .... **CLC 10**
See also CA 1-4R; 103; CANR 29

Heraclitus c. 540B.C.-c. 450B.C. ... **CMLC 22**
See also DLB 176

Herbert, Frank (Patrick)
1920-1986 .... **CLC 12, 23, 35, 44, 85**
See also AAYA 21; BPFB 2; BYA 4, 14; CA 53-56; 118; CANR 5, 43; CDALBS; CPW; DAM POP; DLB 8; INT CANR-5; LAIT 5; MTCW 1, 2; SATA 9, 37; SATA-Obit 47; SCFW 2; SFW 4; YAW

Herbert, George 1593-1633 ...... **LC 24; PC 4**
See also BRW 2; BRWR 2; CDBLB Before 1660; DAB; DAM POET; DLB 126; EXPP; RGEL 2; WP

Herbert, Zbigniew 1924-1998 .... **CLC 9, 43**
See also CA 89-92; 169; CANR 36, 74; CDWLB 4; CWW 2; DAM POET; DLB 232; MTCW 1

Herbst, Josephine (Frey)
1897-1969 .... **CLC 34**
See also CA 5-8R; 25-28R; DLB 9

Herder, Johann Gottfried von
1744-1803 .... **NCLC 8**
See also DLB 97; EW 4

Heredia, Jose Maria 1803-1839
See also HLCS 2; LAW

Hergesheimer, Joseph 1880-1954 ... **TCLC 11**
See also CA 109; 194; DLB 102, 9; RGAL 4

Herlihy, James Leo 1927-1993 .... **CLC 6**
See also CA 1-4R; 143; CAD; CANR 2

Hermogenes fl. c. 175- .... **CMLC 6**

Hernandez, Jose 1834-1886 .... **NCLC 17**
See also LAW; RGWL 2; WLIT 1

Herodotus c. 484B.C.-c. 420B.C. .. **CMLC 17**
See also AW 1; CDWLB 1; DLB 176; RGWL 2

Herrick, Robert 1591-1674 .... **LC 13; PC 9**
See also BRW 2; DA; DAB; DAC; DAM MST, POET; DLB 126; EXPP; PFS 13; RGAL 4; RGEL 2; WP

Herring, Guilles
See Somerville, Edith Oenone

Herriot, James 1916-1995 .... **CLC 12**
See also Wight, James Alfred
See also AAYA 1; BPFB 2; CA 148; CANR 40; CLR 80; CPW; DAM POP; LAIT 3; MAICYA 2; MAICYAS 1; MTCW 2; SATA 86; YAW

Herris, Violet
See Hunt, Violet

Herrmann, Dorothy 1941- .... **CLC 44**
See also CA 107

Herrmann, Taffy
See Herrmann, Dorothy

Hersey, John (Richard) 1914-1993 .... **CLC 1, 2, 7, 9, 40, 81, 97**
See also AAYA 29; BPFB 2; CA 17-20R; 140; CANR 33; CDALBS; CPW; DAM POP; DLB 6, 185; MTCW 1, 2; SATA 25; SATA-Obit 76

Herzen, Aleksandr Ivanovich
1812-1870 .... **NCLC 10, 61**

Herzl, Theodor 1860-1904 .... **TCLC 36**
See also CA 168

Herzog, Werner 1942- .... **CLC 16**
See also CA 89-92

Hesiod c. 8th cent. B.C.- .... **CMLC 5**
See also AW 1; DLB 176; RGWL 2

Hesse, Hermann 1877-1962 ... **CLC 1, 2, 3, 6, 11, 17, 25, 69; SSC 9, 49; WLC**
See also AAYA 43; BPFB 2; CA 17-18; CAP 2; CDWLB 2; DA; DA3; DAB; DAC; DAM MST, NOV; DLB 66; EW 9; EXPN; LAIT 1; MTCW 1, 2; NFS 6, 15; RGWL 2; SATA 50

Hewes, Cady
See De Voto, Bernard (Augustine)

Heyen, William 1940- .... **CLC 13, 18**
See also CA 33-36R; CAAS 9; CANR 98; CP 7; DLB 5

Heyerdahl, Thor 1914-2002 .... **CLC 26**
See also CA 5-8R; CANR 5, 22, 66, 73; LAIT 4; MTCW 1, 2; SATA 2, 52

Heym, Georg (Theodor Franz Arthur)
1887-1912 .... **TCLC 9**
See also CA 106; 181

Heym, Stefan 1913- .... **CLC 41**
See also CA 9-12R; CANR 4; CWW 2; DLB 69

Heyse, Paul (Johann Ludwig von)
1830-1914 .... **TCLC 8**
See also CA 104; DLB 129

Heyward, (Edwin) DuBose
1885-1940 .... **TCLC 59**
See also CA 108; 157; DLB 7, 9, 45, 249; SATA 21

Heywood, John 1497(?)-1580(?) .... **LC 65**
See also DLB 136; RGEL 2

Hibbert, Eleanor Alice Burford
1906-1993 .... **CLC 7**
See also Holt, Victoria
See also BEST 90:4; CA 17-20R; 140; CANR 9, 28, 59; CMW 4; CPW; DAM POP; MTCW 2; RHW; SATA 2; SATA-Obit 74

Hichens, Robert (Smythe)
1864-1950 .... **TCLC 64**
See also CA 162; DLB 153; HGG; RHW; SUFW

Higgins, George V(incent)
1939-1999 .... **CLC 4, 7, 10, 18**
See also BPFB 2; CA 77-80; 186; CAAS 5; CANR 17, 51, 89, 96; CMW 4; CN 7; DLB 2; DLBY 1981, 1998; INT CANR-17; MSW; MTCW 1

Higginson, Thomas Wentworth
1823-1911 .... **TCLC 36**
See also CA 162; DLB 1, 64, 243

Higgonet, Margaret ed. .... **CLC 65**

Highet, Helen
See MacInnes, Helen (Clark)

Highsmith, (Mary) Patricia
1921-1995 .... **CLC 2, 4, 14, 42, 102**
See also Morgan, Claire
See also BRWS 5; CA 1-4R; 147; CANR 1, 20, 48, 62, 108; CMW 4; CPW; DA3; DAM NOV, POP; MSW; MTCW 1, 2

Highwater, Jamake (Mamake)
1942(?)-2001 .... **CLC 12**
See also AAYA 7; BPFB 2; BYA 4; CA 65-68; 199; CAAS 7; CANR 10, 34, 84; CLR 17; CWRI 5; DLB 52; DLBY 1985; JRDA; MAICYA 1, 2; SATA 32, 69; SATA-Brief 30

Highway, Tomson 1951- .... **CLC 92**
See also CA 151; CANR 75; CCA 1; CD 5; DAC; DAM MULT; DFS 2; MTCW 2; NNAL

Hijuelos, Oscar 1951- .... **CLC 65; HLC 1**
See also AAYA 25; AMWS 8; BEST 90:1; CA 123; CANR 50, 75; CPW; DA3; DAM MULT, POP; DLB 145; HW 1, 2; MTCW 2; RGAL 4; WLIT 1

Hikmet, Nazim 1902(?)-1963 .... **CLC 40**
See also CA 141; 93-96

Hildegard von Bingen 1098-1179 . **CMLC 20**
See also DLB 148

Hildesheimer, Wolfgang 1916-1991 .. **CLC 49**
See also CA 101; 135; DLB 69, 124

Hill, Geoffrey (William) 1932- ...... **CLC 5, 8, 18, 45**
See also BRWS 5; CA 81-84; CANR 21, 89; CDBLB 1960 to Present; CP 7; DAM POET; DLB 40; MTCW 1; RGEL 2

Hill, George Roy 1921- .... **CLC 26**
See also CA 110; 122

Hill, John
See Koontz, Dean R(ay)

Hill, Susan (Elizabeth) 1942- ...... **CLC 4, 113**
See also CA 33-36R; CANR 29, 69; CN 7; DAB; DAM MST, NOV; DLB 14, 139; HGG; MTCW 1; RHW

Hillard, Asa G. III .... **CLC 70**

Hillerman, Tony 1925- .... **CLC 62**
See also AAYA 40; BEST 89:1; BPFB 2; CA 29-32R; CANR 21, 42, 65, 97; CMW 4; CPW; DA3; DAM POP; DLB 206; MSW; RGAL 4; SATA 6; TCWW 2; YAW

Hillesum, Etty 1914-1943 .... **TCLC 49**
See also CA 137

Hilliard, Noel (Harvey) 1929-1996 ... **CLC 15**
See also CA 9-12R; CANR 7, 69; CN 7

Hillis, Rick 1956- .... **CLC 66**
See also CA 134

Hilton, James 1900-1954 .... **TCLC 21**
See also CA 108; 169; DLB 34, 77; FANT; SATA 34

Himes, Chester (Bomar) 1909-1984 .. **CLC 2, 4, 7, 18, 58, 108; BLC 2**
See also AFAW 2; BPFB 2; BW 2; CA 25-28R; 114; CANR 22, 89; CMW 4; DAM MULT; DLB 2, 76, 143, 226; MSW; MTCW 1, 2; RGAL 4

Hinde, Thomas .... **CLC 6, 11**
See also Chitty, Thomas Willes

Hine, (William) Daryl 1936- .... **CLC 15**
See also CA 1-4R; CAAS 15; CANR 1, 20; CP 7; DLB 60

Hinkson, Katharine Tynan
See Tynan, Katharine

Hinojosa(-Smith), Rolando (R.) 1929-
See also CA 131; CAAS 16; CANR 62; DAM MULT; DLB 82; HLC 1; HW 1, 2; MTCW 2; RGAL 4

Hinton, S(usan) E(loise) 1950- .. **CLC 30, 111**
See also AAYA 2, 33; BPFB 2; BYA 2, 3; CA 81-84; CANR 32, 62, 92; CDALBS; CLR 3, 23; CPW; DA; DA3; DAB; DAC; DAM MST, NOV; JRDA; LAIT 5; MAICYA 1, 2; MTCW 1, 2; NFS 5, 9, 15; SATA 19, 58, 115; WYA; YAW

Hippius, Zinaida .... **TCLC 9**
See also Gippius, Zinaida (Nikolayevna)

Hiraoka, Kimitake 1925-1970
See Mishima, Yukio
See also CA 97-100; 29-32R; DA3; DAM DRAM; MTCW 1, 2

Hirsch, E(ric) D(onald), Jr. 1928- .... **CLC 79**
See also CA 25-28R; CANR 27, 51; DLB 67; INT CANR-27; MTCW 1

Hirsch, Edward 1950- .... **CLC 31, 50**
See also CA 104; CANR 20, 42, 102; CP 7; DLB 120

Hitchcock, Alfred (Joseph)
1899-1980 .... **CLC 16**
See also AAYA 22; CA 159; 97-100; SATA 27; SATA-Obit 24

Hitchens, Christopher (Eric)
1949- .... **CLC 157**
See also CA 149; CANR 89

Hitler, Adolf 1889-1945 .... **TCLC 53**
See also CA 117; 147

Hoagland, Edward 1932- .... **CLC 28**
See also ANW; CA 1-4R; CANR 2, 31, 57, 107; CN 7; DLB 6; SATA 51; TCWW 2

Hoban, Russell (Conwell) 1925- ... **CLC 7, 25**
See also BPFB 2; CA 5-8R; CANR 23, 37, 66; CLR 3, 69; CN 7; CWRI 5; DAM NOV; DLB 52; FANT; MAICYA 1, 2; MTCW 1, 2; SATA 1, 40, 78; SFW 4

Hobbes, Thomas 1588-1679 .... **LC 36**
See also DLB 151, 252; RGEL 2

Hobbs, Perry
See Blackmur, R(ichard) P(almer)

Hobson, Laura Z(ametkin)
1900-1986 .... **CLC 7, 25**
See also Field, Peter
See also BPFB 2; CA 17-20R; 118; CANR 55; DLB 28; SATA 52

Hoccleve, Thomas c. 1368-c. 1437 ...... **LC 75**
See also DLB 146; RGEL 2

Hoch, Edward D(entinger) 1930-
See Queen, Ellery
See also CA 29-32R; CANR 11, 27, 51, 97; CMW 4; SFW 4

Hochhuth, Rolf 1931- .... **CLC 4, 11, 18**
See also CA 5-8R; CANR 33, 75; CWW 2; DAM DRAM; DLB 124; MTCW 1, 2

Hochman, Sandra 1936- .... **CLC 3, 8**
See also CA 5-8R; DLB 5

Hochwaelder, Fritz 1911-1986 .... **CLC 36**
See also Hochwalder, Fritz
See also CA 29-32R; 120; CANR 42; DAM DRAM; MTCW 1

Hochwalder, Fritz
See Hochwaelder, Fritz
See also RGWL 2

Hocking, Mary (Eunice) 1921- .... **CLC 13**
See also CA 101; CANR 18, 40

Hodgins, Jack 1938- .... **CLC 23**
See also CA 93-96; CN 7; DLB 60

Hodgson, William Hope
1877(?)-1918 .... **TCLC 13**
See also CA 111; 164; CMW 4; DLB 70, 153, 156, 178; HGG; MTCW 2; SFW 4; SUFW

Hoeg, Peter 1957- .... **CLC 95, 156**
See also CA 151; CANR 75; CMW 4; DA3; DLB 214; MTCW 2

Hoffman, Alice 1952- .... **CLC 51**
See also AAYA 37; AMWS 10; CA 77-80; CANR 34, 66, 100; CN 7; CPW; DAM NOV; MTCW 1, 2

Hoffman, Daniel (Gerard) 1923- . **CLC 6, 13, 23**
See also CA 1-4R; CANR 4; CP 7; DLB 5

Hoffman, Stanley 1944- .... **CLC 5**
See also CA 77-80

Hoffman, William 1925- .... **CLC 141**
See also CA 21-24R; CANR 9, 103; CSW; DLB 234

Hoffman, William M(oses) 1939- ..... **CLC 40**
See also CA 57-60; CANR 11, 71

Hoffmann, E(rnst) T(heodor) A(madeus)
1776-1822 .... **NCLC 2; SSC 13**
See also CDWLB 2; DLB 90; EW 5; RGSF 2; RGWL 2; SATA 27; SUFW; WCH

Hofmann, Gert 1931- .... **CLC 54**
See also CA 128

Hofmannsthal, Hugo von
1874-1929 .... **TCLC 11; DC 4**
See also CA 106; 153; CDWLB 2; DAM DRAM; DFS 12; DLB 81, 118; EW 9; RGWL 2

Hogan, Linda 1947- .... **CLC 73; PC 35**
See also AMWS 4; ANW; BYA 12; CA 120; CANR 45, 73; CWP; DAM MULT; DLB 175; NNAL; SATA 132; TCWW 2

Hogarth, Charles
See Creasey, John

Hogarth, Emmett
See Polonsky, Abraham (Lincoln)

Hogg, James 1770-1835 .... **NCLC 4, 109**
See also DLB 93, 116, 159; HGG; RGEL 2; SUFW

Holbach, Paul Henri Thiry Baron
1723-1789 .... **LC 14**

Holberg, Ludvig 1684-1754 .... **LC 6**
See also RGWL 2

Holcroft, Thomas 1745-1809 .... **NCLC 85**
See also DLB 39, 89, 158; RGEL 2

Holden, Ursula 1921- .... **CLC 18**
See also CA 101; CAAS 8; CANR 22

Holderlin, (Johann Christian) Friedrich
1770-1843 .... **NCLC 16; PC 4**
See also CDWLB 2; DLB 90; EW 5; RGWL 2

Holdstock, Robert
See Holdstock, Robert P.

Holdstock, Robert P. 1948- .... **CLC 39**
See also CA 131; CANR 81; DLB 261; FANT; HGG; SFW 4

Holinshed, Raphael fl. 1580- .... **LC 69**
See also DLB 167; RGEL 2

Holland, Isabelle (Christian)
1920-2002 .... **CLC 21**
See also AAYA 11; CA 21-24R, 181; CAAE 181; CANR 10, 25, 47; CLR 57; CWRI 5; JRDA; LAIT 4; MAICYA 1, 2; SATA 8, 70; SATA-Essay 103; SATA-Obit 132; WYA

Holland, Marcus
See Caldwell, (Janet Miriam) Taylor (Holland)

Hollander, John 1929- .... **CLC 2, 5, 8, 14**
See also CA 1-4R; CANR 1, 52; CP 7; DLB 5; SATA 13

Hollander, Paul
See Silverberg, Robert

Holleran, Andrew 1943(?)- .... **CLC 38**
See also Garber, Eric
See also CA 144; GLL 1

Holley, Marietta 1836(?)-1926 .... **TCLC 99**
See also CA 118; DLB 11

Hollinghurst, Alan 1954- .... **CLC 55, 91**
See also CA 114; CN 7; DLB 207; GLL 1

Hollis, Jim
See Summers, Hollis (Spurgeon, Jr.)

Holly, Buddy 1936-1959 .... **TCLC 65**

Holmes, Gordon
See Shiel, M(atthew) P(hipps)

Holmes, John
See Souster, (Holmes) Raymond

Holmes, John Clellon 1926-1988 ...... **CLC 56**
See also CA 9-12R; 125; CANR 4; DLB 16, 237

Holmes, Oliver Wendell, Jr.
1841-1935 .... **TCLC 77**
See also CA 114; 186

Holmes, Oliver Wendell
1809-1894 .... **NCLC 14, 81**
See also AMWS 1; CDALB 1640-1865; DLB 1, 189, 235; EXPP; RGAL 4; SATA 34

Holmes, Raymond
See Souster, (Holmes) Raymond

Holt, Victoria
See Hibbert, Eleanor Alice Burford
See also BPFB 2

Holub, Miroslav 1923-1998 .... **CLC 4**
See also CA 21-24R; 169; CANR 10; CDWLB 4; CWW 2; DLB 232

Homer c. 8th cent. B.C.- .... **CMLC 1, 16; PC 23; WLCS**
See also AW 1; CDWLB 1; DA; DA3; DAB; DAC; DAM MST, POET; DLB 176; EFS 1; LAIT 1; RGWL 2; TWA; WP

Hongo, Garrett Kaoru 1951- .... **PC 23**
See also CA 133; CAAS 22; CP 7; DLB 120; EXPP; RGAL 4

Honig, Edwin 1919- .... **CLC 33**
See also CA 5-8R; CAAS 8; CANR 4, 45; CP 7; DLB 5

Hood, Hugh (John Blagdon) 1928- . **CLC 15, 28; SSC 42**
See also CA 49-52; CAAS 17; CANR 1, 33, 87; CN 7; DLB 53; RGSF 2

Hood, Thomas 1799-1845 .... **NCLC 16**
See also BRW 4; DLB 96; RGEL 2

Hooker, (Peter) Jeremy 1941- .... **CLC 43**
See also CA 77-80; CANR 22; CP 7; DLB 40

hooks, bell .... **CLC 94**
See also Watkins, Gloria Jean
See also DLB 246

Hope, A(lec) D(erwent) 1907-2000 .... **CLC 3, 51**
See also BRWS 7; CA 21-24R; 188; CANR 33, 74; MTCW 1, 2; PFS 8; RGEL 2

Hope, Anthony 1863-1933 .... **TCLC 83**
See also CA 157; DLB 153, 156; RGEL 2; RHW

Hope, Brian
See Creasey, John

Hope, Christopher (David Tully)
1944- .... **CLC 52**
See also AFW; CA 106; CANR 47, 101; CN 7; DLB 225; SATA 62

Hopkins, Gerard Manley
1844-1889 .... **NCLC 17; PC 15; WLC**
See also BRW 5; BRWR 2; CDBLB 1890-1914; DA; DA3; DAB; DAC; DAM MST, POET; DLB 35, 57; EXPP; PAB; RGEL 2; WP

Hopkins, John (Richard) 1931-1998 .. **CLC 4**
See also CA 85-88; 169; CBD; CD 5

Hopkins, Pauline Elizabeth
1859-1930 .... **TCLC 28; BLC 2**
See also AFAW 2; BW 2, 3; CA 141; CANR 82; DAM MULT; DLB 50

Hopkinson, Francis 1737-1791 .... **LC 25**
See also DLB 31; RGAL 4

Hopley-Woolrich, Cornell George 1903-1968
See Woolrich, Cornell
See also CA 13-14; CANR 58; CAP 1; CMW 4; DLB 226; MTCW 2

Horace 65B.C.-8B.C. .... **CMLC 39**
See also AW 2; CDWLB 1; DLB 211; RGWL 2

Horatio
See Proust, (Valentin-Louis-George-Eugene-)Marcel

Horgan, Paul (George Vincent O'Shaughnessy) 1903-1995 .. **CLC 9, 53**
See also BPFB 2; CA 13-16R; 147; CANR 9, 35; DAM NOV; DLB 102, 212; DLBY 1985; INT CANR-9; MTCW 1, 2; SATA 13; SATA-Obit 84; TCWW 2

Horn, Peter
See Kuttner, Henry
Hornem, Horace Esq.
See Byron, George Gordon (Noel)
Horney, Karen (Clementine Theodore Danielsen) 1885-1952 .... **TCLC 71**
See also CA 114; 165; DLB 246; FW
Hornung, E(rnest) W(illiam)
1866-1921 .... **TCLC 59**
See also CA 108; 160; CMW 4; DLB 70
Horovitz, Israel (Arthur) 1939- .... **CLC 56**
See also CA 33-36R; CANR 46, 59; CD 5; DAM DRAM; DLB 7
Horton, George Moses
1797(?)-1883(?) .... **NCLC 87**
See also DLB 50
Horvath, Odon von 1901-1938 .... **TCLC 45**
See also von Horvath, Oedoen
See also CA 118; 194; DLB 85, 124; RGWL 2
Horvath, Oedoen von -1938
See Horvath, Odon von
Horwitz, Julius 1920-1986 .... **CLC 14**
See also CA 9-12R; 119; CANR 12
Hospital, Janette Turner 1942- .... **CLC 42, 145**
See also CA 108; CANR 48; CN 7; RGSF 2
Hostos, E. M. de
See Hostos (y Bonilla), Eugenio Maria de
Hostos, Eugenio M. de
See Hostos (y Bonilla), Eugenio Maria de
Hostos, Eugenio Maria
See Hostos (y Bonilla), Eugenio Maria de
Hostos (y Bonilla), Eugenio Maria de
1839-1903 .... **TCLC 24**
See also CA 123; 131; HW 1
Houdini
See Lovecraft, H(oward) P(hillips)
Hougan, Carolyn 1943- .... **CLC 34**
See also CA 139
Household, Geoffrey (Edward West)
1900-1988 .... **CLC 11**
See also CA 77-80; 126; CANR 58; CMW 4; DLB 87; SATA 14; SATA-Obit 59
Housman, A(lfred) E(dward)
1859-1936 ... **TCLC 1, 10; PC 2; WLCS**
See also BRW 6; CA 104; 125; DA; DA3; DAB; DAC; DAM MST, POET; DLB 19; EXPP; MTCW 1, 2; PAB; PFS 4, 7; RGEL 2; WP
Housman, Laurence 1865-1959 .... **TCLC 7**
See also CA 106; 155; DLB 10; FANT; RGEL 2; SATA 25
Howard, Elizabeth Jane 1923- ..... **CLC 7, 29**
See also CA 5-8R; CANR 8, 62; CN 7
Howard, Maureen 1930- .... **CLC 5, 14, 46, 151**
See also CA 53-56; CANR 31, 75; CN 7; DLBY 1983; INT CANR-31; MTCW 1, 2
Howard, Richard 1929- .... **CLC 7, 10, 47**
See also AITN 1; CA 85-88; CANR 25, 80; CP 7; DLB 5; INT CANR-25
Howard, Robert E(rvin)
1906-1936 .... **TCLC 8**
See also BPFB 2; BYA 5; CA 105; 157; FANT; SUFW
Howard, Warren F.
See Pohl, Frederik
Howe, Fanny (Quincy) 1940- .... **CLC 47**
See also CA 117; CAAE 187; CAAS 27; CANR 70; CP 7; CWP; SATA-Brief 52
Howe, Irving 1920-1993 .... **CLC 85**
See also AMWS 6; CA 9-12R; 141; CANR 21, 50; DLB 67; MTCW 1, 2
Howe, Julia Ward 1819-1910 .... **TCLC 21**
See also CA 117; 191; DLB 1, 189, 235; FW

Howe, Susan 1937- .... **CLC 72, 152**
See also AMWS 4; CA 160; CP 7; CWP; DLB 120; FW; RGAL 4
Howe, Tina 1937- .... **CLC 48**
See also CA 109; CAD; CD 5; CWD
Howell, James 1594(?)-1666 .... **LC 13**
See also DLB 151
Howells, W. D.
See Howells, William Dean
Howells, William D.
See Howells, William Dean
Howells, William Dean 1837-1920 .. **TCLC 7, 17, 41; SSC 36**
See also AMW; CA 104; 134; CDALB 1865-1917; DLB 12, 64, 74, 79, 189; MTCW 2; RGAL 4
Howes, Barbara 1914-1996 .... **CLC 15**
See also CA 9-12R; 151; CAAS 3; CANR 53; CP 7; SATA 5
Hrabal, Bohumil 1914-1997 .... **CLC 13, 67**
See also CA 106; 156; CAAS 12; CANR 57; CWW 2; DLB 232; RGSF 2
Hrotsvit of Gandersheim c. 935-c. 1000 .... **CMLC 29**
See also DLB 148
Hsi, Chu 1130-1200 .... **CMLC 42**
Hsun, Lu
See Lu Hsun
Hubbard, L(afayette) Ron(ald)
1911-1986 .... **CLC 43**
See also CA 77-80; 118; CANR 52; CPW; DA3; DAM POP; FANT; MTCW 2; SFW 4
Huch, Ricarda (Octavia)
1864-1947 .... **TCLC 13**
See also CA 111; 189; DLB 66
Huddle, David 1942- .... **CLC 49**
See also CA 57-60; CAAS 20; CANR 89; DLB 130
Hudson, Jeffrey
See Crichton, (John) Michael
Hudson, W(illiam) H(enry)
1841-1922 .... **TCLC 29**
See also CA 115; 190; DLB 98, 153, 174; RGEL 2; SATA 35
Hueffer, Ford Madox
See Ford, Ford Madox
Hughart, Barry 1934- .... **CLC 39**
See also CA 137; FANT; SFW 4
Hughes, Colin
See Creasey, John
Hughes, David (John) 1930- .... **CLC 48**
See also CA 116; 129; CN 7; DLB 14
Hughes, Edward James
See Hughes, Ted
See also DA3; DAM MST, POET
Hughes, (James Mercer) Langston
1902-1967 .... **CLC 1, 5, 10, 15, 35, 44, 108; BLC 2; DC 3; PC 1; SSC 6; WLC**
See also AAYA 12; AFAW 1, 2; AMWR 1; AMWS 1; BW 1, 3; CA 1-4R; 25-28R; CANR 1, 34, 82; CDALB 1929-1941; CLR 17; DA; DA3; DAB; DAC; DAM DRAM, MST, MULT, POET; DLB 4, 7, 48, 51, 86, 228; EXPP; EXPS; JRDA; LAIT 3; MAICYA 1, 2; MTCW 1, 2; PAB; PFS 1, 3, 6, 10, 15; RGAL 4; RGSF 2; SATA 4, 33; SSFS 4, 7; WCH; WP; YAW
Hughes, Richard (Arthur Warren)
1900-1976 .... **CLC 1, 11**
See also CA 5-8R; 65-68; CANR 4; DAM NOV; DLB 15, 161; MTCW 1; RGEL 2; SATA 8; SATA-Obit 25
Hughes, Ted 1930-1998 . **CLC 2, 4, 9, 14, 37, 119; PC 7**
See also Hughes, Edward James
See also BRWR 2; BRWS 1; CA 1-4R; 171; CANR 1, 33, 66, 108; CLR 3; CP 7; DAB; DAC; DLB 40, 161; EXPP; MAI-

CYA 1, 2; MTCW 1, 2; PAB; PFS 4; RGEL 2; SATA 49; SATA-Brief 27; SATA-Obit 107; YAW
Hugo, Richard
See Huch, Ricarda (Octavia)
Hugo, Richard F(ranklin)
1923-1982 .... **CLC 6, 18, 32**
See also AMWS 6; CA 49-52; 108; CANR 3; DAM POET; DLB 5, 206; RGAL 4
Hugo, Victor (Marie) 1802-1885 .... **NCLC 3, 10, 21; PC 17; WLC**
See also AAYA 28; DA; DA3; DAB; DAC; DAM DRAM, MST, NOV, POET; DLB 119, 192, 217; EFS 2; EW 6; EXPN; GFL 1789 to the Present; LAIT 1, 2; NFS 5; RGWL 2; SATA 47
Huidobro, Vicente
See Huidobro Fernandez, Vicente Garcia
See also LAW
Huidobro Fernandez, Vicente Garcia
1893-1948 .... **TCLC 31**
See also CA 131; HW 1
Hulme, Keri 1947- .... **CLC 39, 130**
See also CA 125; CANR 69; CN 7; CP 7; CWP; FW; INT 125
Hulme, T(homas) E(rnest)
1883-1917 .... **TCLC 21**
See also BRWS 6; CA 117; DLB 19
Hume, David 1711-1776 .... **LC 7, 56**
See also BRWS 3; DLB 104, 252
Humphrey, William 1924-1997 .... **CLC 45**
See also AMWS 9; CA 77-80; 160; CANR 68; CN 7; CSW; DLB 6, 212, 234; TCWW 2
Humphreys, Emyr Owen 1919- .... **CLC 47**
See also CA 5-8R; CANR 3, 24; CN 7; DLB 15
Humphreys, Josephine 1945- ..... **CLC 34, 57**
See also CA 121; 127; CANR 97; CSW; INT 127
Huneker, James Gibbons
1860-1921 .... **TCLC 65**
See also CA 193; DLB 71; RGAL 4
Hungerford, Hesba Fay
See Brinsmead, H(esba) F(ay)
Hungerford, Pixie
See Brinsmead, H(esba) F(ay)
Hunt, E(verette) Howard, (Jr.)
1918- .... **CLC 3**
See also AITN 1; CA 45-48; CANR 2, 47, 103; CMW 4
Hunt, Francesca
See Holland, Isabelle (Christian)
Hunt, Howard
See Hunt, E(verette) Howard, (Jr.)
Hunt, Kyle
See Creasey, John
Hunt, (James Henry) Leigh
1784-1859 .... **NCLC 1, 70**
See also DAM POET; DLB 96, 110, 144; RGEL 2; TEA
Hunt, Marsha 1946- .... **CLC 70**
See also BW 2, 3; CA 143; CANR 79
Hunt, Violet 1866(?)-1942 .... **TCLC 53**
See also CA 184; DLB 162, 197
Hunter, E. Waldo
See Sturgeon, Theodore (Hamilton)
Hunter, Evan 1926- .... **CLC 11, 31**
See also McBain, Ed
See also AAYA 39; BPFB 2; CA 5-8R; CANR 5, 38, 62, 97; CMW 4; CN 7; CPW; DAM POP; DLBY 1982; INT CANR-5; MSW; MTCW 1; SATA 25; SFW 4
Hunter, Kristin 1931-
See Lattany, Kristin (Elaine Eggleston) Hunter

Hunter, Mary
See Austin, Mary (Hunter)
Hunter, Mollie 1922- .... **CLC 21**
See also McIlwraith, Maureen Mollie Hunter
See also AAYA 13; BYA 6; CANR 37, 78; CLR 25; DLB 161; JRDA; MAICYA 1, 2; SAAS 7; SATA 54, 106; WYA; YAW
Hunter, Robert (?)-1734 .... **LC 7**
Hurston, Zora Neale 1891-1960 .. **CLC 7, 30, 61; BLC 2; DC 12; SSC 4; WLCS**
See also AAYA 15; AFAW 1, 2; AMWS 6; BW 1, 3; BYA 12; CA 85-88; CANR 61; CDALBS; DA; DA3; DAC; DAM MST, MULT, NOV; DFS 6; DLB 51, 86; EXPN; EXPS; FW; LAIT 3; MAWW; MTCW 1, 2; NFS 3; RGAL 4; RGSF 2; SSFS 1, 6, 11; TCLC 121; YAW
Husserl, E. G.
See Husserl, Edmund (Gustav Albrecht)
Husserl, Edmund (Gustav Albrecht) 1859-1938 .... **TCLC 100**
See also CA 116; 133
Huston, John (Marcellus) 1906-1987 .... **CLC 20**
See also CA 73-76; 123; CANR 34; DLB 26
Hustvedt, Siri 1955- .... **CLC 76**
See also CA 137
Hutten, Ulrich von 1488-1523 .... **LC 16**
See also DLB 179
Huxley, Aldous (Leonard) 1894-1963 .... **CLC 1, 3, 4, 5, 8, 11, 18, 35, 79; SSC 39; WLC**
See also AAYA 11; BPFB 2; BRW 7; CA 85-88; CANR 44, 99; CDBLB 1914-1945; DA; DA3; DAB; DAC; DAM MST, NOV; DLB 36, 100, 162, 195, 255; EXPN; LAIT 5; MTCW 1, 2; NFS 6; RGEL 2; SATA 63; SCFW 2; SFW 4; YAW
Huxley, T(homas) H(enry) 1825-1895 .... **NCLC 67**
See also DLB 57
Huysmans, Joris-Karl 1848-1907 ... **TCLC 7, 69**
See also CA 104; 165; DLB 123; EW 7; GFL 1789 to the Present; RGWL 2
Hwang, David Henry 1957- .. **CLC 55; DC 4**
See also CA 127; 132; CAD; CANR 76; CD 5; DA3; DAM DRAM; DFS 11; DLB 212, 228; INT CA-132; MTCW 2; RGAL 4
Hyde, Anthony 1946- .... **CLC 42**
See also Chase, Nicholas
See also CA 136; CCA 1
Hyde, Margaret O(ldroyd) 1917- ..... **CLC 21**
See also AAYA 13; CA 1-4R; CANR 1, 36; CLR 23; JRDA; MAICYA 1, 2; SAAS 8; SATA 1, 42, 76
Hynes, James 1956(?)- .... **CLC 65**
See also CA 164; CANR 105
Hypatia c. 370-415 .... **CMLC 35**
Ian, Janis 1951- .... **CLC 21**
See also CA 105; 187
Ibanez, Vicente Blasco
See Blasco Ibanez, Vicente
Ibarbourou, Juana de 1895-1979
See also HLCS 2; HW 1; LAW
Ibarguengoitia, Jorge 1928-1983 ...... **CLC 37**
See also CA 124; 113; HW 1
Ibsen, Henrik (Johan) 1828-1906 ... **TCLC 2, 8, 16, 37, 52; DC 2; WLC**
See also CA 104; 141; DA; DA3; DAB; DAC; DAM DRAM; MST; DFS 15; EW 7; LAIT 2; RGWL 2
Ibuse, Masuji 1898-1993 .... **CLC 22**
See also Ibuse Masuji
See also CA 127; 141; MJW

Ibuse Masuji
See Ibuse, Masuji
See also DLB 180
Ichikawa, Kon 1915- .... **CLC 20**
See also CA 121
Ichiyo, Higuchi 1872-1896 .... **NCLC 49**
See also MJW
Idle, Eric 1943-2000 .... **CLC 21**
See also Monty Python
See also CA 116; CANR 35, 91
Ignatow, David 1914-1997 .... **CLC 4, 7, 14, 40; PC 34**
See also CA 9-12R; 162; CAAS 3; CANR 31, 57, 96; CP 7; DLB 5
Ignotus
See Strachey, (Giles) Lytton
Ihimaera, Witi 1944- .... **CLC 46**
See also CA 77-80; CN 7; RGSF 2
Ilf, Ilya .... **TCLC 21**
See also Fainzilberg, Ilya Arnoldovich
Illyes, Gyula 1902-1983 .... **PC 16**
See also CA 114; 109; CDWLB 4; DLB 215; RGWL 2
Immermann, Karl (Lebrecht) 1796-1840 .... **NCLC 4, 49**
See also DLB 133
Ince, Thomas H. 1882-1924 .... **TCLC 89**
See also IDFW 3, 4
Inchbald, Elizabeth 1753-1821 ...... **NCLC 62**
See also DLB 39, 89; RGEL 2
Inclan, Ramon (Maria) del Valle
See Valle-Inclan, Ramon (Maria) del
Infante, G(uillermo) Cabrera
See Cabrera Infante, G(uillermo)
Ingalls, Rachel (Holmes) 1940- .... **CLC 42**
See also CA 123; 127
Ingamells, Reginald Charles
See Ingamells, Rex
Ingamells, Rex 1913-1955 .... **TCLC 35**
See also CA 167; DLB 260
Inge, William (Motter) 1913-1973 ..... **CLC 1, 8, 19**
See also CA 9-12R; CDALB 1941-1968; DA3; DAM DRAM; DFS 1, 5, 8; DLB 7, 249; MTCW 1, 2; RGAL 4
Ingelow, Jean 1820-1897 .... **NCLC 39, 107**
See also DLB 35, 163; FANT; SATA 33
Ingram, Willis J.
See Harris, Mark
Innaurato, Albert (F.) 1948(?)- ... **CLC 21, 60**
See also CA 115; 122; CAD; CANR 78; CD 5; INT CA-122
Innes, Michael
See Stewart, J(ohn) I(nnes) M(ackintosh)
See also MSW
Innis, Harold Adams 1894-1952 .... **TCLC 77**
See also CA 181; DLB 88
Insluis, Alanus de
See Alain de Lille
Ionesco, Eugene 1912-1994 ... **CLC 1, 4, 6, 9, 11, 15, 41, 86; DC 12; WLC**
See also CA 9-12R; 144; CANR 55; CWW 2; DA; DA3; DAB; DAC; DAM DRAM, MST; DFS 4, 9; EW 13; GFL 1789 to the Present; MTCW 1, 2; RGWL 2; SATA 7; SATA-Obit 79
Iqbal, Muhammad 1877-1938 .... **TCLC 28**
Ireland, Patrick
See O'Doherty, Brian
Irenaeus St. 130- .... **CMLC 42**
Iron, Ralph
See Schreiner, Olive (Emilie Albertina)

Irving, John (Winslow) 1942- ... **CLC 13, 23, 38, 112**
See also AAYA 8; AMWS 6; BEST 89:3; BPFB 2; CA 25-28R; CANR 28, 73; CN 7; CPW; DA3; DAM NOV, POP; DLB 6; DLBY 1982; MTCW 1, 2; NFS 12, 14; RGAL 4
Irving, Washington 1783-1859 . **NCLC 2, 19, 95; SSC 2, 37; WLC**
See also AMW; CDALB 1640-1865; DA; DA3; DAB; DAC; DAM MST; DLB 3, 11, 30, 59, 73, 74, 183, 186, 250, 254; EXPS; LAIT 1; RGAL 4; RGSF 2; SSFS 1, 8; SUFW; WCH; YABC 2
Irwin, P. K.
See Page, P(atricia) K(athleen)
Isaacs, Jorge Ricardo 1837-1895 ... **NCLC 70**
See also LAW
Isaacs, Susan 1943- .... **CLC 32**
See also BEST 89:1; BPFB 2; CA 89-92; CANR 20, 41, 65; CPW; DA3; DAM POP; INT CANR-20; MTCW 1, 2
Isherwood, Christopher (William Bradshaw) 1904-1986 ...... **CLC 1, 9, 11, 14, 44**
See also AMW; CA 13-16R; 117; CANR 35, 97; DA3; DAM DRAM, NOV; DLB 15, 195; DLBY 1986; IDTP; MTCW 1, 2; RGAL 4; RGEL 2; WLIT 4
Ishiguro, Kazuo 1954- .. **CLC 27, 56, 59, 110**
See also BEST 90:2; BPFB 2; BRWS 4; CA 120; CANR 49, 95; CN 7; DA3; DAM NOV; DLB 194; MTCW 1, 2; NFS 13; WLIT 4
Ishikawa, Hakuhin
See Ishikawa, Takuboku
Ishikawa, Takuboku 1886(?)-1912 .... **TCLC 15; PC 10**
See also CA 113; 153; DAM POET
Iskander, Fazil 1929- .... **CLC 47**
See also CA 102
Isler, Alan (David) 1934- .... **CLC 91**
See also CA 156; CANR 105
Ivan IV 1530-1584 .... **LC 17**
Ivanov, Vyacheslav Ivanovich 1866-1949 .... **TCLC 33**
See also CA 122
Ivask, Ivar Vidrik 1927-1992 .... **CLC 14**
See also CA 37-40R; 139; CANR 24
Ives, Morgan
See Bradley, Marion Zimmer
See also GLL 1
Izumi Shikibu c. 973-c. 1034 .... **CMLC 33**
J .... **CLC 8**
See also CA 33-36R; CANR 28, 67; CN 7; DLB 2, 28, 218; DLBY 1980
J .... **TCLC 123**
See also DLB 98
J. R. S.
See Gogarty, Oliver St. John
Jabran, Kahlil
See Gibran, Kahlil
Jabran, Khalil
See Gibran, Kahlil
Jackson, Daniel
See Wingrove, David (John)
Jackson, Helen Hunt 1830-1885 .... **NCLC 90**
See also DLB 42, 47, 186, 189; RGAL 4
Jackson, Jesse 1908-1983 .... **CLC 12**
See also BW 1; CA 25-28R; 109; CANR 27; CLR 28; CWRI 5; MAICYA 1, 2; SATA 2, 29; SATA-Obit 48
Jackson, Laura (Riding) 1901-1991
See Riding, Laura
See also CA 65-68; 135; CANR 28, 89; DLB 48
Jackson, Sam
See Trumbo, Dalton
Jackson, Sara
See Wingrove, David (John)

Jackson, Shirley 1919-1965 . **CLC 11, 60, 87; SSC 9, 39; WLC**
See also AAYA 9; AMWS 9; BPFB 2; CA 1-4R; 25-28R; CANR 4, 52; CDALB 1941-1968; DA; DA3; DAC; DAM MST; DLB 6, 234; EXPS; HGG; LAIT 4; MTCW 2; RGAL 4; RGSF 2; SATA 2; SSFS 1; SUFW

Jacob, (Cyprien-)Max 1876-1944 .... **TCLC 6**
See also CA 104; 193; DLB 258; GFL 1789 to the Present; GLL 2; RGWL 2

Jacobs, Harriet A(nn) 1813(?)-1897 .... **NCLC 67**
See also AFAW 1, 2; DLB 239; FW; LAIT 2; RGAL 4

Jacobs, Jim 1942- .... **CLC 12**
See also CA 97-100; INT 97-100

Jacobs, W(illiam) W(ymark) 1863-1943 .... **TCLC 22**
See also CA 121; 167; DLB 135; EXPS; HGG; RGEL 2; RGSF 2; SSFS 2; SUFW

Jacobsen, Jens Peter 1847-1885 .... **NCLC 34**

Jacobsen, Josephine 1908- .... **CLC 48, 102**
See also CA 33-36R; CAAS 18; CANR 23, 48; CCA 1; CP 7; DLB 244

Jacobson, Dan 1929- .... **CLC 4, 14**
See also AFW; CA 1-4R; CANR 2, 25, 66; CN 7; DLB 14, 207, 225; MTCW 1; RGSF 2

Jacqueline
See Carpentier (y Valmont), Alejo

Jagger, Mick 1944- .... **CLC 17**

Jahiz, al- c. 780-c. 869 .... **CMLC 25**

Jakes, John (William) 1932- .... **CLC 29**
See also AAYA 32; BEST 89:4; BPFB 2; CA 57-60; CANR 10, 43, 66; CPW; CSW; DA3; DAM NOV, POP; DLBY 1983; FANT; INT CANR-10; MTCW 1, 2; RHW; SATA 62; SFW 4; TCWW 2

James I 1394-1437 .... **LC 20**
See also RGEL 2

James, Andrew
See Kirkup, James

James, C(yril) L(ionel) R(obert) 1901-1989 .... **CLC 33; BLCS**
See also BW 2; CA 117; 125; 128; CANR 62; DLB 125; MTCW 1

James, Daniel (Lewis) 1911-1988
See Santiago, Danny
See also CA 174; 125

James, Dynely
See Mayne, William (James Carter)

James, Henry Sr. 1811-1882 .... **NCLC 53**

James, Henry 1843-1916 .... **TCLC 2, 11, 24, 40, 47, 64; SSC 8, 32, 47; WLC**
See also AMW; AMWR 1; BPFB 2; BRW 6; CA 104; 132; CDALB 1865-1917; DA; DA3; DAB; DAC; DAM MST, NOV; DLB 12, 71, 74, 189; DLBD 13; EXPS; HGG; LAIT 2; MTCW 1, 2; NFS 12; RGAL 4; RGEL 2; RGSF 2; SSFS 9; SUFW

James, M. R.
See James, Montague (Rhodes)
See also DLB 156, 201

James, Montague (Rhodes) 1862-1936 .... **TCLC 6; SSC 16**
See also James, M. R.
See also CA 104; HGG; RGEL 2; RGSF 2; SUFW

James, P. D. .... **CLC 18, 46, 122**
See also White, Phyllis Dorothy James
See also BEST 90:2; BPFB 2; BRWS 4; CDBLB 1960 to Present; DLB 87; DLBD 17; MSW

James, Philip
See Moorcock, Michael (John)

James, Samuel
See Stephens, James

James, Seumas
See Stephens, James

James, Stephen
See Stephens, James

James, William 1842-1910 .... **TCLC 15, 32**
See also AMW; CA 109; 193; RGAL 4

Jameson, Anna 1794-1860 .... **NCLC 43**
See also DLB 99, 166

Jameson, Fredric (R.) 1934- .... **CLC 142**
See also CA 196; DLB 67

Jami, Nur al-Din 'Abd al-Rahman 1414-1492 .... **LC 9**

Jammes, Francis 1868-1938 .... **TCLC 75**
See also CA 198; GFL 1789 to the Present

Jandl, Ernst 1925-2000 .... **CLC 34**
See also CA 200

Janowitz, Tama 1957- .... **CLC 43, 145**
See also CA 106; CANR 52, 89; CN 7; CPW; DAM POP

Japrisot, Sebastien 1931- .... **CLC 90**
See also Rossi, Jean Baptiste
See also CMW 4

Jarrell, Randall 1914-1965 .... **CLC 1, 2, 6, 9, 13, 49; PC 41**
See also AMW; BYA 5; CA 5-8R; 25-28R; CABS 2; CANR 6, 34; CDALB 1941-1968; CLR 6; CWRI 5; DAM POET; DLB 48, 52; EXPP; MAICYA 1, 2; MTCW 1, 2; PAB; PFS 2; RGAL 4; SATA 7

Jarry, Alfred 1873-1907 .... **TCLC 2, 14; SSC 20**
See also CA 104; 153; DA3; DAM DRAM; DFS 8; DLB 192, 258; EW 9; GFL 1789 to the Present; RGWL 2

Jarvis, E. K.
See Silverberg, Robert

Jawien, Andrzej
See John Paul II, Pope

Jaynes, Roderick
See Coen, Ethan

Jeake, Samuel, Jr.
See Aiken, Conrad (Potter)

Jean Paul 1763-1825 .... **NCLC 7**

Jefferies, (John) Richard 1848-1887 .... **NCLC 47**
See also DLB 98, 141; RGEL 2; SATA 16; SFW 4

Jeffers, (John) Robinson 1887-1962 .. **CLC 2, 3, 11, 15, 54; PC 17; WLC**
See also AMWS 2; CA 85-88; CANR 35; CDALB 1917-1929; DA; DAC; DAM MST, POET; DLB 45, 212; MTCW 1, 2; PAB; PFS 3, 4; RGAL 4

Jefferson, Janet
See Mencken, H(enry) L(ouis)

Jefferson, Thomas 1743-1826 . **NCLC 11, 103**
See also ANW; CDALB 1640-1865; DA3; DLB 31, 183; LAIT 1; RGAL 4

Jeffrey, Francis 1773-1850 .... **NCLC 33**
See also Francis, Lord Jeffrey

Jelakowitch, Ivan
See Heijermans, Herman

Jellicoe, (Patricia) Ann 1927- .... **CLC 27**
See also CA 85-88; CBD; CD 5; CWD; CWRI 5; DLB 13, 233; FW

Jemyma
See Holley, Marietta

Jen, Gish .... **CLC 70**
See also Jen, Lillian

Jen, Lillian 1956(?)-
See Jen, Gish
See also CA 135; CANR 89

Jenkins, (John) Robin 1912- .... **CLC 52**
See also CA 1-4R; CANR 1; CN 7; DLB 14

Jennings, Elizabeth (Joan) 1926-2001 .... **CLC 5, 14, 131**
See also BRWS 5; CA 61-64; 200; CAAS 5; CANR 8, 39, 66; CP 7; CWP; DLB 27; MTCW 1; SATA 66

Jennings, Waylon 1937- .... **CLC 21**

Jensen, Johannes V. 1873-1950 ...... **TCLC 41**
See also CA 170; DLB 214

Jensen, Laura (Linnea) 1948- .... **CLC 37**
See also CA 103

Jerome, Jerome K(lapka) 1859-1927 .... **TCLC 23**
See also CA 119; 177; DLB 10, 34, 135; RGEL 2

Jerrold, Douglas William 1803-1857 .... **NCLC 2**
See also DLB 158, 159; RGEL 2

Jewett, (Theodora) Sarah Orne 1849-1909 .... **TCLC 1, 22; SSC 6, 44**
See also AMW; CA 108; 127; CANR 71; DLB 12, 74, 221; EXPS; FW; MAWW; NFS 15; RGAL 4; RGSF 2; SATA 15; SSFS 4

Jewsbury, Geraldine (Endsor) 1812-1880 .... **NCLC 22**
See also DLB 21

Jhabvala, Ruth Prawer 1927- . **CLC 4, 8, 29, 94, 138**
See also BRWS 5; CA 1-4R; CANR 2, 29, 51, 74, 91; CN 7; DAB; DAM NOV; DLB 139, 194; IDFW 3, 4; INT CANR-29; MTCW 1, 2; RGSF 2; RGWL 2; RHW

Jibran, Kahlil
See Gibran, Kahlil

Jibran, Khalil
See Gibran, Kahlil

Jiles, Paulette 1943- .... **CLC 13, 58**
See also CA 101; CANR 70; CWP

Jimenez (Mantecon), Juan Ramon 1881-1958 .... **TCLC 4; HLC 1; PC 7**
See also CA 104; 131; CANR 74; DAM MULT, POET; DLB 134; EW 9; HW 1; MTCW 1, 2; RGWL 2

Jimenez, Ramon
See Jimenez (Mantecon), Juan Ramon

Jimenez Mantecon, Juan
See Jimenez (Mantecon), Juan Ramon

Jin, Ha .... **CLC 109**
See also Jin, Xuefei
See also CA 152; DLB 244

Jin, Xuefei 1956-
See Jin, Ha
See also CANR 91

Joel, Billy .... **CLC 26**
See also Joel, William Martin

Joel, William Martin 1949-
See Joel, Billy
See also CA 108

John, Saint 107th cent. -100 .... **CMLC 27**

John of the Cross, St. 1542-1591 ..... **LC 18**
See also RGWL 2

John Paul II, Pope 1920- .... **CLC 128**
See also CA 106; 133

Johnson, B(ryan) S(tanley William) 1933-1973 .... **CLC 6, 9**
See also CA 9-12R; 53-56; CANR 9; DLB 14, 40; RGEL 2

Johnson, Benjamin F., of Boone
See Riley, James Whitcomb

Johnson, Charles (Richard) 1948- .... **CLC 7, 51, 65; BLC 2**
See also AFAW 2; AMWS 6; BW 2, 3; CA 116; CAAS 18; CANR 42, 66, 82; CN 7; DAM MULT; DLB 33; MTCW 2; RGAL 4

Johnson, Denis 1949- .... **CLC 52, 160**
See also CA 117; 121; CANR 71, 99; CN 7; DLB 120

Johnson, Diane 1934- .... **CLC 5, 13, 48**
See also BPFB 2; CA 41-44R; CANR 17, 40, 62, 95; CN 7; DLBY 1980; INT CANR-17; MTCW 1

Johnson, Eyvind (Olof Verner) 1900-1976 .... **CLC 14**
See also CA 73-76; 69-72; CANR 34, 101; DLB 259; EW 12

Johnson, J. R.
See James, C(yril) L(ionel) R(obert)

Johnson, James Weldon 1871-1938 . **TCLC 3, 19; BLC 2; PC 24**
See also AFAW 1, 2; BW 1, 3; CA 104; 125; CANR 82; CDALB 1917-1929; CLR 32; DA3; DAM MULT, POET; DLB 51; EXPP; MTCW 1, 2; PFS 1; RGAL 4; SATA 31

Johnson, Joyce 1935- .... **CLC 58**
See also CA 125; 129; CANR 102

Johnson, Judith (Emlyn) 1936- .... **CLC 7, 15**
See also Sherwin, Judith Johnson
See also CA 25-28R, 153; CANR 34

Johnson, Lionel (Pigot) 1867-1902 .... **TCLC 19**
See also CA 117; DLB 19; RGEL 2

Johnson, Marguerite (Annie)
See Angelou, Maya

Johnson, Mel
See Malzberg, Barry N(athaniel)

Johnson, Pamela Hansford 1912-1981 .... **CLC 1, 7, 27**
See also CA 1-4R; 104; CANR 2, 28; DLB 15; MTCW 1, 2; RGEL 2

Johnson, Paul (Bede) 1928- .... **CLC 147**
See also BEST 89:4; CA 17-20R; CANR 34, 62, 100

Johnson, Robert .... **CLC 70**

Johnson, Robert 1911(?)-1938 .... **TCLC 69**
See also BW 3; CA 174

Johnson, Samuel 1709-1784 .... **LC 15, 52; WLC**
See also BRW 3; BRWR 1; CDBLB 1660-1789; DA; DAB; DAC; DAM MST; DLB 39, 95, 104, 142, 213; RGEL 2; TEA

Johnson, Uwe 1934-1984 .. **CLC 5, 10, 15, 40**
See also CA 1-4R; 112; CANR 1, 39; CDWLB 2; DLB 75; MTCW 1; RGWL 2

Johnston, George (Benson) 1913- ..... **CLC 51**
See also CA 1-4R; CANR 5, 20; CP 7; DLB 88

Johnston, Jennifer (Prudence) 1930- .... **CLC 7, 150**
See also CA 85-88; CANR 92; CN 7; DLB 14

Joinville, Jean de 1224(?)-1317 ..... **CMLC 38**

Jolley, (Monica) Elizabeth 1923- ..... **CLC 46; SSC 19**
See also CA 127; CAAS 13; CANR 59; CN 7; RGSF 2

Jones, Arthur Llewellyn 1863-1947
See Machen, Arthur
See also CA 104; 179; HGG

Jones, D(ouglas) G(ordon) 1929- ..... **CLC 10**
See also CA 29-32R; CANR 13, 90; CP 7; DLB 53

Jones, David (Michael) 1895-1974 .... **CLC 2, 4, 7, 13, 42**
See also BRW 6; BRWS 7; CA 9-12R; 53-56; CANR 28; CDBLB 1945-1960; DLB 20, 100; MTCW 1; PAB; RGEL 2

Jones, David Robert 1947-
See Bowie, David
See also CA 103; CANR 104

Jones, Diana Wynne 1934- .... **CLC 26**
See also AAYA 12; BYA 6, 7, 9, 11, 13; CA 49-52; CANR 4, 26, 56; CLR 23; DLB 161; FANT; JRDA; MAICYA 1, 2; SAAS 7; SATA 9, 70, 108; SFW 4; YAW

Jones, Edward P. 1950- .... **CLC 76**
See also BW 2, 3; CA 142; CANR 79; CSW

Jones, Gayl 1949- ...... **CLC 6, 9, 131; BLC 2**
See also AFAW 1, 2; BW 2, 3; CA 77-80; CANR 27, 66; CN 7; CSW; DA3; DAM MULT; DLB 33; MTCW 1, 2; RGAL 4

Jones, James 1931-1978 ...... **CLC 1, 3, 10, 39**
See also AITN 1, 2; BPFB 2; CA 1-4R; 69-72; CANR 6; DLB 2, 143; DLBD 17; DLBY 1998; MTCW 1; RGAL 4

Jones, John J.
See Lovecraft, H(oward) P(hillips)

Jones, LeRoi .... **CLC 1, 2, 3, 5, 10, 14**
See also Baraka, Amiri
See also MTCW 2

Jones, Louis B. 1953- .... **CLC 65**
See also CA 141; CANR 73

Jones, Madison (Percy, Jr.) 1925- ..... **CLC 4**
See also CA 13-16R; CAAS 11; CANR 7, 54, 83; CN 7; CSW; DLB 152

Jones, Mervyn 1922- .... **CLC 10, 52**
See also CA 45-48; CAAS 5; CANR 1, 91; CN 7; MTCW 1

Jones, Mick 1956(?)- .... **CLC 30**

Jones, Nettie (Pearl) 1941- .... **CLC 34**
See also BW 2; CA 137; CAAS 20; CANR 88

Jones, Preston 1936-1979 .... **CLC 10**
See also CA 73-76; 89-92; DLB 7

Jones, Robert F(rancis) 1934- .... **CLC 7**
See also CA 49-52; CANR 2, 61

Jones, Rod 1953- .... **CLC 50**
See also CA 128

Jones, Terence Graham Parry 1942- .... **CLC 21**
See also Jones, Terry; Monty Python
See also CA 112; 116; CANR 35, 93; INT 116; SATA 127

Jones, Terry
See Jones, Terence Graham Parry
See also SATA 67; SATA-Brief 51

Jones, Thom (Douglas) 1945(?)- .... **CLC 81**
See also CA 157; CANR 88; DLB 244

Jong, Erica 1942- .... **CLC 4, 6, 8, 18, 83**
See also AITN 1; AMWS 5; BEST 90:2; BPFB 2; CA 73-76; CANR 26, 52, 75; CN 7; CP 7; CPW; DA3; DAM NOV, POP; DLB 2, 5, 28, 152; FW; INT CANR-26; MTCW 1, 2

Jonson, Ben(jamin) 1572(?)-1637 .. **LC 6, 33; DC 4; PC 17; WLC**
See also BRW 1; BRWR 1; CDBLB Before 1660; DA; DAB; DAC; DAM DRAM, MST, POET; DFS 4, 10; DLB 62, 121; RGEL 2; WLIT 3

Jordan, June 1936- .... **CLC 5, 11, 23, 114; BLCS; PC 38**
See also Meyer, June
See also AAYA 2; AFAW 1, 2; BW 2, 3; CA 33-36R; CANR 25, 70; CLR 10; CP 7; CWP; DAM MULT, POET; DLB 38; GLL 2; LAIT 5; MAICYA 1, 2; MTCW 1; SATA 4; YAW

Jordan, Neil (Patrick) 1950- .... **CLC 110**
See also CA 124; 130; CANR 54; CN 7; GLL 2; INT 130

Jordan, Pat(rick M.) 1941- .... **CLC 37**
See also CA 33-36R

Jorgensen, Ivar
See Ellison, Harlan (Jay)

Jorgenson, Ivar
See Silverberg, Robert

Joseph, George Ghevarughese .... **CLC 70**

Josephson, Mary
See O'Doherty, Brian

Josephus, Flavius c. 37-100 .... **CMLC 13**
See also AW 2; DLB 176

Josiah Allen's Wife
See Holley, Marietta

Josipovici, Gabriel (David) 1940- ...... **CLC 6, 43, 153**
See also CA 37-40R; CAAS 8; CANR 47, 84; CN 7; DLB 14

Joubert, Joseph 1754-1824 .... **NCLC 9**

Jouve, Pierre Jean 1887-1976 .... **CLC 47**
See also CA 65-68; DLB 258

Jovine, Francesco 1902-1950 .... **TCLC 79**

Joyce, James (Augustine Aloysius) 1882-1941 ... **TCLC 3, 8, 16, 35, 52; DC 16; PC 22; SSC 3, 26, 44; WLC**
See also AAYA 42; BRW 7; BRWR 1; BYA 11, 13; CA 104; 126; CDBLB 1914-1945; DA; DA3; DAB; DAC; DAM MST, NOV, POET; DLB 10, 19, 36, 162, 247; EXPN; EXPS; LAIT 3; MTCW 1, 2; NFS 7; RGSF 2; SSFS 1; WLIT 4

Jozsef, Attila 1905-1937 .... **TCLC 22**
See also CA 116; CDWLB 4; DLB 215

Juana Ines de la Cruz, Sor 1651(?)-1695 ...... **LC 5; HLCS 1; PC 24**
See also FW; LAW; RGWL 2; WLIT 1

Juana Inez de La Cruz, Sor
See Juana Ines de la Cruz, Sor

Judd, Cyril
See Kornbluth, C(yril) M.; Pohl, Frederik

Juenger, Ernst 1895-1998 .... **CLC 125**
See also Junger, Ernst
See also CA 101; 167; CANR 21, 47, 106; DLB 56

Julian of Norwich 1342(?)-1416(?) . **LC 6, 52**
See also DLB 146

Julius Caesar 100B.C.-44B.C.
See Caesar, Julius
See also CDWLB 1; DLB 211

Junger, Ernst
See Juenger, Ernst
See also CDWLB 2; RGWL 2

Junger, Sebastian 1962- .... **CLC 109**
See also AAYA 28; CA 165

Juniper, Alex
See Hospital, Janette Turner

Junius
See Luxemburg, Rosa

Just, Ward (Swift) 1935- .... **CLC 4, 27**
See also CA 25-28R; CANR 32, 87; CN 7; INT CANR-32

Justice, Donald (Rodney) 1925- .. **CLC 6, 19, 102**
See also AMWS 7; CA 5-8R; CANR 26, 54, 74; CP 7; CSW; DAM POET; DLBY 1983; INT CANR-26; MTCW 2; PFS 14

Juvenal c. 60-c. 130 .... **CMLC 8**
See also AW 2; CDWLB 1; DLB 211; RGWL 2

Juvenis
See Bourne, Randolph S(illiman)

Kabakov, Sasha .... **CLC 59**

Kacew, Romain 1914-1980
See Gary, Romain
See also CA 108; 102

Kadare, Ismail 1936- .... **CLC 52**
See also CA 161

Kadohata, Cynthia .... **CLC 59, 122**
See also CA 140

Kafka, Franz 1883-1924 . **TCLC 2, 6, 13, 29, 47, 53, 112; SSC 5, 29, 35; WLC**
See also AAYA 31; BPFB 2; CA 105; 126; CDWLB 2; DA; DA3; DAB; DAC; DAM MST, NOV; DLB 81; EW 9; EXPS; MTCW 1, 2; NFS 7; RGSF 2; RGWL 2; SFW 4; SSFS 3, 7, 12

Kahanovitsch, Pinkhes
See Der Nister

Kahn, Roger 1927- .... **CLC 30**
See also CA 25-28R; CANR 44, 69; DLB 171; SATA 37

Kain, Saul
See Sassoon, Siegfried (Lorraine)

Kaiser, Georg 1878-1945 .... **TCLC 9**
See also CA 106; 190; CDWLB 2; DLB 124; RGWL 2
Kaledin, Sergei .... **CLC 59**
Kaletski, Alexander 1946- .... **CLC 39**
See also CA 118; 143
Kalidasa fl. c. 400-455 .... **CMLC 9; PC 22**
See also RGWL 2
Kallman, Chester (Simon)
1921-1975 .... **CLC 2**
See also CA 45-48; 53-56; CANR 3
Kaminsky, Melvin 1926-
See Brooks, Mel
See also CA 65-68; CANR 16
Kaminsky, Stuart M(elvin) 1934- ..... **CLC 59**
See also CA 73-76; CANR 29, 53, 89; CMW 4
Kandinsky, Wassily 1866-1944 .... **TCLC 92**
See also CA 118; 155
Kane, Francis
See Robbins, Harold
Kane, Henry 1918-
See Queen, Ellery
See also CA 156; CMW 4
Kane, Paul
See Simon, Paul (Frederick)
Kanin, Garson 1912-1999 .... **CLC 22**
See also AITN 1; CA 5-8R; 177; CAD; CANR 7, 78; DLB 7; IDFW 3, 4
Kaniuk, Yoram 1930- .... **CLC 19**
See also CA 134
Kant, Immanuel 1724-1804 ..... **NCLC 27, 67**
See also DLB 94
Kantor, MacKinlay 1904-1977 .... **CLC 7**
See also CA 61-64; 73-76; CANR 60, 63; DLB 9, 102; MTCW 2; RHW; TCWW 2
Kanze Motokiyo
See Zeami
Kaplan, David Michael 1946- .... **CLC 50**
See also CA 187
Kaplan, James 1951- .... **CLC 59**
See also CA 135
Karadzic, Vuk Stefanovic
1787-1864 .... **NCLC 115**
See also CDWLB 4; DLB 147
Karageorge, Michael
See Anderson, Poul (William)
Karamzin, Nikolai Mikhailovich
1766-1826 .... **NCLC 3**
See also DLB 150; RGSF 2
Karapanou, Margarita 1946- .... **CLC 13**
See also CA 101
Karinthy, Frigyes 1887-1938 .... **TCLC 47**
See also CA 170; DLB 215
Karl, Frederick R(obert) 1927- .... **CLC 34**
See also CA 5-8R; CANR 3, 44
Kastel, Warren
See Silverberg, Robert
Kataev, Evgeny Petrovich 1903-1942
See Petrov, Evgeny
See also CA 120
Kataphusin
See Ruskin, John
Katz, Steve 1935- .... **CLC 47**
See also CA 25-28R; CAAS 14, 64; CANR 12; CN 7; DLBY 1983
Kauffman, Janet 1945- .... **CLC 42**
See also CA 117; CANR 43, 84; DLB 218; DLBY 1986
Kaufman, Bob (Garnell) 1925-1986 . **CLC 49**
See also BW 1; CA 41-44R; 118; CANR 22; DLB 16, 41
Kaufman, George S. 1889-1961 ...... **CLC 38; DC 17**
See also CA 108; 93-96; DAM DRAM; DFS 1, 10; DLB 7; INT CA-108; MTCW 2; RGAL 4

Kaufman, Sue .... **CLC 3, 8**
See also Barondess, Sue K(aufman)
Kavafis, Konstantinos Petrou 1863-1933
See Cavafy, C(onstantine) P(eter)
See also CA 104
Kavan, Anna 1901-1968 .... **CLC 5, 13, 82**
See also BRWS 7; CA 5-8R; CANR 6, 57; DLB 255; MTCW 1; RGEL 2; SFW 4
Kavanagh, Dan
See Barnes, Julian (Patrick)
Kavanagh, Julie 1952- .... **CLC 119**
See also CA 163
Kavanagh, Patrick (Joseph)
1904-1967 .... **CLC 22; PC 33**
See also BRWS 7; CA 123; 25-28R; DLB 15, 20; MTCW 1; RGEL 2
Kawabata, Yasunari 1899-1972 ..... **CLC 2, 5, 9, 18, 107; SSC 17**
See also Kawabata Yasunari
See also CA 93-96; 33-36R; CANR 88; DAM MULT; MJW; MTCW 2; RGSF 2; RGWL 2
Kawabata Yasunari
See Kawabata, Yasunari
See also DLB 180
Kaye, M(ary) M(argaret) 1909- .... **CLC 28**
See also CA 89-92; CANR 24, 60, 102; MTCW 1, 2; RHW; SATA 62
Kaye, Mollie
See Kaye, M(ary) M(argaret)
Kaye-Smith, Sheila 1887-1956 .... **TCLC 20**
See also CA 118; DLB 36
Kaymor, Patrice Maguilene
See Senghor, Leopold Sedar
Kazakov, Yuri Pavlovich 1927-1982 . **SSC 43**
See also CA 5-8R; CANR 36; MTCW 1; RGSF 2
Kazan, Elia 1909- .... **CLC 6, 16, 63**
See also CA 21-24R; CANR 32, 78
Kazantzakis, Nikos 1883(?)-1957 .... **TCLC 2, 5, 33**
See also BPFB 2; CA 105; 132; DA3; EW 9; MTCW 1, 2; RGWL 2
Kazin, Alfred 1915-1998 ..... **CLC 34, 38, 119**
See also AMWS 8; CA 1-4R; CAAS 7; CANR 1, 45, 79; DLB 67
Keane, Mary Nesta (Skrine) 1904-1996
See Keane, Molly
See also CA 108; 114; 151; CN 7; RHW
Keane, Molly .... **CLC 31**
See also Keane, Mary Nesta (Skrine)
See also INT 114
Keates, Jonathan 1946(?)- .... **CLC 34**
See also CA 163
Keaton, Buster 1895-1966 .... **CLC 20**
See also CA 194
Keats, John 1795-1821 ... **NCLC 8, 73; PC 1; WLC**
See also BRW 4; BRWR 1; CDBLB 1789-1832; DA; DA3; DAB; DAC; DAM MST, POET; DLB 96, 110; EXPP; PAB; PFS 1, 2, 3, 9; RGEL 2; WLIT 3; WP
Keble, John 1792-1866 .... **NCLC 87**
See also DLB 32, 55; RGEL 2
Keene, Donald 1922- .... **CLC 34**
See also CA 1-4R; CANR 5
Keillor, Garrison .... **CLC 40, 115**
See also Keillor, Gary (Edward)
See also AAYA 2; BEST 89:3; BPFB 2; DLBY 1987; SATA 58
Keillor, Gary (Edward) 1942-
See Keillor, Garrison
See also CA 111; 117; CANR 36, 59; CPW; DA3; DAM POP; MTCW 1, 2
Keith, Carlos
See Lewton, Val
Keith, Michael
See Hubbard, L(afayette) Ron(ald)

Keller, Gottfried 1819-1890 .... **NCLC 2; SSC 26**
See also CDWLB 2; DLB 129; EW; RGSF 2; RGWL 2
Keller, Nora Okja 1965- .... **CLC 109**
See also CA 187
Kellerman, Jonathan 1949- .... **CLC 44**
See also AAYA 35; BEST 90:1; CA 106; CANR 29, 51; CMW 4; CPW; DA3; DAM POP; INT CANR-29
Kelley, William Melvin 1937- .... **CLC 22**
See also BW 1; CA 77-80; CANR 27, 83; CN 7; DLB 33
Kellogg, Marjorie 1922- .... **CLC 2**
See also CA 81-84
Kellow, Kathleen
See Hibbert, Eleanor Alice Burford
Kelly, M(ilton) T(errence) 1947- ...... **CLC 55**
See also CA 97-100; CAAS 22; CANR 19, 43, 84; CN 7
Kelly, Robert 1935- .... **SSC 50**
See also CA 17-20R; CAAS 19; CANR 47; CP 7; DLB 5, 130, 165
Kelman, James 1946- .... **CLC 58, 86**
See also BRWS 5; CA 148; CANR 85; CN 7; DLB 194; RGSF 2; WLIT 4
Kemal, Yashar 1923- .... **CLC 14, 29**
See also CA 89-92; CANR 44; CWW 2
Kemble, Fanny 1809-1893 .... **NCLC 18**
See also DLB 32
Kemelman, Harry 1908-1996 .... **CLC 2**
See also AITN 1; BPFB 2; CA 9-12R; 155; CANR 6, 71; CMW 4; DLB 28
Kempe, Margery 1373(?)-1440(?) ... **LC 6, 56**
See also DLB 146; RGEL 2
Kempis, Thomas a 1380-1471 .... **LC 11**
Kendall, Henry 1839-1882 .... **NCLC 12**
See also DLB 230
Keneally, Thomas (Michael) 1935- ... **CLC 5, 8, 10, 14, 19, 27, 43, 117**
See also BRWS 4; CA 85-88; CANR 10, 50, 74; CN 7; CPW; DA3; DAM NOV; MTCW 1, 2; RGEL 2; RHW
Kennedy, Adrienne (Lita) 1931- ...... **CLC 66; BLC 2; DC 5**
See also AFAW 2; BW 2, 3; CA 103; CAAS 20; CABS 3; CANR 26, 53, 82; CD 5; DAM MULT; DFS 9; DLB 38; FW
Kennedy, John Pendleton
1795-1870 .... **NCLC 2**
See also DLB 3, 248, 254; RGAL 4
Kennedy, Joseph Charles 1929-
See Kennedy, X. J.
See also CA 1-4R; CAAE 201; CANR 4, 30, 40; CP 7; CWRI 5; MAICYA 2; MAICYAS 1; SATA 14, 86; SATA-Essay 130
Kennedy, William 1928- ... **CLC 6, 28, 34, 53**
See also AAYA 1; AMWS 7; BPFB 2; CA 85-88; CANR 14, 31, 76; CN 7; DA3; DAM NOV; DLB 143; DLBY 1985; INT CANR-31; MTCW 1, 2; SATA 57
Kennedy, X. J. .... **CLC 8, 42**
See also Kennedy, Joseph Charles
See also CAAS 9; CLR 27; DLB 5; SAAS 22
Kenny, Maurice (Francis) 1929- ...... **CLC 87**
See also CA 144; CAAS 22; DAM MULT; DLB 175; NNAL
Kent, Kelvin
See Kuttner, Henry
Kenton, Maxwell
See Southern, Terry
Kenyon, Robert O.
See Kuttner, Henry
Kepler, Johannes 1571-1630 .... **LC 45**
Ker, Jill
See Conway, Jill K(er)
Kerkow, H. C.
See Lewton, Val

Kerouac, Jack 1922-1969 ...... **CLC 1, 2, 3, 5, 14, 29, 61; WLC**
See also Kerouac, Jean-Louis Lebris de
See also AAYA 25; AMWS 3; BPFB 2; CDALB 1941-1968; CPW; DLB 2, 16, 237; DLBD 3; DLBY 1995; GLL 1; MTCW 2; NFS 8; RGAL 4; TCLC 117; WP

Kerouac, Jean-Louis Lebris de 1922-1969
See Kerouac, Jack
See also AITN 1; CA 5-8R; 25-28R; CANR 26, 54, 95; DA; DA3; DAB; DAC; DAM MST, NOV, POET, POP; MTCW 1, 2

Kerr, Jean 1923- .... **CLC 22**
See also CA 5-8R; CANR 7; INT CANR-7

Kerr, M. E. .... **CLC 12, 35**
See Meaker, Marijane (Agnes)
See also AAYA 2, 23; BYA 1, 7, 8; CLR 29; SAAS 1; WYA

Kerr, Robert .... **CLC 55**

Kerrigan, (Thomas) Anthony 1918- .. **CLC 4, 6**
See also CA 49-52; CAAS 11; CANR 4

Kerry, Lois
See Duncan, Lois

Kesey, Ken (Elton) 1935-2001 ... **CLC 1, 3, 6, 11, 46, 64; WLC**
See also AAYA 25; BPFB 2; CA 1-4R; CANR 22, 38, 66; CDALB 1968-1988; CN 7; CPW; DA; DA3; DAB; DAC; DAM MST, NOV, POP; DLB 2, 16, 206; EXPN; LAIT 4; MTCW 1, 2; NFS 2; RGAL 4; SATA 66; SATA-Obit 131; YAW

Kesselring, Joseph (Otto) 1902-1967 .... **CLC 45**
See also CA 150; DAM DRAM, MST

Kessler, Jascha (Frederick) 1929- ...... **CLC 4**
See also CA 17-20R; CANR 8, 48

Kettelkamp, Larry (Dale) 1933- .... **CLC 12**
See also CA 29-32R; CANR 16; SAAS 3; SATA 2

Key, Ellen (Karolina Sofia) 1849-1926 .... **TCLC 65**
See also DLB 259

Keyber, Conny
See Fielding, Henry

Keyes, Daniel 1927- .... **CLC 80**
See also AAYA 23; BYA 11; CA 17-20R, 181; CAAE 181; CANR 10, 26, 54, 74; DA; DA3; DAC; DAM MST, NOV; EXPN; LAIT 4; MTCW 2; NFS 2; SATA 37; SFW 4

Keynes, John Maynard 1883-1946 .... **TCLC 64**
See also CA 114; 162, 163; DLBD 10; MTCW 2

Khanshendel, Chiron
See Rose, Wendy

Khayyam, Omar 1048-1131 ... **CMLC 11; PC 8**
See also Omar Khayyam
See also DA3; DAM POET

Kherdian, David 1931- .... **CLC 6, 9**
See also AAYA 42; CA 21-24R; CAAE 192; CAAS 2; CANR 39, 78; CLR 24; JRDA; LAIT 3; MAICYA 1, 2; SATA 16, 74; SATA-Essay 125

Khlebnikov, Velimir .... **TCLC 20**
See also Khlebnikov, Viktor Vladimirovich
See also EW 10; RGWL 2

Khlebnikov, Viktor Vladimirovich 1885-1922
See Khlebnikov, Velimir
See also CA 117

Khodasevich, Vladislav (Felitsianovich) 1886-1939 .... **TCLC 15**
See also CA 115

Kielland, Alexander Lange 1849-1906 .... **TCLC 5**
See also CA 104

Kiely, Benedict 1919- .... **CLC 23, 43**
See also CA 1-4R; CANR 2, 84; CN 7; DLB 15

Kienzle, William X(avier) 1928-2001 .... **CLC 25**
See also CA 93-96; CAAS 1; CANR 9, 31, 59; CMW 4; DA3; DAM POP; INT CANR-31; MSW; MTCW 1, 2

Kierkegaard, Soren 1813-1855 ..... **NCLC 34, 78**
See also EW 6

Kieslowski, Krzysztof 1941-1996 .... **CLC 120**
See also CA 147; 151

Killens, John Oliver 1916-1987 .... **CLC 10**
See also BW 2; CA 77-80; 123; CAAS 2; CANR 26; DLB 33

Killigrew, Anne 1660-1685 .... **LC 4, 73**
See also DLB 131

Killigrew, Thomas 1612-1683 .... **LC 57**
See also DLB 58; RGEL 2

Kim
See Simenon, Georges (Jacques Christian)

Kincaid, Jamaica 1949- ..... **CLC 43, 68, 137; BLC 2**
See also AAYA 13; AFAW 2; AMWS 7; BRWS 7; BW 2, 3; CA 125; CANR 47, 59, 95; CDALBS; CDWLB 3; CLR 63; CN 7; DA3; DAM MULT, NOV; DLB 157, 227; DNFS 1; EXPS; FW; MTCW 2; NCFS 1; NFS 3; SSFS 5, 7; YAW

King, Francis (Henry) 1923- .... **CLC 8, 53, 145**
See also CA 1-4R; CANR 1, 33, 86; CN 7; DAM NOV; DLB 15, 139; MTCW 1

King, Kennedy
See Brown, George Douglas

King, Martin Luther, Jr. 1929-1968 .... **CLC 83; BLC 2; WLCS**
See also BW 2, 3; CA 25-28; CANR 27, 44; CAP 2; DA; DA3; DAB; DAC; DAM MST, MULT; LAIT 5; MTCW 1, 2; SATA 14

King, Stephen (Edwin) 1947- .... **CLC 12, 26, 37, 61, 113; SSC 17**
See also AAYA 1, 17; AMWS 5; BEST 90:1; BPFB 2; CA 61-64; CANR 1, 30, 52, 76; CPW; DA3; DAM NOV, POP; DLB 143; DLBY 1980; HGG; JRDA; LAIT 5; MTCW 1, 2; RGAL 4; SATA 9, 55; SUFW 4; WYAS 1; YAW

King, Steve
See King, Stephen (Edwin)

King, Thomas 1943- .... **CLC 89**
See also CA 144; CANR 95; CCA 1; CN 7; DAC; DAM MULT; DLB 175; NNAL; SATA 96

Kingman, Lee .... **CLC 17**
See also Natti, (Mary) Lee
See also CWRI 5; SAAS 3; SATA 1, 67

Kingsley, Charles 1819-1875 .... **NCLC 35**
See also CLR 77; DLB 21, 32, 163, 178, 190; FANT; MAICYA 2; MAICYAS 1; RGEL 2; WCH; YABC 2

Kingsley, Henry 1830-1876 .... **NCLC 107**
See also DLB 21, 230; RGEL 2

Kingsley, Sidney 1906-1995 .... **CLC 44**
See also CA 85-88; 147; CAD; DFS 14; DLB 7; RGAL 4

Kingsolver, Barbara 1955- . **CLC 55, 81, 130**
See also AAYA 15; AMWS 7; CA 129; 134; CANR 60, 96; CDALBS; CPW; CSW; DA3; DAM POP; DLB 206; INT CA-134; LAIT 5; MTCW 2; NFS 5, 10, 12; RGAL 4

Kingston, Maxine (Ting Ting) Hong 1940- .... **CLC 12, 19, 58, 121; AAL; WLCS**
See also AAYA 8; AMWS 5; BPFB 2; CA 69-72; CANR 13, 38, 74, 87; CDALBS; CN 7; DA3; DAM MULT, NOV; DLB 173, 212; DLBY 1980; FW; INT CANR-13; LAIT 5; MAWW; MTCW 1, 2; NFS 6; RGAL 4; SATA 53; SSFS 3

Kinnell, Galway 1927- ..... **CLC 1, 2, 3, 5, 13, 29, 129; PC 26**
See also AMWS 3; CA 9-12R; CANR 10, 34, 66; CP 7; DLB 5; DLBY 1987; INT CANR-34; MTCW 1, 2; PAB; PFS 9; RGAL 4; WP

Kinsella, Thomas 1928- .... **CLC 4, 19, 138**
See also BRWS 5; CA 17-20R; CANR 15; CP 7; DLB 27; MTCW 1, 2; RGEL 2

Kinsella, W(illiam) P(atrick) 1935- . **CLC 27, 43**
See also AAYA 7; BPFB 2; CA 97-100; CAAS 7; CANR 21, 35, 66, 75; CN 7; CPW; DAC; DAM NOV, POP; FANT; INT CANR-21; LAIT 5; MTCW 1, 2; NFS 15; RGSF 2

Kinsey, Alfred C(harles) 1894-1956 .... **TCLC 91**
See also CA 115; 170; MTCW 2

Kipling, (Joseph) Rudyard 1865-1936 ... **TCLC 8, 17; PC 3; SSC 5, 54; WLC**
See also AAYA 32; BRW 6; BYA 4; CA 105; 120; CANR 33; CDBLB 1890-1914; CLR 39, 65; CWRI 5; DA; DA3; DAB; DAC; DAM MST, POET; DLB 19, 34, 141, 156; EXPS; FANT; LAIT 3; MAI-CYA 1, 2; MTCW 1, 2; RGEL 2; RGSF 2; SATA 100; SFW 4; SSFS 8; SUFW; WCH; WLIT 4; YABC 2

Kirk, Russell (Amos) 1918-1994 .. **TCLC 119**
See also AITN 1; CA 1-4R; 145; CAAS 9; CANR 1, 20, 60; HGG; INT CANR-20; MTCW 1, 2

Kirkland, Caroline M. 1801-1864 . **NCLC 85**
See also DLB 3, 73, 74, 250, 254; DLBD 13

Kirkup, James 1918- .... **CLC 1**
See also CA 1-4R; CAAS 4; CANR 2; CP 7; DLB 27; SATA 12

Kirkwood, James 1930(?)-1989 .... **CLC 9**
See also AITN 2; CA 1-4R; 128; CANR 6, 40; GLL 2

Kirshner, Sidney
See Kingsley, Sidney

Kis, Danilo 1935-1989 .... **CLC 57**
See also CA 109; 118; 129; CANR 61; CDWLB 4; DLB 181; MTCW 1; RGSF 2; RGWL 2

Kissinger, Henry A(lfred) 1923- ...... **CLC 137**
See also CA 1-4R; CANR 2, 33, 66, 109; MTCW 1

Kivi, Aleksis 1834-1872 .... **NCLC 30**

Kizer, Carolyn (Ashley) 1925- ... **CLC 15, 39, 80**
See also CA 65-68; CAAS 5; CANR 24, 70; CP 7; CWP; DAM POET; DLB 5, 169; MTCW 2

Klabund 1890-1928 .... **TCLC 44**
See also CA 162; DLB 66

Klappert, Peter 1942- .... **CLC 57**
See also CA 33-36R; CSW; DLB 5

Klein, A(braham) M(oses) 1909-1972 .... **CLC 19**
See also CA 101; 37-40R; DAB; DAC; DAM MST; DLB 68; RGEL 2

Klein, Joe
See Klein, Joseph

Klein, Joseph 1946- .... **CLC 154**
See also CA 85-88; CANR 55

Klein, Norma 1938-1989 .... **CLC 30**
See also AAYA 2, 35; BPFB 2; BYA 6, 7, 8; CA 41-44R; 128; CANR 15, 37; CLR 2, 19; INT CANR-15; JRDA; MAICYA 1, 2; SAAS 1; SATA 7, 57; WYA; YAW

Klein, T(heodore) E(ibon) D(onald)
1947- .... **CLC 34**
See also CA 119; CANR 44, 75; HGG

Kleist, Heinrich von 1777-1811 ...... **NCLC 2, 37; SSC 22**
See also CDWLB 2; DAM DRAM; DLB 90; EW 5; RGSF 2; RGWL 2

Klima, Ivan 1931- .... **CLC 56**
See also CA 25-28R; CANR 17, 50, 91; CDWLB 4; CWW 2; DAM NOV; DLB 232

Klimentov, Andrei Platonovich
1899-1951 .... **TCLC 14; SSC 42**
See also CA 108

Klinger, Friedrich Maximilian von
1752-1831 .... **NCLC 1**
See also DLB 94

Klingsor the Magician
See Hartmann, Sadakichi

Klopstock, Friedrich Gottlieb
1724-1803 .... **NCLC 11**
See also DLB 97; EW 4; RGWL 2

Knapp, Caroline 1959-2002 .... **CLC 99**
See also CA 154

Knebel, Fletcher 1911-1993 .... **CLC 14**
See also AITN 1; CA 1-4R; 140; CAAS 3; CANR 1, 36; SATA 36; SATA-Obit 75

Knickerbocker, Diedrich
See Irving, Washington

Knight, Etheridge 1931-1991 . **CLC 40; BLC 2; PC 14**
See also BW 1, 3; CA 21-24R; 133; CANR 23, 82; DAM POET; DLB 41; MTCW 2; RGAL 4

Knight, Sarah Kemble 1666-1727 .... **LC 7**
See also DLB 24, 200

Knister, Raymond 1899-1932 .... **TCLC 56**
See also CA 186; DLB 68; RGEL 2

Knowles, John 1926-2001 ... **CLC 1, 4, 10, 26**
See also AAYA 10; BPFB 2; BYA 3; CA 17-20R; CANR 40, 74, 76; CDALB 1968-1988; CN 7; DA; DAC; DAM MST, NOV; DLB 6; EXPN; MTCW 1, 2; NFS 2; RGAL 4; SATA 8, 89; YAW

Knox, Calvin M.
See Silverberg, Robert

Knox, John c. 1505-1572 .... **LC 37**
See also DLB 132

Knye, Cassandra
See Disch, Thomas M(ichael)

Koch, C(hristopher) J(ohn) 1932- .... **CLC 42**
See also CA 127; CANR 84; CN 7

Koch, Christopher
See Koch, C(hristopher) J(ohn)

Koch, Kenneth 1925-2002 .... **CLC 5, 8, 44**
See also CA 1-4R; CAD; CANR 6, 36, 57, 97; CD 5; CP 7; CWP 5; DLB 5; DLBY; INT CANR-36; MTCW 2; SATA 65; WP

Kochanowski, Jan 1530-1584 .... **LC 10**
See also RGWL 2

Kock, Charles Paul de 1794-1871 . **NCLC 16**

Koda Rohan
See Koda Shigeyuki

Koda Rohan
See Koda Shigeyuki
See also DLB 180

Koda Shigeyuki 1867-1947 .... **TCLC 22**
See also Koda Rohan
See also CA 121; 183

Koestler, Arthur 1905-1983 ... **CLC 1, 3, 6, 8, 15, 33**
See also BRWS 1; CA 1-4R; 109; CANR 1, 33; CDBLB 1945-1960; DLBY 1983; MTCW 1, 2; RGEL 2

Kogawa, Joy Nozomi 1935- ...... **CLC 78, 129**
See also CA 101; CANR 19, 62; CN 7; CWP; DAC; DAM MST, MULT; FW; MTCW 2; NFS 3; SATA 99

Kohout, Pavel 1928- .... **CLC 13**
See also CA 45-48; CANR 3

Koizumi, Yakumo
See Hearn, (Patricio) Lafcadio (Tessima Carlos)

Kolmar, Gertrud 1894-1943 .... **TCLC 40**
See also CA 167

Komunyakaa, Yusef 1947- .... **CLC 86, 94; BLCS**
See also AFAW 2; CA 147; CANR 83; CP 7; CSW; DLB 120; PFS 5; RGAL 4

Konrad, George
See Konrad, Gyorgy
See also CWW 2

Konrad, Gyorgy 1933- .... **CLC 4, 10, 73**
See also Konrad, George
See also CA 85-88; CANR 97; CDWLB 4; CWW 2; DLB 232

Konwicki, Tadeusz 1926- .... **CLC 8, 28, 54, 117**
See also CA 101; CAAS 9; CANR 39, 59; CWW 2; DLB 232; IDFW 3; MTCW 1

Koontz, Dean R(ay) 1945- .... **CLC 78**
See also AAYA 9, 31; BEST 89:3; 90:2; CA 108; CANR 19, 36, 52, 95; CMW 4; CPW; DA3; DAM NOV, POP; HGG; MTCW 1; SATA 92; SFW 4; YAW

Kopernik, Mikolaj
See Copernicus, Nicolaus

Kopit, Arthur (Lee) 1937- ...... **CLC 1, 18, 33**
See also AITN 1; CA 81-84; CABS 3; CD 5; DAM DRAM; DFS 7, 14; DLB 7; MTCW 1; RGAL 4

Kops, Bernard 1926- .... **CLC 4**
See also CA 5-8R; CANR 84; CBD; CN 7; CP 7; DLB 13

Kornbluth, C(yril) M. 1923-1958 .... **TCLC 8**
See also CA 105; 160; DLB 8; SFW 4

Korolcnko, V. G.
See Korolenko, Vladimir Galaktionovich

Korolenko, Vladimir
See Korolenko, Vladimir Galaktionovich

Korolenko, Vladimir G.
See Korolenko, Vladimir Galaktionovich

Korolenko, Vladimir Galaktionovich
1853-1921 .... **TCLC 22**
See also CA 121

Korzybski, Alfred (Habdank Skarbek)
1879-1950 .... **TCLC 61**
See also CA 123; 160

Kosinski, Jerzy (Nikodem)
1933-1991 .... **CLC 1, 2, 3, 6, 10, 15, 53, 70**
See also AMWS 7; BPFB 2; CA 17-20R; 134; CANR 9, 46; DA3; DAM NOV; DLB 2; DLBY 1982; HGG; MTCW 1, 2; NFS 12; RGAL 4

Kostelanetz, Richard (Cory) 1940- .. **CLC 28**
See also CA 13-16R; CAAS 8; CANR 38, 77; CN 7; CP 7

Kostrowitzki, Wilhelm Apollinaris de
1880-1918
See Apollinaire, Guillaume
See also CA 104

Kotlowitz, Robert 1924- .... **CLC 4**
See also CA 33-36R; CANR 36

Kotzebue, August (Friedrich Ferdinand) von
1761-1819 .... **NCLC 25**
See also DLB 94

Kotzwinkle, William 1938- ...... **CLC 5, 14, 35**
See also BPFB 2; CA 45-48; CANR 3, 44, 84; CLR 6; DLB 173; FANT; MAICYA 1, 2; SATA 24, 70; SFW 4; YAW

Kowna, Stancy
See Szymborska, Wislawa

Kozol, Jonathan 1936- .... **CLC 17**
See also CA 61-64; CANR 16, 45, 96

Kozoll, Michael 1940(?)- .... **CLC 35**

Kramer, Kathryn 19(?)- .... **CLC 34**

Kramer, Larry 1935- .... **CLC 42; DC 8**
See also CA 124; 126; CANR 60; DAM POP; DLB 249; GLL 1

Krasicki, Ignacy 1735-1801 .... **NCLC 8**

Krasinski, Zygmunt 1812-1859 .... **NCLC 4**
See also RGWL 2

Kraus, Karl 1874-1936 .... **TCLC 5**
See also CA 104; DLB 118

Kreve (Mickevicius), Vincas
1882-1954 .... **TCLC 27**
See also CA 170; DLB 220

Kristeva, Julia 1941- .... **CLC 77, 140**
See also CA 154; CANR 99; DLB 242; FW

Kristofferson, Kris 1936- .... **CLC 26**
See also CA 104

Krizanc, John 1956- .... **CLC 57**
See also CA 187

Krleza, Miroslav 1893-1981 .... **CLC 8, 114**
See also CA 97-100; 105; CANR 50; CDWLB 4; DLB 147; EW 11; RGWL 2

Kroetsch, Robert 1927- .. **CLC 5, 23, 57, 132**
See also CA 17-20R; CANR 8, 38; CCA 1; CN 7; CP 7; DAC; DAM POET; DLB 53; MTCW 1

Kroetz, Franz
See Kroetz, Franz Xaver

Kroetz, Franz Xaver 1946- .... **CLC 41**
See also CA 130

Kroker, Arthur (W.) 1945- .... **CLC 77**
See also CA 161

Kropotkin, Peter (Aleksieevich)
1842-1921 .... **TCLC 36**
See also CA 119

Krotkov, Yuri 1917-1981 .... **CLC 19**
See also CA 102

Krumb
See Crumb, R(obert)

Krumgold, Joseph (Quincy)
1908-1980 .... **CLC 12**
See also BYA 1, 2; CA 9-12R; 101; CANR 7; MAICYA 1, 2; SATA 1, 48; SATA-Obit 23; YAW

Krumwitz
See Crumb, R(obert)

Krutch, Joseph Wood 1893-1970 ..... **CLC 24**
See also ANW; CA 1-4R; 25-28R; CANR 4; DLB 63, 206

Krutzch, Gus
See Eliot, T(homas) S(tearns)

Krylov, Ivan Andreevich
1768(?)-1844 .... **NCLC 1**
See also DLB 150

Kubin, Alfred (Leopold Isidor)
1877-1959 .... **TCLC 23**
See also CA 112; 149; CANR 104; DLB 81

Kubrick, Stanley 1928-1999 .... **CLC 16**
See also AAYA 30; CA 81-84; 177; CANR 33; DLB 26; TCLC 112

Kueng, Hans 1928-
See Kung, Hans
See also CA 53-56; CANR 66; MTCW 1, 2

Kumin, Maxine (Winokur) 1925- ..... **CLC 5, 13, 28; PC 15**
See also AITN 2; AMWS 4; ANW; CA 1-4R; CAAS 8; CANR 1, 21, 69; CP 7; CWP; DA3; DAM POET; DLB 5; EXPP; MTCW 1, 2; PAB; SATA 12

Kundera, Milan 1929- . **CLC 4, 9, 19, 32, 68, 115, 135; SSC 24**
See also AAYA 2; BPFB 2; CA 85-88; CANR 19, 52, 74; CDWLB 4; CWW 2; DA3; DAM NOV; DLB 232; EW 13; MTCW 1, 2; RGSF 2; SSFS 10

Kunene, Mazisi (Raymond) 1930- ... **CLC 85**
See also BW 1, 3; CA 125; CANR 81; CP 7; DLB 117

Kung, Hans .... **CLC 130**
See also Kueng, Hans

Kunikida Doppo 1869(?)-1908
See Doppo, Kunikida
See also DLB 180

Kunitz, Stanley (Jasspon) 1905- .. **CLC 6, 11, 14, 148; PC 19**
See also AMWS 3; CA 41-44R; CANR 26, 57, 98; CP 7; DA3; DLB 48; INT CANR-26; MTCW 1, 2; PFS 11; RGAL 4

Kunze, Reiner 1933- .... **CLC 10**
See also CA 93-96; CWW 2; DLB 75

Kuprin, Aleksander Ivanovich 1870-1938 .... **TCLC 5**
See also CA 104; 182

Kureishi, Hanif 1954(?)- .... **CLC 64, 135**
See also CA 139; CBD; CD 5; CN 7; DLB 194, 245; GLL 2; IDFW 4; WLIT 4

Kurosawa, Akira 1910-1998 ..... **CLC 16, 119**
See also AAYA 11; CA 101; 170; CANR 46; DAM MULT

Kushner, Tony 1957(?)- .... **CLC 81; DC 10**
See also AMWS 9; CA 144; CAD; CANR 74; CD 5; DA3; DAM DRAM; DFS 5; DLB 228; GLL 1; LAIT 5; MTCW 2; RGAL 4

Kuttner, Henry 1915-1958 .... **TCLC 10**
See also CA 107; 157; DLB 8; FANT; SCFW 2; SFW 4

Kuzma, Greg 1944- .... **CLC 7**
See also CA 33-36R; CANR 70

Kuzmin, Mikhail 1872(?)-1936 ...... **TCLC 40**
See also CA 170

Kyd, Thomas 1558-1594 .... **LC 22; DC 3**
See also BRW 1; DAM DRAM; DLB 62; IDTP; RGEL 2; TEA; WLIT 3

Kyprianos, Iossif
See Samarakis, Antonis

Labrunie, Gerard
See Nerval, Gerard de

La Bruyere, Jean de 1645-1696 .... **LC 17**
See also EW 3; GFL Beginnings to 1789

Lacan, Jacques (Marie Emile) 1901-1981 .... **CLC 75**
See also CA 121; 104

Laclos, Pierre Ambroise Francois 1741-1803 .... **NCLC 4, 87**
See also EW 4; GFL Beginnings to 1789; RGWL 2

Lacolere, Francois
See Aragon, Louis

La Colere, Francois
See Aragon, Louis

La Deshabilleuse
See Simenon, Georges (Jacques Christian)

Lady Gregory
See Gregory, Lady Isabella Augusta (Persse)

Lady of Quality, A
See Bagnold, Enid

La Fayette, Marie-(Madelaine Pioche de la Vergne) 1634-1693 .... **LC 2**
See also GFL Beginnings to 1789; RGWL 2

Lafayette, Rene
See Hubbard, L(afayette) Ron(ald)

La Fontaine, Jean de 1621-1695 .... **LC 50**
See also EW 3; GFL Beginnings to 1789; MAICYA 1, 2; RGWL 2; SATA 18

Laforgue, Jules 1860-1887 . **NCLC 5, 53; PC 14; SSC 20**
See also DLB 217; EW 7; GFL 1789 to the Present; RGWL 2

Layamon
See Layamon
See also DLB 146

Lagerkvist, Paer (Fabian) 1891-1974 .... **CLC 7, 10, 13, 54**
See also Lagerkvist, Par
See also CA 85-88; 49-52; DA3; DAM DRAM, NOV; MTCW 1, 2

Lagerkvist, Par .... **SSC 12**
See also Lagerkvist, Paer (Fabian)
See also DLB 259; EW 10; MTCW 2; RGSF 2; RGWL 2

Lagerloef, Selma (Ottiliana Lovisa) 1858-1940 .... **TCLC 4, 36**
See also Lagerlof, Selma (Ottiliana Lovisa)
See also CA 108; MTCW 2; SATA 15

Lagerlof, Selma (Ottiliana Lovisa)
See Lagerloef, Selma (Ottiliana Lovisa)
See also CLR 7; SATA 15

La Guma, (Justin) Alex(ander) 1925-1985 .... **CLC 19; BLCS**
See also AFW; BW 1, 3; CA 49-52; 118; CANR 25, 81; CDWLB 3; DAM NOV; DLB 117, 225; MTCW 1, 2; WLIT 2

Laidlaw, A. K.
See Grieve, C(hristopher) M(urray)

Lainez, Manuel Mujica
See Mujica Lainez, Manuel
See also HW 1

Laing, R(onald) D(avid) 1927-1989 . **CLC 95**
See also CA 107; 129; CANR 34; MTCW 1

Lamartine, Alphonse (Marie Louis Prat) de 1790-1869 .... **NCLC 11; PC 16**
See also DAM POET; DLB 217; GFL 1789 to the Present; RGWL 2

Lamb, Charles 1775-1834 ..... **NCLC 10, 113; WLC**
See also BRW 4; CDBLB 1789-1832; DA; DAB; DAC; DAM MST; DLB 93, 107, 163; RGEL 2; SATA 17

Lamb, Lady Caroline 1785-1828 ... **NCLC 38**
See also DLB 116

Lamming, George (William) 1927- ... **CLC 2, 4, 66, 144; BLC 2**
See also BW 2, 3; CA 85-88; CANR 26, 76; CDWLB 3; CN 7; DAM MULT; DLB 125; MTCW 1, 2; NFS 15; RGEL 2

L'Amour, Louis (Dearborn) 1908-1988 .... **CLC 25, 55**
See also Burns, Tex; Mayo, Jim
See also AAYA 16; AITN 2; BEST 89:2; BPFB 2; CA 1-4R; 125; CANR 3, 25, 40; CPW; DA3; DAM NOV, POP; DLB 206; DLBY 1980; MTCW 1, 2; RGAL 4

Lampedusa, Giuseppe (Tomasi) di .... **TCLC 13**
See also Tomasi di Lampedusa, Giuseppe
See also CA 164; EW 11; MTCW 2; RGWL 2

Lampman, Archibald 1861-1899 ... **NCLC 25**
See also DLB 92; RGEL 2

Lancaster, Bruce 1896-1963 .... **CLC 36**
See also CA 9-10; CANR 70; CAP 1; SATA 9

Lanchester, John .... **CLC 99**
See also CA 194

Landau, Mark Alexandrovich
See Aldanov, Mark (Alexandrovich)

Landau-Aldanov, Mark Alexandrovich
See Aldanov, Mark (Alexandrovich)

Landis, Jerry
See Simon, Paul (Frederick)

Landis, John 1950- .... **CLC 26**
See also CA 112; 122

Landolfi, Tommaso 1908-1979 .... **CLC 11, 49**
See also CA 127; 117; DLB 177

Landon, Letitia Elizabeth 1802-1838 .... **NCLC 15**
See also DLB 96

Landor, Walter Savage 1775-1864 .... **NCLC 14**
See also BRW 4; DLB 93, 107; RGEL 2

Landwirth, Heinz 1927-
See Lind, Jakov
See also CA 9-12R; CANR 7

Lane, Patrick 1939- .... **CLC 25**
See also CA 97-100; CANR 54; CP 7; DAM POET; DLB 53; INT 97-100

Lang, Andrew 1844-1912 .... **TCLC 16**
See also CA 114; 137; CANR 85; DLB 98, 141, 184; FANT; MAICYA 1, 2; RGEL 2; SATA 16; WCH

Lang, Fritz 1890-1976 .... **CLC 20, 103**
See also CA 77-80; 69-72; CANR 30

Lange, John
See Crichton, (John) Michael

Langer, Elinor 1939- .... **CLC 34**
See also CA 121

Langland, William 1332(?)-1400(?) ..... **LC 19**
See also BRW 1; DA; DAB; DAC; DAM MST, POET; DLB 146; RGEL 2; WLIT 3

Langstaff, Launcelot
See Irving, Washington

Lanier, Sidney 1842-1881 .... **NCLC 6**
See also AMWS 1; DAM POET; DLB 64; DLBD 13; EXPP; MAICYA 1; PFS 14; RGAL 4; SATA 18

Lanyer, Aemilia 1569-1645 .... **LC 10, 30**
See also DLB 121

Lao Tzu c. 6th cent. B.C.-3rd cent. B.C. .... **CMLC 7**

Lao-Tzu
See Lao Tzu

Lapine, James (Elliot) 1949- .... **CLC 39**
See also CA 123; 130; CANR 54; INT 130

Larbaud, Valery (Nicolas) 1881-1957 .... **TCLC 9**
See also CA 106; 152; GFL 1789 to the Present

Lardner, Ring
See Lardner, Ring(gold) W(ilmer)
See also BPFB 2; CDALB 1917-1929; DLB 11, 25, 86, 171; DLBD 16; RGAL 4; RGSF 2

Lardner, Ring W., Jr.
See Lardner, Ring(gold) W(ilmer)

Lardner, Ring(gold) W(ilmer) 1885-1933 .... **TCLC 2, 14; SSC 32**
See also Lardner, Ring
See also AMW; CA 104; 131; MTCW 1, 2; TUS

Laredo, Betty
See Codrescu, Andrei

Larkin, Maia
See Wojciechowska, Maia (Teresa)

Larkin, Philip (Arthur) 1922-1985 ... **CLC 3, 5, 8, 9, 13, 18, 33, 39, 64; PC 21**
See also BRWS 1; CA 5-8R; 117; CANR 24, 62; CDBLB 1960 to Present; DA3; DAB; DAM MST, POET; DLB 27; MTCW 1, 2; PFS 3, 4, 12; RGEL 2

Larra (y Sanchez de Castro), Mariano Jose de 1809-1837 .... **NCLC 17**

Larsen, Eric 1941- .... **CLC 55**
See also CA 132

Larsen, Nella 1893-1963 ...... **CLC 37; BLC 2**
See also AFAW 1, 2; BW 1; CA 125; CANR 83; DAM MULT; DLB 51; FW

Larson, Charles R(aymond) 1938- ... **CLC 31**
See also CA 53-56; CANR 4

Larson, Jonathan 1961-1996 .... **CLC 99**
See also AAYA 28; CA 156

Las Casas, Bartolome de 1474-1566 . **LC 31; HLCS**
See also Casas, Bartolome de las
See also LAW

Lasch, Christopher 1932-1994 .... **CLC 102**
See also CA 73-76; 144; CANR 25; DLB 246; MTCW 1, 2

Lasker-Schueler, Else 1869-1945 ... **TCLC 57**
See also CA 183; DLB 66, 124

Laski, Harold J(oseph) 1893-1950 . **TCLC 79**
See also CA 188

Latham, Jean Lee 1902-1995 .... **CLC 12**
See also AITN 1; BYA 1; CA 5-8R; CANR 7, 84; CLR 50; MAICYA 1, 2; SATA 2, 68; YAW

Latham, Mavis
See Clark, Mavis Thorpe

Lathen, Emma .... **CLC 2**
See also Hennissart, Martha; Latsis, Mary J(ane)
See also BPFB 2; CMW 4

Lathrop, Francis
See Leiber, Fritz (Reuter, Jr.)

Latsis, Mary J(ane) 1927(?)-1997
See Lathen, Emma
See also CA 85-88; 162; CMW 4

Lattany, Kristin
See Lattany, Kristin (Elaine Eggleston) Hunter

Lattany, Kristin (Elaine Eggleston) Hunter 1931- .... **CLC 35**
See also AITN 1; BW 1; BYA 3; CA 13-16R; CANR 13, 108; CLR 3; CN 7; DLB 33; INT CANR-13; MAICYA 1, 2; SAAS 10; SATA 12, 132; YAW

Lattimore, Richmond (Alexander) 1906-1984 .... **CLC 3**
See also CA 1-4R; 112; CANR 1

Laughlin, James 1914-1997 .... **CLC 49**
See also CA 21-24R; 162; CAAS 22; CANR 9, 47; CP 7; DLB 48; DLBY 1996, 1997

Laurence, (Jean) Margaret (Wemyss) 1926-1987 . **CLC 3, 6, 13, 50, 62; SSC 7**
See also BYA 13; CA 5-8R; 121; CANR 33; DAC; DAM MST; DLB 53; FW; MTCW 1, 2; NFS 11; RGEL 2; RGSF 2; SATA-Obit 50; TCWW 2

Laurent, Antoine 1952- .... **CLC 50**

Lauscher, Hermann
See Hesse, Hermann

Lautreamont 1846-1870 .. **NCLC 12; SSC 14**
See also Lautreamont, Isidore Lucien Ducasse
See also GFL 1789 to the Present; RGWL 2

Lautreamont, Isidore Lucien Ducasse
See Lautreamont
See also DLB 217

Laverty, Donald
See Blish, James (Benjamin)

Lavin, Mary 1912-1996 . **CLC 4, 18, 99; SSC 4**
See also CA 9-12R; 151; CANR 33; CN 7; DLB 15; FW; MTCW 1; RGEL 2; RGSF 2

Lavond, Paul Dennis
See Kornbluth, C(yril) M.; Pohl, Frederik

Lawler, Raymond Evenor 1922- .... **CLC 58**
See also CA 103; CD 5; RGEL 2

Lawrence, D(avid) H(erbert Richards) 1885-1930 .... **TCLC 2, 9, 16, 33, 48, 61, 93; SSC 4, 19; WLC**
See also Chambers, Jessie
See also BPFB 2; BRW 7; BRWR 2; CA 104; 121; CDBLB 1914-1945; DA; DA3; DAB; DAC; DAM MST, NOV, POET; DLB 10, 19, 36, 98, 162, 195; EXPP; EXPS; LAIT 2, 3; MTCW 1, 2; PFS 6; RGEL 2; RGSF 2; SSFS 2, 6; TEA; WLIT 4; WP

Lawrence, T(homas) E(dward) 1888-1935 .... **TCLC 18**
See also Dale, Colin
See also BRWS 2; CA 115; 167; DLB 195

Lawrence of Arabia
See Lawrence, T(homas) E(dward)

Lawson, Henry (Archibald Hertzberg) 1867-1922 .... **TCLC 27; SSC 18**
See also CA 120; 181; DLB 230; RGEL 2; RGSF 2

Lawton, Dennis
See Faust, Frederick (Schiller)

Laxness, Halldor .... **CLC 25**
See also Gudjonsson, Halldor Kiljan
See also EW 12; RGWL 2

Layamon fl. c. 1200- .... **CMLC 10**
See also Layamon
See also RGEL 2

Laye, Camara 1928-1980 ... **CLC 4, 38; BLC 2**
See also AFW; BW 1; CA 85-88; 97-100; CANR 25; DAM MULT; MTCW 1, 2; WLIT 2

Layton, Irving (Peter) 1912- .... **CLC 2, 15**
See also CA 1-4R; CANR 2, 33, 43, 66; CP 7; DAC; DAM MST, POET; DLB 88; MTCW 1, 2; PFS 12; RGEL 2

Lazarus, Emma 1849-1887 ...... **NCLC 8, 109**

Lazarus, Felix
See Cable, George Washington

Lazarus, Henry
See Slavitt, David R(ytman)

Lea, Joan
See Neufeld, John (Arthur)

Leacock, Stephen (Butler) 1869-1944 .... **TCLC 2; SSC 39**
See also CA 104; 141; CANR 80; DAC; DAM MST; DLB 92; MTCW 2; RGEL 2; RGSF 2

Lead, Jane Ward 1623-1704 .... **LC 72**
See also DLB 131

Lear, Edward 1812-1888 .... **NCLC 3**
See also BRW 5; CLR 1, 75; DLB 32, 163, 166; MAICYA 1, 2; RGEL 2; SATA 18, 100; WCH; WP

Lear, Norman (Milton) 1922- .... **CLC 12**
See also CA 73-76

Leautaud, Paul 1872-1956 .... **TCLC 83**
See also DLB 65; GFL 1789 to the Present

Leavis, F(rank) R(aymond) 1895-1978 .... **CLC 24**
See also BRW 7; CA 21-24R; 77-80; CANR 44; DLB 242; MTCW 1, 2; RGEL 2

Leavitt, David 1961- .... **CLC 34**
See also CA 116; 122; CANR 50, 62, 101; CPW; DA3; DAM POP; DLB 130; GLL 1; INT 122; MTCW 2

Leblanc, Maurice (Marie Emile) 1864-1941 .... **TCLC 49**
See also CA 110; CMW 4

Lebowitz, Fran(ces Ann) 1951(?)- ... **CLC 11, 36**
See also CA 81-84; CANR 14, 60, 70; INT CANR-14; MTCW 1

Lebrecht, Peter
See Tieck, (Johann) Ludwig

le Carre, John .... **CLC 3, 5, 9, 15, 28**
See also Cornwell, David (John Moore)
See also AAYA 42; BEST 89:4; BPFB 2; BRWS 2; CDBLB 1960 to Present; CMW 4; CN 7; CPW; DLB 87; MSW; MTCW 2; RGEL 2

Le Clezio, J(ean) M(arie) G(ustave) 1940- .... **CLC 31, 155**
See also CA 116; 128; DLB 83; GFL 1789 to the Present; RGSF 2

Leconte de Lisle, Charles-Marie-Rene 1818-1894 .... **NCLC 29**
See also DLB 217; EW 6; GFL 1789 to the Present

Le Coq, Monsieur
See Simenon, Georges (Jacques Christian)

Leduc, Violette 1907-1972 .... **CLC 22**
See also CA 13-14; 33-36R; CANR 69; CAP 1; GFL 1789 to the Present; GLL 1

Ledwidge, Francis 1887(?)-1917 .... **TCLC 23**
See also CA 123; DLB 20

Lee, Andrea 1953- .... **CLC 36; BLC 2**
See also BW 1, 3; CA 125; CANR 82; DAM MULT

Lee, Andrew
See Auchincloss, Louis (Stanton)

Lee, Chang-rae 1965- .... **CLC 91**
See also CA 148; CANR 89

Lee, Don L. .... **CLC 2**
See also Madhubuti, Haki R.

Lee, George W(ashington) 1894-1976 .... **CLC 52; BLC 2**
See also BW 1; CA 125; CANR 83; DAM MULT; DLB 51

Lee, (Nelle) Harper 1926- .... **CLC 12, 60; WLC**
See also AAYA 13; AMWS 8; BPFB 2; BYA 3; CA 13-16R; CANR 51; CDALB 1941-1968; CSW; DA; DA3; DAB; DAC; DAM MST, NOV; DLB 6; EXPN; LAIT 3; MTCW 1, 2; NFS 2; SATA 11; WYA; YAW

Lee, Helen Elaine 1959(?)- .... **CLC 86**
See also CA 148

Lee, John .... **CLC 70**

Lee, Julian
See Latham, Jean Lee

Lee, Larry
See Lee, Lawrence

Lee, Laurie 1914-1997 .... **CLC 90**
See also CA 77-80; 158; CANR 33, 73; CP 7; CPW; DAB; DAM POP; DLB 27; MTCW 1; RGEL 2

Lee, Lawrence 1941-1990 .... **CLC 34**
See also CA 131; CANR 43

Lee, Li-Young 1957- .... **PC 24**
See also CA 153; CP 7; DLB 165; PFS 11, 15

Lee, Manfred B(ennington) 1905-1971 .... **CLC 11**
See also Queen, Ellery
See also CA 1-4R; 29-32R; CANR 2; CMW 4; DLB 137

Lee, Shelton Jackson 1957(?)- .... **CLC 105; BLCS**
See also Lee, Spike
See also BW 2, 3; CA 125; CANR 42; DAM MULT

Lee, Spike
See Lee, Shelton Jackson
See also AAYA 4, 29

Lee, Stan 1922- .... **CLC 17**
See also AAYA 5; CA 108; 111; INT 111

Lee, Tanith 1947- .... **CLC 46**
See also AAYA 15; CA 37-40R; CANR 53, 102; DLB 261; FANT; SATA 8, 88; SFW 4; SUFW; YAW

Lee, Vernon .... **TCLC 5; SSC 33**
See also Paget, Violet
See also DLB 57, 153, 156, 174, 178; GLL 1; SUFW

Lee, William
See Burroughs, William S(eward)
See also GLL 1

Lee, Willy
See Burroughs, William S(eward)
See also GLL 1

Lee-Hamilton, Eugene (Jacob) 1845-1907 .... **TCLC 22**
See also CA 117

Leet, Judith 1935- .... **CLC 11**
See also CA 187

Le Fanu, Joseph Sheridan 1814-1873 .... **NCLC 9, 58; SSC 14**
See also CMW 4; DA3; DAM POP; DLB 21, 70, 159, 178; HGG; RGEL 2; RGSF 2; SUFW

Leffland, Ella 1931- .... **CLC 19**
See also CA 29-32R; CANR 35, 78, 82; DLBY 1984; INT CANR-35; SATA 65

Leger, Alexis
See Leger, (Marie-Rene Auguste) Alexis Saint-Leger

Leger, (Marie-Rene Auguste) Alexis Saint-Leger 1887-1975 .. **CLC 4, 11, 46; PC 23**
See also Perse, Saint-John; Saint-John Perse
See also CA 13-16R; 61-64; CANR 43; DAM POET; MTCW 1

Leger, Saintleger
See Leger, (Marie-Rene Auguste) Alexis Saint-Leger

Le Guin, Ursula K(roeber) 1929- ..... **CLC 8, 13, 22, 45, 71, 136; SSC 12**
See also AAYA 9, 27; AITN 1; BPFB 2; BYA 5, 8, 11, 14; CA 21-24R; CANR 9, 32, 52, 74; CDALB 1968-1988; CLR 3, 28; CN 7; CPW; DA3; DAB; DAC; DAM MST, POP; DLB 8, 52, 256; EXPS; FANT; FW; INT CANR-32; JRDA; LAIT 5; MAICYA 1, 2; MTCW 1, 2; NFS 6, 9; SATA 4, 52, 99; SCFW; SFW 4; SSFS 2; SUFW; WYA; YAW

Lehmann, Rosamond (Nina) 1901-1990 .... **CLC 5**
See also CA 77-80; 131; CANR 8, 73; DLB 15; MTCW 2; RGEL 2; RHW

Leiber, Fritz (Reuter, Jr.) 1910-1992 .... **CLC 25**
See also BPFB 2; CA 45-48; 139; CANR 2, 40, 86; DLB 8; FANT; HGG; MTCW 1, 2; SATA 45; SATA-Obit 73; SCFW 2; SFW 4; SUFW

Leibniz, Gottfried Wilhelm von 1646-1716 .... **LC 35**
See also DLB 168

Leimbach, Martha 1963-
See Leimbach, Marti
See also CA 130

Leimbach, Marti .... **CLC 65**
See also Leimbach, Martha

Leino, Eino .... **TCLC 24**
See also Loennbohm, Armas Eino Leopold

Leiris, Michel (Julien) 1901-1990 ..... **CLC 61**
See also CA 119; 128; 132; GFL 1789 to the Present

Leithauser, Brad 1953- .... **CLC 27**
See also CA 107; CANR 27, 81; CP 7; DLB 120

Lelchuk, Alan 1938- .... **CLC 5**
See also CA 45-48; CAAS 20; CANR 1, 70; CN 7

Lem, Stanislaw 1921- ...... **CLC 8, 15, 40, 149**
See also CA 105; CAAS 1; CANR 32; CWW 2; MTCW 1; SCFW 2; SFW 4

Lemann, Nancy 1956- .... **CLC 39**
See also CA 118; 136

Lemonnier, (Antoine Louis) Camille 1844-1913 .... **TCLC 22**
See also CA 121

Lenau, Nikolaus 1802-1850 .... **NCLC 16**

L'Engle, Madeleine (Camp Franklin) 1918- .... **CLC 12**
See also AAYA 28; AITN 2; BPFB 2; BYA 2, 4, 5, 7; CA 1-4R; CANR 3, 21, 39, 66, 107; CLR 1, 14, 57; CPW; CWRI 5; DA3; DAM POP; DLB 52; JRDA; MAICYA 1, 2; MTCW 1, 2; SAAS 15; SATA 1, 27, 75, 128; SFW 4; WYA; YAW

Lengyel, Jozsef 1896-1975 .... **CLC 7**
See also CA 85-88; 57-60; CANR 71; RGSF 2

Lenin 1870-1924
See Lenin, V. I.
See also CA 121; 168

Lenin, V. I. .... **TCLC 67**
See also Lenin

Lennon, John (Ono) 1940-1980 .. **CLC 12, 35**
See also CA 102; SATA 114

Lennox, Charlotte Ramsay 1729(?)-1804 .... **NCLC 23**
See also DLB 39; RGEL 2

Lentricchia, Frank, (Jr.) 1940- .... **CLC 34**
See also CA 25-28R; CANR 19, 106; DLB 246

Lenz, Gunter .... **CLC 65**

Lenz, Siegfried 1926- .... **CLC 27; SSC 33**
See also CA 89-92; CANR 80; CWW 2; DLB 75; RGSF 2; RGWL 2

Leon, David
See Jacob, (Cyprien-)Max

Leonard, Elmore (John, Jr.) 1925- . **CLC 28, 34, 71, 120**
See also AAYA 22; AITN 1; BEST 89:1, 90:4; BPFB 2; CA 81-84; CANR 12, 28, 53, 76, 96; CMW 4; CN 7; CPW; DA3; DAM POP; DLB 173, 226; INT CANR-28; MSW; MTCW 1, 2; RGAL 4; TCWW 2

Leonard, Hugh .... **CLC 19**
See also Byrne, John Keyes
See also CBD; CD 5; DFS 13; DLB 13

Leonov, Leonid (Maximovich) 1899-1994 .... **CLC 92**
See also CA 129; CANR 74, 76; DAM NOV; MTCW 1, 2

Leopardi, (Conte) Giacomo 1798-1837 .... **NCLC 22; PC 37**
See also EW 5; RGWL 2; WP

Le Reveler
See Artaud, Antonin (Marie Joseph)

Lerman, Eleanor 1952- .... **CLC 9**
See also CA 85-88; CANR 69

Lerman, Rhoda 1936- .... **CLC 56**
See also CA 49-52; CANR 70

Lermontov, Mikhail Iur'evich
See Lermontov, Mikhail Yuryevich
See also DLB 205

Lermontov, Mikhail Yuryevich 1814-1841 .... **NCLC 5, 47; PC 18**
See also Lermontov, Mikhail Iur'evich
See also EW 6; RGWL 2

Leroux, Gaston 1868-1927 .... **TCLC 25**
See also CA 108; 136; CANR 69; CMW 4; SATA 65

Lesage, Alain-Rene 1668-1747 .... **LC 2, 28**
See also EW 3; GFL Beginnings to 1789; RGWL 2

Leskov, N(ikolai) S(emenovich) 1831-1895
See Leskov, Nikolai (Semyonovich)

Leskov, Nikolai (Semyonovich) 1831-1895 .... **NCLC 25; SSC 34**
See also Leskov, Nikolai Semenovich

Leskov, Nikolai Semenovich
See Leskov, Nikolai (Semyonovich)
See also DLB 238

Lesser, Milton
See Marlowe, Stephen

Lessing, Doris (May) 1919- ... **CLC 1, 2, 3, 6, 10, 15, 22, 40, 94; SSC 6; WLCS**
See also AFW; BRWS 1; CA 9-12R; CAAS 14; CANR 33, 54, 76; CD 5; CDBLB 1960 to Present; CN 7; DA; DA3; DAB; DAC; DAM MST, NOV; DLB 15, 139; DLBY 1985; EXPS; FW; LAIT 4; MTCW 1, 2; RGEL 2; RGSF 2; SFW 4; SSFS 1, 12; WLIT 2, 4

Lessing, Gotthold Ephraim 1729-1781 . **LC 8**
See also CDWLB 2; DLB 97; EW 4; RGWL 2

Lester, Richard 1932- .... **CLC 20**

Levenson, Jay .... **CLC 70**

Lever, Charles (James) 1806-1872 .... **NCLC 23**
See also DLB 21; RGEL 2

Leverson, Ada 1865(?)-1936(?) .... **TCLC 18**
See also Elaine
See also CA 117; DLB 153; RGEL 2

Levertov, Denise 1923-1997 .. **CLC 1, 2, 3, 5, 8, 15, 28, 66; PC 11**
See also AMWS 3; CA 1-4R, 178; 163; CAAE 178; CAAS 19; CANR 3, 29, 50, 108; CDALBS; CP 7; CWP; DAM POET; DLB 5, 165; EXPP; FW; INT CANR-29; MTCW 1, 2; PAB; PFS 7; RGAL 4; WP

Levi, Jonathan .... **CLC 76**
See also CA 197

Levi, Peter (Chad Tigar) 1931-2000 .... **CLC 41**
See also CA 5-8R; 187; CANR 34, 80; CP 7; DLB 40

Levi, Primo 1919-1987 . **CLC 37, 50; SSC 12**
See also CA 13-16R; 122; CANR 12, 33, 61, 70; DLB 177; MTCW 1, 2; RGWL 2; TCLC 109

Levin, Ira 1929- .... **CLC 3, 6**
See also CA 21-24R; CANR 17, 44, 74; CMW 4; CN 7; CPW; DA3; DAM POP; HGG; MTCW 1, 2; SATA 66; SFW 4

Levin, Meyer 1905-1981 .... **CLC 7**
See also AITN 1; CA 9-12R; 104; CANR 15; DAM POP; DLB 9, 28; DLBY 1981; SATA 21; SATA-Obit 27

Levine, Norman 1924- .... **CLC 54**
See also CA 73-76; CAAS 23; CANR 14, 70; DLB 88

Levine, Philip 1928- .. **CLC 2, 4, 5, 9, 14, 33, 118; PC 22**
See also AMWS 5; CA 9-12R; CANR 9, 37, 52; CP 7; DAM POET; DLB 5; PFS 8

Levinson, Deirdre 1931- .... **CLC 49**
See also CA 73-76; CANR 70

Levi-Strauss, Claude 1908- .... **CLC 38**
See also CA 1-4R; CANR 6, 32, 57; DLB 242; GFL 1789 to the Present; MTCW 1, 2

Levitin, Sonia (Wolff) 1934- .... **CLC 17**
See also AAYA 13; CA 29-32R; CANR 14, 32, 79; CLR 53; JRDA; MAICYA 1, 2; SAAS 2; SATA 4, 68, 119; SATA-Essay 131; YAW

Levon, O. U.
See Kesey, Ken (Elton)

Levy, Amy 1861-1889 .... **NCLC 59**
See also DLB 156, 240

Lewes, George Henry 1817-1878 ... **NCLC 25**
See also DLB 55, 144

Lewis, Alun 1915-1944 .... **TCLC 3; SSC 40**
See also BRW 7; CA 104; 188; DLB 20, 162; PAB; RGEL 2

Lewis, C. Day
See Day Lewis, C(ecil)

Lewis, C(live) S(taples) 1898-1963 .... **CLC 1, 3, 6, 14, 27, 124; WLC**
See also AAYA 3, 39; BPFB 2; BRWS 3; CA 81-84; CANR 33, 71; CDBLB 1945-1960; CLR 3, 27; CWRI 5; DA; DA3; DAB; DAC; DAM MST, NOV, POP; DLB 15, 100, 160, 255; FANT; JRDA; MAICYA 1, 2; MTCW 1, 2; RGEL 2; SATA 13, 100; SCFW; SFW 4; SUFW; WCH; WYA; YAW

Lewis, Cecil Day
See Day Lewis, C(ecil)

Lewis, Janet 1899-1998 .... **CLC 41**
See also Winters, Janet Lewis
See also CA 9-12R; 172; CANR 29, 63; CAP 1; CN 7; DLBY 1987; RHW; TCWW 2

Lewis, Matthew Gregory 1775-1818 .... **NCLC 11, 62**
See also DLB 39, 158, 178; HGG; RGEL 2; SUFW

Lewis, (Harry) Sinclair 1885-1951 . **TCLC 4, 13, 23, 39; WLC**
See also AMW; BPFB 2; CA 104; 133; CDALB 1917-1929; DA; DA3; DAB;

DAC; DAM MST, NOV; DLB 9, 102; DLBD 1; LAIT 3; MTCW 1, 2; NFS 15; RGAL 4

Lewis, (Percy) Wyndham
1884(?)-1957 .. **TCLC 2, 9, 104; SSC 34**
See also BRW 7; CA 104; 157; DLB 15; FANT; MTCW 2; RGEL 2

Lewisohn, Ludwig 1883-1955 .... **TCLC 19**
See also CA 107; DLB 4, 9, 28, 102

Lewton, Val 1904-1951 .... **TCLC 76**
See also CA 199; IDFW 3, 4

Leyner, Mark 1956- .... **CLC 92**
See also CA 110; CANR 28, 53; DA3; MTCW 2

Lezama Lima, Jose 1910-1976 .... **CLC 4, 10, 101; HLCS 2**
See also CA 77-80; CANR 71; DAM MULT; DLB 113; HW 1, 2; LAW; RGWL 2

L'Heureux, John (Clarke) 1934- ...... **CLC 52**
See also CA 13-16R; CANR 23, 45, 88; DLB 244

Liddell, C. H.
See Kuttner, Henry

Lie, Jonas (Lauritz Idemil)
1833-1908(?) .... **TCLC 5**
See also CA 115

Lieber, Joel 1937-1971 .... **CLC 6**
See also CA 73-76; 29-32R

Lieber, Stanley Martin
See Lee, Stan

Lieberman, Laurence (James)
1935- .... **CLC 4, 36**
See also CA 17-20R; CANR 8, 36, 89; CP 7

Lieh Tzu fl. 7th cent. B.C.-5th cent. B.C. .... **CMLC 27**

Lieksman, Anders
See Haavikko, Paavo Juhani

Li Fei-kan 1904-
See Pa Chin
See also CA 105

Lifton, Robert Jay 1926- .... **CLC 67**
See also CA 17-20R; CANR 27, 78; INT CANR-27; SATA 66

Lightfoot, Gordon 1938- .... **CLC 26**
See also CA 109

Lightman, Alan P(aige) 1948- .... **CLC 81**
See also CA 141; CANR 63, 105

Ligotti, Thomas (Robert) 1953- ...... **CLC 44; SSC 16**
See also CA 123; CANR 49; HGG

Li Ho 791-817 .... **PC 13**

Liliencron, (Friedrich Adolf Axel) Detlev von 1844-1909 .... **TCLC 18**
See also CA 117

Lille, Alain de
See Alain de Lille

Lilly, William 1602-1681 .... **LC 27**

Lima, Jose Lezama
See Lezama Lima, Jose

Lima Barreto, Afonso Henrique de
1881-1922 .... **TCLC 23**
See also CA 117; 181; LAW

Lima Barreto, Afonso Henriques de
See Lima Barreto, Afonso Henrique de

Limonov, Edward 1944- .... **CLC 67**
See also CA 137

Lin, Frank
See Atherton, Gertrude (Franklin Horn)

Lincoln, Abraham 1809-1865 .... **NCLC 18**
See also LAIT 2

Lind, Jakov .... **CLC 1, 2, 4, 27, 82**
See also Landwirth, Heinz
See also CAAS 4

Lindbergh, Anne (Spencer) Morrow
1906-2001 .... **CLC 82**
See also BPFB 2; CA 17-20R; 193; CANR 16, 73; DAM NOV; MTCW 1, 2; SATA 33; SATA-Obit 125

Lindsay, David 1878(?)-1945 .... **TCLC 15**
See also CA 113; 187; DLB 255; FANT; SFW 4; SUFW

Lindsay, (Nicholas) Vachel
1879-1931 .... **TCLC 17; PC 23; WLC**
See also AMWS 1; CA 114; 135; CANR 79; CDALB 1865-1917; DA; DA3; DAC; DAM MST, POET; DLB 54; EXPP; RGAL 4; SATA 40; WP

Linke-Poot
See Doeblin, Alfred

Linney, Romulus 1930- .... **CLC 51**
See also CA 1-4R; CAD; CANR 40, 44, 79; CD 5; CSW; RGAL 4

Linton, Eliza Lynn 1822-1898 .... **NCLC 41**
See also DLB 18

Li Po 701-763 .... **CMLC 2; PC 29**
See also WP

Lipsius, Justus 1547-1606 .... **LC 16**

Lipsyte, Robert (Michael) 1938- ...... **CLC 21**
See also AAYA 7; CA 17-20R; CANR 8, 57; CLR 23, 76; DA; DAC; DAM MST, NOV; JRDA; LAIT 5; MAICYA 1, 2; SATA 5, 68, 113; WYA; YAW

Lish, Gordon (Jay) 1934- ... **CLC 45; SSC 18**
See also CA 113; 117; CANR 79; DLB 130; INT 117

Lispector, Clarice 1925(?)-1977 .... **CLC 43; HLCS 2; SSC 34**
See also CA 139; 116; CANR 71; CDWLB 3; DLB 113; DNFS 1; FW; HW 1; LAW; RGSF 2; RGWL 2; WLIT 1

Littell, Robert 1935(?)- .... **CLC 42**
See also CA 109; 112; CANR 64; CMW 4

Little, Malcolm 1925-1965
See Malcolm X
See also BW 1, 3; CA 125; 111; CANR 82; DA; DA3; DAB; DAC; DAM MST, MULT; MTCW 1, 2; NCFS 3

Littlewit, Humphrey Gent.
See Lovecraft, H(oward) P(hillips)

Litwos
See Sienkiewicz, Henryk (Adam Alexander Pius)

Liu, E. 1857-1909 .... **TCLC 15**
See also CA 115; 190

Lively, Penelope (Margaret) 1933- .. **CLC 32, 50**
See also BPFB 2; CA 41-44R; CANR 29, 67, 79; CLR 7; CN 7; CWRI 5; DAM NOV; DLB 14, 161, 207; FANT; JRDA; MAICYA 1, 2; MTCW 1, 2; SATA 7, 60, 101

Livesay, Dorothy (Kathleen)
1909-1996 .... **CLC 4, 15, 79**
See also AITN 2; CA 25-28R; CAAS 8; CANR 36, 67; DAC; DAM MST, POET; DLB 68; FW; MTCW 1; RGEL 2

Livy c. 59B.C.-c. 12 .... **CMLC 11**
See also AW 2; CDWLB 1; DLB 211; RGWL 2

Lizardi, Jose Joaquin Fernandez de
1776-1827 .... **NCLC 30**
See also LAW

Llewellyn, Richard
See Llewellyn Lloyd, Richard Dafydd Vivian
See also DLB 15

Llewellyn Lloyd, Richard Dafydd Vivian
1906-1983 .... **CLC 7, 80**
See also Llewellyn, Richard
See also CA 53-56; 111; CANR 7, 71; SATA 11; SATA-Obit 37

Llosa, (Jorge) Mario (Pedro) Vargas
See Vargas Llosa, (Jorge) Mario (Pedro)

Lloyd, Manda
See Mander, (Mary) Jane

Lloyd Webber, Andrew 1948-
See Webber, Andrew Lloyd
See also AAYA 1, 38; CA 116; 149; DAM DRAM; SATA 56

Llull, Ramon c. 1235-c. 1316 .... **CMLC 12**

Lobb, Ebenezer
See Upward, Allen

Locke, Alain (Le Roy) 1886-1954 . **TCLC 43; BLCS**
See also BW 1, 3; CA 106; 124; CANR 79; RGAL 4

Locke, John 1632-1704 .... **LC 7, 35**
See also DLB 31, 101, 213, 252; RGEL 2; WLIT 3

Locke-Elliott, Sumner
See Elliott, Sumner Locke

Lockhart, John Gibson 1794-1854 .. **NCLC 6**
See also DLB 110, 116, 144

Lockridge, Ross (Franklin), Jr.
1914-1948 .... **TCLC 111**
See also CA 108; 145; CANR 79; DLB 143; DLBY 1980; RGAL 4; RHW

Lodge, David (John) 1935- .... **CLC 36, 141**
See also BEST 90:1; BRWS 4; CA 17-20R; CANR 19, 53, 92; CN 7; CPW; DAM POP; DLB 14, 194; INT CANR-19; MTCW 1, 2

Lodge, Thomas 1558-1625 .... **LC 41**
See also DLB 172; RGEL 2

Loewinsohn, Ron(ald William)
1937- .... **CLC 52**
See also CA 25-28R; CANR 71

Logan, Jake
See Smith, Martin Cruz

Logan, John (Burton) 1923-1987 .... **CLC 5**
See also CA 77-80; 124; CANR 45; DLB 5

Lo Kuan-chung 1330(?)-1400(?) .... **LC 12**

Lombard, Nap
See Johnson, Pamela Hansford

Lomotey (editor), Kofi .... **CLC 70**

London, Jack 1876-1916 ..... **TCLC 9, 15, 39; SSC 4, 49; WLC**
See also London, John Griffith
See also AAYA 13; AITN 2; AMW; BPFB 2; BYA 4, 13; CDALB 1865-1917; DLB 8, 12, 78, 212; EXPS; LAIT 3; NFS 8; RGAL 4; RGSF 2; SATA 18; SFW 4; SSFS 7; TCWW 2; TUS; WYA; YAW

London, John Griffith 1876-1916
See London, Jack
See also CA 110; 119; CANR 73; DA; DA3; DAB; DAC; DAM MST, NOV; JRDA; MAICYA 1, 2; MTCW 1, 2

Long, Emmett
See Leonard, Elmore (John, Jr.)

Longbaugh, Harry
See Goldman, William (W.)

Longfellow, Henry Wadsworth
1807-1882 .... **NCLC 2, 45, 101, 103; PC 30; WLCS**
See also AMW; CDALB 1640-1865; DA; DA3; DAB; DAC; DAM MST, POET; DLB 1, 59, 235; EXPP; PAB; PFS 2, 7; RGAL 4; SATA 19; TUS; WP

Longinus c. 1st cent. - .... **CMLC 27**
See also AW 2; DLB 176

Longley, Michael 1939- .... **CLC 29**
See also CA 102; CP 7; DLB 40

Longus fl. c. 2nd cent. - .... **CMLC 7**

Longway, A. Hugh
See Lang, Andrew

Lonnrot, Elias 1802-1884 .... **NCLC 53**
See also EFS 1

Lonsdale, Roger ed. .... **CLC 65**

Lopate, Phillip 1943- .... **CLC 29**
See also CA 97-100; CANR 88; DLBY 1980; INT 97-100

Lopez, Barry (Holstun) 1945- .... **CLC 70**
See also AAYA 9; ANW; CA 65-68; CANR 7, 23, 47, 68, 92; DLB 256; INT CANR-7, -23; MTCW 1; RGAL 4; SATA 67

Lopez Portillo (y Pacheco), Jose 1920- .... **CLC 46**
See also CA 129; HW 1

Lopez y Fuentes, Gregorio 1897(?)-1966 .... **CLC 32**
See also CA 131; HW 1

Lorca, Federico Garcia
See Garcia Lorca, Federico
See also DFS 4; EW 11; RGWL 2; WP

Lord, Bette Bao 1938- .... **CLC 23; AAL**
See also BEST 90:3; BPFB 2; CA 107; CANR 41, 79; INT CA-107; SATA 58

Lord Auch
See Bataille, Georges

Lord Brooke
See Greville, Fulke

Lord Byron
See Byron, George Gordon (Noel)

Lorde, Audre (Geraldine) 1934-1992 .. **CLC 18, 71; BLC 2; PC 12**
See also Domini, Rey
See also AFAW 1, 2; BW 1, 3; CA 25-28R; 142; CANR 16, 26, 46, 82; DA3; DAM MULT, POET; DLB 41; FW; MTCW 1, 2; RGAL 4

Lord Houghton
See Milnes, Richard Monckton

Lord Jeffrey
See Jeffrey, Francis

Loreaux, Nichol .... **CLC 65**

Lorenzini, Carlo 1826-1890
See Collodi, Carlo
See also MAICYA 1, 2; SATA 29, 100

Lorenzo, Heberto Padilla
See Padilla (Lorenzo), Heberto

Loris
See Hofmannsthal, Hugo von

Loti, Pierre .... **TCLC 11**
See also Viaud, (Louis Marie) Julien
See also DLB 123; GFL 1789 to the Present

Lou, Henri
See Andreas-Salome, Lou

Louie, David Wong 1954- .... **CLC 70**
See also CA 139

Louis, Father M.
See Merton, Thomas

Lovecraft, H(oward) P(hillips) 1890-1937 .... **TCLC 4, 22; SSC 3, 52**
See also AAYA 14; BPFB 2; CA 104; 133; CANR 106; DA3; DAM POP; HGG; MTCW 1, 2; RGAL 4; SCFW; SFW 4; SUFW

Lovelace, Earl 1935- .... **CLC 51**
See also BW 2; CA 77-80; CANR 41, 72; CD 5; CDWLB 3; CN 7; DLB 125; MTCW 1

Lovelace, Richard 1618-1657 .... **LC 24**
See also BRW 2; DLB 131; EXPP; PAB; RGEL 2

Lowell, Amy 1874-1925 ... **TCLC 1, 8; PC 13**
See also AMW; CA 104; 151; DAM POET; DLB 54, 140; EXPP; MAWW; MTCW 2; RGAL 4

Lowell, James Russell 1819-1891 ... **NCLC 2, 90**
See also AMWS 1; CDALB 1640-1865; DLB 1, 11, 64, 79, 189, 235; RGAL 4

Lowell, Robert (Traill Spence, Jr.) 1917-1977 ..... **CLC 1, 2, 3, 4, 5, 8, 9, 11, 15, 37, 124; PC 3; WLC**
See also AMW; CA 9-12R; 73-76; CABS 2; CANR 26, 60; CDALBS; DA; DA3; DAB; DAC; DAM MST, NOV; DLB 5, 169; MTCW 1, 2; PAB; PFS 6, 7; RGAL 4; WP

Lowenthal, Michael (Francis) 1969- .... **CLC 119**
See also CA 150

Lowndes, Marie Adelaide (Belloc) 1868-1947 .... **TCLC 12**
See also CA 107; CMW 4; DLB 70; RHW

Lowry, (Clarence) Malcolm 1909-1957 .... **TCLC 6, 40; SSC 31**
See also BPFB 2; BRWS 3; CA 105; 131; CANR 62, 105; CDBLB 1945-1960; DLB 15; MTCW 1, 2; RGEL 2

Lowry, Mina Gertrude 1882-1966
See Loy, Mina
See also CA 113

Loxsmith, John
See Brunner, John (Kilian Houston)

Loy, Mina .... **CLC 28; PC 16**
See also Lowry, Mina Gertrude
See also DAM POET; DLB 4, 54

Loyson-Bridet
See Schwob, Marcel (Mayer Andre)

Lucan 39-65 .... **CMLC 33**
See also AW 2; DLB 211; EFS 2; RGWL 2

Lucas, Craig 1951- .... **CLC 64**
See also CA 137; CAD; CANR 71, 109; CD 5; GLL 2

Lucas, E(dward) V(errall) 1868-1938 .... **TCLC 73**
See also CA 176; DLB 98, 149, 153; SATA 20

Lucas, George 1944- .... **CLC 16**
See also AAYA 1, 23; CA 77-80; CANR 30; SATA 56

Lucas, Hans
See Godard, Jean-Luc

Lucas, Victoria
See Plath, Sylvia

Lucian c. 125-c. 180 .... **CMLC 32**
See also AW 2; DLB 176; RGWL 2

Lucretius c. 94B.C.-c. 49B.C. .... **CMLC 48**
See also AW 2; CDWLB 1; DLB 211; EFS 2; RGWL 2

Ludlam, Charles 1943-1987 .... **CLC 46, 50**
See also CA 85-88; 122; CAD; CANR 72, 86

Ludlum, Robert 1927-2001 .... **CLC 22, 43**
See also AAYA 10; BEST 89:1, 90:3; BPFB 2; CA 33-36R; 195; CANR 25, 41, 68, 105; CMW 4; CPW; DA3; DAM NOV, POP; DLBY 1982; MSW; MTCW 1, 2

Ludwig, Ken .... **CLC 60**
See also CA 195; CAD

Ludwig, Otto 1813-1865 .... **NCLC 4**
See also DLB 129

Lugones, Leopoldo 1874-1938 .... **TCLC 15; HLCS 2**
See also CA 116; 131; CANR 104; HW 1; LAW

Lu Hsun .... **TCLC 3; SSC 20**
See also Shu-Jen, Chou

Lukacs, George .... **CLC 24**
See also Lukacs, Gyorgy (Szegeny von)

Lukacs, Gyorgy (Szegeny von) 1885-1971
See Lukacs, George
See also CA 101; 29-32R; CANR 62; CD-WLB 4; DLB 215, 242; EW 10; MTCW 2

Luke, Peter (Ambrose Cyprian) 1919-1995 .... **CLC 38**
See also CA 81-84; 147; CANR 72; CBD; CD 5; DLB 13

Lunar, Dennis
See Mungo, Raymond

Lurie, Alison 1926- .... **CLC 4, 5, 18, 39**
See also BPFB 2; CA 1-4R; CANR 2, 17, 50, 88; CN 7; DLB 2; MTCW 1; SATA 46, 112

Lustig, Arnost 1926- .... **CLC 56**
See also AAYA 3; CA 69-72; CANR 47, 102; CWW 2; DLB 232; SATA 56

Luther, Martin 1483-1546 .... **LC 9, 37**
See also CDWLB 2; DLB 179; EW 2; RGWL 2

Luxemburg, Rosa 1870(?)-1919 ..... **TCLC 63**
See also CA 118

Luzi, Mario 1914- .... **CLC 13**
See also CA 61-64; CANR 9, 70; CWW 2; DLB 128

L'vov, Arkady .... **CLC 59**

Lyly, John 1554(?)-1606 .... **LC 41; DC 7**
See also BRW 1; DAM DRAM; DLB 62, 167; RGEL 2

L'Ymagier
See Gourmont, Remy(-Marie-Charles) de

Lynch, B. Suarez
See Borges, Jorge Luis

Lynch, David (K.) 1946- .... **CLC 66**
See also CA 124; 129

Lynch, James
See Andreyev, Leonid (Nikolaevich)

Lyndsay, Sir David 1485-1555 .... **LC 20**
See also RGEL 2

Lynn, Kenneth S(chuyler) 1923-2001 .... **CLC 50**
See also CA 1-4R; 196; CANR 3, 27, 65

Lynx
See West, Rebecca

Lyons, Marcus
See Blish, James (Benjamin)

Lyotard, Jean-Francois 1924-1998 .... **TCLC 103**
See also DLB 242

Lyre, Pinchbeck
See Sassoon, Siegfried (Lorraine)

Lytle, Andrew (Nelson) 1902-1995 ... **CLC 22**
See also CA 9-12R; 150; CANR 70; CN 7; CSW; DLB 6; DLBY 1995; RGAL 4; RHW

Lyttelton, George 1709-1773 .... **LC 10**
See also RGEL 2

Lytton of Knebworth, Baron
See Bulwer-Lytton, Edward (George Earle Lytton)

Maas, Peter 1929-2001 .... **CLC 29**
See also CA 93-96; 201; INT CA-93-96; MTCW 2

Macaulay, Catherine 1731-1791 .... **LC 64**
See also DLB 104

Macaulay, (Emilie) Rose 1881(?)-1958 .... **TCLC 7, 44**
See also CA 104; DLB 36; RGEL 2; RHW

Macaulay, Thomas Babington 1800-1859 .... **NCLC 42**
See also BRW 4; CDBLB 1832-1890; DLB 32, 55; RGEL 2

MacBeth, George (Mann) 1932-1992 .... **CLC 2, 5, 9**
See also CA 25-28R; 136; CANR 61, 66; DLB 40; MTCW 1; PFS 8; SATA 4; SATA-Obit 70

MacCaig, Norman (Alexander) 1910-1996 .... **CLC 36**
See also BRWS 6; CA 9-12R; CANR 3, 34; CP 7; DAB; DAM POET; DLB 27; RGEL 2

MacCarthy, Sir (Charles Otto) Desmond 1877-1952 .... **TCLC 36**
See also CA 167

MacDiarmid, Hugh .... CLC 2, 4, 11, 19, 63; PC 9
See also Grieve, C(hristopher) M(urray)
See also CDBLB 1945-1960; DLB 20; RGEL 2

MacDonald, Anson
See Heinlein, Robert A(nson)

Macdonald, Cynthia 1928- .... CLC 13, 19
See also CA 49-52; CANR 4, 44; DLB 105

MacDonald, George 1824-1905 .... TCLC 9, 113
See also BYA 5; CA 106; 137; CANR 80; CLR 67; DLB 18, 163, 178; FANT; MAICYA 1, 2; RGEL 2; SATA 33, 100; SFW 4; SUFW; WCH

Macdonald, John
See Millar, Kenneth

MacDonald, John D(ann) 1916-1986 .... CLC 3, 27, 44
See also BPFB 2; CA 1-4R; 121; CANR 1, 19, 60; CMW 4; CPW; DAM NOV, POP; DLB 8; DLBY 1986; MSW; MTCW 1, 2; SFW 4

Macdonald, John Ross
See Millar, Kenneth

Macdonald, Ross ..... CLC 1, 2, 3, 14, 34, 41
See also Millar, Kenneth
See also AMWS 4; BPFB 2; DLBD 6; MSW; RGAL 4

MacDougal, John
See Blish, James (Benjamin)

MacDougal, John
See Blish, James (Benjamin)

MacDowell, John
See Parks, Tim(othy Harold)

MacEwen, Gwendolyn (Margaret) 1941-1987 .... CLC 13, 55
See also CA 9-12R; 124; CANR 7, 22; DLB 53, 251; SATA 50; SATA-Obit 55

Macha, Karel Hynek 1810-1846 .... NCLC 46

Machado (y Ruiz), Antonio 1875-1939 .... TCLC 3
See also CA 104; 174; DLB 108; EW 9; HW 2; RGWL 2

Machado de Assis, Joaquim Maria 1839-1908 ..... TCLC 10; BLC 2; HLCS 2; SSC 24
See also CA 107; 153; CANR 91; LAW; RGSF 2; RGWL 2; WLIT 1

Machen, Arthur .... TCLC 4; SSC 20
See also Jones, Arthur Llewellyn
See also CA 179; DLB 156, 178; RGEL 2; SUFW

Machiavelli, Niccolo 1469-1527 ..... LC 8, 36; DC 16; WLCS
See also DA; DAB; DAC; DAM MST; EW 2; LAIT 1; NFS 9; RGWL 2

MacInnes, Colin 1914-1976 .... CLC 4, 23
See also CA 69-72; 65-68; CANR 21; DLB 14; MTCW 1, 2; RGEL 2; RHW

MacInnes, Helen (Clark) 1907-1985 .... CLC 27, 39
See also BPFB 2; CA 1-4R; 117; CANR 1, 28, 58; CMW 4; CPW; DAM POP; DLB 87; MSW; MTCW 1, 2; SATA 22; SATA-Obit 44

Mackay, Mary 1855-1924
See Corelli, Marie
See also CA 118; 177; FANT; RHW

Mackenzie, Compton (Edward Montague) 1883-1972 .... CLC 18
See also CA 21-22; 37-40R; CAP 2; DLB 34, 100; RGEL 2; TCLC 116

Mackenzie, Henry 1745-1831 .... NCLC 41
See also DLB 39; RGEL 2

Mackintosh, Elizabeth 1896(?)-1952
See Tey, Josephine
See also CA 110; CMW 4

MacLaren, James
See Grieve, C(hristopher) M(urray)

Mac Laverty, Bernard 1942- .... CLC 31
See also CA 116; 118; CANR 43, 88; CN 7; INT CA-118; RGSF 2

MacLean, Alistair (Stuart) 1922(?)-1987 .... CLC 3, 13, 50, 63
See also CA 57-60; 121; CANR 28, 61; CMW 4; CPW; DAM POP; MTCW 1; SATA 23; SATA-Obit 50; TCWW 2

Maclean, Norman (Fitzroy) 1902-1990 .... CLC 78; SSC 13
See also CA 102; 132; CANR 49; CPW; DAM POP; DLB 206; TCWW 2

MacLeish, Archibald 1892-1982 ... CLC 3, 8, 14, 68
See also AMW; CA 9-12R; 106; CAD; CANR 33, 63; CDALBS; DAM POET; DFS 15; DLB 4, 7, 45; DLBY 1982; EXPP; MTCW 1, 2; PAB; PFS 5; RGAL 4

MacLennan, (John) Hugh 1907-1990 .... CLC 2, 14, 92
See also CA 5-8R; 142; CANR 33; DAC; DAM MST; DLB 68; MTCW 1, 2; RGEL 2

MacLeod, Alistair 1936- .... CLC 56
See also CA 123; CCA 1; DAC; DAM MST; DLB 60; MTCW 2; RGSF 2

Macleod, Fiona
See Sharp, William
See also RGEL 2; SUFW

MacNeice, (Frederick) Louis 1907-1963 .... CLC 1, 4, 10, 53
See also BRW 7; CA 85-88; CANR 61; DAB; DAM POET; DLB 10, 20; MTCW 1, 2; RGEL 2

MacNeill, Dand
See Fraser, George MacDonald

Macpherson, James 1736-1796 .... LC 29
See also Ossian
See also DLB 109; RGEL 2

Macpherson, (Jean) Jay 1931- .... CLC 14
See also CA 5-8R; CANR 90; CP 7; CWP; DLB 53

Macrobius fl. 430- .... CMLC 48

MacShane, Frank 1927-1999 .... CLC 39
See also CA 9-12R; 186; CANR 3, 33; DLB 111

Macumber, Mari
See Sandoz, Mari(e Susette)

Madach, Imre 1823-1864 .... NCLC 19

Madden, (Jerry) David 1933- .... CLC 5, 15
See also CA 1-4R; CAAS 3; CANR 4, 45; CN 7; CSW; DLB 6; MTCW 1

Maddern, Al(an)
See Ellison, Harlan (Jay)

Madhubuti, Haki R. 1942- . CLC 6, 73; BLC 2; PC 5
See also Lee, Don L.
See also BW 2, 3; CA 73-76; CANR 24, 51, 73; CP 7; CSW; DAM MULT, POET; DLB 5, 41; DLBD 8; MTCW 2; RGAL 4

Maepenn, Hugh
See Kuttner, Henry

Maepenn, K. H.
See Kuttner, Henry

Maeterlinck, Maurice 1862-1949 ..... TCLC 3
See also CA 104; 136; CANR 80; DAM DRAM; DLB 192; EW 8; GFL 1789 to the Present; RGWL 2; SATA 66

Maginn, William 1794-1842 .... NCLC 8
See also DLB 110, 159

Mahapatra, Jayanta 1928- .... CLC 33
See also CA 73-76; CAAS 9; CANR 15, 33, 66, 87; CP 7; DAM MULT

Mahfouz, Naguib (Abdel Aziz Al-Sabilgi) 1911(?)- .... CLC 153
See also Mahfuz, Najib (Abdel Aziz al-Sabilgi)
See also BEST 89:2; CA 128; CANR 55, 101; CWW 2; DA3; DAM NOV; MTCW 1, 2; RGWL 2; SSFS 9

Mahfuz, Najib (Abdel Aziz al-Sabilgi) .... CLC 52, 55
See also Mahfouz, Naguib (Abdel Aziz Al-Sabilgi)
See also AFW; DLBY 1988; RGSF 2; WLIT 2

Mahon, Derek 1941- .... CLC 27
See also BRWS 6; CA 113; 128; CANR 88; CP 7; DLB 40

Maiakovskii, Vladimir
See Mayakovski, Vladimir (Vladimirovich)
See also IDTP; RGWL 2

Mailer, Norman 1923- ... CLC 1, 2, 3, 4, 5, 8, 11, 14, 28, 39, 74, 111
See also AAYA 31; AITN 2; AMW; BPFB 2; CA 9-12R; CABS 1; CANR 28, 74, 77; CDALB 1968-1988; CN 7; CPW; DA; DA3; DAB; DAC; DAM MST, NOV, POP; DLB 2, 16, 28, 185; DLBD 3; DLBY 1980, 1983; MTCW 1, 2; NFS 10; RGAL 4

Maillet, Antonine 1929- .... CLC 54, 118
See also CA 115; 120; CANR 46, 74, 77; CCA 1; CWW 2; DAC; DLB 60; INT 120; MTCW 2

Mais, Roger 1905-1955 .... TCLC 8
See also BW 1, 3; CA 105; 124; CANR 82; CDWLB 3; DLB 125; MTCW 1; RGEL 2

Maistre, Joseph 1753-1821 .... NCLC 37
See also GFL 1789 to the Present

Maitland, Frederic William 1850-1906 .... TCLC 65

Maitland, Sara (Louise) 1950- .... CLC 49
See also CA 69-72; CANR 13, 59; FW

Major, Clarence 1936- . CLC 3, 19, 48; BLC 2
See also AFAW 2; BW 2, 3; CA 21-24R; CAAS 6; CANR 13, 25, 53, 82; CN 7; CP 7; CSW; DAM MULT; DLB 33; MSW

Major, Kevin (Gerald) 1949- .... CLC 26
See also AAYA 16; CA 97-100; CANR 21, 38; CLR 11; DAC; DLB 60; INT CANR-21; JRDA; MAICYA 1, 2; MAICYAS 1; SATA 32, 82; WYA; YAW

Maki, James
See Ozu, Yasujiro

Malabaila, Damiano
See Levi, Primo

Malamud, Bernard 1914-1986 .. CLC 1, 2, 3, 5, 8, 9, 11, 18, 27, 44, 78, 85; SSC 15; WLC
See also AAYA 16; AMWS 1; BPFB 2; CA 5-8R; 118; CABS 1; CANR 28, 62; CDALB 1941-1968; CPW; DA; DA3; DAB; DAC; DAM MST, NOV, POP; DLB 2, 28, 152; DLBY 1980, 1986; EXPS; LAIT 4; MTCW 1, 2; NFS 4, 9; RGAL 4; RGSF 2; SSFS 8, 13

Malan, Herman
See Bosman, Herman Charles; Bosman, Herman Charles

Malaparte, Curzio 1898-1957 .... TCLC 52

Malcolm, Dan
See Silverberg, Robert

Malcolm X .... CLC 82, 117; BLC 2; WLCS
See also Little, Malcolm
See also LAIT 5

Malherbe, Francois de 1555-1628 .... LC 5
See also GFL Beginnings to 1789

Mallarme, Stephane 1842-1898 ...... NCLC 4, 41; PC 4
See also DAM POET; DLB 217; EW 7; GFL 1789 to the Present; RGWL 2

Mallet-Joris, Francoise 1930- .... **CLC 11**
See also CA 65-68; CANR 17; DLB 83; GFL 1789 to the Present

Malley, Ern
See McAuley, James Phillip

Mallowan, Agatha Christie
See Christie, Agatha (Mary Clarissa)

Maloff, Saul 1922- .... **CLC 5**
See also CA 33-36R

Malone, Louis
See MacNeice, (Frederick) Louis

Malone, Michael (Christopher)
1942- .... **CLC 43**
See also CA 77-80; CANR 14, 32, 57

Malory, Sir Thomas 1410(?)-1471(?) . **LC 11; WLCS**
See also BRW 1; BRWR 2; CDBLB Before 1660; DA; DAB; DAC; DAM MST; DLB 146; EFS 2; RGEL 2; SATA 59; SATA-Brief 33; WLIT 3

Malouf, (George Joseph) David
1934- .... **CLC 28, 86**
See also CA 124; CANR 50, 76; CN 7; CP 7; MTCW 2

Malraux, (Georges-)Andre
1901-1976 .... **CLC 1, 4, 9, 13, 15, 57**
See also BPFB 2; CA 21-22; 69-72; CANR 34, 58; CAP 2; DA3; DAM NOV; DLB 72; EW 12; GFL 1789 to the Present; MTCW 1, 2; RGWL 2

Malzberg, Barry N(athaniel) 1939- ... **CLC 7**
See also CA 61-64; CAAS 4; CANR 16; CMW 4; DLB 8; SFW 4

Mamet, David (Alan) 1947- .. **CLC 9, 15, 34, 46, 91; DC 4**
See also AAYA 3; CA 81-84; CABS 3; CANR 15, 41, 67, 72; CD 5; DA3; DAM DRAM; DFS 15; DLB 7; IDFW 4; MTCW 1, 2; RGAL 4

Mamoulian, Rouben (Zachary)
1897-1987 .... **CLC 16**
See also CA 25-28R; 124; CANR 85

Mandelshtam, Osip
See Mandelstam, Osip (Emilievich)
See also EW 10; RGWL 2

Mandelstam, Osip (Emilievich)
1891(?)-1943(?) .... **TCLC 2, 6; PC 14**
See also Mandelshtam, Osip
See also CA 104; 150; MTCW 2

Mander, (Mary) Jane 1877-1949 ... **TCLC 31**
See also CA 162; RGEL 2

Mandeville, Sir John fl. 1350- ...... **CMLC 19**
See also DLB 146

Mandiargues, Andre Pieyre de .... **CLC 41**
See also Pieyre de Mandiargues, Andre
See also DLB 83

Mandrake, Ethel Belle
See Thurman, Wallace (Henry)

Mangan, James Clarence
1803-1849 .... **NCLC 27**
See also RGEL 2

Maniere, J.-E.
See Giraudoux, Jean(-Hippolyte)

Mankiewicz, Herman (Jacob)
1897-1953 .... **TCLC 85**
See also CA 120; 169; DLB 26; IDFW 3, 4

Manley, (Mary) Delariviere
1672(?)-1724 .... **LC 1, 42**
See also DLB 39, 80; RGEL 2

Mann, Abel
See Creasey, John

Mann, Emily 1952- .... **DC 7**
See also CA 130; CAD; CANR 55; CD 5; CWD

Mann, (Luiz) Heinrich 1871-1950 ... **TCLC 9**
See also CA 106; 164, 181; DLB 66, 118; EW 8; RGWL 2

Mann, (Paul) Thomas 1875-1955 ... **TCLC 2, 8, 14, 21, 35, 44, 60; SSC 5; WLC**
See also BPFB 2; CA 104; 128; CDWLB 2; DA; DA3; DAB; DAC; DAM MST, NOV; DLB 66; EW 9; GLL 1; MTCW 1, 2; RGSF 2; RGWL 2; SSFS 4, 9

Mannheim, Karl 1893-1947 .... **TCLC 65**

Manning, David
See Faust, Frederick (Schiller)
See also TCWW 2

Manning, Frederic 1887(?)-1935 ... **TCLC 25**
See also CA 124; DLB 260

Manning, Olivia 1915-1980 .... **CLC 5, 19**
See also CA 5-8R; 101; CANR 29; FW; MTCW 1; RGEL 2

Mano, D. Keith 1942- .... **CLC 2, 10**
See also CA 25-28R; CAAS 6; CANR 26, 57; DLB 6

Mansfield, Katherine .... **TCLC 2, 8, 39; SSC 9, 23, 38; WLC**
See also Beauchamp, Kathleen Mansfield
See also BPFB 2; BRW 7; DAB; DLB 162; EXPS; FW; GLL 1; RGEL 2; RGSF 2; SSFS 2, 8, 10, 11

Manso, Peter 1940- .... **CLC 39**
See also CA 29-32R; CANR 44

Mantecon, Juan Jimenez
See Jimenez (Mantecon), Juan Ramon

Mantel, Hilary (Mary) 1952- .... **CLC 144**
See also CA 125; CANR 54, 101; CN 7; RHW

Manton, Peter
See Creasey, John

Man Without a Spleen, A
See Chekhov, Anton (Pavlovich)

Manzoni, Alessandro 1785-1873 ... **NCLC 29, 98**
See also EW 5; RGWL 2

Map, Walter 1140-1209 .... **CMLC 32**

Mapu, Abraham (ben Jekutiel)
1808-1867 .... **NCLC 18**

Mara, Sally
See Queneau, Raymond

Marat, Jean Paul 1743-1793 .... **LC 10**

Marcel, Gabriel Honore 1889-1973 . **CLC 15**
See also CA 102; 45-48; MTCW 1, 2

March, William 1893-1954 .... **TCLC 96**

Marchbanks, Samuel
See Davies, (William) Robertson
See also CCA 1

Marchi, Giacomo
See Bassani, Giorgio

Marcus Aurelius
See Aurelius, Marcus
See also AW 2

Marguerite
See de Navarre, Marguerite

Marguerite d'Angouleme
See de Navarre, Marguerite
See also GFL Beginnings to 1789

Marguerite de Navarre
See de Navarre, Marguerite
See also RGWL 2

Margulies, Donald 1954- .... **CLC 76**
See also CA 200; DFS 13; DLB 228

Marie de France c. 12th cent. - ...... **CMLC 8; PC 22**
See also DLB 208; FW; RGWL 2

Marie de l'Incarnation 1599-1672 ...... **LC 10**

Marier, Captain Victor
See Griffith, D(avid Lewelyn) W(ark)

Mariner, Scott
See Pohl, Frederik

Marinetti, Filippo Tommaso
1876-1944 .... **TCLC 10**
See also CA 107; DLB 114; EW 9

Marivaux, Pierre Carlet de Chamblain de
1688-1763 .... **LC 4; DC 7**
See also GFL Beginnings to 1789; RGWL 2

Markandaya, Kamala .... **CLC 8, 38**
See also Taylor, Kamala (Purnaiya)
See also BYA 13; CN 7

Markfield, Wallace 1926- .... **CLC 8**
See also CA 69-72; CAAS 3; CN 7; DLB 2, 28

Markham, Edwin 1852-1940 .... **TCLC 47**
See also CA 160; DLB 54, 186; RGAL 4

Markham, Robert
See Amis, Kingsley (William)

Marks, J
See Highwater, Jamake (Mamake)

Marks, J.
See Highwater, Jamake (Mamake)

Marks-Highwater, J
See Highwater, Jamake (Mamake)

Marks-Highwater, J.
See Highwater, Jamake (Mamake)

Markson, David M(errill) 1927- .... **CLC 67**
See also CA 49-52; CANR 1, 91; CN 7

Marley, Bob .... **CLC 17**
See also Marley, Robert Nesta

Marley, Robert Nesta 1945-1981
See Marley, Bob
See also CA 107; 103

Marlowe, Christopher 1564-1593 ...... **LC 22, 47; DC 1; WLC**
See also BRW 1; BRWR 1; CDBLB Before 1660; DA; DA3; DAB; DAC; DAM DRAM, MST; DFS 1, 5, 13; DLB 62; EXPP; RGEL 2; TEA; WLIT 3

Marlowe, Stephen 1928- .... **CLC 70**
See also Queen, Ellery
See also CA 13-16R; CANR 6, 55; CMW 4; SFW 4

Marmontel, Jean-Francois 1723-1799 .. **LC 2**

Marquand, John P(hillips)
1893-1960 .... **CLC 2, 10**
See also AMW; BPFB 2; CA 85-88; CANR 73; CMW 4; DLB 9, 102; MTCW 2; RGAL 4

Marques, Rene 1919-1979 .. **CLC 96; HLC 2**
See also CA 97-100; 85-88; CANR 78; DAM MULT; DLB 113; HW 1, 2; LAW; RGSF 2

Marquez, Gabriel (Jose) Garcia
See Garcia Marquez, Gabriel (Jose)

Marquis, Don(ald Robert Perry)
1878-1937 .... **TCLC 7**
See also CA 104; 166; DLB 11, 25; RGAL 4

Marric, J. J.
See Creasey, John
See also MSW

Marryat, Frederick 1792-1848 .... **NCLC 3**
See also DLB 21, 163; RGEL 2; WCH

Marsden, James
See Creasey, John

Marsh, Edward 1872-1953 .... **TCLC 99**

Marsh, (Edith) Ngaio 1899-1982 .. **CLC 7, 53**
See also CA 9-12R; CANR 6, 58; CMW 4; CPW; DAM POP; DLB 77; MSW; MTCW 1, 2; RGEL 2

Marshall, Garry 1934- .... **CLC 17**
See also AAYA 3; CA 111; SATA 60

Marshall, Paule 1929- .. **CLC 27, 72; BLC 3; SSC 3**
See also AFAW 1, 2; BPFB 2; BW 2, 3; CA 77-80; CANR 25, 73; CN 7; DA3; DAM MULT; DLB 33, 157, 227; MTCW 1, 2; RGAL 4; SSFS 15

Marshallik
See Zangwill, Israel

Marsten, Richard
See Hunter, Evan

Marston, John 1576-1634 .... **LC 33**
See also BRW 2; DAM DRAM; DLB 58, 172; RGEL 2
Martha, Henry
See Harris, Mark
Marti (y Perez), Jose (Julian)
1853-1895 .... **NCLC 63; HLC 2**
See also DAM MULT; HW 2; LAW; RGWL 2; WLIT 1
Martial c. 40-c. 104 .... **CMLC 35; PC 10**
See also AW 2; CDWLB 1; DLB 211; RGWL 2
Martin, Ken
See Hubbard, L(afayette) Ron(ald)
Martin, Richard
See Creasey, John
Martin, Steve 1945- .... **CLC 30**
See also CA 97-100; CANR 30, 100; MTCW 1
Martin, Valerie 1948- .... **CLC 89**
See also BEST 90:2; CA 85-88; CANR 49, 89
Martin, Violet Florence
1862-1915 .... **TCLC 51**
Martin, Webber
See Silverberg, Robert
Martindale, Patrick Victor
See White, Patrick (Victor Martindale)
Martin du Gard, Roger
1881-1958 .... **TCLC 24**
See also CA 118; CANR 94; DLB 65; GFL 1789 to the Present; RGWL 2
Martineau, Harriet 1802-1876 .... **NCLC 26**
See also DLB 21, 55, 159, 163, 166, 190; FW; RGEL 2; YABC 2
Martines, Julia
See O'Faolain, Julia
Martinez, Enrique Gonzalez
See Gonzalez Martinez, Enrique
Martinez, Jacinto Benavente y
See Benavente (y Martinez), Jacinto
Martinez de la Rosa, Francisco de Paula
1787-1862 .... **NCLC 102**
Martinez Ruiz, Jose 1873-1967
See Azorin; Ruiz, Jose Martinez
See also CA 93-96; HW 1
Martinez Sierra, Gregorio
1881-1947 .... **TCLC 6**
See also CA 115
Martinez Sierra, Maria (de la O'LeJarraga
1874-1974 .... **TCLC 6**
See also CA 115
Martinsen, Martin
See Follett, Ken(neth Martin)
Martinson, Harry (Edmund)
1904-1978 .... **CLC 14**
See also CA 77-80; CANR 34; DLB 259
Martyn, Edward 1859-1923 .... **TCLC 121**
See also CA 179; DLB 10; RGEL 2
Marut, Ret
See Traven, B.
Marut, Robert
See Traven, B.
Marvell, Andrew 1621-1678 .... **LC 4, 43; PC 10; WLC**
See also BRW 2; BRWR 2; CDBLB 1660-1789; DA; DAB; DAC; DAM MST, POET; DLB 131; EXPP; PFS 5; RGEL 2; WP
Marx, Karl (Heinrich)
1818-1883 .... **NCLC 17, 114**
See also DLB 129
Masaoka, Shiki .... **TCLC 18**
See also Masaoka, Tsunenori
Masaoka, Tsunenori 1867-1902
See Masaoka, Shiki
See also CA 117; 191

Masefield, John (Edward)
1878-1967 .... **CLC 11, 47**
See also CA 19-20; 25-28R; CANR 33; CAP 2; CDBLB 1890-1914; DAM POET; DLB 10, 19, 153, 160; EXPP; FANT; MTCW 1, 2; PFS 5; RGEL 2; SATA 19
Maso, Carole 19(?)- .... **CLC 44**
See also CA 170; GLL 2; RGAL 4
Mason, Bobbie Ann 1940- ... **CLC 28, 43, 82, 154; SSC 4**
See also AAYA 5, 42; AMWS 8; BPFB 2; CA 53-56; CANR 11, 31, 58, 83; CDALBS; CN 7; CSW; DA3; DLB 173; DLBY 1987; EXPS; INT CANR-31; MTCW 1, 2; NFS 4; RGAL 4; RGSF 2; SSFS 3,8; YAW
Mason, Ernst
See Pohl, Frederik
Mason, Hunni B.
See Sternheim, (William Adolf) Carl
Mason, Lee W.
See Malzberg, Barry N(athaniel)
Mason, Nick 1945- .... **CLC 35**
Mason, Tally
See Derleth, August (William)
Mass, Anna .... **CLC 59**
Mass, William
See Gibson, William
Massinger, Philip 1583-1640 .... **LC 70**
See also DLB 58; RGEL 2
Master Lao
See Lao Tzu
Masters, Edgar Lee 1868-1950 .... **TCLC 2, 25; PC 1, 36; WLCS**
See also AMWS 1; CA 104; 133; CDALB 1865-1917; DA; DAC; DAM MST, POET; DLB 54; EXPP; MTCW 1, 2; RGAL 4; WP
Masters, Hilary 1928- .... **CLC 48**
See also CA 25-28R; CANR 13, 47, 97; CN 7; DLB 244
Mastrosimone, William 19(?)- .... **CLC 36**
See also CA 186; CAD; CD 5
Mathe, Albert
See Camus, Albert
Mather, Cotton 1663-1728 .... **LC 38**
See also AMWS 2; CDALB 1640-1865; DLB 24, 30, 140; RGAL 4
Mather, Increase 1639-1723 .... **LC 38**
See also DLB 24
Matheson, Richard (Burton) 1926- .. **CLC 37**
See also AAYA 31; CA 97-100; CANR 88, 99; DLB 8, 44; HGG; INT 97-100; SCFW 2; SFW 4
Mathews, Harry 1930- .... **CLC 6, 52**
See also CA 21-24R; CAAS 6; CANR 18, 40, 98; CN 7
Mathews, John Joseph 1894-1979 .... **CLC 84**
See also CA 19-20; 142; CANR 45; CAP 2; DAM MULT; DLB 175; NNAL
Mathias, Roland (Glyn) 1915- .... **CLC 45**
See also CA 97-100; CANR 19, 41; CP 7; DLB 27
Matsuo Basho 1644-1694 .... **LC 62; PC 3**
See also Basho, Matsuo
See also DAM POET; PFS 2, 7
Mattheson, Rodney
See Creasey, John
Matthews, (James) Brander
1852-1929 .... **TCLC 95**
See also DLB 71, 78; DLBD 13
Matthews, Greg 1949- .... **CLC 45**
See also CA 135
Matthews, William (Procter III)
1942-1997 .... **CLC 40**
See also AMWS 9; CA 29-32R; 162; CAAS 18; CANR 12, 57; CP 7; DLB 5
Matthias, John (Edward) 1941- .... **CLC 9**
See also CA 33-36R; CANR 56; CP 7

Matthiessen, F(rancis) O(tto)
1902-1950 .... **TCLC 100**
See also CA 185; DLB 63
Matthiessen, Peter 1927- ... **CLC 5, 7, 11, 32, 64**
See also AAYA 6, 40; AMWS 5; ANW; BEST 90:4; BPFB 2; CA 9-12R; CANR 21, 50, 73, 100; CN 7; DA3; DAM NOV; DLB 6, 173; MTCW 1, 2; SATA 27
Maturin, Charles Robert
1780(?)-1824 .... **NCLC 6**
See also DLB 178; HGG; RGEL 2; SUFW
Matute (Ausejo), Ana Maria 1925- .. **CLC 11**
See also CA 89-92; MTCW 1; RGSF 2
Maugham, W. S.
See Maugham, W(illiam) Somerset
Maugham, W(illiam) Somerset
1874-1965 .. **CLC 1, 11, 15, 67, 93; SSC 8; WLC**
See also BPFB 2; BRW 6; CA 5-8R; 25-28R; CANR 40; CDBLB 1914-1945; CMW 4; DA; DA3; DAB; DAC; DAM DRAM, MST, NOV; DLB 10, 36, 77, 100, 162, 195; LAIT 3; MTCW 1, 2; RGEL 2; RGSF 2; SATA 54
Maugham, William Somerset
See Maugham, W(illiam) Somerset
Maupassant, (Henri Rene Albert) Guy de
1850-1893 .... **NCLC 1, 42, 83; SSC 1; WLC**
See also BYA 14; DA; DA3; DAB; DAC; DAM MST; DLB 123; EW 7; EXPS; GFL 1789 to the Present; LAIT 2; RGSF 2; RGWL 2; SSFS 4; SUFW; TWA
Maupin, Armistead (Jones, Jr.)
1944- .... **CLC 95**
See also CA 125; 130; CANR 58, 101; CPW; DA3; DAM POP; GLL 1; INT 130; MTCW 2
Maurhut, Richard
See Traven, B.
Mauriac, Claude 1914-1996 .... **CLC 9**
See also CA 89-92; 152; CWW 2; DLB 83; GFL 1789 to the Present
Mauriac, Francois (Charles)
1885-1970 .... **CLC 4, 9, 56; SSC 24**
See also CA 25-28; CAP 2; DLB 65; EW 10; GFL 1789 to the Present; MTCW 1, 2; RGWL 2
Mavor, Osborne Henry 1888-1951
See Bridie, James
See also CA 104
Maxwell, William (Keepers, Jr.)
1908-2000 .... **CLC 19**
See also AMWS 8; CA 93-96; 189; CANR 54, 95; CN 7; DLB 218; DLBY 1980; INT CA-93-96; SATA-Obit 128
May, Elaine 1932- .... **CLC 16**
See also CA 124; 142; CAD; CWD; DLB 44
Mayakovski, Vladimir (Vladimirovich)
1893-1930 .... **TCLC 4, 18**
See also Maiakovskii, Vladimir; Mayakovsky, Vladimir
See also CA 104; 158; MTCW 2; SFW 4
Mayakovsky, Vladimir
See Mayakovski, Vladimir (Vladimirovich)
See also EW 11; WP
Mayhew, Henry 1812-1887 .... **NCLC 31**
See also DLB 18, 55, 190
Mayle, Peter 1939(?)- .... **CLC 89**
See also CA 139; CANR 64, 109
Maynard, Joyce 1953- .... **CLC 23**
See also CA 111; 129; CANR 64
Mayne, William (James Carter)
1928- .... **CLC 12**
See also AAYA 20; CA 9-12R; CANR 37, 80, 100; CLR 25; FANT; JRDA; MAI-CYA 1, 2; MAICYAS 1; SAAS 11; SATA 6, 68, 122; YAW

Mayo, Jim
See L'Amour, Louis (Dearborn)
See also TCWW 2

Maysles, Albert 1926- .... **CLC 16**
See also CA 29-32R

Maysles, David 1932-1987 .... **CLC 16**
See also CA 191

Mazer, Norma Fox 1931- .... **CLC 26**
See also AAYA 5, 36; BYA 1, 8; CA 69-72; CANR 12, 32, 66; CLR 23; JRDA; MAICYA 1, 2; SAAS 1; SATA 24, 67, 105; WYA; YAW

Mazzini, Guiseppe 1805-1872 .... **NCLC 34**

McAlmon, Robert (Menzies)
1895-1956 .... **TCLC 97**
See also CA 107; 168; DLB 4, 45; DLBD 15; GLL 1

McAuley, James Phillip 1917-1976 .. **CLC 45**
See also CA 97-100; DLB 260; RGEL 2

McBain, Ed
See Hunter, Evan
See also MSW

McBrien, William (Augustine)
1930- .... **CLC 44**
See also CA 107; CANR 90

McCabe, Patrick 1955- .... **CLC 133**
See also CA 130; CANR 50, 90; CN 7; DLB 194

McCaffrey, Anne (Inez) 1926- .... **CLC 17**
See also AAYA 6, 34; AITN 2; BEST 89:2; BPFB 2; BYA 5; CA 25-28R; CANR 15, 35, 55, 96; CLR 49; CPW; DA3; DAM NOV, POP; DLB 8; JRDA; MAICYA 1, 2; MTCW 1, 2; SAAS 11; SATA 8, 70, 116; SFW 4; WYA; YAW

McCall, Nathan 1955(?)- .... **CLC 86**
See also BW 3; CA 146; CANR 88

McCann, Arthur
See Campbell, John W(ood, Jr.)

McCann, Edson
See Pohl, Frederik

McCarthy, Charles, Jr. 1933-
See McCarthy, Cormac
See also CANR 42, 69, 101; CN 7; CPW; CSW; DA3; DAM POP; MTCW 2

McCarthy, Cormac .... **CLC 4, 57, 59, 101**
See also McCarthy, Charles, Jr.
See also AAYA 41; AMWS 8; BPFB 2; CA 13-16R; CANR 10; DLB 6, 143, 256; TCWW 2

McCarthy, Mary (Therese)
1912-1989 .. **CLC 1, 3, 5, 14, 24, 39, 59; SSC 24**
See also AMW; BPFB 2; CA 5-8R; 129; CANR 16, 50, 64; DA3; DLB 2; DLBY 1981; FW; INT CANR-16; MAWW; MTCW 1, 2; RGAL 4

McCartney, (James) Paul 1942- . **CLC 12, 35**
See also CA 146

McCauley, Stephen (D.) 1955- .... **CLC 50**
See also CA 141

McClaren, Peter .... **CLC 70**

McClure, Michael (Thomas) 1932- ... **CLC 6, 10**
See also CA 21-24R; CAD; CANR 17, 46, 77; CD 5; CP 7; WP

McCorkle, Jill (Collins) 1958- .... **CLC 51**
See also CA 121; CSW; DLB 234; DLBY 1987

McCourt, Frank 1930- .... **CLC 109**
See also CA 157; CANR 97; NCFS 1

McCourt, James 1941- .... **CLC 5**
See also CA 57-60; CANR 98

McCourt, Malachy 1932- .... **CLC 119**
See also SATA 126

McCoy, Horace (Stanley)
1897-1955 .... **TCLC 28**
See also CA 108; 155; CMW 4; DLB 9

McCrae, John 1872-1918 .... **TCLC 12**
See also CA 109; DLB 92; PFS 5

McCreigh, James
See Pohl, Frederik

McCullers, (Lula) Carson (Smith)
1917-1967 .... **CLC 1, 4, 10, 12, 48, 100; SSC 9, 24; WLC**
See also AAYA 21; AMW; BPFB 2; CA 5-8R; 25-28R; CABS 1, 3; CANR 18; CDALB 1941-1968; DA; DA3; DAB; DAC; DAM MST, NOV; DFS 5; DLB 2, 7, 173, 228; EXPS; FW; GLL 1; LAIT 3, 4; MAWW; MTCW 1, 2; NFS 6, 13; RGAL 4; RGSF 2; SATA 27; SSFS 5; YAW

McCulloch, John Tyler
See Burroughs, Edgar Rice

McCullough, Colleen 1938(?)- .. **CLC 27, 107**
See also AAYA 36; BPFB 2; CA 81-84; CANR 17, 46, 67, 98; CPW; DA3; DAM NOV, POP; MTCW 1, 2; RHW

McDermott, Alice 1953- .... **CLC 90**
See also CA 109; CANR 40, 90

McElroy, Joseph 1930- .... **CLC 5, 47**
See also CA 17-20R; CN 7

McEwan, Ian (Russell) 1948- ...... **CLC 13, 66**
See also BEST 90:4; BRWS 4; CA 61-64; CANR 14, 41, 69, 87; CN 7; DAM NOV; DLB 14, 194; HGG; MTCW 1, 2; RGSF 2

McFadden, David 1940- .... **CLC 48**
See also CA 104; CP 7; DLB 60; INT 104

McFarland, Dennis 1950- .... **CLC 65**
See also CA 165

McGahern, John 1934- ... **CLC 5, 9, 48, 156; SSC 17**
See also CA 17-20R; CANR 29, 68; CN 7; DLB 14, 231; MTCW 1

McGinley, Patrick (Anthony) 1937- . **CLC 41**
See also CA 120; 127; CANR 56; INT 127

McGinley, Phyllis 1905-1978 .... **CLC 14**
See also CA 9-12R; 77-80; CANR 19; CWRI 5; DLB 11, 48; PFS 9, 13; SATA 2, 44; SATA-Obit 24

McGinniss, Joe 1942- .... **CLC 32**
See also AITN 2; BEST 89:2; CA 25-28R; CANR 26, 70; CPW; DLB 185; INT CANR-26

McGivern, Maureen Daly
See Daly, Maureen

McGrath, Patrick 1950- .... **CLC 55**
See also CA 136; CANR 65; CN 7; DLB 231; HGG

McGrath, Thomas (Matthew)
1916-1990 .... **CLC 28, 59**
See also AMWS 10; CA 9-12R; 132; CANR 6, 33, 95; DAM POET; MTCW 1; SATA 41; SATA-Obit 66

McGuane, Thomas (Francis III)
1939- .... **CLC 3, 7, 18, 45, 127**
See also AITN 2; BPFB 2; CA 49-52; CANR 5, 24, 49, 94; CN 7; DLB 2, 212; DLBY 1980; INT CANR-24; MTCW 1; TCWW 2

McGuckian, Medbh 1950- ... **CLC 48; PC 27**
See also BRWS 5; CA 143; CP 7; CWP; DAM POET; DLB 40

McHale, Tom 1942(?)-1982 .... **CLC 3, 5**
See also AITN 1; CA 77-80; 106

McIlvanney, William 1936- .... **CLC 42**
See also CA 25-28R; CANR 61; CMW 4; DLB 14, 207

McIlwraith, Maureen Mollie Hunter
See Hunter, Mollie
See also SATA 2

McInerney, Jay 1955- .... **CLC 34, 112**
See also AAYA 18; BPFB 2; CA 116; 123; CANR 45, 68; CN 7; CPW; DA3; DAM POP; INT 123; MTCW 2

McIntyre, Vonda N(eel) 1948- .... **CLC 18**
See also CA 81-84; CANR 17, 34, 69; MTCW 1; SFW 4; YAW

McKay, Claude .... **TCLC 7, 41; BLC 3; PC 2; WLC**
See also McKay, Festus Claudius
See also AFAW 1, 2; AMWS 10; DAB; DLB 4, 45, 51, 117; EXPP; GLL 2; LAIT 3; PAB; PFS 4; RGAL 4; WP

McKay, Festus Claudius 1889-1948
See McKay, Claude
See also BW 1, 3; CA 104; 124; CANR 73; DA; DAC; DAM MST, MULT, NOV, POET; MTCW 1, 2

McKuen, Rod 1933- .... **CLC 1, 3**
See also AITN 1; CA 41-44R; CANR 40

McLoughlin, R. B.
See Mencken, H(enry) L(ouis)

McLuhan, (Herbert) Marshall
1911-1980 .... **CLC 37, 83**
See also CA 9-12R; 102; CANR 12, 34, 61; DLB 88; INT CANR-12; MTCW 1, 2

McMillan, Terry (L.) 1951- .... **CLC 50, 61, 112; BLCS**
See also AAYA 21; BPFB 2; BW 2, 3; CA 140; CANR 60, 104; CPW; DA3; DAM MULT, NOV, POP; MTCW 2; RGAL 4; YAW

McMurtry, Larry (Jeff) 1936- .. **CLC 2, 3, 7, 11, 27, 44, 127**
See also AAYA 15; AITN 2; AMWS 5; BEST 89:2; BPFB 2; CA 5-8R; CANR 19, 43, 64, 103; CDALB 1968-1988; CN 7; CPW; CSW; DA3; DAM NOV, POP; DLB 2, 143, 256; DLBY 1980, 1987; MTCW 1, 2; RGAL 4; TCWW 2

McNally, T. M. 1961- .... **CLC 82**

McNally, Terrence 1939- .... **CLC 4, 7, 41, 91**
See also CA 45-48; CAD; CANR 2, 56; CD 5; DA3; DAM DRAM; DLB 7, 249; GLL 1; MTCW 2

McNamer, Deirdre 1950- .... **CLC 70**

McNeal, Tom .... **CLC 119**

McNeile, Herman Cyril 1888-1937
See Sapper
See also CA 184; CMW 4; DLB 77

McNickle, (William) D'Arcy
1904-1977 .... **CLC 89**
See also CA 9-12R; 85-88; CANR 5, 45; DAM MULT; DLB 175, 212; NNAL; RGAL 4; SATA-Obit 22

McPhee, John (Angus) 1931- .... **CLC 36**
See also AMWS 3; ANW; BEST 90:1; CA 65-68; CANR 20, 46, 64, 69; CPW; DLB 185; MTCW 1, 2

McPherson, James Alan 1943- .. **CLC 19, 77; BLCS**
See also BW 1, 3; CA 25-28R; CAAS 17; CANR 24, 74; CN 7; CSW; DLB 38, 244; MTCW 1, 2; RGAL 4; RGSF 2

McPherson, William (Alexander)
1933- .... **CLC 34**
See also CA 69-72; CANR 28; INT CANR-28

McTaggart, J. McT. Ellis
See McTaggart, John McTaggart Ellis

McTaggart, John McTaggart Ellis
1866-1925 .... **TCLC 105**
See also CA 120; DLB 262

Mead, George Herbert 1873-1958 . **TCLC 89**

Mead, Margaret 1901-1978 .... **CLC 37**
See also AITN 1; CA 1-4R; 81-84; CANR 4; DA3; FW; MTCW 1, 2; SATA-Obit 20

Meaker, Marijane (Agnes) 1927-
See Kerr, M. E.
See also CA 107; CANR 37, 63; INT 107; JRDA; MAICYA 1, 2; MAICYAS 1; MTCW 1; SATA 20, 61, 99; SATA-Essay 111; YAW

Medoff, Mark (Howard) 1940- .... **CLC 6, 23**
See also AITN 1; CA 53-56; CAD; CANR 5; CD 5; DAM DRAM; DFS 4; DLB 7; INT CANR-5

Medvedev, P. N.
See Bakhtin, Mikhail Mikhailovich

Meged, Aharon
See Megged, Aharon

Meged, Aron
See Megged, Aharon

Megged, Aharon 1920- .... **CLC 9**
See also CA 49-52; CAAS 13; CANR 1

Mehta, Ved (Parkash) 1934- .... **CLC 37**
See also CA 1-4R; CANR 2, 23, 69; MTCW 1

Melanter
See Blackmore, R(ichard) D(oddridge)

Meleager c. 140B.C.-c. 70B.C. ...... **CMLC 53**

Melies, Georges 1861-1938 .... **TCLC 81**

Melikow, Loris
See Hofmannsthal, Hugo von

Melmoth, Sebastian
See Wilde, Oscar (Fingal O'Flahertie Wills)

Meltzer, Milton 1915- .... **CLC 26**
See also AAYA 8; BYA 2, 6; CA 13-16R; CANR 38, 92, 107; CLR 13; DLB 61; JRDA; MAICYA 1, 2; SAAS 1; SATA 1, 50, 80, 128; SATA-Essay 124; WYA; YAW

Melville, Herman 1819-1891 ..... **NCLC 3, 12, 29, 45, 49, 91, 93; SSC 1, 17, 46; WLC**
See also AAYA 25; AMW; AMWR 1; CDALB 1640-1865; DA; DA3; DAB; DAC; DAM MST, NOV; DLB 3, 74, 250, 254; EXPN; EXPS; LAIT 1, 2; NFS 7, 9; RGAL 4; RGSF 2; SATA 59; SSFS 3

Members, Mark
See Powell, Anthony (Dymoke)

Membreno, Alejandro .... **CLC 59**

Menander c. 342B.C.-c. 293B.C. .... **CMLC 9, 51; DC 3**
See also AW 1; CDWLB 1; DAM DRAM; DLB 176; RGWL 2

Menchu, Rigoberta 1959- .. **CLC 160; HLCS 2**
See also CA 175; DNFS 1; WLIT 1

Mencken, H(enry) L(ouis) 1880-1956 .... **TCLC 13**
See also AMW; CA 105; 125; CDALB 1917-1929; DLB 11, 29, 63, 137, 222; MTCW 1, 2; RGAL 4

Mendelsohn, Jane 1965- .... **CLC 99**
See also CA 154; CANR 94

Mercer, David 1928-1980 .... **CLC 5**
See also CA 9-12R; 102; CANR 23; CBD; DAM DRAM; DLB 13; MTCW 1; RGEL 2

Merchant, Paul
See Ellison, Harlan (Jay)

Meredith, George 1828-1909 ... **TCLC 17, 43**
See also CA 117; 153; CANR 80; CDBLB 1832-1890; DAM POET; DLB 18, 35, 57, 159; RGEL 2

Meredith, William (Morris) 1919- .... **CLC 4, 13, 22, 55; PC 28**
See also CA 9-12R; CAAS 14; CANR 6, 40; CP 7; DAM POET; DLB 5

Merezhkovsky, Dmitry Sergeyevich 1865-1941 .... **TCLC 29**
See also CA 169

Merimee, Prosper 1803-1870 ... **NCLC 6, 65; SSC 7**
See also DLB 119, 192; EW 6; EXPS; GFL 1789 to the Present; RGSF 2; RGWL 2; SSFS 8; SUFW

Merkin, Daphne 1954- .... **CLC 44**
See also CA 123

Merlin, Arthur
See Blish, James (Benjamin)

Merrill, James (Ingram) 1926-1995 .. **CLC 2, 3, 6, 8, 13, 18, 34, 91; PC 28**
See also AMWS 3; CA 13-16R; 147; CANR 10, 49, 63, 108; DA3; DAM POET; DLB 5, 165; DLBY 1985; INT CANR-10; MTCW 1, 2; PAB; RGAL 4

Merriman, Alex
See Silverberg, Robert

Merriman, Brian 1747-1805 .... **NCLC 70**

Merritt, E. B.
See Waddington, Miriam

Merton, Thomas 1915-1968 ..... **CLC 1, 3, 11, 34, 83; PC 10**
See also AMWS 8; CA 5-8R; 25-28R; CANR 22, 53; DA3; DLB 48; DLBY 1981; MTCW 1, 2

Merwin, W(illiam) S(tanley) 1927- ... **CLC 1, 2, 3, 5, 8, 13, 18, 45, 88**
See also AMWS 3; CA 13-16R; CANR 15, 51; CP 7; DA3; DAM POET; DLB 5, 169; INT CANR-15; MTCW 1, 2; PAB; PFS 5, 15; RGAL 4

Metcalf, John 1938- .... **CLC 37; SSC 43**
See also CA 113; CN 7; DLB 60; RGSF 2

Metcalf, Suzanne
See Baum, L(yman) Frank

Mew, Charlotte (Mary) 1870-1928 .. **TCLC 8**
See also CA 105; 189; DLB 19, 135; RGEL 2

Mewshaw, Michael 1943- .... **CLC 9**
See also CA 53-56; CANR 7, 47; DLBY 1980

Meyer, Conrad Ferdinand 1825-1905 .... **NCLC 81**
See also DLB 129; EW; RGWL 2

Meyer, Gustav 1868-1932
See Meyrink, Gustav
See also CA 117; 190

Meyer, June
See Jordan, June
See also GLL 2

Meyer, Lynn
See Slavitt, David R(ytman)

Meyers, Jeffrey 1939- .... **CLC 39**
See also CA 73-76; CAAE 186; CANR 54, 102; DLB 111

Meynell, Alice (Christina Gertrude Thompson) 1847-1922 .... **TCLC 6**
See also CA 104; 177; DLB 19, 98; RGEL 2

Meyrink, Gustav .... **TCLC 21**
See also Meyer, Gustav
See also DLB 81

Michaels, Leonard 1933- .... **CLC 6, 25; SSC 16**
See also CA 61-64; CANR 21, 62; CN 7; DLB 130; MTCW 1

Michaux, Henri 1899-1984 .... **CLC 8, 19**
See also CA 85-88; 114; DLB 258; GFL 1789 to the Present; RGWL 2

Micheaux, Oscar (Devereaux) 1884-1951 .... **TCLC 76**
See also BW 3; CA 174; DLB 50; TCWW 2

Michelangelo 1475-1564 .... **LC 12**
See also AAYA 43

Michelet, Jules 1798-1874 .... **NCLC 31**
See also EW 5; GFL 1789 to the Present

Michels, Robert 1876-1936 .... **TCLC 88**

Michener, James A(lbert) 1907(?)-1997 .. **CLC 1, 5, 11, 29, 60, 109**
See also AAYA 27; AITN 1; BEST 90:1; BPFB 2; CA 5-8R; 161; CANR 21, 45, 68; CN 7; CPW; DA3; DAM NOV, POP; DLB 6; MTCW 1, 2; RHW

Mickiewicz, Adam 1798-1855 . **NCLC 3, 101; PC 38**
See also EW 5; RGWL 2

Middleton, Christopher 1926- .... **CLC 13**
See also CA 13-16R; CANR 29, 54; CP 7; DLB 40

Middleton, Richard (Barham) 1882-1911 .... **TCLC 56**
See also CA 187; DLB 156; HGG

Middleton, Stanley 1919- .... **CLC 7, 38**
See also CA 25-28R; CAAS 23; CANR 21, 46, 81; CN 7; DLB 14

Middleton, Thomas 1580-1627 .... **LC 33; DC 5**
See also BRW 2; DAM DRAM, MST; DLB 58; RGEL 2

Migueis, Jose Rodrigues 1901- .... **CLC 10**

Mikszath, Kalman 1847-1910 .... **TCLC 31**
See also CA 170

Miles, Jack .... **CLC 100**
See also CA 200

Miles, John Russiano
See Miles, Jack

Miles, Josephine (Louise) 1911-1985 .... **CLC 1, 2, 14, 34, 39**
See also CA 1-4R; 116; CANR 2, 55; DAM POET; DLB 48

Militant
See Sandburg, Carl (August)

Mill, Harriet (Hardy) Taylor 1807-1858 .... **NCLC 102**
See also FW

Mill, John Stuart 1806-1873 .... **NCLC 11, 58**
See also CDBLB 1832-1890; DLB 55, 190, 262; FW 1; RGEL 2

Millar, Kenneth 1915-1983 .... **CLC 14**
See also Macdonald, Ross
See also CA 9-12R; 110; CANR 16, 63, 107; CMW 4; CPW; DA3; DAM POP; DLB 2, 226; DLBD 6; DLBY 1983; MTCW 1, 2

Millay, E. Vincent
See Millay, Edna St. Vincent

Millay, Edna St. Vincent 1892-1950 ... **TCLC 4, 49; PC 6; WLCS**
See also Boyd, Nancy
See also AMW; CA 104; 130; CDALB 1917-1929; DA; DA3; DAB; DAC; DAM MST, POET; DLB 45, 249; EXPP; MAWW; MTCW 1, 2; PAB; PFS 3; RGAL 4; WP

Miller, Arthur 1915- .... **CLC 1, 2, 6, 10, 15, 26, 47, 78; DC 1; WLC**
See also AAYA 15; AITN 1; AMW; CA 1-4R; CABS 3; CAD; CANR 2, 30, 54, 76; CD 5; CDALB 1941-1968; DA; DA3; DAB; DAC; DAM DRAM, MST; DFS 1, 3; DLB 7; LAIT 1, 4; MTCW 1, 2; RGAL 4; TUS; WYAS 1

Miller, Henry (Valentine) 1891-1980 .... **CLC 1, 2, 4, 9, 14, 43, 84; WLC**
See also AMW; BPFB 2; CA 9-12R; 97-100; CANR 33, 64; CDALB 1929-1941; DA; DA3; DAB; DAC; DAM MST, NOV; DLB 4, 9; DLBY 1980; MTCW 1, 2; RGAL 4

Miller, Jason 1939(?)-2001 .... **CLC 2**
See also AITN 1; CA 73-76; 197; CAD; DFS 12; DLB 7

Miller, Sue 1943- .... **CLC 44**
See also BEST 90:3; CA 139; CANR 59, 91; DA3; DAM POP; DLB 143

Miller, Walter M(ichael, Jr.) 1923-1996 .... **CLC 4, 30**
See also BPFB 2; CA 85-88; CANR 108; DLB 8; SCFW; SFW 4

Millett, Kate 1934- .... **CLC 67**
See also AITN 1; CA 73-76; CANR 32, 53, 76; DA3; DLB 246; FW; GLL 1; MTCW 1, 2

Millhauser, Steven (Lewis) 1943- .... **CLC 21, 54, 109**
See also CA 110; 111; CANR 63; CN 7; DA3; DLB 2; FANT; INT CA-111; MTCW 2

Millin, Sarah Gertrude 1889-1968 ... **CLC 49**
See also CA 102; 93-96; DLB 225

Milne, A(lan) A(lexander) 1882-1956 .... **TCLC 6, 88**
See also BRWS 5; CA 104; 133; CLR 1, 26; CMW 4; CWRI 5; DA; DA3; DAB; DAC; DAM MST; DLB 10, 77, 100, 160; FANT; MAICYA 1, 2; MTCW 1, 2; RGEL 2; SATA 100; WCH; YABC 1

Milner, Ron(ald) 1938- .... **CLC 56; BLC 3**
See also AITN 1; BW 1; CA 73-76; CAD; CANR 24, 81; CD 5; DAM MULT; DLB 38; MTCW 1

Milnes, Richard Monckton 1809-1885 .... **NCLC 61**
See also DLB 32, 184

Milosz, Czeslaw 1911- ...... **CLC 5, 11, 22, 31, 56, 82; PC 8; WLCS**
See also CANR 23, 51, 91; CD-WLB 4; CWW 2; DA3; DAM MST, POET; DLB 215; EW 13; MTCW 1, 2; RGWL 2

Milton, John 1608-1674 ..... **LC 9, 43; PC 19, 29; WLC**
See also BRW 2; BRWR 2; CDBLB 1660-1789; DA; DA3; DAB; DAC; DAM MST, POET; DLB 131, 151; EFS 1; EXPP; LAIT 1; PAB; PFS 3; RGEL 2; TEA; WLIT 3; WP

Min, Anchee 1957- .... **CLC 86**
See also CA 146; CANR 94

Minehaha, Cornelius
See Wedekind, (Benjamin) Frank(lin)

Miner, Valerie 1947- .... **CLC 40**
See also CA 97-100; CANR 59; FW; GLL 2

Minimo, Duca
See D'Annunzio, Gabriele

Minot, Susan 1956- .... **CLC 44, 159**
See also AMWS 6; CA 134; CN 7

Minus, Ed 1938- .... **CLC 39**
See also CA 185

Miranda, Javier
See Bioy Casares, Adolfo
See also CWW 2

Mirbeau, Octave 1848-1917 .... **TCLC 55**
See also DLB 123, 192; GFL 1789 to the Present

Miro (Ferrer), Gabriel (Francisco Victor) 1879-1930 .... **TCLC 5**
See also CA 104; 185

Misharin, Alexandr .... **CLC 59**

Mishima, Yukio ... **CLC 2, 4, 6, 9, 27; DC 1; SSC 4**
See also Hiraoka, Kimitake
See also BPFB 2; DLB 182; GLL 1; MJW; MTCW 2; RGSF 2; RGWL 2; SSFS 5, 12

Mistral, Frederic 1830-1914 .... **TCLC 51**
See also CA 122; GFL 1789 to the Present

Mistral, Gabriela
See Godoy Alcayaga, Lucila
See also DNFS 1; LAW; RGWL 2; WP

Mistry, Rohinton 1952- .... **CLC 71**
See also CA 141; CANR 86; CCA 1; CN 7; DAC; SSFS 6

Mitchell, Clyde
See Ellison, Harlan (Jay); Silverberg, Robert

Mitchell, James Leslie 1901-1935
See Gibbon, Lewis Grassic
See also CA 104; 188; DLB 15

Mitchell, Joni 1943- .... **CLC 12**
See also CA 112; CCA 1

Mitchell, Joseph (Quincy) 1908-1996 .... **CLC 98**
See also CA 77-80; 152; CANR 69; CN 7; CSW; DLB 185; DLBY 1996

Mitchell, Margaret (Munnerlyn) 1900-1949 .... **TCLC 11**
See also AAYA 23; BPFB 2; BYA 1; CA 109; 125; CANR 55, 94; CDALBS; DA3; DAM NOV, POP; DLB 9; LAIT 2; MTCW 1, 2; NFS 9; RGAL 4; RHW; WYAS 1; YAW

Mitchell, Peggy
See Mitchell, Margaret (Munnerlyn)

Mitchell, S(ilas) Weir 1829-1914 .... **TCLC 36**
See also CA 165; DLB 202; RGAL 4

Mitchell, W(illiam) O(rmond) 1914-1998 .... **CLC 25**
See also CA 77-80; 165; CANR 15, 43; CN 7; DAC; DAM MST; DLB 88

Mitchell, William 1879-1936 .... **TCLC 81**

Mitford, Mary Russell 1787-1855 ... **NCLC 4**
See also DLB 110, 116; RGEL 2

Mitford, Nancy 1904-1973 .... **CLC 44**
See also CA 9-12R; DLB 191; RGEL 2

Miyamoto, (Chujo) Yuriko 1899-1951 .... **TCLC 37**
See also Miyamoto Yuriko
See also CA 170, 174

Miyamoto Yuriko
See Miyamoto, (Chujo) Yuriko
See also DLB 180

Miyazawa, Kenji 1896-1933 .... **TCLC 76**
See also CA 157

Mizoguchi, Kenji 1898-1956 .... **TCLC 72**
See also CA 167

Mo, Timothy (Peter) 1950(?)- ... **CLC 46, 134**
See also CA 117; CN 7; DLB 194; MTCW 1; WLIT 4

Modarressi, Taghi (M.) 1931-1997 ... **CLC 44**
See also CA 121; 134; INT 134

Modiano, Patrick (Jean) 1945- .... **CLC 18**
See also CA 85-88; CANR 17, 40; CWW 2; DLB 83

Mofolo, Thomas (Mokopu) 1875(?)-1948 .... **TCLC 22; BLC 3**
See also AFW; CA 121; 153; CANR 83; DAM MULT; DLB 225; MTCW 2; WLIT 2

Mohr, Nicholasa 1938- .... **CLC 12; HLC 2**
See also AAYA 8; CA 49-52; CANR 1, 32, 64; CLR 22; DAM MULT; DLB 145; HW 1, 2; JRDA; LAIT 5; MAICYA 2; MAIC-YAS 1; RGAL 4; SAAS 8; SATA 8, 97; SATA-Essay 113; WYA; YAW

Mojtabai, A(nn) G(race) 1938- ...... **CLC 5, 9, 15, 29**
See also CA 85-88; CANR 88

Moliere 1622-1673 ..... **LC 10, 28, 64; DC 13; WLC**
See also DA; DA3; DAB; DAC; DAM DRAM, MST; DFS 13; EW 3; GFL Beginnings to 1789; RGWL 2

Molin, Charles
See Mayne, William (James Carter)

Molnar, Ferenc 1878-1952 .... **TCLC 20**
See also CA 109; 153; CANR 83; CDWLB 4; DAM DRAM; DLB 215; RGWL 2

Momaday, N(avarre) Scott 1934- ...... **CLC 2, 19, 85, 95, 160; PC 25; WLCS**
See also AAYA 11; AMWS 4; ANW; BPFB 2; CA 25-28R; CANR 14, 34, 68; CDALBS; CN 7; CPW; DA; DA3; DAB; DAC; DAM MST, MULT, NOV, POP; DLB 143, 175, 256; EXPP; INT CANR-14; LAIT 4; MTCW 1, 2; NFS 10; NNAL; PFS 2, 11; RGAL 4; SATA 48; SATA-Brief 30; WP; YAW

Monette, Paul 1945-1995 .... **CLC 82**
See also AMWS 10; CA 139; 147; CN 7; GLL 1

Monroe, Harriet 1860-1936 .... **TCLC 12**
See also CA 109; DLB 54, 91

Monroe, Lyle
See Heinlein, Robert A(nson)

Montagu, Elizabeth 1720-1800 .... **NCLC 7**
See also FW

Montagu, Mary (Pierrepont) Wortley 1689-1762 .... **LC 9, 57; PC 16**
See also DLB 95, 101; RGEL 2

Montagu, W. H.
See Coleridge, Samuel Taylor

Montague, John (Patrick) 1929- ..... **CLC 13, 46**
See also CA 9-12R; CANR 9, 69; CP 7; DLB 40; MTCW 1; PFS 12; RGEL 2

Montaigne, Michel (Eyquem) de 1533-1592 .... **LC 8; WLC**
See also DA; DAB; DAC; DAM MST; EW 2; GFL Beginnings to 1789; RGWL 2

Montale, Eugenio 1896-1981 ... **CLC 7, 9, 18; PC 13**
See also CA 17-20R; 104; CANR 30; DLB 114; EW 11; MTCW 1; RGWL 2

Montesquieu, Charles-Louis de Secondat 1689-1755 .... **LC 7, 69**
See also EW 3; GFL Beginnings to 1789

Montessori, Maria 1870-1952 ...... **TCLC 103**
See also CA 115; 147

Montgomery, (Robert) Bruce 1921(?)-1978
See Crispin, Edmund
See also CA 179; 104; CMW 4

Montgomery, L(ucy) M(aud) 1874-1942 .... **TCLC 51**
See also AAYA 12; BYA 1; CA 108; 137; CLR 8; DA3; DAC; DAM MST; DLB 92; DLBD 14; JRDA; MAICYA 1, 2; MTCW 2; RGEL 2; SATA 100; WCH; WYA; YABC 1

Montgomery, Marion H., Jr. 1925- .... **CLC 7**
See also AITN 1; CA 1-4R; CANR 3, 48; CSW; DLB 6

Montgomery, Max
See Davenport, Guy (Mattison, Jr.)

Montherlant, Henry (Milon) de 1896-1972 .... **CLC 8, 19**
See also CA 85-88; 37-40R; DAM DRAM; DLB 72; EW 11; GFL 1789 to the Present; MTCW 1

Monty Python
See Chapman, Graham; Cleese, John (Marwood); Gilliam, Terry (Vance); Idle, Eric; Jones, Terence Graham Parry; Palin, Michael (Edward)
See also AAYA 7

Moodie, Susanna (Strickland) 1803-1885 .... **NCLC 14, 113**
See also DLB 99

Moody, Hiram F. III 1961-
See Moody, Rick
See also CA 138; CANR 64

Moody, Minerva
See Alcott, Louisa May

Moody, Rick .... **CLC 147**
See also Moody, Hiram F. III

Moody, William Vaughan 1869-1910 .... **TCLC 105**
See also CA 110; 178; DLB 7, 54; RGAL 4

Mooney, Edward 1951-
See Mooney, Ted
See also CA 130

Mooney, Ted .... **CLC 25**
See also Mooney, Edward

Moorcock, Michael (John) 1939- ...... **CLC 5, 27, 58**
See also Bradbury, Edward P.
See also AAYA 26; CA 45-48; CAAS 5; CANR 2, 17, 38, 64; CN 7; DLB 14, 231, 261; FANT; MTCW 1, 2; SATA 93; SFW 4; SUFW

Moore, Brian 1921-1999 ... **CLC 1, 3, 5, 7, 8, 19, 32, 90**
See also Bryan, Michael
See also CA 1-4R; 174; CANR 1, 25, 42, 63; CCA 1; CN 7; DAB; DAC; DAM MST; DLB 251; FANT; MTCW 1, 2; RGEL 2

Moore, Edward
See Muir, Edwin
See also RGEL 2

Moore, G. E. 1873-1958 .... **TCLC 89**
See also DLB 262

Moore, George Augustus
1852-1933 .... **TCLC 7; SSC 19**
See also BRW 6; CA 104; 177; DLB 10, 18, 57, 135; RGEL 2; RGSF 2

Moore, Lorrie .... **CLC 39, 45, 68**
See also Moore, Marie Lorena
See also AMWS 10; DLB 234

Moore, Marianne (Craig)
1887-1972 .... **CLC 1, 2, 4, 8, 10, 13, 19, 47; PC 4; WLCS**
See also AMW; CA 1-4R; 33-36R; CANR 3, 61; CDALB 1929-1941; DA; DA3; DAB; DAC; DAM MST, POET; DLB 45; DLBD 7; EXPP; MAWW; MTCW 1, 2; PAB; PFS 14; RGAL 4; SATA 20; WP

Moore, Marie Lorena 1957-
See Moore, Lorrie
See also CA 116; CANR 39, 83; CN 7; DLB 234

Moore, Thomas 1779-1852 .... **NCLC 6, 110**
See also DLB 96, 144; RGEL 2

Moorhouse, Frank 1938- .... **SSC 40**
See also CA 118; CANR 92; CN 7; RGSF 2

Mora, Pat(ricia) 1942-
See also CA 129; CANR 57, 81; CLR 58; DAM MULT; DLB 209; HLC 2; HW 1, 2; MAICYA 2; SATA 92

Moraga, Cherrie 1952- .... **CLC 126**
See also CA 131; CANR 66; DAM MULT; DLB 82, 249; FW; GLL 1; HW 1, 2

Morand, Paul 1888-1976 ...... **CLC 41; SSC 22**
See also CA 184; 69-72; DLB 65

Morante, Elsa 1918-1985 .... **CLC 8, 47**
See also CA 85-88; 117; CANR 35; DLB 177; MTCW 1, 2; RGWL 2

Moravia, Alberto .... **CLC 2, 7, 11, 27, 46; SSC 26**
See also Pincherle, Alberto
See also DLB 177; EW 12; MTCW 2; RGSF 2; RGWL 2

More, Hannah 1745-1833 .... **NCLC 27**
See also DLB 107, 109, 116, 158; RGEL 2

More, Henry 1614-1687 .... **LC 9**
See also DLB 126, 252

More, Sir Thomas 1478(?)-1535 .... **LC 10, 32**
See also BRWS 7; DLB 136; RGEL 2; TEA

Moreas, Jean .... **TCLC 18**
See also Papadiamantopoulos, Johannes
See also GFL 1789 to the Present

Moreton, Andrew Esq.
See Defoe, Daniel

Morgan, Berry 1919- .... **CLC 6**
See also CA 49-52; DLB 6

Morgan, Claire
See Highsmith, (Mary) Patricia
See also GLL 1

Morgan, Edwin (George) 1920- .... **CLC 31**
See also CA 5-8R; CANR 3, 43, 90; CP 7; DLB 27

Morgan, (George) Frederick 1922- .. **CLC 23**
See also CA 17-20R; CANR 21; CP 7

Morgan, Harriet
See Mencken, H(enry) L(ouis)

Morgan, Jane
See Cooper, James Fenimore

Morgan, Janet 1945- .... **CLC 39**
See also CA 65-68

Morgan, Lady 1776(?)-1859 .... **NCLC 29**
See also DLB 116, 158; RGEL 2

Morgan, Robin (Evonne) 1941- .... **CLC 2**
See also CA 69-72; CANR 29, 68; FW; GLL 2; MTCW 1; SATA 80

Morgan, Scott
See Kuttner, Henry

Morgan, Seth 1949(?)-1990 .... **CLC 65**
See also CA 185; 132

Morgenstern, Christian (Otto Josef Wolfgang) 1871-1914 .... **TCLC 8**
See also CA 105; 191

Morgenstern, S.
See Goldman, William (W.)

Mori, Rintaro
See Mori Ogai
See also CA 110

Moricz, Zsigmond 1879-1942 .... **TCLC 33**
See also CA 165; DLB 215

Morike, Eduard (Friedrich)
1804-1875 .... **NCLC 10**
See also DLB 133; RGWL 2

Mori Ogai
See Mori Ogai
See also DLB 180

Mori Ogai 1862-1922 .... **TCLC 14**
See also Mori Ogai; Ogai
See also CA 164; TWA

Moritz, Karl Philipp 1756-1793 .... **LC 2**
See also DLB 94

Morland, Peter Henry
See Faust, Frederick (Schiller)

Morley, Christopher (Darlington)
1890-1957 .... **TCLC 87**
See also CA 112; DLB 9; RGAL 4

Morren, Theophil
See Hofmannsthal, Hugo von

Morris, Bill 1952- .... **CLC 76**

Morris, Julian
See West, Morris L(anglo)

Morris, Steveland Judkins 1950(?)-
See Wonder, Stevie
See also CA 111

Morris, William 1834-1896 .... **NCLC 4**
See also BRW 5; CDBLB 1832-1890; DLB 18, 35, 57, 156, 178, 184; FANT; RGEL 2; SFW 4; SUFW

Morris, Wright 1910-1998 .. **CLC 1, 3, 7, 18, 37**
See also AMW; CA 9-12R; 167; CANR 21, 81; CN 7; DLB 2, 206, 218; DLBY 1981; MTCW 1, 2; RGAL 4; TCLC 107; TCWW 2

Morrison, Arthur 1863-1945 .... **TCLC 72; SSC 40**
See also CA 120; 157; CMW 4; DLB 70, 135, 197; RGEL 2

Morrison, Chloe Anthony Wofford
See Morrison, Toni

Morrison, James Douglas 1943-1971
See Morrison, Jim
See also CA 73-76; CANR 40

Morrison, Jim .... **CLC 17**
See also Morrison, James Douglas

Morrison, Toni 1931- . **CLC 4, 10, 22, 55, 81, 87; BLC 3**
See also AAYA 1, 22; AFAW 1, 2; AMWS 3; BPFB 2; BW 2, 3; CA 29-32R; CANR 27, 42, 67; CDALB 1968-1988; CN 7; CPW; DA; DA3; DAB; DAC; DAM MST, MULT, NOV, POP; DLB 6, 33, 143; DLBY 1981; EXPN; FW; LAIT 2, 4; MAWW; MTCW 1, 2; NFS 1, 6, 8, 14; RGAL 4; RHW; SATA 57; SSFS 5; YAW

Morrison, Van 1945- .... **CLC 21**
See also CA 116; 168

Morrissy, Mary 1958- .... **CLC 99**

Mortimer, John (Clifford) 1923- ..... **CLC 28, 43**
See also CA 13-16R; CANR 21, 69, 109; CD 5; CDBLB 1960 to Present; CMW 4; CN 7; CPW; DA3; DAM DRAM, POP; DLB 13, 245; INT CANR-21; MSW; MTCW 1, 2; RGEL 2

Mortimer, Penelope (Ruth)
1918-1999 .... **CLC 5**
See also CA 57-60; 187; CANR 45, 88; CN 7

Mortimer, Sir John
See Mortimer, John (Clifford)

Morton, Anthony
See Creasey, John

Morton, Thomas 1579(?)-1647(?) .... **LC 72**
See also DLB 24; RGEL 2

Mosca, Gaetano 1858-1941 .... **TCLC 75**

Mosher, Howard Frank 1943- .... **CLC 62**
See also CA 139; CANR 65

Mosley, Nicholas 1923- .... **CLC 43, 70**
See also CA 69-72; CANR 41, 60, 108; CN 7; DLB 14, 207

Mosley, Walter 1952- .... **CLC 97; BLCS**
See also AAYA 17; BPFB 2; BW 2; CA 142; CANR 57, 92; CMW 4; CPW; DA3; DAM MULT, POP; MSW; MTCW 2

Moss, Howard 1922-1987 . **CLC 7, 14, 45, 50**
See also CA 1-4R; 123; CANR 1, 44; DAM POET; DLB 5

Mossgiel, Rab
See Burns, Robert

Motion, Andrew (Peter) 1952- .... **CLC 47**
See also BRWS 7; CA 146; CANR 90; CP 7; DLB 40

Motley, Willard (Francis)
1912-1965 .... **CLC 18**
See also BW 1; CA 117; 106; CANR 88; DLB 76, 143

Motoori, Norinaga 1730-1801 .... **NCLC 45**

Mott, Michael (Charles Alston)
1930- .... **CLC 15, 34**
See also CA 5-8R; CAAS 7; CANR 7, 29

Mountain Wolf Woman 1884-1960 .. **CLC 92**
See also CA 144; CANR 90; NNAL

Moure, Erin 1955- .... **CLC 88**
See also CA 113; CP 7; CWP; DLB 60

Mowat, Farley (McGill) 1921- .... **CLC 26**
See also AAYA 1; BYA 2; CA 1-4R; CANR 4, 24, 42, 68, 108; CLR 20; CPW; DAC; DAM MST; DLB 68; INT CANR-24; JRDA; MAICYA 1, 2; MTCW 1, 2; SATA 3, 55; YAW

Mowatt, Anna Cora 1819-1870 ..... **NCLC 74**
See also RGAL 4

Moyers, Bill 1934- .... **CLC 74**
See also AITN 2; CA 61-64; CANR 31, 52

Mphahlele, Es'kia
See Mphahlele, Ezekiel
See also AFW; CDWLB 3; DLB 125, 225; RGSF 2; SSFS 11

Mphahlele, Ezekiel 1919- .... **CLC 25, 133; BLC 3**
See also Mphahlele, Es'kia
See also BW 2, 3; CA 81-84; CANR 26, 76; CN 7; DA3; DAM MULT; MTCW 2; SATA 119

Mqhayi, S(amuel) E(dward) K(rune Loliwe)
1875-1945 .... **TCLC 25; BLC 3**
See also CA 153; CANR 87; DAM MULT

Mrozek, Slawomir 1930- .... **CLC 3, 13**
See also CA 13-16R; CAAS 10; CANR 29; CDWLB 4; CWW 2; DLB 232; MTCW 1

Mrs. Belloc-Lowndes
See Lowndes, Marie Adelaide (Belloc)
M'Taggart, John M'Taggart Ellis
See McTaggart, John McTaggart Ellis
Mtwa, Percy (?)- .... **CLC 47**
Mueller, Lisel 1924- .... **CLC 13, 51; PC 33**
See also CA 93-96; CP 7; DLB 105; PFS 9, 13
Muggeridge, Malcolm (Thomas)
1903-1990 .... **TCLC 120**
See also AITN 1; CA 101; CANR 33, 63; MTCW 1, 2
Muir, Edwin 1887-1959 .... **TCLC 2, 87**
See also Moore, Edward
See also BRWS 6; CA 104; 193; DLB 20, 100, 191; RGEL 2
Muir, John 1838-1914 .... **TCLC 28**
See also AMWS 9; ANW; CA 165; DLB 186
Mujica Lainez, Manuel 1910-1984 ... **CLC 31**
See also Lainez, Manuel Mujica
See also CA 81-84; 112; CANR 32; HW 1
Mukherjee, Bharati 1940- .... **CLC 53, 115; AAL; SSC 38**
See also BEST 89:2; CA 107; CANR 45, 72; CN 7; DAM NOV; DLB 60, 218; DNFS 1, 2; FW; MTCW 1, 2; RGAL 4; RGSF 2; SSFS 7
Muldoon, Paul 1951- .... **CLC 32, 72**
See also BRWS 4; CA 113; 129; CANR 52, 91; CP 7; DAM POET; DLB 40; INT 129; PFS 7
Mulisch, Harry 1927- .... **CLC 42**
See also CA 9-12R; CANR 6, 26, 56
Mull, Martin 1943- .... **CLC 17**
See also CA 105
Muller, Wilhelm .... **NCLC 73**
Mulock, Dinah Maria
See Craik, Dinah Maria (Mulock)
See also RGEL 2
Munford, Robert 1737(?)-1783 .... **LC 5**
See also DLB 31
Mungo, Raymond 1946- .... **CLC 72**
See also CA 49-52; CANR 2
Munro, Alice 1931- .... **CLC 6, 10, 19, 50, 95; SSC 3; WLCS**
See also AITN 1; BPFB 2; CA 33-36R; CANR 33, 53, 75; CCA 1; CN 7; DA3; DAC; DAM MST, NOV; DLB 53; MTCW 1, 2; RGEL 2; RGSF 2; SATA 29; SSFS 5, 13
Munro, H(ector) H(ugh) 1870-1916
See Saki
See also CA 104; 130; CANR 104; CDBLB 1890-1914; DA; DAB; DAC; DAM MST, NOV; DLB 34, 162; EXPS; MTCW 1, 2; RGEL 2; SSFS 15; WLC
Murakami, Haruki 1949- .... **CLC 150**
See also Murakami Haruki
See also CA 165; CANR 102; MJW; SFW 4
Murakami Haruki
See Murakami, Haruki
See also DLB 182
Murasaki, Lady
See Murasaki Shikibu
Murasaki Shikibu 978(?)-1026(?) ... **CMLC 1**
See also EFS 2; RGWL 2
Murdoch, (Jean) Iris 1919-1999 ... **CLC 1, 2, 3, 4, 6, 8, 11, 15, 22, 31, 51**
See also BRWS 1; CA 13-16R; 179; CANR 8, 43, 68, 103; CDBLB 1960 to Present; CN 7; DA3; DAB; DAC; DAM MST, NOV; DLB 14, 194, 233; INT CANR-8; MTCW 1, 2; RGEL 2; TEA; WLIT 4
Murfree, Mary Noailles 1850-1922 ... **SSC 22**
See also CA 122; 176; DLB 12, 74; RGAL 4
Murnau, Friedrich Wilhelm
See Plumpe, Friedrich Wilhelm

Murphy, Richard 1927- .... **CLC 41**
See also BRWS 5; CA 29-32R; CP 7; DLB 40
Murphy, Sylvia 1937- .... **CLC 34**
See also CA 121
Murphy, Thomas (Bernard) 1935- ... **CLC 51**
See also CA 101
Murray, Albert L. 1916- .... **CLC 73**
See also BW 2; CA 49-52; CANR 26, 52, 78; CSW; DLB 38
Murray, James Augustus Henry
1837-1915 .... **TCLC 117**
Murray, Judith Sargent
1751-1820 .... **NCLC 63**
See also DLB 37, 200
Murray, Les(lie Allan) 1938- .... **CLC 40**
See also BRWS 7; CA 21-24R; CANR 11, 27, 56, 103; CP 7; DAM POET; DLBY 01; RGEL 2
Murry, J. Middleton
See Murry, John Middleton
Murry, John Middleton
1889-1957 .... **TCLC 16**
See also CA 118; DLB 149
Musgrave, Susan 1951- .... **CLC 13, 54**
See also CA 69-72; CANR 45, 84; CCA 1; CP 7; CWP
Musil, Robert (Edler von)
1880-1942 .... **TCLC 12, 68; SSC 18**
See also CA 109; CANR 55, 84; CDWLB 2; DLB 81, 124; EW 9; MTCW 2; RGSF 2; RGWL 2
Muske, Carol .... **CLC 90**
See also Muske-Dukes, Carol (Anne)
Muske-Dukes, Carol (Anne) 1945-
See Muske, Carol
See also CA 65-68; CANR 32, 70; CWP
Musset, (Louis Charles) Alfred de
1810-1857 .... **NCLC 7**
See also DLB 192, 217; EW 6; GFL 1789 to the Present; RGWL 2; TWA
Mussolini, Benito (Amilcare Andrea)
1883-1945 .... **TCLC 96**
See also CA 116
My Brother's Brother
See Chekhov, Anton (Pavlovich)
Myers, L(eopold) H(amilton)
1881-1944 .... **TCLC 59**
See also CA 157; DLB 15; RGEL 2
Myers, Walter Dean 1937- .. **CLC 35; BLC 3**
See also AAYA 4, 23; BW 2; BYA 6, 8, 11; CA 33-36R; CANR 20, 42, 67, 108; CLR 4, 16, 35; DAM MULT, NOV; DLB 33; INT CANR-20; JRDA; LAIT 5; MAICYA 1, 2; MAICYAS 1; MTCW 2; SAAS 2; SATA 41, 71, 109; SATA-Brief 27; WYA; YAW
Myers, Walter M.
See Myers, Walter Dean
Myles, Symon
See Follett, Ken(neth Martin)
Nabokov, Vladimir (Vladimirovich)
1899-1977 .... **CLC 1, 2, 3, 6, 8, 11, 15, 23, 44, 46, 64; SSC 11; WLC**
See also AMW; AMWR 1; BPFB 2; CA 5-8R; 69-72; CANR 20, 102; CDALB 1941-1968; DA; DA3; DAB; DAC; DAM MST, NOV; DLB 2, 244; DLBD 3; DLBY 1980, 1991; EXPS; MTCW 1, 2; NFS 9; RGAL 4; RGSF 2; SSFS 6, 15; TCLC 108
Naevius c. 265B.C.-201B.C. .... **CMLC 37**
See also DLB 211
Nagai, Kafu .... **TCLC 51**
See also Nagai, Sokichi
See also DLB 180
Nagai, Sokichi 1879-1959
See Nagai, Kafu
See also CA 117

Nagy, Laszlo 1925-1978 .... **CLC 7**
See also CA 129; 112
Naidu, Sarojini 1879-1949 .... **TCLC 80**
See also RGEL 2
Naipaul, Shiva(dhar Srinivasa)
1945-1985 .... **CLC 32, 39**
See also CA 110; 112; 116; CANR 33; DA3; DAM NOV; DLB 157; DLBY 1985; MTCW 1, 2
Naipaul, V(idiadhar) S(urajprasad)
1932- .... **CLC 4, 7, 9, 13, 18, 37, 105; SSC 38**
See also BPFB 2; BRWS 1; CA 1-4R; CANR 1, 33, 51, 91; CDBLB 1960 to Present; CDWLB 3; CN 7; DA3; DAB; DAC; DAM MST, NOV; DLB 125, 204, 207; DLBY 1985, 2001; MTCW 1, 2; RGEL 2; RGSF 2; WLIT 4
Nakos, Lilika 1899(?)- .... **CLC 29**
Narayan, R(asipuram) K(rishnaswami)
1906-2001 . **CLC 7, 28, 47, 121; SSC 25**
See also BPFB 2; CA 81-84; 196; CANR 33, 61; CN 7; DA3; DAM NOV; DNFS 1; MTCW 1, 2; RGEL 2; RGSF 2; SATA 62; SSFS 5
Nash, (Frediric) Ogden 1902-1971 . **CLC 23; PC 21**
See also CA 13-14; 29-32R; CANR 34, 61; CAP 1; DAM POET; DLB 11; MAICYA 1, 2; MTCW 1, 2; RGAL 4; SATA 2, 46; TCLC 109; WP
Nashe, Thomas 1567-1601(?) .... **LC 41**
See also DLB 167; RGEL 2
Nathan, Daniel
See Dannay, Frederic
Nathan, George Jean 1882-1958 .... **TCLC 18**
See also Hatteras, Owen
See also CA 114; 169; DLB 137
Natsume, Kinnosuke
See Natsume, Soseki
Natsume, Soseki 1867-1916 .... **TCLC 2, 10**
See also Natsume Soseki; Soseki
See also CA 104; 195; RGWL 2
Natsume Soseki
See Natsume, Soseki
See also DLB 180
Natti, (Mary) Lee 1919-
See Kingman, Lee
See also CA 5-8R; CANR 2
Navarre, Marguerite de
See de Navarre, Marguerite
Naylor, Gloria 1950- . **CLC 28, 52, 156; BLC 3; WLCS**
See also AAYA 6, 39; AFAW 1, 2; AMWS 8; BW 2, 3; CA 107; CANR 27, 51, 74; CN 7; CPW; DA; DA3; DAC; DAM MST, MULT, NOV, POP; DLB 173; FW; MTCW 1, 2; NFS 4, 7; RGAL 4
Neff, Debra .... **CLC 59**
Neihardt, John Gneisenau
1881-1973 .... **CLC 32**
See also CA 13-14; CANR 65; CAP 1; DLB 9, 54, 256; LAIT 2
Nekrasov, Nikolai Alekseevich
1821-1878 .... **NCLC 11**
Nelligan, Emile 1879-1941 .... **TCLC 14**
See also CA 114; DLB 92
Nelson, Willie 1933- .... **CLC 17**
See also CA 107
Nemerov, Howard (Stanley)
1920-1991 .... **CLC 2, 6, 9, 36; PC 24; TCLC 124**
See also AMW; CA 1-4R; 134; CABS 2; CANR 1, 27, 53; DAM POET; DLB 5, 6; DLBY 1983; INT CANR-27; MTCW 1, 2; PFS 10, 14; RGAL 4

Neruda, Pablo 1904-1973 .. **CLC 1, 2, 5, 7, 9, 28, 62; HLC 2; PC 4; WLC**
See also CA 19-20; 45-48; CAP 2; DA; DA3; DAB; DAC; DAM MST, MULT, POET; DNFS 2; HW 1; LAW; MTCW 1, 2; PFS 11; RGWL 2; WLIT 1; WP

Nerval, Gerard de 1808-1855 ... **NCLC 1, 67; PC 13; SSC 18**
See also DLB 217; EW 6; GFL 1789 to the Present; RGSF 2; RGWL 2

Nervo, (Jose) Amado (Ruiz de) 1870-1919 .... **TCLC 11; HLCS 2**
See also CA 109; 131; HW 1; LAW

Nesbit, Malcolm
See Chester, Alfred

Nessi, Pio Baroja y
See Baroja (y Nessi), Pio

Nestroy, Johann 1801-1862 .... **NCLC 42**
See also DLB 133; RGWL 2

Netterville, Luke
See O'Grady, Standish (James)

Neufeld, John (Arthur) 1938- .... **CLC 17**
See also AAYA 11; CA 25-28R; CANR 11, 37, 56; CLR 52; MAICYA 1, 2; SAAS 3; SATA 6, 81; SATA-Essay 131; YAW

Neumann, Alfred 1895-1952 .... **TCLC 100**
See also CA 183; DLB 56

Neumann, Ferenc
See Molnar, Ferenc

Neville, Emily Cheney 1919- .... **CLC 12**
See also BYA 2; CA 5-8R; CANR 3, 37, 85; JRDA; MAICYA 1, 2; SAAS 2; SATA 1; YAW

Newbound, Bernard Slade 1930-
See Slade, Bernard
See also CA 81-84; CANR 49; CD 5; DAM DRAM

Newby, P(ercy) H(oward) 1918-1997 .... **CLC 2, 13**
See also CA 5-8R; 161; CANR 32, 67; CN 7; DAM NOV; DLB 15; MTCW 1; RGEL 2

Newcastle
See Cavendish, Margaret Lucas

Newlove, Donald 1928- .... **CLC 6**
See also CA 29-32R; CANR 25

Newlove, John (Herbert) 1938- .... **CLC 14**
See also CA 21-24R; CANR 9, 25; CP 7

Newman, Charles 1938- .... **CLC 2, 8**
See also CA 21-24R; CANR 84; CN 7

Newman, Edwin (Harold) 1919- ...... **CLC 14**
See also AITN 1; CA 69-72; CANR 5

Newman, John Henry 1801-1890 . **NCLC 38, 99**
See also BRWS 7; DLB 18, 32, 55; RGEL 2

Newton, (Sir) Isaac 1642-1727 ...... **LC 35, 53**
See also DLB 252

Newton, Suzanne 1936- .... **CLC 35**
See also BYA 7; CA 41-44R; CANR 14; JRDA; SATA 5, 77

New York Dept. of Ed. .... **CLC 70**

Nexo, Martin Andersen 1869-1954 .... **TCLC 43**
See also DLB 214

Nezval, Vitezslav 1900-1958 .... **TCLC 44**
See also CA 123; CDWLB 4; DLB 215

Ng, Fae Myenne 1957(?)- .... **CLC 81**
See also CA 146

Ngema, Mbongeni 1955- .... **CLC 57**
See also BW 2; CA 143; CANR 84; CD 5

Ngugi, James T(hiong'o) .... **CLC 3, 7, 13**
See also Ngugi wa Thiong'o

Ngugi wa Thiong'o
See Ngugi wa Thiong'o
See also DLB 125

Ngugi wa Thiong'o 1938- .... **CLC 36; BLC 3**
See also Ngugi, James T(hiong'o); Ngugi wa Thiong'o
See also AFW; BW 2; CA 81-84; CANR 27, 58; CDWLB 3; DAM MULT, NOV; DNFS 2; MTCW 1, 2; RGEL 2

Nichol, B(arrie) P(hillip) 1944-1988 . **CLC 18**
See also CA 53-56; DLB 53; SATA 66

Nichols, John (Treadwell) 1940- .... **CLC 38**
See also CA 9-12R; CAAE 190; CAAS 2; CANR 6, 70; DLBY 1982; TCWW 2

Nichols, Leigh
See Koontz, Dean R(ay)

Nichols, Peter (Richard) 1927- .... **CLC 5, 36, 65**
See also CA 104; CANR 33, 86; CBD; CD 5; DLB 13, 245; MTCW 1

Nicholson, Linda ed. .... **CLC 65**

Ni Chuilleanain, Eilean 1942- .... **PC 34**
See also CA 126; CANR 53, 83; CP 7; CWP; DLB 40

Nicolas, F. R. E.
See Freeling, Nicolas

Niedecker, Lorine 1903-1970 ...... **CLC 10, 42**
See also CA 25-28; CAP 2; DAM POET; DLB 48

Nietzsche, Friedrich (Wilhelm) 1844-1900 .... **TCLC 10, 18, 55**
See also CA 107; 121; CDWLB 2; DLB 129; EW 7; RGWL 2

Nievo, Ippolito 1831-1861 .... **NCLC 22**

Nightingale, Anne Redmon 1943-
See Redmon, Anne
See also CA 103

Nightingale, Florence 1820-1910 ... **TCLC 85**
See also CA 188; DLB 166

Nijo Yoshimoto 1320-1388 .... **CMLC 49**
See also DLB 203

Nik. T. O.
See Annensky, Innokenty (Fyodorovich)

Nin, Anais 1903-1977 ..... **CLC 1, 4, 8, 11, 14, 60, 127; SSC 10**
See also AITN 2; AMWS 10; BPFB 2; CA 13-16R; 69-72; CANR 22, 53; DAM NOV, POP; DLB 2, 4, 152; GLL 2; MAWW; MTCW 1, 2; RGAL 4; RGSF 2

Nisbet, Robert A(lexander) 1913-1996 .... **TCLC 117**
See also CA 25-28R; 153; CANR 17; INT CANR-17

Nishida, Kitaro 1870-1945 .... **TCLC 83**

Nishiwaki, Junzaburo 1894-1982 .... **PC 15**
See also Nishiwaki, Junzaburo
See also CA 194; 107; MJW

Nishiwaki, Junzaburo 1894-1982
See Nishiwaki, Junzaburo
See also CA 194

Nissenson, Hugh 1933- .... **CLC 4, 9**
See also CA 17-20R; CANR 27, 108; CN 7; DLB 28

Niven, Larry .... **CLC 8**
See also Niven, Laurence Van Cott
See also AAYA 27; BPFB 2; BYA 10; DLB 8; SCFW 2

Niven, Laurence Van Cott 1938-
See Niven, Larry
See also CA 21-24R; CAAS 12; CANR 14, 44, 66; CPW; DAM POP; MTCW 1, 2; SATA 95; SFW 4

Nixon, Agnes Eckhardt 1927- .... **CLC 21**
See also CA 110

Nizan, Paul 1905-1940 .... **TCLC 40**
See also CA 161; DLB 72; GFL 1789 to the Present

Nkosi, Lewis 1936- .... **CLC 45; BLC 3**
See also BW 1, 3; CA 65-68; CANR 27, 81; CBD; CD 5; DAM MULT; DLB 157, 225

Nodier, (Jean) Charles (Emmanuel) 1780-1844 .... **NCLC 19**
See also DLB 119; GFL 1789 to the Present

Noguchi, Yone 1875-1947 .... **TCLC 80**

Nolan, Christopher 1965- .... **CLC 58**
See also CA 111; CANR 88

Noon, Jeff 1957- .... **CLC 91**
See also CA 148; CANR 83; SFW 4

Norden, Charles
See Durrell, Lawrence (George)

Nordhoff, Charles (Bernard) 1887-1947 .... **TCLC 23**
See also CA 108; DLB 9; LAIT 1; RHW 1; SATA 23

Norfolk, Lawrence 1963- .... **CLC 76**
See also CA 144; CANR 85; CN 7

Norman, Marsha 1947- .... **CLC 28; DC 8**
See also CA 105; CABS 3; CAD; CANR 41; CD 5; CSW; CWD; DAM DRAM; DFS 2; DLBY 1984; FW

Normyx
See Douglas, (George) Norman

Norris, (Benjamin) Frank(lin, Jr.) 1870-1902 .... **TCLC 24; SSC 28**
See also AMW; BPFB 2; CA 110; 160; CDALB 1865-1917; DLB 12, 71, 186; NFS 12; RGAL 4; TCWW 2; TUS

Norris, Leslie 1921- .... **CLC 14**
See also CA 11-12; CANR 14; CAP 1; CP 7; DLB 27, 256

North, Andrew
See Norton, Andre

North, Anthony
See Koontz, Dean R(ay)

North, Captain George
See Stevenson, Robert Louis (Balfour)

North, Captain George
See Stevenson, Robert Louis (Balfour)

North, Milou
See Erdrich, Louise

Northrup, B. A.
See Hubbard, L(afayette) Ron(ald)

North Staffs
See Hulme, T(homas) E(rnest)

Northup, Solomon 1808-1863 ...... **NCLC 105**

Norton, Alice Mary
See Norton, Andre
See also MAICYA 1; SATA 1, 43

Norton, Andre 1912- .... **CLC 12**
See also Norton, Alice Mary
See also AAYA 14; BPFB 2; BYA 4, 10, 12; CA 1-4R; CANR 68; CLR 50; DLB 8, 52; JRDA; MAICYA 2; MTCW 1; SATA 91; SUFW; YAW

Norton, Caroline 1808-1877 .... **NCLC 47**
See also DLB 21, 159, 199

Norway, Nevil Shute 1899-1960
See Shute, Nevil
See also CA 102; 93-96; CANR 85; MTCW 2

Norwid, Cyprian Kamil 1821-1883 .... **NCLC 17**

Nosille, Nabrah
See Ellison, Harlan (Jay)

Nossack, Hans Erich 1901-1978 .... **CLC 6**
See also CA 93-96; 85-88; DLB 69

Nostradamus 1503-1566 .... **LC 27**

Nosu, Chuji
See Ozu, Yasujiro

Notenburg, Eleanora (Genrikhovna) von
See Guro, Elena

Nova, Craig 1945- .... **CLC 7, 31**
See also CA 45-48; CANR 2, 53

Novak, Joseph
See Kosinski, Jerzy (Nikodem)

Novalis 1772-1801 .... **NCLC 13**
See also CDWLB 2; DLB 90; EW 5; RGWL 2

Novis, Emile
See Weil, Simone (Adolphine)

Nowlan, Alden (Albert) 1933-1983 ... **CLC 15**
See also CA 9-12R; CANR 5; DAC; DAM MST; DLB 53; PFS 12

Noyes, Alfred 1880-1958 ...... **TCLC 7; PC 27**
See also CA 104; 188; DLB 20; EXPP; FANT; PFS 4; RGEL 2

Nunn, Kem .... **CLC 34**
See also CA 159

Nwapa, Flora 1931-1993 .... **CLC 133; BLCS**
See also BW 2; CA 143; CANR 83; CDWLB 3; CWRI 5; DLB 125; WLIT 2

Nye, Robert 1939- .... **CLC 13, 42**
See also CA 33-36R; 29, 67, 107; CN 7; CP 7; CWRI 5; DAM NOV; DLB 14; FANT; HGG; MTCW 1; RHW; SATA 6

Nyro, Laura 1947-1997 .... **CLC 17**
See also CA 194

Oates, Joyce Carol 1938- .. **CLC 1, 2, 3, 6, 9, 11, 15, 19, 33, 52, 108, 134; SSC 6; WLC**
See also AAYA 15; AITN 1; AMWS 2; BEST 89:2; BPFB 2; BYA 11; CA 5-8R; CANR 25, 45, 74; CDALB 1968-1988; CN 7; CP 7; CPW; CWP; DA; DA3; DAB; DAC; DAM MST, NOV, POP; DLB 2, 5, 130; DLBY 1981; EXPS; HGG; INT CANR-25; LAIT 4; MAWW; MTCW 1, 2; NFS 8; RGAL 4; RGSF 2; SSFS 1, 8

O'Brian, Patrick 1914-2000 .... **CLC 152**
See also CA 144; 187; CANR 74; CPW; MTCW 2; RHW

O'Brien, Darcy 1939-1998 .... **CLC 11**
See also CA 21-24R; 167; CANR 8, 59

O'Brien, E. G.
See Clarke, Arthur C(harles)

O'Brien, Edna 1936- ...... **CLC 3, 5, 8, 13, 36, 65, 116; SSC 10**
See also BRWS 5; CA 1-4R; CANR 6, 41, 65, 102; CDBLB 1960 to Present; CN 7; DA3; DAM NOV; DLB 14, 231; FW; MTCW 1, 2; RGSF 2; WLIT 4

O'Brien, Fitz-James 1828-1862 ..... **NCLC 21**
See also DLB 74; RGAL 4; SUFW

O'Brien, Flann .... **CLC 1, 4, 5, 7, 10, 47**
See also O Nuallain, Brian
See also BRWS 2; DLB 231; RGEL 2

O'Brien, Richard 1942- .... **CLC 17**
See also CA 124

O'Brien, (William) Tim(othy) 1946- . **CLC 7, 19, 40, 103**
See also AAYA 16; AMWS 5; CA 85-88; CANR 40, 58; CDALBS; CN 7; CPW; DA3; DAM POP; DLB 152; DLBD 9; DLBY 1980; MTCW 2; RGAL 4; SSFS 5, 15

Obstfelder, Sigbjoern 1866-1900 .... **TCLC 23**
See also CA 123

O'Casey, Sean 1880-1964 .... **CLC 1, 5, 9, 11, 15, 88; DC 12; WLCS**
See also BRW 7; CA 89-92; CANR 62; CBD; CDBLB 1914-1945; DA3; DAB; DAC; DAM DRAM, MST; DLB 10; MTCW 1, 2; RGEL 2; TEA; WLIT 4

O'Cathasaigh, Sean
See O'Casey, Sean

Occom, Samson 1723-1792 .... **LC 60**
See also DLB 175; NNAL

Ochs, Phil(ip David) 1940-1976 .... **CLC 17**
See also CA 185; 65-68

O'Connor, Edwin (Greene) 1918-1968 .... **CLC 14**
See also CA 93-96; 25-28R

O'Connor, (Mary) Flannery 1925-1964 .... **CLC 1, 2, 3, 6, 10, 13, 15, 21, 66, 104; SSC 1, 23; WLC**
See also AAYA 7; AMW; BPFB 3; CA 1-4R; CANR 3, 41; CDALB 1941-1968; DA; DA3; DAB; DAC; DAM MST, NOV, DLB 2, 152; DLBD 12; DLBY 1980; EXPS; LAIT 5; MAWW; MTCW 1, 2; NFS 3; RGAL 4; RGSF 2; SSFS 2, 7, 10

O'Connor, Frank .... **CLC 23; SSC 5**
See also O'Donovan, Michael John
See also DLB 162; RGSF 2; SSFS 5

O'Dell, Scott 1898-1989 .... **CLC 30**
See also AAYA 3; BPFB 3; BYA 1, 2, 3, 5; CA 61-64; 129; CANR 12, 30; CLR 1, 16; DLB 52; JRDA; MAICYA 1, 2; SATA 12, 60; WYA; YAW

Odets, Clifford 1906-1963 ..... **CLC 2, 28, 98; DC 6**
See also AMWS 2; CA 85-88; CAD; CANR 62; DAM DRAM; DFS 3; DLB 7, 26; MTCW 1, 2; RGAL 4

O'Doherty, Brian 1928- .... **CLC 76**
See also CA 105; CANR 108

O'Donnell, K. M.
See Malzberg, Barry N(athaniel)

O'Donnell, Lawrence
See Kuttner, Henry

O'Donovan, Michael John 1903-1966 .... **CLC 14**
See also O'Connor, Frank
See also CA 93-96; CANR 84

Oe, Kenzaburo 1935- .. **CLC 10, 36, 86; SSC 20**
See also Oe Kenzaburo
See also CA 97-100; CANR 36, 50, 74; DA3; DAM NOV; DLBY 1994; MTCW 1, 2

Oe Kenzaburo
See Oe, Kenzaburo
See also CWW 2; DLB 182; EWL 3; MJW; RGSF 2; RGWL 2

O'Faolain, Julia 1932- .... **CLC 6, 19, 47, 108**
See also CA 81-84; CAAS 2; CANR 12, 61; CN 7; DLB 14, 231; FW; MTCW 1; RHW

O'Faolain, Sean 1900-1991 ...... **CLC 1, 7, 14, 32, 70; SSC 13**
See also CA 61-64; 134; CANR 12, 66; DLB 15, 162; MTCW 1, 2; RGEL 2; RGSF 2

O'Flaherty, Liam 1896-1984 .... **CLC 5, 34; SSC 6**
See also CA 101; 113; CANR 35; DLB 36, 162; DLBY 1984; MTCW 2; RGEL 2; RGSF 2; SSFS 5

Ogai
See Mori Ogai
See also MJW

Ogilvy, Gavin
See Barrie, J(ames) M(atthew)

O'Grady, Standish (James) 1846-1928 .... **TCLC 5**
See also CA 104; 157

O'Grady, Timothy 1951- .... **CLC 59**
See also CA 138

O'Hara, Frank 1926-1966 .. **CLC 2, 5, 13, 78**
See also CA 9-12R; 25-28R; CANR 33; DA3; DAM POET; DLB 5, 16, 193; MTCW 1, 2; PFS 8; 12; RGAL 4; WP

O'Hara, John (Henry) 1905-1970 . **CLC 1, 2, 3, 6, 11, 42; SSC 15**
See also AMW; BPFB 3; CA 5-8R; 25-28R; CANR 31, 60; CDALB 1929-1941; DAM NOV; DLB 9, 86; DLBD 2; MTCW 1, 2; NFS 11; RGAL 4; RGSF 2

O Hehir, Diana 1922- .... **CLC 41**
See also CA 93-96

Ohiyesa 1858-1939
See Eastman, Charles A(lexander)

Okigbo, Christopher (Ifenayichukwu) 1932-1967 .... **CLC 25, 84; BLC 3; PC 7**
See also AFW; BW 1, 3; CA 77-80; CANR 74; CDWLB 3; DAM MULT, POET; DLB 125; MTCW 1, 2; RGEL 2

Okri, Ben 1959- .... **CLC 87**
See also AFW; BRWS 5; BW 2, 3; CA 130; 138; CANR 65; CN 7; DLB 157, 231; INT CA-138; MTCW 2; RGSF 2; WLIT 2

Olds, Sharon 1942- .. **CLC 32, 39, 85; PC 22**
See also AMWS 10; CA 101; CANR 18, 41, 66, 98; CP 7; CPW; CWP; DAM POET; DLB 120; MTCW 2

Oldstyle, Jonathan
See Irving, Washington

Olesha, Iurii
See Olesha, Yuri (Karlovich)
See also RGWL 2

Olesha, Yuri (Karlovich) 1899-1960 .. **CLC 8**
See also Olesha, Iurii
See also CA 85-88; EW 11

Oliphant, Mrs.
See Oliphant, Margaret (Oliphant Wilson)
See also SUFW

Oliphant, Laurence 1829(?)-1888 .. **NCLC 47**
See also DLB 18, 166

Oliphant, Margaret (Oliphant Wilson) 1828-1897 .... **NCLC 11, 61; SSC 25**
See also Oliphant, Mrs.
See also DLB 18, 159, 190; HGG; RGEL 2; RGSF 2

Oliver, Mary 1935- .... **CLC 19, 34, 98**
See also AMWS 7; CA 21-24R; CANR 9, 43, 84, 92; CP 7; CWP; DLB 5, 193; PFS 15

Olivier, Laurence (Kerr) 1907-1989 . **CLC 20**
See also CA 111; 150; 129

Olsen, Tillie 1912- ... **CLC 4, 13, 114; SSC 11**
See also BYA 11; CA 1-4R; CANR 1, 43, 74; CDALBS; CN 7; DA; DA3; DAB; DAC; DAM MST; DLB 28, 206; DLBY 1980; EXPS; FW; MTCW 1, 2; RGAL 4; RGSF 2; SSFS 1

Olson, Charles (John) 1910-1970 .. **CLC 1, 2, 5, 6, 9, 11, 29; PC 19**
See also AMWS 2; CA 13-16; 25-28R; CABS 2; CANR 35, 61; CAP 1; DAM POET; DLB 5, 16, 193; MTCW 1, 2; RGAL 4; WP

Olson, Toby 1937- .... **CLC 28**
See also CA 65-68; CANR 9, 31, 84; CP 7

Olyesha, Yuri
See Olesha, Yuri (Karlovich)

Omar Khayyam
See Khayyam, Omar
See also RGWL 2

Ondaatje, (Philip) Michael 1943- .... **CLC 14, 29, 51, 76; PC 28**
See also CA 77-80; CANR 42, 74, 109; CN 7; CP 7; DA3; DAB; DAC; DAM MST; DLB 60; MTCW 2; PFS 8; TWA

Oneal, Elizabeth 1934-
See Oneal, Zibby
See also CA 106; CANR 28, 84; MAICYA 1, 2; SATA 30, 82; YAW

Oneal, Zibby .... **CLC 30**
See also Oneal, Elizabeth
See also AAYA 5, 41; BYA 13; CLR 13; JRDA; WYA

O'Neill, Eugene (Gladstone) 1888-1953 .... **TCLC 1, 6, 27, 49; WLC**
See also AITN 1; AMW; CA 110; 132; CAD; CDALB 1929-1941; DA; DA3; DAB; DAC; DAM DRAM, MST; DFS 9, 11, 12; DLB 7; LAIT 3; MTCW 1, 2; RGAL 4; TUS

Onetti, Juan Carlos 1909-1994 ... **CLC 7, 10; HLCS 2; SSC 23**
See also CA 85-88; 145; CANR 32, 63; CDWLB 3; DAM MULT, NOV; DLB 113; HW 1, 2; LAW; MTCW 1, 2; RGSF 2

O Nuallain, Brian 1911-1966
See O'Brien, Flann
See also CA 21-22; 25-28R; CAP 2; DLB 231; FANT

Ophuls, Max 1902-1957 .... **TCLC 79**
See also CA 113

Opie, Amelia 1769-1853 .... **NCLC 65**
See also DLB 116, 159; RGEL 2

Oppen, George 1908-1984 ..... **CLC 7, 13, 34; PC 35**
See also CA 13-16R; 113; CANR 8, 82; DLB 5, 165; TCLC 107

Oppenheim, E(dward) Phillips 1866-1946 .... **TCLC 45**
See also CA 111; 202; CMW 4; DLB 70

Opuls, Max
See Ophuls, Max

Origen c. 185-c. 254 .... **CMLC 19**

Orlovitz, Gil 1918-1973 .... **CLC 22**
See also CA 77-80; 45-48; DLB 2, 5

Orris
See Ingelow, Jean

Ortega y Gasset, Jose 1883-1955 ... **TCLC 9; HLC 2**
See also CA 106; 130; DAM MULT; EW 9; HW 1, 2; MTCW 1, 2

Ortese, Anna Maria 1914- .... **CLC 89**
See also DLB 177

Ortiz, Simon J(oseph) 1941- ..... **CLC 45; PC 17**
See also AMWS 4; CA 134; CANR 69; CP 7; DAM MULT, POET; DLB 120, 175, 256; EXPP; NNAL; PFS 4; RGAL 4

Orton, Joe .... **CLC 4, 13, 43; DC 3**
See also Orton, John Kingsley
See also BRWS 5; CBD; CDBLB 1960 to Present; DFS 3, 6; DLB 13; GLL 1; MTCW 2; RGEL 2; WLIT 4

Orton, John Kingsley 1933-1967
See Orton, Joe
See also CA 85-88; CANR 35, 66; DAM DRAM; MTCW 1, 2

Orwell, George .... **TCLC 2, 6, 15, 31, 51; WLC**
See also Blair, Eric (Arthur)
See also BPFB 3; BRW 7; BYA 5; CDBLB 1945-1960; CLR 68; DAB; DLB 15, 98, 195, 255; EXPN; LAIT 4, 5; NFS 3, 7; RGEL 2; SCFW 2; SFW 4; SSFS 4; WLIT 4; YAW

Osborne, David
See Silverberg, Robert

Osborne, George
See Silverberg, Robert

Osborne, John (James) 1929-1994 .... **CLC 1, 2, 5, 11, 45; WLC**
See also BRWS 1; CA 13-16R; 147; CANR 21, 56; CDBLB 1945-1960; DA; DAB; DAC; DAM DRAM, MST; DFS 4; DLB 13; MTCW 1, 2; RGEL 2

Osborne, Lawrence 1958- .... **CLC 50**
See also CA 189

Osbourne, Lloyd 1868-1947 .... **TCLC 93**

Oshima, Nagisa 1932- .... **CLC 20**
See also CA 116; 121; CANR 78

Oskison, John Milton 1874-1947 ... **TCLC 35**
See also CA 144; CANR 84; DAM MULT; DLB 175; NNAL

Ossian c. 3rd cent. - .... **CMLC 28**
See also Macpherson, James

Ossoli, Sarah Margaret (Fuller) 1810-1850 .... **NCLC 5, 50**
See also Fuller, Margaret; Fuller, Sarah Margaret
See also CDALB 1640-1865; FW; SATA 25

Ostriker, Alicia (Suskin) 1937- .... **CLC 132**
See also CA 25-28R; CAAS 24; CANR 10, 30, 62, 99; CWP; DLB 120; EXPP

Ostrovsky, Alexander 1823-1886 .. **NCLC 30, 57**

Otero, Blas de 1916-1979 .... **CLC 11**
See also CA 89-92; DLB 134

Otto, Rudolf 1869-1937 .... **TCLC 85**

Otto, Whitney 1955- .... **CLC 70**
See also CA 140

Ouida .... **TCLC 43**
See also De La Ramee, (Marie) Louise
See also DLB 18, 156; RGEL 2

Ouologuem, Yambo 1940- .... **CLC 146**
See also CA 111; 176

Ousmane, Sembene 1923- ... **CLC 66; BLC 3**
See also Sembene, Ousmane
See also BW 1, 3; CA 117; 125; CANR 81; CWW 2; MTCW 1

Ovid 43B.C.-17 .... **CMLC 7; PC 2**
See also AW 2; CDWLB 1; DA3; DAM POET; DLB 211; RGWL 2; WP

Owen, Hugh
See Faust, Frederick (Schiller)

Owen, Wilfred (Edward Salter) 1893-1918 ... **TCLC 5, 27; PC 19; WLC**
See also BRW 6; CA 104; 141; CDBLB 1914-1945; DA; DAB; DAC; DAM MST, POET; DLB 20; EXPP; MTCW 2; PFS 10; RGEL 2; WLIT 4

Owens, Rochelle 1936- .... **CLC 8**
See also CA 17-20R; CAAS 2; CAD; CANR 39; CD 5; CP 7; CWD; CWP

Oz, Amos 1939- .... **CLC 5, 8, 11, 27, 33, 54**
See also CA 53-56; CANR 27, 47, 65; CWW 2; DAM NOV; MTCW 1, 2; RGSF 2

Ozick, Cynthia 1928- .... **CLC 3, 7, 28, 62, 155; SSC 15**
See also AMWS 5; BEST 90:1; CA 17-20R; CANR 23, 58; CN 7; CPW; DA3; DAM NOV, POP; DLB 28, 152; DLBY 1982; EXPS; INT CANR-23; MTCW 1, 2; RGAL 4; RGSF 2; SSFS 3, 12

Ozu, Yasujiro 1903-1963 .... **CLC 16**
See also CA 112

Pacheco, C.
See Pessoa, Fernando (Antonio Nogueira)

Pacheco, Jose Emilio 1939-
See also CA 111; 131; CANR 65; DAM MULT; HLC 2; HW 1, 2; RGSF 2

Pa Chin .... **CLC 18**
See also Li Fei-kan

Pack, Robert 1929- .... **CLC 13**
See also CA 1-4R; CANR 3, 44, 82; CP 7; DLB 5; SATA 118

Padgett, Lewis
See Kuttner, Henry

Padilla (Lorenzo), Heberto 1932-2000 .... **CLC 38**
See also AITN 1; CA 123; 131; 189; HW 1

Page, Jimmy 1944- .... **CLC 12**

Page, Louise 1955- .... **CLC 40**
See also CA 140; CANR 76; CBD; CD 5; CWD; DLB 233

Page, P(atricia) K(athleen) 1916- ...... **CLC 7, 18; PC 12**
See also Cape, Judith
See also CA 53-56; CANR 4, 22, 65; CP 7; DAC; DAM MST; DLB 68; MTCW 1; RGEL 2

Page, Stanton
See Fuller, Henry Blake

Page, Stanton
See Fuller, Henry Blake

Page, Thomas Nelson 1853-1922 .... **SSC 23**
See also CA 118; 177; DLB 12, 78; DLBD 13; RGAL 4

Pagels, Elaine Hiesey 1943- .... **CLC 104**
See also CA 45-48; CANR 2, 24, 51; FW

Paget, Violet 1856-1935
See Lee, Vernon
See also CA 104; 166; GLL 1; HGG

Paget-Lowe, Henry
See Lovecraft, H(oward) P(hillips)

Paglia, Camille (Anna) 1947- .... **CLC 68**
See also CA 140; CANR 72; CPW; FW; GLL 2; MTCW 2

Paige, Richard
See Koontz, Dean R(ay)

Paine, Thomas 1737-1809 .... **NCLC 62**
See also AMWS 1; CDALB 1640-1865; DLB 31, 43, 73, 158; LAIT 1; RGAL 4; RGEL 2

Palamas, Kostes 1859-1943 .... **TCLC 5**
See also CA 105; 190; RGWL 2

Palazzeschi, Aldo 1885-1974 .... **CLC 11**
See also CA 89-92; 53-56; DLB 114

Pales Matos, Luis 1898-1959
See Pales Matos, Luis
See also HLCS 2; HW 1; LAW

Paley, Grace 1922- .. **CLC 4, 6, 37, 140; SSC 8**
See also AMWS 6; CA 25-28R; CANR 13, 46, 74; CN 7; CPW; DA3; DAM POP; DLB 28, 218; EXPS; FW; INT CANR-13; MAWW; MTCW 1, 2; RGAL 4; RGSF 2; SSFS 3

Palin, Michael (Edward) 1943- .... **CLC 21**
See also Monty Python
See also CA 107; CANR 35, 109; SATA 67

Palliser, Charles 1947- .... **CLC 65**
See also CA 136; CANR 76; CN 7

Palma, Ricardo 1833-1919 .... **TCLC 29**
See also CA 168; LAW

Pancake, Breece Dexter 1952-1979
See Pancake, Breece D'J
See also CA 123; 109

Pancake, Breece D'J .... **CLC 29**
See also Pancake, Breece Dexter
See also DLB 130

Panchenko, Nikolai .... **CLC 59**

Pankhurst, Emmeline (Goulden) 1858-1928 .... **TCLC 100**
See also CA 116; FW

Panko, Rudy
See Gogol, Nikolai (Vasilyevich)

Papadiamantis, Alexandros 1851-1911 .... **TCLC 29**
See also CA 168

Papadiamantopoulos, Johannes 1856-1910
See Moreas, Jean
See also CA 117

Papini, Giovanni 1881-1956 .... **TCLC 22**
See also CA 121; 180

Paracelsus 1493-1541 .... **LC 14**
See also DLB 179

Parasol, Peter
See Stevens, Wallace

Pardo Bazan, Emilia 1851-1921 .... **SSC 30**
See also FW; RGSF 2; RGWL 2

Pareto, Vilfredo 1848-1923 .... **TCLC 69**
See also CA 175

Paretsky, Sara 1947- .... **CLC 135**
See also AAYA 30; BEST 90:3; CA 125; 129; CANR 59, 95; CMW 4; CPW; DA3; DAM POP; INT CA-129; MSW; RGAL 4

Parfenie, Maria
See Codrescu, Andrei

Parini, Jay (Lee) 1948- .... **CLC 54, 133**
See also CA 97-100; CAAS 16; CANR 32, 87
Park, Jordan
See Kornbluth, C(yril) M.; Pohl, Frederik
Park, Robert E(zra) 1864-1944 ..... **TCLC 73**
See also CA 122; 165
Parker, Bert
See Ellison, Harlan (Jay)
Parker, Dorothy (Rothschild)
1893-1967 .. **CLC 15, 68; PC 28; SSC 2**
See also AMWS 9; CA 19-20; 25-28R; CAP 2; DLB POET; DLB 11, 45, 86; EXPP; FW; MAWW; MTCW 1, 2; RGAL 4; RGSF 2
Parker, Robert B(rown) 1932- .... **CLC 27**
See also AAYA 28; BEST 89:4; BPFB 3; CA 49-52; CANR 1, 26, 52, 89; CMW 4; CPW; DAM NOV, POP; INT CANR-26; MSW; MTCW 1
Parkin, Frank 1940- .... **CLC 43**
See also CA 147
Parkman, Francis, Jr. 1823-1893 .. **NCLC 12**
See also AMWS 2; DLB 1, 30, 183, 186, 235; RGAL 4
Parks, Gordon (Alexander Buchanan)
1912- .... **CLC 1, 16; BLC 3**
See also AAYA 36; AITN 2; BW 2, 3; CA 41-44R; CANR 26, 66; DA3; DAM MULT; DLB 33; MTCW 2; SATA 8, 108
Parks, Tim(othy Harold) 1954- ...... **CLC 147**
See also CA 126; 131; CANR 77; DLB 231; INT CA-131
Parmenides c. 515B.C.-c.
450B.C. .... **CMLC 22**
See also DLB 176
Parnell, Thomas 1679-1718 .... **LC 3**
See also DLB 95; RGEL 2
Parra, Nicanor 1914- ... **CLC 2, 102; HLC 2; PC 39**
See also CA 85-88; CANR 32; CWW 2; DAM MULT; HW 1; LAW; MTCW 1
Parra Sanojo, Ana Teresa de la 1890-1936
See de la Parra, (Ana) Teresa (Sonojo)
See also HLCS 2; LAW
Parrish, Mary Frances
See Fisher, M(ary) F(rances) K(ennedy)
Parshchikov, Aleksei .... **CLC 59**
Parson, Professor
See Coleridge, Samuel Taylor
Parson Lot
See Kingsley, Charles
Parton, Sara Payson Willis
1811-1872 .... **NCLC 86**
See also DLB 43, 74, 239
Partridge, Anthony
See Oppenheim, E(dward) Phillips
Pascal, Blaise 1623-1662 .... **LC 35**
See also EW 3; GFL Beginnings to 1789; RGWL 2
Pascoli, Giovanni 1855-1912 .... **TCLC 45**
See also CA 170; EW 7
Pasolini, Pier Paolo 1922-1975 .. **CLC 20, 37, 106; PC 17**
See also CA 93-96; 61-64; CANR 63; DLB 128, 177; MTCW 1; RGWL 2
Pasquini
See Silone, Ignazio
Pastan, Linda (Olenik) 1932- .... **CLC 27**
See also CA 61-64; CANR 18, 40, 61; CP 7; CSW; CWP; DAM POET; DLB 5; PFS 8
Pasternak, Boris (Leonidovich)
1890-1960 ...... **CLC 7, 10, 18, 63; PC 6; SSC 31; WLC**
See also BPFB 3; CA 127; 116; DA; DA3; DAB; DAC; DAM MST, NOV, POET; EW 10; MTCW 1, 2; RGSF 2; RGWL 2; TWA; WP

Patchen, Kenneth 1911-1972 .... **CLC 1, 2, 18**
See also CA 1-4R; 33-36R; CANR 3, 35; DAM POET; DLB 16, 48; MTCW 1; RGAL 4
Pater, Walter (Horatio) 1839-1894 . **NCLC 7, 90**
See also BRW 5; CDBLB 1832-1890; DLB 57, 156; RGEL 2; TEA
Paterson, A(ndrew) B(arton)
1864-1941 .... **TCLC 32**
See also CA 155; DLB 230; RGEL 2; SATA 97
Paterson, Katherine (Womeldorf)
1932- .... **CLC 12, 30**
See also AAYA 1, 31; BYA 1, 2, 7; CA 21-24R; CANR 28, 59; CLR 7, 50; CWRI 5; DLB 52; JRDA; LAIT 4; MAICYA 1, 2; MAICYAS 1; MTCW 1; SATA 13, 53, 92, 133; WYA; YAW
Patmore, Coventry Kersey Dighton
1823-1896 .... **NCLC 9**
See also DLB 35, 98; RGEL 2; TEA
Paton, Alan (Stewart) 1903-1988 ...... **CLC 4, 10, 25, 55, 106; WLC**
See also AAYA 26; AFW; BPFB 3; BRWS 2; BYA 1; CA 13-16; 125; CANR 22; CAP 1; DA; DA3; DAB; DAC; DAM MST, NOV; DLB 225; DLBD 17; EXPN; LAIT 4; MTCW 1, 2; NFS 3, 12; RGEL 2; SATA 11; SATA-Obit 56; WLIT 2
Paton Walsh, Gillian 1937- .... **CLC 35**
See also Paton Walsh, Jill; Walsh, Jill Paton
See also AAYA 11; CANR 38, 83; CLR 2, 65; DLB 161; JRDA; MAICYA 1, 2; SAAS 3; SATA 4, 72, 109; YAW
Paton Walsh, Jill
See Paton Walsh, Gillian
See also BYA 1, 8
Patton, George S(mith), Jr.
1885-1945 .... **TCLC 79**
See also CA 189
Paulding, James Kirke 1778-1860 ... **NCLC 2**
See also DLB 3, 59, 74, 250; RGAL 4
Paulin, Thomas Neilson 1949-
See Paulin, Tom
See also CA 123; 128; CANR 98; CP 7
Paulin, Tom .... **CLC 37**
See also Paulin, Thomas Neilson
See also DLB 40
Pausanias c. 1st cent. - .... **CMLC 36**
Paustovsky, Konstantin (Georgievich)
1892-1968 .... **CLC 40**
See also CA 93-96; 25-28R
Pavese, Cesare 1908-1950 .. **TCLC 3; PC 13; SSC 19**
See also CA 104; 169; DLB 128, 177; EW 12; RGSF 2; RGWL 2
Pavic, Milorad 1929- .... **CLC 60**
See also CA 136; CDWLB 4; CWW 2; DLB 181
Pavlov, Ivan Petrovich 1849-1936 . **TCLC 91**
See also CA 118; 180
Payne, Alan
See Jakes, John (William)
Paz, Gil
See Lugones, Leopoldo
Paz, Octavio 1914-1998 . **CLC 3, 4, 6, 10, 19, 51, 65, 119; HLC 2; PC 1; WLC**
See also CA 73-76; 165; CANR 32, 65, 104; CWW 2; DA; DA3; DAB; DAC; DAM MST, MULT, POET; DLBY 1990, 1998; DNFS 1; HW 1, 2; LAW; LAWS 1; MTCW 1, 2; RGWL 2; SSFS 13; WLIT 1
p'Bitek, Okot 1931-1982 ..... **CLC 96; BLC 3**
See also AFW; BW 2, 3; CA 124; 107; CANR 82; DAM MULT; DLB 125; MTCW 1, 2; RGEL 2; WLIT 2

Peacock, Molly 1947- .... **CLC 60**
See also CA 103; CAAS 21; CANR 52, 84; CP 7; CWP; DLB 120
Peacock, Thomas Love
1785-1866 .... **NCLC 22**
See also BRW 4; DLB 96, 116; RGEL 2; RGSF 2
Peake, Mervyn 1911-1968 .... **CLC 7, 54**
See also CA 5-8R; 25-28R; CANR 3; DLB 15, 160, 255; FANT; MTCW 1; RGEL 2; SATA 23; SFW 4
Pearce, Philippa
See Christie, Philippa
See also CA 5-8R; CANR 4, 109; CWRI 5; FANT; MAICYA 2
Pearl, Eric
See Elman, Richard (Martin)
Pearson, T(homas) R(eid) 1956- .... **CLC 39**
See also CA 120; 130; CANR 97; CSW; INT 130
Peck, Dale 1967- .... **CLC 81**
See also CA 146; CANR 72; GLL 2
Peck, John (Frederick) 1941- .... **CLC 3**
See also CA 49-52; CANR 3, 100; CP 7
Peck, Richard (Wayne) 1934- .... **CLC 21**
See also AAYA 1, 24; BYA 1, 6, 8, 11; CA 85-88; CANR 19, 38; CLR 15; INT CANR-19; JRDA; MAICYA 1, 2; SAAS 2; SATA 18, 55, 97; SATA-Essay 110; WYA; YAW
Peck, Robert Newton 1928- .... **CLC 17**
See also AAYA 3, 43; BYA 1, 6; CA 81-84, 182; CAAE 182; CANR 31, 63; CLR 45; DA; DAC; DAM MST; JRDA; LAIT 3; MAICYA 1, 2; SAAS 1; SATA 21, 62, 111; SATA-Essay 108; WYA; YAW
Peckinpah, (David) Sam(uel)
1925-1984 .... **CLC 20**
See also CA 109; 114; CANR 82
Pedersen, Knut 1859-1952
See Hamsun, Knut
See also CA 104; 119; CANR 63; MTCW 1, 2
Peeslake, Gaffer
See Durrell, Lawrence (George)
Peguy, Charles (Pierre)
1873-1914 .... **TCLC 10**
See also CA 107; 193; DLB 258; GFL 1789 to the Present
Peirce, Charles Sanders
1839-1914 .... **TCLC 81**
See also CA 194
Pellicer, Carlos 1900(?)-1977
See also CA 153; 69-72; HLCS 2; HW 1
Pena, Ramon del Valle y
See Valle-Inclan, Ramon (Maria) del
Pendennis, Arthur Esquir
See Thackeray, William Makepeace
Penn, William 1644-1718 .... **LC 25**
See also DLB 24
PEPECE
See Prado (Calvo), Pedro
Pepys, Samuel 1633-1703 ... **LC 11, 58; WLC**
See also BRW 2; CDBLB 1660-1789; DA; DA3; DAB; DAC; DAM MST; DLB 101, 213; RGEL 2; WLIT 3
Percy, Thomas 1729-1811 .... **NCLC 95**
See also DLB 104
Percy, Walker 1916-1990 .... **CLC 2, 3, 6, 8, 14, 18, 47, 65**
See also AMWS 3; BPFB 3; CA 1-4R; 131; CANR 1, 23, 64; CPW; CSW; DA3; DAM NOV, POP; DLB 2; DLBY 1980, 1990; MTCW 1, 2; RGAL 4
Percy, William Alexander
1885-1942 .... **TCLC 84**
See also CA 163; MTCW 2

Perec, Georges 1936-1982 .... **CLC 56, 116**
See also CA 141; DLB 83; GFL 1789 to the Present

Pereda (y Sanchez de Porrua), Jose Maria de 1833-1906 .... **TCLC 16**
See also CA 117

Pereda y Porrua, Jose Maria de
See Pereda (y Sanchez de Porrua), Jose Maria de

Peregoy, George Weems
See Mencken, H(enry) L(ouis)

Perelman, S(idney) J(oseph) 1904-1979 .. **CLC 3, 5, 9, 15, 23, 44, 49; SSC 32**
See also AITN 1, 2; BPFB 3; CA 73-76; 89-92; CANR 18; DAM DRAM; DLB 11, 44; MTCW 1, 2; RGAL 4

Peret, Benjamin 1899-1959 .... **TCLC 20; PC 33**
See also CA 117; 186; GFL 1789 to the Present

Peretz, Isaac Loeb 1851(?)-1915 ... **TCLC 16; SSC 26**
See also CA 109

Peretz, Yitzkhok Leibush
See Peretz, Isaac Loeb

Perez Galdos, Benito 1843-1920 ... **TCLC 27; HLCS 2**
See also Galdos, Benito Perez
See also CA 125; 153; HW 1; RGWL 2

Peri Rossi, Cristina 1941- .. **CLC 156; HLCS 2**
See also CA 131; CANR 59, 81; DLB 145; HW 1, 2

Perlata
See Peret, Benjamin

Perloff, Marjorie G(abrielle) 1931- .... **CLC 137**
See also CA 57-60; CANR 7, 22, 49, 104

Perrault, Charles 1628-1703 ... **LC 2, 56; DC 12**
See also BYA 4; CLR 79; GFL Beginnings to 1789; MAICYA 1, 2; RGWL 2; SATA 25; WCH

Perry, Anne 1938- .... **CLC 126**
See also CA 101; CANR 22, 50, 84; CMW 4; CN 7; CPW

Perry, Brighton
See Sherwood, Robert E(mmet)

Perse, St.-John
See Leger, (Marie-Rene Auguste) Alexis Saint-Leger

Perse, Saint-John
See Leger, (Marie-Rene Auguste) Alexis Saint-Leger
See also DLB 258

Perutz, Leo(pold) 1882-1957 .... **TCLC 60**
See also CA 147; DLB 81

Peseenz, Tulio F.
See Lopez y Fuentes, Gregorio

Pesetsky, Bette 1932- .... **CLC 28**
See also CA 133; DLB 130

Peshkov, Alexei Maximovich 1868-1936
See Gorky, Maxim
See also CA 105; 141; CANR 83; DA; DAC; DAM DRAM, MST, NOV; MTCW 2

Pessoa, Fernando (Antonio Nogueira) 1898-1935 ..... **TCLC 27; HLC 2; PC 20**
See also CA 125; 183; DAM MULT; EW 10; RGWL 2; WP

Peterkin, Julia Mood 1880-1961 ...... **CLC 31**
See also CA 102; DLB 9

Peters, Joan K(aren) 1945- .... **CLC 39**
See also CA 158; CANR 109

Peters, Robert L(ouis) 1924- .... **CLC 7**
See also CA 13-16R; CAAS 8; CP 7; DLB 105

Petofi, Sandor 1823-1849 .... **NCLC 21**
See also RGWL 2

Petrakis, Harry Mark 1923- .... **CLC 3**
See also CA 9-12R; CANR 4, 30, 85; CN 7

Petrarch 1304-1374 .... **CMLC 20; PC 8**
See also DA3; DAM POET; EW 2; RGWL 2

Petronius c. 20-66 .... **CMLC 34**
See also AW 2; CDWLB 1; DLB 211; RGWL 2

Petrov, Evgeny .... **TCLC 21**
See also Kataev, Evgeny Petrovich

Petry, Ann (Lane) 1908-1997 ... **CLC 1, 7, 18**
See also AFAW 1, 2; BPFB 3; BW 1, 3; BYA 2; CA 5-8R; 157; CAAS 6; CANR 4, 46; CLR 12; CN 7; DLB 76; JRDA; LAIT 1; MAICYA 1, 2; MAICYAS 1; MTCW 1; RGAL 4; SATA 5; SATA-Obit 94; TCLC 112

Petursson, Hallgrimur 1614-1674 .... **LC 8**

Peychinovich
See Vazov, Ivan (Minchov)

Phaedrus c. 15B.C.-c. 50 .... **CMLC 25**
See also DLB 211

Phelps (Ward), Elizabeth Stuart
See Phelps, Elizabeth Stuart
See also FW

Phelps, Elizabeth Stuart 1844-1911 .... **TCLC 113**
See also Phelps (Ward), Elizabeth Stuart
See also DLB 74

Philips, Katherine 1632-1664 . **LC 30; PC 40**
See also DLB 131; RGEL 2

Philipson, Morris H. 1926- .... **CLC 53**
See also CA 1-4R; CANR 4

Phillips, Caryl 1958- .... **CLC 96; BLCS**
See also BRWS 5; BW 2; CA 141; CANR 63, 104; CBD; CD 5; CN 7; DA3; DAM MULT; DLB 157; MTCW 2; WLIT 4

Phillips, David Graham 1867-1911 .... **TCLC 44**
See also CA 108; 176; DLB 9, 12; RGAL 4

Phillips, Jack
See Sandburg, Carl (August)

Phillips, Jayne Anne 1952- .... **CLC 15, 33, 139; SSC 16**
See also BPFB 3; CA 101; CANR 24, 50, 96; CN 7; CSW; DLBY 1980; INT CANR-24; MTCW 1, 2; RGAL 4; RGSF 2; SSFS 4

Phillips, Richard
See Dick, Philip K(indred)

Phillips, Robert (Schaeffer) 1938- .... **CLC 28**
See also CA 17-20R; CAAS 13; CANR 8; DLB 105

Phillips, Ward
See Lovecraft, H(oward) P(hillips)

Piccolo, Lucio 1901-1969 .... **CLC 13**
See also CA 97-100; DLB 114

Pickthall, Marjorie L(owry) C(hristie) 1883-1922 .... **TCLC 21**
See also CA 107; DLB 92

Pico della Mirandola, Giovanni 1463-1494 .... **LC 15**

Piercy, Marge 1936- .... **CLC 3, 6, 14, 18, 27, 62, 128; PC 29**
See also BPFB 3; CA 21-24R; CAAE 187; CAAS 1; CANR 13, 43, 66; CN 7; CP 7; CWP; DLB 120, 227; EXPP; FW; MTCW 1, 2; PFS 9; SFW 4

Piers, Robert
See Anthony, Piers

Pieyre de Mandiargues, Andre 1909-1991
See Mandiargues, Andre Pieyre de
See also CA 103; 136; CANR 22, 82; GFL 1789 to the Present

Pilnyak, Boris 1894-1938 . **TCLC 23; SSC 48**
See also Vogau, Boris Andreyevich

Pinchback, Eugene
See Toomer, Jean

Pincherle, Alberto 1907-1990 ...... **CLC 11, 18**
See also Moravia, Alberto
See also CA 25-28R; 132; CANR 33, 63; DAM NOV; MTCW 1

Pinckney, Darryl 1953- .... **CLC 76**
See also BW 2, 3; CA 143; CANR 79

Pindar 518(?)B.C.-438(?)B.C. .... **CMLC 12; PC 19**
See also AW 1; CDWLB 1; DLB 176; RGWL 2

Pineda, Cecile 1942- .... **CLC 39**
See also CA 118; DLB 209

Pinero, Arthur Wing 1855-1934 .... **TCLC 32**
See also CA 110; 153; DAM DRAM; DLB 10; RGEL 2

Pinero, Miguel (Antonio Gomez) 1946-1988 .... **CLC 4, 55**
See also CA 61-64; 125; CAD; CANR 29, 90; HW 1

Pinget, Robert 1919-1997 .... **CLC 7, 13, 37**
See also CA 85-88; 160; CWW 2; DLB 83; GFL 1789 to the Present

Pink Floyd
See Barrett, (Roger) Syd; Gilmour, David; Mason, Nick; Waters, Roger; Wright, Rick

Pinkney, Edward 1802-1828 .... **NCLC 31**
See also DLB 248

Pinkwater, Daniel
See Pinkwater, Daniel Manus

Pinkwater, Daniel Manus 1941- .... **CLC 35**
See also AAYA 1; BYA 9; CA 29-32R; CANR 12, 38, 89; CLR 4; CSW; FANT; JRDA; MAICYA 1, 2; SAAS 3; SATA 8, 46, 76, 114; SFW 4; YAW

Pinkwater, Manus
See Pinkwater, Daniel Manus

Pinsky, Robert 1940- .... **CLC 9, 19, 38, 94, 121; PC 27**
See also AMWS 6; CA 29-32R; CAAS 4; CANR 58, 97; CP 7; DA3; DAM POET; DLBY 1982, 1998; MTCW 2; RGAL 4

Pinta, Harold
See Pinter, Harold

Pinter, Harold 1930- .. **CLC 1, 3, 6, 9, 11, 15, 27, 58, 73; DC 15; WLC**
See also BRWR 1; BRWS 1; CA 5-8R; CANR 33, 65; CBD; CD 5; CDBLB 1960 to Present; DA; DA3; DAB; DAC; DAM DRAM, MST; DFS 3, 5, 7, 14; DLB 13; IDFW 3, 4; MTCW 1, 2; RGEL 2

Piozzi, Hester Lynch (Thrale) 1741-1821 .... **NCLC 57**
See also DLB 104, 142

Pirandello, Luigi 1867-1936 ...... **TCLC 4, 29; DC 5; SSC 22; WLC**
See also CA 104; 153; CANR 103; DA; DA3; DAB; DAC; DAM DRAM, MST; DFS 4, 9; EW 8; MTCW 2; RGSF 2; RGWL 2

Pirsig, Robert M(aynard) 1928- ... **CLC 4, 6, 73**
See also CA 53-56; CANR 42, 74; CPW 1; DA3; DAM POP; MTCW 1, 2; SATA 39

Pisarev, Dmitry Ivanovich 1840-1868 .... **NCLC 25**

Pix, Mary (Griffith) 1666-1709 .... **LC 8**
See also DLB 80

Pixerecourt, (Rene Charles) Guilbert de 1773-1844 .... **NCLC 39**
See also DLB 192; GFL 1789 to the Present

Plaatje, Sol(omon) T(shekisho) 1878-1932 .... **TCLC 73; BLCS**
See also BW 2, 3; CA 141; CANR 79; DLB 125, 225

Plaidy, Jean
See Hibbert, Eleanor Alice Burford

Planche, James Robinson
1796-1880 .... NCLC 42
See also RGEL 2

Plant, Robert 1948- .... CLC 12

Plante, David (Robert) 1940- . CLC 7, 23, 38
See also CA 37-40R; CANR 12, 36, 58, 82; CN 7; DAM NOV; DLBY 1983; INT CANR-12; MTCW 1

Plath, Sylvia 1932-1963 ..... CLC 1, 2, 3, 5, 9, 11, 14, 17, 50, 51, 62, 111; PC 1, 37; WLC
See also AAYA 13; AMWS 1; BPFB 3; CA 19-20; CANR 34, 101; CAP 2; CDALB 1941-1968; DA; DA3; DAB; DAC; DAM MST, POET; DLB 5, 6, 152; EXPN; EXPP; FW; LAIT 4; MAWW; MTCW 1, 2; NFS 1; PAB; PFS 1, 15; RGAL 4; SATA 96; WP; YAW

Plato c. 428B.C.-347B.C. ... CMLC 8; WLCS
See also AW 1; CDWLB 1; DA; DA3; DAB; DAC; DAM MST; DLB 176; LAIT 1; RGWL 2

Platonov, Andrei
See Klimentov, Andrei Platonovich

Platt, Kin 1911- .... CLC 26
See also AAYA 11; CA 17-20R; CANR 11; JRDA; SAAS 17; SATA 21, 86; WYA

Plautus c. 254B.C.-c. 184B.C. ...... CMLC 24; DC 6
See also AW 1; CDWLB 1; DLB 211; RGWL 2

Plick et Plock
See Simenon, Georges (Jacques Christian)

Plieksans, Janis
See Rainis, Janis

Plimpton, George (Ames) 1927- .... CLC 36
See also AITN 1; CA 21-24R; CANR 32, 70, 103; DLB 185, 241; MTCW 1, 2; SATA 10

Pliny the Elder c. 23-79 .... CMLC 23
See also DLB 211

Plomer, William Charles Franklin
1903-1973 .... CLC 4, 8
See also AFW; CA 21-22; CANR 34; CAP 2; DLB 20, 162, 191, 225; MTCW 1; RGEL 2; RGSF 2; SATA 24

Plotinus 204-270 .... CMLC 46
See also CDWLB 1; DLB 176

Plowman, Piers
See Kavanagh, Patrick (Joseph)

Plum, J.
See Wodehouse, P(elham) G(renville)

Plumly, Stanley (Ross) 1939- .... CLC 33
See also CA 108; 110; CANR 97; CP 7; DLB 5, 193; INT 110

Plumpe, Friedrich Wilhelm
1888-1931 .... TCLC 53
See also CA 112

Po Chu-i 772-846 .... CMLC 24

Poe, Edgar Allan 1809-1849 ..... NCLC 1, 16, 55, 78, 94, 97; PC 1; SSC 1, 22, 34, 35, 54; WLC
See also AAYA 14; AMW; BPFB 3; BYA 5, 11; CDALB 1640-1865; CMW 4; DA; DA3; DAB; DAC; DAM MST, POET; DLB 3, 59, 73, 74, 248, 254; EXPP; EXPS; HGG; LAIT 2; MSW; PAB; PFS 1, 3, 9; RGAL 4; RGSF 2; SATA 23; SCFW 2; SFW 4; SSFS 2, 4, 7, 8; SUFW; WP; WYA

Poet of Titchfield Street, The
See Pound, Ezra (Weston Loomis)

Pohl, Frederik 1919- .... CLC 18; SSC 25
See also AAYA 24; CA 61-64; CAAE 188; CAAS 1; CANR 11, 37, 81; CN 7; DLB 8; INT CANR-11; MTCW 1, 2; SATA 24; SCFW 2; SFW 4

Poirier, Louis 1910-
See Gracq, Julien
See also CA 122; 126; CWW 2

Poitier, Sidney 1927- .... CLC 26
See also BW 1; CA 117; CANR 94

Polanski, Roman 1933- .... CLC 16
See also CA 77-80

Poliakoff, Stephen 1952- .... CLC 38
See also CA 106; CBD; CD 5; DLB 13

Police, The
See Copeland, Stewart (Armstrong); Summers, Andrew James; Sumner, Gordon Matthew

Polidori, John William 1795-1821 . NCLC 51
See also DLB 116; HGG

Pollitt, Katha 1949- .... CLC 28, 122
See also CA 120; 122; CANR 66, 108; MTCW 1, 2

Pollock, (Mary) Sharon 1936- .... CLC 50
See also CA 141; CD 5; CWD; DAC; DAM DRAM, MST; DFS 3; DLB 60; FW

Polo, Marco 1254-1324 .... CMLC 15

Polonsky, Abraham (Lincoln)
1910-1999 .... CLC 92
See also CA 104; 187; DLB 26; INT 104

Polybius c. 200B.C.-c. 118B.C. ...... CMLC 17
See also AW 1; DLB 176; RGWL 2

Pomerance, Bernard 1940- .... CLC 13
See also CA 101; CAD; CANR 49; CD 5; DAM DRAM; DFS 9; LAIT 2

Ponge, Francis 1899-1988 .... CLC 6, 18
See also CA 85-88; 126; CANR 40, 86; DAM POET; GFL 1789 to the Present; RGWL 2

Poniatowska, Elena 1933- . CLC 140; HLC 2
See also CA 101; CANR 32, 66, 107; CDWLB 3; DAM MULT; DLB 113; HW 1, 2; LAWS 1; WLIT 1

Pontoppidan, Henrik 1857-1943 .... TCLC 29
See also CA 170

Poole, Josephine .... CLC 17
See Helyar, Jane Penelope Josephine
See also SAAS 2; SATA 5

Popa, Vasko 1922-1991 .... CLC 19
See also CA 112; 148; CDWLB 4; DLB 181; RGWL 2

Pope, Alexander 1688-1744 ...... LC 3, 58, 60, 64; PC 26; WLC
See also BRW 3; BRWR 1; CDBLB 1660-1789; DA; DA3; DAB; DAC; DAM MST, POET; DLB 95, 101, 213; EXPP; PAB; PFS 12; RGEL 2; WLIT 3; WP

Popov, Yevgeny .... CLC 59

Porter, Connie (Rose) 1959(?)- .... CLC 70
See also BW 2, 3; CA 142; CANR 90, 109; SATA 81, 129

Porter, Gene(va Grace) Stratton .. TCLC 21
See also Stratton-Porter, Gene(va Grace)
See also BPFB 3; CA 112; CWRI 5; RHW

Porter, Katherine Anne 1890-1980 ... CLC 1, 3, 7, 10, 13, 15, 27, 101; SSC 4, 31, 43
See also AAYA 42; AITN 2; AMW; BPFB 3; CA 1-4R; 101; CANR 1, 65; CDALBS; DA; DA3; DAB; DAC; DAM MST, NOV; DLB 4, 9, 102; DLBD 12; DLBY 1980; EXPS; LAIT 3; MAWW; MTCW 1, 2; NFS 14; RGAL 4; RGSF 2; SATA 39; SATA-Obit 23; SSFS 1, 8, 11

Porter, Peter (Neville Frederick)
1929- .... CLC 5, 13, 33
See also CA 85-88; CP 7; DLB 40

Porter, William Sydney 1862-1910
See Henry, O.
See also CA 104; 131; CDALB 1865-1917; DA; DA3; DAB; DAC; DAM MST; DLB 12, 78, 79; MTCW 1, 2; YABC 2

Portillo (y Pacheco), Jose Lopez
See Lopez Portillo (y Pacheco), Jose

Portillo Trambley, Estela 1927-1998
See Trambley, Estela Portillo
See also CANR 32; DAM MULT; DLB 209; HLC 2; HW 1

Posse, Abel .... CLC 70

Post, Melville Davisson
1869-1930 .... TCLC 39
See also CA 110; 202; CMW 4

Potok, Chaim 1929-2002 ... CLC 2, 7, 14, 26, 112
See also AAYA 15; AITN 1, 2; BPFB 3; BYA 1; CA 17-20R; CANR 19, 35, 64, 98; CN 7; DA3; DAM NOV; DLB 28, 152; EXPN; INT CANR-19; LAIT 4; MTCW 1, 2; NFS 4; SATA 33, 106; YAW

Potter, Dennis (Christopher George)
1935-1994 .... CLC 58, 86, 123
See also CA 107; 145; CANR 33, 61; CBD; DLB 233; MTCW 1

Pound, Ezra (Weston Loomis)
1885-1972 .. CLC 1, 2, 3, 4, 5, 7, 10, 13, 18, 34, 48, 50, 112; PC 4; WLC
See also AMW; AMWR 1; CA 5-8R; 37-40R; CANR 40; CDALB 1917-1929; DA; DA3; DAB; DAC; DAM MST, POET; DLB 4, 45, 63; DLBD 15; EFS 2; EXPP; MTCW 1, 2; PAB; PFS 2, 8; RGAL 4; WP

Povod, Reinaldo 1959-1994 .... CLC 44
See also CA 136; 146; CANR 83

Powell, Adam Clayton, Jr.
1908-1972 .... CLC 89; BLC 3
See also BW 1, 3; CA 102; 33-36R; CANR 86; DAM MULT

Powell, Anthony (Dymoke)
1905-2000 .... CLC 1, 3, 7, 9, 10, 31
See also BRW 7; CA 1-4R; 189; CANR 1, 32, 62, 107; CDBLB 1945-1960; CN 7; DLB 15; MTCW 1, 2; RGEL 2; TEA

Powell, Dawn 1896(?)-1965 .... CLC 66
See also CA 5-8R; DLBY 1997

Powell, Padgett 1952- .... CLC 34
See also CA 126; CANR 63, 101; CSW; DLB 234; DLBY 01

Powell, (Oval) Talmage 1920-2000
See Queen, Ellery
See also CA 5-8R; CANR 2, 80

Power, Susan 1961- .... CLC 91
See also BYA 14; CA 160; NFS 11

Powers, J(ames) F(arl) 1917-1999 ..... CLC 1, 4, 8, 57; SSC 4
See also CA 1-4R; 181; CANR 2, 61; CN 7; DLB 130; MTCW 1; RGAL 4; RGSF 2

Powers, John J(ames) 1945-
See Powers, John R.
See also CA 69-72

Powers, John R. .... CLC 66
See also Powers, John J(ames)

Powers, Richard (S.) 1957- .... CLC 93
See also AMWS 9; BPFB 3; CA 148; CANR 80; CN 7

Pownall, David 1938- .... CLC 10
See also CA 89-92; 180; CAAS 18; CANR 49, 101; CBD; CD 5; CN 7; DLB 14

Powys, John Cowper 1872-1963 ... CLC 7, 9, 15, 46, 125
See also CA 85-88; CANR 106; DLB 15, 255; FANT; MTCW 1, 2; RGEL 2; SUFW

Powys, T(heodore) F(rancis)
1875-1953 .... TCLC 9
See also CA 106; 189; DLB 36, 162; FANT; RGEL 2; SUFW

Prado (Calvo), Pedro 1886-1952 ... TCLC 75
See also CA 131; HW 1; LAW

Prager, Emily 1952- .... CLC 56

Pratolini, Vasco 1913-1991 .... TCLC 124
See also DLB 177; RGWL 2

Pratt, E(dwin) J(ohn) 1883(?)-1964 . **CLC 19**
See also CA 141; 93-96; CANR 77; DAC; DAM POET; DLB 92; RGEL 2

Premchand .... **TCLC 21**
See also Srivastava, Dhanpat Rai

Preussler, Otfried 1923- .... **CLC 17**
See also CA 77-80; SATA 24

Prevert, Jacques (Henri Marie)
1900-1977 .... **CLC 15**
See also CA 77-80; 69-72; CANR 29, 61; DLB 258; GFL 1789 to the Present; IDFW 3, 4; MTCW 1; RGWL 2; SATA-Obit 30

Prevost, (Antoine Francois)
1697-1763 .... **LC 1**
See also EW 4; GFL Beginnings to 1789; RGWL 2

Price, (Edward) Reynolds 1933- ... **CLC 3, 6, 13, 43, 50, 63; SSC 22**
See also AMWS 6; CA 1-4R; CANR 1, 37, 57, 87; CN 7; CSW; DAM NOV; DLB 2, 218; INT CANR-37

Price, Richard 1949- .... **CLC 6, 12**
See also CA 49-52; CANR 3; DLBY 1981

Prichard, Katharine Susannah
1883-1969 .... **CLC 46**
See also CA 11-12; CANR 33; CAP 1; DLB 260; MTCW 1; RGEL 2; RGSF 2; SATA 66

Priestley, J(ohn) B(oynton)
1894-1984 .... **CLC 2, 5, 9, 34**
See also BRW 7; CA 9-12R; 113; CANR 33; CDBLB 1914-1945; DA3; DAM DRAM, NOV; DLB 10, 34, 77, 100, 139; DLBY 1984; MTCW 1, 2; RGEL 2; SFW 4

Prince 1958(?)- .... **CLC 35**

Prince, F(rank) T(empleton) 1912- .. **CLC 22**
See also CA 101; CANR 43, 79; CP 7; DLB 20

Prince Kropotkin
See Kropotkin, Peter (Aleksieevich)

Prior, Matthew 1664-1721 .... **LC 4**
See also DLB 95; RGEL 2

Prishvin, Mikhail 1873-1954 .... **TCLC 75**

Pritchard, William H(arrison)
1932- .... **CLC 34**
See also CA 65-68; CANR 23, 95; DLB 111

Pritchett, V(ictor) S(awdon)
1900-1997 ...... **CLC 5, 13, 15, 41; SSC 14**
See also BPFB 3; BRWS 3; CA 61-64; 157; CANR 31, 63; CN 7; DA3; DAM NOV; DLB 15, 139; MTCW 1, 2; RGEL 2; RGSF 2

Private 19022
See Manning, Frederic

Probst, Mark 1925- .... **CLC 59**
See also CA 130

Prokosch, Frederic 1908-1989 ...... **CLC 4, 48**
See also CA 73-76; 128; CANR 82; DLB 48; MTCW 2

Propertius, Sextus c. 50B.C.-c.
16B.C. .... **CMLC 32**
See also AW 2; CDWLB 1; DLB 211; RGWL 2

Prophet, The
See Dreiser, Theodore (Herman Albert)

Prose, Francine 1947- .... **CLC 45**
See also CA 109; 112; CANR 46, 95; DLB 234; SATA 101

Proudhon
See Cunha, Euclides (Rodrigues Pimenta) da

Proulx, Annie
See Proulx, E(dna) Annie

Proulx, E(dna) Annie 1935- ...... **CLC 81, 158**
See also AMWS 7; BPFB 3; CA 145; CANR 65; CN 7; CPW 1; DA3; DAM POP; MTCW 2

Proust,
(Valentin-Louis-George-Eugene-)Marcel
1871-1922 .... **TCLC 7, 13, 33; WLC**
See also BPFB 3; CA 104; 120; DA; DA3; DAB; DAC; DAM MST, NOV; DLB 65; EW 8; GFL 1789 to the Present; MTCW 1, 2; RGWL 2

Prowler, Harley
See Masters, Edgar Lee

Prus, Boleslaw 1845-1912 .... **TCLC 48**
See also RGWL 2

Pryor, Richard (Franklin Lenox Thomas)
1940- .... **CLC 26**
See also CA 122; 152

Przybyszewski, Stanislaw
1868-1927 .... **TCLC 36**
See also CA 160; DLB 66

Pteleon
See Grieve, C(hristopher) M(urray)
See also DAM POET

Puckett, Lute
See Masters, Edgar Lee

Puig, Manuel 1932-1990 .... **CLC 3, 5, 10, 28, 65, 133; HLC 2**
See also BPFB 3; CA 45-48; CANR 2, 32, 63; CDWLB 3; DA3; DAM MULT; DLB 113; DNFS 1; GLL 1; HW 1, 2; LAW; MTCW 1, 2; RGWL 2; WLIT 1

Pulitzer, Joseph 1847-1911 .... **TCLC 76**
See also CA 114; DLB 23

Purchas, Samuel 1577(?)-1626 .... **LC 70**
See also DLB 151

Purdy, A(lfred) W(ellington)
1918-2000 .... **CLC 3, 6, 14, 50**
See also CA 81-84; 189; CAAS 17; CANR 42, 66; CP 7; DAC; DAM MST, POET; DLB 88; PFS 5; RGEL 2

Purdy, James (Amos) 1923- .... **CLC 2, 4, 10, 28, 52**
See also AMWS 7; CA 33-36R; CAAS 1; CANR 19, 51; CN 7; DLB 2, 218; INT CANR-19; MTCW 1; RGAL 4

Pure, Simon
See Swinnerton, Frank Arthur

Pushkin, Aleksandr Sergeevich
See Pushkin, Alexander (Sergeyevich)
See also DLB 205

Pushkin, Alexander (Sergeyevich)
1799-1837 .... **NCLC 3, 27, 83; PC 10; SSC 27; WLC**
See also DA; DA3; DAB; DAC; DAM DRAM, MST, POET; EW 5; EXPS; RGSF 2; RGWL 2; SATA 61; SSFS 9

P'u Sung-ling 1640-1715 .... **LC 49; SSC 31**

Putnam, Arthur Lee
See Alger, Horatio, Jr.

Puzo, Mario 1920-1999 .... **CLC 1, 2, 6, 36, 107**
See also BPFB 3; CA 65-68; 185; CANR 4, 42, 65, 99; CN 7; CPW; DA3; DAM NOV, POP; DLB 6; MTCW 1, 2; RGAL 4

Pygge, Edward
See Barnes, Julian (Patrick)

Pyle, Ernest Taylor 1900-1945
See Pyle, Ernie
See also CA 115; 160

Pyle, Ernie .... **TCLC 75**
See also Pyle, Ernest Taylor
See also DLB 29; MTCW 2

Pyle, Howard 1853-1911 .... **TCLC 81**
See also BYA 2, 4; CA 109; 137; CLR 22; DLB 42, 188; DLBD 13; LAIT 1; MAICYA 1, 2; SATA 16, 100; WCH; YAW

Pym, Barbara (Mary Crampton)
1913-1980 .... **CLC 13, 19, 37, 111**
See also BPFB 3; BRWS 2; CA 13-14; 97-100; CANR 13, 34; CAP 1; DLB 14, 207; DLBY 1987; MTCW 1, 2; RGEL 2; TEA

Pynchon, Thomas (Ruggles, Jr.)
1937- ...... **CLC 2, 3, 6, 9, 11, 18, 33, 62, 72, 123; SSC 14; WLC**
See also AMWS 2; BEST 90:2; BPFB 3; CA 17-20R; CANR 22, 46, 73; CN 7; CPW 1; DA; DA3; DAB; DAC; DAM MST, NOV, POP; DLB 2, 173; MTCW 1, 2; RGAL 4; SFW 4; TUS

Pythagoras c. 582B.C.-c. 507B.C. . **CMLC 22**
See also DLB 176

Q
See Quiller-Couch, Sir Arthur (Thomas)

Qian, Chongzhu
See Ch'ien, Chung-shu

Qian Zhongshu
See Ch'ien, Chung-shu

Qroll
See Dagerman, Stig (Halvard)

Quarrington, Paul (Lewis) 1953- ...... **CLC 65**
See also CA 129; CANR 62, 95

Quasimodo, Salvatore 1901-1968 ...... **CLC 10**
See also CA 13-16; 25-28R; CAP 1; DLB 114; EW 12; MTCW 1; RGWL 2

Quatermass, Martin
See Carpenter, John (Howard)

Quay, Stephen 1947- .... **CLC 95**
See also CA 189

Quay, Timothy 1947- .... **CLC 95**
See also CA 189

Queen, Ellery .... **CLC 3, 11**
See also Deming, Richard; Dannay, Frederic; Davidson, Avram (James); Fairman, Paul W.; Flora, Fletcher; Hoch, Edward D(entinger); Kane, Henry; Lee, Manfred B(ennington); Marlowe, Stephen; Powell, (Oval) Talmage; Sheldon, Walter J(ames); Sturgeon, Theodore (Hamilton); Tracy, Don(ald Fiske); Vance, John Holbrook
See also BPFB 3; CMW 4; MSW; RGAL 4

Queen, Ellery, Jr.
See Dannay, Frederic; Lee, Manfred B(ennington)

Queneau, Raymond 1903-1976 ..... **CLC 2, 5, 10, 42**
See also CA 77-80; 69-72; CANR 32; DLB 72, 258; EW 12; GFL 1789 to the Present; MTCW 1, 2; RGWL 2

Quevedo, Francisco de 1580-1645 .... **LC 23**

Quiller-Couch, Sir Arthur (Thomas)
1863-1944 .... **TCLC 53**
See also CA 118; 166; DLB 135, 153, 190; HGG; RGEL 2; SUFW

Quin, Ann (Marie) 1936-1973 .... **CLC 6**
See also CA 9-12R; 45-48; DLB 14, 231

Quinn, Martin
See Smith, Martin Cruz

Quinn, Peter 1947- .... **CLC 91**
See also CA 197

Quinn, Simon
See Smith, Martin Cruz

Quintana, Leroy V. 1944- .... **PC 36**
See also CA 131; CANR 65; DAM MULT; DLB 82; HLC 2; HW 1, 2

Quiroga, Horacio (Sylvestre)
1878-1937 .... **TCLC 20; HLC 2**
See also CA 117; 131; DAM MULT; HW 1; LAW; MTCW 1; RGSF 2; WLIT 1

Quoirez, Francoise 1935- .... **CLC 9**
See also Sagan, Francoise
See also CA 49-52; CANR 6, 39, 73; CWW 2; MTCW 1, 2

Raabe, Wilhelm (Karl) 1831-1910 . **TCLC 45**
See also CA 167; DLB 129

Rabe, David (William) 1940- .. **CLC 4, 8, 33; DC 16**
See also CA 85-88; CABS 3; CAD; CANR 59; CD 5; DAM DRAM; DFS 3, 8, 13; DLB 7, 228

Rabelais, Francois 1494-1553 .... **LC 5, 60; WLC**
See also DA; DAB; DAC; DAM MST; EW 2; GFL Beginnings to 1789; RGWL 2

Rabinovitch, Sholem 1859-1916
See Aleichem, Sholom
See also CA 104

Rabinyan, Dorit 1972- .... **CLC 119**
See also CA 170

Rachilde
See Vallette, Marguerite Eymery

Racine, Jean 1639-1699 .... **LC 28**
See also DA3; DAB; DAM MST; EW 3; GFL Beginnings to 1789; RGWL 2

Radcliffe, Ann (Ward) 1764-1823 ... **NCLC 6, 55, 106**
See also DLB 39, 178; HGG; RGEL 2; SUFW; WLIT 3

Radclyffe-Hall, Marguerite
See Hall, (Marguerite) Radclyffe

Radiguet, Raymond 1903-1923 ...... **TCLC 29**
See also CA 162; DLB 65; GFL 1789 to the Present; RGWL 2

Radnoti, Miklos 1909-1944 .... **TCLC 16**
See also CA 118; CDWLB 4; DLB 215; RGWL 2

Rado, James 1939- .... **CLC 17**
See also CA 105

Radvanyi, Netty 1900-1983
See Seghers, Anna
See also CA 85-88; 110; CANR 82

Rae, Ben
See Griffiths, Trevor

Raeburn, John (Hay) 1941- .... **CLC 34**
See also CA 57-60

Ragni, Gerome 1942-1991 .... **CLC 17**
See also CA 105; 134

Rahv, Philip .... **CLC 24**
See also Greenberg, Ivan
See also DLB 137

Raimund, Ferdinand Jakob
1790-1836 .... **NCLC 69**
See also DLB 90

Raine, Craig (Anthony) 1944- .. **CLC 32, 103**
See also CA 108; CANR 29, 51, 103; CP 7; DLB 40; PFS 7

Raine, Kathleen (Jessie) 1908- ..... **CLC 7, 45**
See also CA 85-88; CANR 46, 109; CP 7; DLB 20; MTCW 1; RGEL 2

Rainis, Janis 1865-1929 .... **TCLC 29**
See also CA 170; CDWLB 4; DLB 220

Rakosi, Carl .... **CLC 47**
See also Rawley, Callman
See also CAAS 5; CP 7; DLB 193

Ralegh, Sir Walter
See Raleigh, Sir Walter
See also BRW 1; RGEL 2; WP

Raleigh, Richard
See Lovecraft, H(oward) P(hillips)

Raleigh, Sir Walter 1554(?)-1618 .... **LC 31, 39; PC 31**
See also Ralegh, Sir Walter
See also CDBLB Before 1660; DLB 172; EXPP; PFS 14; TEA

Rallentando, H. P.
See Sayers, Dorothy L(eigh)

Ramal, Walter
See de la Mare, Walter (John)

Ramana Maharshi 1879-1950 .... **TCLC 84**

Ramoacn y Cajal, Santiago
1852-1934 .... **TCLC 93**

Ramon, Juan
See Jimenez (Mantecon), Juan Ramon

Ramos, Graciliano 1892-1953 .... **TCLC 32**
See also CA 167; HW 2; LAW; WLIT 1

Rampersad, Arnold 1941- .... **CLC 44**
See also BW 2, 3; CA 127; 133; CANR 81; DLB 111; INT 133

Rampling, Anne
See Rice, Anne
See also GLL 2

Ramsay, Allan 1686(?)-1758 .... **LC 29**
See also DLB 95; RGEL 2

Ramsay, Jay
See Campbell, (John) Ramsey

Ramuz, Charles-Ferdinand
1878-1947 .... **TCLC 33**
See also CA 165

Rand, Ayn 1905-1982 ...... **CLC 3, 30, 44, 79; WLC**
See also AAYA 10; AMWS 4; BPFB 3; BYA 12; CA 13-16R; 105; CANR 27, 73; CDALBS; CPW; DA; DA3; DAC; DAM MST, NOV, POP; DLB 227; MTCW 1, 2; NFS 10; RGAL 4; SFW 4; YAW

Randall, Dudley (Felker) 1914-2000 . **CLC 1, 135; BLC 3**
See also BW 1, 3; CA 25-28R; 189; CANR 23, 82; DAM MULT; DLB 41; PFS 5

Randall, Robert
See Silverberg, Robert

Ranger, Ken
See Creasey, John

Rank, Otto 1884-1939 .... **TCLC 115**

Ransom, John Crowe 1888-1974 .. **CLC 2, 4, 5, 11, 24**
See also AMW; CA 5-8R; 49-52; CANR 6, 34; CDALBS; DA3; DAM POET; DLB 45, 63; EXPP; MTCW 1, 2; RGAL 4

Rao, Raja 1909- .... **CLC 25, 56**
See also CA 73-76; CANR 51; CN 7; DAM NOV; MTCW 1, 2; RGEL 2; RGSF 2

Raphael, Frederic (Michael) 1931- ... **CLC 2, 14**
See also CA 1-4R; CANR 1, 86; CN 7; DLB 14

Ratcliffe, James P.
See Mencken, H(enry) L(ouis)

Rathbone, Julian 1935- .... **CLC 41**
See also CA 101; CANR 34, 73

Rattigan, Terence (Mervyn)
1911-1977 .... **CLC 7; DC 18**
See also BRWS 7; CA 85-88; 73-76; CBD; CDBLB 1945-1960; DAM DRAM; DFS 8; DLB 13; IDFW 3, 4; MTCW 1, 2; RGEL 2

Ratushinskaya, Irina 1954- .... **CLC 54**
See also CA 129; CANR 68; CWW 2

Raven, Simon (Arthur Noel)
1927-2001 .... **CLC 14**
See also CA 81-84; 197; CANR 86; CN 7

Ravenna, Michael
See Welty, Eudora (Alice)

Rawley, Callman 1903-
See Rakosi, Carl
See also CA 21-24R; CANR 12, 32, 91

Rawlings, Marjorie Kinnan
1896-1953 .... **TCLC 4**
See also AAYA 20; AMWS 10; ANW; BPFB 3; BYA 3; CA 105; 137; CANR 74; CLR 63; DLB 9, 22, 102; DLBD 17; JRDA; MAICYA 1, 2; MTCW 2; RGAL 4; SATA 100; WCH; YABC 1; YAW

Ray, Satyajit 1921-1992 .... **CLC 16, 76**
See also CA 114; 137; DAM MULT

Read, Herbert Edward 1893-1968 ..... **CLC 4**
See also BRW 6; CA 85-88; 25-28R; DLB 20, 149; PAB; RGEL 2

Read, Piers Paul 1941- .... **CLC 4, 10, 25**
See also CA 21-24R; CANR 38, 86; CN 7; DLB 14; SATA 21

Reade, Charles 1814-1884 .... **NCLC 2, 74**
See also DLB 21; RGEL 2

Reade, Hamish
See Gray, Simon (James Holliday)

Reading, Peter 1946- .... **CLC 47**
See also CA 103; CANR 46, 96; CP 7; DLB 40

Reaney, James 1926- .... **CLC 13**
See also CA 41-44R; CAAS 15; CANR 42; CD 5; CP 7; DAC; DAM MST; DLB 68; RGEL 2; SATA 43

Rebreanu, Liviu 1885-1944 .... **TCLC 28**
See also CA 165; DLB 220

Rechy, John (Francisco) 1934- ...... **CLC 1, 7, 14, 18, 107; HLC 2**
See also CA 5-8R; CAAE 195; CAAS 4; CANR 6, 32, 64; CN 7; DAM MULT; DLB 122; DLBY 1982; HW 1, 2; INT CANR-6; RGAL 4

Redcam, Tom 1870-1933 .... **TCLC 25**

Reddin, Keith .... **CLC 67**
See also CAD

Redgrove, Peter (William) 1932- . **CLC 6, 41**
See also BRWS 6; CA 1-4R; CANR 3, 39, 77; CP 7; DLB 40

Redmon, Anne .... **CLC 22**
See also Nightingale, Anne Redmon
See also DLBY 1986

Reed, Eliot
See Ambler, Eric

Reed, Ishmael 1938- .. **CLC 2, 3, 5, 6, 13, 32, 60; BLC 3**
See also AFAW 1, 2; AMWS 10; BPFB 3; BW 2, 3; CA 21-24R; CANR 25, 48, 74; CN 7; CP 7; CSW; DA3; DAM MULT; DLB 2, 5, 33, 169, 227; DLBD 8; MSW; MTCW 1, 2; PFS 6; RGAL 4; TCWW 2

Reed, John (Silas) 1887-1920 .... **TCLC 9**
See also CA 106; 195

Reed, Lou .... **CLC 21**
See also Firbank, Louis

Reese, Lizette Woodworth 1856-1935 . **PC 29**
See also CA 180; DLB 54

Reeve, Clara 1729-1807 .... **NCLC 19**
See also DLB 39; RGEL 2

Reich, Wilhelm 1897-1957 .... **TCLC 57**
See also CA 199

Reid, Christopher (John) 1949- .... **CLC 33**
See also CA 140; CANR 89; CP 7; DLB 40

Reid, Desmond
See Moorcock, Michael (John)

Reid Banks, Lynne 1929-
See Banks, Lynne Reid
See also AAYA 6; CA 1-4R; CANR 6, 22, 38, 87; CLR 24; CN 7; JRDA; MAICYA 1, 2; SATA 22, 75, 111; YAW

Reilly, William K.
See Creasey, John

Reiner, Max
See Caldwell, (Janet Miriam) Taylor (Holland)

Reis, Ricardo
See Pessoa, Fernando (Antonio Nogueira)

Remarque, Erich Maria 1898-1970 . **CLC 21**
See also AAYA 27; BPFB 3; CA 77-80; 29-32R; CDWLB 2; DA; DA3; DAB; DAC; DAM MST, NOV; DLB 56; EXPN; LAIT 3; MTCW 1, 2; NFS 4; RGWL 2

Remington, Frederic 1861-1909 ..... **TCLC 89**
See also CA 108; 169; DLB 12, 186, 188; SATA 41

Remizov, A.
See Remizov, Aleksei (Mikhailovich)

Remizov, A. M.
See Remizov, Aleksei (Mikhailovich)

Remizov, Aleksei (Mikhailovich)
1877-1957 .... **TCLC 27**
See also CA 125; 133

Renan, Joseph Ernest 1823-1892 .. **NCLC 26**
See also GFL 1789 to the Present
Renard, Jules 1864-1910 .... **TCLC 17**
See also CA 117; GFL 1789 to the Present
Renault, Mary .... **CLC 3, 11, 17**
See also Challans, Mary
See also BPFB 3; BYA 2; DLBY 1983; GLL 1; LAIT 1; MTCW 2; RGEL 2; RHW
Rendell, Ruth (Barbara) 1930- .. **CLC 28, 48**
See also Vine, Barbara
See also BPFB 3; CA 109; CANR 32, 52, 74; CN 7; CPW; DAM POP; DLB 87; INT CANR-32; MSW; MTCW 1, 2
Renoir, Jean 1894-1979 .... **CLC 20**
See also CA 129; 85-88
Resnais, Alain 1922- .... **CLC 16**
Reverdy, Pierre 1889-1960 .... **CLC 53**
See also CA 97-100; 89-92; DLB 258; GFL 1789 to the Present
Rexroth, Kenneth 1905-1982 .... **CLC 1, 2, 6, 11, 22, 49, 112; PC 20**
See also CA 5-8R; 107; CANR 14, 34, 63; CDALB 1941-1968; DAM POET; DLB 16, 48, 165, 212; DLBY 1982; INT CANR-14; MTCW 1, 2; RGAL 4
Reyes, Alfonso 1889-1959 .. **TCLC 33; HLCS 2**
See also CA 131; HW 1; LAW
Reyes y Basoalto, Ricardo Eliecer Neftali
See Neruda, Pablo
Reymont, Wladyslaw (Stanislaw)
1868(?)-1925 .... **TCLC 5**
See also CA 104
Reynolds, Jonathan 1942- .... **CLC 6, 38**
See also CA 65-68; CANR 28
Reynolds, Joshua 1723-1792 .... **LC 15**
See also DLB 104
Reynolds, Michael S(hane)
1937-2000 .... **CLC 44**
See also CA 65-68; 189; CANR 9, 89, 97
Reznikoff, Charles 1894-1976 .... **CLC 9**
See also CA 33-36; 61-64; CAP 2; DLB 28, 45; WP
Rezzori (d'Arezzo), Gregor von
1914-1998 .... **CLC 25**
See also CA 122; 136; 167
Rhine, Richard
See Silverstein, Alvin; Silverstein, Virginia B(arbara Opshelor)
Rhodes, Eugene Manlove
1869-1934 .... **TCLC 53**
See also CA 198; DLB 256
R'hoone, Lord
See Balzac, Honore de
Rhys, Jean 1894(?)-1979 ...... **CLC 2, 4, 6, 14, 19, 51, 124; SSC 21**
See also BRWS 2; CA 25-28R; 85-88; CANR 35, 62; CDBLB 1945-1960; CDWLB 3; DA3; DAM NOV; DLB 36, 117, 162; DNFS 2; MTCW 1, 2; RGEL 2; RGSF 2; RHW; TEA
Ribeiro, Darcy 1922-1997 .... **CLC 34**
See also CA 33-36R; 156
Ribeiro, Joao Ubaldo (Osorio Pimentel)
1941- .... **CLC 10, 67**
See also CA 81-84
Ribman, Ronald (Burt) 1932- .... **CLC 7**
See also CA 21-24R; CAD; CANR 46, 80; CD 5
Ricci, Nino 1959- .... **CLC 70**
See also CA 137; CCA 1
Rice, Anne 1941- .... **CLC 41, 128**
See also Rampling, Anne
See also AAYA 9; AMWS 7; BEST 89:2; BPFB 3; CA 65-68; CANR 12, 36, 53, 74, 100; CN 7; CPW; CSW; DA3; DAM POP; GLL 2; HGG; MTCW; YAW

Rice, Elmer (Leopold) 1892-1967 .... **CLC 7, 49**
See also CA 21-22; 25-28R; CAP 2; DAM DRAM; DFS 12; DLB 4, 7; MTCW 1, 2; RGAL 4
Rice, Tim(othy Miles Bindon)
1944- .... **CLC 21**
See also CA 103; CANR 46; DFS 7
Rich, Adrienne (Cecile) 1929- ... **CLC 3, 6, 7, 11, 18, 36, 73, 76, 125; PC 5**
See also AMWS 1; CA 9-12R; CANR 20, 53, 74; CDALBS; CP 7; CSW; CWP; DA3; DAM POET; DLB 5, 67; EXPP; FW; MAWW; MTCW 1, 2; PAB; PFS 15; RGAL 4; WP
Rich, Barbara
See Graves, Robert (von Ranke)
Rich, Robert
See Trumbo, Dalton
Richard, Keith .... **CLC 17**
See also Richards, Keith
Richards, David Adams 1950- .... **CLC 59**
See also CA 93-96; CANR 60; DAC; DLB 53
Richards, I(vor) A(rmstrong)
1893-1979 .... **CLC 14, 24**
See also BRWS 2; CA 41-44R; 89-92; CANR 34, 74; DLB 27; MTCW 2; RGEL 2
Richards, Keith 1943-
See Richard, Keith
See also CA 107; CANR 77
Richardson, Anne
See Roiphe, Anne (Richardson)
Richardson, Dorothy Miller
1873-1957 .... **TCLC 3**
See also CA 104; 192; DLB 36; FW; RGEL 2
Richardson (Robertson), Ethel Florence Lindesay 1870-1946
See Richardson, Henry Handel
See also CA 105; 190; DLB 230; RHW
Richardson, Henry Handel .... **TCLC 4**
See also Richardson (Robertson), Ethel Florence Lindesay
See also DLB 197; RGEL 2; RGSF 2
Richardson, John 1796-1852 .... **NCLC 55**
See also CCA 1; DAC; DLB 99
Richardson, Samuel 1689-1761 ...... **LC 1, 44; WLC**
See also BRW 3; CDBLB 1660-1789; DA; DAB; DAC; DAM MST, NOV; DLB 39; RGEL 2; WLIT 3
Richler, Mordecai 1931-2001 .... **CLC 3, 5, 9, 13, 18, 46, 70**
See also AITN 1; CA 65-68; 201; CANR 31, 62; CCA 1; CLR 17; CWRI 5; DAC; DAM MST, NOV; DLB 53; MAICYA 1, 2; MTCW 1, 2; RGEL 2; SATA 44, 98; SATA-Brief 27
Richter, Conrad (Michael)
1890-1968 .... **CLC 30**
See also AAYA 21; BYA 2; CA 5-8R; 25-28R; CANR 23; DLB 9, 212; LAIT 1; MTCW 1, 2; RGAL 4; SATA 3; TCWW 2; YAW
Ricostranza, Tom
See Ellis, Trey
Riddell, Charlotte 1832-1906 .... **TCLC 40**
See also Riddell, Mrs. J. H.
See also CA 165; DLB 156
Riddell, Mrs. J. H.
See Riddell, Charlotte
See also HGG; SUFW
Ridge, John Rollin 1827-1867 .... **NCLC 82**
See also CA 144; DAM MULT; DLB 175; NNAL
Ridgeway, Jason
See Marlowe, Stephen

Ridgway, Keith 1965- .... **CLC 119**
See also CA 172
Riding, Laura .... **CLC 3, 7**
See also Jackson, Laura (Riding)
See also RGAL 4
Riefenstahl, Berta Helene Amalia 1902-
See Riefenstahl, Leni
See also CA 108
Riefenstahl, Leni .... **CLC 16**
See also Riefenstahl, Berta Helene Amalia
Riffe, Ernest
See Bergman, (Ernst) Ingmar
Riggs, (Rolla) Lynn 1899-1954 .... **TCLC 56**
See also CA 144; DAM MULT; DLB 175; NNAL
Riis, Jacob A(ugust) 1849-1914 ..... **TCLC 80**
See also CA 113; 168; DLB 23
Riley, James Whitcomb
1849-1916 .... **TCLC 51**
See also CA 118; 137; DAM POET; MAICYA 1, 2; RGAL 4; SATA 17
Riley, Tex
See Creasey, John
Rilke, Rainer Maria 1875-1926 .. **TCLC 1, 6, 19; PC 2**
See also CA 104; 132; CANR 62, 99; CDWLB 2; DA3; DAM POET; DLB 81; EW 9; MTCW 1, 2; RGWL 2; WP
Rimbaud, (Jean Nicolas) Arthur
1854-1891 .... **NCLC 4, 35, 82; PC 3; WLC**
See also DA; DA3; DAB; DAC; DAM MST, POET; DLB 217; EW 7; GFL 1789 to the Present; RGWL 2; TWA; WP
Rinehart, Mary Roberts
1876-1958 .... **TCLC 52**
See also BPFB 3; CA 108; 166; RGAL 4; RHW
Ringmaster, The
See Mencken, H(enry) L(ouis)
Ringwood, Gwen(dolyn Margaret) Pharis
1910-1984 .... **CLC 48**
See also CA 148; 112; DLB 88
Rio, Michel 1945(?)- .... **CLC 43**
See also CA 201
Ritsos, Giannes
See Ritsos, Yannis
Ritsos, Yannis 1909-1990 .... **CLC 6, 13, 31**
See also CA 77-80; 133; CANR 39, 61; EW 12; MTCW 1; RGWL 2
Ritter, Erika 1948(?)- .... **CLC 52**
See also CD 5; CWD
Rivera, Jose Eustasio 1889-1928 ... **TCLC 35**
See also CA 162; HW 1, 2; LAW
Rivera, Tomas 1935-1984
See also CA 49-52; CANR 32; DLB 82; HLCS 2; HW 1; RGAL 4; SSFS 15; TCWW 2; WLIT 1
Rivers, Conrad Kent 1933-1968 .... **CLC 1**
See also BW 1; CA 85-88; DLB 41
Rivers, Elfrida
See Bradley, Marion Zimmer
See also GLL 1
Riverside, John
See Heinlein, Robert A(nson)
Rizal, Jose 1861-1896 .... **NCLC 27**
Roa Bastos, Augusto (Antonio)
1917- .... **CLC 45; HLC 2**
See also CA 131; DAM MULT; DLB 113; HW 1; LAW; RGSF 2; WLIT 1
Robbe-Grillet, Alain 1922- .... **CLC 1, 2, 4, 6, 8, 10, 14, 43, 128**
See also BPFB 3; CA 9-12R; CANR 33, 65; DLB 83; EW 13; GFL 1789 to the Present; IDFW 3, 4; MTCW 1, 2; RGWL 2; SSFS 15
Robbins, Harold 1916-1997 .... **CLC 5**
See also BPFB 3; CA 73-76; 162; CANR 26, 54; DA3; DAM NOV; MTCW 1, 2

Robbins, Thomas Eugene 1936-
See Robbins, Tom
See also CA 81-84; CANR 29, 59, 95; CN 7; CPW; CSW; DA3; DAM NOV, POP; MTCW 1, 2

Robbins, Tom .... **CLC 9, 32, 64**
See also Robbins, Thomas Eugene
See also AAYA 32; AMWS 10; BEST 90:3; BPFB 3; DLBY 1980; MTCW 2

Robbins, Trina 1938- .... **CLC 21**
See also CA 128

Roberts, Charles G(eorge) D(ouglas)
1860-1943 .... **TCLC 8**
See also CA 105; 188; CLR 33; CWRI 5; DLB 92; RGEL 2; RGSF 2; SATA 88; SATA-Brief 29

Roberts, Elizabeth Madox
1886-1941 .... **TCLC 68**
See also CA 111; 166; CWRI 5; DLB 9, 54, 102; RGAL 4; RHW; SATA 33; SATA-Brief 27; WCH

Roberts, Kate 1891-1985 .... **CLC 15**
See also CA 107; 116

Roberts, Keith (John Kingston)
1935-2000 .... **CLC 14**
See also CA 25-28R; CANR 46; DLB 261; SFW 4

Roberts, Kenneth (Lewis)
1885-1957 .... **TCLC 23**
See also CA 109; 199; DLB 9; RGAL 4; RHW

Roberts, Michele (Brigitte) 1949- .... **CLC 48**
See also CA 115; CANR 58; CN 7; DLB 231; FW

Robertson, Ellis
See Ellison, Harlan (Jay); Silverberg, Robert

Robertson, Thomas William
1829-1871 .... **NCLC 35**
See also Robertson, Tom
See also DAM DRAM

Robertson, Tom
See Robertson, Thomas William
See also RGEL 2

Robeson, Kenneth
See Dent, Lester

Robinson, Edwin Arlington
1869-1935 .... **TCLC 5, 101; PC 1, 35**
See also AMW; CA 104; 133; CDALB 1865-1917; DA; DAC; DAM MST, POET; DLB 54; EXPP; MTCW 1, 2; PAB; PFS 4; RGAL 4; WP

Robinson, Henry Crabb
1775-1867 .... **NCLC 15**
See also DLB 107

Robinson, Jill 1936- .... **CLC 10**
See also CA 102; INT 102

Robinson, Kim Stanley 1952- .... **CLC 34**
See also AAYA 26; CA 126; CN 7; SATA 109; SCFW 2; SFW 4

Robinson, Lloyd
See Silverberg, Robert

Robinson, Marilynne 1944- .... **CLC 25**
See also CA 116; CANR 80; CN 7; DLB 206

Robinson, Smokey .... **CLC 21**
See also Robinson, William, Jr.

Robinson, William, Jr. 1940-
See Robinson, Smokey
See also CA 116

Robison, Mary 1949- .... **CLC 42, 98**
See also CA 113; 116; CANR 87; CN 7; DLB 130; INT 116; RGSF 2

Rochester
See Wilmot, John
See also RGEL 2

Rod, Edouard 1857-1910 .... **TCLC 52**

Roddenberry, Eugene Wesley 1921-1991
See Roddenberry, Gene
See also CA 110; 135; CANR 37; SATA 45; SATA-Obit 69

Roddenberry, Gene .... **CLC 17**
See also Roddenberry, Eugene Wesley
See also AAYA 5; SATA-Obit 69

Rodgers, Mary 1931- .... **CLC 12**
See also BYA 5; CA 49-52; CANR 8, 55, 90; CLR 20; CWRI 5; INT CANR-8; JRDA; MAICYA 1, 2; SATA 8, 130

Rodgers, W(illiam) R(obert)
1909-1969 .... **CLC 7**
See also CA 85-88; DLB 20; RGEL 2

Rodman, Eric
See Silverberg, Robert

Rodman, Howard 1920(?)-1985 .... **CLC 65**
See also CA 118

Rodman, Maia
See Wojciechowska, Maia (Teresa)

Rodo, Jose Enrique 1871(?)-1917
See also CA 178; HLCS 2; HW 2; LAW

Rodolph, Utto
See Ouologuem, Yambo

Rodriguez, Claudio 1934-1999 .... **CLC 10**
See also CA 188; DLB 134

Rodriguez, Richard 1944- .... **CLC 155; HLC 2**
See also CA 110; CANR 66; DAM MULT; DLB 82, 256; HW 1, 2; LAIT 5; NCFS 3; WLIT 1

Roelvaag, O(le) E(dvart) 1876-1931
See Rolvaag, O(le) E(dvart)
See also CA 117; 171

Roethke, Theodore (Huebner)
1908-1963 .... **CLC 1, 3, 8, 11, 19, 46, 101; PC 15**
See also AMW; CA 81-84; CABS 2; CDALB 1941-1968; DA3; DAM POET; DLB 5, 206; EXPP; MTCW 1, 2; PAB; PFS 3; RGAL 4; WP

Rogers, Samuel 1763-1855 .... **NCLC 69**
See also DLB 93; RGEL 2

Rogers, Thomas Hunton 1927- .... **CLC 57**
See also CA 89-92; INT 89-92

Rogers, Will(iam Penn Adair)
1879-1935 .... **TCLC 8, 71**
See also CA 105; 144; DA3; DAM MULT; DLB 11; MTCW 2; NNAL

Rogin, Gilbert 1929- .... **CLC 18**
See also CA 65-68; CANR 15

Rohan, Koda
See Koda Shigeyuki

Rohlfs, Anna Katharine Green
See Green, Anna Katharine

Rohmer, Eric .... **CLC 16**
See also Scherer, Jean-Marie Maurice

Rohmer, Sax .... **TCLC 28**
See also Ward, Arthur Henry Sarsfield
See also DLB 70; MSW; SUFW

Roiphe, Anne (Richardson) 1935- .. **CLC 3, 9**
See also CA 89-92; CANR 45, 73; DLBY 1980; INT 89-92

Rojas, Fernando de 1475-1541 .... **LC 23; HLCS 1**
See also RGWL 2

Rojas, Gonzalo 1917-
See also CA 178; HLCS 2; HW 2; LAWS 1

Rolfe, Frederick (William Serafino Austin Lewis Mary) 1860-1913 .... **TCLC 12**
See Corvo, Baron
See also CA 107; DLB 34, 156; RGEL 2

Rolland, Romain 1866-1944 .... **TCLC 23**
See also CA 118; 197; DLB 65; GFL 1789 to the Present; RGWL 2

Rolle, Richard c. 1300-c. 1349 .... **CMLC 21**
See also DLB 146; RGEL 2

Rolvaag, O(le) E(dvart) .... **TCLC 17**
See also Roelvaag, O(le) E(dvart)
See also DLB 9, 212; NFS 5; RGAL 4

Romain Arnaud, Saint
See Aragon, Louis

Romains, Jules 1885-1972 .... **CLC 7**
See also CA 85-88; CANR 34; DLB 65; GFL 1789 to the Present; MTCW 1

Romero, Jose Ruben 1890-1952 .... **TCLC 14**
See also CA 114; 131; HW 1; LAW

Ronsard, Pierre de 1524-1585 . **LC 6, 54; PC 11**
See also EW 2; GFL Beginnings to 1789; RGWL 2

Rooke, Leon 1934- .... **CLC 25, 34**
See also CA 25-28R; CANR 23, 53; CCA 1; CPW; DAM POP

Roosevelt, Franklin Delano
1882-1945 .... **TCLC 93**
See also CA 116; 173; LAIT 3

Roosevelt, Theodore 1858-1919 .... **TCLC 69**
See also CA 115; 170; DLB 47, 186

Roper, William 1498-1578 .... **LC 10**

Roquelaure, A. N.
See Rice, Anne

Rosa, Joao Guimaraes 1908-1967 ... **CLC 23; HLCS 1**
See also Guimaraes Rosa, Joao
See also CA 89-92; DLB 113; WLIT 1

Rose, Wendy 1948- .... **CLC 85; PC 13**
See also CA 53-56; CANR 5, 51; CWP; DAM MULT; DLB 175; NNAL; PFS 13; RGAL 4; SATA 12

Rosen, R. D.
See Rosen, Richard (Dean)

Rosen, Richard (Dean) 1949- .... **CLC 39**
See also CA 77-80; CANR 62; CMW 4; INT CANR-30

Rosenberg, Isaac 1890-1918 .... **TCLC 12**
See also BRW 6; CA 107; 188; DLB 20, 216; PAB; RGEL 2

Rosenblatt, Joe .... **CLC 15**
See also Rosenblatt, Joseph

Rosenblatt, Joseph 1933-
See Rosenblatt, Joe
See also CA 89-92; CP 7; INT 89-92

Rosenfeld, Samuel
See Tzara, Tristan

Rosenstock, Sami
See Tzara, Tristan

Rosenstock, Samuel
See Tzara, Tristan

Rosenthal, M(acha) L(ouis)
1917-1996 .... **CLC 28**
See also CA 1-4R; 152; CAAS 6; CANR 4, 51; CP 7; DLB 5; SATA 59

Ross, Barnaby
See Dannay, Frederic

Ross, Bernard L.
See Follett, Ken(neth Martin)

Ross, J. H.
See Lawrence, T(homas) E(dward)

Ross, John Hume
See Lawrence, T(homas) E(dward)

Ross, Martin 1862-1915
See Martin, Violet Florence
See also DLB 135; GLL 2; RGEL 2; RGSF 2

Ross, (James) Sinclair 1908-1996 ... **CLC 13; SSC 24**
See also CA 73-76; CANR 81; CN 7; DAC; DAM MST; DLB 88; RGEL 2; RGSF 2; TCWW 2

Rossetti, Christina (Georgina)
1830-1894 .... **NCLC 2, 50, 66; PC 7; WLC**
See also BRW 5; BYA 4; DA; DA3; DAB; DAC; DAM MST, POET; DLB 35, 163, 240; EXPP; MAICYA 1, 2; PFS 10, 14; RGEL 2; SATA 20; TEA; WCH

Rossetti, Dante Gabriel 1828-1882 . **NCLC 4, 77; WLC**
See also BRW 5; CDBLB 1832-1890; DA; DAB; DAC; DAM MST, POET; DLB 35; EXPP; RGEL 2

Rossi, Cristina Peri
See Peri Rossi, Cristina

Rossi, Jean Baptiste 1931-
See Japrisot, Sebastien
See also CA 201

Rossner, Judith (Perelman) 1935- . **CLC 6, 9, 29**
See also AITN 2; BEST 90:3; BPFB 3; CA 17-20R; CANR 18, 51, 73; CN 7; DLB 6; INT CANR-18; MTCW 1, 2

Rostand, Edmond (Eugene Alexis)
1868-1918 .... **TCLC 6, 37; DC 10**
See also CA 104; 126; DA; DA3; DAB; DAC; DAM DRAM, MST; DFS 1; DLB 192; LAIT 1; MTCW 1; RGWL 2

Roth, Henry 1906-1995 ..... **CLC 2, 6, 11, 104**
See also AMWS 9; CA 11-12; 149; CANR 38, 63; CAP 1; CN 7; DA3; DLB 28; MTCW 1, 2; RGAL 4

Roth, (Moses) Joseph 1894-1939 ... **TCLC 33**
See also CA 160; DLB 85; RGWL 2

Roth, Philip (Milton) 1933- ... **CLC 1, 2, 3, 4, 6, 9, 15, 22, 31, 47, 66, 86, 119; SSC 26; WLC**
See also AMWS 3; BEST 90:3; BPFB 3; CA 1-4R; CANR 1, 22, 36, 55, 89; CDALB 1968-1988; CN 7; CPW 1; DA; DA3; DAB; DAC; DAM MST, NOV, POP; DLB 2, 28, 173; DLBY 1982; MTCW 1, 2; RGAL 4; RGSF 2; SSFS 12

Rothenberg, Jerome 1931- .... **CLC 6, 57**
See also CA 45-48; CANR 1, 106; CP 7; DLB 5, 193

Rotter, Pat ed. .... **CLC 65**

Roumain, Jacques (Jean Baptiste)
1907-1944 .... **TCLC 19; BLC 3**
See also BW 1; CA 117; 125; DAM MULT

Rourke, Constance (Mayfield)
1885-1941 .... **TCLC 12**
See also CA 107; YABC 1

Rousseau, Jean-Baptiste 1671-1741 ..... **LC 9**

Rousseau, Jean-Jacques 1712-1778 .... **LC 14, 36; WLC**
See also DA; DA3; DAB; DAC; DAM MST; EW 4; GFL Beginnings to 1789; RGWL 2

Roussel, Raymond 1877-1933 .... **TCLC 20**
See also CA 117; 201; GFL 1789 to the Present

Rovit, Earl (Herbert) 1927- .... **CLC 7**
See also CA 5-8R; CANR 12

Rowe, Elizabeth Singer 1674-1737 ..... **LC 44**
See also DLB 39, 95

Rowe, Nicholas 1674-1718 .... **LC 8**
See also DLB 84; RGEL 2

Rowlandson, Mary 1637(?)-1678 .... **LC 66**
See also DLB 24, 200; RGAL 4

Rowley, Ames Dorrance
See Lovecraft, H(oward) P(hillips)

Rowling, J(oanne) K(athleen)
1965(?)- .... **CLC 137**
See also AAYA 34; BYA 13, 14; CA 173; CLR 66, 80; SATA 109

Rowson, Susanna Haswell
1762(?)-1824 .... **NCLC 5, 69**
See also DLB 37, 200; RGAL 4

Roy, Arundhati 1960(?)- .... **CLC 109**
See also CA 163; CANR 90; DLBY 1997

Roy, Gabrielle 1909-1983 .... **CLC 10, 14**
See also CA 53-56; 110; CANR 5, 61; CCA 1; DAB; DAC; DAM MST; DLB 68; MTCW 1; RGWL 2; SATA 104

Royko, Mike 1932-1997 .... **CLC 109**
See also CA 89-92; 157; CANR 26; CPW

Rozanov, Vassili 1856-1919 .... **TCLC 104**

Rozewicz, Tadeusz 1921- ...... **CLC 9, 23, 139**
See also CA 108; CANR 36, 66; CWW 2; DA3; DAM POET; DLB 232; MTCW 1, 2

Ruark, Gibbons 1941- .... **CLC 3**
See also CA 33-36R; CAAS 23; CANR 14, 31, 57; DLB 120

Rubens, Bernice (Ruth) 1923- **CLC 19, 31**
See also CA 25-28R; CANR 33, 65; CN 7; DLB 14, 207; MTCW 1

Rubin, Harold
See Robbins, Harold

Rudkin, (James) David 1936- .... **CLC 14**
See also CA 89-92; CBD; CD 5; DLB 13

Rudnik, Raphael 1933- .... **CLC 7**
See also CA 29-32R

Ruffian, M.
See Hasek, Jaroslav (Matej Frantisek)

Ruiz, Jose Martinez .... **CLC 11**
See also Martinez Ruiz, Jose

Rukeyser, Muriel 1913-1980 . **CLC 6, 10, 15, 27; PC 12**
See also AMWS 6; CA 5-8R; 93-96; CANR 26, 60; DA3; DAM POET; DLB 48; FW; GLL 1; MTCW 1, 2; PFS 10; RGAL 4; SATA-Obit 22

Rule, Jane (Vance) 1931- .... **CLC 27**
See also CA 25-28R; CAAS 18; CANR 12, 87; CN 7; DLB 60; FW

Rulfo, Juan 1918-1986 .. **CLC 8, 80; HLC 2; SSC 25**
See also CA 85-88; 118; CANR 26; CDWLB 3; DAM MULT; DLB 113; HW 1, 2; LAW; MTCW 1, 2; RGSF 2; RGWL 2; WLIT 1

Rumi, Jalal al-Din 1207-1273 .... **CMLC 20**
See also RGWL 2; WP

Runeberg, Johan 1804-1877 .... **NCLC 41**

Runyon, (Alfred) Damon
1884(?)-1946 .... **TCLC 10**
See also CA 107; 165; DLB 11, 86, 171; MTCW 2; RGAL 4

Rush, Norman 1933- .... **CLC 44**
See also CA 121; 126; INT 126

Rushdie, (Ahmed) Salman 1947- .... **CLC 23, 31, 55, 100; WLCS**
See also BEST 89:3; BPFB 3; BRWS 4; CA 108; 111; CANR 33, 56, 108; CN 7; CPW 1; DA3; DAB; DAC; DAM MST, NOV, POP; DLB 194; FANT; INT CA-111; MTCW 1, 2; RGEL 2; RGSF 2; WLIT 4

Rushforth, Peter (Scott) 1945- .... **CLC 19**
See also CA 101

Ruskin, John 1819-1900 .... **TCLC 63**
See also BRW 5; BYA 5; CA 114; 129; CDBLB 1832-1890; DLB 55, 163, 190; RGEL 2; SATA 24; TEA; WCH

Russ, Joanna 1937- .... **CLC 15**
See also BPFB 3; CA 5-28R; CANR 11, 31, 65; CN 7; DLB 8; FW; GLL 1; MTCW 1; SCFW 2; SFW 4

Russell, George William 1867-1935
See A.E.; Baker, Jean H.
See also CA 104; 153; CDBLB 1890-1914; DAM POET; RGEL 2

Russell, Jeffrey Burton 1934- .... **CLC 70**
See also CA 25-28R; CANR 11, 28, 52

Russell, (Henry) Ken(neth Alfred)
1927- .... **CLC 16**
See also CA 105

Russell, William Martin 1947-
See Russell, Willy
See also CA 164; CANR 107

Russell, Willy .... **CLC 60**
See also Russell, William Martin
See also CBD; CD 5; DLB 233

Rutherford, Mark .... **TCLC 25**
See also White, William Hale
See also DLB 18; RGEL 2

Ruyslinck, Ward .... **CLC 14**
See also Belser, Reimond Karel Maria de

Ryan, Cornelius (John) 1920-1974 ..... **CLC 7**
See also CA 69-72; 53-56; CANR 38

Ryan, Michael 1946- .... **CLC 65**
See also CA 49-52; CANR 109; DLBY 1982

Ryan, Tim
See Dent, Lester

Rybakov, Anatoli (Naumovich)
1911-1998 .... **CLC 23, 53**
See also CA 126; 135; 172; SATA 79; SATA-Obit 108

Ryder, Jonathan
See Ludlum, Robert

Ryga, George 1932-1987 .... **CLC 14**
See also CA 101; 124; CANR 43, 90; CCA 1; DAC; DAM MST; DLB 60

S. H.
See Hartmann, Sadakichi

S. S.
See Sassoon, Siegfried (Lorraine)

Saba, Umberto 1883-1957 .... **TCLC 33**
See also CA 144; CANR 79; DLB 114; RGWL 2

Sabatini, Rafael 1875-1950 .... **TCLC 47**
See also BPFB 3; CA 162, RHW

Sabato, Ernesto (R.) 1911- .... **CLC 10, 23; HLC 2**
See also CA 97-100; CANR 32, 65; CDWLB 3; DAM MULT; DLB 145; HW 1, 2; LAW; MTCW 1, 2

Sa-Carnieiro, Mario de 1890-1916 . **TCLC 83**

Sacastru, Martin
See Bioy Casares, Adolfo
See also CWW 2

Sacher-Masoch, Leopold von
1836(?)-1895 .... **NCLC 31**

Sachs, Marilyn (Stickle) 1927- .... **CLC 35**
See also AAYA 2; BYA 6; CA 17-20R; CANR 13, 47; CLR 2; JRDA; MAICYA 1, 2; SAAS 2; SATA 3, 68; SATA-Essay 110; WYA; YAW

Sachs, Nelly 1891-1970 .... **CLC 14, 98**
See also CA 17-18; 25-28R; CANR 87; CAP 2; MTCW 2; RGWL 2

Sackler, Howard (Oliver)
1929-1982 .... **CLC 14**
See also CA 61-64; 108; CAD; CANR 30; DFS 15; DLB 7

Sacks, Oliver (Wolf) 1933- .... **CLC 67**
See also CA 53-56; CANR 28, 50, 76; CPW; DA3; INT CANR-28; MTCW 1, 2

Sadakichi
See Hartmann, Sadakichi

Sade, Donatien Alphonse Francois
1740-1814 .... **NCLC 3, 47**
See also EW 4; GFL Beginnings to 1789; RGWL 2

Sadoff, Ira 1945- .... **CLC 9**
See also CA 53-56; CANR 5, 21, 109; DLB 120

Saetone
See Camus, Albert

Safire, William 1929- .... **CLC 10**
See also CA 17-20R; CANR 31, 54, 91

Sagan, Carl (Edward) 1934-1996 .... **CLC 30, 112**
See also AAYA 2; CA 25-28R; 155; CANR 11, 36, 74; CPW; DA3; MTCW 1, 2; SATA 58; SATA-Obit 94

Sagan, Francoise .... **CLC 3, 6, 9, 17, 36**
See also Quoirez, Francoise
See also CWW 2; DLB 83; GFL 1789 to the Present; MTCW 2

Sahgal, Nayantara (Pandit) 1927- .... **CLC 41**
See also CA 9-12R; CANR 11, 88; CN 7

Said, Edward W. 1935- .... **CLC 123**
See also CA 21-24R; CANR 45, 74, 107; DLB 67; MTCW 2

Saint, H(arry) F. 1941- .... **CLC 50**
See also CA 127

St. Aubin de Teran, Lisa 1953-
See Teran, Lisa St. Aubin de
See also CA 118; 126; CN 7; INT 126

Saint Birgitta of Sweden c. 1303-1373 .... **CMLC 24**

Sainte-Beuve, Charles Augustin 1804-1869 .... **NCLC 5**
See also DLB 217; EW 6; GFL 1789 to the Present

Saint-Exupery, Antoine (Jean Baptiste Marie Roger) de 1900-1944 .... **TCLC 2, 56; WLC**
See also BPFB 3; BYA 3; CA 108; 132; CLR 10; DA3; DAM NOV; DLB 72; EW 12; GFL 1789 to the Present; LAIT 3; MAICYA 1, 2; MTCW 1, 2; RGWL 2; SATA 20

St. John, David
See Hunt, E(verette) Howard, (Jr.)

St. John, J. Hector
See Crevecoeur, Michel Guillaume Jean de

Saint-John Perse
See Leger, (Marie-Rene Auguste) Alexis Saint-Leger
See also EW 10; GFL 1789 to the Present; RGWL 2

Saintsbury, George (Edward Bateman) 1845-1933 .... **TCLC 31**
See also CA 160; DLB 57, 149

Sait Faik .... **TCLC 23**
See also Abasiyanik, Sait Faik

Saki .... **TCLC 3; SSC 12**
See also Munro, H(ector) H(ugh)
See also BRWS 6; LAIT 2; MTCW 2; RGEL 2; SSFS 1; SUFW

Sakutaro, Hagiwara
See Hagiwara, Sakutaro

Sala, George Augustus 1828-1895 . **NCLC 46**

Saladin 1138-1193 .... **CMLC 38**

Salama, Hannu 1936- .... **CLC 18**

Salamanca, J(ack) R(ichard) 1922- .. **CLC 4, 15**
See also CA 25-28R; CAAE 193

Salas, Floyd Francis 1931-
See also CA 119; CAAS 27; CANR 44, 75, 93; DAM MULT; DLB 82; HLC 2; HW 1, 2; MTCW 2

Sale, J. Kirkpatrick
See Sale, Kirkpatrick

Sale, Kirkpatrick 1937- .... **CLC 68**
See also CA 13-16R; CANR 10

Salinas, Luis Omar 1937- ... **CLC 90; HLC 2**
See also CA 131; CANR 81; DAM MULT; DLB 82; HW 1, 2

Salinas (y Serrano), Pedro 1891(?)-1951 .... **TCLC 17**
See also CA 117; DLB 134

Salinger, J(erome) D(avid) 1919- .. **CLC 1, 3, 8, 12, 55, 56, 138; SSC 2, 28; WLC**
See also AAYA 2, 36; AMW; BPFB 3; CA 5-8R; CANR 39; CDALB 1941-1968; CLR 18; CN 7; CPW 1; DA; DA3; DAB; DAC; DAM MST, NOV, POP; DLB 2, 102, 173; EXPN; LAIT 4; MAICYA 1, 2; MTCW 1, 2; NFS 1; RGAL 4; RGSF 2; SATA 67; WYA; YAW

Salisbury, John
See Caute, (John) David

Salter, James 1925- .... **CLC 7, 52, 59**
See also AMWS 9; CA 73-76; CANR 107; DLB 130

Saltus, Edgar (Everton) 1855-1921 . **TCLC 8**
See also CA 105; DLB 202; RGAL 4

Saltykov, Mikhail Evgrafovich 1826-1889 .... **NCLC 16**
See also DLB 238:

Saltykov-Shchedrin, N.
See Saltykov, Mikhail Evgrafovich

Samarakis, Antonis 1919- .... **CLC 5**
See also CA 25-28R; CAAS 16; CANR 36

Sanchez, Florencio 1875-1910 .... **TCLC 37**
See also CA 153; HW 1; LAW

Sanchez, Luis Rafael 1936- .... **CLC 23**
See also CA 128; DLB 145; HW 1; WLIT 1

Sanchez, Sonia 1934- .... **CLC 5, 116; BLC 3; PC 9**
See also BW 2, 3; CA 33-36R; CANR 24, 49, 74; CLR 18; CP 7; CSW; CWP; DA3; DAM MULT; DLB 41; DLBD 8; MAICYA 1, 2; MTCW 1, 2; SATA 22; WP

Sand, George 1804-1876 ..... **NCLC 2, 42, 57; WLC**
See also DA; DA3; DAB; DAC; DAM MST, NOV; DLB 119, 192; EW 6; FW; GFL 1789 to the Present; RGWL 2

Sandburg, Carl (August) 1878-1967 . **CLC 1, 4, 10, 15, 35; PC 2, 41; WLC**
See also AAYA 24; AMW; BYA 1, 3; CA 5-8R; 25-28R; CANR 35; CDALB 1865-1917; CLR 67; DA; DA3; DAB; DAC; DAM MST, POET; DLB 17, 54; EXPP; LAIT 2; MAICYA 1, 2; MTCW 1, 2; PAB; PFS 3, 6, 12; RGAL 4; SATA 8; WCH; WP; WYA

Sandburg, Charles
See Sandburg, Carl (August)

Sandburg, Charles A.
See Sandburg, Carl (August)

Sanders, (James) Ed(ward) 1939- .... **CLC 53**
See also Sanders, Edward
See also CA 13-16R; CAAS 21; CANR 13, 44, 78; CP 7; DAM POET; DLB 16, 244

Sanders, Edward
See Sanders, (James) Ed(ward)
See also DLB 244

Sanders, Lawrence 1920-1998 .... **CLC 41**
See also BEST 89:4; BPFB 3; CA 81-84; 165; CANR 33, 62; CMW 4; CPW; DA3; DAM POP; MTCW 1

Sanders, Noah
See Blount, Roy (Alton), Jr.

Sanders, Winston P.
See Anderson, Poul (William)

Sandoz, Mari(e Susette) 1900-1966 .. **CLC 28**
See also CA 1-4R; 25-28R; CANR 17, 64; DLB 9, 212; LAIT 2; MTCW 1, 2; SATA 5; TCWW 2

Saner, Reg(inald Anthony) 1931- .... **CLC 9**
See also CA 65-68; CP 7

Sankara 788-820 .... **CMLC 32**

Sannazaro, Jacopo 1456(?)-1530 .... **LC 8**
See also RGWL 2

Sansom, William 1912-1976 . **CLC 2, 6; SSC 21**
See also CA 5-8R; 65-68; CANR 42; DAM NOV; DLB 139; MTCW 1; RGEL 2; RGSF 2

Santayana, George 1863-1952 .... **TCLC 40**
See also AMW; CA 115; 194; DLB 54, 71, 246; DLBD 13; RGAL 4

Santiago, Danny .... **CLC 33**
See also James, Daniel (Lewis)
See also DLB 122

Santmyer, Helen Hooven 1895-1986 .... **CLC 33**
See also CA 1-4R; 118; CANR 15, 33; DLBY 1984; MTCW 1; RHW

Santoka, Taneda 1882-1940 .... **TCLC 72**

Santos, Bienvenido N(uqui) 1911-1996 .... **CLC 22**
See also CA 101; 151; CANR 19, 46; DAM MULT; RGAL 4

Sapir, Edward 1884-1939 .... **TCLC 108**
See also DLB 92

Sapper .... **TCLC 44**
See also McNeile, Herman Cyril

Sapphire
See Sapphire, Brenda

Sapphire, Brenda 1950- .... **CLC 99**

Sappho fl. 6256th cent. B.C.- ... **CMLC 3; PC 5**
See also CDWLB 1; DA3; DAM POET; DLB 176; RGWL 2; WP

Saramago, Jose 1922- ...... **CLC 119; HLCS 1**
See also CA 153; CANR 96

Sarduy, Severo 1937-1993 .... **CLC 6, 97; HLCS 2**
See also CA 89-92; 142; CANR 58, 81; CWW 2; DLB 113; HW 1, 2; LAW

Sargeson, Frank 1903-1982 .... **CLC 31**
See also CA 25-28R; 106; CANR 38, 79; GLL 2; RGEL 2; RGSF 2

Sarmiento, Domingo Faustino 1811-1888
See also HLCS 2; LAW; WLIT 1

Sarmiento, Felix Ruben Garcia
See Dario, Ruben

Saro-Wiwa, Ken(ule Beeson) 1941-1995 .... **CLC 114**
See also BW 2; CA 142; 150; CANR 60; DLB 157

Saroyan, William 1908-1981 ... **CLC 1, 8, 10, 29, 34, 56; SSC 21; WLC**
See also CA 5-8R; 103; CAD; CANR 30; CDALBS; DA; DA3; DAB; DAC; DAM DRAM, MST, NOV; DLB 7, 9, 86; DLBY 1981; LAIT 4; MTCW 1, 2; RGAL 4; RGSF 2; SATA 23; SATA-Obit 24; SSFS 14

Sarraute, Nathalie 1900-1999 .... **CLC 1, 2, 4, 8, 10, 31, 80**
See also BPFB 3; CA 9-12R; 187; CANR 23, 66; CWW 2; DLB 83; EW 12; GFL 1789 to the Present; MTCW 1, 2; RGWL

Sarton, (Eleanor) May 1912-1995 ..... **CLC 4, 14, 49, 91; PC 39**
See also AMWS 8; CA 1-4R; 149; CANR 1, 34, 55; CN 7; CP 7; DAM POET; DLB 48; DLBY 1981; FW; INT CANR-34; MTCW 1, 2; RGAL 4; SATA 36; SATA-Obit 86; TCLC 120; TUS

Sartre, Jean-Paul 1905-1980 . **CLC 1, 4, 7, 9, 13, 18, 24, 44, 50, 52; DC 3; SSC 32; WLC**
See also CA 9-12R; 97-100; CANR 21; DA; DA3; DAB; DAC; DAM DRAM, MST, NOV; DFS 5; DLB 72; EW 12; GFL 1789 to the Present; MTCW 1, 2; RGSF 2; RGWL 2; SSFS 9

Sassoon, Siegfried (Lorraine) 1886-1967 .... **CLC 36, 130; PC 12**
See also BRW 6; CA 104; 25-28R; CANR 36; DAB; DAM MST, NOV, POET; DLB 20, 191; DLBD 18; MTCW 1, 2; PAB; RGEL 2; TEA

Satterfield, Charles
See Pohl, Frederik

Satyremont
See Peret, Benjamin

Saul, John (W. III) 1942- .... **CLC 46**
See also AAYA 10; BEST 90:4; CA 81-84; CANR 16, 40, 81; CPW; DAM NOV, POP; HGG; SATA 98

Saunders, Caleb
See Heinlein, Robert A(nson)

Saura (Atares), Carlos 1932-1998 .... **CLC 20**
See also CA 114; 131; CANR 79; HW 1

Sauser-Hall, Frederic 1887-1961 ...... **CLC 18**
See also Cendrars, Blaise
See also CA 102; 93-96; CANR 36, 62; MTCW 1

Saussure, Ferdinand de
1857-1913 .... **TCLC 49**
See also DLB 242

Savage, Catharine
See Brosman, Catharine Savage

Savage, Thomas 1915- .... **CLC 40**
See also CA 126; 132; CAAS 15; CN 7; INT 132; TCWW 2

Savan, Glenn (?)- .... **CLC 50**

Sayers, Dorothy L(eigh)
1893-1957 .... **TCLC 2, 15**
See also BPFB 3; BRWS 3; CA 104; 119; CANR 60; CDBLB 1914-1945; CMW 4; DAM POP; DLB 10, 36, 77, 100; MSW; MTCW 1, 2; RGEL 2; SSFS 12; TEA

Sayers, Valerie 1952- .... **CLC 50, 122**
See also CA 134; CANR 61; CSW

Sayles, John (Thomas) 1950- . **CLC 7, 10, 14**
See also CA 57-60; CANR 41, 84; DLB 44

Scammell, Michael 1935- .... **CLC 34**
See also CA 156

Scannell, Vernon 1922- .... **CLC 49**
See also CA 5-8R; CANR 8, 24, 57; CP 7; CWRI 5; DLB 27; SATA 59

Scarlett, Susan
See Streatfeild, (Mary) Noel

Scarron 1847-1910
See Mikszath, Kalman

Schaeffer, Susan Fromberg 1941- ..... **CLC 6, 11, 22**
See also CA 49-52; CANR 18, 65; CN 7; DLB 28; MTCW 1, 2; SATA 22

Schama, Simon (Michael) 1945- ...... **CLC 150**
See also BEST 89:4; CA 105; CANR 39, 91

Schary, Jill
See Robinson, Jill

Schell, Jonathan 1943- .... **CLC 35**
See also CA 73-76; CANR 12

Schelling, Friedrich Wilhelm Joseph von
1775-1854 .... **NCLC 30**
See also DLB 90

Scherer, Jean-Marie Maurice 1920-
See Rohmer, Eric
See also CA 110

Schevill, James (Erwin) 1920- .... **CLC 7**
See also CA 5-8R; CAAS 12; CAD; CD 5

Schiller, Friedrich von
1759-1805 .... **NCLC 39, 69; DC 12**
See also CDWLB 2; DAM DRAM; DLB 94; EW 5; RGWL 2

Schisgal, Murray (Joseph) 1926- .... **CLC 6**
See also CA 21-24R; CAD; CANR 48, 86; CD 5

Schlee, Ann 1934- .... **CLC 35**
See also CA 101; CANR 29, 88; SATA 44; SATA-Brief 36

Schlegel, August Wilhelm von
1767-1845 .... **NCLC 15**
See also DLB 94; RGWL 2

Schlegel, Friedrich 1772-1829 .... **NCLC 45**
See also DLB 90; EW 5; RGWL 2

Schlegel, Johann Elias (von)
1719(?)-1749 .... **LC 5**

Schleiermacher, Friedrich
1768-1834 .... **NCLC 107**
See also DLB 90

Schlesinger, Arthur M(eier), Jr.
1917- .... **CLC 84**
See also AITN 1; CA 1-4R; CANR 1, 28, 58, 105; DLB 17; INT CANR-28; MTCW 1, 2; SATA 61

Schmidt, Arno (Otto) 1914-1979 ...... **CLC 56**
See also CA 128; 109; DLB 69

Schmitz, Aron Hector 1861-1928
See Svevo, Italo
See also CA 104; 122; MTCW 1

Schnackenberg, Gjertrud (Cecelia)
1953- .... **CLC 40**
See also CA 116; CANR 100; CP 7; CWP; DLB 120; PFS 13

Schneider, Leonard Alfred 1925-1966
See Bruce, Lenny
See also CA 89-92

Schnitzler, Arthur 1862-1931 ... **TCLC 4; DC 17; SSC 15**
See also CA 104; CDWLB 2; DLB 81, 118; EW 8; RGSF 2; RGWL 2

Schoenberg, Arnold Franz Walter
1874-1951 .... **TCLC 75**
See also CA 109; 188

Schonberg, Arnold
See Schoenberg, Arnold Franz Walter

Schopenhauer, Arthur 1788-1860 .. **NCLC 51**
See also DLB 90; EW 5

Schor, Sandra (M.) 1932(?)-1990 ..... **CLC 65**
See also CA 132

Schorer, Mark 1908-1977 .... **CLC 9**
See also CA 5-8R; 73-76; CANR 7; DLB 103

Schrader, Paul (Joseph) 1946- .... **CLC 26**
See also CA 37-40R; CANR 41; DLB 44

Schreber, Daniel 1842-1911 .... **TCLC 123**

Schreiner, Olive (Emilie Albertina)
1855-1920 .... **TCLC 9**
See also AFW; BRWS 2; CA 105; 154; DLB 18, 156, 190, 225; FW; RGEL 2; WLIT 2

Schulberg, Budd (Wilson) 1914- .. **CLC 7, 48**
See also BPFB 3; CA 25-28R; CANR 19, 87; CN 7; DLB 6, 26, 28; DLBY 1981, 2001

Schulman, Arnold
See Trumbo, Dalton

Schulz, Bruno 1892-1942 .. **TCLC 5, 51; SSC 13**
See also CA 115; 123; CANR 86; CDWLB 4; DLB 215; MTCW 2; RGSF 2; RGWL 2

Schulz, Charles M(onroe)
1922-2000 .... **CLC 12**
See also AAYA 39; CA 9-12R; 187; CANR 6; INT CANR-6; SATA 10; SATA-Obit 118

Schumacher, E(rnst) F(riedrich)
1911-1977 .... **CLC 80**
See also CA 81-84; 73-76; CANR 34, 85

Schuyler, James Marcus 1923-1991 .. **CLC 5, 23**
See also CA 101; 134; DAM POET; DLB 5, 169; INT 101; WP

Schwartz, Delmore (David)
1913-1966 ... **CLC 2, 4, 10, 45, 87; PC 8**
See also AMWS 2; CA 17-18; 25-28R; CANR 35; CAP 2; DLB 28, 48; MTCW 1, 2; PAB; RGAL 4; TUS

Schwartz, Ernst
See Ozu, Yasujiro

Schwartz, John Burnham 1965- .... **CLC 59**
See also CA 132

Schwartz, Lynne Sharon 1939- .... **CLC 31**
See also CA 103; CANR 44, 89; DLB 218; MTCW 2

Schwartz, Muriel A.
See Eliot, T(homas) S(tearns)

Schwarz-Bart, Andre 1928- .... **CLC 2, 4**
See also CA 89-92; CANR 109

Schwarz-Bart, Simone 1938- . **CLC 7; BLCS**
See also BW 2; CA 97-100

Schwitters, Kurt (Hermann Edward Karl Julius) 1887-1948 .... **TCLC 95**
See also CA 158

Schwob, Marcel (Mayer Andre)
1867-1905 .... **TCLC 20**
See also CA 117; 168; DLB 123; GFL 1789 to the Present

Sciascia, Leonardo 1921-1989 .. **CLC 8, 9, 41**
See also CA 85-88; 130; CANR 35; DLB 177; MTCW 1; RGWL 2

Scoppettone, Sandra 1936- .... **CLC 26**
See also Early, Jack
See also AAYA 11; BYA 8; CA 5-8R; CANR 41, 73; GLL 1; MAICYA 2; MAICYAS 1; SATA 9, 92; WYA; YAW

Scorsese, Martin 1942- .... **CLC 20, 89**
See also AAYA 38; CA 110; 114; CANR 46, 85

Scotland, Jay
See Jakes, John (William)

Scott, Duncan Campbell
1862-1947 .... **TCLC 6**
See also CA 104; 153; DAC; DLB 92; RGEL 2

Scott, Evelyn 1893-1963 .... **CLC 43**
See also CA 104; 112; CANR 64; DLB 9, 48; RHW

Scott, F(rancis) R(eginald)
1899-1985 .... **CLC 22**
See also CA 101; 114; CANR 87; DLB 88; INT CA-101; RGEL 2

Scott, Frank
See Scott, F(rancis) R(eginald)

Scott, Joan .... **CLC 65**

Scott, Joanna 1960- .... **CLC 50**
See also CA 126; CANR 53, 92

Scott, Paul (Mark) 1920-1978 .... **CLC 9, 60**
See also BRWS 1; CA 81-84; 77-80; CANR 33; DLB 14, 207; MTCW 1; RGEL 2; RHW

Scott, Sarah 1723-1795 .... **LC 44**
See also DLB 39

Scott, Sir Walter 1771-1832 .... **NCLC 15, 69, 110; PC 13; SSC 32; WLC**
See also AAYA 22; BRW 4; BYA 2; CDBLB 1789-1832; DA; DAB; DAC; DAM MST, NOV, POET; DLB 93, 107, 116, 144, 159; HGG; LAIT 1; RGEL 2; RGSF 2; SSFS 10; SUFW; WLIT 3; YABC 2

Scribe, (Augustin) Eugene
1791-1861 .... **NCLC 16; DC 5**
See also DAM DRAM; DLB 192; GFL 1789 to the Present; RGWL 2

Scrum, R.
See Crumb, R(obert)

Scudery, Georges de 1601-1667 .... **LC 75**
See also GFL Beginnings to 1789

Scudery, Madeleine de 1607-1701 .. **LC 2, 58**
See also GFL Beginnings to 1789

Scum
See Crumb, R(obert)

Scumbag, Little Bobby
See Crumb, R(obert)

Seabrook, John
See Hubbard, L(afayette) Ron(ald)

Sealy, I(rwin) Allan 1951- .... **CLC 55**
See also CA 136; CN 7

Search, Alexander
See Pessoa, Fernando (Antonio Nogueira)

Sebastian, Lee
See Silverberg, Robert

Sebastian Owl
See Thompson, Hunter S(tockton)

Sebestyen, Igen
See Sebestyen, Ouida

Sebestyen, Ouida 1924- .... **CLC 30**
See also AAYA 8; BYA 7; CA 107; CANR 40; CLR 17; JRDA; MAICYA 1, 2; SAAS 10; SATA 39; WYA; YAW

Secundus, H. Scriblerus
See Fielding, Henry

Sedges, John
See Buck, Pearl S(ydenstricker)

Sedgwick, Catharine Maria
1789-1867 .... **NCLC 19, 98**
See also DLB 1, 74, 183, 239, 243, 254; RGAL 4

Seelye, John (Douglas) 1931- .... **CLC 7**
See also CA 97-100; CANR 70; INT 97-100; TCWW 2

Seferiades, Giorgos Stylianou 1900-1971
See Seferis, George
See also CA 5-8R; 33-36R; CANR 5, 36; MTCW 1

Seferis, George .... **CLC 5, 11**
See also Seferiades, Giorgos Stylianou
See also EW 12; RGWL 2

Segal, Erich (Wolf) 1937- .... **CLC 3, 10**
See also BEST 89:1; BPFB 3; CA 25-28R; CANR 20, 36, 65; CPW; DAM POP; DLBY 1986; INT CANR-20; MTCW 1

Seger, Bob 1945- .... **CLC 35**

Seghers, Anna -1983 .... **CLC 7**
See also Radvanyi, Netty
See also CDWLB 2; DLB 69

Seidel, Frederick (Lewis) 1936- .... **CLC 18**
See also CA 13-16R; CANR 8, 99; CP 7; DLBY 1984

Seifert, Jaroslav 1901-1986 .. **CLC 34, 44, 93**
See also CA 127; CDWLB 4; DLB 215; MTCW 1, 2

Sei Shonagon c. 966-1017(?) .... **CMLC 6**

Sejour, Victor 1817-1874 .... **DC 10**
See also DLB 50

Sejour Marcou et Ferrand, Juan Victor
See Sejour, Victor

Selby, Hubert, Jr. 1928- .... **CLC 1, 2, 4, 8; SSC 20**
See also CA 13-16R; CANR 33, 85; CN 7; DLB 2, 227

Selzer, Richard 1928- .... **CLC 74**
See also CA 65-68; CANR 14, 106

Sembene, Ousmane
See Ousmane, Sembene
See also AFW; CWW 2; WLIT 2

Senancour, Etienne Pivert de
1770-1846 .... **NCLC 16**
See also DLB 119; GFL 1789 to the Present

Sender, Ramon (Jose) 1902-1982 ...... **CLC 8; HLC 2**
See also CA 5-8R; 105; CANR 8; DAM MULT; HW 1; MTCW 1; RGWL 2

Seneca, Lucius Annaeus c. 4B.C.-c. 65 .... **CMLC 6; DC 5**
See also AW 2; CDWLB 1; DAM DRAM; DLB 211; RGWL 2

Senghor, Leopold Sedar 1906-2001 . **CLC 54, 130; BLC 3; PC 25**
See also AFW; BW 2; CA 116; 125; CANR 47, 74; DAM MULT, POET; DNFS 2; GFL 1789 to the Present; MTCW 1, 2; TWA

Senna, Danzy 1970- .... **CLC 119**
See also CA 169

Serling, (Edward) Rod(man)
1924-1975 .... **CLC 30**
See also AAYA 14; AITN 1; CA 162; 57-60; DLB 26; SFW 4

Serna, Ramon Gomez de la
See Gomez de la Serna, Ramon

Serpieres
See Guillevic, (Eugene)

Service, Robert
See Service, Robert W(illiam)
See also BYA 4; DAB; DLB 92

Service, Robert W(illiam)
1874(?)-1958 .... **TCLC 15; WLC**
See also Service, Robert
See also CA 115; 140; CANR 84; DA; DAC; DAM MST, POET; PFS 10; RGEL 2; SATA 20

Seth, Vikram 1952- .... **CLC 43, 90**
See also CA 121; 127; CANR 50, 74; CN 7; CP 7; DA3; DAM MULT; DLB 120; INT 127; MTCW 2

Seton, Cynthia Propper 1926-1982 .. **CLC 27**
See also CA 5-8R; 108; CANR 7

Seton, Ernest (Evan) Thompson
1860-1946 .... **TCLC 31**
See also ANW; BYA 3; CA 109; CLR 59; DLB 92; DLBD 13; JRDA; SATA 18

Seton-Thompson, Ernest
See Seton, Ernest (Evan) Thompson

Settle, Mary Lee 1918- .... **CLC 19, 61**
See also BPFB 3; CA 89-92; CAAS 1; CANR 44, 87; CN 7; CSW; DLB 6; INT 89-92

Seuphor, Michel
See Arp, Jean

Sevigne, Marie (de Rabutin-Chantal)
1626-1696 .... **LC 11**
See also GFL Beginnings to 1789

Sewall, Samuel 1652-1730 .... **LC 38**
See also DLB 24; RGAL 4

Sexton, Anne (Harvey) 1928-1974 ..... **CLC 2, 4, 6, 8, 10, 15, 53, 123; PC 2; WLC**
See also AMWS 2; CA 1-4R; 53-56; CABS 2; CANR 3, 36; CDALB 1941-1968; DA; DA3; DAB; DAC; DAM MST, POET; DLB 5, 169; EXPP; FW; MAWW; MTCW 1, 2; PAB; PFS 4, 14; RGAL 4; SATA 10

Shaara, Jeff 1952- .... **CLC 119**
See also CA 163; CANR 109

Shaara, Michael (Joseph, Jr.)
1929-1988 .... **CLC 15**
See also AITN 1; BPFB 3; CA 102; 125; CANR 52, 85; DAM POP; DLBY 1983

Shackleton, C. C.
See Aldiss, Brian W(ilson)

Shacochis, Bob .... **CLC 39**
See also Shacochis, Robert G.

Shacochis, Robert G. 1951-
See Shacochis, Bob
See also CA 119; 124; CANR 100; INT 124

Shaffer, Anthony (Joshua)
1926-2001 .... **CLC 19**
See also CA 110; 116; 200; CBD; CD 5; DAM DRAM; DFS 13; DLB 13

Shaffer, Peter (Levin) 1926- .. **CLC 5, 14, 18, 37, 60; DC 7**
See also BRWS 1; CA 25-28R; CANR 25, 47, 74; CBD; CD 5; CDBLB 1960 to Present; DA3; DAB; DAM DRAM, MST; DFS 5, 13; DLB 13, 233; MTCW 1, 2; RGEL 2; TEA

Shakey, Bernard
See Young, Neil

Shalamov, Varlam (Tikhonovich)
1907(?)-1982 .... **CLC 18**
See also CA 129; 105; RGSF 2

Shamlu, Ahmad 1925-2000 .... **CLC 10**
See also CWW 2

Shammas, Anton 1951- .... **CLC 55**
See also CA 199

Shandling, Arline
See Berriault, Gina

Shange, Ntozake 1948- .... **CLC 8, 25, 38, 74, 126; BLC 3; DC 3**
See also AAYA 9; AFAW 1, 2; BW 2; CA 85-88; CABS 3; CAD; CANR 27, 48, 74; CD 5; CP 7; CWD; CWP; DA3; DAM DRAM, MULT; DFS 2, 11; DLB 38, 249; FW; LAIT 5; MTCW 1, 2; NFS 11; RGAL 4; YAW

Shanley, John Patrick 1950- .... **CLC 75**
See also CA 128; 133; CAD; CANR 83; CD 5

Shapcott, Thomas W(illiam) 1935- .. **CLC 38**
See also CA 69-72; CANR 49, 83, 103; CP 7

Shapiro, Jane 1942- .... **CLC 76**
See also CA 196

Shapiro, Karl (Jay) 1913-2000 ...... **CLC 4, 8, 15, 53; PC 25**
See also AMWS 2; CA 1-4R; 188; CAAS 6; CANR 1, 36, 66; CP 7; DLB 48; EXPP; MTCW 1, 2; PFS 3; RGAL 4

Sharp, William 1855-1905 .... **TCLC 39**
See also Macleod, Fiona
See also CA 160; DLB 156; RGEL 2

Sharpe, Thomas Ridley 1928-
See Sharpe, Tom
See also CA 114; 122; CANR 85; INT CA-122

Sharpe, Tom .... **CLC 36**
See also Sharpe, Thomas Ridley
See also CN 7; DLB 14, 231

Shatrov, Mikhail .... **CLC 59**

Shaw, Bernard
See Shaw, George Bernard
See also DLB 190

Shaw, G. Bernard
See Shaw, George Bernard

Shaw, George Bernard 1856-1950 .. **TCLC 3, 9, 21, 45; WLC**
See also Shaw, Bernard
See also BRW 6; BRWR 2; CA 104; 128; CDBLB 1914-1945; DA; DA3; DAB; DAC; DAM DRAM, MST; DFS 1, 3, 6, 11; DLB 10, 57; LAIT 2; MTCW 1, 2; RGEL 2; TEA; WLIT 4

Shaw, Henry Wheeler 1818-1885 .. **NCLC 15**
See also DLB 11; RGAL 4

Shaw, Irwin 1913-1984 .... **CLC 7, 23, 34**
See also AITN 1; BPFB 3; CA 13-16R; CANR 21; CDALB 1941-1968; CPW; DAM DRAM, POP; DLB 6, 102; DLBY 1984; MTCW 1, 21

Shaw, Robert 1927-1978 .... **CLC 5**
See also AITN 1; CA 1-4R; 81-84; CANR 4; DLB 13, 14

Shaw, T. E.
See Lawrence, T(homas) E(dward)

Shawn, Wallace 1943- .... **CLC 41**
See also CA 112; CAD; CD 5

Shchedrin, N.
See Saltykov, Mikhail Evgrafovich

Shea, Lisa 1953- .... **CLC 86**
See also CA 147

Sheed, Wilfrid (John Joseph) 1930- . **CLC 2, 4, 10, 53**
See also CA 65-68; CANR 30, 66; CN 7; DLB 6; MTCW 1, 2

Sheldon, Alice Hastings Bradley
1915(?)-1987
See Tiptree, James, Jr.
See also CA 108; 122; CANR 34; INT 108; MTCW 1

Sheldon, John
See Bloch, Robert (Albert)

Sheldon, Walter J(ames) 1917-1996
See Queen, Ellery
See also AITN 1; CA 25-28R; CANR 10

Shelley, Mary Wollstonecraft (Godwin)
1797-1851 ...... **NCLC 14, 59, 103; WLC**
See also AAYA 20; BPFB 3; BRW 3; BRWS 3; BYA 5; CDBLB 1789-1832; DA; DA3; DAB; DAC; DAM MST, NOV; DLB 110, 116, 159, 178; EXPN; HGG; LAIT 1; NFS 1; RGEL 2; SATA 29; SCFW; SFW 4; TEA; WLIT 3

Shelley, Percy Bysshe 1792-1822 .. **NCLC 18, 93; PC 14; WLC**
See also BRW 4; BRWR 1; CDBLB 1789-1832; DA; DA3; DAB; DAC; DAM MST, POET; DLB 96, 110, 158; EXPP; PAB; PFS 2; RGEL 2; WLIT 3; WP

Shepard, Jim 1956- .... **CLC 36**
See also CA 137; CANR 59, 104; SATA 90

Shepard, Lucius 1947- .... **CLC 34**
See also CA 128; 141; CANR 81; HGG; SCFW 2; SFW 4

Shepard, Sam 1943- .... **CLC 4, 6, 17, 34, 41, 44; DC 5**
See also AAYA 1; AMWS 3; CA 69-72; CABS 3; CAD; CANR 22; CD 5; DA3; DAM DRAM; DFS 3, 6, 7, 14; DLB 7, 212; IDFW 3, 4; MTCW 1, 2; RGAL 4

Shepherd, Michael
See Ludlum, Robert

Sherburne, Zoa (Lillian Morin)
1912-1995 .... **CLC 30**
See also AAYA 13; CA 1-4R; 176; CANR 3, 37; MAICYA 1, 2; SAAS 18; SATA 3; YAW

Sheridan, Frances 1724-1766 .... **LC 7**
See also DLB 39, 84

Sheridan, Richard Brinsley
1751-1816 ..... **NCLC 5, 91; DC 1; WLC**
See also BRW 3; CDBLB 1660-1789; DA; DAB; DAC; DAM DRAM, MST; DFS 15; DLB 89; WLIT 3

Sherman, Jonathan Marc .... **CLC 55**

Sherman, Martin 1941(?)- .... **CLC 19**
See also CA 116; 123; CANR 86

Sherwin, Judith Johnson
See Johnson, Judith (Emlyn)
See also CANR 85; CP 7; CWP

Sherwood, Frances 1940- .... **CLC 81**
See also CA 146

Sherwood, Robert E(mmet)
1896-1955 .... **TCLC 3**
See also CA 104; 153; CANR 86; DAM DRAM; DFS 15; DLB 7, 26, 249; IDFW 3, 4; RGAL 4

Shestov, Lev 1866-1938 .... **TCLC 56**

Shevchenko, Taras 1814-1861 .... **NCLC 54**

Shiel, M(atthew) P(hipps)
1865-1947 .... **TCLC 8**
See also Holmes, Gordon
See also CA 106; 160; DLB 153; HGG; MTCW 2; SFW 4; SUFW

Shields, Carol 1935- .... **CLC 91, 113**
See also AMWS 7; CA 81-84; CANR 51, 74, 98; CCA 1; CN 7; CPW; DA3; DAC; MTCW 2

Shields, David 1956- .... **CLC 97**
See also CA 124; CANR 48, 99

Shiga, Naoya 1883-1971 ..... **CLC 33; SSC 23**
See also Shiga Naoya
See also CA 101; 33-36R; MJW

Shiga Naoya
See Shiga, Naoya
See also DLB 180

Shilts, Randy 1951-1994 .... **CLC 85**
See also AAYA 19; CA 115; 127; 144; CANR 45; DA3; GLL 1; INT 127; MTCW 2

Shimazaki, Haruki 1872-1943
See Shimazaki Toson
See also CA 105; 134; CANR 84

Shimazaki Toson .... **TCLC 5**
See also Shimazaki, Haruki
See also DLB 180

Sholokhov, Mikhail (Aleksandrovich)
1905-1984 .... **CLC 7, 15**
See also CA 101; 112; MTCW 1, 2; RGWL 2; SATA-Obit 36

Shone, Patric
See Hanley, James

Shreve, Susan Richards 1939- .... **CLC 23**
See also CA 49-52; CAAS 5; CANR 5, 38, 69, 100; MAICYA 1, 2; SATA 46, 95; SATA-Brief 41

Shue, Larry 1946-1985 .... **CLC 52**
See also CA 145; 117; DAM DRAM; DFS 7

Shu-Jen, Chou 1881-1936
See Lu Hsun
See also CA 104

Shulman, Alix Kates 1932- .... **CLC 2, 10**
See also CA 29-32R; CANR 43; FW; SATA 7

Shusaku, Endo
See Endo, Shusaku

Shuster, Joe 1914-1992 .... **CLC 21**

Shute, Nevil .... **CLC 30**
See also Norway, Nevil Shute
See also BPFB 3; DLB 255; NFS 9; RHW; SFW 4

Shuttle, Penelope (Diane) 1947- .... **CLC 7**
See also CA 93-96; CANR 39, 84, 92, 108; CP 7; CWP; DLB 14, 40

Sidney, Mary 1561-1621 .... **LC 19, 39**
See also Sidney Herbert, Mary

Sidney, Sir Philip 1554-1586 . **LC 19, 39; PC 32**
See also BRW 1; BRWR 2; CDBLB Before 1660; DA; DA3; DAB; DAC; DAM MST, POET; DLB 167; EXPP; PAB; RGEL 2; TEA; WP

Sidney Herbert, Mary
See Sidney, Mary
See also DLB 167

Siegel, Jerome 1914-1996 .... **CLC 21**
See also CA 116; 169; 151

Siegel, Jerry
See Siegel, Jerome

Sienkiewicz, Henryk (Adam Alexander Pius)
1846-1916 .... **TCLC 3**
See also CA 104; 134; CANR 84; RGSF 2; RGWL 2

Sierra, Gregorio Martinez
See Martinez Sierra, Gregorio

Sierra, Maria (de la O'LeJarraga) Martinez
See Martinez Sierra, Maria (de la O'LeJarraga)

Sigal, Clancy 1926- .... **CLC 7**
See also CA 1-4R; CANR 85; CN 7

Sigourney, Lydia H.
See Sigourney, Lydia Howard (Huntley)
See also DLB 73, 183

Sigourney, Lydia Howard (Huntley)
1791-1865 .... **NCLC 21, 87**
See also Sigourney, Lydia H.; Sigourney, Lydia Huntley
See also DLB 1

Sigourney, Lydia Huntley
See Sigourney, Lydia Howard (Huntley)
See also DLB 42, 239, 243

Siguenza y Gongora, Carlos de
1645-1700 .... **LC 8; HLCS 2**
See also LAW

Sigurjonsson, Johann 1880-1919 ... **TCLC 27**
See also CA 170

Sikelianos, Angelos 1884-1951 ...... **TCLC 39; PC 29**
See also RGWL 2

Silkin, Jon 1930-1997 .... **CLC 2, 6, 43**
See also CA 5-8R; CAAS 5; CANR 89; CP 7; DLB 27

Silko, Leslie (Marmon) 1948- .... **CLC 23, 74, 114; SSC 37; WLCS**
See also AAYA 14; AMWS 4; ANW; BYA 12; CA 115; 122; CANR 45, 65; CN 7; CP 7; CPW 1; CWP; DA; DA3; DAC; DAM MST, MULT, POP; DLB 143, 175, 256; EXPP; EXPS; LAIT 4; MTCW 2; NFS 4; NNAL; PFS 9; RGAL 4; RGSF 2; SSFS 4, 8, 10, 11

Sillanpaa, Frans Eemil 1888-1964 ... **CLC 19**
See also CA 129; 93-96; MTCW 1

Sillitoe, Alan 1928- .. **CLC 1, 3, 6, 10, 19, 57, 148**
See also AITN 1; BRWS 5; CA 9-12R; CAAE 191; CAAS 2; CANR 8, 26, 55; CDBLB 1960 to Present; CN 7; DLB 14, 139; MTCW 1, 2; RGEL 2; RGSF 2; SATA 61

Silone, Ignazio 1900-1978 .... **CLC 4**
See also CA 25-28; 81-84; CANR 34; CAP 2; EW 12; MTCW 1; RGSF 2; RGWL 2

Silone, Ignazione
See Silone, Ignazio

Silva, Jose Asuncion
See da Silva, Antonio Jose
See also LAW

Silver, Joan Micklin 1935- .... **CLC 20**
See also CA 114; 121; INT 121

Silver, Nicholas
See Faust, Frederick (Schiller)
See also TCWW 2

Silverberg, Robert 1935- .... **CLC 7, 140**
See also AAYA 24; BPFB 3; BYA 7, 9; CA 1-4R; 186; CAAE 186; CAAS 3; CANR 1, 20, 36, 85; CLR 59; CN 7; CPW; DAM POP; DLB 8; INT CANR-20; MAICYA 1, 2; MTCW 1, 2; SATA 13, 91; SATA-Essay 104; SCFW 2; SFW 4

Silverstein, Alvin 1933- .... **CLC 17**
See also CA 49-52; CANR 2; CLR 25; JRDA; MAICYA 1, 2; SATA 8, 69, 124

Silverstein, Virginia B(arbara Opshelor)
1937- .... **CLC 17**
See also CA 49-52; CANR 2; CLR 25; JRDA; MAICYA 1, 2; SATA 8, 69, 124

Sim, Georges
See Simenon, Georges (Jacques Christian)

Simak, Clifford D(onald) 1904-1988 . **CLC 1, 55**
See also CA 1-4R; 125; CANR 1, 35; DLB 8; MTCW 1; SATA-Obit 56; SFW 4

Simenon, Georges (Jacques Christian)
1903-1989 .... **CLC 1, 2, 3, 8, 18, 47**
See also BPFB 3; CA 85-88; 129; CANR 35; CMW 4; DA3; DAM POP; DLB 72; DLBY 1989; EW 12; GFL 1789 to the Present; MSW; MTCW 1, 2; RGWL 2

Simic, Charles 1938- .... **CLC 6, 9, 22, 49, 68, 130**
See also AMWS 8; CA 29-32R; CAAS 4; CANR 12, 33, 52, 61, 96; CP 7; DA3; DAM POET; DLB 105; MTCW 2; PFS 7; RGAL 4; WP

Simmel, Georg 1858-1918 .... **TCLC 64**
See also CA 157

Simmons, Charles (Paul) 1924- .... **CLC 57**
See also CA 89-92; INT 89-92

Simmons, Dan 1948- .... **CLC 44**
See also AAYA 16; CA 138; CANR 53, 81; CPW; DAM POP; HGG

Simmons, James (Stewart Alexander)
1933- .... **CLC 43**
See also CA 105; CAAS 21; CP 7; DLB 40

Simms, William Gilmore
1806-1870 .... **NCLC 3**
See also DLB 3, 30, 59, 73, 248, 254; RGAL 4

Simon, Carly 1945- .... **CLC 26**
  See also CA 105
Simon, Claude 1913-1984 ... **CLC 4, 9, 15, 39**
  See also CA 89-92; CANR 33; DAM NOV; DLB 83; EW 13; GFL 1789 to the Present; MTCW 1
Simon, Myles
  See Follett, Ken(neth Martin)
Simon, (Marvin) Neil 1927- ... **CLC 6, 11, 31, 39, 70; DC 14**
  See also AAYA 32; AITN 1; AMWS 4; CA 21-24R; CANR 26, 54, 87; CD 5; DA3; DAM DRAM; DFS 2, 6, 12; DLB 7; LAIT 4; MTCW 1, 2; RGAL 4
Simon, Paul (Frederick) 1941(?)- ..... **CLC 17**
  See also CA 116; 153
Simonon, Paul 1956(?)- .... **CLC 30**
Simonson, Rick ed. .... **CLC 70**
Simpson, Harriette
  See Arnow, Harriette (Louisa) Simpson
Simpson, Louis (Aston Marantz) 1923- .... **CLC 4, 7, 9, 32, 149**
  See also AMWS 9; CA 1-4R; CAAS 4; CANR 1, 61; CP 7; DAM POET; DLB 5; MTCW 1, 2; PFS 7, 11, 14; RGAL 4
Simpson, Mona (Elizabeth) 1957- ... **CLC 44, 146**
  See also CA 122; 135; CANR 68, 103; CN 7
Simpson, N(orman) F(rederick) 1919- .... **CLC 29**
  See also CA 13-16R; CBD; DLB 13; RGEL 2
Sinclair, Andrew (Annandale) 1935- . **CLC 2, 14**
  See also CA 9-12R; CAAS 5; CANR 14, 38, 91; CN 7; DLB 14; FANT; MTCW 1
Sinclair, Emil
  See Hesse, Hermann
Sinclair, Iain 1943- .... **CLC 76**
  See also CA 132; CANR 81; CP 7; HGG
Sinclair, Iain MacGregor
  See Sinclair, Iain
Sinclair, Irene
  See Griffith, D(avid Lewelyn) W(ark)
Sinclair, Mary Amelia St. Clair 1865(?)-1946
  See Sinclair, May
  See also CA 104; HGG; RHW
Sinclair, May .... **TCLC 3, 11**
  See also Sinclair, Mary Amelia St. Clair
  See also CA 166; DLB 36, 135; RGEL 2; SUFW
Sinclair, Roy
  See Griffith, D(avid Lewelyn) W(ark)
Sinclair, Upton (Beall) 1878-1968 ..... **CLC 1, 11, 15, 63; WLC**
  See also AMWS 5; BPFB 3; BYA 2; CA 5-8R; 25-28R; CANR 7; CDALB 1929-1941; DA; DA3; DAB; DAC; DAM MST, NOV; DLB 9; INT CANR-7; LAIT 3; MTCW 1, 2; NFS 6; RGAL 4; SATA 9; YAW
Singer, Isaac
  See Singer, Isaac Bashevis
Singer, Isaac Bashevis 1904-1991 .. **CLC 1, 3, 6, 9, 11, 15, 23, 38, 69, 111; SSC 3, 53; WLC**
  See also AAYA 32; AITN 1, 2; AMW; BPFB 3; BYA 1, 4; CA 1-4R; 134; CANR 1, 39, 106; CDALB 1941-1968; CLR 1; CWRI 5; DA; DA3; DAB; DAC; DAM MST, NOV; DLB 6, 28, 52; DLBY 1991; EXPS; HGG; JRDA; LAIT 3; MAICYA 1, 2; MTCW 1, 2; RGAL 4; RGSF 2; SATA 3, 27; SATA-Obit 68; SSFS 2, 12; TUS; TWA
Singer, Israel Joshua 1893-1944 .... **TCLC 33**
  See also CA 169

Singh, Khushwant 1915- .... **CLC 11**
  See also CA 9-12R; CAAS 9; CANR 6, 84; CN 7; RGEL 2
Singleton, Ann
  See Benedict, Ruth (Fulton)
Singleton, John 1968(?)- .... **CLC 156**
  See also BW 2, 3; CA 138; CANR 67, 82; DAM MULT
Sinjohn, John
  See Galsworthy, John
Sinyavsky, Andrei (Donatevich) 1925-1997 .... **CLC 8**
  See also Tertz, Abram
  See also CA 85-88; 159
Sirin, V.
  See Nabokov, Vladimir (Vladimirovich)
Sissman, L(ouis) E(dward) 1928-1976 .... **CLC 9, 18**
  See also CA 21-24R; 65-68; CANR 13; DLB 5
Sisson, C(harles) H(ubert) 1914- .... **CLC 8**
  See also CA 1-4R; CAAS 3; CANR 3, 48, 84; CP 7; DLB 27
Sitwell, Dame Edith 1887-1964 ..... **CLC 2, 9, 67; PC 3**
  See also BRW 7; CA 9-12R; CANR 35; CDBLB 1945-1960; DAM POET; DLB 20; MTCW 1, 2; RGEL 2; TEA
Siwaarmill, H. P.
  See Sharp, William
Sjoewall, Maj 1935- .... **CLC 7**
  See also Sjowall, Maj
  See also CA 65-68; CANR 73
Sjowall, Maj
  See Sjoewall, Maj
  See also BPFB 3; CMW 4; MSW
Skelton, John 1460(?)-1529 ..... **LC 71; PC 25**
  See also BRW 1; DLB 136; RGEL 2
Skelton, Robin 1925-1997 .... **CLC 13**
  See Zuk, Georges
  See also AITN 2; CA 5-8R; 160; CAAS 5; CANR 28, 89; CCA 1; CP 7; DLB 27, 53
Skolimowski, Jerzy 1938- .... **CLC 20**
  See also CA 128
Skram, Amalie (Bertha) 1847-1905 .... **TCLC 25**
  See also CA 165
Skvorecky, Josef (Vaclav) 1924- ...... **CLC 15, 39, 69, 152**
  See also CA 61-64; CAAS 1; CANR 10, 34, 63, 108; CDWLB 4; DA3; DAC; DAM NOV; DLB 232; MTCW 1, 2
Slade, Bernard .... **CLC 11, 46**
  See Newbound, Bernard Slade
  See also CAAS 9; CCA 1; DLB 53
Slaughter, Carolyn 1946- .... **CLC 56**
  See also CA 85-88; CANR 85; CN 7
Slaughter, Frank G(ill) 1908-2001 ... **CLC 29**
  See also AITN 2; CA 5-8R; 197; CANR 5, 85; INT CANR-5; RHW
Slavitt, David R(ytman) 1935- ...... **CLC 5, 14**
  See also CA 21-24R; CAAS 3; CANR 41, 83; CP 7; DLB 5, 6
Slesinger, Tess 1905-1945 .... **TCLC 10**
  See also CA 107; 199; DLB 102
Slessor, Kenneth 1901-1971 .... **CLC 14**
  See also CA 102; 89-92; DLB 260; RGEL 2
Slowacki, Juliusz 1809-1849 .... **NCLC 15**
Smart, Christopher 1722-1771 . **LC 3; PC 13**
  See also DAM POET; DLB 109; RGEL 2
Smart, Elizabeth 1913-1986 .... **CLC 54**
  See also CA 81-84; 118; DLB 88
Smiley, Jane (Graves) 1949- ...... **CLC 53, 76, 144**
  See also AMWS 6; BPFB 3; CA 104; CANR 30, 50, 74, 96; CN 7; CPW 1; DA3; DAM POP; DLB 227, 234; INT CANR-30

Smith, A(rthur) J(ames) M(arshall) 1902-1980 .... **CLC 15**
  See also CA 1-4R; 102; CANR 4; DAC; DLB 88; RGEL 2
Smith, Adam 1723(?)-1790 .... **LC 36**
  See also DLB 104, 252; RGEL 2
Smith, Alexander 1829-1867 .... **NCLC 59**
  See also DLB 32, 55
Smith, Anna Deavere 1950- .... **CLC 86**
  See also CA 133; CANR 103; CD 5; DFS 2
Smith, Betty (Wehner) 1904-1972 .... **CLC 19**
  See also BPFB 3; BYA 3; CA 5-8R; 33-36R; DLBY 1982; LAIT 3; RGAL 4; SATA 6
Smith, Charlotte (Turner) 1749-1806 .... **NCLC 23, 115**
  See also DLB 39, 109; RGEL 2
Smith, Clark Ashton 1893-1961 .... **CLC 43**
  See also CA 143; CANR 81; FANT; HGG; MTCW 2; SCFW 2; SFW 4; SUFW
Smith, Dave .... **CLC 22, 42**
  See also Smith, David (Jeddie)
  See also CAAS 7; DLB 5
Smith, David (Jeddie) 1942-
  See Smith, Dave
  See also CA 49-52; CANR 1, 59; CP 7; CSW; DAM POET
Smith, Florence Margaret 1902-1971
  See Smith, Stevie
  See also CA 17-18; 29-32R; CANR 35; CAP 2; DAM POET; MTCW 1, 2
Smith, Iain Crichton 1928-1998 .... **CLC 64**
  See also CA 21-24R; 171; CN 7; CP 7; DLB 40, 139; RGSF 2
Smith, John 1580(?)-1631 .... **LC 9**
  See also DLB 24, 30; TUS
Smith, Johnston
  See Crane, Stephen (Townley)
Smith, Joseph, Jr. 1805-1844 .... **NCLC 53**
Smith, Lee 1944- .... **CLC 25, 73**
  See also CA 114; 119; CANR 46; CSW; DLB 143; DLBY 1983; INT CA-119; RGAL 4
Smith, Martin
  See Smith, Martin Cruz
Smith, Martin Cruz 1942- .... **CLC 25**
  See also BEST 89:4; BPFB 3; CA 85-88; CANR 6, 23, 43, 65; CMW 4; CPW; DAM MULT, POP; HGG; INT CANR-23; MTCW 2; NNAL; RGAL 4
Smith, Mary-Ann Tirone 1944- .... **CLC 39**
  See also CA 118; 136
Smith, Patti 1946- .... **CLC 12**
  See also CA 93-96; CANR 63
Smith, Pauline (Urmson) 1882-1959 .... **TCLC 25**
  See also DLB 225
Smith, Rosamond
  See Oates, Joyce Carol
Smith, Sheila Kaye
  See Kaye-Smith, Sheila
Smith, Stevie .... **CLC 3, 8, 25, 44; PC 12**
  See also Smith, Florence Margaret
  See also BRWS 2; CA DLB 20; MTCW 2; PAB; PFS 3; RGEL 2
Smith, Wilbur (Addison) 1933- .... **CLC 33**
  See also CA 13-16R; CANR 7, 46, 66; CPW; MTCW 1, 2
Smith, William Jay 1918- .... **CLC 6**
  See also CA 5-8R; CANR 44, 106; CP 7; CSW; CWRI 5; DLB 5; MAICYA 1, 2; SAAS 22; SATA 2, 68
Smith, Woodrow Wilson
  See Kuttner, Henry
Smith, Zadie 1976- .... **CLC 158**
  See also CA 193
Smolenskin, Peretz 1842-1885 .... **NCLC 30**

Smollett, Tobias (George) 1721-1771 ... **LC 2, 46**
See also BRW 3; CDBLB 1660-1789; DLB 39, 104; RGEL 2; TEA

Snodgrass, W(illiam) D(e Witt)
1926- .... **CLC 2, 6, 10, 18, 68**
See also AMWS 6; CA 1-4R; CANR 6, 36, 65, 85; CP 7; DAM POET; DLB 5; MTCW 1, 2; RGAL 4

Snow, C(harles) P(ercy) 1905-1980 ... **CLC 1, 4, 6, 9, 13, 19**
See also BRW 7; CA 5-8R; 101; CANR 28; CDBLB 1945-1960; DAM NOV; DLB 15, 77; DLBD 17; MTCW 1, 2; RGEL 2; TEA

Snow, Frances Compton
See Adams, Henry (Brooks)

Snyder, Gary (Sherman) 1930- . **CLC 1, 2, 5, 9, 32, 120; PC 21**
See also AMWS 8; ANW; CA 17-20R; CANR 30, 60; CP 7; DA3; DAM POET; DLB 5, 16, 165, 212, 237; MTCW 2; PFS 9; RGAL 4; WP

Snyder, Zilpha Keatley 1927- .... **CLC 17**
See also AAYA 15; BYA 1; CA 9-12R; CANR 38; CLR 31; JRDA; MAICYA 1, 2; SAAS 2; SATA 1, 28, 75, 110; SATA-Essay 112; YAW

Soares, Bernardo
See Pessoa, Fernando (Antonio Nogueira)

Sobh, A.
See Shamlu, Ahmad

Sobol, Joshua 1939- .... **CLC 60**
See also Sobol, Yehoshua
See also CA 200; CWW 2

Sobol, Yehoshua 1939-
See Sobol, Joshua
See also CWW 2

Socrates 470B.C.-399B.C. .... **CMLC 27**

Soderberg, Hjalmar 1869-1941 ...... **TCLC 39**
See also DLB 259; RGSF 2

Soderbergh, Steven 1963- .... **CLC 154**
See also AAYA 43

Sodergran, Edith (Irene) -1923
See Soedergran, Edith (Irene)
See also CA 202; DLB 259; EW 11; RGWL 2

Soedergran, Edith (Irene)
1892-1923 .... **TCLC 31**
See also Sodergran, Edith (Irene)

Softly, Edgar
See Lovecraft, H(oward) P(hillips)

Softly, Edward
See Lovecraft, H(oward) P(hillips)

Sokolov, Raymond 1941- .... **CLC 7**
See also CA 85-88

Sokolov, Sasha .... **CLC 59**

Solo, Jay
See Ellison, Harlan (Jay)

Sologub, Fyodor .... **TCLC 9**
See also Teternikov, Fyodor Kuzmich

Solomons, Ikey Esquir
See Thackeray, William Makepeace

Solomos, Dionysios 1798-1857 .... **NCLC 15**

Solwoska, Mara
See French, Marilyn

Solzhenitsyn, Aleksandr I(sayevich)
1918- .. **CLC 1, 2, 4, 7, 9, 10, 18, 26, 34, 78, 134; SSC 32; WLC**
See also AITN 1; BPFB 3; CA 69-72; CANR 40, 65; DA; DA3; DAB; DAC; DAM MST, NOV; EW 13; EXPS; LAIT 4; MTCW 1, 2; NFS 6; RGSF 2; RGWL 2; SSFS 9

Somers, Jane
See Lessing, Doris (May)

Somerville, Edith Oenone
1858-1949 .... **TCLC 51**
See also CA 196; DLB 135; RGEL 2; RGSF 2

Somerville & Ross
See Martin, Violet Florence; Somerville, Edith Oenone

Sommer, Scott 1951- .... **CLC 25**
See also CA 106

Sondheim, Stephen (Joshua) 1930- . **CLC 30, 39, 147**
See also AAYA 11; CA 103; CANR 47, 67; DAM DRAM; LAIT 4

Song, Cathy 1955- .... **PC 21**
See also AAL; CA 154; CWP; DLB 169; EXPP; FW; PFS 5

Sontag, Susan 1933- .... **CLC 1, 2, 10, 13, 31, 105**
See also AMWS 3; CA 17-20R; CANR 25, 51, 74, 97; CN 7; CPW; DA3; DAM POP; DLB 2, 67; MAWW; MTCW 1, 2; RGAL 4; RHW; SSFS 10

Sophocles 496(?)B.C.-406(?)B.C. .... **CMLC 2, 47, 51; DC 1; WLCS**
See also AW 1; CDWLB 1; DA; DA3; DAB; DAC; DAM DRAM, MST; DFS 1, 4, 8; DLB 176; LAIT 1; RGWL 2

Sordello 1189-1269 .... **CMLC 15**

Sorel, Georges 1847-1922 .... **TCLC 91**
See also CA 118; 188

Sorel, Julia
See Drexler, Rosalyn

Sorokin, Vladimir .... **CLC 59**

Sorrentino, Gilbert 1929- .. **CLC 3, 7, 14, 22, 40**
See also CA 77-80; CANR 14, 33; CN 7; CP 7; DLB 5, 173; DLBY 1980; INT CANR-14

Soseki
See Natsume, Soseki
See also MJW

Soto, Gary 1952- ... **CLC 32, 80; HLC 2; PC 28**
See also AAYA 10, 37; BYA 11; CA 119; 125; CANR 50, 74, 107; CLR 38; CP 7; DAM MULT; DLB 82; EXPP; HW 1, 2; INT CA-125; JRDA; MAICYA 2; MAICYAS 1; MTCW 2; PFS 7; RGAL 4; SATA 80, 120; WYA; YAW

Soupault, Philippe 1897-1990 .... **CLC 68**
See also CA 116; 147; 131; GFL 1789 to the Present

Souster, (Holmes) Raymond 1921- .... **CLC 5, 14**
See also CA 13-16R; CAAS 14; CANR 13, 29, 53; CP 7; DA3; DAC; DAM POET; DLB 88; RGEL 2; SATA 63

Southern, Terry 1924(?)-1995 .... **CLC 7**
See also BPFB 3; CA 1-4R; 150; CANR 1, 55, 107; CN 7; DLB 2; IDFW 3, 4

Southey, Robert 1774-1843 .... **NCLC 8, 97**
See also BRW 4; DLB 93, 107, 142; RGEL 2; SATA 54

Southworth, Emma Dorothy Eliza Nevitte
1819-1899 .... **NCLC 26**
See also DLB 239

Souza, Ernest
See Scott, Evelyn

Soyinka, Wole 1934- .... **CLC 3, 5, 14, 36, 44; BLC 3; DC 2; WLC**
See also AFW; BW 2, 3; CA 13-16R; CANR 27, 39, 82; CD 5; CDWLB 3; CN 7; CP 7; DA; DA3; DAB; DAC; DAM DRAM, MST, MULT; DFS 10; DLB 125; MTCW 1, 2; RGEL 2; WLIT 2

Spackman, W(illiam) M(ode)
1905-1990 .... **CLC 46**
See also CA 81-84; 132

Spacks, Barry (Bernard) 1931- .... **CLC 14**
See also CA 154; CANR 33, 109; CP 7; DLB 105

Spanidou, Irini 1946- .... **CLC 44**
See also CA 185

Spark, Muriel (Sarah) 1918- ..... **CLC 2, 3, 5, 8, 13, 18, 40, 94; SSC 10**
See also BRWS 1; CA 5-8R; CANR 12, 36, 76, 89; CDBLB 1945-1960; CN 7; CP 7; DA3; DAB; DAC; DAM MST, NOV; DLB 15, 139; FW; INT CANR-12; LAIT 4; MTCW 1, 2; RGEL 2; WLIT 4; YAW

Spaulding, Douglas
See Bradbury, Ray (Douglas)

Spaulding, Leonard
See Bradbury, Ray (Douglas)

Spelman, Elizabeth .... **CLC 65**

Spence, J. A. D.
See Eliot, T(homas) S(tearns)

Spencer, Elizabeth 1921- .... **CLC 22**
See also CA 13-16R; CANR 32, 65, 87; CN 7; CSW; DLB 6, 218; MTCW 1; RGAL 4; SATA 14

Spencer, Leonard G.
See Silverberg, Robert

Spencer, Scott 1945- .... **CLC 30**
See also CA 113; CANR 51; DLBY 1986

Spender, Stephen (Harold)
1909-1995 .... **CLC 1, 2, 5, 10, 41, 91**
See also BRWS 2; CA 9-12R; 149; CANR 31, 54; CDBLB 1945-1960; CP 7; DA3; DAM POET; DLB 20; MTCW 1, 2; PAB; RGEL 2

Spengler, Oswald (Arnold Gottfried)
1880-1936 .... **TCLC 25**
See also CA 118; 189

Spenser, Edmund 1552(?)-1599 ..... **LC 5, 39; PC 8; WLC**
See also BRW 1; CDBLB Before 1660; DA; DA3; DAB; DAC; DAM MST, POET; DLB 167; EFS 2; EXPP; PAB; RGEL 2; WLIT 3; WP

Spicer, Jack 1925-1965 .... **CLC 8, 18, 72**
See also CA 85-88; DAM POET; DLB 5, 16, 193; GLL 1; WP

Spiegelman, Art 1948- .... **CLC 76**
See also AAYA 10; CA 125; CANR 41, 55, 74; MTCW 2; SATA 109; YAW

Spielberg, Peter 1929- .... **CLC 6**
See also CA 5-8R; CANR 4, 48; DLBY 1981

Spielberg, Steven 1947- .... **CLC 20**
See also AAYA 8, 24; CA 77-80; CANR 32; SATA 32

Spillane, Frank Morrison 1918-
See Spillane, Mickey
See also CA 25-28R; CANR 28, 63; DA3; MTCW 1, 2; SATA 66

Spillane, Mickey .... **CLC 3, 13**
See also Spillane, Frank Morrison
See also BPFB 3; CMW 4; DLB 226; MSW; MTCW 2

Spinoza, Benedictus de 1632-1677 .. **LC 9, 58**

Spinrad, Norman (Richard) 1940- ... **CLC 46**
See also BPFB 3; CA 37-40R; CAAS 19; CANR 20, 91; DLB 8; INT CANR-20; SFW 4

Spitteler, Carl (Friedrich Georg)
1845-1924 .... **TCLC 12**
See also CA 109; DLB 129

Spivack, Kathleen (Romola Drucker)
1938- .... **CLC 6**
See also CA 49-52

Spoto, Donald 1941- .... **CLC 39**
See also CA 65-68; CANR 11, 57, 93

Springsteen, Bruce (F.) 1949- .... **CLC 17**
See also CA 111

Spurling, Hilary 1940- .... **CLC 34**
See also CA 104; CANR 25, 52, 94

Spyker, John Howland
See Elman, Richard (Martin)

Squires, (James) Radcliffe
1917-1993 .... **CLC 51**
See also CA 1-4R; 140; CANR 6, 21

Srivastava, Dhanpat Rai 1880(?)-1936
See Premchand
See also CA 118; 197

Stacy, Donald
See Pohl, Frederik

Stael
See Stael-Holstein, Anne Louise Germaine Necker
See also EW 5; RGWL 2

Stael, Germaine de
See Stael-Holstein, Anne Louise Germaine Necker
See also DLB 119, 192; FW; GFL 1789 to the Present; TWA

Stael-Holstein, Anne Louise Germaine Necker 1766-1817 .... **NCLC 3, 91**
See also Stael; Stael, Germaine de

Stafford, Jean 1915-1979 .. **CLC 4, 7, 19, 68; SSC 26**
See also CA 1-4R; 85-88; CANR 3, 65; DLB 2, 173; MTCW 1, 2; RGAL 4; RGSF 2; SATA-Obit 22; TCWW 2

Stafford, William (Edgar)
1914-1993 .... **CLC 4, 7, 29**
See also CA 5-8R; 142; CAAS 3; CANR 5, 22; DAM POET; DLB 5, 206; EXPP; INT CANR-22; PFS 2, 8; RGAL 4; WP

Stagnelius, Eric Johan 1793-1823 . **NCLC 61**

Staines, Trevor
See Brunner, John (Kilian Houston)

Stairs, Gordon
See Austin, Mary (Hunter)
See also TCWW 2

Stairs, Gordon 1868-1934
See Austin, Mary (Hunter)

Stalin, Joseph 1879-1953 .... **TCLC 92**

Stancykowna
See Szymborska, Wislawa

Stannard, Martin 1947- .... **CLC 44**
See also CA 142; DLB 155

Stanton, Elizabeth Cady
1815-1902 .... **TCLC 73**
See also CA 171; DLB 79; FW

Stanton, Maura 1946- .... **CLC 9**
See also CA 89-92; CANR 15; DLB 120

Stanton, Schuyler
See Baum, L(yman) Frank

Stapledon, (William) Olaf
1886-1950 .... **TCLC 22**
See also CA 111; 162; DLB 15, 255; SFW 4

Starbuck, George (Edwin)
1931-1996 .... **CLC 53**
See also CA 21-24R; 153; CANR 23; DAM POET

Stark, Richard
See Westlake, Donald E(dwin)

Staunton, Schuyler
See Baum, L(yman) Frank

Stead, Christina (Ellen) 1902-1983 ... **CLC 2, 5, 8, 32, 80**
See also BRWS 4; CA 13-16R; 109; CANR 33, 40; DLB 260; FW; MTCW 1, 2; RGEL 2; RGSF 2

Stead, William Thomas
1849-1912 .... **TCLC 48**
See also CA 167

Stebnitsky, M.
See Leskov, Nikolai (Semyonovich)

Steele, Sir Richard 1672-1729 .... **LC 18**
See also BRW 3; CDBLB 1660-1789; DLB 84, 101; RGEL 2; WLIT 3

Steele, Timothy (Reid) 1948- .... **CLC 45**
See also CA 93-96; CANR 16, 50, 92; CP 7; DLB 120

Steffens, (Joseph) Lincoln
1866-1936 .... **TCLC 20**
See also CA 117

Stegner, Wallace (Earle) 1909-1993 .. **CLC 9, 49, 81; SSC 27**
See also AITN 1; AMWS 4; ANW; BEST 90:3; BPFB 3; CA 1-4R; 141; CAAS 9; CANR 1, 21, 46; DAM NOV; DLB 9, 206; DLBY 1993; MTCW 1, 2; RGAL 4; TCWW 2

Stein, Gertrude 1874-1946 .... **TCLC 1, 6, 28, 48; PC 18; SSC 42; WLC**
See also AMW; CA 104; 132; CANR 108; CDALB 1917-1929; DA; DA3; DAB; DAC; DAM MST, NOV, POET; DLB 4, 54, 86, 228; DLBD 15; EXPS; GLL 1; MAWW; MTCW 1, 2; RGAL 4; RGSF 2; SSFS 5; WP

Steinbeck, John (Ernst) 1902-1968 ... **CLC 1, 5, 9, 13, 21, 34, 45, 75, 124; SSC 11, 37; WLC**
See also AAYA 12; AMW; BPFB 3; BYA 2, 3, 13; CA 1-4R; 25-28R; CANR 1, 35; CDALB 1929-1941; DA; DA3; DAB; DAC; DAM DRAM, MST, NOV; DLB 7, 9, 212; DLBD 2; EXPS; LAIT 3; MTCW 1, 2; NFS 1, 5, 7; RGAL 4; RGSF 2; RHW; SATA 9; SSFS 3, 6; TCWW 2; WYA; YAW

Steinem, Gloria 1934- .... **CLC 63**
See also CA 53-56; CANR 28, 51; DLB 246; FW; MTCW 1, 2

Steiner, George 1929- .... **CLC 24**
See also CA 73-76; CANR 31, 67, 108; DAM NOV; DLB 67; MTCW 1, 2; SATA 62

Steiner, K. Leslie
See Delany, Samuel R(ay), Jr.

Steiner, Rudolf 1861-1925 .... **TCLC 13**
See also CA 107

Stendhal 1783-1842 .. **NCLC 23, 46; SSC 27; WLC**
See also DA; DA3; DAB; DAC; DAM MST, NOV; DLB 119; EW 5; GFL 1789 to the Present; RGWL 2; TWA

Stephen, Adeline Virginia
See Woolf, (Adeline) Virginia

Stephen, Sir Leslie 1832-1904 .... **TCLC 23**
See also BRW 5; CA 123; DLB 57, 144, 190

Stephen, Sir Leslie
See Stephen, Sir Leslie

Stephen, Virginia
See Woolf, (Adeline) Virginia

Stephens, James 1882(?)-1950 .... **TCLC 4; SSC 50**
See also CA 104; 192; DLB 19, 153, 162; FANT; RGEL 2; SUFW

Stephens, Reed
See Donaldson, Stephen R(eeder)

Steptoe, Lydia
See Barnes, Djuna
See also GLL 1

Sterchi, Beat 1949- .... **CLC 65**

Sterling, Brett
See Bradbury, Ray (Douglas); Hamilton, Edmond

Sterling, Bruce 1954- .... **CLC 72**
See also CA 119; CANR 44; SCFW 2; SFW 4

Sterling, George 1869-1926 .... **TCLC 20**
See also CA 117; 165; DLB 54

Stern, Gerald 1925- .... **CLC 40, 100**
See also AMWS 9; CA 81-84; CANR 28, 94; CP 7; DLB 105; RGAL 4

Stern, Richard (Gustave) 1928- ... **CLC 4, 39**
See also CA 1-4R; CANR 1, 25, 52; CN 7; DLB 218; DLBY 1987; INT CANR-25

Sternberg, Josef von 1894-1969 .... **CLC 20**
See also CA 81-84

Sterne, Laurence 1713-1768 .... **LC 2, 48; WLC**
See also BRW 3; CDBLB 1660-1789; DA; DAB; DAC; DAM MST, NOV; DLB 39; RGEL 2

Sternheim, (William Adolf) Carl
1878-1942 .... **TCLC 8**
See also CA 105; 193; DLB 56, 118; RGWL 2

Stevens, Mark 1951- .... **CLC 34**
See also CA 122

Stevens, Wallace 1879-1955 ...... **TCLC 3, 12, 45; PC 6; WLC**
See also AMW; AMWR 1; CA 104; 124; CDALB 1929-1941; DA; DA3; DAB; DAC; DAM MST, POET; DLB 54; EXPP; MTCW 1, 2; PAB; PFS 13; RGAL 4; WP

Stevenson, Anne (Katharine) 1933- .. **CLC 7, 33**
See also BRWS 6; CA 17-20R; CAAS 9; CANR 9, 33; CP 7; CWP; DLB 40; MTCW 1; RHW

Stevenson, Robert Louis (Balfour)
1850-1894 ...... **NCLC 5, 14, 63; SSC 11, 51; WLC**
See also AAYA 24; BPFB 3; BRW 5; BRWR 1; BYA 1, 2, 4, 13; CDBLB 1890-1914; CLR 10, 11; DA; DA3; DAB; DAC; DAM MST, NOV; DLB 18, 57, 141, 156, 174; DLBD 13; HGG; JRDA; LAIT 1, 3; MAICYA 1, 3; NFS 11; RGEL 2; RGSF 2; SATA 100; SUFW; TEA; WCH; WLIT 4; WYA; YABC 2; YAW

Stewart, J(ohn) I(nnes) M(ackintosh)
1906-1994 .... **CLC 7, 14, 32**
See also Innes, Michael
See also CA 85-88; 147; CAAS 3; CANR 47; CMW 4; MTCW 1, 2

Stewart, Mary (Florence Elinor)
1916- .... **CLC 7, 35, 117**
See also AAYA 29; BPFB 3; CA 1-4R; CANR 1, 59; CMW 4; CPW; DAB; FANT; RHW; SATA 12; YAW

Stewart, Mary Rainbow
See Stewart, Mary (Florence Elinor)

Stifle, June
See Campbell, Maria

Stifter, Adalbert 1805-1868 .. **NCLC 41; SSC 28**
See also CDWLB 2; DLB 133; RGSF 2; RGWL 2

Still, James 1906-2001 .... **CLC 49**
See also CA 65-68; 195; CAAS 17; CANR 10, 26; CSW; DLB 9; DLBY 01; SATA 29; SATA-Obit 127

Sting 1951-
See Sumner, Gordon Matthew
See also CA 167

Stirling, Arthur
See Sinclair, Upton (Beall)

Stitt, Milan 1941- .... **CLC 29**
See also CA 69-72

Stockton, Francis Richard 1834-1902
See Stockton, Frank R.
See also CA 108; 137; MAICYA 1, 2; SATA 44; SFW 4

Stockton, Frank R. .... **TCLC 47**
See also Stockton, Francis Richard
See also BYA 4, 13; DLB 42, 74; DLBD 13; EXPS; SATA-Brief 32; SSFS 3; SUFW; WCH

Stoddard, Charles
See Kuttner, Henry

Stoker, Abraham 1847-1912
See Stoker, Bram
See also CA 105; 150; DA; DA3; DAC; DAM MST, NOV; HGG; SATA 29; TEA

Stoker, Bram .... **TCLC 8; WLC**
See also Stoker, Abraham
See also AAYA 23; BPFB 3; BRWS 3; BYA 5; CDBLB 1890-1914; DAB; DLB 36, 70, 178; RGEL 2; SUFW; WLIT 4

Stolz, Mary (Slattery) 1920- .... **CLC 12**
See also AAYA 8; AITN 1; CA 5-8R; CANR 13, 41; JRDA; MAICYA 1, 2; SAAS 3; SATA 10, 71, 133; YAW

Stone, Irving 1903-1989 .... **CLC 7**
See also AITN 1; BPFB 3; CA 1-4R; 129; CAAS 3; CANR 1, 23; CPW; DA3; DAM POP; INT CANR-23; MTCW 1, 2; RHW; SATA 3; SATA-Obit 64

Stone, Oliver (William) 1946- .... **CLC 73**
See also AAYA 15; CA 110; CANR 55

Stone, Robert (Anthony) 1937- ... **CLC 5, 23, 42**
See also AMWS 5; BPFB 3; CA 85-88; CANR 23, 66, 95; CN 7; DLB 152; INT CANR-23; MTCW 1

Stone, Zachary
See Follett, Ken(neth Martin)

Stoppard, Tom 1937- ... **CLC 1, 3, 4, 5, 8, 15, 29, 34, 63, 91; DC 6; WLC**
See also BRWR 2; BRWS 1; CA 81-84; CANR 39, 67; CBD; CD 5; CDBLB 1960 to Present; DA; DA3; DAB; DAC; DAM DRAM, MST; DFS 2, 5, 8, 11, 13; DLB 13, 233; DLBY 1985; MTCW 1, 2; RGEL 2; WLIT 4

Storey, David (Malcolm) 1933- . **CLC 2, 4, 5, 8**
See also BRWS 1; CA 81-84; CANR 36; CBD; CD 5; CN 7; DAM DRAM; DLB 13, 14, 207, 245; MTCW 1; RGEL 2

Storm, Hyemeyohsts 1935- .... **CLC 3**
See also CA 81-84; CANR 45; DAM MULT; NNAL

Storm, Theodor 1817-1888 .... **SSC 27**
See also CDWLB 2; RGSF 2; RGWL 2

Storm, (Hans) Theodor (Woldsen) 1817-1888 .... **NCLC 1; SSC 27**
See also DLB 129; EW

Storni, Alfonsina 1892-1938 .. **TCLC 5; HLC 2; PC 33**
See also CA 104; 131; DAM MULT; HW 1; LAW

Stoughton, William 1631-1701 .... **LC 38**
See also DLB 24

Stout, Rex (Todhunter) 1886-1975 ..... **CLC 3**
See also AITN 2; BPFB 3; CA 61-64; CANR 71; CMW 4; MSW; RGAL 4

Stow, (Julian) Randolph 1935- ... **CLC 23, 48**
See also CA 13-16R; CANR 33; CN 7; DLB 260; MTCW 1; RGEL 2

Stowe, Harriet (Elizabeth) Beecher 1811-1896 .... **NCLC 3, 50; WLC**
See also AMWS 1; CDALB 1865-1917; DA; DA3; DAB; DAC; DAM MST, NOV; DLB 1, 12, 42, 74, 189, 239, 243; EXPN; JRDA; LAIT 2; MAICYA 1, 2; NFS 6; RGAL 4; YABC 1

Strabo c. 64B.C.-c. 25 .... **CMLC 37**
See also DLB 176

Strachey, (Giles) Lytton 1880-1932 .... **TCLC 12**
See also BRWS 2; CA 110; 178; DLB 149; DLBD 10; MTCW 2

Strand, Mark 1934- .... **CLC 6, 18, 41, 71**
See also AMWS 4; CA 21-24R; CANR 40, 65, 100; CP 7; DAM POET; DLB 5; PAB; PFS 9; RGAL 4; SATA 41

Stratton-Porter, Gene(va Grace) 1863-1924
See Porter, Gene(va Grace) Stratton
See also ANW; CA 137; DLB 221; DLBD 14; MAICYA 1, 2; SATA 15

Straub, Peter (Francis) 1943- ... **CLC 28, 107**
See also BEST 89:1; BPFB 3; CA 85-88; CANR 28, 65, 109; CPW; DAM POP; DLBY 1984; HGG; MTCW 1, 2

Strauss, Botho 1944- .... **CLC 22**
See also CA 157; CWW 2; DLB 124

Streatfeild, (Mary) Noel 1897(?)-1986 .... **CLC 21**
See also CA 81-84; 120; CANR 31; CLR 17; CWRI 5; DLB 160; MAICYA 1, 2; SATA 20; SATA-Obit 48

Stribling, T(homas) S(igismund) 1881-1965 .... **CLC 23**
See also CA 189; 107; CMW 4; DLB 9; RGAL 4

Strindberg, (Johan) August 1849-1912 ... **TCLC 1, 8, 21, 47; DC 18; WLC**
See also CA 104; 135; DA; DA3; DAB; DAC; DAM DRAM, MST; DFS 4, 9; DLB 259; EW 7; IDTP; MTCW 2; RGWL 2

Stringer, Arthur 1874-1950 .... **TCLC 37**
See also CA 161; DLB 92

Stringer, David
See Roberts, Keith (John Kingston)

Stroheim, Erich von 1885-1957 ..... **TCLC 71**

Strugatskii, Arkadii (Natanovich) 1925-1991 .... **CLC 27**
See also CA 106; 135; SFW 4

Strugatskii, Boris (Natanovich) 1933- .... **CLC 27**
See also CA 106; SFW 4

Strummer, Joe 1953(?)- .... **CLC 30**

Strunk, William, Jr. 1869-1946 ...... **TCLC 92**
See also CA 118; 164

Stryk, Lucien 1924- .... **PC 27**
See also CA 13-16R; CANR 10, 28, 55; CP 7

Stuart, Don A.
See Campbell, John W(ood, Jr.)

Stuart, Ian
See MacLean, Alistair (Stuart)

Stuart, Jesse (Hilton) 1906-1984 ... **CLC 1, 8, 11, 14, 34; SSC 31**
See also CA 5-8R; 112; CANR 31; DLB 9, 48, 102; DLBY 1984; SATA 2; SATA-Obit 36

Stubblefield, Sally
See Trumbo, Dalton

Sturgeon, Theodore (Hamilton) 1918-1985 .... **CLC 22, 39**
See also Queen, Ellery
See also BPFB 3; BYA 9, 10; CA 81-84; 116; CANR 32, 103; DLB 8; DLBY 1985; HGG; MTCW 1, 2; SCFW; SFW 4; SUFW

Sturges, Preston 1898-1959 .... **TCLC 48**
See also CA 114; 149; DLB 26

Styron, William 1925- .... **CLC 1, 3, 5, 11, 15, 60; SSC 25**
See also AMW; BEST 90:4; BPFB 3; CA 5-8R; CANR 6, 33, 74; CDALB 1968-1988; CN 7; CPW; CSW; DA3; DAM NOV, POP; DLB 2, 143; DLBY 1980; INT CANR-6; LAIT 2; MTCW 1, 2; NCFS 1; RGAL 4; RHW

Su, Chien 1884-1918
See Su Man-shu
See also CA 123

Suarez Lynch, B.
See Bioy Casares, Adolfo; Borges, Jorge Luis

Suassuna, Ariano Vilar 1927-
See also CA 178; HLCS 1; HW 2; LAW

Suckling, Sir John 1609-1642 . **LC 75; PC 30**
See also BRW 2; DAM POET; DLB 58, 126; EXPP; PAB; RGEL 2

Suckow, Ruth 1892-1960 .... **SSC 18**
See also CA 193; 113; DLB 9, 102; RGAL 4; TCWW 2

Sudermann, Hermann 1857-1928 .. **TCLC 15**
See also CA 107; 201; DLB 118

Sue, Eugene 1804-1857 .... **NCLC 1**
See also DLB 119

Sueskind, Patrick 1949- .... **CLC 44**
See also Suskind, Patrick

Sukenick, Ronald 1932- .... **CLC 3, 4, 6, 48**
See also CA 25-28R; CAAS 8; CANR 32, 89; CN 7; DLB 173; DLBY 1981

Suknaski, Andrew 1942- .... **CLC 19**
See also CA 101; CP 7; DLB 53

Sullivan, Vernon
See Vian, Boris

Sully Prudhomme, Rene-Francois-Armand 1839-1907 .... **TCLC 31**
See also GFL 1789 to the Present

Su Man-shu .... **TCLC 24**
See also Su, Chien

Summerforest, Ivy B.
See Kirkup, James

Summers, Andrew James 1942- .... **CLC 26**

Summers, Andy
See Summers, Andrew James

Summers, Hollis (Spurgeon, Jr.) 1916- .... **CLC 10**
See also CA 5-8R; CANR 3; DLB 6

Summers, (Alphonsus Joseph-Mary Augustus) Montague 1880-1948 .... **TCLC 16**
See also CA 118; 163

Sumner, Gordon Matthew .... **CLC 26**
See also Police, The; Sting

Surtees, Robert Smith 1805-1864 .. **NCLC 14**
See also DLB 21; RGEL 2

Susann, Jacqueline 1921-1974 .... **CLC 3**
See also AITN 1; BPFB 3; CA 65-68; 53-56; MTCW 1, 2

Su Shi
See Su Shih
See also RGWL 2

Su Shih 1036-1101 .... **CMLC 15**
See also Su Shi

Suskind, Patrick
See Sueskind, Patrick
See also BPFB 3; CA 145; CWW 2

Sutcliff, Rosemary 1920-1992 .... **CLC 26**
See also AAYA 10; BYA 1, 4; CA 5-8R; 139; CANR 37; CLR 1, 37; CPW; DAB; DAC; DAM MST, POP; JRDA; MAICYA 1, 2; MAICYAS 1; RHW; SATA 6, 44, 78; SATA-Obit 73; WYA; YAW

Sutro, Alfred 1863-1933 .... **TCLC 6**
See also CA 105; 185; DLB 10; RGEL 2

Sutton, Henry
See Slavitt, David R(ytman)

Suzuki, D. T.
See Suzuki, Daisetz Teitaro

Suzuki, Daisetz T.
See Suzuki, Daisetz Teitaro

Suzuki, Daisetz Teitaro 1870-1966 .... **TCLC 109**
See also CA 121; 111; MTCW 1, 2

Suzuki, Teitaro
See Suzuki, Daisetz Teitaro

Svevo, Italo .... **TCLC 2, 35; SSC 25**
See also Schmitz, Aron Hector
See also EW 8; RGWL 2

Swados, Elizabeth (A.) 1951- .... **CLC 12**
See also CA 97-100; CANR 49; INT 97-100

Swados, Harvey 1920-1972 .... **CLC 5**
See also CA 5-8R; 37-40R; CANR 6; DLB 2

Swan, Gladys 1934- .... **CLC 69**
See also CA 101; CANR 17, 39

Swanson, Logan
See Matheson, Richard (Burton)

Swarthout, Glendon (Fred)
1918-1992 .... **CLC 35**
See also CA 1-4R; 139; CANR 1, 47; LAIT 5; SATA 26; TCWW 2; YAW

Sweet, Sarah C.
See Jewett, (Theodora) Sarah Orne

Swenson, May 1919-1989 ...... **CLC 4, 14, 61, 106; PC 14**
See also AMWS 4; CA 5-8R; 130; CANR 36, 61; DA; DAB; DAC; DAM MST, POET; DLB 5; EXPP; GLL 2; MTCW 1, 2; SATA 15; WP

Swift, Augustus
See Lovecraft, H(oward) P(hillips)

Swift, Graham (Colin) 1949- ...... **CLC 41, 88**
See also BRWS 5; CA 117; 122; CANR 46, 71; CN 7; DLB 194; MTCW 2; RGSF 2

Swift, Jonathan 1667-1745 .. **LC 1, 42; PC 9; WLC**
See also AAYA 41; BRW 3; BRWR 1; BYA 5, 14; CDBLB 1660-1789; CLR 53; DA; DA3; DAB; DAC; DAM MST, NOV, POET; DLB 39, 95, 101; EXPN; LAIT 1; NFS 6; RGEL 2; SATA 19; WCH; WLIT 3

Swinburne, Algernon Charles
1837-1909 ... **TCLC 8, 36; PC 24; WLC**
See also BRW 5; CA 105; 140; CDBLB 1832-1890; DA; DA3; DAB; DAC; DAM MST, POET; DLB 35, 57; PAB; RGEL 2

Swinfen, Ann .... **CLC 34**
See also CA 202

Swinnerton, Frank Arthur
1884-1982 .... **CLC 31**
See also CA 108; DLB 34

Swithen, John
See King, Stephen (Edwin)

Sylvia
See Ashton-Warner, Sylvia (Constance)

Symmes, Robert Edward
See Duncan, Robert (Edward)

Symonds, John Addington
1840-1893 .... **NCLC 34**
See also DLB 57, 144

Symons, Arthur 1865-1945 .... **TCLC 11**
See also CA 107; 189; DLB 19, 57, 149; RGEL 2

Symons, Julian (Gustave)
1912-1994 .... **CLC 2, 14, 32**
See also CA 49-52; 147; CAAS 3; CANR 3, 33, 59; CMW 4; DLB 87, 155; DLBY 1992; MSW; MTCW 1

Synge, (Edmund) J(ohn) M(illington)
1871-1909 .... **TCLC 6, 37; DC 2**
See also BRW 6; BRWR 1; CA 104; 141; CDBLB 1890-1914; DAM DRAM; DLB 10, 19; RGEL 2; WLIT 4

Syruc, J.
See Milosz, Czeslaw

Szirtes, George 1948- .... **CLC 46**
See also CA 109; CANR 27, 61; CP 7

Szymborska, Wislawa 1923- .... **CLC 99**
See also CA 154; CANR 91; CDWLB 4; CWP; CWW 2; DA3; DLB 232; DLBY 1996; MTCW 2; PFS 15

T. O., Nik
See Annensky, Innokenty (Fyodorovich)

Tabori, George 1914- .... **CLC 19**
See also CA 49-52; CANR 4, 69; CBD; CD 5; DLB 245

Tagore, Rabindranath 1861-1941 ... **TCLC 3, 53; PC 8; SSC 48**
See also CA 104; 120; DA3; DAM DRAM, POET; MTCW 1, 2; RGEL 2; RGSF 2; RGWL 2

Taine, Hippolyte Adolphe
1828-1893 .... **NCLC 15**
See also EW 7; GFL 1789 to the Present

Talese, Gay 1932- .... **CLC 37**
See also AITN 1; CA 1-4R; CANR 9, 58; DLB 185; INT CANR-9; MTCW 1, 2

Tallent, Elizabeth (Ann) 1954- .... **CLC 45**
See also CA 117; CANR 72; DLB 130

Tally, Ted 1952- .... **CLC 42**
See also CA 120; 124; CAD; CD 5; INT 124

Talvik, Heiti 1904-1947 .... **TCLC 87**

Tamayo y Baus, Manuel
1829-1898 .... **NCLC 1**

Tammsaare, A(nton) H(ansen)
1878-1940 .... **TCLC 27**
See also CA 164; CDWLB 4; DLB 220

Tam'si, Tchicaya U
See Tchicaya, Gerald Felix

Tan, Amy (Ruth) 1952- .... **CLC 59, 120, 151; AAL**
See also AAYA 9; AMWS 10; BEST 89:3; BPFB 3; CA 136; CANR 54, 105; CDALBS; CN 7; CPW 1; DA3; DAM MULT, NOV, POP; DLB 173; EXPN; FW; LAIT 3, 5; MTCW 2; NFS 1, 13; RGAL 4; SATA 75; SSFS 9; YAW

Tandem, Felix
See Spitteler, Carl (Friedrich Georg)

Tanizaki, Jun'ichiro 1886-1965 ... **CLC 8, 14, 28; SSC 21**
See also Tanizaki Jun'ichiro
See also CA 93-96; 25-28R; MJW; MTCW 2; RGSF 2; RGWL 2

Tanizaki Jun'ichiro
See Tanizaki, Jun'ichiro
See also DLB 180

Tanner, William
See Amis, Kingsley (William)

Tao Lao
See Storni, Alfonsina

Tarantino, Quentin (Jerome)
1963- .... **CLC 125**
See also CA 171

Tarassoff, Lev
See Troyat, Henri

Tarbell, Ida M(inerva) 1857-1944 . **TCLC 40**
See also CA 122; 181; DLB 47

Tarkington, (Newton) Booth
1869-1946 .... **TCLC 9**
See also BPFB 3; BYA 3; CA 110; 143; CWRI 5; DLB 9, 102; MTCW 2; RGAL 4; SATA 17

Tarkovsky, Andrei (Arsenyevich)
1932-1986 .... **CLC 75**
See also CA 127

Tartt, Donna 1964(?)- .... **CLC 76**
See also CA 142

Tasso, Torquato 1544-1595 .... **LC 5**
See also EFS 2; EW 2; RGWL 2

Tate, (John Orley) Allen 1899-1979 .. **CLC 2, 4, 6, 9, 11, 14, 24**
See also AMW; CA 5-8R; 85-88; CANR 32, 108; DLB 4, 45, 63; DLBD 17; MTCW 1, 2; RGAL 4; RHW

Tate, Ellalice
See Hibbert, Eleanor Alice Burford

Tate, James (Vincent) 1943- ...... **CLC 2, 6, 25**
See also CA 21-24R; CANR 29, 57; CP 7; DLB 5, 169; PFS 10, 15; RGAL 4; WP

Tauler, Johannes c. 1300-1361 ...... **CMLC 37**
See also DLB 179

Tavel, Ronald 1940- .... **CLC 6**
See also CA 21-24R; CAD; CANR 33; CD 5

Taviani, Paolo 1931- .... **CLC 70**
See also CA 153

Taylor, Bayard 1825-1878 .... **NCLC 89**
See also DLB 3, 189, 250, 254; RGAL 4

Taylor, C(ecil) P(hilip) 1929-1981 .... **CLC 27**
See also CA 25-28R; 105; CANR 47; CBD

Taylor, Edward 1642(?)-1729 .... **LC 11**
See also AMW; DA; DAB; DAC; DAM MST, POET; DLB 24; EXPP; RGAL 4; TUS

Taylor, Eleanor Ross 1920- .... **CLC 5**
See also CA 81-84; CANR 70

Taylor, Elizabeth 1932-1975 ..... **CLC 2, 4, 29**
See also CA 13-16R; CANR 9, 70; DLB 139; MTCW 1; RGEL 2; SATA 13

Taylor, Frederick Winslow
1856-1915 .... **TCLC 76**
See also CA 188

Taylor, Henry (Splawn) 1942- .... **CLC 44**
See also CA 33-36R; CAAS 7; CANR 31; CP 7; DLB 5; PFS 10

Taylor, Kamala (Purnaiya) 1924-
See Markandaya, Kamala
See also CA 77-80; NFS 13

Taylor, Mildred D(elois) 1943- .... **CLC 21**
See also AAYA 10; BW 1; BYA 3, 8; CA 85-88; CANR 25; CLR 9, 59; CSW; DLB 52; JRDA; LAIT 3; MAICYA 1, 2; SAAS 5; SATA 15, 70; WYA; YAW

Taylor, Peter (Hillsman) 1917-1994 .. **CLC 1, 4, 18, 37, 44, 50, 71; SSC 10**
See also AMWS 5; BPFB 3; CA 13-16R; 147; CANR 9, 50; CSW; DLB 218; DLBY 1981, 1994; EXPS; INT CANR-9; MTCW 1, 2; RGSF 2; SSFS 9

Taylor, Robert Lewis 1912-1998 .... **CLC 14**
See also CA 1-4R; 170; CANR 3, 64; SATA 10

Tchekhov, Anton
See Chekhov, Anton (Pavlovich)

Tchicaya, Gerald Felix 1931-1988 .. **CLC 101**
See also CA 129; 125; CANR 81

Tchicaya U Tam'si
See Tchicaya, Gerald Felix

Teasdale, Sara 1884-1933 .... **TCLC 4; PC 31**
See also CA 104; 163; DLB 45; GLL 1; PFS 14; RGAL 4; SATA 32

Tegner, Esaias 1782-1846 .... **NCLC 2**

Teilhard de Chardin, (Marie Joseph) Pierre
1881-1955 .... **TCLC 9**
See also CA 105; GFL 1789 to the Present

Temple, Ann
See Mortimer, Penelope (Ruth)

Tennant, Emma (Christina) 1937- ... **CLC 13, 52**
See also CA 65-68; CAAS 9; CANR 10, 38, 59, 88; CN 7; DLB 14; SFW 4

Tenneshaw, S. M.
See Silverberg, Robert

Tennyson, Alfred, Lord
1809-1892 ..... **NCLC 30, 65, 115; PC 6; WLC**
See also BRW 4; CDBLB 1832-1890; DA; DA3; DAB; DAC; DAM MST, POET; DLB 32; EXPP; PAB; PFS 1, 2, 4, 11, 15; RGEL 2; TEA; WLIT 4; WP

Teran, Lisa St. Aubin de .... **CLC 36**
See also St. Aubin de Teran, Lisa

Terence c. 184B.C.-c. 159B.C. ...... **CMLC 14; DC 7**
See also AW 1; CDWLB 1; DLB 211; RGWL 2

Teresa de Jesus, St. 1515-1582 .... **LC 18**

Terkel, Louis 1912-
See Terkel, Studs
See also CA 57-60; CANR 18, 45, 67; DA3; MTCW 1, 2

Terkel, Studs .... **CLC 38**
See also Terkel, Louis
See also AAYA 32; AITN 1; MTCW 2

Terry, C. V.
See Slaughter, Frank G(ill)

Terry, Megan 1932- .... **CLC 19; DC 13**
See also CA 77-80; CABS 3; CAD; CANR 43; CD 5; CWD; DLB 7, 249; GLL 2

Tertullian c. 155-c. 245 .... **CMLC 29**

Tertz, Abram
See Sinyavsky, Andrei (Donatevich)
See also CWW 2; RGSF 2

Tesich, Steve 1943(?)-1996 .... **CLC 40, 69**
See also CA 105; 152; CAD; DLBY 1983

Tesla, Nikola 1856-1943 .... **TCLC 88**

Teternikov, Fyodor Kuzmich 1863-1927
See Sologub, Fyodor
See also CA 104

Tevis, Walter 1928-1984 .... **CLC 42**
See also CA 113; SFW 4

Tey, Josephine .... **TCLC 14**
See also Mackintosh, Elizabeth
See also DLB 77; MSW

Thackeray, William Makepeace
1811-1863 ..... **NCLC 5, 14, 22, 43; WLC**
See also BRW 5; CDBLB 1832-1890; DA; DA3; DAB; DAC; DAM MST, NOV; DLB 21, 55, 159, 163; RGEL 2; SATA 23; TEA; WLIT 3

Thakura, Ravindranatha
See Tagore, Rabindranath

Thames, C. H.
See Marlowe, Stephen

Tharoor, Shashi 1956- .... **CLC 70**
See also CA 141; CANR 91; CN 7

Thelwell, Michael Miles 1939- .... **CLC 22**
See also BW 2; CA 101

Theobald, Lewis, Jr.
See Lovecraft, H(oward) P(hillips)

Theocritus c. 310B.C.- .... **CMLC 45**
See also AW 1; DLB 176; RGWL 2

Theodorescu, Ion N. 1880-1967
See Arghezi, Tudor
See also CA 116

Theriault, Yves 1915-1983 .... **CLC 79**
See also CA 102; CCA 1; DAC; DAM MST; DLB 88

Theroux, Alexander (Louis) 1939- .... **CLC 2, 25**
See also CA 85-88; CANR 20, 63; CN 7

Theroux, Paul (Edward) 1941- ..... **CLC 5, 8, 11, 15, 28, 46**
See also AAYA 28; AMWS 8; BEST 89:4; BPFB 3; CA 33-36R; CANR 20, 45, 74; CDALBS; CN 7; CPW 1; DA3; DAM POP; DLB 2, 218; HGG; MTCW 1, 2; RGAL 4; SATA 44, 109

Thesen, Sharon 1946- .... **CLC 56**
See also CA 163; CP 7; CWP

Thespis fl. 6th cent. B.C.- .... **CMLC 51**

Thevenin, Denis
See Duhamel, Georges

Thibault, Jacques Anatole Francois
1844-1924
See France, Anatole
See also CA 106; 127; DA3; DAM NOV; MTCW 1, 2

Thiele, Colin (Milton) 1920- .... **CLC 17**
See also CA 29-32R; CANR 12, 28, 53, 105; CLR 27; MAICYA 1, 2; SAAS 2; SATA 14, 72, 125; YAW

Thomas, Audrey (Callahan) 1935- .... **CLC 7, 13, 37, 107; SSC 20**
See also AITN 2; CA 21-24R; CAAS 19; CANR 36, 58; CN 7; DLB 60; MTCW 1; RGSF 2

Thomas, Augustus 1857-1934 .... **TCLC 97**

Thomas, D(onald) M(ichael) 1935- . **CLC 13, 22, 31, 132**
See also BPFB 3; BRWS 4; CA 61-64; CAAS 11; CANR 17, 45, 75; CDBLB 1960 to Present; CN 7; CP 7; DA3; DLB 40, 207; HGG; INT CANR-17; MTCW 1, 2; SFW 4

Thomas, Dylan (Marlais)
1914-1953 ... **TCLC 1, 8, 45, 105; PC 2; SSC 3, 44; WLC**
See also BRWS 1; CA 104; 120; CANR 65; CDBLB 1945-1960; DA; DA3; DAB; DAC; DAM DRAM, MST, POET; DLB 13, 20, 139; EXPP; LAIT 3; MTCW 1, 2; PAB; PFS 1, 3, 8; RGEL 2; RGSF 2; SATA 60; WLIT 4; WP

Thomas, (Philip) Edward
1878-1917 .... **TCLC 10**
See also BRW 6; BRWS 3; CA 106; 153; DAM POET; DLB 19, 98, 156, 216; PAB; RGEL 2

Thomas, Joyce Carol 1938- .... **CLC 35**
See also AAYA 12; BW 2, 3; CA 113; 116; CANR 48; CLR 19; DLB 33; INT CA-116; JRDA; MAICYA 1, 2; MTCW 1, 2; SAAS 7; SATA 40, 78, 123; WYA; YAW

Thomas, Lewis 1913-1993 .... **CLC 35**
See also ANW; CA 85-88; 143; CANR 38, 60; MTCW 1, 2

Thomas, M. Carey 1857-1935 .... **TCLC 89**
See also FW

Thomas, Paul
See Mann, (Paul) Thomas

Thomas, Piri 1928- .... **CLC 17; HLCS 2**
See also CA 73-76; HW 1

Thomas, R(onald) S(tuart)
1913-2000 .... **CLC 6, 13, 48**
See also CA 89-92; 189; CAAS 4; CANR 30; CDBLB 1960 to Present; CP 7; DAB; DAM POET; DLB 27; MTCW 1; RGEL 2

Thomas, Ross (Elmore) 1926-1995 .. **CLC 39**
See also CA 33-36R; 150; CANR 22, 63; CMW 4

Thompson, Francis (Joseph)
1859-1907 .... **TCLC 4**
See also BRW 5; CA 104; 189; CDBLB 1890-1914; DLB 19; RGEL 2; TEA

Thompson, Francis Clegg
See Mencken, H(enry) L(ouis)

Thompson, Hunter S(tockton)
1937(?)- .... **CLC 9, 17, 40, 104**
See also BEST 89:1; BPFB 3; CA 17-20R; CANR 23, 46, 74, 77; CPW; CSW; DA3; DAM POP; DLB 185; MTCW 1, 2

Thompson, James Myers
See Thompson, Jim (Myers)

Thompson, Jim (Myers)
1906-1977(?) .... **CLC 69**
See also BPFB 3; CA 140; CMW 4; CPW; DLB 226; MSW

Thompson, Judith .... **CLC 39**
See also CWD

Thomson, James 1700-1748 .... **LC 16, 29, 40**
See also BRWS 3; DAM POET; DLB 95; RGEL 2

Thomson, James 1834-1882 .... **NCLC 18**
See also DAM POET; DLB 35; RGEL 2

Thoreau, Henry David 1817-1862 .. **NCLC 7, 21, 61; PC 30; WLC**
See also AAYA 42; AMW; ANW; BYA 3; CDALB 1640-1865; DA; DA3; DAB; DAC; DAM MST; DLB 1, 183, 223; LAIT 2; NCFS 3; RGAL 4; TUS

Thorndike, E. L.
See Thorndike, Edward L(ee)

Thorndike, Edward L(ee)
1874-1949 .... **TCLC 107**
See also CA 121

Thornton, Hall
See Silverberg, Robert

Thucydides c. 455B.C.-c. 395B.C. . **CMLC 17**
See also AW 1; DLB 176; RGWL 2

Thumboo, Edwin Nadason 1933- .... **PC 30**
See also CA 194

Thurber, James (Grover)
1894-1961 .. **CLC 5, 11, 25, 125; SSC 1, 47**
See also AMWS 1; BPFB 3; BYA 5; CA 73-76; CANR 17, 39; CDALB 1929-1941; CWRI 5; DA; DA3; DAB; DAC; DAM DRAM, MST, NOV; DLB 4, 11, 22, 102; EXPS; FANT; LAIT 3; MAICYA 1, 2; MTCW 1, 2; RGAL 4; RGSF 2; SATA 13; SSFS 1, 10; SUFW

Thurman, Wallace (Henry)
1902-1934 .... **TCLC 6; BLC 3**
See also BW 1, 3; CA 104; 124; CANR 81; DAM MULT; DLB 51

Tibullus c. 54B.C.-c. 18B.C. .... **CMLC 36**
See also AW 2; DLB 211; RGWL 2

Ticheburn, Cheviot
See Ainsworth, William Harrison

Tieck, (Johann) Ludwig
1773-1853 .... **NCLC 5, 46; SSC 31**
See also CDWLB 2; DLB 90; EW 5; IDTP; RGSF 2; RGWL 2; SUFW

Tiger, Derry
See Ellison, Harlan (Jay)

Tilghman, Christopher 1948(?)- .... **CLC 65**
See also CA 159; CSW; DLB 244

Tillich, Paul (Johannes)
1886-1965 .... **CLC 131**
See also CA 5-8R; 25-28R; CANR 33; MTCW 1, 2

Tillinghast, Richard (Williford)
1940- .... **CLC 29**
See also CA 29-32R; CAAS 23; CANR 26, 51, 96; CP 7; CSW

Timrod, Henry 1828-1867 .... **NCLC 25**
See also DLB 3, 248; RGAL 4

Tindall, Gillian (Elizabeth) 1938- .... **CLC 7**
See also CA 21-24R; CANR 11, 65, 107; CN 7

Tiptree, James, Jr. .... **CLC 48, 50**
See also Sheldon, Alice Hastings Bradley
See also DLB 8; SCFW 2; SFW 4

Tirso de Molina
See Tirso de Molina
See also RGWL 2

Tirso de Molina 1580(?)-1648 ..... **LC 73; DC 13; HLCS 2**
See also Tirso de Molina

Titmarsh, Michael Angelo
See Thackeray, William Makepeace

Tocqueville, Alexis (Charles Henri Maurice Clerel Comte) de 1805-1859 .. **NCLC 7, 63**
See also EW 6; GFL 1789 to the Present

Tolkien, J(ohn) R(onald) R(euel)
1892-1973 .... **CLC 1, 2, 3, 8, 12, 38; WLC**
See also AAYA 10; AITN 1; BPFB 3; BRWS 2; CA 17-18; 45-48; CANR 36; CAP 2; CDBLB 1914-1945; CLR 56; CPW 1; CWRI 5; DA; DA3; DAB; DAC; DAM MST, NOV, POP; DLB 15, 160, 255; EFS 2; FANT; JRDA; LAIT 1; MAICYA 1, 2; MTCW 1, 2; NFS 8; RGEL 2; SATA 2, 32, 100; SATA-Obit 24; SFW 4; SUFW; TEA; WCH; WYA; YAW

Toller, Ernst 1893-1939 .... **TCLC 10**
See also CA 107; 186; DLB 124; RGWL 2

Tolson, M. B.
See Tolson, Melvin B(eaunorus)
Tolson, Melvin B(eaunorus)
1898(?)-1966 .... **CLC 36, 105; BLC 3**
See also AFAW 1, 2; BW 1, 3; CA 124; 89-92; CANR 80; DAM MULT, POET; DLB 48, 76; RGAL 4
Tolstoi, Aleksei Nikolaevich
See Tolstoy, Alexey Nikolaevich
Tolstoi, Lev
See Tolstoy, Leo (Nikolaevich)
See also RGSF 2; RGWL 2
Tolstoy, Alexey Nikolaevich
1882-1945 .... **TCLC 18**
See also CA 107; 158; SFW 4
Tolstoy, Leo (Nikolaevich)
1828-1910 .. **TCLC 4, 11, 17, 28, 44, 79; SSC 9, 30, 45, 54; WLC**
See also Tolstoi, Lev
See also CA 104; 123; DA; DA3; DAB; DAC; DAM MST, NOV; DLB 238; EFS 2; EW 7; EXPS; IDTP; LAIT 2; NFS 10; SATA 26; SSFS 5
Tolstoy, Count Leo
See Tolstoy, Leo (Nikolaevich)
Tomasi di Lampedusa, Giuseppe 1896-1957
See Lampedusa, Giuseppe (Tomasi) di
See also CA 111; DLB 177
Tomlin, Lily .... **CLC 17**
See also Tomlin, Mary Jean
Tomlin, Mary Jean 1939(?)-
See Tomlin, Lily
See also CA 117
Tomlinson, (Alfred) Charles 1927- .... **CLC 2, 4, 6, 13, 45; PC 17**
See also CA 5-8R; CANR 33; CP 7; DAM POET; DLB 40
Tomlinson, H(enry) M(ajor)
1873-1958 .... **TCLC 71**
See also CA 118; 161; DLB 36, 100, 195
Tonson, Jacob
See Bennett, (Enoch) Arnold
Toole, John Kennedy 1937-1969 ..... **CLC 19, 64**
See also BPFB 3; CA 104; DLBY 1981; MTCW 2
Toomer, Eugene
See Toomer, Jean
Toomer, Eugene Pinchback
See Toomer, Jean
Toomer, Jean 1892-1967 .... **CLC 1, 4, 13, 22; BLC 3; PC 7; SSC 1, 45; WLCS**
See also AFAW 1, 2; AMWS 3, 9; BW 1; CA 85-88; CDALB 1917-1929; DA3; DAM MULT; DLB 45, 51; EXPP; EXPS; MTCW 1, 2; NFS 11; RGAL 4; RGSF 2; SSFS 5
Toomer, Nathan Jean
See Toomer, Jean
Toomer, Nathan Pinchback
See Toomer, Jean
Torley, Luke
See Blish, James (Benjamin)
Tornimparte, Alessandra
See Ginzburg, Natalia
Torre, Raoul della
See Mencken, H(enry) L(ouis)
Torrence, Ridgely 1874-1950 .... **TCLC 97**
See also DLB 54, 249
Torrey, E(dwin) Fuller 1937- .... **CLC 34**
See also CA 119; CANR 71
Torsvan, Ben Traven
See Traven, B.
Torsvan, Benno Traven
See Traven, B.
Torsvan, Berick Traven
See Traven, B.
Torsvan, Berwick Traven
See Traven, B.
Torsvan, Bruno Traven
See Traven, B.
Torsvan, Traven
See Traven, B.
Tourneur, Cyril 1575(?)-1626 .... **LC 66**
See also BRW 2; DAM DRAM; DLB 58; RGEL 2
Tournier, Michel (Edouard) 1924- .... **CLC 6, 23, 36, 95**
See also CA 49-52; CANR 3, 36, 74; DLB 83; GFL 1789 to the Present; MTCW 1, 2; SATA 23
Tournimparte, Alessandra
See Ginzburg, Natalia
Towers, Ivar
See Kornbluth, C(yril) M.
Towne, Robert (Burton) 1936(?)- ...... **CLC 87**
See also CA 108; DLB 44; IDFW 3, 4
Townsend, Sue .... **CLC 61**
See also Townsend, Susan Elaine
See also AAYA 28; CBD; CWD; SATA 55, 93; SATA-Brief 48
Townsend, Susan Elaine 1946-
See Townsend, Sue
See also CA 119; 127; CANR 65, 107; CD 5; CPW; DAB; DAC; DAM MST; INT 127; YAW
Townshend, Pete
See Townshend, Peter (Dennis Blandford)
Townshend, Peter (Dennis Blandford)
1945- .... **CLC 17, 42**
See also CA 107
Tozzi, Federigo 1883-1920 .... **TCLC 31**
See also CA 160
Tracy, Don(ald Fiske) 1905-1970(?)
See Queen, Ellery
See also CA 1-4R; 176; CANR 2
Trafford, F. G.
See Riddell, Charlotte
Traill, Catharine Parr 1802-1899 .. **NCLC 31**
See also DLB 99
Trakl, Georg 1887-1914 .... **TCLC 5; PC 20**
See also CA 104; 165; EW 10; MTCW 2; RGWL 2
Transtroemer, Tomas (Goesta)
1931- .... **CLC 52, 65**
See also CA 117; 129; CAAS 17; DAM POET
Transtromer, Tomas
See Transtroemer, Tomas (Goesta)
See also DLB 257
Transtromer, Tomas Gosta
See Transtroemer, Tomas (Goesta)
Traven, B. 1882(?)-1969 .... **CLC 8, 11**
See also CA 19-20; 25-28R; CAP 2; DLB 9, 56; MTCW 1; RGAL 4
Trediakovsky, Vasilii Kirillovich
1703-1769 .... **LC 68**
See also DLB 150
Treitel, Jonathan 1959- .... **CLC 70**
Trelawny, Edward John
1792-1881 .... **NCLC 85**
See also DLB 110, 116, 144
Tremain, Rose 1943- .... **CLC 42**
See also CA 97-100; CANR 44, 95; CN 7; DLB 14; RGSF 2; RHW
Tremblay, Michel 1942- .... **CLC 29, 102**
See also CA 116; 128; CCA 1; CWW 2; DAC; DAM MST; DLB 60; GLL 1; MTCW 1, 2
Trevanian .... **CLC 29**
See also Whitaker, Rod(ney)
Trevor, Glen
See Hilton, James
Trevor, William .. **CLC 7, 9, 14, 25, 71, 116; SSC 21**
See also Cox, William Trevor
See also BRWS 4; CBD; CD 5; CN 7; DLB 14, 139; MTCW 2; RGEL 2; RGSF 2; SSFS 10
Trifonov, Iurii (Valentinovich)
See Trifonov, Yuri (Valentinovich)
See also RGWL 2
Trifonov, Yuri (Valentinovich)
1925-1981 .... **CLC 45**
See also Trifonov, Iurii (Valentinovich)
See also CA 126; 103; MTCW 1
Trilling, Diana (Rubin) 1905-1996 . **CLC 129**
See also CA 5-8R; 154; CANR 10, 46; INT CANR-10; MTCW 1, 2
Trilling, Lionel 1905-1975 .... **CLC 9, 11, 24**
See also AMWS 3; CA 9-12R; 61-64; CANR 10, 105; DLB 28, 63; INT CANR-10; MTCW 1, 2; RGAL 4
Trimball, W. H.
See Mencken, H(enry) L(ouis)
Tristan
See Gomez de la Serna, Ramon
Tristram
See Housman, A(lfred) E(dward)
Trogdon, William (Lewis) 1939-
See Heat-Moon, William Least
See also CA 115; 119; CANR 47, 89; CPW; INT CA-119
Trollope, Anthony 1815-1882 .... **NCLC 6, 33, 101; SSC 28; WLC**
See also BRW 5; CDBLB 1832-1890; DA; DA3; DAB; DAC; DAM MST, NOV; DLB 21, 57, 159; RGEL 2; RGSF 2; SATA 22
Trollope, Frances 1779-1863 .... **NCLC 30**
See also DLB 21, 166
Trotsky, Leon 1879-1940 .... **TCLC 22**
See also CA 118; 167
Trotter (Cockburn), Catharine
1679-1749 .... **LC 8**
See also DLB 84, 252
Trotter, Wilfred 1872-1939 .... **TCLC 97**
Trout, Kilgore
See Farmer, Philip Jose
Trow, George W. S. 1943- .... **CLC 52**
See also CA 126; CANR 91
Troyat, Henri 1911- .... **CLC 23**
See also CA 45-48; CANR 2, 33, 67; GFL 1789 to the Present; MTCW 1
Trudeau, G(arretson) B(eekman) 1948-
See Trudeau, Garry B.
See also CA 81-84; CANR 31; SATA 35
Trudeau, Garry B. .... **CLC 12**
See also Trudeau, G(arretson) B(eekman)
See also AAYA 10; AITN 2
Truffaut, Francois 1932-1984 ... **CLC 20, 101**
See also CA 81-84; 113; CANR 34
Trumbo, Dalton 1905-1976 .... **CLC 19**
See also CA 21-24R; 69-72; CANR 10; DLB 26; IDFW 3, 4; YAW
Trumbull, John 1750-1831 .... **NCLC 30**
See also DLB 31; RGAL 4
Trundlett, Helen B.
See Eliot, T(homas) S(tearns)
Truth, Sojourner 1797(?)-1883 .... **NCLC 94**
See also DLB 239; FW; LAIT 2
Tryon, Thomas 1926-1991 .... **CLC 3, 11**
See also AITN 1; BPFB 3; CA 29-32R; 135; CANR 32, 77; CPW; DA3; DAM POP; HGG; MTCW 1
Tryon, Tom
See Tryon, Thomas
Ts'ao Hsueh-ch'in 1715(?)-1763 .... **LC 1**
Tsushima, Shuji 1909-1948
See Dazai Osamu
See also CA 107

Tsvetaeva (Efron), Marina (Ivanovna)
1892-1941 .... **TCLC 7, 35; PC 14**
See also CA 104; 128; CANR 73; EW 11; MTCW 1, 2; RGWL 2

Tuck, Lily 1938- .... **CLC 70**
See also CA 139; CANR 90

Tu Fu 712-770 .... **PC 9**
See also Du Fu
See also DAM MULT; WP

Tunis, John R(oberts) 1889-1975 ..... **CLC 12**
See also BYA 1; CA 61-64; CANR 62; DLB 22, 171; JRDA; MAICYA 1, 2; SATA 37; SATA-Brief 30; YAW

Tuohy, Frank .... **CLC 37**
See also Tuohy, John Francis
See also DLB 14, 139

Tuohy, John Francis 1925-
See Tuohy, Frank
See also CA 5-8R; 178; CANR 3, 47; CN 7

Turco, Lewis (Putnam) 1934- ..... **CLC 11, 63**
See also CA 13-16R; CAAS 22; CANR 24, 51; CP 7; DLBY 1984

Turgenev, Ivan (Sergeevich)
1818-1883 .... **NCLC 21, 37; DC 7; SSC 7; WLC**
See also DA; DAB; DAC; DAM MST, NOV; DFS 6; DLB 238; EW 6; RGSF 2; RGWL 2

Turgot, Anne-Robert-Jacques
1727-1781 .... **LC 26**

Turner, Frederick 1943- .... **CLC 48**
See also CA 73-76; CAAS 10; CANR 12, 30, 56; DLB 40

Turton, James
See Crace, Jim

Tutu, Desmond M(pilo) 1931- .... **CLC 80; BLC 3**
See also BW 1, 3; CA 125; CANR 67, 81; DAM MULT

Tutuola, Amos 1920-1997 ...... **CLC 5, 14, 29; BLC 3**
See also AFW; BW 2, 3; CA 9-12R; 159; CANR 27, 66; CDWLB 3; CN 7; DA3; DAM MULT; DLB 125; DNFS 2; MTCW 1, 2; RGEL 2; WLIT 2

Twain, Mark .... **TCLC 6, 12, 19, 36, 48, 59; SSC 34; WLC**
See also Clemens, Samuel Langhorne
See also AAYA 20; AMW; BPFB 3; BYA 2, 3, 11, 14; CLR 58, 60, 66; DLB 11; EXPN; EXPS; FANT; LAIT 2; NFS 1, 6; RGAL 4; RGSF 2; SFW 4; SSFS 1, 7; SUFW; WCH; WYA; YAW

Tyler, Anne 1941- . **CLC 7, 11, 18, 28, 44, 59, 103**
See also AAYA 18; AMWS 4; BEST 89:1; BPFB 3; BYA 12; CA 9-12R; CANR 11, 33, 53, 109; CDALBS; CN 7; CPW; CSW; DAM NOV, POP; DLB 6, 143; DLBY 1982; EXPN; MAWW; MTCW 1, 2; NFS 2, 7, 10; RGAL 4; SATA 7, 90; YAW

Tyler, Royall 1757-1826 .... **NCLC 3**
See also DLB 37; RGAL 4

Tynan, Katharine 1861-1931 .... **TCLC 3**
See also CA 104; 167; DLB 153, 240; FW

Tyutchev, Fyodor 1803-1873 .... **NCLC 34**

Tzara, Tristan 1896-1963 ..... **CLC 47; PC 27**
See also CA 153; 89-92; DAM POET; MTCW 2

Uhry, Alfred 1936- .... **CLC 55**
See also CA 127; 133; CAD; CD 5; CSW; DA3; DAM DRAM, POP; DFS 15; INT CA-133

Ulf, Haerved
See Strindberg, (Johan) August

Ulf, Harved
See Strindberg, (Johan) August

Ulibarri, Sabine R(eyes) 1919- .... **CLC 83; HLCS 2**
See also CA 131; CANR 81; DAM MULT; DLB 82; HW 1, 2; RGSF 2

Unamuno (y Jugo), Miguel de
1864-1936 .. **TCLC 2, 9; HLC 2; SSC 11**
See also CA 104; 131; CANR 81; DAM MULT, NOV; DLB 108; EW 8; HW 1, 2; MTCW 1, 2; RGSF 2; RGWL 2

Undercliffe, Errol
See Campbell, (John) Ramsey

Underwood, Miles
See Glassco, John

Undset, Sigrid 1882-1949 ..... **TCLC 3; WLC**
See also CA 104; 129; DA; DA3; DAB; DAC; DAM MST, NOV; EW 9; FW; MTCW 1, 2; RGWL 2

Ungaretti, Giuseppe 1888-1970 ... **CLC 7, 11, 15**
See also CA 19-20; 25-28R; CAP 2; DLB 114; EW 10; RGWL 2

Unger, Douglas 1952- .... **CLC 34**
See also CA 130; CANR 94

Unsworth, Barry (Forster) 1930- .... **CLC 76, 127**
See also BRWS 7; CA 25-28R; CANR 30, 54; CN 7; DLB 194

Updike, John (Hoyer) 1932- . **CLC 1, 2, 3, 5, 7, 9, 13, 15, 23, 34, 43, 70, 139; SSC 13, 27; WLC**
See also AAYA 36; AMW; AMWR 1; BPFB 3; BYA 12; CA 1-4R; CABS 1; CANR 4, 33, 51, 94; CDALB 1968-1988; CN 7; CP 7; CPW 1; DA; DA3; DAB; DAC; DAM MST, NOV, POET, POP; DLB 2, 5, 143, 218, 227; DLBD 3; DLBY 1980, 1982, 1997; EXPP; HGG; MTCW 1, 2; NFS 12; RGAL 4; RGSF 2; SSFS 3

Upshaw, Margaret Mitchell
See Mitchell, Margaret (Munnerlyn)

Upton, Mark
See Sanders, Lawrence

Upward, Allen 1863-1926 .... **TCLC 85**
See also CA 117; 187; DLB 36

Urdang, Constance (Henriette)
1922-1996 .... **CLC 47**
See also CA 21-24R; CANR 9, 24; CP 7; CWP

Uriel, Henry
See Faust, Frederick (Schiller)

Uris, Leon (Marcus) 1924- .... **CLC 7, 32**
See also AITN 1, 2; BEST 89:2; BPFB 3; CA 1-4R; CANR 1, 40, 65; CN 7; CPW 1; DA3; DAM NOV, POP; MTCW 1, 2; SATA 49

Urista, Alberto H. 1947- .... **PC 34**
See also Alurista
See also CA 45-48, 182; CANR 2, 32; HLCS 1; HW 1

Urmuz
See Codrescu, Andrei

Urquhart, Guy
See McAlmon, Robert (Menzies)

Urquhart, Jane 1949- .... **CLC 90**
See also CA 113; CANR 32, 68; CCA 1; DAC

Usigli, Rodolfo 1905-1979
See also CA 131; HLCS 1; HW 1; LAW

Ustinov, Peter (Alexander) 1921- .... **CLC 1**
See also AITN 1; CA 13-16R; CANR 25, 51; CBD; CD 5; DLB 13; MTCW 2

U Tam'si, Gerald Felix Tchicaya
See Tchicaya, Gerald Felix

U Tam'si, Tchicaya
See Tchicaya, Gerald Felix

Vachss, Andrew (Henry) 1942- .... **CLC 106**
See also CA 118; CANR 44, 95; CMW 4

Vachss, Andrew H.
See Vachss, Andrew (Henry)

Vaculik, Ludvik 1926- .... **CLC 7**
See also CA 53-56; CANR 72; CWW 2; DLB 232

Vaihinger, Hans 1852-1933 .... **TCLC 71**
See also CA 116; 166

Valdez, Luis (Miguel) 1940- ..... **CLC 84; DC 10; HLC 2**
See also CA 101; CAD; CANR 32, 81; CD 5; DAM MULT; DFS 5; DLB 122; HW 1; LAIT 4

Valenzuela, Luisa 1938- .... **CLC 31, 104; HLCS 2; SSC 14**
See also CA 101; CANR 32, 65; CDWLB 3; CWW 2; DAM MULT; DLB 113; FW; HW 1, 2; LAW; RGSF 2

Valera y Alcala-Galiano, Juan
1824-1905 .... **TCLC 10**
See also CA 106

Valery, (Ambroise) Paul (Toussaint Jules)
1871-1945 .... **TCLC 4, 15; PC 9**
See also CA 104; 122; DA3; DAM POET; DLB 258; EW 8; GFL 1789 to the Present; MTCW 1, 2; RGWL 2

Valle-Inclan, Ramon (Maria) del
1866-1936 .... **TCLC 5; HLC 2**
See also CA 106; 153; CANR 80; DAM MULT; DLB 134; EW 8; HW 2; RGSF 2; RGWL 2

Vallejo, Antonio Buero
See Buero Vallejo, Antonio

Vallejo, Cesar (Abraham)
1892-1938 .... **TCLC 3, 56; HLC 2**
See also CA 105; 153; DAM MULT; HW 1; LAW; RGWL 2

Valles, Jules 1832-1885 .... **NCLC 71**
See also DLB 123; GFL 1789 to the Present

Vallette, Marguerite Eymery
1860-1953 .... **TCLC 67**
See also CA 182; DLB 123, 192

Valle Y Pena, Ramon del
See Valle-Inclan, Ramon (Maria) del

Van Ash, Cay 1918- .... **CLC 34**

Vanbrugh, Sir John 1664-1726 .... **LC 21**
See also BRW 2; DAM DRAM; DLB 80; IDTP; RGEL 2

Van Campen, Karl
See Campbell, John W(ood, Jr.)

Vance, Gerald
See Silverberg, Robert

Vance, Jack .... **CLC 35**
See also Vance, John Holbrook
See also DLB 8; FANT; SCFW 2; SFW 4; SUFW

Vance, John Holbrook 1916-
See Queen, Ellery; Vance, Jack
See also CA 29-32R; CANR 17, 65; CMW 4; MTCW 1

Van Den Bogarde, Derek Jules Gaspard Ulric Niven 1921-1999 .... **CLC 14**
See also Bogarde, Dirk
See also CA 77-80; 179

Vandenburgh, Jane .... **CLC 59**
See also CA 168

Vanderhaeghe, Guy 1951- .... **CLC 41**
See also BPFB 3; CA 113; CANR 72

van der Post, Laurens (Jan)
1906-1996 .... **CLC 5**
See also AFW; CA 5-8R; 155; CANR 35; CN 7; DLB 204; RGEL 2

van de Wetering, Janwillem 1931- ... **CLC 47**
See also CA 49-52; CANR 4, 62, 90; CMW 4

Van Dine, S. S. .... **TCLC 23**
See also Wright, Willard Huntington
See also MSW

Van Doren, Carl (Clinton)
1885-1950 .... **TCLC 18**
See also CA 111; 168

Van Doren, Mark 1894-1972 .... **CLC 6, 10**
See also CA 1-4R; 37-40R; CANR 3; DLB 45; MTCW 1, 2; RGAL 4

Van Druten, John (William)
1901-1957 .... **TCLC 2**
See also CA 104; 161; DLB 10; RGAL 4

Van Duyn, Mona (Jane) 1921- ...... **CLC 3, 7, 63, 116**
See also CA 9-12R; CANR 7, 38, 60; CP 7; CWP; DAM POET; DLB 5

Van Dyne, Edith
See Baum, L(yman) Frank

van Itallie, Jean-Claude 1936- .... **CLC 3**
See also CA 45-48; CAAS 2; CAD; CANR 1, 48; CD 5; DLB 7

Van Loot, Cornelius Obenchain
See Roberts, Kenneth (Lewis)

van Ostaijen, Paul 1896-1928 .... **TCLC 33**
See also CA 163

Van Peebles, Melvin 1932- .... **CLC 2, 20**
See also BW 2, 3; CA 85-88; CANR 27, 67, 82; DAM MULT

van Schendel, Arthur(-Francois-Emile)
1874-1946 .... **TCLC 56**

Vansittart, Peter 1920- .... **CLC 42**
See also CA 1-4R; CANR 3, 49, 90; CN 7; RHW

Van Vechten, Carl 1880-1964 .... **CLC 33**
See also AMWS 2; CA 183; 89-92; DLB 4, 9; RGAL 4

van Vogt, A(lfred) E(lton) 1912-2000 . **CLC 1**
See also BPFB 3; BYA 13, 14; CA 21-24R; 190; CANR 28; DLB 8, 251; SATA 14; SATA-Obit 124; SCFW; SFW 4

Varda, Agnes 1928- .... **CLC 16**
See also CA 116; 122

Vargas Llosa, (Jorge) Mario (Pedro)
1936- .... **CLC 3, 6, 9, 10, 15, 31, 42, 85; HLC 2**
See also Llosa, (Jorge) Mario (Pedro) Vargas
See also BPFB 3; CA 73-76; CANR 18, 32, 42, 67; CDWLB 3; DA; DA3; DAB; DAC; DAM MST, MULT, NOV; DLB 145; DNFS 2; HW 1, 2; LAIT 5; LAW; LAWS 1; MTCW 1, 2; RGWL 2; SSFS 14; TWA; WLIT 1

Vasiliu, George
See Bacovia, George

Vasiliu, Gheorghe
See Bacovia, George
See also CA 123; 189

Vassa, Gustavus
See Equiano, Olaudah

Vassilikos, Vassilis 1933- .... **CLC 4, 8**
See also CA 81-84; CANR 75

Vaughan, Henry 1621-1695 .... **LC 27**
See also BRW 2; DLB 131; PAB; RGEL 2

Vaughn, Stephanie .... **CLC 62**

Vazov, Ivan (Minchov) 1850-1921 . **TCLC 25**
See also CA 121; 167; CDWLB 4; DLB 147

Veblen, Thorstein B(unde)
1857-1929 .... **TCLC 31**
See also AMWS 1; CA 115; 165; DLB 246

Vega, Lope de 1562-1635 .... **LC 23; HLCS 2**
See also EW 2; RGWL 2

Vendler, Helen (Hennessy) 1933- ... **CLC 138**
See also CA 41-44R; CANR 25, 72; MTCW 1, 2

Venison, Alfred
See Pound, Ezra (Weston Loomis)

Verdi, Marie de
See Mencken, H(enry) L(ouis)

Verdu, Matilde
See Cela, Camilo Jose

Verga, Giovanni (Carmelo)
1840-1922 .... **TCLC 3; SSC 21**
See also CA 104; 123; CANR 101; EW 7; RGSF 2; RGWL 2

Vergil 70B.C.-19B.C. .... **CMLC 9, 40; PC 12; WLCS**
See also Virgil
See also AW 2; DA; DA3; DAB; DAC; DAM MST, POET; EFS 1

Verhaeren, Emile (Adolphe Gustave)
1855-1916 .... **TCLC 12**
See also CA 109; GFL 1789 to the Present

Verlaine, Paul (Marie) 1844-1896 .. **NCLC 2, 51; PC 2, 32**
See also DAM POET; DLB 217; EW 7; GFL 1789 to the Present; RGWL 2

Verne, Jules (Gabriel) 1828-1905 ... **TCLC 6, 52**
See also AAYA 16; BYA 4; CA 110; 131; DA3; DLB 123; GFL 1789 to the Present; JRDA; LAIT 2; MAICYA 1, 2; RGWL 2; SATA 21; SCFW; SFW 4; WCH

Verus, Marcus Annius
See Aurelius, Marcus

Very, Jones 1813-1880 .... **NCLC 9**
See also DLB 1, 243; RGAL 4

Vesaas, Tarjei 1897-1970 .... **CLC 48**
See also CA 190; 29-32R; EW 11

Vialis, Gaston
See Simenon, Georges (Jacques Christian)

Vian, Boris 1920-1959 .... **TCLC 9**
See also CA 106; 164; DLB 72; GFL 1789 to the Present; MTCW 2; RGWL 2

Viaud, (Louis Marie) Julien 1850-1923
See Loti, Pierre
See also CA 107

Vicar, Henry
See Felsen, Henry Gregor

Vicker, Angus
See Felsen, Henry Gregor

Vidal, Gore 1925- ...... **CLC 2, 4, 6, 8, 10, 22, 33, 72, 142**
See Box, Edgar
See also AITN 1; AMWS 4; BEST 90:2; BPFB 3; CA 5-8R; CAD; CANR 13, 45, 65, 100; CD 5; CDALBS; CN 7; CPW; DA3; DAM NOV, POP; DFS 2; DLB 6, 152; INT CANR-13; MTCW 1, 2; RGAL 4; RHW

Viereck, Peter (Robert Edwin)
1916- .... **CLC 4; PC 27**
See also CA 1-4R; CANR 1, 47; CP 7; DLB 5; PFS 9, 14

Vigny, Alfred (Victor) de
1797-1863 .... **NCLC 7, 102; PC 26**
See also DAM POET; DLB 119, 192, 217; EW 5; GFL 1789 to the Present; RGWL 2

Vilakazi, Benedict Wallet
1906-1947 .... **TCLC 37**
See also CA 168

Villa, Jose Garcia 1914-1997 .... **PC 22**
See also AAL; CA 25-28R; CANR 12; EXPP

Villarreal, Jose Antonio 1924-
See also CA 133; CANR 93; DAM MULT; DLB 82; HLC 2; HW 1; LAIT 4; RGAL 4

Villaurrutia, Xavier 1903-1950 ...... **TCLC 80**
See also CA 192; HW 1; LAW

Villehardouin, Geoffroi de
1150(?)-1218(?) .... **CMLC 38**

Villiers de l'Isle Adam, Jean Marie Mathias Philippe Auguste 1838-1889 ... **NCLC 3; SSC 14**
See also DLB 123, 192; GFL 1789 to the Present; RGSF 2

Villon, Francois 1431-1463(?) . **LC 62; PC 13**
See also DLB 208; EW 2; RGWL 2

Vine, Barbara .... **CLC 50**
See also Rendell, Ruth (Barbara)
See also BEST 90:4

Vinge, Joan (Carol) D(ennison)
1948- .... **CLC 30; SSC 24**
See also AAYA 32; BPFB 3; CA 93-96; CANR 72; SATA 36, 113; SFW 4; YAW

Viola, Herman J(oseph) 1938- .... **CLC 70**
See also CA 61-64; CANR 8, 23, 48, 91; SATA 126

Violis, G.
See Simenon, Georges (Jacques Christian)

Viramontes, Helena Maria 1954-
See also CA 159; DLB 122; HLCS 2; HW 2

Virgil
See Vergil
See also CDWLB 1; DLB 211; LAIT 1; RGWL 2; WP

Visconti, Luchino 1906-1976 .... **CLC 16**
See also CA 81-84; 65-68; CANR 39

Vittorini, Elio 1908-1966 .... **CLC 6, 9, 14**
See also CA 133; 25-28R; EW 12; RGWL 2

Vivekananda, Swami 1863-1902 .... **TCLC 88**

Vizenor, Gerald Robert 1934- .... **CLC 103**
See also CA 13-16R; CAAS 22; CANR 5, 21, 44, 67; DAM MULT; DLB 175, 227; MTCW 2; NNAL; TCWW 2

Vizinczey, Stephen 1933- .... **CLC 40**
See also CA 128; CCA 1; INT 128

Vliet, R(ussell) G(ordon)
1929-1984 .... **CLC 22**
See also CA 37-40R; 112; CANR 18

Vogau, Boris Andreyevich 1894-1937(?)
See Pilnyak, Boris
See also CA 123

Vogel, Paula A(nne) 1951- ... **CLC 76; DC 18**
See also CA 108; CAD; CD 5; CWD; DFS 14; RGAL 4

Voigt, Cynthia 1942- .... **CLC 30**
See also AAYA 3, 30; BYA 1, 3, 6, 7, 8; CA 106; CANR 18, 37, 40, 94; CLR 13, 48; INT CANR-18; JRDA; LAIT 5; MAICYA 1, 2; MAICYAS 1; SATA 48, 79, 116; SATA-Brief 33; WYA; YAW

Voigt, Ellen Bryant 1943- .... **CLC 54**
See also CA 69-72; CANR 11, 29, 55; CP 7; CSW; CWP; DLB 120

Voinovich, Vladimir (Nikolaevich)
1932- .... **CLC 10, 49, 147**
See also CA 81-84; CAAS 12; CANR 33, 67; MTCW 1

Vollmann, William T. 1959- .... **CLC 89**
See also CA 134; CANR 67; CPW; DA3; DAM NOV, POP; MTCW 2

Voloshinov, V. N.
See Bakhtin, Mikhail Mikhailovich

Voltaire 1694-1778 .... **LC 14, 79; SSC 12; WLC**
See also BYA 13; DA; DA3; DAB; DAC; DAM DRAM, MST; EW 4; GFL Beginnings to 1789; NFS 7; RGWL 2

von Aschendrof, Baron Ignatz 1873-1939
See Ford, Ford Madox

von Daeniken, Erich 1935- .... **CLC 30**
See also AITN 1; CA 37-40R; CANR 17, 44

von Daniken, Erich
See von Daeniken, Erich

von Hartmann, Eduard
1842-1906 .... **TCLC 96**

von Hayek, Friedrich August
See Hayek, F(riedrich) A(ugust von)

von Heidenstam, (Carl Gustaf) Verner
See Heidenstam, (Carl Gustaf) Verner von

von Heyse, Paul (Johann Ludwig)
See Heyse, Paul (Johann Ludwig von)

von Hofmannsthal, Hugo
See Hofmannsthal, Hugo von

von Horvath, Odon
See Horvath, Odon von

von Horvath, Odon
See Horvath, Odon von

von Horvath, Oedoen
See Horvath, Odon von
See also CA 184

von Liliencron, (Friedrich Adolf Axel) Detlev
See Liliencron, (Friedrich Adolf Axel) Detlev von

Vonnegut, Kurt, Jr. 1922- . **CLC 1, 2, 3, 4, 5, 8, 12, 22, 40, 60, 111; SSC 8; WLC**
See also AAYA 6; AITN 1; AMWS 2; BEST 90:4; BPFB 3; BYA 3, 14; CA 1-4R; CANR 1, 25, 49, 75, 92; CDALB 1968-1988; CN 7; CPW 1; DA; DA3; DAB; DAC; DAM MST, NOV, POP; DLB 2, 8, 152; DLBD 3; DLBY 1980; EXPN; EXPS; LAIT 4; MTCW 1, 2; NFS 3; RGAL 4; SCFW; SFW 4; SSFS 5; TUS; YAW

Von Rachen, Kurt
See Hubbard, L(afayette) Ron(ald)

von Rezzori (d'Arezzo), Gregor
See Rezzori (d'Arezzo), Gregor von

von Sternberg, Josef
See Sternberg, Josef von

Vorster, Gordon 1924- .... **CLC 34**
See also CA 133

Vosce, Trudie
See Ozick, Cynthia

Voznesensky, Andrei (Andreievich) 1933- .... **CLC 1, 15, 57**
See also CA 89-92; CANR 37; CWW 2; DAM POET; MTCW 1

Waddington, Miriam 1917- .... **CLC 28**
See also CA 21-24R; CANR 12, 30; CCA 1; CP 7; DLB 68

Wagman, Fredrica 1937- .... **CLC 7**
See also CA 97-100; INT 97-100

Wagner, Linda W.
See Wagner-Martin, Linda (C.)

Wagner, Linda Welshimer
See Wagner-Martin, Linda (C.)

Wagner, Richard 1813-1883 .... **NCLC 9**
See also DLB 129; EW 6

Wagner-Martin, Linda (C.) 1936- .... **CLC 50**
See also CA 159

Wagoner, David (Russell) 1926- .... **CLC 3, 5, 15; PC 33**
See also AMWS 9; CA 1-4R; CAAS 3; CANR 2, 71; CN 7; CP 7; DLB 5, 256; SATA 14; TCWW 2

Wah, Fred(erick James) 1939- .... **CLC 44**
See also CA 107; 141; CP 7; DLB 60

Wahloo, Per 1926-1975 .... **CLC 7**
See also BPFB 3; CA 61-64; CANR 73; CMW 4; MSW

Wahloo, Peter
See Wahloo, Per

Wain, John (Barrington) 1925-1994 . **CLC 2, 11, 15, 46**
See also CA 5-8R; 145; CAAS 4; CANR 23, 54; CDBLB 1960 to Present; DLB 15, 27, 139, 155; MTCW 1, 2

Wajda, Andrzej 1926- .... **CLC 16**
See also CA 102

Wakefield, Dan 1932- .... **CLC 7**
See also CA 21-24R; CAAS 7; CN 7

Wakefield, Herbert Russell 1888-1965 .... **TCLC 120**
See also CA 5-8R; CANR 77; HGG; SUFW

Wakoski, Diane 1937- ...... **CLC 2, 4, 7, 9, 11, 40; PC 15**
See also CA 13-16R; CAAS 1; CANR 9, 60, 106; CP 7; CWP; DAM POET; DLB 5; INT CANR-9; MTCW 2

Wakoski-Sherbell, Diane
See Wakoski, Diane

Walcott, Derek (Alton) 1930- .... **CLC 2, 4, 9, 14, 25, 42, 67, 76, 160; BLC 3; DC 7**
See also BW 2; CA 89-92; CANR 26, 47, 75, 80; CBD; CD 5; CDWLB 3; CP 7; DA3; DAB; DAC; DAM MST, MULT, POET; DLB 117; DLBY 1981; DNFS 1; EFS 1; MTCW 1, 2; PFS 6; RGEL 2

Waldman, Anne (Lesley) 1945- .... **CLC 7**
See also CA 37-40R; CAAS 17; CANR 34, 69; CP 7; CWP; DLB 16

Waldo, E. Hunter
See Sturgeon, Theodore (Hamilton)

Waldo, Edward Hamilton
See Sturgeon, Theodore (Hamilton)

Walker, Alice (Malsenior) 1944- ... **CLC 5, 6, 9, 19, 27, 46, 58, 103; BLC 3; PC 30; SSC 5; WLCS**
See also AAYA 3, 33; AFAW 1, 2; AMWS 3; BEST 89:4; BPFB 3; BW 2, 3; CA 37-40R; CANR 9, 27, 49, 66, 82; CDALB 1968-1988; CN 7; CPW; CSW; DA; DA3; DAB; DAC; DAM MST, MULT, NOV, POET, POP; DLB 6, 33, 143; EXPN; EXPS; FW; INT CANR-27; LAIT 3; MAWW; MTCW 1, 2; NFS 5; RGAL 4; RGSF 2; SATA 31; SSFS 2, 11; YAW

Walker, David Harry 1911-1992 ...... **CLC 14**
See also CA 1-4R; 137; CANR 1; CWRI 5; SATA 8; SATA-Obit 71

Walker, Edward Joseph 1934-
See Walker, Ted
See also CA 21-24R; CANR 12, 28, 53; CP 7

Walker, George F. 1947- .... **CLC 44, 61**
See also CA 103; CANR 21, 43, 59; CD 5; DAB; DAC; DAM MST; DLB 60

Walker, Joseph A. 1935- .... **CLC 19**
See also BW 1, 3; CA 89-92; CAD; CANR 26; CD 5; DAM DRAM, MST; DFS 12; DLB 38

Walker, Margaret (Abigail) 1915-1998 .... **CLC 1, 6; BLC; PC 20**
See also AFAW 1, 2; BW 2, 3; CA 73-76; 172; CANR 26, 54, 76; CN 7; CP 7; CSW; DAM MULT; DLB 76, 152; EXPP; FW; MTCW 1, 2; RGAL 4; RHW

Walker, Ted .... **CLC 13**
See also Walker, Edward Joseph
See also DLB 40

Wallace, David Foster 1962- ..... **CLC 50, 114**
See also AMWS 10; CA 132; CANR 59; DA3; MTCW 2

Wallace, Dexter
See Masters, Edgar Lee

Wallace, (Richard Horatio) Edgar 1875-1932 .... **TCLC 57**
See also CA 115; CMW 4; DLB 70; MSW; RGEL 2

Wallace, Irving 1916-1990 .... **CLC 7, 13**
See also AITN 1; BPFB 3; CA 1-4R; 132; CAAS 1; CANR 1, 27; CPW; DAM NOV, POP; INT CANR-27; MTCW 1, 2

Wallant, Edward Lewis 1926-1962 ... **CLC 5, 10**
See also CA 1-4R; CANR 22; DLB 2, 28, 143; MTCW 1, 2; RGAL 4

Wallas, Graham 1858-1932 .... **TCLC 91**

Walley, Byron
See Card, Orson Scott

Walpole, Horace 1717-1797 .... **LC 2, 49**
See also BRW 3; DLB 39, 104, 213; HGG; RGEL 2; SUFW; TEA

Walpole, Hugh (Seymour) 1884-1941 .... **TCLC 5**
See also CA 104; 165; DLB 34; HGG; MTCW 2; RGEL 2; RHW

Walser, Martin 1927- .... **CLC 27**
See also CA 57-60; CANR 8, 46; CWW 2; DLB 75, 124

Walser, Robert 1878-1956 .... **TCLC 18; SSC 20**
See also CA 118; 165; CANR 100; DLB 66

Walsh, Gillian Paton
See Paton Walsh, Gillian

Walsh, Jill Paton .... **CLC 35**
See also Paton Walsh, Gillian
See also CLR 2, 65; WYA

Walter, Villiam Christian
See Andersen, Hans Christian

Walton, Izaak 1593-1683 .... **LC 72**
See also BRW 2; CDBLB Before 1660; DLB 151, 213; RGEL 2

Wambaugh, Joseph (Aloysius, Jr.) 1937- .... **CLC 3, 18**
See also AITN 1; BEST 89:3; BPFB 3; CA 33-36R; CANR 42, 65; CMW 4; CPW 1; DA3; DAM NOV, POP; DLB 6; DLBY 1983; MSW; MTCW 1, 2

Wang Wei 699(?)-761(?) .... **PC 18**
See also TWA

Ward, Arthur Henry Sarsfield 1883-1959
See Rohmer, Sax
See also CA 108; 173; CMW 4; HGG

Ward, Douglas Turner 1930- .... **CLC 19**
See also BW 1; CA 81-84; CAD; CANR 27; CD 5; DLB 7, 38

Ward, E. D.
See Lucas, E(dward) V(errall)

Ward, Mrs. Humphry 1851-1920
See Ward, Mary Augusta
See also RGEL 2

Ward, Mary Augusta 1851-1920 ... **TCLC 55**
See also Ward, Mrs. Humphry
See also DLB 18

Ward, Peter
See Faust, Frederick (Schiller)

Warhol, Andy 1928(?)-1987 .... **CLC 20**
See also AAYA 12; BEST 89:4; CA 89-92; 121; CANR 34

Warner, Francis (Robert le Plastrier) 1937- .... **CLC 14**
See also CA 53-56; CANR 11

Warner, Marina 1946- .... **CLC 59**
See also CA 65-68; CANR 21, 55; CN 7; DLB 194

Warner, Rex (Ernest) 1905-1986 .... **CLC 45**
See also CA 89-92; 119; DLB 15; RGEL 2; RHW

Warner, Susan (Bogert) 1819-1885 .... **NCLC 31**
See also DLB 3, 42, 239, 250, 254

Warner, Sylvia (Constance) Ashton
See Ashton-Warner, Sylvia (Constance)

Warner, Sylvia Townsend 1893-1978 .... **CLC 7, 19; SSC 23**
See also BRWS 7; CA 61-64; 77-80; CANR 16, 60, 104; DLB 34, 139; FANT; FW; MTCW 1, 2; RGEL 2; RGSF 2; RHW

Warren, Mercy Otis 1728-1814 ...... **NCLC 13**
See also DLB 31, 200; RGAL 4

Warren, Robert Penn 1905-1989 .. **CLC 1, 4, 6, 8, 10, 13, 18, 39, 53, 59; PC 37; SSC 4; WLC**
See also AITN 1; AMW; BPFB 3; BYA 1; CA 13-16R; 129; CANR 10, 47; CDALB 1968-1988; DA; DA3; DAB; DAC; DAM MST, NOV, POET; DLB 2, 48, 152; DLBY 1980, 1989; INT CANR-10; MTCW 1, 2; NFS 13; RGAL 4; RGSF 2; RHW; SATA 46; SATA-Obit 63; SSFS 8

Warshofsky, Isaac
See Singer, Isaac Bashevis
Warton, Thomas 1728-1790 .... **LC 15**
See also DAM POET; DLB 104, 109; RGEL 2
Waruk, Kona
See Harris, (Theodore) Wilson
Warung, Price .... **TCLC 45**
See also Astley, William
See also DLB 230; RGEL 2
Warwick, Jarvis
See Garner, Hugh
See also CCA 1
Washington, Alex
See Harris, Mark
Washington, Booker T(aliaferro)
1856-1915 .... **TCLC 10; BLC 3**
See also BW 1; CA 114; 125; DA3; DAM MULT; LAIT 2; RGAL 4; SATA 28
Washington, George 1732-1799 .... **LC 25**
See also DLB 31
Wassermann, (Karl) Jakob
1873-1934 .... **TCLC 6**
See also CA 104; 163; DLB 66
Wasserstein, Wendy 1950- .. **CLC 32, 59, 90; DC 4**
See also CA 121; 129; CABS 3; CAD; CANR 53, 75; CD 5; CWD; DA3; DAM DRAM; DFS 5; DLB 228; FW; INT CA-129; MTCW 2; SATA 94
Waterhouse, Keith (Spencer) 1929- . **CLC 47**
See also CA 5-8R; CANR 38, 67, 109; CBD; CN 7; DLB 13, 15; MTCW 1, 2
Waters, Frank (Joseph) 1902-1995 .. **CLC 88**
See also CA 5-8R; 149; CAAS 13; CANR 3, 18, 63; DLB 212; DLBY 1986; RGAL 4; TCWW 2
Waters, Mary C. .... **CLC 70**
Waters, Roger 1944- .... **CLC 35**
Watkins, Frances Ellen
See Harper, Frances Ellen Watkins
Watkins, Gerrold
See Malzberg, Barry N(athaniel)
Watkins, Gloria Jean 1952(?)-
See hooks, bell
See also BW 2; CA 143; CANR 87; MTCW 2; SATA 115
Watkins, Paul 1964- .... **CLC 55**
See also CA 132; CANR 62, 98
Watkins, Vernon Phillips
1906-1967 .... **CLC 43**
See also CA 9-10; 25-28R; CAP 1; DLB 20; RGEL 2
Watson, Irving S.
See Mencken, H(enry) L(ouis)
Watson, John H.
See Farmer, Philip Jose
Watson, Richard F.
See Silverberg, Robert
Waugh, Auberon (Alexander)
1939-2001 .... **CLC 7**
See also CA 45-48; 192; CANR 6, 22, 92; DLB 14, 194
Waugh, Evelyn (Arthur St. John)
1903-1966 .. **CLC 1, 3, 8, 13, 19, 27, 44, 107; SSC 41; WLC**
See also BPFB 3; BRW 7; CA 85-88; 25-28R; CANR 22; CDBLB 1914-1945; DA; DA3; DAB; DAC; DAM MST, NOV, POP; DLB 15, 162, 195; MTCW 1, 2; NFS 13; RGEL 2; RGSF 2; TEA; WLIT 4
Waugh, Harriet 1944- .... **CLC 6**
See also CA 85-88; CANR 22
Ways, C. R.
See Blount, Roy (Alton), Jr.
Waystaff, Simon
See Swift, Jonathan

Webb, Beatrice (Martha Potter)
1858-1943 .... **TCLC 22**
See also CA 117; 162; DLB 190; FW
Webb, Charles (Richard) 1939- .... **CLC 7**
See also CA 25-28R
Webb, James H(enry), Jr. 1946- ...... **CLC 22**
See also CA 81-84
Webb, Mary Gladys (Meredith)
1881-1927 .... **TCLC 24**
See also CA 182; 123; DLB 34; FW
Webb, Mrs. Sidney
See Webb, Beatrice (Martha Potter)
Webb, Phyllis 1927- .... **CLC 18**
See also CA 104; CANR 23; CCA 1; CP 7; CWP; DLB 53
Webb, Sidney (James) 1859-1947 .. **TCLC 22**
See also CA 117; 163; DLB 190
Webber, Andrew Lloyd .... **CLC 21**
See also Lloyd Webber, Andrew
See also DFS 7
Weber, Lenora Mattingly
1895-1971 .... **CLC 12**
See also CA 19-20; 29-32R; CAP 1; SATA 2; SATA-Obit 26
Weber, Max 1864-1920 .... **TCLC 69**
See also CA 109; 189
Webster, John 1580(?)-1634(?) .... **LC 33; DC 2; WLC**
See also BRW 2; CDBLB Before 1660; DA; DAB; DAC; DAM MST; DLB 58; IDTP; RGEL 2; WLIT 3
Webster, Noah 1758-1843 .... **NCLC 30**
See also DLB 1, 37, 42, 43, 73, 243
Wedekind, (Benjamin) Frank(lin)
1864-1918 .... **TCLC 7**
See also CA 104; 153; CDWLB 2; DAM DRAM; DLB 118; EW 8; RGWL 2
Wehr, Demaris .... **CLC 65**
Weidman, Jerome 1913-1998 .... **CLC 7**
See also AITN 2; CA 1-4R; 171; CAD; CANR 1; DLB 28
Weil, Simone (Adolphine)
1909-1943 .... **TCLC 23**
See also CA 117; 159; EW 12; FW; GFL 1789 to the Present; MTCW 2
Weininger, Otto 1880-1903 .... **TCLC 84**
Weinstein, Nathan
See West, Nathanael
Weinstein, Nathan von Wallenstein
See West, Nathanael
Weir, Peter (Lindsay) 1944- .... **CLC 20**
See also CA 113; 123
Weiss, Peter (Ulrich) 1916-1982 .. **CLC 3, 15, 51**
See also CA 45-48; 106; CANR 3; DAM DRAM; DFS 3; DLB 69, 124; RGWL 2
Weiss, Theodore (Russell) 1916- ... **CLC 3, 8, 14**
See also CA 9-12R; CAAE 189; CAAS 2; CANR 46, 94; CP 7; DLB 5
Welch, (Maurice) Denton
1915-1948 .... **TCLC 22**
See also CA 121; 148; RGEL 2
Welch, James 1940- .... **CLC 6, 14, 52**
See also CA 85-88; CANR 42, 66, 107; CN 7; CP 7; CPW; DAM MULT, POP; DLB 175, 256; NNAL; RGAL 4; TCWW 2
Weldon, Fay 1931- . **CLC 6, 9, 11, 19, 36, 59, 122**
See also BRWS 4; CA 21-24R; CANR 16, 46, 63, 97; CDBLB 1960 to Present; CN 7; CPW; DAM POP; DLB 14, 194; FW; HGG; INT CANR-16; MTCW 1, 2; RGEL 2; RGSF 2
Wellek, Rene 1903-1995 .... **CLC 28**
See also CA 5-8R; 150; CAAS 7; CANR 8; DLB 63; INT CANR-8
Weller, Michael 1942- .... **CLC 10, 53**
See also CA 85-88; CAD; CD 5

Weller, Paul 1958- .... **CLC 26**
Wellershoff, Dieter 1925- .... **CLC 46**
See also CA 89-92; CANR 16, 37
Welles, (George) Orson 1915-1985 .. **CLC 20, 80**
See also AAYA 40; CA 93-96; 117
Wellman, John McDowell 1945-
See Wellman, Mac
See also CA 166; CD 5
Wellman, Mac .... **CLC 65**
See also Wellman, John McDowell; Wellman, John McDowell
See also CAD; RGAL 4
Wellman, Manly Wade 1903-1986 ... **CLC 49**
See also CA 1-4R; 118; CANR 6, 16, 44; FANT; SATA 6; SATA-Obit 47; SFW 4; SUFW
Wells, Carolyn 1869(?)-1942 .... **TCLC 35**
See also CA 113; 185; CMW 4; DLB 11
Wells, H(erbert) G(eorge)
1866-1946 .... **TCLC 6, 12, 19; SSC 6; WLC**
See also AAYA 18; BPFB 3; BRW 6; CA 110; 121; CDBLB 1914-1945; CLR 64; DA; DA3; DAB; DAC; DAM MST, NOV; DLB 34, 70, 156, 178; EXPS; HGG; LAIT 3; MTCW 1, 2; RGEL 2; RGSF 2; SATA 20; SCFW; SFW 4; SSFS 3; SUFW; WCH; YAW
Wells, Rosemary 1943- .... **CLC 12**
See also AAYA 13; BYA 7, 8; CA 85-88; CANR 48; CLR 16, 69; CWRI 5; MAICYA 1, 2; SAAS 1; SATA 18, 69, 114; YAW
Welsh, Irvine 1958- .... **CLC 144**
See also CA 173
Welty, Eudora (Alice) 1909-2001 .. **CLC 1, 2, 5, 14, 22, 33, 105; SSC 1, 27, 51; WLC**
See also AMW; AMWR 1; BPFB 3; CA 9-12R; 199; CABS 1; CANR 32, 65; CDALB 1941-1968; CN 7; CSW; DA; DA3; DAB; DAC; DAM MST, NOV; DLB 2, 102, 143; DLBD 12; DLBY 1987, 2001; EXPS; HGG; LAIT 3; MAWW; MTCW 1, 2; NFS 13, 15; RGAL 4; RGSF 2; RHW; SSFS 2, 10
Wen I-to 1899-1946 .... **TCLC 28**
Wentworth, Robert
See Hamilton, Edmond
Werfel, Franz (Viktor) 1890-1945 ... **TCLC 8**
See also CA 104; 161; DLB 81, 124; RGWL 2
Wergeland, Henrik Arnold
1808-1845 .... **NCLC 5**
Wersba, Barbara 1932- .... **CLC 30**
See also AAYA 2, 30; BYA 6, 12, 13; CA 29-32R; 182; CAAE 182; CANR 16, 38; CLR 3, 78; DLB 52; JRDA; MAICYA 1, 2; SAAS 2; SATA 1, 58; SATA-Essay 103; WYA; YAW
Wertmueller, Lina 1928- .... **CLC 16**
See also CA 97-100; CANR 39, 78
Wescott, Glenway 1901-1987 .. **CLC 13; SSC 35**
See also CA 13-16R; 121; CANR 23, 70; DLB 4, 9, 102; RGAL 4
Wesker, Arnold 1932- .... **CLC 3, 5, 42**
See also CA 1-4R; CAAS 7; CANR 1, 33; CBD; CD 5; CDBLB 1960 to Present; DAB; DAM DRAM; DLB 13; MTCW 1; RGEL 2
Wesley, Richard (Errol) 1945- .... **CLC 7**
See also BW 1; CA 57-60; CAD; CANR 27; CD 5; DLB 38
Wessel, Johan Herman 1742-1785 .... **LC 7**
West, Anthony (Panther)
1914-1987 .... **CLC 50**
See also CA 45-48; 124; CANR 3, 19; DLB 15

West, C. P.
See Wodehouse, P(elham) G(renville)

West, Cornel (Ronald) 1953- .... **CLC 134; BLCS**
See also CA 144; CANR 91; DLB 246

West, Delno C(loyde), Jr. 1936- .... **CLC 70**
See also CA 57-60

West, Dorothy 1907-1998 .... **TCLC 108**
See also BW 2; CA 143; 169; DLB 76

West, (Mary) Jessamyn 1902-1984 ... **CLC 7, 17**
See also CA 9-12R; 112; CANR 27; DLB 6; DLBY 1984; MTCW 1, 2; RHW; SATA-Obit 37; TUS; YAW

West, Morris L(anglo) 1916-1999 ..... **CLC 6, 33**
See also BPFB 3; CA 5-8R; 187; CANR 24, 49, 64; CN 7; CPW; MTCW 1, 2

West, Nathanael 1903-1940 .... **TCLC 1, 14, 44; SSC 16**
See also AMW; BPFB 3; CA 104; 125; CDALB 1929-1941; DA3; DLB 4, 9, 28; MTCW 1, 2; RGAL 4

West, Owen
See Koontz, Dean R(ay)

West, Paul 1930- .... **CLC 7, 14, 96**
See also CA 13-16R; CAAS 7; CANR 22, 53, 76, 89; CN 7; DLB 14; INT CANR-22; MTCW 2

West, Rebecca 1892-1983 ... **CLC 7, 9, 31, 50**
See also BPFB 3; BRWS 3; CA 5-8R; 109; CANR 19; DLB 36; DLBY 1983; FW; MTCW 1, 2; RGEL 2; TEA

Westall, Robert (Atkinson)
1929-1993 .... **CLC 17**
See also AAYA 12; BYA 2, 6, 7, 8, 9; CA 69-72; 141; CANR 18, 68; CLR 13; FANT; JRDA; MAICYA 1, 2; MAICYAS 1; SAAS 2; SATA 23, 69; SATA-Obit 75; WYA; YAW

Westermarck, Edward 1862-1939 . **TCLC 87**

Westlake, Donald E(dwin) 1933- . **CLC 7, 33**
See also BPFB 3; CA 17-20R; CAAS 13; CANR 16, 44, 65, 94; CMW 4; CPW; DAM POP; INT CANR-16; MSW; MTCW 2

Westmacott, Mary
See Christie, Agatha (Mary Clarissa)

Weston, Allen
See Norton, Andre

Wetcheek, J. L.
See Feuchtwanger, Lion

Wetering, Janwillem van de
See van de Wetering, Janwillem

Wetherald, Agnes Ethelwyn
1857-1940 .... **TCLC 81**
See also CA 202; DLB 99

Wetherell, Elizabeth
See Warner, Susan (Bogert)

Whale, James 1889-1957 .... **TCLC 63**

Whalen, Philip 1923- .... **CLC 6, 29**
See also CA 9-12R; CANR 5, 39; CP 7; DLB 16; WP

Wharton, Edith (Newbold Jones)
1862-1937 ... **TCLC 3, 9, 27, 53; SSC 6; WLC**
See also AAYA 25; AMW; AMWR 1; BPFB 3; CA 104; 132; CDALB 1865-1917; DA; DA3; DAB; DAC; DAM MST, NOV; DLB 4, 9, 12, 78, 189; DLBD 13; EXPS; HGG; LAIT 2, 3; MAWW; MTCW 1, 2; NFS 5, 11, 15; RGAL 4; RGSF 2; RHW; SSFS 6, 7; SUFW

Wharton, James
See Mencken, H(enry) L(ouis)

Wharton, William (a pseudonym) . **CLC 18, 37**
See also CA 93-96; DLBY 1980; INT 93-96

Wheatley (Peters), Phillis
1753(?)-1784 ... **LC 3, 50; BLC 3; PC 3; WLC**
See also AFAW 1, 2; CDALB 1640-1865; DA; DA3; DAC; DAM MST, MULT, POET; DLB 31, 50; EXPP; PFS 13; RGAL 4

Wheelock, John Hall 1886-1978 .... **CLC 14**
See also CA 13-16R; 77-80; CANR 14; DLB 45

White, Babington
See Braddon, Mary Elizabeth

White, E(lwyn) B(rooks)
1899-1985 .... **CLC 10, 34, 39**
See also AITN 2; AMWS 1; CA 13-16R; 116; CANR 16, 37; CDALBS; CLR 1, 21; CPW; DA3; DAM POP; DLB 11, 22; FANT; MAICYA 1, 2; MTCW 1, 2; RGAL 4; SATA 2, 29, 100; SATA-Obit 44

White, Edmund (Valentine III)
1940- .... **CLC 27, 110**
See also AAYA 7; CA 45-48; CANR 3, 19, 36, 62, 107; CN 7; DA3; DAM POP; DLB 227; MTCW 1, 2

White, Hayden V. 1928- .... **CLC 148**
See also CA 128; DLB 246

White, Patrick (Victor Martindale)
1912-1990 ...... **CLC 3, 4, 5, 7, 9, 18, 65, 69; SSC 39**
See also BRWS 1; CA 81-84; 132; CANR 43; DLB 260; MTCW 1; RGEL 2; RGSF 2; RHW

White, Phyllis Dorothy James 1920-
See James, P. D.
See also CA 21-24R; CANR 17, 43, 65; CMW 4; CN 7; CPW; DA3; DAM POP; MTCW 1, 2

White, T(erence) H(anbury)
1906-1964 .... **CLC 30**
See also AAYA 22; BPFB 3; BYA 4, 5; CA 73-76; CANR 37; DLB 160; FANT; JRDA; LAIT 1; MAICYA 1, 2; RGEL 2; SATA 12; SUFW; YAW

White, Terence de Vere 1912-1994 ... **CLC 49**
See also CA 49-52; 145; CANR 3

White, Walter
See White, Walter F(rancis)

White, Walter F(rancis)
1893-1955 .... **TCLC 15; BLC 3**
See also BW 1; CA 115; 124; DAM MULT; DLB 51

White, William Hale 1831-1913
See Rutherford, Mark
See also CA 121; 189

Whitehead, Alfred North
1861-1947 .... **TCLC 97**
See also CA 117; 165; DLB 100, 262

Whitehead, E(dward) A(nthony)
1933- .... **CLC 5**
See also CA 65-68; CANR 58; CBD; CD 5

Whitehead, Ted
See Whitehead, E(dward) A(nthony)

Whitemore, Hugh (John) 1936- .... **CLC 37**
See also CA 132; CANR 77; CBD; CD 5; INT CA-132

Whitman, Sarah Helen (Power)
1803-1878 .... **NCLC 19**
See also DLB 1, 243

Whitman, Walt(er) 1819-1892 .. **NCLC 4, 31, 81; PC 3; WLC**
See also AAYA 42; AMW; AMWR 1; CDALB 1640-1865; DA; DA3; DAB; DAC; DAM MST, POET; DLB 3, 64, 224, 250; EXPP; LAIT 2; PAB; PFS 2, 3, 13; RGAL 4; SATA 20; WP; WYAS 1

Whitney, Phyllis A(yame) 1903- .... **CLC 42**
See also AAYA 36; AITN 2; BEST 90:3; CA 1-4R; CANR 3, 25, 38, 60; CLR 59; CMW 4; CPW; DA3; DAM POP; JRDA; MAICYA 1, 2; MTCW 2; RHW; SATA 1, 30; YAW

Whittemore, (Edward) Reed (Jr.)
1919- .... **CLC 4**
See also CA 9-12R; CAAS 8; CANR 4; CP 7; DLB 5

Whittier, John Greenleaf
1807-1892 .... **NCLC 8, 59**
See also AMWS 1; DLB 1, 243; RGAL 4

Whittlebot, Hernia
See Coward, Noel (Peirce)

Wicker, Thomas Grey 1926-
See Wicker, Tom
See also CA 65-68; CANR 21, 46

Wicker, Tom .... **CLC 7**
See also Wicker, Thomas Grey

Wideman, John Edgar 1941- ...... **CLC 5, 34, 36, 67, 122; BLC 3**
See also AFAW 1, 2; AMWS 10; BPFB 4; BW 2, 3; CA 85-88; CANR 14, 42, 67, 109; CN 7; DAM MULT; DLB 33, 143; MTCW 2; RGAL 4; RGSF 2; SSFS 6, 12

Wiebe, Rudy (Henry) 1934- .. **CLC 6, 11, 14, 138**
See also CA 37-40R; CANR 42, 67; CN 7; DAC; DAM MST; DLB 60; RHW

Wieland, Christoph Martin
1733-1813 .... **NCLC 17**
See also DLB 97; EW 4; RGWL 2

Wiene, Robert 1881-1938 .... **TCLC 56**

Wieners, John 1934- .... **CLC 7**
See also CA 13-16R; CP 7; DLB 16; WP

Wiesel, Elie(zer) 1928- .... **CLC 3, 5, 11, 37; WLCS**
See also AAYA 7; AITN 1; CA 5-8R; CAAS 4; CANR 8, 40, 65; CDALBS; DA; DAB; DAC; DAM MST, NOV; DLB 83; DLBY 1987; INT CANR-8; LAIT 4; MTCW 1, 2; NFS 4; SATA 56; YAW

Wiggins, Marianne 1947- .... **CLC 57**
See also BEST 89:3; CA 130; CANR 60

Wiggs, Susan .... **CLC 70**
See also CA 201

Wight, James Alfred 1916-1995
See Herriot, James
See also CA 77-80; SATA 55; SATA-Brief 44

Wilbur, Richard (Purdy) 1921- ..... **CLC 3, 6, 9, 14, 53, 110**
See also AMWS 3; CA 1-4R; CABS 2; CANR 2, 29, 76, 93; CDALBS; CP 7; DA; DAB; DAC; DAM MST, POET; DLB 5, 169; EXPP; INT CANR-29; MTCW 1, 2; PAB; PFS 11, 12; RGAL 4; SATA 9, 108; WP

Wild, Peter 1940- .... **CLC 14**
See also CA 37-40R; CP 7; DLB 5

Wilde, Oscar (Fingal O'Flahertie Wills)
1854(?)-1900 ...... **TCLC 1, 8, 23, 41; DC 17; SSC 11; WLC**
See also BRW 5; BRWR 2; CA 104; 119; CDBLB 1890-1914; DA; DA3; DAB; DAC; DAM DRAM, MST, NOV; DFS 4, 8, 9; DLB 10, 19, 34, 57, 141, 156, 190; EXPS; FANT; RGEL 2; RGSF 2; SATA 24; SSFS 7; SUFW; TEA; WCH; WLIT 4

Wilder, Billy .... **CLC 20**
See also Wilder, Samuel
See also DLB 26

Wilder, Samuel 1906-2002
See Wilder, Billy
See also CA 89-92

Wilder, Stephen
See Marlowe, Stephen

Wilder, Thornton (Niven)
1897-1975 .. **CLC 1, 5, 6, 10, 15, 35, 82; DC 1; WLC**
See also AAYA 29; AITN 2; AMW; CA 13-16R; 61-64; CAD; CANR 40; CDALBS; DA; DA3; DAB; DAC; DAM DRAM, MST, NOV; DFS 1, 4; DLB 4, 7, 9, 228; DLBY 1997; LAIT 3; MTCW 1, 2; RGAL 4; RHW; WYAS 1

Wilding, Michael 1942- ...... **CLC 73; SSC 50**
See also CA 104; CANR 24, 49, 106; CN 7; RGSF 2

Wiley, Richard 1944- .... **CLC 44**
See also CA 121; 129; CANR 71

Wilhelm, Kate .... **CLC 7**
See Wilhelm, Katie (Gertrude)
See also AAYA 20; CAAS 5; DLB 8; INT CANR-17; SCFW 2

Wilhelm, Katie (Gertrude) 1928-
See Wilhelm, Kate
See also CA 37-40R; CANR 17, 36, 60, 94; MTCW 1; SFW 4

Wilkins, Mary
See Freeman, Mary E(leanor) Wilkins

Willard, Nancy 1936- .... **CLC 7, 37**
See also BYA 5; CA 89-92; CANR 10, 39, 68, 107; CLR 5; CWP; CWRI 5; DLB 5, 52; FANT; MAICYA 1, 2; MTCW 1; SATA 37, 71, 127; SATA-Brief 30

William of Ockham 1290-1349 ...... **CMLC 32**

Williams, Ben Ames 1889-1953 ..... **TCLC 89**
See also CA 183; DLB 102

Williams, C(harles) K(enneth) 1936- .... **CLC 33, 56, 148**
See also CA 37-40R; CAAS 26; CANR 57, 106; CP 7; DAM POET; DLB 5

Williams, Charles
See Collier, James Lincoln

Williams, Charles (Walter Stansby) 1886-1945 .... **TCLC 1, 11**
See also CA 104; 163; DLB 100, 153, 255; FANT; RGEL 2; SUFW

Williams, (George) Emlyn 1905-1987 .... **CLC 15**
See also CA 104; 123; CANR 36; DAM DRAM; DLB 10, 77; MTCW 1

Williams, Hank 1923-1953 .... **TCLC 81**

Williams, Hugo 1942- .... **CLC 42**
See also CA 17-20R; CANR 45; CP 7; DLB 40

Williams, J. Walker
See Wodehouse, P(elham) G(renville)

Williams, John A(lfred) 1925- ..... **CLC 5, 13; BLC 3**
See also AFAW 2; BW 2, 3; CA 53-56; CAAE 195; CAAS 3; CANR 6, 26, 51; CN 7; CSW; DAM MULT; DLB 2, 33; INT CANR-6; RGAL 4; SFW 4

Williams, Jonathan (Chamberlain) 1929- .... **CLC 13**
See also CA 9-12R; CAAS 12; CANR 8, 108; CP 7; DLB 5

Williams, Joy 1944- .... **CLC 31**
See also CA 41-44R; CANR 22, 48, 97

Williams, Norman 1952- .... **CLC 39**
See also CA 118

Williams, Sherley Anne 1944-1999 . **CLC 89; BLC 3**
See also AFAW 2; BW 2, 3; CA 73-76; 185; CANR 25, 82; DAM MULT; POET; DLB 41; INT CANR-25; SATA 78; SATA-Obit 116

Williams, Shirley
See Williams, Sherley Anne

Williams, Tennessee 1911-1983 . **CLC 1, 2, 5, 7, 8, 11, 15, 19, 30, 39, 45, 71, 111; DC 4; WLC**
See also AAYA 31; AITN 1, 2; AMW; CA 5-8R; 108; CABS 3; CAD; CANR 31; CDALB 1941-1968; DA; DA3; DAB; DAC; DAM DRAM, MST; DFS 1, 3, 7, 12; DLB 7; DLBD 4; DLBY 1983; GLL 1; LAIT 4; MTCW 1, 2; RGAL 4

Williams, Thomas (Alonzo) 1926-1990 .... **CLC 14**
See also CA 1-4R; 132; CANR 2

Williams, William C.
See Williams, William Carlos

Williams, William Carlos 1883-1963 .... **CLC 1, 2, 5, 9, 13, 22, 42, 67; PC 7; SSC 31**
See also AMW; AMWR 1; CA 89-92; CANR 34; CDALB 1917-1929; DA; DA3; DAB; DAC; DAM MST, POET; DLB 4, 16, 54, 86; EXPP; MTCW 1, 2; PAB; PFS 1, 6, 11; RGAL 4; RGSF 2; WP

Williamson, David (Keith) 1942- ..... **CLC 56**
See also CA 103; CANR 41; CD 5

Williamson, Ellen Douglas 1905-1984
See Douglas, Ellen
See also CA 17-20R; 114; CANR 39

Williamson, Jack .... **CLC 29**
See also Williamson, John Stewart
See also CAAS 8; DLB 8; SCFW 2

Williamson, John Stewart 1908-
See Williamson, Jack
See also CA 17-20R; CANR 23, 70; SFW 4

Willie, Frederick
See Lovecraft, H(oward) P(hillips)

Willingham, Calder (Baynard, Jr.) 1922-1995 .... **CLC 5, 51**
See also CA 5-8R; 147; CANR 3; CSW; DLB 2, 44; IDFW 3, 4; MTCW 1

Willis, Charles
See Clarke, Arthur C(harles)

Willy
See Colette, (Sidonie-Gabrielle)

Willy, Colette
See Colette, (Sidonie-Gabrielle)
See also GLL 1

Wilmot, John 1647-1680 .... **LC 75**
See Rochester
See also BRW 2; DLB 131; PAB

Wilson, A(ndrew) N(orman) 1950- .. **CLC 33**
See also BRWS 6; CA 112; 122; CN 7; DLB 14, 155, 194; MTCW 2

Wilson, Angus (Frank Johnstone) 1913-1991 . **CLC 2, 3, 5, 25, 34; SSC 21**
See also BRWS 1; CA 5-8R; 134; CANR 21; DLB 15, 139, 155; MTCW 1, 2; RGEL 2; RGSF 2

Wilson, August 1945- ... **CLC 39, 50, 63, 118; BLC 3; DC 2; WLCS**
See also AAYA 16; AFAW 2; AMWS 8; BW 2, 3; CA 115; 122; CAD; CANR 42, 54, 76; CD 5; DA; DA3; DAB; DAC; DAM DRAM, MST, MULT; DFS 15; DLB 228; LAIT 4; MTCW 1, 2; RGAL 4

Wilson, Brian 1942- .... **CLC 12**

Wilson, Colin 1931- .... **CLC 3, 14**
See also CA 1-4R; CAAS 5; CANR 1, 22, 33, 77; CMW 4; CN 7; DLB 14, 194; HGG; MTCW 1; SFW 4

Wilson, Dirk
See Pohl, Frederik

Wilson, Edmund 1895-1972 .. **CLC 1, 2, 3, 8, 24**
See also AMW; CA 1-4R; 37-40R; CANR 1, 46; DLB 63; MTCW 1, 2; RGAL 4

Wilson, Ethel Davis (Bryant) 1888(?)-1980 .... **CLC 13**
See also CA 102; DAC; DAM POET; DLB 68; MTCW 1; RGEL 2

Wilson, Harriet
See Wilson, Harriet E. Adams
See also DLB 239

Wilson, Harriet E. Adams 1827(?)-1863(?) .... **NCLC 78; BLC 3**
See also Wilson, Harriet
See also DAM MULT; DLB 50, 243

Wilson, John 1785-1854 .... **NCLC 5**

Wilson, John (Anthony) Burgess 1917-1993
See Burgess, Anthony
See also CA 1-4R; 143; CANR 2, 46; DA3; DAC; DAM NOV; MTCW 1, 2; NFS 15

Wilson, Lanford 1937- .... **CLC 7, 14, 36**
See also CA 17-20R; CABS 3; CAD; CANR 45, 96; CD 5; DAM DRAM; DFS 4, 9, 12; DLB 7; TUS

Wilson, Robert M. 1944- .... **CLC 7, 9**
See also CA 49-52; CAD; CANR 2, 41; CD 5; MTCW 1

Wilson, Robert McLiam 1964- .... **CLC 59**
See also CA 132

Wilson, Sloan 1920- .... **CLC 32**
See also CA 1-4R; CANR 1, 44; CN 7

Wilson, Snoo 1948- .... **CLC 33**
See also CA 69-72; CBD; CD 5

Wilson, William S(mith) 1932- .... **CLC 49**
See also CA 81-84

Wilson, (Thomas) Woodrow 1856-1924 .... **TCLC 79**
See also CA 166; DLB 47

Wilson and Warnke eds. .... **CLC 65**

Winchilsea, Anne (Kingsmill) Finch 1661-1720
See Finch, Anne
See also RGEL 2

Windham, Basil
See Wodehouse, P(elham) G(renville)

Wingrove, David (John) 1954- .... **CLC 68**
See also CA 133; SFW 4

Winnemucca, Sarah 1844-1891 ..... **NCLC 79**
See also DAM MULT; DLB 175; NNAL; RGAL 4

Winstanley, Gerrard 1609-1676 .... **LC 52**

Wintergreen, Jane
See Duncan, Sara Jeannette

Winters, Janet Lewis .... **CLC 41**
See also Lewis, Janet
See also DLBY 1987

Winters, (Arthur) Yvor 1900-1968 .... **CLC 4, 8, 32**
See also AMWS 2; CA 11-12; 25-28R; CAP 1; DLB 48; MTCW 1; RGAL 4

Winterson, Jeanette 1959- .... **CLC 64, 158**
See also BRWS 4; CA 136; CANR 58; CN 7; CPW; DA3; DAM POP; DLB 207, 261; FANT; FW; GLL 1; MTCW 2; RHW

Winthrop, John 1588-1649 .... **LC 31**
See also DLB 24, 30

Wirth, Louis 1897-1952 .... **TCLC 92**

Wiseman, Frederick 1930- .... **CLC 20**
See also CA 159

Wister, Owen 1860-1938 .... **TCLC 21**
See also BPFB 3; CA 108; 162; DLB 9, 78, 186; RGAL 4; SATA 62; TCWW 2

Witkacy
See Witkiewicz, Stanislaw Ignacy

Witkiewicz, Stanislaw Ignacy 1885-1939 .... **TCLC 8**
See also CA 105; 162; CDWLB 4; DLB 215; EW 10; RGWL 2; SFW 4

Wittgenstein, Ludwig (Josef Johann) 1889-1951 .... **TCLC 59**
See also CA 113; 164; DLB 262; MTCW 2

Wittig, Monique 1935(?)- .... **CLC 22**
See also CA 116; 135; CWW 2; DLB 83; FW; GLL 1

Wittlin, Jozef 1896-1976 .... **CLC 25**
See also CA 49-52; 65-68; CANR 3

Wodehouse, P(elham) G(renville) 1881-1975 ... **CLC 1, 2, 5, 10, 22; SSC 2**
See also AITN 2; BRWS 3; CA 45-48; 57-60; CANR 3, 33; CDBLB 1914-1945; CPW 1; DA3; DAB; DAC; DAM NOV; DLB 34, 162; MTCW 1, 2; RGEL 2; RGSF 2; SATA 22; SSFS 10; TCLC 108

Woiwode, L.
See Woiwode, Larry (Alfred)

Woiwode, Larry (Alfred) 1941- ... **CLC 6, 10**
See also CA 73-76; CANR 16, 94; CN 7; DLB 6; INT CANR-16

Wojciechowska, Maia (Teresa)
1927- .... **CLC 26**
See also AAYA 8; BYA 3; CA 9-12R, 183; CAAE 183; CANR 4, 41; CLR 1; JRDA; MAICYA 1, 2; SAAS 1; SATA 1, 28, 83; SATA-Essay 104; YAW

Wojtyla, Karol
See John Paul II, Pope

Wolf, Christa 1929- .... **CLC 14, 29, 58, 150**
See also CA 85-88; CANR 45; CDWLB 2; CWW 2; DLB 75; FW; MTCW 1; RGWL 2; SSFS 14

Wolf, Naomi 1962- .... **CLC 157**
See also CA 141; FW

Wolfe, Gene (Rodman) 1931- .... **CLC 25**
See also AAYA 35; CA 57-60; CAAS 9; CANR 6, 32, 60; CPW; DAM POP; DLB 8; FANT; MTCW 2; SATA 118; SCFW 2; SFW 4

Wolfe, George C. 1954- .... **CLC 49; BLCS**
See also CA 149; CAD; CD 5

Wolfe, Thomas (Clayton)
1900-1938 ...... **TCLC 4, 13, 29, 61; SSC 33; WLC**
See also AMW; BPFB 3; CA 104; 132; CANR 102; CDALB 1929-1941; DA; DA3; DAB; DAC; DAM MST, NOV; DLB 9, 102, 229; DLBD 2, 16; DLBY 1985, 1997; MTCW 1, 2; RGAL 4

Wolfe, Thomas Kennerly, Jr.
1930- .... **CLC 147**
See also Wolfe, Tom
See also CA 13-16R; CANR 9, 33, 70, 104; DA3; DAM POP; DLB 185; INT CANR-9; MTCW 1, 2; TUS

Wolfe, Tom .... **CLC 1, 2, 9, 15, 35, 51**
See also Wolfe, Thomas Kennerly, Jr.
See also AAYA 8; AITN 2; AMWS 3; BEST 89:1; BPFB 3; CN 7; CPW; CSW; DLB 152; LAIT 5; RGAL 4

Wolff, Geoffrey (Ansell) 1937- .... **CLC 41**
See also CA 29-32R; CANR 29, 43, 78

Wolff, Sonia
See Levitin, Sonia (Wolff)

Wolff, Tobias (Jonathan Ansell)
1945- .... **CLC 39, 64**
See also AAYA 16; AMWS 7; BEST 90:2; BYA 12; CA 114; 117; CAAS 22; CANR 54, 76, 96; CN 7; CSW; DA3; DLB 130; INT CA-117; MTCW 2; RGAL 4; RGSF 2; SSFS 4, 11

Wolfram von Eschenbach c. 1170-c. 1220 .... **CMLC 5**
See also CDWLB 2; DLB 138; EW 1; RGWL 2

Wolitzer, Hilma 1930- .... **CLC 17**
See also CA 65-68; CANR 18, 40; INT CANR-18; SATA 31; YAW

Wollstonecraft, Mary 1759-1797 ..... **LC 5, 50**
See also BRWS 3; CDBLB 1789-1832; DLB 39, 104, 158, 252; FW; LAIT 1; RGEL 2; TEA; WLIT 3

Wonder, Stevie .... **CLC 12**
See also Morris, Steveland Judkins

Wong, Jade Snow 1922- .... **CLC 17**
See also CA 109; CANR 91; SATA 112

Woodberry, George Edward
1855-1930 .... **TCLC 73**
See also CA 165; DLB 71, 103

Woodcott, Keith
See Brunner, John (Kilian Houston)

Woodruff, Robert W.
See Mencken, H(enry) L(ouis)

Woolf, (Adeline) Virginia
1882-1941 .. **TCLC 1, 5, 20, 43, 56, 101, 123; SSC 7; WLC**
See also BPFB 3; BRW 7; BRWR 1; CA 104; 130; CANR 64; CDBLB 1914-1945; DA; DA3; DAB; DAC; DAM MST, NOV; DLB 36, 100, 162; DLBD 10; EXPS; FW; LAIT 3; MTCW 1, 2; NCFS 2; NFS 8, 12; RGEL 2; RGSF 2; SSFS 4, 12; TEA; WLIT 4

Woollcott, Alexander (Humphreys)
1887-1943 .... **TCLC 5**
See also CA 105; 161; DLB 29

Woolrich, Cornell .... **CLC 77**
See also Hopley-Woolrich, Cornell George
See also MSW

Woolson, Constance Fenimore
1840-1894 .... **NCLC 82**
See also DLB 12, 74, 189, 221; RGAL 4

Wordsworth, Dorothy 1771-1855 .. **NCLC 25**
See also DLB 107

Wordsworth, William 1770-1850 .. **NCLC 12, 38, 111; PC 4; WLC**
See also BRW 4; CDBLB 1789-1832; DA; DA3; DAB; DAC; DAM MST, POET; DLB 93, 107; EXPP; PAB; PFS 2; RGEL 2; TEA; WLIT 3; WP

Wotton, Sir Henry 1568-1639 .... **LC 68**
See also DLB 121; RGEL 2

Wouk, Herman 1915- .... **CLC 1, 9, 38**
See also BPFB 2, 3; CA 5-8R; CANR 6, 33, 67; CDALBS; CN 7; CPW; DA3; DAM NOV, POP; DLBY 1982; INT CANR-6; LAIT 4; MTCW 1, 2; NFS 7

Wright, Charles (Penzel, Jr.) 1935- .. **CLC 6, 13, 28, 119, 146**
See also AMWS 5; CA 29-32R; CAAS 7; CANR 23, 36, 62, 88; CP 7; DLB 165; DLBY 1982; MTCW 1, 2; PFS 10

Wright, Charles Stevenson 1932- ... **CLC 49; BLC 3**
See also BW 1; CA 9-12R; CANR 26; CN 7; DAM MULT, POET; DLB 33

Wright, Frances 1795-1852 .... **NCLC 74**
See also DLB 73

Wright, Frank Lloyd 1867-1959 .... **TCLC 95**
See also AAYA 33; CA 174

Wright, Jack R.
See Harris, Mark

Wright, James (Arlington)
1927-1980 .... **CLC 3, 5, 10, 28; PC 36**
See also AITN 2; AMWS 3; CA 49-52; 97-100; CANR 4, 34, 64; CDALBS; DAM POET; DLB 5, 169; EXPP; MTCW 1, 2; PFS 7, 8; RGAL 4; WP

Wright, Judith (Arundell)
1915-2000 .... **CLC 11, 53; PC 14**
See also CA 13-16R; 188; CANR 31, 76, 93; CP 7; CWP; DLB 260; MTCW 1, 2; PFS 8; RGEL 2; SATA 14; SATA-Obit 121

Wright, L(aurali) R. 1939- .... **CLC 44**
See also CA 138; CMW 4

Wright, Richard (Nathaniel)
1908-1960 .... **CLC 1, 3, 4, 9, 14, 21, 48, 74; BLC 3; SSC 2; WLC**
See also AAYA 5, 42; AFAW 1, 2; AMW; BPFB 3; BW 1; BYA 2; CA 108; CANR 64; CDALB 1929-1941; DA; DA3; DAB; DAC; DAM MST, MULT, NOV; DLB 76, 102; DLBD 2; EXPN; LAIT 3, 4; MTCW 1, 2; NCFS 1; NFS 1, 7; RGAL 4; RGSF 2; SSFS 3, 9, 15; YAW

Wright, Richard B(ruce) 1937- .... **CLC 6**
See also CA 85-88; DLB 53

Wright, Rick 1945- .... **CLC 35**

Wright, Rowland
See Wells, Carolyn

Wright, Stephen 1946- .... **CLC 33**

Wright, Willard Huntington 1888-1939
See Van Dine, S. S.
See also CA 115; 189; CMW 4; DLBD 16

Wright, William 1930- .... **CLC 44**
See also CA 53-56; CANR 7, 23

Wroth, Lady Mary 1587-1653(?) .... **LC 30; PC 38**
See also DLB 121

Wu Ch'eng-en 1500(?)-1582(?) .... **LC 7**

Wu Ching-tzu 1701-1754 .... **LC 2**

Wurlitzer, Rudolph 1938(?)- .... **CLC 2, 4, 15**
See also CA 85-88; CN 7; DLB 173

Wyatt, Sir Thomas c. 1503-1542 . **LC 70; PC 27**
See also BRW 1; DLB 132; EXPP; RGEL 2; TEA

Wycherley, William 1640-1716 .... **LC 8, 21**
See also BRW 2; CDBLB 1660-1789; DAM DRAM; DLB 80; RGEL 2

Wylie, Elinor (Morton Hoyt)
1885-1928 .... **TCLC 8; PC 23**
See also AMWS 1; CA 105; 162; DLB 9, 45; EXPP; RGAL 4

Wylie, Philip (Gordon) 1902-1971 ... **CLC 43**
See also CA 21-22; 33-36R; CAP 2; DLB 9; SFW 4

Wyndham, John .... **CLC 19**
See also Harris, John (Wyndham Parkes Lucas) Beynon
See also DLB 255; SCFW 2

Wyss, Johann David Von
1743-1818 .... **NCLC 10**
See also JRDA; MAICYA 1, 2; SATA 29; SATA-Brief 27

Xenophon c. 430B.C.-c. 354B.C. ... **CMLC 17**
See also AW 1; DLB 176; RGWL 2

Yakumo Koizumi
See Hearn, (Patricio) Lafcadio (Tessima Carlos)

Yamamoto, Hisaye 1921- .... **SSC 34; AAL**
See also DAM MULT; LAIT 4; SSFS 14

Yanez, Jose Donoso
See Donoso (Yanez), Jose

Yanovsky, Basile S.
See Yanovsky, V(assily) S(emenovich)

Yanovsky, V(assily) S(emenovich)
1906-1989 .... **CLC 2, 18**
See also CA 97-100; 129

Yates, Richard 1926-1992 .... **CLC 7, 8, 23**
See also CA 5-8R; 139; CANR 10, 43; DLB 2, 234; DLBY 1981, 1992; INT CANR-10

Yeats, W. B.
See Yeats, William Butler

Yeats, William Butler 1865-1939 .... **TCLC 1, 11, 18, 31, 93, 116; PC 20; WLC**
See also BRW 6; BRWR 1; CA 104; 127; CANR 45; CDBLB 1890-1914; DA; DA3; DAB; DAC; DAM DRAM, MST, POET; DLB 10, 19, 98, 156; EXPP; MTCW 1, 2; NCFS 3; PAB; PFS 1, 2, 5, 7, 13, 15; RGEL 2; TEA; WLIT 4; WP

Yehoshua, A(braham) B. 1936- ... **CLC 13, 31**
See also CA 33-36R; CANR 43, 90; RGSF 2

Yellow Bird
See Ridge, John Rollin

Yep, Laurence Michael 1948- .... **CLC 35**
See also AAYA 5, 31; BYA 7; CA 49-52; CANR 1, 46, 92; CLR 3, 17, 54; DLB 52; FANT; JRDA; MAICYA 1, 2; MAICYAS 1; SATA 7, 69, 123; WYA; YAW

Yerby, Frank G(arvin) 1916-1991 . **CLC 1, 7, 22; BLC 3**
See also BPFB 3; BW 1, 3; CA 9-12R; 136; CANR 16, 52; DAM MULT; DLB 76; INT CANR-16; MTCW 1; RGAL 4; RHW

Yesenin, Sergei Alexandrovich
See Esenin, Sergei (Alexandrovich)

Yevtushenko, Yevgeny (Alexandrovich)
1933- ...... **CLC 1, 3, 13, 26, 51, 126; PC 40**
See also Evtushenko, Evgenii Aleksandrovich
See also CA 81-84; CANR 33, 54; CWW 2; DAM POET; MTCW 1

Yezierska, Anzia 1885(?)-1970 .... **CLC 46**
See also CA 126; 89-92; DLB 28, 221; FW; MTCW 1; RGAL 4; SSFS 15

Yglesias, Helen 1915- .... **CLC 7, 22**
See also CA 37-40R; CAAS 20; CANR 15, 65, 95; CN 7; INT CANR-15; MTCW 1

Yokomitsu, Riichi 1898-1947 .... **TCLC 47**
See also CA 170

Yonge, Charlotte (Mary)
1823-1901 .... **TCLC 48**
See also CA 109; 163; DLB 18, 163; RGEL 2; SATA 17; WCH

York, Jeremy
See Creasey, John

York, Simon
See Heinlein, Robert A(nson)

Yorke, Henry Vincent 1905-1974 ..... **CLC 13**
See also Green, Henry
See also CA 85-88; 49-52

Yosano Akiko 1878-1942 .... **TCLC 59; PC 11**
See also CA 161

Yoshimoto, Banana .... **CLC 84**
See also Yoshimoto, Mahoko
See also NFS 7

Yoshimoto, Mahoko 1964-
See Yoshimoto, Banana
See also CA 144; CANR 98

Young, Al(bert James) 1939- . **CLC 19; BLC 3**
See also BW 2, 3; CA 29-32R; CANR 26, 65, 109; CN 7; CP 7; DAM MULT; DLB 33

Young, Andrew (John) 1885-1971 ...... **CLC 5**
See also CA 5-8R; CANR 7, 29; RGEL 2

Young, Collier
See Bloch, Robert (Albert)

Young, Edward 1683-1765 .... **LC 3, 40**
See also DLB 95; RGEL 2

Young, Marguerite (Vivian)
1909-1995 .... **CLC 82**
See also CA 13-16; 150; CAP 1; CN 7

Young, Neil 1945- .... **CLC 17**
See also CA 110; CCA 1

Young Bear, Ray A. 1950- .... **CLC 94**
See also CA 146; DAM MULT; DLB 175; NNAL

Yourcenar, Marguerite 1903-1987 ... **CLC 19, 38, 50, 87**
See also BPFB 3; CA 69-72; CANR 23, 60, 93; DAM NOV; DLB 72; DLBY 1988; EW 12; GFL 1789 to the Present; GLL 1; MTCW 1, 2; RGWL 2

Yuan, Chu 340(?)B.C.-278(?)B.C. . **CMLC 36**

Yurick, Sol 1925- .... **CLC 6**
See also CA 13-16R; CANR 25; CN 7

Zabolotsky, Nikolai Alekseevich
1903-1958 .... **TCLC 52**
See also CA 116; 164

Zagajewski, Adam 1945- .... **PC 27**
See also CA 186; DLB 232

Zalygin, Sergei -2000 .... **CLC 59**

Zamiatin, Evgenii
See Zamyatin, Evgeny Ivanovich
See also RGSF 2; RGWL 2

Zamiatin, Yevgenii
See Zamyatin, Evgeny Ivanovich

Zamora, Bernice (B. Ortiz) 1938- .. **CLC 89; HLC 2**
See also CA 151; CANR 80; DAM MULT; DLB 82; HW 1, 2

Zamyatin, Evgeny Ivanovich
1884-1937 .... **TCLC 8, 37**
See also Zamiatin, Evgenii
See also CA 105; 166; EW 10; SFW 4

Zangwill, Israel 1864-1926 ... **TCLC 16; SSC 44**
See also CA 109; 167; CMW 4; DLB 10, 135, 197; RGEL 2

Zappa, Francis Vincent, Jr. 1940-1993
See Zappa, Frank
See also CA 108; 143; CANR 57

Zappa, Frank .... **CLC 17**
See also Zappa, Francis Vincent, Jr.

Zaturenska, Marya 1902-1982 ...... **CLC 6, 11**
See also CA 13-16R; 105; CANR 22

Zeami 1363-1443 .... **DC 7**
See also DLB 203; RGWL 2

Zelazny, Roger (Joseph) 1937-1995 . **CLC 21**
See also AAYA 7; BPFB 3; CA 21-24R; 148; CANR 26, 60; CN 7; DLB 8; FANT; MTCW 1, 2; SATA 57; SATA-Brief 39; SCFW; SFW 4; SUFW

Zhdanov, Andrei Alexandrovich
1896-1948 .... **TCLC 18**
See also CA 117; 167

Zhukovsky, Vasilii Andreevich
See Zhukovsky, Vasily (Andreevich)
See also DLB 205

Zhukovsky, Vasily (Andreevich)
1783-1852 .... **NCLC 35**
See also Zhukovsky, Vasilii Andreevich

Ziegenhagen, Eric .... **CLC 55**

Zimmer, Jill Schary
See Robinson, Jill

Zimmerman, Robert
See Dylan, Bob

Zindel, Paul 1936- .... **CLC 6, 26; DC 5**
See also AAYA 2, 37; BYA 2, 3, 8, 11, 14; CA 73-76; CAD; CANR 31, 65, 108; CD 5; CDALBS; CLR 3, 45; DA; DA3; DAB; DAC; DAM DRAM, MST, NOV; DFS 12; DLB 7, 52; JRDA; LAIT 5; MAICYA 1, 2; MTCW 1, 2; NFS 14; SATA 16, 58, 102; WYA; YAW

Zinov'Ev, A. A.
See Zinoviev, Alexander (Aleksandrovich)

Zinoviev, Alexander (Aleksandrovich)
1922- .... **CLC 19**
See also CA 116; 133; CAAS 10

Zoilus
See Lovecraft, H(oward) P(hillips)

Zola, Emile (Edouard Charles Antoine)
1840-1902 ...... **TCLC 1, 6, 21, 41; WLC**
See also CA 104; 138; DA; DA3; DAB; DAC; DAM MST, NOV; DLB 123; EW 7; GFL 1789 to the Present; IDTP; RGWL 2

Zoline, Pamela 1941- .... **CLC 62**
See also CA 161; SFW 4

Zoroaster 628(?)B.C.-551(?)B.C. ... **CMLC 40**

Zorrilla y Moral, Jose 1817-1893 .... **NCLC 6**

Zoshchenko, Mikhail (Mikhailovich)
1895-1958 .... **TCLC 15; SSC 15**
See also CA 115; 160; RGSF 2

Zuckmayer, Carl 1896-1977 .... **CLC 18**
See also CA 69-72; DLB 56, 124; RGWL 2

Zuk, Georges
See Skelton, Robin
See also CCA 1

Zukofsky, Louis 1904-1978 ... **CLC 1, 2, 4, 7, 11, 18; PC 11**
See also AMWS 3; CA 9-12R; 77-80; CANR 39; DAM POET; DLB 5, 165; MTCW 1; RGAL 4

Zweig, Paul 1935-1984 .... **CLC 34, 42**
See also CA 85-88; 113

Zweig, Stefan 1881-1942 .... **TCLC 17**
See also CA 112; 170; DLB 81, 118

Zwingli, Huldreich 1484-1531 .... **LC 37**
See also DLB 179

Literary Criticism Series
Cumulative Topic Index

This index lists all topic entries in Gale's *Classical and Medieval Literature Criticism, Contemporary Literary Criticism, Drama Criticism, Literature Criticism from 1400 to 1800, Nineteenth-Century Literature Criticism,* and *Twentieth-Century Literary Criticism.*

The Aesopic Fable LC 51: 1-100
  the British Aesopic Fable, 1-54
  the Aesopic tradition in non-English-speaking cultures, 55-66
  political uses of the Aesopic fable, 67-88
  the evolution of the Aesopic fable, 89-99

Age of Johnson LC 15: 1-87
  Johnson's London, 3-15
  aesthetics of neoclassicism, 15-36
  "age of prose and reason," 36-45
  clubmen and bluestockings, 45-56
  printing technology, 56-62
  periodicals: "a map of busy life," 62-74
  transition, 74-86

Age of Spenser LC 39: 1-70
  overviews and general studies, 2-21
  literary style, 22-34
  poets and the crown, 34-70

AIDS in Literature CLC 81: 365-416

Alcohol and Literature TCLC 70: 1-58
  overview, 2-8
  fiction, 8-48
  poetry and drama, 48-58

American Abolitionism NCLC 44: 1-73
  overviews and general studies, 2-26
  abolitionist ideals, 26-46
  the literature of abolitionism, 46-72

American Autobiography TCLC 86: 1-115
  overviews and general studies, 3-36
  American authors and autobiography, 36-82
  African-American autobiography, 82-114

American Black Humor Fiction TCLC 54: 1-85
  characteristics of black humor, 2-13
  origins and development, 13-38
  black humor distinguished from related literary trends, 38-60
  black humor and society, 60-75
  black humor reconsidered, 75-83

American Civil War in Literature NCLC 32: 1-109
  overviews and general studies, 2-20
  regional perspectives, 20-54
  fiction popular during the war, 54-79
  the historical novel, 79-108

American Frontier in Literature NCLC 28: 1-103
  definitions, 2-12
  development, 12-17
  nonfiction writing about the frontier, 17-30
  frontier fiction, 30-45
  frontier protagonists, 45-66
  portrayals of Native Americans, 66-86
  feminist readings, 86-98
  twentieth-century reaction against frontier literature, 98-100

American Humor Writing NCLC 52: 1-59
  overviews and general studies, 2-12
  the Old Southwest, 12-42
  broader impacts, 42-5
  women humorists, 45-58

American Mercury, The TCLC 74: 1-80

American Popular Song, Golden Age of TCLC 42: 1-49
  background and major figures, 2-34
  the lyrics of popular songs, 34-47

American Proletarian Literature TCLC 54: 86-175
  overviews and general studies, 87-95
  American proletarian literature and the American Communist Party, 95-111
  ideology and literary merit, 111-7
  novels, 117-36
  Gastonia, 136-48
  drama, 148-54
  journalism, 154-9
  proletarian literature in the United States, 159-74

American Romanticism NCLC 44: 74-138
  overviews and general studies, 74-84
  sociopolitical influences, 84-104
  Romanticism and the American frontier, 104-15
  thematic concerns, 115-37

American Western Literature TCLC 46: 1-100
  definition and development of American Western literature, 2-7
  characteristics of the Western novel, 8-23
  Westerns as history and fiction, 23-34
  critical reception of American Western literature, 34-41
  the Western hero, 41-73
  women in Western fiction, 73-91
  later Western fiction, 91-9

American Writers in Paris TCLC 98: 1-156
  overviews and general studies, 2-155

Anarchism NCLC 84: 1-97
  overviews and general studies, 2-23
  the French anarchist tradition, 23-56
  Anglo-American anarchism, 56-68
  anarchism: incidents and issues, 68-97

Animals in Literature TCLC 106: 1-120
  overviews and general studies, 2-8
  animals in American literature, 8-45
  animals in Canadian literature, 45-57
  animals in European literature, 57-100
  animals in Latin American literature, 100-06
  animals in women's literature, 106-20

Antebellum South, Literature of the NCLC 112:1-188
  overviews, 4-55
  culture of the Old South, 55-68
  antebellum fiction: pastoral and heroic romance, 68-120
  role of women: a subdued rebellion, 120-59
  slavery and the slave narrative, 159-85

The Apocalyptic Movement TCLC 106: 121-69

Aristotle CMLC 31:1-397
  philosophy, 3-100
  poetics, 101-219
  rhetoric, 220-301
  science, 302-397

Art and Literature TCLC 54: 176-248
  overviews and general studies, 176-93
  definitions, 193-219
  influence of visual arts on literature, 219-31
  spatial form in literature, 231-47

Arthurian Literature CMLC 10: 1-127
  historical context and literary beginnings, 2-27
  development of the legend through Malory, 27-64
  development of the legend from Malory to the Victorian Age, 65-81
  themes and motifs, 81-95
  principal characters, 95-125

Arthurian Revival NCLC 36: 1-77
  overviews and general studies, 2-12
  Tennyson and his influence, 12-43
  other leading figures, 43-73
  the Arthurian legend in the visual arts, 73-6

Australian Literature TCLC 50: 1-94
  origins and development, 2-21
  characteristics of Australian literature, 21-33
  historical and critical perspectives, 33-41

poetry, 41-58
fiction, 58-76
drama, 76-82
Aboriginal literature, 82-91

Beat Generation, Literature of the TCLC 42: 50-102
overviews and general studies, 51-9
the Beat generation as a social phenomenon, 59-62
development, 62-5
Beat literature, 66-96
influence, 97-100

The Bell Curve Controversy CLC 91: 281-330

Bildungsroman **in Nineteenth-Century Literature** NCLC 20: 92-168
surveys, 93-113
in Germany, 113-40
in England, 140-56
female *Bildungsroman,* 156-67

Bloomsbury Group TCLC 34: 1-73
history and major figures, 2-13
definitions, 13-7
influences, 17-27
thought, 27-40
prose, 40-52
and literary criticism, 52-4
political ideals, 54-61
response to, 61-71

The Blues in Literature TCLC 82: 1-71

Bly, Robert, *Iron John: A Book about Men and Men's Work* CLC 70: 414-62

The Book of J CLC 65: 289-311

British Ephemeral Literature LC 59: 1-70
overviews and general studies, 1-9
broadside ballads, 10-40
chapbooks, jestbooks, pamphlets, and newspapers, 40-69

Buddhism and Literature TCLC 70: 59-164
eastern literature, 60-113
western literature, 113-63

Businessman in American Literature TCLC 26: 1-48
portrayal of the businessman, 1-32
themes and techniques in business fiction, 32-47

The Calendar LC 55: 1-92
overviews and general studies, 2-19
measuring time, 19-28
calendars and culture, 28-60
calendar reform, 60-92

Catholicism in Nineteenth-Century American Literature NCLC 64: 1-58
overviews, 3-14
polemical literature, 14-46
Catholicism in literature, 47-57

Celtic Mythology CMLC 26: 1-111
overviews and general studies, 2-22
Celtic myth as literature and history, 22-48
Celtic religion: Druids and divinities, 48-80
Fionn MacCuhaill and the Fenian cycle, 80-111

Celtic Twilight See Irish Literary Renaissance

Chartist Movement and Literature, The NCLC 60: 1-84
overview: nineteenth-century working-class fiction, 2-19
Chartist fiction and poetry, 19-73
the Chartist press, 73-84

Child Labor in Nineteenth-Century Literature NCLC 108: 1-133
overviews, 3-10
climbing boys and chimney sweeps, 10-16
the international traffic in children, 16-45
critics and reformers, 45-82
fictional representations of child laborers, 83-132

Children's Literature, Nineteenth-Century NCLC 52: 60-135
overviews and general studies, 61-72
moral tales, 72-89
fairy tales and fantasy, 90-119
making men/making women, 119-34

Christianity in Twentieth-Century Literature TCLC 110: 1-79
overviews and general studies, 2-31
Christianity in twentieth-century fiction, 31-78

The City and Literature TCLC 90: 1-124
overviews and general studies, 2-9
the city in American literature, 9-86
the city in European literature, 86-124

Civic Critics, Russian NCLC 20: 402-46
principal figures and background, 402-9
and Russian Nihilism, 410-6
aesthetic and critical views, 416-45

The Cockney School NCLC 68: 1-64
overview, 2-7
Blackwood's Magazine and the contemporary critical response, 7-24
the political and social import of the Cockneys and their critics, 24-63

Colonial America: The Intellectual Background LC 25: 1-98
overviews and general studies, 2-17
philosophy and politics, 17-31
early religious influences in Colonial America, 31-60
consequences of the Revolution, 60-78
religious influences in post-revolutionary America, 78-87
colonial literary genres, 87-97

Colonialism in Victorian English Literature NCLC 56: 1-77
overviews and general studies, 2-34
colonialism and gender, 34-51
monsters and the occult, 51-76

Columbus, Christopher, Books on the Quincentennial of His Arrival in the New World CLC 70: 329-60

Comic Books TCLC 66: 1-139
historical and critical perspectives, 2-48
superheroes, 48-67
underground comix, 67-88
comic books and society, 88-122
adult comics and graphic novels, 122-36

Connecticut Wits NCLC 48: 1-95
overviews and general studies, 2-40
major works, 40-76
intellectual context, 76-95

Crime in Literature TCLC 54: 249-307
evolution of the criminal figure in literature, 250-61
crime and society, 261-77
literary perspectives on crime and punishment, 277-88
writings by criminals, 288-306

The Crusades CMLC 38: 1-144
history of the Crusades, 3-60
literature of the Crusades, 60-116
the Crusades and the people: attitudes and influences, 116-44

Cyberpunk TCLC 106: 170-366
overviews and general studies, 171-88
feminism and cyberpunk, 188-230
history and cyberpunk, 230-70
sexuality and cyberpunk, 270-98
social issues and cyberpunk, 299-366

Czechoslovakian Literature of the Twentieth Century TCLC 42:103-96
through World War II, 104-35
de-Stalinization, the Prague Spring, and contemporary literature, 135-72
Slovak literature, 172-85
Czech science fiction, 185-93

Dadaism TCLC 46: 101-71
background and major figures, 102-16
definitions, 116-26
manifestos and commentary by Dadaists, 126-40
theater and film, 140-58
nature and characteristics of Dadaist writing, 158-70

Darwinism and Literature NCLC 32: 110-206
background, 110-31
direct responses to Darwin, 131-71
collateral effects of Darwinism, 171-205

Death in American Literature NCLC 92: 1-170
overviews and general studies, 2-32
death in the works of Emily Dickinson, 32-72
death in the works of Herman Melville, 72-101
death in the works of Edgar Allan Poe, 101-43
death in the works of Walt Whitman, 143-70

Death in Nineteenth-Century British Literature NCLC 68: 65-142
overviews and general studies, 66-92
responses to death, 92-102
feminist perspectives, 103-17
striving for immortality, 117-41

Death in Literature TCLC 78:1-183
fiction, 2-115
poetry, 115-46
drama, 146-81

de Man, Paul, Wartime Journalism of CLC 55: 382-424

Detective Fiction, Nineteenth-Century NCLC 36: 78-148
origins of the genre, 79-100
history of nineteenth-century detective fiction, 101-33
significance of nineteenth-century detective fiction, 133-46

Detective Fiction, Twentieth-Century TCLC 38: 1-96
genesis and history of the detective story, 3-22
defining detective fiction, 22-32
evolution and varieties, 32-77
the appeal of detective fiction, 77-90

Dime Novels NCLC 84: 98-168
overviews and general studies, 99-123
popular characters, 123-39
major figures and influences, 139-52
socio-political concerns, 152-167

Disease and Literature TCLC 66: 140-283
overviews and general studies, 141-65
disease in nineteenth-century literature, 165-81
tuberculosis and literature, 181-94
women and disease in literature, 194-221
plague literature, 221-53
AIDS in literature, 253-82

El Dorado, The Legend of See Legend of El Dorado, The

The Double in Nineteenth-Century Literature NCLC 40: 1-95
genesis and development of the theme, 2-15
the double and Romanticism, 16-27
sociological views, 27-52
psychological interpretations, 52-87
philosophical considerations, 87-95

Dramatic Realism NCLC 44: 139-202
 overviews and general studies, 140-50
 origins and definitions, 150-66
 impact and influence, 166-93
 realist drama and tragedy, 193-201

Drugs and Literature TCLC 78: 184-282
 overviews and general studies, 185-201
 pre-twentieth-century literature, 201-42
 twentieth-century literature, 242-82

Eastern Mythology CMLC 26: 112-92
 heroes and kings, 113-51
 cross-cultural perspective, 151-69
 relations to history and society, 169-92

Eighteenth-Century British Periodicals LC 63: 1-123
 rise of periodicals, 2-31
 impact and influence of periodicals, 31-64
 periodicals and society, 64-122

Eighteenth-Century Travel Narratives LC 77: 252-355
 overviews and general studies, 254-79
 eighteenth-century European travel narratives, 279-334
 non-European eighteenth-century travel narratives, 334-55

Electronic "Books": Hypertext and Hyperfiction CLC 86: 367-404
 books vs. CD-ROMS, 367-76
 hypertext and hyperfiction, 376-95
 implications for publishing, libraries, and the public, 395-403

Eliot, T. S., Centenary of Birth CLC 55: 345-75

Elizabethan Drama LC 22: 140-240
 origins and influences, 142-67
 characteristics and conventions, 167-83
 theatrical production, 184-200
 histories, 200-12
 comedy, 213-20
 tragedy, 220-30

Elizabethan Prose Fiction LC 41: 1-70
 overviews and general studies, 1-15
 origins and influences, 15-43
 style and structure, 43-69

Enclosure of the English Common NCLC 88: 1-57
 overviews and general studies, 1-12
 early reaction to enclosure, 12-23
 nineteenth-century reaction to enclosure, 23-56

The Encyclopedists LC 26: 172-253
 overviews and general studies, 173-210
 intellectual background, 210-32
 views on esthetics, 232-41
 views on women, 241-52

English Caroline Literature LC 13: 221-307
 background, 222-41
 evolution and varieties, 241-62
 the Cavalier mode, 262-75
 court and society, 275-91
 politics and religion, 291-306

English Decadent Literature of the 1890s NCLC 28: 104-200
 fin de siècle: the Decadent period, 105-19
 definitions, 120-37
 major figures: "the tragic generation," 137-50
 French literature and English literary Decadence, 150-7
 themes, 157-61
 poetry, 161-82
 periodicals, 182-96

English Essay, Rise of the LC 18: 238-308
 definitions and origins, 236-54
 influence on the essay, 254-69
 historical background, 269-78
 the essay in the seventeenth century, 279-93
 the essay in the eighteenth century, 293-307

English Mystery Cycle Dramas LC 34: 1-88
 overviews and general studies, 1-27
 the nature of dramatic performances, 27-42
 the medieval worldview and the mystery cycles, 43-67
 the doctrine of repentance and the mystery cycles, 67-76
 the fall from grace in the mystery cycles, 76-88

The English Realist Novel, 1740-1771 LC 51: 102-98
 overviews and general studies, 103-22
 from Romanticism to Realism, 123-58
 women and the novel, 159-175
 the novel and other literary forms, 176-197

English Revolution, Literature of the LC 43: 1-58
 overviews and general studies, 2-24
 pamphlets of the English Revolution, 24-38
 political sermons of the English Revolution, 38-48
 poetry of the English Revolution, 48-57

English Romantic Hellenism NCLC 68: 143-250
 overviews and general studies, 144-69
 historical development of English Romantic Hellenism, 169-91
 influence of Greek mythology on the Romantics, 191-229
 influence of Greek literature, art, and culture on the Romantics, 229-50

English Romantic Poetry NCLC 28: 201-327
 overviews and reputation, 202-37
 major subjects and themes, 237-67
 forms of Romantic poetry, 267-78
 politics, society, and Romantic poetry, 278-99
 philosophy, religion, and Romantic poetry, 299-324

The Epistolary Novel LC 59: 71-170
 overviews and general studies, 72-96
 women and the Epistolary novel, 96-138
 principal figures: Britain, 138-53
 principal figures: France, 153-69

Espionage Literature TCLC 50: 95-159
 overviews and general studies, 96-113
 espionage fiction/formula fiction, 113-26
 spies in fact and fiction, 126-38
 the female spy, 138-44
 social and psychological perspectives, 144-58

European Debates on the Conquest of the Americas LC 67: 1-129
 overviews and general studies, 3-56
 major Spanish figures, 56-98
 English perceptions of Native Americans, 98-129

European Romanticism NCLC 36: 149-284
 definitions, 149-77
 origins of the movement, 177-82
 Romantic theory, 182-200
 themes and techniques, 200-23
 Romanticism in Germany, 223-39
 Romanticism in France, 240-61
 Romanticism in Italy, 261-4
 Romanticism in Spain, 264-8
 impact and legacy, 268-82

Exile in Literature TCLC 122: 1-129
 overviews and general studies, 2-33
 exile in fiction, 33-92
 German literature in exile, 92-129

Existentialism and Literature TCLC 42: 197-268
 overviews and definitions, 198-209
 history and influences, 209-19
 Existentialism critiqued and defended, 220-35
 philosophical and religious perspectives, 235-41
 Existentialist fiction and drama, 241-67

Familiar Essay NCLC 48: 96-211
 definitions and origins, 97-130
 overview of the genre, 130-43
 elements of form and style, 143-59
 elements of content, 159-73
 the Cockneys: Hazlitt, Lamb, and Hunt, 173-91
 status of the genre, 191-210

The Faust Legend LC 47: 1-117

Fear in Literature TCLC 74: 81-258
 overviews and general studies, 81
 pre-twentieth-century literature, 123
 twentieth-century literature, 182

Feminism in the 1990s: Commentary on Works by Naomi Wolf, Susan Faludi, and Camille Paglia CLC 76: 377-415

Feminist Criticism in 1990 CLC 65: 312-60

Fifteenth-Century English Literature LC 17: 248-334
 background, 249-72
 poetry, 272-315
 drama, 315-23
 prose, 323-33

Film and Literature TCLC 38: 97-226
 overviews and general studies, 97-119
 film and theater, 119-34
 film and the novel, 134-45
 the art of the screenplay, 145-66
 genre literature/genre film, 167-79
 the writer and the film industry, 179-90
 authors on film adaptations of their works, 190-200
 fiction into film: comparative essays, 200-23

Finance and Money as Represented in Nineteenth-Century Literature NCLC 76: 1-69
 historical perspectives, 2-20
 the image of money, 20-37
 the dangers of money, 37-50
 women and money, 50-69

Folklore and Literature TCLC 86: 116-293
 overviews and general studies, 118-144
 Native American literature, 144-67
 African-American literature, 167-238
 folklore and the American West, 238-57
 modern and postmodern literature, 257-91

Food in Literature TCLC 114: 1-133
 food and children's literature, 2-14
 food as a literary device, 14-32
 rituals invloving food, 33-45
 food and social and ethnic identity, 45-90
 women's relationship with food, 91-132

Food in Nineteenth-Century Literature NCLC 108: 134-288
 overviews, 136-74
 food and social class, 174-85
 food and gender, 185-219
 food and love, 219-31
 food and sex, 231-48
 eating disorders, 248-70
 vegetarians, carnivores, and cannibals, 270-87

French Drama in the Age of Louis XIV LC 28: 94-185
 overview, 95-127
 tragedy, 127-46
 comedy, 146-66
 tragicomedy, 166-84

French Enlightenment LC 14: 81-145
  the question of definition, 82-9
  le siècle des lumières, 89-94
  women and the salons, 94-105
  censorship, 105-15
  the philosophy of reason, 115-31
  influence and legacy, 131-44

French New Novel TCLC 98: 158-234
  overviews and general studies, 158-92
  influences, 192-213
  themes, 213-33

French Realism NCLC 52: 136-216
  origins and definitions, 137-70
  issues and influence, 170-98
  realism and representation, 198-215

French Revolution and English Literature NCLC 40: 96-195
  history and theory, 96-123
  romantic poetry, 123-50
  the novel, 150-81
  drama, 181-92
  children's literature, 192-5

Futurism, Italian TCLC 42: 269-354
  principles and formative influences, 271-9
  manifestos, 279-88
  literature, 288-303
  theater, 303-19
  art, 320-30
  music, 330-6
  architecture, 336-9
  and politics, 339-46
  reputation and significance, 346-51

Gaelic Revival See **Irish Literary Renaissance**

Gates, Henry Louis, Jr., and African-American Literary Criticism CLC 65: 361-405

Gay and Lesbian Literature CLC 76: 416-39

German Exile Literature TCLC 30: 1-58
  the writer and the Nazi state, 1-10
  definition of, 10-4
  life in exile, 14-32
  surveys, 32-50
  Austrian literature in exile, 50-2
  German publishing in the United States, 52-7

German Expressionism TCLC 34: 74-160
  history and major figures, 76-85
  aesthetic theories, 85-109
  drama, 109-26
  poetry, 126-38
  film, 138-42
  painting, 142-7
  music, 147-53
  and politics, 153-8

The Gilded Age NCLC 84: 169-271
  popular themes, 170-90
  Realism, 190-208
  Aestheticism, 208-26
  socio-political concerns, 226-70

***Glasnost* and Contemporary Soviet Literature** CLC 59: 355-97

Gothic Novel NCLC 28: 328-402
  development and major works, 328-34
  definitions, 334-50
  themes and techniques, 350-78
  in America, 378-85
  in Scotland, 385-91
  influence and legacy, 391-400

The Governess in Nineteenth-Century Literature NCLC 104: 1-131
  overviews and general studies, 3-28
  social roles and economic conditions, 28-86
  fictional governesses, 86-131

Graphic Narratives CLC 86: 405-32
  history and overviews, 406-21
  the "Classics Illustrated" series, 421-2
  reviews of recent works, 422-32

Graveyard Poets LC 67: 131-212
  origins and development, 131-52
  major figures, 152-75
  major works, 175-212

Greek Historiography CMLC 17: 1-49

Greek Mythology CMLC 26: 193-320
  overviews and general studies, 194-209
  origins and development of Greek mythology, 209-29
  cosmogonies and divinities in Greek mythology, 229-54
  heroes and heroines in Greek mythology, 254-80
  women in Greek mythology, 280-320

Greek Theater CMLC 51: 1-58
  criticism, 2-58

Hard-Boiled Fiction TCLC 118: 1-109
  overviews and general studies, 2-39
  major authors, 39-76
  women and hard-boiled fiction, 76-109

Harlem Renaissance TCLC 26: 49-125
  principal issues and figures, 50-67
  the literature and its audience, 67-74
  theme and technique in poetry, fiction, and drama, 74-115
  and American society, 115-21
  achievement and influence, 121-2

Havel, Václav, Playwright and President CLC 65: 406-63

Historical Fiction, Nineteenth-Century NCLC 48: 212-307
  definitions and characteristics, 213-36
  Victorian historical fiction, 236-65
  American historical fiction, 265-88
  realism in historical fiction, 288-306

Hollywood and Literature TCLC 118: 110-251
  overviews and general studies, 111-20
  adaptations, 120-65
  socio-historical and cultural impact, 165-206
  theater and hollywood, 206-51

Holocaust and the Atomic Bomb: Fifty Years Later CLC 91: 331-82
  the Holocaust remembered, 333-52
  Anne Frank revisited, 352-62
  the atomic bomb and American memory, 362-81

Holocaust Denial Literature TCLC 58: 1-110
  overviews and general studies, 1-30
  Robert Faurisson and Noam Chomsky, 30-52
  Holocaust denial literature in America, 52-71
  library access to Holocaust denial literature, 72-5
  the authenticity of Anne Frank's diary, 76-90
  David Irving and the "normalization" of Hitler, 90-109

Holocaust, Literature of the TCLC 42: 355-450
  historical overview, 357-61
  critical overview, 361-70
  diaries and memoirs, 370-95
  novels and short stories, 395-425
  poetry, 425-41
  drama, 441-8

Homosexuality in Nineteenth-Century Literature NCLC 56: 78-182
  defining homosexuality, 80-111
  Greek love, 111-44
  trial and danger, 144-81

Hungarian Literature of the Twentieth Century TCLC 26: 126-88
  surveys of, 126-47
  Nyugat and early twentieth-century literature, 147-56
  mid-century literature, 156-68
  and politics, 168-78
  since the 1956 revolt, 178-87

Hysteria in Nineteenth-Century Literature NCLC 64: 59-184
  the history of hysteria, 60-75
  the gender of hysteria, 75-103
  hysteria and women's narratives, 103-57
  hysteria in nineteenth-century poetry, 157-83

Image of the Noble Savage in Literature LC 79: 136-252
  overviews and development, 136-76
  the Noble Savage in the New World, 176-221
  Rousseau and the French Enlightenment's view of the noble savage, 221-51

Imagism TCLC 74: 259-454
  history and development, 260
  major figures, 288
  sources and influences, 352
  Imagism and other movements, 397
  influence and legacy, 431

Immigrants in Nineteenth-Century Literature, Representation of NCLC 112: 188-298
  overview, 189-99
  immigrants in America, 199-223
  immigrants and labor, 223-60
  immigrants in England, 260-97

Incest in Nineteenth-Century American Literature NCLC 76: 70-141
  overview, 71-88
  the concern for social order, 88-117
  authority and authorship, 117-40

Incest in Victorian Literature NCLC 92: 172-318
  overviews and general studies, 173-85
  novels, 185-276
  plays, 276-84
  poetry, 284-318

Indian Literature in English TCLC 54: 308-406
  overview, 309-13
  origins and major figures, 313-25
  the Indo-English novel, 325-55
  Indo-English poetry, 355-67
  Indo-English drama, 367-72
  critical perspectives on Indo-English literature, 372-80
  modern Indo-English literature, 380-9
  Indo-English authors on their work, 389-404

The Industrial Revolution in Literature NCLC 56: 183-273
  historical and cultural perspectives, 184-201
  contemporary reactions to the machine, 201-21
  themes and symbols in literature, 221-73

The Irish Famine as Represented in Nineteenth-Century Literature NCLC 64: 185-261
  overviews and general studies, 187-98
  historical background, 198-212
  famine novels, 212-34
  famine poetry, 234-44
  famine letters and eye-witness accounts, 245-61

Irish Literary Renaissance TCLC 46: 172-287
  overview, 173-83
  development and major figures, 184-202

influence of Irish folklore and mythology, 202-22
Irish poetry, 222-34
Irish drama and the Abbey Theatre, 234-56
Irish fiction, 256-86

Irish Nationalism and Literature NCLC 44: 203-73
the Celtic element in literature, 203-19
anti-Irish sentiment and the Celtic response, 219-34
literary ideals in Ireland, 234-45
literary expressions, 245-73

Irish Novel, The NCLC 80: 1-130
overviews and general studies, 3-9
principal figures, 9-22
peasant and middle class Irish novelists, 22-76
aristocratic Irish and Anglo-Irish novelists, 76-129

Israeli Literature TCLC 94: 1-137
overviews and general studies, 2-18
Israeli fiction, 18-33
Israeli poetry, 33-62
Israeli drama, 62-91
women and Israeli literature, 91-112
Arab characters in Israeli literature, 112-36

Italian Futurism See Futurism, Italian

Italian Humanism LC 12: 205-77
origins and early development, 206-18
revival of classical letters, 218-23
humanism and other philosophies, 224-39
humanism and humanists, 239-46
the plastic arts, 246-57
achievement and significance, 258-76

Italian Romanticism NCLC 60: 85-145
origins and overviews, 86-101
Italian Romantic theory, 101-25
the language of Romanticism, 125-45

Jacobean Drama LC 33: 1-37
the Jacobean worldview: an era of transition, 2-14
the moral vision of Jacobean drama, 14-22
Jacobean tragedy, 22-3
the Jacobean masque, 23-36

Jazz and Literature TCLC 102: 3-124

Jewish-American Fiction TCLC 62: 1-181
overviews and general studies, 2-24
major figures, 24-48
Jewish writers and American life, 48-78
Jewish characters in American fiction, 78-108
themes in Jewish-American fiction, 108-43
Jewish-American women writers, 143-59
the Holocaust and Jewish-American fiction, 159-81

Jews in Literature TCLC 118: 252-417
overviews and general studies, 253-97
representing the Jew in literature, 297-351
the Holocaust in literature, 351-416

Journals of Lewis and Clark, The NCLC 100: 1-88
overviews and general studies, 4-30
journal-keeping methods, 30-46
Fort Mandan, 46-51
the Clark journal, 51-65
the journals as literary texts, 65-87

Kabuki LC 73: 118-232
overviews and general studies, 120-40
the development of Kabuki, 140-65
major works, 165-95
Kabuki and society, 195-231

Kit-Kat Club, The LC 71: 66-112
overviews and general studies, 67-88
major figures, 88-107
attacks on the Kit-Kat Club, 107-12

Knickerbocker Group, The NCLC 56: 274-341
overviews and general studies, 276-314
Knickerbocker periodicals, 314-26
writers and artists, 326-40

Lake Poets, The NCLC 52: 217-304
characteristics of the Lake Poets and their works, 218-27
literary influences and collaborations, 227-66
defining and developing Romantic ideals, 266-84
embracing Conservatism, 284-303

Larkin, Philip, Controversy CLC 81: 417-64

Latin American Literature, Twentieth-Century TCLC 58: 111-98
historical and critical perspectives, 112-36
the novel, 136-45
the short story, 145-9
drama, 149-60
poetry, 160-7
the writer and society, 167-86
Native Americans in Latin American literature, 186-97

Legend of El Dorado, The LC 74: 248-350
overviews, 249-308
major explorations for El Dorado, 308-50

The Levellers LC 51: 200-312
overviews and general studies, 201-29
principal figures, 230-86
religion, political philosophy, and pamphleteering, 287-311

Literary Prizes TCLC 122: 130-203
overviews and general studies, 131-34
the Nobel Prize in Literature, 135-83
the Pulitzer Prize, 183-203

Literature and Millenial Lists CLC 119: 431-67
The Modern Library list, 433
The Waterstone list, 438-439

Literature of the American Cowboy NCLC 96: 1-60
overview, 3-20
cowboy fiction, 20-36
cowboy poetry and songs, 36-59

Literature of the California Gold Rush NCLC 92: 320-85
overviews and general studies, 322-24
early California Gold Rush fiction, 324-44
Gold Rush folklore and legend, 344-51
the rise of Western local color, 351-60
social relations and social change, 360-385

Living Theatre, The DC 16: 154-214

Madness in Nineteenth-Century Literature NCLC 76: 142-284
overview, 143-54
autobiography, 154-68
poetry, 168-215
fiction, 215-83

Madness in Twentieth-Century Literature TCLC 50: 160-225
overviews and general studies, 161-71
madness and the creative process, 171-86
suicide, 186-91
madness in American literature, 191-207
madness in German literature, 207-13
madness and feminist artists, 213-24

Magic Realism TCLC 110: 80-327
overviews and general studies, 81-94
magic realism in African literature, 95-110
magic realism in American literature, 110-32
magic realism in Canadian literature, 132-46
magic realism in European literature, 146-66
magic realism in Asian literature, 166-79
magic realism in Latin-American literature, 179-223
magic realism in Israeli literature and the novels of Salman Rushdie, 223-38
magic realism in literature written by women, 239-326

The Masque LC 63: 124-265
development of the masque, 125-62
sources and structure, 162-220
race and gender in the masque, 221-64

Medical Writing LC 55: 93-195
colonial America, 94-110
enlightenment, 110-24
medieval writing, 124-40
sexuality, 140-83
vernacular, 185-95

Memoirs of Trauma CLC 109: 419-466
overview, 420
criticism, 429

Metaphysical Poets LC 24: 356-439
early definitions, 358-67
surveys and overviews, 367-92
cultural and social influences, 392-406
stylistic and thematic variations, 407-38

Missionaries in the Nineteenth-Century, Literature of NCLC 112: 299-392
history and development, 300-16
uses of ethnography, 316-31
sociopolitical concerns, 331-82
David Livingstone, 382-91

Modern Essay, The TCLC 58: 199-273
overview, 200-7
the essay in the early twentieth century, 207-19
characteristics of the modern essay, 219-32
modern essayists, 232-45
the essay as a literary genre, 245-73

Modern French Literature TCLC 122: 205-359
overviews and general studies, 207-43
French theater, 243-77
gender issues and French women writers, 277-315
ideology and politics, 315-24
modern French poetry, 324-41
resistance literature, 341-58

Modern Irish Literature TCLC 102: 125-321
overview, 129-44
dramas, 144-70
fiction, 170-247
poetry, 247-321

Modern Japanese Literature TCLC 66: 284-389
poetry, 285-305
drama, 305-29
fiction, 329-61
western influences, 361-87

Modernism TCLC 70: 165-275
definitions, 166-184
Modernism and earlier influences, 184-200
stylistic and thematic traits, 200-229
poetry and drama, 229-242
redefining Modernism, 242-275

Muckraking Movement in American Journalism TCLC 34: 161-242
development, principles, and major figures, 162-70
publications, 170-9
social and political ideas, 179-86
targets, 186-208
fiction, 208-19
decline, 219-29
impact and accomplishments, 229-40

Multiculturalism in Literature and Education CLC 70: 361-413

Music and Modern Literature TCLC 62: 182-329
  overviews and general studies, 182-211
  musical form/literary form, 211-32
  music in literature, 232-50
  the influence of music on literature, 250-73
  literature and popular music, 273-303
  jazz and poetry, 303-28

Native American Literature CLC 76: 440-76

Natural School, Russian NCLC 24: 205-40
  history and characteristics, 205-25
  contemporary criticism, 225-40

Naturalism NCLC 36: 285-382
  definitions and theories, 286-305
  critical debates on Naturalism, 305-16
  Naturalism in theater, 316-32
  European Naturalism, 332-61
  American Naturalism, 361-72
  the legacy of Naturalism, 372-81

Negritude TCLC 50: 226-361
  origins and evolution, 227-56
  definitions, 256-91
  Negritude in literature, 291-343
  Negritude reconsidered, 343-58

New Criticism TCLC 34: 243-318
  development and ideas, 244-70
  debate and defense, 270-99
  influence and legacy, 299-315

The New World in Renaissance Literature LC 31: 1-51
  overview, 1-18
  utopia vs. terror, 18-31
  explorers and Native Americans, 31-51

New York Intellectuals and *Partisan Review* TCLC 30: 117-98
  development and major figures, 118-28
  influence of Judaism, 128-39
  Partisan Review, 139-57
  literary philosophy and practice, 157-75
  political philosophy, 175-87
  achievement and significance, 187-97

The New Yorker TCLC 58: 274-357
  overviews and general studies, 274-95
  major figures, 295-304
  New Yorker style, 304-33
  fiction, journalism, and humor at *The New Yorker*, 333-48
  the new *New Yorker*, 348-56

Newgate Novel NCLC 24: 166-204
  development of Newgate literature, 166-73
  Newgate Calendar, 173-7
  Newgate fiction, 177-95
  Newgate drama, 195-204

Nigerian Literature of the Twentieth Century TCLC 30: 199-265
  surveys of, 199-227
  English language and African life, 227-45
  politics and the Nigerian writer, 245-54
  Nigerian writers and society, 255-62

Nihilism and Literature TCLC 110: 328-93
  overviews and general studies, 328-44
  European and Russian nihilism, 344-73
  nihilism in the works of Albert Camus, Franz Kafka, and John Barth, 373-92

Nineteenth-Century Captivity Narratives NCLC 80:131-218
  overview, 132-37
  the political significance of captivity narratives, 137-67
  images of gender, 167-96
  moral instruction, 197-217

Nineteenth-Century Euro-American Literary Representations of Native Americans NCLC 104: 132-264
  overviews and general studies, 134-53
  Native American history, 153-72
  the Indians of the Northeast, 172-93
  the Indians of the Southeast, 193-212
  the Indians of the West, 212-27
  Indian-hater fiction, 227-43
  the Indian as exhibit, 243-63

Nineteenth-Century Native American Autobiography NCLC 64: 262-389
  overview, 263-8
  problems of authorship, 268-81
  the evolution of Native American autobiography, 281-304
  political issues, 304-15
  gender and autobiography, 316-62
  autobiographical works during the turn of the century, 362-88

Norse Mythology CMLC 26: 321-85
  history and mythological tradition, 322-44
  Eddic poetry, 344-74
  Norse mythology and other traditions, 374-85

Northern Humanism LC 16: 281-356
  background, 282-305
  precursor of the Reformation, 305-14
  the Brethren of the Common Life, the Devotio Moderna, and education, 314-40
  the impact of printing, 340-56

Novel of Manners, The NCLC 56: 342-96
  social and political order, 343-53
  domestic order, 353-73
  depictions of gender, 373-83
  the American novel of manners, 383-95

Novels of the Ming and Early Ch'ing Dynasties LC 76: 213-356
  overviews and historical development, 214-45
  major works—overview, 245-85
  genre studies, 285-325
  cultural and social themes, 325-55

Nuclear Literature: Writings and Criticism in the Nuclear Age TCLC 46: 288-390
  overviews and general studies, 290-301
  fiction, 301-35
  poetry, 335-8
  nuclear war in Russo-Japanese literature, 338-55
  nuclear war and women writers, 355-67
  the nuclear referent and literary criticism, 367-88

Occultism in Modern Literature TCLC 50: 362-406
  influence of occultism on literature, 363-72
  occultism, literature, and society, 372-87
  fiction, 387-96
  drama, 396-405

Opium and the Nineteenth-Century Literary Imagination NCLC 20:250-301
  original sources, 250-62
  historical background, 262-71
  and literary society, 271-9
  and literary creativity, 279-300

Orientalism NCLC 96: 149-364
  overviews and general studies, 150-98
  Orientalism and imperialism, 198-229
  Orientalism and gender, 229-59
  Orientalism and the nineteenth-century novel, 259-321
  Orientalism in nineteenth-century poetry, 321-63

The Oxford Movement NCLC 72: 1-197
  overviews and general studies, 2-24
  background, 24-59
  and education, 59-69
  religious responses, 69-128
  literary aspects, 128-178
  political implications, 178-196

The Parnassian Movement NCLC 72: 198-241
  overviews and general studies, 199-231
  and epic form, 231-38
  and positivism, 238-41

Pastoral Literature of the English Renaissance LC 59: 171-282
  overviews and general studies, 172-214
  principal figures of the Elizabethan period, 214-33
  principal figures of the later Renaissance, 233-50
  pastoral drama, 250-81

Periodicals, Nineteenth-Century British NCLC 24: 100-65
  overviews and general studies, 100-30
  in the Romantic Age, 130-41
  in the Victorian era, 142-54
  and the reviewer, 154-64

Picaresque Literature of the Sixteenth and Seventeenth Centuries LC 78: 223-355
  context and development, 224-71
  genre, 271-98
  the picaro, 299-326
  the picara, 326-53

Plath, Sylvia, and the Nature of Biography CLC 86: 433-62
  the nature of biography, 433-52
  reviews of *The Silent Woman,* 452-61

Political Theory from the 15th to the 18th Century LC 36: 1-55
  overview, 1-26
  natural law, 26-42
  empiricism, 42-55

Polish Romanticism NCLC 52: 305-71
  overviews and general studies, 306-26
  major figures, 326-40
  Polish Romantic drama, 340-62
  influences, 362-71

Politics and Literature TCLC 94: 138-61
  overviews and general studies, 139-96
  Europe, 196-226
  Latin America, 226-48
  Africa and the Caribbean, 248-60

Popular Literature TCLC 70: 279-382
  overviews and general studies, 280-324
  "formula" fiction, 324-336
  readers of popular literature, 336-351
  evolution of popular literature, 351-382

The Portrayal of Jews in Nineteenth-Century English Literature NCLC 72: 242-368
  overviews and general studies, 244-77
  Anglo-Jewish novels, 277-303
  depictions by non-Jewish writers, 303-44
  Hebraism versus Hellenism, 344-67

The Portrayal of Mormonism NCLC 96: 61-148
  overview, 63-72
  early Mormon literature, 72-100
  Mormon periodicals and journals, 100-10
  women writers, 110-22
  Mormonism and nineteenth-century literature, 122-42
  Mormon poetry, 142-47

Postcolonialism TCLC 114: 134-239
  overviews and general studies, 135-153
  African postcolonial writing, 153-72
  Asian/Pacific literature, 172-78
  postcolonial literary theory, 178-213
  postcolonial women's writing, 213-38

Postmodernism TCLC 90:125-307
  overview, 126-166
  criticism, 166-224
  fiction, 224-282
  poetry, 282-300
  drama, 300-307

Pre-Raphaelite Movement NCLC 20: 302-401
    overview, 302-4
    genesis, 304-12
    Germ and *Oxford and Cambridge Magazine,* 312-20
    Robert Buchanan and the "Fleshly School of Poetry," 320-31
    satires and parodies, 331-4
    surveys, 334-51
    aesthetics, 351-75
    sister arts of poetry and painting, 375-94
    influence, 394-9

Pre-romanticism LC 40: 1-56
    overviews and general studies, 2-14
    defining the period, 14-23
    new directions in poetry and prose, 23-45
    the focus on the self, 45-56

Pre-Socratic Philosophy CMLC 22: 1-56
    overviews and general studies, 3-24
    the Ionians and the Pythagoreans, 25-35
    Heraclitus, the Eleatics, and the Atomists, 36-47
    the Sophists, 47-55

Protestant Reformation, Literature of the LC 37: 1-83
    overviews and general studies, 1-49
    humanism and scholasticism, 49-69
    the reformation and literature, 69-82

Psychoanalysis and Literature TCLC 38: 227-338
    overviews and general studies, 227-46
    Freud on literature, 246-51
    psychoanalytic views of the literary process, 251-61
    psychoanalytic theories of response to literature, 261-88
    psychoanalysis and literary criticism, 288-312
    psychoanalysis as literature/literature as psychoanalysis, 313-34

The Quarrel between the Ancients and the Moderns LC 63: 266-381
    overviews and general studies, 267-301
    Renaissance origins, 301-32
    Quarrel between the Ancients and the Moderns in France, 332-58
    Battle of the Books in England, 358-80

Rap Music CLC 76: 477-50

Renaissance Natural Philosophy LC 27: 201-87
    cosmology, 201-28
    astrology, 228-54
    magic, 254-86

Representations of the Devil in Nineteenth-Century Literature NCLC 100: 89-223
    overviews and general studies, 90-115
    the Devil in American fiction, 116-43
    English Romanticism: the satanic school, 143-89
    Luciferian discourse in European literature, 189-222

Restoration Drama LC 21: 184-275
    general overviews and general studies, 185-230
    Jeremy Collier stage controversy, 230-9
    other critical interpretations, 240-75

Revenge Tragedy LC 71: 113-242
    overviews and general studies, 113-51
    Elizabethan attitudes toward revenge, 151-88
    the morality of revenge, 188-216
    reminders and remembrance, 217-41

Revising the Literary Canon CLC 81: 465-509

Revising the Literary Canon TCLC 114: 240-84
    overviews and general studies, 241-85

    canon change in American literature, 285-339
    gender and the literary canon, 339-59
    minority and third-world literature and the canon, 359-84

Revolutionary Astronomers LC 51: 314-65
    overviews and general studies, 316-25
    principal figures, 325-51
    Revolutionary astronomical models, 352-64

Robin Hood, Legend of LC 19: 205-58
    origins and development of the Robin Hood legend, 206-20
    representations of Robin Hood, 220-44
    Robin Hood as hero, 244-56

Rushdie, Salman, *Satanic Verses* **Controversy** CLC 55: 214-63; 59:404-56

Russian Nihilism NCLC 28: 403-47
    definitions and overviews, 404-17
    women and Nihilism, 417-27
    literature as reform: the Civic Critics, 427-33
    Nihilism and the Russian novel: Turgenev and Dostoevsky, 433-47

Russian Thaw TCLC 26: 189-247
    literary history of the period, 190-206
    theoretical debate of socialist realism, 206-11
    Novy Mir, 211-7
    Literary Moscow, 217-24
    Pasternak, *Zhivago,* and the Nobel prize, 224-7
    poetry of liberation, 228-31
    Brodsky trial and the end of the Thaw, 231-6
    achievement and influence, 236-46

Salem Witch Trials LC 38: 1-145
    overviews and general studies, 2-30
    historical background, 30-65
    judicial background, 65-78
    the search for causes, 78-115
    the role of women in the trials, 115-44

Salinger, J. D., Controversy Surrounding *In Search of J. D. Salinger* CLC 55: 325-44

Science and Modern Literature TCLC 90: 308-419
    overviews and general studies, 295-333
    fiction, 333-95
    poetry, 395-405
    drama, 405-19

Science in Nineteenth-Century Literature NCLC 100: 224-366
    overviews and general studies, 225-65
    major figures, 265-336
    sociopolitical concerns, 336-65

Science Fiction, Nineteenth-Century NCLC 24: 241-306
    background, 242-50
    definitions of the genre, 251-56
    representative works and writers, 256-75
    themes and conventions, 276-305

Scottish Chaucerians LC 20: 363-412

Scottish Poetry, Eighteenth-Century LC 29: 95-167
    overviews and general studies, 96-114
    the Scottish Augustans, 114-28
    the Scots Vernacular Revival, 132-63
    Scottish poetry after Burns, 163-66

Sea in Literature, The TCLC 82: 72-191
    drama, 73-9
    poetry, 79-119
    fiction, 119-91

Sea in Nineteenth-Century English and American Literature, The NCLC 104: 265-362
    overviews and general studies, 267-306

    major figures in American sea fiction—Cooper and Melville, 306-29
    American sea poetry and short stories, 329-45
    English sea literature, 345-61

Sensation Novel, The NCLC 80: 219-330
    overviews and general studies, 221-46
    principal figures, 246-62
    nineteenth-century reaction, 262-91
    feminist criticism, 291-329

Sentimental Novel, The NCLC 60: 146-245
    overviews and general studies, 147-58
    the politics of domestic fiction, 158-79
    a literature of resistance and repression, 179-212
    the reception of sentimental fiction, 213-44

Sex and Literature TCLC 82: 192-434
    overviews and general studies, 193-216
    drama, 216-63
    poetry, 263-87
    fiction, 287-431

Sherlock Holmes Centenary TCLC 26: 248-310
    Doyle's life and the composition of the Holmes stories, 248-59
    life and character of Holmes, 259-78
    method, 278-79
    Holmes and the Victorian world, 279-92
    Sherlockian scholarship, 292-301
    Doyle and the development of the detective story, 301-07
    Holmes's continuing popularity, 307-09

The Silver Fork Novel NCLC 88: 58-140
    criticism, 59-139

Slave Narratives, American NCLC 20: 1-91
    background, 2-9
    overviews and general studies, 9-24
    contemporary responses, 24-7
    language, theme, and technique, 27-70
    historical authenticity, 70-5
    antecedents, 75-83
    role in development of Black American literature, 83-8

The Slave Trade in British and American Literature LC 59: 283-369
    overviews and general studies, 284-91
    depictions by white writers, 291-331
    depictions by former slaves, 331-67

Social Conduct Literature LC 55: 196-298
    overviews and general studies, 196-223
    prescriptive ideology in other literary forms, 223-38
    role of the press, 238-63
    impact of conduct literature, 263-87
    conduct literature and the perception of women, 287-96
    women writing for women, 296-98

Socialism NCLC 88: 141-237
    origins, 142-54
    French socialism, 154-83
    Anglo-American socialism, 183-205
    Socialist-Feminism, 205-36

Southern Literature of the Reconstruction NCLC 108: 289-369
    overview, 290-91
    reconstruction literature: the consequences of war, 291-321
    old south to new: continuities in southern culture, 321-68

Spanish Civil War Literature TCLC 26: 311-85
    topics in, 312-33
    British and American literature, 333-59
    French literature, 359-62
    Spanish literature, 362-73
    German literature, 373-75
    political idealism and war literature, 375-83

CUMULATIVE TOPIC INDEX

Spanish Golden Age Literature LC 23: 262-332
  overviews and general studies, 263-81
  verse drama, 281-304
  prose fiction, 304-19
  lyric poetry, 319-31

Spasmodic School of Poetry NCLC 24: 307-52
  history and major figures, 307-21
  the Spasmodics on poetry, 321-7
  Firmilian and critical disfavor, 327-39
  theme and technique, 339-47
  influence, 347-51

Sports in Literature TCLC 86: 294-445
  overviews and general studies, 295-324
  major writers and works, 324-402
  sports, literature, and social issues, 402-45

Steinbeck, John, Fiftieth Anniversary of *The Grapes of Wrath* CLC 59: 311-54

Sturm und Drang NCLC 40: 196-276
  definitions, 197-238
  poetry and poetics, 238-58
  drama, 258-75

Supernatural Fiction in the Nineteenth Century NCLC 32: 207-87
  major figures and influences, 208-35
  the Victorian ghost story, 236-54
  the influence of science and occultism, 254-66
  supernatural fiction and society, 266-86

Supernatural Fiction, Modern TCLC 30: 59-116
  evolution and varieties, 60-74
  "decline" of the ghost story, 74-86
  as a literary genre, 86-92
  technique, 92-101
  nature and appeal, 101-15

Surrealism TCLC 30: 334-406
  history and formative influences, 335-43
  manifestos, 343-54
  philosophic, aesthetic, and political principles, 354-75
  poetry, 375-81
  novel, 381-6
  drama, 386-92
  film, 392-8
  painting and sculpture, 398-403
  achievement, 403-5

Symbolism, Russian TCLC 30: 266-333
  doctrines and major figures, 267-92
  theories, 293-8
  and French Symbolism, 298-310
  themes in poetry, 310-4
  theater, 314-20
  and the fine arts, 320-32

Symbolist Movement, French NCLC 20: 169-249
  background and characteristics, 170-86
  principles, 186-91
  attacked and defended, 191-7
  influences and predecessors, 197-211
  and Decadence, 211-6
  theater, 216-26
  prose, 226-33
  decline and influence, 233-47

Television and Literature TCLC 78: 283-426
  television and literacy, 283-98
  reading vs. watching, 298-341
  adaptations, 341-62
  literary genres and television, 362-90
  television genres and literature, 390-410
  children's literature/children's television, 410-25

Theater of the Absurd TCLC 38: 339-415
  "The Theater of the Absurd," 340-7
  major plays and playwrights, 347-58
  and the concept of the absurd, 358-86
  theatrical techniques, 386-94
  predecessors of, 394-402
  influence of, 402-13

Tin Pan Alley See American Popular Song, Golden Age of

Tobacco Culture LC 55: 299-366
  social and economic attitudes toward tobacco, 299-344
  tobacco trade between the old world and the new world, 344-55
  tobacco smuggling in Great Britain, 355-66

Transcendentalism, American NCLC 24: 1-99
  overviews and general studies, 3-23
  contemporary documents, 23-41
  theological aspects of, 42-52
  and social issues, 52-74
  literature of, 74-96

Travel Writing in the Nineteenth Century NCLC 44: 274-392
  the European grand tour, 275-303
  the Orient, 303-47
  North America, 347-91

Travel Writing in the Twentieth Century TCLC 30: 407-56
  conventions and traditions, 407-27
  and fiction writing, 427-43
  comparative essays on travel writers, 443-54

Tristan and Isolde Legend CMLC 42: 311-404

True-Crime Literature CLC 99: 333-433
  history and analysis, 334-407
  reviews of true-crime publications, 407-23
  writing instruction, 424-29
  author profiles, 429-33

***Ulysses* and the Process of Textual Reconstruction** TCLC 26:386-416
  evaluations of the new *Ulysses,* 386-94
  editorial principles and procedures, 394-401
  theoretical issues, 401-16

Utilitarianism NCLC 84: 272-340
  J. S. Mill's Utilitarianism: liberty, equality, justice, 273-313
  Jeremy Bentham's Utilitarianism: the science of happiness, 313-39

Utopianism NCLC 88: 238-346
  overviews: Utopian literature, 239-59
  Utopianism in American literature, 259-99
  Utopianism in British literature, 299-311
  Utopianism and Feminism, 311-45

Utopian Literature, Nineteenth-Century NCLC 24: 353-473
  definitions, 354-74
  overviews and general studies, 374-88
  theory, 388-408
  communities, 409-26
  fiction, 426-53
  women and fiction, 454-71

Utopian Literature, Renaissance LC 32: 1-63
  overviews and general studies, 2-25
  classical background, 25-33
  utopia and the social contract, 33-9
  origins in mythology, 39-48
  utopia and the Renaissance country house, 48-52
  influence of millenarianism, 52-62

Vampire in Literature TCLC 46: 391-454
  origins and evolution, 392-412
  social and psychological perspectives, 413-44
  vampire fiction and science fiction, 445-53

Vernacular Bibles LC 67: 214-388
  overviews and general studies, 215-59
  the English Bible, 259-355
  the German Bible, 355-88

Victorian Autobiography NCLC 40: 277-363
  development and major characteristics, 278-88
  themes and techniques, 289-313
  the autobiographical tendency in Victorian prose and poetry, 313-47
  Victorian women's autobiographies, 347-62

Victorian Fantasy Literature NCLC 60: 246-384
  overviews and general studies, 247-91
  major figures, 292-366
  women in Victorian fantasy literature, 366-83

Victorian Hellenism NCLC 68: 251-376
  overviews and general studies, 252-78
  the meanings of Hellenism, 278-335
  the literary influence, 335-75

Victorian Novel NCLC 32: 288-454
  development and major characteristics, 290-310
  themes and techniques, 310-58
  social criticism in the Victorian novel, 359-97
  urban and rural life in the Victorian novel, 397-406
  women in the Victorian novel, 406-25
  Mudie's Circulating Library, 425-34
  the late-Victorian novel, 434-51

Vietnamese Literature TCLC 102: 322-386

Vietnam War in Literature and Film CLC 91: 383-437
  overview, 384-8
  prose, 388-412
  film and drama, 412-24
  poetry, 424-35

Violence in Literature TCLC 98: 235-358
  overviews and general studies, 236-74
  violence in the works of modern authors, 274-358

Vorticism TCLC 62: 330-426
  Wyndham Lewis and Vorticism, 330-8
  characteristics and principles of Vorticism, 338-65
  Lewis and Pound, 365-82
  Vorticist writing, 382-416
  Vorticist painting, 416-26

Well-Made Play, The NCLC 80: 331-370
  overviews and general studies, 332-45
  Scribe's style, 345-56
  the influence of the well-made play, 356-69

Women's Autobiography, Nineteenth Century NCLC 76: 285-368
  overviews and general studies, 287-300
  autobiographies concerned with religious and political issues, 300-15
  autobiographies by women of color, 315-38
  autobiographies by women pioneers, 338-51
  autobiographies by women of letters, 351-68

Women's Diaries, Nineteenth-Century NCLC 48: 308-54
  overview, 308-13
  diary as history, 314-25
  sociology of diaries, 325-34
  diaries as psychological scholarship, 334-43
  diary as autobiography, 343-8
  diary as literature, 348-53

Women in Modern Literature TCLC 94: 262-425
  overviews and general studies, 263-86

American literature, 286-304
other national literatures, 304-33
fiction, 333-94
poetry, 394-407
drama, 407-24

Women Writers, Seventeenth-Century LC 30: 2-58
overview, 2-15
women and education, 15-9
women and autobiography, 19-31
women's diaries, 31-9
early feminists, 39-58

World War I Literature TCLC 34: 392-486
overview, 393-403
English, 403-27
German, 427-50
American, 450-66
French, 466-74
and modern history, 474-82

Yellow Journalism NCLC 36: 383-456
overviews and general studies, 384-96
major figures, 396-413

Young Playwrights Festival
1988 CLC 55: 376-81
1989 CLC 59: 398-403
1990 CLC 65: 444-8

NCLC Cumulative Nationality Index

AMERICAN

Adams, John **106**
Alcott, Amos Bronson **1**
Alcott, Louisa May **6, 58, 83**
Alger, Horatio Jr. **8, 83**
Allston, Washington **2**
Apess, William **73**
Audubon, John James **47**
Barlow, Joel **23**
Beecher, Catharine Esther **30**
Bellamy, Edward **4, 86**
Bird, Robert Montgomery **1**
Brackenridge, Hugh Henry **7**
Brentano, Clemens (Maria) **1**
Brown, Charles Brockden **22, 74**
Brown, William Wells **2, 89**
Brownson, Orestes Augustus **50**
Bryant, William Cullen **6, 46**
Calhoun, John Caldwell **15**
Channing, William Ellery **17**
Child, Lydia Maria **6, 73**
Chivers, Thomas Holley **49**
Cooke, John Esten **5**
Cooke, Rose Terry **110**
Cooper, James Fenimore **1, 27, 54**
Cranch, Christopher Pearse **115**
Crèvecoeur, Michel Guillaume Jean de **105**
Crockett, David **8**
Dana, Richard Henry Sr. **53**
Delany, Martin Robinson **93**
Dickinson, Emily (Elizabeth) **21, 77**
Douglass, Frederick **7, 55**
Dunlap, William **2**
Dwight, Timothy **13**
Emerson, Mary Moody **66**
Emerson, Ralph Waldo **1, 38, 98**
Field, Eugene **3**
Foster, Hannah Webster **99**
Foster, Stephen Collins **26**
Frederic, Harold **10**
Freneau, Philip Morin **1, 111**
Hale, Sarah Josepha (Buell) **75**
Halleck, Fitz-Greene **47**
Hamilton, Alexander **49**
Hammon, Jupiter **5**
Harris, George Washington **23**
Hawthorne, Nathaniel **2, 10, 17, 23, 39, 79, 95**
Hayne, Paul Hamilton **94**
Holmes, Oliver Wendell **14, 81**
Horton, George Moses **87**
Irving, Washington **2, 19, 95**
Jackson, Helen Hunt **90**
Jacobs, Harriet A(nn) **67**
James, Henry Sr. **53**
Jefferson, Thomas **11, 103**
Kennedy, John Pendleton **2**
Kirkland, Caroline M. **85**
Lanier, Sidney **6**
Lazarus, Emma **8, 109**
Lincoln, Abraham **18**
Longfellow, Henry Wadsworth **2, 45, 101, 103**
Lowell, James Russell **2, 90**
Melville, Herman **3, 12, 29, 45, 49, 91, 93**
Mowatt, Anna Cora **74**
Murray, Judith Sargent **63**
Parkman, Francis Jr. **12**
Parton, Sara Payson Willis **86**
Paulding, James Kirke **2**
Pinkney, Edward **31**
Poe, Edgar Allan **1, 16, 55, 78, 94, 97**
Rowson, Susanna Haswell **5, 69**
Sedgwick, Catharine Maria **19, 98**
Shaw, Henry Wheeler **15**
Sheridan, Richard Brinsley **5, 91**
Sigourney, Lydia Howard (Huntley) **21, 87**
Simms, William Gilmore **3**
Smith, Joseph Jr. **53**
Solomon, Northup **105**
Southworth, Emma Dorothy Eliza Nevitte **26**
Stowe, Harriet (Elizabeth) Beecher **3, 50**
Taylor, Bayard **89**
Thoreau, Henry David **7, 21, 61**
Timrod, Henry **25**
Trumbull, John **30**
Truth, Sojourner **94**
Tyler, Royall **3**
Very, Jones **9**
Warner, Susan (Bogert) **31**
Warren, Mercy Otis **13**
Webster, Noah **30**
Whitman, Sarah Helen (Power) **19**
Whitman, Walt(er) **4, 31, 81**
Whittier, John Greenleaf **8, 59**
Wilson, Harriet E. Adams **78**
Winnemucca, Sarah **79**

ARGENTINIAN

Echeverria, (Jose) Esteban (Antonino) **18**
Hernández, José **17**

AUSTRALIAN

Adams, Francis **33**
Clarke, Marcus (Andrew Hislop) **19**
Gordon, Adam Lindsay **21**
Harpur, Charles **114**
Kendall, Henry **12**

AUSTRIAN

Grillparzer, Franz **1, 102**
Lenau, Nikolaus **16**
Nestroy, Johann **42**
Raimund, Ferdinand Jakob **69**
Sacher-Masoch, Leopold von **31**
Stifter, Adalbert **41**

CANADIAN

Crawford, Isabella Valancy **12**
Haliburton, Thomas Chandler **15**
Lampman, Archibald **25**
Moodie, Susanna (Strickland) **14, 113**
Richardson, John **55**
Traill, Catharine Parr **31**

COLOMBIAN

Isaacs, Jorge Ricardo **70**
Silva, José Asunción **114**

CUBAN

Avellaneda, Gertrudis Gómez de **111**
Martí (y Pérez), José (Julian) **63**

CZECH

Macha, Karel Hynek **46**

DANISH

Andersen, Hans Christian **7, 79**
Grundtvig, Nicolai Frederik Severin **1**
Jacobsen, Jens Peter **34**
Kierkegaard, Søren **34, 78**

ENGLISH

Ainsworth, William Harrison **13**
Arnold, Matthew **6, 29, 89**
Arnold, Thomas **18**
Austen, Jane **1, 13, 19, 33, 51, 81, 95**
Bagehot, Walter **10**
Barbauld, Anna Laetitia **50**
Barham, Richard Harris **77**
Barnes, William **75**
Beardsley, Aubrey **6**
Beckford, William **16**
Beddoes, Thomas Lovell **3**
Bentham, Jeremy **38**
Blake, William **13, 37, 57**
Borrow, George (Henry) **9**
Bowles, William Lisle **103**
Brontë, Anne **4, 71, 102**
Brontë, Charlotte **3, 8, 33, 58, 105**
Brontë, Emily (Jane) **16, 35**
Brontë, (Patrick) Branwell **109**
Browning, Elizabeth Barrett **1, 16, 61, 66**
Browning, Robert **19, 79**
Bulwer-Lytton, Edward (George Earle Lytton) **1, 45**
Burney, Fanny **12, 54, 107**
Burton, Richard F(rancis) **42**
Byron, George Gordon (Noel) **2, 12, 109**
Carlyle, Thomas **22, 70**
Clare, John **9, 86**
Clough, Arthur Hugh **27**
Cobbett, William **49**
Coleridge, Hartley **90**
Coleridge, Samuel Taylor **9, 54, 99, 111**
Coleridge, Sara **31**
Collins, (William) Wilkie **1, 18, 93**
Cowper, William **8, 94**
Crabbe, George **26**
Craik, Dinah Maria (Mulock) **38**
Darwin, Charles **57**
Darwin, Erasmus **106**
De Quincey, Thomas **4, 87**

Dickens, Charles (John Huffam) **3, 8, 18, 26, 37, 50, 86, 105, 113**
Disraeli, Benjamin **2, 39, 79**
Dobell, Sydney Thompson **43**
Du Maurier, George **86**
Eden, Emily **10**
Eliot, George **4, 13, 23, 41, 49, 89**
FitzGerald, Edward **9**
Forster, John **11**
Froude, James Anthony **43**
Gaskell, Elizabeth Cleghorn **5, 70, 97**
Gilpin, William **30**
Godwin, William **14**
Gore, Catherine **65**
Hallam, Arthur Henry **110**
Hays, Mary **114**
Hazlitt, William **29, 82**
Hemans, Felicia **29, 71**
Holcroft, Thomas **85**
Hood, Thomas **16**
Hopkins, Gerard Manley **17**
Hunt, (James Henry) Leigh **1, 70**
Huxley, T(homas) H(enry) **67**
Inchbald, Elizabeth **62**
Ingelow, Jean **39, 107**
Jefferies, (John) Richard **47**
Jerrold, Douglas William **2**
Jewsbury, Geraldine (Endsor) **22**
Keats, John **8, 73**
Keble, John **87**
Kemble, Fanny **18**
Kingsley, Charles **35**
Kingsley, Henry **107**
Lamb, Charles **10, 113**
Lamb, Lady Caroline **38**
Landon, Letitia Elizabeth **15**
Landor, Walter Savage **14**
Lear, Edward **3**
Lennox, Charlotte Ramsay **23**
Lewes, George Henry **25**
Lewis, Matthew Gregory **11, 62**
Linton, Eliza Lynn **41**
Macaulay, Thomas Babington **42**
Marryat, Frederick **3**
Martineau, Harriet **26**
Mayhew, Henry **31**
Mill, Harriet (Hardy) Taylor **102**
Mill, John Stuart **11, 58**
Mitford, Mary Russell **4**
More, Hannah **27**
Morris, William **4**
Newman, John Henry **38, 99**
Norton, Caroline **47**
Oliphant, Laurence **47**
Opie, Amelia **65**
Paine, Thomas **62**
Pater, Walter (Horatio) **7, 90**
Patmore, Coventry Kersey Dighton **9**
Peacock, Thomas Love **22**
Percy, Thomas **95**
Piozzi, Hester Lynch (Thrale) **57**
Planché, James Robinson **42**
Polidori, John William **51**
Radcliffe, Ann (Ward) **6, 55, 106**
Reade, Charles **2, 74**
Reeve, Clara **19**
Robertson, Thomas William **35**
Robinson, Henry Crabb **15**
Rogers, Samuel **69**
Rossetti, Christina (Georgina) **2, 50, 66**
Rossetti, Dante Gabriel **4, 77**
Sala, George Augustus **46**
Shelley, Mary Wollstonecraft (Godwin) **14, 59, 103**
Shelley, Percy Bysshe **18, 93**
Smith, Charlotte (Turner) **23, 115**
Southey, Robert **8, 97**
Surtees, Robert Smith **14**
Symonds, John Addington **34**
Tennyson, Alfred **30, 65, 115**
Thackeray, William Makepeace **5, 14, 22, 43**
Trelawny, Edward John **85**
Trollope, Anthony **6, 33, 101**
Trollope, Frances **30**
Wordsworth, Dorothy **25**
Wordsworth, William **12, 38, 111**

FILIPINO

Rizal, Jose **27**

FINNISH

Kivi, Aleksis **30**
Lonnrot, Elias **53**
Runeberg, Johan **41**

FRENCH

Augier, Emile **31**
Balzac, Honoré de **5, 35, 53**
Banville, Théodore (Faullain) de **9**
Barbey d'Aurevilly, Jules-Amédée **1**
Baudelaire, Charles **6, 29, 55**
Becque, Henri **3**
Beranger, Pierre Jean de **34**
Bertrand, Aloysius **31**
Borel, Pétrus **41**
Chamisso, Adelbert von **82**
Chateaubriand, François René de **3**
Comte, Auguste **54**
Constant (de Rebecque), (Henri) Benjamin **6**
Corbière, Tristan **43**
Crèvecoeur, Michel Guillaume Jean de **105**
Daudet, (Louis Marie) Alphonse **1**
Desbordes-Valmore, Marceline **97**
Dumas, Alexandre (fils) **9**
Dumas, Alexandre (pere) **11, 71**
Du Maurier, George **86**
Feuillet, Octave **45**
Flaubert, Gustave **2, 10, 19, 62, 66**
Fourier, Charles **51**
Fromentin, Eugène (Samuel Auguste) **10**
Gaboriau, émile **14**
Gautier, Théophile **1, 59**
Gobineau, Joseph-Arthur **17**
Goncourt, Edmond (Louis Antoine Huot) de **7**
Goncourt, Jules (Alfred Huot) de **7**
Hugo, Victor (Marie) **3, 10, 21**
Joubert, Joseph **9**
Kock, Charles Paul de **16**
Laclos, Pierre Ambroise François **4, 87**
Laforgue, Jules **5, 53**
Lamartine, Alphonse (Marie Louis Prat) de **11**
Lautréamont **12**
Leconte de Lisle, Charles-Marie-René **29**
Maistre, Joseph **37**
Mallarmé, Stéphane **4, 41**
Maupassant, (Henri René Albert) Guy de **1, 42, 83**
Mérimée, Prosper **6, 65**
Michelet, Jules **31**
Musset, (Louis Charles) Alfred de **7**
Nerval, Gérard de **1, 67**
Nodier, (Jean) Charles (Emmanuel) **19**
Pixérécourt, (René Charles) Guilbert de **39**
Renan, Joseph Ernest **26**
Rimbaud, (Jean Nicolas) Arthur **4, 35, 82**
Sade, Donatien Alphonse François **3, 47**
Sainte-Beuve, Charles Augustin **5**
Sand, George **2, 42, 57**
Scribe, (Augustin) Eugène **16**
Senancour, Etienne Pivert de **16**
Staël-Holstein, Anne Louise Germaine Necker **3**
Stendhal **23, 46**
Sue, Eugene **1**
Taine, Hippolyte Adolphe **15**
Tocqueville, Alexis (Charles Henri Maurice Clérel Comte) de **7, 63**
Vallès, Jules **71**
Verlaine, Paul (Marie) **2, 51**
Vigny, Alfred (Victor) de **7, 102**
Villiers de l'Isle Adam, Jean Marie Mathias Philippe Auguste **3**

GERMAN

Arnim, Achim von (Ludwig Joachim von Arnim) **5**
Arnim, Bettina von **38**
Bonaventura **35**
Büchner, (Karl) Georg **26**
Chamisso, Adelbert von **82**
Claudius, Matthias **75**
Droste-Hülshoff, Annette Freiin von **3**
Eichendorff, Joseph **8**
Engels, Friedrich **85, 114**
Fichte, Johann Gottlieb **62**
Fontane, Theodor **26**
Fouqué, Friedrich (Heinrich Karl) de la Motte **2**
Freytag, Gustav **109**
Goethe, Johann Wolfgang von **4, 22, 34, 90**
Grabbe, Christian Dietrich **2**
Grimm, Jacob Ludwig Karl **3, 77**
Grimm, Wilhelm Karl **3, 77**
Hebbel, Friedrich **43**
Hegel, Georg Wilhelm Friedrich **46**
Heine, Heinrich **4, 54**
Herder, Johann Gottfried von **8**
Hoffmann, E(rnst) T(heodor) A(madeus) **2**
Hölderlin, (Johann Christian) Friedrich **16**
Immermann, Karl (Lebrecht) **4, 49**
Jean Paul **7**
Kant, Immanuel **27, 67**
Kleist, Heinrich von **2, 37**
Klinger, Friedrich Maximilian von **1**
Klopstock, Friedrich Gottlieb **11**
Kotzebue, August (Friedrich Ferdinand) von **25**
Ludwig, Otto **4**
Marx, Karl (Heinrich) **17, 114**
Meyer, Conrad Ferdinand **81**
Mörike, Eduard (Friedrich) **10**
Novalis **13**
Schelling, Friedrich Wilhelm Joseph von **30**
Schiller, Friedrich von **39, 69**
Schlegel, August Wilhelm von **15**
Schlegel, Friedrich **45**
Schleiermacher, Friedrich **107**
Schopenhauer, Arthur **51**
Storm, (Hans) Theodor (Woldsen) **1**
Tieck, (Johann) Ludwig **5, 46**
Wagner, Richard **9**
Wieland, Christoph Martin **17**

GREEK

Foscolo, Ugo **8, 97**
Solomos, Dionysios **15**

HUNGARIAN

Arany, Janos **34**
Madach, Imre **19**
Petofi, Sándor **21**

INDIAN

Chatterji, Bankim Chandra **19**
Dutt, Toru **29**

IRISH

Allingham, William **25**
Banim, John **13**
Banim, Michael **13**
Boucicault, Dion **41**
Carleton, William **3**
Croker, John Wilson **10**
Darley, George **2**
Edgeworth, Maria **1, 51**
Ferguson, Samuel **33**
Griffin, Gerald **7**
Jameson, Anna **43**
Le Fanu, Joseph Sheridan **9, 58**
Lever, Charles (James) **23**

Maginn, William **8**
Mangan, James Clarence **27**
Maturin, Charles Robert **6**
Merriman, Brian **70**
Moore, Thomas **6, 110**
Morgan, Lady **29**
O'Brien, Fitz-James **21**
Sheridan, Richard Brinsley **5, 91**

ITALIAN

Alfieri, Vittorio **101**
Collodi, Carlo **54**
Foscolo, Ugo **8, 97**
Gozzi, (Conte) Carlo **23**
Leopardi, Giacomo **22**
Manzoni, Alessandro **29, 98**
Mazzini, Guiseppe **34**
Nievo, Ippolito **22**

JAPANESE

Ichiyō, Higuchi **49**
Motoori, Norinaga **45**

LITHUANIAN

Mapu, Abraham (ben Jekutiel) **18**

MEXICAN

Lizardi, Jose Joaquin Fernandez de **30**

NORWEGIAN

Collett, (Jacobine) Camilla (Wergeland) **22**
Wergeland, Henrik Arnold **5**

POLISH

Fredro, Aleksander **8**
Krasicki, Ignacy **8**
Krasiński, Zygmunt **4**
Mickiewicz, Adam **3, 101**
Norwid, Cyprian Kamil **17**
Slowacki, Juliusz **15**

ROMANIAN

Eminescu, Mihail **33**

RUSSIAN

Aksakov, Sergei Timofeyvich **2**
Bakunin, Mikhail (Alexandrovich) **25, 58**
Baratynsky, Evgenii Abramovich **103**
Bashkirtseff, Marie **27**
Belinski, Vissarion Grigoryevich **5**
Chernyshevsky, Nikolay Gavrilovich **1**
Dobrolyubov, Nikolai Alexandrovich **5**
Dostoevsky, Fedor Mikhailovich **2, 7, 21, 33, 43**
Gogol, Nikolai (Vasilyevich) **5, 15, 31**
Goncharov, Ivan Alexandrovich **1, 63**
Granovsky, Timofei Nikolaevich **75**
Herzen, Aleksandr Ivanovich **10, 61**
Karamzin, Nikolai Mikhailovich **3**
Krylov, Ivan Andreevich **1**
Lermontov, Mikhail Yuryevich **5, 47**
Leskov, Nikolai (Semyonovich) **25**
Nekrasov, Nikolai Alekseevich **11**
Ostrovsky, Alexander **30, 57**
Pisarev, Dmitry Ivanovich **25**
Pushkin, Alexander (Sergeyevich) **3, 27, 83**
Saltykov, Mikhail Evgrafovich **16**
Smolenskin, Peretz **30**
Turgenev, Ivan **21, 37**
Tyutchev, Fyodor **34**
Zhukovsky, Vasily (Andreevich) **35**

SCOTTISH

Baillie, Joanna **2**
Beattie, James **25**
Blair, Hugh **75**
Campbell, Thomas **19**
Carlyle, Thomas **22, 70**
Ferrier, Susan (Edmonstone) **8**
Galt, John **1, 110**
Hogg, James **4, 109**
Jeffrey, Francis **33**
Lockhart, John Gibson **6**
Mackenzie, Henry **41**
Oliphant, Margaret (Oliphant Wilson) **11, 61**
Scott, Walter **15, 69, 110**
Stevenson, Robert Louis (Balfour) **5, 14, 63**
Thomson, James **18**
Wilson, John **5**
Wright, Frances **74**

SERBIAN

Karadžić, Vuk Stefanović **115**

SPANISH

Alarcon, Pedro Antonio de **1**
Bécquer, Gustavo Adolfo **106**
Caballero, Fernan **10**
Castro, Rosalia de **3, 78**
Espronceda, Jose de **39**
Larra (y Sanchez de Castro), Mariano Jose de **17**
Martínez de la Rosa, Francisco de Paula **102**
Tamayo y Baus, Manuel **1**
Zorrilla y Moral, Jose **6**

SWEDISH

Almqvist, Carl Jonas Love **42**
Bremer, Fredrika **11**
Stagnelius, Eric Johan **61**
Tegner, Esaias **2**

SWISS

Amiel, Henri Frederic **4**
Burckhardt, Jacob (Christoph) **49**
Charriere, Isabelle de **66**
Gotthelf, Jeremias **115**
Keller, Gottfried **2**
Meyer, Conrad Ferdinand **81**
Wyss, Johann David Von **10**

UKRAINIAN

Shevchenko, Taras **54**

NCLC-115 Title Index

"The American Pantheon" (Cranch) **115**:22, 41
"The Ancient Sage" (Tennyson) **115**:257, 335, 348
"The Ant Hills" (Cranch) **115**:47
Ariel and Caliban (Cranch) **115**:18, 23, 35, 37, 39, 42, 55
"Ariel and Caliban" (Cranch) **115**:35
"Armageddon" (Tennyson) **115**:247
"Ars Longa Vita Brevis" (Cranch) **115**:10
"The Artist" (Cranch) **115**:40, 67
"Audley Court" (Tennyson) **115**:335
"Audley End" (Tennyson) **115**:240
"Autobiography" (Cranch) **115**:23
"Balin and Balan" (Tennyson) **115**:335
"The Balloon" (Cranch) **115**:47
The Banished Man (Smith) **115**:144, 147, 149-50, 158, 166-68, 207, 211
"Banović Strahinja" (Karadžić) **115**:91-92
Beachy Head, with Other Poems (Smith) **115**:134, 211, 217
"Beachy Head" (Smith) **115**:118, 126, 129-35, 206, 209
"Beauty and Truth" (Cranch) **115**:5
The Bird and the Bell, with Other Poems (Cranch) **115**:17, 22-23, 26, 40, 55
"The Bird and the Bell" (Cranch) **115**:15, 17, 22, 27, 35
"Bird Language" (Cranch) **115**:41, 43
"The Birds on the Wires" (Cranch) **115**:43
"Blackwood" (Tennyson) **115**:235
"The Blind Seer" (Cranch) **115**:9, 40
"Bobolinks" (Cranch) **115**:41, 43
"The Brook" (Tennyson) **115**:358
"Burley-bones" (Cranch) **115**:57-58
"Captain Leka's Sister" (Karadžić) **115**:92
Celestina (Smith) **115**:123, 146, 157-58, 160, 222-23
"Childe Christopher" (Cranch) **115**:13, 38, 54
"A Chinese Story" (Cranch) **115**:57
"The Coal-Imp" (Cranch) **115**:58
"College Lyfe" (Cranch) **115**:3, 6
"Commonplace Book" (Cranch) **115**:68
"Composed during a walk on the Downs, in November 1787" (Smith)
    See "Sonnet 42"
Conversations for the Use of Children and Young Persons (Smith) **115**:119
"Correspondences" (Cranch) **115**:9, 22, 35-36, 54, 67
"Crossing the Bar" (Tennyson) **115**:239
"De Profundis" (Tennyson) **115**:341
"The Death of Oenone" (Tennyson) **115**:337
Desmond: A Novel (Smith) **115**:126, 134, 136, 140, 142, 144-47, 158-64, 167-68, 207, 210-11, 223-26
"Doctor Theophilus" (Cranch)
    See "The Legend of Doctor Theophilus: or, The Enchanted Clothes"
"Dreams" (Cranch) **115**:50
"Duties and Responsibilities of Unitarian Christians" (Cranch) **115**:47

Elegiac Sonnets, and Other Essays (Smith) **115**:120, 122-23, 125, 135, 152, 154-56, 165-66, 174-75, 199-204, 207, 209-12, 215, 217, 223
Elegiac Sonnets, and Other Poems (Smith) **115**:180
"Elegies" (Tennyson) **115**:236
"Emerson's Limitations as a Poet" (Cranch) **115**:33
The Emigrants (Smith) **115**:126, 129, 133-34, 158, 164, 166, 168, 195-97, 199, 204, 206-11, 218
"The Emigrants" (Smith) **115**:121
Emmeline, The Orphan of the Castle (Smith) **115**:136-42, 144-46, 150, 153, 187-90, 192, 210, 221-24
"Endymion" (Cranch) **115**:5
"Enosis" (Cranch) **115**:5, 13-14, 22, 27-29, 32, 35, 54, 67
Ethelinde (Smith) **115**:149
"Field Notes" (Cranch) **115**:66
"The Fireplace" (Cranch) **115**:42
"Flora" (Smith) **115**:119
"Four Charades" (Cranch) **115**:58
"A Friend" (Cranch) **115**:26
"The Garden" (Cranch) **115**:9-10, 31, 35
"Glimmerings" (Cranch) **115**:51
"Gnosis" (Cranch) **115**:8
"The Golden Year" (Tennyson) **115**:240
Grammar of the Serbian Language (Karadžić)
    See *Pismenica serbskoga iezika*
"Grandfather's Spectacles" (Cranch) **115**:51
Heroic Songs of the Recent Times of the War for Freedom (Karadžić)
    See *Pjesme junačke srednjijeh vrema*
History of England, from the earliest records, to the peace of Amiens; in a series of letters to a young lady at school (Smith) **115**:126, 130
"Horologe of the Fields, addressed to a Young Lady, on seeing at the house of an acquaintance a magnificent French Time-piece" (Smith) **115**:119
"How Willie Coasted by Moonlight" (Cranch) **115**:58
"The Humming Bird" (Cranch) **115**:40
Idylls of the King (Tennyson) **115**:269, 275, 309, 341
"Idylls of the King" (Tennyson) **115**:235
"If Life Be Final" (Cranch) **115**:18
In Memoriam (Tennyson) **115**:231-381
"In Memoriam" (Tennyson) **115**:235-41, 313, 318
"In the Garden at Swainston" (Tennyson) **115**:341
"In the Valley of Cauteretz" (Tennyson) **115**:341
"Inworld" (Cranch) **115**:35
Kobboltozo: A Sequel to The Last of the Huggermuggers (Cranch) **115**:16-17, 54-59
"Lady of Shallott" (Tennyson) **115**:335, 358
The Last of the Huggermuggers (Cranch) **115**:16-17, 54-59

"Leaves from My Omnibus Book" (Cranch) **115**:50
"The Legend of Doctor Theophilus: or, The Enchanted Clothes" (Cranch) **115**:54, 57-59
"Letter on travelling, & c" (Cranch) **115**:48
The Letters of a Solitary Wanderer (Smith) **115**:124, 221-22
Letters (Tennyson) **115**:360
"The Lightning and the Lantern" (Cranch) **115**:49
"Lines on the Death of an Aged Relative" (Cranch) **115**:8
Little Slaveno-Serbian Songbook for the Common Folk (Karadžić)
    See *Mala prostonarodnja slaveno-serbska pjesnarica*
A Little Slaveno-Serbian Songbook (Karadžić)
    See *Mala prostonarodnja slaveno-serbska pjesnarica*
Locksley Hall (Tennyson) **115**:263
"Locksley Hall" (Tennyson) **115**:252, 359
"The Lotos Eaters" (Tennyson) **115**:235-36, 275, 305
"Lucretius" (Tennyson) **115**:335
"Luna Through a Lorgnette" (Cranch) **115**:41
Lycidas (Tennyson) **115**:258
Mala prostonarodnja slaveno-serbska pjesnarica (Karadžić) **115**:77, 82, 100-101, 105, 110
Marchmont (Smith) **115**:148
"Mariana" (Tennyson) **115**:358
"Marko Kraljević and Demo of the Mountain" (Karadžić) **115**:91
"Marko Kraljević and Lujutica Bogdan" (Karadžić) **115**:91
"Marko Kraljević and Musa Kesedžij" (Karadžić) **115**:91
"Marko Kraljević and the Daughter of the Arab King" (Karadžić) **115**:91
"Marko Kraljević Knows His Father's Sword" (Karadžić) **115**:91
Maud (Tennyson) **115**:252, 269, 275, 341, 359
"Maud" (Tennyson) **115**:237
"Memorial to Robert Browning" (Cranch) **115**:22
"Middleton Sonnet" (Smith)
    See "Sonnet 44"
Minor Morals, interspersed with sketchs of natural history, historical anecdotes, and original stories (Smith) **115**:129
Montalbert (Smith) **115**:145
"Morning" (Cranch) **115**:5
"Morte d'Arthur" (Tennyson) **115**:235
"The Music of Nature" (Cranch) **115**:67
"Musings of a Recluse" (Cranch) **115**:32, 51
"My Thoughts" (Cranch) **115**:15
Narodna srbska pjesnarica (Karadžić) **115**:77, 110-11
A Narrative of the Loss of the Catherine, Venus, and Piedmont Transports, and the Thomas, Golden Grove, and Æolus Merchant Ships, Near Weymouth, on

TITLE INDEX

Wednesday the 18th of November Last (Smith) **115**:126
The Natural History of Birds (Smith) **115**:126, 211
"New Philosophy Scrapbook" (Cranch) **115**:54
"New School" (Cranch) **115**:40
"Night and the Soul" (Cranch) **115**:5
"The Ocean" (Cranch) **115**:5, 67
"The Ode to Memory" (Tennyson) **115**:358
"Oeneone" (Tennyson) **115**:235, 258
The Old Manor House (Smith) **115**:133, 145, 147-50, 166, 174, 207, 211, 222-24
Oldest Heroic Songs (Karadžić)
  See *Pjesme junačke najstarije*
"On being cautioned against walking on an headland overlooking the sea, because it was frequented by a lunatic" (Smith)
  See "Sonnet 70"
"On the Ideal in Art" (Cranch) **115**:68
"Ormuzd and Ahriman" (Cranch) **115**:23
"Outworld" (Cranch) **115**:35
"The Painter's Scarecrow" (Cranch) **115**:57
"The Palace of Art" (Tennyson) **115**:237, 279, 335
"Personal Reminiscences" (Cranch) **115**:27
"Phaeton" (Cranch) **115**:58
"The Pines and the Sea" (Cranch) **115**:18
Pismenica serbskoga iezika (Karadžić) **115**:83, 105
Pjesme junačke najstarije (Karadžić) **115**:112
Pjesme junačke srednjijeh vrema (Karadžić) **115**:112
Poems (Cranch) **115**:15, 22, 26, 28, 34, 40, 42, 55
Poems of Charlotte Smith (Smith) **115**:172, 176-78, 180, 182
"Poems of the War" (Cranch) **115**:23
Poems (Tennyson) **115**:246
"The Poet" (Cranch) **115**:5, 40-41
"The Poet's Soliloquy" (Cranch) **115**:43
"Prayer Without Ceasing" (Cranch) **115**:50
The Princess (Tennyson) **115**:255
"The Princess" (Tennyson) **115**:237, 240
"The Printing Press" (Cranch) **115**:42
"The Prophet Unveiled" (Cranch) **115**:39, 41
Prvi srpski bukvar (Karadžić) **115**:106
"Quarterly" (Tennyson) **115**:235
"Ralph Waldo Emerson" (Cranch) **115**:33, 39
"Rape of Proserpine" (Tennyson) **115**:337
"A Ride over the Mountains" (Cranch) **115**:48
The Ring and the Book (Tennyson) **115**:269
"The Ring and the Book" (Tennyson) **115**:235
"The Ring" (Tennyson) **115**:247
"The River of Death" (Cranch) **115**:49
Rječnik (Karadžić) **115**:77, 104
Rural Walks (Smith) **115**:173, 210
"Saint Monica" (Smith) **115**:119, 121
Satan: A Libretto (Cranch) **115**:17-18, 23, 26, 35-36, 55
"The Sea View" (Smith)
  See "Sonnet 83"
A Serbian Book of Folk Songs (Karadžić)
  See *Narodna srbska pjesnarica*
Serbian Dictionary (Karadžić)
  See *Srpski rječnik*
Serbian Grammar (Karadžić)
  See *Srpska gramatika*

"The Seven Wonders of the World" (Cranch) **115**:42
"Sign from the West" (Cranch) **115**:51
"Sonnet" (Cranch) **115**:6
"Sonnet 1" (Smith) **115**:152, 156
"Sonnet 2" (Smith) **115**:124, 204-5, 215
"Sonnet 3" (Smith) **115**:153
"Sonnet 4" (Smith) **115**:153, 173, 177, 180, 202-3
"Sonnet 5" (Smith) **115**:154, 177-78
"Sonnet 9" (Smith) **115**:156
"Sonnet 10" (Smith) **115**:177
"Sonnet 12" (Smith) **115**:154, 218
"Sonnet 26" (Smith) **115**:178
"Sonnet 27" (Smith) **115**:177
"Sonnet 30" (Smith) **115**:178
"Sonnet 31" (Smith) **115**:206
"Sonnet 32" (Smith) **115**:152, 178, 215
"Sonnet 33" (Smith) **115**:178
"Sonnet 34" (Smith) **115**:177
"Sonnet 36" (Smith) **115**:125, 154
"Sonnet 42" (Smith) **115**:206
"Sonnet 44" (Smith) **115**:123, 153-54, 197-99, 205
"Sonnet 45" (Smith) **115**:178
"Sonnet 47" (Smith) **115**:153, 176-77
"Sonnet 48" (Smith) **115**:154, 182
"Sonnet 55" (Smith) **115**:177
"Sonnet 57" (Smith) **115**:212, 217
"Sonnet 62" (Smith) **115**:217
"Sonnet 66" (Smith) **115**:176-77, 216
"Sonnet 67" (Smith) **115**:216
"Sonnet 68" (Smith) **115**:152
"Sonnet 70" (Smith) **115**:199
"Sonnet 77" (Smith) **115**:153
"Sonnet 79" (Smith) **115**:177, 218-19
"Sonnet 83" (Smith) **115**:210
"Sonnet 84" (Smith) **115**:177, 182
"Sonnet 89" (Smith) **115**:216
"Sonnet 90" (Smith) **115**:153, 216
"Sonnet 91" (Smith) **115**:216
"Sonnet 92" (Smith) **115**:210, 216
"Sonnet on the Mexican War" (Cranch) **115**:22
Srpska gramatika (Karadžić) **115**:83
Srpske narodne pjesme (Karadžić) **115**:77-80, 100, 112
Srpske narodne poslovice (Karadžić) **115**:78-79
Srpski rječnik (Karadžić) **115**:83
"'St. Agnes Eve'" (Tennyson) **115**:235
"Stanzas" (Cranch) **115**:32, 35
"The Star Gazer" (Cranch) **115**:5, 40
"Studies by the Sea" (Smith) **115**:119
"Supposed Confessions of a Second-rate Sensitive Mind not in unity with itself" (Tennyson) **115**:237, 239
"The Swallow" (Smith) **115**:119
"Symbolism and Language" (Cranch) **115**:9
"Tears, Idle Tears" (Tennyson) **115**:364, 366
"The Telegraph and Telephone" (Cranch) **115**:42
"The Three Mountains" (Cranch) **115**:49
"The Thrush in a Gilded Cage" (Cranch) **115**:41
"Thunder-gust" (Cranch) **115**:5
"Tithonus" (Tennyson) **115**:237, 240
"To a Nightingale" (Smith)
  See "Sonnet 3"

"To Dependence" (Smith)
  See "Sonnet 57"
"To Fancy" (Smith)
  See "Sonnet 47"
"To Hope" (Smith) **115**:156
"To J[ames] R[ussell] L[owell] on his Fiftieth Birthday (Cranch) **115**:35
"To Melancholy" (Smith)
  See "Sonnet 32"
"To My Lyre" (Smith) **115**:155-56
"To Oblivion" (Smith)
  See "Sonnet 90"
"To the Aurora Borealis" (Cranch) **115**:8, 32, 54
"To the Goddess of Botany" (Smith)
  See "Sonnet 79"
"To the Magnolia Grandiflora" (Cranch) **115**:46
"To the Moon" (Smith)
  See "Sonnet 4"
"To the South Downs" (Smith)
  See "Sonnet 5"
"To the Sun" (Smith)
  See "Sonnet 89"
"Transcendentalism" (Cranch) **115**:32, 64
"The True in Dreams" (Cranch) **115**:22
"The Two Voices" (Tennyson) **115**:236-37, 252, 256-57, 261
"Ulysses" (Tennyson) **115**:235, 240, 275
"The Unconscious Life" (Cranch) **115**:68
"Vastness" (Tennyson) **115**:341-42
"Veils" (Cranch) **115**:26-29, 35
"The Violin" (Cranch) **115**:6
"The Vision of Sin" (Tennyson) **115**:236
"Walking to the Mail" (Tennyson) **115**:240
The Wanderings of Warwick (Smith) **115**:166
"Way of the Soul" (Tennyson) **115**:313
"The Wedding of Maksim Crnojević" (Karadžić) **115**:92
"The Wedding of Marko Kraljevič" (Karadžić) **115**:91
Women's Songs (Karadžić)
  See *Ženske pjesme*
"Written at Bignor Park in Sussex, in August, 1799" (Smith)
  See "Sonnet 92"
"Written at Exmouth, midsummer 1795" (Smith)
  See "Sonnet 68"
"Written at the Close of Spring" (Smith)
  See "Sonnet 2"
"Written in a tempestuous night, on the coast of Sussex" (Smith)
  See "Sonnet 66"
"Written in Farm Wood, South Downs, in May 1784" (Smith)
  See "Sonnet 31"
"Written in the Church-Yard at Middleton in Sussex" (Smith)
  See "Sonnet 44"
"Written on the sea shore.—October, 1784" (Smith)
  See "Sonnet 12"
The Young Philosopher (Smith) **115**:136, 144, 147-48
Ženske pjesme (Karadžić) **115**:112
Zivot i obicaji naroda srpska (Karadžić) **115**:79

ISBN 0-7876-5979-7